DATE DUE			

Encyclopedia
of the
American Presidency

Editorial Board

Encyclopedia
of the
American Presidency

Editors

LEONARD W. LEVY
LOUIS FISHER

Volume 1

SIMON & SCHUSTER

A Paramount Communications Company

New York London Toronto Sydney Tokyo Singapore

Simon & Schuster
Academic Reference Division
15 Columbus Circle
New York, New York 10023

A Paramount Communications Company

Printed in the United States of America

printing number
2   3   4   5   6   7   8   9   10

Library of Congress Cataloging-in-Publication Data

Encyclopedia of the American presidency

Leonard W. Levy, Louis Fisher, editors.
v. cm.

Includes bibliographical references and index.

1. Presidents—United States—Encyclopedias.   2.
Presidents—United States—Biography.   I. Levy, Leonard
Williams, 1923–   .   II. Fisher, Louis.
JK511.E53 1994   353.03'13'03—dc20   93-13574 CIP

ISBN 0-13-275983-7 (Set)
0-13-276197-1 (Vol. 1)

The paper used in this publication meets the minimum
requirements of the American National Standard for
Information Sciences—Permanence of Paper for Printed Library
Materials ANSI Z39.48-1984.

About the Editors

Leonard W. Levy is Andrew W. Mellon All-Claremont Professor of Humanities, Emeritus, Claremont Graduate School. Previously he was Earl Warren Professor of American Constitutional History at Brandeis University, where he also served as Dean of the Faculty of Arts and Sciences. He has been a Guggenheim Fellow, a Fellow of the American Council of Learned Societies, a Senior Fellow of the National Endowment for the Humanities, and a Legal Merit Fellow of the American Bar Association. He has held endowed lectureships at the University of Chicago Law School and other law schools. His books include *The Law of the Commonwealth and Chief Justice Shaw* (1957); *Legacy of Suppression* (1960, Sigma Delta Chi award); *Origins of the Fifth Amendment: The Right against Self-Incrimination* (1968, Pulitzer Prize); *Against the Law: The Nixon Court and Criminal Justice* (1974, Commonwealth Club Prize); *Emergence of a Free Press* (1985, ALA award for best book on intellectual freedom); *The Establishment Clause* (1986); *Original Intent and the Framers' Constitution* (1988); and *Blasphemy: Verbal Offense against the Sacred* (1993). He was senior editor of *Encyclopedia of the American Constitution* (4 vols. 1986; supp. 1992; Dartmouth Medal for best reference work). He has written several other books, edited nineteen others, and has published numerous articles. He is a graduate of Columbia University (B.S., 1946; M.A., 1947; Ph.D., 1951).

Louis Fisher is Senior Specialist in Separation of Powers with the Congressional Research Service of the Library of Congress and adjunct professor at the School of Law, Catholic University of America. He is a Fellow of the National Academy of Public Administration and testifies frequently before Congress on such issues as executive privilege, the item veto, the pocket veto, presidential reorganization authority, executive spending discretion, and presidential impoundment powers. In 1987 he served as research director of the House Iran-Contra Committee and wrote major sections of the final report. His books include *President and Congress* (1972), *Presidential Spending Power* (1975, Louis Brownlow Book Award), *The Constitution between Friends: Congress, the President, and the Law* (1978); *The Politics of Shared Power: Congress and the Executive* (3d ed., 1991); *Constitutional Dialogues* (1988, Louis Brownlow Book Award); *American Constitutional Law* (1990); *Constitutional Conflicts between Congress and the President* (3d ed., 1991); and *Political Dynamics of Constitutional Law* (1992, with Neal Devins). Author of more than 150 articles, he has participated actively with the American Bar Association in providing assistance to constitution-drafters in eastern Europe and in Russia. He is a graduate of the College of William and Mary (B.S., 1956) and the New School for Social Research (Ph.D., 1967).

Editorial and Production Staff

Publisher
Charles E. Smith

Editorial Director
Paul Bernabeo

Senior Project Editor
Stephen Wagley

Manuscript Editors
Geoffrey Gneuhs   James Waller
Susan M. Carini   Jerilyn Seife Famighetti   Maria Montenegro
Vincent Montenegro   Susan Converse Winslow

Proofreaders
Katharyn Dunham   Mary Flower

Executive Assistant
Glady Villegas Delgado

Assistant Project Editors
Stephen Garrett   Sara Simon

Compositor
ATLIS Graphics and Design
Mechanicsburg, Pennsylvania

Indexer
Katharyn Dunham
ParaGraphs

Case Designer
Mike McIver

Production Supervisor
Winston Sukhnanand

Contents

Preface

In a flight of fancy, William Gladstone in 1878 described the American Constitution as "the most wonderful work ever struck off at a given time by the brain and purpose of man." The framers at the Philadelphia Convention did not create from whole cloth either Congress or the Supreme Court. In establishing those branches they borrowed openly from British precedents, the experience under the Continental Congress, the American state constitutions, and other sources.

Gladstone's remark, however, has merit when applied to the American Presidency, an office both unique and experimental. Precisely what the framers had wrought was unclear from the beginning. In creating an office with broad and ill-defined powers, they took some comfort in assuming that the first incumbent would be George Washington. It was America's good fortune to have his solid judgment and character shape the early and critical precedents for executive power.

What would come after Washington was less reassuring. On 15 March 1789, one month before Washington's inauguration, Thomas Jefferson wrote to James Madison, "The tyranny of the legislatures is the most formidable dread at present, and will be for long years. That of the executive will come in its turn, but it will be at a remote period." The American presidency would later pass through many troubling and contradictory stages: serving as champion of the national interest at one moment, posing a threat to individual liberties at others; acting as leader of the free world but also invading sovereign countries; professing a truncated theory of executive power in one administration, only to push the boundaries to the fullest in the next.

There is no comparable encyclopedia of the American presidency. This work seeks to fill the need for a single comprehensive reference work that treats the subject in a multidisciplinary way. It was pointed out to us that a more accurate title would have been "Encyclopedia of the President of the United States," to differentiate it from presidents in Central and South America, but we concluded that our title is justified by the tests of common usage and brevity.

This Encyclopedia, containing 1,011 articles by 335 contributors from all regions of the country, representing many disciplines and institutions, captures the origin, evolution, and constant unfolding of the American presidency. When we began planning, we knew that the book had to satisfy the interests of historians, lawyers, practitioners, librarians, political scientists, students, and the general public. As a first step, we prepared a tentative list of topics, allocating the number of words for each subject. We began with biographies on each of the Presidents and Vice Presidents and selected First Ladies, also-rans, executive officials, and members of the judiciary. Biographical sketches of Presidents emphasize the individual's presidential years, rather than his entire life; biographical sketches of others focus on an individual's relationship to the presidency.

We added articles on the powers and prerogatives of the office, including appointments and removals, vetoes and pardons, foreign affairs and the war power, reorganization authority and rulemaking, budgetary and economic duties, impeachments and scandals. We sought to include articles on the multiple roles of the President: Chief Executive, Commander in Chief, chief of state, chief diplomat, party leader, leader of the nation, manager of the federal bureaucracy, governor of the economy, and spokesman of the bully pulpit who provides moral leadership or what President George Bush called "the vision thing." The executive branch required close scrutiny: the White House, the Executive Office of the President, the Cabinet, departments and agencies, bureaucracy, civil service, inspectors general, independent counsels, independent commissions, and government corporations.

We included entries on relationships with Congress and the judiciary. Congress relates to the executive through the powers of investigation, oversight, legislative veto, contempt, and impeachment; there are articles on each of these topics. Liaison between Congress and the executive branch is closely examined. Legal dimensions called for essays on major court cases, appointment of judges, and constitutional issues. Separate articles deal with statutes that add to presidential power and those that constrict it. Significant executive orders and proclamations receive individual treatment. We commissioned dozens of articles on public policies that demand presidential attention: international trade, arms control, civil rights, law enforcement, health, abortion, women's rights, immigration, education, transportation, agriculture, and many others. The President's responsibility as party leader is covered in articles on the major and minor parties, party platforms, slogans and pledges, primaries, nomination and election, the Electoral College, inauguration, and campaign financing. Other political influences on the President are dealt with in essays on the media, the press, public opinion, issue networks, and interest groups.

We wanted the Encyclopedia to help readers understand contemporary events. If the President asks Congress to grant him "fast-track" authority to implement trade agreements, the reader can find an article that explains the elements of that authority. Other articles explain budget terms (appropriations riders, continuing resolutions, entitlements, and reconciliation), bureaucratic positions (Schedule C and Senior Executive Service), and prominent arms control treaties (AMB, CFE, INF, SDI, and START).

In preparing an A-to-Z list to encompass these diverse subjects, we slogged through a succession of drafts and later received suggestions from our editorial advisory board, contributors, and colleagues. As we began reading manuscripts we saw the need for other topics. Such was the design, beginning with core concepts of the presidency and hammered out incrementally thereafter.

In commissioning articles, we reached out to historians, political scientists, law professors, economists, jurists, journalists, experts within the executive branch, and other specialists. We attracted prominent names and younger scholars who have published important works. We made a concerted effort to maintain a balance of views among conservatives, moderates, and liberals. To assure fair treatment, subjects are generally analyzed by more than one author. We believe that a certain level of redundancy or overlap is appropriate to give voice to rival interpretations. In asking authors to cover the basic facts and concepts of a subject, we urged them to express their own opinions and judgments.

Starting with the primitive drafts of what belonged in the A-to-Z plan, we watched with delight as our skeletal outline gained flesh. Scholars under great demand from other publishers found the time, and interest, to write essays that are enlightening and painstakingly accurate. A number of authors tackled subjects on which little has been written. It was our pleasure to work with men and women who maintained remarkably high standards, displayed a capacity to produce under pressure, and retained the all-important qualities of patience and good humor. Our collective thanks goes to them.

Cross-references operate in three ways: as internal cross-references, as end-references, and as blind entires. Internal cross-references appear as words set in small capitals within the body of an article; they direct the reader to related articles that expand on a topic. For example, small capitals in the article on "War, declaration of" (e.g., CALEB CUSHING, WAR POWER, LITTLE v. BARREME, QUASI-WAR WITH FRANCE) indicate that there are articles on these topics. End-references appear in brackets at the end of entires. Blind entires direct the reader from an alternate form of an entry term to the entry itself. For example, a blind entry for "Blacks" tells the reader to look under "Slavery" and "Fugitive Slavery" for the period before the Civil War and under "Affirmative Action," "Civil Rights Policy," and particular civil rights acts for the period after the Civil War and the late twentieth century. The blind entry "Wiretapping" points to the article "Electronic Surveillance."

The word order of a cross-reference is not necessarily the word order of the entry; this is the case for all personal names (to find Caleb Cushing, for example, the reader should look under "Cushing, Caleb"), Cabinet departments (as in "State, Department of"), and for some articles with "presidential" or "White House" in the entry term. Topics that we assume most readers will expect to find in the Encyclopedia are not cross-referenced within articles. Presidents and presidential elections (which are discussed in articles titled "Election, presidential, 1788," through "Election, presidential, 1992") are not usually cross-referenced, though very rarely an election article is cross-referenced if it contains a particularly relevant discussion.

A bibliography at the end of each article recommends books, articles, and government documents for further study.

Tables within articles on Cabinet departments and executive-branch organizations list secretaries and officials; there are also tables on events (e.g., assassinations), salaries, election campaign funds, and relations between the executive and the other two branches (e.g., Supreme Court Justices; vetoes). At the end of Volume 4 are comprehensive tables that list personal information about the Presidents, the complete Cabinet for each administration, other officers, and election results.

Volume 4 also contains a synoptic outline to which the reader can turn for a systematic overview of the contents of the Encyclopedia, a case index listing all court cases mentioned in the Encyclopedia with their citations, and a general index.

We are pleased to acknowledge our gratitude to Stephen Wagley, Senior Project Editor at Simon & Schuster, who was a pleasure to work with and an asset to the enterprise in many ways.

Finally, we enthusiastically dedicate this encyclopedia to our publisher, Charles E. Smith. He shares responsibility for the existence of the work and has our respect, appreciation, and affection.

This encyclopedia is designed to satisfy a variety of needs. Some readers will use it to check specific facts, or to gain an initial orientation in studying some issue. Others will pursue cross-references and sources listed in the bibliographies to reach a more sophisticated understanding of a topic. We hope that these volumes, whether used for small tasks or for ambitious projects, enrich the reader's knowledge of the presidency and stimulate additional research into a political institution that continues to have worldwide impact.

LEONARD W. LEVY and LOUIS FISHER

Tables

Directory of Contributors

A

Richard H. Abbott
Department of History
Eastern Michigan University
WILSON, HENRY

Elie Abel
Department of Communication
Stanford University
CUBAN MISSILE CRISIS

Henry J. Abraham
Department of Government
University of Virginia
COURT-PACKING PLAN
JUDGES, APPOINTMENT OF

Richard M. Abrams
Department of History
University of California, Berkeley
BALLINGER-PINCHOT AFFAIR
BULLY PULPIT
NEW FREEDOM
PROGRESSIVE (BULL MOOSE) PARTY
PROGRESSIVE PARTY, 1924

Walter Adams
Department of Economics
Michigan State University
ANTITRUST POLICY
CLAYTON ACT
SHERMAN ANTITRUST ACT

David Gray Adler
Department of Political Science
Idaho State University
AMNESTY
COMMANDER IN CHIEF
GOLDWATER V. CARTER
PARDON POWER
TREATY TERMINATION
UNITED STATES V. CURTISS-WRIGHT
  EXPORT CORP.
WAR POWERS
WAR POWERS RESOLUTION

Herbert E. Alexander
Department of Political Science
University of Southern California
CAMPAIGN FINANCES
CONSULTANTS
FEDERAL ELECTION COMMISSION

Dean Alfange, Jr.
Department of Politcial Science
University of Massachusetts
BOWSHER V. SYNAR (1986)
INDEPENDENT COMMISSIONS
MISTRETTA V. UNITED STATES (1989)

James B. Allen
Department of History
Brigham Young University
MORMONS

Stephen E. Ambrose
Eisenhower Center
University of New Orleans
EISENHOWER, DWIGHT D.
EISENHOWER DOCTRINE
ELECTION, PRESIDENTIAL, 1972
HAGERTY, JAMES
MILITARY-INDUSTRIAL COMPLEX

Lloyd E. Ambrosius
Department of History
University of Nebraska
FOURTEEN POINTS
LEAGUE OF NATIONS
TREATY OF VERSAILLES
WORLD WAR I

Charles D. Ameringer
Department of History
Pennsylvania State University
COLONIALISM
DOMINICAN REPUBLIC

Harry Ammon
Department of History
Southern Illinois University at
  Carbondale
ELECTION, PRESIDENTIAL, 1816
ERA OF GOOD FEELINGS
MONROE, JAMES

David L. Anderson
Department of History
University of Indianapolis
VIETNAM WAR

Donald F. Anderson
Department of Social Sciences
University of Michigan—Dearborn
TAFT, WILLIAM HOWARD

Martin Anderson
Hoover Institution
Stanford University
PRESIDENT'S FOREIGN INTELLIGENCE
  ADVISORY BOARD
PRESIDENT'S INTELLIGENCE OVERSIGHT
  BOARD
SUPPLY-SIDE ECONOMICS

William G. Andrews
Department of Political Science
State University of New York,
  College at Brockport
PRESIDENCY, PRESIDENTIAL
  CONCEPTIONS OF THE

Peri E. Arnold
Department of Government and
  International Studies
University of Notre Dame
ADMINISTRATIVE REFORMS OF THE
  PRESIDENCY
COMMENTATORS ON THE PRESIDENCY
DOCKERY-COCKRELL COMMISSION
KEEP COMMISSION
REORGANIZATION POWER
TAFT COMMISSION

Raymond O. Arsenault
Department of History
University of South Florida
CIVIL RIGHTS ACT OF 1875
FORCE ACT

Herbert B. Asher
Department of Political Science
Ohio State University
POLLS AND POPULARITY

B

Nancy V. Baker
Department of Government
New Mexico State University
ATTORNEY GENERAL
ATTORNEY GENERAL'S SUBVERSIVES
  LIST
BROWNELL, HERBERT
CLARK, RAMSEY
JUSTICE, DEPARTMENT OF
MITCHELL, JOHN

Howard Ball
Department of Political Science
University of Vermont
EXECUTIVE PRIVILEGE
NEW YORK TIMES CO. V. UNITED
  STATES (1971)
NIXON V. ADMINISTRATOR OF GENERAL
  SERVICES (1977)
UNITED STATES V. NIXON (1974)

Lance Banning
Department of History
University of Kentucky
ELECTION, PRESIDENTIAL, 1788
ELECTION, PRESIDENTIAL, 1792

Edwin C. Bearss
National Park Service
INTERIOR, DEPARTMENT OF THE

David Z. Beckler
American Museum of Natural History
SCIENCE ADVISER
SCIENCE POLICY

Michal Belknap
California Western School of Law
CIVIL RIGHTS ACT OF 1968

John M. Belohlavek
Department of History
University of South Florida
DALLAS, GEORGE MIFFLIN
EAST FLORIDA
ELECTION, PRESIDENTIAL, 1864
FREE-SOIL PARTY
INTERNAL IMPROVEMENTS
NULLIFICATION
PINCKNEY'S TREATY
WILMOT PROVISO

Michael Les Benedict
Department of History
Ohio State University
ELECTION, PRESIDENTIAL, 1856
ELECTION, PRESIDENTIAL, 1868
ELECTION, PRESIDENTIAL, 1872
ELECTORAL COMMISSION
IMPEACHMENT OF ANDREW JOHNSON

Paul H. Bergeron
Department of History
University of Tennessee, Knoxville
POLK, JAMES K.

Edward D. Berkowitz
Department of History
George Washington University
SOCIAL SECURITY
WELFARE POLICY

Larry Berman
Department of Political Science
University of California, Davis
GULF OF TONKIN RESOLUTION
LIBRARIES, PRESIDENTIAL

Irving Bernstein
Department of Political Science
University of California, Los Angeles
KENNEDY, JOHN F.
NEW FRONTIER

Maurice R. Berube
Department of Education
Old Dominion University
EDUCATION, DEPARTMENT OF
EDUCATION POLICY

George Athan Billias
Department of History, Emeritus
Clark University
GERRY, ELBRIDGE

G. Robert Blakey
School of Law
University of Notre Dame
WARREN COMMISSION

Tim A. Blessing
Department of History
Pennsylvania State University, Berks
  Campus
RATINGS, SCHOLARLY

Sidney Blumenthal
The New Yorker
ELECTION, PRESIDENTIAL, 1992

Nicholas Aharon Boggioni
Toledo, Ohio
CIVILIAN CONSERVATION CORPS
HOMESTEAD ACT
LA FOLLETTE, ROBERT M.
MORRILL LAND GRANT ACT
NATIONAL ORIGINS ACT
WORKS PROGRESS ADMINISTRATION

Vaughn Davis Bornet
Department of History, Emeritus
Southern Oregon State College
ELECTION, PRESIDENTIAL, 1964
ELECTION, PRESIDENTIAL, 1968

Douglas E. Bowers
United States Department of
  Agriculture
AGRICULTURE, DEPARTMENT OF
AGRICULTURE ADJUSTMENT ACTS
FREEMAN, ORVILLE

John Braeman
Department of History
University of Nebraska
BANK HOLIDAY
ELECTION, PRESIDENTIAL, 1932
ELECTION, PRESIDENTIAL, 1940
PERKINS, FRANCES
ROOSEVELT, FRANKLIN D.

Kinley Brauer
Department of History
University of Minnesota
GADSDEN PURCHASE
HAWAII, ANNEXATION OF
OPEN DOOR
OREGON TREATY
TEXAS, ANNEXATION OF

James W. Brock
Department of Economics
Richard T. Farmer School of Business
  Administration
Miami University
ANTITRUST POLICY
CLAYTON ACT
SHERMAN ANTITRUST ACT

Harold H. Bruff
National Law Center
George Washington University
ADMINISTRATIVE PROCEDURE ACT
EXECUTIVE ORDER 12291
EXECUTIVE ORDER 12498
FEDERAL REGISTER ACT
IMMUNITY, PRESIDENTIAL
MINISTERIAL DUTIES
NIXON V. FITZGERALD (1982)
OFFICE OF INFORMATION AND
    REGULATORY AFFAIRS
REGULATORY POLICY
RULEMAKING POWER

Gary C. Bryner
Department of Political Science
Brigham Young University
COMPETITIVENESS COUNCIL
DELEGATION OF LEGISLATIVE POWER
HAMPTON & CO. V. UNITED STATES
    (1928)
PERSONAL PRESIDENT
RULEMAKING, CONGRESSIONAL CONTROL
    OF
SUBDELEGATION
YAKUS V. UNITED STATES (1944)

John P. Burke
Department of Political Science
University of Vermont
PRESIDENTIAL STRATEGIES (VIETNAM)

David Burner
Department of History
State University of New York,
    Stony Brook
ELECTION, PRESIDENTIAL, 1920
ELECTION, PRESIDENTIAL, 1924
HARDING, WARREN G.

James MacGregor Burns
Department of Political Science
Williams College
PRESIDENTIAL LEADERSHIP

C
―

Joseph A. Califano, Jr.
Center on Addiction and Substance
    Abuse New York
HEALTH AND HUMAN SERVICES,
    DEPARTMENT OF
HEALTH POLICY

Lou Cannon
The Washington Post
REAGAN, RONALD

Milton Cantor
Department of History
University of Massachusetts
RADICALISM

Betty Boyd Caroli
Department of History
Kingsborough Community College
ADAMS, ABIGAIL
BUSH, BARBARA
CARTER, ROSALYNN
CLINTON, HILLARY RODHAM
EISENHOWER, MAMIE
FIRST LADIES
FIRST LADY'S OFFICE
FORD, BETTY
JOHNSON, LADY BIRD
KENNEDY, JACQUELINE
LINCOLN, MARY TODD
MADISON, DOLLEY
NIXON, PAT
REAGAN, NANCY
WASHINGTON, MARTHA

Albert Castel
Department of History
Western Michigan University
JOHNSON, ANDREW

James Ceaser
Department of Government and
    Foreign Affairs
University of Virginia
ELECTORAL REFORM
NOMINATING PRESIDENTIAL CANDIDATES
SEPARATION OF POWERS

James E. Cebula
Department of History
University of Cincinnati
COX, JAMES M.

Peter Chandler
Alexandria, Virginia
COMMERCE, DEPARTMENT OF

Erwin Chemerinsky
School of Law,
University of Southern California
SUPREME COURT DECISIONS ON THE
    PRESIDENCY

Americo R. Cinquegrana
Central Intelligence Agency
ELECTRONIC SURVEILLANCE
FOREIGN INTELLIGENCE SURVEILLANCE
    ACT
KATZ V. UNITED STATES (1967)
OLMSTEAD V. UNITED STATES (1928)
UNITED STATES V. UNITED STATES
    DISTRICT COURT (1972)

Diane Shaver Clemens
Department of History
University of California, Berkeley
YALTA CONFERENCE

Jeffrey E. Cohen
Department of Political Science
University of Kansas
CABINET

Wayne S. Cole
Department of History, Emeritus
University of Maryland
ISOLATIONISM

Paolo E. Coletta
Department of History
United States Naval Academy
BRYAN, WILLIAM JENNINGS
SHERMAN, JAMES S.

Ellen C. Collier
Congressional Research Service
Library of Congress
AREA RESOLUTIONS
NATIONAL COMMITMENTS RESOLUTION

John Milton Cooper, Jr.
Department of History
University of Wisconsin, Madison
NEW NATIONALISM
ROOSEVELT, THEODORE

Phillip J. Cooper
Department of Public Administration
University of Kansas
EXECUTIVE ORDERS
OFFICE OF FEDERAL PROCUREMENT
    POLICY
PROCLAMATIONS

Robert J. Cottrol
School of Law
Rutgers University
CIVIL RIGHTS ACT OF 1957
CIVIL RIGHTS ACT OF 1960
CIVIL RIGHTS ACT OF 1964

Thomas E. Cronin
Department of Political Science
Colorado College
TWENTY-SECOND AMENDMENT

D

Lori Fisler Damrosch
School of Law
Columbia University
CONNALLY AMENDMENT
LOGAN ACT
UNITED NATIONS PARTICIPATION ACT

Roger Daniels
Department of History
University of Cincinnati
ALIENS, EXCLUSION OF
CHINESE EXCLUSION ACTS
IMMIGRATION ACT
IMMIGRATION POLICY

Roger H. Davidson
Department of Government and Politics
University of Maryland
IRON TRIANGLES
PRESIDENTIAL-CONGRESSIONAL RELATIONS

William C. Davis
Mechanicsburg, Pennsylvania
DAVIS, JEFFERSON

Alexander DeConde
Department of History, Emeritus
University of California, Santa
Barbara
JAY'S TREATY
LOUISIANA PURCHASE

George M. Dennison
Department of History
University of Montana
DORR WAR

Marshall L. DeRosa
Department of Political Science
Florida Atlantic University
CONFEDERATE CONSTITUTION

Vincent DeSantis
Department of History, Emeritus
University of Notre Dame
CLEVELAND, GROVER
REPUBLICAN PARTY

I. M. Destler
Department of Public Affairs
University of Maryland
OFFICE OF THE U.S. TRADE
  REPRESENTATIVE
TRADE EXPANSION ACT
TRADE POLICY

James I. Deutsch
Department of American Studies
George Washington University
FILMS, PRESIDENTS IN

Neal Devins
School of Law
College of William and Mary
AFFIRMATIVE ACTION
APPROPRIATION RIDERS
CIVIL RIGHTS ACT OF 1991
CONTINUING RESOLUTION
PHILADELPHIA PLAN

Leonard Dinnerstein
Department of History
University of Arizona
ELECTION, PRESIDENTIAL, 1892
KU KLUX KLAN

John M. Dobson
Department of History
Iowa State University
ELECTION, PRESIDENTIAL, 1888

Justus D. Doenecke
Division of Social Sciences
University of South Florida
ARTHUR, CHESTER A.

Norman Dorsen
School of Law
New York University
FLAG DESECRATION

Davison M. Douglas
School of Law
College of William and Mary
FAIR EMPLOYMENT PRACTICE
  COMMITTEE

Elizabeth Drew
Washington, D.C.
CLINTON, BILL
GORE, AL
PEROT, ROSS

Melvyn Dubofsky
Department of History
State University of New York at
Binghampton
CHILD LABOR
LABOR POLICY

Craig R. Ducat
Department of Political Science
Northern Illinois University
BUCKLEY V. VALEO (1976)
EXECUTIVE ORDER 10340
YOUNGSTOWN SHEET & TUBE CO. V.
  SAWYER (1952)

E

George C. Edwards III
Center for Presidential Studies
Texas A&M University
BIPARTISANSHIP, CONGRESS AND
COATTAILS EFFECT
CONGRESS, WHITE HOUSE INFLUENCE
  ON
DARK HORSES
HONEYMOON PERIOD
LEGISLATIVE LEADERSHIP
PUBLIC OPINION
RATINGS, PUBLIC

Douglas R. Egerton
Department of History
Le Moyne College
BURR, AARON

Stephen L. Elkin
Department of Government and Politics
University of Maryland
IRAN-CONTRA AFFAIR

Richard E. Ellis
Department of History
State University of New York at
Buffalo
ANTI-MASONIC PARTY
ELECTION, PRESIDENTIAL, 1824
ELECTION, PRESIDENTIAL, 1832

Richard J. Ellis
Department of Political Science
Willamette University
PRESIDENTIAL GREATNESS AND
  CULTURAL DILEMMAS

Robert Ernst
Department of History, Emeritus
Adelphi University
KING, RUFUS

Paul D. Escott
Department of History
Wake Forest University
BELL, JOHN
CIVIL WAR
SLAVERY

F

John D. Feerick
School of Law
Fordham University
DISABILITY, PRESIDENTIAL
TWENTY-FIFTH AMENDMENT
TWENTY-FOURTH AMENDMENT
TWENTY-THIRD AMENDMENT

Bruce L. Felknor
Lake Bluff, Illinois
DIRTY TRICKS

E. James Ferguson
Department of History, Emeritus
City University of New York and
    Queens College
HAMILTON, ALEXANDER

Robert H. Ferrell
Department of History
Indiana University
ACHESON, DEAN
CLAYTON-BULWER TREATY
COOLIDGE, CALVIN
DULLES, JOHN FOSTER
FAIR DEAL
FORDNEY-McCUMBER TARIFF ACT
HEALTH, PRESIDENTIAL
STIMSON, HENRY
TRUMAN, BESS

Paul Finkelman
Department of History
Virginia Polytechnic Institute and State
    University
ABOLITIONISM AND ANTISLAVERY
BRECKINRIDGE, JOHN C.
CASS, LEWIS
CLINTON, DeWITT
CUSHING, CALEB
DOUGLAS, STEPHEN A.
ELECTION, PRESIDENTIAL, 1800
FUGITIVE SLAVERY
HARRISON, WILLIAM HENRY
INDEPENDENT TREASURY
KNOW-NOTHING (AMERICAN) PARTY
LIBERTY PARTY
SCOTT, WINFIELD
TYLER, JOHN

Edwin Firmage
School of Law
University of Utah
WAR, DECLARATION OF

Ronald Fischer
Blacksburg, Virginia
INDEPENDENT TREASURY

Louis Fisher
Congressional Research Service
Library of Congress
BAKER ACCORD
CHECKS AND BALANCES
COMPTROLLER GENERAL
FISCAL CORPORATION BILL
GAG ORDERS
GENERAL ACCOUNTING OFFICE
IMPOUNDMENT
IMPOUNDMENT CONTROL ACT
INCOMPATIBILITY CLAUSE
INELIGIBILITY CLAUSE
INS v. CHADHA (1983)
LEGISLATIVE VETO
LOBBYING WITH APPROPRIATED
    MONEY ACT
QUASI-WAR WITH FRANCE
SPENDING POWER
UNVOUCHERED EXPENSES

David Flitner, Jr.
Methuen, Massachusetts
COMMISSIONS, PRESIDENTIAL

Anita P. Folsom
Paducah Community College
MELLON, ANDREW

Burton W. Folsom, Jr.
Department of History
Murray State University
MELLON, ANDREW

Ben A. Franklin
McGraw-Hill Nuclear Publications
VETERANS AFFAIRS, DEPARTMENT OF
VETERANS POLICY

Steve Fraser
Basic Books
New York
ELECTION, PRESIDENTIAL, 1944
FAIR LABOR STANDARDS ACT

Tony Freyer
School of Law
University of Alabama
COOPER v. AARON (1958)
LITTLE ROCK CRISIS

Jaime B. Fuster
Supreme Court of Puerto Rico
PUERTO RICO

G

Gilbert J. Gall
Department of Labor Studies and
    Industrial Relations
Pennsylvania State University
TAFT-HARTLEY ACT
WAGNER ACT

Larry Gara
Department of History, Emeritus
Wilmington College
KING, WILLIAM RUFUS
PIERCE, FRANKLIN

Rogelio Garcia
Congressional Research Service
Library of Congress
EXECUTIVE RESIDENCE STAFF
VICE PRESIDENT'S RESIDENCE

Mark I. Gelfand
Department of History
Boston College
ALSO-RANS
CAMPAIGN PLEDGES
CAMPAIGN SLOGANS

Michael A. Genovese
Department of Political Science
Loyola Marymount University
CRISIS MANAGEMENT

James N. Giglio
Department of History
Southwest Missouri State University
ALLIANCE FOR PROGRESS
SORENSEN, THEODORE

Michael L. Gillette
Center for Legislative Archives
National Archives
DUKAKIS, MICHAEL
ELECTION, PRESIDENTIAL, 1988

Donna Giordano
Stony Brook, New York
HARDING, WARREN G.

Betty Glad
Department of Government and
    International Affairs
University of South Carolina
PSYCHOLOGICAL PRESIDENCY

Michael J. Glennon
School of Law
University of California, Davis
ANZUS TREATY
LITTLE V. BARREME (1804)
NATO TREATY
RIO TREATY
SEATO TREATY
TREATIES, MUTUAL SECURITY

William T. Golden
American Museum of Natural History
SCIENCE ADVISER
SCIENCE POLICY

Joel K. Goldstein
Goldstein and Price
Saint Louis
BARKLEY, ALBEN W.
CURTIS, CHARLES
FAIRBANKS, CHARLES W.
GARNER, JOHN NANCE
HENDRICKS, THOMAS A.
HOBART, GARRET A.
MARSHALL, THOMAS R.
TWELFTH AMENDMENT
TWENTIETH AMENDMENT
VICE PRESIDENT

Court E. Golumbic
Richardson, Berlin & Morvillo
Washington, D.C.
CONTEMPT OF CONGRESS
INVESTIGATIONS, CONGRESSIONAL

Paul Goodman
Department of History
University of California, Davis
ELECTION, PRESIDENTIAL, 1796
ELECTION, PRESIDENTIAL, 1804

Lawrence C. Goodwyn
Department of History
Duke University
WEAVER, JAMES B.

Lewis L. Gould
Department of History
University of Texas at Austin
ELECTION, PRESIDENTIAL, 1896
ELECTION, PRESIDENTIAL, 1900
ELECTION, PRESIDENTIAL, 1904
ELECTION, PRESIDENTIAL, 1908
FEDERALISM
MCKINLEY, WILLIAM
PARKER, ALTON B.
WILSON, EDITH

John C. Grabow
Richardson, Berlin & Morvillo
Washington, D.C.
CONTEMPT OF CONGRESS
INVESTIGATIONS, CONGRESSIONAL

Norman Graebner
Department of History, Emeritus
University of Virginia
ANNEXATION BY JOINT RESOLUTION
ATLANTIC ALLIANCE
ATLANTIC CHARTER
BERLIN CRISIS
FISH, HAMILTON
FOUR FREEDOMS
HAY-PAUNCEFOTE TREATY
IMPERIALISM
LEND-LEASE ACT
MANIFEST DESTINY
MEXICAN WAR
MONROE DOCTRINE
POLK DOCTRINE
QUEBEC CONFERENCE
SLIDELL'S MISSION
TREATY OF GUADELUPE HIDALGO
TREATY OF WASHINGTON (1871)

Henry F. Graff
Department of History
Columbia University
GREAT SOCIETY
JOHNSON, LYNDON BAINES
RETREATS, PRESIDENTIAL
WHITE HOUSE SECRETARIES

Hugh D. Graham
Department of History
Vanderbilt University
VOTING RIGHTS

Otis L. Graham, Jr.
Department of History
University of California
ELECTION, PRESIDENTIAL, 1936
NATIONAL INDUSTRIAL RECOVERY ACT
NEW DEAL
TENNESSEE VALLEY AUTHORITY ACT

Fred I. Greenstein
Woodrow Wilson School of Public and
    International Affairs
Princeton University
ADAMS, SHERMAN
HIDDEN-HAND PRESIDENT

James O. Horton
*Department of History and American
    Civilization*
George Washington University
CIVIL RIGHTS ACT OF 1866
FREEDMEN'S BUREAU

H. Draper Hunt, III
Department of History
University of Southern Maine
HAMLIN, HANNIBAL

I

Allan P. Ides
School of Law
Washington and Lee University
ATOMIC ENERGY COMMISSION
FIRST USE OF NUCLEAR WEAPONS
MANHATTAN PROJECT
NUCLEAR FREEZE
NUCLEAR TESTING
NUCLEAR WEAPONS

Patricia W. Ingraham
Department of Public Administration
Syracuse University
CIVIL SERVICE REFORM
CIVIL SEVICE REFORM ACT
MERIT SYSTEMS PROTECTION BOARD
SENIOR EXECUTIVE SERVICE

Dennis S. Ippolito
Department of Political Science
Southern Methodist University
ANTIDEFICIENCY ACT
BUDGET AND ACCOUNTING ACT
FISCAL POLICY
GRAMM-RUDMAN-HOLLINGS ACTS
RECONCILIATION BILLS

J

Gary Jeffrey Jacobsohn
Department of Government
Williams College
STATES' RIGHTS

Kathleen Hall Jamieson
Annenberg School of Communications
University of Pennsylvania
ACCEPTANCE SPEECHES
DEBATES, PRESIDENTIAL
STATE OF THE UNION MESSAGES

Robert C. Jeffrey
Department of Political Science
Emory University
GOLDWATER, BARRY

Loch K. Johnson
Department of Political Science
University of Georgia
CASE ACT
CENTRAL INTELLIGENCE AGENCY
CHURCH COMMITTEE
CLARK AMENDMENT
COOPER-CHURCH AMENDMENT
FINDING, PRESIDENTIAL
INTELLIGENCE COMMUNITY
PIKE COMMITTEE
STATEMENT AND ACCOUNT CLAUSE
UNITED STATES V. RICHARDSON (1974)

Howard Jones
Department of History
University of Alabama
MARSHALL PLAN
NEUTRALITY
PROCLAMATION OF NEUTRALITY
TRUMAN DOCTRINE
WEBSTER-ASHBURTON TREATY

K

Frederick M. Kaiser
Congressional Research Service
Library of Congress
ASSASSINATIONS, PRESIDENTIAL
CLASSIFIED INFORMATION
CLASSIFIED INFORMATION PROCEDURES
    ACT
CZOLGOSZ, LEON F.
INFORMATION SECURITY OVERSIGHT
    OFFICE
INSPECTORS GENERAL
OSWALD, LEE HARVEY
PROTECTION OF PRESIDENTS
SECRET SERVICE
SECURITY CLEARANCES

Laura Kalman
Department of History
University of California, Santa Barbara
FORTAS, ABE

John Kaminski
Department of History
University of Wisconsin
CLINTON, GEORGE

Burton Kaufman
Department of History
*Virginia Polytechnic Institute and State
    University*
CAMP DAVID
CAMP DAVID ACCORDS
CARTER, JIMMY
CARTER DOCTRINE
CRISIS OF CONFIDENCE SPEECH
KOREAN WAR
POINT FOUR PROGRAM

Barbara Kellerman
SmartDecisions
Westport, Connecticut
KINFOLK, PRESIDENTIAL
LEADERSHIP SKILLS

Michael P. Kelly
Stony Brook, New York
ELECTION, PRESIDENTIAL, 1920

Edward Keynes
Department of Political Science
Pennsylvania State University
LEBANESE RESOLUTION
MARQUE AND REPRISAL
WAR, UNDECLARED

Richard S. Kirkendall
Department of American History
University of Washington
ELECTION, PRESIDENTIAL, 1948

Maury Klein
Honors Center
University of Rhode Island
CRÉDIT MOBILIER SCANDAL
WHISKEY RING

Edward Knight
Congressional Research Service
Library of Congress
COUNCIL OF ECONOMIC ADVISERS
EMPLOYMENT ACT
NATIONAL ECONOMIC COUNCIL

Elizabeth Koed
Department of History
University of California, Santa Barbara
ELECTION, PRESIDENTIAL, 1936
NATIONAL INDUSTRIAL RECOVERY ACT
NEW DEAL
TENNESSEE VALLEY AUTHORITY ACT

Louis W. Koenig
C. W. Post Center
Long Island University
COUDERT RESOLUTION
GREAT DEBATE OF 1951
HOT-LINE AGREEMENT
LITERALIST PRESIDENT
MEREDITH CASE
MISSISSIPPI V. JOHNSON (1867)
PARLIAMENTARY SYSTEM
PRIZE CASES (1863)
STEWARDSHIP THEORY
STRONG PRESIDENT

Harold Hongju Koh
Yale Law School
BOLAND AMENDMENTS
DESERT ONE
IRANIAN HOSTAGE CRISIS
TOWER COMMISSION

David A. Koplow
Georgetown University Law Center
ABM (ANTIBALLISTIC MISSILE SYSTEM) TREATY
CFE (CONVENTIONAL FORCES IN EUROPE) TREATY
CHEMICAL WEAPONS CONVENTION
INF (INTERMEDIATE-RANGE NUCLEAR FORCES) TREATY
OPEN SKIES TREATY
SALT (STRATEGIC ARMS LIMITATION TALKS)
SDI (STRATEGIC DEFENSE INITIATIVE)
START (STRATEGIC ARMS REDUCTION TALKS)

Martha Kumar
Department of Political Science
Towson State University
INTEREST GROUPS, PRESIDENTS AND
OFFICE OF PUBLIC LIAISON
PRESS CONFERENCES
SPEECHWRITERS, PRESIDENTIAL
WHITE HOUSE PHOTOGRAPHER

Stephen G. Kurtz
Department of History
American University
ADAMS, JOHN
FRIES REBELLION

Stanley I. Kutler
Department of History
University of Wisconsin–Madison
MARSHALL, JOHN

David E. Kyvig
Department of History
University of Akron
PROHIBITION
PROHIBITION PARTY

L

John R. Labovitz
Steptoe & Johnson
Washington, D.C.
HIGH CRIMES AND MISDEMEANORS
IMPEACHMENT

L. Bruce Laingen
American Academy of Diplomacy
FOREIGN SERVICE

Lester D. Langley
Department of History
University of Georgia
BAY OF PIGS INVASION
CUBA
GUNBOAT DIPLOMACY
HAITI
PANAMA
PANAMA CANAL

John A. Larkin
Department of History
State University of New York, Buffalo
PHILIPPINES

William Lasser
Department of Political Science
Clemson University
BIDDLE, FRANCIS
BRAIN TRUST
BYRNES, JAMES F.
COHEN, BENJAMIN V.
CORCORAN, THOMAS
DAUGHERTY, HARRY M.
FARLEY, JAMES A.
FIRESIDE CHATS
ICKES, HAROLD
JACKSON, ROBERT
KATZENBACH, NICHOLAS DEB.

KENNEDY, ROBERT
MOLEY, RAYMOND
PUBLIC UTILITY HOLDING COMPANY ACT
PUBLIC WORKS ADMINISTRATION
ROSENMAN, SAMUEL
WIRT, WILLIAM

Richard B. Latner
Department of History
Tulane University
AMERICAN SYSTEM
ELECTION, PRESIDENTIAL, 1828
ELECTION, PRESIDENTIAL, 1836

Mary C. Lawton
Office of Intelligence Policy and Review
United States Department of Justice
OFFICE OF LEGAL COUNSEL

Lance LeLoup
Public Policy Research Centers
University of Missouri, Saint Louis
BUDGET POLICY
CONGRESSIONAL BUDGET AND IMPOUNDMENT CONTROL ACT

William E. Leuchtenburg
Department of History
University of North Carolina
HUMPHREY'S EXECUTOR V. UNITED STATES (1935)
PANAMA REFINING CO. V. RYAN (1935)
SCHECHTER POULTRY CORP. V. UNITED STATES (1935)

Leonard W. Levy
Graduate Faculty of History, Emeritus
Claremont Graduate School
EMBARGO ACTS
FOREIGN AFFAIRS: ORIGINAL INTENT
KNOX, PHILANDER
MARBURY V. MADISON (1803)
MIDNIGHT JUDGES
MORRIS, GOUVERNEUR
OLNEY, RICHARD
PULLMAN STRIKE
RANDOLPH, EDMUND
WHISKEY REBELLION

Paul C. Light
Hubert H. Humphrey School
University of Minnesota
AGENDA, PRESIDENT'S
POLICY, PRESIDENTIAL

Robert D. Linder
Department of History
Kansas State University
CIVIL RELIGION, PRESIDENT AND

Arthur S. Link
Papers of Woodrow Wilson
Princeton University
ELECTION, PRESIDENTIAL, 1912
ELECTION, PRESIDENTIAL, 1916
WILSON, WOODROW

John E. Little
Papers of Woodrow Wilson
Princeton University
BAKER, NEWTON D.
HOUSE, EDWARD M.
HUGHES, CHARLES EVANS

Jules Lobel
School of Law
University of Pittsburgh
COVERT OPERATIONS
HUGHES-RYAN AMENDMENT
INTELLIGENCE OVERSIGHT ACT
INTERNATIONAL LAW, PRESIDENT AND

Mark M. Lowenthal
Congressional Research Service
Library of Congress
JOINT CHIEFS OF STAFF
NATIONAL SECURITY ACT
NATIONAL SECURITY ADVISER
NATIONAL SECURITY COUNCIL
NATIONAL SECURITY POLICY

Richard Lowitt
Department of History
University of Oklahoma
CONSERVATION POLICY

M

Forrest McDonald
Department of History
University of Alabama
EXECUTIVE PREROGATIVE
GALLATIN, ALBERT
WASHINGTON, GEORGE

George McJimsey
Department of History
Iowa State University
CUMMINGS, HOMER
EARLY, STEPHEN
ELECTION, PRESIDENTIAL, 1852
ELECTION, PRESIDENTIAL, 1876
HOPKINS, HARRY
HOWE, LOUIS MCHENRY

G. Calvin MacKenzie
Department of American Government
Colby College
ADVICE AND CONSENT
APPOINTMENT POWER
HUMPHREY, HUBERT H.
RECESS APPOINTMENTS
VACANCIES ACT

Judson E. MacLaury
United States Department of Labor
LABOR, DEPARTMENT OF

Kim McQuaid
Department of History
Lake Erie College
BUSINESS POLICY
FULL EMPLOYMENT

John Anthony Maltese
Department of Political Science
University of Georgia
WHITE HOUSE OFFICE OF
COMMUNICATIONS

Leon Mann
Graduate School of Management
University of Melbourne
GROUPTHINK

Thomas R. Marshall
Department of Political Science
University of Texas at Arlington
CAUCUSES, PRESIDENTIAL

Brian Wells Martin
History Associates, Inc.
Rockville, Maryland
ENERGY, DEPARTMENT OF

Kate Martin
National Securities Litigation Project
American Civil Liberties Union
Foundation
HAIG V. AGEE (1981)
REGAN V. WALD (1984)
TRAVEL, RIGHT TO

Jack Maskell
Congressional Research Service
Library of Congress
GIFTS TO PRESIDENTS

John Massaro
Department of Political Science
State University of New York,
Potsdam College
SUPREME COURT NOMINEES NOT
CONFIRMED

Daniel A. Mazmanian
Center for Politics and Policy
Claremont Graduate School
THIRD PARTIES

Robert L. Messer
Department of History
University of Illinois at Chicago
ATOMIC BOMB, USE OF

Sidney M. Milkis
Department of Politics
Brandeis University
PARTY LEADER, PRESIDENT AS

Ralph Mitzenmacher
Department of History
Claremont Graduate School
DINGLEY TARIFF ACT
ECONOMIC STABILIZATION ACT
ESCH-CUMMINS TRANSPORTATION ACT
FEDERAL TRADE COMMISSION ACT
FIELD V. CLARK (1891)
MCKINLEY TARIFF ACT
MILLS TARIFF ACT
MORRILL TARIFF ACT
NATIONAL HOUSING ACT
PAYNE-ALDRICH TARIFF ACT
PUMP PRIMING
SMOOT-HAWLEY TARIFF ACT
TARIFF ACT OF 1789
TARIFF ACT OF 1816
TARIFF ACT OF 1857
TARIFF POLICY
UNDERWOOD TARIFF ACT
WALKER TARIFF ACT
WILSON-GORMAN TARIFF ACT

Ronald C. Moe
Congressional Research Service
Library of Congress
ASH COUNCIL
BROWNLOW COMMITTEE
EXECUTIVE DEPARTMENTS
GOVERNMENT CORPORATIONS
GOVERNMENT-SPONSORED ENTERPRISES
HOOVER COMMISSIONS
PRIVATIZATION

H. Wayne Morgan
Department of History
University of Oklahoma
BLAINE, JAMES G.
ELECTION, PRESIDENTIAL, 1880
GREENBACK PARTY
SHERMAN, JOHN
STEVENSON, ADLAI E. (1835–1914)
TILDEN, SAMUEL J.

Ruth P. Morgan
Office of the Provost
Southern Methodist University
EXECUTIVE ORDER 9981
EXECUTIVE ORDER 11063
EXECUTIVE ORDER 11246

Joseph S. Murphy
Department of International and
    Worker Education
City University of New York
PEACE CORPS

N

Michael V. Namorato
Department of History
University of Mississippi
TUGWELL, REXFORD G.

R. William Nary
United States Arms Control and
    Disarmament Agency
ARMS CONTROL AND DISARMAMENT
    AGENCY

Steve Neal
Chicago Sun-Times
WILLKIE, WENDELL

Mark E. Neely, Jr.
Department of History
Saint Louis University
BATES, EDWARD
BOOTH, JOHN WILKES
ELECTION, PRESIDENTIAL, 1860
EMANCIPATION PROCLAMATION
GETTYSBURG ADDRESS
HABEAS CORPUS, SUSPENSION OF
HAY, JOHN
LINCOLN, ABRAHAM
MERRYMAN, EX PARTE (1861)
SECESSION
SEWARD, WILLIAM H.

Michael Nelson
Department of Political Science
Rhodes College
CREATION OF THE PRESIDENCY
PRESIDENTIAL CHARACTER
QUALIFICATIONS FOR PRESIDENT
TERM AND TENURE

Chester A. Newland
School of Public Administration
University of Southern California,
    Sacramento Center
FAITHFUL EXECUTION CLAUSE

John Niven
Department of History
Claremont Graduate School
CALHOUN, JOHN
VAN BUREN, MARTIN

O

David M. O'Brien
Department of Government and
    Foreign Affairs
University of Virginia
FRANKFURTER, FELIX
JUDICIARY, FEDERAL
SUPREME COURT JUSTICES' PERSONAL
    RELATIONS WITH PRESIDENT

Karen O'Connor
Department of Political Science
Emory University
ABORTION
EQUAL RIGHTS AMENDMENT
FERRARO, GERALDINE
WOMEN'S RIGHTS

Morris S. Ogul
Department of Political Science
University of Pittsburgh
OVERSIGHT, CONGRESSIONAL

James S. Olson
Department of History
Sam Houston State University
RECONSTRUCTION FINANCE
    CORPORATION

Sean O'Neill
Department of History
Grand Valley State University
INDIANS

William L. O'Neill
Department of History
Rutgers University
STEVENSON, ADLAI E. (1900-1965)

Norman Ornstein
American Enterprise Institute for
    Public Policy Research
CONGRESSIONAL INFLUENCE ON
    PRESIDENT
THEORIES OF THE PRESIDENCY

Shari L. Osborn
Stony Brook, New York
ELECTION, PRESIDENTIAL, 1924

David Oshinsky
Department of History
Rutgers University
MCCARTHYISM
PALMER RAIDS

P

Chester J. Pach, Jr.
Department of History
Ohio University
ELECTION, PRESIDENTIAL, 1952
ELECTION, PRESIDENTIAL, 1956

Herbert S. Parmet
Graduate School and University Center
City University of New York
ELECTION, PRESIDENTIAL, 1960

Bradley H. Patterson, Jr.
Bethesda, Maryland
OPTION PAPERS
WHITE HOUSE ADVISERS
WHITE HOUSE BUREAUCRACY
WHITE HOUSE SITUATION ROOMS

Jordan J. Paust
School of Law
University of Houston
MAYAGUEZ INCIDENT

Paul Pavlich
Department of Political Science
Southern Oregon State University
WHISTLE-BLOWERS

Michael D. Pearlman
U.S. Army Command and General
   Staff College
Fort Leavenworth, Kansas
SQUARE DEAL

Thomas E. Pennington
89th Airlift Wing
Andrews Air Force Base
AIRCRAFT, PRESIDENTIAL

Michael Perman
Department of History
University of Illinois at Chicago
COMPROMISE OF 1850
COPPERHEADS
KANSAS-NEBRASKA ACT
MCCLELLAN, GEORGE B.
RADICAL REPUBLICANS
RECONSTRUCTION

Elisabeth Israels Perry
Department of History
Vanderbilt University
ROOSEVELT, ELEANOR

Allan Peskin
Department of History
Cleveland State University
GARFIELD, JAMES A.
GUITEAU, CHARLES
HANCOCK, WINFIELD

James P. Pfiffner
Department of Government and Politics
George Mason University
DEPARTMENTAL SECRETARIES
DIVIDED GOVERNMENT
GULF WAR
MANAGERIAL PRESIDENCY
OFFICE OF PERSONNEL MANAGEMENT
OFFICE OF PRESIDENTIAL PERSONNEL
PATRONAGE
SCHEDULE C POSITIONS
STRATEGIC PRESIDENCY
TRANSITIONS, PRESIDENTIAL

Richard V. Pierard
Department of History
Indiana State University
CIVIL RELIGION, PRESIDENT AND

Richard M. Pious
Department of Political Science
Barnard College and Graduate
   Faculties, Columbia University
ACCOUNTABILITY, PRESIDENTIAL
DECISION OF 1789
DOMESTIC PROGRAM INNOVATION
KENDALL V. UNITED STATES (1838)
MYERS V. UNITED STATES (1926)
NATIONAL TREASURY EMPLOYEES
UNION V. NIXON (1974)
REMOVAL POWER
TENURE OF OFFICE ACT
WIENER V. UNITED STATES (1958)

Donald Pisani
Department of History
University of Oklahoma
ENVIRONMENTAL POLICY

John J. Pitney, Jr.
Department of Government
Claremont McKenna College
CONSERVATISM

Elmer Plischke
Department of Government and
   Politics, Emeritus
University of Maryland
DIPLOMAT IN CHIEF
FULBRIGHT RESOLUTION
ORGANIZATION OF AMERICAN STATES
PRESIDENT (TITLE)
PRIVATE ENVOYS
PROTOCOL, PRESIDENTIAL
SAINT LAWRENCE SEAWAY
UNITED NATIONS DECLARATION

Forrest C. Pogue
Arlington, Virginia
MARSHALL, GEORGE C.

Michla Pomerance
Department of International Relations
Hebrew University of Jerusalem
HUMAN RIGHTS

Gerald M. Pomper
Department of Political Science
Rutgers University
ELECTION, PRESIDENTIAL, 1984
PLATFORMS, PARTY

Richard G. Powers
Department of History
City University of New York, College of
   Staten Island
FEDERAL BUREAU OF INVESTIGATION

Vladimir N. Pregelj
Congressional Research Service
Library of Congress
FAST-TRACK AUTHORITY
GATT (GENERAL AGREEMENT ON
   TARIFFS AND TRADE)
RECIPROCAL TRADE AGREEMENTS

C. Herman Pritchett
Department of Political Science,
   Emeritus
University of California, Santa Barbara
MILLIGAN, EX PARTE (1866)
NEAGLE, IN RE (1890)
TWO-TERM TRADITION

R

Jack N. Rakove
Department of History
Stanford University
ANTI-FEDERALISTS
CONSTITUTIONAL CONVENTION
FEDERALIST, THE
HELVIDIUS-PACIFICUS DEBATES
JAY, JOHN

Kenneth C. Randall
School of Law
University of Alabama
AMBASSADORS, RECEIVING AND
   APPOINTING
MISSOURI V. HOLLAND (1920)
NEGOTIATION, POWER OF
RECOGNITION POWER
SOFAER DOCTRINE
TREATY-MAKING POWER
TREATY REINTERPRETATION

A. James Reichley
Governmental Studies Program,
   Retired
Brookings Institution
FORD, GERALD

Robert D. Reischauer
Congressional Budget Office
CONGRESSIONAL BUDGET OFFICE

Harold C. Relyea
Congressional Research Service
Library of Congress
EMERGENCY POWERS
FREEDOM OF INFORMATION ACT
INTERNATIONAL EMERGENCY ECONOMIC
   POWERS ACT
NATIONAL EMERGENCIES ACT
NATIONAL SECURITY
NATIONAL-SECURITY DIRECTIVES
OFFICE FOR EMERGENCY MANAGEMENT
OFFICE OF WAR MOBILIZATION
PAPERS, PRESIDENTIAL
PAPERWORK REDUCTION ACT
POLYGRAPH TESTS
PRESIDENTIAL RECORDS ACT
PUBLIC PAPERS OF THE PRESIDENTS
WEEKLY COMPILATION OF PRESIDENTIAL
   DOCUMENTS

Robert V. Remini
Department of History
University of Illinois at Chicago
BANK OF THE UNITED STATES
BLAIR, FRANCIS PRESTON
CLAY, HENRY
CRAWFORD, WILLIAM H.
FORCE BILL
JACKSON, ANDREW
SPECIE CIRCULAR
TANEY, ROGER B.
TARIFF ACT OF 1832
TARIFF ACT OF 1833
TARIFF OF ABOMINATIONS

Donald L. Robinson
Department of Government
Smith College
CONSTITUTIONAL REFORM

Raymond H. Robinson
Department of History
Northeastern University
ELECTION, PRESIDENTIAL, 1820
ELECTION, PRESIDENTIAL, 1848

Bert A. Rockman
Department of Political Science
University of Pittsburgh
Brookings Institution
CYCLES, PRESIDENTIAL

David H. Rosenbloom
Department of Public Administration
American University
CIVIL SERVICE
CIVIL SERVICE ACT
EXECUTIVE ORDER 9835
HATCH ACT
LLOYD-LAFOLLETTE ACT
LOYALTY-SECURITY PROGRAMS
UNITED STATES V. LOVETT (1946)

Ralph A. Rossum
Claremont McKenna College
WILSON, JAMES

Eugene V. Rostow
National Defense University
IMPLIED POWERS
JAPANESE AMERICANS, TREATMENT OF

Alfred Runte
Seattle, Washington
UDALL, STEWART

Robert A. Rutland
Department of History, Emeritus
University of Virginia
DEMOCRATIC PARTY
ELECTION, PRESIDENTIAL, 1808
ELECTION, PRESIDENTIAL, 1812
MADISON, JAMES
MONTPELIER
PINCKNEY, CHARLES COTESWORTH

S

Nick Salvatore
Department of Industrial and Labor
   Relations
Cornell University
DEBS, EUGENE V.
DEBS, IN RE

M. Elizabeth Sanders
Department of Government
Cornell University
AGRICULTURAL POLICY

Elsa M. Santoyo
Congressional Research Service
Library of Congress
OLD EXECUTIVE OFFICE BUILDING

Edward L. Schapsmeier
Department of History
Illinois State University
PROGRESSIVE PARTY, 1948
WALLACE, HENRY A.

Allen Schick
Brookings Institution
Bureau of Government Research
University of Maryland
BUDGET ENFORCEMENT ACT
BUDGET SUMMITS
ENTITLEMENTS
SEQUESTRATION

Arthur Schlesinger, Jr.
Graduate School and University Center
City University of New York
IMPERIAL PRESIDENCY

John R. Schmidhauser
Department of Political Science,
Emeritus
University of Southern California
CIVIL LIBERTIES
COLE V. YOUNG (1956)
CONSTITUTION, PRESIDENT IN THE
GREENE V. MCELROY (1959)
PETERS V. HOBBY (1955)
SNEPP V. UNITED STATES (1980)

James C. Schneider
Department of History
University of Texas
INTERVENTIONISM

Jeffrey D. Schultz
Department of Government
Georgetown University
BRINKMANSHIP
CLIFFORD, CLARK
EMERGENCY BANKING ACT
LAIRD, MELVIN R.
LANDON, ALFRED M.
MCNAMARA, ROBERT S.
PETS, PRESIDENTIAL
REGAN, DONALD T.
RELIGIONS, PRESIDENTIAL
VACATION SPOTS, PRESIDENTIAL
WATT, JAMES

Robert D. Schulzinger
Department of History
University of Colorado at Boulder
CASABLANCA CONFERENCE
COLD WAR
CONTAINMENT
DETENTE
DOLLAR DIPLOMACY
FOREIGN AID
GRENADA INVASION
KELLOG-BRIAND PACT
KISSINGER, HENRY
NIXON DOCTRINE
RUSK, DEAN
SHULTZ, GEORGE
TEHERAN CONFERENCE
U-2 INCIDENT

Jordan A. Schwarz
Department of History
Northern Illinois University
BARUCH, BERNARD

William Seale
The White House
BLAIR HOUSE
HOMES, PRESIDENTIAL
OVAL OFFICE
WHITE HOUSE (BUILDING)

James E. Sefton
Department of History
California State University, Northridge
COLFAX, SCHUYLER
DRED SCOTT V. SANDFORD (1857)
GRANT, ULYSSES S.

Gerald F. Seib
The Wall Street Journal
Washington, D.C.
BUSH, GEORGE

Robert E. Shalhope
Department of History
University of Oklahoma at Norman
ELECTION, PRESIDENTIAL, 1844

Peter M. Shane
School of Law
University of Iowa
DAMES & MOORE V. REGAN
EXECUTIVE AGREEMENTS
INDEPENDENT COUNSEL
MORRISON V. OLSON (1988)
UNITED STATES V. BELMONT (1937)
UNITED STATES V. PINK (1942)

David L. Shapiro
Harvard Law School
SOLICITOR GENERAL

Eugene Sheridan
Department of History
Princeton University
JEFFERSON, THOMAS

Steven A. Shull
Department of Political Science
University of New Orleans
TWO PRESIDENCIES

Hugh Sidey
Time, Inc.
WHITE HOUSE PRESS CORPS

Joel H. Silbey
Department of History
Cornell University
ELECTION, PRESIDENTIAL, 1840
KITCHEN CABINET
MISSOURI COMPROMISE
TOMPKINS, DANIEL D.
WHIG PARTY

William E. Simon
John M. Olin Foundation
New York
TREASURY, DEPARTMENT OF THE

Harvard Sitkoff
Department of History
University of New Hampshire
ELECTION, PRESIDENTIAL, 1976
ELECTION, PRESIDENTIAL, 1980

Shlomo Slonim
Department of American Studies
Hebrew University of Jerusalem
ELECTORAL COLLEGE
LODGE-GOSSETT PLAN

Elbert B. Smith
Department of History, Emeritus
University of Maryland
BUCHANAN, JAMES
FILLMORE, MILLARD
FRÉMONT, JOHN C.
TAYLOR, ZACHARY

James Morton Smith
Winterthur Museum and Gardens
ALIEN AND SEDITION ACTS

Marcia S. Smith
Congressional Research Service
Library of Congress
SPACE POLICY

Abraham D. Sofaer
Hughes Hubbard & Reed
Washington, D.C.
INHERENT POWERS
STATE, DEPARTMENT OF

Frank J. Sorauf
Department of Political Science
University of Minnesota
PACs (POLITICAL ACTION
    COMMITTEES)
PRESIDENTIAL ELECTION CAMPAIGN FUND

Allan B. Spetter
Department of History
Wright State University
HARRISON, BENJAMIN
MORTON, LEVI PARSONS

Robert J. Spitzer
Department of Political Science
State University of New York, College
    at Cortland
COUNCIL ON ENVIRONMENTAL QUALITY
OFFICE OF INTERGOVERNMENTAL
    RELATIONS
PRESENTATION CLAUSE
SIGNING STATEMENTS, PRESIDENTIAL
VETO, ITEM
VETO, POCKET
VETO, REGULAR

Stephen W. Stathis
Congressional Research Service
Library of Congress
COINS, PRESIDENTS DEPICTED ON
FLAG, PRESIDENTIAL
HYDE PARK
INAUGURAL ADDRESSES
INAUGURATION
MEDALS, PRESIDENTIAL
MONUMENTS, PRESIDENTIAL
MOUNT RUSHMORE
OATH OF OFFICE, PRESIDENTIAL
PRESIDENTIAL SUCCESSION ACT
SALUTE, PRESIDENTIAL
SEAL, PRESIDENTIAL
STAMPS COMMEMORATING PRESIDENTS
SUCCESSION, PRESIDENTIAL
TYLER PRECEDENT
WITNESSES, PRESIDENTS AND FORMER
    PRESIDENTS AS
YACHTS, PRESIDENTIAL

James L. Sundquist
Brookings Institution
SIX-YEAR PRESIDENTIAL TERM

T

Duane Tananbaum
Department of History
Lehman College, City University of
    New York
BRICKER AMENDMENT
REID V. COVERT (1957)
SEERY V. UNITED STATES (1955)
UNITED STATES V. GUY W. CAPPS,
    INC. (1955)

John Tebbel
Southbury, Connecticut
PRESS AND THE PRESIDENCY, HISTORY OF

Athan G. Theoharis
Department of History
Marquette University
HOOVER, J. EDGAR

Norman C. Thomas
Department of Political Science
University of Cincinnati
CHIEF EXECUTIVE

Kenneth W. Thompson
Miller Center
University of Virginia
PRESIDENTS AND MORAL PHILOSOPHY

Eugene P. Trani
Department of History
Virginia Commonwealth University
TEAPOT DOME SCANDAL

David F. Trask
Washington, D.C.
SPANISH-AMERICAN WAR

Roger R. Trask
General Accounting Office
DEFENSE POLICY
DEFENSE, DEPARTMENT OF
WAR, DEPARTMENT OF

Phillip R. Trimble
School of Law
University of California, Los Angeles
ARMS CONTROL

Jeffery K. Tulis
Department of Government
University of Texas at Austin
RHETORICAL PRESIDENCY

Michael Turner
Department of Applied Social Sciences
University of Paisley, Scotland
ROCKEFELLER, NELSON A.

Mark Tushnet
Georgetown University Law Center
CIVIL RIGHTS POLICY

Dorothy Twohig
Papers of George Washington
University of Virginia
MOUNT VERNON

U

Gerald F. Uelmen
School of Law
Santa Clara University
CAPITAL PUNISHMENT

V

Brian VanDeMark
Department of History
United States Naval Academy
BRETTON WOODS AGREEMENT
DESTROYERS FOR BASES
GOOD NEIGHBOR POLICY
HULL, CORDELL
JAPANESE PEACE TREATY
PEARL HARBOR
POTSDAM CONFERENCE
VANDENBERG RESOLUTION

James M. Verdier
Indiana Family and Social Services
    Administration
TAX POLICY

W

Samuel Walker
Department of Criminal Justice
University of Nebraska at Omaha
LAW ENFORCEMENT

John F. Walsh
Department of History
Claremont McKenna College
ALASKA PURCHASE TREATY
CHASE, SALMON P.
COXEY'S ARMY
GREELEY, HORACE
JOHNSON, RICHARD M.
KENDALL, AMOS
MCCARTHY, EUGENE
MONDALE, WALTER F.
ROOT, ELIHU
SEYMOUR, HORATIO
STANTON, EDWIN M.
STASSEN, HAROLD
THIRD-PARTY CANDIDATES
THOMAS, NORMAN

Richard A. Watson
Department of Political Science,
   Emeritus
University of Missouri–Columbia
CAMPAIGN STRATEGY
PRIMARIES, PRESIDENTIAL

Stephen J. Wayne
Department of Government
Georgetown University
BOXSCORES, PRESIDENTIAL
CONGRESS, WHITE HOUSE LIAISON WITH
LAME-DUCK PRESIDENTS

David M. Welborn
Department of Political Science
University of Tennessee, Knoxville
DEREGULATION

Robert F. Wesser
Department of History
State University of New York, Albany
SMITH, ALFRED E.

John G. West, Jr.
Discovery Institute
Seattle, Washington
BAKER, JAMES A., III
BARBARY WAR
CHENEY, DICK
FAREWELL ADDRESS
MCGOVERN, GEORGE
MEESE, EDWIN III
QUAYLE, DAN
RELIGION, POLICY ON
THANKSGIVING PROCLAMATIONS
WEINBERGER, CASPAR W.

Marcia Lynn Whicker
Department of Public Administration
Rutgers University
CABINET COUNCILS
OFFICE OF PRICE ADMINISTRATION
WHITE HOUSE CHIEF OF STAFF
WHITE HOUSE COUNSEL
WHITE HOUSE-DEPARTMENTAL
   RELATIONS

Aaron Wildavsky
Department of Political Science
University of California, Berkeley
PRESIDENTIAL GREATNESS AND
   CULTURAL DILEMMAS

Theodore A. Wilson
Department of History
University of Kansas
WORLD WAR II

Jules Witcover
The Baltimore Sun
AGNEW, SPIRO T.

Peter Woll
Department of Politics
Brandeis University
EXECUTIVE POWER

Robert C. Wood
Department of Government
Wesleyan University
HOUSING AND URBAN DEVELOPMENT,
   DEPARTMENT OF HOUSING POLICY

J. David Woodard
Department of Political Science
Clemson University
TELEVISION AND PRESIDENTIAL POLITICS
THURMOND, STROM
WALLACE, GEORGE

G. Thomas Woodward
Congressional Research Service
Library of Congress
SAVINGS AND LOAN DEBACLE

John T. Woolley
Department of Political Science
University of California, Santa
   Barbara, Washington Center
FEDERAL RESERVE SYSTEM
MONETARY POLICY
QUADRIAD

Margaret Jane Wyszomirski
National Endowment for the Arts
ADMINISTRATIVE PRESIDENCY
DOMESTIC POLICY ADVISER
INSTITUTIONAL PRESIDENCY
OFFICE OF POLICY DEVELOPMENT
OFFICE OF SCIENCE AND TECHNOLOGY
   POLICY
POSTMODERN PRESIDENT
TEXTBOOK PRESIDENCY
WHITE HOUSE OFFICE OF
   ADMINISTRATION

Z

Franklin E. Zimring
School of Law
University of California, Berkeley
CRIME, POLICY ON

Alphabetical List of Entries

Abbreviations Used in This Work

Ala. Alabama
Ariz. Arizona
Ark. Arkansas
Art. Article
b. born
c. circa, about, approximately
Calif. California
cf. confer, compare
chap. chapter (pl., chaps.)
CIO Congress of Industrial Organizations
Cong. Congress
Colo. Colorado
Conn. Connecticut
d. died
D Democrat, Democratic
D.C. District of Columbia
Del. Delaware
diss. dissertation
DR Democratic-Republican
ed. editor (pl., eds); edition
e.g. exempli gratia, for example
enl. enlarged
esp. especially
et al. et alii, and others
etc. et cetera, and so forth

exp. expanded
f. and following (pl., ff.)
F Federalist
Fla. Florida
Ga. Georgia
GOP Grand Old Party (Republican Party)
H.R. House of Representatives
I Independent
ibid. ibidem, in the same place (as the one immediately preceding)
Ida. Idaho
i.e. id est, that is
Ill. Illinois
Ind. Indiana
IRS Internal Revenue Service
Kan. Kansas
Ky. Kentucky
La. Louisiana
M.A. Master of Arts
Mass. Massachusetts
Me. Maine
Mich. Michigan
Minn. Minnesota

Miss. Mississippi
Mo. Missouri
Mont. Montana
n. note
N.C. North Carolina
n.d. no date
N.Dak. North Dakota
Neb. Nebraska
Nev. Nevada
N.H. New Hampshire
N.J. New Jersey
N.Mex. New Mexico
no. number (pl., nos.)
n.p. no place
n.s. new series
N.Y. New York
Okla. Oklahoma
Ore. Oregon
p. page (pl., pp.)
Pa. Pennsylvania
pt. part (pl., pts.)
R Republican
rev. revised
R.I. Rhode Island
S. Senate
S.C. South Carolina

S.Dak. South Dakota
sec. section (pl., secs.)
ser. series
ses. session
supp. supplement
Tenn. Tennessee
Tex. Texas
U.N. United Nations
U.S. United States, United States Reports
USA United States Army
USAF United States Air Force
USN United States Navy
U.S.S.R. Union of Soviet Socialist Republics
v. versus
Va. Virginia
vol. volume (pl., vols.)
Vt. Vermont
W Whig
Wash. Washington
Wis. Wisconsin
W.Va. West Virginia
Wyo. Wyoming

Encyclopedia
of the
American Presidency

A

ABM (ANTIBALLISTIC MISSILE SYSTEM) TREATY. A permanent-duration agreement between the United States and the Soviet Union limiting their activities in the field of strategic defensive systems, the ABM treaty was signed in 1972 by President Richard M. Nixon as part of the SALT (STRATEGIC ARMS LIMITATION TALKS) I package of agreements and overwhelmingly endorsed by the U.S. Senate. The treaty limited each country to maintaining no more than two antiballistic missile sites, each one of which could contain no more than one hundred interceptor missiles and launchers. (A subsequent protocol, concluded in 1974, reduced the permitted level to a single facility in each country.) The treaty also limited the types and locations of ABM-related radar facilities that each country could deploy.

The ABM treaty figured in two prominent controversies. First, in the early 1980s, the Soviet Union began construction of a modern "phased array" radar facility near the Siberian town of Krasnoyarsk, and the Ronald Reagan administration alleged that this activity was a violation of the treaty. Controversy about the capability of the installation and the appropriate mechanism for resolving the problem lingered for years, until the Mikhail Gorbachev government acknowledged the impropriety of the U.S.S.R.'s action and undertook to dismantle the offending facility.

Second, beginning in 1983, the ABM treaty became embroiled in the tumult surrounding President Reagan's SDI (STRATEGIC DEFENSE INITIATIVE). The purpose of SDI was to pursue novel technologies for performing the mission of intercepting incoming missile warheads, a function apparently prohibited by the ABM treaty. Executive branch officials then developed a "new interpretation" of the treaty, under which its constraints were greatly relaxed for defensive systems relying on high-energy beams instead of interceptor missiles. This proposed alteration in the meaning of the treaty triggered a new round of controversy, with the administration insisting that the TREATY REINTERPRETATION was legally correct and substantively preferable and various critics charging that departure from the traditional understanding was both unwise and unconstitutional.

BIBLIOGRAPHY

Chayes, Antonia Handler, and Paul Doty, eds. *Defending Deterrence: Managing the ABM Treaty Regime into the 21st Century.* 1989.
Garthoff, Raymond L. *Policy versus Law: The Reinterpretation of the ABM Treaty.* 1987.

DAVID A. KOPLOW

ABOLITIONISM AND ANTISLAVERY. During and after the Revolution, opponents of SLAVERY formed abolition societies in most of the North and in the upper South. These societies initially pushed for an end to slavery in their own states. In the 1790s various abolition societies petitioned Congress to curb the African slave trade, thus raising the specter of slavery as disruptive to national harmony.

After the adoption of gradual emancipation statutes (or outright abolition) in the North and the federal abolition of the slave trade in 1808, the early abolition societies focused their energies on protecting and educating free blacks in their own states and for the most part avoided national politics. In 1831 a new antislavery movement arose, led by William Lloyd Garrison. Initially the movement focused on petitioning Congress on such issues as ending slavery in federal territories and the District of Columbia and not allowing any new slave states into the Union. Southerners, who dominated the DEMOCRATIC PARTY in the 1830s, pushed through a gag rule that prevented Congressmen from reading abolitionist petitions on the floor of the House. From 1836 to 1844 Congress annually adopted a gag, which was opposed by former President John Quincy Adams and others who were generally anathema to their own parties' view of slavery as an issue that threatened to undermine the Union. Presidential candidates during this period tried to avoid being tarred as sympathetic to abolitionism, although sometimes they simultaneously tried to avoid alienating the growing number of northern voters who opposed slavery. No major party presidential candidate openly sought the antislavery vote until the emergence of the Republicans in 1856.

Well before the formation of the REPUBLICAN PARTY antislavery voters had alternatives to the Whigs and Democrats. In 1840 the LIBERTY PARTY emerged, nominating James Gillespie Birney, a former slave owner turned abolitionist, for President. The Garrisonian abolitionists despised the Liberty Party because it challenged their disunionist, antipolitical stance. In the late 1830s Garrison declared the Constitution to be a proslavery compact, a "covenant with death," and many of his followers refused to take part in politics. In 1840 the abolitionist movement suffered schisms over political activities and the role of women. In 1843 Garrison and his lieutenant Wendell Phillips advocated the expulsion of the slave states from the Union. This and other radical proposals kept Garrisonians on the fringes of American society. But from that position they were able to influence politics by keeping pressure on all opponents of slavery. Phillips's trenchant critique of the American Constitution as a proslavery compact brought few people to abandon politics, but ironically it probably led many antislavery people to take a more active role in the Liberty Party and later the FREE-SOIL PARTY.

A single-issue candidate, Birney initially attracted little support in 1840, winning only about seven thousand votes. In 1844 the Liberty Party again nominated Birney, who won about sixty-two thousand votes, over 2 percent of all votes cast. The party received at least some votes in four-fifths of the counties in the North, suggesting the breadth of antislavery sentiment. More importantly, the Liberty Party won some sixteen thousand votes in New York. James K. Polk, who won the election, carried New York by only five thousand votes. The New York vote indicates the importance of antislavery voters. Had most of the Liberty Party votes gone to Whig Henry Clay, he would have carried New York and with it the election. Many Whigs blamed the loss of the election on the abolitionists who had voted for the Liberty Party.

There is no reason to believe Liberty voters would have supported Clay, a slaveholder, over Polk, also a slaveholder. These voters had clearly rejected the major parties, which had for too long tried to ignore or finesse the issue of slavery. The abolitionist movement had pulled at least 2 percent of the voters from the major parties.

In 1848 the Democrats learned the dangers of ignoring the growing power of antislavery voters. Senator John P. Hale initially accepted the Liberty Party nomination, but then withdrew in favor of former President Martin Van Buren, who ran on the Free-Soil Party. Most Liberty Party supporters also voted for Van Buren, whose running mate was Charles Francis Adams, the son and grandson of Presidents and a leading antislavery Whig. While he carried no states, most of Van Buren's 291,263 votes came at the expense of the Democratic Party. Although most Liberty men voted for Van Buren, the radical abolitionists (who voted at all) cast a mere 2,545 votes for Gerrit Smith, running as the candidate of the National Liberty Party.

By 1856 abolitionist voters had moved into the Republican Party. Democrats in 1856 and 1860 tried to cast the Republicans as dangerous abolitionist radicals, which was an exaggeration. While opposed to slavery, most Republicans, unlike abolitionists, did not advocate an end to slavery where it existed. Nevertheless, political abolitionists like Charles Sumner, Salmon P. Chase, and John P. Hale, found a congenial home in the new party. Even the acerbic Wendell Phillips admitted that a Republican President would have one hand "on the jugular of the slave system." With the outbreak of the CIVIL WAR, Garrisonian abolitionists entered the Republican Party as respected prophets while political abolitionists like Chase and Sumner had secured important offices and policy-making roles.

Lincoln's election forever changed the relationship between abolitionism and politics. Early in his administration Lincoln proclaimed that the Civil War was not over slavery. He insisted that he only wanted to maintain the union, and that he would free no slaves, some slaves, or all the slaves to achieve that goal. Nevertheless, antislavery Republicans constantly pressured Lincoln, and the Congress, to take steps to end slavery.

Early in the war Lincoln countermanded orders of General JOHN C. FRÉMONT, who attempted to free all the slaves in the loyal state of Missouri. However, Lincoln urged loyal border state slaveowners to accept compensated emancipation. In the summer of 1862 Lincoln decided to issue a general emancipation proclamation, but waited until a Union victory to do so. The preliminary proclamation, issued after the battle of Antietam in September 1862, declared that in one hundred days (1 January 1863) all slaves owned in the Confederacy would be free. This was a war measure, issued under Lincoln's authority as COMMANDER IN CHIEF. Under the EMANCIPATION PROCLAMATION—which was effectively implemented by the armies of Grant and Sherman—most southern slaves gained their freedom. Meanwhile, Congress ended slavery in the District of Columbia and the federal territories, and thousands of slaves in the border states joined the Union army. In 1865 Congress sent the Thirteenth Amendment to the states. When ratified, December 1865, it ended all slavery in the United States. After the war most abolitionists retreated from social reform, although many continued to work with former slaves or take up other causes, especially WOMEN'S RIGHTS and labor reform.

BIBLIOGRAPHY

Barnes, Gilbert Hobbs. *The Antislavery Impulse, 1830–1844*. 1933.
Dillon, Merton. *The Abolitionists: The Growth of a Dissenting Minority*. 1974.
Finkelman, Paul, ed. *Articles on American Slavery*. Vol. 9: *Antislavery*. 1989.
Sewell, Richard. *Ballots for Freedom: Antislavery Politics in the United States, 1837–1860*. 1976.
Stewart, James Brewer. *Holy Warriors*. 1976.
Stewart, James Brewer. *Wendell Phillips: Liberty's Hero*. 1986.

PAUL FINKELMAN

ABORTION. Before the 1960s the topic of abortion was not widely discussed in the United States, although there were some denunciations of the practice of abortion. Even Margaret Sanger, one of the first to call for women's access to birth control, publicly spoke out against abortion. But in the 1960s a series of events combined to lead many to recognize the need to change restrictive state abortion laws. In *Griswold v. Connecticut* (1965) the U.S. Supreme Court ruled that a Connecticut statute prohibiting the dissemination of birth-control information was unconstitutional. In reaching its landmark decision, the Court ruled that the decision to use birth control was the exercise of a fundamental freedom. This right to privacy, which included the right to be free from governmental interference in matters of contraception, was said to be found in various specific constitutional provisions including the First, Fourth, and Fourteenth Amend-

ments. Soon groups, including the newly formed National Organization for Women (NOW), were calling for a total repeal of all restrictive state abortion laws. Building on *Griswold*, a number of lawsuits challenging state abortion restrictions were initiated.

In 1973, the Supreme Court handed down *Roe v. Wade*, a decision that, ironically, was bumped from the headlines by the death of former President Lyndon B. Johnson. In *Roe*, a case involving a challenge to the constitutionality of an abortion statute in Johnson's home state of Texas, the Court ruled that a woman's decision to terminate her pregnancy was a fundamental freedom protected by the U.S. Constitution. The seven-member majority concluded that the privacy doctrine enunciated in *Griswold* included the right to terminate a pregnancy, thereby invalidating all restrictive state abortion laws.

The *Roe* decision came within days of Richard M. Nixon's second inauguration. Although Nixon had no comments on *Roe* at the time, he had earlier rescinded an EXECUTIVE ORDER allowing abortions on U.S. military bases and had publicly stated his opposition to abortion as a method of birth control. He also rejected the recommendation of his own Commission on Population Growth that restrictive abortion laws be liberalized.

Despite Nixon's stated policy preference, when *Roe* was accepted for argument before the Supreme Court, his administration took no action, even though it is hardly unusual for the government to file a brief advocating a position on so important a matter. Perhaps Nixon believed that the Court, which included four of his own appointees, shared his views. In fact, Justice Harry Blackmun, one of those appointees, wrote the majority opinion in *Roe*.

Until his wife, BETTY FORD, publicly announced her support for *Roe*, Gerald Ford, Nixon's successor, made no comments on abortion rights. In his first public utterance on abortion, he voiced support for a constitutional amendment that would allow the individual states to regulate abortion policy. Ford made no efforts to restrict abortion during his term in office. In 1976 he vetoed the Labor-HEW appropriations bill, which contained the Hyde Amendment restricting the use of federal funds for some medically necessary abortions for indigent women. His veto, however, was based on excessive appropriations, not the Hyde Amendment. His veto message explained, "I agree with the restriction on the use of Federal funds for abortion." Congress overrode his veto. Ford's administration declined to take any position on the challenges to restrictive state abortion laws that were being heard by the U.S. Supreme Court.

Abortion first became an issue in a presidential campaign in 1976. Ford, the incumbent and eventual Republican nominee, noted his belief that there should be some flexibility on the issue and that abortion should be permitted in situations where the health of the mother was endangered or where pregnancy had resulted from rape or incest. During his primary campaign he even portrayed his opponent, Ronald Reagan, as an antiabortion extremist.

Jimmy Carter, who defeated Ford, refused to support a constitutional amendment to restrict abortion but he did little to advance the prochoice cause. He opposed federal funding for abortions even though the Democratic Party platform on which he ran supported federal funding, and in *Harris v. McRae* (1980) his administration successfully defended the constitutionality of a new version of the Hyde Amendment in court.

The Reagan administration, however, mounted a concerted effort to ban abortions and to convince the Supreme Court to overrule *Roe v. Wade*. With the strong support of the antiabortion movement that had arisen to counter *Roe*, Reagan successfully ran on a platform calling for a constitutional amendment to end abortion and containing a plank that called for the President to appoint to the federal courts only judges who supported strong family values and who opposed abortion. In fact, Reagan's first appointee to the Supreme Court, Sandra Day O'Connor, was criticized because prolife forces feared that she would not be a vote to overrule *Roe*. Their fears were somewhat assuaged in *Akron v. Akron Center for Reproductive Health* (1983). *Akron* was the first case in which a President used his Justice Department to advance a prolife position, claiming that "the time [had] come to call a halt" to judicial limitation on state regulation of abortion. Nevertheless, in a 6-to-3 opinion, the Court struck down a vast majority of the restrictions at issue and dealt a stunning blow to the Reagan administration. O'Connor, Reagan's lone appointment to that date, did, however, join the dissenters. Eventually, through Reagan's appointment of several Justices to the Supreme Court plus his elevation of William H. Rehnquist to the position of Chief Justice, the scope of *Roe* was slowly whittled away. The Reagan administration continually appeared in Court to urge the Justices to limit *Roe* or to overrule it completely.

The effort to overrule *Roe* judicially picked up during the George Bush administration. During Bush's 1988 campaign for the presidency, he urged "adoption not abortion" as a solution to unwanted pregnancies and he called for the passage of a constitutional amendment to ban abortions. As President, Bush maintained the antiabortion policies of the Reagan administration, including bans on abortions at military installations and on fetal-tissue research and the elimination of Medicaid funding for poor women's abortions in cases of rape and incest. Abortion became a much more highly publicized issue during Bush's first term. His Justice Department defended the so-called gag rule—a 1988 federal regulation barring federally funded family-planning clinics from providing clients with any information about abortions, even if a woman requested it or the pregnancy was likely to endanger the woman's health.

Changes in the composition of the Supreme Court and the political climate during the Bush administration led many to believe that *Roe v. Wade* would soon be overruled or severely limited. In *Webster v. Reproductive Health Services* (1989), for example, it appeared that *Roe* was in real jeopardy when four Justices—Reagan appointees Antonin Scalia and Anthony Kennedy as well as Chief Justice Rehnquist and Byron White, who had both dissented in *Roe*—seemed willing to overrule *Roe*.

Webster mobilized forces on both sides of the abortion controversy. Marches were held around the country, and even sitting Justices began to voice their fears about a post-*Roe* nation. In 1990, Bush appointed David Souter to the Court to replace retiring Justice William Brennan, and in 1991 the liberal, prochoice Thurgood Marshall resigned from the Court and was replaced by Bush appointee Clarence Thomas. With the addition of two Bush appointees, most Court watchers believed that *Roe* would not remain on the books for long. But in *Planned Parenthood v. Casey* (1992), a challenge to Pennsylvania's restrictive abortion statutes, the Court in another closely divided opinion upheld several state restrictions on abortions but stopped short of overruling *Roe*.

The election of avowedly prochoice Bill Clinton in 1992 was a major turning point in the abortion debate. The Democratic Party platform on which he ran called for a strict adherence to the standards originally set out in *Roe v. Wade* and supported public funding of abortions. After taking office, Clinton showed his commitment to abortion rights by repealing the gag rule (which had been upheld by the Supreme Court in *Rust v. Sullivan* [1991]), ending the bans on abortions on military bases and on fetal-tissue research, and asking the Food and Drug Administration to reconsider its ban on RU-487, the French "morning-after" abortion pill. He also promised to support the Freedom of Choice Act. Perhaps most importantly, he pledged to appoint to the Supreme Court Justices who support a constitutional right to privacy, the under-pinning of *Roe v. Wade*.

BIBLIOGRAPHY

Baer, Judith A. *Women in American Law.* 1991.
O'Connor, Karen, and Lee Epstein. "Abortion Policy." In *The Reagan Administration and Human Rights.* Edited by Tinsley E. Yarbrough. 1985.

KAREN O'CONNOR

ACCEPTANCE SPEECHES. What we know as acceptance speeches at party conventions were origi-nally letters dispatched by the nominated candidate in response to a letter notifying him of the offered honor. The first candidate notified under this procedure was Democratic vice presidential nominee Martin Van Buren in 1832. Early notification letters were mailed.

In 1852 Franklin Pierce was notified in person by a delegation sent from the convention. With represen-tatives of the party and the candidate now in one place, a formal ceremony could occur. Typically such cere-monies took place six weeks to two months after the convention. In 1856, James Buchanan took the pro-cess a step further by delivering an oral acceptance statement. The CIVIL WAR then interrupted the prac-tice. No notification ceremonies occurred in 1860 and 1864.

In the last decade of the nineteenth century and the first quarter of the twentieth, notification ceremonies increased in size and rhetorical significance. So, for example, Grover Cleveland's 1892 acceptance was held in Madison Square Garden. Where once the candidate was assumed to stand on the party platform, candidates began to use the opportunity provided by the ceremony to define and detail the issues of impor-tance to the campaign. In 1908, the ceremonies re-placed the notification letters altogether.

In 1912, newsreels shown in movie theaters carried Woodrow Wilson's acceptance address to a national audience. In 1924, radio gave the message the imme-diacy of live broadcast. Beginning in 1928, the candi-dates of both major parties scheduled their acceptan-ces for evening hours in order to reach radio's largest audiences.

To dramatize the urgency of the times and his eagerness to address the issues before the country, in 1932 the Democratic nominee, Franklin D. Roosevelt, flew to Chicago to deliver his acceptance in person at the convention. Under the wartime conditions of 1940 and 1944, his speeches were carried live to the conven-tion by radio.

The acceptance address identifies the argumenta-tive terrain on which the candidate wishes to contest for votes. By so doing, it forecasts the discourse of the campaign itself. Indeed in 1968, 1972, 1984, 1988, and 1992, political ads were clipped directly from the acceptance speech.

Only the audience for presidential debates exceeds that of the acceptance speeches. In 1960, for example, John F. Kennedy's acceptance speech reached 35 mil-lion; the first Kennedy-Nixon PRESIDENTIAL DEBATE reached 100 million.

Since the acceptance addresses usually reach the largest audience of any speech of the campaign, they play an important role in defining the candidate, his agenda, and the issues he sees as decisive. As a result, the convention organizers work hard to ensure that the speech airs in prime time in all three time zones of the continental United States. The one candidate in the television age who failed to speak in prime time sacrificed an important opportunity to define himself and his agenda. Had George McGovern delivered his 1972 acceptance speech at 10:00 P.M., he would have reached an audience of just over 17 million. By 2:48 A.M. when it actually began, the audience had dropped to just over 3.5 million.

When the nominee is an incumbent, the speech highlights the presumed successes of his term. At the same time, it argues that important work remains unfinished, and it invites the assembled partisans and the viewing audience to commit themselves to this agenda and the candidacy of its champion. When the nominee is a challenger, the speech identifies the failures of the incumbent's administration and fore-casts an alternative vision.

Acceptance speeches are not usually memorable. The exceptions are noteworthy. In 1964, BARRY GOLD-WATER uttered what he thought was an uncontrover-sial sentiment: "Extremism in the defense of liberty is no vice. Moderation in the pursuit of justice is no virtue." Throughout the fall campaign, Democrats pilloried him for the statement. By contrast, George Bush's central convention claim became a pillar of his campaign discourse. "Read my lips, no new taxes," Bush told the assembled Republicans. Four years later, an opponent in the Republican primaries was reminding voters that Bush had betrayed that pledge.

Where the conventions once determined the iden-tity of the party nominee, that decision now usually has been made by the end of the season of PRESIDENTIAL

PRIMARIES. Second ballots are now a thing of the past. And when the putative nominee enters the convention with the votes needed to capture the nomination, the other function of conventions, adopting a PARTY PLATFORM, becomes similarly ritualistic.

As a result, the drama of party conventions has shifted from disputes over the platform and determination of the nominee to revelation of the vice presidential nominee. Although the person with the majority of committed delegates shapes the convention and its platform, the putative nominee officially assumes the role of standard bearer for the party in the acceptance speech.

[*See also* NOMINATING PRESIDENTIAL CANDIDATES.]

BIBLIOGRAPHY

Farrell, Thomas B. "Political Conventions as Legitimation Ritual." *Communication Monographs* 45 (1978): 293–325.
Ritter, Kurt W. "American Political Rhetoric and the Jeremiad Tradition: Presidential Nomination Acceptance Addresses, 1960–1976." *Central States Speech Journal* (1980): 153–171.

KATHLEEN HALL JAMIESON

ACCOUNTABILITY, PRESIDENTIAL. The concept of presidential accountability has several dimensions: *electoral accountability*, which requires the President or his party's nominee to defend his performance in the next election; *executive accountability*, which places the ultimate responsibility for actions by presidential appointees with the President himself; and, finally, *legal and constitutional accountability*, which holds the President responsible for the discharge of his own statutory and constitutional duties. There are no provisions for mechanisms of presidential accountability in the Constitution of 1787. The Framers concentrated on SEPARATION OF POWERS to increase the efficiency of government, provisions of reelection to ensure dependence on the people's will; and CHECKS AND BALANCES to guard against abuses of power. Attempts to increase presidential accountability inevitably run up against, and require trade-offs with, these higher constitutional values.

The Framers provided for electoral accountability based on the state legislatures, which controlled the ELECTORAL COLLEGE. In the early nineteenth century Presidents also became accountable to their congressional parties through congressional nominating caucuses, but by the 1830s congressional influence gave way to state parties that controlled both the national nominating conventions and the Electoral College vote. The modern transformation of conventions into a registering device for the preferences of a party's electorate in the PRESIDENTIAL PRIMARIES, combined with public financing of campaigns and candidate-centered campaign organizations, has loosened the bonds between President and party leaders, which in turn has created a plebiscitary presidency. To the extent that there is electoral accountability it is to the primary voters during the renomination contest and then to that part (about half) of the eligible electorate that actually votes in the general election. But the TWENTY-SECOND AMENDMENT has eliminated presidential electoral accountability in the second term and proposals for a SIX-YEAR PRESIDENTIAL TERM with no reeligibility would have the effect of eliminating altogether this aspect of accountability.

Presidential electoral accountability has also been lessened because DIVIDED GOVERNMENT rather than party government has been the prevailing partisan pattern in the twentieth century. Only during the administrations of Theodore Roosevelt, Warren G. Harding, Calvin Coolidge, Franklin D. Roosevelt, John F. Kennedy, and Lyndon Baines Johnson were Congresses always controlled by the party that occupied the White House. Since the 1950s Republican Presidents have first railed and then run against "do-nothing" or "irresponsible" Congresses that have refused to pass their programs while Democratic congressional leaders have blamed the Republican Presidents for inaction or ineptitude. Those arguing that a presidential election mandate should be respected have proposed to amend the Constitution so that one chamber by a two-thirds vote should be able to pass a bill to be sent to the President, even if the other house fails to pass the measure. Another idea is that the Senate should consent to treaties by a three-fifths rather than a two-thirds vote. Such reforms would allow Presidents to get their way with Congress more easily, increasing the electoral accountability of the President at the expense of checks and balances.

Another proposal is to provide Presidents with automatic congressional majorities, for instance, by the automatic election of an at-large slate of candidates for the House of Representatives sufficient to ensure the winning presidential candidate a majority in that chamber. Or the weak presidential coattails could be strengthened if House and Senate members had four-year terms and there were party tickets so that a single ballot cast for President would also automatically be cast for the local House and Senate candidates of the President's party. While maximizing the prospects for responsible party government and electoral accountability, these reforms would also erode the independence of the congressional parties and the effectiveness of checks and balances.

Several proposals borrowed from parliamentary systems would increase the influence of Congress at the expense of the presidency. In 1974, Representative Henry Reuss of Wisconsin proposed a constitutional amendment that would have permitted three-fifths of the members of each chamber of Congress to vote a resolution of no confidence in the President. Congress would then fix a date to call special elections for President, Vice President, Representatives, and Senators. CABINET government has also been proposed. In 1879, Senator George Pendleton offered a bill providing that "the principal officers of each of the Executive Departments may occupy seats on the floor of the Senate and House of Representatives" and participate in debates, and in the 1880s Gamaliel Bradford suggested that Cabinet secretaries be subject to question periods. Similar proposals were endorsed by President William Howard Taft in his last message to Congress in 1913 and by President Harding in 1921. The fullest exposition of the doctrine of Cabinet government was developed by Woodrow Wilson, who as a senior at Princeton University in 1879 proposed in an article submitted to the *International Review* (accepted for publication by its editor, Henry Cabot Lodge) that the President select members of his Cabinet from the legislature. They would retain their seats in Congress and have the power to initiate legislation and would be prepared to resign should Congress reject their programs.

Most proposals since Wilson's have called for some sort of joint council of legislators and Cabinet secretaries to coordinate government policies. Edward Corwin, a Princeton University professor of constitutional law, in 1940 called for an advisory joint cabinet consisting of all the DEPARTMENTAL SECRETARIES as well as the chairs of appropriate standing legislative committees. In 1945 Thomas Finletter, Secretary of the Air Force, called for a "joint cabinet of Congress" consisting of nine committee chairs in each chamber; nine of these chairs along with nine cabinet secretaries would constitute a "joint executive-legislative cabinet." A constitutional amendment would provide the President with power to dissolve the government in case of deadlock between Congress and the joint cabinet. In 1979 Henry Reuss proposed a constitutional amendment to permit members of Congress to serve in key executive-branch offices. Section 1 of his amendment proposed that "Congress shall have the power by law to designate officers of the Executive Branch, not to exceed 50 in number, to which Members of the Senate and the House of Representatives would be eligible for nomination and appointment . . . without being required to vacate their offices in the Senate or House of Repre-

sentatives." All these ideas would make Presidents and their Cabinets more accountable to Congress; at the same time, joint executive-legislative decision making would erode institutional lines of responsibility and make it even more difficult for the electorate to hold a President accountable for public policy during his term of office. All, it should be added, would be unworkable in periods of divided government.

Presidents have argued that their accountability is strengthened when the chain of command in the bureaucracy runs from the Oval Office down to subordinates in "the executive branch" without legislative or judicial interference. Not surprisingly, presidential study commissions such as the Commission on Economy and Efficiency in the Taft administration, the BROWNLOW COMMITTEE in the Franklin Roosevelt presidency, and the two HOOVER COMMISSIONS in the Harry S. Truman and Dwight D. Eisenhower presidencies, have all endorsed this view. Presidential budgeting, legislative and regulatory clearance, and management oversight have all increased at the expense of departmental autonomy. The Supreme Court has accepted presidential separation-of-powers claims over congressionalist arguments based on checks and balances in cases such as MYERS V. UNITED STATES (1926), which recognized presidential REMOVAL POWER; INS V. CHADHA (1983), which invalidated legislative vetoes of administrative acts; BUCKLEY V. VALEO (1976), in which the Court refused to recognize rule-making powers of officials not appointed in conformity with the appointments clause; and BOWSHER V. SYNAR (1986), which limited the power of the COMPTROLLER GENERAL to instruct the President to make certain expenditure cuts that might be required by a statute. While the High Court required judicial in camera inspection of presidential claims of EXECUTIVE PRIVILEGE in UNITED STATES V. NIXON (1974), a lower court sustained the claim of executive privilege against a congressional committee investigating crimes associated with the WATERGATE AFFAIR.

At times Congress has passed framework statutes that require the executive to report and wait before taking action (in matters such as arms sales) or that require presidential consultation with Congress before action is taken (as in the use of armed forces in hostilities). Alternatively, to ensure that lines of accountability are clear in NATIONAL SECURITY matters, the laws can require PRESIDENTIAL FINDINGS so that Presidents cannot later deny that actions (such as schemes to assassinate foreign leaders or destabilize and overthrow foreign governments) were taken without their knowledge. The finding requirement is designed to end the practice of plausible deniability, which shields top members of the administration from having to take responsibility for the consequences of their actions. Unfortunately, in many instances Presidents have not complied with either the spirit or the letter of framework legislation. They have argued that the WAR POWERS RESOLUTION (1973) is unconstitutional and have evaded its provisions. In the IRAN-CONTRA AFFAIR the INTELLIGENCE OVERSIGHT ACT (1980) was flouted: President Ronald Reagan issued findings orally or even retroactively, and no notification was ever given to Congress by the Director of Central Intelligence or the President that arms were being sold to Iran, leaving presidential accountability for major decisions in the affair subject to plausible deniability.

In spite of numerous attempts by Congress to legislate frameworks that provide for both collaborative decision making and procedures to prevent abuses of power, presidential legal and constitutional accountability remains weak. The Ethics in Government Act (1978) provides for the appointment of an INDEPENDENT COUNSEL to investigate and prosecute high-level government officials where it appears the DEPARTMENT OF JUSTICE might have a conflict of interest. The ATTORNEY GENERAL conducts a preliminary investigation and then may request appointment of independent counsel by a special panel of federal judges. The statute itself came under attack by Colonel Oliver North in the Iran-contra affair but was upheld by the Supreme Court in MORRISON V. OLSON (1988). But the difficulty in bringing presidential subordinates to justice was underlined by the dismissal of North's conviction by an appeals court on the grounds that his right to a fair trial had been prejudiced by congressional hearings into the Iran-contra affair. The effort to ensure the political accountability of the President before Congress and the American public had interfered with the subsequent attempts to provide for the legal accountability of the President's agents, and this pattern is likely to be repeated.

"All the officers of the government, from the highest to the lowest, are creatures of the law and are bound to obey it," Justice Samuel F. Miller said in *United States v. Lee* (1882). But while in office a President's accountability to the courts is minimal. Presidents take the language of Article I, Section 5, clause 7—that "judgment in cases of IMPEACHMENT shall not extend further than to removal from Office"—to mean that a President must be impeached and removed from office before he is subject to judicial sanctions. While federal judges can be indicted prior to being removed from office it is doubtful that such a precedent would apply to the President (unless he were charged with something like murder). The Wa-

tergate grand jury wished to indict President Richard M. Nixon for obstruction of justice, but special prosecutor Leon Jaworski thought it might not be upheld by the courts and had the jury settle instead for naming Nixon an unindicted co-conspirator.

In civil cases presidential immunity from suit is absolute. The Supreme Court in NIXON V. FITZGERALD (1982) ruled that the President has absolute immunity from civil damages liability for his official acts, an immunity that goes well beyond the qualified or functional immunity granted to other government officials. In its sweeping language the Court held that immunity attaches to the office of President, extends to the outer perimeters of the powers of that office, and includes all official acts, whether constitutionally mandated or not. Lawsuits, Chief Justice Warren Burger held, would violate separation of powers.

The impeachment clause makes the President accountable to Congress for "Treason, Bribery, and other High Crimes and Misdemeanors." The IMPEACHMENT OF ANDREW JOHNSON involved a debate about the meaning of "High Crimes and Misdemeanors," with Republicans arguing that abuse of power could be the standard for conviction and Democrats insisting that conviction required proof that laws of the United States had been violated. The same issues were revisited in the impeachment proceedings against Nixon, but this time the party positions switched: Democrats insisted that "usurpation or abuse of power or a serious breach of trust" would be an impeachable offense while Republicans followed Nixon, who argued that "a criminal offense on the part of the President is the requirement for impeachment." Nixon's resignation prior to impeachment by the House left these issues unsettled, though it seems in both cases that "abuse of power" was a sufficient standard to initiate impeachment proceedings.

The political and executive models of accountability, in which an energetic CHIEF EXECUTIVE takes decisive action and then holds himself accountable to the electorate, prevailed through most of the twentieth century. The model of constitutional accountability, which emphasizes protection against presidential abuses of power, seemed outdated until the Watergate crisis, when it became clear that some of the executive's decisive actions were designed to subvert electoral accountability itself, thus requiring what James Madison would have termed auxiliary precautions. Since then, reformers have divided, with some continuing to emphasize electoral and administrative accountability and doctrines of party and Cabinet government while others concentrate on strengthening institutional checks and balances and providing improved framework legislation to promote collaborative decision making, especially in national security affairs. Neither group, it should be noted, as yet has had much success.

BIBLIOGRAPHY

Committee on the Constitutional System. *Report and Recommendations of the Committee on the Constitutional System. A Bicentennial Analysis of the American Political Structure.* 1987. Pp. 1–20.

Cutler, Lloyd N. "To Form a Government." *Foreign Affairs* 59 (1980): 126–143.

Danielson, George. "Presidential Immunity from Criminal Prosecution." *Georgetown Law Journal* 63 (1975): 1065–1069.

Harriger, Katy J. *Independent Justice*: *The Federal Special Prosecutor in American Politics.* 1992.

Lindbeck, Kathryn. "Presidential Immunity—Supreme Court Attaches Absolute Immunity to the Presidential Office, *Nixon v. Fitzgerald*, 102 S. Ct. 2690." *Southern Illinois University Law Journal* (1983): 109–126.

Petracca, Mark P. "Proposals for Constitutional Reform: An Evaluation of the Committee on the Constitutional System." *Presidential Studies Quarterly* 20 (1990): 503–532.

Robinson, Donald, ed. *Reforming American Government: The Bicentennial Papers of the Committee on the Constitutional System.* 1985.

Wilson, Woodrow. "Cabinet Government in the United States." *International Review* 7 (1879): 146–163.

RICHARD M. PIOUS

ACHESON, DEAN (1893–1971), Secretary of State. Dean G. Acheson was born in Middletown, Connecticut, and attended Yale University and Harvard Law School. He clerked for Justice Louis D. Brandeis of the Supreme Court and in 1921 entered the Washington, D.C., firm of Covington, Burling and Rublee, with which he, when not in public office, was associated for the rest of his life. In 1933 he became Under Secretary of the Treasury but resigned over the decision of President Franklin D. Roosevelt to take the country off the gold standard. Roosevelt was miffed but understanding and later told friends that Acheson resigned like a gentleman. After the outbreak of WORLD WAR II, Acheson in 1941 accepted an assistant secretaryship in the State Department, taking such assignments as he could obtain, including congressional relations under Secretary Edward R. Stettinius, Jr., in 1944–1945. With the appointment of JAMES F. BYRNES as Secretary of State, Acheson's star quickly rose, as President Harry S. Truman needed someone to manage the department while Byrnes was out of the country (Byrnes traveled frequently). Truman became well acquainted with Acheson. The two men might have seemed opposites, and indeed were in background, but they re-

joiced in direct approaches to all problems and worked easily together. GEORGE C. MARSHALL replaced Byrnes as Secretary of State in 1947, and Acheson remained for half a year—the time of the announcement of the TRUMAN DOCTRINE and the MARSHALL PLAN.

On Marshall's resignation in early 1949, Acheson returned as Secretary of State and remained for the rest of the Truman administration. No secretary in the twentieth century, and perhaps from the beginning of the Republic, worked so closely with a President. When Senator Joseph R. McCarthy and other members of the Senate demanded Acheson's resignation, Truman refused. Acheson's affection for the President turned to devotion, and years later he dedicated his memoirs to Truman.

As Secretary of State Acheson gave first attention to European economic recovery and rearmament and steadily refused to make concessions to the Soviet Union. He maintained that one could not deal with the Soviets from a position of weakness and that only putting together a North Atlantic Treaty Organization military force of size and quality, achieved by the time he left office, could ensure European peace. In pursuing his NATO policy he would make no promises over German reunification; in 1952 the Soviets offered to reunify Germany if Germany were neutralized—that is, if all foreign troops were withdrawn—but Acheson would have none of it. The secretary had complete support of the President.

Like Truman, Acheson was thunderstruck by the outbreak of the KOREAN WAR. The President had given up on a solution for China, and like Acheson underrated what the Soviet Union and Communist China, which supported the North Koreans, might do. Both Truman and Acheson were surprised by Chinese intervention in the war. Both showed steel in steadying the jittery Far East commander, General Douglas MacArthur, and such United Nations allies as Great Britain.

Acheson and Truman agreed over what they considered the inconsequence of Latin America and disagreed, albeit with little discussion (for recognition occurred in 1948), over the independence of Israel and what it might mean for the Middle East.

During his years of retirement Acheson carried on a detailed correspondence with Truman, both men commiserating over the failure of national Democratic politics during the Dwight D. Eisenhower administration. They believed the thirty-fourth President a "captive hero," in the hands of businessmen and the military. In matters of foreign policy they beheld a dangerous drift toward force at just the time when the Soviets were becoming militarily dangerous because of possession of nuclear weapons and ballistic missiles.

Acheson became increasingly conservative, especially in regard to the Vietnam War, although in 1968, as an elder statesman, he advised President Lyndon Baines Johnson to get out of Vietnam. When the Democrats lost the national election that year, Acheson toyed with some sort of approach to President Richard M. Nixon, perhaps in hope of guiding his foreign policy.

To the end, Acheson was defiant of critics. His historical position is not yet clear, but he probably will rank with such illustrious predecessors as Hamilton Fish, John Hay, and Charles Evans Hughes. His successes came because of his close relationship with President Truman.

BIBLIOGRAPHY

Acheson, Dean. *Present at the Creation.* 1969.
Brinkley, Douglas. *Dean Acheson: The Cold War Years, 1953–71.* 1992.
McLellan, David S. *Dean Acheson.* 1976.
Smith, Gaddis. *Dean Acheson.* 1972.

ROBERT H. FERRELL

ACT OF STATE DOCTRINE. The Supreme Court expressed the act of state doctrine in *Underhill v. Hernandez* (1897) as follows:

> Every sovereign State is bound to respect the independence of every other sovereign State, and the courts of one country will not sit in judgment on the acts of the government of another done within its own territory. Redress of grievances by reason of such acts must be obtained through the means open to be availed of by sovereign powers as between themselves.

The Court restated the doctrine and gave it new vigor in 1964 in Banco Nacional de Cuba v. Sabbatino. In that case the Court gave effect to a nationalization by Cuba of properties of U.S. nationals without just compensation, though the expropriation was alleged to be in violation of international law.

In its effect, the act of state doctrine may be seen as a special principle of the law governing the conflict of laws. In circumstances in which a court in the United States would ordinarily apply and give effect to foreign law, the court is generally free not to do so where the foreign law contravenes U.S. (or local) public policy. The act of state doctrine, where it applies, requires the court to give effect to the laws of the foreign state regardless of any domestic public policy.

The Supreme Court established the act of state doctrine on its own authority, under an inherent judicial power to make rules for the guidance of the courts. The Court also declared the doctrine to be a federal principle binding on the courts of the states of the United States.

In *Sabbatino*, the Court identified the constitutional underpinnings of the doctrine as reflecting "a basic choice regarding the competence and function of the Judiciary and the National Executive in ordering our relationships with other members of the international community" and in making "decisions in the area of international relations." The Court saw the act of state doctrine as an expression of judicial deference to executive diplomacy [*see* Diplomat in Chief] and a reflection of doubt as to the competence of the judiciary to address issues of possible diplomatic sensitivity. For these reasons courts have commonly honored a "Bernstein letter" (deriving its appellation from *Bernstein v. Van Heyghen Freres, S.A.* [1947, 1949, 1954]), in which the executive branch declares that it has no objection to the court's refusing effect to an act of a foreign state in the particular case. However, in *First National City Bank of New York v. Banco Nacional de Cuba* (1972), a majority of the Justices declared that the doctrine was judicial policy and that the judiciary was not bound to follow executive dictate in the matter.

Lower courts have been unanimous in refusing to give effect to an act of a foreign state applied outside its territory. In 1984, the executive branch supported another exception asking the court not to apply the doctrine where the act of the foreign state violated a provision in a treaty with the United States; a court of appeals adopted that exception in *Kalamazoo Spice Extraction Co. v. Provisional Military Government of Socialist Ethiopia* (1984) but it has not been considered by the Supreme Court. Courts have also refused to apply the doctrine to acts of torture or other gross violations of human rights by foreign officials as in *Filartiga v. Pena Irala* (1980) and *Forti v. Suarez-Mason* (1987). In *Alfred Dunhill of London, Inc. v. Republic of Cuba* (1976), four Justices of the Supreme Court suggested that the act of state doctrine should not apply to acts of state of a commercial character, an exception akin to that recognized in the application of the doctrine of state sovereign immunity.

The act of state doctrine applies not only to legislative acts of foreign states but also to other state policies and state involvements. It applies only to acts of the state, not to those of foreign private persons or other entities. In *Kirkpatrick & Co. v. Environmental Tectonics Corp.* (1990), a case involving allegations of bribery in the awarding of Nigerian government contracts, the Supreme Court held that the act of state doctrine does not apply where the U.S. court is not required to rule directly on the validity of an act of state even if adjudication may require the court to impute improper motives to foreign officials and to establish that foreign officials had made an illegal contract.

The act of state doctrine is sometimes confused with the principle of state sovereign immunity. Both are based on considerations of respect for the independence and equality of states, but the doctrines are independent of each other and differ in important ways. Sovereign immunity is an undisputed principle of customary international law; the act of state doctrine is not a principle of international law but only of the law of the United States (though some other states have also adopted such a doctrine.) By the principle of sovereign immunity, a state cannot be sued in and is otherwise immune from the jurisdiction of courts of another state; the act of state doctrine applies whether or not the foreign state is itself a party to the case before the court. Act of state does not deny the court's jurisdiction but limits the scope of judicial inquiry and may direct the court as to how to decide the case or an issue before it.

The act of state doctrine has been a subject of controversy. At the time of *Sabbatino* (1964), the Johnson administration appeared to favor the act of state doctrine. Later administrations, however, tended to favor limitations and exceptions to the doctrine in response to business interests that wanted the opportunity to challenge the validity of foreign acts of state in U.S. courts rather than be relegated to the fruits of diplomatic negotiations. Some segments of the business community and of the bar have favored the doctrine, apparently fearing that its abolition would create uncertainty in trade and financial markets. Immediately after *Sabbatino*, Congress in the second HICKENLOOPER AMENDMENT declared the doctrine inapplicable to foreign acts confiscating properties of U.S. nationals without the required compensation unless the President determined that application of the doctrine in a particular case was required by the national interest. By implication Congress thereby gave legislative support to the judge-made act of state doctrine for all cases where the Hickenlooper Amendment does not apply.

[*See also* INTERNATIONAL LAW, PRESIDENT AND.]

BIBLIOGRAPHY

American Law Institute. *Restatement (Third) of the Foreign Relations Law of the United States.* 1987. Secs. 443–444.
Mooney, Eugene F. *Foreign Seizures: Sabbatino and the Act of State Doctrine.* 1967.

LOUIS HENKIN

ADAMS, ABIGAIL (1744–1818), First Lady, wife of John Adams. Although frequently absent from her husband's side while he was President (illness and family matters detained her in Massachusetts), Abigail Smith Adams, who was intellectually outstanding, was thought by her contemporaries to be highly influential in his presidency. Numerous letters between them attest to his reliance on her judgment, and both their biographers have concluded that she served as "minister without portfolio."

Although she spoke admiringly of MARTHA WASHINGTON's tenure as First Lady, Abigail Adams approached the job more aggressively. In many letters written to her relatives and friends, she lamented verbal attacks on her family, especially her son and her husband, and she favored legal constraints against making such disparaging criticisms. She complained about the pro-French bent of the opposition and leveled strong, personal attacks on her husband's critics. Her willingness to voice an opinion and her partisan views earned her both opponents and admirers. Ridiculed as "Mrs. President" by her husband's enemies, she was recognized by others as an appropriate model for strong women.

In November 1800, Abigail Adams moved with her husband to the newly constructed President's House in Washington. Although in her letters she criticized the building for its poor setting and its lack of comforts, nevertheless she followed those patterns set by her predecessor before moving in, thus helping to establish the President's House as a social and cultural center. On 1 January 1801, she opened the mansion for a public reception, and invited the Marine Band to perform, beginning a tradition that survived for more than a century and increased the President's accessibility to the public.

BIBLIOGRAPHY

Gelles, Edith B. "The Abigail Industry." *William and Mary Quarterly* 3d ser., 45 (1988): 656–683.
Levin, Phyllis Lee. *Abigail Adams.* 1987.
Smith, Page. *John Adams.* 2 vols. 1962–63.

BETTY BOYD CAROLI

ADAMS, JOHN (1735–1826), second President of the United States (1797–1801). In the first partisan presidential contest, Adams was chosen over Thomas Jefferson by three electoral votes to succeed George Washington. To ABIGAIL ADAMS he had privately described himself as "heir apparent," and Jefferson virtually agreed when he urged his friends to support Adams in the event of a tie vote on the simple grounds that Adams was senior to him. In 1796, neither Adams, clearly the choice of the Federalists, nor Jefferson, supported by the Democratic-Republicans, campaigned for election or made any effort to oppose the other. Adams's record after more than twenty years of public service was well known and had made him a logical successor to Washington.

Adams, who was born in the village of Braintree near Boston on 19 October 1735, was elected to the First Continental Congress in 1775; the next year he returned for the duration of the War of Independence. No delegate worked harder or gained a higher reputation for patriotism than Adams, whose service on fifty committees (twenty-five of which he chaired) won him honor and accolade as the "Atlas" or "Colossus" of the independence movement. Between 1778 and 1788 Adams was endowed with great trust when he was selected, first, as minister to negotiate peace with Great Britain and then to serve as the American minister to the Court of St. James's. His diplomatic appointments proved frustrating and lonely, however, for he lived for years apart from his beloved wife Abigail and their children John Quincy, Thomas, Charles, and Abby, and was constantly thwarted by the French foreign minister, who found Adams uncooperative, suspicious, and independent-minded. Adams made significant contributions to American success, however, both in treating with Britain and in securing a Dutch loan that kept the faltering Confederation government in Philadelphia in business.

Although largely overlooked by British officials he represented his country with dignity as the first American minister. After his European experience, Adams typically vacillated between exaggerating and denigrating his accomplishments. It was with great surprise that Adams found himself honored and praised on his return to Massachusetts. He was New England's candidate for high office in the new United States government in 1788, and even through the obscurity of his vice presidency under Washington and the turmoil of his own presidency Adams managed to retain the loyalty of his region.

Political Philosophy. By 1796 Adams's reputation as a political thinker and writer was well established. No one among the nation's founders was more widely read in history and politics; none had published as much. Adams was the brain trust of the patriot faction during the prerevolutionary struggle, but it was as a member of the Second Continental Congress, when his pamphlet *Thoughts on Government* circulated as a blueprint of republican government, that Adams gained a wide reputation for his political views.

In 1779, Adams was elected to the Massachusetts constitutional convention. He dominated the committee charged with preparing the new state constitution and himself largely drafted the document. In these early writings Adams reflected nearly orthodox Whig positions. He favored a bicameral legislature, with a popularly elected lower house and a property-based upper house. He stressed the value of a strong executive armed with the veto power somewhat earlier than most of his colleagues in public life and was considered a republican in every way until 1787, when his three-volume *Defence of the Constitutions* was published.

Adams scholars see this learned but repetitious work as proof that Adams had grown increasingly critical of popular government during his years in Europe. Adams's contemporaries would have agreed with this assessment. The *Defence* was a serious attack on what he considered to be the simplistic ideas of government represented by Pennsylvania's unicameral, assembly-dominated constitution. Adams advocated CHECKS AND BALANCES, the representation of aristocratic property holders in an upper house of great power and prestige, and a very powerful executive armed with an absolute veto. Adams denied that he was any less republican than the members of the Philadelphia CONSTITUTIONAL CONVENTION whose deliberations he had rushed to influence, but suspicions lingered despite his protestations. In 1791 he published a series of essays, *Discourses on Davila*, which warned the world against the kind of extremism the French had shown in eliminating their powerful monarchy and aristocracy. His insistence that France would turn to a military tyranny before its revolutionary zeal was extinguished linked him with ALEXANDER HAMILTON and the Federalists, who in reaction against the revolution in France supported an increasingly pro-British orientation.

Like other public men of his generation, Adams was opposed to political parties. Perhaps because of his isolation from the play of politics imposed by his diplomatic and vice presidential posts, he was never during Washington's two administrations an insider in Federalist ranks. He was known to have opposed both the BANK OF THE UNITED STATES and the assumption by the new government of the revolutionary war debt. His main objection to Hamiltonian economic policy was that it spawned speculation, which Adams, like a good Jeffersonian, labeled "stock jobbing," or gambling. Adams's writings, however, reveal no sustained economic thinking whatsoever. In his disapproval of the new financiers—a "monied aristocracy" in Adams's parlance—and in his fondness and respect for agricultural pursuits Adams was in harmony with the Democratic-Republicans.

Adams's administrative principles, however, were decidedly more Hamiltonian than Jeffersonian. These were a belief in a powerful executive independent of faction or party and armed with the veto and control over armed forces and foreign affairs and a belief in the necessity of giving the propertied class a special place in the legislative process lest they intrigue against popular liberties. But, unlike other leaders of the party with which he would be forever linked, he never became cynical or bitter against popularly elected representative bodies. In this last regard, Adams has undoubtedly been misunderstood, for the rock-hard foundation of his system was neither monarchical executive power nor aristocratic hegemony (with checks upon it) but rather honest, free, and frequent elections that truly reflected the popular will. For Adams, even more than for Washington, loyalty to, dependence on, or consultation with a political faction or party was forbidden. He was proud to state in March 1797 that he came to the presidency without obligation to anyone, and, like Jefferson (who may have meant it), Adams had declared his indifference to the election's outcome. If he was bitter that his ELECTORAL COLLEGE victory was by so slim a margin, he did not show it and appeared to commence his duties without rancor.

He would have had good cause for anger. Adams was well aware that Hamilton had again, as in 1792, attempted to deflect enough electoral votes from him to elect a more pliable man (in 1796 Hamilton favored Thomas Pinckney of South Carolina), but outwardly at least Adams maintained cordial relations with Hamilton and Hamilton's friends for the first three years of his administration. Contrary to his reputation for jealousy and impetuosity, President Adams exercised extraordinary forbearance in dealing with those who contested his will. Whether this was a reflection of deliberate dissimulation or of benevolence is an intriguing question. Adams believed that politics was a science, and he was sure that he had discovered many of the laws of this science—for example, that to be effective the executive must mask his intentions, must arrive at decisions independently and secretly, and must act with suddenness so as to immobilize his opponents. It has been argued that Adams acted erratically, often contrary to what he had led others to expect, because he dreaded face-to-face confrontations with men whom he mistrusted and disliked, particularly Hamilton and Benjamin Franklin, but his pattern of often acting in direct opposition to advice that he had requested, debated, and seemingly accepted may well be explained as a reflection of his political science.

Presidency. The major crises of Adams's administration originated in foreign relations. He maintained strong control over foreign policy, and his decisions have been judged wise even though he utterly failed to work with the FEDERALIST PARTY or to reach accommodation with those who might have assured his reelection in 1800.

As a major neutral maritime nation the United States was caught between the demands of the world's strongest naval power, Great Britain, and the volatile French Republic, which pressed for recognition of rights and privileges guaranteed under the Franco-American alliance of 1778. By the terms of their commercial treaty France and the United States upheld a narrow definition of wartime contraband under the doctrine of freedom of the seas. Britain justified its practice of constant search and seizure of other nations' vessels by adhering to a very broad definition of contraband. In 1794 Washington had sent Chief Justice JOHN JAY to London to settle differences that, had they been left to fester, could have provoked war. While peace was momentarily assured and the means to settle mutual claims established, the price was humiliating for the United States. France and its partisans in the United States viewed JAY'S TREATY as an abject surrender to brute force, an abandonment of free-trade principles, and ample justification for working to unseat the American administration. The immediate consequence was French intervention in the presidential election of 1796 on the side of the Democratic-Republicans. In November the French minister to the United States, Pierre Adet, announced the suspension of diplomatic relations, and as Pennsylvanians went to the polls he published announcements that the election of Jefferson would restore cordial relations between the world's two foremost republics. In the meantime orders went out to French naval vessels and privateers to begin attacks on American shipping. These orders became known soon after the election.

In the two-month interval between these events and his inauguration Adams made clear that he wanted to renew his friendship with Jefferson, which had been close during their European missions of the late 1780s. Adams suggested appointing either Jefferson or James Madison to serve the new administration as minister plenipotentiary to France. Jefferson refused consideration but promised to approach Madison informally on the matter of a French mission. Federalists learned of these manifestations of political independence and were nervous. Adams alarmed them further in his inaugural address by emphasizing his desire to settle differences with France as rapidly as possible and by alluding to his friendly feelings for the people of France. This promising rapprochement ended abruptly when, on 16 May 1797, Adams called Congress into joint session to make the stunning announcement that France had broken off commercial relations once more, had ordered American Minister CHARLES COTESWORTH PINCKNEY to leave Paris, and would not treat officially until the United States had addressed French grievances arising from the Jay treaty. Adams denounced France and requested that Congress authorize defense measures for harbor fortification, for the purchase of a dozen vessels that could be armed and readied at once for naval duty, for the completion of the three frigates under construction, for the mustering of additional regular army regiments, and for authorization to call a reserve army into being in the event of an invasion threat.

Conflicts with Hamilton. Federalists celebrated while Democratic-Republicans sought an explanation for this dramatic and unsettling reversal in the influence of Adams's department heads. Jefferson had earlier guessed that Adams must have faced opposition in considering Madison for a French mission since it was never again proposed. In fact, Adams had been confronted with threats of resignation by his three principal advisers if he insisted on Madison. Adams did not take up the challenge, backed down, and retained all four of the Cabinet-level advisers appointed by Washington. One of them, Attorney General Charles Lee of Virginia, served Adams well, but the three department heads, Timothy Pickering of Massachusetts (State), Oliver Wolcott, Jr., of Connecticut (Treasury), and James McHenry of Maryland (War), were devoted to Hamilton, to whom in varying degrees they were wont to turn for advice on policy matters. To his eventual detriment Adams retained them despite warnings from friends of their divided loyalties. He did so, however, for reasons that to him were compelling. First, he was opposed to rotation on principle, for it implied acceptance of either a PATRONAGE, or spoils, system or loyalty to party or faction. Second, he was well aware that Washington had suffered embarrassment in trying to persuade strong political figures to take Cabinet posts. Jefferson, Hamilton, and EDMUND RANDOLPH had all gone deeply into debt trying to live and entertain on the modest salaries they were paid. No one of consequence wanted the positions. Third, Adams viewed his advisers with polite regard but with little awe. In his eyes they were senior clerks who would do his bidding as required, carry out routine duties, and who, when asked, would render advice that he was prepared to overlook. Adams on more than one occasion stated bluntly that he knew more of the world than did any of them. Finally, it is entirely likely that Adams kept Pickering, Wolcott, and McHenry on rather than split with the Hamiltonians. In response to

one warning about Hamilton's influence over the Cabinet, Adams simply replied that they were as loyal as he wished. For nearly three years he was careful not to confront Hamilton directly, and for the first two years there was little reason to do so, for both the President and Hamilton believed in a policy of defiance and readiness while avoiding a declared war. Hamilton urged the department heads to support the appointment of a prominent Democratic-Republican for a new French mission on the grounds that its likely failure would further weaken the opposition.

The XYZ affair. In speaking of peace with honor and in calling for an arms buildup, Adams won the ardent support of Federalists, many of whom assumed that a call for war would follow. When he nominated John Marshall of Virginia and Francis Dana, chief justice of Massachusetts, to join Pinckney in France the mission was uniformly Federalist and showed no sensitivity to the doubts and suspicions of Jefferson and his colleagues. When Dana declined appointment, however, Adams named ELBRIDGE GERRY of Massachusetts to replace him over the strong objections of his Cabinet advisers, for Gerry's opposition to Hamiltonian measures was well known. He was nonpartisan in his own view but a strong supporter of his old friend Adams. Once the commissioners had been instructed, Adams left the capital, Philadelphia, for his Braintree, Massachusetts, farm. Federalist Senators complained that he was showing irresolution in the Gerry appointment and in his failure to remain in Philadelphia with them as they debated and passed bills enlarging the army well beyond what the President had requested.

When Congress convened in early December, no authoritative word had been received from the American emissaries, but rumors circulated that the mission had stalled. Adams once more sounded a note of defiance in his speech opening the session and asked that the defense program he had advocated be carried through. The most that Congress would authorize, however, was a bill allowing the arming of merchant vessels, which carried only with the tie-breaking vote of the Speaker of the House. Faced with having to vote for taxes to pay for defense, Congress drew back. By the end of 1797 no majority had developed for an aggressive response to French bullying.

The situation was radically altered in March 1798, when the President announced the failure of the mission and the humiliation suffered by the envoys in the process. The French foreign minister Talleyrand-Périgord had refused to receive the Americans officially, had contacted them through agents described in the dispatches simply as Messrs. X, Y, and Z, and had demanded a guarantee of a large loan to France and a handsome under-the-table advance for Talleyrand himself as the price of negotiation. Vice President Jefferson testified that the rumor of his own complicity in the so-called XYZ affair had already begun to circulate hours after the announcement from the President. Several days later he noted that the antiadministration Philadelphia newspaper *Aurora* was likely to close down as sales and subscriptions fell sharply. Republican Congressmen packed and left for home. By contrast Adams and the Federalists enjoyed the praise and support of thousands. Hamiltonians now saw Adams as a distinguished patriot and statesman. A report from Boston, which gave the President great satisfaction, testified that at a meeting of Federalist leaders he had been praised as having "immortalized himself."

In the spring of 1798 resolutions of public support from civic groups and private organizations flooded into Philadelphia and were presented to Adams. He responded to them with energy and passion, making each reply specific and writing the drafts himself. That France was in the grip of corrupt men whose sympathizers in the United States were blind to the truth was a repeated theme. In at least one instance, Adams suggested that those who persisted in excusing France might prefer to join the French in the event of an invasion. The outburst of resentment in March grew into hysteria by summer.

The 1790s have frequently been viewed by historians as a decade of deep suspicions and unparalleled partisanship, "An Age of Passion," as one scholar labeled his study. For thousands the XYZ crisis seemed to come as a welcome release from the tensions that the French Revolution had produced in America. That France had proclaimed republican principles was attractive to Americans, but France's denunciation of religion and use of terror as a weapon against its own citizens was abhorrent. Slowly it became clear to many Americans that, like it or not, Britain stood as the champion of the ordered liberty they themselves espoused.

In 1798 Americans' ambivalence over the conflict between their rejected motherland and an alien republic gave way to ardent support for their own country. Suspicions aroused by those who persisted in excusing France hardened into open displays of hostility. In Philadelphia and other coastal towns streetfighting between supporters and opponents of France broke out, incited, according to Federalists, by mobs of recent Irish immigrants. During June a dozen ships carrying frightened French nationals left Philadelphia. The President became so alarmed that he ordered arms delivered to the executive mansion for the use of his own household. In the midst of turmoil Adams drafted a war message but then thought better of it. As July approached, many in the Senate and House, without prompting from the President, pressed for debate on a war resolution and hoped to produce a declaration on Bastille Day (14 July).

Preparations for war. Without declaring war the Federalist-dominated Fifth Congress prepared for one, going well beyond the defense measures the President had suggested. The treaties of alliance with France were abrogated, the Department of the Navy and Marine Corps were established, authorization was given to increase the regular army by twelve additional regiments (three times what Adams had asked for), and a reserve force of thirty thousand men was authorized to be called up when and if the President declared a national emergency. Intent on intimidating their political opponents the Federalist majority adopted the ALIEN AND SEDITION ACTS, which increased the naturalization period from five to fourteen years, authorized the executive to deport aliens considered dangerous to NATIONAL SECURITY (and in a national emergency to deport all aliens), and made it a crime punishable by fine and imprisonment to defame the government of the United States. Later, in retirement, Adams attributed the harsh program of the 1798 crisis to the most extreme of the Federalists, but while it was true that he drew criticism for making almost no use of the alien controls granted him and less use of the Sedition Act than some extreme Federalists believed was warranted, Adams showed no disapproval of these laws. He did much to create the hostile atmosphere in which they were conceived and tolerated, and the government prosecuted fifteen editors, of whom ten were convicted of seditious libel. Adams never asked for the Alien and Sedition Acts, but he acquiesced in them.

The ardent leaders of the House and Senate, Congressmen Joshua Coit of Connecticut, Robert Goodloe Harper of South Carolina, and Senator James Lloyd of Maryland, gave the President the naval force he had repeatedly requested, but in legislating what amounted to a very large military establishment they followed the desires of Hamilton, not Adams. The entire program was shockingly expensive. Between 1798 and 1800 the federal budget doubled to $12 million. Taxes were levied on property, including slaves, and for immediate needs the Treasury in 1798 was authorized to borrow $7 million at 6 percent interest. While some Democratic-Republicans supported the defense program and voted for heavy taxes, this was essentially a Federalist financing scheme. Adams was quick to object to expenditures of such magnitude, predicting their unpopularity, and Jefferson, taking comfort where he could, wrote that the XYZ "fever" would soon be cured by the effects of taxes, especially those that came to be known as stamp and window taxes.

In the summer of 1798 the President and the Hamiltonian Federalists developed serious policy differences. For the first time since Adams had taken office the antagonism that he and Hamilton had long cultivated became central to presidential decisions. Neither Hamilton nor the President favored a declaration of war, neither opposed the Alien and Sedition Acts, and both favored vigorous defense of national rights and sovereignty, but their ideas of what constituted an effective armaments program differed fundamentally.

Adams had had no military experience and turned at once to former President Washington for aid and comfort. He went so far as to admit that if it were possible he would gladly resign in favor of his predecessor during the emergency and offered Washington virtually carte blanche in military matters if he would come out of retirement and take command. With great reluctance Washington consented but horrified Adams when he insisted that his serving was to be contingent on Hamilton's appointment as second-in-command. Adams had already made clear his intention of ranking the general officers below Washington according to the seniority they had at the end of the War of Independence, but in Washington's view Henry Knox and Benjamin Lincoln were too old; he needed a younger man to take over the daily duties and said he would resign if his wishes were not heeded.

Hamilton had made it clear to his political friends that he wanted an active and prominent role in developing the new army, and Adams and Washington found out quickly that most leading Federalists favored Hamilton's appointment. Their ardor was fed by a breathtaking vision of new possibilities that Hamilton brashly promoted. The stakes were high. From Madrid, London, and Paris came rumors that France would force Spain to cede the Floridas and Louisiana. It was as clear in 1798 as it would be to Jefferson five years later that a revival of French imperial ambitions in North America would force the United States into a close official or unofficial alliance with Britain, an event much to be desired in Hamilton's scheme. RUFUS KING, the American minister in London and a former Senator and a close friend of Hamilton's, advised the President and Secretary of State that possibilities of cooperation with Great Britain in such a partnership were being encouraged by the king's ministers. In July, Robert Liston, Britain's

minister to the United States, journeyed to Adams's farm to press the advantages of pursuing an understanding—the opportunity to acquire sugar-producing Caribbean islands for Britain and the Floridas and the Mississippi Valley for the United States.

Rejection of alliance with Britain. Adams clearly was tempted but ultimately decided against the alliance. The scheme assumed that American energies and resources would concentrate on a military buildup and leave the United States dependent on the British navy for protection of its shipping. Adams pointed out that Britain had made peace with France before and might well do so again, leaving the United States without an effective naval shield. He also made an issue of morality; the United States had only recently settled its differences with Spain and had no justification for invading its territories. And what was to be said to those who pointed out that as between French bullying and British bullying there was little to choose? British seizures of American cargoes and, above all, the policy of impressment were very sore points. The most humiliating incident of the so-called QUASI-WAR WITH FRANCE was actually a British attack on an American naval vessel, the sloop *Baltimore*, in November 1798. The President was intent upon a swift deployment of naval vessels in the Caribbean, where France was most vulnerable to American power. His new Secretary of the Navy, Benjamin Stoddert, a former merchant, was proving to be hardworking and efficient, and the flow of letters between them in the summers of 1798 and 1799 clearly indicate that Adams had opted against dependence on British seapower. He directed naval officers to cooperate with their British counterparts, but he would not be pressured into an alliance. Soon after his return to Philadelphia in the fall of 1798, he bluntly told McHenry that, in any contest between the army and the navy over priorities, he would side with Stoddert and the navy.

Adams's reasons for rejecting the British alliance and for opposing the Hamiltonian Federalists with increasing directness at the end of 1798 centered on Hamilton's ambitions and Adams's fear of having a large standing army under Hamilton's command. Despite great pressure to settle the seniority question, Adams stalled until September before commissioning Hamilton as major general ahead of Knox and Lincoln, and he waited to issue the necessary authority to recruit the new forces for five months more. By February 1799 it became difficult to recruit, however, since by then, the President had nearly destroyed the reasons for the army's existence. Also, by the time Hamilton received his commission, news of Nelson's great victory over the French at the Battle of the Nile had reached American shores. Adams and the Federalists in Congress had maintained that the enlarged army was to be raised as a protection against a potential French invasion, but Nelson had removed any possibility of a French invasion of the United States.

If a large, expensive force was to be raised and maintained it could be justified and made palatable to the people only so long as war remained a possibility. Hamilton and his close circle wished to keep that possibility alive as long as possible, perhaps even until the presidential election of 1800. In the interval a large military force could prove useful. Adams, however, gradually became alarmed. His study of history had left him convinced that standing armies invariably threaten popular liberties. He acted to destroy the military establishment because he believed that it threatened to become the cause of internal violence. Repeatedly, he explained the decisions he made in 1799 and 1800 as dictated by the need to avert civil war.

Hamilton's political views were well known. Ever since the Constitutional Convention of 1787 he had admitted his preference for monarchical and aristocratic safeguards against the power and sovereignty of the majority. He had never been discreet in his critique of American republicanism, which in his view required a constant check that only a powerful executive willing to make use of the armed forces could provide. He had persuaded Washington to move with overwhelming force against tax evaders during the WHISKEY REBELLION of 1794. In 1798, as Virginia and its satellite, Kentucky, raised serious objection to the legality of the Alien and Sedition Acts in their famous STATES' RIGHTS resolutions, Hamilton became convinced that the time to assert the authority of the central government and to weaken that of the states was ripe. When the Virginia legislature provided revenue for the purchase of arms at the same time he saw it as provocation as well as proof. He challenged the Federalist leadership to seize an opportunity to create a stronger Union, to vastly extend its borders, and to subdue their Democratic-Republican opponents—invariably described in Federalist correspondence as "Jacobins" or "mobocrats." In January 1799 he audaciously laid out his proposals to the new Speaker and the recently retired Speaker of the House of Representatives: strengthen the federal courts, make more use of the Sedition Act, move the Army into the south (toward the borders of the Spanish territories), and, as he phrased it in writing to former Speaker Jonathan Dayton, "put Virginia to the test of resistance" and, finally, divide the large southern states into smaller ones.

Whether Hamilton would have carried out these plans had he been given the opportunity and whether he genuinely believed that Jefferson, Madison, and their allies were threatening the integrity of the Union cannot be answered with certainty. His closest friends believed that, as one of them afterward stated, Hamilton was convinced that "the great crisis of the Union had arrived." Adams was convinced that Hamilton was prepared to take advantage of the situation to achieve his own ends, and by the end of 1798 he resolved to oppose him. Adams threatened to resign the presidency, turning it over to Jefferson; he procrastinated giving necessary orders; he nominated scores of field-grade officers—including AARON BURR and other recognized Democratic-Republicans—for commissions; and he let it be known that he was open to the possibility of renewing discussions with France. As he said to Attorney General Charles Lee, he might be overwhelmed by "combinations of Senators, generals, and heads of departments" and even forced from office, but he would first see what the powers of the presidency enabled him to do.

Resumption of relations with France. Even as the President was stirring public indignation against France in the summer of 1798 he was also listening to the firsthand report of John Marshall, the first of the three envoys to return from Paris. He learned that French behavior toward the United States was not unique. The new government of the Directory was notoriously venal and pinched for funds. Military successes had at the same time produced a heady arrogance as one after another of France's small neighbors became satellite states. In effect, Marshall suggested, Talleyrand had overplayed his hand, was clearly surprised at the vehemence of the American reaction, and in persuading Elbridge Gerry to remain longer in Paris was not only attempting to exploit American political divisions but was also trying to reopen negotiations. Adams was impressed, and even as he once more called for defense measures in conveying Marshall's report to Congress, he mentioned the possibility of renewing diplomatic relations. Friends and political opponents alike noted the belligerent nature of Adams's message. Overlooked as window dressing was the statement that he would not send another envoy unless assured that the envoy would be treated "as the representative of a great, free, respected, and independent nation."

During the fall and early winter of 1798-1799 the President and the Secretary of State received reliable communications from Europe that Talleyrand and the French government wished to settle differences with the United States. Returning home, Gerry was at first spurned by Adams as well as by Pickering, but in face-to-face sessions with the President at Braintree Gerry convinced him of his own good intentions and of Talleyrand's desire to find a way of apologizing that was more convincing than his insistence that "X," "Y," and "Z" had acted without his knowledge. Massachusetts Senator Harrison Otis, a Hamiltonian, gave Adams the testimonial of a trusted business associate in Paris that French authorities wanted a settlement. Dispatches from William Vans Murray, American minister at The Hague, described overtures from Talleyrand through Louis André Pichon, the French chargé, that indicated a reversal of policy toward the United States. And letters arrived from John Quincy Adams, minister to Prussia, that testified to the reliability of the Pichon-Murray discussions as a reflection of French intentions. Notably, the President in reply urged his son to write to him at length and to send his letters by private conveyance but to be guarded in his reports to Pickering. On the eve of his return to Philadelphia in November, Adams relayed Murray's reports, noted that he was impressed with them, and asked his secretaries to debate the merits of reopening negotiations or of declaring war before he arrived to consult with them. He enclosed a list of candidates for a second mission for them to consider.

The discussions Adams held with his Cabinet in late November appear to have been the most extensive of his presidency. McHenry urged that in his December message the President admit his deep concern for the future of the Spanish borderlands, but with this exception the advice of his three Hamiltonian secretaries and of Stoddert and Lee was uniformly to maintain the status quo, neither to negotiate nor to declare war. Pickering was not opposed to war; he simply believed that the public was not ready to support it. Wolcott at once asked Hamilton to prepare a response to the President's questions, but it is not clear whether he acted only in his own behalf or in that of his colleagues as well. Hamilton's formula, as Wolcott conveyed it largely verbatim, was to reject discussions with France until France took the initiative by sending a special envoy to Philadelphia.

On 8 December, however, Adams in his annual address repeated what he had stated previously, that he would reopen discussions only with assurances of good conduct by France and that in the meantime defense preparations would continue. A month later, contrary again to the advice of his secretaries, Adams sent Gerry's reports of his discussions with Talleyrand to Congress, a dramatic gesture considering Federalist disdain for a man many regarded as a traitor. In doing this Adams reflected the decision he had apparently

already made: as far as he was concerned, Talleyrand had apologized and had submitted to Adams's sole demand, for a dispatch from Murray had arrived that relayed Talleyrand's assurance to Pichon that a new American negotiator would be received as representing "a free, powerful, and independent nation." On 15 February 1799 Adams announced that France had rescinded its decree authorizing capture of American merchant ships, and on 18 February, without giving anyone prior notice, he sent to the Senate the nomination of William Murray to serve as minister plenipotentiary to negotiate with France.

Adams's sudden announcement astonished friend and enemy alike. The Hamiltonians, including Secretary of State Pickering, protested loudly that they had been misled, that Adams had acted insanely and without cause, that he had sacrificed political advantage as well as national honor, and that he had acted entirely alone. While Adams had always stated that new negotiations were possible, he had coupled the statement with renewed demands for defense measures so that his posture seemed more aggressive than pacific. Clearly he intended to shock the political world on 18 February. His reason for doing so was not spelled out: was it because he wished to avoid further acrimony, because he was following his administrative precepts, or because he wished to throw down a dramatic challenge to the ardent Hamiltonians? *Why* he did it is clear even if the reason for acting in such secrecy is not. He would later defend his peace decision as having been disinterested and as the most important of his long career—"a diamond in my crown," as he immodestly insisted. His explanation was simply that the threat of civil war had grown dangerous and that the best means open to quash it was to destroy the army's raison d'être. He argued that there were many signs that the people were growing tired of the talk of war and the reality of taxes. And what he did not admit openly was that he had received a letter from George Washington conveying a notice of Talleyrand's good intentions, which Washington had recently received; Washington's letter ended with the brief comment that people appeared weary of war measures.

Evidence that Adams's decision was influenced by concern over internal unrest rather than by considerations of diplomacy is provided by his decisions after 18 February. When a delegation of leading Federalists came to him to argue that Murray was too young and inexperienced for the diplomatic role Adams wanted him to play—an attempt, as Adams interpreted it, to delay the negotiations—he listened and agreed to their request that older, more trustworthy men be added to the delegation. He named Governor William R. Davie of North Carolina and Chief Justice Oliver Ellsworth, both of them acceptable to his critics, but he made no move to prepare instructions for their departure before he left for Massachusetts where he would remain with his very ill wife from May well into October. George Cabot, of the so-called Essex Junto, an influential Boston Federalist group, called on Adams and found him angry and argumentative. He defended his decision, complained that high-toned Federalists were attempting to dictate to him, and predicted that public support would prove him wise. For a time it looked as if he might be correct. Spring elections in 1799 produced an astonishing crop of Federalist supporters in Virginia, North Carolina, South Carolina, and Georgia. Election returns in New York and in Massachusetts could also be seen as reflecting approval of administration policies and disapproval of pro-French, states' rights Democratic-Republicanism. Gradually, a significant group of Federalist leaders, including Marshall and Otis, began openly to support the President. Yet he made no move against the Hamiltonians or Pickering, McHenry, and Wolcott, whose anguish over his second mission was clear. To the contrary, he showed interest in arguments put forward by Pickering that the overthrow of the Directory in France by a group backed by Napoleon Bonaparte's army had created such confusion as to justify delaying the mission. Adams concurred.

The President's primary concern in the summer of 1799 was with naval affairs. His correspondence with Secretary of the Navy Stoddert was detailed and frequent, heavier in volume than all Adams's other correspondence combined. His policy of armed resistance was at last nearing completion. In early September he approved final orders to the commanders of the four American squadrons in Caribbean waters off French islands. There, American power was effectively concentrated to produce maximum pressure on France to respect American rights.

In late September Adams prepared to journey to Trenton, New Jersey, where government offices had moved during Philadelphia's yellow-fever season. Stoddert and Attorney General Lee urged his return so that he might deal directly with attempts to postpone the mission to France indefinitely. They made it clear that Adams's three senior department heads were deeply involved. This obvious case of insubordination justified dismissal, but Adams instead showed no hostility; he met for long discussions with them and Major General Hamilton, who argued that the possibility of a Bourbon restoration as well as the disfavor of Great Britain at the prospect of American negotiations with France ought to justify postponement. Adams

dismissed such arguments out of hand and immediately afterwards worked with his Cabinet on the wording of final instructions for Ellsworth and Davie. With the same unexpected suddenness that had marked the Murray nomination, Adams ordered the peace envoys to sail for France in two weeks, leaving Hamilton and Pickering to complain bitterly of his rashness.

With the martial spirit of the country rapidly diminishing, the Navy secure at its Caribbean stations, and the mission en route to France the significant work of Adams's administration was complete. Almost as an afterthought (it seemed), McHenry's resignation was accepted and Pickering's demanded as soon as election returns from New York in May 1800 revealed that the Federalists had been defeated there, guaranteeing the Republicans that state's electoral vote. Wolcott, who for months had been complaining of military expenses, was spared the President's ire. Later, he would be rewarded by appointment to the federal bench. John Marshall succeeded Pickering, and Samuel Dexter, a moderate Federalist from Massachusetts, replaced McHenry.

The Ellsworth mission received a warm welcome from a new French government dominated by Napoleon. Napoleon instructed his brother, Joseph Bonaparte, the chief French negotiator, and Talleyrand, to reach an amicable understanding with the United States. The Treaty of Alliance of 1778 was officially ended by the Convention of Mortefontaine, but the issues that had plagued the administrations of Washington and Adams were mostly just swept under the rug and would reemerge five years later for Jefferson and Madison. The Senate at first rejected the convention but accepted it a year later when it was resubmitted by President Jefferson.

Finally, one may ask whether John Adams, largely outside and isolated from the party system that took firm shape during his administration, accomplished anything of note. Or was he, as Hamilton charged, an obstructionist without an understanding of realities? The response rests upon our judgment of Hamilton's power and the seriousness of his intention when he challenged the President's leadership. Over the ensuing twenty-five years Adams repeatedly argued that he had destroyed a dangerous threat to the nation's internal peace. He lived to renew his friendship with Jefferson and to see his son chosen President before his death on 4 July 1826.

BIBLIOGRAPHY

Brown, Ralph A. *The Presidency of John Adams.* 1975.
Dauer, Manning J. *The Adams Federalists.* 1953.
DeConde, Alexander. *The Quasi-War.* 1966.

Howe, John R. *The Changing Political Thought of John Adams.* 1966.
Kohn, Richard H. *Eagle and Sword.* 1975.
Kurtz, Stephen G. *The Presidency of John Adams.* 1957.
McDonald, Forrest. *Alexander Hamilton.* 1979.
Miller, John C. *The Federalist Era.* 1960.
Shaw, Peter. *The Character of John Adams.* 1976.
Smith, James M. *Freedom's Fetters.* 1956.
Smith, Page. *John Adams.* 1962.
Stinchcombe, William. *The X,Y,Z Affair.* 1980.

STEPHEN G. KURTZ

ADAMS, JOHN QUINCY (1767–1848), sixth President of the United States (1825–1829). Recognized historically as perhaps the nation's greatest Secretary of State (1817–1825), Adams was also the only President who subsequently resumed public life as a member of Congress, where for seventeen more years he remained a leading proponent of national as opposed to the developing sectional interests.

Early Career. The eldest son of President John Adams, John Quincy Adams was born at Braintree, Massachusetts, and reared amid the political controversy of the American Revolution. When his father was sent to France as a negotiator for the new nation in 1778, John Quincy Adams accompanied him, attended schools in Paris and Holland, and served as secretary to Francis Dana during negotiations in Saint Petersburg and to the elder Adams during the framing of the Treaty of Paris. He returned to America in 1785, graduated from Harvard College, read law, and set up practice in Boston in 1790.

Despite his youth he was appointed minister to the Hague in 1794. He was transferred to Berlin in 1797, but following his father's failure to win reelection in 1800 young Adams resumed legal practice in Boston. He was elected to the Massachusetts senate as a Federalist in 1801 and sought election to Congress as an independent the following year. Although defeated in his congressional bid, he was named to the United States Senate in 1803. There his independence in voting to support the LOUISIANA PURCHASE and the EMBARGO ACT following the British attack on the *Chesapeake* so angered Massachusetts political leaders that they voted to replace him. When in 1809 he then accepted appointment by the Jeffersonian Republican President James Madison as minister to Saint Petersburg, he was widely denounced for apostasy.

Adams became an intermediary in Tsar Alexander I's efforts to effect peace between the United States and Britain during the WAR OF 1812. While that intercession was rejected, it led to direct negotiations at Ghent, with Adams as one of the American commissioners. There his proposal to extend British naviga-

tion rights on the Mississippi River in exchange for American fishing rights off Newfoundland was sharply opposed by the Kentuckian HENRY CLAY in a dispute that split the American delegation. The resulting TREATY OF GHENT deferred settlement of both issues. The commercial convention, negotiated by the same commissioners at London in 1815, proved similarly unsatisfactory to Adams when it failed to gain American access to trade with the British West Indies.

Secretary of State. Transferred as minister to London in 1815, Adams was recalled two years later to become Secretary of State. In that office he achieved agreements with Great Britain in 1818 that granted the United States access to the Newfoundland fisheries, established general boundaries between Canada and the United States, and provided for joint occupation of the Oregon Country. In 1819 he induced the Spanish to cede the Floridas and to define the western boundary of the Louisiana Purchase—the latter action entailing American relinquishment of vague claims to Texas and incurring further criticism of Adams by Clay and his western supporters. This opposition was heightened when, in an effort to induce reluctant Spanish authorities to ratify the treaty, Adams opposed recognizing the independence of the newly formed Latin American republics, which Clay had long championed.

With the ratification of the treaty with Spain completed, however, Adams extended recognition to the new Latin American states and adopted a policy setting forth the leadership of the United States as guardian in closing the New World to further foreign colonization. Enunciated by President James Monroe in his annual message of 1823, this MONROE DOCTRINE established the concept of two spheres, with that of the West committed to republican government in contrast to the monarchies of Europe. At the same time, it renounced any desire on the part of the United States to interfere with Europe's existing colonies or to intervene in Europe's internal affairs.

The Election of 1824. As Monroe's presidency neared its end, three CABINET members—Adams, Secretary of War JOHN C. CALHOUN, and Secretary of the Treasury WILLIAM H. CRAWFORD—vied with Clay, the Speaker of the House of Representatives, for the presidency. All had served prominently in the national government for more than a dozen years. They were surprised when Gen. Andrew Jackson emerged as a candidate in the spring of 1822. Jackson had held national civil office for only brief periods, as a Representative in 1796 and 1797, as a Senator from September 1797 to April 1798, and as territorial governor of Florida from July to October 1821. He had relinquished each post with distaste for such employment. His summary actions against the Tennessee and Kentucky militias in events related to the Battle of New Orleans (1815) and his subsequent prolongation of martial law in that city, as well as his assault on the Spanish outposts in Florida, had indicated ruthless disregard for civil authority and civil rights. His military prowess, however, held immense popular appeal in the years approaching the nation's jubilee.

Old party affiliations were disintegrating during the social and economic adjustments that followed the War of 1812, and established political leaders lost support. By the spring of 1823, division in the Jeffersonian Republican Party had so fragmented Calhoun's base in Pennsylvania that a meeting scheduled for his nomination resulted in the endorsement of Jackson. Crawford, stricken with paralysis in the fall of that year, won nomination by a congressional caucus that included only 66 of 216 Republicans. In New York the state senate endorsed Crawford; the assembly, Adams. With a joint ballot necessary to resolve the division of electoral delegates, a split ticket of Adams and Clay supporters opposing the caucus system agreed in the assembly to provide sufficient votes to rank Clay rather than Crawford among the top three candidates to be brought to vote before the United States House of Representatives in the event that no one attained a majority in the ELECTORAL COLLEGE. Instead, three Adams supporters scattered their votes so that Crawford, not Clay, joined Jackson and Adams as the nominees brought before Congress.

This was one more among many reasons Clay might have had to support Jackson or Crawford instead of Adams in the House vote. But at least as early as October 1824, Clay had informed friends of his decision to endorse Adams if he himself were eliminated. He announced that decision to Adams on 9 January, a week before news reached Washington that members of the so-called relief movement, then holding a lame-duck majority in the Kentucky legislature, had instructed the state's congressional delegation to support Jackson. Clay ignored the instruction on the ground that he represented a constituency that had not only opposed the relief forces but for over twenty years had sustained—and, indeed, never rejected—his leadership.

Despite their occasionally differing sectional concerns, Adams and Clay shared a commitment to national goals that set them apart from the increasingly states' rights positions of Crawford, Calhoun, and Jackson. In domestic concerns Adams had early advocated federal aid for internal improvements and measures for commercial development that Clay and his Ohio Valley supporters found essential for economic growth. In his belated recognition of Latin American independence and espousal of the Monroe Doctrine, Adams had also moved close to diplomatic views that Clay espoused. In mid December Clay's friend Robert P. Letcher had resolved the differences with Adams related to the Ghent negotiations. On the other hand, Clay had been one of Jackson's severest critics in congressional discussion of the general's foray into Spanish Florida. Clay believed such autocratic tendencies threatened republican institutions.

Even with Clay's endorsement, Adams required the votes of at least two additional state delegations to attain the requisite majority in the House of Representatives. He won the vote of Illinois on the basis of his support for politically ostracized Illinois leaders who had attacked Crawford, and he won Maryland through a carefully worded assurance that Federalists would no longer be proscribed from holding office. As Adams noted in his diary, his knowledge that he had not been elected "by the unequivocal suffrages of a majority of the people" was embarrassing. He identified his political efforts as evidence of excessive ambition, and he recognized that the defeated candidates would coalesce in opposition.

That opposition was underway before the House chose Adams. As soon as Clay's support for Adams was publicly known, followers of Calhoun and Jackson warned of violent protest if Clay were put in the Cabinet. Clay demanded congressional inquiry into charges of corrupt bargaining, but when the accuser explained that he had not intended to imply "corruption or dishonor" and refused to testify before the investigating committee, the issue was tabled. Adams subsequently offered Clay the post of Secretary of State, and after much deliberation Clay accepted.

Foreign Policy. The nationalism of the administration's program took form in what was called the AMERICAN SYSTEM, programs applicable to both foreign and domestic policy. In foreign affairs they embraced concern to extend and safeguard United States commerce and to protect the independence of the New World republics established through revolt against European monarchies. Because of his own background Adams centered his attention on foreign affairs and focused particularly on U.S. commercial interests. Agents of the government were directed to seek reimbursement, with interest, for seizures from Americans during the War of 1812 and the Napoleonic Wars. Accordingly, American slaveowners were reimbursed for slaves and property taken by the British in raids on southern coastal areas. The Swedish government agreed to a compromise for goods seized and sold under restrictive decrees in Pomerania; Denmark paid damages for detention of vessels at Kiel; and Russia provided reimbursement for seizures in the Gulf of Smyrna and at Corfu. While such payments generally fell short of full reimbursement and usually recompensed insurance companies rather than the individual claimants, the governmental efforts underscored the national commitment to maintenance of the rights of neutrals.

Similar efforts were successfully directed to protection of American shipping as blockades were decreed, property seized, and seamen mistreated during the war between Brazil and Buenos Aires that began in 1825. To safeguard American shipping from the privateering and piracy that accompanied the conflicts marking the breakup of the Spanish empire, a naval squadron was assigned to patrol the coasts of the warring states. Security in trade was upheld as a basic principle of New World relationships, whether at sea or on land. When a Mexican trader was robbed by Osage Indians along the Arkansas River in 1825, the United States promptly extended indemnity.

More important was the administration's action in concluding nine general commercial treaties, more than in any comparable period prior to the CIVIL WAR. Following congressional instructions applied in the 1815 convention with Britain and incorporated in a general invitation for trade enacted in 1824, the arrangements centered on reciprocity, a distinction from the most-favored-nation concept then prevalent in that reciprocity allowed for preferential differences in privileges. Already a concern in Franco-American relations, such differences delayed settlement of claims dating from Napoleonic depredations, and commercial relations with France remained tenuous until 1828, when a barter arrangement provided preferential tariffs as an offsetting consideration.

The showpiece of the administration's effort to base commercial arrangements on reciprocity was the treaty signed with the Central American Federation in December 1825. Designed as a model for commercial conduct in the New World, much of the agreement concerned the opening of relations that would permit United States shipping to operate under terms as favorable as had existed between the former European colonies and their mother country. The Central American treaty provided for both reciprocity and most-favored-nation treatment, with a stipulation that favors granted to any other nations should become common if the concessions were freely given or should rest on compensation if the concessions were conditioned on reciprocal favors. The definition of reciprocal navigation privileges was drawn so as to permit indirect trade, including reexport to any foreign country in vessels of either the United States or the Central American Federation under the same bounties, duties, and drawbacks, whatever the nationality of the cargo. The agreement bound the parties to protect neutral rights, set forth the principle that the nationality of the ship covered the nationality of the cargo (free ships make free goods), narrowly defined blockade and contraband, and extended generous freedoms to citizens of either party when under jurisdiction of the other.

The administration's efforts to resolve the impasse on commerce with the British West Indies were far less successful. Hoping to force Britain to admit American vessels to the traffic, the United States Congress in 1818 had enacted countervailing legislation, a form of negative reciprocity, barring British vessels from trade between the islands and the United States. Confronted with protests from West Indies planters who depended upon American provisions, Britain had revised its regulations in 1822 so as to permit direct commerce under reciprocal arrangements, but only subject to protective duties and limited to designated ports and specified articles, excluding fish and salted provisions, which were predominantly products of New England. In drafting legislative proposals for the American response, Adams had called for admission of American vessels and goods without payment of duties or other charges higher than those on British vessels and for the privilege of indirect traffic. The controversy, thus centering largely upon mercantile concerns, hung in abeyance.

Because the British proposal had at least offered a market as an outlet for direct trade in agricultural produce, primarily from American farmers of the Chesapeake Bay and Ohio Valley regions, who had been experiencing severe depression, Clay consulted congressional leaders in the spring of 1825 concerning possible policy concessions. The response indicated strong disagreement between shipping and agricultural interests, but a year later the administration instructed its newly appointed minister in London to accept in large part the British terms, relinquishing all claim to participate in the indirect trade between the islands and the mother country. The American negotiator found instead that Britain had recently instituted a new policy without formal notification to the United States. While liberalizing its trade arrangements with the new Latin American states, Britain had ordered closure of its West Indies to American shipping even under the existing restrictions.

This action had grown out of misunderstanding on both sides of the Atlantic, but it owed much to American political disagreements, which had afforded encouragement for the British retaliatory action. Farmers of the Middle Atlantic states and the Ohio Valley were informed by Jacksonian publicists that their economic hardship was being prolonged in order to uphold potential benefits for New England shipping interests. In actuality, the Caribbean trade declined only slightly, since increased exports to other islands in the area largely offset the loss of those to the British West Indies. More serious was the decline in American commerce with much of Latin America as British and European capital investment entered into the competition in that region.

Adams was manifestly concerned to develop commerce with the new Latin American states, but he also showed surprising interest in encouraging friendly relations with those governments as a gesture of commitment to democracy. The decision to demonstrate the nation's goodwill through U.S. participation in what has been called the first Pan-American congress, called by Simón Bolivar to meet at PANAMA in the spring of 1826, precipitated the opening of political attack upon the administration and provided the rallying base for organizing the opposition. During the course of congressional debate challenging Adams's authority to appoint ministers to the congress, an insulting remark by Virginia Senator John Randolph concerning the association of Adams and Clay led the Secretary of State to demand "personal satisfaction." In the ensuing duel neither man was physically injured, but the moral revulsion of Adams's New England supporters embarrassed the administration. Ultimately Congress approved the sending and funding of the ministers. Meanwhile, however, U.S. participation had been so delayed that the onset of the unhealthy summer season in Panama led to adjournment of the assembly before the ministers' arrival. The presence of a British representative, who exploited the Americans' absence to foster suspicion regarding their objectives, counteracted whatever favorable influence had been achieved in the effort.

The problem of CUBA's continued colonial relationship to Spain posed other difficulties in the administration's hemispheric diplomacy. Warning of the danger that Mexico and Colombia, either jointly or separately, might expand their war with Spain by attacking Cuba, Adams and Clay urged the Russian tsar to encourage Spanish recognition of the independence of the already lost colonies. Revolutionary movements in Cuba had several times sought aid from the United States, but fear that weakened authority on the island would lead to a massive slave uprising had divided U.S. opinion. Adams believed that American

intervention would precipitate European or British intervention, resulting in a more hostile trading policy than existed under Spanish authority. At the same time, he realized that the threat of military invasion of the island by Mexico or Colombia was serious. Since the Monroe Doctrine had renounced action by the United States against the existing possessions of European powers in the New World, the possibility of warfare against Spanish control of Cuba by states covered, however tenuously, by the assurance of that pronouncement was alarming. Desire to exert some restraint on such action was evident in the instructions drafted for the American ministers to the Panama congress.

The tsar did inform the other European powers of the American warning, but their response was not what the Americans had anticipated. The French moved their fleet into the Caribbean during the summer of 1825. The Spanish reinforced their garrison on the island the following October. Subsequently political upheavals in both Colombia and Mexico removed the Latin American threat to Cuba; but those states, as well as warring Brazil and Buenos Aires, each of whom sought American support, learned that the ideological pronouncements of the Monroe Doctrine, the assertion of an American System in foreign affairs, depended operationally upon pragmatic and nationalistic determinants.

Domestic Policy. The Adams administration's domestic policy was similarly definable as a nationalistic American System. One component of it was INTERNAL IMPROVEMENTS. Adams took pride that as early as 1807 he had introduced a Senate resolution asserting the power of the general government to engage in such improvements. He knew that proponents of strict construction of the Constitution had challenged that view as recently as the Monroe presidency, but in outlining his agenda in his inaugural address he expressed hope that patient deliberation would remove such objections. Support for internal improvements as a means of consolidating diverse sectional interests was one of the major bonds in the Adams-Clay relationship. Utilizing the planning and construction skills of the Army Corps of Engineers, and in some cases with public funding of state and local undertakings, projects for road and canal construction, removal of stream obstructions, and harbor works from the Great Lakes around the Atlantic coast to the Gulf of Mexico encouraged the growth of internal commerce, which was one of the most dynamic economic trends of the pre–Civil War period.

A second component of the American System was a sound and stable financial system based on the BANK OF

THE UNITED STATES as a national institution of credit control. Both Adams and Clay had long advocated enactment of a national bankruptcy law, applicable particularly to merchants who engaged in interstate activity. The political opposition countered with a proposal to extend the measure to agricultural interests. After prolonged debate, however, a large number of those who had called for such an extension voted against both versions, and the legislation was rejected.

Partisan obstructionism also defeated efforts by the Secretary of the Treasury to refinance the national debt so as to reduce the interest burden. Largely because earlier sales of securities for such purposes had depended heavily on purchase by the Bank of the United States, although at low interest rates, the proposal generated bitter criticism. Opponents argued that the action had led to contraction of the bank's loans to state and local institutions in order to avert specie exports in meeting the requirements of federal debt repayment. The debate marked the opening round of the Jacksonian war against the bank.

TARIFF POLICY was a third component of the American System as domestically applied. Clay had long supported protective legislation; but Adams, considering New England's commercial interests, had been less outspoken on the issue. As New England's economic concerns broadened by the mid 1820s, however, President Adams acclaimed his administration's tariff measure as a benefit to "the planter and the merchant and the shepherd and the husbandman . . . thriving in their occupations under the duties imposed for the protection of domestic manufactures." The agricultural depression that had stricken rural districts earlier in the decade had generated support for the view that industrial growth would open a home market for domestic farm produce. In arguing for tariff legislation, Secretary of the Treasury Richard Rush advised that a quarter of the cotton produced in the South was already being sold domestically. Such sectional linkage appeared as yet another contribution to national development.

Like so much of the administration-backed legislation, however, the effect was vitiated. Jackson supporters controlling Congress in 1828 proposed to aid farmers more directly through an expanded list of protected goods. Sheep raisers were to have rates that added to the cost of woolens; sugar and molasses producers were to receive duties hurtful to wine and rum making; hemp growers were to gain a tariff that would increase the price of bagging. Fearful that tariff barriers would hurt sales of American cotton in Europe, southern leaders nevertheless entered into the plan by resisting moderating amendments. So unsatis-factory to so many interests that it was called the TARIFF OF ABOMINATIONS, the measure was designed in the expectation that Adams's friends would reject their own program, thus making the administration liable to charges of inconsistency in an election year. The maneuver failed when administration leaders supported the bill. At election time, with the measure enacted, South Carolina spokesmen were threatening NULLIFICATION.

Adams had rejected active pursuit of reelection. He rarely permitted ceremonial honors in his behalf when he traveled home for his annual vacations, and he could not understand why such electioneering tactics were pursued by other members of his Cabinet. While he occasionally yielded to partisan pressures in making new appointments to office, he refused to dismiss incumbents for hostile political views or even, in notable instances, for activity damaging to his administration. Despite the dangers inherent in a sweeping assertion of federal authority, at the beginning of his presidency he had stubbornly enunciated a broad agenda of public improvements, including, in addition to the measures of the American System, establishment of a naval academy, a national university, a national program of geographic and astronomical exploration, and reform of the militia system and of policy concerning the Indians. All these proposals incurred strong criticism that challenged their constitutionality, and only the measures for localized benefits of well-distributed public works gained majority approval.

In the end, Jackson defeated Adams in the election of 1828. The growth of the West had opened politics to a new style of leadership. Liberalization of voting requirements and disintegration of old political alignments had brought a broader based electorate to power. The New Englander had little popular appeal in the Ohio Valley, where Clay's support had eroded. Many voters there did not like the administration's ties to the Bank of the United States, its opposition to graduated reduction of public land prices, its defense of Indian treaty stipulations, or its proposal to establish a permanent Indian territory. While they approved the governmental aid for internal improvements and the protection afforded by the tariff of 1828, they did not believe that Jackson himself opposed those programs. They cared little about the fundamental ideological policy commitments.

Historically, however, Adams's defeat represented more than the personality difference between the intellectuality of the New Englander and the activism of the dynamic military leader. That difference took form in contrasting conceptions of the functions of government. Adams believed that the national government had a responsibility to develop generalized programs for the long-run growth of the country and for the development of its stature internationally. He warned members of Congress that in this effort they should not be "palsied" by the special interests of their constituents. Jackson, on the other hand, looked upon government as a simpler, more direct response to constituent concerns. Believing the incumbent officials corrupt, he sought primarily a changing of the bureaucracy and a redistribution of the governmental favors. Sectional, even local, particularism were to have new channels for expression.

Congressman. Adams was not content in retirement. He accepted nomination for election to the House of Representatives in 1831 and as the only President ever to reenter Congress continued to voice his policy concerns for another seventeen years. As chairman of the House Committee on Manufactures he proposed tariff revisions in 1832 [see TARIFF ACT OF 1832] that generally restored the moderate levels prior to 1828, but when southern leaders demanded still further reductions, he protested vehemently against the compromise TARIFF ACT OF 1833. As Jackson moved against the Bank of the United States, Adams prepared a bitter committee report, filed as a minority of one, in defense of that institution. His commitment to federal aid for internal improvements was long-lasting: in 1842 he even opposed Whig tariff legislation when it entailed elimination of such funding.

Adams contended that, with the failure of these measures, national honor and wealth were being cast aside by efforts to placate the sectional particularism of the South and West. From 1835, when he initiated a nine-year protest against the tabling of antislavery petitions, his efforts became increasingly directed toward opposing slaveholding interests. He led the resistance in Congress to the ANNEXATION OF TEXAS and the resulting MEXICAN WAR. He appeared before the Supreme Court in 1841 to defend, successfully, thirty-nine slaves on trial for revolt aboard the Spanish slave ship *Amistad*. During his long struggle against slavery he won distinction and the title "Old Man Eloquent" for his caustic sarcasm and slashing argument.

Already handicapped by severe palsy, Adams suffered a stroke while in Boston during the summer of 1846. Although he recovered sufficiently to return to Congress for another year, he was stricken again and died on the floor of the House of Representatives on 23 February 1848.

Adams had attained greater popular acclaim as a sectional and humanitarian congressional spokesman than as President, but neither of those particularistic

concerns fundamentally motivated his actions. He believed that the southern commitment to preserve the institution of slavery and the western desire for access to cheap public land formed the basis for consolidation of a political alliance hostile to legislation for the promotion of general national development. His administration was the last before Lincoln's to set forth a cohesive program for such growth. Modified to appease the land hunger of the West, it shaped the agenda for maturation of the national economy after the CIVIL WAR—a foreign policy of active pursuit of foreign trade, including reassertion of the Monroe Doctrine, and a domestic program of federal aid for internal improvements, commitment to a sound currency, and a high protective tariff.

BIBLIOGRAPHY

Adams, John Quincy. *Memoirs . . . , Comprising Portions of His Diary from 1795 to 1848.* Edited by Charles Francis Adams. 12 vols. 1874–1877.

Bemis, Samuel Flagg. *John Quincy Adams and the Foundations of American Foreign Policy.* 1949.

Bemis, Samuel Flagg. *John Quincy Adams and the Union.* 1956.

Burton, Theodore E. "Henry Clay, Secretary of State." In vol. 4 of *The American Secretaries of State and Their Diplomacy.* Edited by Samuel Flagg Bemis. 17 vols. 1927–1967.

Hargreaves, Mary W. M. *The Presidency of John Quincy Adams.* 1985.

Hecht, Marie B. *John Quincy Adams: A Personal History of an Independent Man.* 1972.

Lipsky, George A. *John Quincy Adams: His Theory and Ideas.* 1950.

Nagel, Paul C. *Descent from Glory: Four Generations of the John Adams Family.* 1983.

Perkins, Dexter, "John Quincy Adams." In vol. 4 of *The American Secretaries of State and Their Diplomacy.* Edited by Samuel Flagg Bemis. 17 vols. 1927–1967.

Richards, Leonard L. *The Life and Times of Congressman John Quincy Adams.* 1986.

MARY W. M. HARGREAVES

ADAMS, SHERMAN (1899–1966), aide in the Eisenhower administration. A former New Hampshire governor and a central figure in winning Eisenhower the presidential nomination, Adams served as what in effect was the first WHITE HOUSE CHIEF OF STAFF in the history of the presidency. Officially designated the Assistant to the President (so as to avoid the military connotations of the term *chief of staff*), Adams coordinated Eisenhower's domestic policy.

Adams was noted for his brusk, laconic manner. He was intensely hard-working and made little effort to ingratiate himself on the Washington scene. Working for a President who was widely, though incorrectly, viewed as passive [see HIDDEN-HAND PRESIDENT], Adams was commonly considered the architect of the Eisenhower administration's domestic policy, just as Secretary of State JOHN FOSTER DULLES was viewed as the creator of that administration's foreign policy. Once the archives of the Eisenhower presidency were opened for research, historians discovered that neither interpretation was true, and that in fact Eisenhower retained control of his administration's policies. This evidence also disproved the contemporary view that Adams insulated Eisenhower from outside influence.

Adams resigned under pressure in 1958 after attempting to weather a controversy over a pattern of gift giving between his family and that of New England manufacturer Bernard Goldfine, in whose favor he had intervened in matters bearing on the Federal Trade Commission and the Securities and Exchange Commission. The controversies attending Adams's conduct of his responsibilities may have contributed to the decision by Eisenhower's two immediate successors not to appoint a White House Chief of Staff. Later Presidents, however, appear to have concluded that a Chief of Staff is essential to the conduct of the modern presidency. Such an official, whether or not so-named, has served in every modern White House from that of Richard Nixon to that of Bill Clinton, with the exception of those of Gerald Ford in his first few months in office and Jimmy Carter in his first three years in office.

BIBLIOGRAPHY

Adams, Sherman. *First-Hand Report: The Story of the Eisenhower Presidency.* 1961.

Greenstein, Fred I. *The Hidden-Hand Presidency: Eisenhower as Leader.* 1982.

Kernell, Samuel, and Samuel Popkin. *The Chief of Staff: Twenty-Five Years of Managing the Presidency.* 1986.

FRED I. GREENSTEIN

ADMINISTRATIVE PRESIDENCY. The term administrative presidency was coined by Richard P. Nathan to describe the managerial emphasis of the second term of President Richard M. Nixon. It implies that an acceptable role for the President is to serve as de facto manager of the executive branch with the goal of advancing the presidential policy agenda through administrative channels—that is, using the implementation of existing laws to advance objectives rather than enacting new legislation.

The administrative President uses his executive powers and domestic policy apparatus to exercise tight control over the bureaucracy and domestic policy implementation. During President Nixon's first term, when his primary focus was on Congress and the pursuit of a legislative agenda, he came to perceive the bureaucracy as thwarting implementation of presidential objectives. Thus, at the start of his second term, he shifted to an administrative strategy to centralize management and control.

The five main elements that define an administrative presidency, according to Nathan, are as follows: first, selecting a CABINET whose views closely follow those of the President; second, selecting sub-Cabinet officials who share the President's policy objectives; third, motivating Cabinet and sub-Cabinet officials to give attention to agency operations and administrative processes; fourth, using the budget process as the primary framework for policy making; and fifth, avoiding overreliance on centralized White House clearance and control systems.

A cornerstone of this administrative approach is that the President must establish a managerial support network. President Nixon accomplished this by appointing individuals of proven personal loyalty and little national standing to high executive branch positions, at both Cabinet and sub-Cabinet levels, replacing the more independent executives of his first term. Continuing contact with these officials was maintained, often symbolically, through invitations to meetings or state dinners, press conference attributions, budget decisions, and phone calls and personal notes designed to reinforce presidential objectives and ensure staff support. A paradox of the administrative presidency, experienced by President Nixon, is that efficient administrative control requires delegation. The President must de-emphasize the White House bureaucracy, creating an unimpeded chain of action between him and his Cabinet. He also must rely upon his Cabinet to implement policy, rather than introducing White House oversight. The penetration of officials into administrative processes cannot be directly supervised by the President.

Although the administrative presidency was initially developed as a conceptual description of the Nixon administration, elements of this management style are also evident in the administration of Ronald Reagan. President Reagan's commitment to retrenchment in the size and scope of government involvement in domestic affairs created a climate conducive to an administrative strategy. This strategy was pursued in conjunction with a legislative agenda and focused primarily on sub-Cabinet officials.

BIBLIOGRAPHY

Nathan, Richard P. *The Administrative Presidency.* 1983.

Nathan, Richard P. *The Plot that Failed: Nixon and the Administrative Presidency.* 1975.

MARGARET JANE WYSZOMIRSKI

ADMINISTRATIVE PROCEDURE ACT (1946).

The act (APA) is the most important statute that Congress has enacted to control policy-making procedures in the executive branch. In many ways it serves as an administrative constitution, setting forth basic principles and procedures for a wide variety of government functions. The APA, which is located in Title 5 of the United States Code, applies to almost all executive agencies, except that military and foreign-affairs functions receive various exemptions from its strictures. The text of the APA does not specify whether the act applies directly to the President. The Supreme Court has never decided this issue, but courts often use the APA to control the President indirectly by applying it to acts he performs through subordinates.

The APA was enacted against a background of dissatisfaction with bureaucratic irregularities that occurred in the rapidly expanding agencies of the NEW DEAL. Today, the APA remains much as it was originally written, except for the addition of a series of provisions controlling public access to agency records and meetings: the FREEDOM OF INFORMATION ACT, the Privacy Act, and the Government in the Sunshine Act. The courts have adapted the APA to changing conditions during the four decades of its existence by glossing its rather terse text in a fashion that resembles judicial interpretation of the Constitution itself.

The original APA focused on three aspects of administration that needed clarification or improvement. First, it specified a simple process for exercising the RULEMAKING POWER. Agencies were to give public notice of proposed rules, receive and consider written comments on the proposals, and then publish final rules in the Federal Register. Over the years, this process has become a somewhat more formal interchange with affected interests. The result for most final rules is a record of fact and opinion that undergoes judicial review.

Second, the APA provided a process for agency adjudication of case-by-case decisions. This procedure has always resembled a civil trial, but with no jury and relaxed rules of evidence. Decisions are made on a formal record that is compiled before an administrative law judge. Responding to early practices that excessively combined prosecutorial and adjudicative functions, the APA forbids the judges to work under the supervision of prosecuting personnel. The courts review the records of these formal adjudications and have developed methods to review less formal case-by-case decisions that are not required to follow the APA's procedures.

Third, the APA codified existing doctrines defining judicial review of administrative action. These doctrines grew out of common-law methods for controlling executive officers. Under them, courts seek a reasonable basis for the agency's decision in fact, law, and procedure, but avoid invading the agency's policy-making discretion. The APA, through these doctrines, also defines the limits of judicial power to review the merits of administrative decisions. Thus, the APA has left room for courts to continue their traditional process of crafting administrative law to serve the nation's needs.

BIBLIOGRAPHY

Pierce, Richard A., Jr., Sidney A. Shapiro, and Paul R. Verkuil. *Administrative Law and Process.* 2d ed. 1992.
Schwartz, Bernard. *Administrative Law.* 3d ed. 1991.

HAROLD H. BRUFF

ADMINISTRATIVE REFORMS OF THE PRESIDENCY.

In the twentieth century Presidents became administrative reformers: ten twentieth-century Presidents initiated large-scale administrative reform. In the nineteenth century Congress dominated the executive branch, but in the early twentieth century Presidents asserted responsibility for administrative reform. This article traces that development and describes the related expansion of the presidency.

Four goals in administrative reform are central to the modern presidency. First, in pursuing administrative reform, Presidents tried to create a more manageable executive branch by organizing departments by purpose. Second, they sought a unified budgetary authority over the executive branch. Third, they sought expansion of WHITE HOUSE STAFF. Finally, they sought greater influence over the higher CIVIL SERVICE. The history of executive reform can be organized into four different phases: the three decades prior to the NEW DEAL; the reform efforts of the New Deal, culminating in the BROWNLOW COMMITTEE; the post–WORLD WAR II period of congressional resurgence; and the modern period, from Dwight D. Eisenhower through Jimmy Carter. In what follows, these periods will be discussed with attention to their reform-planning initiatives and goals.

Presidents Take the Initiative (1905–1932). President Theodore Roosevelt broke Congress's monopoly on administrative reform by appointing a five-member commission to improve administration. Chaired by Assistant Secretary of the Treasury Charles Keep, it was called the KEEP COMMISSION. Roosevelt instructed the commission to seek reforms that would not require congressional action for their adoption. The Keep Commission produced eleven reports addressing such matters as the management of public records, the purchase of government supplies, and the administration of government statistical information.

Following Roosevelt, President William Howard Taft appointed Dr. Frederick Cleveland, an expert on public administration, as his consultant for administrative reform. In 1911 Taft created the six-member Commission on Economy and Efficiency, better known as the TAFT COMMISSION, with Cleveland as chairperson. Unlike the Keep Commission, the Taft Commission addressed the overall structure of the executive branch. It found that the executive branch lacked rational organization and severely criticized the absence of a budget system for the government. The commission thought that organizing the executive branch more rationally would make it more manageable. It proposed unifying CABINET-level departments by purpose. It also recommended that the President prepare for Congress an annual executive budget. Such a budget would give the President a capacity to set priorities among competing claims. To support its recommended budget system, the commission also recommended a budgetary-staff organization for the President.

Although the Taft Commission's recommendations were not immediately adopted, it did establish the modern administrative-reform agenda. Thereafter, the ideal of rationally organized Cabinet departments guided reformers, and nine years after the commission proposed an executive budget, Congress passed the BUDGET AND ACCOUNTING ACT of 1921, initiating an executive budget and creating the Bureau of the Budget.

Before the 1920 presidential election, Congress created a Joint Congressional Committee on Reorganization. When President Warren G. Harding took office, he requested that Congress amend the committee's structure to allow the President to appoint an additional member who would also chair the committee. Congress consented, creating the anomalous situation of a congressional joint committee chaired by a presidential appointee. Harding appointed Walter F. Brown, who also served as Harding's assistant for administrative efficiency. Brown organized a reform-planning process based in the Cabinet departments, and the joint committee later approved the plan with few changes. Thus what was intended to be a legislative reform initiative became a presidential initiative.

The Harding administration–joint committee report proposed a series of department-level reorganizations that would join agencies on the basis of shared purposes. But the joint committee's most important innovation was to recommend that, after the adoption of large-scale changes in the executive branch, the President should have authority to initiate reforms as they became necessary—in effect, that the President be given reorganization authority. Only a few of the committee's recommendations for departmental reform were adopted, but the recommendation for presidential REORGANIZATION POWERS was eventually incorporated in the Economy Act of 1932.

The New Deal and Administrative Management (1933–1939). Franklin D. Roosevelt's policy initiatives overwhelmed the administrative capacities of the executive branch. The presidency was not equipped to direct a massive executive-branch bureaucracy, which grew from 609,746 civilian employees in 1931 to 953,891 in 1939. The President's effort to increase his capacity as manager drew on the existing agenda for administrative reform and, at the same time, expanded that agenda. In doing so, Roosevelt also created the organizational system that remains the basic anatomy of the modern presidency.

After several failed attempts at Cabinet-level coordination, Roosevelt created a committee of three administrative experts to design a program of administrative reform. Formed in early 1936, the committee, chaired by Louis Brownlow, was officially called the President's Committee on Administrative Management, but it is better known as the BROWNLOW COMMITTEE. Brownlow was head of the Public Administration Clearing House in Chicago. The committee assembled a staff of thirty specialists who would, in Brownlow's words, skim "the cream off the top of their own memories." The committee's recommendations incorporated the administrative-reform agenda that had evolved over the previous three decades. But the existing reform agenda proved insufficient, and the committee ultimately fixed on the need to strengthen the presidency itself—recommending, for example, the addition of six new presidential assistants and the establishment of presidential staff organizations to be housed within a new EXECUTIVE OFFICE OF THE PRESIDENT.

Roosevelt submitted the report of the Brownlow Committee to Congress in January 1937. Over the next two years Congress rejected bills conveying the committee's recommendations, but in 1939 Congress finally passed a Reorganization Act creating the recommended six White House assistants and delegating reorganization authority to the President for a two-year period. Under that authority Roosevelt issued Reorganization Plan No. 1 of 1939 to establish the Executive Office of the President, which included the Bureau of the Budget, the Central Statistical Board, and the National Resources Planning Board.

Congress Retakes the Initiative (1947–1955). After WORLD WAR II, Congress created two commissions meant to capture the initiative in administrative reform. Both were headed by former President Herbert Hoover, and they are popularly known as the HOOVER COMMISSIONS. The first, the Commission on the Organization of the Executive Branch, was created in 1947 by the Republican-dominated Eightieth Congress. It had twelve members, with the President, President Pro Tem of the Senate, and Speaker of the House each selecting four members on a bipartisan basis. In 1953 another Republican Congress created the second Hoover Commission, also called the Commission on the Organization of the Executive Branch and also with twelve members (who were, however, appointed without regard to bipartisanship, four each by the President, President Pro Tem of the Senate, and Speaker of the House).

Its sponsors intended the first Hoover Commission to prepare the transition for a Republican President after the election of 1948, but President Harry S. Truman's unexpected victory changed the commission's situation. Hoover chose to cooperate with the Truman administration and wrote a report on management in the executive branch that echoed the themes of the earlier Brownlow report. By its own count, at least 100 of the commission's 277 recommendations were adopted.

The second Hoover commission was more hampered by partisanship than the first had been. Neglected by President Eisenhower, who had established his own mechanism for administrative reform, the second commission delivered its reports in 1955 to a skeptical Democratic Congress. The commission's partisan recommendations in areas such as water resources and medical services were rejected, but many of recommendations that proposed nonpartisan, technical reforms were adopted. A 1958 Senate report found that 61 percent of the commission's 519 recommendations had been adopted.

Parallel to the second commission, the Eisenhower administration had created the President's Advisory Committee for Government Organization (PACGO) to provide him with guidance on administrative issues. It had three members—the President's brother Milton Eisenhower, Arthur Flemming, a Republican member of the Hoover Commissions, and NELSON A. ROCKEFELLER, who served as the committee's chair.

The President's committee signified that administrative reform was becoming a routine part of the organized presidency. Simultaneously, the Bureau of the Budget expanded its role in administrative issues. With expanding staff, the bureau supported presidential concerns regarding administration; during the eight years of the Eisenhower administration, PACGO and the bureau worked hand in hand—the pattern for future administrative reform, in contrast to the procedure presented by the Hoover Commissions.

Administrative Reform in the Late Twentieth Century. After 1955 the presidency dominated administrative reform, and reform efforts meshed with the staff system of the modern presidency. Furthermore, routine congressional delegation of reorganization authority to the President further weighted initiative toward the executive. Since 1960 three Presidents have sought large-scale administrative reform: Lyndon Baines Johnson, Richard M. Nixon, and Jimmy Carter.

Johnson initiated two task forces for administrative reform. In 1964, he created the ten-member Task Force on Government Reorganization, chaired by Professor Don K. Price of Harvard University. With staff support from the Bureau of the Budget, the Price task force submitted its report on 6 November 1964. It recommended a number of departmental reorganizations, improvements in the Executive Office of the President, and reforms in the upper levels of the civil service. The task force introduced one major innovation in the reform agenda, calling for the addition of a capacity for policy evaluation (using modern analytic techniques) to the Executive Office. There is no evidence that Johnson chose to adopt any of the task force's recommendations.

In his 1966 STATE OF THE UNION MESSAGE, Johnson said that the GREAT SOCIETY required the elimination of "administrative arrangements which have not kept pace with changing needs." In September 1966, Johnson again initiated reform planning with the Task Force on Governmental Organization, chaired by Chicago businessman Ben Heineman. It had eleven members, including the President's budget director, Kermit Gordon, Secretary of Defense ROBERT MCNAMARA, and former National Security Assistant McGeorge Bundy. The Heineman task force worked more directly with the White House than had the Price task force and was assigned several specific tasks to address, such as the organization of Great Society programs. The Heineman task force added one new concept to the agenda of administration reform, conceiving of departmental reorganization as combining related activities into very large organizational conglomerates, or "superdepartments." Additionally, it expanded on the Price task force's concern with public policy and proposed the creation of a unit to coordinate public policy in the Executive Office of the President. Although some of the Heineman task force's recommendations were incorporated in the Equal Opportunity Act of 1967, its major recommendations were issued in the waning days of the Johnson presidency, when the VIETNAM WAR—not domestic policy—preoccupied the administration. But, the major concerns of the two Johnson-administration task forces outlived the Johnson presidency and were incorporated in Nixon-administration reform initiatives.

President Nixon created the Advisory Council on Government Organization in April 1969. He asked the council to address organizational problems arising from the huge scale of the executive branch. The council, which was known as the ASH COUNCIL because it was headed by Roy Ash, the president of Litton Industries, was composed of six members, all but one of whom held major positions in American business. The Ash Council was located within the Executive Office of the President. Its first recommendations addressed the President's staff system itself, reorganizing and renaming the Bureau of the Budget and, in a way that echoed the Price and Heineman task forces, creating a new council to coordinate and plan in the arena of domestic policy. Nixon adopted these recommendations, implementing them through Reorganization Plan No. 2 of 1970, which renamed the budget bureau as the OFFICE OF MANAGEMENT AND BUDGET (OMB) and expanded the bureau's managerial and policy coordinating functions. Within the Executive Office the plan also created a Domestic Policy Council—a domestic version of the NATIONAL SECURITY COUNCIL, with a staff headed by a presidential assistant.

Next, the Ash Council addressed regulatory reform and the organization of the Cabinet departments—the latter making the largest impact. Adopting the Heineman task force's concept of superdepartments, the council recommended that most of the existing domestic agencies be reformed into four new departments: natural resources, economic affairs, human resources, and community development. President Nixon proposed these new departments in his 1971 state of the union address, but Congress approved none of the superdepartments, and after his 1972 reelection Nixon attempted to reorganize the Cabinet through administrative fiat, restructuring Cabinet relationships to subordinate some department heads under cabinet overseers for broad policy areas, such as natural resources. This was the administration's last

effort at administrative reform, as political survival soon became paramount in the Nixon administration.

Jimmy Carter won the presidency in 1976, associating administrative reform with responsive government. Carter's primary vehicle for administrative reform was called the President's Reorganization Project and was integrated into the Office of Management and Budget as a new division. Its head, Harrison Wellford, was executive associate director of OMB for reorganization and management. The project focused study teams on policy areas such as energy and natural resources, economic development, and national security and international affairs. Its total personnel reached three hundred people, most of whom were from outside government or borrowed from other agencies. Simultaneously, the Carter administration also sought budget reform and reform in the personnel system. No President had ever attempted such an array of reforms as Carter, nor had any President created so large a reform-planning mechanism.

Carter effected budget reform with a 1977 order from OMB instructing agencies to adopt a budgeting format called zero-base budgeting, which asked agencies to set their objectives and plan expenditures each year, starting from scratch. Carter's personnel reform aimed at giving the President more flexibility over policy-related roles in the bureaucracy; the project was conducted by the Personnel Management Project (PMP), with a staff of 118 people. PMP proposed a SENIOR EXECUTIVE SERVICE, with increased rewards for career employees and more flexibility for political officials. It was passed into law in 1979. Carter also abolished the Civil Service Commission and created the OFFICE OF PERSONNEL MANAGEMENT and the MERIT SYSTEMS PROTECTION BOARD through Reorganization Plan No. 2 of 1978.

The President's Reorganization Project itself focused on structural reforms on the executive branch. In line with the recommendations of the Heineman task force and the Ash Council, the project in 1978 developed proposals for four superdepartments: natural resources, developmental assistance, food and nutrition, and trade and technology. At the same time that the project was pursuing that goal, however, the Carter administration successfully proposed two departments based on narrow domains: Energy in 1977 and Education in 1979. In his 1979 state of the union address Carter adopted recommendations for major departmental reorganizations and expansion in the areas of economic development and natural resources, but the administration only submitted legislation for a department of natural resources, and it died in Congress.

Having invested more resources in administrative reform than any predecessor, Carter met with mixed success. In budget reform he continued a quest that had begun with the Taft Commission—a quest to make appropriation requests more rational. In his success in civil-service reform he achieved goals that had first been proposed by the Brownlow Committee. But in his grand plan to reorganize the executive branch, Carter met with the same results as the Heineman task force and the Ash Council. Since Carter, no President has initiated administrative reform on a broad scale. The administrations of Presidents Ronald Reagan and George Bush were characterized by another approach to controlling government, an approach using ideological tests in appointment and increasing centralization of review processes in the executive branch to achieve presidential purposes. That approach has been characterized as the ADMINISTRATIVE PRESIDENCY strategy. American government remains a government of great scale and complexity, however, and concerns with rationalizing organization cannot long be ignored by elected officials.

BIBLIOGRAPHY

Arnold, Peri E. *Making the Managerial Presidency*. 1986.

Karl, Barry. *Executive Reorganization and Reform in the New Deal*. 1963.

Mansfield, Harvey C. "Federal Executive Reorganization: Thirty Years' Experience." *Public Administration Review* 29(1969):332–345.

Nathan, Richard. *The Administrative Presidency*. 1982.

Seidman, Harold, and Robert Gilmour. *Politics, Position, and Power*. 1986.

Sundquist, James. *The Decline and Resurgence of Congress*. 1981.

PERI E. ARNOLD

ADVICE AND CONSENT. The Senate's formal role in the appointment process derives from the language of Article II, Section 2, of the Constitution: The President "shall nominate, and by and with the Advice and Consent of the Senate, shall appoint Ambassadors, other public Ministers and Consuls, Judges of the Supreme Court, and all other Officers of the United States, whose Appointments are not herein otherwise provided for, and which shall be established by Law."

The Framers of this language only provided a framework for the sharing of the APPOINTMENT POWER. They left many technical questions unanswered: What does "advice and consent" mean? What is an "officer"? May the Senate reverse its judgment after confirming an appointment? Is the Senate also entitled to advise and consent on executive removals, or only on appointments? Over time many of these technical questions have been sources of heated dispute between the Senate and the President.

The Framers of the Constitution wrote before political parties had emerged and before the government had grown to its enormous contemporary proportions. Those changes have placed great pressures on the constitutional design of the advice and consent clause.

Historical Background. ALEXANDER HAMILTON argued in FEDERALIST 76, that the Senate's role would be largely reactive and corrective, that the appointment power ultimately belonged to the President.

> Every advantage to be expected from such an arrangement would in substance be derived from the power of *nomination*, which is proposed to be conferred upon [the President].... In the act of nomination, his judgment alone would be exercised; and as it would be his sole duty to point out the man who, with the approbation of the Senate should fill an office, his responsibility would be as complete as if he were to make the final appointment. There can, in this view, be no difference between nominating and appointing. The same motives which would influence a proper discharge of his duty in one case, would exist in the other. And as no man could be appointed but on his previous nomination, every man who might be appointed would be, in fact, his choice.

This view held little sway in the Senate. From the First Congress, members of the Senate sought to play a partnership role in filling positions in the federal government. When George Washington nominated Benjamin Fishbourn to be naval officer for the port of Savannah, Georgia, the two Senators from that state objected and the Senate rejected Fishbourn's appointment. That action established a precedent: that the Senate would not confirm appointees whose work would be confined to the jurisdiction of a single state without the approval of the Senators of that state. This practice came to be known as senatorial courtesy. When political parties later emerged, the courtesy was typically extended only to those Senators of the President's party.

Also in that First Congress, President George Washington established a precedent that limited the interpretation of the "advice" portion of the advice-and-consent clause. He chose to submit his nominations in writing to the Senate, rather than to visit that body and confer with its members.

The Senate also initiated the practice, followed with rare exceptions since then, of passing its final judgment on appointments by viva voce vote. It further instituted the procedure, finally abandoned in 1929, of considering all nominations in executive session. Before 1929, the division of Senate confirmation votes was not made public.

In the years that followed the earliest Congress, the Senate's role in the appointment process developed inconsistently. All Presidents have had the bulk of their appointments confirmed by the Senate, usually with little controversy or opposition. But periods of tension between the President and the Senate have usually affected the appointment process and caused Presidents heightened difficulty in getting their nominees approved. A clique of opponents in the Senate frequently interfered with James Madison's efforts to fill his administration. Ulysses S. Grant suffered similar difficulties and indignities. John Tyler was probably the least successful President in dealing with the Senate on appointments. Four of Tyler's Cabinet nominations and four to the Supreme Court were rejected by the Senate. Richard M. Nixon and Ronald Reagan in the final year of their administrations experienced significant difficulty in getting a Senate controlled by the opposition party to consider, let alone confirm, many of their nominees.

The problems Presidents sometimes experience in securing the advice and consent of the Senate are often the result, not of deficiencies in the credentials of particular appointees, but of efforts by members of the Senate to use appointments as leverage in policy or political disputes with the President. In the 1980s, for example, Senator Jesse Helms of North Carolina, a Republican, often held up the confirmation of individuals nominated by President Ronald Reagan, a fellow Republican, to positions in the STATE DEPARTMENT or other foreign affairs agencies. Helms's concern was less often with the individual nominees than with Reagan administration policies. He sought to delay or deny confirmation until those policies were changed to his satisfaction.

In the 1970s, a significant change began to occur in the Senate's exercise of the confirmation power. Prior to that time, despite brief periods of obstinacy, the typical pattern of Senate behavior had been deference to the President and acquiescence in his personnel nominations. But the 1970s initiated a long period of DIVIDED GOVERNMENT that coincided with the rapid loss of influence by national political parties. At the same time, the internal operations of the Senate were becoming increasingly decentralized, individual Senators were attaining a greater degree of independence, and growth in staff and other resources were affording Senate committees enhanced opportunities for investigating judicial- and executive-branch nominees. Many of the old constraints on the confirmation process were loosened, and Senate activism began to grow.

An important consequence of these changes in the Senate was that Presidents could no longer take con-firmation for granted. In response, administrations became more assertive and consistent in consulting with relevant Senators before designating their appointees. Following what some scholars have called the law of anticipated reactions, presidential personnel assistants sought to identify potential Senate opposition before it became public and sometimes to bypass a potential nominee who was likely to incur significant opposition in the confirmation process.

As the operation of the appointment process became more formalized in the White House, prior clearance of potential nominees with relevant Senators became part of the routine. This was not an entirely novel invention by any means. Informal consultation with individual Senators, to one degree or another, had been a component of the nominee selection process in every administration. What changed in the years after 1970 was the extent to which this became the norm, the extent to which it was institutionalized in the increasingly structured procedures of nominee selection. As a result, the "advice" language of the advice-and-consent clause is now more important than it has ever been before. Presidents do not always follow the advice they acquire in their Senate consultations, but they seek that advice consistently and weigh it carefully in the calculus of appointment decisions.

The Advice-and-consent Process. When nominations go to the Senate, they follow a process of review that is defined in Senate rules and the procedures of individual committees with confirmation jurisdiction. The formalities of the confirmation process are simple and routine. Presidents transmit their nominations by message to the Senate. Upon arrival there, the message is read on the Senate floor, received by the parliamentarian, and assigned a consecutive number by the executive clerk. Nominations are then referred to an individual committee (or, in a few cases, to several committees) for review. These referrals are based on precedent and the subject matter for which the committees are responsible.

The procedures for committee review are established by individual committees and vary widely. Most nominees offer to meet individually with committee members prior to their confirmation hearings. Some Senators welcome the opportunity for these meetings; others regard them as a burden on their time. These meetings are usually brief and largely social occasions for getting acquainted. Sometimes, however, Senators will use these opportunities to raise substantive questions.

Many committees routinely ask Senators for their views on nominees from their states. Since those home-state senators have normally been consulted by the White House in advance of the nomination, the response is usually affirmative. Typically, in fact, Senators often introduce nominees from their states at confirmation hearings.

Most of the interaction the nominee has with the committee is with the committee staff. Staffs administer questionnaires about the nominee's policy views and his or her relevant experience. All Senate committees now also make detailed inquiries into nominees' personal finances to ensure that no potential conflicts of interest exist. Once the written materials have been filed and reviewed, a hearing is scheduled.

Most confirmation hearings are routine and pro forma. Nominees answer a few questions about their plans and priorities, are welcomed by the committee, and then sent on their way to unanimous confirmation in the Senate. The occasional controversial nominee is likely to be subject to much more vigorous scrutiny. The confirmation of Supreme Court nominees since the late 1960s, for example, has become almost ritualistic, with television coverage and extensive and detailed questioning by every member of the Judiciary Committee. Sometimes the hearings become blistering and abusive as they did for EDWIN MEESE III, whom Ronald Reagan had nominated to be Attorney General, and for John Tower, George Bush's unsuccessful nominee for Secretary of Defense.

After their own review, the committees report nominations favorably or unfavorably to the full Senate. These reports are filed with the legislative clerk and then assigned an executive calendar number by the executive clerk. On a number of occasions a committee will refuse to act at all, forcing the President to withdraw the nominee and submit another.

In general, nominations are considered by the full Senate on the first day they appear on the executive calendar. Nearly all are approved by the Senate, usually with little debate and by unanimous consent. On appointment confirmations, extensive floor debate and roll call votes are rarities.

Senate Rule XXXI governs floor procedures on nominations. Confirmation requires a vote of approval by a majority of the Senators present and voting. After the full Senate has acted, the secretary of the Senate attests to a resolution of confirmation (or rejection), and the resolution is transmitted to the White House. If the nomination has been approved by the Senate, the President completes the appointment process by issuing a certificate that commissions the appointee.

The increasing thoroughness of Senate review of nominees has slowed the process of confirmation. It now typically takes six to eight weeks from the time a nomination is announced by the President to its confirmation by the Senate.

Criticisms of the Senate. Because of the ambiguity of the constitutional language that defines the confirmation power and the Framers' uncertainty about the proper division of appointment authority, the Senate's responsibilities have never been entirely clear. Debate continues, and the Senate has often been criticized for the manner in which it fulfilled its duty to advise and consent on presidential appointments. Ironically, the criticism has come from two quite opposite directions.

One group of critics has accused the Senate of failing to act with significant vigilance, of being a rubber stamp for the President. The view that underlies this criticism is that the Senate should force the President to choose nominees with care and to appoint only those with appropriate skills and credentials for the difficult jobs they are undertaking. The Senate properly exercises its responsibilities, in this view, only by giving careful attention to each nominee and by rejecting those who fail to measure up.

Another group of critics takes the position that the appointment power is largely the President's to exercise and that the Senate should intervene only on those very rare occasions when the President nominates a clearly unqualified candidate. If the Senate seeks a larger role, it diminishes presidential accountability by denying the President a free choice of advisers and subordinates, and it burdens the recruitment process by scaring off potential nominees who do not wish to submit themselves to brutal confirmation hearings.

Both these criticisms have often been heard, their volume magnified by the frequency of divided partisan control of the Senate and the White House. Partisans of the President find much to dislike in Senate efforts to prolong the confirmation process. To the President's supporters this looks like a concerted effort to deny the President the rightful authority of his office. To partisans of the Senate majority, vigor in the confirmation process is an appropriate check on what they see as the misguided selection of nominees who are unqualified or whose policy views seem deeply threatening.

The confirmation process has been brought into the mainstream of the natural antagonism between the President and the Senate. It is a site of disputes not simply and not merely over the qualifications of individual nominees, but over the whole range of public-policy issues on which Presidents and members of the Senate may disagree. The advice-and-consent clause affords Senators some leverage in their dealings with the President on policy matters. The confirmation process thus can be inconsistent, sometimes unfair, and occasionally even cruel. But in a government that divides power between the executive and the legislature, it is not surprising that legislators should use every filament of their authority to impose their will on the CHIEF EXECUTIVE or at least to blunt his initiatives.

BIBLIOGRAPHY

Fisher, Louis. *Constitutional Conflicts between Congress and the President.* 1991.

Harris, Joseph. *The Advice and Consent of the Senate.* 1953.

Mackenzie, G. Calvin. *The Politics of Presidential Appointments.* 1981.

Mann, Dean E. *The Assistant Secretaries: Problems and Processes of Appointment.* 1965.

U.S. Senate. *Confirmation Hearings on Federal Appointments: Hearings before the Committee on the Judiciary.* 99th Cong., 2d Sess. 1986.

G. CALVIN MACKENZIE

ADVISERS, PRESIDENTIAL. See WHITE HOUSE ADVISERS.

AFFIRMATIVE ACTION. Courts, regulators, and legislators at both the state and federal level sometimes demand that race (and occasionally gender) be considered a positive factor in governmental decision making. The manner in which government may affirmatively recognize an individual based on such immutable traits as race and gender has divided the nation. On one side, defenders of affirmative action argue —in the words of Supreme Court Justice Harry Blackmun in *Regents of the University of California v. Bakke* (1978)—that "in order to get beyond racism, we must first take account of race. There is no other way." For these individuals, preferential treatment is an equalizer—responsive to past and present discrimination. On the other side, opponents of benign racial classifications fear that substituting group identity for individual identity is a harbinger of a return to the days of "separate but equal." For these individuals, affirmative action runs contrary to Justice John Harlan's admonition in *Plessy v. Ferguson* (1896) that "our constitution is color-blind, and neither knows nor tolerates classes among citizens."

Federal Efforts. Federal affirmative action efforts have been launched in all three branches. Congress has authorized programs that use racial preference to allocate government funds and benefits in the Small Business Administration, the DEPARTMENT OF TRANSPORTATION, and the Federal Communications Commission. The Supreme Court endorsed court-initiated hiring and promotion plans to remedy illegal discrimination. While these legislative and judicial initiatives are significant, federal affirmative action efforts are principally the province of the executive branch. Through EXECUTIVE ORDERS and agency initiatives, affirmative-action programs have been established within the departments of Commerce, Defense, Labor, and Transportation as well as at the Equal Employment Opportunity Commission (EEOC), Federal Communications Commission (FCC), and Small Business Administration. The Department of Justice, moreover, plays a critical role in advancing the government's position on affirmative action before the courts. Affirmative action is also a factor in presidential appointments, including APPOINTMENT OF JUDGES. Finally, through the power to recommend and veto legislation, the President has also played an instrumental role in defining legislative initiatives in this area. Although executive-branch efforts are, of course, subject to judicial review and legislative oversight, neither Congress nor the courts have been especially active in checking the executive. For example, no executive-initiated affirmative action plan designed to increase minority business ownership has been successfully challenged in either Congress or the courts.

Federal affirmative action programs date back to the efforts of the Reconstruction Congress to assist former slaves to become freedmen. Remarkably, Congress's 1866 debates over these measures are strikingly similar to debates in the 1990s. Opponents called the measures "class legislation" and argued that rather than promoting "equality before the law," they "overleap the mark and land on the other side." Proponents argued that it would be a "cruel mockery" "not [to] provide for those among us who have been held in bondage all their lives" and that therefore the "true object of [such race-specific legislation] is the amelioration of the condition of the colored people."

One hundred years later, affirmative action battles began with President Lyndon B. Johnson's historic June 1965 Howard University commencement address. Speaking of the "devastating heritage of long years of slavery," the President "pledged not just to open the gates of opportunity" but to see to it that "all our citizens have the ability to walk through those gates." For example, the Johnson administration—pursuant to EXECUTIVE ORDER 11246—established an Office of Federal Contract Compliance within the Department of Labor and launched the so-called PHILADELPHIA PLAN of withholding federal contract awards from employers with inadequate minority representation. The Nixon administration, although technically opposed to race preferences, expanded upon these efforts. In addition to institutionalizing Executive Order 11246 programs, President Richard M. Nixon created the Office of Minority Business Enterprise within the Department of Commerce and issued three executive orders to "help establish and promote minority business."

During the Carter years, federal departments and agencies strengthened existing affirmative-action programs (especially in the Small Business Administration and the Office of Federal Contract Compliance) and launched numerous race- and gender-conscious initiatives. Carter initiatives included efforts to demand adequate minority student representation in tax-exempt private schools, the granting of preferences to minority and women broadcasters, the establishment of a minority business set-aside for Department of Transportation highway programs, and EEOC efforts to balance the workplace. The Carter Justice Department also defended private, state, and federal affirmative-action initiatives before the Supreme Court in *United Steelworkers of America v. Weber* (1979) (upholding a private company's one-minority for one-nonminority promotion scheme), *Regents of U. of Calif. v. Bakke* (1978) (invalidating a minority student quota at a California medical school), and *Fullilove v. Klutznick* (1980) (upholding a minority business set-aside for a federal public works employment program).

Challenges under Reagan. Ronald Reagan ran on a platform in 1980 that disavowed the Carter administration's reliance on "quotas, ratios, and numerical requirements to exclude some individuals in favor of others." His Assistant Attorney General for Civil Rights, William Bradford Reynolds, argued that race and gender preferences are "as offensive to standards of human decency today as it was some 84 years ago when countenanced under Plessy v. Ferguson." In court, the administration persistently subscribed to this view. The Reagan Justice Department challenged affirmative-action programs before the Supreme Court in such cases as *Wygant v. Jackson Board of Education* (1986), invalidating a collective bargaining agreement that allowed for senior nonminority teachers to be laid off ahead of junior minority teachers; *Sheet Metal Works v. EEOC* (1986), approving a court-ordered affirmative-action plan in a statutory employment discrimination lawsuit; and *Richmond (City of) v. J. A. Croson Co..* (1989), invalidating a municipal set-aside plan for city-funded construction.

Outside of court, however, the Reagan administration record is less clear. On one hand, the President opposed numerical proofs of discrimination in voting rights and other legislation, appointed numerous individuals who questioned affirmative-action programs, and supported the Justice Department's fron-

tal assault on affirmative action. On the other hand, the administration left in place several of its predecessors' most controversial programs and policies. For example, after the Supreme Court rejected Department of Justice efforts to dismantle affirmative-action programs, the administration reluctantly embraced Executive Order 11246. More striking, President Reagan strongly backed Small Business Administration and other executive-initiated set-aside programs.

The Bush administration has generally supported affirmative-action programs. Bush appointees at the Civil Rights Commission and the FCC, for example, disavowed Reagan administration efforts to dismantle affirmative action. President George Bush also spoke of his "commitment to affirmative action" in criticizing efforts at the Department of Education to limit minority scholarships. Finally, the Bush administration supported minority set-asides. At the same time, President Bush claimed to be a strong opponent of quota hiring. Moreover, the Bush Department of Justice unsuccessfully opposed Bush FCC appointees before the Supreme Court in *Metro Broadcasting Inc. v. Federal Communications Commission* (1990), upholding the granting of preferences to minority broadcasters.

Debate over Affirmative Action. Apparent inconsistencies in the Bush administration's handling of preferential treatment help explain why the affirmative action debate appears intractable. Proponents and opponents of preferences both advance strong arguments why their position is essential to the eradication of artificial line drawing on the basis of race and gender. The Carter administration, for example, viewed affirmative action programs "an essential component of our commitment to expanding civil rights protections" because "racism pervades every aspect of social activity." In contrast, the Reagan administration characterized "bureaucratic numerical regulations" as "inherently discriminatory" because the "obvious and not-so-obvious barriers that once marked blacks as inferior and second-class citizens largely have been eliminated."

Affirmative action remains divisive because neither the Carter nor the Reagan vision predominates. Witness the struggle over the CIVIL RIGHTS ACT OF 1991, which demanded that an employer must demonstrate "business necessity" whenever its employment practices disproportionately burden women and minorities. Proponents of the bill claimed that racism and sexism are cloaked, not explicit, and therefore numerical proofs are needed to ward off illegal pernicious discrimination. Opponents of the bill—most notably George Bush—dubbed the measure a quota bill since employers would rather hire on the basis of race and gender than be embroiled in costly controversial litigation. Bush vetoed the bill in 1990 on that ground. Ironically, in the wake of his controversial appointment of an African American, Clarence Thomas, to the Supreme Court, President Bush capitulated in 1991 and signed the bill after Congress had modified it slightly.

The affirmative action wars seems destined to continue. The inability of the Reagan administration to challenge effectively executive-branch-sponsored race and gender preference demonstrates that these programs are extraordinarily well entrenched. At the same time, opposition to quota hiring too is extraordinarily strong. As the battle over the Civil Rights Act of 1991 reveals, the line separating undesirable quotas from desirable antidiscrimination measures is quite murky. With feelings running so strong on both sides, this murkiness suggests that consensus is unlikely to form. Instead, the struggle over affirmative action will likely remain a prominent feature of political conflict.

BIBLIOGRAPHY

Amaker, Norman. *Civil Rights and the Reagan Administration.* 1988.
Belz, Herman. *Equality Transformed.* 1991.
Graham, Hugh Davis. *The Civil Rights Era.* 1990.

NEAL DEVINS

AFRICAN AMERICANS. For discussion of presidential policy toward African Americans in the period before the Civil War, see SLAVERY; for the period after the Civil War and for the late twentieth century, see AFFIRMATIVE ACTION; CIVIL RIGHTS POLICY; particular CIVIL RIGHTS ACTS; EXECUTIVE ORDER 9981; FAIR EMPLOYMENT PRACTICE COMMITTEE; FREEDMEN'S BUREAU.

AGENDA, PRESIDENT'S. The CHIEF EXECUTIVE'S policy proposals constitute his agenda. Agenda proposals are typically divided into two categories, legislative and administrative. Legislative agendas are most easily found in Presidents' INAUGURAL ADDRESSES and annual STATE OF THE UNION MESSAGES, while administrative agendas are most directly represented by EXECUTIVE ORDERS. Because some proposals offered in a state of the union address or an executive order are merely symbolic gestures, some scholars restrict the President's agenda to include only those proposals on the so-called "must list" that the President and WHITE HOUSE STAFF aggressively pursue. This list can be identified through OFFICE OF MANAGEMENT AND BUDGET (OMB) legislative clearance records, legislative liaison activities, presidential press releases, and other announcements that indicate a President's interests in national policy. Although Presidents also pursue judicial agendas by bringing specific cases to court and by nominating judges, the judicial avenue is rarely a President's first choice for securing action on a policy program. Courts move at their own speed and are unpredictable instruments of executive policy.

Resources. The President's agenda uses two kinds of resources: the internal, organizational resources of time, energy, information, and expertise; and the external, political capital of public support, seats in Congress, and electoral margin. These resources are distributed unevenly across the life of an administration and create the cycles that determine when the agenda is set. First is the cycle of *increasing effectiveness.* Presidents who, during their previous careers, were governors or other "outsiders" often start their terms with little knowledge about the ways things work in Washington, D.C. Depending on how quickly their staffs learn, these Presidents do better at agenda-setting later in their terms. Outsider Presidents can compensate by recruiting seasoned Washington insiders as senior aides and CABINET officers, but this strategy may work against innovative proposals and undermine public support, particularly if a President was elected by running against the entrenched elite in Washington.

Second is the cycle of *decreasing influence.* Presidents can start their terms at the highest point of their influence and use their political capital with each new agenda proposal, spending it down, as Vice President WALTER MONDALE once explained, like a checking account. A President rarely ends the first term of office with the same level of public approval he began with, and the President's party almost inevitably loses seats in Congress in the midterm elections. This cycle of decreasing influence puts great pressure on the agenda, driving a President to act early, even if these proposals are deficient or knowledge is insufficient. Given this tendency, pragmatists will push Presidents to move quickly, lest they squander their scarce capital. Idealists, however, suggest a more deliberative process, arguing for long-term patience even at the price of short-term popularity.

The Agenda-Setting Process. Regardless of when the agenda gets set, it is usually the product of specific choices about problems, alternatives, and priorities. Decisions do not always fall in sequence. Sometimes Presidents identify solutions long before they analyze problems. Presidents may establish their legislative and administrative agendas during the early months of transition. Three discrete steps determine the agenda.

In the first step, the President and White House staff select the problems that they believe demand attention. The list of problems requiring action can come from a variety of sources: the campaign, the party platform, the President's own experiences, the staff, or from task forces, commissions, or White House study groups. However, most of the problems Presidents choose to address arise from sources outside the White House. Congress, current events, and the executive branch are the primary sources of presidential thinking about what problems matter most.

This reliance on outside sources, particularly Congress and the bureaucracy, varies greatly depending on the President's party and ideology. Whereas Democrats such as John F. Kennedy and Lyndon Baines Johnson could rely on Congress and the bureaucracy as stable sources of ideas, Republicans such as Richard M. Nixon, Ronald Reagan, and George Bush had to turn elsewhere. Because during these Presidents' terms the Democrats controlled the House of Representatives and usually the Senate as well, these Republicans developed alternative sources of ideas, perhaps explaining the prominent role of conservative think tanks, such as the Washington, D.C.–based Heritage Foundation, in the 1980s.

When it comes time to choose which problems will be addressed, Democratic and Republican Presidents make choices the same way: on the basis of perceived benefits. Although crisis events often force action, Presidents nevertheless retain a fair amount of discretion in selecting the agenda topics. In doing so, they emphasize both their personal goals and the political benefits of each given issue. The connection between goals and benefits is implicit in that goals attach to the individual President, while benefits attach to specific issues. Thus, a President interested in reelection as a primary goal would tend to seek problems that emerge from PUBLIC OPINION or that generate high electoral benefits.

Presidents have three basic goals that shape agenda choice: reelection, historical achievement, and good policy. There is no doubt that every first-term President cares about reelection to a certain extent, and even second-term Presidents read the polls. Presidents also care deeply about earning a place in history and improving the world as they see it. One or another of these goals may weigh more heavily on the President at a given point in time. (In theory, reelection should dissipate as a goal in the second, and final, term.) At the second step in the agenda-setting process, a President endeavors to match problems to specific solutions. Selecting alternative solutions may be the single most important step in the presidential policy-setting

process. Programmatic content and political benefits are set at this point. More than any other choice, the choice of alternatives determines who gets what, where, and how.

Not all alternatives involve substantive policy, however. Presidents can always decide to do nothing about a given problem, letting history take its course or adopting a wait-and-see posture. Presidents can also choose a symbolic alternative, substituting rhetoric or a study commission for legislative proposals or administrative action.

Once a President decides to act, at least five specific choices must be made, all of which are constrained by the availability of political capital. First, the President must decide whether to offer a specific proposal or to oppose, or even veto, a competing legislative initiative. Second, the President must decide whether to use a legislative, administrative, or, more rarely, judicial alternative. Third, the President must choose between proposing an entirely new program that has never been tested and proposing an expansion of an existing initiative that already has an established coalition of support. Fourth, the President must decide on the size of the program being proposed. Fifth, the President must choose a "tool of government"—for example, direct services, grants, tax expenditures, regulation, or another option—for implementing his objectives.

Obviously, some choices are more politically expensive than others. Doing something about a problem costs more than doing nothing; passing a bill costs more than sustaining a veto; legislative proposals cost more than administrative; large-scale more than small-scale; new more than old; and spending initiatives cost more than tax expenditures or regulation—an especially important consideration in an era of tight federal budgets. Political capital thus shapes both size and scope of each item on the President's agenda, even as it restricts the absolute number of proposals a President can pursue.

In the 1980s and early 1990s, the choice of alternatives expanded somewhat to include questions of packaging, especially when legislation is involved. All Presidents are concerned about how to present their proposals to maximize the chances of congressional enactment. The 1980s and early 1990s saw increasing use of omnibus packages for everything from SOCIAL SECURITY reform (a 1983 package contained a massive new Medicare cost-containment proposal alongside a multitrillion-dollar social security rescue bill) to budget cuts (a 1981 package, for example, contained literally thousands of policy changes).

At the third step, the President assigns a priority to each proposal, placing the item on the "must list" or relegating it to lesser status. This is of particular importance for legislative proposals. A President cannot have so many priorities that there effectively are none, a lesson Jimmy Carter learned in 1977 when he overwhelmed Congress with one "priority" after another. The priority-setting decision is essentially one of balancing the President's personal commitment to a given proposal against its real chance for congressional or administrative success.

Three factors move items up or down the list over time. First, Congress may signal that a given proposal is either ripe for passage (thereby inviting presidential leadership) or doomed to defeat. Second, a given event—for example, a scandal, an economic crisis, or a highly visible media investigation—may accelerate action on a proposal, creating a window of opportunity that may not have existed previously. Third, depending in particular on the state of the economy, the cost of a spending proposal may skyrocket out of the range of the acceptable, or, conversely, may become particularly attractive as a solution to an economic downturn.

Changes in the Agenda-Setting Process. The three steps of agenda-setting became more difficult during the latter half of the twentieth century. A general decentralization of congressional committees increased the number of potential opponents to the President's agenda. A reduction in the quality and quantity of policy analysis and evaluation in government limited the sources of alternatives as Presidents went about the business of building their agendas. And, finally, a weakening of voter attachment to the political system, represented by declines in party identification, made public support more volatile and less effective as a lever for prodding Congress. These changes may have created an agenda-setting process more prone to stalemate than in earlier eras of presidential policy-making.

BIBLIOGRAPHY

Edwards, George, III. *At the Margins: Presidential Leadership of Congress.* 1989.
Light, Paul C. *The President's Agenda: Domestic Policy Choice from Kennedy to Reagan.* 1991.
Peterson, Mark. *Legislating Together: The White House and Capitol Hill from Eisenhower to Reagan.* 1991.
James P. Pfiffner. *The Strategic Presidency.* 1988.
Richard Rose. *The Postmodern President: The White House Meets the World.* 1991.

PAUL C. LIGHT

AGNEW, SPIRO T. (b. 1918), thirty-ninth Vice President of the United States (1969-1973). Little known when the Republican presidential nominee of 1968, Richard M. Nixon, selected him as his running mate, Spiro Theodore Agnew had a meteoric rise as a national figure and a sudden and cataclysmic fall. Accused of taking illegal payments from Maryland contractors as governor of the state and later as Vice President, Agnew was forced to resign to avoid prison. His position at the head of the line of presidential succession at the time the WATERGATE AFFAIR was threatening to remove Nixon from office had raised the real possibility that a man indicated as a felon might succeed to the presidency. As a result, a concerted effort was undertaken to oust him before that could happen.

Regarded for most of his years as Baltimore County Executive and then governor as a moderate, Agnew in 1968 sought to draft a fellow governor, NELSON A. ROCKEFELLER of New York, for the Republican presidential nomination. When Rockefeller unexpectedly took himself out of the running, Agnew was quickly recruited by the Nixon forces, in part because he had lately demonstrated strong conservative tendencies in dealing harshly with black protesters at a predominantly black state college and with discontented black leaders in Baltimore.

When public-opinion polls by the Nixon campaign indicated that no prominent Republican would help Nixon in the fall election, he decided to pick a man with little public recognition on grounds that at least he would not detract from the ticket. After the narrow Republican victory over the Democratic ticket of HUBERT H. HUMPHREY and Edmund S. Muskie, however, Agnew became an outspoken critic of all aspects of the domestic society that took issue with the Nixon administration, particularly in regard to its conduct of the VIETNAM WAR.

With the assistance of White House speechwriters, Agnew went on the attack against war protesters, student radicals, and the news media with colorfully vindictive rhetoric that came to be known as "Agnewisms." He railed against "an effete corps of impudent snobs who characterize themselves as intellectuals" and against the "nattering nabobs of negativism" in the press, and in the process won a nationwide coterie of support, particularly among white blue-collar workers. Agnew took on the role of political hatchet man that Nixon had played as Vice President under Dwight D. Eisenhower and was considered by 1973 to be a strong prospect for the Republican presidential nominee in 1976.

In the summer of 1973, however, as revelations of a White House cover-up in the Watergate break-in threatened the Nixon presidency, Agnew faced a political crisis of his own. Federal investigators in Baltimore, with the assistance of informants, built a solid case that the Vice President had taken illegal payments as governor and even as Vice President. For a time, Nixon was so occupied with the Watergate scandal that his Attorney General, Elliot L. Richardson, delayed informing him of the developing case against Agnew. Nixon and his political advisers in fact regarded Agnew as an "insurance policy" of sorts against IMPEACHMENT, in the belief that the Democrats who controlled Congress, and would have the political power to impeach him, would hesitate to take action against Nixon because it would result in putting Agnew, despised by most Democrats, in the Oval Office in Nixon's place.

Agnew for his part denied the allegations against him when they were made public in August 1973. He vowed to fight them, but when he realized the strength of the case the Justice Department was prepared to make, he sought a political arena that might be more favorable to him. He requested Speaker of the House Carl Albert to initiate "a full inquiry" of the charges, arguing that a Vice President could not be indicted and could be removed from office only by the impeachment procedures specified in the Constitution. While Agnew did not directly ask that impeachment proceedings be undertaken, the request amounted to that, and came to be known as "the impeachment track" on which Agnew hoped to extricate himself.

This challenge was of great concern to Nixon and his advisers, who feared that impeachment of the Vice President might make it easier for the House then to take comparable measures against the President. However, a brief by the Solicitor General ordered by Richardson held that a Vice President could be indicted but a President could not. It argued that removal of a Vice President, unlike the removal of a President, would not immobilize the conduct of the executive branch. The brief effectively cast Agnew afloat on his own, and the Vice President, in his desperation, launched a bitter attack on the Nixon administration itself. He publicly charged that "individuals in the upper professional echelons of the Department of Justice have been severely stung by their ineptness in the prosecution of the Watergate case" and were "trying to recoup their reputation at my expense." This allegation sealed Agnew's fate with the Nixon White House. Intermediaries for Nixon called on him to resign, and when he continued to decline, the Internal Revenue Service stepped up its investigation based on Agnew's net worth, with charges of income-tax evasion the clear objective. The investigatory circle was closing rapidly on the Vice President.

Imperative to Richardson was the removal of Agnew from the line of presidential succession before a vacancy in the presidency occurred as a result of the Watergate investigation. The Attorney General and his aides entered into negotiations with Agnew's lawyers, and in secret plea-bargaining meetings with the federal judge in the case, Walter E. Hoffman, a tentative deal was struck. Agnew would resign the vice presidency and then plead nolo contendere (no contest) to a single count of tax evasion, with a lengthy summary of the charges of illegal payments included in the presentation to the court. Richardson in return would recommend that Agnew not be incarcerated. Hoffman finally agreed, giving Agnew a three-year suspended sentence and a fine of $10,000. Agnew, now a private citizen, walked out of the courtroom on 10 October 1973 a disgraced, but free, man.

With Agnew purged from the line of succession, Nixon nominated and Congress confirmed Gerald R. Ford, Jr., as the nation's first unelected Vice President. On 9 August 1974, upon the resignation of Nixon, Ford, became the country's first unelected President, proclaiming the end of a "national nightmare" that constituted one of the most sordid periods in the history of American presidential politics.

BIBLIOGRAPHY

Cohen, Richard M., and Jules Witcover. *A Heartbeat Away: The Investigation and Resignation of Vice President Spiro T. Agnew.* 1974.
Lippman, Theodore, Jr. *Spiro Agnew's America.* 1972.
Witcover, Jules. *White Knight: The Rise of Spiro Agnew.* 1972.

JULES WITCOVER

AGRICULTURAL ADJUSTMENT ACTS (1933, 1938). The Agricultural Adjustment Acts of 1933 and 1938 were the NEW DEAL's response to low agricultural prices during the Great Depression. The agricultural crisis had begun with a severe price break in 1920. When surplus production kept prices low through the 1920s, farmers and their developing organizations began demanding that the government step in. Direct federal action to shore up prices was a new idea that drew on the experience of the government's strong economic authority during WORLD WAR I. Farmers argued for government assistance because they had less control over production and marketing than did industry. Several plans circulated during the 1920s, most importantly the McNary-Haugen bill, which would have sold surpluses abroad to support domestic prices. President Calvin Coolidge twice vetoed the bill. President Herbert Hoover supported the Agricultural Marketing Act of 1929, which established the Federal

Farm Board to buy up surplus production. The severity of the depression, however, along with the disintegration of international trade in the 1930s, doomed the Board's efforts.

By the time Franklin D. Roosevelt took office in 1932, many agricultural economists had concluded that farm prices could be stabilized only by a strong government effort to put a floor under prices and take land out of production. Roosevelt also saw farm aid as a means of stimulating the broader economy, since farm families then made up 25 percent of the population. The Agricultural Adjustment Act (AAA) of 12 May 1933 was hastily pushed through Congress during the so-called Hundred Days. At first seen as only an emergency measure, the act embodied what had become known as the voluntary domestic allotment plan. Guided by the Agricultural Adjustment Administration and local committees of farmers, growers took surplus acreage out of production in return for payments funded by a tax on processors of food and fibers. Reflecting the experimental approach of the early Roosevelt administration, the act also provided for a number of other methods of price support, including nonrecourse loans and marketing agreements. In practice, almost all the basic commodities covered—corn, wheat, hogs, cotton, rice, tobacco, and milk—were given their own price-support programs. In 1934 and 1935 several other commodities were added. Amendments in 1935 permitted export subsidies and import quotas on agricultural products. The act succeeded in raising prices from their 1932 depression lows, but prices also received some help from a drought in the mid-1930s.

In 1936 the Supreme Court struck down AAA processing taxes in its *Hoosac-Mills* decision. The Roosevelt administration countered with the Soil Conservation and Domestic Allotment Act of 29 February 1936, which reestablished production controls under the banner of soil conservation. This act also explicitly introduced the goal of parity income to ensure that farm commodities would have the same purchasing power they enjoyed in the prosperous period of 1909 to 1914.

The Agricultural Adjustment Act of 1938, approved on 16 February 1938, was a more permanent replacement for the 1933 AAA and, along with the Agricultural Act of 1949, forms the legal basis for modern farm programs. Under the 1938 AAA, producers of basic crops followed voluntary acreage allotments in return for minimum price protection and possible income supplements. When the Secretary of Agriculture estimated that surplus stocks of a commodity would exceed a predetermined level, the program

imposed mandatory marketing quotas subject to a two-thirds vote by producers. The 1938 act also established four regional research laboratories to find new uses for surplus crops.

The Agricultural Adjustment Acts of 1933 and 1938 and their amendments brought unprecedented government intervention in agriculture. In the wide variety of options they provided were the seeds of many ideas that became more important later, such as payments in kind, crop insurance, and payment limitations.

BIBLIOGRAPHY

Hamilton, David E. *From New Day to New Deal: American Farm Policy from Hoover to Roosevelt, 1928–1933.* 1991.

Nourse, Edwin G., et al. *Three Years of the Agricultural Adjustment Administration.* 1937.

Saloutos, Theodore. *The American Farmer and the New Deal.* 1982.

DOUGLAS E. BOWERS

AGRICULTURAL POLICY. The significance of agricultural policy for the presidency has three aspects: domestic electoral needs and party building; foreign-policy goals; and overall economic policy.

The nation's most marginal farmers, in the South and Great Plains, were traditionally the strongest claimants for government intervention in agriculture. In the nineteenth century the REPUBLICAN PARTY cultivated midwestern and western farmers with such programs as the HOMESTEAD ACT for inexpensive land, the MORRILL LAND GRANT ACT for agricultural colleges, the HATCH ACT, for extension services, and the creation of the U.S. DEPARTMENT OF AGRICULTURE (USDA). Before the NEW DEAL, the impetus for such aid typically came from Congress, with Presidents playing a more passive or conservative role. President Grover Cleveland, for example, vetoed a modest appropriation for free seed for drought-stricken Texas farmers, and Woodrow Wilson at first resisted congressional demands for credit programs and abolition of commodity futures speculation. In the 1920s President Calvin Coolidge twice vetoed the ambitious McNary-Haugen plans developed by the congressional farm bloc and agricultural groups, which provided for government maintenance of domestic prices and sale of surplus crops abroad.

Wilson and Roosevelt. In the twentieth century the goal of building a rural clientele for an expanded federal government through large-scale, publicly provided income maintenance and services has been preeminently a Democratic, not a Republican, project. The Democrats' response to the farmers' needs made agricultural policy central to the state-building projects of Wilson and Franklin D. Roosevelt. Wilson and his Secretary of Agriculture, David Houston, met the southern and western farmers' radical demands for government action with moderate programs of banking, regulation, and services that tempered agrarian radicalism while significantly expanding the power of the federal government (and the size of the USDA). The entrepreneurial USDA had thus become a reservoir of respected bureaucratic expertise attaching farmers to the federal government even before the New Deal.

By 1933, President Roosevelt and the agricultural economists in the USDA were convinced that government-mandated production controls were the solution to the farm crisis. They were able to persuade rural spokesmen to support proposals by the executive branch that became the AGRICULTURAL ADJUSTMENT ACT (AAA). As farm laborers and tenant farmers were not well organized and, in the South, largely excluded from the electorate, the AAA was oriented toward larger commercial farmers. The lack of attention to the condition of poor farm workers, only partially remedied by subsequent AAA regulations and the 1937 Farm Security Act for tenant farmers, rendered the administration's policy less effective as a mechanism for raising incomes and purchasing power in the rural sector, but it reflected political reality in the Democratic coalition, as well as the preference of the New Deal BRAIN TRUST to get marginal farmers and surplus labor off the land and into industrial jobs.

The New Deal created a government-farmer nexus that became entrenched, bolstered by the typical IRON TRIANGLE of organized farm groups, USDA units, and House and Senate agricultural committees. Once so institutionalized, the dynamic center of these networks tended to reside in Congress, in committees dominated, until the late 1970s, by southern Democrats. This situation made the New Deal policy system less useful to subsequent Democratic Presidents (and, of course, to Republicans) than it had been to Roosevelt. In the late 1940s the administration of the narrowly elected Harry S. Truman, faced with open southern Democratic rebellion and the rising demands of labor and civil rights groups, attempted to make a reformed agricultural policy the centerpiece of a transformed Democratic Party—one that better reflected the President's electoral coalition.

Roosevelt had taken societal interests as he found them and melded often incongruous interests into a coalition that traded votes in Congress. By the late 1930s, however, the northern urban wing of the Democratic Party complained bitterly that the southerners

who dominated the committee system were unwilling to give as much as they got. Having secured their farm-price supports with the aid of northern votes, the southern Democrats often joined the Republicans in opposing labor, public works, and urban social legislation.

Truman's Program. In 1949 Truman endorsed a new farm program designed by his Secretary of Agriculture, Charles Brannan. Brannan and his aides developed the program with little or no collaboration from the major farm groups or congressional committee leaders. It was, however, endorsed by the Farmers' Union, the Congress of Industrial Organizations (CIO), and Americans for Democratic Action. In contrast with the New Deal system, which relied on production and marketing controls to boost farm prices and disproportionately benefited large commercial farmers, Brannan proposed to let the prices of perishable commodities reach their natural (market) level and to indemnify family farmers with direct income support (limited to about $20,000 per farm). While protecting small and medium-size farmers, the plan would benefit the urban working and middle classes with lower food prices. The CIO hoped to trade its Brannan-plan support for repeal of the TAFT-HARTLEY ACT. Thus, the Truman administration would preside over the construction of a new farmer-labor coalition whose interests were better integrated by greater class coherence and interdependence. The proposal would, it was hoped, permanently solidify the support of midwestern farmers who had delivered a surprisingly strong Democratic presidential vote in 1948. The plan was opposed by the Republicans, who foresaw a potent coalition built around the Brannan proposal, and by the conservative Farm Bureau Federation and congressional southern Democrats. As a result of this opposition, the Brannan plan received little attention in 1949 as Congress prepared its own farm bill relying on traditional mechanisms. Support for the new plan appeared to be growing in 1950, amid declining farm prices, and the administration hoped to make it an issue in the congressional elections. However, the outbreak of the KOREAN WAR brought rising commodity prices, necessitated a new political strategy focused on COLD WAR calculations, and drew the President's attention away from domestic reform and party building.

Captives of the System. Since 1949, agricultural policy has evolved incrementally. Republican Presidents have rhetorically condemned the entrenched dependence of the farmers on the federal government and urged the dismantling of the New Deal system, but, in practice, they have yielded to its continuation and even, in the 1980s, to a dramatic expansion of agricultural expenditures by, and farmer dependence on, the government. Democratic Presidents since Truman have sought only minor changes, although they became, in the 1960s, increasingly sensitive to non-producer interests in food policy. John F. Kennedy, Lyndon B. Johnson, and Jimmy Carter encouraged an expansion of the food stamp program, and Carter gave strong backing to consumer and environmental interests in agricultural policy. This policy evolution was supported by congressional committee and seniority reform and by demographic changes and reapportionment that reduced the number of farm-oriented House districts and required farmer representatives to bargain more assiduously with spokesmen for poor and urban Americans.

The largely incremental addition of these new claimants, and the inability of Republican Presidents to effect a significant reduction of the government's role in agriculture suggests that, while Roosevelt could be said to have captured farmers for the state, subsequent Presidents have themselves been captives of agricultural policy system. It is a less closed system than before, and urban Democrats are in a stronger position to bargain for food stamps and environmental protection; thus the development of agriculture policy has been more contentious since the 1970s. The President, however, is only one player among many. He can threaten a veto if his perspective is not accommodated, but it is unlikely that Presidents of either party will risk antagonizing a still very potent farm bloc. Farm-belt electoral losses during the tenures of Dwight D. Eisenhower in 1958, Carter in 1978 and in 1980, and Ronald Reagan in 1986 (which cost the Republicans control of the Senate) were painful reminders of the price of alienating the vigilant, politically mobilized farmers.

The farm bloc, then, has proven remarkably resilient, and the government's massive intervention in agricultural markets quite resistant to presidentially induced changes. In recognition of this weakness, Presidents have devoted few of their energies to agriculture, and the Secretary of Agriculture has not, since Roosevelt's first term, been an important presidential adviser. While allowing the price-support and income-support system to continue, Presidents have often made agricultural concerns subservient to the larger economic and foreign-policy interests that occupy much more of their attention. Neither the farm lobby nor its advocates in USDA were able to dissuade the Carter and Reagan administrations from monetary policies that priced U.S. agricultural goods out of world markets, nor were they able to prevent grain

embargoes by the administrations of Richard M. Nixon, Gerald Ford, and Carter. These were imposed to serve the Presidents' greater domestic goals (of containing food price inflation) or foreign-policy objectives (as in the 1980 grain embargo to punish the Soviet Union for its invasion of Afghanistan). While low-cost food sales or grants have utility as a foreign-policy strategy, and export subsidies may serve as bargaining chips in international trade negotiations, unilateral U.S. embargoes have proved self-defeating. The targets easily found other sources and the perceived unreliability of U.S. delivery led an array of customers to seek alternative suppliers. Thus the 1980 embargo merely succeeded in damaging U.S. farmers and handing Reagan an effective issue with which to win the midwestern farm vote.

Agricultural policy has inevitably figured in presidential strategy for dealing with inflation and the growing budget deficits of the post-1973 era. But presidential talk of reducing farm subsidies has only threatened to alienate rural voters, with little ultimate impact on the policy system. Reagan and George Bush ultimately swallowed most of their ideological principles rather than continue a futile quest to "take the government out of agriculture." The most that Republican Presidents have been able to accomplish has been more administrative flexibility in fixing loan rates and target prices (setting the latter low enough to make U.S. exports competitive in world markets), allowing more freedom to plant crops currently in demand, and reducing surpluses and storage costs by offering government-owned commodities as payments in kind for taking land out of production. In the Reagan and Bush administrations these policies did reduce surpluses and help farmers to regain lost markets. But the price paid for these accomplishments was huge outlays for income support via deficiency payments representing the difference between federally set target prices and the market price or government loan rate. Not only did government expenditures in support of agriculture reach historic highs in the mid-1980s (rising to almost $26 billion in 1986, from a pre-1981 average of under $3 billion), but record acreage-reduction programs and export subsidies contributed to making the Reagan-Bush years the most interventionist era ever for U.S. agriculture.

BIBLIOGRAPHY

Benedict, Murray R. *Farm Policies of the United States, 1790–1950.* 1953.

Hamby, Alonzo L. *Beyond the New Deal: Harry S. Truman and American Liberalism.* 1973.

Kirkendall, Richard S. *Social Scientists and Farm Politics in the Age of Roosevelt.* 1966.

Rapp, David. *How the U.S. Got into Agriculture and Why It Can't Get Out.* 1988.

Skocpol, Theda, and Kenneth Feingold. "State Capacity and Economic Intervention in the Early New Deal." *Political Science Quarterly* 97 (1982): 255–278.

M. ELIZABETH SANDERS

AGRICULTURE, DEPARTMENT OF. The U.S. Department of Agriculture (USDA) is the sixth-largest CABINET department, with about ninety-five thousand permanent, full-time employees. Organizationally, it has forty-two separate agencies reporting to nine assistant secretaries and other subcabinet officials. During most administrations AGRICULTURAL POLICY has been considered a specialized issue, receiving less White House attention than some others. This has left Secretaries of Agriculture with relatively large discretion in formulating policy.

Early History. USDA was established as an independent agency in 1862, during the presidency of Abraham Lincoln. It was the first department of the federal government devoted to a particular economic interest. Previously, most federal assistance to farmers had been indirect, for example, through the rapid sale of federal lands and transportation subsidies. In 1839, Patent Office commissioner Oliver Ellsworth obtained a small appropriation to assist in distributing seeds to farmers from promising crop varieties collected by diplomats overseas. The appropriation also provided for the collection of agricultural statistics. Subsequent Patent Office reports became compendiums of agricultural information from voluntary reporters in different states. Scientific work began with a small propagating garden in Washington, D.C. By the 1850s pressure was growing, both in Congress and in the newly formed United States Agricultural Society, to establish a formal agriculture department. This, along with the creation of the land-grant college system and the HOMESTEAD ACT, which provided 160 acres of free land those who would farm it, became possible after the Southern states withdrew from Congress during the CIVIL WAR. On 15 May 1862 Lincoln signed the act creating as a separate Department of Agriculture with nine employees headed by a commissioner.

The new department continued the seed-distribution and information work that had been done by the Patent Office. The first commissioner, Isaac Newton, soon expanded the government's research to include plants, animals, soils, and fertilizers. Statistics were systematized and collected on a more rigorous basis.

During the department's first quarter-century it expanded rapidly, reaching 488 employees by 1889. That year, USDA's significant role was recognized in the granting of Cabinet status. President Grover Cleveland appointed Norman J. Colman to be the first secretary.

By the turn of the century the Department of Agriculture was reaching out into a number of new areas. It began regulatory work, including the inspection and grading of food, the quarantining of foreign animals, and the investigation of adulterated food. It began to assist farmers in marketing crops at home and abroad, forecasted the weather, took charge of the nation's forest reserves, and between 1893 and 1939 served as the government's road-building agency. Research expanded greatly after the Hatch Experiment Station Act of 1887 began sponsoring cooperative federal-state experiment stations at land-grant colleges. Influential new research began on nutrition and diet. Statistical activities also improved, and the department began to hire economists to analyze the data. During this period the department's organization developed, with bureaus covering such scientific disciplines as soil, chemistry, entomology, and plant and animal industry. By 1900, USDA had 3,128 employees.

By 1914 the department had begun to look for a more efficient means of delivering the results of its research to farmers. That year the Smith-Lever Act set up the USDA Extension Service, which put extension agents in nearly every county in the nation to bring the latest in research information directly to farmers. The department's combination of local, state, and federal initiative and funding became a model of federalism. WORLD WAR I brought new, though temporary, regulatory powers to USDA to control prices and encourage production of food for the war effort. In this period USDA also began to regulate futures trading and stockyards and to provide long-term credit for farmers.

A sharp decline in commodity prices in 1920, following the collapse of wartime demand, led to a long-term depression in agriculture and to demands for direct government intervention in the agricultural economy to support farm prices. American farmers were able to produce considerably more than they could sell domestically or overseas. Congressional efforts to do this in the 1920s were vetoed by President Calvin Coolidge. The Federal Farm Board was created in 1929 to buy surplus production but found the problem too big to solve with its limited resources.

The New Deal and After. With the full-scale depression that followed the stock market crash of 1929, demands for action by the government grew more

Secretaries of Agriculture

President	Secretary of Agriculture
22 Cleveland	Norman J. Coleman, 1889
23 B. Harrison	Jeremiah M. Rusk, 1889–1893
24 Cleveland	Julius Sterling Morton, 1893–1897
25 McKinley	James Wilson, 1897–1901
26 T. Roosevelt	James Wilson, 1901–1909
27 Taft	James Wilson, 1909–1913
28 Wilson	David F. Houston, 1913–1920 Edwin T. Meredith, 1920–1921
29 Harding	Henry C. Wallace, 1921–1923
30 Coolidge	Henry C. Wallace, 1923–1924 Howard M. Gore, 1924–1925 William M. Jardine, 1925–1929
31 Hoover	Arthur M. Hyde, 1929–1933
32 F. D. Roosevelt	Henry A. Wallace, 1933–1940 Claude R. Wickard, 1940–1945
33 Truman	Claude R. Wickard, 1945 Clinton P. Anderson, 1945–1948 Charles F. Brannan, 1948–1953
34 Eisenhower	Ezra Taft Benson, 1953–1961
35 Kennedy	Orville L. Freeman, 1961–1963
36 L. B. Johnson	Orville L. Freeman, 1963–1969
37 Nixon	Clifford M. Hardin, 1969–1971 Earl L. Butz, 1971–1974
38 Ford	Earl L. Butz, 1974–1976 John A. Knebel, 1976–1977
39 Carter	Bob S. Bergland, 1977–1981
40 Reagan	John R. Block, 1981–1986 Richard E. Lyng, 1986–1989
41 Bush	Clayton Yeutter, 1989–1991 Edward R. Madigan, 1991–1993
42 Clinton	Mike Espy, 1993–

urgent. Farm prices fell to a low point in 1932, sending many farmers into bankruptcy. After Franklin D. Roosevelt's election in 1932, the new administration saw agricultural relief as a means of stimulating the whole economy. During the NEW DEAL USDA attained its modern form, undertaking many new programs and expanded its work force four times by 1940.

The New Deal's first agricultural priority under Secretary HENRY A. WALLACE was to raise farm prices and remove burdensome surpluses from the market. The AGRICULTURAL ADJUSTMENT ACTS of 1933 and 1938 and their amendments inaugurated government price-support and acreage-reduction programs, encouraged farmers to practice proper soil conservation, and began export subsidies, import quotas, and crop insurance. Food relief assisted the unemployed. To improve the quality of rural life, USDA subsidized rural electric power cooperatives and stepped up road-building activities. Many farmers on drought-stricken or other marginal land were resettled in more productive areas. Laboratories were built to find new uses for farm products. Several new rural credit programs appeared. Most of these programs spawned new agencies to administer them.

During WORLD WAR II the department was given even more emergency control over agriculture than it had had during the previous war. Through such agencies as the War Food Administration, USDA helped ration food, stimulated production, allocated scarce resources needed by farmers, encouraged gardening, established labor importation programs, and educated the public on food conservation and other wartime themes. The department's research emphasized finding agricultural alternatives to scarce products that could no longer be imported. High price supports kept production near record levels.

Following World War II the department returned to its peacetime orientation. New Deal programs, which had often originated as reform ideas, entered the mainstream, except for some of the more unconventional plans, such as farmer resettlement and greenbelt towns. Farming went through a major transformation in the two decades after the war. Farms became larger, more specialized, more heavily capitalized, and fewer in number. With the growing use of chemical fertilizers and pesticides, productivity soared. Fearing that the return of farm surpluses would lead to a price collapse like that which had occurred after World War I, the department grappled with ways to use or dispose of excess commodities. Marketing received renewed emphasis from the Agricultural Market Act of 1946. Beginning in 1954, the Food for Peace (P.L. 480) program sought to combine assistance to hungry nations with a reduction in surplus commodities. The Dwight D. Eisenhower administration began a rural development program to revitalize rural communities that lost population as farm families left for the cities.

From Kennedy to Bush. The administrations of John F. Kennedy and Lyndon B. Johnson put new emphasis on alleviating hunger. The Food Stamp Act of 1964 was joined by school lunch subsidies and other assistance targeted to poor children and mothers. The department cooperated in enforcing the CIVIL RIGHTS ACT OF 1964, an assignment made difficult by the persistence of racist mores in many local USDA offices. Rural development was expanded nationwide in cooperation with other agencies active in Johnson's War on Poverty. In the 1960s many older price-support programs were replaced with a voluntary system of relatively low supports supplemented by income payments.

In the 1970s farmers enjoyed a period of prosperity stimulated by a rapid increase in exports of major field crops such as wheat, corn, and soybeans. Rural development activities were enhanced by the Rural Development Act of 1972. Food programs expanded to become the major item in the USDA budget. Many nonagricultural groups became interested in USDA programs, encouraging the department to place greater emphasis on consumer issues such as food safety.

American agriculture suffered another reverse in the 1980s. Exports peaked in 1981 and then fell because of a rising dollar and lower foreign demand. Farm prices followed. Many farmers had gone deeply into debt in order to expand their operations. When commodity and farmland prices began to decline in the early 1980s, many farmers suffered financial hardship. The Ronald Reagan administration proposed sharp cuts in farm programs to stem their rising costs. Congress sustained the programs, but the administration did succeed in cutting back in some areas. The 1985 Food Security Act stimulated exports with lower price supports and export subsidies while the administration's General Agreement on Tariffs and Trade (GATT) proposals in the Uruguay round of negotiations attempted to eliminate subsidies from world trade. The 1985 act also showed a new interest in conservation with its provision for a conservation reserve to remove erodible land from production. The 1990 Food, Agriculture, Conservation, and Trade Act continued in the same direction, with strong conservation provisions. In the 1980s, USDA also took a more important role on other environmental issues, such as organic farming and pollution from agricultural chemicals.

The Department of Agriculture remains active in its traditional areas of research, forestry, marketing, inspection, disease control, and price supports. But its mandate now covers much more than agriculture per se. More than half of the department's 1992 budget of $62 billion was allocated for food programs, and the department plays an active role in areas such as the environment, recreation, consumer education, nutrition, and rural housing. About 90 percent of its employees are in field locations.

BIBLIOGRAPHY

Baker, Gladys L., et al. *Century of Service: The First 100 Years of the United States Department of Agriculture.* 1963.

Fite, Gilbert C. *American Farmers: The New Minority.* 1981.

Gaus, John M., and Leon O. Wolcott. *Public Administration and the United States Department of Agriculture.* 1940.

Harding, T. Swann. *Some Landmarks in the History of the Department of Agriculture.* Rev. ed. 1951.

Rasmussen, Wayne D., and Gladys L. Baker. *The Department of Agriculture.* 1972.

Saloutos, Theodore. *The American Farmer and the New Deal.* 1982.

DOUGLAS E. BOWERS

AIRCRAFT, PRESIDENTIAL. Presidential air transport began 3 February 1945, when a Douglas C-54 (DC-4) Skymaster—unofficially named the Sacred Cow—was used by President Franklin D. Roosevelt. A special electric hoist was installed in the rear of the aircraft to accommodate the President's wheelchair. The next aircraft used, the *Independence*, a Douglas C-118 (DC-6) Liftmaster, transported President Harry S. Truman from 1947 to 1953. President Dwight D. Eisenhower traveled aboard the *Columbine II* and *Columbine III*, both Lockheed L-749 Constellations (C-121) from 1953 to 1961.

The call sign *Air Force One* was first used in September 1961, identifying President John F. Kennedy flying aboard a C-118 aircraft. On 10 November 1962, the first jet aircraft for presidential travel—a Boeing C-137, tail number 26000—was used by President Kennedy. Having transported seven Presidents, it may have the most historical significance of the presidential aircraft. Aircraft 26000 is noted for carrying President Kennedy to Dallas, Texas on 22 November 1963, and returning his body to Washington, D.C., following his assassination. That same day, Lyndon B. Johnson was sworn into office on board 26000 at Love Field in Dallas. This aircraft was also used to return President Johnson's body to Texas following his state funeral on 24 January 1973.

Tail number 27000—another C-137—was received on 23 December 1972, replacing 26000 as the primary presidential aircraft. It was used to fly former Presidents Richard M. Nixon, Gerald R. Ford, and Jimmy Carter to Cairo, Egypt on 19 October 1981, to attend the funeral of Egyptian president Anwar Sadat.

A Boeing 747-200B (VC-25A), tail number 28000, first flew as *Air Force One* on 6 September 1990, when President George Bush was flown to Kansas and Florida and back to Washington D.C. A sister plane, tail number 29000, is used as a backup to 28000. The two VC-25A aircraft will be used for presidential travel well into the twenty-first century upholding the distinction of transporting the President of the United States under the call sign of *Air Force One*.

BIBLIOGRAPHY

Mikesh, Robert C. "Presidential Aircraft." *American Aviation Historical Society Journal* 8, no. 2 (Summer 1963): 84.

Pennington, Thomas E. *History of the 89th Military Airlift Wing—1990.* 1991.

THOMAS E. PENNINGTON

ALASKA PURCHASE TREATY. Marking the end of the Russian presence in North America, Andrew Johnson's administration purchased Alaska for $7.2 million from the imperial government. Secretary of State WILLIAM H. SEWARD negotiated for the United States. The treaty was signed on 30 March 1867 in Washington, D.C. On 9 April 1867 the Senate voted to ratify, and Congress passed the appropriations necessary on 14 July 1868. Maj. Gen. Lovell Rousseau took possession of the territory on 16 October 1867.

Immediate impetus for the Alaska purchase came from the Russian side. With Baron Stoeckl, the Russian minister to the United States, as its chief negotiator, the imperial government privately announced to Seward its willingness to sell the Alaska territory. Seward, who had spoken publicly about American expansion north into British North America, leapt at the opportunity. Seward recognized the strategic utility of Alaska in American hands: it at once withdrew the Russian empire from the continent and placed the British, in British Columbia, on the defensive. The British ambassador Sir Frederick Bruce objected to the purchase.

Attaining congressional appropriations was no easy matter. Enmity against the extremely unpopular Andrew Johnson, mistrust of Seward and his imperialist designs, and support for Benjamin Perkins's claim against the Russian government slowed progress in Congress. Although the Senate ratified quickly after Sen. Charles Sumner's endorsement (Sumner first called the territory Alaska), Congress held off with the appropriations necessary. In late March 1868, just prior to the trial for the IMPEACHMENT OF ANDREW JOHNSON the House of Representatives voted to delay consideration of the appropriations bill for two months. This placed the United States in violation of the 20 April 1868 deadline for payment prescribed by the treaty. Intense lobbying by Seward, Thaddeus Stevens, Sumner, and Stoeckl (rumored to have bribed Congressmen), finally won out in July 1868.

Reaction to the purchase was mixed. Anti-Johnson newspapers called it "Seward's folly." A report issued by the Smithsonian Institution (at Seward's request), however, revealed the territory's true natural value. Its strategic value was more apparent, though an American presence in Alaska failed to set off an annexationist movement in British North America, as Seward had vaguely hoped. In 1867, British North America be-came Canada; British Columbia entered the confederation in 1870. British anger was neither serious nor long-lasting. The TREATY OF WASHINGTON of 1871 set the pattern for Anglo-American-Canadian relations into the next century. Johnson and Seward managed no further imperial acquisitions.

BIBLIOGRAPHY

Castel, Albert E. *The Presidency of Andrew Johnson.* 1979.
Paolino, Ernest. *The Foundations of the American Empire: William Henry Seward and U.S. Foreign Policy.* 1973.
Trefousse, Hans L. *Andrew Johnson.* 1989.
Van Deusen, Glyndon G. *William Henry Seward.* 1967.

JOHN F. WALSH

ALIEN AND SEDITION ACTS. Passed in 1798 by a Federalist-dominated Congress, the Alien and Sedition Acts were part of a national defense and internal security system during the QUASI-WAR WITH FRANCE. The administration of President John Adams and the FEDERALIST PARTY established a preparedness program that carried the United States into a state of undeclared war with France. In recommending the defense measures, Adams asked Congress to act with unanimity, a clear indication that political opposition would be viewed as disloyal.

Thus was the stage set for legislation to deal with what the Federalists called the "internal foe," the Democratic-Republican Party headed by Vice President Thomas Jefferson. Rallying their forces behind patriotic slogans and political orthodoxy, the Federalists quickly enacted an internal security system designed to cripple, if not destroy, the Jeffersonian Republicans.

Enacting the Measures. This program of political intolerance was inaugurated by the Naturalization Act of 1798 (1 Stat. 566), a move designed to cut off an increasingly important source of Democratic-Republican strength: French and Irish immigrants. Unable to prevent the Jeffersonians from recruiting former aliens into their ranks, the Federalists slowed the process of enlistment by nearly tripling the time required for immigrants to become citizens.

The Act Concerning Aliens (1 Stat. 570) allowed the President to deport all aliens whom he judged to be dangerous to the peace and safety of the United States or whom he suspected of being engaged in "any treasonable or secret machinations against the government." Although Adams signed several blank warrants in case offenders should be seized, no aliens were actually deported under the law's provisions.

The second alien act, the Alien Enemies Law (1 Stat. 577), was enacted with bipartisan support and authorized the imprisonment or banishment of aliens who were citizens of an enemy nation in time of war. Since Congress did not declare war with France, the law was not enforced during the quasi-war, but it has remained a fundamental part of American wartime policy ever since.

The Sedition Act (1 Stat. 596), the capstone of the internal security program of the Federalist Party, was designed to deal with domestic disaffection during the crisis with France. The Federalists first linked the Democratic-Republican Party with the French and then treated opposition to administration measures as nearly traitorous. The law made it a federal crime for anyone to conspire to impede governmental measures or to write or publish "any false, scandalous, and malicious" criticism of the federal government, Congress, or the President, or to bring them into contempt or disrepute by exciting against them "the hatred of the good people of the United States." Thus the Federalists construed criticism of the administration as opposition to the government and subversion of the Constitution.

Debating the Acts. Neither the Naturalization Act nor the Alien Enemies Act raised any controversial constitutional issues, but the Democratic-Republicans attacked both the Act Concerning Aliens and the Sedition Law as arbitrary, unnecessary, and unconstitutional. The Federalists argued that the original Constitution gave Congress jurisdiction over sedition, including seditious words, and that the Bill of Rights had not removed that authority. They claimed that the federal government had an inherent power to protect itself against sedition that endangered its existence. It, therefore, followed that all means calculated to endanger the government were criminal. Although the Constitution did not delegate the power to punish sedition to the government, Congress could make all laws "necessary and proper" to protect its delegated powers. Finally, the Federalists asserted that the Constitution conferred common law jurisdiction on the federal courts, and they defined freedom of speech and press according to English common law—as an exemption from all previous restraints or censorship. According to the Federalists, subsequent punishment of words was therefore no violation of this freedom, and the Sedition Act did not restrict the liberty of the press but was instead aimed at its licentiousness.

The Democratic-Republicans rejected the Federalist arguments. If the federal courts had a common law jurisdiction over seditious libel, why was it necessary to pass a law conferring that jurisdiction on them? More importantly, they denied that there was a federal common law. Even if the common law of one of the states or of England had been adopted by the Constitution, it could only be changed by constitutional amendment, not by law.

According to ALBERT GALLATIN, the leading Democratic-Republican in Congress, the Federalists had failed to prove that a sedition law was necessary and proper because they had not shown which specific power given to Congress or the President would be carried into effect by a law against seditious libels. The clause did not give Congress the power either arbitrarily to create offenses against the government or to take cognizance of cases that were exclusively under the jurisdiction of the state courts. What new danger, asked Gallatin, now threatened such that federal laws would not be executed unless there was a sedition statute on the books? Finally, the Republicans argued for a broad definition of the First Amendment, claiming that it guaranteed free discussion. Counterargument, not coercion, was the Republican answer for calumny.

After Congress passed the Sedition Law by a narrow margin, it was vigorously enforced by the Federalist administration and the courts, always against Jeffersonian printers or spokesmen. There were twenty-five arrests, twenty-one indicments, twelve trails, eleven convictions, and one acquittal. Those convicted included Republican Congressmen and editors of leading Republican newspapers. All were fined up to $1,000 and imprisoned up to eighteen months in federal jail. The repressive legislation expired on 3 March 1801, the day preceding the inauguration of President Thomas Jefferson, the law's leading opponent. The new President quickly pardoned those still in jail and dismissed all prosecutions still pending under the expired law.

BIBLIOGRAPHY

Miller, John C. *Crisis in Freedom: The Alien and Sedition Acts.* 1951.
Smith, James Morton. *Freedom's Fetters: The Alien and Sedition Laws and American Civil Liberties.* 1956.

JAMES MORTON SMITH

ALIENS, EXCLUSION OF. Although the short-lived Aliens Act of 1798 [*see* ALIEN AND SEDITION ACTS] authorized excluding aliens, President John Adams did not exercise that option and no aliens were actually excluded by federal action until the Chinese Exclusion Act of 1882 barred all Chinese laborers. Since that time there has been a steady accretion of reasons for exclusion, such as, in the 1980s and early 1990s, testing positive for AIDS.

By 1917 immigration law had established seven major grounds for exclusion: Asians (except for Japanese and Filipinos), criminals, persons who failed to meet certain moral standards, certain poor persons, certain sick persons, certain radicals, and illiterates. Beginning with Ulysses S. Grant, most late-nineteenth- and early-twentieth-century Presidents urged Congress to restrict immigration in one way or another, although there was sometimes conflict over methods, such as that which led to President Chester A. Arthur's veto of an early version of the Chinese Exclusion Act, which he eventually signed. The only immigration issue which seriously divided Presidents and the Congress was the literacy test, which was successfully vetoed by Presidents Cleveland, Taft, and Wilson before being enacted over the latter's second veto in 1917.

The so-called "quota acts" of 1921 and 1924 [*see* IMMIGRATION ACT OF 1924] supported enthusiastically by Presidents Harding and Coolidge, and the requirement that all immigrants have valid visas issued by American consuls abroad greatly reduced the volume of immigration. From that time, the denial of a visa abroad rather than rejection at an American port of entry or deportation was the most numerically significant, if largely untabulated, form of positive exclusion. How many potential immigrants were discouraged from even applying is unknowable.

Nearly 650,000 aliens have been excluded at ports of entry since 1892, the vast majority of them prior to 1941. Between 1892 and 1920 the majority of the 300,000 exclusions were under the l.p.c. (likely to become a public charge) clause. From 1921 to 1950, the majority of the 290,000 exclusions were for improper documents as were most of the 62,000 exclusions were between 1951 and 1990. Those two categories have accounted for nearly two-thirds of all exclusions. Some 80,000 were kept out because of mental or physical defects, 40,000 as contract laborers, 16,000 as criminals, 13,000 as illiterates, and 8,000 on one of the morals categories. 1,420 persons were excluded as subversives. In 1990 2,845 persons were excluded, three-quarters of them for lack of papers.

The incidence of exclusion at ports of entry rose steadily from an almost insignificant level of seven per thousand immigrants in the 1890s to almost thirteen per hundred immigrants—better than one in eight—in the 1930s and has dropped to less than two per thousand since the 1950s. Most exclusion now takes place abroad. Obviously a vague criterion, at best, the l.p.c. clause was transformed administratively by President Hoover from one that had kept out persons who seemed incapable of earning a living to one that kept out poor persons who might wind up on relief. In the years between Hoover's order and 1965,

when there were no quotas on immigrants from independent, New World nations, the l.p.c. clause was used largely to keep out poor Mexicans.

The first ideological barriers were raised in 1891 when polygamists—MORMONS were the target—were added to the excluded classes. In 1903, partly in reaction to the assassination of President McKinley by a native-born Polish American, Congress ordered the exclusion of "anarchists, or persons who believe in or advocate the overthrow by force or violence of the Government of the United States or of all government or of all forms of law." These and similar exclusions enacted during the post-WORLD WAR I red scare [*see* PALMER RAIDS] and the so-called McCarthy era of the COLD WAR years [see MCCARTHYISM] actually kept out few immigrants but were more significant as causes for deportation. In addition, parts of the 1952 MCCARRAN-WALTER ACT excluded not only immigrants but also visiting professors, lecturers, and performers whose politics failed to pass the political litmus tests applied by the State Department and the Immigration and Naturalization Service.

In 1993, grounds for exclusion included persons with physical and mental defects and diseases, drug addicts and alcoholics, sexual deviants, paupers, beggars, vagrants and persons likely to become a public charge, prostitutes or procurers, illiterates, persons without proper documents, previously convicted criminals, anarchists, communists and other political subversives, Nazi war criminals, and graduates of a foreign medical school.

[*See also* IMMIGRATION POLICY].

BIBLIOGRAPHY

Daniels, Roger. *Coming to America: A History of Immigration and Ethnicity in American Life*. 1990.

Hutchinson, E. P. *Legislative History of American Immigration Policy, 1798–1965*. 1981.

Miller, John C. *Crisis in Freedom: The Alien and Sedition Acts*. 1952.

Preston, William. *Aliens and Dissenters: Federal Suppression of Radicals, 1903–1933*. 1963.

ROGER DANIELS

ALLIANCE FOR PROGRESS. During the 1960 presidential campaign, John F. Kennedy called for a dramatic new foreign policy for Latin America. The Alliance for Progress was designed to meet the social and economic needs of oppressed Latin Americans who viewed the United States as a counterrevolutionary bully and who seemed vulnerable to the appeal of communism as introduced in CUBA by Fidel Castro. President Kennedy proposed an Alliance for Progress to Latin American officials in March 1961, outlining three components: economic assistance, land and tax reform, and political democratization. The latter two facets represented an idealistic and dramatic effort to change the ossified political, social, and economic structure of Latin America. No American President had ever sought such monumental restructuring.

The U.S. government provided the financial incentive at the August 1961 conference at Punta del Este, Uruguay, when it promised Latin American delegates $1 billion during the first year and $10 billion of a proposed $20 billion in public and private moneys over the next ten years to transform the social and economic landscape. In return, recipient countries were expected to institute comprehensive plans to effect changes.

The Alliance for Progress made modest improvements in economic conditions. It ensured the construction of schools, hospitals, roads, low-cost housing, and electrical power plants, but it suffered from financial shortcomings. Contributing to these shortfalls was the fact that American assistance often came in the form of loans, not grants. Moreover, the net disbursement for the promised $10 billion in assistance was only $4.8 billion from 1961 to 1969, as funds remained in the United States to defray Latin American debts. The administration also insisted that some of the money be used to purchase U.S. commodities at U.S. prices. Perhaps the biggest problem, however, was the population explosion in Latin America, which prevented the alliance from meeting its stated annual per capita economic growth rate of 2.5 percent.

At the same time, the Kennedy administration fallaciously believed that it could simply will social and political changes in Latin America. Few questioned the dubitable premise that middle-class progressives introducing land and other reforms could supplant oligarchical regimes. Kennedy supporters initially placed far too much confidence in that leadership and in the concept of democratic revolution. They also overemphasized the strengths of constitutionalism in a period that saw military leaders topple six popularly elected presidents in Latin America. Finally, as the Kennedy administration became more concerned about protecting U.S. corporate interests in Latin America, it rejected expropriations. It also became less willing to favor popularly elected left-wing parties. For these reasons, it wavered on comprehensive reform.

In the end, the Kennedy administration seemed more concerned about containing Castro than helping poor Latin Americans. It increased military aid to Latin America by 50 percent and created an Office of Public Safety to train Latin American police officers in mob control and counterinsurgency. The Alliance for Progress produced an ambiguous legacy largely because of the administration's unfulfilled and contradictory objectives. What survived was as much a military as an economic aid program. Even so, the alliance provided a modicum of hope and better relations with many Latin American countries.

BIBLIOGRAPHY

Giglio, James N. *The Presidency of John F. Kennedy*. 1991.
Levinson, Jerome, and Juan de Onis. *The Alliance that Lost the Way*. 1970.
Schlesinger, Arthur, Jr. "The Alliance for Progress: A Retrospective." In *Latin America: The Search for a New International Role*. Edited by Ronald G. Hellman and H. Jan Rosenbaum. 1975.

JAMES N. GIGLIO

ALSO-RANS. As of 1993, forty-one men had held the office of President; scores more have been acknowledged contenders for the position and several of these men—some of greater distinction than those who gained the presidency—have come close to winning it. No single explanation—simple or otherwise—can separate the also-rans from the victors, but some general themes can be identified.

Good economic times favor incumbents, while making life difficult for challengers. WILLIAM JENNINGS BRYAN in 1900, JOHN W. DAVIS in 1924, ALFRED E. SMITH in 1928, ADLAI E. STEVENSON in 1956, and WALTER MONDALE in 1984, Democrats all, were victims of the prosperity voters associated with the Republican incumbents in those years. Each had other liabilities that dragged down their candidacies, but with the economic issue working clearly in the Republicans' favor, they started at a disadvantage. Interestingly, Democratic management of the economy directly redounded to their favor only in 1936—conditions under Franklin D. Roosevelt were not great, but they seemed far better than the way Herbert Hoover had left them in 1933—when ALFRED M. LANDON was buried in the Roosevelt–NEW DEAL landslide. (In 1964, Republican BARRY GOLDWATER also lost badly amid an economy shaking off the lethargy of the previous decade.)

Until the last half of the twentieth century, war and the prospect of war placed challengers in awkward situations. To criticize the way a war already underway was being waged was to risk the charge of undermining the combat effort, while to question the direction of administration policies when war appeared imminent ran the danger of alienating either (perhaps both) those who fervently wanted peace or those who demanded the protection of American interests. The election of 1812 demonstrated the difficulties of seeking the presidency with a war going on. Finding widespread unhappiness with the lack of adequate preparations for the war and considerable opposition to the war itself, DEWITT CLINTON tried to have it all ways: as someone who would more effectively prosecute the war and thereby achieve peace sooner. This appearance of opportunism—not yet standard practice in American politics—earned Clinton the scorn of many of his contemporaries, but, in the closest election since 1800, he almost unseated President James Madison.

Similar confusion marked the 1864 campaign of General GEORGE B. MCCLELLAN. With the CIVIL WAR in its fourth year, the Democrats adopted a platform calling for an immediate end to hostilities without any assurances that the Union would be preserved; but their candidate, McClellan, insisted he would carry on the fight until the South agreed to rejoin the Union. Republicans feared that this combination of a warrior running on a peace platform would prove popular, but a series of Union victories played well at the polls and McClellan won only three states.

In 1916 and 1940 the nation was confronted with wars it hoped to avoid, and in both elections the Democratic incumbents stressed their success in keeping the country out of foreign conflicts. The Republican candidate in 1916, CHARLES EVANS HUGHES, never developed a coherent alternative to Woodrow Wilson's policies, or at least one that satisfied the widespread desire for the United States to remain a nonbelligerent. In 1940 the Republican WENDELL WILLKIE portrayed Franklin Roosevelt as a warmonger and promised not "to fight anybody else's war," but Roosevelt matched Willkie's pledge and emphasized his experience in leading the country through perilous times. Willkie made a contest of it, but Roosevelt had built up too many credits with the voters over the previous eight years for the untested Willkie to prevail. PEARL HARBOR turned WORLD WAR II into an American war, and Roosevelt sought a fourth term in 1944—with Allied forces advancing in Europe and the Pacific—on his record as COMMANDER IN CHIEF and proven diplomatic skills. Republican THOMAS E. DEWEY, just two years into his first term as governor of New York and with no foreign policy credentials, offered voters no compelling reasons to dispense with Roosevelt's leadership.

The COLD WAR distorted the Constitution's WAR POWERS provisions and led to overseas conflicts with no clear-cut resolution, thereby allowing challengers in the second half of the twentieth century to use the war issue to their advantage. Adlai Stevenson in 1952 had to defend the unpopular KOREAN WAR policy of the incumbent Democratic administration, a situation parallel to the one faced by HUBERT H. HUMPHREY in 1968 in regard to the VIETNAM WAR—both lost to Republican outsiders who said they had better ways to end the fighting while maintaining American power and honor. As Democrat GEORGE MCGOVERN found out in 1972, however, the challenger did not necessarily have the upper hand. By calling for the immediate and unconditional withdrawal of American troops from Indochina, McGovern alienated voters unprepared to see their country "cut and run." Claims by the Richard M. Nixon administration shortly before election day that "peace was at hand" also demonstrated how the incumbent could use the power of office to manipulate events; McGovern lost in a landslide.

Some also-rans have run into towering individuals who effectively blocked their path to the White House. JOHN CALHOUN, HENRY CLAY, and DANIEL WEBSTER suffered from the misfortune of reaching their political primes in the 1820s and 1830s, when the popular Andrew Jackson dominated presidential elections and defined the issues of the day. For a variety of personal and policy reasons, Jackson became the bitter enemy of each and thwarted their pursuit of the presidency. In 1912 former President Theodore Roosevelt's campaign on the PROGRESSIVE (BULL MOOSE) PARTY to retake the White House derailed the candidacy of progressive Republican, ROBERT M. LA FOLLETTE. The Wisconsin Senator had carried the brunt of the battle against President William Howard Taft over the previous four years, but once the far more charismatic Roosevelt threw his hat into the ring, La Follette's support evaporated.

Alf Landon, Wendell Willkie, and Thomas Dewey all fell victim to Franklin Roosevelt's remaking of American politics, and Adlai Stevenson experienced the sting of Dwight D. Eisenhower's amazing rapport with the American people. Although Stevenson had an appealing style of his own, it was no match for Eisenhower's, and he was decisively beaten in 1952 and 1956. Ronald Reagan's reshaping of the political universe not only defeated Walter Mondale in 1984 but also MICHAEL DUKAKIS in 1988, when the Republican candidate was George Bush, who had been Reagan's Vice President.

Jackson and Eisenhower were examples of military heroes who gained the White House, and besides Calhoun, Clay, Webster, and Stevenson, two other also-rans gained that distinction by having to contest elections against popular generals. Flush from his victories in the MEXICAN WAR, Zachary Taylor was the choice of the ideologically bankrupt Whigs in 1848, and he narrowly defeated veteran Democratic politician LEWIS CASS. Another veteran Democrat, HORATIO SEYMOUR, was a reluctant candidate against the Civil War hero Ulysses S. Grant in 1868, but Seymour ran a surprisingly good race.

Some other military leaders did not make it. WINFIELD SCOTT, who shared Mexican War honors with Taylor, lacked Taylor's popularity. Nicknamed "Old Fuss and Feathers," Scott was a vain and pompous man. The Whigs nominated him in 1852 solely because of his distinguished military record, but the Democratic split that had allowed Taylor to prevail in 1848 did not recur and Scott carried only four states. The Democrats found a general with a familiar name to carry their banner in 1880: WINFIELD SCOTT HANCOCK, a hero at Gettysburg. Hancock shielded the party from the charges of disloyalty under which it long suffered and came close to breaking the Republican's twenty-year lock on the White House. In 1952, Douglas MacArthur, a hero of World War II, waited for the REPUBLICAN PARTY to call, but its leaders were more comfortable with Eisenhower, a known team player. As former President Hoover wrote privately, MacArthur "had a Napoleonic bent to put through the ideas which he holds very strongly."

Images, whether consciously adopted by the candidate or forced on him, have contributed to the making of also-rans. William Jennings Bryan's strident crusade for free silver and rural America in 1896 allowed the well-financed Republican opposition to portray him as a radical who would upset the nation's march toward progress. The Democrat moderated his tone in his campaigns in 1900 and 1908, but the image of 1896 persisted and contributed to Bryan's defeat both times. In 1928, Al Smith's thoroughly urban campaign, highlighted by his New York accent, his call for the repeal of PROHIBITION, and his Roman Catholicism, did not play well in rural America, including the traditionally Democratic south. Barry Goldwater in 1964 offered voters "a choice, not an echo" with his conservative views, but because of his own loose rhetoric and the barrage leveled against him by Democrats, Goldwater was identified as an extremist. He received less than 40 percent of the vote, about the same as George McGovern received in 1972, after the latter had been labeled the candidate of "acid [i.e., LSD], abortion and amnesty" by the Republicans.

If too clear an image can inflict fatal damage on a candidacy, so too can the lack of a distinct identity. The 1916 campaign of Charles Evans Hughes, whom Theodore Roosevelt called "a bearded iceberg," floundered on the Republican's inability to reach out to and inspire audiences. Blandness was also the undoing of two other leading Republicans: Thomas Dewey and Robert Taft. If Dewey's defeat in 1944 was explained by Franklin Roosevelt's name on the ballot, his loss in 1948 was much more his own doing. Having a stiff public manner to begin with, Dewey was lulled into waging a restrained campaign by public opinion polls that showed him far ahead. The initiative passed to the hell-raising incumbent, Harry S. Truman, and Dewey lost in the biggest upset in presidential politics. Taft was Dewey's archrival in the Republican Party and was the leading contender for the party's nomination in 1952, but like Dewey he had an aloof personality on the campaign trail, and after the debacle of 1948, Republicans preferred the much warmer Eisenhower. The Democrats in 1988 nominated Michael Dukakis, who disdained ideology and offered himself as a competent manager. Republicans, whose own candidate, George Bush, had long been derided as a wimp, jumped all over the colorless Dukakis, who made only a feeble response.

Some also-rans have been the victims of serious divisions within their own party. Democrats Lewis Cass in 1848 and STEPHEN A. DOUGLAS in 1860 lost because the SLAVERY controversy led to the formation of splinter parties that sundered the usual Democratic majorities. JAMES G. BLAINE suffered Republican defections from two directions in 1884: Mugwumps (reformers) disgusted by his use of public office for private gain, and Stalwarts (spoilsmen) unhappy with Blaine's distribution of patronage. Despite this, Blaine, who was one of the few genuinely popular politicians of the Gilded Age, almost won. The American Independent Party of GEORGE WALLACE complicated Hubert Humphrey's campaign in 1968 but may have actually made the results closer than they might have been otherwise.

Also-rans have made mistakes in timing. By not taking himself out of the running when the electoral tally of 1800 threw the election into the House of Representatives, AARON BURR miscalculated his own strength and the enmity that his failure to stand aside would arouse in Jefferson and his supporters. Whatever chance Burr had of succeeding Jefferson was destroyed. Conversely, WILLIAM H. CRAWFORD let an opportunity to become President in 1816 slip by in the expectation that the prize would be his as a matter of course in 1824. But when 1824 arrived, Crawford was seriously ill and the political system in operation in 1816 had disappeared. In a four-man field, Crawford finished fourth in the popular vote and a badly beaten third in the electoral vote.

Small incidents—or so they may have seemed at the

time—have turned likely winners into also-rans. Despite the defections in his own ranks and the damage inflicted on his candidacy by charges of scandal, Blaine probably would have won in 1884 if it had not been for some unfortunate remarks made by a supporter at a New York campaign rally a week before election day. A minister referred to the Democrats as the party of "Rum, Romanism, and Rebellion," a statement that Blaine neglected to repudiate and that, when circulated in Irish and other Catholic neighborhoods, turned out a large vote for Blaine's opponent, Grover Cleveland, who took New York by a narrow margin and won the White House. Similarly, with all the weaknesses of the Hughes campaign in 1916, he almost certainly would have won if he had not snubbed—unintentionally—the leading Republican in California, Hiram Johnson, when both were staying at the same hotel. Hughes lost California and the election.

One additional also-ran deserves mention: SAMUEL J. TILDEN. In all likelihood, Tilden had the election of 1876 stolen from him.

BIBLIOGRAPHY

Schlesinger, Arthur M., Jr., ed. *History of American Presidential Elections, 1789–1968.* 4 vols. 1971.
Southwick, Leslie H. *Presidential Also-Rans and Running Mates, 1788–1980.* 1984.

MARK I. GELFAND

AMBASSADORS, RECEIVING AND APPOINTING.

The President's authority to receive and appoint ambassadors is an important part of his foreign affairs powers. Article II, Section 2, of the Constitution says that the President "shall nominate, and by and with the Advice and Consent of the Senate, shall appoint Ambassadors, other public Ministers and Consuls." Article II, Section 3, says that the President "shall receive Ambassadors and other public Ministers." Hence, the presidential power to appoint ambassadors is subject to senatorial oversight, while the power to receive ambassadors is not. The reception and appointment of ambassadors helps the executive branch to communicate with other nations and to supervise the United States' international relations. In modern times, the power to appoint and receive ambassadors has not, standing alone, been as controversial as some of the President's other international powers (e.g., the TREATY-MAKING POWER and the power to command the armed forces). But when combined with all the President's express and implied international powers, the authority to receive and appoint ambassadors is enmeshed in the larger SEPARATION OF POWERS dispute between the executive and legislative branches over the governance of foreign affairs.

Appointing Ambassadors. The United States sends one ambassador to most of the foreign governments it recognizes. An ambassador serves as the nation's highest ranking diplomat, representing the United States in its regular dealings with the other country. The United States also sends an ambassador to the UNITED NATIONS. Presidential nominations of these individuals normally fall into one of three categories: the nomination of a career diplomat, that is, someone who has dedicated his professional life to foreign service and normally has been educated for the position and moved up through the diplomatic ranks; the nomination of someone with more domestic government experience, that is, a Washington insider, who may be chosen due to the current circumstances in a particular country and his ability to deal successfully with that specific situation; and, finally, the nomination of a significant political benefactor, that is, someone with neither foreign affairs nor government expertise, who has contributed a large sum of money to or helped to manage the President's successful campaign for the White House. Unfortunately, Presidents have recently nominated as ambassadors more and more individuals who fall into this final category, putting presidential politics above the nation's foreign affairs needs. The Senate and the public have sometimes criticized Presidents for making such nominations, although virtually all of these nominees have been confirmed; perhaps such nominations are relatively harmless if the ambassador is appointed to a smaller and less significant foreign country. Sometimes an ambassador will continue to serve the United States even when a new President takes over. Ambassadors have no particular tenure in office and may resign or be recalled by the President at any time without senatorial approval being necessary.

Under Article II of the Constitution, the Senate's consent is necessary not only when the President nominates an ambassador, but also when he nominates a consul. A consul's diplomatic duties are more narrow than an ambassador's. An ambassador may carry the President's message to the foreign sovereign on a panoply of issues and may also assume ceremonial functions; but a consul's primary job historically has been to represent the commercial interests of United States citizens in a foreign country. Apart from ambassadors and consuls, however, Presidents have traditionally appointed lesser and temporary diplomats without seeking the Senate's consent. For example, in 1791 President George Washington authorized GOU-

VERNEUR MORRIS of New York to negotiate with the British government concerning both the treaty of peace and the potential for a new commercial treaty. In doing so, Washington acted upon the counsel of Thomas Jefferson, who advised that the President did not need senatorial consent except when nominating ambassadors and consuls. President Washington and his successors often unilaterally appointed diplomatic agents to further a particular foreign relations goal or to draft a treaty with another nation. Presidents occasionally have even conferred the ambassadorial rank on someone temporarily, without the Senate's approval. In 1917, for instance, President Woodrow Wilson unilaterally named ELIHU ROOT as ambassador to Russia on a special mission. The legislative branch has tried to control the President's enlargement of his diplomatic cadre, requiring congressional authorization of new ministerial posts and regulating the diplomatic corps' expenditures. But where confidentiality or dispatch is needed—as when President Grover Cleveland sent J. H. Blount to Hawaii in 1893—Presidents have regularly prevailed in sending their PRIVATE ENVOY abroad with little senatorial oversight. In his renowned study *The President*, Edward Corwin refers to the executive's "long . . . conceded right to employ in the discharge of his diplomatic function so-called 'special,' 'personal,' or 'secret' agents in whose designation the Senate has no voice."

Receiving Ambassadors. The President's control over foreign affairs also derives from his reception of ambassadors and other ministers from foreign countries. Diplomatic relations are generally reciprocal in nature, so that the executive receives an ambassador from any country to which he has appointed an ambassador. The President and his delegatees may have regular contact with foreign diplomats who reside in embassies in Washington, D.C. Such contacts may range from being ceremonial in nature to being very significant in times of international exigency. Under international law, foreign ambassadors should abide by the United States' laws and regulations; but they nevertheless usually have immunity from prosecution if they violate the United States' laws. In such instances, the executive branch has the authority to declare that the foreign ambassador is no longer welcome in the United States and must return to his own country (hopefully to be prosecuted there). Such scenarios may lead to diplomats being recalled by both nations and to strained foreign relations. The Senate has no say in these matters.

In *Federalist* 69, ALEXANDER HAMILTON downplayed the significance of the President's power to receive ambassadors. He called it "more a matter of dignity than of authority." Viewing this executive power to be merely ceremonial in nature, Hamilton said that "it was far more convenient that it should be arranged in this manner than that there should be a necessity of convening the legislature, or one of its branches, upon every arrival of a foreign minister, though it were merely to take the place of a departed predecessor." Hamilton, however, was interested in allaying fears that the executive branch would become too powerful; and he probably was incorrect so to demean the President's power to receive ambassadors. First, the executive branch's communications with foreign dignitaries has become an integral part of the President's growing domination of foreign affairs within the federal government; the legislative branch is not part of such communications and its influence and expertise in foreign affairs suffers as a result.

Second, the power to receive ambassadors has helped to establish the President's important authority to recognize foreign governments. It is now established that the President has the authority to decide whether to recognize a foreign government, whether that government is part of a new country or is competing with another regime for an older country's governance. The Constitution does not explicitly give the President the RECOGNITION POWER. Instead, the recognition power has been inferred from the President's power to receive ambassadors. By implication, if the President has the ability to receive a foreign diplomat, he impliedly also has the power to decide from which foreign governments he will receive those diplomats. Hence, the reception of ambassadors has become a power more important than Hamilton had originally indicated; Hamilton himself recognized this point when later arguing against James Madison and in favor of presidential supremacy in foreign affairs.

BIBLIOGRAPHY

Corwin, Edward S. *The President*. 5th ed. 1984.
Henkin, Louis. *Foreign Affairs and the Constitution*. 1972. Chapter 2.
Stein, Bruce. "Justiciability and the Limits of Presidential Foreign Policy Power." *Hofstra Law Review* 11(1982): 413, 463–466.
Taft, William Howard. *The President and His Powers*. 1916. Chapter 3.

KENNETH C. RANDALL

AMERICAN INDIANS. See INDIANS.

AMERICAN PARTY. See KNOW-NOTHING (AMERICAN) PARTY.

AMERICAN SYSTEM. The American System was a term applied to an integrated set of policies that employed the powers of the national government to promote economic development. In 1824, HENRY CLAY, who was called the Father of the American System, used the term in arguing that American prosperity depended on "modifying our foreign policy, and . . . adopting a genuine American System" of promoting manufacturing. First explicitly associated with protective tariffs, the American System also encompassed government support of INTERNAL IMPROVEMENTS and a national bank. The term was somewhat elastic, however, and other policies sponsored by Clay, such as the distribution of land revenues to the states, were often considered as components.

Reflecting the nationalistic aspirations of Americans after the WAR OF 1812, the American System sought to guarantee prosperity and to establish economic independence by creating a diversified economy that balanced commerce, manufacturing, and agriculture. Its reliance on government action challenged the prevailing assumptions of British laissez-faire economics, which Clay argued would keep the United States weak and subservient to the British. The program promised to harmonize sectional and class tensions. Each section would specialize in certain productions and exchange these for the products of other sections. Similarly, a growing economy would diffuse wealth among all groups in society.

During the administrations of James Madison, James Monroe, and John Quincy Adams, a number of elements of the American System were enacted into law, including a new national bank, protective tariffs, and increased expenditures for internal improvements. The program became identified with the National Republican Party and the WHIG PARTY. But in the years after Andrew Jackson's election in 1828, the American System fell victim to political and sectional opposition. Jackson and his followers labeled it a "British System" of power and privilege, at odds with America's republican tradition of limited government and individual rights. Local and sectional interests either categorically rejected the program or sought their own advantage so that measures were considered on an ad hoc, piecemeal basis, rather than as part of a system of national development.

Ironically, the American System also suffered at the hands of Clay himself and of the Whig Party. Clay abandoned the principle of tariff protection when offering a compromise tariff to end the NULLIFICATION crisis. Years later, the Whig President John Tyler vetoed bills for a national bank and distribution. With Clay's defeat in the presidential election of 1844, the American System as a political program was virtually dead. However, its influence persisted among those who, like Abraham Lincoln, sought to carry on Clay's political ideals.

BIBLIOGRAPHY

Howe, Daniel Walker. *The Political Culture of the American Whigs.* 1979.
Peterson, Merrill D. *The Great Triumvirate: Webster, Clay, and Calhoun.* 1987.
Remini, Robert V. *Henry Clay: Statesman for the Union.* 1991.

RICHARD B. LATNER

AMNESTY. Amnesty is an act of mercy that exempts a group of persons from the punishment the law inflicts for the commission of what is typically a political offense against the state. The Supreme Court has acknowledged that there may be a "philological" difference between amnesties, which overlook or forget offenses, and pardons, which repeal or remit sanctions. Amnesty exhibits characteristics of a legislative act rather than of an executive act since it applies to a defined class of persons and not to a particular individual. In spite of these differences, the terms have been treated as synonyms in judicial decisions and scholarly discourse. Amnesty may be issued anytime after an offense has been committed, either before legal proceedings have been commenced or after conviction and judgment, and it may be conferred absolutely or conditionally, provided the conditions are constitutional. Under the Constitution, the President shares with Congress the power to grant amnesties, a power that is limited to offenses against the United States. The Court has held that the presidential PARDON POWER includes the authority to issue amnesties. Congress may grant general amnesties pursuant to its authority under the necessary and proper clause.

There is no doubt that the CONSTITUTIONAL CONVENTION intended to vest the President with authority to issue general amnesties. In the context of their debate on the issue of whether the President should be empowered to confer pardons for treasonous activities, the Framers were persuaded to do so, as ALEXANDER HAMILTON explained in the FEDERALIST 74 by the argument that such a power might be critical to halting rebellions and restoring domestic tranquillity. Without the offer of a general amnesty, rebels might choose to die in the battlefields rather than at the gallows.

In 1795, President George Washington initiated the use of the power when he issued a proclamation of amnesty to participants in the WHISKEY REBELLION. President Thomas Jefferson granted amnesty in 1801 to persons convicted or charged under the ALIEN AND SEDITION ACTS. During the CIVIL WAR and its aftermath, some two hundred thousand Southern rebels benefitted from amnesties issued by Presidents Abraham Lincoln and Andrew Johnson. But Congress was concerned about the exercise of the power and sought to limit it through legislation. In 1862, Congress passed a statute that "authorized" the President to issue amnesties. But since Lincoln and Johnson believed the Constitution empowered the President to issue amnesties, they regarded the act as meaningless and made no reference to it in granting clemency. In 1867, Congress responded by enacting legislation that annulled the political benefits of the pardons already extended by denying recipients the rights to vote, hold office, and own property. The conflict hinged on the severity of punishment to be inflicted on the Confederates, and it required the intervention of the Supreme Court. In 1867, in the *Test Oath Cases*, the Court declared the law unconstitutional on the grounds that the President's pardon power may not be restricted by legislation. Presidents Franklin D. Roosevelt and Harry S. Truman issued general amnesties to classes of convicts and deserters.

The end of the Vietnam War brought renewed calls for amnesty for draft-law violators. On 16 September 1974, President Gerald R. Ford issued a conditional amnesty to military deserters and draft evaders of the war. The Presidential Clemency Board was established to direct applicants to alternative public service for up to a period of two years. On 21 January 1977, one day after his inaugural address, President Jimmy Carter granted an unconditional pardon to draft evaders. However, deserters from the armed services were not affected by the amnesty and were to be considered on a case-by-case basis.

BIBLIOGRAPHY

Corwin, Edward S. *The President: Office and Power, 1787–1984: A History and Analysis of Practice and Opinion.* 5th rev. ed. 1984.

Dorris, Jonathan T. *Pardon and Amnesty Under Lincoln and Johnson.* 1953.

Duker, William. "The President's Power to Pardon: A Constitutional History." *William and Mary Law Review* 18 (1977): 475–535.

Humbert, W. H. *The Pardoning Power of the President.* 1941.

Kurland, Philip. *Watergate and the Constitution.* 1978.

DAVID GRAY ADLER

ANNEXATION BY JOINT RESOLUTION.

Annexation by joint resolution of both houses of Congress emerged in the 1840s as an alternative for procedure for annexing territory when political opposition prevented a treaty from winning the required two-thirds vote in the Senate. Although the Senate had overwhelmingly approved earlier treaties annexing Louisiana and Florida, the Texas annexation treaty of April 1844 faced strong conservative and antislavery opposition [*see* TEXAS, ANNEXATION OF]. Thomas Hart Benton of Missouri led the attack on the treaty, declaring that annexation would bring a presidential war with Mexico. On 8 June the Senate voted down the treaty, 35 to 16. During the subsequent presidential campaign western Democrats successfully nationalized the Texas issue with appeals to MANIFEST DESTINY and forced it on the DEMOCRATIC PARTY. When Congress reconvened in December, President John Tyler reminded Congress that Texas annexation now touched the interests of every state in the Union. Early in January 1845 the House turned to the proposal of C. J. Ingersoll, chairman of the House Foreign Affairs Committee, for annexation by joint resolution. On 25 January the House approved by an almost straight party vote, 120 to 98, a resolution providing that Texas would enter the Union as a state with whatever boundary it claimed.

Meanwhile Benton discovered that his Missouri constituents favored annexation. During December he took up the issue in the Senate but insisted on negotiations among the United States, Texas, and Mexico to settle the boundary question prior to U.S. annexation. He proposed a compromise boundary line; if Mexico rejected it, he would accept annexation on Texas's terms. By February Benton was prepared to retreat to the House position. Late that month the expansionist Robert J. Walker of Mississippi, troubled that the Senate would not accept the House resolution with its disregard for the boundary question, proposed an amendment that would permit the President to select either the House resolution or a new Texas negotiation. Benton voted for Walker's resolution, which narrowly passed the Senate, 27 to 25. The House readily concurred. Tyler exercised his choice without delay. On 3 March he instructed the U.S. chargé d'affaires in Texas to press for immediate annexation. A week later James Knox Polk, the new President, lent his support to Tyler's action.

Much of American expansionism in the 1890s focused on Hawaii, a cluster of islands in the Pacific under the control of American settlers who favored annexation [*see* HAWAII, ANNEXATION OF]. In June 1897 Secretary of State John Sherman negotiated an annexation treaty with Hawaiian commissioners. Senate anti-imperialists overwhelmingly defeated the treaty, but annexationists such as Vice President Theodore Roosevelt refused to let the issue die. Suddenly, on 1 May 1898, Commodore George Dewey's destruction of the Spanish squadron in Manila Bay during the

SPANISH-AMERICAN WAR unleashed an expansionist mood that sealed Hawaii's fate. On 4 May expansionists in Congress introduced a joint resolution for Hawaii's annexation. Within a month the resolution had gone through committee and onto the floors of both houses. Requiring only a bare majority, the measure passed the House, 209 to 91, with 49 abstentions. The Senate concurred by a vote of 42 to 21, enough to approve a treaty.

BIBLIOGRAPHY

Kuykendall, Ralph S. *The Hawaiian Kingdom.* 1967.
Smith, Justin H. *The Annexation of Texas.* 1911.
Tate, Merze. *The United States and the Hawaiian Kingdom.* 1965.

NORMAN A. GRAEBNER

ANTIBALLISTIC MISSILE SYSTEM TREATY.

See ABM (ANTIBALLISTIC MISSILE SYSTEM) TREATY.

ANTIDEFICIENCY ACT (1905).

This act was a 1905 attempt by Congress to curb deliberate overspending of appropriated funds by executive departments and agencies and thereby to limit the necessity for additional or deficiency appropriations within a given fiscal year. The original legislation was rewritten in 1906 and 1950, in both instances with the goal of strengthening congressional control over agency spending.

The Antideficiency Acts of 1905 and 1906 were part of a broader effort by Congress to strengthen its budgetary procedures and to counter pressures to create a national, or presidential, budget. After the CIVIL WAR, Congress had tightened controls over agency spending. Some agencies then circumvented these controls, spending all of their appropriations before the fiscal year was over and leaving Congress no option but to enact additional appropriations to cover these "coercive deficiencies."

The 1905 Antideficiency Act sought to curtail coercive deficiencies by requiring monthly or other allotments of general appropriations. Executive department heads were allowed, however, to waive or modify these allotments, and routine use of this authority led Congress to rewrite antideficiency legislation in 1906, limiting waivers and modifications to "extraordinary emergency or unusual circumstance which could not be anticipated." Continued high levels of deficiency funding, and occasional flagrant abuses, led Congress to rewrite the Antideficiency Act once again in 1950, this time by authorizing agencies to set aside reserves to cover unanticipated expenses and by sanctioning deficiency appropriations only for limited purposes.

As controls on coercive deficiencies were tightened, other difficulties surfaced. One was a growing pattern of deliberate underfunding by Congress, with the expectation of supplemental funding later in the fiscal year. A second, more contentious, issue arose when the administration of Richard M. Nixon used the "other developments" clause in the 1950 Antideficiency Act to impound funds. Congress attempted to deal with these problems in the 1974 budget act, which instituted IMPOUNDMENT controls, deleted the "other developments" clause, and formally integrated supplemental appropriations into the presidential and congressional budget processes.

During the 1980s, the use of supplemental appropriations declined sharply, in large part because of new legislative requirements and executive branch restrictions that raised the threshold for additional appropriations. In addition, the BUDGET ENFORCEMENT ACT of 1990 further tightened controls over discretionary spending, for which annual appropriations are required. Neither coercive nor deliberate deficiencies were major budget control problems by the 1990s, although either may cause occasional disturbances in PRESIDENTIAL-CONGRESSIONAL RELATIONS.

BIBLIOGRAPHY

Congressional Budget Office. *Supplemental Appropriations in the 1980s.* 1990.
Fisher, Louis. *Presidential Spending Power.* 1975.

DENNIS S. IPPOLITO

ANTI-FEDERALISTS.

Those who opposed ratifying the Constitution proposed by the CONSTITUTIONAL CONVENTION of 1787 were not happy when the label "Anti-Federalists" stuck to them. They argued that they were defending the true federal system that the framers of the Constitution meant to replace with a national government verging on a consolidation of the states. But they have been known as Anti-Federalists ever since. As dissenters, they were under less pressure to agree on the lines of their attack on the Constitution than its supporters were in defining common positions around which to rally its defense. Federalists then, and scholars since, have accordingly argued that different groups of Anti-Federalists often took positions inconsistent with each other. On issues of executive power, however, the main lines of their criticism of the Constitution were fairly clear if not always consistent. Many of their objections predictably derived from—and also sought to exploit—the habitual fear of executive power that informed so much of the political culture and thinking of Englishmen and Americans in the seventeenth and eighteenth centuries.

To a significant extent, the origins of Anti-Federalist criticism of Article II can be traced to the three members of the Constitutional Convention who refused to sign the completed Constitution. At one time or another, George Mason and EDMUND RANDOLPH of Virginia, and ELBRIDGE GERRY of Massachusetts, all objected strongly to particular aspects of the presidency as it evolved over the course of the deliberations. Randolph and Mason were both critical of the fundamental concept of a unitary executive; Gerry had offered several typically idiosyncratic suggestions for electing the executive. All three men worried about the potential domination of the President by an "aristocratic" Senate. After the Convention adjourned on 17 September 1787, these three dissenters took a prominent role in formulating and publicizing initial objections to the Constitution. Mason was first in the field: his objections to the Constitution were quickly circulating among Anti-Federalists throughout the country.

For Mason, the principal flaw in the design of the executive lay in the likelihood either that the President would become "a tool to the Senate" or that the heads of the departments would evolve into a cabinet that would be effectively screened from either presidential control or congressional inquiry. His own favored solution to this dilemma was the creation of a six-member council that would effectively serve to buttress the authority and independence of the President. In stressing the danger that the President might prove prey to the Senate, Mason and other Anti-Federalists who took the same position revealed their support for the same principle of executive independence to which the framers of the Constitution were also attached. If the Constitution was to prove too "aristocratic," as they often alleged, the source of danger was perceived to lie more in the Senate than in the executive. Through their joint exercise of appointive and diplomatic powers, the upper house of Congress and the President would be drawn into a collusive partnership. Whether the executive would be more the victim in this collusion or a happy conspirator ultimately mattered little.

Anti-Federalist arguments about the presidency ranged more widely than this, however. The structure of debate and the problematic quality of all predictions about how the Constitution would work in practice left nearly every clause open to indictment. The executive veto could be faulted for making the judgment of a single individual equivalent to the considered thought of two houses of Congress. Presidential power as COMMANDER IN CHIEF raised the specter of an ambitious demagogue deploying his legions to subvert the government. Through the APPOINTMENT POWER the President could prove equally adept at gathering pliant officeholders to do his corrupt bidding. And through the TREATY-MAKING POWER the President would be well positioned to betray the entire country to foreign power.

Beneath all these particular objections, images of the old regime still figured prominently in the Anti-Federalist critique of the presidency. If too strong, the proposed executive would evolve into a monarch; if too weak, into a creature of the aristocracy or oligarchy that would reign in the Senate. Within the broader matrix of Anti-Federalist thought, however, it is impossible to calculate the precise influence that issues of executive power exerted over the opposition to ratification. Because in every state the debate over the Constitution ultimately took the form of a simple vote in favor of approval or rejection—rather than a clause-by-clause evaluation of all its provisions—Anti-Federalists had a natural incentive to convert every innovation in the text into a threat to liberty. As perhaps the most innovative aspect of the Constitution, the presidency received its full share of objections.

BIBLIOGRAPHY

Main, Jackson Turner. *The Anti-Federalists: Critics of the Constitution, 1781–1788.* 1961.

Storing, Herbert J., ed. *The Complete Anti-Federalist.* Vol. 1: *What the Anti-Federalists Were For.* 1981.

JACK N. RAKOVE

ANTI-MASONIC PARTY. The Anti-Masonic Party had its origins in the mysterious disappearance of William Morgan of Batavia, New York, in September 1826. He was a former Freemason who had threatened to publish the secrets of the Masonic order. The rumor quickly spread that he had been murdered, and widespread popular indignation led to an official investigation and several trials, but nothing conclusive ever came of them. Since many of the state's most important officeholders were Freemasons, many people believed that the order had used its influence to obstruct the inquiry about Morgan's fate. In reaction there developed by 1830 a political party known as the Anti-Masons that was particularly strong in western New York. Playing upon traditional American fears of the role of secret societies and conspiracies and espousing an evangelical Protestantism, the movement spread with particular force into New England, especially Massachusetts and Vermont, and into Pennsylvania, Ohio, and Michigan.

The Anti-Masons played an active role in the presidential election of 1832. They vociferously opposed the reelection of Andrew Jackson, who was a Mason, and they were unenthusiastic about his National Republican opponent, HENRY CLAY, a lapsed member of the order who refused to renounce it. To select their own candidates, the Anti-Masons held a special convention in Baltimore in September 1831 and nominated WILLIAM WIRT of Maryland for President and Amos Ellmaker of Pennsylvania for Vice President. The Anti-Masons became the first THIRD PARTY in American history, and the first party to hold a national nominating convention. Moreover, like most third parties they stressed a single issue: opposition to secret societies, especially the Society of Free Masons. In the presidential election of 1832, the Anti-Masonic Party carried only one state: Vermont (seven electoral votes). While it received scattered support in a number of other states, Jackson was easily reelected, and would have been even if all the votes cast in favor of the Anti-Masonic candidate had gone to Clay.

By 1836 the party had begun to disintegrate and it was no longer a force in national politics. Its most important leaders, WILLIAM H. SEWARD, Thurlow Weed, and Thaddeus Stevens tended to go into the WHIG PARTY. What happened to most of its followers is less clear.

BIBLIOGRAPHY

Goodman, Paul. *Towards a Christian Republic: Anti-Masonry and the Great Transition in New England, 1826–1836.* 1988.

Vaughn, William Preston. *The Anti-Masonic Party in The United States, 1826–1843.* 1983.

RICHARD E. ELLIS

ANTITRUST POLICY. The primary purpose of antitrust policy is to perpetuate and preserve a system of governance for a competitive free-enterprise economy. Like the political framework prescribed by the Constitution, antitrust policy calls for the dispersion of power, buttressed by built-in CHECKS AND BALANCES, to guard against the abuse of power and to preserve not only individual freedom but, more importantly, a free economic system.

Antitrust policy's philosophic rationale was best stated by Supreme Court Justice William O. Douglas. In *United States v. Columbia Steel Company* (1948), Douglas wrote that concentrated power should be jealously watched:

> In the final analysis, [it] is the measure of the power of a handful of men over our economy. That power can be utilized with

lightning speed. It can be benign or it can be dangerous. The philosophy of the [antitrust laws] is that it should not exist. For all power tends to develop into a government in itself. Power that controls the economy should be in the hands of elected representatives of the people, not in the hands of an industrial oligarchy. Industrial power should be decentralized. It should be scattered into many hands so that the fortunes of the people will not be dependent on the whim or caprice, the political prejudices, the emotional stability of a few self-appointed men. The fact that they are not vicious men but respectable and social-minded is irrelevant. That is the philosophy and the command of [antitrust].

The Sherman Act. The trust problem first became a major political issue in the 1880s, triggered by the wave of corporate mergers, combinations, and monopolies ("trusts") that enveloped the newly industrialized American economy. Such consolidations as the meat-packing trust, the Standard Oil trust, the cotton seed-oil trust, the whiskey trust, the sugar trust, the lead trust, and the tobacco trust seemed to demonstrate the self-destructiveness of laissez-faire, the demise of Adam Smith's system of "natural" competition, and the emergence of a new kind of economic feudalism.

The options for dealing with the problem were four. First, the government could decide on a do-nothing policy of laissez-faire grounded in social-economic Darwinism. ("The growth of a large business is merely a survival of the fittest," offered John D. Rockefeller, father of the Standard Oil trust.) Second, the government could permit trusts and monopolies to form but then control them by direct regulation (such as the INTERSTATE COMMERCE ACT, passed in 1887 to regulate the railroads). Third, trusts that arose in important fields like transportation and energy could be nationalized. Or, fourth, the government could adopt the antitrust approach of dissolving monopolies and cartels and maintaining the competitive market as a free-enterprise system's prime instrument for regulating economic affairs.

Following his successful 1888 campaign, President Benjamin Harrison urged Congress to confront the monopoly problem. He urged Congress to give

> Earnest attention . . . to a consideration of the question how far the restraint of those combinations of capital commonly called "trusts" is a matter of Federal jurisdiction. . . . When organized, as they often are, to crush out all healthy competition and to monopolize the production or sale of an article of commerce and general necessity, they are dangerous conspiracies against the public good, and should be made the subject of prohibitory and even penal legislation.

The nation formally adopted the antitrust approach when on 2 July 1890, President Harrison signed into law the SHERMAN ANTITRUST ACT, named for its leading sponsor in Congress, Ohio's Senator JOHN SHERMAN. Section 1 of the Sherman Act is an anticartel provision, prohibiting "contracts, combinations and conspiracies in restraint of trade," while section 2 addresses concentrated market structures by prohibiting "monopolization" and "attempts to monopolize" trade or commerce. Underscoring the broad purpose of the act, Senator Sherman characterized it as an economic "charter of liberty"—an economic bill of rights insuring that "occupations were to be kept open to all those who wished to try their luck, that the individual was to be protected in his 'common right' to choose his calling and that hindrances to equal opportunity were to be eliminated."

Immediately after its enactment, however, the Sherman Act slumped into a decade-long somnolence during the Harrison, Grover Cleveland, and William McKinley administrations. On the rare occasions it was enforced, it was deployed against labor as often as big business. It was further undercut by the Supreme Court's 1895 decision in the sugar-trust case of *United States v. E. C. Knight*, in which the Court declared "manufacturing" to be local in character, thereby rendering mergers and monopolies beyond the constitutional power of the federal government to regulate interstate trade. That decision, in conjunction with the strong anticartel policy enunciated by the Supreme Court in *Addyston Pipe & Steel Co. v. United States* (1898), precipitated another wave of corporate consolidations at the turn of the century, as firms eschewed cartels in favor of mergers, finding refuge in the seemingly safe harbor of monopoly formation.

Roosevelt and Wilson. It was President Theodore Roosevelt who rejuvenated the Sherman Act—although he privately held the view that concentration and corporate bigness reflected the technological dictates of modern industry, that the competitively structured market system had become obsolete as an effective social regulator of business affairs, and that direct public-utility-type supervision by the government afforded a better instrument for regulating modern business. Despite these reservations, and with evolving support in the courts and follow-through by his successor, William Howard Taft, Roosevelt launched some forty antitrust suits against some of the most powerful monopolies of the day, including Standard Oil, the United States Steel Corporation, the American Tobacco Company, E. I. DuPont de Nemours and Company, the Beef trust, and the Eastman Kodak Company, as well as the Northern Pacific, Great Northern, and Union Pacific railroad interests. In the eyes of the public, Roosevelt came to be regarded as the great trustbuster.

The framework of American government-business relations again became a major point of debate in the 1912 presidential campaign. The contrasting visions presented by Roosevelt and Woodrow Wilson were fundamental and far-reaching: regulated monopoly versus regulated competition. Leading his PROGRESSIVE (BULL MOOSE) PARTY, Roosevelt advocated the view that corporate bigness was the embodiment of industrial progress, strength, and efficiency—and that monopolies, therefore, should be regulated, not banned. Wilson rejected this notion, maintaining instead that monopolies were artificial products of a lust for power that undermined efficiency and innovation, that preserving competitive markets would protect economic freedom for all, that decentralization of economic power would compel good economic performance, and that government-business cooperation along Roosevelt's lines would invite the capture of government by powerful private interests.

Following his election, Wilson pushed two measures through Congress to bolster the Sherman Act and reinvigorate antitrust: The CLAYTON ACT (1914) prohibited a number of specific business practices—price discrimination, tie-in sales and exclusive dealership agreements, mergers and acquisitions, and interlocking corporate directorships—where the effect might be "substantially to lessen competition or to tend to create a monopoly." The FEDERAL TRADE COMMISSION ACT (also 1914) created the Federal Trade Commission as an expert body charged with compiling and evaluating evidence concerning the operation of American business; section 5 of the act also prohibited "unfair methods" of competition.

Enforcement and Desuetude. Despite these advances, antitrust suffered another setback as a result of the laissez-faire philosophy regnant during the Warren G. Harding, Calvin Coolidge, and Herbert Hoover administrations of the 1920s and the national trauma of the Great Depression of the 1930s. But the failure of Franklin D. Roosevelt's procartel policy of industrial "self-government" under the NATIONAL INDUSTRIAL RECOVERY ACT during the early 1930s and the subsequent failure of his flirtation with national tripartite planning among industry, labor, and government produced a resurgence in antitrust enforcement by the late 1930s. Concluding that corporate bigness and industrial concentration constituted an important part of the nation's economic problem, not its solution, the Roosevelt administration launched a number of major Sherman act suits under the direction of Attorney General Thurman Arnold—a thrust generally sustained through the 1950s and 1960s, with a number of important legal (if not always economically effective) victories.

After the 1970s, antitrust again fell into desuetude. The faltering performance of the American economy beginning in the 1970s and the challenge of foreign competition led some to revert to faith in bigness and consolidation as correctives for the nation's economic malaise—despite the fact that some of America's most troubled industries (e.g., auto, steel) have long been dominated by a few large firms. The reemergence of a new economic Darwinism (the Chicago school) advocating a return to laissez-faire also attracted a considerable number of adherents—despite the fact that it was a laissez-faire policy that had precipitated the trust problem ninety years earlier. These movements combined to dominate government policy during the presidency of Ronald Reagan. With the exception of its breakup of the telecommunications monopoly of American Telephone and Telegraph, the Reagan administration presided over an era of megamergers and consolidation not seen since the turn of the century. It mercilessly enforced section 1 of the Sherman Act against small-business price-fixers while ignoring anticompetitive combinations between corporate giants in oil, steel, airlines, retailing, appliance, and food processing. It also permitted, and even encouraged, cooperative joint ventures between American big business and its largest foreign rivals in a number of industries, including automobiles.

Viewed in perspective, then, the history of American antitrust policy is one of stubborn persistence—a record of ebb and flow, of assertion, demise, and resurgence. Perhaps this is, as Walton Hamilton and Irene Till once reflected, because antitrust

> is a symbol of democracy. It is an assertion that every industry is affected with a public interest. Quite apart from its operation, it keeps alive within law and public policy a value which must not be sacrificed or abridged. It asserts the firm, the trade, the economy to be the instrument of the general welfare."

"If the fact falls short of the ideal," they concluded, the call eventually arises "to amend the fact rather than abandon the ideal."

[*See also* BUSINESS POLICY.]

BIBLIOGRAPHY

Adams, Walter, and James W. Brock. *Antitrust Economics on Trial: A Dialogue on the New Laissez-Faire.* 1991.
Adams, Walter, and James W. Brock. *The Bigness Complex: Industry, Labor and Government in the American Economy.* 1986.
Fox, Eleanor M., and Lawrence A. Sullivan. *Cases and Materials on Antitrust.* 1989.
Hamilton, Walton, and Irene Till. *Antitrust in Action.* 1940.
Hawley, Ellis B. *The New Deal and the Problem of Monopoly.* 1966.
Kovaleff, Theodore P., ed. "Symposium on the 100th Anniversary of the Sherman Act and the 75th Anniversary of the Clayton Act." *Antitrust Bulletin* 35 (1990).
Millon, David. "The Sherman Act and the Balance of Power." *Southern California Law Review* 61 (1988): 1219–1292.
Thorelli, Hans B. *The Federal Antitrust Policy: Origination of an American Tradition.* 1955.

WALTER ADAMS and JAMES W. BROCK

ANZUS TREATY. The Security Treaty Between Australia, New Zealand, and the United States (ANZUS) was ratified on 1 September 1951. Article IV of the treaty states that each party "recognizes that an armed attack in the Pacific Area on any of the Parties would be dangerous to its own peace and safety and declares that it would act to meet the common danger in accordance with its constitutional processes." That article further provides that any such armed attack and all measures taken as a result of the attack shall be immediately reported to the Security Council of the UNITED NATIONS and that retaliatory measures shall be terminated when the Security Council has taken the measures necessary to restore and maintain international peace and security.

U.S. negotiators occasionally tried to soft-pedal the significance of the "constitutional processes" language when explaining its significance to their foreign counterparts—in terms that would surely have raised alarm had they been used before the U.S. Senate. In a meeting with the foreign ministers of Australia and New Zealand, Ambassador JOHN FOSTER DULLES was asked what was meant by "constitutional processes." In reply, he said that the phrase did not "impose any serious limitation" on U.S. assistance to its allies. In a top secret dispatch to General Douglas MacArthur, however, Dulles candidly described the unfettered discretion the United States reserved for itself: "While [the draft treaty] commits each party to take action (presumably go to war) it does not commit any nation to action in any particular part of the world. In other words, the United States can discharge its obligations by action against the common enemy in any way and in any area that it sees fit." In testimony before the Senate Foreign Relations Committee in 1952, Dulles said that each party to the treaty would have to decide what action was appropriate "in the light of the fact that there is recognition that it is a common danger," and "that each will act in accordance with its constitutional processes to meet that danger." The subject of the United States' commitment to action was not pursued as closely at these hearings as it was during hearings on the NATO TREATY and RIO TREATY. Dulles's statement was repeated in the committee report, and discussion of the issue on the Senate floor was cursory. It was widely understood that the parties were not automatically committed to provide military forces in the event of an armed attack.

In 1986, the United States suspended its obligations to New Zealand under the ANZUS Treaty after then–Prime Minister David Lange called for a halt to visits by nuclear-armed U.S. warships.

BIBLIOGRAPHY

Glennon, Michael J. *Constitutional Diplomacy.* 1990.
Glennon, Michael J. "United States Mutual Security Treaties: The Commitment Myth." *Columbia Journal of Transnational Law* 24 (1986): 509–552.

MICHAEL J. GLENNON

APPOINTMENT OF JUDGES. See JUDGES, APPOINTMENT OF.

APPOINTMENT POWER. Disagreement prevailed among the framers of the Constitution over the proper manner of selecting federal judges, ambassadors, and executive-branch officials. Some of them, like ALEXANDER HAMILTON and JAMES WILSON, believed that this was inherently an executive function and ought to be assigned to the President alone. In their view, this would minimize intrigue and cabal in the selection process and focus accountability on the person solely responsible for selection.

Others, including John Rutledge and Luther Martin, disagreed, arguing that personnel selection was too important to be left to one person. To prevent an undesirable concentration of power, in their view, it was necessary to assign appointment responsibility to the legislature, whose members would have a broad acquaintance with the leading citizens of the country and whose debates would ensure careful consideration of qualifications.

When neither view prevailed, the CONSTITUTIONAL CONVENTION resolved the disagreement with the compromise that came to reside in Article II, Section 2, of the Constitution: the President "shall nominate, and by and with the ADVICE AND CONSENT of the Senate, shall appoint Ambassadors, other public Ministers and Consuls, Judges of the supreme Court, and all other Officers of the United States, whose Appointments are not herein otherwise provided for, and which shall be established by Law." The President and the Senate would share the appointment power.

Historical Overview. And so they have, with varying degrees of formality and informality, comity and hostility. The constitutional language was only a starting point in this long relationship. It did not envision the emergence of political parties before the end of the eighteenth century, the development of standing congressional committees in the nineteenth, or the vast growth of the executive and judicial branches in the twentieth. Nor could it possibly have envisioned the extended period of divided party control of the federal government in the years since WORLD WAR II [*see* DIVIDED GOVERNMENT]. All these changes have added new dimensions and new strains to the appointment process.

Over time, there has been remarkably little litigation to alter or interpret the constitutional limits on the appointment power. In 1932, in *United States v. Smith,* the Supreme Court decided that the Senate could not revoke its consent to a nomination once an appointee had been installed in office. In 1976, in BUCKLEY V. VALEO, the Court found unconstitutional a provision of the 1974 federal campaign act amendments that provided for the appointments of four of the six members of the FEDERAL ELECTION COMMISSION by the president pro tempore of the Senate and the Speaker of the House. The Court held that because this commission was an administrative agency with significant authority to make and enforce rules, its members had to be appointed by the President as specified in Article II.

Greater confusion has resulted from the recess appointments clause of Article II. The language states that "The President shall have Power to fill up all Vacancies that may happen during the Recess of the Senate, by granting Commissions which shall expire at the End of the next Session." For much of the early history of the country, congressional sessions lasted only a few months, and Presidents often made recess appointments during the long periods when Congress was in recess or adjournment. This raised technical questions about such matters as when a recess actually occurred and whether a recess appointee could continue to serve even after his or her appointment was rejected by the Senate. Congress has enacted legislation to restrict the President's use of RECESS APPOINTMENTS.

A separate issue concerns vacancies that result from the death, absence, or sickness of the heads of EXECUTIVE DEPARTMENTS. Such vacancies can occur throughout the year, whether the Senate is in session or in recess, and require the President to make temporary appointments subject to restrictions placed in the VACANCIES ACT.

Through much of American history, the selection by the President of nominees for executive or judicial positions was a process without much structure and often without much rationality. For most of the thousands of positions that came to be presidential appointments, Presidents relied on their parties to propose nominees. Most of these were PATRONAGE appointments such as local postmasters, customs collectors, and revenue agents. They commanded little presidential attention. In the vast majority of cases, in fact, Presidents nominated candidates suggested by Senators of their own party from the state in which the position was located. This practice quickly acquired the veneer of custom when the Senate rejected George Washington's appointment of Benjamin Fishbourn to be naval officer for the port of Savannah, Georgia. Fishbourn was fully qualified for the post, but the two Senators from Georgia preferred another candidate and succeeded in convincing their colleagues to reject the Fishbourn nomination. Hence was born the concept of senatorial courtesy by which Senators are granted significant influence over presidential appointments within their home states. When parties later emerged, the courtesy was usually granted only to Senators of the President's party.

For higher-level positions in the executive branch and for appointments to the Courts of Appeal and the Supreme Court, Presidents often selected personal acquaintances or leading federal or state office-holders in their party. It was a common practice up through the early decades of the twentieth century, for example, for presidential CABINETS to include representatives of all of the major factions of the President's party.

The Senate, for its part, adopted a dual posture toward presidential appointments. It expected to be consulted, and in most cases deferred to, on appointments to lower-level positions operating within the home states of individual Senators. Over positions of this sort, it is fair to say, the Senate dominated. On the other hand, the Senate—with a few notable exceptions—usually acquiesced to the President's choices on Cabinet and other top-level positions in the executive branch. From 1789 to 1993, only nine Cabinet nominees were rejected by the Senate. The consensus in the Senate throughout much of American history was that the President was entitled to work closely with people of his own choosing.

The one set of positions about which the President and the Senate did disagree with some frequency was appointments to the Supreme Court. Recognizing that such appointees often served for very long terms and that their decisions directly affected the shape of public policy, the Senate objected to Supreme Court nominations more than to any others. From 1789 through 1991, 106 individuals served on the Supreme Court. In that same period, the Senate rejected 27 nominees for the Court, more than 1 in 5 overall [see SUPREME COURT NOMINEES NOT CONFIRMED].

The Early Twentieth Century. In the first third of the twentieth century the appointment process varied little from what it had been in the second half of the nineteenth. The positions outside the CIVIL SERVICE were filled by a process in which political parties played an important role, and appointments were viewed as a reward for political services.

This is not to suggest that all presidential appointees lacked substantive qualifications for federal service. Many of those who had been party activists had also built impressive records of public service and would have merited high-level positions even without party sponsorship. Names like CHARLES EVANS HUGHES and WILLIAM JENNINGS BRYAN would have appeared on most lists of highly qualified eligibles for Cabinet or other top positions in government. And Presidents also retained the latitude to select some appointees who had no significant record of party service, whose primary qualification was their talent or experience. In this category were people like Josephus Daniels and ANDREW W. MELLON.

But partisan pressures in the appointment process were ever-present. In putting together their Cabinets, for example, Presidents felt constrained to select people who represented different factions or regional elements in their party. In this sense, Woodrow Wilson's Cabinet was not very different from Abraham Lincoln's. Though strong-willed and independent leaders, both felt compelled to respect partisan concerns in staffing the top positions in their administrations.

Throughout this period, the national party organizations played an important role in identifying candidates for presidential appointments. It was quite common, in fact, for the head of the President's party to hold a position in the Cabinet, usually as POSTMASTER GENERAL. This made sense, not only because the POST OFFICE DEPARTMENT was the principal source of patronage appointments, but also because a Cabinet post provided a vantage point from which the party leader could work with the President and other Cabinet secretaries to ensure a steady flow of partisan loyalists into federal posts throughout the government.

The party role was critical to the functioning of the government because there was at the time no alternative source of candidates for appointment. Each Cabinet secretary had his own acquaintances and contacts, but few of them knew enough politicians to fill all the available positions in their departments with people who would be loyal to the administration, pass muster with appropriate members of Congress, and satisfy the political litmus tests of party leaders in the states and cities where they might serve. The party could help with all of that.

If some of those the parties brought forward to fill appointive positions were unqualified political hacks—and some surely were—the parties performed valuable functions as well. Many of the appointees who came through the party channel were skilled and qualified. More importantly, partisan control of this process usually guaranteed the construction of an administration that was broadly representative of the elements of the President's party and thus, in some important ways, in touch with the American people it was intended to serve. Equally important, the parties served as an employment agency upon which the government was heavily reliant. They provided a steady stream of politically approved candidates for federal offices. That was a function of no small significance in a government that lacked any other tested means of recruitment for positions outside the civil service.

Following the pattern of his predecessors, Franklin Roosevelt appointed JAMES A. FARLEY, the leader of the DEMOCRATIC PARTY, to serve as Postmaster General and superintend the selection of lower-level appointments in the first Roosevelt administration. Farley directed a patronage operation that bore close resemblance to those of the previous half century.

New Deal Transformations. Despite the familiar look of Roosevelt's patronage operation, however, three changes were set in motion by the NEW DEAL that would have lasting consequences for staffing presidential administrations. The first was the very nature of the politics of the New Deal. The coalition that brought Franklin Roosevelt to office was composed of a broad divergence of groups and views. It provided him a sweeping victory by drawing support from Americans who disagreed with each other about important matters yet agreed on the need to elect a President of their own party. But the New Deal coalition soon proved as useless for running a government as it had been useful for winning elections. Even with the most delicate kind of balancing act, it was no small task to construct an administration of intellectuals and union members, northern liberals and southern conservatives, progressives and racists. The task was complicated all the more by the intensity of the new administration's efforts, not merely to redirect, but to reconstruct public policy in the United States. It simply

could not be reliably assumed that Democratic appointees would fully support all the dimensions of the President's program.

Hence Roosevelt and his senior advisers began increasingly to evade the Democratic Party patronage system in filling key positions in the government. More and more the people closest to the President—James Rowe, LOUIS MCHENRY HOWE, HARRY HOPKINS, and others—began to operate their own recruitment programs. Typically they would identify bright young people already serving in government or anxious to do so and cultivate them with the kind of ad hoc assignments that prepared them for more important managerial positions. While these were either life-long or recently converted Democrats, they tended not to be people with any history of party activism. It was the passions of the time and their commitment to the New Deal that inspired their interest in politics, not a pattern of service to local or state political machines.

The need for such people grew increasingly apparent as the consequence of a second change wrought by the New Deal. The government was growing. Total federal employment was 604,000 in 1933. It nearly doubled by the end of that decade. The New Deal seemed to spawn new agencies and programs almost daily. This created a voracious need not merely for people to fill newly created slots, but for skilled managers and creative program specialists to attend to problems at least as complicated as any the federal government had ever before tackled. This, too, had the effect of diminishing the importance of the party patronage system as a source of appointees. It became increasingly apparent that the party faithful did not always include the kinds of people required to operate technical agencies like the Securities and Exchange Commission and the Agriculture Adjustment Administration. So Roosevelt turned to other sources, even occasionally risking the wrath of party leaders in so doing.

A third change in the New Deal years fed the momentum of the first two. That was the growing importance of the WHITE HOUSE STAFF. As the energy of the federal government came to be centered in the President—and it did dramatically during the New Deal—the need for more support for the President became increasingly apparent. In 1936, Roosevelt appointed a committee headed by his friend Louis Brownlow to study the organization of the executive branch and make recommendations. The report of the BROWNLOW COMMITTEE described the need for vigorous executive leadership to make a modern democracy work. But it also pointed out that "the President needs help" in this enterprise. It went on to recommend the creation of an EXECUTIVE OFFICE OF THE PRESIDENT (EOP) and the creation of presidential authority to appoint a small personal staff to assist in the management of the government. In 1939, the Congress acted affirmatively on most of the recommendations of the Brownlow Committee.

Presidents had previously had little choice but to rely on their party's patronage operation because they lacked the staff necessary to run a personnel recruitment operation of their own. With the creation of the EOP that began to change. Embedded in the recommendations of the Brownlow Committee was a philosophy of public management that also threatened the importance of party patronage. Political control of the government, in the view of Brownlow and his many supporters in the schools of public administration, had come to mean policy control, not merely party control. It was no longer enough for a President to staff his administration with members of his own party and let them work with copartisans in Congress to superintend the routines of government. Instead, the President needed managerial support through broader control of the budget, government organization, and personnel selection to move public policy in the direction that he set and which had earned the endorsement of the American electorate.

This gradual evolution in management philosophy clearly suggested the need for the President and his personal staff to play a larger role in recruiting appointees who supported his policy priorities and who possessed the skills and creativity necessary to develop and implement them. In that scheme, government jobs could not be viewed primarily as rewards for party loyalty, and recruitment could not be left primarily to party patronage operations.

None of these changes took place overnight, but they slowly found their way into the operations of the presidency. Loyal Democrats continued to claim positions in the Roosevelt and later the Truman administration. The pressure to fill vacancies with the party faithful did not abate. The Democratic National Committee continued to operate a full-service employment agency. But few of the appointments to important positions came via this route any longer.

The strains on the patronage operation grew more acute after Roosevelt's death. The enormous expansion that the New Deal and World War II wrought in the size and responsibility of the government put new pressures on the appointment process. With more departments and agencies to staff, Presidents could no longer rely on personal acquaintances for their nominees. And, when political parties went into decline, they were no longer the useful pipeline of candidates

for appointment they had once been. In response, Presidents began to construct new sets of procedures for identifying, recruiting, clearing, and nominating candidates for appointment. The creation of the EOP in 1939 also gave Presidents, for the first time, resources of their own to use in taking fuller command of the appointment power.

The White House Personnel Office. Harry S. Truman was the first President to assign one staff member, Donald Dawson, to work nearly full-time on appointments and to serve as his administration's principal overseer for recruitment. In the administration of Dwight D. Eisenhower, more staff members were added to this function, and by 1958 Eisenhower had created an Office of Special Assistant for Executive Appointments that formalized the personnel function in the EOP.

John F. Kennedy came to office promising to establish a "ministry of talent," and realizing the need for a more sophisticated personnel operation than ever before existed. He assigned to Dan H. Fenn, Jr., responsibility for assessing presidential needs and for setting up a White House personnel office to supply the administration with a steady stream of talented candidates for appointment. Under Fenn—and later in the administration of Lyndon B. Johnson under the leadership of John W. Macy, Jr.—the personnel office in the White House developed procedures for identifying candidates from many sources, some traditional and political, others not. The office took the lead in recruiting candidates and managed the politically necessary task of clearing potential appointees with leading figures in the states and in Congress before their nominations were announced. From 1958 to 1970 the personnel selection process in the White House became increasingly formalized and institutionalized.

The administration of Richard M. Nixon was committed to getting control of the federal bureaucracy, many of whose employees it thought to be burdened by enduring loyalties to the Democratic Party. The Nixon administration regarded firm and efficient control of the appointment power as a critical part of its efforts. Only by recruiting and appointing people who were loyal to the President and sufficiently competent to impose Nixon's policy preferences on recalcitrant bureaucrats could the Nixon imprimatur be placed on public policy.

In 1970, Frederic V. Malek was brought from the subcabinet to the White House to analyze and then reorganize the White House personnel operation. What emerged was a comparatively large (more than sixty people at its peak), segmented, and functionally specialized professional recruiting operation. When a vacancy occurred, a position profile was prepared describing the functions of the office and the kinds of skills and experience it required. A staff of professional personnel recruiters would then reach out through carefully woven networks of contacts to identify candidates for the position. When this list was shortened, one or more of the candidates would be contacted and asked about their interest in serving. When a favorite was identified, his or her name would be circulated in the White House and among relevant members of Congress to ensure that there were no strong objections to going forward with the nomination. After successful clearance and approval by the President and his top aides (see below), the nomination would be announced.

This process, with minor variations, has remained essentially intact since the early 1970s. The OFFICE OF PRESIDENTIAL PERSONNEL is now a regular component of the White House Office and its director is usually an assistant to the President, the highest rank among presidential aides.

Prenomination Clearances. In 1993 the President has direct appointment authority for slightly more than four thousand positions. Some of these require the consent of the Senate and are usually designated as PAS (presidential appointment with Senate confirmation) positions; others do not require confirmation and are called PA (presidential appointment) positions. Cabinet secretaries, ambassadors, and the members of independent regulatory commissions are examples of PAS positions. Part-time members of most of the federal advisory boards and commissions are examples of PA positions. As of 4 March 1992, the totals in each category within the executive branch (not including military appointments) were: PAS full-time, 1,971; PAS part-time, 505; PA full-time, 24; and PA part-time, 1,584. In addition to these 4,084 appointees, 438 members of the White House staff serve at the pleasure of the President.

Once the President has designated a candidate of choice for a position in his administration, and once that candidate has agreed to serve if appointed, a series of clearances is initiated to ensure the candidate's fitness for the job. In most cases, these clearances are completed before the formal announcement of the nomination. They include a congressional clearance, a FEDERAL BUREAU OF INVESTIGATION full field investigation, and an examination of the potential nominee's background and personal finances by the Office of the Counsel to the President.

Congressional clearance. Congress is a prominent feature on any President's political landscape, and the selection of appointees is an important component of

PRESIDENTIAL-CONGRESSIONAL RELATIONS. Sensitivity to congressional concerns in the appointment process can often strengthen the President's working relations with important congressional leaders. Hence routine efforts are made to inform members of Congress of the progress of a personnel search and to allow them opportunities to express their reactions to the candidates under consideration. Among those most often consulted on appointments are: the leaders of the President's party in the House and Senate, the Senators and influential Representatives from the candidate's home state who are members of the President's party, and the leaders of the committees and subcommittees with jurisdiction over the agency in which the nominee will serve.

Most of the contact with members of Congress on appointment matters is handled by the White House Office of Congressional Relations, the presidential aides who work with Congress every day. Members of Congress generally recognize that the appointment power belongs to the President and that by "clearing" a nomination with them, the White House is not offering an opportunity for a veto, only for a reaction. This is essentially a process of information exchange and, except in a few cases, not much more. It would normally require a major objection, strongly expressed by a member of Congress, to stop a nomination at this point. In reality, the vast majority of congressional clearances result in pro forma approval.

FBI full field investigation. The full field investigation is a comprehensive inquiry designed to turn up information that might disqualify a candidate from holding high office or that might embarrass the President were it to become public. The requirement for a full field investigation on all candidates for presidential appointment originated with President Eisenhower's Executive Order 10450 in 1953.

Most full field investigations are conducted by a unit of the Criminal Investigation Division of the FBI that handles special inquiries from the White House, the so-called SPIN Unit. SPIN investigations are given high priority by FBI special agents. The thrust of the investigation is summarized by the acronym CARL: character, associations, reputation, loyalty. The background investigation covers the candidate's entire adult life with emphasis on the recent past. Those interviewed by FBI agents are told that the candidate is being considered for a government position, but the position is not identified. In some cases, the FBI may not know what the position is.

If the FBI develops information of alleged misconduct or obtains unfavorable information about a potential nominee, the FBI, after contact with the White

House, may arrange for an interview with the nominee in an attempt to resolve suitability or access issues or to make as part of an official record that person's response to the allegations. The FBI also makes a significant effort to uncover any evidence that exculpates the candidate. Both sides of the allegation are fully explored and reported. The FBI does not evaluate the information it uncovers. Its role is to furnish as complete a record as possible to the White House, where the actual judgments are made.

Full field investigations are scheduled for completion in twenty-five to thirty-five days, but may take substantially longer if there are delays in receipt of records and reports from other agencies, if the need arises for follow-up inquiries after the first level of interviews and review, or for other reasons that may be difficult to anticipate or predict. Once completed, the results of the full field investigation are sent to the WHITE HOUSE COUNSEL for evaluation. Routine and favorable information is summarized by the FBI and sent to the White House, but the complete results of interviews of individuals who provide derogatory information are included so that the White House can make its own assessment. The counsel usually examines the file and reports the general results to the Presidential Personnel Office. Only if there is reason for particular concern does the President or his top aides examine the contents of the file.

The records of the full field investigation are protected by the Privacy Act and are generally exempt from release under the FREEDOM OF INFORMATION ACT. The results are provided only to the White House. With the President's authorization, the record may also be shared with specific Senators and staff members on the committee responsible for confirmation of the appointment.

Personal background review. The third clearance that takes place before a nomination is announced is a thorough examination of the potential nominee's personal background and financial situation, supervised by the Office of the Counsel to the President.

This begins with the completion by the nominee of a personal data statement, a lengthy list of questions on such matters as the previous involvement of the candidate in criminal or civil litigation, the candidate's business associations, controversial public statements made by the candidate, and any other information that, if made public, might prove harmful or embarrassing to the nominee or the President. All this information is for internal White House use only; none of it is made public. Once this statement has been completed, it is submitted to the counsel's office, where it is subject to careful review. The candidate

may well be asked to clarify any information that seems incomplete or potentially troublesome.

The counsel's office also works with nominees to help them complete a draft of SF 278, the Executive Personnel Financial Disclosure Report. This allows the counsel's office to determine whether the potential nominee is likely to encounter serious conflict-of-interest problems and to begin the process of resolving those problems before the nomination is announced.

If each of these clearances is completed without producing information that causes a reconsideration of the President's choice, there soon follows a formal announcement. If the position requires Senate confirmation, the nomination is transmitted to the Senate. If the President is the sole appointing authority, a certificate is issued and the appointee's service begins.

New Burdens on the Appointment Power. Changes in the laws affecting presidential appointees and in the public environment in the early 1990s have made it increasingly difficult for Presidents to recruit the individuals they prefer for positions in the executive branch. Each passing year, in fact, seems to add more encumbrances to the task of the executive recruiters who work for the President of the United States. Especially notable among those are relatively low government salaries, an increasingly intrusive press, and ever more rigid conflict-of-interest restrictions.

There have been few, if any, times in American history when the salaries paid to executives in the federal government equaled those for equivalent work in the private sector. Since the early 1970s, however, the gap has expanded. Salary levels for the five executive ranks in the federal pay structure have grown slowly over time. At the same time, the salaries of corporate executives, partners in large law firms, medical and technical specialists, and professors have grown dramatically. [*See table accompanying* SALARIES, EXECUTIVE.]

For most of the people the Presidential Personnel Office seeks to recruit, acceptance of a position in government requires a financial sacrifice. Some students of this process suggest that the sacrifice is short-term, and that government executives return to the private sector in more prestigious jobs at higher salaries than the ones they held before entering government. While that is true in some cases, experiences differ widely. Many departing government executives find that their federal service has added little to their employability in the private sector, especially if the President they served has been replaced by one from the opposition party. And some government jobs—like arms-control negotiation or management of welfare programs—have few analogs in private industry where high salaries are most available.

Many private-sector leaders look with trepidation on the visibility of executive jobs in government. Even those who have run large corporations are unlikely to have had the experience in dealing with the communications media, special-interest groups, and congressional committees that are part of the daily routines of many government executives.

The visibility attendant to public life is two-edged. It has made some people famous and added to their reputations. But others have had less happy experiences, their reputations diminished or destroyed while the nation watched. Investigative reporting has been very much a growth industry since the 1970s. In many ways, it has helped to improve the integrity and accountability of government. But it has not been without excess or cost. And its costs are felt most fully by the President's executive recruiters in their efforts to overcome the fears that many potential appointees hold about risking their reputations and their futures in the glare of the public eye.

One of the largest impediments that presidential personnel officers face is the burden of educating the people they are trying to recruit about the growing body of federal ethics law. There were good reasons for many of these laws, and they provide some important new safeguards against conflicts of interest, but they have made it harder to recruit people to government from the private sector. Part of the problem is simply misunderstanding. Many of those outside of government believe the ethics laws more restrictive than they are in fact. But the impediment to recruiting is not just perceptual. Compliance with conflict-of-interest legislation has required a number of new government executives to rearrange their personal finances, sometimes at significant cost.

To many potential government executives, one of the most troubling aspects of the ethics laws is the financial-disclosure requirement. Under the Ethics in Government Act of 1978, all senior government executives must, at the time of their appointment and annually thereafter, make full public disclosure of their personal finances: sources and amounts of income (within broad categories), assets, investments, and significant liabilities. In addition, much of this information must be disclosed for the executive's spouse and minor children. Some of those whom Presidents have sought to recruit have declined appointments simply because they thought the public disclosure requirement too great an intrusion into their personal lives.

The appointment power has become an increasingly important tool of PRESIDENTIAL LEADERSHIP in the second half of the twentieth century. With many large and complex enterprises to run in the federal government, modern Presidents require lots of talented help. As it has become more important, however, the appointment process has become more formal, more institutionalized, more conflictual, and more burdened by rules and procedural constraints. The appointment power has become simultaneously a more valuable and a more cumbersome instrument of executive leadership.

BIBLIOGRAPHY

Fenno, Richard F. *The President's Cabinet*. 1959.
Fisher, Louis. *Constitutional Conflicts between Congress and the President*. 3d ed. 1991.
Heclo, Hugh. *A Government of Strangers*. 1977.
Mackenzie, G. Calvin, ed. *The In and Outers*. 1987.
Mackenzie, G. Calvin. "Partisan Presidential Leadership: The President's Appointees." In *The Parties Respond: Changes in the American Party System*. Edited by L. Sandy Maisel. 1990.
Mackenzie, G. Calvin. *The Politics of Presidential Appointments*. 1981.
Mann, Dean E. *The Assistant Secretaries: Problems and Processes of Appointment*. 1965.
Pfiffner, James P. *The Strategic Presidency: Hitting the Ground Running*. 1988.
Twentieth Century Fund. *Judicial Roulette: The Report of the Twentieth Century Fund Task Force on the Appointment of Federal Judges*. 1988.

G. CALVIN MACKENZIE

APPOINTMENTS, RECESS. See RECESS APPOINTMENTS.

APPROPRIATION RIDERS. One of the most controversial and frequently used devices of appropriations-based policy-making is the rider. Appropriation riders, which are amendments tacked onto an appropriation bill, take one of two forms. Legislative riders are nongermane amendments that change existing law, impose additional duties on government, or require judgments and determinations not otherwise required by law. Congressional rules prohibit such riders in order to keep authorizations separate and apart from appropriations. Limitation riders, in contrast, are presumptively germane amendments to an appropriations bill that specifically prohibit the use of funds for designated activities.

The History of Riders. Congress's use of and presidential opposition to appropriation riders dates back to the 1830s. Indeed, by 1837, delays in the enactment of appropriation bills caused by the attachment of legislative riders led the House to adopt a rule prohibiting the appropriation "for any expenditure not previously authorized by law." Legislative riders were still enacted, however. In 1879, President Rutherford B. Hayes attacked such riders as improperly interfering with EXECUTIVE PREROGATIVE. Through a series of veto messages, Hayes claimed that Congress effectively negated the President's veto power by attaching nongermane riders to appropriations. In language strikingly similar to both late twentieth-century attacks on continuing resolutions and justifications for the ITEM VETO, Hayes argued that the "executive will no longer be what the framers of the Constitution intended" because Congress's attachment of nongermane riders to necessary appropriation measures made it impossible for the President to use the veto power without "stopping all of the operations of the Government."

The Constitution does not distinguish between Congress's power to appropriate funds and its other lawmaking powers. The Constitution, moreover, does not demand that all provisions in a bill be pertinent to the bill's purpose. Legislative riders therefore are not constitutionally foreclosed. House and Senate rules, however, prohibit such riders. Limitation riders, which are not affected by these rules, have also had an enormous impact and remain extremely controversial. Military activities in Southeast Asia, public funding of ABORTION, air bags for automobiles, tax-exemptions for discriminatory schools, religious activities in the public schools, and public funding of school desegregation are but some of the areas affected by limitation riders.

Congress has been attaching limitation riders to appropriation bills since the 1870s. Nineteenth-century riders involved WAR POWERS, federal supervision of elections, and extensions of the Constitution and revenue laws to territories. By the 1970s, limitation riders became one of Congress's principal policy-making tools. From 1971 to 1977, 225 limitation amendments (31 percent of all amendments) were offered to appropriations bills. By 1980, limitation riders accounted for over 40 percent of all amendments. These riders, moreover, frequently addressed volatile policy disputes. Fiscal year 1980 riders, for example, included restrictions on nondiscrimination enforcement by the Internal Revenue Service (IRS), the Department of Education, and the Department of Justice; Occupational Safety and Health Administration (OSHA) enforcement of safety standards in small businesses; Department of Housing and Urban Development financial assistance to student aliens; the distribution of government publications to CUBA, Iran, and the Soviet Union; and possible Department of Education efforts to prevent voluntary prayer in the public schools.

Limitation riders have also proved critically important during the Reagan and Bush presidencies. The IRAN-CONTRA AFFAIR, for example, centered on the refusal of Reagan administration officials to comply with a limitation rider prohibiting federal assistance to the contra rebels in Nicaragua. Other 1980s and 1990s riders affected abortion funding, Federal Communications Commission (FCC) affirmative action guidelines, and communications between executive agencies and congressional oversight committees.

Debate over Riders. The controversial nature of limitation riders is not simply an outgrowth of the controversial subjects addressed by such riders. Limitation riders also affect congressional relations with both the courts and the executive. Critics of limitation riders, for example, claim that since most appropriations are enacted every year, agencies frequently do not know whether to view limitation riders as permanent changes or temporary measures. Also, courts do not know whether to view limitation riders as amendments to the underlying authorization bill. For example, does the annual reenactment (since 1977) of riders prohibiting Medicaid-supported abortions relieve the states of their abortion-related Medicaid cost-sharing responsibilities?

Critics also argue that Congress disrupts the balance of powers by using limitation riders to micromanage executive agencies. Specifically, these critics point to limitation riders prohibiting funding of regulatory initiatives, proposed reexaminations of agency policy, agency supervision of contacts between agency employees and members and committees of Congress and their staff, and White House review of agency orders. In 1990, pointing to such measures, Bush administration Attorney General Dick Thornburgh attacked such riders as "clearly eroding the President's constitutional responsibility to supervise the affairs of the executive branch as he sees fit." Some critics have extended this attack to argue that Congress cannot use its appropriations powers to prevent the President from performing the duties and exercising the prerogatives given him by Article II of the Constitution. Furthermore, since limitation riders are often attached to omnibus funding bills, critics also argue that the President cannot effectively use the veto power to check legislative interference.

Supporters of Congress's use of limitation riders, in contrast, argue that appropriations-based restrictions on agency action may be the only realistic way to stop the executive from launching administrative initiatives that Congress disfavors. Claiming that the appropriations clause empowers Congress to control the level of executive-branch enforcement or execution of the law, supporters of Congress's use of limitation riders also reject opponents' constitutional objections. Indeed, for supporters, rather than a mechanism to oversee every detail of executive implementation, limitation riders enable Congress to defend against executive intrusions into Congress's lawmaking powers. For example, in response to IRS efforts during the Carter administration to deny tax-exempt status to private schools with inadequate minority enrollments, Congress enacted limitation riders as a stopgap measure to allow the appropriate legislative committees a chance to evaluate the proposal. Similarly, after the FCC sought to reexamine its affirmative action guidelines during the Reagan administration, Congress sought to check this "unwarranted" initiative through a limitation rider first enacted in 1987. That Congress used limitation riders to check both Carter and Reagan initiatives demonstrates that this device is neither liberal nor conservative, Republican nor Democratic.

Congress's use of limitation riders as a policy-making device extends well beyond appropriations-based oversight of the executive. Another controversial use of limitation riders concerns elected government responses to Supreme Court decisions. Unlike constitutional amendments and statutory challenges to Supreme Court decisions, funding restrictions do not seek to overturn Court decisions. Instead, elected government expresses its disagreement with the Court by refusing to appropriate funds that help effectuate Court rulings. For example, since fiscal year 1977, appropriations bills for the DEPARTMENT OF HEALTH AND HUMAN SERVICES (formerly Department of Health, Education, and Welfare) have contained language prohibiting federal funding of abortion in almost all circumstances. These limitation riders have been supported, at various times and to varying degrees, by both the Congress and the White House. The Reagan and Bush administrations, for example, strongly backed these measures and vetoed appropriations bills that attempted to liberalize abortion funding.

The debate over the propriety of riders is likely to continue. Congress has strong incentive to use this power. Appropriation riders are easier to enact than substantive legislation. Riders too are an effective mechanism to check both the executive and the Supreme Court. That the benefits of Congress's use of appropriation riders may strain the policy-making process does not matter. Congress is unlikely to abandon a policy tool that is as convenient as it is potent. Presidents too are unlikely to abandon appropriation riders as a mechanism to keep in check court rulings and government programs that they disfavor.

BIBLIOGRAPHY

Devins, Neal. "Appropriations Redux: A Critical Look at the Fiscal Year 1988 Continuing Resolution." *Duke Law Journal* (1988): 389–421.
U.S. General Accounting Office. *Appropriations: Continuing Resolutions and an Assessment of Automatic Funding Approaches.* Report to the Chairman. Committee on Rules. House of Representatives. 1986.

NEAL DEVINS

ARCHIVES, PRESIDENTIAL. See LIBRARIES, PRESIDENTIAL.

AREA RESOLUTIONS. From 1955 through 1964 Congress adopted five significant resolutions supporting Presidential foreign policy during crises in specific geographic areas. These were the Formosa, Middle East, Cuban, Berlin, and Gulf of Tonkin resolutions. The trend started when President Dwight D. Eisenhower recognized the domestic importance of congressional authorization for military action and requested the Formosa and Middle East resolutions. The resolutions also served the international purpose of demonstrating unity and clarifying U.S. intentions.

The Formosa Resolution (P.L. 84-4, H.J. Res. 159), signed on 29 January 1955, authorized the President to employ the U.S. Armed Forces "as he deems necessary for the specific purpose of securing and protecting Formosa and the Pescadores against armed attack." The Nationalist Chinese government of Chiang Kai-shek had fled to Formosa (Taiwan) when the communists had gained control of mainland China. After a long series of military threats against Chiang Kai-shek, Chinese communist forces seized a small Nationalist-held island north of Formosa and concern mounted that they would attack Formosa. On 24 January 1955, Eisenhower asked Congress to make clear the unified intentions of the United States to protect Formosa and to fight if necessary. The House passed the resolution by a vote of 310 to 3 on 25 January, and the Senate by a vote of 75 to 3 on January 28. Later, some members of Congress contended that the resolution failed to spell out the precise geographic area that the United States would defend. The Formosa Resolution was repealed in 1974 by Public Law 93-475.

The Middle East Resolution (P.L. 85-7, H.J. Res. 117), signed on 9 March 1957, responded to the declining power of Great Britain and France in the Middle East after the Suez crisis of 1956. On 5 January 1957, President Eisenhower urged a congressional resolution to support a policy that became known as the EISENHOWER DOCTRINE. The resolution, which passed by votes of 72 to 19 in the Senate and 370 to 60 in the House, stated the United States "regards as vital to the national interest and world peace the preservation of the independence and integrity of the nations of the Middle East." It declared that the United States was prepared to use armed forces to assist nations against armed aggression from any communist-controlled country. It also authorized the President to extend military and economic aid to Middle Eastern nations.

The Cuban Resolution (P.L. 87-733, S.J. Res. 230), signed on 3 October 1962, did not authorize action but rather expressed the determination of the United States to prevent "by whatever means may be necessary, including the use of arms, the Marxist-Leninist regime in CUBA from extending its aggressive or subversive activities to any part of this hemisphere" and to stop the creation of an externally supported military capability in Cuba endangering U.S. security. The resolution, a product of legislative-executive interaction after reports of Soviet missiles in Cuba, was adopted on 20 September 1962 by votes of 86 to 1 in the Senate and 384 to 7 in the House. On 22 October 1962, President John F. Kennedy demanded that Soviet leader Nikita Khrushchev withdraw the missiles from Cuba [see also CUBAN MISSILE CRISIS].

On 10 October 1962, Congress also passed the Berlin Resolution (House Con. Res. 570), which stated that the United States was "determined to prevent by whatever means may be necessary, including the use of arms" any violation of American, British, and/or French rights in occupied Berlin. The Berlin Resolution differed from the other four area resolutions in that it was a concurrent resolution stating the sense of the Congress (and thus was nonbinding) and had not been requested by the President. Construction of the Berlin Wall had begun in 1961 and the major crisis was over, but Rep. Clement Zablocki (D-Wis.) sponsored the resolution because, he said, Congress had not yet officially declared its support of President Kennedy's position on the Berlin issue.

The GULF OF TONKIN RESOLUTION, also known as the Southeast Asia Resolution (P.L. 88-408, H.J. Res. 1145), signed on 10 August 1964, was adopted by votes of 414 to 0 in the House and 88 to 2 in the Senate. President Lyndon B. Johnson had requested the resolution on 5 August, citing military incidents against U.S. ships in the Gulf of Tonkin. The resolution stated that the United States was "prepared, as the President determines, to take all necessary steps, including the use of armed force" to assist certain states in Southeast Asia. Later, Johnson administration officials referred to the resolution as the moral equivalent of a declaration of the VIETNAM WAR, but members of Congress criticized it as having amounted to a "blank check." The resolution was repealed by Public Law 91-672, signed on 12 January 1971.

Many in Congress came to see some of these resolutions as having been adopted too hastily and with inadequate information and too much pressure. Congress became more cautious in the use of area resolutions and eventually, in the WAR POWERS RESOLUTION, called for explicit congressional authorization for uses of force in hostilities.

BIBLIOGRAPHY

Eisenhower, Dwight D. *The White House Years: Mandate for Change, 1953–1956.* 1963.
U.S. House of Representatives. *Authorizing the President to Undertake Economic and Military Cooperation with Nations in the General Area of the Middle East.* 85th Cong., 1st sess. 1957.
U.S. Senate. *Situation in Cuba.* 87th Cong., 2d sess. 1962.

ELLEN C. COLLIER

ARMS CONTROL. The history of U.S. government participation in international arms control goes back to the Rush-Bagehot agreement of 1817, which eliminated naval deployments on the Great Lakes, and includes such prominent landmarks as the failed TREATY OF VERSAILLES, as well as the temporarily successful WASHINGTON TREATY of 1922 and the London Naval Treaty of 1930 limiting naval ships among the major powers. Nevertheless, only in recent decades has arms control became a significant and enduring objective of U.S. foreign policy. As the COLD WAR flourished, then moderated and waned, arms control became centrally important in U.S.-Soviet relations, as well as a prominent force in American domestic politics. Throughout the history of arms control efforts, the President has dominated the agenda in the United States political culture.

Presidents and Agreements. In partisan political terms, the liberal end of the political spectrum and the DEMOCRATIC PARTY have been more vigorously supportive of arms control. At the same time the conservative wing of the populace and the REPUBLICAN PARTY have been more conspicuously supportive of increased defense spending. Because the Democratic Party has often been portrayed as insufficiently supportive of strong defense, Democratic Presidents have been notably less successful than Republicans in concluding arms control agreements, although of course they have held office for only eighteen of the forty-six years between 1946 and 1992. Nevertheless, most conservatives have supported some arms control measures, and arms control has been generally popular with the public at large. This public popularity has often produced vigorous congressional proponents of arms control, but the President has provided the leadership necessary to elevate the subject to a priority position, not only in the public mind, but also in the government bureaucracy.

The President sets the agenda for arms control negotiations. He decides what subjects to negotiate and when. He makes the inevitable compromises in the course of a negotiation. And he decides how to effectuate the results of a negotiation, for example, deciding whether a policy or agreed norm should be made legally binding as a matter of international law and, if so, whether and how to secure congressional support. From the 1970s to the 1990s Presidents have decided to make important arms control measures politically binding, thereby avoiding the inflexibility of legally binding rules (and perhaps the public expectations of strict compliance with them) and avoiding the necessity of congressional participation in their conclusion. For example, President Gerald Ford avoided parliamentary difficulty in this manner when signing the 1975 Helsinki Accords, which were developed at the Conference on Security and Cooperation in Europe (CSCE). Since then important measures following up the CSCE, embodied in the Stockholm Declaration and the 1992 Vienna Document affecting conventional arms and military maneuvers in Europe, have been treated as politically binding. Finally, once an agreement is reached, the President decides, at least initially, how to interpret its ambiguous provisions, whether and how to react to breaches by others, and how to settle compliance controversies.

NUCLEAR WEAPONS have provided the principal focus of public attention. Nuclear test ban negotiations started during the Eisenhower administration, and every American President since then has negotiated or concluded a nuclear arms control agreement. John F. Kennedy personally directed the negotiation of the Limited Test Ban Treaty, the first agreement to deal explicitly with nuclear issues. Lyndon B. Johnson presided over the conclusion of the Outer Space Treaty, which banned nuclear weapons in space, and the preparation of the Nuclear Nonproliferation Treaty. Johnson also laid the groundwork for SALT (STRATEGIC ARMS LIMITATION TALKS). Richard M. Nixon signed the SALT I interim agreement and the ABM (ANTIBALLISTIC MISSILE SYSTEM) TREATY, the foundation for a new era of DETENTE between the United States and the Soviet Union. Gerald Ford continued the SALT negotiations, nearly completing an agreement at the Vladivostok summit (1974), and he also sent two treaties dealing with nuclear testing to the Senate for its advice and consent to ratification. Jimmy Carter made arms control the centerpiece of his Soviet policy with the negotiation of the SALT II Treaty.

Although Ronald Reagan vociferously opposed SALT II, and for a while the entire arms control process as well, he eventually proposed radically sweeping arms reductions at a summit meeting with Mikhail Gorbachev at Reykjavic, Iceland (1986), and ultimately concluded the INF (INTERMEDIATE RANGE NUCLEAR FORCES) TREATY, which was the first agreement to eliminate an entire class of nuclear missiles and which included unprecedented verification features that served as a model for subsequent treaties. George Bush carried on the process, completing START (STRATEGIC ARMS REDUCTION TALKS), which built upon SALT II, and extending it, with nonproliferation commitments, to four former constituent republics of the Soviet Union. As the Soviet Union disintegrated, Bush concluded nuclear-testing restrictions with sweeping verification controls, concluded the CFE (CONVENTIONAL FORCES IN EUROPE) TREATY, limiting levels of conventional forces in Europe, signed a bilateral chemical weapons agreement with the Soviet Union, and agreed with the new Russian Republic to cut back dramatically nuclear weapons to approximately one-third of existing levels. Bush also elevated nuclear nonproliferation to center stage, taking dramatic steps in the UNITED NATIONS to enforce nonproliferation obligations against a recalcitrant Iraq. He pushed for successful conclusion of the multilateral CHEMICAL WEAPONS CONVENTION, achieved a politically binding series of commitments regarding military maneuvers in Europe, secured agreement on ballistic missile technology transfer, and used unilateral measures to advance the goals of nuclear, chemical, and biological weapons nonproliferation.

Reaching Agreements. In order to conclude an agreement, the President must not only successfully negotiate with foreign states through his ambassador or other representative, but must also guide and force the complex bureaucratic process within the executive branch. The resistance to change created by that process has often been as difficult to overcome as opposing positions presented by negotiating partners. For example, Kennedy's personal attention was important in overcoming the opposition of the ATOMIC ENERGY COMMISSION and military services, whose voices carry significant weight in the interagency, bureaucratic decision-making process within the executive branch.

An international negotiation involves several interlocking processes, intragovernmental as well as international. Initially, the government bureaucracies involved formulate positions through intricate interagency negotiations. The President may also discuss the issues with congressional committees and affected nongovernmental interests, such as the nuclear weapons laboratories. Each agency has a distinctive perspective from which it views the process and that influences the position it advocates. For example, in a negotiation regarding strategic nuclear missiles, the DEPARTMENT OF DEFENSE and the JOINT CHIEFS OF STAFF (JCS) have usually proposed a position that accommodates current production plans. Arms control proponents in the ARMS CONTROL AND DISARMAMENT AGENCY (ACDA) may prefer a position calling for elimination of certain weapons systems or radical cuts in the existing levels of weapons, but they also have an interest in keeping the process of negotiation going. The DEPARTMENT OF STATE is concerned with improvement of the overall political relationship between the parties to the negotiations and may therefore also want to reach an agreement that can contribute to the maintenance of a good relationship. In this light it is likely to look to what is open to negotiation and thus favor a result that accommodates both sides' interests. The CENTRAL INTELLIGENCE AGENCY (CIA) may want an agreement that can be monitored easily. Some members of Congress may want to ensure that any proposed position does not foreclose production of a favored weapons system that is important to their constituencies. The weapons laboratories may favor a position that requires the development of new warheads.

All these interests must either be accommodated, compromised, or overridden by the President before a position can even be put on the negotiating table. Moreover, since the resulting agreement may have to be approved by the full Congress or the Senate, Presidents have often been reluctant to override a strong congressional preference or the position of the Pentagon or JCS, whose views carry great weight in Congress.

Constitutional Authority. In the course of concluding arms control agreements, the constitutional authority of the President has been exercised, tested, and perhaps even expanded. The authority of the President to conduct foreign policy rests on an inherent or implied constitutional foreign affairs power that is based on a mix of constitutional text, original intent, and historical practice. His authority to define policy (such as that supporting nuclear nonproliferation), to initiate a negotiation, to determine the course of the negotiation, and to act on the basis of its results is exclusively a presidential power. Of course Congress may influence the President, as it did in forcing the advocacy of human rights on reluctant executive branch officials and in halting the illegal war in Nicaragua, but congressional influence is sporadic, episodic, and often resisted on constitutional grounds. Despite that executive-branch resistance, however, as the VIETNAM WAR and the IRAN-CONTRA AFFAIR illustrated, Congress can eventually prevail through its control of appropriations and the legislative process, including, most importantly, its political power that forces Presidents to compromise.

Once a negotiation is concluded, the President, in conjunction with his negotiating partners, decides on the form in which the agreement will be expressed. This decision can have international and domestic legal effects. The results may be expressed as an agreed policy, with no intended legal effect, or they may be politically binding, in which case some level of compliance short of strict compliance is expected, but the parties do not expect to invoke even the scant remedies available under international law. Often an agreement is concluded in this form in order to avoid the requirement of congressional approval, as was the case in the Helsinki Accords. Finally, the agreement may be legally binding as a matter of international law. In that case the President must decide, taking into consideration domestic constitutional law, whether to seek approval of the agreement from the full Congress or the Senate prior to ratification of the accord by the United States.

Article II of the Constitution authorizes the President to make treaties with the ADVICE AND CONSENT of the Senate, provided two-thirds of the Senators present concur. This formal act (or ratification) is separate from the act of signing the treaty and is accomplished pursuant to an instrument executed by the President. Accordingly, the Article II TREATY-MAKING POWER is a presidential power that requires Senate participation prior to its exercise. However, the President is not constitutionally required to follow the process specified in Article II. Historical practice has confirmed that there are additional sources of authority for presidential conclusion of an international agreement on behalf of the United States. The President chooses the most appropriate basis in domestic constitutional law for bringing the agreement into force. Most important, the President may seek congressional authorization of an international agreement by joint resolution or act of Congress, passed by majority vote of both houses, or he may use existing legislation as a basis for ratification of the agreement. The use of these congressional-executive agreements, as an alternative to the Article II procedure, seems to have been accepted as constitutionally equivalent to the Article II procedure.

An international agreement may also be concluded on the basis of the President's FOREIGN AFFAIRS power or the COMMANDER IN CHIEF power. Many arms control treaties have been concluded on the basis of this authority, although these treaties tend to deal with consultation, notification, and relatively routine or noncontroversial matters. Nevertheless, those treaties, known as EXECUTIVE AGREEMENTS, have the same effect internationally as an Article II treaty or a congressional-executive agreement.

The decision by the President as to which form to choose is essentially a political choice. Historically, international agreements dealing with arms control have normally been submitted to the Senate as Article II treaties. Nevertheless, the record suggests that there is no strict constitutional requirement to that effect. Important commitments, such as the ANNEXATION OF TEXAS and the ANNEXATION OF HAWAII, the decision to join the International Labor Organization, and the SALT I interim agreement, were all congressional-executive agreements. Most significant, when Congress established the Arms Control and Disarmament Agency within the executive branch, it stated that no arms reduction could be accomplished except pursuant to Article II or an act of Congress, thereby implying the constitutional equivalence of the two forms. Although obviously the weight of tradition and the strong preference of the Senate for the Article II process no doubt constrains the President's choice as a political matter, he still claims to have the choice, at least as a matter of formal law. In a departure from the general pattern of past practice, the Bush administration initially decided to treat the 1990 U.S.-Soviet chemical weapons agreement as a congressional-executive agreement. The Senate has expressed its disapproval in the form of understandings attached to its ratification resolutions covering the CFE and START treaties. The political struggle over presidential authority to decide the form of an agreement will no doubt continue.

Interpretation and Reinterpretation. Once a treaty has been ratified, the President has the power to interpret it, unilaterally or in agreement with treaty partners, pursuant to the President's foreign affairs power. The courts of course may issue definitive interpretations of treaties that come before them, but even the courts normally give great weight to an executive branch interpretation. If the President goes beyond interpretation and attempts to amend a treaty in a major respect without congressional approval, the matter may become controversial, as when President Reagan attempted to change a fundamental provision of the ABM Treaty (see SOFAER DOCTRINE). In addition, the President normally does not commit the interpretation of treaties to third-party dispute resolution, such as arbitration or adjudication by the International Court of Justice, without congressional acquiescence or approval. Moreover, if the President changes an earlier treaty interpretation, Congress may use its legislative and appropriations powers to force the President to reconsider, as it did in connection with the ABM Treaty.

The TREATY REINTERPRETATION controversy involving the ABM Treaty is a good example of this phenomenon. When the President sent the ABM Treaty to the Senate for its advice and consent to ratification as an Article II treaty, executive branch officials told the Senate that the treaty prohibited the development and testing of space-based ABM systems based on "other physical principles" than those existing in 1972, such as lasers. The Reagan administration reinterpreted the treaty to permit the development and testing of those space-based ABM systems, contrary to the earlier interpretations of the treaty provided to the Senate and contrary to the Soviet understanding of the treaty. Congress used its legislative and appropriation powers to force the executive branch to limit development and testing of ABM systems to activities permitted under the original interpretation and challenged the President's constitutional power to reinterpret or amend the treaty in this way. The Senate debated the issue on three occasions. It declined to adopt a general solution disavowing presidential authority to change all interpretations of a treaty, but it conditioned the Senate's ratification of the INF Treaty on presidential agreement not to reinterpret that treaty without congressional declaration. In its resolution approving ratification of the CFE Treaty, the Senate attached a declaration purporting to apply to all treaties. The President expressly disputed the constitutionality of the INF condition but did not react to the CFE counterpart. The controversy does not seem to have been settled.

Most commentators would probably agree that the President may not reinterpret fundamental treaty provisions in major respects, even with the agreement of a treaty partner, without seeking congressional consent. Such a change would properly be classified as a major amendment to the treaty and, as such, would require that consent. As to supplemental agreements contemplated by a treaty, they would seem to be implicitly approved; this point seems to have been uncontroversial. It would also seem that minor reinterpretations, as well as minor amendments, can be made by the President with congressional acquiescence. If Congress disagrees with a presidential interpretation, it may demonstrate its nonacquiescence by the use of its legislative or appropriations power. Finally, conditions formally adopted, like that to the INF Treaty, should bind the President if he chooses to ratify the treaty.

BIBLIOGRAPHY

Caldwell, D. *The Dynamics of Domestic Politics and Arms Control.* 1991.

Krepon, M., and D. Caldwell, eds. *The Politics of Arms Control.* 1991.

Newhouse, J. *Cold Dawn: The Story of SALT.* 1973.

Seaborg, G. *Kennedy, Khrushchev, and the Test Ban.* 1981.

Seaborg, G., and B. Loeb. *Stemming the Tide: Arms Control in the Johnson Years.* 1987.

Smith, G. *Doubletalk: The Story of SALT I.* 1980.

Talbot, S. *Deadly Gambits.* 1984.

Talbot, S. *Endgame: The Inside Story of SALT II.* 1979.

Trimble, Phillip R. "Arms Control and International Negotiation Theory." *Stanford Journal of International Law* 25 (1989).

Trimble, Phillip R. "Beyond Verification: The Next Stop in Arms Control." *Harvard Law Review* 102 (1991).

Trimble, Phillip R., and J. Weiss. "The Role of the President, the Senate, and Congress with Respect to Arms Control Treaties Concluded by the United States." *University of Chicago–Kent Law Review* 67 (1992).

PHILLIP R. TRIMBLE

ARMS CONTROL AND DISARMAMENT AGENCY. The U.S. Arms Control and Disarmament Agency (ACDA) was established by Congress as an independent agency in the executive branch of the U.S. government. President John F. Kennedy signed the ACDA Act into law on 26 September 1961 in New York City. Before then, except for two years (1955–1957) when there was an Office of the Special Assistant to the President for Disarmament in the White House, the DEPARTMENT OF STATE had responsibility for ARMS CONTROL and disarmament matters.

The ACDA Act stipulated that the agency's Director would serve as the principal adviser to the Secretary of State and the President on arms control and disarmament and, under the direction of the Secretary of State, would have primary responsibility for those matters.

The Committee of Principals during the Kennedy-Johnson administrations (1961–1969) and the NATIONAL SECURITY COUNCIL (NSC) and its various committees since then have been the administrative bodies through which ACDA's Director has advised the President and Secretary of State (and the heads of other government agencies). In 1975, the Director became the principal adviser on arms control and disarmament to the NSC, and in 1983 he was designated to be in attendance at its meetings involving not only arms control and disarmament matters but also weapons procurement, arms sales, and the defense budget.

The ACDA Act also charged the agency with preparing for and managing U.S. participation in international negotiations, conducting research, and disseminating public information on arms control and disarmament. Amendments to the act have charged the agency with preparation of various reports and studies, including an annual report on compliance with arms control agreements that the President submits to the Congress.

ACDA has been involved with many international negotiating forums. During the 1960s, an international body meeting in Geneva called the Eighteen Nation Disarmament Committee (ENDC) was the only one. It still functions as the principal forum for multilateral negotiations. Having been enlarged and having changed its name three times, it is now known as the Conference on Disarmament (CD) and has thirty-nine members.

The following international agreements were negotiated in whole or in part in the ENDC-CD: the Limited Test Ban Treaty (1963), the Nuclear Non-Proliferation Treaty (1968), the Seabed Arms Control Treaty (1971), the Biological Weapons Convention (1972), the Environmental Modification Convention (1977), and the CHEMICAL WEAPONS CONVENTION (1992). This last agreement had been under negotiation there since the late 1960s. In 1984, then Vice President George Bush submitted to the conference a draft convention that was used thereafter as the basis for negotiations.

Since 1969, other forums have been used as well. Bilateral talks between the United States and the Soviet Union have reached agreements limiting strategic arms: the Anti-Ballistic Missile Treaty (1972), the Interim Agreement on Strategic Offensive Arms (1972), the Strategic Arms Limitation Treaty (1979), and the Strategic Arms Reduction Treaty (1991). They produced agreements limiting underground nuclear tests (1974, 1976, 1990). They achieved the Intermediate-Range Nuclear Forces Treaty (1987) that eliminated an entire class of nuclear missiles. They resulted in a series of agreements designed to reduce the risk of war by accident, among them the three HOT-LINE AGREEMENTS (1963, 1971, and 1984) establishing and then modernizing direct communications links between Washington and Moscow. They also led to a bilateral agreement to destroy chemical weapons stocks (1990).

Multilateral negotiations begun in Helsinki in 1973 among thirty-three states of Europe plus the United States and Canada have led to a series of agreements on confidence- and security-building measures (in 1975, 1986, 1990, and 1992), such as advance notice of military maneuvers and movements, to reduce the likelihood of military attack, particularly by surprise. Negotiations in 1989 and 1990 among the twenty-two nations of NATO and the former Warsaw Pact led to the Treaty on Conventional Armed Forces in Europe (1990) reducing various types of conventional weapons—tanks, armored personnel vehicles, artillery, and certain types of aircraft and helicopters. Succeeding negotiations produced agreements in 1992 providing for an aerial inspection regime to promote openness and transparency in military activities and for reductions in conventional forces personnel.

Significantly, these arms-control agreements have included increasingly intrusive verification provisions, agreed to at U.S. insistence and designed to create confidence in compliance by deterring cheating and detecting it before it threatens security. Also important have been their provisions for review conferences and for the creation, beginning with the first strategic-arms-limitation agreements (1972), of a series of commissions, consisting of representatives of the parties to the agreements, charged with considering questions of compliance and proposals for increasing the agreements' viability.

ACDA representatives have been on the U.S. delegations to these disarmament negotiations. Some delegation leaders have been ACDA officials. For many delegations, ACDA has supplied a significant portion of the diplomatic, advisory, and administrative personnel. It has also chaired or played a leading role in the day-to-day interagency committees in Washington that have supported the delegations.

In discharging its research function, ACDA has sponsored an external research program which in some of the earliest years accounted for half of its budget and now amounts to about $1.5 million annually. To inform the public about its activities, ACDA has issued annual reports, collections of documents, data on world military expenditures and arms transfers, and other information items. Its officials have given numerous interviews to journalists and spoken before many groups of interested citizens.

Since the end of the COLD WAR, the United States has been shifting emphasis from measures to obtain military balance to measures to further reduce levels of weapons, prevent the proliferation of weapons of mass destruction, and promote regional arms control.

Most ACDA offices have been located in the Department of State building in the Foggy Bottom section of Washington, D.C. The ACDA staff has usually numbered some 200 to 250 people. In addition to its Director and Deputy Director, ACDA's four bureau heads are presidential appointees.

BIBLIOGRAPHY

United States Arms Control and Disarmament Agency. *Annual Report to the Congress.* Annual, 1961– .

United States Arms Control and Disarmament Agency. *Arms Control and Disarmament Agreements: Texts and Histories of Negotiations.* 6th ed. 1990.

United States Arms Control and Disarmament Agency. *Documents on Disarmament.* Issued by ACDA annually, 1961–1986.

United States Arms Control and Disarmament Agency. *The U.S. Control and Disarmament Agency: Thirty Years Promoting a Secure Peace.* 1991.

United States Arms Control and Disarmament Agency. *World Military Expenditures and Arms Transfers.* Issued by ACDA periodically, 1968–1989.

R. WILLIAM NARY

ARMS SALES. Although Congress has displayed continuing interest in arms sales and transfers issues since the 1960s, only since the rapid growth of the foreign military sales (FMS) cash and credit program in the early 1970s has it focused intensively on this subject. Congressional concerns in this area were stimulated by the increasing tendency in the executive branch to use arms sales as an instrument in support of American foreign policy goals. Concurrent with the growing congressional interest in arms sales issues has been a parallel interest in obtaining greater oversight over the transfers of major items of American weaponry.

Before 1974, consultations between the executive and the legislative branches on arms sales were limited generally to briefings of foreign policy committee members and discussions that developed during hearings on security assistance legislation in the wake of news media reports of major sales. The explosive growth of major sales of weapons to less developed nations—especially those in the oil-rich but politically volatile Middle East and Persian Gulf region—stimulated a growing congressional desire for both additional consultation and more complete information on sales that might have serious consequences for American national interests. Congressional concerns about arms sales were also enhanced by mistrust of the executive branch in the wake of the VIETNAM WAR and the WATERGATE AFFAIR.

Congress in the early 1970s received very limited information on the policy rationale behind executive branch decisions on specific arms sales. For example, the Nixon administration's massive buildup of Iran's military forces through major sales occurred with minimal congressional involvement. Further, once Congress learned of a prospective arms sale or transfer—usually through press accounts—it was generally too late for it to reverse the decision that had been made. Congress could exercise its option to place restrictions on sales or transfers to a specific country or region through amendments to pertinent legislation, but such efforts are exceptionally hard to advance successfully and are always subject to a presidential veto.

In this context, Congress in late 1974 passed legislation that established its right to receive notice of and to veto, by a concurrent resolution, major sales of defense articles and services. Originally enacted as part of the Foreign Assistance Act of 1974, this LEGISLATIVE VETO was subsequently incorporated into section 36(b) of the Arms Export Control Act, created through the enactment of the International Security Assistance and Arms Export Control Act of 1976. The veto and its related reporting requirements, the House Foreign Affairs Committee argued in a 1974 report, would provide the legislative branch with an institutionalized mechanism that would "give the Congress the opportunity to study the circumstances surrounding each major [arms] sale, and to assess the foreign policy impact of each such transaction." Sen. Gaylord Nelson reiterated this perspective during Senate debate on the issue in 1974. He observed:

> Despite the serious policy issues raised by this tremendous increase in Government arms sales, these transactions are made with little regard for congressional or public opinion. The DEPARTMENT OF DEFENSE is consulted. The manufacturers of weapons and providers of military services are consulted. The foreign purchasers are involved. But Congress is hardly informed of these transactions, much less consulted as to their propriety. As it stands now, the executive branch simply presents Congress and the public with the accomplished facts.

Senator Nelson concluded therefore that Congress was in need of a "review process" to keep up with the "galloping growth" of the U.S. arms sales program. Congress had to obtain the "necessary information on and oversight authority over proposed foreign military sales to exercise its responsibility in this crucial area."

As perfected by the 1976 legislation and by later amendments to it, the legislative veto in section 36(b) of the Arms Export Control Act (AECA) required, in part, that Congress be given thirty calendar days to review any proposed sale of defense articles or services (as defined under the act) valued at $50 million or more, or of any major defense equipment valued at $14 million or more. If, within the thirty-calendar-day period, a majority of both houses of Congress voted to block the proposed sales by a concurrent resolution, then it could not proceed. The 1976 act, as amended, also expanded the authority of Congress to obtain by request additional detailed information related to any arms sales proposal submitted to it pursuant to section 36(b). The Department of Defense also agreed in 1976 to an informal procedure to provide Congress with a "preliminary notification" of possible arms sales that would ultimately be submitted for congressional review under section 36(b) of the Arms Export Control Act.

Because of the tendency of the executive branch to use arms sales as an instrument in support of American foreign policy, the prospect for differences over them has been heightened when Congress has disagreed with elements of an administration's foreign policy. On the other hand, there are literally scores of arms cases formally submitted to Congress each year under the applicable statutory requirements, the vast bulk of which are noncontroversial and clear Congressional review without formal committee hearings even being held.

The Supreme Court's decisions in INS V. CHADHA (1983) and in related cases invalidated the use of a concurrent resolution of disapproval by Congress to block an arms sale. As a result, Congress subsequently passed legislation, enacted on 12 February 1986, that allowed the veto of arms sales through passage and enactment of a joint resolution of disapproval, which, unlike the concurrent resolution, would be subject to a presidential veto.

Because of the existence of the legislative veto, consultations on controversial arms sales invariably involve negotiations between the executive and the legislative branches regarding the appropriateness and the content of the particular sale proposal. The veto compels the executive branch to deal with Congress in a systematic way. It does not, however, require the executive branch to accept the advice or approach recommended by Congress to deal with a given arms sale if an administration is prepared to run the risks of defying strong congressional opposition to that sale.

Moreover, the executive branch, on balance, has almost always found ways of finessing detailed discussions and negotiations with Congress on major arms sales until it has made its basic decision to sell. As a result, the executive branch has made it very difficult for Congress to influence the final shape of a prospective arms sale. In particular, the President's ability to use the powers and the prestige of his office to define or redefine the terms or emphasis of the public debate on a major arms sale makes it difficult for Congress to overrule his decision. The President can overcome serious criticism of an arms sales proposal by arguing that NATIONAL SECURITY and bilateral relations with an important client state may be notably damaged if the specific sale is vetoed. This basic power of the presidency to influence the outcome of a sale is further enhanced by the institutional difficulty in Congress of achieving consensus on the proper course to take when confronted with a controversial sale.

In the absence of a strong majority in both houses of Congress supporting legislation to block or modify a prospective arms sale, the practical and procedural obstacles to passing such a law—whether a freestanding measure or one within the existing framework of the Arms Export Control Act—are great. Even if Congress can pass the requisite legislation to work its will on an arms sale, the President need only veto it and secure the support of one-third plus one of the members of either the Senate or the House to have his veto sustained.

Congress has never successfully blocked a proposed arms sale by use of a joint resolution of disapproval, although it has come close to doing so (as in the sales of missiles to Saudi Arabia in 1986). Nevertheless, Congress has—by expressing strong opposition to prospective arms sales during consultations with the executive branch—affected the timing and the composition of some arms sales and may have dissuaded the President from formally proposing certain arms sales.

BIBLIOGRAPHY

Franck, Thomas M., and Edward Weisband. *Foreign Policy by Congress.* 1979.

Gibson, Martha Liebler. *Weapons of Influence: The Legislative Veto, American Foreign Policy, and the Irony of Reform.* 1992.

Gilmour, Robert S., and Barbara Hinkson Craig. "After the Congressional Veto: Assessing the Alternatives." *Journal of Policy Analysis and Management* 3 (1984): 373–392.

Schwartz, Bernard. "Congressional Veto in the Conduct of Foreign Policy." In *The Tethered Presidency: Congressional Restraints on Executive Power.* Edited by Thomas M. Franck. 1981.

U.S. House of Representatives. Committee on Foreign Affairs. *Executive-Legislative Consultation on U.S. Arms Sales.* Congress and Foreign Policy Series, no. 7. 1982.

RICHARD F. GRIMMETT

ARTHUR, CHESTER A. (1829–1886), twenty-first President of the United States (1881–1885).

Chester Alan Arthur was born in Fairfield, Vermont, on 5 October 1829, the son of an itinerant Baptist minister. After graduating from Union College in Schenectady, New York, in 1848, he spent several years as a school teacher and school principal. In 1854 he was admitted to the bar. He participated in the *Lemmon Slave Case* (1858), which concerned the liberation of eight slaves passing through New York City; the young lawyer also served in a test case that led to the integration of the city's streetcar system. In 1859, he married Ellen ("Nell") Lewis Herndon of Virginia.

Early Political Career. A Whig as far back as 1844, Arthur soon joined the newly organized Republican Party as a protégé of a wealthy merchant, Edwin D. Morgan, who, as governor of New York, appointed Arthur the state's engineer in chief. When the CIVIL WAR broke out, Arthur represented the quartermaster general's office in New York, overseeing the feeding, housing, and equipping of troops. In July 1862, he became quartermaster general of the New York State militia.

After Morgan was defeated for reelection in 1862, Arthur lost his commission, and he did not reenlist for military service. He may have been influenced in this decision by his wife, who had close relatives fighting for the Confederacy; he may not have wanted to see the war turn into an antislavery crusade. Perhaps he simply needed more money.

He was closely affiliated with the conservative wing of the REPUBLICAN PARTY, headed by Thurlow Weed and WILLIAM H. SEWARD, serving as a collector of assessments (that is, compulsory contributions) in the 1864 election. In the late 1860s he rose in the party hierarchy, but in 1869—his law practice slipping—he became counsel to the New York City tax commission through the influence of the Democratic boss, William M. Tweed. His role in the tax commission remains cloudy; he resigned the post in 1870.

By now Arthur was becoming the chief lieutenant of Sen. Roscoe Conkling, the ruthless boss of the New York Republican machine. In 1871, President Ulysses S. Grant appointed Arthur collector of the New York Customhouse, the largest single federal office and the greatest source of political PATRONAGE in the nation; the collector was the highest-paid federal official. Arthur tolerated, and at times encouraged, the illegal conduct that made the office a national scandal, discreetly bypassing civil-service rules to give party supporters lucrative positions. For the now corpulent, elegantly dressed Arthur, the world was, in the words of his biographer, Thomas C. Reeves, one "of expensive Havana cigars, Tiffany silver, fine carriages, and grand balls; the 'real' world where men manipulated, plotted, and stole for power and prestige and the riches that brought both."

Arthur supported Conkling for the Republican presidential nomination in 1876, but threw himself into the campaign of Rutherford B. Hayes, engaging in his usual drive for assessments and possibly assisting Republican leaders in influencing the outcome of the disputed election. Although Arthur might have expected continued support from the White House, Hayes ordered an investigation of customs corruption, suspending Arthur in mid 1878. He returned to collecting assessments for the New York party. Despite the glitter, Arthur's life was becoming marred by tragedy. A son, William Lewis Herndon Arthur, had died in 1863 and his wife died in 1880.

Vice Presidency. Arthur returned to national visibility at the Republican convention of 1880. As a member of the Conkling, or Stalwart, faction, he helped lead the forces that sought to nominate Grant for a third term. When Sen. James A. Garfield was nominated instead, his backers offered Arthur the vice presidential nomination, which he accepted over the objections of Conkling, who was embittered by Grant's defeat. He may have seen the chance to run on a national ticket as a vindication of his conduct as customs collector and hence a rebuke to Hayes; his candidacy would also revive the fortunes of the highly factionalized Stalwarts and compensate for Conkling's declining stature in the Senate and in New York State. Garfield acquiesced in Arthur's nomination, realizing the need of Stalwart cooperation.

In his letter of acceptance, Arthur presented his first public statement on national issues. He supported suffrage for blacks, praised Hayes's vetoes of army bills, and lauded fitness for office in general while opposing civil-service examinations in particular. In the campaign, he served the party well, coordinating rallies and managing tours by Conkling and Grant; indeed, he may be seen as the first advance man in American history. As chairman of the New York State Republican committee, he collected assessments from city, state, and federal employees, building a secret fund intended to ensure a Republican victory in Indiana.

On 2 November 1880, Arthur was elected Vice President of the United States. The event did not cause him to abandon the Conkling machine but rather strengthened his ties to it. He made efforts to bolster Stalwart power, journeying to Albany to engage in intrafactional intrigue centering on a Senate slot. He tastelessly boasted of his role in winning Indiana for the Republicans. And he sat in silence while Conkling personally lambasted Garfield over the appointment of the Postmaster General. Arthur's behavior might be criticized, but he lived by a code in which factional loyalty was everything.

Once Garfield and Arthur were inaugurated on 4 March 1881, Arthur presided over the Senate. Here he used his strategic position to the benefit of his party, twice breaking ties and thereby enabling the Republicans to control Senate committees. Trouble came when Garfield appointed William H. Robertson to the collectorship of the New York Customhouse. Robertson, who was president pro tem of the New York Senate, was a Half-Breed, that is, a member of the rival party faction headed by Senator James G. Blaine of Maine. When the Robertson appointment was announced, Conkling and the other New York senator, Thomas Platt, resigned from the Senate on the grounds that senatorial courtesy had been violated. Arthur supported Conkling in every possible way: he personally begged Garfield to drop the nomination, lent his home for Stalwart strategy meetings, urged businessmen to sign petitions criticizing Robertson's record as a state legislator, and attempted in vain to cajole the New York legislature to send Conkling and Platt back to Washington. Few Vice Presidents had ever undercut their superior so blatantly, but for Arthur genuinely loyalty belonged to Conkling. Besides, if the Stalwarts won the fight, Arthur's own power would be enhanced, not decreased.

Such partisan maneuvering was suddenly cut short when, on the morning of 2 July, the crazed Charles Guiteau, a disappointed office-seeker and a Stalwart, shot Garfield. A bullet lodged in Garfield's spinal column, and he grew steadily weaker. Secretary of State Blaine was a bitter personal enemy of Conkling, but, fearing that the country would lack direction, he reportedly wanted Arthur to serve as acting president. Arthur turned the proposal down, finding it improper. Fortunately for all concerned, Congress was not in session and the President only had to sign one paper. For the moment, all went smoothly.

While Garfield lay dying, eyes were turned on the Vice President, and many were apprehensive. His long record of unsavory maneuvering, capped by disloyalty to the President, was now backfiring with a vengeance. The resignation of Conkling and Platt had given the Democrats a majority in the Senate, but Arthur—fearing that a Democrat, Thomas Bayard, would be elected president pro tem—refused to vacate his chair. Hence the man who would soon be President lacked any constitutional successor.

Domestic Policy. On 19 September, Garfield died, and at 2:15 A.M. the following day Arthur took the oath of office. On 22 September, he gave a brief inaugural address, referring to Garfield's "example and achievements" and the "pathos of his death." The new President called attention to the nation's prosperity and, as a hard-money man, praised its "well-grounded" fiscal policy. He found "no demand for speedy legislation"; as President he never would.

Arthur realized he had an unsavory reputation to overcome. Throughout the country, the almost universal response to Arthur's elevation to the nation's highest office was amazement. "Chet Arthur, President of the United States! Good God," the historian Henry Adams noted; "We are going to have a nasty *chopping-sea* in politics." But, as Reeves notes, Arthur "had never coveted the office of Chief Executive, and was overwhelmed by the prospect of filling the highest office in the land; he was stunned by the cruel circumstances that brought him to Washington and crushed by the savage attacks in the nation's press."

Few guessed that Arthur would turn out to be one of the nation's great political surprises or that a man of his obvious limitations would do a decent, even somewhat commendable job. One of those few was Charles Foster, governor of Ohio, who said that "the people and the politicians will find that Vice-President Arthur and President Arthur are different men."

Upon becoming President, Arthur did much to change his image as spoilsman. He made some able appointments, including Frederick T. Frelinghuysen as Secretary of State, Chief Justice Charles J. Folger of the New York State supreme court as Secretary of the Treasury, and Pennsylvania's former attorney general Benjamin Harris Brewster as Attorney General. Arthur sought prosecution of a postal scandal, the Star Route affair, knowing that former cronies were culpable. (When the courts found the defendants not guilty, Arthur was extremely embarrassed.) While still welcoming the Stalwarts to sumptuous White House feasts, he refrained from favors to such a degree that Conkling found the Hayes administration "reputable, if not heroic," by comparison. As one of his old customhouse cronies commented, "He isn't 'Chet' Arthur any more; he's the president."

In his first annual message, Arthur called for CIVIL-SERVICE REFORM. He repeated his earlier pledge, given while Vice President, that the civil service should be conducted like a "successful private business," and the new President specifically mentioned "fitness" for the position, stable tenure of office, and prompt investigation of abuses. Arthur—the former spoilsman—even proposed that a central examining board should make certain nominations. He objected to competitive examinations, voicing the fear that immature college youths might monopolize appointments, yet he prom-

ised to support any civil-service bill the Congress might pass, even were it to prescribe such exams. And he said that if Congress failed to act, he would seek to reactivate the dormant Civil Service Commission.

It was not Arthur's endorsement, however, nor even the assassination of Garfield by a "disappointed office-seeker" that led to civil-service legislation. Rather it was the congressional elections of 1882, in which the Democrats won the House and almost captured the Senate. The lame-duck Republican Congress realized the wisdom of immediately supporting the civil-service bill introduced by Senator George Hunt Pendleton, a Democrat. By acting quickly, the Republicans hoped to convince their constituents of their reform sentiments while protecting the tenure of their own incumbent officeholders. Arthur joined the reform chorus, and in his second annual message the spoilsman came out for competitive examination and the banning of assessments. (Indeed, he claimed to have always opposed forced contributions.)

On 18 January 1883, President Arthur signed the CIVIL SERVICE (Pendleton) ACT. Given his past record, he was obviously acting more out of expediency—in this case fear of national outrage—than out of firm conviction. The act provided for a five-member Civil Service Examination Board with authority to hold competitive examinations for positions on a classified list. In reality, however, the act was extremely limited in scope, applying only to officials in Washington and employees in major customhouses and post offices. The vast majority of federal employees and all municipal and state workers were still not covered. In fact, only 11 percent of the nation's federal employees, some 14,000 out of a total of 131,000, came under the scope of the law. And, as incumbent officeholders were excluded, one Democratic senator, Joseph E. Brown of Georgia, aptly called the measure "a bill to perpetuate in office the Republicans who now control the patronage of the Government."

The President's successive annual messages contained a host of proposals, ranging from establishing a government for Alaska to constructing a building to house the Library of Congress. Reporting a large surplus in the Treasury, Arthur sought repeal of all internal taxes save excise duties on tobacco and liquor. He wanted an ITEM VETO whereby a President could block certain portions of a bill while keeping others, and he went so far as to suggest a constitutional amendment on the subject. He asked Congress to consider the entire matter of PRESIDENTIAL SUCCESSION so as to avoid the kind of political limbo that existed just before Garfield's death. He also requested that Congress decide who was to count the electoral votes to prevent the kind of confusion that had existed during the presidential election of 1876. Accusing the railroads of price collusion and rate discrimination, Arthur endorsed the regulation of interstate commerce. Before 1883, Republican majorities in both houses of Congress were slim, however, and Congress retained its focus upon favor and patronage, feeling little compunction about ignoring such suggestions.

Arthur did have some successes, and in some ways he was a better President than has long been thought. In addition to signing the Pendleton Act, he successfully vetoed a Chinese exclusion bill. The bill, introduced in 1882 by Republican Senator John F. Miller, would have excluded Chinese laborers for twenty years and denied American citizenship to Chinese residents. In his veto message, Arthur did claim that unrestricted Chinese labor might threaten American institutions and some American livelihoods but argued that twenty years—"nearly a generation"—was an unreasonable length of time. Moreover, he pointed out that the bill violated a treaty made with China in 1880 and would be "a breach of our national faith." Furthermore, Arthur declared that the Chinese had made a major contribution to the American economy, pointing specifically to their labor on the transcontinental railroad. The veto message also stressed Asia's commercial potential. Any exclusion policy, if not handled skillfully, might "have a direct tendency to repel Oriental nations from us and to drive their trade and commerce into more friendly hands."

New England Brahmins, with their commitment to racial tolerance and tradition of free immigration, welcomed Arthur's veto. Labor groups throughout the nation, however, denounced the President. In San Francisco, the center of much exclusionist sentiment, flags were hung at half-staff, and merchants draped their stores as if in mourning. When Congress revised the bill, reducing the term of exclusion to ten years, Arthur signed it into law. [See CHINESE EXCLUSION ACTS.]

Arthur promoted naval development, so much so that he could be called one of the founders of the modern navy. In his annual message of 1881, he denied that the United States faced danger from abroad. It did, however, have to be ever-ready to defend its harbors and protect its citizens. Undoubtedly Arthur's experience as collector of the Port of New York encouraged him to mention what he called "the highways of commerce, the varied interests of our foreign trade." Similarly, his role as inspector general and quartermaster general in Civil War mobilization undoubtedly helped inspire his comment that "we must be prepared to enforce any policy we think wise to adopt."

To help carry through his vision, Arthur appointed William E. Chandler as Secretary of the Navy. Chandler, a ruthless Republican Party organizer from New Hampshire, instituted a surprising number of reforms, ranging from establishing the much-needed Naval War College at Newport, Rhode Island, to closing down superfluous navy yards at Pensacola, Florida, and New London, Connecticut. Chandler established a new naval advisory board, headed by a prominent explorer, Commodore Robert W. Shufeldt, that recommended the construction of armor-plated cruisers. In March 1883, Arthur signed the bill that brought the nation its first three steel-plated cruisers and a new dispatch boat as well. Nonetheless, not all naval policy embodied reform, for Chandler administered shipyards in a highly partisan fashion.

Arthur also vetoed a steamboat safety bill, claiming that its wording contained several serious technical errors; Congress redrafted the measure as he suggested. He endorsed the establishment of a tariff commission, thereby advancing the cause of scientific rates, even though the resulting tariff of 1883 embodied little reform.

In some areas, Arthur revealed his limitations. His belief in laissez-faire left him unable to cope with a declining economy. His call for individual Indian landholding was unwise, leading to further degradation by causing many Indians to lose their personal holdings. It was, however, the solution advocated by leading reformers.

Arthur's record toward African Americans was mixed. He would make personal gestures of sympathy, such as contributing funds to a black church or personally awarding diplomas at a black high school graduation in Washington, D.C. More important was Arthur's reaction when the Supreme Court struck down the CIVIL RIGHTS ACT OF 1875, a law that provided that all persons, regardless of race, were entitled to "the full and equal enjoyment of the accommodations, advantages, facilities and privileges of inns, public conveyances on land or water, theaters, and other places of public amusement." In his third annual message, the President said he would unhesitatingly support any "right, privilege, and immunity of citizenship" that Congress might pass, asserting that "it was the special purpose of [the Fourteenth] amendment to insure to members of the colored race the full enjoyment of civil and political rights." In addition, he called for federal aid to education, and he particularly stressed the need to combat illiteracy among African Americans. His overtures to white southern independents—despite controversy—won major black endorsement.

Yet Arthur was certainly not in the forefront of black advancement. At a time when the status of African Americans was declining, Arthur made no reference to blacks in his inaugural address, spoke only of educational needs in his annual messages, and was silent concerning discrimination such as was embodied in the Eight-Box Ballot Law of South Carolina, which instituted a confusing series of ballot boxes and ballots for each office. He told a delegation of white Republicans from Georgia that he found white office-holders more helpful to the Republican Party; southern blacks, he said, excelled only in "office begging." When congressional Republicans introduced five different bills to replace the defunct 1875 civil rights act, Arthur offered little support.

Foreign Policy. Arthur had his share of setbacks. Congress, for example, overrode his veto of a rivers and harbors bill. Moreover, his foreign policy involved much failure. The Arthur administration was unable to mediate a war between Peru and Chile, a conflict that had begun in April 1879. At first, Arthur retained James G. Blaine as Secretary of State, who early in December 1881 convinced Arthur to send a special mission to the belligerents. The diplomat William Henry Trescot was chosen. Chile's peace demands, Blaine said, should be limited to financial indemnity and not territory, and he offered the good offices of the United States in resolving the dispute. A threat was included: if Chile did not release Peruvian leader Francisco García Calderón from captivity, the United States would sever diplomatic relations. Continued Chilean recalcitrance, the secretary added, would lead the United States to appeal to other republics in the hemisphere, asking them to apply pressure on Chile.

In January 1882, Arthur's new Secretary of State, Frederick Theodore Frelinghuysen, cabled Trescot, currently in Peru. The United States, said Frelinghuysen, frowned on Chile's demands—which included a high indemnity, the cession of Tarapacá, and the ten-year's occupation of Tacna, Arica, and the Lobos Islands. However, it had no intention of dictating terms, much less severing relations with Chile. By refusing to continue Blaine's efforts to create general pressure on Latin America, the Arthur administration blunted what might have been the only diplomatic weapon the United States possessed.

Problems also existed concerning the Isthmus of Panama. Frelinghuysen had suggested total abrogation of the CLAYTON-BULWER TREATY, an agreement made in 1850 with Great Britain that recognized British rights over any canal built through any part of Central America. In a letter to the American minister in London, James Russell Lowell, Frelinghuysen de-

nied that the treaty ever applied to PANAMA, claimed that joint rights were calculated to "breed dissension," and endorsed the establishment of a lone United States protectorate over any canal built across the Isthmus. Britain's foreign secretary, Lord Granville, patiently responded that the terms of the 1850 treaty remained in force.

The Arthur administration was also unable to secure Senate passage of a treaty with Nicaragua giving the United States co-ownership over a canal strip there. When the agreement came before the Senate in December 1884, it met with a variety of objections: Britain and France would get the most benefit, perhaps being able to dominate Pacific commerce; the cost would far outweigh any advantage; confrontation with Great Britain would result; holding land in any foreign country was unconstitutional as were efforts to turn Nicaragua into a United States "colony." When the Senate voted on 29 January 1885, the bill fell nine votes short of the two-thirds needed for ratification and Arthur's successor, Grover Cleveland, withdrew the treaty soon after he entered the White House.

Another issue concerned German bans on American pork. Acting out of both sanitary and protectionist motives, Germany claimed that American pigs were stricken with trichinosis. Arthur established an impartial commission to examine American packing plants. However, this body found that the United States might still be exporting diseased meat, and Germany continued its ban until 1891.

Reciprocity efforts concerning Mexico, CUBA, PUERTO RICO, and the DOMINICAN REPUBLIC lay stillborn. Most treaties came before a lame-duck Senate after James G. Blaine, the Republican standbearer in 1884, had made the high tariff a keynote of his campaign and the Democrats had captured the presidency. Arthur never pushed for the agreements.

Arthur also failed to draw significant support for the Berlin agreement of 1885, a treaty that formally recognized the Congo Free State. On paper, the agreement pledged religious freedom, free trade, free navigation on the Congo and Niger rivers, and the abolition of the slave trade. In reality King Leopold II of Belgium secured personal control of some 900,000 square miles. In February 1885, John A. Kasson, American minister to Germany and delegate at the conference, signed the treaty but it still needed Senate approval. Defenders claimed that the conference contributed to the causes of peace and humanitarianism and, in his last annual message, Arthur referred to "the rich prospective trade of the Kongo valley." Critics, however, suspected Leopold's materialistic motives, feared involvement in any African war, and doubted whether Central Africa would ever provide a good market. The administration did not submit the Berlin convention to the Senate until Arthur's last day in office, and President Cleveland took no steps to secure its passage.

Part of Arthur's weakness lay in the fact that he could not totally escape his shady past. Secretary of the Navy Chandler was perceived as a typical spoilsman. So was Timothy O. Howe, Arthur's first Postmaster General. Arthur's removal of Silas Burt, naval officer to the New York Customhouse, was a petty act of spite against a man of proven competence, and certain other appointments—such as Randolph DeB. Keim, Arthur's first choice for chief examiner of the Civil Service Commission—aroused the ire of reformers.

Arthur always conducted himself regally. Indeed, few Presidents have been as concerned with the ceremonial and the symbolic. He renovated the WHITE HOUSE on a grand scale, supervising the project himself. With his youngest sister serving as surrogate FIRST LADY, he entertained in a grand manner, dressed elegantly, and bowed to all he met. He seldom put in a full day's work and reserved Sundays and Mondays to himself.

Much of his apparent lethargy was caused by Bright's disease, a fatal kidney ailment. Although he learned of his illness in 1882, a year during which he was often sick, his deteriorating condition was probably the best-kept secret of his administration. Yet all the time he was failing, he carried on his official duties, refusing to go into seclusion.

In fact, in 1884 he made a nominal bid for a second term, doing so in the realization that retreat would raise suspicions about his health, competence, and courage. After James G. Blaine received the Republican nomination, Arthur spent his final days in office on ceremonial matters such as dedicating the Washington Monument. After leaving the White House, he moved to New York City, accepting the position of counsel to his old law firm. During the last year of his life he was an invalid. He died in New London, Connecticut, on 17 November 1886.

BIBLIOGRAPHY

Doenecke, Justus D. *The Presidency of James A. Garfield and Chester A. Arthur.* 1981.

Hoogenboom, Ari. *Outlawing the Spoils: A History of the Civil Service Reform Movement, 1865–1883.* 1961.

Howe, George Frederick. *Chester A. Arthur: A Quarter-Century of Machine Politics.* 1935.

Morgan, H. Wayne. *From Hayes to McKinley: National Party Politics, 1877–1896.* 1969.

Peskin, Allan. *Garfield.* 1978.

Pletcher, David M. *The Awkward Years: American Foreign Policy under Garfield and Arthur.* 1962.

Reeves, Thomas C. *Gentleman Boss: The Life of Chester Alan Arthur.* 1975.

JUSTUS D. DOENECKE

ASH COUNCIL. In 1969, President Richard M. Nixon appointed a six-member advisory council chaired by the businessman Roy L. Ash. Officially called the President's Council on Executive Organization but better known as the Ash Council, the body concluded that the executive branch had become too fragmented, resulting in a lack of effective coordination in meeting public problems. To address this fragmentation, the council proposed more centralized and politically responsible lines of authority within the executive branch. The council advocated a package approach to reorganization combining various elements of the New Federalism (e.g., revenue sharing) with executive-branch reorganization. The council also recommended a change in the organization, role, and name of the Bureau of the Budget.

The council's memorandums to the President formed the basis for legislative proposals to reorganize much of the executive branch, which the President submitted to Congress in 1971. These bills proposed to reorganize seven existing departments and several independent agencies into four, "super" departments of Human Resources, Community Development, Natural Resources, and Economic Affairs. Each department would be headed by a secretary assisted by a small number of staff officers having departmentwide responsibilities. To provide for a rational grouping of the large bureaus and programs to be inherited by the new departments, the concept of the "Administration" was introduced as a first-tier device for program direction. These organizations, patterned after the operating administrations in the then-new DEPARTMENT OF TRANSPORTATION (1966), were envisioned as management centers—each with a major segment of the department's administrative program. Administrators would head these basic units within the department and would report directly to the secretary.

The combined use of cross-cutting staff officers concerned with functions affecting all elements of the department and program administrators charged with directing important segments of the department's operating responsibilities was expected to facilitate decentralized management while simultaneously providing for more effective secretarial control and department cohesion.

It was a dramatic proposal, the logical conclusion of the orthodox public administration values embodied in the earlier BROWNLOW COMMITTEE and HOOVER COMMISSIONS reports. Lines of accountability to the President would be made direct, agency-head authority was to be commensurate with responsibility, and policy-making was to be integrated around comprehensive subject matter. Congress was not persuaded and rejected all four pieces of legislation. Only a lesser proposal to reorganize the EXECUTIVE OFFICE OF THE PRESIDENT was passed by Congress, and that with misgivings.

With the failure of Nixon's strategy to reorganize the executive branch according to orthodox public administration principles, the commission and report approach to organizational management fell into disrepute. After 1970 no President sought to promote a presidential commission with a comprehensive organizational mandate, nor have Presidents expressed support for orthodox public-administration principles of organization.

BIBLIOGRAPHY

Arnold, Peri. *Making the Managerial Presidency: Comprehensive Reorganization Planning, 1905–1980.* 1986

Berman, Larry. "The Office of Management and Budget That Almost Wasn't." *Political Science Quarterly* 92 (1977): 281–303.

U.S. Executive Office of the President, Office of Management and Budget. *Papers Relating to the President's Departmental Reorganization Program.* 1971.

RONALD C. MOE

ASSASSINATIONS, PRESIDENTIAL.

Assassinations, direct assaults on Presidents and candidates, and other forms of violence and threats against the CHIEF EXECUTIVE increased in the twentieth century. Overall, assassinations and direct attempts on the life of the President since the founding of the Republic through early 1993 affected eight of the forty-two Presidents while they were in office. Such attacks, though, have escalated since 1950, involving four of the nine incumbents. Four Presidents (Abraham Lincoln, James Garfield, William McKinley, and John F. Kennedy) have been shot to death, while another four have been exposed either to assailants' bullets (Andrew Jackson, Gerald R. Ford, and Ronald Reagan) or to an armed attack on their official residence (Harry S. Truman at BLAIR HOUSE, while the White House was being renovated). Only one President (Ford) has been the target of more than one assassination attempt.

In addition, assaults have occurred against a President-elect (Franklin D. Roosevelt) and a former President (Theodore Roosevelt, while he was campaigning for the PROGRESSIVE [BULL MOOSE] PARTY nomination in

1912). Thus, of the seventeen men to serve in the White House from 1900 to 1992, seven were the victims of direct assaults: five as incumbents, one as a President-elect, and one as a candidate. Two other candidates for the presidency have been killed (ROBERT F. KENNEDY) or wounded (GEORGE WALLACE).

No incumbent Vice President, incidentally, has been subject to a direct attack, probably reflecting this office's limited political power and low visibility, at least by comparison to the President.

Different interpretations of the assailants and their motivation have evolved over the years. Although the evidence is limited, the assassins and would-be assassins appear to be a more diverse and heterogeneous lot than had long been thought. The range of their motives, reasons for acting, state of rationality (or irrationality), and background characteristics mean that there is no archetypal presidential assassin. The 1969 report of the National Commission on the Causes and Prevention of Violence, produced in the aftermath of the assassination of Robert F. Kennedy as a presidential candidate, tried to develop a profile of the archetypal assassin. Based on the evidence available until that time, the report projected the following "attributes" of future assailants: An assailant would generally come from a broken home, with the father absent or unresponsive to the child; would be withdrawn, a loner, without girl friends, either unmarried or a failure at marriage; would be unable to work steadily in the year or so before the assault; would be white, male, foreign-born or with parents foreign-born, and would be short, and slight of build; would be a zealot for a political, religious, or other cause, but not a member of an organized movement; would commit the attack in the name of a specific issue, related to the principles or philosophy of his cause; would choose a handgun as his weapon; and would select a moment when the President is appearing amid a crowd.

One problem with such projections is that many of the characteristics apply to any number of individuals, not just potential assassins. Indeed, the SECRET SERVICE, which has principal responsibility for presidential protection, has noted that there is no consistent profile of a potential assassin. The service added that its sponsorship of at least sixteen studies of relevant behavioral or attitudinal characteristics failed to produce any meaningful consensus.

A second problem with the 1969 listing is that some of the characteristics have proven wrong or unreliable. Ford's two assailants, for example, were both women, whereas all the previous attackers were men. Reagan's attacker was not a zealot on behalf of a cause and not from a broken home, and neither the assailant

Assassination and Assaults

Date of Assault	Victim	Location	Method of Attack and Result	Assailant, Professed or Alleged Reason, and Result
30 Jan 1835	Andrew Jackson	Washington, D.C.	pistol, misfired	Richard Lawrence said Jackson was preventing him from obtaining large sums of money; declared insane
14 Apr 1865	Abraham Lincoln	Washington, D.C.	pistol, killed	John Wilkes Booth revenge for defeat of Confederacy; killed
2 Jul 1881	James A. Garfield	Washington, D.C.	pistol, killed	Charles Guiteau disgruntled office seeker; convicted and executed
6 Sep 1901	William McKinley	Buffalo, N.Y.	pistol, killed	Leon F. Czolgosz anarchist ideology; convicted and executed
14 Oct 1912	Theodore Roosevelt candidate	Milwaukee, Wis.	pistol, wounded	John Schrank had vision that McKinley wanted him to avenge his death; declared insane
15 Feb 1933	Franklin D. Roosevelt President-elect	Miami, Fla.	pistol, missed but killed Anton Cermak, mayor of Chicago	Giuseppe Zangara hated rulers and capitalists; convicted
1 Nov 1950	Harry S. Truman	Washington, D.C.	automatic weapons, prevented from shooting at Truman	Oscar Collazo and Griselio Torresola espoused Puerto Rican independence; convicted and imprisoned
22 Nov 1963	John F. Kennedy	Dallas Tex.	rifle, killed	Lee Harvey Oswald motive unknown; killed
4 Jun 1968	Robert F. Kennedy candidate	Los Angeles, Cal.	pistol, killed	Sirhan Sirhan opposed Kennedy's stand on Arab-Israeli conflict; convicted and imprisoned
15 May 1972	George C. Wallace candidate	Laurel, Md.	pistol, wounded	Arthur Bremer motive unknown; convicted and imprisoned
5 Sep 1975	Gerald Ford	Sacramento, Cal.	pistol, misfired	Lynette Alice Fromme follower of Charles Manson; convicted and imprisoned
22 Sep 1975	Gerald Ford	San Francisco, Cal.	pistol, missed	Sara Jane Moore revolutionary ideology; convicted and imprisoned
30 Mar 1981	Ronald Reagan	Washington, D.C.	pistol, wounded	John W. Hinkley, Jr. motive unknown; found not guilty by reason of insanity; confined to mental institution

SOURCES: James E. Kirkham et al., *Assassination and Political Violence* (1969), p. 22; Frederick M. Kaiser, "Presidential Assassinations and Assaults," *Presidential Studies Quarterly* 11 (1981), p. 547.
Prepared by Frederick M. Kaiser.

nor his parents were born abroad. The attribute of being foreign-born or having foreign-born parents is less meaningful now than in earlier eras, when such groupings comprised a larger percentage of the population. Significantly, none of the four assaults since 1969 involved an immigrant or first-generation American.

An analysis by James W. Clarke, author of *American Assassins* (1990), also concludes that there are too many exceptions to the rules postulated by the 1969 Commission on Violence. As an alternative to the (nonexistent) assassin-archetype approach, Clarke employs a fourfold typology based upon the assailants' motives, rationality, criminal culpability, and contextual framework (that is, the array of political, social, economic, and cultural forces that can influence behavior). Clark's four categories (and the assailants who fall into them) are these: Type I—extremists and zealots willing to sacrifice self for a political cause (JOHN WILKES BOOTH; LEON CZOLGOSZ; Oscar Collazo and Griselio Torresola, who tried to kill Truman; and Sirhan Sirhan, the assassin of Robert Kennedy); Type II—persons with overwhelming and aggressive egocentric needs for acceptance, recognition, and status (LEE HARVEY OSWALD and the two women who tried to kill Ford, Lynette Alice "Squeaky" Fromme and Sara Jane Moore); Type III—psychopaths or sociopaths who believe that the condition of their lives is so intolerably meaningless and without purpose that destruction of society and themselves is desirable for its own sake (Joseph Zangara, who killed Chicago mayor Anton Cermak while aiming at Franklin D. Roosevelt, and John W. Hinkley, Jr., who shot Reagan); and Type IV—irrational or insane persons who manifest severe emotional and cognitive distortion that is expressed in hallucinations and delusions of persecution and/or grandeur and perceive their acts as mystically or divinely inspired (Richard Lawrence, who attacked Jackson; CHARLES GUITEAU; and John Schrank, who shot Theodore Roosevelt).

Besides direct assaults, Presidents have been exposed to other types of violence and threats of harm. John Quincy Adams, for instance, was accosted by a court-martialed army sergeant who was demanding reinstatement by the Commander in Chief. When the President refused, his life was threatened; the sergeant later recanted the threat, insisting it had been a jest. During John Tyler's administration, the White House was the site of several disquieting episodes, and Tyler himself was once pelted by rocks thrown by an intoxicated painter.

Other more recent incidents reveal a wide range of possible attacks on the President, direct and indirect. One planned assault—by Samuel Byck against Richard M. Nixon—however, never got off the ground, literally or figuratively. Byck's bizarre attempt to hijack a plane and crash it into the White House was aborted at the airport, when Byck, wounded by a security guard, committed suicide. During the Ford administration, moreover, a man wired with explosives and threatening to take "actions against the government" crashed his car through the White House gates. Later, an intruder scaled the security fence surrounding the Executive Mansion; armed with what appeared to be a bomb, he was killed by a security guard.

In addition to these assaults, other threatening behavior has raised concerns for the safety of the President and others. In 1992, for instance, an individual was convicted for threatening to kill Bill Clinton, then a presidential candidate; an explosive device was also discovered in a hall where vice presidential candidate AL GORE was scheduled to speak. The Secret Service estimates that annually it requests preliminary psychiatric examinations for approximately three hundred persons who exhibit erratic behavior in their unusually intense attempts to contact the President, his advisers, or CABINET officers. In addition to these in-person acts, other threats come by way of telephone calls or letters. Anxiety about some White House visitors, moreover, is not confined to the late twentieth century era of stricter security and less accessible Chief Executives. In 1906, for example, the Washington Metropolitan Police, then responsible for White House security, forcibly removed a woman who had "shrieked her refusal" to leave the building and "threw herself on the ground" when informed that she could not see the President.

Nonetheless, by comparison to earlier periods, the late twentieth century has experienced a higher number and frequency of assaults and threats against Presidents and candidates. Among other things, this reflects the sizable increase in the U.S. population, which simply means that there are more potential threats than before, along with the heightened public visibility and political power of individual Presidents, which makes them more inviting targets for different types of would-be assassins.

BIBLIOGRAPHY

Clarke, James W. *American Assassins: The Darker Side of Politics.* 2d rev. ed. 1990.

Clarke, James W. *On Being Mad or Merely Angry: John W. Hinckley, Jr., and Other Dangerous People.* 1990.

Crotty, William J. ed. *Assassinations and the Political Order.* 1971.

Kaiser, Frederick M. "Presidential Assassinations and Assaults: Characteristics and Impact on Protective Procedures." *Presidential Studies Quarterly* 11 (1981): 545–558.

Kirkham, James E., et al. *Assassination and Political Violence: A Report to the National Commission on the Causes and Prevention of Violence.* 1969.

U.S. National Commission on the Causes and Prevention of Violence. *To Establish Justice, To Insure Domestic Tranquility: Final Report.* 1969.

FREDERICK M. KAISER

ATLANTIC ALLIANCE. Europe emerged in the late 1940s as the key to international peace and prosperity. U.S. leaders had embodied that conviction in the MARSHALL PLAN for Western Europe, as well as in their determination to integrate a unified and reconstructed West Germany into the European economy. At the London Foreign Ministers Conference of December 1947, the Soviet Foreign Minister, V. M. Molotov, evinced again the troubling Soviet intransigence toward Western plans for Germany. At the close of the conference the British Foreign Secretary, Ernest Bevin, convinced that the Western powers could achieve no agreement in the foreseeable future, admonished President Harry S. Truman's Secretary of State, GEORGE C. MARSHALL, that Western salvation now depended on "some form of union, formal or informal in character, in Western Europe backed by the United States and the Dominions." Bevin followed that suggestion with his historic speech in Parliament on 22 January 1948, in which he concluded that the time was ripe for "the consolidation of Western Europe."

State Department officials disagreed on the nature of both an adequate defense for Europe and the U.S. role in rendering it effective. John D. Hickerson, director of the Office of European Affairs, advised Marshall that an alliance without the United States would be ineffective. George Kennan, chairman of the Policy Planning Staff, argued that no existing Soviet menace required such involvement. Bevin believed American support essential, yet saw that Washington would not act unless Europe took the lead. The communist overthrow of the Czech government on 25 February broke the pattern of indecision; the Soviet takeover of Czechoslovakia seemed to endanger other areas of Europe as well. Britain, France, and the three Benelux countries responded to the Prague coup by signing the Brussels Pact against aggression. Truman immediately informed Congress that the pact demanded U.S. support. On 11 June the Senate approved the Vandenberg Resolution, committing the Senate to collective security, by a vote of 64 to 4. In subsequent talks American officials assured France and other countries that the United States would defend Europe against Soviet encroachments.

The formal negotiations for an Atlantic Alliance began with Truman's election in November. In April 1949 Britain, France, the Benelux countries, the United States, Canada, Denmark, Iceland, Norway, Italy, and Portugal signed the North Atlantic Treaty with appropriate ceremonies in Washington. After extensive debate the Senate approved the treaty in July, 82 to 13.

BIBLIOGRAPHY

Henderson, Nicholas. *The Birth of NATO.* 1983.
Henrikson, Alan K. "The Creation of the North Atlantic Alliance." In *American Defense Policy.* Edited by John F. Reichart and Steven R. Sturm. 1982.
Reid, Escott. *Time of Fear and Hope: The Making of the North Atlantic Treaty, 1947–1949.* 1977.

NORMAN A. GRAEBNER

ATLANTIC CHARTER. Behind the Atlantic Conference of 9–12 August 1941, which produced the Atlantic Charter, was Franklin D. Roosevelt's long quest for a meeting with Prime Minister Winston Churchill to clarify the principles that would guide the countries fighting Hitler in the making of peace. On July 11 he sent HARRY HOPKINS to London to arrange a meeting with Churchill that would focus exclusively on the problems of postwar reconstruction. The subsequent Atlantic Conference took place aboard the U.S. heavy cruiser *Augusta* and the British battleship *Prince of Wales* in Placentia Bay off Argentia, Newfoundland. Roosevelt made clear at the outset that he wanted no more of Churchill than "a joint declaration laying down certain broad principles which should guide our policies along the same road."

Determined to avoid a quarrel over the application of self-determination to the countries of the British Empire, Roosevelt asked Churchill to prepare the initial statement of principles. On the second morning Churchill produced a draft that disavowed any Anglo-American territorial ambitions, proclaimed the principle that all territorial changes reflect the will of the peoples concerned, recognized the right of all people to governments of their own choice as well as to freedom of speech and thought, and advocated an effective international organization that would guarantee the security of all states, including their right to freedom of the seas. Two days of discussion among Roosevelt, Undersecretary of State Sumner Welles, Churchill, and Sir Alexander Cadogan, Permanent Undersecretary for Foreign Affairs, produced the declaration that the President sought.

The Atlantic Charter, as the document was soon called, began with a preamble that expressed the intention of the two Western leaders "to make known certain common principles . . . on which they base their hopes for a better future for the world." The first of the eight articles that followed comprised an Anglo-American renunciation of territorial or other aggrandizement. The second and third articles expressed opposition to territorial changes contrary to the wishes of the people directly concerned and declared the right of all peoples to choose their own form of government. The fourth article offered support, with the necessary respect for existing obligations, for the easing of trade restrictions and the granting of equal access to raw materials. Churchill preferred a less specific declaration that would not contradict the Ottawa Agreements (the system of imperial preferences adopted in July–August 1932) and their designation of special trading privileges for members of the British Commonwealth. Roosevelt and Welles wanted an unqualified endorsement of equal economic opportunity and the elimination of all artificial barriers to the free flow of commerce. Roosevelt compromised by accepting the phrase, "with due respect for their existing obligations."

The fifth article proclaimed support for cooperative efforts to improve the economic status, labor standards, and social security of the peoples of the world. The sixth article anticipated a postwar peace that would guarantee all peoples freedom from want and fear. The seventh and eighth articles addressed the issue of freedom of the seas and, pending the establishment of a permanent peace structure, that of disarming aggressor nations and relieving the peaceful states of the unwanted burden of armaments. Roosevelt, fearing adverse isolationist reaction, objected to Churchill's suggestion of an "effective international organization," but accepted, in deference to American internationalists, the "establishment of a wider and permanent system of general security."

Roosevelt hoped that the Atlantic Charter, released to the public on 14 August along with the revelation of the Argentia conference itself, would reinforce the notion of a common Anglo-American civilization with its contrasting values to those of Hitler's Germany. At a press conference on 16 August he described in detail the religious service aboard the *Prince of Wales* on the previous Sunday morning. He noted the intermingling of U.S. and British servicemen, all of whom joined in the singing of three hymns; the two chaplains, one English and one American; and the ship's altar draped with American and British flags. It was, Churchill recalled, "a deeply moving expression of the unity of faith of our two peoples." Unfortunately for Roosevelt, the Atlantic Charter had no effect on isolationist sentiment except to affirm the conviction that the President was unneutral and a threat to peace. Polls revealed that three-fourths of Americans still opposed any involvement in the European war. Still on 24 September fifteen nations fighting Hitler, including the U.S.S.R., adopted the Atlantic Charter as the standard against which they would measure the postwar reconstruction of Europe.

BIBLIOGRAPHY

Dallek, Robert. *Franklin D. Roosevelt and American Foreign Policy, 1932–1945.* 1979.

Drummond, Donald F. *The Passing of American Neutrality, 1937–41.* 1955.

Langer, William L., and S. Everett Gleason. *The Undeclared War, 1940–1941.* 1953.

Stone, Julius. *The Atlantic Charter: New Worlds for Old.* 1945.

Wilson, Theodore A. *The First Summit: Roosevelt and Churchill at Placentia Bay, 1941.* 1969.

NORMAN A. GRAEBNER

ATOMIC BOMB, USE OF. The decision to drop atomic bombs on the Japanese cities of Hiroshima and Nagasaki in August 1945 was a defining event in the history of the world and of the American presidency. The arsenal that began with these first two crude prototypes used at the end of WORLD WAR II made any American President the most powerful human being on earth. The bomb was a major factor in the rise of what has been called the IMPERIAL PRESIDENCY.

The use of the atomic bombs is often depicted as the action of one man, President Harry S. Truman, who as COMMANDER IN CHIEF gave the order. Some have argued, however, that Truman had little or nothing to do with an action that was determined by larger political and bureaucratic forces. In some sense the decision whether to use the bomb was a foregone conclusion, a given implicit in Franklin D. Roosevelt's 1941 decision to build such a "winning weapon." But how, when and where the bomb was used were all very much up to the President and his closest advisers. Truman, and those on whom he relied for guidance, were indeed the key actors in one of history's greatest dramas.

Truman never denied personal responsibility for the bombings. As a former WORLD WAR I artillery officer he had no hesitation nor any second thoughts about using this new more powerful and efficient weapon. At the time he justified his decision on the grounds that using the bomb shortened the war and saved "thousands and thousands" of American lives. Later, he estimated the number of American lives saved at between a quarter- and a half-million. To this total he added the lives of several million Japanese who would have been killed had the Allied invasion of Japan, scheduled to begin in November 1945, occurred. This became the official and widely accepted explanation of why the bomb was used. Public opinion polls taken just after the bombings showed that most Americans (54 percent) endorsed Truman's action. For every American who then opposed any use of the new weapon (5 percent), more than four times as many (23 percent) were disappointed that more atomic bombs had not been used before Japan was able to surrender.

It is now possible to reconstruct from Truman's contemporary personal records what he did and did not know about the bomb when he made his historic decision. That record shows that Truman, to a much greater degree than Roosevelt, was dependent on a few key advisers for advice and even the most basic information about the bomb. Foremost among these advisers were Secretary of War HENRY L. STIMSON and Truman's immediate choice as Secretary of State, JAMES F. BYRNES. In effect, the bomb decision was made by Truman, Stimson, and Byrnes.

Truman's dependence on these advisers derived from the circumstances of his newly formed presidency. Until very late in the process, Truman, first as a Senator and then as Vice President, had been deliberately kept uninformed regarding the top-secret project referred to by a very select group of insiders only as "S-1." In this and many other matters of high policy Truman was among American history's least-informed Vice Presidents. He was clearly overwhelmed by the weight of the office suddenly thrust upon him and by his lack of preparation.

The day after taking the oath as Roosevelt's successor on 12 April 1945, Truman was told by Byrnes about a new bomb that might "destroy the whole world." Ten days later, in the new President's first formal briefing about the bomb project, Stimson told him that an atomic fission bomb powerful enough to "destroy a city" would be ready for testing sometime that summer.

At Stimson's suggestion Truman immediately appointed a committee to advise him on how best to use the new weapon. This committee was dominated by Stimson, its chairman, and Byrnes, Truman's personal representative. As the battle for Okinawa raged this committee decided how to use the bomb for "maximum psychological effect" on what seemed a fanatical, even suicidal, Japanese leadership. The committee's report, submitted to Truman in early June, recommended using the bomb without warning on an industrial target surrounded by civilian housing.

Stimson and the military decided where the bomb should be used. The military commander of the bomb project, General Leslie Groves, compiled a list of a half-dozen suitable target cities, which deliberately had been left unscathed by conventional bombing attacks.

The only remaining question for Truman was when to use the bomb. His seemingly simple answer—as soon as possible—resulted from a combination of military, diplomatic, and political factors. Truman shared the wartime perception of the Japanese as "savages, ruthless, merciless and fanatic," who responded only to brute force. He was aware through American intelligence sources of Japanese efforts to negotiate an end to the war through neutral third countries, chief among them the Soviet Union. Truman also knew that Stalin had promised Roosevelt at the YALTA CONFERENCE in February 1945 that, in return for a sphere of influence in China, the Soviet Union would declare war on Japan three months after the defeat of Germany (approximately 8 August). Finally, Truman, whose political reputation and elevation to Vice President rested largely on his work as the Senate's "billion dollar watch dog" over wartime expenditures, was particularly sensitive to the enormous costs of the bomb project. The $2 billion allotted to the mysterious MANHATTAN PROJECT was the single most expensive weapons-development appropriation in history. It was important to everyone involved that the bomb prove its worth by helping to end the war.

Until just days before he gave his approval to use the bomb, Truman still could not be sure what the bomb was, or even if it worked at all. Only the results of the so-called Trinity test at Alamogordo, New Mexico, sent to Truman in a series of reports in mid July, finally made the bomb real to him. Yet these reports were incomplete and misleading. Nowhere in these reports or the earlier briefings was Truman made aware of the lethal effects of radioactivity—the single qualitative difference between the atomic bomb and other explosives. Everything Truman was told about the bomb emphasized its destructive power in terms of TNT equivalence, something the old artilleryman could understand.

The news from Alamogordo was exhilarating. Truman needed this boost in his sense of confidence. He was the midst of the difficult and frustrating POTSDAM CONFERENCE with British Prime Minister Winston Churchill and Soviet leader Joseph Stalin on the outskirts of Soviet-occupied Berlin. The bomb gave Truman an entirely new sense of confidence in his diplomacy. It was, as he put it, his "ace in the hole" in dealing with the other leaders.

The bomb's impact on Truman's timetable for ending the war with Japan is revealed in his diary entries and letters to BESS TRUMAN during the Potsdam Conference. After his first meeting with Stalin, on 17 July, Truman recorded his conviction that a Soviet declaration of war would seal Japan's fate, or, as he put it, "Fini Japs when that comes about." The next day he wrote to his wife hailing Stalin's renewed commitment to enter the war as signaling an early end to the fighting, shortening the war by a full year. "Think of the kids who won't be killed!" he added. But on receiving the full descriptions of the bomb test, Truman immediately revised his estimate of how the war would end, and expressed his belief that once the bomb was used Japan would "fold up" before Soviet entry. Suddenly the bomb, with its unexpected power, provided an alternative to sharing victory with the Soviet Union. As Byrnes put it at the time, the point was "to outmaneuver Stalin on China" and end the war with the bomb before the Soviets could "get in so much on the kill."

The evidence of Truman's own diary and letters undercuts his public explanation of the bomb's use.

His own inner doubts are suggested in a diary entry recorded on the night he received the first news of the successful Trinity test. He noted that "machines are ahead of morals by some centuries," that humans are but "termites on a planet" and that should they bore too deeply there someday might be "a reckoning. Who knows?" Perhaps for Truman the reckoning came with the actual bombings.

The first bomb was exploded over Hiroshima on the morning of 6 August. Three days later Nagasaki was bombed. Some 200,000 people died, either instantly or of injuries and radiation sickness in the ensuing months. The Soviet Union, apparently accelerating its plans in light of the bombings, declared war on Japan on 8 August. Within hours of these successive shocks the Japanese government expressed its willingness to surrender, with the condition that the emperor be protected from punishment. The Allies agreed to this condition, and the war ended. The day after the Nagasaki bombing Truman told his Cabinet that there would be no more atomic attacks, in part because the thought of killing another 100,000 people—including "all those kids"—was simply "too horrible." A few months later he told an aide that he doubted if he could ever use the bomb again. Fortunately, all Presidents since then have shared Truman's belated recognition of the bomb's horror.

BIBLIOGRAPHY

Alperovitz, Gar. *Atomic Diplomacy: Hiroshima and Potsdam.* Rev. ed. 1985.

Bernstein, Barton J. *The Atomic Bomb: The Crucial Issues.* 1976.

Feis, Herbert. *The Atomic Bomb and the End of World War II.* 1966.

Messer, Robert L. "New Evidence on Truman's Decision." *Bulletin of Atomic Scientists* 41 (1985): 50–56.

Pacific War Research Society. *The Day Man Lost: Hiroshima, 6 August 1945.* 1972.

Rhodes, Richard, *The Making of the Atomic Bomb.* 1986.

Sherwin, Martin J. *A World Destroyed: The Atomic Bomb and the Grand Alliance.* 1975.

Wells, Samuel J. "The Decision to Use the Bomb: A Historiographical Update." *Diplomatic History* 14 (1990): 97–114.

ROBERT L. MESSER

ATOMIC ENERGY COMMISSION. The atomic age thrust itself upon a largely unsuspecting world when the United States detonated two atomic bombs on the Japanese cities of Hiroshima and Nagasaki in August of 1945 (*see* ATOMIC BOMB, USE OF). These weapons of unprecedented explosive force were the creation of the Manhattan Engineer District (the MANHATTAN PROJECT), the United States' secret program for the creation of an atomic bomb. The devastating explo-sions ended WORLD WAR II and at the same time catalyzed a debate over the future of atomic energy. The military possibilities of nuclear fission had been dramatically demonstrated; but a potential for peaceful use of it was also apparent. With the specific mission of the Manhattan Engineer District accomplished, it was clear that the United States needed to develop a more comprehensive program to oversee the development and use of atomic energy.

On 3 October 1945, President Harry S. Truman sent a special message to Congress on the subject of atomic energy. Truman urged Congress to create an atomic energy commission, the purpose of which would be "to control all sources of atomic energy and all activities connected with its development and use in the United States." Among other things the commission would promote scientific investigation and the development of practical applications for the use of atomic energy. The President's message also informed Congress that he intended to open discussions with foreign nations regarding the international control of atomic energy, particularly with respect to NUCLEAR WEAPONS.

An intense debate ensued. From a NATIONAL SECURITY perspective, the need for strict secrecy and control over the secrets of atomic energy seemed evident; from the academic perspective, the importance of uninhibited scientific research and free dissemination of information seemed equally evident. A number of leading scientists also argued for complete disclosure of all scientific discoveries in order to ensure and promote international control over atomic energy. The result of this debate was the Atomic Energy Act of 1946, which President Truman signed into law on 1 August 1946.

The act created the Atomic Energy Commission, a five-person board appointed by the President with the ADVICE AND CONSENT of the Senate. The Commission was vested with broad authority to oversee the development and production of atomic energy, including research and development of military applications. To this end, ownership of Manhattan Engineer District production facilities and laboratories was transferred to the commission. The express purpose of the commission was to encourage scientific progress, to promote and control the dissemination and reciprocal sharing of scientific and technical information, and to oversee governmental research and development, all with an eye toward safeguarding "the common defense and security." In addition, the commission was to oversee and control the production, ownership and use of all fissionable material, later defined as special nuclear material, within the United States. A fundamental premise of the act was that the authority of the commission would be limited by any subsequent international agreements regarding atomic energy entered by the United States.

The rapid development of nuclear physics over the next few decades, as well as the international proliferation of nuclear technology, led to various amendments to the act. These amendments were designed to enhance security over sensitive data, to keep the commission's authority abreast of current developments in nuclear physics, and to promote more aggressively the development of peaceful uses of nuclear energy. Eventually, the commission was also given the authority to license and regulate privately owned nuclear power plants. In addition, between the years 1946 and 1974, the commission oversaw a wide-ranging program of weapons testing and development. Not coincidentally, the vast network of commission-owned production facilities and laboratories expanded dramatically during that period.

The Atomic Energy Commission was abolished by the Energy Reorganization Act of 1974. The licensing and regulatory functions of the commission were transferred to the newly created Nuclear Regulatory Commission. The research and development functions, including both military and nonmilitary uses, were transferred to the Energy Research and Development Administration. During the administration of President Jimmy Carter, the research and development functions were placed in the newly created DEPARTMENT OF ENERGY.

BIBLIOGRAPHY

Hewlett, Richard G., and Oscar E. Anderson, Jr. *The New World, 1939/1946. A History of the United States Atomic Energy Commission,* vol. 1. 1962.

Hewlett, Richard G. and Francis Duncan. *Atomic Shield, 1947/1952. A History of the United States Atomic Energy Commission,* vol. 2. 1969.

Miller, Richard L. *Under the Cloud: The Decades of Nuclear Testing.* 1986.

Truman, Harry S. *Public Papers of the Presidents (1945).* 1961.

ALLAN IDES

ATTORNEY GENERAL. The chief law officer of the national government, a key presidential adviser, a member of the CABINET since 1792, and the head of the DEPARTMENT OF JUSTICE since its creation in 1870, the Attorney General is appointed by the President with the ADVICE AND CONSENT of the Senate. Hearings on the Attorney General's confirmation are held by the Senate Judiciary Committee. As of 1993, seventy-eight men and one women had served as Attorney General. EDMUND RANDOLPH, the first, joined the Washington administration in 1790. The burdens on the incumbent have increased heavily since then, significantly so since the 1940s as executive branch responsibilities, federal legislation, and court activity have increased.

Functions. The oldest function of the office is to represent the government in court, a function that dates from fourteenth-century England. Originally, the U.S. Attorney General argued cases before the Supreme Court, a task now delegated to the SOLICITOR GENERAL. In the lower federal courts, U.S. attorneys represent the government. The Solicitor General, working with the Attorney General, determines what cases will be appealed to the Supreme Court or other appellate courts and what position (if any) the government will take as an amicus curiae ("friend of the court") in cases to which it is not a party. Generally, the Attorney General expresses broad administration perspectives in making these decisions. On occasion, however, the Justice Department has clashed with the White House over Supreme Court litigation issues.

The Attorney General's second most venerable function—with antecedents in seventeenth-century England and the American colonies—is to provide legal advice to the CHIEF EXECUTIVE. By defining the scope and meaning of the law, the Attorney General assists the President in fulfilling his constitutional obligation to "take care that the laws be faithfully executed." This advisory role has been widely regarded as quasi-judicial. Today, much of the responsibility for writing opinions is delegated to the OFFICE OF LEGAL COUNSEL (OLC). As a legal adviser, the Attorney General faces competition from other persons and agencies in government, particularly the WHITE HOUSE COUNSEL and the legal staffs in the various executive departments.

The third function of the Attorney General is to administer the large bureaucracy of the Department of Justice. The Attorney General supervises much of the government's legal work, overseeing the department's six divisions involved in litigation (antitrust, civil, criminal, civil rights, tax, and environment and natural resources), the Solicitor General's office, the ninety-five U.S. attorneys, and the Office of Legal Counsel. In addition, the Attorney General supervises several nonlawyering offices, including the Immigration and Naturalization Service, the Bureau of Prisons, the U.S. Parole Commission, and the U.S. Marshals Service. The FEDERAL BUREAU OF INVESTIGATION (FBI), created in 1924 out of a small detective staff formed in 1908, also falls within his administrative jurisdiction. Another investigative unit, the Drug Enforcement Administration, was added to the Justice Department in 1973.

Besides providing legal counsel, the Attorney General often serves as a political adviser to the President, offering policy and political advice in three capacities. First, as a department head the Attorney General is constitutionally required to provide policy advice to the President on matters relating to the Justice Department, including departmental priorities, policies, and budget requests. He participates in formulating legislation related to the Justice Department and the federal court system, and he testifies before Congress. The Attorney General assists the President in recommending and screening nominees to the federal bench [see JUDGES, APPOINTMENT OF].

Secondly, as a Cabinet member, the Attorney General may be involved in policy decisions that reach beyond his department—for example, decisions affecting EDUCATION POLICY or NATIONAL SECURITY. He may be required to lobby Congress on measures that are only tangentially related (if at all) to the Justice Department. Whether the Attorney General plays this role depends on how the President uses the Cabinet.

Finally, some Attorneys General have been friends and political allies of their Presidents. As such, they have helped to plan campaign strategy, to organize partisan activities, and to frame broad administration policy goals. A minority have become trusted presidential advisers on a wide range of issues.

Unlike his colleagues in the executive branch, the Attorney General has responsibilities that are distinctly legal in character. On one hand, he is the chief law officer of the nation and an officer of the court. Yet he is also a political actor, an appointed official who is accountable to an elected chief executive. This legal-political duality makes his position a singular one. Obligated to serve the President, who is, in a sense, his client, the Attorney General must also exhibit "a proper loyalty . . . to the idea of law itself," as former Attorney General and legal scholar Edward Levi put it during his 1975 Senate confirmation hearings. These dual responsibilities, while not necessarily conflicting, create the potential for tension between loyalty to the law and loyalty to the President. Many Attorneys General have experienced little difficulty responding to these dual demands. Some have defined their office primarily as that of the President's advocate; others have stressed its quasi-judicial character. But, periodically, Attorneys General have been charged with manipulating their legal opinions to suit political needs. Among the legal opinions that have been cited as examples of politics prevailing over law are ROBERT JACKSON's support for Franklin D. Roosevelt's DESTROYERS FOR BASES exchange in the early days of WORLD WAR II, and ROBERT F. KENNEDY's interpretation of the Cuban quarantine during the 1962 CUBAN MISSILE CRISIS as an act short of war, an interpretation that ran contrary to international law.

Public sensitivity to the dual nature of the office may be heightened because most Attorneys General have been politically active prior to appointment. Many have held elective office on state and national levels. A few have had presidential ambitions, although as of 1993 none had become President or Vice President. A further factor is that Presidents tend to name partisans and political campaigners to the post. With the exception of Lyndon B. Johnson, Gerald Ford, Jimmy Carter, and George Bush, every President from 1933 to 1992 named either a campaign manager, campaign aide, or national party chairman as Attorney General sometime during his administration. Notable examples include Robert Kennedy in the John F. Kennedy administration, JOHN MITCHELL in the Richard M. Nixon administration, and EDWIN MEESE III in the Ronald Reagan administration. Nonpolitical law officers have been appointed on occasion, but they are the exception, generally chosen by Presidents who, in the wake of predecessors' scandals, are under pressure by Congress or the public to select law officers from outside politics. Both Ford and Carter felt constrained in their choices by the need to rebuild public confidence in the Justice Department in the wake of the WATERGATE AFFAIR. Bill Clinton may have felt a similar pressure when he named Janet Reno as Attorney General. For one thing, controversy about the Attorney General's political role resurfaced during the Reagan-Bush years. Further, Clinton's earlier nominees—Zoe Baird and Kimba Wood—were unsuccessful precisely because of legal and/or ethical questions. Reno, in contrast, has been highly praised for her integrity during her fifteen years as Miami's top prosecutor, a quality that is essential to public confidence. Clinton's choices of Baird, Wood, and Reno may also reflect a new dynamic constraining presidential Cabinet selections, as women's groups put pressure on the White House to name a woman to Justice, one of the top four Cabinet positions.

History. The history of the office of attorney general in America extends back to the colonial period, when attorneys general served as delegates of the English law officer, charged with overseeing the crown's interests. They provided legal advice and courtroom advocacy for pioneer governments in Virginia, Rhode Island, Pennsylvania, and Maryland. The system was so well established that it continued with little interruption as colonial governments evolved into state governments. However, no national law officer existed under the Articles of Confederation. The issue was debated briefly by the Continental Congress in 1781 but was left unresolved. Instead, Congress hired private attorneys to prosecute on its behalf in state courts.

Attorneys General

President	Attorney General
1 Washington	Edmund Randolph, 1789–1794 William Bradford, 1794–1795 Charles Lee, 1795–1797
2 J. Adams	Charles Lee, 1797–1801 Theophilus Parsons, 1801
3 Jefferson	Levi Lincoln, 1801–1804 Robert Smith, 1805 John Breckinridge, 1805–1806 Caesar A. Rodney, 1807–1809
4 Madison	Caesar A. Rodney, 1809–1811 William Pinckney, 1811–1814 Richard Rush, 1814–1817
5 Monroe	Richard Rush, 1817 William Wirt, 1817–1825
6 J. Q. Adams	William Wirt, 1825–1829
7 Jackson	John M. Berrien, 1829–1831 Roger B. Taney, 1831–1833 Benjamin F. Butler, 1833–1837
8 Van Buren	Benjamin F. Butler, 1837–1838 Felix Grundy, 1838–1840 Henry D. Gilpin, 1840–1841
9 W. H. Harrison	John J. Crittenden, 1841
10 Tyler	John J. Crittenden, 1841 Hugh S. Legaré, 1841–1843 John Nelson, 1843–1845

President	Attorney General
11 Polk	John Y. Mason, 1845–1846 Nathan Clifford, 1846–1848 Isaac Toucey, 1848–1849
12 Taylor	Reverdy Johnson, 1849–1850
13 Fillmore	John J. Crittenden, 1850–1853
14 Pierce	Caleb Cushing, 1853–1857
15 Buchanan	Jeremiah S. Black, 1857–1860 Edwin M. Stanton, 1860–1861
16 Lincoln	Edward Bates, 1861–1863 Titian J. Coffey, 1863 James Speed, 1864–1865
17 A. Johnson	James Speed, 1865–1866 Henry Stanbery, 1866–1868 William M. Everts, 1868–1869
18 Grant	Rockwood Hoar, 1869–1870 Amos T. Akerman, 1870–1871 George H. Williams, 1871–1875 Edwards Pierrepont, 1875–1876 Alphonso Taft, 1877
19 Hayes	Charles Devens, 1877–1881
20 Garfield	Wayne MacVeagh, 1881
21 Arthur	Wayne MacVeagh, 1881 Benjamin H. Brewster, 1882–1885
22 Cleveland	Augustus H. Garland, 1885–1889

Neither the U.S. Constitution nor the debates of the Framers mentions an attorney general, but the office is a natural outgrowth of the Constitution. By setting up a national government, the Framers prepared the way for a national law office. National institutions, not existing state machinery, were to be developed to handle national functions.

The office of Attorney General was created by the First Congress in the Judiciary Act of 1789, which established the federal court system and the system of U.S. attorneys and marshals. The Attorney General, who served only on a part-time basis, had two primary tasks: handling litigation for the federal government and giving legal advice to the President and, in certain cases, DEPARTMENTAL SECRETARIES. The bill faced opposition from ANTI-FEDERALISTS who saw it as an effort by Federalists to centralize the nation's legal affairs. Consequently, it did not pass as quickly as the statutes that created the departments of War, Treasury, and State. The Attorney General was therefore the fourth executive office created and is recognized as such in the order of PRESIDENTIAL SUCCESSION outlined in 1886.

Congress itself was dissatisfied with the Judiciary Act and almost immediately ordered Randolph, the first Attorney General, to report on possible improvements. He proposed two reforms: first, that he be given authority over U.S. attorneys to better serve government interests in the lower courts, and, second, that he be given a transcribing clerk to record his opinions. Legislation came out of committee but then died on the floor of Congress. It was the first of many attempts by various Attorneys General and Presidents to secure a more centralized operation, but even the request for a clerk went unheeded for twenty-seven years.

Finally, in 1819, Attorney General WILLIAM WIRT received funding for one clerk. Wirt further institutionalized the office by beginning to keep records of his official opinions, an onerous task avoided by his predecessors. Serving longer than any other Attorney General, Wirt was the first to comprehend the need for an administrative structure. Yet change came slowly; efforts during Andrew Jackson's presidency to expand the Attorney General's authority, staff, and salary met congressional resistance. Presidents James K. Polk and Franklin Pierce also unsuccessfully sought greater centralization. Instead, Congress began to create other government legal offices that were not answerable to the Attorney General. In time, the departments of State, Treasury, Interior, Commerce, Labor, Agriculture, Navy, Post Office, and Internal Revenue maintained their own legal staffs. The result

Attorneys General (continued)

President	Attorney General
23 B. Harrison	William H. H. Miller, 1889–1893
24 Cleveland	Richard Olney, 1893–1895
	Judson Harmon, 1895–1897
25 McKinley	Joseph McKenna, 1897–1898
	John W. Griggs, 1898–1901
	Philander C. Knox, 1901
26 T. Roosevelt	Philander C. Knox, 1901–1904
	William H. Moody, 1904–1906
	Charles J. Bonaparte, 1906–1909
27 Taft	George W. Wickersham, 1909–1913
28 Wilson	James C. McReynolds, 1913–1914
	Thomas W. Gregory, 1914–1919
	A. Mitchell Palmer, 1919–1921
29 Harding	Harry M. Daugherty, 1921–1923
30 Coolidge	Harry M. Daugherty, 1923–1924
	Harlan F. Stone, 1924–1925
	John G. Sargent, 1925–1929
31 Hoover	William D. Mitchell, 1929–1933
32 F. D. Roosevelt	Homer S. Cummings, 1933–1939
	Frank Murphy, 1939–1940
	Robert H. Jackson, 1940–1941
	Francis Biddle, 1941–1945
33 Truman	Francis Biddle, 1945
	Thomas C. Clark, 1945–1949

President	Attorney General
	J. Howard McGrath, 1949–1952
	James P. McGranery, 1952–1953
34 Eisenhower	Herbert Brownell, Jr., 1953–1958
	William P. Rogers, 1958–1961
35 Kennedy	Robert F. Kennedy, 1961–1963
36 L. B. Johnson	Robert F. Kennedy, 1963–1965
	Nicholas deB. Katzenbach, 1965–1967
	Ramsey Clark, 1967–1969
37 Nixon	John N. Mitchell, 1969–1972
	Richard G. Kleindienst, 1972–1973
	Elliot L. Richardson, 1973
	William B. Saxbe, 1974
38 Ford	William B. Saxbe, 1974–1975
	Edward H. Levi, 1975–1977
39 Carter	Griffin B. Bell, 1977–1979
	Benjamin R. Civiletti, 1979–1981
40 Reagan	William French Smith, 1981–1985
	Edwin Meese III, 1985–1988
	Richard Thornburgh, 1988–1989
41 Bush	Richard Thornburgh, 1989–1991
	William P. Barr, 1991–1993
42 Clinton	Janet Reno, 1993–

of this fragmentation was near anarchy in the nation's legal affairs.

Institutionalization of the office of Attorney General was slow in part because until 1853 Attorneys General were part-time officials and not required to reside in the capital. The Attorney General received half the salary of other Cabinet officers; the federal government was simply one client, paying an annual retainer for legal services. Attorneys General were expected to supplement their incomes with private practice. Far from being seen as a potential conflict of interest, private practice was encouraged as a means of honing legal skills and keeping abreast of the law. For the first sixty years, therefore, Attorneys General maintained their hometown residences, traveling to the capital only when necessary. This meant that they were not readily available to provide advice to the President.

The Attorney General's salary was finally increased to that of other Cabinet members in 1853. This led to two developments: the law officer relinquished his outside legal practice, and he moved his residence to Washington. As a full-time Cabinet member, the Attorney General was now more accessible to the President. This gave the office a stronger identification with the executive branch and a more distinctly political character. The first Attorney General to benefit from these changes was CALEB CUSHING, who further

developed the office by actively seeking expanded responsibilities. Cushing had both the time and personal inclination to become involved in a broad range of governmental affairs, including international relations.

Despite rapid developments during the nation's first century, the attorney generalship remained relatively unaltered. Sixty years after the Judiciary Act, the office still housed only four staff members: the Attorney General himself, two clerks, and a messenger. Cushing succeeded in getting two more clerks. In the 1860s, Congress provided for two Assistant Attorneys General and a law clerk, and, in 1861, the U.S. attorneys were made subordinate to the Attorney General, although they maintain a tradition of independence.

Congressional action to create a consolidated law department was not taken until after the CIVIL WAR, which produced a monumental increase in government litigation in courts all across the country. Because the Attorney General's office could not handle the demand, executive departments had to hire outside counsel at high professional rates. As a cost-saving measure, Congress finally passed the Judiciary Act of 1870, which established the Department of Justice and added two assistants and a Solicitor General to the Attorney General's staff. The act still did not create a centralized system, however. While nominally brought under the Attorney General's supervision, the legal staffs of other departments remained autonomous. Later legislative efforts to rectify this situation failed, and the practice of executive departments maintaining their own law offices continues today. Generally, these staffs are restricted to rendering legal advice on matters of concern to their departments alone. Most of the government's litigation now is under Justice Department control.

BIBLIOGRAPHY

Baker, Nancy V. *Conflicting Loyalties: Law and Politics in the Attorney General's Office, 1789–1990.* 1992.

Bell, Griffin. *Taking Care of the Law.* 1982.

Clayton, Cornell. *The Politics of Justice: The Attorney General and the Making of Legal Policy.* 1992.

Cummings, Homer, and Carl McFarland. *Federal Justice: Chapters in the History of Justice and the Federal Executive.* 1937; rpt. 1970.

Huston, Luther. *The Department of Justice.* 1967.

Learned, Henry B. *The President's Cabinet.* 1912.

Meador, Daniel J. *The President, the Attorney General, and the Department of Justice.* 1980.

NANCY V. BAKER

ATTORNEY GENERAL'S SUBVERSIVES LIST.

As part of President Harry S. Truman's federal employee LOYALTY-SECURITY PROGRAM, the Attorney General was authorized in 1947 to compile a list of both foreign and domestic groups that he deemed "totalitarian, fascist, communist or subversive, or as having adopted a policy of advocating or approving the commission of acts of force or violence to deny others their rights under the Constitution of the United States, or as seeking to alter the form of government of the United States by unconstitutional means" (EXECUTIVE ORDER 9835). The list was then sent to the government's Loyalty Review Board, which forwarded it to all departments and agencies. A civilian employee who was a member of a designated group could be dismissed, because membership alone constituted "reasonable grounds" to believe he or she was disloyal.

During the first year, Attorney General Tom C. Clark identified 123 subversive organizations. Over time, some were deleted but others were added, bringing the total by late 1950 to 197. These organizations were permitted no administrative opportunity to challenge their inclusion. Three alleged "communist" organizations brought suit seeking to have their names removed; they argued that they were not communist. Lower federal courts dismissed the complaints on technical grounds, but in 1951 the U.S. Supreme Court reversed and remanded. The Justices held that government attorneys, by seeking the dismissal on technical grounds, implicitly had accepted the inno-

cence asserted by the organizations. In a 5 to 3 ruling in *Joint Anti-Fascist Refugee Committee v. McGrath*, the majority found that the groups had been included in a purely "arbitrary and unauthorized" way, outside the scope of the executive order. While the majority opinion did not address CIVIL LIBERTIES per se, the concurring opinions did, criticizing the list as tantamount to an executive bill of attainder, which denied due process and chilled free speech.

Truman had created the loyalty program because he was genuinely concerned about possible communist infiltration of the U.S. government. Furthermore, he hoped that his program would protect loyal employees against false accusations. Politically, he also had to respond to Republican allegations that he was soft on communism, particularly from the House Committee on Un-American Activities and later Senator Joseph McCarthy [see MCCARTHYISM]. Under Truman's program, twelve hundred federal employees were dismissed and six thousand resigned, many to save themselves the legal expense and emotional cost that came with fighting the charges.

Constitutional questions were raised from the beginning. The accused were not informed of specific charges, and informants could remain confidential. Too often, mere accusation was taken as evidence of guilt. Certain departmental loyalty review boards targeted minority groups, particularly black and Jewish workers.

On the other hand, Truman did not go as far as many demanded. Critics argued the program failed to eradicate Moscow's "fifth columnists" from government service. Truman further angered anticommunists when he refused to release FBI files to congressional investigative committees. He also vetoed the MCCARRAN INTERNAL SECURITY ACT in 1950; it passed over his veto.

The loyalty program and Attorney General's list were maintained under the Eisenhower administration, which made a great show of cleansing leftover subversives from the government. Truman was angered, but Dwight D. Eisenhower was partly responding to congressional pressures. Most of those eliminated during this time were dismissed on security grounds and not on loyalty grounds, a fact that the Eisenhower administration downplayed.

BIBLIOGRAPHY

Bontecou, Eleanor. *The Federal Loyalty-Security Program.* 1953.

Harper, Alan D. *The Politics of Loyalty: The White House and the Communist Issue, 1946–1952.* 1969.

Kutler, Stanley I. *The American Inquisition: Justice and Injustice in the Cold War.* 1982.

NANCY V. BAKER

B

BAKER, JAMES A., III (b. 1930), White House Chief of Staff, Secretary of the Treasury, Secretary of State. A lawyer from Texas, James Baker was a long-time personal friend of George Bush. He ran Bush's unsuccessful campaign for the Senate in 1970, and on Bush's recommendation he was appointed Under Secretary of Commerce in the Ford administration. He then served as chairman for Ford's election bid in 1976. By 1979, he was back at the side of Bush, running Bush's campaign for the Republican presidential nomination. After Bush was picked as Ronald Reagan's running mate, Baker moved over to the Reagan-Bush campaign, and Reagan eventually selected him as his first WHITE HOUSE CHIEF OF STAFF. A hard-worker (often putting in thirteen- to sixteen-hour-days), Baker was renowned as a political tactician and as a master of public relations. He is also known as a pragmatist, with no defined political philosophy. As he himself acknowledged in 1982: "I don't consider myself as one who has deeply held views on specific issues."

Baker's tenure in the Reagan administration was stormy. He won high marks for helping to get Reagan's legislative program through Congress, but he was criticized by conservatives for limiting access to Reagan in order to steer the President away from some of his conservative positions. He was also accused of using leaks to the media to discredit his opponents within the administration, an accusation that he denied.

Friend and foe alike praised Baker's ability to work out deals behind the scenes. But on occasion his deals could backfire. In 1983, Baker tried to have himself appointed NATIONAL SECURITY ADVISER, succeeding William Clark, who decided to resign after a series of anony-mous White House leaks attacking him. Baker attempted to secure his appointment to the post without consulting President Reagan's senior advisers in the area of NATIONAL SECURITY. Baker's plan was thwarted when Reagan's other advisers discovered it and counseled the President to reject the scheme, which he did.

During Reagan's second term, Baker traded places with Secretary of the Treasury DONALD T. REGAN. As Treasury Secretary, Baker's two major initiatives were tax reform and third world debt relief. A tax reform package had already been devised by Regan before he left Treasury, but Baker revised it and helped push it through Congress. Baker's plan for debt relief, meanwhile, sought to avert an international monetary crisis by offering new loans to already debt-ridden developing countries.

Baker left the Treasury Department to become chairman of George Bush's successful 1988 campaign for the presidency. Bush then appointed Baker as his Secretary of State. Baker's tenure at the STATE DEPARTMENT occurred during a time of great instability in the international scene. He had to deal with the breakup of the Soviet Union, the crisis in PANAMA, the crackdown against dissent in China, and the invasion of Kuwait by Iraq, and the resulting GULF WAR. Baker also sponsored peace negotiations between the Israelis and Arabs.

In 1992 Baker resigned as Secretary of State in order to run President Bush's unsuccessful reelection campaign.

BIBLIOGRAPHY

Anderson, Jim. "The President's Man in the State Department." *Foreign Service Journal.* (December 1989): 30–37.

Baker, James A., III. "America and the Collapse of the Soviet Empire: What Has to be Done." *Vital Speeches*. (1 January 1992): 162–168.

Solomon, Burt. "The President's Peer." *National Journal*. (7 January 1989): 6–10.

JOHN G. WEST, JR.

BAKER, NEWTON D. (1871–1937), Secretary of War. Born and raised in West Virginia, Newton Diehl Baker earned his bachelor's degree from Johns Hopkins University in 1892 and a law degree from Washington and Lee University in 1894. After serving several years as private secretary to Postmaster General William Lyne Wilson, Baker began the practice of law. He became a protégé of the reform mayor of Cleveland, Tom Loftin Johnson, and in 1903 was elected city solicitor. Baker was elected mayor in 1911. He continued Johnson's reform program during his two terms in office and was chiefly responsible for a new home-rule charter for the city and for the building of a municipal electric power plant.

Baker had studied under the then professor Woodrow Wilson at Johns Hopkins. Wilson was impressed by Baker's record as mayor and grateful for his support in the presidential campaign of 1912. The President-elect offered Baker the Cabinet post of Secretary of the Interior but the latter preferred to remain mayor of Cleveland. In March 1916, following the resignation of the then Secretary of War, Lindley Miller Garrison, in a dispute over military preparedness, Wilson offered that position to Baker and Baker reluctantly accepted. Baker, with his intellectual and philosophical inclinations, soon became one of Wilson's most intimate and trusted advisers; his influence extended far beyond military matters.

A mild-mannered little man with pronounced antimilitaristic and pacifistic views prior to American entry into WORLD WAR I, Baker as Secretary of War was often blamed for the glaring deficiencies of the War Department in the early stages of American participation in the great conflict. However, he had inherited an antiquated department that oversaw an army of 5,800 officers and 122,000 enlisted men in April 1917, just prior to the DECLARATION OF WAR by Congress. Baker presided over the expansion of this force within a period of two-and-one-half years to a peak wartime strength of 3.7 million men. He implemented a highly successful selective service system. Though very tardy in reforming the outmoded administrative system of the department and the army, he ultimately did so, partly under the pressure of a congressional investigation. Baker brought in highly competent officials, such as General Peyton C. March, who became chief of staff in early 1918. He strongly supported General John J. Pershing, the commander of the American Expeditionary Force in Europe, especially in the latter's determination to preserve his army as an independent fighting force. In the later stages of the war, Baker proved himself an able diplomat in dealing with his European counterparts in the military coalition. Finally he dealt competently with the difficult task of demobilizing the army after the armistice of November 1918.

Baker returned to his Cleveland law practice at the conclusion of the Wilson administration in March 1921 and remained an active, though increasingly conservative, figure in the DEMOCRATIC PARTY until his death.

BIBLIOGRAPHY

Beaver, Daniel R. *Newton D. Baker and the American War Effort, 1917–1919*. 1966.

Cramer, Clarence H. *Newton D. Baker: A Biography*. 1961.

Ferrell, Robert H. *Woodrow Wilson and World War I, 1917–1921*. 1985.

JOHN E. LITTLE

BAKER ACCORD (1989). A proposal by Secretary of State JAMES A. BAKER III in 1989 illustrates the persistence of the informal LEGISLATIVE VETO that permits Congress to control executive actions without having to pass a public law. The informal, nonstatutory character of this type of agreement between the two branches eliminates any constitutional challenge under INS V. CHADHA (1983), which invalidated the legislative veto.

After President George Bush took office in 1989, administration officials wanted Congress to appropriate humanitarian assistance to the contra rebels fighting the Marxist Sandinista government in Nicaragua. Baker understood that the IRAN-CONTRA AFFAIR had so soured relations between Congress and the President that it was unrealistic to expect legislators fully to trust administration promises that the money would be spent properly. Congress had experienced repeated problems during the administration of Ronald Reagan, when it had provided humanitarian funds to the contras only to discover later that the administration used some of the funds to provide weapons to the contras.

Secretary of State Baker decided on a compromise. If Congress agreed to appropriate $50 million for the contras, the administration would accept a procedure that kept some portion of that amount in reserve while

Congress decided whether the administration could keep its word. If the administration behaved properly, the withheld funds would be released on the approval of certain congressional committees and party leaders.

White House Counsel C. Boyden Gray objected that the Baker Accord would permit Congress to become involved in the administration of FOREIGN AFFAIRS and that it relied on what seemed to Gray a clear use of the forbidden legislative veto. Former federal judge Robert H. Bork regarded the Baker proposal as "even more objectionable" than the legislative veto at issue in *Chadha*, because the Bush administration had agreed to legislative control by committees rather than a one-house or two-house veto.

Despite this opposition, Baker (with the blessing of President Bush) proceeded with his idea. In a letter to Congress on 28 April 1989, he set forth the essentials of the Baker Accord. Humanitarian assistance would be given to the contras through 28 February 1990. This assistance, however, would not continue beyond 30 November 1989 without the approval of the Senate majority and minority leaders, the Speaker of the House, the House majority and minority leaders, and the relevant authorization and appropriations committees. Baker called the bipartisan accord "a unique agreement" between the branches that "in no way establishes any precedent for the Executive or the Legislative Branch regarding the authorization and appropriation process." After the administration convinced Congress of its good faith, the congressional committees and party leaders agreed on 30 November 1989 to release the balance of the money.

Chadha applies only to legislative vetoes included in bills that become law. As noted by a federal court in *Burton v. Baker* (1989), the Baker Accord was purely informal and nonstatutory and therefore outside the reach of *Chadha*. There are no legal hurdles to administration officials deciding to enter into informal arrangements that permit certain committees or leaders of Congress to share in administrative decisions.

BIBLIOGRAPHY

Felton, John. "Cush, Hill Agree to Provide Contras with New Aid." *Congressional Quarterly Weekly Report* (25 March 1989): 655–657.

Glennon, Michael J. "The Good Friday Accords: Legislative Veto by Another Name?" *American Journal of International Law* 83 (1989): 544–546.

LOUIS FISHER

BALLINGER-PINCHOT AFFAIR. The Ballinger-Pinchot scandal broke during the first year of William Howard Taft's presidency (1909–1913). It turned on a dispute between Richard Ballinger, Taft's Secretary of the Interior, and Ballinger's subordinate, Chief Forester Gifford Pinchot. Pinchot, an outstanding pioneer in the conservation movement, had first been appointed to his office by Taft's predecessor, Theodore Roosevelt, in whose administration the first major program for the conservation of natural resources had got under way. Roosevelt would come to regard conservation as the prize domestic achievement of his administration, and many of the gains in that regard were the result of the energy and imagination of Pinchot. Ballinger on the other hand, represented precisely the interests that Pinchot sought to restrain.

The conservation movement developed largely through the efforts of easterners who had reflected on the cruel wasting of forests, grasslands, and other depletable resources by entrepreneurs interested only in maximizing short-term profits. Westerners, who resented restraints placed on the profit opportunities available to them in the still rich wildernesses in the West, counted among the fiercer opponents of the movement. Taft, an easterner, generally sympathized with the conservationists. On taking office, he retained most of the conservationists appointed by Roosevelt, including Pinchot. But he was an inept administrator who was insensitive to the fine points of politics, especially the politics of group-interest rivalry.

The temperamentally conservative Taft never liked Pinchot. He thought him "a radical and a crank." He felt impelled to reappoint him because he recognized that to much of the public Pinchot symbolized the entire conservation cause. But in an effort to establish his independence of Roosevelt, his patron and predecessor, Taft replaced James Garfield, TR's distinguished Secretary of the Interior, with Ballinger, a decidedly undistinguished Seattle businessman, who in fact had some years before left his subordinate position in the DEPARTMENT OF THE INTERIOR because of policy differences with Pinchot.

Taft appears to have been eager to win support from westerners by appointing one of their own to that key Cabinet post, believing that Ballinger was reasonable on regulating profit-seeking ventures on pubic lands. But Taft failed to reckon with the fact that what was reasonable to westerners like Ballinger typically included the unimpaired right of businesses to make profits from public resources. As the governor of Ballinger's home state of Washington saw it, conservationists were enemies of progress; Pinchot in particular, he said, "had done more to retard the growth and development of the Northwest than any other man." Taft, typically, failed to grasp the issues at stake. Ballinger soon gave him an education.

First, he persuaded Taft that TR had illegally withdrawn millions of acres of land and hundreds of water-power sites. He acted promptly to restore those resources to use for profit. The Supreme Court would later uphold Roosevelt's view of the law, but Taft followed Ballinger's view. More troubling, Ballinger quickly acted to validate certain claims to Alaskan coal fields in which his own business associates had substantial interests and which former Interior Secretary Garfield had found to be tainted with fraud. When the Department's own investigator, Louis Glavis, protested the validation, Ballinger removed him from the case. Glavis contacted Pinchot, and the widely popular Pinchot went public through *Collier's Magazine*.

Taft did not trouble to look into the details of the case but acted precipitously in support of Ballinger. It was enough for him that Glavis and Pinchot were insubordinate and engaging in common muckraking behavior. He fired them. He did not expect the ensuing outcry. Congress launched public hearings on Glavis's charges that Ballinger had a conflict of interest in the Alaska case and that fraud was involved. The renowned attorney Louis Brandeis, acting as counsel for Glavis and for *Collier's*, was able to prove that the internal report on which President Taft claimed to have based his exoneration of Ballinger had been predated and that the President had in fact relied entirely on a preliminary report drafted by Ballinger himself.

The scandal was only one of several political calamities that befell William Howard Taft during his single term in office. The irony is that Taft genuinely favored conservationist objectives. Eventually persuaded that Ballinger did not share those objectives, Taft forced his resignation and appointed a Pinchot associate, Walter Fischer, to succeed him. He also wrested from Congress the power, denied to Roosevelt, to withdraw public lands from private use by EXECUTIVE ORDER; ultimately, Taft protected more land than Roosevelt had been able to. But the Ballinger-Pinchot affair tarred Taft as unfriendly to the conservation cause. As with several other issues that arose during his term, Taft proved unable to comprehend the nature of the contest among rival interests, while his misplaced loyalties and clumsy personal style further foiled his own intentions and crippled his administration.

BIBLIOGRAPHY

Abrams, Richard M. *The Burdens of Progress.* 1978.
Harbaugh, William H. *The Life and Times of Theodore Roosevelt.* 1975.
Hays, Samuel P. *Conservation and the Gospel of Efficiency.* 1959.

RICHARD M. ABRAMS

BANCO NACIONAL DE CUBA v. SABBATINO

376 U.S. 398 (1964). The *Sabbatino* case reaffirmed and established the ACT OF STATE DOCTRINE, giving it new vitality.

The Cuban government had nationalized sugar owned by U.S. interests without providing just compensation. Later, CUBA sought to sell the sugar on the U.S. market. When Banco Nacional de Cuba, the official bank of Cuba, sought to recover the proceeds of a sale of sugar, representatives of the original owners challenged the Cuban government's title to the sugar on the ground that it had been acquired in violation of international law. The lower courts denied the Cuban government's title but the Supreme Court reversed. Applying the act of state doctrine, the Supreme Court ruled that courts in the United States should give effect to the act of a foreign state within its territory, "in the absence of a treaty or other unambiguous agreement regarding controlling legal principles, even if the complaint alleges that the taking violates customary international law."

In an extended essay in its opinion, the Court found constitutional underpinnings for the act of state doctrine in a consideration of the SEPARATION OF POWERS, stating that there is a "basic choice regarding the competence and function of the Judiciary and the National Executive in ordering our relations with other members of the international community" and in making "decisions in the area of international relations." The Court declared the doctrine to be federal law binding on state courts. Implicitly, *Sabbatino* also affirmed the power of the courts to make foreign affairs law interstitially at least as in the case of the act of state doctrine, law for the special guidance of the courts.

Sabbatino and the act of state doctrine represent judicial deference to the executive branch, leaving certain private claims against foreign states to diplomatic resolution. This posture of judicial deference to the executive, however, has generally led courts to respond favorably to so-called Bernstein letters, indicating that the executive would have no objection if the court made an exception to the act of state doctrine in the particular case.

The result in *Sabbatino* was overruled by act of Congress in the second HICKENLOOPER AMENDMENT, which instructed the courts not to apply the act of state doctrine to foreign confiscations of property of U.S. nationals without just compensation, unless the President determined that application of the doctrine in a particular case is required by the national interest. However, the *Sabbatino* case established the act of state doctrine generally, and the doctrine remains in full effect (subject to some exceptions developed by the courts), and indeed has legislative support, for cases in which the second Hickenlooper Amendment does not apply.

[*See also* INTERNATIONAL LAW, PRESIDENT AND.]

BIBLIOGRAPHY

Mooney, Eugene F. *Foreign Seizures: Sabbatino and the Act of State Doctrine.* 1967.

LOUIS HENKIN

BANK HOLIDAY OF 1933.

The roots of the bank holiday of 1933 lay in the ramshackle structure of American banking. Even in the prosperous 1920s, bank failures occurred at a high rate. The stock market crash of October 1929 aggravated the situation by devaluing bank assets while undercutting depositor confidence. By the time of President Franklin D. Roosevelt's inauguration on 4 March 1933, more than half the states (including the nation's financial center, New York) had closed their banks.

Lame-duck President Herbert Hoover and President-elect Roosevelt had failed to agree on action to deal with the crisis because of Hoover's efforts to commit Roosevelt to support the gold standard, sound money, and the balanced budget. Roosevelt's optimistic reassurance in his inaugural address that "the only thing we have to fear is fear itself" had a tremendous psychological impact. On 5 March, he called Congress into special session and issued an EXECUTIVE ORDER imposing a national bank holiday and halting transactions in gold. When Congress met on 9 March Roosevelt submitted a plan, which had been prepared by Treasury Department officials during the Hoover administration, to extend emergency assistance to enable the sounder banks to reopen. Swift approval by the lawmakers ended the immediate crisis by restoring public confidence. To promote the future stability of the banking system, Congress adopted the Glass-Steagall Banking Act in June 1933. The act strengthened the power of the Federal Reserve over member banks and separated commercial and investment banking. Roosevelt was personally doubtful about the act's most important stabilizer—federal deposit insurance—but he gave way to Congress's demand for its inclusion. In the years that followed, the number of bank failures declined sharply.

BIBLIOGRAPHY

Badger, Anthony J. *The New Deal: The Depression Years, 1933–40.* 1989.

Burns, Helen M. *The American Banking Community and New Deal Banking Reforms, 1933–1935.* 1974.
Kennedy, Susan E. *The Banking Crisis of 1933.* 1973.

JOHN BRAEMAN

BANK OF THE UNITED STATES.

ALEXANDER HAMILTON, first Secretary of the Treasury under President George Washington, proposed the creation of a national bank as part of a fiscal program to place the new nation on a firm financial footing.

He envisioned a central-banking system created by Congress, with a parent bank in Philadelphia and branch banks in all the major cities of the nation. The bank would be chartered for twenty years; four-fifths of its capital stock would be purchased by private investors and one-fifth by the United States government, which would control one-fifth of the bank's board. The bank would act as a depository for government funds and serve as an agent for the collection of taxes; it could also issue notes, redeemable in specie and acceptable in the payment of taxes.

The bill creating this central banking system passed Congress in 1791, but strict constructionists argued that it was unconstitutional. Washington asked for written opinions from Thomas Jefferson, his Secretary of State, who judged the enactment of a bank bill an exercise of power unwarranted by the Constitution, and from Hamilton, who argued that the "necessary and proper" clause of the Constitution justified the legislation. Agreeing with Hamilton, Washington signed the bill.

The Bank improved the credit and currency of the nation, but continuing political opposition by strict constructionists, strengthened by opposition from state-chartered banks, resulted in the failure of the effort to recharter the bank in 1811. The WAR OF 1812, however, demonstrated the importance of the Bank to the nation. Consequently, a new national bank bill was passed and signed into law by President James Madison in 1816. This Second Bank of the United States was similar to the first, except that the capital stock was increased and the Bank would pay the government a bonus.

When President Andrew Jackson took office in 1829, he expressed reservations about the Bank. HENRY CLAY, believing he could defeat Jackson in the next election on the bank issue, persuaded the Bank to apply early for an extension of its charter. The recharter bill passed Congress, but Jackson vetoed it, incensed in part by the Bank's attempt to influence elections. The election of 1832 was largely fought over this issue, and Jackson resoundingly defeated Clay.

The President then removed the government's deposits and placed them in state ("pet") banks. The operation of the Bank was investigated, and the House passed resolutions on 4 April 1834, against renewing the charter. The Bank of the United States went out of existence in 1836.

BIBLIOGRAPHY

Catterall, Ralph C. H. *The Second Bank of the United States.* 1903.
Hammond, Bray. *Banks and Politics in America from the Revolution to the Civil War.* 1957.

ROBERT V. REMINI

BARBARY WAR. The Barbary War (1815–1816) was the sequel to the War with Tripoli of 1801–1805. The Barbary powers—Algiers, Morocco, Tunis, and Tripoli—resumed their piracy of American ships, and President James Madison asked for a DECLARATION OF WAR. Congress authorized military action in 1815. Madison thereupon dispatched two squadrons to the region, the first led by Stephen Decatur, the hero of the Tripolitan conflict. Decatur captured two Algerian ships and blockaded Algiers. He then planned to demolish the port and destroy the rest of the Algerian fleet unless the dey of Algiers returned the American sailors he had enslaved, paid reparations for an American ship captured in 1812, and abolished the bribes heretofore extracted from the United States as protection money against Algerian piracy. When the dey acceded to these demands in a treaty, Decatur proceeded to Tunis and Tripoli and procured similar agreements.

A year later the dey attempted to repudiate Decatur's treaty, refusing to sign it after it had been ratified by the United States Senate. In response, American forces prepared to attack Algiers by night and destroy the Algerian military threat once and for all. A French frigate warned the dey beforehand, however, and the attack was called off.

When President Madison learned of the dey's defiance, he issued an ultimatum: "The United States, whilst they wish for war with no nation, will buy peace with none. It is a principle incorporated into the settled policy of America, that as peace is better than war, war is better than tribute." The dey then relented. In fact, he had little choice. Great Britain had reduced his defenses to rubble in a bombardment a few months earlier. Decatur's treaty thus went into effect, and for the most part, America's problems with the Barbary powers came to an end.

The Barbary War illustrates the different models of EXECUTIVE POWER that had already arisen in America during the early national period. A stickler for constitutional procedures, President Madison sought congressional sanction before taking any action in the Mediterranean. By contrast, President Thomas Jefferson had launched his earlier response to Tripoli without congressional authorization, sending in warships with orders to blockade the ports of the offending powers and to sink their ships "wherever you shall find them." Only after an American warship had actually captured a Tripolitan vessel did Jefferson seek congressional permission for further measures. The differing interpretations of executive power displayed during the two conflicts have continued to resurface in debates over the presidency's role in foreign affairs.

BIBLIOGRAPHY

Allen, Gardner. *Our Navy and the Barbary Corsairs.* 1905.
Irwin, Ray W. *The Diplomatic Relations of the United States with the Barbary Powers, 1776–1816.* 1931.

JOHN G. WEST, JR.

BARKLEY, ALBEN W. (1877–1956), thirty-fifth Vice President of the United States (1949–1953). Few people who never served as nor were nominated to run for President were associated for so long with that office as Alben W. Barkley. By the time Barkley unsuccessfully sought the Democratic presidential nomination in 1952, he had figured prominently in presidential government and politics for more than a quarter century.

Born on 24 November 1877 in Graves County, Kentucky, Barkley entered the House of Representatives on 4 March 1913, the day Woodrow Wilson became President. Politically and temperamentally suited to supporting the activist leadership of progressive Presidents, Barkley revered Wilson. Yet his most important service came during the terms of Wilson's two Democratic successors, Franklin D. Roosevelt and Harry S. Truman. Elected to the Senate in 1926, Barkley became majority leader in 1937 in a 38 to 37 vote over Sen. Byron Patton (Pat) Harrison. Although Barkley championed Roosevelt's domestic and foreign policy, the most memorable moment of his nine and one-half years as majority leader came when he chastised the President on the Senator floor in early 1944. Irate at Roosevelt's strongly worded veto of a revenue measure, Barkley denounced the President, called for the Senate to override his veto (it did) and resigned as majority leader (only to be reelected unanimously the following day).

Barkley long figured in Democratic presidential politics, as a delegate to Democratic conventions from

1920 to 1952, as permanent chairman in 1940 and 1944, as keynoter in 1932, 1936, and 1948, and as a possible vice-presidential candidate from 1928 on. He did not secure that nomination until 1948, and only then after Truman's first choice, Justice William O. Douglas, elected to remain on the Supreme Court rather than join Truman in what appeared a quixotic quest. Although Barkley's age (seventy) and political characteristics—he and Truman came from border states and the same wing of the party—worked against his vice presidential prospects, his upbeat and effective keynote speech advanced his campaign. Faced with rising sentiment for Barkley and lacking an alternative, Truman agreed to run with him. Barkley became the first major party candidate to travel widely by plane, using his DC-3 to cover 150,000 miles in thirty-six states.

Barkley was the oldest man ever elected Vice President. Roosevelt had ignored Truman during the latter's brief tenure as Vice President. Perhaps due to that experience and to his close relationship with Barkley, Truman took steps to include Barkley in presidential affairs. He persuaded Congress to make the Vice President a statutory member of the NATIONAL SECURITY COUNCIL. In that capacity, Barkley participated in deliberations over the KOREAN WAR and the removal of General Douglas MacArthur. Barkley also met with the CABINET, attended weekly legislative conferences with Truman, and performed the constitutional role of presiding over the Senate. Truman ordered that a vice-presidential seal and flag be designed and was generous in his public praise of Barkley. Yet significantly the portion of Barkley's autobiography on his vice-presidential years focuses almost entirely on his courtship of his second wife, not on substantive contributions as Vice President. The word "Veep" was first used in reference to Barkley, a shorthand developed due to his grandson's inability to pronounce his full title.

Barkley had deferred his presidential ambitions, blocked for much of his career by Roosevelt and by the unexpected ascendance of Truman. After Truman decided not to run in 1952, Barkley, then nearly seventy-five, declared his availability, and when Gov. ADLAI E. STEVENSON (1900–1965) of Illinois, Barkley's distant cousin, initially refused to run, Barkley became the candidate of the administration and Democratic legislative leaders. He appeared well-positioned to compete for the nomination until he suffered a series of setbacks when the convention opened. The announcement that Truman backed Barkley created a backlash among delegates who thought the party's nominee needed to distance himself from the unpop-

ular President. At the same time, the draft-Stevenson movement gained momentum. Labor leaders, notwithstanding their long association with Barkley, announced they would not support him due to his age. Stunned, Barkley withdrew from the race. His address to the 1952 convention was framed by ovations that exceeded thirty minutes. The emotional response rekindled some interest in a Barkley candidacy and indeed friends nominated him. By then, his time had passed and he could not compete with the enthusiastic support building for Stevenson.

Barkley was reelected to the Senate in 1954. He died on 30 April 1956 in Lexington, Virginia, when he collapsed while delivering a speech to a mock political convention at Washington and Lee University.

BIBLIOGRAPHY

Barkley, Alben W. *That Reminds Me—The Autobiography of the Veep.* 1954.

Claussen, E. Neal. "Alben Barkley's Rhetorical Victory in 1948." *Southern Speech Communication Journal* 45 (Fall 1979): 79–92.

Davis, Polly Ann. *Alben W. Barkley: Senate Majority Leader and Vice President.* 1979.

Libbey, James K. *Dear Alben: Mr. Barkley of Kentucky.* 1979.

Wallace, H. Lew. "Alben Barkley and the Democratic Convention of 1948." *Filson Club History Quarterly* 55 (July 1981): 231–252.

JOEL K. GOLDSTEIN

BARUCH, BERNARD (1870–1965), financier. The American press in the 1940s and 1950s frequently dubbed Bernard Baruch an adviser to Presidents, but he freely conceded that Presidents usually did not heed his advice.

Woodrow Wilson, however, sought Baruch's financial contribution for the campaign of 1912 and followed his advice on economic matters. Wilson appointed Baruch to the Council of National Defense in 1916 and the War Industries Board (WIB) in 1917, making him the chairperson of the WIB in 1918. Baruch made himself a czar of American industry, and Wilson took him to the Paris Peace Conference of 1919 as one of his economic advisers. Baruch's performances in 1918–1919 sealed his reputation as an economic sage.

In the 1920s Baruch advised farm organizations, the press, and numerous Democratic Senators on economic problems involving agricultural overproduction and foreign debts. But, as a Democrat, he was unwelcome in Republican White Houses until Herbert Hoover consulted him about the RECONSTRUCTION FINANCE CORPORATION in 1932. In 1932, he sat on the fence until Franklin D. Roosevelt won the party's nomination; then he contributed thousands of dollars to the campaign and his associate, Hugh Johnson, to Roosevelt's BRAIN TRUST.

Many people believed that Baruch heavily influenced the early NEW DEAL because two former aides, Johnson and George Peek, ran the National Recovery Administration and Agricultural Adjustment Administration respectively. In truth, Baruch had mixed feelings concerning the New Deal—approving its pump priming as justified by the depression but rejecting its welfare and redistributive measures such as the undistributed profits tax. Roosevelt, who recognized Baruch's influence in Washington, sought to avoid confrontations with him. Nevertheless, Baruch and Roosevelt remained friendly adversaries. During WORLD WAR II, Baruch became the "Park Bench Statesman" of Lafayette Park because Roosevelt refused to use his administrative experiences from WORLD WAR I.

President Harry S. Truman appointed Baruch the American representative at the UNITED NATIONS Atomic Energy Commission to present the Baruch plan on international atomic energy development as a sop to public and congressional opinion. But Truman considered him something of a troublemaker. He rejected Baruch's advice on price stabilization during the KOREAN WAR. Baruch was closer to Dwight D. Eisenhower, the only Republican he backed for the presidency, and Eisenhower actually solicited some of Baruch's economic advice; but Baruch's increasing advocacy of statist controls upon inflation clashed with Eisenhower's inclination to curb inflation by manipulating market forces. Not wanting Baruch to endorse Richard M. Nixon, in 1960 John F. Kennedy sent the economist John Kenneth Galbraith to solicit the ninety-year-old Baruch's advice principally because political lore had it that it was safer politically to assuage Baruch than to antagonize him. It was a rule that even Lyndon Baines Johnson followed—thereby making him the seventh President Baruch had "advised."

BIBLIOGRAPHY

Schwarz, Jordan A. *The Speculator: Bernard M. Baruch in Washington, 1917–1965.* 1981.

JORDAN A. SCHWARZ

BATES, EDWARD (1793–1869), Attorney General. Born in Virginia but a resident of St. Louis, Missouri, from 1814 on, Edward Bates became a lawyer and a dedicated Whig politician. He joined the KNOW-NOTHING (AMERICAN) PARTY when the American party system began to collapse in 1854. He can be characterized as a reluctant Republican—not until 1860 did Bates affirm publicly, "I am opposed to the extension of SLAVERY." Nevertheless, he was a major contender for the Party's presidential nomination the same year. He gained 48 votes on the first ballot at the convention in Chicago, but never got nearer the 233 necessary to gain nomination. He endorsed Abraham Lincoln but did not campaign actively.

In keeping with his policy of recruiting the strongest men for his Cabinet, Lincoln chose his political rival Bates as Attorney General. The Missourian took over modest offices occupying a wing of the Treasury building and containing only an assistant secretary, six clerks, and a black laborer. In August Congress increased the size and authority of Bates's domain, which also included federal district courts, U.S. attorneys' offices, and marshals' offices across the country. His son Richard served as a clerk in Bates's office.

Bates was arguably the most conservative member of Lincoln's Cabinet. Though he loyally supported all important administration measures from the provisioning of Fort Sumter to emancipation and the employment of black soldiers, Bates hated RADICAL REPUBLICANS and retained his Know-Nothing dislike of im- migrants, especially German Americans. None of his opinions rendered as the President's legal adviser was of great import.

Bates suffered a stroke in May 1864 and resigned in November to be replaced by James Speed, the brother of an old friend of Lincoln's. Bates was feeling old and irrelevant. "I belong to no party," he said. "When the WHIG PARTY committed suicide, . . . I died with it."

BIBLIOGRAPHY

Beale, Howard K. ed. *The Diary of Edward Bates, 1859–1866* Vol. IV of the Annual Report of the American Historical Association for the Year 1930. 1933.

Cain, Marvin R. *Lincoln's Attorney General Edward Bates of Missouri.* 1965.

MARK E. NEELY, JR.

BAY OF PIGS INVASION. The unsuccessful April 1961 invasion of CUBA at Playa Girón by a band of fourteen hundred Cuban exiles trained by the CENTRAL INTELLIGENCE AGENCY (CIA) represented the first major foreign policy setback of the administration of John F. Kennedy. The origins of this catastrophe lay in the determination of the Eisenhower administration to contain communism in the Western Hemisphere. In 1954, the CIA had undermined the leftist government of President Jacobo Arbenz in Guatemala on the grounds that it was dominated by communist influence.

The triumph of the revolutionary guerrilla fighters led by Fidel Castro over the U.S.-supported government of Fulgencio Batista in Cuba in 1959 constituted a new challenge to U.S. policy. Determined to deny Castro's revolutionary nationalism in a country that held $3 billion in U.S. investments and that was widely believed to be thoroughly Americanized, the Eisenhower administration initiated planning for Castro's overthrow even as the first U.S. ambassador to revolutionary Cuba, Philip Bonsal, tried to adjust U.S. policy to deal with a government committed to the "de-Americanization" of the island, its politics, economy, society, and culture.

One persistent myth about the Bay of Pigs invasion holds that Kennedy was trapped into supporting the effort by the force of events. In reality, Kennedy, who took a hard-line position on Cuba in the 1960 election, had resolved to get rid of Castro even as he called for a "peaceful revolution" in Latin America and committed the United States to the ALLIANCE FOR PROGRESS, a far-reaching U.S. and Latin American commitment to democracy, economic development, and social progress. As Kennedy touted the goals of the Alliance, high-level planning for the invasion, code-named Operation Zapata, was well under way in Washington, Miami, and Central America. Anti-Castro political leaders in the United States who wanted to emulate Castro's guerrilla success by dispatching the invaders into the eastern portion of the island were intimidated by U.S. officials and especially by CIA operatives. Naively, the Cubans retained a faith that Kennedy would not let the invasion fail.

The invasion force departed from Puerto Cabezas, Nicaragua, on 17 April 1961, landing at Playa Girón, a sparsely populated region on Cuba's south coast. A raid by B-26s on 15 April failed to knock out Castro's air force. As Castro's forces isolated the beleaguered invaders, his planes sank one of the supply ships. A second air strike by the invaders was called off. Although Kennedy had publicly stated that no U.S. personnel would be involved in the invasion, he did authorize a third strike of B-26s, this one to be manned by U.S. pilots, but Castro's planes shot them down. During the fighting, 114 of the invaders died and 1,189 were captured.

Only a major invasion could have succeeded against Castro's forces. Kennedy publicly took responsibility for the failure but privately resolved to bring down the Cuban leader through COVERT OPERATIONS, propaganda, diplomatic pressures, and economic retaliation. Among the tactics considered were the so-called Operation Mongoose, a plan for raids against Cuba, and CIA-hatched assassination plots against Castro (of

which Kennedy may not have known). In meetings of the ORGANIZATION OF AMERICAN STATES, the United States used its political and economic influence to isolate Cuba in the hemisphere and to impose an economic boycott of the island.

Castro's reputation among the Latin American left did not diminish. More important, Castro was able to use the Bay of Pigs to persuade the U.S.S.R. to step up its economic support for the revolution and to supply military support for its defense. The CUBAN MISSILE CRISIS of October 1962 stemmed directly from the failure of the Bay of Pigs; had Kennedy done nothing or done everything necessary to get rid of Castro, it was sometimes said, Nikita Khrushchev would have understood and would probably not have committed the U.S.S.R. to Cuba's defense by sending offensive nuclear weapons to the island.

In the last few months of his life, Kennedy was quietly responding to Cuban overtures for an easing of the tension. Earlier in 1963, Kennedy had concluded that the numerous raids against Cuba by exiles were accomplishing little. But even as private talks were under way, Kennedy still talked menacingly about Cuba and Castro. A French correspondent, Jean Daniel, carried a conciliatory message to Castro, and was talking with Castro on 22 November 1963 when news of Kennedy's death arrived in Havana. Because the putative assassin, LEE HARVEY OSWALD, had been active in the Fair Play for Cuba movement, Castro correctly anticipated that some North Americans would blame him for Kennedy's assassination, even though several investigations concluded that the Cuban leader played no part in the shooting.

In the immediate aftermath of the Bay of Pigs, Kennedy blamed his own stupidity for the disaster. Yet his obsession with removing Castro, his preoccupation with winning a COLD WAR victory, his understandable apprehension that a canceled invasion would have long-standing political repercussions, and, most critical, the poor planning by the CIA explain the administration's most embarrassing foreign policy venture. Skeptics participated in the critical meetings on the operation but hesitated to speak up for fear of losing favor with a President ill disposed to tolerate dissent in a moment of action [see GROUPTHINK]. The argument that direct U.S. support would have achieved victory, however, is flawed. Castro was unpopular, undoubtedly, but he had already marshaled an army and a militia capable of withstanding anything short of a massive invasion. Castro had studied the Guatemalan operation of 1954, where the United States brought down a leftist government by supporting a Guatemalan revolutionary movement. There was no need to commit U.S. troops. He correctly sensed that no U.S. President would send U.S. troops if Cuban exiles failed to bring down the Cuban revolution. The cost in U.S. lives would have been too great. As an aide to ADLAI E. STEVENSON (1900–1965) told Kennedy, "Mr. President, it could have been worse. . . . It might have succeeded."

BIBLIOGRAPHY

Halperin, Maurice. *The Rise and Decline of Fidel Castro.* 1972.
Higgins, Trumbell. *The Perfect Failure.* 1987.
Morley, Morris. *Imperial State and Revolution: The United States and Revolution, 1952–1987.* 1987.
Operation Zapata: The Ultrasensitive Report and Testimony of the Board of Inquiry on the Bay of Pigs. 1981.
Welch, Richard E., Jr. *Response to Revolution: The United States and the Cuban Revolution, 1959–1961.* 1985.
Wyden, Peter. *Bay of Pigs.* 1979.

LESTER D. LANGLEY

BELL, JOHN (1796–1869), Speaker of the House, Senator, and Constitutional Union Party presidential nominee in 1860. A Tennessee lawyer, Bell became a U.S. Congressman in 1827 and served for fourteen years, including a term as Speaker from 1834 to 1835. Bell was Secretary of War for a brief period under Presidents William Henry Harrison and John Tyler. In 1847 he won election to the U.S. Senate for the first of three terms; there he became a leader of Tennessee's Whigs and contested many battles against James K. Polk and other Democrats.

Bell's congressional career was notable for its moderation amid the deepening sectional crisis. During the NULLIFICATION crisis, he cautiously supported Jackson's FORCE BILL. In 1836, when southern congressmen proposed a gag rule to table abolitionist petitions without discussion [see ABOLITIONISM], Bell withheld his support and did not vote; the next year he argued against the rule's readoption and in 1838 voted against it. In the 1840s and 1850s, when the issue of SLAVERY in the territories was dominant, Bell frequently departed from orthodox southern positions. Although Bell was a large slaveholder, he supported President Zachary Taylor's proposal to admit California as a state without requiring it to pass through a territorial stage. When the COMPROMISE OF 1850 came to a vote, Bell supported most of its elements and even expressed a willingness to abolish slavery in the District of Columbia, with hopes that it would quiet sectional strife. While most southerners in Congress fought tenaciously for the KANSAS-NEBRASKA ACT, he opposed it as an unwise stimulus to divisive issues and became the only south-

ern Whig in the Senate to vote against it. In 1858 he defied numerous critics in Tennessee and opposed Kansas's admission to the Union under the proslavery Lecompton Constitution.

Bell had pondered the formation of a Union party composed of moderate voters from both North and South as early as 1851, and later the idea of an alliance between moderate Republicans and southern Whigs did not seem impossible to him. In 1860, when sectional disputes clearly were on the verge of destroying the Union, more than two dozen old Whigs or American party leaders from the upper South called for the formation of a new party to save the Union. In May delegates from twenty-three states met in Baltimore to form the Constitutional Union Party and nominate Bell with Edward Everett of Massachusetts as his running mate.

Supporters of the Constitutional Union Party organized colorful demonstrations featuring noisy "Bell ringers" while their candidate, following tradition, stayed close to home and made few statements. The desire somehow to preserve the Union was fairly widespread, but to most voters an appeal to the Union and the Constitution held no solution to controversies over slavery. Others who shared Bell's hopes feared that the efforts of his party were futile.

On election day Bell did well only in the upper South, where his strength in traditionally Whig districts brought victory in Virginia, Kentucky, and Tennessee. Bell won 13 percent of the vote in Massachusetts but less than 5 percent in the free states as a whole, and in the lower South he was overwhelmed by JOHN BRECKINRIDGE, candidate of the Southern Rights Democrats. The existence of fusion arrangements among parties in some states makes it impossible to determine Bell's vote total precisely, but estimates approach 600,000 votes, or nearly 13 percent of the electorate.

The 1860 campaign ended John Bell's public career. Although he disapproved of SECESSION, he advised Tennesseans to ally with the Confederacy if the federal government attempted to coerce the seceded states. After the CIVIL WAR began he looked on with sadness and, according to family tradition, died a heartbroken man in 1869.

BIBLIOGRAPHY

Crofts, Daniel. *Reluctant Confederates.* 1989.
Parks, Joseph Howard. *John Bell of Tennessee.* 1950.
Potter, David M. *The Impending Crisis, 1848–1861.* 1976.

PAUL D. ESCOTT

BENEFITS, PRESIDENTIAL. In addition to a salary of $200,000 per year, the President of the

United States and his family are eligible for benefits that confer security and ease the burdens of office. Of these benefits, only one is monetary: an annual, taxable allowance of $50,000. There are no constraints on spending this allowance, other than that it be used for expenses.

The WHITE HOUSE is the official residence of the President. The second-floor family quarters are largely furnished, though each First Family brings its personal touches to these rooms. The family is required to provide the food eaten by its members and personal guests, as well as to pay for services such as personal long-distance telephone calls and laundry. Most of the WHITE HOUSE STAFF is employed by the government. The President must pay the salary of any personal service staff, however. The White House itself and the grounds are often changed, to varying degrees, to fit the needs and desires of the incumbent. In addition to the major restoration and remodeling of 1952, there have been additions such as a swimming pool, tennis courts, a movie theater, a putting green, a horseshoe pit, and, within weeks of Bill Clinton's taking office, a jogging track, which was privately funded.

Most First Families have considered the White House a constraining environment in which to live, despite its comfort. Because the White House is a public building and a workplace, the President's family has little privacy, unlike the families of most heads of government. Security considerations severely restrict the movements of the President and all members of the First Family outside the White House.

Personal security for the President and his family is provided by the U.S. SECRET SERVICE. The size of the detail depends on whether the President is traveling or in Washington.

CAMP DAVID, a naval facility in the Catoctin Mountains of Maryland, has served several Presidents as a rustic retreat. The U.S. Marine Corps provides security and the Navy Corps of Engineers administers, maintains, and services the facility. Camp David has several guest cabins, making it possible to use the site for meetings. The level of use has varied from administration to administration.

The Secret Service and the General Services Administration are responsible for altering the President's personal home site(s) to make it, or them, acceptable in terms of security and communication access. Whenever possible, these alterations are not permanent, and the homes are returned to to their previous condition when the President leaves office.

The President is eligible to enroll in the contributory Federal Employees Health Benefits program. However, a personal physician, selected by the President, maintains an office in the White House. The White House medical office is staffed by military medical personnel, and the President and the immediate family are eligible for medical care in military hospitals, a benefit available to the President as COMMANDER IN CHIEF of the armed forces.

The communication system available to the President is one of the most sophisticated in the world. Regardless of location, the President can be in voice communication with almost anywhere in the world within a matter of seconds.

The President travels principally by automobile, airplane, and helicopter. Several presidential limousines have been customized for security and comfort and are used for short local trips. Often when the President travels, one of the limousines is flown to the destination for his ground transportation.

The President is transported by helicopter to and from Camp David and Andrews Air Force Base just outside Washington, D.C. (Rarely is a motorcade used for these purposes). The helicopter in which the President flies is designated Marine One.

Air Force One is the radio designation given to any aircraft on which the President flies. Generally, Air Force One is either of two Boeing 747 aircraft that in 1990 replaced the 707s. These PRESIDENTIAL AIRCRAFT are supported by the 89th Military Airlift Wing and are based at Andrews Air Force Base. Air Force One is equipped with state-of-the-art electronics for operation and communications and incorporates sophisticated safeguards against attack. On board are the President's quarters, two galleys, several bathrooms, and seating and accommodations for a crew of twenty-three and seventy passengers. The plane's office facilities include conference rooms, computers, copy machines, and banks of communications equipment.

Under statute, the President has $100,000 available to him for travel expenses. In reality, that amount comes nowhere near answering the costs of Presidential travel. Most of the vehicle-related expenses are covered in the budgets of the agencies responsible for maintaining and operating the vehicles. The actual total cost of the support of the President of the United States is probably not calculable. Although the annual cost of operating the White House physical plant can be determined by reading the U.S. government budget, there are many hidden costs. The military services, the National Park Service, and the General Services Administration bear much of the responsibility and costs for the support provided to the White House. The Navy and the Marine Corps do not publish the costs of maintaining and operating Camp

David, largely because of the security involved. Most of the other security cots are borne by the DEPARTMENT OF THE TREASURY, the parent agency of the Secret Service.

BIBLIOGRAPHY

Aikman, Lonnelle. *The Living White House.* 1991.
Boyd, Betty. *Inside the White House.* 1992.
Ter Horst, J. F., and Ralph Albertazzie. *The Flying White House.* 1979.

SHARON STIVER GRESSLE

BENEFITS TO FORMER PRESIDENTS. To what extent should a former President be required to earn a living after having served in the highest office in the nation? Are there occupations or activities that would be considered inappropriate or unseemly for a former President of the United States? For decades these questions were intermittently raised as former Presidents, who did not have significant personal wealth, left office with no pension provision and the necessity of "earning" a living.

Congress addressed these questions in 1873 when it voted to increase the presidential salary from $25,000 to $50,000. The support for the increase reflected the opinion that there should be sufficient financial provision while in office to preclude the necessity of seeking money-making pursuits after serving as President. Several of the nineteenth-century former Presidents died in various stages of poverty.

The Former Presidents Act of 1958 (72 Stat. 838) established a systematic pension payment for former Presidents, as well as other benefits. As amended, the provisions now require that each former President be paid an annual taxable pension, which is equal to the salary rate paid at Executive level I (Cabinet-level positions) of the executive salary schedule. Widows of Presidents or former Presidents are paid a pension of $20,000 per annum.

For the purposes of the act, a former President is defined as "an individual who shall have held the office of President of the United States, whose service in such office shall have been terminated other than by removal pursuant to section 4 Article II, of the Constitution" (3 U.S.C. 102, note). Thus, although he left office by resigning, Richard M. Nixon remained eligible for all benefits available to former Presidents.

A former President is eligible to receive funds under the Presidential Transitions Effectiveness Act of 1988 (102 Stat. 985). Up to $1.5 million may be appropriated for the use of the outgoing President and Vice President. There are provisions for a diminution of that amount if the outgoing Vice President is the newly elected President. Unused funds are to be returned to the general treasury. The General Services Administration (GSA) is authorized to provide the President with adequate services and facilities to be available from one month prior to, and for a period of six months from the date of, the expiration of the term of office.

The GSA in addition to administering the Former Presidents Act pension provisions is authorized to provide the former President with staff. The annual compensation for such staff may not exceed $150,000 during the initial thirty-month period and thereafter, the aggregate staff compensation is limited to $96,000 per annum. A former President may supplement staff hire and compensation through nonfederal funds. The statute also requires that GSA shall provide for each former President furnished office space at a location within the United States chosen by the former President.

As a general rule, travel funds are available through the GSA support activities for the former President and no more than two staff members. The GSA provides to the oversight committees, upon request, information on those travel expenses.

The former Presidents and the surviving spouse may use the franking privilege. Nonpolitical mail may be sent within the United States, its territories, and possessions. To some extent nonpolitical mail may also be sent internationally at no fee.

Former Presidents, their spouses, widows, and minor children hold the status of secretarial designees with regard to eligibility for care in military service health facilities. They receive care on a minimally reimbursable basis. These same individuals are eligible to enroll in and contribute to the group health plans available to federal employees.

SECRET SERVICE protection is available to former Presidents and to their families. Originally, in 1962, it was available to former Presidents only for a period of six months. In 1963 the Secret Service was authorized to protect the widow and minor children of President John F. Kennedy. Since 1965, Secret Service protection has been extended to include lifetime protection for former Presidents and their spouses. Surviving spouses are covered until remarriage and minor children receive protection until age sixteen. Congress determined, in 1984, that former Presidents or their dependents should be allowed to decline protective services. Former President and Mrs. Richard M. Nixon declined the Secret Service protection pursuant to that statute.

PRESIDENTIAL LIBRARIES serve as the depositories for the papers and historical materials related to specific presidencies. These institutions are becoming important centers for scholarly research. Presidential libraries, while planned, developed, and constructed with private funds, must meet certain federal guidelines. The subsequent maintenance of the libraries is a federal responsibility.

BIBLIOGRAPHY

Hecht, Marie B. *Beyond the Presidency.* 1976.

U.S. House of Representatives. Committee on the Judiciary. *Salaries of Executive, Judicial, and Legislative Officers.* 42d Cong., 3d Sess. 1873. H. Rep. No. 59.

U.S. House of Representatives. Committee on Post Office and Civil Service. *Retirement, Staff Assistants, and Mailing Privileges for Former Presidents and Annuities for Widows of Former Presidents.* 85th Cong., 2d sess. 1958. H. Rept. 2200.

U.S. Senate. Committee on the Judiciary. *Providing Continuing Authority for the Protection of Former Presidents.* 89th Cong., 1st sess. 1965. S. Rept. 89–611.

U.S. Senate. Subcommittees of the Committee on Appropriations and Committee on Governmental Affairs. *Cost of Former Presidents to U.S. Taxpayers.* 96th Cong., 1st sess. 1980. Hearings.

SHARON STIVER GRESSLE

BERLIN CRISIS (1961). Long before the Berlin crisis of 1961 that city had become symbolic of a divided, yet stabilized Europe during the COLD WAR. For that reason the Western allies were determined to maintain their presence, based on international agreement, in the isolated city. Soviet leader Nikita Khrushchev initiated a crisis over Berlin when, in late 1958, he threatened unilaterally to change the city's status. Sen. John F. Kennedy exclaimed in an interview in December 1959: "They're fighting for New York and Paris when they struggle for Berlin." As President in March 1961, Kennedy responded to the ongoing Soviet threat by seeking the advice of former Secretary of State DEAN ACHESON. Acheson reaffirmed the new President's fears. Any change in the status of Berlin, he warned, would reshape the global alignment of power. Acheson recommended a huge increase in the military budget. In Vienna, on 4 June, Khrushchev warned Kennedy that unless the Western powers accepted the conversion of West Berlin into a free city, the U.S.S.R. would assign control of the access routes to the East German government. Kennedy retorted that the Western powers intended to maintain their positions in West Berlin even at the risk of war. At a NATO meeting on 4 August 1961, the allies agreed to defend West Berlin's freedom and viability with force.

Anticipating a crisis, the East German government, in July, began to restrict the exodus of East Germans into West Berlin. The resulting anxiety sent a flood of East Germans across the line, including hundreds of

professionals. During the first twelve days of August forty-seven thousand East Germans fled to the West. On the night of 12 August the Communists sealed the border between East and West Berlin. Beginning with a barricade of barbed wire, they eventually divided the city totally with a wall. Germans watched in despair. Western governments complained that the barricade broke the four-power agreement on Berlin but shrank from the risk of initiating a war. In a gesture of defiance President Kennedy sent a U.S. battle group from Mannheim down the autobahn through the East German checkpoints into West Berlin. The Berlin crisis continued until October 1961 when Khrushchev announced that he would withdraw his 31 December deadline if the Western powers revealed a willingness to negotiate. The Berlin crisis of 1961 died like those that preceded it, with the Soviets reluctant to fight for change in Berlin's status and the Western powers unwilling to compromise their commitment to West Berlin's freedom. For the Soviets the Berlin Wall, by halting the drain on East Germany, had in large measure resolved the Berlin question.

BIBLIOGRAPHY

Schlesinger, Arthur M., Jr. *A Thousand Days: John F. Kennedy in the White House.* 1965.

Sorenson, Theodore C. *Kennedy.* 1965.

Walton, Richard J. *Cold War and Counterrevolution: The Foreign Policy of John F. Kennedy.* 1972.

NORMAN A. GRAEBNER

BIDDLE, FRANCIS (1896–1968), Solicitor General, Attorney General. A progressive aristocrat, Francis Beverly Biddle attended Harvard Law School and from 1911 to 1912 served as law clerk to Justice Oliver Wendell Holmes. After nearly two decades in private practice and a stint as an assistant U.S. attorney, he went to Washington, D.C., in 1934 and held several NEW DEAL positions. President Franklin D. Roosevelt named him to the U.S. Circuit Court of Appeals in 1939. A year later Biddle resigned his seat to become SOLICITOR GENERAL. In 1941 he became ATTORNEY GENERAL, a post he held until 1945.

At the Justice Department, Biddle struggled to reconcile his progressive attitudes on CIVIL LIBERTIES issues with the increasingly intolerant atmosphere during WORLD WAR II. He supported the administration's policies on alien registration and supervised the relocation and internment of Japanese Americans. He helped write the President's message supporting the Smith Act, which was later used to prosecute members of the American Communist Party. Yet he also spoke out against intolerance toward aliens and denounced congressional attempts to deport Harry Bridges, the head of the West Coast longshoremen's union. Years later Biddle expressed regret for his part in the TREAT-MENT OF JAPANESE AMERICANS, explaining that as a new member of the CABINET he did not feel confident enough to stand up to Secretary of War HENRY STIMSON.

At President Harry S. Truman's request, Biddle resigned as Attorney General in 1945 to make way for Tom Clark. He was then appointed as a member of the International Military Tribunal in Nuremberg, Germany. Later—possibly to atone for his part in the violation of civil liberties during World War II—Biddle served as head of Americans for Democratic Action and as an adviser to the American Civil Liberties Union; he also wrote several books on liberal themes.

BIBLIOGRAPHY

"Biddle, Francis (Beverly)." *Current Biography 1941.* 1941. Pp. 76–78.
Obituary. *New York Times.* 5 October 1968. P. 35.

WILLIAM LASSER

BIPARTISANSHIP, CONGRESS AND. Despite a President's advantage in dealing with members of his party in Congress, he is often forced to solicit bipartisan support. In the first place, the opposition party may control one or both houses of Congress. Even if Presidents received total support from all members of their parties, they would still require support from some members of the opposition. For instance, between 1953 and 1992 there were twenty years during which the Republicans controlled the executive branch while the Democrats controlled the legislative branch (1955–1961, 1969–1977, and 1987–1993). From 1981 to 1987, the Republicans had a majority in the Senate only.

A successful bipartisan approach depends upon restraining partisanship to avoid alienating the opposition. The President must subordinate his role as a party leader to that of his role as a coalition leader. President Dwight D. Eisenhower, who faced a Democratic Congress in six of his eight years as President and who was not inclined toward overt partisanship, consciously attempted to follow such an approach, as did his staff, as he cultivated Democratic votes, especially on foreign policy.

President Richard M. Nixon and President Gerald R. Ford also faced Congresses controlled by Democrats. They tried to steer a middle course between Eisenhower's soft sell and the more partisan ap-

proaches of John F. Kennedy and Lyndon B. Johnson. They wanted to make the most of Republican strength while appealing to conservative Democrats by taking an issue-oriented, ideological line as well as a party line. Ronald Reagan and George Bush have followed a similar strategy.

A second reason for bipartisanship is that no matter how large the representation of the President's party in Congress, he cannot always depend on it for support, for members of the President's own party frequently oppose him. This is especially true of southern Democrats. In the 1950s and 1960s their inconsistent support of Democratic Presidents was especially evident in the area of civil rights legislation. Southern Democrats overwhelmingly opposed important pieces of civil rights legislation, and the President would have lost the vote on each of these without the support of some Republicans.

Civil rights is not the only area in which Democratic Presidents have needed Republican support. For example, Lyndon Johnson realized at the beginning of his presidency that as a progressive President he would need help from the leaders of both parties to pass his domestic legislation. Thus he regularly consulted Republican congressional leaders and restrained evidence of partisanship in public forums.

Republican Presidents have also had trouble gaining support from members of their party in Congress, furthering their need for a bipartisan strategy. President Eisenhower had trouble gaining support from the basically conservative congressional Republicans for his internationalist foreign policy and his moderate domestic policies. President Nixon went to the highly unusual step of helping to defeat Sen. Charles Goodell of New York, a Republican, in the election of 1970 because of the liberal senator's opposition to the President's policies.

In their efforts to secure bipartisan support, Republican Presidents may exploit divisions within the DEMOCRATIC PARTY. What is a problem for Democratic Presidents is an opportunity for Republican ones. Given the essentially conservative orientation of Republican Presidents and southern Democratic members of Congress, one should not be surprised that on the average southern Democrats have supported Republican Presidents about as often as they do Presidents of their own party. This is changing somewhat, however, as southern Democrats become more moderate and thus more consistent in their voting record with other Democrats in Congress.

Not only do partisan strategies often fail for lack of numbers or reliability of party cohorts, but they may also provoke the other party into a more unified posture of opposition. Where there is confrontation, there can be no consensus, and consensus is often required to legislate on important issues. Some observers believe President Reagan hurt his chances of obtaining Democratic support for some of his proposals by his steadfast unwillingness to compromise with them early in his term.

The President is also inhibited in his partisanship by pressures to be President of all the people rather than a highly partisan figure. This expectation that they be somewhat above the political fray undoubtedly constrains Presidents in their role as party leader and further fuels the need for a bipartisan approach.

Despite the frequent necessity of a bipartisan strategy, it is not without costs. Bipartisanship often creates a strain with the extremists within the President's party, as a Republican President tries to appeal to the left for Democratic votes and a Democratic President to the right for Republican votes. Although the Republican right wing and Democratic left wing may find it difficult to forge a coalition in opposition to their own President's policies, it is not true that they must therefore support the President. Instead, they may complicate a President's strategy by joining those who oppose his policies.

It is not only in matters of ideology that a President following a bipartisan approach to coalition building may irritate his fellow partisans. Providing discrete benefits to members of the opposition instead of to members of his own party may have the same effect.

Bipartisanship may also be hindered by the leaders of the President's party in Congress. Speaker Tip O'Neill and Senate Majority Leader Robert Byrd let Jimmy Carter know they would be upset if he dealt with Republicans in Congress frequently. To avoid offending the Democratic Party leaders, Carter therefore had fewer contacts with Republicans than he otherwise might have.

The ultimate limitation on a bipartisan strategy, especially for a liberal Democratic President, is that the opposition party is generally not fertile ground for obtaining policy support. Johnson's White House, for example, directly sought Republican support only rarely, because Republicans were not often movable. Sometimes the isolation from the opposition was complete.

The Democrats are not the only ones who find it difficult to obtain bipartisan support. The task is not easy for the Republicans either. For example, only twenty-three House Democrats supported Ronald Reagan on both the budget and tax votes in 1981, despite the President's persuasive efforts and the pull of ideology.

Any discussion of bipartisanship must devote special attention to foreign policy. The consensus during the Truman and Eisenhower administrations of opposition to communism generated by the COLD WAR did not, however, cause partisan differences in Congress to be set aside when foreign policy matters were considered. Instead, foreign policy debates in Congress were typically characterized by bitter, partisan, and generally consensus-free debate. Subsequent administrations have witnessed no change in this pattern.

Eisenhower's internationalist foreign policies did elicit support from liberal Democrats. The hawkish foreign policies of later Republican Presidents, however, did not appeal to many Democrats. Liberal Democratic Presidents similarly received low support on foreign policy from Republicans, who remained overwhelmingly conservative.

[See also LEGISLATIVE LEADERSHIP; CONGRESS, WHITE HOUSE INFLUENCE ON.]

BIBLIOGRAPHY

Collier, Ellen C. *Bipartisanship and the Making of Foreign Policy.* 1991.
Edwards, George C., III. *At the Margins: Presidential Leadership of Congress.* 1989.
Mayhew, David R. *Divided We Govern.* 1992.
McCormick, James M., and Eugene R. Wittkopf. "Bipartisanship, Partisanship, and Ideology in Congressional-Executive Foreign Policy Relations." *Journal of Politics* 52 (1990): 1077–1100.
Oldfield, Duane M., and Aaron Wildavsky. "Reconsidering the Two Presidencies." *Society* 26 (1989): 54–59.
Shull, Steven A., ed. *The Two Presidencies.* 1991.
Warburg, Gerald Felix. *Conflict and Consensus.* 1989.

GEORGE C. EDWARDS III

BLACKS. For discussion of presidential policy toward African Americans in the period before the Civil War, see SLAVERY and FUGITIVE SLAVERY; for the period after the Civil War and for the late twentieth century, see AFFIRMATIVE ACTION; CIVIL RIGHTS POLICY; particular CIVIL RIGHTS ACTS.

BLAINE, JAMES G. (1830–1893), Representative, Senator, Republican presidential nominee in 1884. James Gillespie Blaine was born in western Pennsylvania when the area was still a frontier. A precocious youth, he received a solid grounding in English and the classics. Blaine taught for a time in Kentucky, but he disliked the South and moved to Philadelphia to study law. The law yielded to journalism when family connections allowed him to undertake newspaper work in Augusta, Maine, in the mid 1850s. In 1854, he abandoned the WHIG PARTY and urged friends to join him in the new REPUBLICAN PARTY, to whose first convention in 1856 he was a delegate. He based his allegiance to the party on the Republican belief in economic development, opposition to SLAVERY, and nationalism.

Blaine left journalism and local politics to represent Maine in the House of Representatives from 1863 to 1876 (he was Speaker from 1869 to 1876) and in the Senate from 1876 to 1881. He was generally moderate on the issues that arose during and after the CIVIL WAR, while opposing any restoration of southern rule. He made few lasting enemies, and even people who did not like or trust him often found him fascinating. He understood intuitively that the electorate expected to see and hear political leaders as extensions of themselves. He knew that much of mass politics was theater, in which candidates had to express the aspirations and anxieties of ordinary voters. He shrewdly used all the contemporary publicity methods—the formal set speech to denote statesmanship, the informal story to indicate individuality, and the purely personal notice that made him seem real to potential voters. He became "the magnetic man"; wags said that people went mad over him, half for and half against.

Such a person was bound to become presidential timber. Blaine was a leading contender for the Republican nomination in 1876, but he was unable to overcome the suspicions of personal wrongdoing revealed in the so-called Mulligan Letters. These missives seemed to show that Blaine had done legislative favors for an Arkansas railroad and had profited from selling its bonds. Blaine denied the charges, but suspicion hung on him like the odor of smoke, and the nod went to Governor Rutherford B. Hayes of Ohio. Blaine was again a logical choice in 1880, but he cheerfully supported the final selection, James A. Garfield of Ohio, who won the national election. Blaine entered Garfield's CABINET in 1881 as Secretary of State and hoped to widen United States influence in Latin America. Garfield's assassination brought Chester A. Arthur, an apparent enemy, to the White House, and Blaine retired to write the first volume of his memoirs and prepare to run for the presidency in 1884.

That year marked the apogee of his fame. His bitter personal quarrel with New York's Senator Roscoe Conkling had divided the Republicans into two factions: the Stalwarts, who took former President Ulysses S. Grant and residual war issues as their guides, and the Half-Breeds, who favored Blaine and concentrated on new industrial issues in their platform. Blaine easily won the nomination on the first ballot in 1884. The campaign that followed against Grover Cleveland was bitter. Blaine lost the election narrowly;

a change of six hundred votes in New York would have reversed the results. The postmortem was as confused as the campaign. The narrow margin made every group of voters seem critical. Blaine might have repudiated the bigots who made him seem anti-Catholic more quickly; he could have mollified dissident Republicans; he should have played his ethnic cards better. Every explanation made some sense; together, all were probably correct, and impossible to attain. One lesson of the campaign was ironic: to succeed, charisma needed to seem unimpeachably trustworthy.

Supporters brought his name forward in 1888, but he yielded easily to Indiana's Benjamin Harrison, who was elected. The following year he returned as Secretary of State, still committed to Pan-Americanism, RECIPROCAL TRADE AGREEMENTS, and expanded overseas markets. To Blaine and his followers, these were legitimate and farsighted goals. Economic development, in this view, would both benefit the United States and its trading partners, producing affluence and political stability. But Blaine was uncomfortable with the chilly, aloof Harrison and resigned just before the Republican convention in 1892. There was talk of a last hurrah, but by now Blaine was aging, unwell, and probably not interested in presidential politics. He died suddenly on 27 January 1893.

Blaine's appeal was manifest, but his legacy was difficult to assess. His name adorned no major legislation, treaty, or manifesto. Perhaps his greatest legacy was an understanding that politics must become personal and that parties must speak to people in realistic ways. In that sense, and with the passage of time that made new issues seem familiar, he helped lay the groundwork for his party's long-term success after 1896.

BIBLIOGRAPHY

Blaine, James G. *Twenty Years of Congress.* 2 vols. 1884–1886.
Hamilton, Gail. *The Biography of James G. Blaine.* 1895.
Muzzey, David S. *James G. Blaine: A Political Idol of Other Days.* 1934.

H. WAYNE MORGAN

BLAIR, FRANCIS P. (1791–1876), journalist, politician. As editor of the Washington *Globe*, Blair sought to explain the presidential policies of Andrew Jackson to the country. Born in Abingdon, Virginia, Blair migrated to Kentucky and was graduated from Transylvania University. He served as treasurer of the Bank of the Commonwealth and became active in Kentucky politics. An assistant to AMOS KENDALL, editor of the *Argus of Western America*, he supported the Relief Party, which sponsored stay laws against foreclosures and favored abolishing imprisonment for debt. He subsequently joined the DEMOCRATIC PARTY, helped Andrew Jackson win Kentucky in the election of 1828, and was brought to Washington by President Jackson in 1830 to found and edit a newspaper to serve as a mouthpiece for the administration. Under his excellent editorship, the Washington *Globe* became an important, hardhitting and dynamic journal, the major source of information for members of the Democratic Party. Blair met virtually every day with Jackson to learn the presidential will and interpret it to the *Globe*'s many readers around the country. The *Globe* became a valuable instrument for winning presidential elections, especially in the 1830s.

Blair was one of the earliest members of the so-called KITCHEN CABINET, which regularly offered Jackson advice on national issues. His greatest editorial work and the one issue that engaged his keenest interest and involvement developed over the war against the Second BANK OF THE UNITED STATES. Along with Kendall he probably did more than any other man to convince the President to kill the bank. He was forced to sell his interest in the *Globe* in 1845 because he incurred the displeasure of President James K. Polk. The *Globe* ceased publication on 30 April 1845. Later Blair joined the REPUBLICAN PARTY and supported Lincoln in the presidential election of 1860. His son, Montgomery Blair, served as Lincoln's Postmaster General. But Blair opposed Radical RECONSTRUCTION after the Civil War and eventually returned to the Democratic Party.

BIBLIOGRAPHY

Smith, Elbert B. *Francis Preston Blair*. 1980.
Smith, William E. *The Francis Preston Blair Family in Politics*. 2 vols. 1933.

ROBERT V. REMINI

BLAIR HOUSE. The "guest house of the President," located across Pennsylvania Avenue from the WHITE HOUSE, is actually a complex of two nineteenth-century houses heavily remodeled into facilities for visiting dignitaries and their staffs who will interact directly with the White House. Blair House is equipped with kitchens, meeting rooms, bedrooms, dressing rooms, sitting rooms, dining rooms, bathrooms, garages, and a highly protected enclosed courtyard garden; it can house extensive entourages of foreign visitors.

The house on the east, built in 1824, was occupied during the administration of Andrew Jackson by the pro-Jackson newspaperman FRANCIS PRESTON BLAIR.

The house on the west, the Samuel Phillips Lee house, built in 1858, belonged to Blair's married daughter.

Blair moved to Washington from Kentucky in 1830 to establish *The Globe*, to rival the anti-Jackson *National Intelligencer*. Possessed of political fervor and sharp journalistic ability, he prospered, and in 1836, he bought the house from the estate of Dr. Joseph Lovell. It provided the setting for a glittering social life which lasted until the CIVIL WAR and after. The hospitality of the Blairs and the Lees naturally produced great moments in their high-ceilinged parlors. The most notable was the meeting that F. P. Blair and Gen. WINFIELD SCOTT called there with Robert E. Lee, at President Abraham Lincoln's behest, in 1861, to try and convince Lee to take up the Union cause.

Descendants of the family still occupied the houses in 1942 when the federal government moved to take over the property for office sites. Laws passed during the administration of Herbert Hoover authorized the condemnation of all property around Lafayette Park. President Franklin D. Roosevelt, however, halted any plans to demolish the houses and determined to use them as guest facilities to relieve the overburdened White House. The two houses, which had long been connected, gained new lives under the name Blair House.

Harry S. Truman moved from his apartment to Blair House for about two weeks in 1945, the day after his swearing-in as President, and he returned in 1948 when the rebuilding of the White House began; the work lasted until 1952. On 1 November 1950 two Puerto Rican nationalists made an unsuccessful attempt to enter Blair House and assassinate President Truman. During the ensuing shoot-out, one of the assailants and a member of the SECRET SERVICE were killed. Plaques affixed to the iron fence of Blair House recount the incident.

Blair House was extensively remodeled and highly decorated in the late 1980s, converting what had seemed two private houses into something more like a stylish bed-and-breakfast inn. It is under the jurisdiction of the Protocol Office, State Department.

BIBLIOGRAPHY

Froneck, Thomas, ed. *An Illustrated History of the City of Washington*. 1977.
Tayloe, Benjamin Ogle. *Our Neighbors on Lafayette Square*. 1972.
Templeman, Eleanor Lee. *The Blair House: Guest House of the President*. 1980.

WILLIAM SEALE

BOLAND AMENDMENTS (1982–1986). Between 1982 and 1986, Congress enacted amendments to successive appropriations bills that expressly barred any "agency or entity of the United States involved in intelligence activities" from spending funds "available" to it "to support military or paramilitary operations in Nicaragua." These amendments, named after their sponsor, Rep. Edward Boland of Massachusetts, became controversial during the IRAN-CONTRA AFFAIR. In late 1986, it came to light that Reagan administration officials and private individuals—directed by national security adviser Vice Adm. John Poindexter and deputy director for political-military affairs Lt. Col. Oliver North—had, while the Boland amendments were in effect, diverted profits from the illegal arms sales to Iran to the contras—Nicaraguan military forces seeking to overthrow the communist Sandinista government.

The Boland amendments were only one example of congressional invocation of its appropriations power to harness executive funding of secret war making. During the VIETNAM WAR, Congress considered the COOPER-CHURCH AMENDMENT and the Hatfield-McGovern bill to cut off funds for military efforts in Southeast Asia. In 1973 and 1974, Congress enacted seven separate provisions denying the use of authorized or appropriated funds to support United States military or paramilitary forces in Vietnam, Cambodia, or Laos. The Boland amendments' direct forerunner was the CLARK AMENDMENT to the Arms Export Control Act of 1976, which for nearly ten years barred aid to private groups that would have the purpose or effect of aiding military or paramilitary operations in Angola.

Following televised congressional hearings held during the summer of 1987, the House and Senate select committees investigating the Iran-contra affair concluded that the staff of the NATIONAL SECURITY COUNCIL had violated the Boland amendments. "[T]he diversion of arms sales proceeds to the Contras' war effort," they wrote, "was an evasion of the Boland Amendment no matter how narrowly that noncriminal statute is construed." The crucial point, they found, was that the full purchase price from the arms sales was "available" to the CENTRAL INTELLIGENCE AGENCY and thus could not be lawfully diverted to the contras. Moreover, the congressional hearings revealed that the only contemporaneous executive branch legal opinion approving the diversion had been based upon a faulty legal analysis and a cursory review of facts conducted by a government attorney who had failed the bar examination four times.

Against this conclusion, the defenders of the Iran-contra affair argued that the amendments' language had changed so many times as to render it impossible for executive officials to determine whether particular activities were proscribed at particular times. In his congressional testimony, Oliver North argued that the Boland amendments had hamstrung U.S. support to democratic resistance movements in Nicaragua. Moreover, Reagan supporters argued that the Boland amendments did not apply to the staff of the National Security Council, which was not technically an intelligence agency. In any event, they claimed, the amendments placed overly strict conditions upon presidential expenditure of authorized funds and thereby encroached unconstitutionally upon the executive's "inherent" authority to conduct foreign affairs.

The Boland amendments became obsolete when the Sandinistas were voted out of power in Nicaragua in 1989. The Supreme Court, however, may yet consider the underlying constitutional question: whether a duly enacted appropriations statute may constitute an unconstitutional exercise of Congress's power of the purse because it impinges upon the President's unenumerated constitutional authority over foreign affairs.

BIBLIOGRAPHY

Koh, Harold H. *The National Security Constitution: Sharing Power After the Iran-Contra Affair*. 1990.

Note. "The Boland Amendments and Foreign Affairs Deference." *Columbia Law Review* 8 (1988): 1535.

U.S. Congress. House Select Committee to Investigate Covert Arms Transactions with Iran and Senate Select Committee on Secret Military Assistance to Iran and the Nicaraguan Opposition. *Report of the Congressional Committees Investigating the Iran-Contra Affair*, 100th Cong., 1st sess., 1987. H. Rept. 433, S. Rept. 216.

HAROLD HONGJU KOH

BONUS ARMY. In 1931 in the midst of the Great Depression, Congress overrode President Herbert Hoover's veto of a bill allowing servicemen to borrow up to 50 percent of the value of their veterans' certificates from WORLD WAR I. Not satisfied with this action, in 1932 approximately ten thousand veterans, known as the Bonus Army, or Bonus Expeditionary Force (BEF), gathered in Washington, D.C., to demand full, immediate redemption of their certificates. On 17 June the Senate refused their request, and all but two thousand accepted the offer of free transportation home. At this point Hoover appeared to have won the battle with the BEF—only to lose it a few days later.

The President did not order the action taken by U.S. Army forces under the direction of Gen. Douglas MacArthur to rout the remaining veterans and their families from various encampments in and around the nation's capital. Hoover specifically told MacArthur to hold the veterans in check at their major camp, Bonus

City, in the Anacostia Flats just outside Washington. Instead, on 28 July 1932 MacArthur commanded a force of tanks, a thousand soldiers, and even a machine-gun contingent to drive the BEF from the flats, leaving the encampment in flames.

Rather than publicly denounce MacArthur for disobeying orders, Hoover took full responsibility for the incident, accepting MacArthur's and Secretary of War Patrick J. Hurley's explanations about "subversive influences" in this remnant of the Bonus Army. When he published his presidential memoirs in the early 1950s, Hoover stressed the purported criminal rather than the communist makeup of the BEF, acknowledging for the first time that he had not ordered the rout. He died, however, without ever satisfactorily explaining why he had not charged MacArthur with insubordination rather than suffer extreme public criticism for an action he had not ordered and that exacerbated his already heartless image.

BIBLIOGRAPHY

Daniels, Roger. *The Bonus March: An Episode in the Great Depression.* 1971.

Lisio, Donald J. *The President and Protest: Hoover, Conspiracy, and the Bonus Riot.* 1974.

JOAN HOFF

BOOTH, JOHN WILKES (1838–1865), assassin of

President Abraham Lincoln. A native of Maryland and the son of a slave-owning actor, Booth had a successful stage career, but his violent political opinions led him in 1864 to plan to kidnap the President en route to or from the Soldiers' Home, where he slept during the hot season. Like many other Marylanders, Booth regarded Lincoln as a tyrant who crushed CIVIL LIBERTIES in the state, and he believed fervently that "This country was formed for the *white*, not for the black man." Hoping to seize Lincoln and carry him to Richmond to exchange him for Confederate prisoners of war, Booth began to recruit a band of like-minded Confederate sympathizers. He traveled to Montreal, a town rife with Confederate agents, but no one, despite many efforts, has ever been able to prove that the Confederate government engineered Booth's plot.

President Lincoln was lightly guarded at best, but Booth's plan took a discouraging turn when recruitment of accomplices carried him into winter, which took away his opportunity. He began to scheme to capture the President while he watched a play, but some, thinking this too dangerous, dropped out of the plot.

Now with too few men and faced as well with the fall of Richmond in April, Booth decided to kill Lincoln and have accomplices murder the Vice President, Andrew Johnson, and the Secretary of State, WILLIAM H. SEWARD. He must have thought that the removal of such key figures in the government might cause a revolution that would save the Confederacy.

On 14 April, Booth shot Lincoln while the President watched *Our American Cousin*, an English comedy, at Ford's Theatre in Washington, D.C. There was no attempt on Johnson, but Seward was badly injured in a knife attack. Lincoln died the next morning. Booth was killed in flight by Union soldiers on 26 April.

BIBLIOGRAPHY

Hanchett, William. *The Lincoln Murder Conspiracies.* 1983.

MARK E. NEELY, JR.

BOWSHER v. SYNAR 478 U.S. 714 (1986). *Bowsher*

involved a challenge to the delegation to the COMPTROLLER GENERAL of authority to determine the size of federal spending reductions required by the GRAMM-RUDMAN-HOLLINGS ACT of 1985. That much publicized act was an utterly ineffectual attempt to control the federal deficit by providing for automatic SEQUESTRATION of federal appropriations whenever projected expenditures for a fiscal year exceeded estimated revenues by more than a specified amount. The final estimates of expenditures and revenues and the determination of the size of the necessary spending reductions were to be made by the Comptroller General, who was chosen because he was regarded as politically independent. The Comptroller General is appointed by the President for a nonrenewable fifteen-year term and is removable only for specified cause by joint resolution of Congress which, since it is subject to veto, would require a two-thirds majority in both houses if the President did not concur.

The constitutionality of the sequestration provisions was immediately challenged by dissenting members of the House of Representatives, (including Mike Synar, D-Okla.) and a federal employees' union, whose principal concern was that Congress had improperly delegated authority over spending reductions to administrative officers, thereby evading responsibility for cutting funds for popular programs. A subsidiary argument was that the law violated the SEPARATION OF POWERS by giving executive responsibilities to an officer responsible to, and removable by, Congress. The United States was a nominal defendant, but although the Reagan administration defended against the delegation claim, it joined the plaintiffs in arguing that the delegation of executive authority to Comptroller General Charles A. Bowsher was unconstitutional. It vigorously contended that the decision in HUMPHREY'S EXECUTOR V. UNITED STATES (1935), which had affirmed Congress's power to provide that the President could remove members of an INDEPENDENT COMMISSION only for cause, should be drastically narrowed, if not overruled. It maintained that *Humphrey's Executor* should be understood to authorize limitations on the President's power to remove officers performing executive functions only when those functions are ancillary to carrying out adjudicatory responsibilities (that is, acting in a judicial capacity to resolve specific disputes), for, otherwise, the President could not discharge the constitutional duty to "take care that the laws be faithfully executed."

A three-judge district court, one of whose members was Antonin Scalia, issued a per curiam opinion rejecting the plaintiffs' delegation claim but upholding the separation-of-powers claim. It disparaged *Humphrey's Executor* for sanctioning a " 'headless fourth branch' " of government under a Constitution providing only for three but contented itself with ruling that the sequestration provisions were invalid because they gave executive duties to an official removable by Congress and thus under "here-and-now subservience" to the legislative branch. On appeal, the Supreme Court addressed only the separation-of-powers issue. The original draft of Chief Justice Warren Burger's majority opinion repeated much of the administration's argument, stressing the vital importance of the President's REMOVAL POWER as a means of ensuring his capacity to perform his constitutional duties. This draft was rejected, however, by a majority of the Justices, who saw that its language could be read as repudiating *Humphrey's Executor* and threatening the constitutional status of the independent commissions. The Court's ultimate opinion dealt only with the narrow issue of whether executive authority could be given to an officer removable by Congress and thus did not implicate in any way the constitutionality of the commissions.

The majority held that Congress could not constitutionally grant executive authority to an officer under its control and agreed with the district court that the fact that the Comptroller General was removable for cause by joint resolution placed him under "here-and-now subservience" to Congress. This conclusion was widely regarded as patently absurd, particularly since it is the very fact that the President can only remove commissioners for cause that is understood to make the regulatory commissions independent of his control. From the outset, the Comptroller General has been looked upon as virtually unremovable—as he was intended to be so that the auditing functions of the office could be carried out without political interference.

Four Justices rejected the Court's conclusion that the removal procedure gave Congress control over the office. Two—John Paul Stevens and Thurgood Marshall—nevertheless concurred in the result because they concluded that the various statutory duties of the Comptroller General in aid of the legislative process rendered him an agent of Congress, thereby making him ineligible to exercise policy-making authority. Justice Byron R. White dissented because the fact that removal of the Comptroller General is authorized only for specified cause and that a removal resolution may be vetoed by the President guaranteed that he will not be subservient to Congress. Justice Harry A. Blackmun also dissented, concluding that it would have been preferable to nullify Congress's never used and essentially unusable power to remove the Comptroller General than to invalidate a key provision of important legislation on a critical national issue.

By denying Congress power to participate in the removal of an officer with executive responsibilities, *Bowsher v. Synar* provided a basis for reconciling *Humphrey's Executor* with MYERS V. UNITED STATES (1926), which invalidated a statutory requirement that the Senate concur in the President's removal of a postmaster. As is now all but universally recognized, *Myers* and *Humphrey's Executor* cannot be reconciled, as the Court in *Humphrey's Executor* tried to do, by regarding a postmaster, but not a commissioner, as an official exercising executive power. But they can be reconciled on the ground that Congress gave itself a role in the removal of postmasters but not commissioners, and distinguishing the cases on that ground would neither undercut *Humphrey's Executor* nor restrict the power of Congress to place substantive limitations on the President's ability to remove an official exercising executive power whenever the nature of that official's duties makes it appropriate to provide protection from political control. In MORRISON V. OLSON (1988), the independent-counsel case, the Supreme Court explicitly distinguished the decisions on this basis. Thus, ironically, although *Bowsher* was originally seen by the administration as an opportunity to obtain judicial abandonment of *Humphrey's Executor* and its acceptance of illimitable presidential removal power, the decision actually played a significant part in the Court's subsequent reaffirmation of the holding of *Humphrey's Executor* that presidential removal power is subject to congressional limitation.

BIBLIOGRAPHY

Banks, William C., and Jeffrey D. Straussman. "*Bowsher v. Synar*: The Emerging Judicialization of the Fisc." *Boston College Law Review* 28 (1987): 659–688.

Elliott, E. Donald. "Regulating the Deficit after *Bowsher v. Synar*." *Yale Journal on Regulation* 4 (1987): 317–362.

Entin, Jonathan L. "The Removal Power and the Federal Deficit: Form, Substance, and Administrative Independence." *Kentucky Law Journal* 75 (1986–1987): 699–792.

Schwartz, Bernard. "An Administrative Law Might Have Been— Chief Justice Burger's *Bowsher v. Synar* Draft." *Administrative Law Review* 42 (1990): 221–249.

Synar, Mike, Vincent LoVoi, and Donald R. C. Pongrace. "Congressional Perspective on the Balanced Budget and Emergency Deficit Control Act of 1985." *Pace Law Review* 7 (1987): 675–694.

DEAN ALFANGE, JR.

BOXSCORES, PRESIDENTIAL. Designed to indicate the level of presidential support in Congress, presidential boxscores reveal the extent to which members of Congress take the same position as the President when they vote on legislation. The most frequently cited boxscore is the *Congressional Quarterly*'s presidential support score. These scores, which the *Congressional Quarterly* has calculated since 1953, measure the percentage of time each member of Congress votes in accordance with the stated position of the President. The *Quarterly* aggregates such scores for the entire Congress for each session, by voting blocs within the Congress (primarily by section—southern and nonsouthern—and by party), and by the legislation's subject (foreign and domestic) to indicate how effective the President has been in attracting congressional support.

Overall congressional support scores have ranged from a high of 93 percent in 1965, when Lyndon B. Johnson was President, to a low of 43.5 percent in 1987, when Ronald Reagan was President. The average score for a single session of Congress from 1953 through 1991 was 69.6 percent.

In addition to determining presidential support scores, the *Congressional Quarterly* also devised a measure called a presidential boxscore. It was designed to measure the percentage of presidentially initiated legislative proposals that were enacted into law during each session of Congress. The journal, however, discontinued computing the boxscore after 1975 because this measure was not sensitive to the time it takes to enact legislation, which is usually longer than a single session of Congress. Also, the measure did not reflect the modifications that are frequently made to the President's proposals during the course of congressional deliberations, and the boxscores were often misleading, giving cautious, programmatically conservative Presidents higher "batting averages" because they introduced fewer new proposals than more legislatively active Presidents.

The presidential support score has also been subject to considerable criticism as an indicator of presidential influence in Congress. One problem has to do with its failure to discriminate between roll calls. All votes on all substantive bills on which the President has taken a position are counted equally. (Procedural bills and appropriations bills are generally excluded from the tally.) Thus priority presidential issues are weighted the same as trivial and unimportant ones; similarly, unanimous, near unanimous, and controversial roll-call votes are lumped together. This system of measurement ignores the fact that, with a limited amount of time, energy, and political capital available, Presidents naturally focus their attention on major legislation and on the controversial votes in which their intervention can make a difference.

To overcome this problem, the *Congressional Quarterly* has also begun to calculate presidential support on key votes. However, this measure includes only a small number of votes, and the range of issues covered by these votes may be very narrow, particularly if more than one of these key votes concerns the same issue. Generalizing on the basis of these key votes can also be hazardous.

There are other problems. The presidential support score will not be sensitive to individualized presidential efforts. Aggregate analysis is not likely to detect the exercise of legislative skills by individual Presidents. Nor is the measure sensitive to other situational variables, such as presidential popularity, that might help explain congressional voting.

Finally, roll-call voting occurs at the final stage of the legislative process, but presidential influence is often exerted earlier. This early influence may be very important to the final disposition and composition of the legislation. Moreover, a vote has to be recorded for it to be analyzed, which means that the method misses voice voting, which the Senate utilizes far more often than the House. Thus, any generalization about presidential influence in Congress made on the basis of presidential support scores must be seen as being limited to recorded votes at the final stage of the legislative process.

Given these limitations, why are presidential support scores employed so frequently by political scientists? There are several reasons. They are easy to compute. They are based on quantitative data that are available in sufficiently large numbers to yield testable hypotheses. Moreover, they enable scholars to take a longitudinal perspective and compare presidential success over time.

One of the most sophisticated studies to utilize presidential support scores is George C. Edwards III's

At the Margins (1989). Edwards examines presidential support in Congress from 1953 to 1986 by computing the support each member of Congress gave the President during this period on all recorded votes, on all nonunanimous votes, on the most important nonunanimous votes, and on the key votes. He concludes that party and, to a much lesser extent, popularity contribute to a President's effectiveness in Congress, but that Presidents' legislative skills have been overrated as a critical factor affecting congressional voting.

Another important quantitative study is Jon R. Bond and Richard Fleisher's *The President in the Legislative Arena* (1990), in which the authors analyze conflictual and important roll-call votes to examine the conditions in which Presidents succeed in congressional floor votes. They reach similar conclusions to Edwards', finding that members' party and ideology are more strongly related to presidential success than are the legislative skills of individual Presidents. Members are more influenced by their own dispositions and attitudes than by the President's actions. Bond and Fleisher did not, however, find presidential popularity to have a major impact on legislative success.

A third study, Mark A. Peterson's *Legislating Together* (1990), attempts to overcome the shortcomings of the boxscores by refining the *Congressional Quarterly*'s technique. Peterson examines new presidential domestic proposals to Congress from 1953 to 1984, determines what happens to them, and then tries to explain this outcome on the basis of the "contexts" of congressional decision making. He concludes that these contexts are influenced by the institutional, political, and economic settings in which they occur as well as by the kind of policy proposal made. Nevertheless, he did find that Presidents can have an impact—that their exercise of legislative skills does matter.

Roll-call votes cannot reveal the scope of the President's legislative involvement, measure the extent of his legislative influence, nor evaluate the effectiveness of his leadership in Congress. They only indicate how successful Presidents are at the final stage of voting and which members are most and least supportive of the President on these votes.

[*See also* LEGISLATIVE LEADERSHIP.]

BIBLIOGRAPHY

Bond, Jon R., and Richard Fleisher. *The President in the Legislative Arena.* 1990.

Edwards, George C. III. *At the Margins.: Presidential Leadership of Congress.* 1989.

King, Gary, and Lyn Ragsdale. *The Elusive Executive.* 1988.

Peterson, Mark A. *Legislating Together.* 1990.

Wayne, Stephen J. *The Legislative Presidency.* 1978. Pp. 168–172.

STEPHEN J. WAYNE

BRAIN TRUST. The term "brain trust" (originally "brains trust") was first applied by the journalist James Kieran to the informal group of academics and policy experts gathered around Franklin D. Roosevelt during the 1932 presidential campaign. Later the term was used less precisely to refer to Roosevelt's informal advisers in general, and still later it was applied to any group of intellectuals gathered around a President.

The first brain trust was organized by RAYMOND MOLEY, a professor of public law at Columbia University, at the suggestion of Governor Roosevelt's counsel, SAMUEL I. ROSENMAN. Moley recruited REXFORD G. TUGWELL, a professor of economics at Columbia; Adolf A. Berle, Jr., also of Columbia and a professor of law; and three men whose expertise was more political than academic: Senators JAMES F. BYRNES of South Carolina and Key Pittman of Nevada, and Hugh Johnson, who later became the head of the National Recovery Agency.

The brain trust set up operations in the Roosevelt Hotel in New York City for the duration of the 1932 campaign. Its primary function was speech writing, though because these speeches were the primary mechanism for the development and announcement of Roosevelt's campaign positions its members were highly involved in determining the substance of the campaign and, later, of the new administration. The activities of Moley's group were strictly separated from those of Roosevelt's personal and political staff.

After the inauguration the original brain trust was disbanded, though all of its members went on to play key roles in NEW DEAL Washington. The pattern established by the original group—the involvement of academics and policy experts in the making of policy, often by committee and often through the medium of speech writing, persisted, though the personnel changed frequently. In later years the term "brain trust" was used in a broader way, and included such figures as FELIX FRANKFURTER, BENJAMIN V. COHEN, THOMAS CORCORAN, HARRY HOPKINS, and others. Critics of the Roosevelt administration took to using the term pejoratively, suggesting the domination of the Roosevelt administration by left-leaning academics and reformers.

After the Roosevelt presidency, the term "brain trust" was frequently used in regard to John F. Kennedy's advisers, among whom were many academics. These included the historian Arthur M. Schlesinger, Jr., and the economist John Kenneth Galbraith, both of Harvard; and Theodore Sorensen, McGeorge Bundy, and Walter W. Rostow. Kennedy, as Schlesinger put it, "carried Roosevelt's brain-trust conception further than it had ever been carried before. The intellectual was no longer merely consultant or adviser but responsible official." Though no subsequent administration has featured so close a connection between the academy and the government as Kennedy's the involvement of academics in Washington power circles is now a routine aspect of American government.

BIBLIOGRAPHY

Moley, Raymond. *The First New Deal.* 1966.
Rosenman, Samuel I. *Working with Roosevelt.* 1952.
Schlesinger, Arthur M., Jr. *A Thousand Days: John F. Kennedy in the White House.* 1965.

WILLIAM LASSER

BRECKINRIDGE, JOHN C. (1821–1875), fourteenth Vice President of the United States (1857–1861), presidential candidate in 1860, Confederate general, Confederate Secretary of War. John Cabell Breckinridge's paternal grandfather, John Breckinridge, introduced the Kentucky Resolutions in the state legislature and was later a U.S. Senator and President Thomas Jefferson's Attorney General. His maternal grandfather and great-grandfather were both presidents of the College of New Jersey (Princeton).

Breckinridge graduated from Centre College in 1839 and studied at the College of New Jersey and Transylvania College before entering law practice in the Iowa Territory. Two years later he then returned to Kentucky, fought in the MEXICAN WAR, and entered politics, serving in Congress from 1851 to 1855. He supported western expansion, backed Senator STEPHEN A. DOUGLAS's plans for a transcontinental railroad, and was a key figure in drafting the final language of the KANSAS-NEBRASKA ACT, insisting on a repeal of all restrictions on SLAVERY in the territories. His role in guiding the Kansas-Nebraska Act through the House of Representatives made him a politician of natural stature. Unlike many southerners, he opposed the Clayton Amendment prohibiting unnaturalized immigrants from voting and holding office in the territories. Similarly, unlike most other southerners, after the Kansas-Nebraska Act opened new territory to slavery, he supported a homestead bill to help settle the West.

In the 1856 Democratic convention Breckinridge initially supported Franklin Pierce, but then switched to Douglas. When Douglas withdrew from consideration, the convention chose James Buchanan, and quite unexpectedly, nominated Breckinridge for the vice presidency after only two ballots. He then became the youngest man ever elected Vice President.

As Vice President, Breckinridge remained a staunch supporter of STATES' RIGHTS, slavery, and the expansion of slavery into the territories. He defended the decision in DRED SCOTT V. SANDFORD and strongly supported the Lecompton Constitution and the admission of Kansas as a slave state.

By 1860 Breckinridge was a leading voice for southern interests in the DEMOCRATIC PARTY. He defended the idea of a federal slave code for the territories while attacking Republicans for their belief in racial equality. A potential Democratic presidential candidate, Breckinridge was openly feuding with his former ally, Stephen A. Douglas. Breckinridge had strong support throughout the South and in some parts of the North. However, because his fellow Kentuckian James Guthrie was openly seeking the nomination, Breckinridge refused to be a candidate. The party's April convention in Charleston was a fiasco. Six southern delegations walked out to protest the platform. Douglas had the most support, but after fifty-seven ballots he could not secure the two-thirds majority needed to win nomination. The convention then adjourned, reconvening in Baltimore in mid June. At the chaotic Baltimore convention members of twenty-two different delegations walked out and the remaining shadow of the party nominated Douglas. The seceding delegates met elsewhere in Baltimore, adopted a platform endorsing a federal slave code in the territories, and unanimously nominated Breckinridge, with Senator Joseph Lane of Oregon as his running mate.

Breckinridge's opponents charged he was a stalking horse for southern secessionists. Breckinridge denied any disunionist goals, claiming he stood firmly for "the Union on the principles of the Constitution." But Breckinridge never disassociated himself from fire-eaters like William Yancey and JEFFERSON DAVIS, and when given the opportunity to denounce secession in the event of Lincoln's election, he refused to do so. However many of his supporters, including EDWIN M. STANTON, who would be President Abraham Lincoln's Secretary of War, and Benjamin F. Butler, a future Union general, believed that Breckinridge was the only candidate who could hold the Union together. Breckinridge won more popular votes in the free states than he did in the deep South, but, in a four-way race Breckinridge carried only eleven slave states. Had he won, or even thrown the election into the House of Representatives, secession would probably not have occurred in 1860–1861.

After the presidential election Breckinridge participated in peace negotiations during the SECESSION crisis; he became a U.S. Senator from Kentucky in March 1861. In the Senate, Breckinridge opposed almost all war measures and was universally considered to be a Confederate sympathizer. Although he claimed to support the Union, Breckinridge maintained contacts with Confederates, including writing a letter of recommendation to Jefferson Davis on behalf of a Confederate patronage seeker and visiting Confederate prisoners of war. In September 1861 Breckinridge left Kentucky for Virginia, soon to return to his home state as a Confederate general. Meanwhile a federal grand jury in Kentucky indicted him for treason and in December the Senate expelled him from that body, although he had in fact already resigned his position. In February 1865 Breckinridge, now a major general, became the Confederate Secretary of War. In May 1965 Breckinridge abandoned Richmond and a month later arrived in CUBA on a small boat. He remained in exile until 1869, then returned to Kentucky, where he practiced law and became involved in railroad development.

BIBLIOGRAPHY

Davis, William C. *Breckinridge: Statesman and Soldier Symbol.* 1974.
Heck, Frank H. *Proud Kentuckian: John C. Breckinridge, 1821–1875.* 1976.

PAUL FINKELMAN

BRETTON WOODS AGREEMENT. The series of multilateral economic accords promoted by the administration of Franklin D. Roosevelt and signed at the United Nations Monetary and Financial Conference at Bretton Woods, New Hampshire, in July 1944, sought to encourage economic prosperity and political stability around the world through free trade, monetary cooperation, and development. Major institutions created as a result of the Bretton Woods Agreement included the International Bank for Reconstruction and Development (IBRD, also known as the World Bank) and the International Monetary Fund (IMF).

President Franklin D. Roosevelt came to believe during the 1940s that the economic isolationism and protectionism of the 1930s helped cause WORLD WAR II. He resolved to avert future conflicts by creating a free-trade system that surmounted destructive economic and political nationalism.

President Roosevelt personally welcomed delegates to the Bretton Woods Conference by declaring that "commerce is the life blood of a free society" and that "we must see to it that the arteries which carry that blood stream are not clogged again, as they have been in the past, by artificial barriers created through senseless economic rivalries." The vision that Roosevelt articulated marked a major attempt by the United States to restructure the world economy, symbolized America's commitment to expanded free trade, and committed Washington to restoring world order through a massive aid program.

BIBLIOGRAPHY

Eckes, Alfred E., Jr. *A Search for Solvency: Bretton Woods and the International Monetary System, 1944–71.* 1979.
Gardner, Richard N. *Sterling-Dollar Diplomacy: The Origins and Prospects of Our International Economic Order.* Rev. ed. 1969.

BRIAN VANDEMARK

BRICKER AMENDMENT (1951). In 1951, Senator John Bricker, a conservative Republican from Ohio, introduced a constitutional amendment to limit the use and effects of treaties and EXECUTIVE AGREEMENTS within the United States. Bricker and the leaders of the American Bar Association feared that the federal government would use the UNITED NATIONS Charter, the Genocide Convention, and the U.N.'s draft covenant on human rights to encroach further on the reserved powers of the states in social and economic matters. They also resented the President's growing dominance over Congress in FOREIGN AFFAIRS, symbolized by Franklin D. Roosevelt's wartime agreements with Joseph Stalin and Winston Churchill at the YALTA CONFERENCE. Basically, the Bricker Amendment sought to prevent any extension of the liberal domestic policies, internationalism, and executive power associated with Roosevelt. By 1953, the amendment had sixty-four cosponsors in the Senate, including almost all the Republicans, conservative Democrats, and isolationists of both parties.

As approved by the Senate Judiciary Committee in June 1953, the Bricker Amendment reiterated the Constitution's supremacy over treaties; required implementing legislation "which would be valid in the absence of treaty" before a treaty would go into effect within the United States; and gave Congress the power to regulate all executive agreements. If adopted, the Bricker Amendment would have weakened the authority of the President and the federal government to enter into and carry out both treaties and executive agreements.

President Dwight D. Eisenhower and his advisers opposed the Bricker Amendment because they feared it would limit the President's authority and flexibility in foreign affairs. The administration realized that most Republicans favored the amendment, however, so Eisenhower moved very carefully in opposing the measure. The President praised Bricker's stated goal of ensuring that treaties and executive agreements were subservient to the Constitution, and administration officials met repeatedly with the Senator to try to draft a compromise amendment. Secretary of State JOHN FOSTER DULLES also sought to weaken the amendment's support by promising during the Senate hearings on the measure that the Eisenhower administration would neither sign nor seek approval of the covenant on human rights, the Genocide Convention, or any other international agreements that might involve domestic matters within the United States.

When the administration and Senator Bricker failed to resolve their differences, the President tried to work with Sen. Walter George (D-Ga.) and the Democrats to draft a bipartisan compromise, which would then be substituted for Bricker's amendment. They could not reach an agreement either, however, and in January 1954, George introduced his own amendment, which restated the Constitution's supremacy over treaties and executive agreements and required implementing legislation for executive agreements—but not for treaties—to take effect within the United States. Treaties would be unaffected by the George amendment as long as they did not violate the Constitution.

Eisenhower and his aides urged their supporters in the Senate to oppose both the Bricker Amendment and the George substitute, asserting that the proposed amendments would violate the traditional SEPARATION OF POWERS, impair the President's ability to conduct the nation's foreign affairs, and take the United States back to the days under the Articles of Confederation when the national government could not force the states to comply with duly ratified treaties.

The President's opposition to the Bricker and George amendments led the Senate to reject both measures in February 1954. The Bricker Amendment failed to win even a simple majority, but the George Amendment came within one vote of the two-thirds majority required for approval. Liberal Democrats led by Senator Thomas Hennings of Missouri joined with the Eisenhower administration's staunchest supporters to provide the crucial votes to defeat the George Amendment. Bricker kept proposing revised versions of his amendment until 1958, but he never won the administration's support, and the measure never again reached the floor of the Senate.

Eisenhower's actions during the Bricker Amendment controversy support the revisionist view of him as a more active, involved, and knowledgeable President who operated behind the scenes. Even though he was intimately involved in the administration's discussions and decisions concerning the Bricker Amendment, Eisenhower stated that his opposition to the measure was based on Dulles's analysis, and Bricker always blamed Dulles, not Eisenhower, for the President's opposition to his amendment.

Even though the Bricker Amendment was never adopted, the debate over the measure made the Eisenhower administration much more aware of Congress's resentment over the executive branch's encroachments on the legislature's authority in foreign affairs and led the administration to consult more closely with Congress in formulating American policy for Vietnam in 1954, Formosa in 1955, and the Middle East in 1957–1958 [see AREA RESOLUTIONS]. The whole controversy also made Senators more aware of the domestic effects of international agreements and delayed American ratification of the Genocide Convention until 1986.

BIBLIOGRAPHY

Cathal, Nolan. "The Last Hurrah of Conservative Isolationism: Eisenhower, Congress, and the Bricker Amendment." *Presidential Studies Quarterly* 22 (1992): 337–349.

Reichard, Gary. "Eisenhower and the Bricker Amendment." *Prologue* 6 (1974): 88–99.

Tananbaum, Duane. *The Bricker Amendment Controversy: A Test of Eisenhower's Political Leadership.* 1988.

Tananbaum, Duane. "The Bricker Amendment Controversy: Its Origins and Eisenhower's Role." *Diplomatic History* 9 (1985): 73–93.

DUANE TANANBAUM

BRINKMANSHIP. Brinkmanship is a foreign policy tactic in which there is the deliberate creation of the risk of war. It is the escalation of a conflict by one side in order to create an intolerable situation for the other side. In this way, the opposition is forced to accommodate demands or risk war.

Brinkmanship along with the concept of massive retaliation were the two prongs of a new foreign policy approach known as deterrence. This new approach by the Eisenhower administration replaced the Truman administration policy of CONTAINMENT.

These terms are attributed to President Dwight D. Eisenhower's Secretary of State JOHN FOSTER DULLES. Brinkmanship was coined after an interview in which Dulles maintained that America must be willing to go to the brink of war if it was to have peace. Dulles in an interview in *Life* magazine (16 January 1956) stated, "If you try to run away from it [war], if you are scared to go to the brink, you are lost."

According to Dulles, this strategy was employed many times throughout the Eisenhower administration. The policy proved successful in dealing with various potential conflicts in Korea (June 1953), Indochina (April 1954), and Formosa Straits (1954–1955). For Dulles, "The ability to get to the verge without getting into war is the necessary art."

There was sharp criticism of the Secretary of State for his comments. Several foreign governments denied that events had taken place as Dulles described. Additionally, the press was relentless in its attack on Dulles for suggesting that the Eisenhower administration was deliberately putting the American people on the brink of war. Sensing that his Secretary of State had lost all credibility, President Eisenhower in 1956 issued a statement defending Dulles as "the best Secretary I have ever known."

Despite the uproar and public rejection of the policy, it was employed in 1958 when the United States sent the Fleet into the Formosa Straits to show Communist China that the United States was willing to fight.

BIBLIOGRAPHY

Capitanchik, David B. *The Eisenhower Presidency and American Foreign Policy.* 1969.
Mosley, Leonard. *Dulles: A Biography of Eleanor, Allen, and John Foster Dulles and their Family Network.* 1978.
Schelling, Thomas. *The Conflict of Strategy.* 1981.

JEFFREY D. SCHULTZ

BROWNELL, HERBERT (b. 1904), Attorney General. Herbert Brownell, a former New York state legislator, was campaign manager for THOMAS E. DEWEY in 1944 and 1948, chairman of the Republican National Committee, and adviser in Dwight D. Eisenhower's 1952 race. He helped Eisenhower select his first-term Cabinet appointees and traveled with the President-elect to assess the military situation in Korea in late 1952.

As ATTORNEY GENERAL from 1953 to 1957, Brownell shared many of the anticommunist sentiments of the time. He helped create the administration's LOYALTY-SECURITY PROGRAM, supported the 1953 execution of the Rosenbergs for espionage, and revived a case against an alleged communist spy who had worked in the Treasury Department during the Truman administration. But he and Eisenhower opposed the inquisitorial methods of Senator Joseph McCarthy. Arguing EXECUTIVE PRIVILEGE, Brownell strongly resisted releasing FBI files to McCarthy's subcommittee.

Brownell was the driving force in framing and advancing the administration's civil rights agenda. Believing that school segregation was unconstitutional, he convinced the reluctant President that the government should file an amicus curiae brief supporting the black child who served as plaintiff in *Brown v. Board of Education* (1954). He persuaded Eisenhower to keep a statement supporting school desegregation in the 1956 Republican platform. In addition, Brownell drafted the first civil rights bill since RECONSTRUCTION and succeeded in getting it passed in 1957

despite strong congressional opposition. The bill reportedly was tougher than Eisenhower wanted. In its final version, the CIVIL RIGHTS ACT OF 1957 was weaker than Brownell's draft but did do three things: it created a Civil Rights Commission, established the Civil Rights Division in the Justice Department, and gave the Attorney General power to seek an injunction when the right to vote was violated. Brownell also helped to handle the administration's major civil rights crisis, the LITTLE ROCK CRISIS. In September 1957, Governor Orval Faubus used the Arkansas National Guard to block the entry of nine black students to Little Rock's Central High School, despite a federal court desegregation order. The Attorney General closely monitored the crisis and advised Eisenhower, who eventually used federal troops to enforce the court order.

BIBLIOGRAPHY

Ambrose, Stephen E. *Eisenhower: The President.* 1984.
Anderson, John. *Eisenhower, Brownell, and the Congress: The Tangled Origins of the Civil Rights Bill of 1956-57.* 1964.

NANCY V. BAKER

BROWNLOW COMMITTEE. At the close of his first term (1933–1937), President Franklin D. Roosevelt sought to improve the management of the executive branch, and incidentally to enhance his institutional capacity to govern, through structural reorganization. Roosevelt was persuaded that what was needed was an academic theory and treatise to buttress a comprehensive reorganization strategy. He appointed Louis Brownlow, a noted public administrator, and two others to write a report with recommendations.

On 1 January 1937, the President's Committee on Administrative Management (the official name of the Brownlow Committee) submitted its fifty-five-page report to the President along with a number of supporting studies. The report emphasized three principal points: first, that the President is constitutionally the head of the executive branch and, therefore, chief administrator; second, that the President requires institutional assistance to perform his managerial functions; and, finally, that a hierarchical principle of organization with clear lines of authority and accountability is necessary for the efficient performance of governmental activities.

The committee recommended the creation of an EXECUTIVE OFFICE OF THE PRESIDENT with several managerial offices, the creation of two additional departments (of public works and of public welfare), and the reintegration into the departmental structures of most existing independent agencies, regulatory commissions, and government corporations. The report was particularly critical of independent regulatory commissions, referring to them as the "headless fourth branch of government."

The report of the committee has been characterized as the "high noon of orthodoxy" because of its advocacy of clear lines of accountability, departmentalism, and the doctrine that responsibility for making policy and setting standards ought to reside in the President and DEPARTMENTAL SECRETARIES rather than being devolved to the agency level.

In 1937 Roosevelt submitted a bill embodying many of the recommendations of the committee. The bill was debated in Congress in 1938 but was under consideration at the same time as the COURT-PACKING PLAN, and the reorganization bill was seen by many to be part of an effort by Roosevelt to establish a "presidential dictatorship," a perception sufficient in credibility to sink the reorganization bill.

In 1939, still smarting from the defeat suffered the previous year, Roosevelt submitted another, much more modest, reorganization bill. The 1939 bill contained only two of the major proposals recommended by the Brownlow Committee. The bill authorized the President to appoint six administrative assistants and to submit reorganization plans to alter executive-branch organization, such plans being subject to a LEGISLATIVE VETO by concurrent resolution of Congress. While considerable concern was expressed regarding the constitutionality of the procedures outlined for approving reorganization plans, the House and Senate passed the bill and it was signed by the President on 3 April 1939 (53 Stat. 561).

In direct legislative accomplishments, the Brownlow Committee's work produced relatively little. The two most important results were the passage of the Reorganization Act of 1939 and the establishment, by way of Reorganization Plan No. 1 of 1939, of the Executive Office of the President. The committee's greatest accomplishment, however, lay in the refinement of the concept of presidential administrative management, much of which would find fruition in the accepted recommendations of the first of the HOOVER COMMISSIONS.

BIBLIOGRAPHY

Emmerich, Herbert. *Federal Organization and Administrative Management.* 1971.
Fisher, Louis, and Ronald C. Moe. "Presidential Reorganization Authority: Is It Worth the Cost?" *Political Science Quarterly* 96 (1981): 301–318.
Karl, Barry. *Executive Reorganization and Reform in the New Deal: The Genesis of Administrative Management, 1900–1939.* 1963.
Polenberg, Richard. *Reorganizing Roosevelt's Government: The Controversy over Executive Reorganization, 1936–1939.* 1966.
U.S. President's Committee on Administrative Management. *Report with Special Studies.* 1937.

RONALD C. MOE

BRYAN, WILLIAM JENNINGS (1860–1925), Democratic presidential nominee in 1896, 1900, and 1908, Secretary of State. Born of religious parents and raised on the moral values of the *McGuffey Reader,* Bryan represented agrarian America. Finding law practice in Illinois unrewarding, he removed to Lincoln, Nebraska, in 1887. The state was Republican, but his demands for tariff, banking, and currency reform and railroad regulation sat well with Populists as well as Democrats and won him a seat in the U.S. House of Representatives in 1890.

During his two terms (1891–1895) Bryan won national acclaim for his tariff reform views and demands for an income tax amendment to the Constitution but particularly for his demand for free silver at the ratio of 16 to 1 with gold, which by inflating the currency could increase farm prices and enable mortgaged farmers to pay off their indebtedness.

Fearing that his demands for free silver made his reelection to the House of Representatives improbable in 1894, Bryan used his mellifluous and persuasive baritone voice to win control of the DEMOCRATIC PARTY from conservative Grover Cleveland. He also sought support from Populists and free-silver groups. At the Democratic national convention in 1896, held in Chicago, he delivered his "Cross of Gold" speech, which many historians believe won him the presidential nomination. He lost the election in part because conservatives opposed him and working people could not see how inflated farm prices would help them. More importantly, with full coffers, raised by Mark Hanna, William McKinley's campaign manager, Republicans sent out much more literature and many more speakers than did the Democrats. In addition, as the *Omaha World-Herald* put it, "The McKinley [Mark] Hanna combine" was guilty of "coercion, bulldozing, intimidation, false representation, suppression of facts, debauchery of purchasable votes and forced ballots."

Bryan erred in endorsing President McKinley's demand for a free CUBA in 1898 and supporting the SPANISH-AMERICAN WAR; although he served in the Nebraska Volunteers, he resigned in December 1898 because of McKinley's "imperialism." After his defeat in the presidential election of 1900, which he called a "solemn referendum" on his policies, he bided his time. After the Democrats were swamped in 1904, Bryan regained party leadership and offered a "bold new program" of progressive reforms, many of which Theodore Roosevelt advocated during his presidency—to the degree that in 1908 Bryan, again the Democratic nominee, claimed that he, rather than Republican William Howard Taft, was the legatee of Roosevelt's policies; nevertheless, Taft won easily.

From 1909 to 1912 Bryan worked for passage of the Sixteenth and Seventeenth amendments to the Constitution. With Bryan's support Woodrow Wilson won the Democratic nomination and the election in 1912. Wilson appointed Bryan Secretary of State. Bryan promoted the passage of Wilson's NEW FREEDOM reforms. His greatest contribution to world peace were thirty conciliation treaties—signatories would seek to resolve their differences for a year prior to using military force. However, his demand that nations in the Southern Hemisphere use democratic methods resulted in making the Caribbean, at least, an American lake. Fearing that Wilson's handling of the sinking of the *Lusitania* would drag the United States into WORLD WAR I, Bryan resigned on 8 June 1915.

Nevertheless, Bryan helped Wilson win reelection in 1916 and became a political force in Florida, where he moved in 1921. The paramount issue of the latter part of his life was his defense of revealed religion. At the famous Scopes trial held in Dayton, Tennessee, in July 1925, Bryan helped in the successful prosecution of high school biology teacher John T. Scopes for having violated the law prohibiting the teaching of evolution in the public schools.

For forty years Bryan sought measures that would allow the people rather than special political and economic interests to rule. His uniqueness lay in his double dedication, first to his God, second to the ideal of imbuing America's domestic and foreign relations with Christian ethics and morality.

BIBLIOGRAPHY

Ashley, LeRoy. *William Jennings Bryan: Champion of Democracy.* 1987.

Cherny, Robert W. *A Righteous Cause: The Life of William Jennings Bryan.* 1985.

Clements, Kendrick. *William Jennings Bryan: Missionary Isolationist.* 1982.

Coletta, Paolo E. *William Jennings Bryan.* 3 vols. (1964–1969).

Koenig, Louis W. *Bryan: A Political Biography of William Jennings Bryan.* 1985.

PAOLO E. COLETTA

BUCHANAN, JAMES (1791–1868), fifteenth President of the United States (1857–1861). Born near Mercersburg, Pennsylvania, to relatively humble parents of Scotch-Irish Presbyterian descent, he graduated from Dickinson College in Carlisle, Pennsylvania, in 1809 and studied law at Lancaster. As an able attorney and investor he amassed a large fortune. In 1819 his fiancée died shortly after they had quarreled, and he vowed to remain a bachelor. This may have affected his political principles because as a Congressman and Senator he shared bachelor quarters with southerners who became his closest personal friends.

Early Career. Buchanan served in the Pennsylvania legislature from 1814 to 1816 and in the U.S. House of Representatives from 1821 to 1831. He began as a strong Federalist, but after 1824 he easily shifted into the new DEMOCRATIC PARTY headed by Andrew Jackson. As minister to Russia from 1832 to 1833, he negotiated an important commercial treaty. He served in the U.S. Senate from 1834 to 1845. As he grew older, Buchanan became more committed to Jacksonian laissez-faire economics while such principles were growing weaker, even among Democrats. He opposed homesteads, river and harbor improvements, land grants for schools, and tariffs, even though he represented a manufacturing state. His Pennsylvania home, Wheatland, near Lancaster, was a manorial estate, and this may have influenced his economic principles, which usually agreed with those of his southern friends.

Buchanan had a remarkable talent for being on the winning side of controversial issues. He expressed regret that SLAVERY existed, but he defended the right of postmasters to censor abolition literature. In 1844 he supported the ANNEXATION OF TEXAS on the grounds that the border states were abandoning slavery and that Texas could become a new home for slaves who might otherwise become free and inundate the North. As James K. Polk's Secretary of State (1845–1849), he opposed Polk's demand for 54°40′ as the northern boundary of the Oregon Territory, then prepared a brilliant argument in favor of 54°40′, then refused to support his own argument and advocated a compromise, and finally insisted that 54°40′ was correct and refused to prepare the message submitting the Oregon Treaty, with 49° as the boundary, to the Senate. During the MEXICAN WAR he advocated only limited annexations, opposed Polk's efforts to send a peace commission for fear it would not demand enough territory, and finally opposed submission of the peace treaty to the Senate because it did not annex enough territory. He emerged from the bitterly controversial Polk administration with no serious political scars.

In retirement, from 1849 to 1853, Buchanan supported the COMPROMISE OF 1850 and opposed the WILMOT PROVISO. From 1853 to 1857 he performed creditably as minister to England, but again displayed his attachment to southern interests and the ideas of MANIFEST DESTINY. Along with the ministers to Spain and France, both southerners, he issued the Ostend Manifesto calling for the purchase of CUBA from Spain if possible and annexation by force if Spain would not sell. Stressing the danger that slavery might be abolished in Cuba, they insisted that this must be prevented as a mortal threat to the South.

Domestic Policies. As the 1856 Democratic candidate for President, Buchanan considered himself the savior of the nation from the disunionist free-soil Republican "fanatics," and he always believed that they were responsible for the CIVIL WAR. His greatest weaknesses in the White House were his strong emotional attachment to the South and his Southern friends and his insensitivity to Northern public opinion.

During the 1856 election campaign, numerous southern leaders and editors advocated secession if the REPUBLICAN PARTY candidate, JOHN C. FREMONT, should win. The greatest danger to the Union in 1860 would be the election of a Republican President, and to prevent this Buchanan should have been as anxious to placate Northern public opinion as Southern. Instead, he made meaningless concessions to the South that were of no practical benefit and served only to strengthen the Republican Party in the North. Upon election, he selected a Cabinet of four slaveholding Southerners and three Northerners, one of whom was senile, one of whom was pro-Southern, and one of whom would be pro-Southern on legal grounds until SECESSION.

In dispensing patronage, Buchanan and his Southern cabinet favored their friends and ignored the followers of STEPHEN A. DOUGLAS, the powerful senator from Illinois, who was the one Democratic leader capable of maintaining the party coalition of Northwest and South that would be necessary for a presidential victory in 1860. Douglas had worked hard for Buchanan's election and claimed to have spent $40,000 for that purpose. Buchanan, however, ardently disliked Douglas personally and gave the patronage in the Northwest to Jesse Bright of Indiana, who owned plantations and slaves in Kentucky.

Buchanan had been out of office for eight years and out of the country for four, and he was quite oblivious to changes in public opinion that had occurred. His Cabinet members and their families were a substitute for the wife and family he lacked and provided him with the companionship and affection he very much needed. Some historians have described his administration as a directory in which the President was dominated by his Cabinet, but Buchanan had selected the Cabinet members because he agreed with them, and he usually reached the same conclusions they did without any undue persuasion.

The 1856 Democratic platform had recommended the Douglas principle of popular sovereignty, whereby the people in the territories would decide for themselves about slavery, but it conveniently failed to specify whether the decision would be made when territorial government should be established or at the point of statehood. Northerners preferred the former, while Southerners insisted upon the latter, which would at least give slavery a chance to fail for economic rather than moral reasons. Buchanan had avoided the issue, but in his inaugural address he announced that the question would soon be settled by the Supreme Court. He knew what this decision would be because he had influenced Justice Robert C. Grier of Pennsylvania to vote with the five Southern justices to avoid a purely Southern verdict. In DRED SCOTT v. SANDFORD (1857) the Court by a 6 to 3 margin ruled that slavery was protected by the federal Constitution in all territories and that neither the federal nor any territorial government could bar slavery from any territory. Buchanan thought this would placate the South without disturbing the North, since no territories economically fit for slavery remained. Most Northerners, however, saw only that all of the western territories had been opened to slavery with no legal power existing to keep it out, and the resulting public outcry was a godsend for the Republican Party.

Almost immediately, Buchanan's belief that slavery could not expand was challenged when a small pro-Southern minority in Kansas met at Lecompton and wrote a state constitution. Probably to minimize voting by opponents of slavery, the convention refused to submit the entire Lecompton Constitution to the electorate and instead allowed the Kansas voters to decide only whether or not the constitution would protect slavery. This violated American political traditions, and for various reasons most Kansans did not vote at all. The result was a vote for slavery that represented only a small fraction of the Kansas population, but nonetheless Kansas would become a slave state if Congress accepted it. Buchanan theorized that if Kansas could be admitted as a slave state, it could amend its constitution and abolish slavery later, even though the constitution barred any amendments before 1865. Ignoring the advice of Robert J. Walker, governor of Kansas, Buchanan announced that Kansas was as much a slave state as Georgia or South Carolina and urged the Congress to accept the new state immediately. After a long and bitter debate the Senate accepted the Lecompton Constitution by a vote of 33 to 25, despite the angry opposition of Douglas. The House, however, after an even more acrimonious debate marked by physical violence, adopted a compromise that gave Kansas citizens another chance to vote. This time the constitution was defeated by a 6 to 1 margin. Angry Southern leaders everywhere now felt that Kansas had been stolen after they had won it fairly in Kansas, at the White House, and in the Senate. Equally important, the affair left Northern voters feeling that the slave power represented by Buchanan was dominating the country. This caused still more former Democratic voters to switch to the Republicans.

During 1857–1858 the United States went through a serious, though brief, economic depression for which Buchanan offered no solutions beyond scolding the nation for the speculation and inflationary activities that had caused it. As a result, the midterm elections of 1858 went heavily Republican in many parts of the North. Southerners, however, interpreted these results entirely as a vote for the party that opposed slavery.

The Coming of the Civil War. Nonetheless, sectional passions appeared to be subsiding until October 1859 when John Brown led a tiny army of twenty-one men in a raid against the federal arsenal at Harpers Ferry, Virginia. Brown hoped to arm the slaves of the surrounding countryside and start a race war throughout the South. No slaves revolted, the effort was quickly defeated, and Brown was captured, tried, and hanged. Most Northerners were horrified by Brown's intentions, but the affair greatly strengthened the Southern secessionist fire-eaters, who could use Brown as proof in their efforts to convince the non-slaveholding white majority in the South that Northerners really were plotting to abolish slavery through violence and mass bloodshed. This set the stage for the presidential election of 1860.

The radical Southerners came to Charleston, South Carolina, for the Democratic national convention in 1860 determined to split the party and ensure the election of a Republican President. Other Southerners hoped for the election of one of their own as President. The only candidate with a significant following in both North and South was Stephen A. Douglas, who had accomplished the repeal of the Missouri Compromise, and was clearly no enemy of slavery.

In his famous debates with Abraham Lincoln in 1858, Douglas had been forced to reconcile his popular sovereignty doctrine with the *Dred Scott* decision by arguing that while territorial governments could not pass laws barring slavery, they were not obligated to pass positive legislation protecting slavery, and no one would take slaves to a territory where such laws did not exist. It was a reasonable position, but the Southern radicals and President Buchanan were determined to prevent Douglas's nomination. Many of the delegates from the Northeast were federal officeholders over whom Buchanan wielded great power; they supported the radical Southerners on every issue of the presidential convention.

In the Southern environment of Charleston, the radicals, led by the great orator William Lowndes Yancey and cheered on by the galleries, countered the Douglas position with the Alabama platform demanding federal protection for slavery in all territories, regardless of the wishes of the inhabitants. No Northern delegate could endorse this principle and survive politically at home. Thus, after long and bitter debate and after various unsuccessful efforts by moderates to get the President to try to persuade the Southern radicals to accept a more reasonable position, the Alabama platform was defeated. As expected, the delegates from seven Southern states immediately bolted the convention. Buchanan's handpicked chairman ruled that a nominee must receive two-thirds of the original number of delegates, which meant that no candidate could be nominated. The convention reconvened in Baltimore a few weeks later, but the Southerners again bolted on the issue of whether those who had walked out in Charleston should be readmitted as delegates. The Northern delegates nominated Douglas for President, while a Southern convention nominated JOHN C. BRECKINRIDGE of Kentucky, who was at the time Vice President. The Republicans nominated Abraham Lincoln, while the Constitutional Union Party nominated JOHN BELL of Tennessee. The Democratic split had been partially engineered and was fully supported by President Buchanan, and the White House served as the campaign headquarters for Breckinridge. Buchanan had contributed significantly to a situation that made the election of Lincoln inevitable.

With Lincoln elected and seven Southern states preparing to secede, Buchanan's annual message to Congress endorsed the wildest arguments of the Southern radicals. He blamed the crisis entirely upon "the long, continued and intemperate interference of the Northern people with the question of slavery." Efforts to exclude slavery from the territories and prevent the execution of the fugitive slave law might have been endured, but "the violent agitation of the slavery question [had] produced its malign influence on the slaves, and inspired them with vague notions of freedom. . . . Hence . . . many a matron throughout the South retires at night in dread of what might befall herself and her children before the morning. . . . No political union, however fraught with blessings and benefits [could endure] if the necessary consequence be to render the homes and firesides of nearly half the parties to it habitually and hopelessly insecure."

Having agreed with the truth of the South's announced reasons for secession, Buchanan then argued that the South was in no real danger from Lincoln. A President, he said, could execute but not make the laws; moreover, no Congress had ever threatened slavery and Lincoln would enforce the fugitive slave laws. If, however, the state legislatures did not repeal their personal liberty laws (designed to hamper efforts of Southerners to recapture escaped slaves), the "injured States . . . would be justified in revolutionary resistance to the government of the Union." Secession, he insisted, was unconstitutional but was justified if called a revolution. And finally, Buchanan asked Congress to call a national convention to enact a constitutional amendment that would state the duty of the federal government to protect slavery in all territories throughout their territorial status, reconfirm the right of masters to have escaped slaves returned, and declare all Northern state laws hindering this process to be null and void. Thus, Buchanan defended the Southerners' excuses for secession, denied them any such right, announced his unwillingness to coerce them, and declared that secession could be prevented only by Northern concessions that every Southerner knew would never be made. The impact of this message upon Southerners still debating the issue of secession may have been considerable.

During the next several weeks, congressional committees and an ad hoc national committee tried desperately to frame an acceptable compromise, and Buchanan gave every support he could to these efforts. The Congress ultimately did pass a thirteenth amendment denying Congress any right to deal with slavery, and if the attack on Fort Sumter had not occurred this effort might have been ratified.

Despite his Southern sympathies, however, Buchanan flatly rejected Southern efforts to bargain for the three critical Southern federal forts: Pickens, Taylor, and Sumter. He would not recognize the Confederacy as a nation qualified to negotiate. He strengthened the first two, and they remained intact throughout the Civil War. Sumter, however, was inside Charleston harbor and very vulnerable to shore batteries. It was no threat to Charleston and of no great value to the Union, but its symbolic significance was obvious. Major Robert Anderson, in command at Sumter, was a

Southern Unionist. On several occasions he reported that his command was safe, but the ultimate danger was clear.

In a highly contradictory public letter, the army chief, General WINFIELD SCOTT, urged Buchanan to strengthen the forts, but pointed out that no forces were available for doing it. Scott also announced that a union that could be preserved only by force was not worth saving, and suggested that the United States should be divided into four separate nations. At one point Buchanan was ready to send reinforcements to Sumter on the powerful warship *Brooklyn*, but Scott persuaded him to substitute the shallow-draft unarmed sidewheeler *Star of the West* because the *Brooklyn* would be more likely to run aground in Charleston harbor. The Confederate shore batteries attacked the ship, which had no alternative but to depart. Scott would later condemn Buchanan for not sending the *Brooklyn*, even though Scott had made this decision himself. Buchanan was more ready than Scott to defend the fort, and four ships for that purpose were already assembled in New York when Lincoln took office.

Buchanan's final days in office were exacerbated further by a serious financial scandal caused by the inefficiency of John Floyd, the Secretary of War, in dealing with contractors and by Floyd's efforts to transfer a large quantity of arms from Pittsburgh to Texas. Floyd, a Virginian, resigned ostensibly to protest Buchanan's refusal to remove Anderson's command from Fort Sumter.

On the morning of Lincoln's inauguration, Buchanan received word from Anderson that twenty thousand men would be required to save Fort Sumter. The shocked President presented Lincoln with all the communications and decisions regarding Sumter and explained the presence of the naval force in readiness in New York. To his credit, he had handed Lincoln a Fort Sumter still intact.

Foreign Affairs. While the sectional conflict occupied most of Buchanan's attention, he also conducted an imperialistic foreign policy checked only by congressional disapproval. He sent an army under Colonel Albert Sydney Johnston to suppress the MORMONS in Utah, and only the skilled intervention of diplomat Thomas L. Kane prevented serious bloodshed. At one point he offered to buy Alaska as a haven for the Mormons, but the Russians refused his tentative $5 million offer.

Buchanan had a prolonged dispute with the British over Central America. Fortunately, the British had decided that U.S. expansion there would not hurt their interests and finally settled for the right to keep

British Honduras. Buchanan also sent General Scott with a small force to uphold American interests in a dispute with the British over the Canadian border in Puget Sound. U.S.-British relations were complicated further by British efforts to stop the African slave trade. Since traders would often run up an American flag to avoid search, the British claimed the right to inspect suspicious looking vessels regardless of their flags. The United States was committed by treaty to assist the British in this effort, but this obligation was ignored, and Buchanan ordered every available vessel to the Gulf of Mexico to protect American ships "from search or detention by the vessels . . . of any other nation."

Adventurer William Walker's private government in Nicaragua had been recognized by President Franklin Pierce but overthrown by other Central American countries. When Walker again sailed for Nicaragua with his own self-styled army, he was arrested by Commodore Hiram Paulding of the U.S. Navy. Buchanan, however, ordered Walker released and reprimanded Paulding for invading Nicaraguan territory. Walker insisted that Buchanan had secretly ordered him to take Nicaragua. Nicaraguan and Costa Rican leaders echoed the charge and proclaimed themselves to be under the protection of Britain, France, and Sardinia. Buchanan answered that the United States would resist any such European intervention and threatened to exact reparations for their insulting accusations. In each of his annual messages, Buchanan applied unsuccessfully to Congress for troops to quell violence and protect Americans in Central America.

In Mexico several leaders were struggling for power and the French were threatening to intervene. Buchanan asked Congress for the money to establish a protectorate or perhaps buy northern Mexico. Congress refused. In 1859 he asked Congress for authority to invade Mexico and obtain "indemnity for the past and security for the future," but Congress was busy investigating John Brown. In 1860 he signed a treaty giving Mexico $4 million for U.S. transit rights from the Gulf of Mexico to the Pacific and the right to police the route, but the Senate rejected it.

In 1859, Buchanan's close friend John Slidell introduced a bill in Congress to provide $30 million for negotiations with Spain for Cuba. The Southerners supported this, but after an angry sectional debate it was defeated. If Buchanan actually meant everything he said and was not merely trying to unify the country against some common enemy, he was prepared to annex everything from the Rio Grande to Colombia if Congress had been willing. No foreign insult, real or imagined, escaped Buchanan's attention. When a Paraguayan sniper killed an American sailor on the Parana River, the President sent nineteen warships carrying two hundred guns and twenty-five hundred sailors and marines to seek redress. Paraguay paid the sailor's family $10,000, apologized, and signed a useless trade treaty.

Buchanan had longed for a peaceful retirement, but the partisan press, fueled by the false statements of General Scott and Thurlow Weed, charged that he had been responsible for the fall of Fort Sumter and had deliberately sabotaged efforts to prepare the North for war. Those who could have defended him had either accepted appointments from Lincoln or were too frightened to speak out. Congress abolished his franking privileges for mailing letters, and various editors charged that he was trying to get foreign governments to support the Confederacy. Others made charges of personal corruption. His portrait had to be removed from the Capitol rotunda to keep it from being defaced.

The attacks at first made Buchanan violently ill, but at every opportunity he supported Lincoln's war effort. He took sharp issue with the peace plank in the 1864 Democratic platform. He opposed the EMANCIPATION PROCLAMATION, however, and advocated an offer to the Confederates "that they might return to the Union just as they were when they left it." In 1862 he demolished General Scott's charges in a series of public letters, and in 1866 he published his memoirs. He established a firm base of innocence of wrongdoing for future biographers and restored his own peace of mind, but his belief that Northern fanatics had provoked the war remained strong. He insisted that slavery should have been tolerated for the same reason that Christians were not using force to destroy Islam, and Catholics and Protestants were no longer warring against each other.

BIBLIOGRAPHY

Auchampaugh, Philip G. *James Buchanan and His Cabinet on the Eve of Secession.* 1926.

Buchanan, James. *Mr. Buchanan's Administration on the Eve of the Rebellion.* 1866.

Curtis, George T. *Life of James Buchanan.* 1883.

Klein, Philip S. *President James Buchanan.* 1962.

Moore, John B. *The Works of James Buchanan.* 12 vols. 1960.

Smith, Elbert B. *The Presidency of James Buchanan.* 1975.

ELBERT B. SMITH

BUCKLEY v. VALEO 424 U.S. 1 (1976). In *Buckley v. Valeo,* the Supreme Court addressed several constitutional challenges to the Federal Election Campaign Act of 1971 (86 Stat. 3), as amended by the Federal Election Campaign Act Amendments of 1974 (88 Stat. 1263). These statutes put in place comprehensive legislation governing the selection of the President, Vice President, and members of Congress, and implemented seven major reforms. These laws limited political contributions by individuals and groups to $1,000 each and by political committees to $5,000 each for any single candidate in any one election and imposed an annual ceiling of $25,000 on any individual contributor; prohibited individuals and groups from independently spending more than $1,000 "relative to a clearly identified candidate" in any one election; imposed ceilings (which vary with the office) on personal campaign contributions by a candidate and members of his or her family; set limits on overall primary and general-election expenditures by a candidate in any one election according to the office sought; required PACs (POLITICAL ACTION COMMITTEES) to keep detailed contribution and expenditure records that disclose the identity of contributors; amended the Internal Revenue Code to provide some public financing of primary and general election campaigns for major party, minor party, and new party candidates on a proportional and dollar-matching basis; and created an eight-member FEDERAL ELECTION COMMISSION to oversee enforcement of these regulations.

Senator James Buckley (Cons.-N.Y.), former Senator and presidential candidate EUGENE MCCARTHY, various major and minor political parties, and several political organizations brought suit to enjoin Francis Valeo (Secretary of the Senate) and the Clerk of the House of Representatives—both in their official capacities and as members of the Federal Election Commission—the commission itself, the ATTORNEY GENERAL, and the COMPTROLLER GENERAL from enforcing the many provisions of these statutes. The plaintiffs attacked these statutory provisions as abridging their free speech and associational rights under the First Amendment and questioned the legitimacy of the commission as a violation of the President's APPOINTMENT POWERS under Article II, Section 2, clause 2 of the Constitution. The government defended the legislation as essential to prevent the appearance or actuality of corruption, to broaden political influence, to equalize financial resources among competing candidates and interests, and to put a lid on the spiraling costs of primary and election campaigns.

The Court upheld the constitutionality of the general limitations on campaign contributions, the disclosure and reporting provisions, and the public-financing scheme. However, it accepted the plaintiffs'

argument that campaign expenditures constituted a form of political speech within the meaning of the First Amendment and held that—when weighed against prevention of the appearance or actuality of corruption, the only justification offered by the government that could be accepted as a compelling interest—the various spending limitations were either void for vagueness or else fatally overbroad. In the words of Justice Byron White, one of the decision's sternest critics, the Court's rulings in this and subsequent cases had the effects of elevating the old adage that "money talks" to the status of a constitutional principle and "transform[ing] a coherent regulatory scheme into a nonsensical, loophole-ridden patchwork." (*Federal Election Commission v. National Conservative Political Action Committee*, [1985], dissenting opinion.)

From the vantage point of the presidency, *Buckley* is important for testing the constitutionality of the Federal Election Commission. The plaintiffs argued that the composition of the commission violated the appointments clause of Article II because the Chief Executive was empowered to nominate only two of the commission's eight members. In addition to the two to be named by the President, two members of the commission were to be nominated by the president pro tempore of the Senate and two by the Speaker of the House. All were to be confirmed by both Houses of Congress. The Secretary of the Senate and Clerk of the House, serving ex officio, were to round out the panel.

Although the Court was deeply divided in its disposition of most of the other questions presented in this case, it held unanimously that the Federal Election Commission was illegally constituted. Since it was undoubtedly true that members of the commission were "Officers of the United States" because they held an office under the government, their appointment was inconsistent with the procedure prescribed in the Constitution. The appointments clause specifies in relevant part that the President "shall nominate, and by and with the Advice and Consent of the Senate, shall appoint . . . all other Officers of the United States, whose Appointments are not herein otherwise provided for, and which shall be established by Law: but the Congress may by Law vest the Appointment of such inferior Officers, as they think proper, in the President alone, in the Courts of Law, or in the Heads of Departments." Two constitutional flaws were therefore apparent in the statutory procedures governing the selection of the commission members. As the Court explained in *Buckley*:

Although two members of the Commission are initially selected by the President, his nominations are subject to confirmation not merely by the Senate, but by the House of Representatives as well.

The remaining four voting members of the Commission are appointed by the President *pro tempore* of the Senate and by the Speaker of the House. While the second part of the Clause authorizes Congress to vest the appointment of the officers described in that part in "the Courts of Law, or in the Heads of Departments," neither the Speaker of the House nor the President *pro tempore* of the Senate comes within this language.

In the Court's view, nothing justified departing from such explicit constitutional language. Rejecting the contention that Congress's authority to oversee federal elections entitled it to impose an election commission of its own choosing, the Court observed, "The position that because Congress has been given explicit and plenary authority to regulate a field of activity, it must therefore have the power to appoint those who are to administer the regulatory statute is both novel and contrary to the language of the Appointments Clause." Moreover, it found the charge that the President could not be trusted with commission nominations "since the administration of the Act would undoubtedly have a bearing on any incumbent President's campaign for re-election" entirely unpersuasive. "Congressmen might have equally good reason to fear a Commission which was unduly responsive to members of Congress whom they were seeking to unseat."

Finally, the Court noted that the intended independence of the commission from presidential control also was insufficient to justify a departure from the prescriptions of the appointments clause. Citing its ruling in HUMPHREY's EXECUTOR v. UNITED STATES (1935), which upheld limitations on the President's REMOVAL POWER over members of the independent regulatory commissions, the Court emphasized that in that case it "was careful to note that it was dealing with an agency intended to be independent of executive authority *except in its selection*'" (emphasis in original).

Although the Court conceded that Congress could construct whatever commission it wanted if its functions were "essentially of an investigative and informative nature," the Federal Election Commission could not be deemed simply an appendage of Congress's legislative function. Said the Court:

> The Commission's enforcement power, exemplified by its discretionary power to seek judicial relief, is authority that cannot possibly be regarded as merely in aid of the legislative function of Congress. A lawsuit is the ultimate remedy for a breach of the law, and it is to the President, and not to Congress, that the Constitution entrusts the responsibility to "take Care that the Laws be faithfully executed."

Insofar, then, as commission members engaged in anything beyond information-gathering, the tribunal was improperly constituted.

Congress responded to the Court's decision in *Buckley v. Valeo* by passing the Federal Election Campaign Act Amendments of 1976 (90 Stat. 475), section 101(a) of which amended the original statute to provide that all six voting members of the commission be nominated by the President and confirmed by the Senate. The amended statute also specified that no more than three members of the commission could have the same political-party affiliation.

BIBLIOGRAPHY

Bierman, Michael T. "Federal Election Reform: An Examination of the Constitutionality of the Federal Election Commission." *Notre Dame Lawyer* 51 (1976): 451–466.

"Congressional Power under the Appointments Clause after *Buckley v. Valeo*." Note. *Michigan Law Review* 75 (1977): 627–648.

Corwin, Edward S. *The President: Office and Powers, 1787–1984*. 5th ed. Revised by Randall W. Bland, Theodore T. Hindson, and Jack W. Peltason. 1984.

Miller, Arthur S. *Presidential Power in a Nutshell*. 1977.

Mutch, Robert E. *Campaigns, Congress, and the Courts: The Making of Federal Campaign Finance Law*. 1988.

CRAIG R. DUCAT

BUDGET AND ACCOUNTING ACT (1921).

This act established a national budget system for the federal government, conferring formal responsibility on the President to prepare a unified, comprehensive executive budget. The act also established a Bureau of the Budget, to provide staff and technical expertise to the President, and the GENERAL ACCOUNTING OFFICE, headed by the COMPTROLLER GENERAL, to examine and audit the expenditure of appropriated funds.

Passage of the 1921 budget act was an extremely important step in the evolution of the modern presidency, and it reflected a clear, if reluctant, admission by Congress that presidential leadership was necessary if the federal government expected to exercise strong, effective fiscal discipline, particularly control over spending. Congress would retain authority to revise or reject presidential budgetary proposals, but the President would first scrutinize all of the requests by spending agencies and revise those requests in accordance with a coherent program. Indeed, the statutory language directed the President to prepare spending proposals necessary "in his judgment" for the government's operations. Behind this injunction was the belief that personal responsibility was uniquely congruent with the institutional character and political accountability of the President.

The willingness of Congress to legitimize presidential budgeting in 1921 did not come easily. Congress had jealously guarded its power of the purse during the nineteenth century, rejecting requests to grant the President statutory authority to review and revise spending requests from executive departments. Instead, these requests, along with estimates and plans for government revenues, were submitted to the Congress without formal presidential review. Presidents and secretaries of the Treasury occasionally attempted to influence departmental requests, but there was no formal executive budget process nor a national budget.

During the nineteenth century, federal budgets were small and usually balanced. Congress was thus able to handle financial matters satisfactorily through its committee system, although it was occasionally forced to revise that system and related budgetary procedures. By the 1890s, however, a gradual erosion of congressional spending controls resulted in mounting deficits that continued into the early twentieth century. Faced with mounting criticism of its financial performance, Congress first attempted to revise its controls over executive agencies, but the costs and debt arising from World War I made a modern budget system necessary, and Congress finally agreed that the starting point for economy and efficiency in government spending was a presidential budget.

The basic framework of the 1921 budget act, along with its central assumptions about institutional capabilities, remained intact for several decades. Occasional changes were enacted in the content and format of the President's budget, but these were usually designed to improve its programmatic focus. The Bureau of the Budget (reorganized into the Office of Management and Budget [OMB] in 1970) was transferred to the Executive Office of the President from the Treasury in 1939, and its staff and advisory capabilities continued to expand. Over this same period, the federal budget's political importance was increasing dramatically, as the federal government assumed new responsibilities for fiscal policy management, National security, social welfare programs, and domestic improvements. By the 1960s, the President's budget had evolved into a highly significant and influential document.

The subsequent decline of the President's budget, and erosion of presidential responsibility for fiscal results, can be traced to unplanned changes in the composition of the federal budget and to deliberate alterations in the federal budget process. The former have reduced the comprehensiveness and coherence of the President's budget. The latter have resulted in competing congressional and presidential budgets, obscuring the accountability of both branches and undercutting the distinctive institutional responsibilities that were integrated into the 1921 budget act. Further, as deficit problems have become more and more serious, the executive branch and Congress have tried to restore a semblance of fiscal control, through balanced budget statutes and the Budget Enforcement Act of 1990, but these complex statutory solutions have not proved effective.

Since the early 1960s, the share of the federal budget devoted to entitlements and mandatory spending and to interest on the federal debt has increased from approximately one-third to about 60 percent. The share devoted to discretionary programs, defense and nondefense, has declined by a roughly corresponding amount. As a result, the President's budget is dominated by spending programs (and revenue sources tied to these programs) that do not require annual legislative actions by Congress. Since no action is required, the President's normal leverage in the legislative process is weakened.

Congress has added to this difficulty by further diminishing the significance of the President's budget. Under the 1974 Congressional Budget and Impoundment Control Act, Congress formulates annual budget resolutions that serve as alternatives to the President's spending priorities, tax program, and fiscal policy choices. Thus, two budgets are debated each year, but neither directly controls the fastest-growing spending programs, particularly entitlements.

The rise of uncontrollable spending, in the form of entitlement, coupled with multiple budgets, has resulted in the worst deficit record in the nation's history. The Gramm-Rudman-Hollings Acts of 1985 and 1987, which sought to force the President and Congress to balance the budget, failed in that task. The Budget Enforcement Act of 1990, which attempts to constrain spending and tax policy changes that would make deficits worse, has left the deficit at record levels.

The act does provide a modest boost to the President's budget, specifying that unless Congress adopts its own budget resolution by 15 April, the President's budget will be used in allocating spending ceilings to the appropriations committees. It also gives the OMB considerable discretion over the economic assumptions and spending and revenue estimates on which the act's enforcement procedures are based. All of this, however, is far removed from the fundamental principle of the 1921 budget act, which made the President personally responsible for the budget, with the corollary being that the President would also be held politically accountable. Budgeting in the 1980s and 1990s, by comparison, appeared to be more sophisticated and complex, yet its results were universally deplored, and there was neither institutional responsibility or political accountability for the failures.

BIBLIOGRAPHY

Ippolito, Dennis S. *Congressional Spending*. 1981.
Schick, Allen. *Congress and Money*. 1980.
Wildavsky, Aaron. *The New Politics of the Budgetary Process*. 1988.

DENNIS S. IPPOLITO

BUDGET ENFORCEMENT ACT (1990). The Budget Enforcement Act (BEA) established rules and procedures governing legislation that would have an impact on the budget during fiscal years 1991 through 1995. It superseded the GRAMM-RUDMAN-HOLLINGS ACT and introduced revised deficits targets, limits on discretionary expenditures, and pay-as-you-go (PAYGO) rules for direct spending and revenues. BEA also revised SEQUESTRATION procedures for excess deficits. Although it was initially effective for only a five-year period, some provisions of BEA had the potential to become ongoing features of federal budgeting.

BEA shifted from the fixed-deficit targets set by the Gramm-Rudman-Hollings law to flexible targets that could be adjusted to changing economic conditions and other factors. Gramm-Rudman's fixed targets had failed to produce promised deficit reductions, with the actual deficit exceeding the target in every year from 1986 through 1990. In most of these years, the gap between the projected and targeted deficit was sufficiently small that the President and Congress could avoid a sequester by using optimistic economic and budget forecasts. The projected gap for fiscal 1991 was so large, however, that it could not be closed by unrealistic forecasts.

BEA raised the deficit targets and allowed them to be further adjusted to take account of revised economic and technical assumptions and other variables. Spending increases resulting from past legislation permitted an upward adjustment in the deficit target, but those resulting from new legislation did not, with certain exceptions, raise the target.

BEA also recognized in law a distinction that, during the previous decade, had emerged in practice between discretionary spending controlled by annual appropriations and "direct spending" (principally for entitlement) controlled by other legislation. Discretionary spending was capped at predetermined levels, but with adjustments permitted for emergency appropriations and certain other items. For fiscal years 1991 through 1993, BEA set separate caps for defense, international, and discretionary domestic spending. For 1994 and 1995, BEA imposed caps only on total budget authority and outlays. BEA barred underspending in one category in order to apply the surplus to another.

Director spending was not capped, but PAYGO rules provided that legislation that increased expenditures had to be offset by legislated cuts in other direct spending, by legislation that would raise revenues, or by the sequestration of certain direct spending. These rules did not pertain to spending increases deriving from existing law and they could be waived by designating new legislation as an emergency measure.

The federal deficit rose sharply in the years immediately after the enactment of BEA, exceeding previous records in both the 1991 and 1992 fiscal years. While the rise was largely caused by a prolonged recession, BEA's flexible deficit targets meant that neither the President nor Congress had to take any action on the burgeoning deficit. Thus, Congress did not consider reconciliation legislation in either its 1991 or 1992 session, but the shift to flexible targets did spur Congress and the President to make more realistic deficit forecasts than they had under Gramm-Rudman.

BEA had only limited success in controlling expenditures. The caps on defense spending did keep it at approximately the same level, without any adjustment for inflation, for fiscal years 1991 through 1993. But, given the collapse of the Soviet Union and the democratization of its former satellites in Eastern Europe, defense spending would have receded even without BEA, possibly to levels below the caps. Discretionary domestic spending was capped at a cumulative level $40 billion above baseline for fiscal years 1991 through 1993, thus providing for substantial increases in annual appropriations.

BEA did restrain the enactment of new mandatory expenditures, but it had no impact on the built-in increase in entitlement spending under existing law. Despite BEA, in 1993 these expenditures were more than $200 billion above the 1990 level.

BEA was enacted pursuant to the 1990 BUDGET SUMMIT agreement between the President and congressional leaders. Both sides anticipated some advantages in the new rules. The House and Senate appropriations committees insulated their spending bills from the relentless rise in entitlements, while authorizing committees gained some respite from annual cutback drives. The President won higher defense spending than would otherwise have ensued and control of the scorekeeping process for estimating the cost of legislation. This power proved to be a mixed blessing, however. The new rules made it difficult for the President to propose legislative initiatives, but he was nevertheless impelled to accommodate some congressional initiatives by supplying favorable cost estimates. The power to keep score became in some cases the power to go along, even if doing so required some questionable estimates.

BIBLIOGRAPHY

Joyce, Philip G., and Robert D. Reischauer. "Deficit Budgeting: The Federal Budget Process and Budget Reform." *Harvard Journal on Legislation* 29 (1992): 429–453.
Kosters, Marvin H., ed. *Fiscal Politics and the Budget Enforcement Act.* 1992.
U.S. Congressional Research Service. *Manual on the Federal Budget Process.* 1991.

ALLEN SCHICK

BUDGET POLICY. Since 1921, one of the most important powers of the presidency has been the formulation of the budget of the United States and its submission to Congress, a process that involves both symbol and substance. The budget is a plan for the nation's finances and therefore a statement of national priorities. As such, it dictates how much money goes to defense or domestic needs and whether or not taxes should be raised or lowered, all the while being balanced or in deficit. The budget provides an opportunity to influence the nation's economy, adjusting taxing and spending to spur growth or restrain inflationary surges. Symbolically, the budget reflects a President's values and leadership abilities, whether in proposing bold new spending initiatives, offering sweeping tax cuts, or resolving to reduce the budget deficit.

Despite its importance for the presidency, budget policy also presents difficult, often intractable problems to an administration. The President does not operate alone under the constitutional system on matters of taxing and spending; the Constitution grants Congress the greater share of taxing and spending powers. Since 1974, with the passage of the CONGRESSIONAL BUDGET AND IMPOUNDMENT CONTROL ACT, Congress has been particularly assertive and able to compete with the President as a coequal partner in determining budget policy. Budgets have become increasingly inflexible in recent decades, reducing presidential control. Most budget outlays are mandatory because of previous commitments such as SOCIAL SECURITY, Medicare, federal retirement, or interest on the national debt. Since the 1980s, chronic budget deficits have constrained the presidency in terms of policy options. Because the budget is built on estimates and assumptions, it is vulnerable to external factors such as the performance of the economy or increases in health care costs. For example, the deficit can increase by as much as $30 billion if unemployment rises only a single percentage point higher than was estimated. Finally, the President is constrained by other liabilities of the federal government, such as loan guarantees and government insurance programs. When savings and loan institutions failed in large numbers, the President had no choice but to ask for hundreds of billions of additional monies to reimburse depositors [see SAVINGS AND LOAN SCANDALS]. While the budget offers some potential for presidential leadership, it also is fraught with political pitfalls.

Components of Budget Policy. To understand both the opportunities and the potential problems that budgeting presents the President, it is necessary to identify the budget numbers that Presidents and the public watch most closely and to examine the composition of spending.

Budget totals. Presidents are frequently most concerned with the overall budget aggregates that will often be the basis for judging their requests to Congress. Particularly important are total outlays, total revenues, and the size of the deficit—the amount that spending exceeds tax receipts in a given year. Total spending indicates the size and scope of government, particularly when measured as a proportion of gross domestic product (GDP). For example, in late 1963 President Lyndon B. Johnson retired to his Texas ranch to make cuts so he would not be the first President to send a $100 billion budget to Congress. In 1974, President Gerald Ford did the same thing to keep total spending below $400 billion. In more recent years, Presidents have been as concerned with the deficit as with total spending. Also of concern to budget makers is the size of the public debt, the sum total of the budget deficits over the years. All Presidents must be concerned with controlling spending, but controlling spending is more difficult with certain categories of outlays than others.

Entitlements. The largest and fastest-growing component of federal outlays consists of mandatory spending for ENTITLEMENTS, that is, statutory guarantees that benefits will be paid to all those who qualify for them. The largest entitlement program is Social Security, followed by Medicare, Medicaid, and civilian and military retirement programs. These programs cannot be cut by appropriating less money but only by changing the law that defines eligibility. In 1960, entitlements made up less than a quarter of the budget. By 1990, they approached half of all outlays.

Defense spending. Historically, defense has been one of the largest and most important components of federal spending. During wartime, as much as 85 percent of the budget has gone to defense. By the early 1990s, it had approached 20 percent of annual outlays. Determining how much to spend on national defense is a critical question for the President, but it takes many years to expand or reduce the size of the military establishment. In the post–COLD WAR era, pressures have increased to reduce defense spending in favor of other needs.

Interest on the national debt. This expense, representing the third-largest component of spending in the early 1990s, is the most uncontrollable since the credit of the federal government depends on meeting its borrowing obligations.

Domestic discretionary spending. This category, although smaller than the other three, often consumes the most time and attention by the administration and Congress. It includes hundreds of programs in health, education, agriculture, environmental protection, housing, and a host of other activities.

Revenues. A budget includes an accounting of where the money will come from as well as where it will go. Decisions on raising or lowering taxes are among the most important policy decisions a President and Congress make. The largest source of federal revenue is the individual income tax, followed by social insurance payroll taxes, corporate income taxes, and excise taxes.

Making Budget Policy. The BUDGET AND ACCOUNTING ACT of 1921 created the national budget and gave the President responsibility for submitting requests from agencies and departments in a single package. To help accomplish this task, the Bureau of the Budget (BOB) was created within the DEPARTMENT OF THE TREASURY. Although Congress did not intend to abdicate its constitutional authority in taxing and spending, the Budget and Accounting Act shifted budgetary power toward the President. This budgetary authority became even more important in the 1930s under President Franklin D. Roosevelt, as the government took a more active role in managing the economy. Under the Keynesian economic theory employed by the Roosevelt administration, the budget became the primary tool for stimulating or restraining the economy. Reflecting its growing importance, BOB was moved in 1939 to the newly created EXECUTIVE OFFICE OF THE PRESIDENT (EOP), where BOB was directly responsible to the President and took a leading role in formulating budget policy. The BOB grew in importance in the ensuing decades and became responsible for assembling the President's legislative program. In 1970, President Richard M. Nixon reorganized the BOB into the OFFICE OF MANAGEMENT AND BUDGET (OMB),

giving the new agency both management and budgetary functions. In the 1980s, President Ronald Reagan gave OMB additional responsibilities in reviewing federal regulations.

Despite the importance of the President's budget office, many other executive-branch officials play key roles in making budget policy. The budget involves literally thousands of large and small decisions, from individual salaries to the amount going to national defense. The executive budget is actually a compendium of budget requests for the government's departments, agencies, bureaus, and public corporations. The federal fiscal year runs from 1 October through 30 September, three months ahead of the calendar year. The executive budget process begins almost eighteen months before the start of the fiscal year, when agencies and departments review their spending needs for the coming years. The busiest time of the year is the fall, when OMB examiners review agency requests and begin to assemble the massive budget document. The President gives the budget director broad guidelines concerning priorities, new initiatives, and areas to cut. Because agencies usually seek additional funding for their programs, OMB generally reduces their requests in order to control spending.

The process involves much more than paring and assembling agency requests, however, since discretionary spending now constitutes a relatively small share of total outlays. The President's budget, built on a series of estimates and projections, is shaped by the data of various administration officials. First, revenues and entitlements will rise or fall automatically depending on the performance of the economy during the fiscal year. The president's COUNCIL OF ECONOMIC ADVISERS prepares economic projections of GDP, unemployment, inflation, and interest rates. These will determine estimates of tax revenues and spending on unemployment compensation, welfare, and other automatic programs. The Treasury Department estimates revenues under existing tax laws and the consequences of any changes the President may propose in the budget. OMB works with agencies such as The DEPARTMENT OF HEALTH AND HUMAN SERVICES to estimate changes in the number of eligible recipients, healthcare cost increases, and other factors that determine outlays. This information is reviewed by the President, the CABINET, and a handful of close advisers in late December as the budget nears final preparation. The budget is printed and delivered to Capitol Hill in late January, eight months before the start of the fiscal year.

Presidents' involvement in budgeting varies, but in most cases the President enters the process only at the highest levels of decision-making. Most Presidents are particularly active in their first year in office as they try to leave their imprint on the nation's most important policy document. Because the budget has important political consequences as well as policy implications, Presidents must consider the potential outcomes of their budget requests. Within these overall bounds, some Presidents take a more active role in making budget policy, depending on their interests and abilities. President Jimmy Carter, for example, spent a great deal of time early in his administration on the details of the budget. He reviewed massive briefing books summarizing hundreds of policy decisions throughout the federal government. In contrast, President Reagan avoided detail altogether, issuing broad instructions and delegating the implementation to the staff. Excessive attention to detail is extremely time-consuming for a President and can obscure the big picture. Conversely, an overly detached approach can result in serious miscalculations by subordinates and can obscure accountability.

Whatever the President's personal role in developing the executive budget, it bears his name and represents his vision of the country's needs for the coming year. The President has various means to develop political support for his budget proposals as they wend their way through Congress. The first is the message that accompanies the budget when it is submitted to Congress. Directed to both Congress and the American public, the budget message is a political appeal that the administration's proposals are best for the country. The STATE OF THE UNION MESSAGE, delivered close to the same time, gives the President another chance to lobby for his budget priorities. The Economic Report of the President explains the administration's economic assumptions and explains how the budget requests relate to the nation's fiscal and monetary policy. Throughout the year, the President may deliver special messages to Congress, introduce new tax packages, or hold press conferences to lobby for budget proposals. At critical junctures, the President may address the nation to argue for the program. In 1981, for example, President Reagan successfully went on television to build public support for his defense buildup, tax cut, and domestic spending reductions. In 1990, President George Bush similarly took to the airwaves but was unable to convince a restive Congress to pass the bipartisan budget agreement that had been worked out with Democratic congressional leaders.

From the 1980s on, as controversy over the budget and the deficit increased, BUDGET SUMMITS between the executive and legislative branch became more important in determining final budget numbers. These involved closed-door negotiations and lobbying between the President's surrogates and top legislative leaders. In addition to negotiations and lobbying by the President and key administration officials, the President may take direct actions to affect budget policy. Before 1974, Presidents could impound funds—that is, refuse to spend monies appropriated by Congress on the grounds that such spending was not necessary. Because of large impoundments by President Nixon, Congress banned IMPOUNDMENT by enacting the Congressional Budget and Impoundment Control Act of 1974. Instead of impoundment, the President may request a deferral to temporarily delay spending; this action takes effect unless Congress votes not to accept it. The President may also request a rescission to eliminate spending permanently; this action does not take effect unless Congress votes to affirm it within forty-five days. Finally, the President may veto appropriations bills, tax bills, or other legislation that affects spending. This does not guarantee that the administration's proposals will be adopted, but it does send Congress back to the drawing board. Dissatisfied with their budgetary powers, Presidents Reagan, Bush, and Clinton requested a constitutional amendment for an ITEM VETO, a power enjoyed by most state governors, that would allow the President to veto parts of a spending bill without rejecting the entire bill.

When the budget is finally approved, the executive branch is responsible for the execution of the budget. OMB and the Treasury work together to disburse monies to various agencies and programs and to coordinate tax collection and borrowing. The executive branch is also responsible for managing programs and auditing various agencies. The GENERAL ACCOUNTING OFFICE, an arm of Congress, also has responsibility for auditing federal spending.

Trends in Budget Policy. The nature of federal budgeting and the composition of revenues and expenditures have changed dramatically since WORLD WAR II. Yet some themes, such as balancing the budget or choosing the proper balance between defense and domestic spending have remained constant. Total outlays were slashed in half as the nation demobilized in the 1940s, but by the early 1950s, defense spending still constituted more than half of the budget. President Dwight D. Eisenhower was willing to use the budget to help stimulate the economy, but balancing the budget remained his highest budgetary principle. Eisenhower had a balanced budget three out of eight years—the last President to do so more than once. His efforts to balance the budget during an economic downturn, however, worsened the recession, and Richard Nixon believed those policies hurt his campaign for the presidency in 1960.

Defense spending first declined in real terms following the end of the KOREAN WAR, then leveled off after 1955. Despite Eisenhower's military background, John F. Kennedy during the 1960 presidential campaign accused the Eisenhower administration of creating a missile gap with the Soviet Union. But defense spending did not begin to rise significantly again until after Lyndon Johnson assumed the presidency and the United States became more deeply involved in the VIETNAM WAR.

Other budget policy issues that dominated the Kennedy-Johnson era included taxes and domestic spending initiatives. Enacted in 1964, a tax cut designed to stimulate the economy was widely acclaimed: unemployment was low, economic growth was robust, and inflation was modest. This provided a fiscal dividend to support new government programs, particularly the Johnson administration's war on poverty and GREAT SOCIETY programs. As spending increased because of the Vietnam War and new social programs, budgetary problems began to increase. Inflation heated up and budget deficits became more troublesome. The Johnson administration was forced to opt for guns over butter and to propose a tax increase, finally enacted in 1968, to curb inflation.

The budget itself began to change under Presidents Nixon, Ford, and Carter. New entitlements such as Medicare, Medicaid, and food stamps, all enacted in the mid-to-late 1960s, commanded a larger share of budget outlays. Increases in Social Security benefits, by as much as 20 percent in a single year, sharply increased the cost of that program. At the same time, economic growth did not match its performance in the 1960s, resulting in revenues that were not growing as fast as expenditures. The post-Vietnam reductions in defense spending from 1970 to 1980 freed some money for domestic uses, but not enough to balance the budget. The last balanced budget occurred in 1969, during the Nixon administration. During the 1970s, total federal spending rose to around 22 percent of GDP, up from 18 percent in 1965. The composition of the budget changed as well. In 1970, defense constituted 43 percent of spending and entitlements 28 percent. By 1980, defense had fallen to 23 percent while entitlements shot up to 42 percent of outlays. Presidents Ford and Carter struggled with stagflation—simultaneously high levels of unemployment and inflation—as well as growing budget deficits. These developments set the stage for the 1980 election of Ronald Reagan, who would make the most dramatic changes in budget policy in a generation.

Reagan campaigned on a platform that defense spending had grown dangerously low, that domestic spending was too high, and that taxes needed to be cut. In 1981, the administration was successful in getting its sweeping budget proposals adopted. A rapid defense buildup—of $1.8 trillion over five years—was initiated. Income taxes were cut 25 percent across the board. Domestic spending was cut, but not enough to compensate for additional defense spending and reduced revenues. The result was an explosion of budget deficits that would become the dominant constraint on budget policy. Defense spending increased to 25 percent of outlays and entitlements to 45 percent, but the largest increase was in interest payments on the growing debt: 15 percent of all outlays by 1990. The category that fell most sharply was discretionary domestic spending, which dropped from 26 percent of the budget to 15 percent.

Taxes have been a crucial element of budget policy in recent years. The 1981 Reagan tax cut lowered the top marginal tax rate to 50 percent; the rate on the wealthiest taxpayers had been as high as 90 percent in the 1950s. Rates fell again in 1986 when President Reagan and Congress adopted the landmark Tax Reform Act that lowered the top marginal rate to 31 percent. Taxes and the deficit were key elements of budget controversies during the administration of President George Bush. Despite the 1985 adoption of the GRAMM-RUDMAN-HOLLINGS ACT, a mandatory deficit reduction plan, by 1990 deficits stood at record levels. After a divisive summit with congressional Democrats, the President broke his 1988 campaign promise ("Read by lips, no new taxes") agreeing to raise taxes to help cut the deficit. Despite the package of tax increases and spending cuts, however, deficits continued to run as high as $300 billion annually. When he took office, President Bill Clinton proposed a massive deficit reduction package of nearly $500 billion over five years that included an increase in the top marginal income tax rate for wealthier households.

Budget policy remains one of the most critical challenges of the American presidency. Making the budget involves extremely difficult choices between competing goals: keeping taxes low and providing adequate spending for domestic and defense needs while trying to reduce large deficits and keep the economy out of recession. The President faces many constraints in trying to manage the nation's budget from a powerful Congress to the continued rapid growth of entitlements. Yet despite the obstacles, the budget will continue to be the most important policy statement of government and a challenge to presidential leadership.

BIBLIOGRAPHY

Fisher, Louis. *Presidential Spending Power.* 1975.
Ippolito, Dennis S. *Uncertain Legacies: Federal Budget Policy from Roosevelt through Reagan.* 1990.
Kettl, Donald E. *Deficit Politics: Public Budgeting in its Institutional and Historical Context.* 1992.
LeLoup, Lance T. *Budgetary Politics.* 1988.
Schick, Allen. *The Capacity to Budget.* 1990.

LANCE T. LELOUP

BUDGET SUMMITS. Negotiations between presidential aides and congressional leaders for the purpose of formulating a deficit-reduction package acceptable to the two sides are known as budget summits. The President sometimes participates in such discussions, but he usually stands apart from the day-to-day negotiations which, in some years, have taken a month or more to complete. If agreement is reached, implementing legislation is enacted in an omnibus measure such as a reconciliation bill.

The first budget summit took place in 1980. It was followed by frequent interbranch negotiations during the next decade, some of which broke up in disagreement. In some years, however, the summit agreement displaced the President's budget as the principal guideline for revenue and spending legislation.

Summits began on a modest scale in the spring of 1980, when President Jimmy Carter, alarmed by panic in financial markets, withdrew the budget he had submitted to Congress two months earlier and prepared a new one in negotiations with congressional Democrats. In 1982, high-level negotiations were held between a congressional group—the so-called Gang of Seventeen—and President Ronald Reagan's advisers, but the talks ended in disagreement. The White House and Senate Republican leaders held extensive discussions in 1983 but were unable to put together an encompassing agreement.

Presidential aides and Senate Republicans returned to the bargaining table in 1984 and negotiated the so-called Rose Garden agreement on the budget. This was followed the next year by the so-called Oak Tree agreement between the President and House Democrats. The next summit, which took place after the 1987 stock market crash, produced a two-year deal with sufficient reduction in the estimated deficit to avoid a sequester under the GRAMM-RUDMAN-HOLLINGS ACT. The 1989 summit was also geared toward avoiding SEQUESTRATION, but its terms were limited to one year. The most ambitious summit during the period under review took place in 1990, when President George Bush and congressional leaders concluded prolonged negotiations with a five-year package that pared an estimated $450 billion from the projected budget deficits for fiscal years 1991 through 1995 and produced the BUDGET ENFORCEMENT ACT of 1990.

Summits are arrangements of convenience. They cannot be programmed in advance, nor does their outcome follow a prescribed course. They occur only when the respective negotiators want them to, and on terms agreed to by both sides. Each year's circumstances determine whether and when the negotiations take place, who participates, the agenda, and the rules of negotiation. If one side or the other feels it would be disadvantaged by negotiations, it can refrain from entering them; if it perceives delay to be advantageous, the talks will be postponed. Sometimes the negotiators are drawn from a single political party; sometimes, conflict between the two parties brings Democrats and Republicans to the bargaining table. Some agreements have been in force for only one year, but the 1990 agreement covered five years. Some negotiations have been conducted in the spring, shortly after the President's budget has been issued; some have taken place in the fall, when the new fiscal year is underway.

Yet the frequency with which budget summits took place during the 1980s suggests the presence of factors impelling the two sides to cooperation. DIVIDED GOVERNMENT—with the Democrats controlling one or both houses of Congress and the Republicans controlling the White House—induced the two branches to seek new means of accommodation, especially in the budget arena, where the need to enact annual appropriations made protracted stalemate unacceptable. Chronic deficits and the need to cut expenditures or add to revenues gave each party and branch a strong incentive to negotiate with the other. The threat of sequestration reinforced the impulse to negotiate, for this threat could be removed only by joint action of the two branches.

Outcomes have varied from summit to summit. Some have produced minimal deficit relief (as little as has been needed to avert a sequester), but the 1990 summit yielded what some hoped would be sufficient savings to put an end to chronic deficit crises. Success at a budget summit is measured in terms of whether a deal has been negotiated and whether Congress has followed through with implementing legislation. Substantive criteria, such as the deal's impact on the deficit, are of less import.

Recourse to summits in the 1980s attested to a fundamental change in the political status of the President's budget. Where once it was an authoritative statement of government policy, now it was just one of a number of plans, including one prepared by Congress's own budget makers. Presidents had to seek at budget summits what they could not obtain through means that had served them so well in the past, when Congress had computed its budget actions according to the President's request. The summit process made Congress more than the President's equal, for it had the final say, not only in enacting the summit-approved package but in carrying through with appropriations and other measures. The summit relied on baseline projections, largely produced by the Congressional Budget Office, to calculate the impact of the summit agreement on the deficit. As a measure of current policy, the baseline was not at all affected by the President's budget; what he initially wanted became almost irrelevant at the summit.

Summits speak to the interdependence of the two branches, with neither being able to prevail on budget matters without cooperation from the other and each needing the other's support to shelter it against criticism for raising taxes or cutting programs. Interdependence arose out of a simple fact of budgetary life in the 1980s: each branch could block adoption of the other's policy preferences. But the interdependence that impelled them to the summit also impelled them to settle for less rather than more.

BIBLIOGRAPHY

Dauster, William G. "Budget Emergencies." *Journal of Legislation* 18 (1992): 249–315.
Schick, Allen. *The Capacity to Budget.* 1990.

ALLEN SCHICK

BULL MOOSE PARTY. See Progressive (Bull Moose) Party.

BULLY PULPIT. It is more than a textbook convenience to refer to the first decade of the twentieth century as the Era of Theodore Roosevelt. Teddy Roosevelt, or TR, as he was popularly called, virtually imprinted his own personality on his times, perhaps because his times so well reflected his own personality. "He is not an American," one contemporary commented, "he is America." Youth, expansiveness, self-confidence, optimism, moralism—TR embodied all these qualities, as did the nation he came to lead at the age of forty-two, the youngest person ever to become President. In achieving the presidency, TR fulfilled many an American boy's ambition, but it was his further ambition, more than anything else, to use the presidency to raise the nation's moral sensibilities. For such

purposes he found the office, as he put it in his robust style, a bully pulpit.

By the time he became President, Roosevelt had already become something of a model American hero, with an extraordinarily broad range of accomplishments. With his education, his political and administrative experience in New York and Washington, his international travel and acquaintances, his scholarly publications, his patrician background, and his sense of disinterested social responsibility, Roosevelt entered the presidency better qualified and better prepared than any man since John Quincy Adams. But in addition to such elite qualities, TR's experiences with real, live cowboys and Indians in the still-wild West and his victorious engagement in heavy combat in Cuba with the Rough Riders, a volunteer cavalry unit during the Spanish-American War, gave substance to virtually every young American's daydream of heroic perfection.

This background, and TR's ebullient style, attracted the nation's attention and mobilized Americans in support of progressive causes as no President had since Andrew Jackson. Most particularly, he removed from social reform the stigma of effeteness that had attached to it during the rough and tumble, crude and cruel age of the robber barons. In fulfilling his personal ambition to "gain access to the governing class," as he put it, he also regained it, for a time, for the patrician class to which he belonged. More than that, he helped make politics, for the next few generations at least, an attractive career for the talented, the educated, the earnest, and the goodwilled. And the publicity he craved, and won, elevated the stature of the federal government as never before. Altogether, with the aid of the bully pulpit, Roosevelt did more than anyone else in the country's history to infuse reform with respectability, to reestablish popular respect for the federal government as an effective instrument for the public welfare, to bring a national focus to the diffuse reform energies at large, and to call the nation's attention to the domestic and international implications of its industrial growth.

BIBLIOGRAPHY

Harbaugh, William H. *The Life and Times of Theodore Roosevelt.* Rev. ed. 1975.

RICHARD M. ABRAMS

BUREAU OF THE BUDGET. See Office of Management and Budget.

BURR, AARON (1756–1836), third Vice President of the United States (1801–1805). Born in New Jersey,

Burr attended Princeton, where he studied for the ministry. Shortly after his graduation in 1772 he turned to the law. During the Revolution, Burr followed Colonel Benedict Arnold through the wilderness of Maine to Quebec. Rising quickly to the rank of major, Burr transferred to the staff of George Washington, although the Virginian's demands for deference clashed with Burr's innate air of superiority. He resigned from the army in early 1779 following strenuous campaigns at Valley Forge, Pennsylvania, and Westchester County, New York.

The fall of 1783 found Burr practicing law in New York City. His considerable abilities caught the eye of Governor GEORGE CLINTON, who in 1789 appointed him state attorney general. His deft handling of the political marriage between the Clinton and Livingston factions, together with his opposition to ALEXANDER HAMILTON's bank (Burr had scant comment on the more explosive policies of funding and assumption) brought about Burr's elevation to the U.S. Senate in 1791. Clinton's temporary retirement from the political wars served to advance Burr as a potential running mate for Thomas Jefferson in 1796, since Jefferson's Virginia-based Democratic-Republican Party required a northern candidate for balance. Although the Democratic-Republican caucus adjourned without making a formal decision for Vice President, most northern electors agreed to cast their lot with Burr. Southern electors, however, failed to adhere to this unofficial agreement: North Carolina gave him only six votes compared to eleven for Jefferson, and Virginia almost shut him out, giving Burr only one vote to Jefferson's twenty. In all, Burr received a mere thirty votes compared to the fifty-nine won by Thomas Pinckney, the candidate the Federalists favored for Vice President.

Retired from the Senate, Burr labored to secure New York—which John Adams, the winner of the 1796 presidential contest, had carried—for the Democratic-Republican camp in 1800. Because the state legislature chose the twelve New York electors, the Democratic-Republican strategy required the party to capture a majority of seats in the spring elections. The key was New York City. Showing extraordinary organizational skill, Burr pieced together a popular slate of eleven candidates, headed by the ancient enemies George Clinton and Brockholst Livingston, for the state legislature. Burr's machine carried the city by more than four hundred votes. With the election of his entire ticket, the closely balanced state assembly tipped to the Democratic-Republican side.

Burr's extraordinary labors again earned him the right to stand as Jefferson's running mate on the national ticket. Clinton wanted the nomination, but more as a recognition of past service than from any desire to serve; Clinton informed ALBERT GALLATIN that if elected he "would be at liberty to resign." Armed with these peculiar conditions, Burr's supporters successfully advanced his name at the Democratic-Republican caucus on 11 May 1800. Because Burr believed he had been "deceived" by the southern electors four years before, the caucus endorsed a compact pledging all electors to vote equally for Jefferson and Burr. This would, if successful result in a tie for the presidency, with the final decision being made in the House of Representatives, but the caucus regarded that course as less dangerous than trying to give Jefferson the edge by instructing one elector throw his second vote away. (The Federalist caucus, which nominated John Adams and CHARLES COTESWORTH PINCKNEY, forged a similar compact.)

As the Democratic-Republicans expected, Jefferson and Burr tied in the electoral college with seventy-three votes each; the election would be decided by the lame-duck Federalist House. Burr promptly responded by informing Samuel Smith of Maryland that he "utterly disclaim[ed] all competition." Many Federalists, however, had no intention of turning the executive mansion over to Jefferson. As an urbane, northern man from a mercantile state, Burr was preferable to most Federalists to the agrarian "visionary" from Virginia. With realistic hopes of obtaining the presidency suddenly within his grasp, Burr grew quiet and stubbornly refused to publicly state that if elected he would decline to serve—a pledge many Democratic-Republicans urged him to make. Yet neither did Burr pursue the office. As Federalist Congressman William Cooper lamented, "Had Burr done anything for himself he would long ere this have been president." On the thirty-sixth ballot, James A. Bayard of Delaware—to the anguished cries of "Deserter!"—broke with his party and cast his ballot for Jefferson.

Never close to Jefferson, Burr's silence during the House debates won him the permanent enmity of the President. His estrangement from the Democratic-Republican Party became complete when he hesitated to use his authority as Vice President to cast the tie-breaking vote over the Judiciary Act of 1801. At the party caucus in early 1804, Burr's spot on the ticket was turned over to George Clinton. Burr had prepared for such a contingency by having his friends in the New York assembly nominate him for governor. Hamilton worked to see that Burr enjoyed no Federalist support, and at a private dinner expounded on Burr's "despicable" public and private conduct. When Burr lost the election to the regular Republican candidate, he sought his revenge on Hamilton, challenging him to a duel. The two rivals met at Weehawken, New Jersey, on 11 July 1804. Hamilton planned to hold his fire, although his pistol went off as Burr's ball struck him in the abdomen. Hamilton died the next day.

His political career in the East at an end, Burr turned his energies to the frontier. Rumors of his fantastic schemes to detach some of the western states from the Union twice brought him before a federal grand jury in Kentucky. Acquitted both times, Burr journeyed to Nashville, where he began to lay plans for an invasion of Spanish Mexico. When the plot threatened to become more than bold words, Burr's confederate, General James Wilkinson, who was secretly in the pay of Spain, determined to betray him to federal authorities. Burr raced south toward Pensacola but was captured near the border and carried to Richmond. Burr was charged with treason. His trial began in May 1807. JOHN MARSHALL, acting as judge of the U.S. Circuit Court, ruled that the Constitution defined treason only as the actual act of "levying war" against the Republic. As no "overt act" could be found, the jury had no choice but to acquit. Shortly thereafter, Burr sailed for Britain in hopes of obtaining aid in fomenting revolution in Mexico. As his plans grew wilder—he tried to interest Napoleon Bonaparte in a plan to precipitate war between Britain and the United States—his purse grew thinner. On returning to New York in 1812, Burr resumed his legal career but failed to end his chronic insolvency. Shortly after his second wife, Eliza Bowen Jumel, sued for divorce to protect her rapidly diminishing estate, Burr suffered a stroke. On 14 September 1836—the date of his death—the divorce became final.

BIBLIOGRAPHY

Abernethy, Thomas. *The Burr Conspiracy.* 1954.
Kline, Mary-Jo, and Joanne Wood Ryan, eds. *Political Correspondence and Public Papers of Aaron Burr.* 2 vols. 1983.
Lomask, Milton. *Aaron Burr.* 2 vols. 1979–1982.
Pancake, John S. "Aaron Burr: Would-Be Usurper." *William and Mary Quarterly* 3d ser., 8 (1951): 209–211.

DOUGLAS R. EGERTON

BUSH, BARBARA (b.1925), First Lady, wife of George Bush. After dropping out of Smith College following her freshman year, Barbara Pierce married George Bush on 6 January 1945. She spent her adult life as a traditional wife and mother, following her husband from one job to another in the United States and abroad, first in private business and then in government. Outside her own family, her major interests centered on volunteer efforts in several fields, with special emphasis on organizations devoted to improving literacy and health. As FIRST LADY, she followed a more traditional path than that taken by some of her immediate predecessors and refused to take public stands on controversial issues or to make known her preferences on presidential appointees. Popular with Americans who appreciated her undisguised matronly appearance, she frequently made jokes at her own expense. Her book, *Millie's Book: As Dictated to Barbara Bush*, purported to tell the story of the family dog, Millie, and became a best seller, producing nearly $800,000 in royalties in 1991. The First Lady's share of the proceeds (after taxes) amounted to far more than the President earned that year and were donated to the Barbara Bush Foundation for Family Literacy.

BIBLIOGRAPHY

Bush, Mildred Kerr. *Millie's Book: As Dictated to Barbara Bush.* 1990.
Radcliffe, Donnie. *Simply Barbara Bush: A Portrait of America's Candid First Lady.* 1989.

BETTY BOYD CAROLI

BUSH, GEORGE (b. 1924), forty-first President of the United States (1989–1993). As much as any President, George Herbert Walker Bush came to office shaped by the American experience of the COLD WAR with the Soviet Union and the institutions that arose during the cold war period. He began his adult life as a U.S. Navy bomber pilot in WORLD WAR II, served in the U.S. House of Representatives, and represented the U.S. both as ambassador to the UNITED NATIONS and as envoy to China. He then directed the CENTRAL INTELLIGENCE AGENCY (CIA) and served as Vice President for eight years while President Ronald Reagan, to counter the Soviet threat, ordered the largest peacetime military buildup in American history.

Yet Bush's central task as President was to oversee the end of the cold war and the demise of the Soviet Union. The Berlin Wall came down, Germany was reunited, the Warsaw Pact military alliance collapsed, and agreements were reached that radically reduced the nuclear arsenals of the superpowers. Many of these momentous changes were pushed along by the deft, highly personalized diplomacy conducted by Bush.

Paradoxically, Bush reaped little political benefit from these gratifying developments abroad or from his successful prosecution of the GULF WAR to drive the occupying Iraqi army out of Kuwait. Instead, by the end of this term his once-formidable popularity had seriously eroded because of a lackluster U.S. economy and a growing sense among voters that he had little of the enthusiasm for addressing domestic problems that he had shown in addressing foreign crises. With few deeply held ideological views, Bush never promised an expansion social agenda. Instead, he once pledged simply to be the "follow-on President" who consolidated and rounded out the accomplishments of his predecessor, Reagan.

Bush achieved legislative successes early in his term, but never fully conquered a Congress controlled by Democrats. Instead, he spent much of his time simply trying to keep Congress in check, chiefly by use of the veto; he cast thirty-five vetoes before Congress finally overrode one just a month before he stood for reelection. An economic recovery he had promised the nation turned out to be anemic. He broke a well-publicized promise never to raise taxes in order to negotiate a budget deal with Democrats that proved unsuccessful at either closing the budget deficit or sparking a healthier economic recovery. Ultimately, the end of the cold war left Americans feeling it was safe to make a change, and Bush suffered a sound defeat when he sought reelection.

Early Life. George Bush was born on 12 June 1924, in Massachusetts. His father, Prescott Bush, was a successful businessman who later became a U.S. Senator from Connecticut. On his eighteenth birthday, just after World War II broke out, Bush became the youngest pilot in the U.S. Navy. In September 1944, Bush's plane was shot down by Japanese antiaircraft fire, but Bush was rescued from the water by an American submarine. After he was ordered home from the war in late 1944, he married Barbara Pierce, the daughter of a New York publishing executive [see BUSH, BARBARA].

Bush earned a degree in economics from Yale University in 1948 and moved to Texas, where he became modestly wealthy in the oil business. Along the way, Bush began dabbling in REPUBLICAN PARTY politics. He became a county chairman in 1962. In 1964, he ran for the U.S. Senate but lost to Ralph Yarborough. In 1966, he ran for the U.S. House of Representatives from his Houston district and won easily. In the House, he made a mark in 1968 by voting for the CIVIL RIGHTS ACT OF 1968, much to the dismay of some of his constituents.

After two terms in the House, Bush decided to make another run for the Senate, calculating that he would again face the liberal Yarborough. But instead he faced a more conservative Democrat, Lloyd Bentsen, who defeated him in a close race.

To show his gratitude to Bush for trying to claim the Senate seat for the Republicans, President Richard M.

Nixon appointed him U.S. ambassador to the United Nations—the first of the series of prestigious posts to which Bush would be appointed. After the 1972 election, Nixon made Bush chairman of the Republican National Committee, a post Bush assumed just as the WATERGATE AFFAIR was engulfing the party. Then, in 1974, President Gerald Ford made him the U.S. envoy to China. After just a year, Ford brought Bush home to become Director of Central Intelligence.

On the strength of this impressive résumé, Bush decided to run for President in 1980. He presented himself as a moderate Republican who favored some government activism to address social problems. He belittled as "voodoo economics" the plan put forth by the more conservative Reagan to sharply cut tax rates while also significantly increasing defense spending. Bush broke away from the Republican pack early and won the Iowa caucuses. But Reagan came back to win a strong victory in the New Hampshire primary and capitalized on his strength among conservatives in the South and West to drive Bush from the race. Despite some philosophical differences and Bush's harsh words about his economic ideas, Reagan picked Bush to be his running mate in an attempt to present a more ideologically balanced ticket. The Reagan-Bush team won the 1980 election in a landslide over Jimmy Carter and WALTER F. MONDALE.

Vice Presidency. Bush became a competent and moderately influential Vice President who kept a low public profile. He used the vice presidency to satisfy his growing interest in foreign affairs, traveling abroad to more than seventy countries to represent the Reagan administration. Bush was the first administration official to hold a meeting with the Soviet Union's new and vibrant leader, Mikhail Gorbachev, in 1985. As Vice President, Bush also took on some specific domestic duties, including heading a task force to reduce federal regulations and another that attempted to stanch the flow of illegal drugs into the United States.

As Bush began his effort to run for President to succeed Reagan, he increasingly sought to assume some credit for the Reagan administration's accomplishments. But his involvement in the Reagan White House's inner workings ultimately turned into a source of controversy for Bush because of the IRAN-CONTRA AFFAIR of 1986. Bush later claimed that he never knew all the details of arms sales to Iran, and he ardently maintained he was "out of the loop" and was never told of the diversion of funds to the Nicaraguan rebels. No evidence emerged to shake his claim, but the issue dogged Bush through his 1988 campaign for President and beyond.

The 1988 presidential campaign was the culmination of a quarter-century's preparation by Bush. He hoped to capitalize on his connection to Reagan's political coalition of Republicans and conservative Democrats and to broaden the coalition by promising to do more than Reagan had on selected issues such as the environment and education. The enormous, 508-point fall in the Dow Jones industrial average in October 1987 had raised some doubts about the financial condition of the country after six years of rising federal budget deficits. Still, Reagan remained generally popular, and Bush hoped to capitalize on this popularity. Above all, Bush argued that at a time when potentially momentous changes were taking shape in the Soviet Union, the United States should be guided by someone, like him, with broad experience in foreign affairs.

The Bush campaign received an early shock when, largely because of dissatisfaction over a sluggish farm economy, he trailed Kansas Senator Robert Dole in the Iowa caucuses. But Bush won the New Hampshire primary and ultimately captured the Republican nomination. Going into the Republican convention, Bush trailed Democratic nominee MICHAEL DUKAKIS of Massachusetts by as much as 17 points in opinion polls. At the convention, Bush surprised even his closest advisers by picking a young, relatively unknown Senator from Indiana, DAN QUAYLE, to be his running mate.

At the convention Bush laid out the successful themes for his general election campaign. He promised to build a "kinder, gentler" nation by giving more energy and money to selected social and environmental programs. And, uttering words that would return to haunt him, Bush told Republicans that when Democrats pressed him for higher taxes, he would reply, "Read my lips, no new taxes." Bush defeated Dukakis comfortably, with 53.4 percent of the popular vote to 45.6 percent for the Democrat. Bush had won a personal mandate, but his party had not. Democrats controlled the Senate, 57 to 43, and the House, 262 to 173.

Bush's Appointments. Bush filled his Cabinet with experienced, mainstream Republicans, many of whom had served with him in the Ford administration. He made his close friend and political adviser JAMES A. BAKER III Secretary of State, and retained another old friend, Nicholas Brady, as Secretary of the Treasury. Brent Scowcroft, who had been national security adviser for Ford, again took that job.

But Bush got an early sign of how difficult it would be to handle Congress when the Senate defeated his nomination of former Senator John Tower to be Secretary of Defense. Bush quickly recovered by picking as Tower's replacement Representative DICK CHENEY, who proved to be one of his most competent Cabinet officers. But the episode signaled the political difficulties Bush would face with Congress despite his desire to operate in a more bipartisan way than had Reagan.

Domestic and Economic Policy. Though he made no dramatic breaks with Reagan's legacy, Bush edged domestic policy away from his predecessor's more ideological positions. Almost immediately after assuming office, Bush had to propose a plan to bail out the nation's sickly savings and loan industry, which was in deep trouble because of a heavy load of bad debt accumulated in the deregulated climate of the 1980s [*see* SAVINGS AND LOAN DEBACLE]. Bush also quickly moved to end the ongoing problem of developing countries' indebtedness to American and other Western banks by shifting away from a policy of encouraging more lending to one of debt reduction.

Bush veered away from Reagan policies by suspending imports of the semiautomatic rifles that were proliferating among drug dealers, though that move hardly satisfied those who wanted such weapons outlawed entirely. In an attempt to make good on his promise to be the "education President," Bush proposed a package of spending increases on some education programs, particularly those for the youngest children, and summoned all the nation's governors to a summit conference to establish a set of education goals for the nation's schoolchildren.

He proposed raising the minimum wage if Congress would also establish a lower, six-month "training wage" for young workers. After vetoing one bill, Bush got and signed a measure raising the minimum wage to $4.25 and instituting the training wage he wanted. He also began scaling back the Reagan defense program by dropping its call for annual 2 percent inflation-adjusted spending increases, a bow to both fiscal reality and the fact that the Soviet threat was fading amid new democratic reforms there. From the outset, Bush also began pushing for a cut in the capital gains tax rate, something he was to seek unsuccessfully throughout his term.

Bush championed legislation to expand federal help for child care. By the midpoint of his term, Bush had pushed through Congress the Americans with Disabilities Act, which gave broad new rights to disabled Americans. But perhaps his biggest domestic accomplishment came in the fall of 1990, when Congress passed a comprehensive new Clean Air Act. The measure enacted tighter controls on auto emissions, accelerated the use of cleaner-burning fuel, capped emissions by utility plants, and cut allowable emissions of hazardous gases by industrial plants. It was estimated that the bill would cost American businesses more than $20 billion annually. Taken together, the Americans with Disabilities Act and the Clean Air Act illustrate the great paradox of Bush policies: though he railed against government overregulation, Bush championed two laws that imposed significant new regulatory requirements.

Foreign Policy. As time went on, Bush was spending an increasing amount energy managing relations with the rapidly changing Soviet Union. He entered office proclaiming skepticism about the depth of the economic and political reforms proclaimed by Soviet leader Gorbachev. He ordered a review of U.S. policy toward the Soviet Union. This frustrated Gorbachev and raised doubts about whether Bush would continue to honor the personal ties that had developed between Reagan and Gorbachev.

End of the cold war. But, by the summer of 1989, Bush began moving to engage Gorbachev, proposing a summit conference on Malta. The timing of the meeting turned out to be fortuitous, because the Soviets' Eastern European empire was just beginning to crack. Increasingly emboldened by Gorbachev's calls for political reform, Poland and Hungary had started to free themselves of the Soviet grip. In short order, Hungary called free elections, Czechoslovakia's communist leadership resigned, and Bulgaria's communist leader quit amid growing popular demands for change. Most dramatically, East Germany's communist leadership was collapsing as well.

Bush and Gorbachev virtually declared that the cold war was over. Bush offered Gorbachev a long list of steps to increase economic ties if the Soviets continued their move away from communism and toward free markets. The two leaders also pledged to finish agreements slashing strategic nuclear and conventional-arms arsenals in Europe within a year. An important milestone, the summit created a strong bond between Bush and Gorbachev and led the Soviet leader to conclude that Bush would support his reforms and not embarrass him if he let Eastern Europe to go its own way.

Bush and Gorbachev met again in six months, this time in Washington, to agree on the outlines of a deal cutting strategic nuclear arsenals by more than a third and to discuss the evolving situation in Germany. That meeting was followed by months of intensive U.S. diplomacy over German unification, led by Secretary of State Baker, during which Gorbachev was persuaded to let a newly united Germany to become part of the Western military alliance.

Bush's attention was pulled back to the historic changes in the Soviet Union in the summer and autumn of 1991. Gorbachev's hold over his country was steadily loosening, as the Baltic republics and others pulled away from Moscow's control and his adversary Boris Yeltsin became the first popularly elected leader of the Russian Republic. When Gorbachev allowed the Soviet military to crack down on the Baltics to keep them in the fold, Bush and Baker exerted strong pressure on him to pull the army back. Gorbachev eased up enough to clear the way for another Bush-Gorbachev summit meeting at the end of July 1991 in Washington, where they signed a formal treaty ensuring deep cuts in strategic nuclear arsenals.

But within weeks, while Bush was vacationing at his summer home in Kennebunkport, Maine, a badly organized coalition of Gorbachev aides, KGB leaders, and military officers detained Gorbachev and attempted a coup. Bush reacted cautiously, calling the coup attempt "extraconstitutional" but keeping open the possibility of working with the coup leaders if they ultimately consolidated control. But it quickly became clear that Boris Yeltsin would step forward to lead popular resistance to the coup. Bush quickly threw his support behind Yeltsin's charismatic leadership. When it became clear that Soviet soldiers and KGB units would not move against Yeltsin and his Russian supporters, the coup collapsed, and, as it did, so did the Soviet Communist Party. Gorbachev returned to Moscow, but he had lost public support to Yeltsin. Republics began pulling away, and Bush recognized the independence of the Baltic states on 2 September. Gorbachev and Bush met once more, at the 30 October opening of a Middle East peace conference, but the Soviet Union's end was near. On Christmas Day 1991, Gorbachev called Bush to tell him he was resigning as Soviet leader and disbanding the Soviet state.

Bush quickly turned to building relations with Yeltsin. In early 1992, Bush and Baker hosted an international conference to generate aid to help the new nations of the former Soviet Union through the difficult process of building free-market economies. By spring 1992, Bush and other leaders of the industrialized world had agreed on a $24-billion package of assistance, though disbursement of the aid was slowed by the erratic pace of economic reforms in Moscow. And Bush and Yeltsin quickly agreed on a second round of dramatic cuts in strategic nuclear weapons, reducing superpower arsenals to just a third their former size.

Panama and China. Bush invested his time on other foreign policy initiatives as well. After a few American soldiers in PANAMA were harassed and one was killed, he ordered American troops to invade the country on 20 December 1989. Their mission was to capture

Panama's leader, General Manuel Noriega, who was wanted in the United States on drug-trafficking charges. Noriega gave himself up on 3 January 1990 and was flown to Miami, Florida. The Panama invasion, ordered without congressional approval, helped Bush recover from an earlier embarrassing episode in which Panamanian officers had mounted a failed attempt to oust Noriega—without receiving the U.S. support they had evidently expected.

Bush's policy toward China, where he had years before served a happy stint as envoy, sparked public controversy. After China's communist leaders crushed a prodemocracy uprising in Beijing in mid 1989, Bush announced a cutoff of high-level official exchanges in protest. But a month later, he secretly sent National Security Adviser Scowcroft and Deputy Secretary of State Lawrence Eagleburger to Beijing for talks aimed at convincing the Chinese to liberalize their system. The two aides returned for another visit in December, when their diplomatic activities were disclosed. The visits produced no wholesale changes in Chinese policies, however.

Persian Gulf War. Bush's most dramatic challenge overseas began on 2 August 1990, when Iraqi troops and tanks overran and occupied the small Persian Gulf oil sheikdom of Kuwait and threatened to move on to the world's largest oil fields in adjoining Saudi Arabia.

Bush reacted swiftly. Within a week of the invasion, he had ordered the deployment of some 100,000 U.S. troops and a large contingent of warplanes to Saudi Arabia. The U.S. and its allies pushed a series of resolutions through the United Nations Security Council ordering Iraq to leave Kuwait and slapping a total economic embargo on Iraq until it complied. U.S. ships were used to enforce the embargo, and nations in the region were persuaded to cut off Iraqi oil pipelines. Bush and Baker also began a diplomatic drive to convince other countries to send military forces to Saudi Arabia, an effort that eventually led more than twenty nations to contribute troops or equipment to the effort. Crucially, the Soviet Union was persuaded to break with Iraq, its longtime ally, and forcefully to oppose the occupation of Kuwait. Bush and Gorbachev held a special summit meeting specifically to discuss the crisis in Helsinki, Finland, on 9 September 1990.

The standoff turned into a showdown between Bush and Iraq's Saddam Hussein, whom Bush portrayed as the personification of the evil forces that had to be contained in a post–cold war world. Just after the November 1990 congressional elections, Bush ordered American troop presence expanded to more than 400,000 and instructed his military commanders

to prepare plans for offensive operations. He also insisted he did not require approval from Congress to launch military action against Iraq because such action would be aimed at fulfilling America's obligations to help enforce U.N. resolutions. But Bush realized that seeking U.N. approval to start a war without seeking the same approval from the U.S. Congress put him in an awkward position, so he belatedly sought a congressional resolution authorizing military action if necessary. It passed easily in the House, and, after a day of dramatic debate, narrowly passed the Senate on 12 January.

The U.N. Security Council set a deadline of 15 January 1991 for Iraqi forces to evacuate Kuwait. Iraq did not budge. So on 17 January 1991, Bush ordered U.S. warplanes, with help from British and French allied forces, to launch a massive bombing campaign against Iraqi troop positions in Kuwait and military and economic targets throughout Iraq. In late February, Bush ordered U.S. and allied ground troops to move into Kuwait to drive out the Iraqis. The allies quickly sliced through the battered Iraqi defenses and soon had Iraqi occupying troops encircled. After just a hundred hours of ground fighting, with Iraqi troops fleeing Kuwait in a mad rush and American casualties startlingly low, Bush ordered an end to the conflict.

Kuwait had been liberated, Iraq's military embarrassed, and Bush's determination vindicated. But Saddam Hussein himself had survived, a fact that prompted critics to question whether Bush had ended the war too soon. Bush and his aides heatedly replied that U.N. resolutions had authorized only the liberation of Kuwait and that any attempt to root out Saddam could have entangled the U.S. in Iraq for years. Thus, when Shiite Muslims in southern Iraq and Kurdish rebels in northern Iraq rose up against Saddam shortly after the war's conclusion, the Bush administration decided against coming to their aid. Instead, Bush came to rely on continued U.N. economic sanctions and restrictions on Saddam's actions against his Kurdish and Shiite subjects to keep Iraq in check.

Postwar Problems. The Persian Gulf victory sent Bush's popularity soaring to unprecedented heights, with his job approval reaching nearly 90 percent in some polls. But Bush failed to turn the victory abroad into significant action at home. He appeared before a cheering joint session of Congress and announced a new Middle East peace initiative, which by fall 1991 had brought ISRAEL and its Arab neighbors together for the first-ever direct peace talks. But Bush failed to propose any significant new domestic initiatives.

Worse, it became clear that the economy, which had been growing at a 4.4 percent annual rate when Bush won the presidency, slipped into a recession at about the time Iraq invaded Kuwait in the summer of 1990. That compelled Bush to make a fateful decision. In the fall of 1990 he authorized his aides to try to negotiate a deficit-cutting budget deal with Congress and to accept tax increases as part of the deal. His goal was to reach an agreement that would appear certain to cut the deficit in coming years, in hopes that a cut in federal borrowing to finance the debt would lower interest rates and spark a solid economic recovery. Bush did achieve a budget deal designed to cut the deficit by $500 billion over five years (in part by raising top individual tax rates as well as taxes on gasoline, beer, and luxury items), but the vibrant economic recovery never came. In part this was because the financial markets remained unconvinced that the terms of the the budget deal would be followed. And because the sluggish economy kept down tax receipts, the deficit did not shrink, either. In the meantime, Bush had broken his vow never to raise taxes, angering conservative supporters and raising questions about his trustworthiness.

By 1991, Bush also was juggling simultaneous problems on civil rights legislation and the controversy that followed his nomination of a black conservative to replace retiring Supreme Court Justice Thurgood Marshall. Bush's nominee, Clarence Thomas, was a controversial figure in the African American community because of his conservative legal views. Still, he appeared to be heading toward Senate confirmation when Anita Hill, a former employee of Thomas's at the Education Department and the Equal Employment Opportunity Commission, accused Thomas of having sexually harassed her. Thomas emphatically denied the charges and was narrowly confirmed by the divided Senate by a 52-to-48 vote on 15 October 1991 amid an erupting national debate about sexual harassment.

In the aftermath of the Thomas trauma, Bush faced an equally sensitive decision over a new civil rights bill designed to reverse the effects of a Supreme Court decision that had made it more difficult for women and minorities to prove discrimination in the workplace. When Congress passed such a bill in October 1990, Bush vetoed it, claiming it would impose unacceptable hiring quotas. By late 1991 Congress was about to pass the legislation again. In the wake of the Thomas hearings, and with his reelection campaign on the horizon, Bush and his advisers were loath to wade into another social controversy with another veto of civil rights legislation. This time, Bush's aides and Republican Senator John Danforth of Missouri negotiated some changes in the legislation, and Bush signed

it when it passed in November. He thus managed to anger both sides of the debate: conservatives and business interests were upset that Bush refused to veto the bill, and liberals and civil-rights leaders were angered because Bush's White House signaled its intention to use a narrow, conservative interpretation in enforcing the law.

Presidential Election of 1992. Increasingly, Bush pulled back from international affairs to counter criticism that he had been neglecting the home front. Bush's own Attorney General, Richard Thornburgh, who had left the Cabinet to run against Democrat Harris Wofford in a special race to fill a vacant Senate seat in Pennsylvania, suffered a stunning upset loss. Wofford won by attacking Republicans for ignoring the everyday economic woes of Americans, particularly the exploding cost of health care. The Thornburgh defeat sent shock waves through the Bush camp. The President promptly postponed a long-scheduled trip to Japan and Australia to stay at home to push for tax cuts and investment credits designed to improve the economy. When Bush rescheduled his trip to Japan three months later, he tried to tie it to domestic affairs by taking along a group of U.S. auto executives and other businessmen, an initiative that came off appearing clumsy and cynical.

At the outset of 1992 Bush again tried to inject some life into the economy by announcing measures to cut withholding-tax rates, to accelerate federal spending, and to freeze federal regulations. By this time, however, Bush was facing an unwelcome challenge from within his own party by conservative television and newspaper commentator Patrick Buchanan. The challenge was never serious, but it forced Bush to play to his party's right wing at a time when he would have preferred to concentrate on winning the support of wavering moderate voters from both parties. Buchanan never won a primary and by spring had to pull out of the race for lack of money. Bush's renomination was secure.

The economy provided Bush with an intractable problem. The recession was over, and the American economy was actually growing and even performing better than the economies of several other industrialized nations, but Bush's advisers were unable to find the formula to spark the vibrant recovery Americans wanted. Instead, there were troubling signs that the economy might slip back into recession. In the first quarter of 1992, the economy grew at a 2.9 percent rate, then fell back to a 1.5-percent growth rate in the second quarter. By the time the summer convention season arrived, there was a popular sense that the economy was in the doldrums and that the Bush administration did not know what to do about it. In one attempt to show that he had a long-term vision for economic growth, Bush emphasized his philosophy of negotiating free-trade agreements around the globe. The centerpiece of this effort was the North American Free-trade Agreement among the United States, Canada, and Mexico, which Bush and his counterparts in those nations completed in late 1992.

Meanwhile, Democrat Bill Clinton was sewing up the Democratic nomination and laying the groundwork for a campaign in which he promised a more activist government, a far more intense effort to improve the domestic economy, and programs to invest in new technologies to prepare the country to compete in the global marketplace of the 1990s. Above all, Clinton skillfully portrayed himself as a youthful and forward-looking leader, by implication casting Bush as a tired thinker still focused on the fading foreign-policy issues of the cold war. To complicate Bush's political fortune further, an unexpected challenge arose from an independent candidate, the irascible Texas billionaire, H. ROSS PEROT. "Change" became the most potent campaign theme for both Clinton and Perot, and the combination worked against Bush.

Amid growing press scrutiny of his business practices and of his penchant for secrecy and intrigue, Perot pulled out of the race just as the Democrats were formally nominating Clinton. Perot voters surged toward Clinton, who almost overnight opened up a twenty-point lead over Bush in opinion polls. Bush tried to recover by painting Clinton as "just another tax and spend Democrat" and hinting that Clinton could not be trusted to handle NATIONAL SECURITY affairs because of his role in organizing demonstrations against the VIETNAM WAR in the 1960s. In the final weeks of the campaign, Perot decided to reenter the race, but his reappearance effected no dramatic change in the contours of the competition between Bush and Clinton.

In the end, Clinton won, taking 43 percent of the popular vote and carrying thirty-two states; Bush won just 38 percent of the popular vote—the lowest for an incumbent President in eighty years—and carried eighteen states. Although Perot did not win any states, he got a healthy 19 percent of the popular vote.

During his presidency, George Bush changed the way American leaders conduct foreign policy. More than any of his predecessors, he eschewed traditional foreign-policy channels and used modern communications technology—including frequent phone calls—to conduct personal diplomacy directly with other heads of state. He also labored steadily, but with limited success, to preserve and expand the power of the presidency. He battled congressional efforts to force him to impose trade restrictions on China; he invaded Panama without advance congressional authorization; and he declared he could have moved against Iraq on his own authority as well. He consistently fought for an ITEM VETO that would have given him the power to strike individual spending projects out of catchall spending bills, though he never won congressional approval. Bush also tried to deemphasize the packaging of the presidency, worrying far less about carefully staged television images or dramatic speeches than did President Reagan. Ultimately, though, this disdain for image may have deprived him of opportunities to relay messages about his achievements and contributed to the political problems that cost him a second term.

BIBLIOGRAPHY

Bartley, Robert L. *The Seven Fat Years*. 1992.

Beschloss, Michael R., and Strobe Talbott. *At the Highest Levels*. 1993.

Bush, George, with Victor Gold. *Looking Forward: An Autobiography*. 1987.

Cramer, Richard Ben. *What It Takes: The Way to the White House*. 1992.

Duffy, Michael, and Dan Goodgame. *Marching in Place: The Status Quo Presidency of George Bush*. 1992.

Germond, Jack W., and Jules Witcover. *Whose Broad Stripes and Bright Stars: The Trivial Pursuit of the Presidency 1988*. 1989.

King, Nicholas. *George Bush: A Biography*. 1980.

Wead, Doug. *George Bush: Man of Integrity*. 1988.

Woodward, Bob. *The Commanders*. 1991.

GERALD F. SEIB

BUSINESS POLICY. Through its business policy government attempts to influence or control the economic or social activities of private firms. Few Presidents enter office with unequivocal business policies, but every President affects a diverse business community in much that he does. Modern Presidents have powerfully influenced business interests via fiscal (taxing and spending) policy, economic controls, technology subsidies, financial guarantees, international trade agreements, and social and economic regulations.

The Shift to Activism. Before 1900, presidential activism regarding business was rare. Congress and the states created what regulation existed (as, for example, with the INTERSTATE COMMERCE COMMISSION ACT of 1887 and the SHERMAN ANTITRUST ACT of 1890). When Presidents Theodore Roosevelt, William Howard Taft, and Woodrow Wilson strongly enforced antitrust laws, they violated the long-established federal tradition of laissez faire. Theodore Roosevelt's support for national pure food and drug laws and the conservation of natural resources on federal lands was unconventional. Roosevelt, Taft, and Wilson, however, changed America's laissez faire tradition relatively little. The real shift toward Presidential activism began during the depression of the 1930s and continued through WORLD WAR II and the COLD WAR because of changes in popular expectations of Presidents and because of subsequent changes in the structure and operations of the executive branch.

Franklin D. Roosevelt helped create more national business policies than all his predecessors combined; he brokered scores of congressional and executive-branch reforms and became an unprecedented national arbiter of industrial equity and economic justice. Before Franklin Roosevelt, Presidents had usually asked businessmen to regulate themselves in the public interest or had simply underwritten them on their own terms. Roosevelt, too, underwrote business. The greatly expanded Reconstruction Finance Corporation, first established under Herbert Hoover, became a multibillion-dollar lender of last resort for banks and for capital-intensive railroads and utilities, and the abortive NATIONAL INDUSTRIAL RECOVERY ACT gave trade associations a chance to set prices and apportion markets. But Roosevelt's NEW DEAL also provided novel federal protections for three other groups—the unemployed, industrial workers, and the elderly—alienating almost all American businessmen in the process. For millions of jobless, the federal government became a depression-decade employer of last resort. For workers, the WAGNER ACT established federally guaranteed rights to unionize. For the elderly and the unemployed, the Social Security Act established SOCIAL SECURITY and welfare programs either fully or partially financed by employers. Before Roosevelt, Presidents seldom had an impact on business; after Roosevelt, America's central government and business shared economic power.

World War II accelerated presidential business policy activism. Roosevelt and Harry S. Truman received wide-ranging EMERGENCY POWERS as COMMANDERS IN CHIEF to wage global industrial war. Prices and wages were controlled, and production bans affected everything from automobiles to nylon stockings. The federal government speedily became the biggest single customer American industry had ever had. By the war's end, 60 percent of all manufacturing output was going to the military. The government spent more in four wartime years than it had from 1789 to 1940. The President often made the decision as to what wartime business would build—for example, the mammoth and supersecret MANHATTAN PROJECT that created nu-

clear weapons—and federal fiscal policy during the war was presidentially determined. Washington not only spent more than twenty-five times more in 1945–1946 than it had in 1933, but it raised more than fifteen times as much revenue in taxes. Ten percent of the total U.S. wartime productive capacity came from federally purchased plant and equipment. Aviation, chemicals, and electrical manufacturing were among the industries transformed by emergency presidential defense policies.

Domestic presidential business policy activism diminished in the postwar period. Truman initially controlled wages and prices. In 1946, he defeated a nationwide rail shutdown by threatening to draft strikers into the military. Congress's and Truman's own qualms, however, soon undermined most major emergency economic controls. Truman helped eviscerate full-employment legislation that would have made New Deal jobs programs permanent. A national health insurance drive failed. The Wagner Act was strategically weakened when Congress passed the TAFT-HARTLEY ACT over Truman's veto in 1947. The corporate economic controls that Truman established after the onset of the KOREAN WAR in 1950 were weak imitations of those imposed during World War II. Truman's lame-duck effort to nationalize eighty-five steel companies in 1952 to avoid strikes and lockouts that might hinder war production failed after the Supreme Court, for the first time since Pearl Harbor, voided presidential claims to emergency powers in YOUNGSTOWN SHEET & TUBE CO. V. SAWYER (1952). Internationally, Truman did help chart important policy directions. The BRETTON WOODS AGREEMENT on the international monetary system and the MARSHALL PLAN of foreign aid for Western Europe boosted levels of global economic recovery and trade to help contain communism.

Cold-war Business Policy. Dwight D. Eisenhower's business policy accommodated federal regulatory and other arrangements he inherited. Even so, he reluctantly expanded presidential activism. As cold war Commander in Chief, for example, Eisenhower presided over a federal establishment that financed half (or more) of all scientific research and technological development undertaken in America in every year after 1955. Missiles, supercomputers, and space satellites were among the results. Not only did federal money subsidize industry to research and develop new technologies, but federal dollars also purchased the products that were created. Eisenhower's administration had by its close spent annual amounts equivalent to that of Roosevelt's during the war—over half of it for the military. The "military-industrial complex" was the term that a concerned Eisenhower used to describe such state-financed, science-driven cold war business policy in his final state of the union address.

John F. Kennedy expanded military-industrial networks. The space race complemented the arms race. Kennedy also elaborated Truman- and Eisenhower-era precedents by taking power away from Congress on international trade policy-making. Tariff reductions, after 1962, became primarily presidential initiatives. Keynesian economics and voluntary anti-inflationary wage-price guidelines were Kennedy's most contentious policies. The guidelines soured corporate relationships after Kennedy jawboned a temporary rollback of steel industry price increases in 1962. Kennedy's tax policies, however, revived corporate investments. Most came to fruition under his successor, Lyndon B. Johnson. Tax rates were cut to increase economic growth rates. Kennedy and Johnson were the first Democratic presidential income-tax cutters of the twentieth century. They were also the first to advertise deficit financing as a permanent and essential tool in the presidential business policy arsenal. Corporate-oriented tax cuts, boom times, and promises of further government spending led most big-business leaders to support Johnson over Republican traditionalist Barry Goldwater in 1964—the first time such a shift in business political allegiance took place since the New Deal.

Such presidentially orchestrated partisan realignments soon withered. Johnson controlled neither military spending (to fight the Vietnam War) nor domestic spending (to establish major new Great Society programs such as Medicare and Medicaid) in ways business liked. Deficits rose. The political failure of Keynesian fiscal policy showed itself in the war-fueled inflationary boom, which Johnson did not stop through high-enough tax increases or deep-enough spending reductions. Johnson's decision to fight the war in Southeast Asia without any compulsory economic controls (except Kennedy's increasingly ineffective and unenforceable wage-price guidelines) further worsened the situation.

Controls and Deregulation. By 1968, accordingly, business shifted back to Republican Presidents. Johnson's Keynesian political failures gave Richard M. Nixon increased freedom to mend worsening inflationary problems. In 1971, Nixon used emergency powers Congress had awarded him to begin the first "peacetime" wage, price, and interest-rate controls program in U.S. history. Simultaneously, his main Treasury appointees, including John Connally and Paul Volcker, took the United States off the intergovernmental gold standard, devalued the dollar, ended the system of fixed international monetary exchange

rates that Truman's administration implemented at the end of World War II, and levied temporary import "surcharges" on foreign goods. Such decisive presidential initiatives had proved ineffective domestically by the time controls ended in 1974, but they profoundly changed the structure of the world industrial economy. The United States was no longer the dominant financial policeman of the planet. "Stagflation"—increasing inflation combined with unemployment—was the final business policy challenge Nixon faced, after the low-cost-energy era ended in the wake of the oil embargo by Arab members of OPEC in 1973–1974. Nixon reluctantly supported oil price controls, a move that turned American oilmen into belated fans of laissez-faire.

Nixon's successor, Gerald R. Ford, was in office too briefly to do more than veto many bills on business interests' behalf and to grudgingly participate in the occasional bailout program that major banks desired (e.g., that of New York City in 1975). Jimmy Carter entered office in 1977 committed to selective deregulation, tax reform, deficit reduction, spending control, and other business policies that made him briefly tolerable to corporate leaders.

Carter's regulatory program, however, soon bred widespread business opposition. Though strongly and successfully committed to price deregulation of specific industries (including oil, airlines, finance, telecommunications, and rail and truck transport), Carter also supported the many new social regulations that Congress had gradually imposed on business from 1964 to 1974. These new social regulations particularly governed equal employment, environmental protection, worker health and safety, and consumer product safety standards. American companies had not seen the like since the labor, social welfare, and securities regulations of the New Deal. The new Equal Employment Opportunity Commission, for example, regulated hiring and promotion procedures to open hitherto restricted or closed occupational precincts to women and minorities. Because such new regulatory agencies' evolving standards enforced proliferating compliance costs on almost all industries, they became very unpopular with almost all employers. Carter's unwillingness to use his presidential APPOINTMENT POWER and administrative power to limit the expansion of environmental regulation and other rule making within the executive branch doomed his relations with business leaders. His failure to chart a national course out of the stagflationary economy—with American heavy industry decisively threatened by foreign competition in U.S. markets for the first time in a century—doomed his presidency.

Reagan's Policies. Ronald Reagan's business policy was a pre–New Deal conservatism arrayed in a New Right economic idiom. Like Eisenhower and Kennedy, he unleashed a flood of military spending for new technologies, such as SDI (STRATEGIC DEFENSE INITIATIVE). In defense, at least, government was not the problem; it remained the solution. Otherwise, Reagan continued deregulating industry and tried to weaken industrywide social regulations. Presidential legislative efforts failed, but, via appointment and budgeting moves, Reaganites selectively rolled back industrywide mandates, including long-established collective bargaining regulations, by administrative means. Reagan's most decisive policy was to cut income taxes: the largest tax cuts yet seen for corporations and individuals. A miracle of economic growth was supposed to ensue. But the other business policies tolerated by Reagan, particularly the high interest rates engineered by the Federal Reserve Board to squeeze inflation out of the economy, instead produced the recession of 1981 to 1983, the worst since 1938.

Recovery, afterwards, was slow and spotty. Reagan championed nonmilitary spending reductions to control growing deficits. This policy failed, and total national debt levels tripled in a decade. By 1985, an increasingly polarized economy existed. Some business sectors, including computers and aerospace, boomed. Others, such as key areas of banking and finance, engaged in increasingly risky entrepreneurship to maintain or improve profits. Yet others, steel and automobiles among them, languished.

Undeniable economic and industrial instability led the second Reagan administration to shift emphasis. The first Reagan term produced huge tax cuts, while the second produced tax reforms that closed loopholes to achieve lower general rate structures. Instead of hands-off business deregulation, there were hands-on financial bailouts for financial institutions. In 1984, for instance, Reagan's chastened regulators even temporarily nationalized one of the nation's ten largest banks to avoid global financial panic. Shortly afterwards, Reagan further expanded the financial-guarantor responsibilities that Presidents had possessed since Franklin Roosevelt, as half of America's savings and loan institutions (S&Ls) faced bankruptcy because of overspeculation in real estate and energy. By 1987, a $500 billion federal bailout was underway—the most expensive business salvage operation ever undertaken by Washington [see SAVINGS AND LOAN DEBACLE].

The gargantuan S&L bailout, which George Bush and his successors inherited, speaks to the enduring importance of presidential business policy since 1933. Every President chooses differently regarding fiscal policy, economic controls, technology subsidies, financial guarantees, trade agreements, and social and economic regulation. All these presidential decisions powerfully affect business. Presidents remain the primary national arbiters of industrial equity and economic justice, as they have since Franklin Roosevelt began the modern activist presidency.

BIBLIOGRAPHY

McConnell, Grant. *Private Power and American Democracy.* 1966.
McQuaid, Kim. *Big Business and Presidential Power: From F.D.R. to Reagan.* 1982.
Stein, Herbert. *Presidential Economics: Economics Policy, Roosevelt to Reagan and Beyond.* 1988.
Vietor, Richard H. K. *Energy Policy in America since 1945: A Study of Business-Government Relations.* 1984.
Vogel, David. *Fluctuating Fortunes: The Political Power of Business in America.* 1989.

KIM MCQUAID

BYRNES, JAMES F. (1879–1972), Representative, Senator, Associate Justice of the Supreme Court, director of Economic Stabilization, director of War Mobilization, Secretary of State, governor of South Carolina. In his long public career, James Francis ("Jimmy") Byrnes worked with many Presidents, both formally and informally. William Howard Taft was President when Byrnes came to Congress in 1911; Dwight D. Eisenhower was in office when Byrnes left public service. Byrnes's greatest contributions, however, came under Presidents Franklin D. Roosevelt and Harry S. Truman.

Byrnes was elected to the Senate in 1930 and was an early supporter of Roosevelt's presidential candidacy. In 1933 he was already identified as a key administration supporter in the Senate, and it was even rumored that Roosevelt wanted Byrnes to displace Joe Robinson as majority leader. He played a major role in developing and supporting several early NEW DEAL measures. Though he later clashed with Roosevelt over various issues, Byrnes remained close to the President; he served as Roosevelt's floor manager during the nomination fight at the 1940 Democratic national convention, and in 1941 Roosevelt appointed him to the Supreme Court.

The pressures of WORLD WAR II, particularly after PEARL HARBOR, frequently distracted Byrnes's attention from his role on the Court. He advised Roosevelt frequently on pending emergency legislation, war production issues, staffing problems, and political matters. Finally, the President asked Byrnes to take a leave of absence from the Court to serve as the director of the Office of Economic Stabilization (OES)—a post mainly concerned with fighting wartime inflation (Byrnes never did return to the Court). In addition to Byrnes's performing official duties, however, Roosevelt wanted him to serve as an "assistant President," taking charge of domestic affairs so as to free Roosevelt's time for foreign policy and military affairs. To underscore the importance of Byrnes's informal role, Roosevelt ensconced him in an office in the White House.

In 1943 Byrnes decided that his inflation-fighting duties at OES were interfering with his other duties as "assistant President" and convinced Roosevelt to make him director of the OFFICE OF WAR MOBILIZATION (OWM). The EXECUTIVE ORDER establishing this agency delegated broad power to Byrnes in both war-production matters and other areas of domestic affairs. Byrnes also played a key role as a liaison to Congress and as an informal adviser. He was briefly considered as a possible vice presidential candidate in 1944 but lost out to Truman.

Despite Byrnes's broad domestic responsibilities, his concerns turned to foreign policy after Roosevelt invited him to attend the postwar conference leading to the YALTA CONFERENCE in 1945. After Roosevelt's death, President Truman asked Byrnes to become Secretary of State, a post he assumed in July 1945. In the meantime he served as a representative on the interim committee that recommended that the ATOMIC BOMB be dropped on Japan "without specific warning and as soon as practicable."

For the next eighteen months, Byrnes pursued the complex task of negotiating the postwar order. As he did so his relationship with Truman worsened. Ironically, Byrnes was seen as a hard bargainer with the Soviet Union (especially after he clashed with HENRY A. WALLACE during the POTSDAM CONFERENCE) but was later characterized as "soft on communism" by Truman. The truth is more complex and is further clouded by both Byrnes's and Truman's later attempts to polish their historical reputations.

In retrospect it seems clear that Byrnes was ill equipped to take on the enormous challenges facing the Secretary of State at the close of the war. He had neither foreign policy experience nor exposure to other cultures. Still, his difficulties after the war should not detract from his contributions to the New Deal and the war effort.

BIBLIOGRAPHY

Byrnes, James F. *All in One Lifetime*. 1958.

Messer, Robert L. *The End of an Alliance: James F. Byrnes, Roosevelt, Truman, and the Origins of the Cold War*. 1982.

WILLIAM LASSER

C

CABINET. The United States generally insists on having a constitutional rationale to justify public actions, so it is odd that the Cabinet is not mentioned in the Constitution. The only reference to a cabinet is the provision that the President "may require the Opinion, in writing, of the principal Officer in each of the executive Departments, upon any Subject relating to the Duties of their respective Offices" (Article II, Section 2, clause 1). But this reference is to the individuals who serve as secretaries of the EXECUTIVE DEPARTMENTS, not to a collective entity, or cabinet, in which the secretaries would come together as a group to discuss and help formulate public policies. The Framers of the Constitution did not question that the President would need advice, but they did not consider that these advisers might come together in formal body from which to offer that advice.

Defining the Cabinet. There are two ways to define the Cabinet. The first focuses on the people who direct the executive departments, the DEPARTMENTAL SECRETARIES. These persons are nominated by the President, subject to Senate confirmation, and serve only through the duration of the administration and at the pleasure of the President. (Legally, Cabinet secretaries may serve for one month after a President leaves office, to smooth the transition for the new department secretary. In practice, Cabinet secretaries tender their resignations just prior to the outgoing President's departure from office.)

The second way of defining the Cabinet focuses on the Cabinet as a collective body, that is, the group formed when the Cabinet secretaries meet formally together. Because the Cabinet lacks constitutional or statutory foundation, there has been confusion over its membership, as officials who do not head departments may attend Cabinet meetings. For instance, the ATTORNEY GENERAL was not initially accorded secretarial status. The DEPARTMENT OF JUSTICE was not elevated to departmental status until 1870, and therefore it was not until that year that the Attorney General's salary reached the level of the department secretaries' pay. Nevertheless, the Attorney General was recognized as a member of George Washington's Cabinet.

In recent years, other officials who are not departmental heads have also attended Cabinet meetings. It is now common practice for the VICE PRESIDENT and the Director of the CENTRAL INTELLIGENCE AGENCY (CIA), neither of whom is a departmental head, to attend Cabinet sessions, although the CIA Director's attendance is usually limited to meetings concerning NATIONAL SECURITY issues.

Creating even more conceptual confusion is the idea of a KITCHEN CABINET. Andrew Jackson, who often ignored the departmental secretaries, was the first to employ a kitchen cabinet. Jackson's kitchen cabinet was composed of close personal friends and advisers, people he felt he could trust and rely on. All Presidents have had some type of informal group of close advisers who have played such a role. The limitations and weaknesses of the Cabinet, detailed below, have given rise to kitchen cabinets and other kinds of non-Cabinet presidential advisory systems.

Weakness of the Cabinet. The Cabinet's weakness stems partly from its lack of a constitutional foundation. As a result, it had little institutional authority and cannot issue binding group decisions. While the modern Cabinet does possess some institutional resources, such as a secretary, a modest staff, and a record of

Cabinet Departments, 1789–1993

1789	1798	1829	1849	1862	1870	1889	1903	1913
State	State	State	State	State	State	State	State	State
Treasury	Treasury	Treasury	Treasury	Treasury	Treasury	Treasury	Treasury	Treasury
War	War	War	War	War	War	War	War	War }
	Navy	Navy	Navy	Navy	Navy	Navy	Navy	Navy }
Attorney General	Attorney General	Attorney General	Attorney General	Attorney General	Justice[a]	Justice	Justice	Justice
(Postmaster General)[b]	(Postmaster General)	Postmaster General	Postmaster General	Postmaster General	Postmaster General	Postmaster General	Postmaster General	Postmaster General
			Interior	Interior	Interior	Interior	Interior	Interior
				(Agriculture)[c]	(Agriculture)	Agriculture	Agriculture	Agriculture
							Commerce and Labor	{ Commerce Labor

[a]The Attorney General became head of the Justice Department when the department was created in 1870.

[b]Positions in parentheses are heads of departments but not members of the Cabinet. The Postmaster General was not added to the Cabinet until 1829; the Postmaster General was dropped from the Cabinet in 1971, when the United States Postal Service replaced the United States Post Office.

[c]The Department of Agriculture was created in 1862; the Secretary of Agriculture was added to the Cabinet in 1889.

meetings, only the forces of tradition and expectation give the Cabinet power.

The Cabinet is totally reliant on the President and subject to each President's preference concerning how to employ it. At best it is only advisory to the President; at worst it will be completely ignored. Moreover, the Cabinet's utility to the President is limited by the fact that others, particularly Congress and INTEREST GROUPS, have some influence over who is named a Cabinet secretary.

Each President decides for himself how to use the Cabinet. For example, meetings are called at the discretion of the President. Some Presidents, like Dwight D. Eisenhower, have called meetings frequently and relied on the advice generated at such meetings. Others, like John F. Kennedy, have found little utility in the collective Cabinet. Still others, like Abraham Lincoln, have felt compelled to call meetings but have not felt obligated to heed the advice of their secretaries. In one famous story, Lincoln called a vote of the Cabinet.

The result was a unanimous "nay," which Lincoln overrode with his solitary "aye."

Creation of the Cabinet. Two constitutional decisions affect the Cabinet: first, the system of SEPARATION OF POWERS and CHECKS AND BALANCES and, second, the decision to have a unitary and strong presidency. Other factors also influenced the Framers ideas about a cabinet, including the United States' British heritage, the experience of the Continental Congress during the Revolutionary War, and the congressional experience during the Articles of Confederation period.

British Heritage. The word *cabinet* was first used in seventeenth-century Britain. The king would consult with members of the privy council, but, because that body's membership was quite numerous, the king would often retreat with a select number of counselors to a smaller room, adjacent to the king's room, called the cabinet. Thus the "cabinet council" to the king was established.

The cabinet council, soon simply referred to as the

Cabinet Departments, 1789–1993 (Continued)

1947	1953	1965	1966	1971	1977	1979	1980	1988
State	State	State	State	State	State	State	State	State
Treasury	Treasury	Treasury	Treasury	Treasury	Treasury	Treasury	Treasury	Treasury
Defense	Defense	Defense	Defense	Defense	Defense	Defense	Defense	Defense
Justice	Justice	Justice	Justice	Justice	Justice	Justice	Justice	Justice
Postmaster General	Postmaster General	Postmaster General	Postmaster General					
Interior	Interior	Interior	Interior	Interior	Interior	Interior	Interior	Interior
Agriculture	Agriculture	Agriculture	Agriculture	Agriculture	Agriculture	Agriculture	Agriculture	Agriculture
Commerce	Commerce	Commerce	Commerce	Commerce	Commerce	Commerce	Commerce	Commerce
Labor	Labor	Labor	Labor	Labor	Labor	Labor	Labor	Labor
						Education	Education	Education
	Health, Education, & Welfare	Health, Education, & Welfare	Health, Education, & Welfare	Health, Education, & Welfare	Health, Education, & Welfare		Health and Human Services	Health and Human Services
		Housing and Urban Development	Housing and Urban Development	Housing and Urban Development	Housing and Urban Development	Housing and Urban Development	Housing and Urban Development	Housing and Urban Development
			Transportation	Transportation	Transportation	Transportation	Transportation	Transportation
					Energy	Energy	Energy	Energy
								Veterans Affairs

cabinet, was initially only advisory, but by the late nineteenth century it had evolved into the modern British cabinet system, with the cabinet as a decision-making body with strong ties to the majority party in Parliament. In effect, the new, more powerful British cabinet became the seat of government.

The British cabinet influenced American thinking, but the American Cabinet is not a direct copy of the British one. When the U.S. Constitution was being written, the British governmental model was still developing, and the American Cabinet came more to resemble the earlier, advisory, less-powerful cabinet rather than the parliamentary cabinet that was to emerge later.

Preconstitutional American experiences. The Continental Congress's experience with executive departments during the Revolutionary War also helped set a foundation for the American Cabinet. At first, the Congress conducted affairs through committees of its members. Among the most important of these were the committees of correspondence to agents of several of the colonies, then in England. These early agents, through their contact with the Continental Congress,

in effect became the seeds of the FOREIGN SERVICE and diplomatic corps. In time, these committees were reorganized as the Committee of Foreign Affairs.

In 1781, the Congress found it necessary to have a formal channel for conducting foreign affairs and created the first Department of Foreign Affairs. Importantly, that department was headed by a single secretary, which the Congress felt to be an improvement over the past practice, administration by committee. Soon after, three more executive offices were created: the Superintendent of Finance, the Secretary of War, and the Secretary of Marine. By this time, the idea of executive offices headed by a single executive had been firmly planted, setting a precedent for the later Cabinet departments. During the period of the Articles of Confederation, these departments operated under congressional supervision and direction because the government under the Articles did not include an executive.

Impact of constitutional design. The decisions of the Constitutional Convention to provide for a unitary, strong presidency and the system of separations and checks and balances had lasting impact on the Cabinet.

A unitary executive. The decision to create a unitary executive with relatively strong powers stifled any effort at institutionalizing an advisory body, such as a cabinet, in the executive branch. The Framers feared that creating an advisory council in the executive branch could not only give the President a group to hide behind but could potentially dissipate presidential powers. It might become an alternative power center in the executive, dividing the executive and depriving it of the "energy," "unity," and "vigor" that ALEXANDER HAMILTON, the major proponent of a strong executive, sought. Executive responsibility was to lie solely with the President. Thus, no collective advisory body or cabinet was created.

Separation of powers. The second important constitutional decision was the formal separation of government institutions, which, in turn, are bound together through the system of checks and balances. The separation-of-powers system drove a wedge between the executive and legislative branches. One consequence of this system was that incumbents of one branch could not sit in the other [*see* INCOMPATIBILITY CLAUSE]. Thus, no parliamentary-style cabinet could develop, and this separation limited the interaction between an executive cabinet and Congress as well. Discussion arose in early Congresses about allowing (or requiring) departmental secretaries to sit in Congress and participate in floor deliberations. Legislators decided, however, that such participation would violate the spirit of the Constitution's wall of separation between the branches.

Lastly, the separation between the branches obstructed President Washington's early attempts to seek personal counsel and advice from both the legislative and judicial branches.

This turn of events occurred very early on, in 1789. Washington was trying to fashion a treaty with the INDIANS. At first he sought advice from the Senate, but the Senate rebuffed his attempt to establish the Senate as a consultative body. Then he turned for legal advice to the Supreme Court, then headed by JOHN JAY, who like Washington, was a Federalist. Jay also refused to extend advice. With both the legislative and judicial branches personally unapproachable, Washington turned to his Cabinet secretaries for policy advice and to his Attorney General for legal counsel, although he continued to consult with Congress in writing.

Checks and balances. The system of checks and balances raised questions of how much and in what ways the Congress and the Cabinet would interact. Three issues stood out. First, the Senate was constitutionally empowered to confirm presidential nominations for departmental secretaries, giving the Senate the power to deny the President his choices. The second issue was whether the Congress could remove a secretary from office. The third was whether Congress could question Cabinet secretaries, and, if so, in what ways. The last two issues remained unsettled at the Constitutional Convention and required resolution at a later date. In the case of the REMOVAL POWER, that resolution came nearly a century later.

The removal debate. Congress was cautious about its power to remove Cabinet secretaries from office. In the act creating the Department of State, Congress laid no claim to removal, allowing that power to reside with the President. It acknowledged the same presidential removal power over the Secretary of the Treasury and the Secretary of War.

The proponents of exclusive presidential power to remove secretaries cited executive control over personnel as critical to the constitutional operation of the executive office. Without this power, they maintained, the President would have limited ability to direct the bureaucracy and would not be able to "faithfully execute the laws," as the Constitution mandated. Advocates of a congressional role, however, cited the congressional power to investigate, its power to impeach, and the fact that each department was a creation of Congress. They contended that if Congress could eliminate a department through legislative action—which would have the effect of removing the secretary from office—then it also should possess the power to remove a secretary from office without having to dismantle the department.

Cabinet interactions with Congress. The other unresolved issue, concerning congressional interaction with Cabinet secretaries, arose from the congressional power to investigate. Early congressional actions established that Cabinet secretaries could not sit in the halls of Congress but could be questioned by Congress—and that they should answer Congress in writing, not in person. Furthermore, though President Washington and some of his secretaries felt that all queries should be submitted through the President, Secretary of the Treasury Hamilton's position carried the day. Hamilton wanted to allow direct communication, though written inquiry, from Congress to a secretary without presidential mediation. Hamilton, who had a very active style as secretary, found this direct contact useful in promoting his economic policies in Congress.

Development of the Cabinet. The Cabinet continued to evolve long after the Constitution was ratified and early precedents were established. Importantly, the Cabinet began to take on a collective identity through meetings with the President. The issue of congressional power over the suspension and removal of secretaries from office finally came to a head during the Andrew Johnson administration. And throughout the nineteenth and twentieth centuries the Cabinet expanded as particular interests pressed for representation at the highest levels of the executive branch.

Evolution of Cabinet meetings. Early in his administration George Washington named several people to serve as departmental secretaries: Thomas Jefferson as Secretary of State, Alexander Hamilton as Secretary of the Treasury, Henry Knox as Secretary of War, EDMUND RANDOLPH as Attorney General, and Samuel Osgood as POSTMASTER GENERAL.

The idea of holding meetings in which all departmental secretaries would convene commenced in 1791, when Washington suggested that the Vice President and the departmental secretaries should meet during Washington's absence from the capital city. Such a meeting did take place, but without the Attorney General, presumably because he was not yet of Cabinet rank.

Thereafter, such meetings (with Washington present) became more common. During the spring of 1793, a period of political crisis, the secretaries met with Washington almost daily. This frequency led James Madison to call the group a cabinet, the first time the term was specifically applied in the American context.

Washington quickly learned the limited usefulness of such meetings, however. His primary problem was the political battle between the Federalist Secretary of the Treasury, Hamilton, and the Democratic-Republican Secretary of State, Jefferson. Their conflict undermined the utility of Cabinet meetings, and Washington increased the political stakes and tensions by calling for Cabinet votes. Washington seems to have been bent on using Cabinet votes to decide policy, perhaps to depersonalize the presidency and build a sense of collective governing. It was not long, however, before Hamilton and Jefferson left the Cabinet and Washington's voting innovation was dropped. The political incompatibility of secretaries would plague other Presidents, undermining their Cabinets' utility as well.

The removal power controversy. The IMPEACHMENT OF ANDREW JOHNSON was precipitated in part by the unresolved issue of the power of Congress to monitor and control the removal of Cabinet secretaries. In 1867, Congress passed the TENURE OF OFFICE ACT, which required that the Senate had to confirm a successor before the President could remove a Cabinet secretary from office. Moreover, the act granted the President the power to suspend a secretary while the Senate was in recess, requiring the President to report to the Senate the evidence and reasons for the suspension once its session recommenced. If the Senate concurred with the suspension, the secretary would be removed, while the secretary would resume his official duties if the Senate refused to concur. In effect, the Senate could keep a secretary in office over presidential objections by refusing to confirm a new nominee. The political intention behind the act was to ensure that Johnson would follow the dictates of congressional RADICAL REPUBLICANS with respect to RECONSTRUCTION policy.

Johnson's Secretary of War, EDWIN M. STANTON, who was aligned with the congressional Republicans, was authorized to administer the Reconstruction program. A bitter dispute between Johnson and Stanton erupted, whereupon Johnson suspended Stanton. The Senate refused to concur with the suspension once it reconvened. Johnson countered by removing Stanton from office, an action that increased tensions with the Senate. Johnson's tactic failed, however, as Stanton regained his office. Soon thereafter, Congress initiated impeachment proceedings against Johnson, spurred on very much by the Stanton incident.

For the twenty years after its enactment, every President urged repeal of the law every year in his STATE OF THE UNION MESSAGE. In 1887, Congress repealed the act, giving the President sole power to remove Cabinet secretaries from office and settling the issue of the President's removal power at the Cabinet level.

Expansion and political representation. Though the Cabinet was not able to develop into a decision-making body whose actions were binding, it did acquire some political importance for the President. The President could use Cabinet appointments to build support coalitions and repay past supporters for their backing. In effect, the Cabinet became a place in the administration for the representation of important political interests.

The push to represent particular interests on the Cabinet has come in several waves. In the first wave, departments generally considered to be concerned with a single economic interest were added to the Cabinet. The second wave saw Cabinet status for departments concerned with multiple interests, often social in nature. A third wave of Cabinet expansion in the 1970s and 1980s embraced both patterns.

Thus, in 1849 the INTERIOR DEPARTMENT was created at the behest of interests concerned with development of the west and control of native populations. In 1889, agricultural interests gained representation in the newly formed AGRICULTURE DEPARTMENT, and in 1903 business interests were recognized with establishment of the Department of Commerce and Labor. Ten years later, labor interests secured a seat when commerce and labor concerns were separated into two new departments, the DEPARTMENT OF LABOR and the DEPARTMENT OF COMMERCE.

The multipurpose Cabinet departments that constitute the second wave, which began after WORLD WAR II, included the Department of Health, Education, and Welfare (HEW), established in 1953, the DEPARTMENT OF HOUSING AND URBAN DEVELOPMENT (1966) and the DEPARTMENT OF TRANSPORTATION (1967).

A third wave of Cabinet expansion occurred in the late 1970s and 1980s. First, as a consequence of the energy crises of the 1970s, energy-related programs and agencies were consolidated into the DEPARTMENT OF ENERGY in 1977. Next, HEW was reorganized in 1979 by separating education from health and welfare programs, thus creating two new departments, the DEPARTMENT OF EDUCATION and the DEPARTMENT OF HEALTH AND HUMAN SERVICES. Finally, in 1988, the Veterans Administration was elevated to Cabinet rank as the DEPARTMENT OF VETERANS AFFAIRS.

Other Cabinet Developments. Beginning in the 1930s, the already institutionally weak Cabinet began a trend of further decline. This came about because of the growth of government, the shift of public expectations and government power to the presidency, and the institutionalization of a presidential advisory system separate from the Cabinet.

Public expectations about government and the presidency underwent a fundamental transformation during the 1930s. The ethic of limited government gave way to a push for greater government involvement in directing the economy. The President played the leading role in this expansion.

This increase in presidential policy responsibility and leadership could have transformed the Cabinet into an important policy adviser to the President, since, at the time, it was the only government institution that could have played this role. Instead, the Cabinet's weaknesses, its lack of collective responsibility, and its sensitivity to the demands of special interest groups and other nonpresidential interests (e.g., Congress) motivated the President to develop policy advisement along a different path.

The President institutionalized advice through the EXECUTIVE OFFICE OF THE PRESIDENT (EOP), created in 1939. In time, EOP developed units to provide advice free of, or at least less encumbered with, interest-group demands. In time, three of these units—the COUNCIL OF ECONOMIC ADVISERS, the NATIONAL SECURITY ADVISER, and the Domestic Policy Group—assumed the primary presidential advisement role. The Bureau of the Budget (later the OFFICE OF MANAGEMENT AND BUDGET) also came to take on a major policy advising role,

sometimes eclipsing the three EOP staffs in importance. This development pushed the Cabinet further away from the President, lessening its policy influence.

Eisenhower attempted to reverse the Cabinet's decline by providing it with some institutional resources, such as a secretary, and by calling frequent and regular meetings, but the Cabinet continued its decline under Kennedy, who rarely called Cabinet meetings. But the increasing complexity of government and the perceived failure of government effectively to implement its many programs led some later Presidents to try to integrate the Cabinet into the policy-making process at the White House.

Richard M. Nixon made the first major reform proposal in 1971 with his plan to create four new "superdepartments" of human resources, community development, natural resources, and economic affairs from the more numerous existing departments responsible for those activities. Nixon wanted to reorganize the Cabinet around functional rather than interest-group lines, hoping that this would both tie the Cabinet more closely to the policy-making process at the White House and weaken the bonds between the departments and interest groups. As expected, Congress balked at the plan because it would have disrupted established networks among Congress, the departments, and important interest groups. The WATERGATE AFFAIR eventually destroyed Nixon's position with Congress as he sought the reorganization.

The second major attempt at Cabinet–White House integration came during the 1980s under the Ronald Reagan administration. Close attention to the appointment process and the creation of CABINET COUNCILS were the devices that Reagan used. In paying close mind to the appointment process, Reagan wanted to ensure that Cabinet secretaries would be loyal to him. Extensive background checks were conducted prior to nomination, and, once appointed, the new secretaries were taught about their jobs and departments by White House staff rather than by career departmental personnel. The aim was to create a sense of identification with the administration and to loosen secretaries' ties to their departments and to the long-serving bureaucrats and special-interest groups.

The second aspect of Reagan's approach involved the establishment and use of Cabinet councils. In 1981 and 1982, seven Cabinet councils were created: Economic Affairs, Commerce and Trade, Food and Agriculture, Human Resources, Natural Resources and the Environment, Legal Policy, and Management and Administration. Membership on the councils was composed of departmental secretaries and their aides, as well as White House personnel responsible for particular policy areas. Staff worked up policy proposals, which were later refined at the secretarial level, and finally a meeting, sometimes with the President attending, culminated the policy decision process.

For the first two years of the Reagan administration, the councils were quite active, but they quickly fell into disuse. Again, the lack of a firm institutional sanction, either constitutional or statutory, probably accounts for the decline of the Cabinet council system.

Nixon's proposal to reorganize the Cabinet and Reagan's use of Cabinet councils were the most important attempts at Cabinet–White House integration. Both attempts failed in the end, but they probably herald a trend in presidential management of the White House, the Cabinet, and the policy process in which the Cabinet will take on a more important advisory and policy-making role in the highest chambers of the executive.

BIBLIOGRAPHY

Cohen, Jeffrey E. *The Politics of the U.S. Cabinet: Representation in the Executive Branch, 1789–1984.* 1988.
Fenno, Richard F. *The President's Cabinet: An Analysis of the Period from Wilson to Eisenhower.* 1959.
Hart, James. *The American Presidency in Action 1789.* 1948.
Hinsdale, Mary L. *A History of the President's Cabinet.* 1911.
Horn, Stephen. *The Cabinet and Congress.* 1960.
Learned, Henry B. *The President's Cabinet.* 1912.
Smith, William Henry. *History of the Cabinet of the United States.* 1925.

JEFFREY E. COHEN

CABINET COUNCILS. During his first term in office, Ronald Reagan and his White House advisers experimented with an intermediate form of group advisory structure called the Cabinet council. The Cabinet council structure lay between the typical method by which Cabinet secretaries function as autonomous managers of their departments and individual advisers to the President and a wished-for ideal structure in which the entire CABINET would work together as a cohesive group to make decisions and provide policy advice.

In actuality, the Cabinet rarely functions as a cohesive or coherent body. Rather, each departmental secretary maintains vertical relationships with the President and the White House staff, above, and with other departmental political appointees and career bureaucrats, below. Incentives for lateral coordination among secretaries across functional areas are weak. The diversity of policy areas covered by the Cabinet further undercuts its cohesiveness, and the large number of Cabinet officers (eighteen at the start of the Reagan presidency) also impedes effective group in-

teraction). In most administrations, the Cabinet does not function as an advisory group to the President, although individual members may serve as advisers. Typically, the President relies on advisers within the White House and views Cabinet secretaries' loyalties as divided between their own departments and the Presidents' priorities.

Cabinet councils were subsets of the larger Cabinet, and each was oriented toward a broad policy area. Cabinet councils provided forums for participation and discussion of issues that cut across Cabinet departments, excluding secretaries not affected by the policies being deliberated. The councils were designed to allow for policy integration at a level broader than that of individual departments. Such integration, it was thought, would avoid the strains of interdepartmental competition felt in previous administrations, which had sometimes impeded and undermined major policy initiatives.

Several Cabinet councils were established to provide advice on economic issues; most important of these was the Cabinet Council on Economic Affairs (CCEA). Other councils established in 1981 included those on Commerce and Trade (CCCT), Human Resources (CCHR), National Resources and Environment (CCNRE), and Food and Agriculture (CCFA). In 1982, Cabinet councils on Legal Policy (CCLP) and Management and Administration (CCMA) were created. Each Cabinet council had between six and eleven Cabinet members. Meetings were chaired by the President, and other interested Cabinet members were invited to attend.

Reagan delegated issues to the councils, stipulating that issues of concern were to be discussed there first and not brought bilaterally to the President. Despite complaints by Secretary of State Alexander M. Haig, Jr., and other secretaries that this system permitted White House domination of the Cabinet, it initially worked well in implementing Reagan's agenda. The councils operated in conjunction with the so-called troika—the three major presidential advisers, each of whom had policy and functional specialization, who together filled the role of a WHITE HOUSE CHIEF OF STAFF during Reagan's first term. The system did require an atmosphere of trust between the White House and Cabinet officials, however, and that trust was undermined during Reagan's second term, when DONALD T. REGAN replaced JAMES A. BAKER III as the functional chief of staff. Virtually all the Cabinet secretaries were replaced at that time, and during Reagan's second term the council system collapsed under its own weight.

The Cabinet council system did have a number of advantages. It allowed Cabinet secretaries with common policy interests to discuss issues in a meaningful format without involving and wasting the time of secretaries whose policy interests were far removed. It facilitated coordination across organizational boundaries and held the promise of diminishing bureaucratic turf wars. It encouraged secretaries to take a broader functional approach to issues rather than falling into a pattern of responding primarily to clients and the special interests served by their own departments.

During the time in which the councils functioned successfully, the White House exerted great control over departmental budgets and sub-Cabinet appointments. The Cabinet council system provided some compensation to secretaries for loss of control over budgetary and personnel matters by enabling them to provide policy advice. The Cabinet council system also discouraged secretaries from lobbying the White House individually.

But the system's disadvantages and weaknesses eventually overwhelmed it. Admittedly, some Cabinet councils were more successful than others. But while the CCEA, for example, met 271 times during Reagan's first term, the next busiest council, the CCCT, met only 91 times. The CCNR met 66 times, and the CCLP met only 15 times during its existence. While activity is not synonymous with influence, Cabinet councils that were not very active had little impact on administration policy.

A second problem was that the Cabinet council system created additional decision-making layers through which departmental concerns had to pass, requiring additional preparation and meeting time and, hence, delay. Some critics contended that Cabinet councils were more easily manipulated by the White House than was the full Cabinet and that they merely served as instruments for administration policy implementation. (Proponents of Reagan administration policy, of course, viewed this as a strength, not a weakness.)

Most crucially, however, the Cabinet council system did not replace the President's reliance on White House advisers, who did not require Senate confirmation and were shielded by the principle of EXECUTIVE PRIVILEGE from being forced to testify before Congress. Cabinet councils, then, briefly served as an instrument for policy implementation and never became a source of ongoing and regularized presidential advisement.

BIBLIOGRAPHY

Hill, Dilys M., Raymond A. Moore, and Phil Williams, eds. *The Reagan Presidency: An Incomplete Revolution?* 1990.
Pffifner, James P. *The Strategic Presidency*. 1988.
Stockman, David. *The Triumph of Politics*. 1986.

MARCIA LYNN WHICKER

CALHOUN, JOHN C. (1782–1850), Congressman, Secretary of War, Senator, seventh Vice President of the United States (1825–1832). Calhoun was born of Scotch-Irish stock in South Carolina. His father, Patrick Calhoun, a self-made man, was of one of the wealthiest planters in the back country of the state. But young Calhoun, like others of his class and background, worked the fields along with the family's slaves.

Considered unusually talented by his mother and brothers, Calhoun was sent off to Georgia to study with his brother-in-law, a minister and an autodidact of formidable learning. Calhoun's older brothers struck out on careers of their own in Charleston and the tidewater region of South Carolina. Thus, Calhoun, though still an adolescent, had to interrupt his education to return home and manage the family's properties when his father died.

After a year or so as a planter, Calhoun was again sent by his mother and brothers off to Georgia, where he continued his education under his brother-in-law. They also made it possible for him to gain a college degree. In 1802, he entered Yale. After graduating in 1804, Calhoun studied law at the famous Tapping Reeve law school in Litchfield, Connecticut. He completed his law training in Charleston and for a time practiced law in South Carolina.

Following his 1811 marriage to the heiress of a wealthy planter family, Calhoun entered politics. After serving briefly in the South Carolina legislature, he was elected as a representative to the Twelfth Congress. Almost immediately he took a commanding place in Congress. An ardent nationalist, he became a member of the small group known as the War Hawks, which pushed President James Madison toward war with Great Britain.

After the TREATY OF GHENT ended the WAR OF 1812, Calhoun drafted much of the nationalist legislation that Congress and the Madison administration approved, including a protective tariff and the law that chartered the second BANK OF THE UNITED STATES. But he failed to get the President's approval for government support of a nationwide system of INTERNAL IMPROVEMENTS. His dynamic personal qualities, his proven ability and industry, and the fact that he was a southerner prompted President Monroe, who was also seeking sectional balance, to appoint him Secretary of War.

As anticipated, Calhoun proved to be an able secretary, reorganizing the WAR DEPARTMENT for greater efficiency and economy in the face of a congress bent on retrenchment and proposing scientific expeditions into the far west. He also developed an INDIAN policy that halted some of the worst abuses of the fur trade with Indian tribes. His program necessarily involved him in Washington politics, and its success kindled his ambition to be President.

Unable to match the sectional popularity of HENRY CLAY, John Quincy Adams, or Andrew Jackson, he accepted the vice presidential nomination in 1824. He served nearly eight years as Vice President in the administrations of John Quincy Adams and Jackson.

Calhoun was a model presiding officer of the Senate. Well versed in parliamentary procedure, he was careful not to overstep the limits of the office as he interpreted the Senate rules of debate and the constitutional limitations of a VICE PRESIDENT. Yet he was enough of a politician to recognize that popular and political trends were running strongly against the Adams administration and its tilt toward Hamiltonian doctrines of federal power [see HAMILTON, ALEXANDER]. Thus, he allowed such opponents of the Adams administration as John Randolph a full range of attack.

Calhoun was challenged in a series of articles signed "Patrick Henry" that appeared in the administration's Washington paper, the National Journal. These essays were able, learned pieces and may well have been written by President Adams himself. "Patrick Henry's" first article, highly critical of Calhoun's interpretation of the Senate rules, used a wealth of precedents to argue that, because the Vice President was elected by the people, he was responsible to the public at large, not the Senate. Calhoun responded using the pseudonym "Onslow" (the name of a noted speaker of the British Parliament). Calhoun maintained that, as presiding officer of a deliberative body but not a member of that body, he had to conform narrowly to its rules. The Senate itself, not the Vice President, was the arbiter of debate. Broadening the basic point of the Vice President's inherent powers as presiding officer in the Senate, subsequent articles took up an extended discussion of the essence of government, the respective positions of the various branches, and the ultimate issue of liberty versus power.

The five articles by "Patrick Henry" closely followed the administration's policy of broad national power for the public good as expressed in Adams's inaugural address and his first annual message. Calhoun's six responses indicated a retreat from the nationalist position he had held earlier and drew him closer to the STATES' RIGHTS school of John Randolph of Virginia, John Taylor of South Carolina, and Nathaniel Macon of North Carolina, though it was obvious that Calhoun was using his position to embarrass the administration and to make himself acceptable to the Jacksonians. His papers foreshadowed his later fears for the future of his region, in particular the tariff legislation of 1824 and 1828.

At first Calhoun supported the tariff of 1828 because he thought that, although it protected emerging northern industry, the rates were too low for manufacturing interests to accept. When Congress approved the measure, however, and it became law, South Carolina planters were outraged. Calhoun responded to their pressure and denounced the so-called TARIFF OF ABOMINATIONS, but he did not side with the South Carolina extremists who threatened SECESSION from the Union.

Rather, he drafted a series of resolutions and an explanation (called the "Exposition") of why his state should nullify the tariff, declaring it a prime example of special-interest legislation [see NULLIFICATION]. He argued that the Constitution was a compact entered into by sovereign states that chose the federal government as their agent. The states, however, retained their original sovereignty, and, if the agent broke the contract in any given instance, the injured party not only could but should refuse to recognize its action. Calhoun's "Exposition" defined the right of a minority to protect what it considered vital to its economic and social well-being against a transient majority driven by an organized special-interest group.

Openly associating himself with Jackson and his emerging DEMOCRATIC PARTY, Calhoun was again elected Vice President in 1828. He found himself isolated politically by Secretary of State Martin Van Buren, a position that became untenable for him when it was learned in Washington that he had drafted the pronullification "Exposition." Calhoun resigned on 28 December 1830 and was then elected U.S. Senator from South Carolina.

From that position, except for a brief period in which he served as Secretary of State in the John Tyler administration, he defended his state and his region for the rest of his life. Always a unionist, he sought vainly to fit the southern plantation culture, dependent on SLAVERY, within a nation that included industrializing states. Late in his life he drafted two treatises on government, The Discourse on the Constitution (1851) and The Disquisition on Government (1851). In these works, Calhoun argued for a pluralistic approach to politics as the only sure way to guarantee individual and minority rights while at the same time preserving the framework and many of the powers of a central government. In some respects Calhoun's ideas—a dual executive, for example—were impractical, Calhoun's recognition that many different communities make up a nation-state and form the basis for government is an original contribution to political theory.

In intellectual and logical power Calhoun surpassed the other two outstanding statesmen of the antebellum period, Henry Clay and DANIEL WEBSTER. Together, the three Senators, known as the Great Triumvirate, dominated American political life for almost half a century. Very near the end of his life, Calhoun finally despaired that the South, with its agrarian culture and its institution of slavery, could coexist with northern industry and free labor in a unified nation. He predicted that the federal union would break up "within twelve years or three presidential terms. . . . The probability is, it will explode in a presidential election." Calhoun died on 31 March 1850, shortly after making this prophetic statement.

BIBLIOGRAPHY

Capers, Gerald. *John C. Calhoun, Opportunist: A Reappraisal.* 1960.

Coit, Margaret. *John C. Calhoun: An American Portrait.* 1950.

Current, Richard N. *John C. Calhoun.* 1963.

Niven, John. *John C. Calhoun and the Price of Union.* 1988.

Peterson, Merrill. *The Great Triumvirate: Webster, Clay and Calhoun.* 1987.

Wiltse, Charles M. *John C. Calhoun.* 3 vols. 1944–1951.

JOHN NIVEN

CAMPAIGN FINANCES. Presidential campaigns have become vast spectacles. Modern presidential campaigns contrast with the view of John Quincy Adams, who wrote in 1828, "The presidency of the United States was an office neither to be sought nor declined. To pay money for securing it, directly or indirectly, was in my opinion incorrect in principle." Despite Adams's lofty sentiment, candidates in every election since George Washington first assumed the office in 1789 have spent money to secure the presidency. From torchlight parades to television presentations, someone has had to pay the expenses.

The substantial—and ever-increasing—expense of running for President results from a variety of factors, many of which have evolved since the Republic was founded: the development of competitive political parties; the democratization of the presidency; the extension of suffrage; the introduction of national nominating conventions and PRESIDENTIAL PRIMARIES; and the development of costly communications media and campaign technologies, with their attendant hosts of expensive political consultants.

Many Americans now worry that the escalating costs

and greater reliance on mass media are having a deleterious effect on the presidential selection process. In response to periodic public concern, federal law has sought ways to reduce the perceived influence of monied interests, while also seeking to protect the democratic ideals of free speech and assembly.

Early Presidential Elections. Since the Republic's founding, the cost of printing has been the most basic campaign expense. In 1791, Thomas Jefferson started the *National Gazette*, the subsidized organ of the ANTI-FEDERALISTS. The FEDERALIST PARTY had been financing its own paper, the *Gazette of the United States*, with money from ALEXANDER HAMILTON and RUFUS KING and from printing subsidies. Newspapers vilified candidates mercilessly, and various factions spun off their own papers. During the early 1800s, books, pamphlets, and even newspapers were handed from person to person until they were no longer readable.

By 1840, pictures, buttons, banners, and novelty items had appeared. William Henry Harrison's campaign that year arranged for conventions and mass meetings; scheduled parades and processions with banners and floats; produced long speeches on the log-cabin theme, log-cabin song books and log-cabin newspapers; distributed Harrison pictures; and introduced Tippecanoe handkerchiefs and badges. Each item and activity cost money, though some brought revenues to the campaign.

Presidential candidates did not always actively campaign. Andrew Jackson retired to his home, the Hermitage, after he was nominated, although his supporters held torchlight parades and hickory-pole raisings.

STEPHEN A. DOUGLAS decided to barnstorm the country in his 1860 campaign against Abraham Lincoln, a practice not tried again until 1896, when WILLIAM JENNINGS BRYAN traveled eighteen thousand miles giving some six hundred speeches to a total of at least five million people. By contrast, his opponent, William McKinley, sat on his front porch and let the people come to him; special trains were run to his hometown of Canton, Ohio, with the railroads cooperating by cutting fares. McKinley did not have to travel because his friend, the wealthy industrialist and Republican national committee chairman Marcus A. Hanna, organized fourteen hundred surrogates to speak on his behalf. Hanna also spent money to publish and distribute more than 120 million pieces of McKinley campaign literature.

Twentieth-Century Developments. In the twentieth century, broadcasting became the most effective means by which candidates could get their messages across to voters. Presidential and other federal candidates first used radio broadcasts in the 1924 campaign.

Public Subsidies in Presidential Elections, 1976–1992

Election Period	1976		1980			1984			1988			1992		
	Dem.	Rep.	Dem.	Rep.	Other	Dem.	Rep.	Other	Dem.	Rep.	Other	Dem.	Rep.	Other
Prenom-ination	$14.6[a] (13)[b]	$ 9.1 (2)	$10.6 (4)	$19.2 (6)	—	$26.2 (9)	$ 9.8 (1)	$0.2(C) (1)	$30.8 (8)	$35.5 (6)	$0.9(NA) (1)	$24.6 (7)	$15.9 (2)	$1.9(NA) 0.1(NLP)
National conventions	2.0	1.6	3.7	4.4	—	8.1	8.1	—	9.2	9.2	—	11.0	11.0	—
General election	21.8	21.8	29.4	29.2	4.2(NU)	40.4	40.4	—	46.1	46.1	—	55.2	55.2	—
Total (party)	$38.4	$32.5	$43.7	$52.8	$4.2	$74.7	$58.3	$0.2	$86.1	$90.8	$0.9	$90.8	$82.1	$2.0
Grand total	$70.9		$100.7			$133.1			$177.8			$174.9		

[a] Dollar amounts are in millions.
[b] Number of contenders for nomination.
Abbreviations: C, Citizens (Barry Commoner); NA, National Alliance (Lenora Fulani); NLP, Natural Law Party (John Hagelin); NU, National Unity (John Anderson).
Prepared by Joseph E. Cantor, Congressional Research Service, based on data supplied by the Federal Election Commission and Citizens Research Foundation.

Ever since, candidates have devoted more and more time and money to honing their campaign messages to fit the broadcasting formats. Presidential contenders started using televised advertising in 1952. Generally, such advertising is used minimally during the early prenomination period, which is marked by retail politics and small-state campaigning, but expands dramatically in larger states and in the general election period. Over time, the microphone and the camera came to be the main means through which presidential candidates conveyed their messages.

Television has added new dimensions to campaigning by encouraging PRESIDENTIAL DEBATES and forums among candidates and also by focusing campaign strategy, influencing campaign managers to seek out photo opportunities and coverage on free news broadcasts. The costly national nominating conventions are now timed to reach the largest possible audiences.

As the size of the U.S. population expanded and the technology of campaigning became increasingly complex, the costs of campaigning for political office grew correspondingly. In 1860, Lincoln's victorious general election campaign was said to have cost about $100,000, while the cost of his opponent Douglas's campaign was reportedly $50,000. One hundred years later, the leading two presidential candidates—John F. Kennedy and Richard M. Nixon—spent nearly $20 million to finance their hotly contested race, one of the most competitive in U.S. history.

The 1988 presidential contest was the fourth in which public funds were provided to cover part of the campaign costs. No incumbent was running, and costs were especially high in both major party campaigns. In the general election campaign, the Republican ticket

of George Bush and DAN QUAYLE spent (and had spent on its behalf) about $93.7 million, including a public grant of $46.1 million. Democratic Party candidates MICHAEL DUKAKIS and Lloyd Bentsen spent (and had spent on their behalf) about $106.5 million, also including a public grant of $46.1 million. The 1988 campaign marked the first time in the twentieth century that the Republicans and their allies were outspent by the Democrats and their allies.

The price of electing a President—some $500 million altogether—represented about 20 percent of the $2.7 billion Americans spent on all politics at the federal, state, and local levels in the 1987–1988 election cycle. When calculated for each phase of the presidential selection process, the costs were approximately $234 million in the prenomination period, $40 million for the conventions, and $208 million in the general election. Of course, candidates seeking nomination are entrepreneurs, building their own fundraising, organizational and media campaigns; some spending on their behalf by organized labor, delegates, and independent individuals and groups is factored into the calculations. Once a candidate has been nominated, significant supplemental roles are played in the general election by the political parties and their allies. Amounts spent in party support, "soft money," communication costs, parallel labor spending, and independent expenditures during the postnomination period are included in the figures that indicate the amounts spent by the presidential candidates, on their behalf, or in support of party tickets.

In the early days of presidential campaigning, funds were raised through collections from candidates and assessments from officeholders. The money raised through these two sources was at first sufficient, but as campaign costs escalated, candidates had to find other sources.

In the early nineteenth century, candidates began raising money by rewarding campaign contributors with favors and government jobs—the spoils system of PATRONAGE. The system proved increasingly productive for candidates by the end of the CIVIL WAR in 1865, when corporations and wealthy individuals began paying a major portion of presidential campaign costs. After Congress enacted the CIVIL SERVICE ACT of 1883, contributions from corporations and from wealthy individuals became an even larger source of presidential campaign funds. The act prohibited officers and employees of the United States, with some exceptions, from seeking or receiving political contributions from one another.

In the hotly contested 1896 campaign between Republican candidate McKinley and Democrat-Populist candidate Bryan, for example, Mark Hanna, the manager of McKinley's campaign, collected $3.5 million for the general election campaign effort, mainly from the largesse of corporations, such as the Standard Oil Company, which gave $250,000. In that race, several banks agreed to give McKinley campaign donations in amounts equal to a quarter of 1 percent of their capital.

As restrictions on funding sources mounted, political candidates were forced to devise new methods of raising money and to rely more heavily on particular sources of campaign gifts. When corporate gifts were banned in 1907, candidates responded by seeking more contributions from wealthy individuals, including many corporate stockholders and executives. Some candidates' families were generous; for example, Charles P. Taft contributed more than $200,000 to his brother William Howard Taft's campaign in 1912. And when the HATCH ACT of 1939 and its 1940 amendment restricted the size of contributions to political committees, candidates and political parties began to find other ways of raising funds, including holding fund-raising dinners and events. When labor gifts were banned, PACS (POLITICAL ACTION COMMITTEES) were established to solicit voluntary contributions from members and their families; later, corporations and ideological groups also established PACs.

Candidates also have tried to raise big money in small sums from a great number of individual contributors, but their efforts have not been uniformly successful. In 1964, Republican candidate BARRY GOLDWATER raised large amounts from small contributions solicited through the use of direct mail. Other candidates who had success with direct-mail solicitations

include independent candidate GEORGE WALLACE in 1968, Democratic nominee GEORGE MCGOVERN in 1972, and Republican Ronald Reagan in his 1976 and 1980 prenomination campaigns. All these candidates who successfully built large financial constituencies were factional party leaders or outside the mainstream of American politics; direct mail has not been notably productive for centrist candidates. In 1992, Edmund G. (Jerry) Brown, Jr., a contender for the Democratic nomination, received a generous response to appeals for contributions not exceeding $100 each, utilizing an "800" (toll-free) telephone number.

An incumbent President is normally the biggest attraction in political fund-raising. If not raising funds for reelection, the President, as party leader, usually devotes considerable amounts of time to speaking at political-party events and at dinners and events on behalf of party candidates throughout the country.

Efforts at Reform. Following CIVIL-SERVICE REFORM, growing public concern led Congress to enact a number of ELECTORAL REFORM laws that were designed to lessen any undue influence of large donations in presidential and other federal election campaigns.

In 1907, Congress passed the first law, the Tillman Act, that made it illegal for any corporation or national bank to make a "money contribution in connection with any election" of candidates for federal office.

The first laws requiring House and Senate candidates to file campaign finance disclosure reports were enacted in 1910 and 1911. The latter act extended disclosure to include primary, convention, and preelection financial statements. While neither law specified authority over presidential campaigns, the House committee report accompanying the 1910 bill stated that because presidential electors were elected at the same time as representatives, they were presumed to be covered by the law.

In 1925, Congress codified and revised all previous campaign finance legislation by enacting the Federal Corrupt Practices Act, which remained basic federal campaign law until 1972. The act required all Senate and House candidates and certain political committees to disclose their campaign receipts and expenditures. It also required any political committees conducting their activities in two or more states (mainly national party committees and committees seeking to influence the election of presidential electors) to file disclosure reports. Presidential candidates were not covered until the 1971 Federal Election Campaign Act (FECA).

The Hatch Act of 1939 imposed further constraints on government employees by extending restrictions on political activity to all but about four thousand top policy-making employees in the executive branch of the federal government. The act, along with its 1940 amendments, also sought to reduce the influence of wealthy individuals by limiting the amount that could be contributed to $5,000; multiple contributions up to $5,000 could, however, be contributed to a series of committees supporting the same candidate. This system was ended following the WATERGATE AFFAIR, when it was revealed that the Nixon campaign in 1972 had benefited from contributions as high as $2 million from a single individual, though distributed among numerous supporting committees. The financing of the 1972 election was investigated thoroughly by a Senate committee and special counsel, so more was learned about the financing of that campaign than had been known about any previous campaign.

In 1943, the Smith-Connally War Labor Disputes Act prohibited labor unions from making contributions to federal election campaigns, just as corporate contributions had been banned in 1907. That law was codified by the TAFT-HARTLEY ACT of 1947.

Public Funding. The 1970s witnessed a resurgence of the political reform movement, which was the impetus for a wide array of campaign finance laws passed at both the federal and state levels. At the federal level, these reform efforts were embodied in the Federal Election Campaign Act of 1971, the Revenue Act of 1971, and the FECA Amendments of 1974, 1976, and 1979. The 1971 and 1974 laws contained special provisions relating to presidential elections, providing public financing (starting in 1976) and limiting the amounts that could be contributed and spent. The newly established FEDERAL ELECTION COMMISSION administered the law and certified the disbursement of the public funds. Public funds are government subsidies provided for presidential campaigns and derived from a federal income tax checkoff. The checkoff had started in 1972; amounts were aggregated over a four-year period, and the first payouts in the public-funding program were made in 1976, representing a dramatic departure from the entirely privately funded campaigns up to that time.

Three kinds of public funding are available for different phases of a presidential campaign. During the prenomination period, matching funds are provided for qualifying candidates seeking the nomination for President; expenditure limits (adjusted for inflation) are imposed for the entire prenomination period and for spending in each primary and caucus state. Grants (adjusted for inflation) are made to each of the major parties to arrange for and hold their national nominating conventions. Lesser amounts can be provided for qualifying minor party conventions, but, as of 1992, none had ever proved eligible. For the general election period, a flat grant (adjusted for inflation) is given to each major party candidate; the amount also serves as the candidates' expenditure limit. Smaller amounts are available for minor party or independent candidates if they receive 5 percent or more of the vote; in 1980, independent candidate John Anderson qualified for such a grant.

Federal election law provides optional public funds only for presidential candidates who agree to abide by expenditure limitations. To qualify for matching funds during the prenomination period, candidates must raise $5,000 in contributions of $250 or less in each of twenty states. The federal government then matches each contribution made by an individual to a qualified candidate, up to a limit of $250 per contributor. The federal subsidies may not exceed half the prenomination campaign spending limit, which was $27.6 million in 1992. As noted, the federal government also finances the national nominating conventions of the two major political parties. In 1992, each of the parties received $11 million for this purpose.

The major party presidential candidates also are eligible to receive public treasury grants to fund their general election campaigns; $55.2 million was given to each major party candidate in 1992.

The intentions behind public funding are to help supply serious candidates with the money they need to present themselves and their qualifications, to help keep the process competitive, to diminish or eliminate candidates' need to solicit contributions from wealthy donors and interest groups, and to encourage candidates for nomination to broaden their bases of support by requiring them to seek out large numbers of small individual contributions.

Since its inception, public financing of presidential campaigns has been dependent on taxpayers' willingness to earmark a small portion of their tax liabilities—$1 for individual returns and $2 for married persons filing jointly—for the PRESIDENTIAL ELECTION CAMPAIGN FUND. Through the 1992 election, the checkoff system has been adequate to cover the costs of providing public financing. The Federal Election Commission certified a total of $70.9 million in public funds for the presidential selection process in 1976, $100.6 million in 1980, $133.1 million in 1984, and $177.8 million in 1988. Thus the federal government became the largest contributor to presidential campaigns.

As of 1992, Congress had not increased the $1 federal income tax checkoff even though the value of the U.S. dollar had eroded since public financing was established in 1971. Tax checkoff participation reached its peak in 1981, when about 29 percent of all

Americans filing personal federal income tax returns supported the income tax checkoff. By 1990, that amount of support had diminished to just under 20 percent of taxpayers. Unless remedied, the diminishing support for the checkoff meant that the fund would face a deficit by the 1996 election.

Along with public financing, Congress enacted legislation imposing contribution and expenditure limits on all federal election campaigns. In 1976, however, the Supreme Court ruled in BUCKLEY V. VALEO that spending limits are permissible only in publicly financed campaigns. Since presidential election contests are the only federal elections in which public funds are available to candidates, spending limits pertain only to presidential candidates and their election committees. The law also limits to $50,000 per election the amount of personal funds that publicly financed presidential candidates and their immediate families may use for their own campaigns. A presidential candidate, such as H. ROSS PEROT in 1992, can spend unlimited amounts of money in his or her campaign if he or she does not choose public funding and the accompanying expenditure limits.

Continuing Financing Controversies. Even though public funding and its related expenditure limits attempt to control presidential campaign spending, there are still several legal ways that private funds can be spent to influence the outcome of a presidential election. For example, under the *Buckley v. Valeo* decision, individuals and groups can make unlimited independent expenditures in presidential and other federal campaigns to advocate the election or defeat of any particular candidate, so long as the spending takes place without the consultation or coordination of the candidate's campaign committee.

Individuals and groups also may contribute to elections by making donations to political parties, which, in turn, may spend the money on behalf of their parties' presidential tickets. Some direct spending by the national party is permitted by law, but some so-called soft money expenditures have become controversial because federal election law allows state and local political parties (if permitted by state law) to raise money for such party-building activities as voter registration and get-out-the-vote campaigns from sources that are normally barred from making contributions to federal elections, such as labor unions and corporations. And because these soft-money contributions are not counted against a candidate's expenditure limit and are not subject to federal law, their prevalence in presidential campaigns have become controversial.

Although labor organizations are prohibited from making contributions to presidential campaigns in general election campaigns, their PACs make notable contributions through parallel campaigning among their membership. In addition, labor groups conduct voter registration and get-out-the-vote drives of their own.

The challenge and potential conflict in regulating political finance is to protect the integrity of the election process, usually by limiting or restricting certain monies or activities, while also respecting the rights of free speech and association guaranteed by the First Amendment to the Constitution. Federal election law and its attendant regulations have not been able to curb spending increases in presidential campaigns. The current system of presidential campaign financing is an experiment that, like the system of American democracy itself, is subject to change. It is likely to be further modified in the years to come.

BIBLIOGRAPHY

Alexander, Herbert E., and Monica Bauer. *Financing the 1988 Election.* 1991.

Heard, Alexander. *The Costs of Democracy.* 1960.

Overacker, Louise. *Money in Elections.* 1932.

Roseboom, Eugene. *A History of Presidential Elections.* 1957.

Shannon, Jasper B. *Money and Politics.* 1959.

HERBERT E. ALEXANDER

CAMPAIGN PLEDGES. Until the rise of mass politics and parties in the 1830s, it was considered a mockery of republican principles for presidential aspirants to make promises or pledges to voters. Candidates were supposed to be judged on their characters and records—and nothing else. Because candidates did not personally campaign and no central party organization existed during the early decades of the new nation, there was actually very little opportunity for the making of commitments.

With the democratization of politics, appeals to self-interest became acceptable and in the election of 1832 there appeared new mechanisms and strategies to promote these appeals. The ANTI-MASONIC PARTY held the first national convention (September 1831) to select a presidential candidate; this body also issued an "Address to the People," setting forth the party's general principles. The first PARTY PLATFORM emerged from a National Republican convention of young men that met in May 1832; it included support for specific proposals, including "adequate protection of American industry," and a "uniform system of INTERNAL IMPROVEMENTS." The 1832 contest was also the first to present voters with a clear choice on a specific issue: if Jackson and the Democrats won, their campaign against the Second BANK OF THE UNITED STATES would continue; while if HENRY CLAY and the National Republicans were victorious, the bank would be protected. Jackson achieved a convincing triumph and the bank was destroyed.

Party platforms and pledges became commonplace starting in the 1840s (although the WHIG PARTY often found it advisable to steer clear of both), and most campaign promises—dealing with such narrow issues as tariff rates, farm prices, and monetary policy—have been eminently forgettable. Several stand out, however, as helping to decide an election or shaping the future.

In 1844, the architects of the Democratic platform, hoping to defuse the controversy over Texas, combined support for the ANNEXATION OF TEXAS with support for the reoccupation of the "whole" of Oregon. This plank helped James Polk win, but as President he decided to cut a deal with England on the Oregon border [see OREGON TREATY]. Combined with Polk's insistence on defending American claims in regard to the Texas boundary, leading to the MEXICAN WAR, the compromise on Oregon alienated a segment of northern Democrats. The party would split in 1848 and lose the White House.

The Union would dissolve in 1860 as a consequence of Abraham Lincoln's refusal to compromise his party's stand on the question of the extension of SLAVERY. When, after Lincoln's victory and the SECESSION of the Deep South, various proposals were under consideration that would undermine the REPUBLICAN PARTY platform's vow to confine slavery to the states where it already existed, the President-elect told his followers: "Have none of it. The tug has come, and better now than later."

A pledge Franklin Roosevelt made in 1932 came back to haunt him four years later. In a speech in Pittsburgh, candidate Roosevelt denounced the budget deficits run up by the Hoover administration and promised to slash federal spending. As President Roosevelt prepared to return to Pittsburgh in the 1936 campaign, he was sensitive to the fact—and repeated Republican reminders—that the red ink on federal ledgers had flowed even heavier under his stewardship. Roosevelt instructed his chief PRESIDENTIAL SPEECHWRITER to draft a "good and convincing explanation" of what he had meant in 1932, but he was told that the only explanation he could offer was "to deny categorically that you ever made it." The address Roosevelt delivered avoided direct mention of the earlier speech and argued that benevolence required that relief and recovery take precedence over a balanced budget. Voters in Pittsburgh and elsewhere agreed.

The 1932 pledge surfaced again in another context in the 1940 campaign. Alluding to Roosevelt's fiscal promise and the 1940 Democratic platform pledge "not to participate in foreign wars," Republican challenger WENDELL WILLKIE told a California audience, "I hope and pray that he remembers the pledge of the 1940 platform better than he did the one of 1932. If he does not, you better get ready to get on the transports." With Willkie harping on this theme of Roosevelt as a warmonger, the President responded with a declaration in Boston to the mothers and fathers of America: "I have said this before, but I shall say it again and again and again: Your boys are not going to be sent into any foreign wars." Roosevelt's assurances seemed to have satisfied the voters, but thirteen months later the Japanese attack on PEARL HARBOR turned WORLD WAR II into an American conflict.

Another war—the KOREAN WAR—brought a pledge in 1952 from the five-star general turned presidential candidate, Dwight D. Eisenhower. Playing upon the public's frustration with the stalemated conflict in Asia, Eisenhower announced that "I shall go to Korea," in order to bring an end to the war. Eisenhower's Democratic opponent, ADLAI E. STEVENSON (1900–1965), had considered issuing a similar pledge, but had rejected it as lacking substance. It probably would not have worked for the governor of Illinois, but the military hero's declaration went over very well with the voters, and he kept his pledge.

In 1960, John F. Kennedy pledged that with a "stroke of the Presidential pen" he would end discrimination in federally assisted housing. This was an important element of Kennedy's appeal to black voters, but once in office Kennedy procrastinated in signing the EXECUTIVE ORDER. Civil rights groups organized a "pens for Jack" campaign, which flooded the White House with writing implements to remind the President of his promise. Embarrassed, but still afraid of the political consequences of the order, Kennedy waited until November 1962 before issuing a limited ban on discrimination.

Campaigning in the shadow of the WATERGATE AFFAIR, Jimmy Carter promised in 1976 that "I will never tell a lie to the American people." Candidate Carter's commitment to candor led him to admit having sinned by looking upon women "with lust," but as President, Carter's self-righteousness made him a poor communicator and negotiator. By 1980, Americans were less interested in a President who would not lie than in one who could lead.

In 1984, Democratic candidate WALTER MONDALE pledged to raise taxes to bring the soaring federal deficit under control. After Mondale was buried in

Ronald Reagan's reelection landslide and the deficit grew even larger, George Bush told a cheering 1988 Republican convention, "Read my lips: No New Taxes." That promise figured heavily in his success in November, but in the fall of 1990, faced with higher than expected budget deficits, Bush agreed to the imposition of new taxes. That action brought a crescendo of criticism upon Bush from conservatives in his own party and a challenge to his renomination in 1992. Although Bush overcame that insurgency, he found it necessary to apologize for reneging on his pledge.

BIBLIOGRAPHY

Rosenman, Samuel I. *Working with Roosevelt.* 1952.

Schlesinger, Arthur M., Jr., ed. *History of American Presidential Elections, 1789–1968.* 4 vols. 1971.

Troy, Gil. *See How They Ran: The Changing Role of the Presidential Candidate.* 1991.

MARK I. GELFAND

CAMPAIGN SLOGANS. Long before late-twentieth-century observers of political campaigns started bemoaning "packaged candidates," "attack ads," and "thirty-second sound bites," aspirants for the White House and their supporters had developed a technique to get their message across quickly and simply: the campaign slogan. With just a few words it was possible to highlight a candidate's personality or stand on issues or to attack those of an opponent. Sometimes substantive, sometimes inane, political campaign slogans were forerunners and contemporaries of the jingles and phrases devised to sell consumer products in the twentieth century.

Campaign slogans came into use as a feature of the new democratic politics of the 1830s and 1840s. Most of the earlier contests for the presidency had been played before a small electorate, had been restrained by a sense of decorum, and had been marked by a lack of competitiveness. Given those conditions, attempts to reduce men and issues to a catchphrase were both undignified and unnecessary. But with the rise of a mass electorate, politicians and political parties, and all-out battles for the White House, campaign slogans developed as an important weapon for winning votes.

Slogans made their initial appearance in the Whig campaign of 1840. Convinced they could not deny Democratic incumbent Martin Van Buren a second term with an issue-based campaign, Whig leaders decided to rely on personality, symbols, and organization. From this emphasis on voter involvement came the first—and perhaps most remembered—campaign

slogan: "Tippecanoe and Tyler, too!" The references were to the battle against Indians fought almost thirty years earlier by the party's presidential candidate, William Henry Harrison, and to his running mate, John Tyler. By highlighting Harrison's military record and suggesting the regional balance of the Whig ticket, the slogan might be said to have had some substance to it, but its alliterative and rhyming qualities were paramount then and are responsible for its popular durability. The 1840 Whig campaign also featured the first negative slogan: "Van, Van is a used-up man." In view of the hard economic times the nation experienced during his tenure, Van Buren would probably have lost anyway, but the techniques utilized by the Whigs in 1840 became the norm for presidential campaigns.

Only a few elections have produced winning campaign slogans; matching a handful of words to the temper of the times or to a particular individual has required inspiration and luck. For example, the Whigs tried to duplicate their 1840 success four years later by raising doubts about the stature of their Democratic opponent with the question, "Who is James K. Polk?" Enough voters felt comfortable with the DARK-HORSE CANDIDATE to put him in the White House.

Progressives and liberals have held a monopoly on memorable titles used to identify campaign programs: NEW FREEDOM (Woodrow Wilson, 1912), NEW NATIONALISM (Theodore Roosevelt, 1912), NEW DEAL (Franklin D. Roosevelt, 1932), FAIR DEAL (Harry S. Truman, 1948), NEW FRONTIER (John F. Kennedy, 1960), and GREAT SOCIETY (Lyndon Baines Johnson, 1964). Believing in smaller government, conservatives have either not tried to devise labels or have come up with phrases that failed to capture attention, for example, New Beginning (Ronald Reagan, 1980).

Labels aside, Republicans have fared better with economic-based slogans than have Democrats. The 1896 election pitted the Democratic slogan calling for the "Free and Unlimited Coinage of Silver" against the Republican slogan of "McKinley and the Full Dinner Pail," with the Republicans prevailing. An economic revival allowed the Republicans to return in 1900 with "Four More Years of the Full Dinner Pail," and to triumph again. In 1928, riding another wave of prosperity, Republicans talked of "A Chicken for Every Pot" and of the choice before the voters: "Hoover and Happiness or [ALFRED E.] SMITH and Soup Houses: Which Shall It Be?" With Herbert Hoover and soup kitchens the reality in 1932, however, Republican claims that "Prosperity Is Just Around the Corner" and "The Worst Is Past" fell on deaf ears; the Democratic promise of a "New Deal" was what voters wanted to hear. Democrats, having finally captured the economic issue from their adversaries, successfully ran with it four more times consecutively, but their streak ended in 1952, when "Korea, Communism, and Corruption" ("K_1C_2") overwhelmed the Democratic assertion that "You've Never Had It So Good." Good times were evident in 1956, and the incumbent Republicans proudly declared, "Everything's Booming But the Guns." In 1980 and 1984, Ronald Reagan asked voters, "Are You Better Off Than You Were Four Years Ago?" Their response put him in the White House. Tackling a question that had become one of the hottest in the 1980s, George Bush told the electorate in 1988 to "Read My Lips: No New Taxes"; despite record federal budget deficits, Bush won the presidency. (Bush was, it turned out, unable to keep his promises.)

War and, more often, peace have been the themes of campaign slogans. In 1864, supporters of President Abraham Lincoln advised Union troops to "Vote as You Shoot." Running for the White House four years later, the former commander of the Union army, Ulysses S. Grant, declared, "Let Us Have Peace." Woodrow Wilson held on to the presidency in 1916 in large part because "He Kept Us Out of War"; five months after his reelection, Wilson asked Congress for a declaration of war. Another slogan used by Democrats that year noted: "You Are Working, Not Fighting." The continuing KOREAN WAR was a key element in the K_1C_2 formula used by Republicans in 1952, and the end of American involvement in the VIETNAM WAR permitted Gerald Ford to campaign in 1976, albeit vainly, on the slogan, "Not a Single American Is Fighting or Dying."

Corruption has been a recurring problem in American government and numerous campaign slogans have been targeted at this issue. Liberal Republicans, disgusted by the scandals of the Grant administration, urged voters in 1872 to "Throw the Rascals Out." They did not, but in 1876 both major party candidates—Rutherford B. Hayes and SAMUEL J. TILDEN— presented themselves as foes of Grantism: "Hurrah! For Hayes and Honest Ways!" and "Tilden and Reform!" Ironically, the election was perhaps the most tainted in the nation's history. In 1884, both contenders had character problems that made them vulnerable to barbs. Democrat Grover Cleveland had fathered a child out of wedlock, leading Republicans to chant: "Ma! Ma! Where's My Pa?" But their standard-bearer, JAMES G. BLAINE, had been implicated in a series of shady dealings, which prompted Democrats to proclaim Blaine, "The Continental Liar from the State of Maine." Cleveland, who ran also on the slogan "Public Office is a Public Trust," gained a narrow victory. Republicans took advantage of the Truman scandals

in 1952 with "Clean Up the Mess in Washington." In 1968 Democrat HUBERT H. HUMPHREY's slogan, "He's a Man You Can Trust," sought to remind voters of Richard M. Nixon's "Tricky Dick" reputation, and in 1976, after Nixon had been forced to resign in disgrace, Jimmy Carter presented himself as "Tested and Trustworthy" against Republican incumbent Gerald Ford.

The natural desire of incumbents to hold on to power and of outsiders to gain it produced campaign slogans that sometimes were recycled. In 1800, a Democratic-Republican leaflet asked: "Is It Not High Time for a CHANGE?" This question was raised at least implicitly in almost every subsequent election but was presented most pointedly in 1952 by Republicans ("Time for a Change!") seeking to end twenty years of uninterrupted Democratic control of the White House. Incumbents have used various formulations to persuade voters to keep them where they are. "Don't Swap Horses in the Middle of the Stream," an expression Lincoln had used in a letter, was popular among Republicans in 1864. The Republicans campaigned for a second term for McKinley in 1900 on the slogan, "Let Well Enough Alone." Roles were reversed in 1940, when Franklin D. Roosevelt ran for an unprecedented third term, with Democrats saying simply, "Stick with Roosevelt," while Republicans claimed that "No Man Is Good Three Times." Trying to point up the skills he had acquired as Vice President, Nixon's 1960 slogan was "Experience Counts."

Some of the most effective campaign slogans have been the simplest. "Keep Cool with Coolidge" (1924) and "I Like Ike" (1952) captured the essence of the candidates' relationship to the voters. The effort of ADLAI E. STEVENSON's supporters in 1952 to counter with "Madly for Adlai" met a tepid response. John F. Kennedy's New Frontier was combined in 1960 with a vague promise to "Get the Country Moving Again." Jimmy Carter fared well in 1976 with "Why Not the Best?" and when Ronald Reagan in 1984 declared "We Brought America Back," the people believed him.

Other slogans have been turned around and used with devastating effect against their creators. Democrats seized upon Blaine's failure to repudiate a supporter's characterization of the Democrats as the party of "Rum, Romanism, and Rebellion" to whip up strong feelings against the Republican; it may have been enough to cost Blaine the election. BARRY GOLDWATER in 1964 offered the voters "A Choice, Not an Echo," and his ads proclaimed, "In Your Heart, You Know He's Right!" Democrats had a ready retort to the latter statement: "Yes—Extreme Right!" Eight years later, GEORGE MCGOVERN's plea to "Come Home, America" got lost in the Republican barrage that labeled the Democrat a most un-American candidate of "Acid [i.e., LSD], Abortion, and Amnesty."

The linkage of campaign slogans to consumer advertising was demonstrated most vividly in the Democratic primary battle of 1984 when front-runner WALTER F. MONDALE, purloining the punchline of a television commercial for a fast-food chain, demanded to know "Where's the Beef?" in primary opponent Gary Hart's pledge to move the nation in new directions. Hart's challenge, which heretofore had been gaining strength, never recovered from Mondale's use of the phrase.

BIBLIOGRAPHY

Boller, Paul F., Jr. *Presidential Campaigns*. 1984.

Jamieson, Kathleen Hall. *Packaging the Presidency: A History and Criticism of Presidential Campaign Advertising*. 2d ed. 1992.

Schlesinger, Arthur M., Jr., ed. *History of American Presidential Elections, 1789–1968*. 4 vols. 1971.

Shankle, George Earlie. *American Mottoes and Slogans*. 1941.

Troy, Gil. *See How They Ran: The Changing Role of the Presidential Candidate*. 1991.

MARK I. GELFAND

CAMPAIGN STRATEGY. After a candidate wins a party's nomination, a shift must be made to a new phase of the presidential campaign—the campaign for the general election. Voter participation in this second contest is much greater than that in the primary elections and party convention, so the candidate must try to figure some means to obtain the votes of people who did not take part in the nomination campaign at all. Among people who did participate in the nomination campaign are three other groups that offer potential votes in the general campaign: people who cast their ballots for losers in the nomination contest of the candidate's own party, people who expressed their preference for candidates in the other political party who were also defeated in the nomination contest, and even possibly those who voted in that contest for the other party's nominee. Together these groups constitute a considerable range of potential support.

The general election campaign generally begins around Labor Day, but circumstances can alter that date. Because he had the Republican nomination wrapped up early in both 1980 and 1984, Ronald Reagan launched his campaigns before Labor Day in order to deflect some of the favorable publicity that the Democrats received at their national conventions in those years. (New York governor Mario Cuomo gave a speech designed to electrify the party faithful at the 1984 convention.) In contrast, incumbent President Gerald Ford, who experienced a hotly contested nomination contest in 1976 against challenger Ronald Reagan, waited until the week after Labor Day to launch his campaign because he wanted to reorganize his forces for the campaign ahead.

Political Appeals. For incumbent Presidents there are obvious advantages in the quest for reelection. Incumbents are generally much more familiar to the voters than their opponents, even though the latter may have acquired a great deal of publicity during the long nomination campaign. (One problem for the challenger is that he or she typically shares that publicity with the other, non-nominated candidates in the out-of-power party, whereas an incumbent President generally faces few rivals.) The incumbent also often plays the role of statesman, too busy with the affairs of the nation and the world to take part in a demeaning partisan contest. Journalist Timothy Crouse, commenting on the 1972 contest between President Richard M. Nixon and challenger GEORGE MCGOVERN, said, "Around the White House it bordered on treason to call Nixon a candidate." Also, incumbent Presidents are free to employ the "Rose Garden gambit"—gathering favorable publicity by receiving visitors at the White House or signing bills and calling brief press conferences to make public announcements. While the President is playing the role of statesman, others—such as vice presidential nominees—can be assigned the task of carrying out political attacks against the opposition, as HUBERT H. HUMPHREY did for Lyndon Johnson in 1964 and Robert Dole did for Gerald Ford in 1976.

Presidents can also use the prerogatives of their office to build support during the campaign. In 1980 Jimmy Carter announced his support of water projects in Kentucky and Tennessee that he had previously opposed. In 1984 Reagan allowed the Soviet Union to purchase extra grain, a move that provided financial assistance to American farmers.

While incumbents who run for reelection have certain advantages, it should be noted that they also carry some disadvantages. If the country is experiencing difficulties, the opposition party is free to blame them for all the nation's ills. The fact that Carter had been unable to resolve the IRANIAN HOSTAGE CRISIS was used to good effect by the Republicans in the 1980 campaign.

The character and personality that a candidate projects are also sources of political appeal. One strategy is to adapt one's image to counteract that of one's opponent. In 1976 Ford portrayed himself as a person of experience to counteract Carter's new face and outsider image; in 1980 Reagan painted himself as a decisive leader who could handle the nation's problems to counteract Carter's image of uncertainty and his tendency to blame the nation's problems on what he called in his CRISIS OF CONFIDENCE SPEECH the "spirit of malaise of the American people."

Beginning in the 1980s, candidates became more inclined to engage in highly negative attacks on their opponents. In 1980 Carter suggested that a Reagan presidency would divide Americans "black from white, Jew from Christian, North from South, rural from urban," and that Reagan could "well lead the nation to war." In 1988 the campaign strategists of George Bush painted Massachusetts Governor MICHAEL DUKAKIS as a "card-carrying member of the ACLU" (American Civil Liberties Union). Independent political action committees also used TV commercials to draw attention to the case of Willy Horton, a prison inmate, who after being furloughed under a Massachusetts program, committed a rape in Maryland—an act for which, the ads implied, Dukakis was responsible.

Over the years there has been a tendency to link broad social and economic issues with presidential candidates. The classic example was the Democrats' blaming Herbert Hoover for the Great Depression and maintaining that association for years. Meanwhile, Republicans pointed out that Democrats were in power at the time of WORLD WAR I and WORLD WAR II, as well as the KOREAN WAR and the VIETNAM WAR. Circumstances change, however, the poor economic record of the late 1970s led Republican Reagan to focus on that issue in 1980, while that same year Democrat Carter tried to portray Reagan as a man who could not be trusted to keep the peace abroad. Typically such attacks and counterattacks are general in nature, and candidates are not specific about what they would do to rectify the problems they identify. In 1960 John F. Kennedy asked voters to grant him the opportunity "to get the nation moving again," but he gave no concrete plans as to how he would do that. Nor in 1968 did Nixon indicate how he would extricate the United States from Vietnam. On occasion, however, candidates do provide definite proposals. In 1972 George McGovern suggested that the defense budget be cut by 30 percent and that everyone, regardless of need, be given a $1,000 government grant; in 1984 WALTER MONDALE called for cuts in defense, health, and agriculture and an increase in taxes for upper-income individuals and corporations. (It should be noted that both candidates went down to crushing defeats.)

Partisan appeals are still available in presidential campaigns, but they are less effective than they were at the time when Democrats (benefiting from the memory of Franklin D. Roosevelt) were clearly the majority party and voters thought primarily in partisan terms. Republicans have managed to diminish that appeal by running popular candidates such as Dwight D. Eisenhower and, later, Reagan; by inviting Democrats to "come home," as Nixon did in 1972; and by linking their candidacies with former Democratic Presidents, as Ford did with Roosevelt, Harry S. Truman, and Kennedy.

Another kind of appeal in presidential campaigns is that directed at a particular social group. From the days of Franklin Roosevelt, Democratic candidates have aimed their campaigns at certain constituencies, particularly racial and ethnic groups, organized labor, Catholics, Jews, intellectuals, and in the past, big city bosses. At the same time, they painted Republicans as the party of big business and the rich. Republicans had been less inclined to focus on social groups, but that changed in the 1960s. Nixon aimed his 1968 campaign at the "forgotten Americans," who did not break the law, paid their taxes, went to school, and loved their country. Four years later, the Nixon campaign produced campaign letters for thirty different ethnic groups, and in 1980 Ronald Reagan courted the Polish vote by meeting on Labor Day with Boleslaw Walesa, the father of Lech Walesa, who led the Solidarity union's strike against the Polish government. Other social groups have become targets for presidential candidates in recent years. In the 1980s Democrats made appeals to women based on Reagan's being "trigger-happy" and unsympathetic to the plight of the poor. Republicans in 1984 and again in 1988 sought the support of fundamentalist Christians by emphasizing their party's support of prayer in the public schools and opposition to ABORTION. Young voters constitute another group sought by both parties—in seeking their support, Republicans have emphasized economic opportunities and patriotism; Democrats have stressed the fear of nuclear war and have made idealistic appeals encouraging young people to help those less fortunate than themselves.

Communicating Political Appeals. Since the number of people voting in general elections is twice as large as that participating in the nomination phase, candidates place heavy emphasis on the use of the mass media during the general election campaign. In 1984 Reagan and Mondale each spent more than half his $40 million subsidy from the national government on television, radio, and print advertisements. Of the three media, television is the most important because more people get their news from it than from newspapers or radio and because people are more inclined to believe what they see on television than what they read in the newspaper. Moreover, television is more dramatic than radio.

Over the years, television commercials have used a variety of formats. Some commercials are very brief, lasting thirty seconds or less: one commercial of Nixon's in 1972 showed a hand sweeping away toy soldiers and miniature ships and planes to symbolize McGovern's proposed cuts in defense. (In contrast, McGovern chose to concentrate on much longer speeches in which he talked about Vietnam and the issue of political corruption.) Some commercials include celebrities: in 1976 Ford appeared in an ad that amounted to an informal television interview with television celebrity and former baseball player Joe Garagiola, who tossed him gopher-ball questions such as "How many foreign leaders have you met with, Mr. President?" to which Ford responded, "One hundred and twenty-four, Joe." Or television ads may incorporate scenic or symbolic backdrops: in 1984 the Republicans broadcast a film of Reagan astride his horse, walking on a hilltop with his wife, Nancy, speaking at the Normandy beaches, and taking the oath of office. That same year the Reagan campaign aired commercials illustrating the theme of "It's morning in America again." These ads showed the sun shining on San Francisco Bay, people hurrying to work, and a bride and groom kissing while a mellifluous voice asked, "Why would we ever want to go back to four short years ago?" The Democrats retaliated with a picture of a roller coaster climbing its tracks (suggesting the danger of rising U.S. deficits), with a voice intoning, "If you're thinking of voting for Ronald Reagan in 1984, think what will happen in 1985."

The institution of televised PRESIDENTIAL DEBATES, beginning with the Nixon-Kennedy debates in 1960, introduced a new dimension to campaign communications. That year Congress repealed legislation requiring that equal time be provided to all candidates, including those representing minor parties, and the two major candidates went head-to-head in four separate encounters. The first was the most crucial: Kennedy appeared confident while Nixon's uncertain demeanor and heavy beard were thought to have a negative effect on television viewers. After that first debate, Kennedy's campaign gained more enthusiasm, and he himself credited the debate for his victory.

After a hiatus during the 1964, 1968, and 1972 campaigns, the debates resumed in 1976. The candidates, Ford and Carter, squared off under the auspices of the League of Women Voters, which sponsored the debates as news events. The second of the debates appeared to be the crucial one, as Ford stated in answer to a question by a reporter that he did not consider Eastern Europe, particularly Yugoslavia, Romania, and Poland, to be under Soviet domination. To make matters worse, the President refused to retract the statement after the startled questioner gave him the chance to do so. Many political observers regard that gaffe to be the turning point of the campaign, reversing the decline in public support for Carter.

The debates of the 1980, 1984, and 1988 presidential campaigns had some interesting features, but none appears to have played as major a role in the election as the debates of 1960 and 1976. Only one debate was held between the two major candidates in 1980 (Jimmy Carter refused to participate in the first one, in which the third-party candidate, John Anderson, participated). Reagan was regarded as having won his debate with Carter on style, not substance. In 1984 there were two debates between Reagan and Walter Mondale. Reagan did poorly in the first debate, with Mondale pointing out that although Reagan had implied in his 1980 debate with Carter that he would not cut Medicare, he had in fact tried to cut the program by $20 billion. In the second debate, Reagan scored the cleverest quip, dispatching the issue of his age (he was seventy-three) by saying to Mondale that he did not intend to "exploit my opponent's youth and inexperience." The 1988 debates between Bush and Michael Dukakis were sponsored by the Commission on Debates, a nonprofit, bipartisan organization supported by both national party committees (the League of Women Voters withdrew its sponsorship of the last debate because of disagreements over the format of the debates). The general consensus was that the result of the debates was inconclusive: Dukakis was not able to reverse the momentum of the campaign, which had swung to Bush.

A third source of communication in presidential campaigns is the news and editorial coverage provided by television, radio, newspapers, and magazines. While important, this source is not as significant during the general election campaign as during the process of NOMINATING PRESIDENTIAL CANDIDATES, when there are typically several candidates vying for attention, especially in the out-of-power party.

There are some similarities between the kinds of coverage given the primary and general-election campaigns. Most (but not all) commentators and reporters focus on the election game—that is, on which candidate is leading in opinion polls, on the hoopla of campaign rallies, and so on. They also tend to stress campaign (rather than policy) issues—such as Carter's remark in a *Playboy* magazine interview during the 1976 campaign that he had "lusted after women in his heart." Only a small percentage of newspaper articles mentioned Mondale's accusation that Reagan's tax cuts benefited the rich and none reported Mondale's own progressive tax plan.

Despite the dominance of television, the other media have some advantages. Newspapers and magazines can cover the issues in more detail than is possible on television and can also endorse candidates. The radio can be used to reach commuting drivers, as Ford did in 1976. (Nixon had used radio in 1972 because he felt he came across better there than on television.)

Managing the Campaign. While decisions concerning what kinds of political appeals to use and how they should be communicated are to some degree national in scope, the vastness of the United States means that candidates must also target their messages to specific portions of the electorate. The candidates' task is clear: to win the presidency the candidate must win 270 of the 538 votes in the ELECTORAL COLLEGE. In 1992, a candidate could capture the presidency by winning only the eleven largest states, even if he lost the remaining thirty-nine. This means that the largest states become the main battleground of the campaign.

Of course, candidates also take into account how competitive the various states have been in recent years. Both parties stay away from the sure states. The party in control does not think it is necessary to waste money there, and the opposition party is unlikely to expend much effort in what is considered to be a losing cause.

One major strategy problem since the 1960s has been that American politics has become so politically fluid that there are no longer many sure states. The Solid South, once considered the bastion of the DEMO-CRATIC PARTY, played an important role in the victories of Kennedy in 1960 and Carter in 1976, but since 1980 it has become a Republican stronghold in presidential elections. The regions that have become the most competitive are the Mid-Atlantic states of New York, Pennsylvania, and New Jersey and the Midwest states of Ohio, Michigan, Illinois, and Missouri. In 1988 Bush concentrated on the southern and Rocky Mountain states, along with Ohio and New Jersey; Dukakis concentrated his efforts in eighteen states and ultimately barely lost in Illinois, California, Maryland, and Pennsylvania, all of which were crucial to his victory plan.

A final dimension of managing a presidential campaign is the assemblage of an army of participants to handle various aspects of the operation. This army naturally includes those who helped out in the nomination campaign, but it may also include those who opposed the nominee (Humphrey, for example, worked for McGovern in 1972). Party regulars are one source of workers, but so are those whose loyalties are particular candidates and issues. State and local party organizations form another potential pool of recruiters, particularly since 1980, when the law was changed to permit them to spend money for any purposes other than campaign advertising or hiring outside personnel. Leaders and members of labor unions have also contributed to a number of Democratic campaigns. In recent elections, both political parties have focused their efforts in mobilizing potential new voters—the Democrats concentrating on African Americans, women, Hispanics, and the poor, and the Republicans on white southerners and, in some cases, Hispanics as well.

Specialization has become a distinct feature of presidential campaign strategies. Public-opinion pollsters tap the pulse of Americans to see what they like and dislike about the candidates and where the voters themselves stand on the issues. Media experts coach the candidates on dress, posture, and how to look into the camera. Fund-raisers and allocators help candidates determine how best to solicit and spend contributions while staying within the complex legal provisions regarding how money can be gotten and used. And computer experts assist in targeting lists of potential campaign participants through the use of direct mail.

BIBLIOGRAPHY

Asher, Herbert. *Presidential Elections in American Politics.* 5th ed. 1992.

Chubb, John, and Paul Peterson. *The New Directions in American Politics.* 1985.

Kessel, John. *Presidential Campaign Politics.* 4th ed. 1992.

Nimmo, Dan. *The Political Persuaders: The Techniques of Modern Political Campaigns.* 1970.

Robinson, Michael, and Margaret Sheehan. *Over the Wire and on TV: CBS and UPI in Campaign.* 1980.

Wayne, Stephen. *The Road to the White House.* 5th ed. 1992.

RICHARD A. WATSON

CAMP DAVID. Camp David is a two hundred-acre presidential retreat located in a heavily wooded area of Catoctin Mountain Park in Frederick County, Maryland, approximately seventy miles northwest of Washington, D.C. The camp is administered by the Office of the Military Assistant to the President and is operated by the U.S. Navy. Armed guards from the U.S. Marine Corps patrol the camp, which is surrounded by a high security fence and is not open to the public.

The camp was established in 1942 by President Franklin Roosevelt as a weekend retreat from Washington's summer heat. He called the camp Shangri-La, the name of a mountain kingdom in a novel, *Lost Horizon*, by the British author James Hilton. In 1945, President Harry S. Truman made Shangri-La the official presidential retreat. In 1953, President Dwight D. Eisenhower renamed the camp for his grandson David Eisenhower.

The camp originally consisted of a simple woodland lodge with four bedrooms, a living and dining room that also served as the only office, and a screened porch overlooking the Catoctin Valley. In addition to the main lodge, there was also a swimming pool and separate cottages for the Secret Service, secretaries, telephone exchange, and other support services. A Marine training camp surrounded the place.

During WORLD WAR II, President Roosevelt read many of the messages he received from other wartime leaders and wrote out replies from the one large living room. He also relaxed by working on his stamp collection on the porch. Although the camp still retains its rustic character, the facilities have since been upgraded. A presidential office and meeting room have been added to the main lodge, and in 1953 President Eisenhower installed a pitch-and-putt golf green.

Many world leaders have been presidential guests at Camp David. During World War II, Roosevelt held meetings there with Prime Minister Winston Churchill of Great Britain. In 1959, Eisenhower conferred at Camp David with the Soviet premier, Nikita Khrushchev. In 1978, President Jimmy Carter conducted thirteen days of peace talks between Prime Minister Menachem Begin of Israel and President Anwar al-Sadat of Egypt that resulted in the historic CAMP DAVID ACCORDS. Most of the Presidents since Roosevelt have also used Camp David as a retreat for their staffs and to entertain congressional leaders. In 1980, President Carter held an economic summit in which he brought together prominent people from business, government, labor, and the academic and religious communities. An invitation to Camp David has come to confer a special distinction upon a guest.

BIBLIOGRAPHY

Eisenhower, Dwight D. *Mandate for Change, 1953–1956*. 1963.
Sherwood, Robert E. *Roosevelt and Hopkins*. 1948.

BURTON KAUFMAN

CAMP DAVID ACCORDS. President Jimmy Carter's most significant foreign policy success as President occurred at CAMP DAVID on 17 September 1978 when President Anwar Sadat of Egypt and Prime Minister Menachem Begin of ISRAEL signed the Camp David accords establishing a framework of peace for the Middle East and promising to end thirty years of hostilities between Israel and its Arab neighbors. The agreement was hailed in the United States and throughout the world as not only a monumental diplomatic accomplishment but a personal achievement for Carter, who had brought Sadat and Begin together and who had been instrumental in hammering out the accords.

The Camp David meeting had been a gamble for the President. Chances of success were not good. Ever since taking office, Carter had made the settlement of the Arab-Israeli dispute one of his highest priorities. In a dramatic gesture, Sadat had traveled to Israel in November 1977 and had addressed the Israeli parliament, the Knesset, in a call for peace. But little progress was made on the two major issues preventing an agreement: the Israeli occupation of Arab lands seized during the Six-Day War of 1967 and self-determination for Palestinians living on the West Bank of the Jordan River and in the Gaza Strip. In December 1977, Begin agreed to allow limited home rule for the West Bank and Gaza for three to five years, after which Israel would review the arrangement to see how it was working. But he refused to promise eventual autonomy, even after Sadat agreed to allow Israel to maintain security forces in these territories during a transitional period.

Afraid of renewed conflict in the Middle East, Carter sought to bridge the chasm separating Egypt and Israel. Despite several failed attempts by the administration to mediate an agreement, both Sadat and Begin indicated in the summer of 1978 that they would welcome a new American initiative. For his part, Carter concluded that, while many ideas had been floated for a settlement between Egypt and Israel, the only way an agreement could be reached was to bring the principals together for as long as it took to work out their differences. Once that was achieved, the way would be open for a general Middle East settlement.

Although both Begin and Sadat almost immediately accepted the President's invitation to come to Camp David for talks, the negotiations, which began on 4 September, got off to a poor start. The chemistry between Carter and Begin, whom the President described as rigid and unimaginative, was not good. His meetings with Sadat also went poorly. Despite the fact that Carter admired the Egyptian leader, with whom he had developed a warm personal relationship, he was disappointed at Sadat's insistence that Israel would have to withdraw from all the occupied lands before an agreement would be possible.

At first, the President met with the two leaders together, but, because they did not get along, he began conferring with them separately. The critical moment in the negotiations came on 15 September, after Begin rejected a proposal, agreed to by Sadat, providing for return of the Sinai Peninsula (which Israel had seized in the Six-Day War) to Egypt in exchange for an Egyptian-Israeli peace treaty. In response, Sadat announced that he was returning to Egypt that day. In a final effort to keep the talks going, Carter warned the Egyptian leader that the American people would hold him responsible for the failure of the Camp David summit and that Egyptian-American relations would deteriorate. Shaken by the force of Carter's argument, Sadat agreed to continue the negotiations.

Events then moved quickly. Subject to the approval of the Knesset, Begin agreed to an offer by Carter to help Israel build new airfields in the Negev Desert if the Israelis would give up their airfields and settlements in the Sinai and return that occupied territory to Egypt. The President then persuaded Sadat to accept this formulation. No progress, however, was made on the other issues preventing a Middle East settlement, most notably the Palestinian problem and the Israeli occupation of the West Bank and Gaza. Instead, Sadat and Begin finessed these matters by agreeing to an ambiguous "framework for peace," which Carter had prepared a week earlier when it had looked as if the summit was about to fall apart.

On 17 September, Carter publicly announced the agreements. The signing of the Camp David accords, at a White House ceremony, was carried by all the major television networks. Although the agreements were widely hailed as a glowing success for the President, they were seriously flawed. There was nothing in the "framework for peace" about the building of new Israeli settlements on the West Bank and Gaza, which continued even after the accords were signed. It was also assumed that Jordan and the Palestinians living in the occupied lands would participate in the negotiations over the West Bank and Gaza. But King Hussein of Jordan had stated several times that he would not enter into the peace process until Israel agreed to return East Jerusalem to Jordan, a condition that the Israelis refused to accept. Without Jordan's participation, any agreement on the occupied territories or on Palestinian autonomy would be virtually meaningless. Furthermore, the two accords signed at Camp David were replete with ambiguous terms and provisions, which would make future negotiations extremely difficult.

Notwithstanding public appearances, Sadat was keenly disappointed by the results of Camp David. He returned to Egypt with little to offer any of the other Arab leaders, every one of whom rejected the Camp David agreements. Even Egypt and Israel failed to sign a final peace treaty until March 1979, three months after the deadline agreed to at Camp David. Nevertheless, the Camp David accords did lead to the evacuation of the Sinai Peninsula by Israel and the establishment of diplomatic and economic relations between Egypt and Israel.

BIBLIOGRAPHY

Brzezinski, Zbigniew. *Power and Principle: Memoirs of the National Security Adviser, 1977–1981.* 1983.
Carter, Jimmy. *Keeping Faith: Memoirs of a President.* 1982.
Kaufman, Burton I. *The Presidency of James Earl Carter, Jr.* 1993.
McClellan, David S. *Cyrus Vance.* 1985.
Quandt, William B. *Camp David: Peacemaking and Politics.* 1986.
Smith, Gaddis. *Morality, Reason, and Power: American Diplomacy in the Carter Years.* 1986.
Vance, Cyrus. *Hard Choices: Critical Years in American's Foreign Policy.* 1983.

BURTON KAUFMAN

CAPITAL PUNISHMENT. The issue of capital punishment reappears with regularity in the history of the American presidency, most often in the form of a dramatic plea for a presidential pardon on behalf of a notorious condemned prisoner. Although the presidential PARDON POWER extends only to those convicted of federal crimes or sentenced by military tribunals, this limited jurisdiction included two PRESIDENTIAL ASSASSINATIONS. The conspirators convicted of the plot to assassinate President Abraham Lincoln were sentenced to death by a military tribunal in the District of Columbia. Five of the nine officers on the tribunal recommended that President Andrew Johnson commute the death sentence of Mary Surratt, proprietress of the boarding house where the conspirators met, but Johnson refused to meet with Mrs. Surratt's daughter, who came to the White house to plead for her mother's life, and on 7 July 1865 Mrs. Surratt was hanged. Two years later, when the tribunal's recommendation was publicly revealed, Johnson claimed he had never seen it, and fired Secretary of War EDWIN M. STANTON, who would have been responsible for the concealment. The firing of Stanton led directly to the IMPEACHMENT OF ANDREW JOHNSON.

Because the assassination of President James A. Garfield took place in the District of Columbia, it also fell within federal jurisdiction, although that jurisdiction was unsuccessfully challenged on the grounds that Garfield died in New Jersey. CHARLES GUITEAU was executed after President Chester Arthur turned down a last-minute commutation plea.

In a number of celebrated cases, pleas for presidential commutation of death sentences were more successful. President Woodrow Wilson commuted the death sentence of Robert Stroud in 1919. Stroud, a federal prisoner, was tried three times for fatally stabbing a prison guard. At his second trial, the jury made a binding recommendation of life imprisonment. After that conviction was set aside on appeal, on retrial another jury recommended death. The U.S. Supreme Court upheld the verdict, rejecting a claim that it violated the double jeopardy clause. Wilson then intervened, and Stroud lived another forty-three years, becoming world-famous as the Birdman of Alcatraz.

In 1935, President Franklin D. Roosevelt intervened minutes before the scheduled execution of Charles Bernstein for a District of Columbia murder. Bernstein had been convicted despite the testimony of six witnesses that he was in New York at the time of the crime. President Roosevelt's commutation of the death sentence was later expanded to an unconditional pardon by President Harry S. Truman.

On occasion, presidential commutations have not been welcome. In 1925, a federal prisoner serving a twenty-five year sentence escaped and, while at large, committed a murder in Connecticut. After a Connecticut court sentenced him to death, he asked to be returned to federal prison to serve out his twenty-five year sentence before being executed. President Calvin Coolidge promptly commuted his federal sentence to expedite his execution by the state. Federal courts ruled that the commutation was valid even though the prisoner neither requested or accepted it.

From 1930 to 1957, a total of thirty federal civilian prisoners were executed, including eight convicted of espionage during wartime. The most famous case was that of Julius and Ethel Rosenberg, who were electrocuted in Sing Sing prison in Ossining, New York, in 1953 after President Dwight D. Eisenhower turned down a last-minute plea for commutation.

John F. Kennedy was the last U.S. President to preside over a federal execution, with the hanging of Victor Feguer for kidnapping and murder in 1963. The federal law making the interstate transportation of kidnap victims a capital offense had been enacted in the wake of the kidnapping and murder of the infant son of the world-renowned aviator Charles Lindbergh in 1932. A total of six persons were executed by federal authorities for kidnappings, all of which had resulted in deaths of the victims.

Furman v. Georgia, the 1972 United States Supreme Court decision invalidating state death penalty procedures, was widely construed as invalidating federal and military death penalty procedures as well, although the U.S. Supreme Court never directly ruled on the point. A 1976 ruling upholding death penalty laws under which jury discretion was guided, led to the restoration of death penalty laws in thirty-nine states. No new death penalty law was enacted on the federal level, however, until 1988. The Omnibus Crime Bill of 1988, signed by President Ronald Reagan, provided capital punishment for intentional killings which are linked to major drug offenses. From 1988 to 1992, eight defendants were tried under this law, but only one, David R. Chandler, was sentenced to death. His sentence has been appealed on several grounds, including the failure of Congress to specify the means of execution. The administration of President George Bush has proposed legislation to impose the death penalty for a list of fifty-three crimes, but the proposal stalled over controversies on unrelated issues such as gun control and habeas corpus reform. Meanwhile, the government has utilized pre-1972 death penalty laws in several pending prosecutions, arguing that they comply with all post-*Furman* constitutional requirements.

Eleven military death sentences were imposed under federal law from 1976 to 1992. Five of those sentenced were still on death row in 1992. The last execution of a soldier sentenced under military law was in 1961.

Capital punishment first became a presidential campaign issue in 1968, when Richard M. Nixon strongly advocated use and extension of death penalty laws, and GEORGE C. WALLACE also made it part of his agenda. President Nixon denounced the *Furman* decision in 1972, and vowed to appoint Supreme Court Justices who were more favorably disposed to the death penalty. President Ronald Reagan was also a strong advocate of capital punishment, and in 1988, Bush made his support for the death penalty a major issue in the campaign against Massachusetts governor MICHAEL DUKAKIS, an opponent of capital punishment. The 1992 Democratic nominee, Governor Bill Clinton, was an advocate of capital punishment and presided over several executions in Arkansas.

The popularity of the death penalty in America may deter governors with presidential ambitions from exercising their pardon or commutation powers. From 1961 to 1970, when 135 state executions took place, American governors commuted another 183 death sentences. From 1979 to 1988, 104 executions took place, but only 61 death sentences were commuted. From 1988 to 1990, while 37 executions occurred, only 7 commutations were reported, most by lame-duck governors.

BIBLIOGRAPHY

Amnesty International Publications. *United States of America: The Death Penalty.* 1987.

Bedau, Hugo Adam. *The Death Penalty in America.* 1964.

GERALD F. UELMEN

CARTER, JIMMY (b. 1924), thirty-ninth President of the United States (1977–1981). James Earl Carter, Jr., was born on 1 October 1924 in Plains, Georgia. His father, Earl, was a successful local businessman who operated a brokerage business in peanuts; his mother, Lillian Gordon, was a registered nurse. Jimmy had two sisters, Gloria, born in 1926, and Ruth, born in 1929, and a much younger brother, Billy, born in 1937. Bright, disciplined, and self-directed, Jimmy graduated from high school in 1941 near the top of his class. After spending the next two years at Georgia Southwestern College and at the Georgia Institute of Technology, he was admitted to the U.S. Naval Academy in 1943. In 1946, he graduated from the Academy and married Rosalynn Smith [see ROSALYNN CARTER], also from Plains. He spent the next seven years in the Navy, most of the time working for Captain Hyman Rickover on the *Seawolf*, a prototype of the nuclear submarine.

Early Career. In 1953, following the death of his father, Carter resigned from the Navy and returned to Plains, where he turned his father's faltering peanut business around and became a successful businessman and community leader. In 1962, he ran successfully for the Georgia Senate and quickly established a reputation as a moderate progressive supporting "good government" measures and educational reform. In 1966, he gave up his seat to run for governor. Finishing third, Carter went through a period of deep depression, which was lifted only by the solace he found as a born-again Christian.

In 1970, he made a second bid for governor, this time winning by appealing to segregationist and white supremacist elements in the state. After assuming office, however, he established a reputation as a racial moderate and a reform leader. He increased the number of black state employees, improved services for the mentally handicapped, and worked successfully for environmental and consumer protection and for tax, welfare, and judicial reform—all programs that would receive high priority during the Carter presidency. But his main effort as governor was to reorganize state government and to introduce zero-based budgeting in order to make government more efficient and cost-effective.

By the end of his second year in office, Carter had established a solid record of achievement; in 1971,

Time featured him on its cover as representative of a new, progressive leadership in the South. The next year, Carter decided to prepare for a run for the presidency. Despite the fact that he was virtually unknown outside Georgia, he was persuaded to seek the 1976 Democratic nomination by Dr. Peter Bourne, who headed Georgia's drug-abuse program, and by Hamilton Jordan, who had worked in Carter's gubernatorial campaign and who quickly became one of his shrewdest political advisers. Bourne and Jordan realized that, because of rule changes that made the process of selecting delegates to the national party's nominating convention more democratic, Carter could win by winning the early primaries and building up political momentum. Given a widespread distrust of politics and politicians among Americans, they also sensed a real advantage in the fact that Carter was a political outsider. The plan Jordan developed for the campaign worked almost to perfection. During the next two years, Carter traveled throughout the country, remaining purposely vague on the issues but speaking out instead on the importance in government of values such as honesty, integrity, and compassion. In 1976 he won key victories in the Iowa caucuses and in the New Hampshire, Florida, and Pennsylvania primaries, which gave him the political momentum to win in other states. Even in states he lost, he gained enough delegates to ensure his nomination at the Democratic convention in July 1976.

As Carter began the fall campaign against his Republican opponent, President Gerald Ford, he enjoyed a comfortable lead in the polls. He lost most of this lead because of his vagueness on the issues. But the assertion by Ford during a PRESIDENTIAL DEBATE with Carter that Eastern Europe was not dominated by the Soviet Union hurt the President badly, and in November Carter managed a narrow victory, receiving 40.8 million votes (50.1 percent) to Ford's 39.1 million votes (48 percent).

Expectations of the New President. The narrowness of Carter's victory had important implications for his presidency. First, the President-elect lacked a political mandate from the American people. Second, because of the closeness of the vote, different constituencies, including blacks, labor, and senior citizens, with sometimes conflicting programs, claimed credit for his victory and anticipated his strong backing for their particular interests. Compounding Carter's problems were a cynical electorate, a sluggish economy with high unemployment, and an independent-minded Congress determined to redress what it considered an imbalance between the executive and the legislative branches of government.

Other developments, however, worked to the new President's advantage. The polls showed that the American people trusted Carter and thought he would bring a new way of doing business to government. On Capitol Hill, the Democratic caucus had narrowed the power of committee chairs and had increased the power of the top Democratic leadership. As a result, a Democratic President willing to work with congressional leaders in establishing legislative priorities had a good chance of getting his program through the House and the Senate.

Unfortunately for the new President, he quickly alienated Congress. Instead of establishing close political ties with Congress, he told legislative leaders even before he took office that if he did not get his way on Capitol Hill, he would take his case immediately to the American people. His decision to pardon VIETNAM WAR draft evaders and his unpopular nomination of THEODORE SORENSEN, a former aide to President John F. Kennedy, to head the CENTRAL INTELLIGENCE AGENCY (CIA) further exacerbated tensions between the White House and Congress, as did his action in cutting from the budget a series of water projects being promoted on Capitol Hill. Although most of these were pork-barrel projects that could not be justified economically, pork-barrel politics had been sacrosanct for decades, and Carter's unilateral action stunned and angered lawmakers. Then, the President announced that he had decided against a $50 rebate for every American taxpayer, even though he had promised such a rebate during the campaign and the Democratic leadership had reluctantly agreed to support it.

The new President also angered many Democrats who had voted for him by his economic program. Carter's proposals reflected his own fiscal conservatism and focused more on avoiding a reacceleration of inflation through fiscal restraint than on dealing with high unemployment by creating more public sector jobs (although he did support a limited increase in jobs programs as part of an economic stimulus package). As early as March 1977, organized labor was in open rebellion against the administration, not only because it disliked Carter's economic program but also because the White House failed to support labor on a number of issues. Among these was an increase in the minimum wage from $2.30 to $3.00 an hour.

Despite warnings from his own staff about the importance of setting priorities in developing his legislative program, the new President also presented the ninety-fifth Congress with a complex legislative agenda whose passage would have taxed the political skills of any President, much less one as inexperienced as Carter. During his first six months in office, Carter submitted proposals on executive reorganization, urban and welfare reform, energy, hospital cost containment, taxation, ethics in government, and SOCIAL SECURITY. By August, all but one of these major initiatives had become stalled on Capitol Hill; only Carter's request for authority to reorganize the executive branch was approved.

In September, the President suffered a major political blow when he was forced to accept the resignation of Bert Lance, the director of the Office of Management and Budget and his closest friend. Lance got into political trouble following public revelations that he had engaged in questionable business practices while a banker in Georgia, including running up huge overdrafts on the bank that his family controlled. Instead of asking for Lance's resignation, Carter stood loyally by him, declaring publicly that Lance was "a man of honesty, trustworthiness [and] integrity" and that he was "proud" of him. The Lance affair, which dominated the headlines for weeks, struck at the very credibility of the administration. Carter's unfailing support of his friend raised questions not only about his political judgment but also about his publicly stated commitment to the highest ethical standards in government.

Meanwhile, the economy, which had shown signs of recovery during the first half of 1977 and was the issue that most concerned voters, started to turn downward once more. The rate of economic growth declined from 6.8 percent during the first six months of 1977 to about 4.0 percent by year's end. Unemployment and inflation also began to rise again. As Carter's first year in office came to a close, therefore, it appeared that the outsider from Georgia, to whom voters had looked with high expectations, was stumbling.

Foreign Policy. Carter devoted considerable time during his first year in office to issues of foreign policy. But here, too, his administration seemed to be floundering. From the time Carter entered the White House, he intended to take charge of his own foreign policy. His Secretary of State, Cyrus Vance, a former Deputy Secretary of Defense, would be the diplomat transacting the nation's business abroad. But the President would establish priorities, set directions, and be the final decision maker, assisted by his NATIONAL SECURITY ADVISER, Zbigniew Brzezinski, a former Columbia University professor, whom Carter expected to provide a comprehensive overview of international developments. Diplomacy would be conducted more openly than during the administrations of Richard Nixon and Ford, and a strong commitment would be made to promoting HUMAN RIGHTS. More attention would be paid to Western Europe than under the previous administrations. The White House would seek to continue a policy of DETENTE with the Soviet Union, but not at the expense of its commitment to human rights. Nor would foreign policy continue to focus on the COLD WAR rivalry between Washington and Moscow.

Almost as soon as the new administration took office, problems developed in implementing its foreign policy. The President's public support of Soviet dissidents and his proposals for the STRATEGIC ARMS LIMITATIONS TALKS (SALT II), which were to supersede the 1972 SALT I agreement, angered President Leonid Brezhnev of the Soviet Union. (One proposal would have forced the Soviets to make far greater cuts in their strategic weapons than the United States.) Brezhnev abruptly canceled a round of negotiations in March with Vance. Although the talks resumed in Geneva two months later, the two sides remained far apart on the specifics of an agreement. Carter's human rights campaign also remained a major sore point in Soviet-American relations.

In the Middle East, Carter decided to use American influence to settle the long-standing Arab-Israeli dispute. In November 1977, a major breakthrough in the peace process took place when the Egyptian President, Anwar Sadat, went to Israel and, in an emotional address to the Israeli parliament, the Knesset, called for a new round of negotiations on the Middle East. But other Arab leaders refused to join in the talks, and Menachim Begin, the Israeli prime minister, continued to pursue a hard line on the return of Arab lands seized during the 1967 Six-Day War and on Palestinian autonomy, the two major issues preventing a peace settlement. Meanwhile, President Carter angered Israeli leaders and the influential American Jewish community by courting Arab leaders and by speaking in support of a Palestinian homeland.

Closer to home, the President won a major victory in March 1978, when the Senate ratified the PANAMA CANAL treaties, ceding the Panama Canal to PANAMA at the end of 1999 but giving the United States the right to use military force if necessary to keep the waterway open and guaranteeing its neutrality. The President's effort to conclude such a treaty between the United States and Panama had run into so much opposition that, without an intense White House lobbying campaign and the President's successful courting of the Senate minority leader, Howard Baker of Tennessee, the two treaties would never have gained the two-thirds vote necessary for ratification. But Carter's achievement gained him little favor with American voters. Although he was persuaded that relinquishing the Canal not only was morally right but was needed to avoid violence in Panama, most Americans believed

the act amounted to giving away one of the nation's great treasures.

In September 1978, Carter recorded the most important foreign policy achievement of his administration when Sadat and Begin signed the CAMP DAVID ACCORDS, promising an end to thirty years of hostilities between Israel and Egypt. During the first six months of 1978, the President had tried unsuccessfully to get the Mideast peace process started again by acting as an intermediary between Egypt and Israel. Afraid of a renewed conflict in the Mideast, he decided in the summer to take the bold move of inviting both Begin and Sadat to a summit meeting at CAMP DAVID and to keep them there for as long as it took to work out their differences. Once that was achieved, he thought the way would be open for a general Mideast settlement.

At first the President met with the two leaders together. But because they did not get along, he soon began conferring with them separately. Through sheer tenacity, he kept the negotiations alive. At one point, Sadat even began packing his bags to return to Egypt, only to be talked into staying by his host. After thirteen days, Carter was able to announce an agreement calling for the signing of a peace treaty between Egypt and Israel. The accord provided the framework for a settlement of the Mideast problem that had eluded peacemakers for more than three decades. The signing of the Camp David accords at a White House ceremony was carried by all the major television networks, and Carter was singled out for plaudits.

Economic Problems. The President followed the Camp David agreement with an important domestic victory the next month, when lawmakers on Capitol Hill approved an energy program that had been stalled in Congress for nearly eighteen months. Except for the economy, no domestic matter had concerned the President more than the need for a program to deal with the nation's worsening energy crisis. Since 1973, America's dependency on foreign oil had grown from about 35 percent to 53 percent, while oil prices had doubled from about $6 a barrel to $12 a barrel. The brutal winter of 1976–1977 underscored just how critical the nation's energy shortage had become. In April 1977, Carter announced a comprehensive energy program designed to reduce the nation's energy consumption. The program relied on the imposition of a crude oil equalization tax (COET) intended to raise the price of domestically produced oil to the level of world prices, an increase in the price of natural gas, a standby gasoline tax, and various tax credits and penalties to encourage energy conservation. Almost immediately the program met organized opposition from lawmakers from oil-producing states, from the oil lobby, and from other special interest groups opposed to higher energy costs.

Although the House passed most of Carter's energy program in August, the Senate virtually emasculated the President's program and then locked horns with the House in conference committee. For more than a year, the committee failed to reach a compromise. But in October 1978, Congress finally passed a measure that the President had helped broker. Based on the principle of energy conservation through deregulation rather than through taxation, the legislation was radically different from what Carter had originally proposed and included a provision for the phased deregulation of natural gas, something Carter had at one time strongly opposed. But by deregulating natural gas and establishing a single price structure for intra- and interstate gas, Congress had taken an important step toward conserving gas and distributing it more rationally. It also encouraged energy conservation and the expanded use of nonfossil fuels through various tax credits.

The political capital won by the administration as a result of the President's success on Capitol Hill and of the Camp David accords, however, was short-lived. The economy continued to worsen, and the rate of inflation approached 12 percent. Carter's proposal to deal with inflation through budget cuts and a voluntary system of wage and price controls met with widespread skepticism and opposition on Capitol Hill from Democrats afraid of drastic cuts in domestic programs. Already there was considerable talk among Democratic liberals about replacing Carter with Sen. Edward Kennedy of Massachusetts as the party's standard-bearer in 1980. Although Kennedy denied being a candidate, his relations with Carter had been strained for more than a year over the Senator's proposal for comprehensive national health insurance, which the President supported in principle but said had to be phased in, beginning with coverage for catastrophic illness.

The downward spiral in Carter's popularity among voters continued throughout the rest of the year, as the nation experienced "stagflation," slow economic growth, high unemployment, and high inflation. The signing of an Israeli-Egyptian peace settlement in March 1979 provided some political relief for Carter, who had gone to the Mideast in a final, successful effort to save the peace process. But the problem of inflation, fed by skyrocketing oil prices resulting from a revolution in Iran that ended a worldwide glut of oil, refused to go away. Figures released in May revealed that inflation was growing at an annual rate of about 14 percent and that the economy had entered a slump.

Other figures showed that Americans no longer had confidence in the ability of the White House to deal with the country's problems. Although Kennedy continued to disavow presidential ambitions, he sounded more and more like a candidate, and a Gallup poll in May showed him beating Carter among Democrats 54 percent to 31 percent.

Public discontent with the Carter administration intensified in July following a sequence of unusual events. A presidential speech on energy was postponed without explanation; leaders from a broad cross-section of American society trekked to Camp David for discussions with the President, and five members of Carter's Cabinet resigned. The catalyst for these incidents was an announcement by the Organization of Petroleum Exporting Countries (OPEC) of its fourth and largest price increase in five months. In response, Carter decided to speak to the nation on energy. But he then abruptly canceled his planned address, spending the next eleven days instead at Camp David, where he conferred with prominent people from business, government, labor, and the academic and religious communities. When he finally came down from Camp David and gave his long-delayed address on 15 July, he subordinated the energy crisis and the nation's other economic ills to what he referred to as a "crisis of spirit." Although the President never used the term *malaise*, it rapidly became the catchword for his message (*see* CRISIS OF CONFIDENCE SPEECH).

The President's speech was well-received. But a few days later, he undermined his improved standing with the American public by accepting the forced resignations of five members of his Cabinet. The suddenness and sweep of his action raised questions about the very stability of his administration. His decision to choose the energy crisis as the tinder on which to rekindle the American spirit also hurt him with the American people, for there was no more divisive issue in 1979 than energy. Moreover, his proposals for dealing with the crisis—decontrolling oil and then imposing a windfall profits tax to keep the oil industry from making inordinate profits—were widely perceived as stoking the flames of inflation. To many observers, therefore, Carter appeared unlikely even to win renomination in 1980. Ready to replace him at the head of the Democratic ticket was Kennedy, who ended months of speculation by announcing his candidacy in November.

Crises Foreign and Domestic. Developments in Iran and Afghanistan at the end of 1979 changed the political landscape dramatically. In Iran, the Shah had been overthrown the previous January in a revolution led by the Ayatollah Ruhollah Khomeini, a fundamentalist Muslim cleric committed to establishing an Islamic republic in that country. In February, Khomeini's followers briefly occupied the American embassy in Tehran. Although relations between the United States and Iran then returned to a state of normalcy, Iranian militants again seized the embassy on 4 November, taking sixty American hostages, after learning that the Shah had been allowed into the United States to receive medical treatment. They vowed to hold onto the hostages until the United States returned the Shah to Iran and paid financial damages for the crimes it had allegedly committed against the Iranian people. The next month, the Soviet Union sent 85,000 troops into Afghanistan to install and support a Marxist regime under Babrak Karmal.

President Carter responded to the seizure of the hostages by trying to gain their release through diplomatic channels. He responded to the Afghan invasion by announcing the CARTER DOCTRINE and by imposing a grain embargo on the Soviet Union, barring the sale of high technology to the Soviets, and asking the Senate to delay consideration of the SALT II agreement that had been reached earlier that year and signed by Carter and Brezhnev on 18 June 1979. Carter also indicated that the United States might boycott the 1980 Summer Olympics scheduled for Moscow. The American public gave Carter high marks for his handling of these two crises. He took a commanding lead over Kennedy in the presidential preference polls and in January 1980 beat the Senator in the Iowa caucuses. The next month he won the New Hampshire primary. Although Kennedy remained in the race until the Democratic convention in mid August and defeated Carter in a number of important primaries, he was never able to overcome the lead the President had taken.

Yet the IRANIAN HOSTAGE CRISIS, together with the slumping economy, helped defeat Carter's bid for reelection in November. In the early morning of 25 April 1980, the President went on television to announce that a military effort to rescue the hostages, DESERT ONE, had failed and that eight members of the rescue mission had died in a helicopter crash. Although initial reaction to the hapless mission was supportive of the President, as details of the botched plan were revealed, it became another entry in a long list of failures that many Americans attributed to the President.

Indeed, Carter's whole foreign policy seemed in disarray in mid 1980. The Soviets remained in Afghanistan. Efforts to build on the Egyptian-Israeli peace treaty in the Middle East went nowhere. The country's growing dependence on oil imports and a decline in the value of the dollar left the United States increasingly exposed to the whiplashes of the international economy. And sharp differences existed between Carter and European leaders, especially the West German chancellor, Helmut Schmidt, on a variety of issues, including international economic policy and Carter's handling of the Iranian crisis and the Afghan invasion. When Vance, who had opposed the Iranian rescue mission, announced that he was resigning as Secretary of State, the news media seized on the announcement as evidence that the President's foreign policy was in a quagmire.

The President's most serious problem with the electorate, however, remained the economy. Unemployment lines continued to lengthen, and the prime interest and inflation rates neared 20 percent. The nation's two most important industries, housing and automobiles, virtually collapsed. Housing starts in March were down 42 percent and car sales down 24 percent compared to the rates a year earlier. During the spring and summer, some progress was made in bringing inflation under control, and the prime interest rate dropped to 13 percent. But the recession continued, and unemployment replaced inflation as the nation's most serious economic problem. The Department of Labor set the number of jobless in July at 8.2 million, up a startling 1.9 million since February. Even Carter's own economists predicted that the unemployment rate of 7.8 percent would reach 8.5 percent by the end of the year and stay that way through most of 1981.

In July, the President responded to the nation's economic woes by calling for a tax cut, something the Republican presidential candidate, Ronald Reagan, had been advocating but which Carter had resisted in his effort to hold down the budget deficit. But Carter's latest economic recovery program received a mixed response on Capitol Hill and from the business and financial communities. Even though Carter was renominated for President in August, his prospects for reelection were not good. All the polls showed him substantially behind Reagan, a former governor of California. In a Gallup poll taken in early August, Carter received an approval rating of only 21 percent, three points lower than Richard Nixon's rating during the depths of the WATERGATE AFFAIR and the worst rating of any American President in the history of polling.

The Election of 1980. What is surprising, in fact, is not that Carter lost the election but how close he came to winning, running even or ahead of Reagan throughout most of the campaign. He nearly won the election by making Reagan's fitness to be President the major issue. A series of political gaffes on Reagan's part, including calling the Vietnam War "a noble cause," expressing personal doubts about the theory of evolution, and proposing that Social Security be made voluntary, underscored the doubts Carter was raising. The President was also able to put his opponent on the defensive by pounding the theme that a Reagan presidency would be more likely to lead the nation into war than would a second Carter administration. Meanwhile, the campaign of Rep. John Anderson of Illinois, a Republican maverick who was running as an independent candidate and who at one time promised to be an important factor in the election, fizzled as his standing in the polls dropped dramatically. By the middle of October, the momentum of the campaign had shifted in Carter's favor. Even Reagan's own pollsters reported that, for the first time in the race, the President had moved ahead of Reagan by two points.

Reagan was able to snatch victory from defeat, however, by dispelling doubts about his presidential qualifications and then refocusing the campaign on Carter's own record as President. In a debate with Carter in October, he effectively undermined the single concern that had propelled the President into a virtual tie with him in the polls—that he was not up to the job of Chief Executive. But the masterful stroke of the debate came at the end, when Reagan returned to the two issues—the economy and America's position in the world—that had surfaced in the polls more than all others save Reagan's own fitness to be President. Asking the American people whether they felt better off economically or thought the United States was safer and more respected in the world than when Carter took office, he concluded by remarking that the answers to these questions should determine "who you'll vote for." With seven days remaining in the campaign, he had returned the attention of the American voters to the issues on which Carter was most vulnerable. Once more the election had become a referendum on the Carter presidency.

On the Sunday before the election, the President alienated some voters by indicating in a televised address that a breakthrough in the hostage crisis might be near. Although the President made his announcement on the basis of an optimistic communication he had received from the Tehran government, many voters were suspicious of the motivations behind his announcement, especially since the Republicans had been warning for some time against such an October surprise. Furthermore, the hostages were not released, so the President's message served only to highlight his inability to secure their release.

On 4 November, the voters rejected Carter's bid for reelection. Reagan received 51 percent of the vote to Carter's 41 percent and Anderson's 7 percent. In the ELECTORAL COLLEGE, Reagan's victory was even more decisive. He won 489 electoral votes to Carter's 49. The American public's repudiation of Carter and the DEMOCRATIC PARTY was overwhelming. For the first time in twenty-eight years, Republicans gained control of the Senate. They also picked up thirty-three seats in the House. On the state level, Republicans ended with a net gain of four governorships.

Final Acts as President. After his defeat, Carter demonstrated that he was still President for the next ten weeks and that he had an agenda to pursue, regardless of the election's outcome. On the top of his agenda, of course, was the release of the hostages. Although the news from Iran continued to be encouraging, negotiations were long and complex. Having spent most of his last year as President preoccupied with the hostage crisis, Carter was eager to see their liberation. But he was denied this consolation prize. The Iranians completed a deal involving the transfer to Iran of $9 billion in frozen assets in return for the hostages only a few minutes after Reagan had taken the oath of office on 20 January 1981.

A week after the election, Congress met in an unusual postelection session. In addition to bargaining for the hostages' freedom, Carter busied himself in the remaining weeks of his presidency by lobbying on Capitol Hill for several of his high-priority measures—a youth jobs bill, a superfund to clean up toxic wastes, and an Alaskan lands bill. Determined to keep Democrats in the lame-duck Congress from enacting any last-minute legislation before Reagan assumed office, Republicans managed to prevent passage of the youth jobs bill, which Carter had been pushing for two years.

The President had better luck in persuading Congress to approve two pieces of environmental legislation. The first of these, establishing a $1.6 billion toxic waste superfund, had been in the drafting stage since 1977 when residents of the Love Canal neighborhood near Niagara Falls had been forced to abandon their homes after it was learned that the houses had been built on the site of a former chemical dump. Although Carter lobbied hard for a measure that would extend the superfund to include oil spills, the legislation he finally signed applied only to chemical contamination.

Passage on 12 November of the Alaskan lands bill represented a more significant victory for the President, who had been fighting for the measure since 1978. Over the opposition of oil, gas, mineral, and timber interests and of Alaska's two senators, who wanted to open the land for development, lawmakers set aside 104 million acres, or about one-third of Alaskan lands, from development. Environmentalists were still unhappy with the protection afforded calving grounds for caribou and habitat for migratory birds and disliked a provision allowing seismic exploration of certain parts of Alaska's North Slope. But the measure was one of the most significant pieces of environmental legislation ever approved by Congress and one of the most noteworthy accomplishments of the Carter administration.

Postpresidential Years. Immediately following Reagan's inauguration on 20 January, Carter, Rosalynn, and their daughter, Amy, returned to Plains. The next day, at President Reagan's invitation, Carter flew to Germany to welcome back to freedom the Iranian hostages. It was an exhilarating moment for Carter, but it was followed by a difficult period of transition from President to private citizen. Carter had not recovered from the shock of his defeat, and he was faced with serious financial problems. His principal financial asset, his peanut warehouse business, which had been in a blind trust while he was President, was broke, and he was deeply in debt. After a few months, however, the Carters settled into a new routine. They sold the warehouse business, and both Carters signed lucrative book contracts, thereby ensuring their financial security.

During the first half of the 1980s, the former President all but vanished from the national political scene, failing even to attend the 1984 Democratic presidential convention, which nominated his former vice president, WALTER MONDALE, as its standard-bearer. In forced retirement, Carter spent most of his time writing his memoirs, teaching at Emory University, and raising funds for the Jimmy Carter Library, Museum, and Presidential Center in Atlanta.

Determined that the Carter complex be more than a monument to his presidency, the former President has made the Center a locus of research and social and political activism, with programs on such diverse problems as human rights, preventive health care, the world environment, and conflict resolution in the Middle East, Latin America, and Africa. To further its work, he has traveled throughout the world, promoting improved agricultural methods and better health care in the world's most poverty-stricken countries, especially in Africa. In addition, he has been increasingly active in Habitat for Humanity, a charitable organization started in 1973 to provide housing for the poor.

Since the mid 1980s, Carter has also been publicly

and politically more visible. Beginning around 1985, he began to speak out more frequently on national issues and to criticize the Reagan administration's policies and programs, such as its SDI (STRATEGIC DEFENSE INITIATIVE) and its policy of "constructive engagement" with South Africa. He has also played an increasingly important role as an elder statesman, attempting to mediate the long-running war in Ethiopia between that country's Marxist government and Eritrean rebels (1989) and monitoring elections in Panama (1989) and in Nicaragua (1990).

But the Middle East remained the region of most concern to Carter. As he watched the promise of the Camp David accords of 1978 go largely unfulfilled, he became publicly critical of Israel for its refusal to stop building settlements on the West Bank and to grant Palestinians greater autonomy. He was also a proponent of an international peace conference to mediate the Arab-Israeli dispute and spoke out strongly against military intervention in the Persian Gulf following Iraq's invasion of Kuwait in 1990.

As Carter has become publicly more active, the media have paid more attention to his activities as a private citizen, and he has gained a degree of popularity and stature with the American people that would have been hard to imagine when he left office in 1981. In May 1990, he was awarded the Liberty Medal and a $100,000 prize for his involvement in "issues of liberty around the world." Commentators frequently refer to him as a model of a successful former President, and his reputation as one of the nation's best ex-Presidents continues to grow.

BIBLIOGRAPHY

Carter, Jimmy. *Keeping Faith: Memoirs of a President.* 1982.

Fink, Gary. *Prelude to the Presidency: The Political Character and Legislative Leadership Style of Governor Jimmy Carter.* 1980.

Germond, Jack W., and Jules Witcover. *Blue Smoke and Mirrors: How Reagan Won and Why Carter Lost the Election of 1980.* 1981.

Glad, Betty. *Jimmy Carter: In Search of the White House.* 1980.

Hargrove, Erwin C. *Jimmy Carter as President: Leadership and the Politics of the Public Good.* 1988.

Abernathy, Glenn, Dilys M. Hill, and Phil Williams, eds. *The Carter Years: The President and Policy Making.* 1984.

Jones, Charles O. *The Trustee Presidency: Jimmy Carter and the United States Congress.* 1988.

Kaufman, Burton I. *The Presidency of James Earl Carter, Jr.* 1993.

Miller, William Lee. *Yankee from Georgia: The Emergence of Jimmy Carter.* 1978.

Smith, Gaddis. *Morality, Reason, and Power: American Diplomacy in the Carter Years.* 1986.

Witcover, Jules. *Marathon: The Pursuit of the Presidency, 1972–1976.* 1977.

BURTON KAUFMAN

CARTER, ROSALYNN (b. 1927), First Lady, wife of Jimmy Carter. When she set out to campaign for her husband in early 1975, Rosalynn Smith Carter had little experience in national politics. Nonetheless, her activity in that race was generally regarded as an asset. Unlike most of her predecessors, she campaigned full-time and spoke on substantive matters. In the WHITE HOUSE, she enlarged the definition of a First Lady's role, keeping an office in the East Wing, attending Cabinet meetings, speaking often of her "partnership" with her husband, and publicizing her "working lunches" in the Oval Office.

For her trip to the Caribbean and Latin America in summer 1977, Rosalynn Carter tutored with presidential advisers and became the first President's wife to serve as her husband's emissary in discussing defense and trade policy with other nations' leaders in their own countries. Her work on behalf of the Equal Rights Amendment, resettlement of Cambodian refugees, and mental health reforms involved traveling, public speaking, and (in the case of mental health reforms) testifying before a Senate committee—something that no previous First Lady, except Eleanor Roosevelt, had done.

BIBLIOGRAPHY

Carter, Rosalynn. *First Lady from Plains.* 1984.
Jensen, Faye Lind. "An Awesome Responsibility: Rosalynn Carter as First Lady." *Presidential Studies Quarterly* 20 (1990): 769–775.
Jensen, Faye Lind. " 'These Are Precious Years': The Papers of Rosalynn Smith Carter." In *Modern First Ladies: Their Documentary Legacy.* Edited by Nancy Kegan Smith and Mary C. Ryan. 1989.

BETTY BOYD CAROLI

CARTER DOCTRINE. The Carter Doctrine was a warning from President Jimmy Carter to the Soviet Union in his STATE OF THE UNION MESSAGE of 23 January 1980, in which he said that any "attempt by an outside force to gain control of the Persian Gulf region will be regarded as an assault on the vital interests of the United States of America, and such an assault will be repelled by any means necessary, including military force." The President delivered his threat in response to the Soviet Union's decision in December 1979 to send eighty-five thousand troops to Afghanistan. The Soviet invasion of Afghanistan had caught the President off guard, even though he had been warned by his NATIONAL SECURITY ADVISER, Zbigniew Brzezinski, that the Soviets might invade the country. Before the invasion, Moscow had deployed between five thousand and ten thousand military advisers in Afghanistan and provided other military aid to the Marxist government of Hafizulah Amin. Despite the aid, Amin failed to suppress an insurgency against his government. Distrustful of Amin, the Soviets executed him and installed a puppet regime headed by Babrak Karmal.

At the time the Soviet Union invaded Afghanistan, much of the Islamic world, including the vital Persian Gulf region, was in turmoil. The fervor of Islamic revolution, which had resulted in the overthrow of the Shah of Iran in January 1979, appeared to be spreading throughout the region. In Saudi Arabia, a small but fanatic Muslim sect seized the Grand Mosque in Mecca, Islam's holiest shrine, holding hundreds of pilgrims as hostages. After two weeks of bloodshed, in which as many as two hundred pilgrims and three hundred guerrillas died, Saudi forces were finally able to gain complete control of the shrine. In Pakistan, twenty thousand Muslim rioters stormed and burned the American embassy in Islamabad and murdered two Americans after rumors circulated that the United States and Israel had been responsible for the raid on the Grand Mosque in Mecca.

With so much of the Middle East in turmoil, the President feared that, unless he took a firm stand against the Afghan invasion, the entire region would be vulnerable to Soviet attack. He was worried especially about the Soviet threat to the rich oil fields of the Persian Gulf region and to the waterways through which oil-laden tankers had to pass. The Carter Doctrine was intended to make clear to the Soviet Union the United States's determination to prevent further Soviet expansion toward the Gulf region, even if some form of military response was required. In addition to enunciating the Carter Doctrine, the President imposed a grain embargo on the Soviet Union, barred Soviet access to American high technology and other strategic items, and asked the Senate to postpone indefinitely consideration of the SALT (STRATEGIC ARMS LIMITATION TALKS) II agreement, which had been signed in June. He also raised the possibility that the United States might boycott the 1980 Summer Olympics scheduled to take place in Moscow. "We will deter aggression, we will protect our nation's security, and we will preserve the peace," he declared to the nation.

BIBLIOGRAPHY

Kaufman, Burton I. *The Presidency of James Earl Carter, Jr.* 1993.
Smith, Gaddis. *Morality, Reason, and Power: American Diplomacy in the Carter Years.* 1986.

BURTON KAUFMAN

CASABLANCA CONFERENCE. President Franklin D. Roosevelt met with British Prime Minister Winston Churchill in the Moroccan coastal city of Casablanca from 14 to 25 January 1943 during WORLD WAR II. Convened in the aftermath of the successful Anglo-American invasion of North Africa, the conference planned future Allied wartime strategy. Assuming that their armed forces would defeat the Germans in North Africa in the spring of 1943, the two leaders agreed to attack Sicily next in order eventually to force Italy out of the war. The decision to continue operations in the Mediterranean, rather than directly assault Europe, distressed Soviet leader Josef Stalin, who desperately wanted an early Anglo-American invasion of Europe across the English Channel. In order to allay Stalin's concerns, Roosevelt and Churchill set up a planning commission for a cross-Channel assault to take place in 1944. The two leaders also tried to decide on a leader of Free French forces. Roosevelt, who could not stand the haughty Free French General Charles de Gaulle, sponsored General Henri Giraud. Churchill also found de Gaulle personally difficult, but considered Giraud's antagonism toward Britain even worse. Accordingly, Roosevelt and Churchill forced de Gaulle and Giraud into a short-lived marriage of convenience. While Roosevelt worked closely with Churchill on many issues, the President took the lead on the most far-reaching decision taken at Casablanca—the announcement at the final press conference that the Allies would insist on the unconditional surrender of Germany, Italy, and Japan. Roosevelt wanted to avoid repetition of claims by German nationalists that betrayal by domestic democrats, not defeat on the battlefield, had ended WORLD WAR I. Moreover, the participants at Casablanca expected that demanding unconditional surrender would persuade Stalin that the United States and Great Britain were reliable allies, unwilling to make a separate peace with the Axis.

BIBLIOGRAPHY

Dallek, Robert. *Franklin D. Roosevelt and American Foreign Policy, 1932–1945.* 1979.

Kimball, Warren F. *The Juggler: Franklin Roosevelt as Wartime Statesman.* 1991.

O'Connor, Raymond G. *Diplomacy for Victory: FDR and Unconditional Surrender.* 1971.

ROBERT D. SCHULZINGER

CASE ACT (1972). Every year, hundreds of international agreements are signed between agencies of the U.S. government and their counterparts in other nations. The range of these agreements has been wide and varied, from regulating strawberry trade with Mexico and building a satellite tracking station with Canada to the construction of military bases in, for example, South Korea and Honduras. Members of Congress have had a difficult time keeping track of all the international commitments entered into by agencies of the executive branch; this was especially true of commitments in Indochina during the VIETNAM WAR (1964–1975). In frustration, legislators passed the Case Act of 1972, known more formally as the Case-Zablocki Act after its chief sponsors, Sen. Clifford Case (R-N.J.) and Rep. Clement Zablocki (D-Wis.). The law required executive agencies to report to Congress on all international agreements within sixty days of their signing.

The purpose of the Case Act was to improve congressional monitoring of America's commitments abroad. A report from the Senate Foreign Relations Committee explained, "The principle of mandatory reporting of agreements with foreign countries to the Congress is more than desirable; it is, from a constitutional standpoint, crucial and indispensable. . . . If Congress is to meet its responsibilities in the formulation of foreign policy, no information is more crucial than the fact and content of agreements with foreign nations."

Critics of the Case Act complained that the reporting requirement was flawed, allowing the executive agencies to inform Congress two months after commitments had already been signed. This left legislators with the option of either going along with the initiative or wrecking the agreement after the fact by shutting off funding or otherwise barring implementation.

Many agencies in the executive branch were slow to report under the sixty-day provision, sometimes forwarding information about agreements more than a year after their signing. Even more aggravating to legislators, some agencies failed to report at all on their international agreements. In 1976, for instance, an investigation by Congress's GENERAL ACCOUNTING OFFICE (GAO) disclosed that Department of Defense never reported agreements with the government of South Korea involving the joint use of Taegu Air Base and the transfer of $37.6 million worth of military equipment to Korean troops.

Angered by this flouting of the law, Congress moved in 1978 to tighten the provisions of the original Case Act. In this amended Case-Zablocki Act, all oral international agreements (used by some agencies to bypass formal reporting requirements) had to be reduced to writing and submitted to Congress. Moreover, any agreement reported late (beyond the sixty-day limit) required a written presidential explanation. Finally, Congress increased the Department of State's control over agreement making throughout the executive branch by mandating that every agency consult with that department before signing an international agreement. These reforms produced improved compliance by executive officials, but some reports continued to arrive past the deadline.

From 1976 to 1978, some members of Congress sought even more stringent reporting requirements. They proposed a "treaty-powers resolution" that would have required all "significant" international agreements to be submitted to the Senate as treaties, in advance of implementation and subject to a two-thirds vote of approval by the Senate. This initiative failed to garner majority support, but it did prompt the Carter administration to promise more regular consultation with the Senate Foreign Relations Committee on future international commitments.

BIBLIOGRAPHY

Franck, Thomas M., and Edward Weisband. *Foreign Policy by Congress.* 1979.

Glennon, Michael J. *Constitutional Diplomacy.* 1990.

Johnson, Loch K. *The Making of International Agreements: Congress Confronts the Executive* 1984.

LOCH K. JOHNSON

CASS, LEWIS (1782–1866), Secretary of War, Secretary of State, Democratic presidential nominee in 1848. Cass was a soldier, territorial governor, cabinet member, diplomat, senator, and presidential nominee. He was Secretary of War under Andrew Jackson, Democratic presidential candidate in 1848, and Secretary of State under James Buchanan. His career was marked by nationalism, support for western expansion, hostility to Great Britain, and fidelity to the DEMOCRATIC PARTY.

Born in New Hampshire, Cass began practicing law in Ohio at age twenty. By this time he was already an avid Jeffersonian Democrat. A general in the WAR OF 1812, he served as Michigan territorial governor from 1813 to 1831. In 1831 Cass became Secretary of War, supervising the Black Hawk War, the first Seminole War, and the beginning of the Cherokee removal. Cass helped defuse NULLIFICATION with a strong show of restrained force and shrewd diplomatic overtures to southern Democrats. In 1836 Cass became minister to France. In 1842 he influenced France to oppose the Quintuple Treaty, designed to suppress the international slave trade. Cass's opposition stemmed from the treaty's implicit support for British searches of American ships on the high seas. He later criticized Secretary of State DANIEL WEBSTER for the WEBSTER-ASHBURTON TREATY, because that treaty did not prohibit British

interdiction and searches of American ships. In late 1842 he resigned his diplomatic position, and returned to the United States to begin a long-range campaign for the presidency, advocating MANIFEST DESTINY and the ANNEXATION OF TEXAS. At the 1844 Democratic Party convention Cass led Martin Van Buren after seven ballots, but on the eighth ballot Cass's opponents proposed James K. Polk of Tennessee. On the next ballot Cass's supporters withdrew his name and Polk gained the nomination. A Democratic Party stalwart, Cass campaigned actively for Polk. In 1845 the Michigan legislature elected Cass to the United States Senate.

In the Senate Cass was an avid expansionist, pushing for annexation of Oregon to the fifty-fourth parallel, even if it meant war with England, and enthusiastically supported the MEXICAN WAR. The Mexican War reopened the issue of SLAVERY in the territories, which had been effectively stifled by the MISSOURI COMPROMISE in 1820. Cass opposed the WILMOT PROVISO. Like many Northern Democrats, Cass wanted nothing—including slavery—to interfere with western expansion and the growth of the nation. In 1847 an obscure Tennessee politician, A. O. P. Nicholson wrote Cass, asking what would happen to slavery in the territories if the Wilmot Proviso was defeated. Cass's response, "the Nicholson letter," outlined that the settlers of the territories should be allowed to decide the slavery issue for themselves. This was the beginning of popular sovereignty, a policy Democrats would advocate throughout the 1850s.

In 1848 Cass won the Democratic presidential nomination on the fourth ballot, bringing vast experience with him. He had been a successful politician most of his life, holding office at all important levels of government. Following Polk's successful administration and facing General Zachary Taylor, a political novice, the experienced Cass seemed likely to win. He was a northerner with strong southern support, while his opponent headed a sharply divided party.

However, in August members of the small abolitionist LIBERTY PARTY joined forces with antislavery Democrats to form the FREE-SOIL PARTY, with ex-President Martin Van Buren as its candidate. In the election Taylor carried 163 electoral votes to Cass's 127. Taylor outpolled Cass by 141,000 votes, but Van Buren carried over 291,000 votes. A change of 5,000 popular votes in the right places would have elected Cass.

In January 1849 Cass returned to the Senate, filling the seat he had resigned when he ran for the presidency. In 1850 Cass supported the compromise measures. Cass symbolized the northern democratic Party—which wanted to ignore slavery, defer to popular sovereignty in the territories, and keep the Union together. In 1851 Cass won a second six-year Senate term. The next year he half-heartedly sought the Democratic nomination for President, which went to Franklin Pierce. Cass remained in the Senate. He supported the KANSAS-NEBRASKA ACT, which embodied his concept of popular sovereignty, but denied that it would lead to slavery in those territories. Nevertheless, he seriously underestimated the opposition to the act in Michigan and the North.

In 1856 the Republicans swept Michigan and Cass was not reelected to the Senate. However, President-elect Buchanan nominated him as Secretary of State. As in 1842, Cass opposed British attempts to suppress the illegal African slave trade by interdicting and searching American ships. Cass was not so much proslavery—he continued to publicly oppose the institution to the displeasure of the South—as he was intent on preserving American sovereignty. In 1860 Cass resigned from Buchanan's Cabinet when the President refused to resupply southern forts threatened by secessionists in South Carolina. Ultimately Cass's unionism outweighed his devotion to the Democratic Party and his willingness to compromise. Although aged and enfeebled, he attended Union rallies after the CIVIL WAR began. His last important public act was to advise WILLIAM H. SEWARD and Abraham Lincoln during the *Trent* affair. Consistent with his lifelong opposition to British interference with American ships, Cass successfully urged the administration to give up the two Confederate diplomats taken from the British vessel.

BIBLIOGRAPHY

Woodford, Frank B. *Lewis Cass: The Last Jeffersonian.* 1973.

PAUL FINKELMAN

CAUCUSES, PRESIDENTIAL. Caucuses have long been a fixture in American presidential selection politics. From 1796 until 1824, presidential nominees were chosen in congressional party caucuses. Even after the rise of national nominating conventions in 1832, most national convention delegates were hand-picked in closed caucus-convention meetings by local and statewide party leaders; rank-and-file party supporters had little or no effective opportunity to influence the choice of their state's convention delegates. Since the 1970s, both Republican and Democratic Party rules have required that caucuses and conventions be open to all interested party supporters. Modern caucus meetings typically begin with local (usually precinct) caucus meetings scheduled on a specific date to select delegates for later district and state conventions.

Although PRESIDENTIAL PRIMARIES receive the bulk of media attention, candidates' personal time, and campaign dollars, caucus-convention states remain an important part of the presidential nomination process. In 1988, some nineteen state Democratic parties and seventeen state Republican parties relied on the caucus-convention system to select part or all their national convention delegates. Smaller, less populous, less urban states more often use the caucus-convention, versus presidential primary system. In 1988 and 1992, almost one-fifth of all national party convention delegates in either party were chosen in caucus-convention states. As a result, no serious presidential contender can afford to ignore the caucus-convention states, which differ from primary states in turnout, media coverage, momentum, costs, and occasionally, representation.

Presidential contenders should not expect a heavy turnout in most caucus-convention states. On the average, only 4 percent of voting-age adults attend local caucus meetings in caucus-convention states—compared to nearly 24 percent of voting-age Americans who vote in states with a presidential primary. Although turnout in caucus-convention states is typically low, considerable variation occurs from one state to another. In 1988, for example, the best-attended, first-in-the-nation Iowa caucuses drew 11 percent of that state's voting-age public. By contrast, barely 1 percent of the voting-age public attended the 1988 Hawaii, Nevada, or Wyoming local caucuses. Turnout in caucus-convention states typically rises when the first-round meetings are early and well-publicized, when candidates spend personal time in the state, when the nominations contest is close and competitive, and when the candidates differ considerably in their policy and ideological views. Although one-third to one-half of first-round caucus attenders may be first-time participants, caucus attenders are more often long-term party supporters, strongly committed candidate supporters, or interest group members.

Until the 1980s, caucus-convention states were typically less costly, delegate-for-delegate, than presidential primary states. Campaign costs were usually lower in caucus-convention states because radio and television ads were unnecessary, and because party loyalists and interest group members were easier and cheaper to target.

In 1976, for example, the three major GOP and Democratic contenders (Gerald Ford, Ronald Reagan, and Jimmy Carter) reported spending only 27 percent as much, per delegate available, in caucus-convention states as in presidential primary states. Over time, however, this difference shrank. By 1980 and 1984, seven major GOP and Democratic contenders averaged 62 percent as much, per delegate available, in caucus-convention states as in primary states. By 1988, the three major contenders (George Bush, MICHAEL DUKAKIS, and Jesse Jackson) spent slightly more (102 percent as much), per delegate available, in caucus-convention states. These spending changes may have resulted from the early scheduling of first-round caucus meetings.

Caucus-convention states rarely produce the media attention and resulting momentum that come from a well-covered presidential primary state win. Caucus-convention states are more difficult for journalists to cover because vote tallies are often slow to be reported and the delegates themselves are not allocated until district or state conventions, usually held several weeks after the first-round precinct caucuses. During the 1970s and 1980s, caucus-convention states won far less media attention than did primary states.

When a caucus-convention state is well-covered, however, a well-publicized victory can boost a presidential contender's nationwide poll standings just as a well-publicized primary win does. After the 1976 Iowa caucuses, for example, Jimmy Carter's first-place plurality win led to an 8 percent jump among Democrats in the national polls. Similarly, in 1980, George Bush's first-place Iowa caucus finish led to a nearly 20 percent jump among Republicans in the national polls.

Presidential candidates usually find that caucus-convention attenders are generally more affluent, better educated, and more loyal to their party than nonattending party supporters. Overall, caucus-state attenders may represent their state party's rank-and-file identifiers slightly less well than do presidential primary voters in those states. At recent national party conventions, caucus-convention state delegates have seldom voted very differently than presidential primary state delegates—controlling for a state's urban-rural, racial, regional, and liberal-conservative differences. In a few instances (such as the 1988 Democratic national convention) these differences may be larger if a well-organized, ideologically extreme, or charismatic candidate can turn out supporters at otherwise little-attended caucuses. Overall, however, there is little evidence that holding a caucus-convention system, versus a presidential primary, made large differences in the quality of grass-roots representation during the 1970s and 1980s.

[See also NOMINATING PRESIDENTIAL CANDIDATES.]

BIBLIOGRAPHY

Abramowitz, Alan, and Walter Stone. *Nomination Politics: Party Activists and Presidential Choice.* 1984.
Marshall, Thomas R. "Measuring Reform in the Presidential Nomination Process." *American Politics Quarterly* 7 (1979): 155–174.
Marshall, Thomas R. *Presidential Nominations in a Reform Age.* 1981.

THOMAS R. MARSHALL

CENTRAL INTELLIGENCE AGENCY (CIA). In the midst of two hundred well-guarded acres of forested land in Langley, Virginia, twelve miles from Washington, D.C., along the Potomac River, stands the headquarters of the Central Intelligence Agency. Known more informally by insiders as the Pickle Factory, the Company, or simply the Agency, the CIA is the United States' premier secret intelligence agency, founded by the NATIONAL SECURITY ACT of 1947 (with key strengthening amendments in 1949).

Organization. Organizationally, the CIA is divided into six major divisions: the Office of the Director and, beneath that office, five directorates. The Director wears two hats, serving both as Director of the CIA (DCIA) and as Director of Central Intelligence (DCI). As the DCIA, the Director is the chief executive officer for the Central Intelligence Agency, with all the managerial and planning responsibilities that attend the top position in an executive agency. The CIA chief is assisted by a Deputy Director of the Central Intelligence Agency (DDCIA), the second-in-command and for all practical purposes the top day-to-day administrator at the agency.

Director of Central Intelligence. As the DCI, the Director is in charge of the National Foreign Intelligence Program, which in addition to the CIA and its operations includes all satellite and airplane reconnaisance programs and other remote surveillance operations; intelligence codemaking and codebreaking activities; strategic intelligence programs carried out by intelligence entities in the departments of State, Defense, Treasury, Energy, and Justice (which, together with the CIA, comprise the so-called INTELLIGENCE COMMUNITY); and the overseas counterintelligence responsibilities of the Department of Defense. Above the DCI in the chain of command is the nation's primary decision-making forum for national security and intelligence policy—the NATIONAL SECURITY COUNCIL (NSC), whose key statutory members include the President, the Vice President, and the secretaries of State and Defense.

The vast majority of all intelligence-policy proposals recommended to the NSC originate with the CIA. These proposals, approved by the President on the advice and counsel of the other NSC members and the DCI, take the form of National Security Council Intelligence Directives (NSCIDs, pronounced "n-skids"). These are the broad marching orders for important intelligence operations; the operational specifics are worked out by CIA officials at Langley and at the CIA's stations around the world.

Assisting the DCI is a series of subsidiary units within the Office of the Director at CIA Headquarters: the Office of General Counsel, home of the agency's litigants; the Public Affairs Office, the public relations branch of the CIA; the Office of Congressional Affairs to handle relations with Congress; the Comptroller's Office for budgetary control; and the Office of Inspector General, expected to investigate major allegations of unlawfulness or impropriety by agency officials. Also reporting to the DCI is the National Intelligence Council (NIC), home to the sixteen National Intelligence Officers (NIOs) who work hand in hand with senior analysts throughout the community to prepare major analytic papers, on which policymakers often base their decisions regarding how the United States should react to world developments.

The DCI is further assisted by the Intelligence Community Staff (ICS), an organization designed to assist in the coordination of the various intelligence agencies. Several key ICS interagency committees have been established to aid the DCI in this work of coordination, including panels on human intelligence (i.e., classic espionage); signals intelligence, a generic term for the interception and analysis of communications intelligence as well as other electronic intelligence and telemetry intelligence (chiefly missile emissions); counterintelligence; photographic intelligence; long-range intelligence community planning; and budget coordination.

The DCI is expected not only to run the CIA but also to coordinate and generally supervise every other major intelligence agency in the community—a total of eleven other organizations. Indeed, the budget of the CIA accounts for less than 15 percent of the community's total personnel and annual expenditures (some $30 billion).

Director of the CIA. The DCIA runs the CIA chiefly through its five directorates. The largest and most controversial of these is the Directorate of Operations (DO), home to what insiders refer to as the "spooks"—the Agency's spy-handlers and officers responsible for "dirty tricks" (COVERT OPERATIONS) abroad. Roughly two-thirds of the personnel in the Directorate of Operations are involved in espionage, counterintelligence, and liaison relations with intelligence services in allied nations. The rest are engaged in some form of covert action, such as mounting paramilitary operations or secretly financing friendly politicians overseas. One unit of the DO, the National Collection Division (NCD), operates inside the United States to gather information from foreign visitors and to debrief selected American travelers on their return to the United States. Another DO unit, the Foreign Resources Division (FRD), attempts to recruit foreigners living or traveling in the United States as agents (i.e., spies).

The Directorate of Operations is also subdivided into geographic units (the former Soviet republics, Near East, Europe, East Asia, Africa, and the Western Hemisphere) and other specialized staffs, among them the Covert Action Staff, the Counterintelligence Staff, the Counternarcotics Staff, and the Counterterrorism Staff. Out in the field, the top CIA person in each foreign nation is called the chief-of-station (COS). Beneath the COS are the agency's "case officers," each of whom is in charge of a team of native spies.

The Directorate of Science and Technology (DS&T) is devoted to the improved application of technology to espionage, notably through spy satellites and airplanes. It works closely with the National Reconnaissance Office (NRO), an independent agency that coordinates America's high-altitude spying and reports directly to the DCI. Among other units, the Foreign Broadcast Information Service (FBIS) is lodged in this directorate; the FBIS is responsible for monitoring foreign radio and television broadcasts. The Office of Technical Assistance (OTA), one of the most well-hidden units in the CIA, is also a part of DS&T, providing clandestine eavesdropping capability for the U.S. government overseas. Occasionally, the capabilities of OTA have been misused, as in the WATERGATE AFFAIR, when the "burglars" obtained their disguises from OTA for the infamous attempted theft of documents from the Democratic National Committee headquarters, an action authorized by officials in the Nixon administration.

The Directorate of Administration (DA) handles the CIA's housekeeping, hiring, training, computer processing, worldwide communications, and logistics. It also houses the Office of Security (OS), which is responsible for the physical protection of agency facilities and personnel at home and abroad. This directorate has also been misused on occasion. At the request of White House officials, the surveillance skills of its officers were turned against U.S. antiwar protesters during the VIETNAM WAR era; these activities, called Operation CHAOS, were in violation of the agency's statutory prohibition against spying on U.S. citizens.

The Directorate for Planning and Coordination (DPC), established in 1989, is the newest of the directorates. Its purpose is to conduct long-range planning for the CIA and the broader intelligence community. Its instructions are to map out U.S. intelligence agencies' responses to the new international situation following the end of the COLD WAR.

Finally, the Directorate of Intelligence (DI) is where the agency's research is conducted—the refining, sorting, and interpretation of data from around the world that constitute the essence of the intelligence mission. The CIA has the largest analytic staff of any of the agencies in the intelligence community. Its reports to policymakers, warning them about dangers confronting the United States, represent the primary reason that the CIA and the other intelligence agencies were created in the first place—above all, to guard the nation against another surprise attack like the Japanese bombing of PEARL HARBOR on 7 December 1941.

Purposes and Tasks. The core purpose of this elaborate organizational apparatus has been—and will continue to be in the post–cold war era—the collection, analysis, coordination, and dissemination of information about threats and opportunities affecting the United States abroad (this objective is called collection-and-analysis, for short).

About 75 percent of the information gathered by the CIA and the other intelligence agencies has tended to come from public sources (scientific magazines, for instance). The remaining 25 percent has been obtained through secret sources and methods (though this percentage has shrunk as the Soviet Union has disappeared and its republics have become more open to outside scrutiny). The secret collection of information abroad depends, first, on modern (and expensive) surveillance devices, such as satellites and reconnaissance airplanes—so-called intelligence platforms. These machines, which function at astonishingly high levels of scientific competence, are the key components of the United States' National Technical Means (NTM)—the technical component of intelligence collection. Second, collection continues to rely on more old-fashioned and less costly approaches to espionage—the human intelligence component.

The attack on Pearl Harbor taught the United States the danger of blindness to foreign threats and provided the rationale for the creation of the CIA. In the post–cold war era, almost 90 percent of the CIA's resources are devoted to collection-and-analysis. This represents a significant increase over earlier decades, when this task often took a back seat to counterintelligence and covert action.

The term *counterintelligence* (CI) refers to a range of methods designed to protect the United States against aggressive operations perpetrated by foreign intelligence agencies, including attempts by foreign nations to infiltrate U.S. intelligence agencies through the use of double agents, penetration agents (moles), and false defectors. Counterintelligence employs two approaches: security and counterespionage. Security is the defensive side of counterintelligence—physically guarding U.S. personnel, installations, and operations against hostile nations and terrorist groups. Among the defenses employed by CIA security officers are codes, alarms, watchdogs, fences, document classifications, polygraphs, and restricted areas. Counterespionage represents the more aggressive side of counter intelligence, involving, for instance, infiltrating (penetrating) a foreign intelligence service with a U.S. agent.

Covert action, known more euphemistically as special activities, is the most controversial of the operations carried out by the CIA. It consists of aiming secret propaganda at foreign nations, as well as using political, economic, and paramilitary operations to influence, disrupt, or even overthrow their governments (as in Iran in 1953 and Guatemala in 1954). The objective of covert action is secretly to mold events overseas (insofar as possible) in support of U.S. foreign-policy goals. Since the late 1980s, less than 5 percent of the CIA's resources have been earmarked for covert action. This represents a decrease from the roughly 20 percent allocated during the early years of the Reagan administration, and a steep decline from the 1960s, when a majority of the agency's budget was expended in support of the robust use of covert actions against communist regimes (notably in Southeast Asia).

Supervision. The supervision of the CIA and the other intelligence agencies has presented congressional oversight committees with a difficult challenge. In response to abuses of power by the CIA (Operation CHAOS foremost among them), legislators have created an exceptional approach to the problem of restraining the United States' secret agencies—an approach characterized by an openness that most other nations (even other democracies) find astonishing and inappropriate.

From 1947 until 1975, the CIA, like other intelligence agencies throughout the world, enjoyed almost complete freedom from serious external review. Reports of CIA abuses (Operation CHAOS and other transgressions) in the *New York Times* in December 1974 abruptly altered this situation. The House and Senate, as well as President Gerald Ford, created investigative committees to examine the charges.

These probes culminated in the creation of intelligence oversight committees in both chambers of Congress as well as new instruments of accountability within the executive branch (including an Intelligence Oversight Board in the White House). After decades of isolation from the rest of the government, the CIA and the other intelligence agencies—accustomed to operating on the dark side of U.S. foreign policy—suddenly found themselves, to their great discomfort, bathed in torchlight from Capitol Hill. Since 1975, both branches have struggled to find the proper balance between legislative supervision, on the one hand, and executive discretion, on the other. With the deeply troubling exception of the IRAN-CONTRA AFFAIR (when in the mid 1980s the Reagan administration chose to violate the new intelligence oversight rules), the Congress and the CIA seemed to have arrived at a workable balance between the two important values of accountability and security.

BIBLIOGRAPHY

Colby, William, and Peter Forbath. *Honorable Men: My Life in the CIA.* 1978.
Jeffreys-Jones, Rhodri. *The CIA and American Democracy.* 1989.
Johnson, Loch K. *America's Secret Power: The CIA in a Democratic Society.* 1989.
Ranelagh, John. *The Agency: The Rise and Decline of the CIA.* 1986.
Ransom, Harry Howe. *The Intelligence Establishment.* 1970.
Smist, Frank J., Jr. *Congress Oversees the United States Intelligence Community, 1947–1989.* 1990.
Treverton, Gregory F. *Covert Action: The Limits of Intervention in the Postwar World.* 1987.
Turner, Stansfield. *Secrecy and Democracy: The CIA in Transition.* 1985.

LOCH K. JOHNSON

CFE (CONVENTIONAL FORCES IN EUROPE) TREATY.

Many of the most prominent modern ARMS CONTROL accords have dealt with NUCLEAR WEAPONS or other weapons of mass destruction. The weapons that have been used most often in actual combat and that have resulted in the highest levels of military spending in anticipation of future wars, however, are "conventional" forces, including armaments such as tanks, aircraft, and the like. Europe, in particular, has been a focus of attention, as the point of origin of both devastating world wars.

Throughout the 1970s and 1980s, diplomats from affected states regularly met in the Mutual and Balanced Force Reduction (MBFR) talks, a multilateral effort to reduce the size and the threatening posture of NATO and Warsaw Pact forces in Europe. These negotiations were consistently unsuccessful; the parties were never able to agree on even the basic data regarding existing forces, let alone on a formula for decreasing them.

By the late 1980s, however, the realignment of global politics produced new opportunities for discussion, and new forums were established for dealing with the issues of conventional forces. Formal CFE negotiations opened in March 1989 and proceeded with astonishing speed. In less than two years, broad-ranging agreement was reached to regulate each participating state's arsenals of key military hardware, including tanks, artillery pieces, armored personnel carriers, attack helicopters, and combat aircraft. Even before the CFE treaty was ratified, however, the George Bush administration had to deal with hard-line attempts by the Soviet military to undercut it by evading certain technical counting rules regarding marine combat units and by removing a quantity of excess hardware from the reductions area instead of dismantling it.

In 1992, it was anticipated that the next phases of CFE negotiations would embrace military personnel (in talks dubbed CFE IA, because troop strength was originally intended to be a part of the first treaty, too) and further reductions in the key categories of weapons permitted to each party (CFE II).

BIBLIOGRAPHY

Graham, Thomas, Jr. "The CFE Story: Tales from the Negotiating Table." *Arms Control Today* 22 (January/February 1991): 9–11.
Moodie, Michael. "The Treaty on Conventional Armed Forces in Europe." *Disarmament* 14 (1991): 11–23.

DAVID A. KOPLOW

CHASE, SALMON P.

(1808–1873), Senator, Secretary of the Treasury, governor of Ohio, Chief Justice of the United States, presidential candidate. Salmon Portland Chase was born in Cornish, N.H., on 13 January 1808. A staunch moralist and antislavery advocate, Chase was also an extremely ambitious politician.

Chase grew up in Ohio and graduated from Dartmouth College in 1826. He read law with William Wirt in Washington, D.C., and set up practice in Ohio in 1830.

Chase emerged as an important member of the political antislavery movement in the 1840s. In the *Matilda* and *Van Zandt* cases, he made two important proabolitionist legal arguments. Chase joined the LIBERTY PARTY in 1840, supporting fellow Ohioan James Birney. In 1848, Chase played a key role in the FREE-

SOIL PARTY's formation. He helped to draft the party's provision excluding SLAVERY from the territories and became Senator from Ohio in that year.

Chase opposed the COMPROMISE OF 1850 and disavowed STEPHEN A. DOUGLAS's idea of popular sovereignty. Quickly joining the new Republican coalition, Chase was elected governor of Ohio in 1855; he was reelected in 1857. At the 1856 and 1860 national conventions he hoped for the REPUBLICAN PARTY's presidential nomination, failing both times.

Elected again Senator from Ohio, Chase resigned in March 1861 to become Lincoln's Secretary of the Treasury, a pivotal wartime post. Initially, Chase financed the war effort by floating bonds and securing loans. In February 1863, a reluctant Chase introduced a federal banking system based on reliable national bank notes (greenbacks), a practice he would as chief justice declare unconstitutional.

Chase emerged as the principal leader of the RADICAL REPUBLICANS in the Cabinet. Battling with Secretary of State WILLIAM SEWARD, a frequent rival, Chase became increasingly impatient with Lincoln's prosecution of the CIVIL WAR. In 1864, the so-called Pomeroy circular, sent by Senator Samuel Clarke Pomeroy of Kansas to Radical Republicans, attempted to gain support for a Chase presidential nomination. Publication of this secret circular embarrassed Chase, placed him in poor standing with Lincoln, and forced Lincoln to manage an early Republican (Union) nominating convention. In late spring, Chase resigned from the Cabinet over a relatively slight matter that Lincoln himself had trumped up.

After reelection, Lincoln chose Chase to become Chief Justice. The political battles over RECONSTRUCTION placed adjudication between the executive and the legislature, potentially, within the Court's purview. The Chase court generally chose not to intercede between Presidents Andrew Johnson and Ulysses S. Grant and Congress. In *Texas v. White* (1869), Chase upheld Lincoln's contention that the Union was indivisible. In MISSISSIPPI V. JOHNSON (1867) and *Georgia v. Stanton* (1868), the court did not enjoin the executive from enforcing the loyalty oath.

Even after becoming Chief Justice, Chase maintained his presidential ambitions. He solicited the Democratic nomination in 1868. In 1872, he attempted to head the Liberal Republican revolt against Grant. The nomination instead went to HORACE GREELEY. Chase died on 7 May 1873.

BIBLIOGRAPHY

Blue, Frederick. *Salmon P. Chase: A Life in Politics.* 1987.
Hart, Albert B. *Salmon P. Chase.* 1899.
Schuckner, Jacob W. *The Life and Public Services of Salmon P. Chase.* 1874.

JOHN F. WALSH

CHECKS AND BALANCES. By the late 1780s, after the failure of the Continental Congress was obvious, the doctrine of a strict SEPARATION OF POWERS had lost ground to the more practical idea of checks and balances. The Framers of the Constitution decided that each branch should share many of the powers of the other branches. The President would nominate appointees and submit treaties, but the Senate would have to give its consent. The President gained the power to veto bills, although Congress could override him. The House of Representatives could impeach federal officers, with trial and conviction requiring a two-thirds vote in the Senate. The power to declare war was vested in Congress, but the President served as COMMANDER IN CHIEF.

The Theory of Checks and Balances. A contemporary of the Framers, publishing his views in 1788, ridiculed the separation doctrine as a "hackneyed principle" and a "trite maxim." In THE FEDERALIST, numbers 37, 47, and 48, James Madison explained the reasons for adopting overlapping powers instead of strict separation. In *Federalist* 47, Madison wrote that the "celebrated Montesquieu" had been misinterpreted, because his model of government, the British Constitution, did not "totally separate" the legislative, executive, and judicial branches. According to Madison, Montesquieu did not mean that the branches of government "ought to have no *partial agency* in, or no *control* over, the acts of each other. His meaning . . . can amount to no more than this, that where the *whole* power of one department is exercised by the same hands which possess the *whole* power of another department, the fundamental principles of a free constitution are subverted." Madison also noted that in the constitutions of the American states "there is not a single instance in which the several departments of power have been kept absolutely separate and distinct."

Having explained the political systems of England and the American states, Madison in *Federalist* 48 emphasized the reason for allowing some overlapping of power: unless the branches "be so far connected and blended as to give to each a constitutional control over the others, the degree of separation which the maxim requires, as essential to a free government, can never in practice be duly maintained." To remain separate, the branches had to overlap. Only a strong system of checks and balances would keep the branches coequal and independent, for without these checks the branches would lack the essential means to combat encroachments. Madison feared that mere "parchment barriers" placed in the Constitution to indicate the boundaries of the three branches would be easily penetrated by ambition and power.

In *Federalist* 66, ALEXANDER HAMILTON argued that the true meaning of the separation maxim was "entirely compatible with a partial intermixture" and that overlapping was not only "proper, but necessary to the mutual defence of the several members of the government, against each other." A merely nominal separation, he warned in *Federalist* 71, was futile "if both the executive and the judiciary are so constituted as to be at the absolute devotion of the legislative." Hamilton reacted with irritation to critics who complained about the treaty process because it mixed the executive with the Senate. This level of debate he found plainly annoying, dismissing it in *Federalist* 75 as "the trite topic of the intermixture of powers."

The Proposed Separation Clause. Despite Madison's and Hamilton's explanations, several delegates at the state ratifying conventions expressed shock at the degree to which the Constitution had mingled the departments. "How is the executive," cried one delegate at the Virginia ratifying convention, "contrary to the opinion of all the best writers, blended with the legislative? We have asked for bread, and they have given us a stone." The Constitution was attacked at the North Carolina ratifying convention for violating the maxim that the three branches "ought to be forever separate and distinct from each other." The overlapping of the branches' powers also provoked criticism in Pennsylvania. Opponents of the Constitution insisted that the Senate's judicial power in IMPEACHMENT, as well as the executive's legislative power in making treaties, constituted an "undue and dangerous mixture of the powers of government." A lengthy quotation from Montesquieu was introduced into the record of the Pennsylvania debate over ratification to demonstrate the dependence of freedom and liberty on a separation of powers.

These three states demanded that a separation clause be added to the national bill of rights. Virginia's recommendations in June 1788 included the clause: "legislative, executive, and judiciary powers of Government should be separate and distinct," while Pennsylvania and North Carolina offered their own versions of a separation clause. In 1789, Congress compiled a tentative list of restrictions on the national government, among which was the following: "The powers delegated by this constitution are appropriated to the departments to which they are respectively distributed: so that the legislative department shall never exercise the powers vested in the executive or judicial, nor the executive exercise the powers vested in the legislative or judicial, nor the judicial exercise the powers vested in the legislative or executive departments."

Madison supported the clause, but not because he had suddenly embraced the notion of pure separation. He feared that additional blending, resulting from encroachment, would benefit the legislature at the expense of the executive. In the House debates in 1789, he opposed Senate participation in the REMOVAL POWER because that might reduce presidential power to a "mere vapor." So concerned was Madison about the independence of the executive branch that he began to use the kind of abstract phrases he had earlier rejected. He now declared, "If there is a principle in our constitution, indeed in any free constitution, more sacred than another, it is that which separates the legislative, executive, and judicial powers." From the context of this remark, however, it is clear that Madison had the more modest objective of opposing legislative participation in the designation of officers, which he regarded as a presidential responsibility.

The separation clause was among seventeen constitutional amendments sent to the Senate. The Senators struck it from the list of proposed amendments on 7 September 1789. A substitute amendment that would have made the three departments "separate and distinct" and ensured that the legislative and executive departments would be restrained from oppression by "feeling and participating in the public burthens" through regular elections was also voted down. Three members of the House, Madison among them, met with the Senate in conference to reconcile their different lists of amendments. In the days that followed, the list of seventeen was cut to twelve, with ten of those becoming Bill of Rights. Among the deleted amendments was the separation clause.

BIBLIOGRAPHY

Fisher, Louis. "The Efficiency Side of Separated Powers." *Journal of American Studies* 5 (1971): 113–131.

Gwyn, W. B. *The Meaning of the Separation of Powers.* 1965.

Vile, M. J. *Constitutionalism and the Separation of Powers.* 1967.

Wood, Gordon S. *The Creation the American Republic, 1776–1787.* 1969.

LOUIS FISHER

CHEMICAL WEAPONS CONVENTION. Intended as a comprehensive multilateral treaty prohibiting the production, development, possession, and use of lethal chemical agents in international combat, the Chemical Weapons Convention (CWC) complements the 1972 Biological Weapons Convention, negotiated under President Richard M. Nixon, to ensure that all these exotic armaments—long regarded as particularly loathsome and inhumane—will be abolished.

As of 1992, the CWC had been under negotiation for over a decade. George Bush, as Vice President, went to Geneva in 1984 to offer a proposed text of the treaty, which then served as the basis for the negotiations. During the 1988 presidential campaign, Bush stressed the personal importance he attached to solving the problem of chemical weapons. For several years, however, rigid American positions on key issues of verification, the scope of the treaty, and the timing of the dismantling of existing stockpiles delayed agreement. In 1992, negotiators appeared close to a resolution of the problems, a proposed treaty had been sent to the United Nations General Assembly for its consideration, and a final text was expected to be available for signature in January 1993.

The problem of chemical weapons achieved increased international saliency during the 1980s, when Iraq used chemical weapons extensively in its war with Iran and when Libya appeared to be constructing a covert chemical weapons production facility. Fears of proliferation of these arms, together with the long-standing specter of substantial deployments by Soviet and Warsaw Pact forces in Europe, gave new impetus to the negotiations, even as the United States was beginning the development of a new generation of more reliable, safer, "binary" chemical weapons.

The problem of chemical weapons is unique in ARMS CONTROL, because many of the same substances that are useful in the production of lethal weaponry are simultaneously essential for a wide range of plastics, paints, and other substances of critical importance to the civilian economy. The challenge, therefore, is to ensure that the weapons applications are closed off without unduly impeding legitimate international business. This "dual use" phenomenon has led negotiators to craft a verification apparatus of surpassing delicacy: the procedures must ensure that particular chemical substances are accounted for and not diverted without excessively burdening commercial enterprises through an elaborate array of intrusive inspections and data-reporting requirements. The need to preserve the confidentiality of private manufacturing facilities while providing adequate confidence that the terms of the treaty are being honored has therefore consumed a substantial amount of time and text. In addition, the negotiators in such a high-technology field must take care that the regulations they draft today can survive the likely innovation and experimentation of future chemical experts.

BIBLIOGRAPHY

Adams, Valerie. *Chemical Warfare, Chemical Disarmament.* 1990.
Burck, Gordon M., and Charles C. Flowerree. *International Handbook on Chemical Weapons Proliferation.* 1991.
Stockholm International Peace Research Institute. *Chemical and Biological Warfare Studies.* Ongoing series.

DAVID A. KOPLOW

CHENEY, DICK (b.1941). Deputy Assistant to the President (1974–1975), White House Chief of Staff (1975–1977), Congressman, Secretary of Defense (1989–1993). Richard Cheney began his executive branch service in the area of economics, first becoming Special Assistant to the Director of the Office of Economic Opportunity in the Nixon White House. In 1970, he became a deputy to presidential counselor Donald Rumsfeld; and from 1971 to March 1973, he served as Assistant Director for Operations of the Cost of Living Council. He left the latter position for the private sector, but returned to the White House after Gerald Ford assumed the presidency in 1974. Eventually becoming Ford's WHITE HOUSE CHIEF OF STAFF, Cheney purposely cut a low profile in the new administration. Nevertheless, he was actively involved in approving the administration's political appointments and in managing the information flow to the President.

After Ford's defeat in the 1976 election, Cheney chose to run for Congress, where he served for ten years. Cheney had served on the House Permanent Select Committee on Intelligence and was the ranking Republican on the House Select Committee to Investigate Covert Arms Deals with Iran. In 1989, President Bush nominated Cheney for Secretary of Defense after Sen. John Tower failed to win confirmation for the post because of doubts about his personal character. Well-liked by his colleagues in the House, he won an easy—and unanimous—confirmation in the Senate.

Cheney came to the DEFENSE DEPARTMENT during a period of rapid change in the international arena. The unexpected dissolution of the Soviet Union required that American defense strategy be revised at the most fundamental levels, and Cheney was charged by President Bush to rethink both the role and the requirements of the American military in the post-COLD WAR world. Cheney eventually called for cutbacks in both manpower and current weapons systems in order to redirect more funds into research and development for new military technologies, which he believed would continue to guarantee America's fighting edge in the years to come. As for the broader question of America's role in the international arena, Cheney maintained that America would continue to bear the primary burden of keeping the world safe and stable, rather than multinational bodies such as the United Nations.

At a more practical level, Cheney as Defense Secretary had to oversee two of the largest military operations in recent American history. In 1989, the United States invaded PANAMA in order to remove dictator Manuel Noriega; and in 1991, the United States turned back Iraq's invasion of Kuwait in the GULF WAR. Both operations were resounding military successes, but they raised the vexing question of how far the executive branch can go in sponsoring military action without direct congressional assent. Despite his ten years in Congress, Cheney argued for an extremely expansive view of the executive power in FOREIGN AFFAIRS. Regarding the Iraqi conflict, even before the war began, he made the astonishing claim that the President could go to war with Iraq without specific approval by Congress.

BIBLIOGRAPHY

Borger, Gloria. "The Politician at the Pentagon." *U.S. News and World Report* (2 October 1989): 24–25.
Cheney, Richard. "Legislative-Executive Relations in National Security: Work Together to Govern." *Vital Speeches* (15 March 1990): 334–336.
"Cheney, Richard." *Current Biography Yearbook, 1989.* 1989. 102–106.

JOHN G. WEST, JR.

CHIEF EXECUTIVE. One of the most important roles of the President is that of Chief Executive. The President's executive role is grounded in Article II of the Constitution. In ambiguous language the Constitution vests "the executive Power" in the President and directs him to "take Care that the laws be Faithfully executed." He may also "require the Opinion, in writing, of the principal Officer in each of the executive Departments" and "grant reprieves and pardons." He derives substantial power from his designation as "COMMANDER IN CHIEF of the Army and Navy." Modern Presidents have tended to interpret these constitutional provisions broadly and have derived from them substantial additional powers. In addition to their constitutionally based powers, Presidents have received extensive delegations of authority from Congress.

Most modern Presidents, however, have encountered difficulty in their efforts to direct the executive branch. President Franklin D. Roosevelt complained about the independence of the navy, President John F. Kennedy lamented the inertia of the State Department, and President Ronald Reagan made his campaign attack on an overgrown federal bureaucracy one of the enduring themes of his presidency.

There is an apparent paradox in, on the one hand, the President's considerable formal legal powers and his position as head of a vast, complex bureaucracy and, on the other hand, his limited ability to direct that bureaucracy toward the achievement of his policy goals. That paradox results, at least in part, from the constitutional relationship of the presidency to the legislative and judicial branches of government and the nature of the federal bureaucracy and the President's relationship to it.

The Constitution not only created the executive branch, with the President as its head, but also established the legislative and judicial branches and prescribed a sharing of powers among those separate institutions. The President is dependent on congressional cooperation to carry out his executive responsibilities. Only Congress can authorize government programs, establish administrative agencies to implement them, and appropriate funds to finance them. There are also occasions when the exercise of presidential power must be approved by the judiciary, as when the Supreme Court in 1952 disallowed President Harry S. Truman's seizure of U.S. steel mills to forestall a strike during the Korean War (YOUNGSTOWN SHEET & TUBE CO. V. SAWYER). The point is that presidential power is not self-executing and it is subject to restraint.

The President's task as the nation's Chief Executive is much more, therefore, than issuing commands. Nor is the job mainly that of finding ways to bring a large and complex bureaucracy under his operational control. Rather, he must secure congressional cooperation while suppressing the executive branch's natural tendencies toward conflict with the legislative branch, and he must give direction to the bureaucracy.

Ideally, Presidents should use the WHITE HOUSE STAFF and other units of the EXECUTIVE OFFICE OF THE PRESIDENT to help them define their objectives, convert them into operating programs, allocate resources to the agencies that administer the programs, and coordinate the implementation of programs within the federal government and among federal, state, and local governments. Department executives should direct the work of career civil servants, coordinate the operations of their component bureaus, and develop and maintain links with other federal departments and agencies and with state and local governments. Presidents discover, however, that the reality of their relations with the federal bureaucracy bears little resemblance to the idealized vision just described.

Dealing with the Bureaucracy. There is an inherent tension between the White House, which favors centralized presidential control, and the bureaucracy, which strives for autonomy, that has been present in every modern administration. It exists, at least in part, because of the difference between political leadership of the bureaucracy and bureaucratic power. The direction and effectiveness of the political leadership the President provides depend on the personality, leadership style, and values of the President as well as on external events and conditions. In contrast, bureaucratic power is relatively permanent and does not depend on personalities and transitory political and environmental factors.

At least five general factors contribute to bureaucratic power and present obstacles to presidential control of the federal bureaucracy: the size, complexity, and dispersion of the executive branch; bureaucratic inertia and momentum; the personnel of the executive branch; the legal position of the executive branch; and the susceptibility of executive branch units to external political influence.

Size. By 1993 the federal budget reached $1.5 trillion and there were more than 2.9 million civilian and 2.5 million military employees. The domestic activities of the federal government extended into every community of the nation and touched the lives of individuals from birth to death. Considerations of NATIONAL SECURITY projected U.S. military and foreign policy activities around the world. Providing leadership and direction to the federal bureaucracy is a difficult task.

The multiplicity of agencies and programs creates an additional obstacle to presidential leadership of the executive branch. The complexity that results from overlapping jurisdictions leads to duplication of efforts and complicates the President's job. It places a premium on coordination by the presidency. Bureaucratic complexity also stems from the interdependence of many federal activities. Policy goals in one area are often affected by objectives in other areas. The difficult trade-off between energy policy and ENVIRONMENTAL POLICY, which became acute in the 1970s, illustrates policy interdependence. Efforts to conserve energy and reduce foreign oil imports were at variance with attempts to reduce air and water pollution.

The great size of the federal bureaucracy further frustrates presidential efforts at direction and control because its activities are so widely dispersed. Presidents are at the center of government. The people who operate programs, deliver services to individuals, and regulate the conduct of businesses and other organizations are at the periphery. These people, almost all of whom are civil servants, were there when the President and his staff took office, and they will be there after the political executives have departed. They control many of the resources, human and material, that are needed to implement programs successfully. Their position, at the point of delivery, is the source of much of their power.

Inertia. Because of bureaucratic inertia it is hard to get a new government activity started, and once under way, it is even more difficult to stop or significantly change the activity. Two important factors contributing to bureaucratic inertia are organizational routines: prescribed operating procedures that have worked successfully in the past and the support of interest groups for programs that benefit them and in which they have a material stake.

The aspect of bureaucratic inertia primarily responsible for presidential frustration is the momentum of ongoing programs. The degree of that momentum is revealed in the number of activities to which the government is committed by public laws, the amount of money allocated for those activities in annual appropriations, and the number of employees who carry out the activities. "Uncontrollable" expenditures that the government was obligated to make constituted about 75 percent of President George Bush's proposed 1993 budget. The principal uncontrollable items include interest on the national debt; entitlement programs such as SOCIAL SECURITY, Medicare and Medicaid, Food Stamps, federal retirement and veterans' benefits; and contractual obligations to pay for such things as weapons systems and public facilities. Even the "controllable" portion of the budget is highly resistant to cuts because of support from groups that benefit from those expenditures. Presidents can influence the shape of the federal budget, but major changes usually require several years to be implemented. From one year to the next, Presidents tend to be limited to incremental changes. [*See* BUDGET POLICY.]

Personnel. The large number of career federal employees also commits the President to maintain ongoing programs. Major reductions in personnel or redirection of their activities are economically and politically costly. People will oppose actions that threaten to deprive them of their jobs or require them to move, or reduce their sense of security and importance. Most Presidents can make only modest adjustments in the size and mission of the federal work force.

The personnel—political and career officials—

CHIEF EXECUTIVE 193

upon whom Presidents depend to operate the bureaucracy are the third aspect of bureaucratic power that impedes presidential control of the executive branch. Political executives often are amateurs in the precarious world of Washington politics. They often lack the political knowledge and substantive skills needed to perform their jobs effectively. They quickly discover their dependence on career executives and other lower-ranking civil servants for the information and advice they need. That support comes at a price: loyalty to the agency and support for its programs within the administration, before Congress, and with the public.

Political executives in the bureaucracy are torn between looking upward to the President for support and direction and downward to the permanent government for support and services. In such a position they are imperfect instruments for presidential control of the bureaucracy. They can best serve the President by winning the trust of the careerists who compose the permanent government, but to do so they find it expedient to maintain a considerable degree of independence from the White House.

Career executives and other civil servants provide the institutional resources, such as political experience, substantive knowledge, and technical competence, required to accomplish an agency's mission. They are aware of political problems the agency faces and of its political resources. They have established links with its clientele and with the congressional committees that oversee it through legislative and appropriations powers [*see* IRON TRIANGLES]. They also have a vested interest in their agencies and their programs. Their loyalties are based on norms of bureaucratic and occupational professionalism. They recognize the legitimacy of the President's position and of the claims of political executives for the support, but they will not hesitate to use their substantial capacity to resist the directives of their political superiors.

Legal position. The legal position of the executive branch is ambiguous. All departments and agencies are established by Congress and derive their authority to operate from statutes. Although Presidents act through subordinates, they do so principally through persuasion because of the nature and source of their legal authority and that of their subordinates.

Although the Constitution requires the President to "take care" that the laws are faithfully executed, his legal position as Chief Executive is somewhat unclear because Congress has—with presidential approval—delegated authority to and imposed duties directly on various administrative officials. In some cases, such as independent regulatory commissions, the President has no formal power to direct agency actions or set agency policy. His influence upon these units is based on his budgetary and appointment powers and on his persuasive abilities. For Cabinet members, heads of independent agencies, and other political executives with operating authority to whom Congress has directly delegated power, the situation is not clearly defined. The Supreme Court long ago ruled that the President may not interfere with the performance of a "purely ministerial" duty that does not involve the exercise of discretion or judgment (KENDALL v. UNITED STATES [1838]).

External influence. Susceptibility to external influence and pressure derives in part from the inability of American political parties to provide administrative units with political support and to link party programs with the pursuit of presidential goals. If partisan and presidential support for an agency is lacking, the agency must look elsewhere for help in maintaining its authority, funding, and personnel. It looks for support particularly to the individuals and groups who are affected by its programs and to the congressional committees or subcommittees with jurisdiction over its legislative authorizations and appropriations. An agency without support from such entities is in a precarious position. But to the extent that agencies succeed in the quest for external support presidential control is frustrated.

Presidential Powers. However, Presidents are not without resources to cope with the obstacles to their control of the executive branch. They have substantial powers granted by the Constitution, delegated by Congress, and derived from the nature of their office. The most important are the APPOINTMENT POWER and the REMOVAL POWER, the power to issue EXECUTIVE ORDERS, and the power to prepare the annual federal budget and regulate expenditures.

Appointments and removal. As critical as the appointment and removal powers are to the President's executive responsibilities, they are subject to limitation by Congress. The Constitution makes high-ranking officials subject to senatorial confirmation and Congress determines whether an appointment must be confirmed by the Senate. In addition, it can narrow the President's discretion in making appointments by establishing detailed qualifications for various offices. Congress cannot, however, give itself the power to appoint executive officials that have enforcement or adjudicatory duties. (BUCKLEY v. VALEO [1976]). The President's appointive powers also are constrained by political considerations and practices, such as senatorial courtesy whereby the President gives the Senators of his own party a veto over certain administrative and judicial appointments in the states.

The Senate generally has given Presidents considerable leeway in the appointment of top-level political executives, but confirmation is not automatic, and the Senate has used rejections to express disapproval of specific individuals or particular practices. Since the WATERGATE AFFAIR of 1972–1974, the Senate has tended to be more careful and procedurally consistent in examining the backgrounds, qualifications, and relevant policy views of presidential nominees. However, the confirmation process has become more demanding and time-consuming for the nominees.

The removal power is the logical complement of the appointment power. The ability to remove subordinate officials on performance or policy grounds is fundamental to presidential control of the executive branch. Without the removal power, the President cannot be held fully responsible for the actions of his subordinates or for failure of departments and agencies to achieve his objectives. The Constitution is silent, however, concerning the removal of executive officials other than through IMPEACHMENT, a cumbersome process that is limited to instances of "Treason, Bribery, or other high Crimes and Misdemeanors."

The Supreme Court has dealt directly with the removal power in a decision involving a challenge to President Woodrow Wilson's summary removal of a postmaster. In MYERS V. UNITED STATES (1926), the Court invalidated an 1876 law that required senatorial consent for the removal of postmasters. It held that the Constitution gave the removal power to the President and that Congress could not place restrictions on its exercise. Nine years later, however, the Court upheld the provisions of the Federal Trade Commission Act, which limited the grounds for removal of its members. In HUMPHREY'S EXECUTOR V. UNITED STATES (1935), the Court ruled that the President's unqualified power of removal is limited to "purely executive offices" and that Congress may prescribe conditions for the removal of officials performing "quasi-legislative" and "quasi-judicial" functions. However, the Court has not clarified fully the meaning of those terms.

Although there are some statutory and judicial restrictions on the removal power, its precise limits remain somewhat undefined. Moreover, the President may be able through informal means to force officials from office for reasons other than statutory cause. The President can call publicly for an official's resignation, or he may revoke authority he has delegated to an official as a means of indicating displeasure and lack of confidence.

Legislative power. Under a strict interpretation of the SEPARATION OF POWERS, the President has no direct legislative authority. Established practice, however, based on liberal interpretations of the Constitution by Presidents and the Supreme Court, has vested substantial authority in him to issue executive orders that have the force of law. From the beginnings of the Republic, Presidents have issued orders and directives on the basis of Article II. Executive orders have been a primary means of exercising this broad presidential prerogative power. Presidents also have used them in making public policy in crucial areas such as civil rights, economic stabilization, and national security.

It is generally recognized that executive orders must find their authority in the Constitution or in an act of Congress. The Supreme Court has upheld DELEGATIONS OF LEGISLATIVE POWER to the executive branch provided Congress establishes "intelligible" standards to guide administrative officials in the exercise of their authority in HAMPTON & CO. V. UNITED STATES (1928). In reviewing challenges to statutory delegations, however, the Court has consistently adopted a presumption in favor of statutes authorizing executive action by order or rule.

Financial powers. Presidents have substantial financial powers, delegated by Congress, which they use in their efforts to control the bureaucracy. The most important of these powers is the budget, which is an annual plan for spending by federal departments and agencies. The budget also establishes the President's spending priorities, sets the timing of program initiatives, and distributes rewards to and imposes sanctions on executive branch units. By controlling the total amount of the budget, the President can attempt to influence the performance of the economy.

Presidential use of the executive budget is a twentieth-century development. The BUDGET AND ACCOUNTING ACT of 1921 made the President responsible for compiling department and agency estimates and for submitting them annually to Congress in the form of a budget. The departments and agencies were prohibited from submitting their requests directly to Congress as they had done previously.

The initial emphasis in the development of the budget process was on the control of expenditures and the prevention of administrative abuses. The focus of the budget was on objects of expenditure, that is, personnel, supplies, and equipment. During the NEW DEAL period, in the 1930s, the emphasis shifted from control to management. The budget became a means of evaluating and improving administrative performance. The focus of the budget shifted from objects of expenditure to the work and activities of departments and agencies. The third stage in the development of budgeting is its orientation toward planning, which began in the 1960s. This stage has featured attempts to link annual budgeting, geared to the appropriations process in Congress, to long-range planning of government objectives. The focus is on the relationship of long-term policy goals to current and future spending decisions.

The limited utility of the budget as a means of incorporating planning in presidential decision making stems from the incremental nature of the budget process and from restrictions and conditions imposed by Congress. Budgeting is inherently incremental because it is done annually. Decision makers in Congress and the executive branch are concerned primarily with how large an increase or decrease will be made in a department's or an agency's budget and they focus on spending for the forthcoming fiscal year. Pressures are intense, and the stakes are high. There is little opportunity for consideration of long-range objectives and costs or for examining the effects of different spending levels for specific activities.

In addition to budgeting, Presidents have certain discretionary spending powers that increase their leverage over the bureaucracy. They have substantial nonstatutory authority, based on understandings with congressional appropriations committees, to shift funds within an appropriation and from one program to another. Presidents also have exercised some degree of expenditure control through the practice of impounding or returning appropriated funds to the Treasury. Since George Washington, Presidents have routinely impounded funds as a means of saving when expenditures fall short of appropriations. They have also withheld funds when authorized to do so by Congress and have, on occasion, impounded funds that Congress had added, over their objections, to various appropriations. [See IMPOUNDMENT; SPENDING POWER.]

Managerial Tools. Beyond their formal powers, modern Presidents have relied on managerial tools in their efforts to coordinate and direct executive-branch operations. Three major tools—staffing, reorganization, and planning—have been employed with mixed results. The limited success of presidential efforts to manage the federal bureaucracy more effectively stems primarily from the political character of the administration of the executive branch. The President must rely more on persuasion than command to achieve his objectives, and departments and agencies have substantial autonomy. This is not to argue that the public sector is inhospitable to modern management techniques, but to suggest that their use is significantly affected by political forces.

Staff and Cabinet. The presidency has grown steadily as Presidents have turned to staff support as a means of discharging their many roles and of directing the executive branch. The roles of presidential staff in program implementation and of the CABINET in advising the President have varied in recent administrations, but the tendency has been toward reliance on a strong, sizable, and centralized White House staff to protect the political interests of the President, to act as his principal policy advisers, and to direct (as opposed to monitor and coordinate) the implementation of his priorities by the bureaucracy. Critics of this structure argue that it has undercut the advisory potential of the Cabinet, narrowed the President's perspective on policy choices, and inhibited effective and responsive bureaucratic performance. Experience under President Richard M. Nixon, in the Watergate scandal, and President Ronald Reagan, in the IRAN-CONTRA AFFAIR, indicates that excessive reliance on staffing can be disastrous. Yet, both Presidents Gerald Ford and Jimmy Carter tried a decentralized model of White House staffing and abandoned it in favor of hierarchical arrangements, which President George Bush also utilized. Increasingly, the demands and expectations that Presidents confront lead them to rely on a centralized White House staff run by a strong White House Chief of Staff.

Reorganization. It has been almost an article of faith among political leaders and public administration theorists that executive reorganization can increase presidential power over the bureaucracy. Organizational structure and administrative arrangements are significant because they reflect values and priorities and because they affect access to decision makers. The location and status of an administrative unit—as a department, an independent agency, or a component of a department—symbolize the importance of its goals and the interests it serves. Administrative arrangements also can contribute to or frustrate the achievement of accountability to Congress and the public. Reorganizing, however, does not necessarily result in increased efficiency of operation, greater program effectiveness, or enhanced public accountability. This is true because there is no ideal form for a government agency or a consistent set of prescriptions for organizing the executive branch. Experience has shown that although the rationale for reorganization is couched in the rhetoric of economy and efficiency, the crucial factors in decisions to reorganize and the results of reorganizations are power, policy, and symbolic significance. [See REORGANIZATION POWER.]

Planning. Planning is current action designed to achieve future conditions. It is a rational process that operates on the assumption that objectives are known and accepted. The task is to select the best means appropriate to the achievement of the desired ends. Conflict and disagreement do not interfere because the planners know what is desired. However, planning takes place in an uncertain world. Planners do not have adequate knowledge of the future and their predictions often are fallible.

In addition to the intellectual limitations of all planning, public planning is limited by politics. Public planners do not have the power to command acceptance of their choices. Public choices are made on the basis of the preferences of individuals and groups through a process of bargaining and compromise. The agreements reached in the process of political decision making determine the objectives of public planners. There is no correct result because political preferences are continually changing. As a consequence, political planners shorten their time frames (usually extending them no further into the future than the next election), thus reducing the need for prediction, and offer their plans as proposals or suggestions rather than as directives. The result is that political factors tend to dominate planning and planning tends to blend with regular political decision making. Presidents have engaged in long-range planning with only limited success.

Can the President lead the executive branch? There are reasons to doubt that he can. It is apparent that although the President has substantial formal powers and managerial resources, he is by no means fully in control of his own branch of government. His capacity to direct its many departments and agencies in the implementation of his policies is constrained by bureaucratic complexity and fragmentation, conflict between the presidency and the bureaucracy, congressional and other external pressures and influences on the bureaucracy, and the extreme difficulty of establishing an effective management system within the government.

BIBLIOGRAPHY

Arnold, Peri E. *Making the Managerial Presidency.* 1986.
Berman, Larry. *The Office of Management and Budget and the Presidency.* 1979.
Campbell, Colin. *Managing the Presidency: Carter, Reagan, and the Search for Executive Harmony.* 1986.
Cohen, Jeffrey E. *The Politics of the U.S. Cabinet: Representation in the Executive Branch, 1789–1984.* 1988.
Cronin, Thomas E. *The State of the Presidency.* 2d ed. 1980.
Fisher, Louis. *Constitutional Conflicts between Congress and the President.* 3d ed., rev. 1991.
Hart, John. *The Presidential Branch.* 1987.
Hess, Stephen. *Organizing the Presidency.* 2d ed. 1988.
Mackenzie, G. Calvin. *The Politics of Presidential Appointments.* 1981.
Mackenzie, G. Calvin, ed. *The In-and-Outers.* 1987.
Nathan, Richard P. *The Administrative Presidency.* 1983.
Pfiffner, James P. *The Strategic Presidency.* 1988.
Seidman, Harold, and Robert Gilmour. *Politics, Position, and Power.* 4th ed. 1986.
Wildavsky, Aaron. *The New Politics of the Budgetary Process.* 2d ed. 1992.

NORMAN C. THOMAS

CHIEF OF STAFF, WHITE HOUSE. See White House Chief of Staff.

CHILD LABOR. Not until early in the twentieth century did the child labor question generate much concern among federal officials. Children and adolescents had customarily worked in agrarian and preindustrial societies, the reality in the United States for most of its first century. Prevailing constitutional understandings and judicial interpretations, moreover, left the regulation of work to the separate states not to the national government.

Because the states had widely varying regulations governing the labor of children, social reformers organized in the National Child Labor Committee (NCLC) began to lobby for uniform national regulations. A bill to limit child labor was defeated by a combination of southern congressional resistance (southern states had the nation's weakest child labor laws) and constitutional barriers. Instead, the reformers had to be satisfied with the establishment of a Children's Bureau in the Department of Commerce and Labor in 1912 during the final year of William Howard Taft's presidency. The bureau, which later became a part of the independent Department of Labor in 1913, served solely as an investigative and educational agency.

Because the Children's Bureau lacked the authority to regulate child labor, reformers continued to stress the need for uniform national legislation. During the election of 1912, Theodore Roosevelt's Progressive (Bull Moose) Party, which attracted the support of many social reformers, adopted a platform demanding the regulation of child labor. Soon after the election, reformers urged the new President, Woodrow Wilson, to support federal regulation of child labor. Owing to his dependence on southerners in Congress and his own constitutional scruples, Wilson, at first, opposed federal regulation. By 1916, however, as a result of election-year realities and his own shifting conception of federal power, Wilson endorsed a congressional bill to regulate child labor. With the President's support, the bill (Keating-Owen) passed Congress, only to be declared unconstitutional by the Supreme Court in 1918 (*Hammer v. Dagenhart*) because only the states had the power to regulate manufacturing. In 1919, Congress, again with presidential endorsement, sought to regulate child labor by placing a tax on goods moving in interstate commerce. The Supreme Court also declared this law unconstitutional because the commerce clause did not allow the federal government to use its tax power to regulate manufacturing (*Bailey v. Drexel Furniture Company* [1922]).

With Republicans in political power in the 1920s, the national government undertook few initiatives concerning child labor. Reformers instead sought to eliminate constitutional barriers to federal regulation of child labor through an amendment to the constitution. The campaign to pass such an amendment also failed.

The Great Depression and the ensuing triumph of the NEW DEAL brought success to child labor reformers. One of the first major pieces of New Deal legislation, the NATIONAL INDUSTRIAL RECOVERY ACT (NIRA) of 1933, authorized the President to negotiate codes of fair competition with business groups that included among their provisions the elimination of child labor. Although the Supreme Court declared the NIRA unconstitutional in 1935, three years later, at President Franklin D. Roosevelt's urging, Congress passed the FAIR LABOR STANDARDS ACT, which abolished many forms of child labor and established the principle of federal regulation of working conditions. In *United States v. Darby* (1941) the Supreme Court found this law constitutional, ruling that manufacturing is subject to federal regulation under the commerce clause. After 1938 the federal government expanded the categories of child labor subject to regulation.

[*See also* LABOR POLICY.]

BIBLIOGRAPHY

Felt, Jeremy P. *Hostages of Fortune: Child Labor Reform in New York State*. 1965.

Trattner, Walter I. *Crusade for the Children: A History of the National Child Labor Committee and Child Labor Reform in America*. 1970.

Wood, Stephen B. *Constitutional Politics in the Progressive Era*. 1968.

MELVYN DUBOFSKY

CHINESE EXCLUSION ACTS. The policy of Chinese exclusion was a source of conflict between Presidents and Congress, with the executives concerned not with the human rights of Chinese but with the effects of discrimination on commerce and diplomacy. In 1879 Rutherford B. Hayes vetoed a so-called fifteen-passenger bill, which would have limited the number of Chinese on a single U.S.-bound vessel to fifteen, but he assured Congress that diplomacy could achieve a better result. China agreed in 1880 that the United States could "regulate, limit or suspend" the immigration of Chinese laborers. Congress then passed legislation that would have suspended such immigration for twenty years, but Chester A. Arthur vetoed the bill, insisting that "a shorter experiment" was wiser. Congress then enacted a ten-year suspension, which Arthur signed on 6 May 1882.

Although called the Chinese Exclusion Act, the law exempted teachers, students, merchants, and "travellers for pleasure" and specifically denied Chinese persons the right of naturalization. Benjamin Harrison agreed to the law's extension for ten years in 1892, and Theodore Roosevelt signed an act making Chinese exclusion "permanent" in 1902. The IMMIGRATION ACT of 1924 ended the legal immigration of any Chinese aliens by barring all "aliens ineligible to citizenship."

In 1943, with China and the United States allied in fighting Japan, Franklin D. Roosevelt asked Congress to repeal the fifteen separate statutes that effected Chinese exclusion. Congress agreed, and the era of exclusion came to an end on 17 December 1943. The statute established an annual quota of 105 Chinese immigrants and made Chinese aliens eligible for naturalization.

In retrospect, both Chinese exclusion and its repeal can be seen as the hinges on which American IMMIGRATION POLICY turned. The 1882 act was the first significant curtailment of the once free and unrestricted national immigration policy. Its repeal, sixty-one years later, marked the beginning of a less rigorous restrictive policy that has continued to the present day.

BIBLIOGRAPHY

Daniels, Roger. *Asian America: Chinese and Japanese in the United States Since 1850*. 1988.

Riggs, Fred. *Pressures on Congress: A Study of the Repeal of Chinese Exclusion*. 1950.

Sandmeyer, Elmer C. *The Anti-Chinese Movement in California*. Rev. ed. 1991.

ROGER DANIELS

CHURCH COMMITTEE. On 27 January 1975, the U.S. Senate voted (82 to 4) in favor of establishing a special committee to conduct a nine-month, $750,000 investigation of America's INTELLIGENCE COMMUNITY. The Senate Majority Leader, Mike Mansfield (D-Mont.), selected Frank Church (D-Idaho) to chair the special committee. The House of Representatives established a companion committee, the Pike Committee, chaired by Otis Pike (D-N.Y.).

Congress created these committees in response to a public outcry over a series of articles published in the *New York Times* in December 1974, charging abuse of power by the secret intelligence agencies. Written by *Times* correspondent Seymour M. Hersh, the articles accused the CENTRAL INTELLIGENCE AGENCY (CIA) of "massive" spying and other illegal covert operations directed against anti-VIETNAM WAR activists and other American dissidents. Sources within the CIA quoted by Hersh claimed that the agency had compiled files on more than ten thousand American citizens, despite the language of the NATIONAL SECURITY ACT of 1947 (which established the CIA) barring its involvement in security or police functions within the United States. Arriving on the heels of the WATERGATE AFFAIR, this news of intelligence skullduggery directed against American citizens brought calls for a thorough investigation. President Gerald Ford initiated a separate inquiry, chaired by Vice President NELSON A. ROCKEFELLER (the Rockefeller Commission). Over the next sixteen months, the Church Committee, the Pike Committee, and the Rockefeller Commission subjected the CIA and its sister agencies to an exhaustive investigation that resulted in a long list of recommended reforms.

The Church Committee's probe was the most extensive of the three inquiries, in terms of the time and money spent, the length and scope of its published findings, and the number of recommended reforms. The committee also exerted the greatest influence toward establishing new statutory procedures for the closer monitoring of intelligence policy. The membership of the Church Committee consisted of six Democrats and five Republicans.

The committee's professional staff numbered more than 150 investigators and research personnel, led by New York attorney F. A. O. Schwarz, Jr., who served as chief counsel, and William G. Miller, a former Foreign Service officer and aide to Senator Charles McC. Mathias, Jr. (R-Md.), who served as staff director. The committee was organized into five major units: eleven "designees"—personal staff aides each chosen by and serving each member on the committee; a Command-and-Control Task Force, to examine ties between the White House and the intelligence agencies; a CIA Task Force, to examine this centerpiece agency; a Military Intelligence Task Force, to examine the National Security Agency (NSA) and other agencies within the U.S. military establishment; and a Domestic Intelligence Task Force, to examine the intelligence activities of the FEDERAL BUREAU OF INVESTIGATION (FBI)

and other intelligence entities with missions inside the United States. At the staff level, Schwarz, Miller, the designees, and the four task-force directors shaped the course of the investigation, under the guidance and direction of the committee members—most notably, the panel's official leaders, Senators Church and John G. Tower (R-Tex.).

Beneath the formal hierarchy, the Church Committee—like all congressional investigations—found itself buffeted internally and externally by sharp disagreements over how to proceed. The liberals on the committee, led by Senators Church and WALTER MONDALE (D-Minn.), wished to see strong new regulations that would make the intelligence agencies more accountable to Congress; the conservatives, led by Senators Tower, Howard H. Baker, Jr. (R-Tenn.), and BARRY GOLDWATER (R-Ariz.), generally sided with the Republican White House in opposing new regulations. With these institutional conflicts came the further complication of personal ambition, as individuals on the committee (including the chairperson himself) positioned themselves to become candidates in the 1976 presidential elections. At the staff level, intraparty disputes—as well as a difference of opinion between attorneys and social scientists on how to conduct the inquiry—added to the tensions.

Despite the inevitable internal bickering, the Church Committee ranks as one of the most significant inquiries conducted by the Senate. It provided the first serious examination into America's secret intelligence agencies and set in motion forces that would revolutionize intelligence policy-making in the government. Its multivolume published reports offered citizens valuable information about the dark side of government; and, most important, legislators adopted in 1976 the committee's central recommendation that the Senate create a permanent oversight committee for intelligence. A year later, the House followed suit. These committees have been imperfect vehicles for accountability; neither prevented the IRAN-CONTRA AFFAIR in 1987. Nevertheless, their efforts to help keep the secret agencies operating within the framework of the Constitution and the rule of law have been generally effective. Since the revelations of the Church Committee confirmed the abuse of power reported by the *Times* and disclosed many more improprieties, the United States is unlikely to return to an era when its intelligence agencies were permitted to conduct their operations free of legislative supervision.

BIBLIOGRAPHY

Colby, William, and Peter Forbath. *Honorable Men: My Life in the CIA.* 1978.

Commager, Henry Steele. "Intelligence: The Constitution Betrayed." *The New York Review of Books*, 30 September 1976, pp. 32–37.

Johnson, Loch K. *A Season of Inquiry: The Senate Intelligence Investigation.* 1985.

Smist, Frank J., Jr. *Congress Oversees the United States Intelligence Community, 1947–1989.* 1990.

Treverton, Gregory F. "Intelligence: Welcome to the American Government." In *A Question of Balance: The President, the Congress, and Foreign Policy.* Edited by Thomas E. Mann. 1990.

LOCH K. JOHNSON

CIVILIAN CONSERVATION CORPS. The Civilian Conservation Corps (CCC), one of the NEW DEAL's initial programs to confront widespread unemployment, enrolled men ages eighteen to twenty-five to engage in reforestation, dam and reservoir construction, and park restoration. President Franklin D. Roosevelt, a self-described conservationist, originated the idea for the CCC and drafted the bill himself during his first week as President. Congress responded quickly with the Civilian Conservation Corps Reforestation Relief Act on 31 March 1933. Roosevelt, treating the CCC as his personal agency, actively designed its operational structure and established specific goals.

Unlike other New Deal employment programs, the CCC generated little criticism. Organized labor protested that the $30-per-month pay scale was too low; however, after politically acute Roosevelt appointed Robert Fechner, American Federation of Labor vice president, as agency director, labor's protests faded.

By 1935 the CCC employed more than a half-million men in twenty-five hundred camps; in its nine-year tenure, the CCC employed approximately 2.5 million men. Despite Roosevelt's vision of luring city dwellers into the fresh air of rural America, however, the CCC failed to benefit many of the urban unemployed. Moreover, although the CCC was open to all races, Director Fechner's policies, reflecting his southern orientation, led to segregated camps. Nevertheless, 200,000 blacks did enroll, although they had to await openings in the black camps. Nearly 15,000 American INDIANS participated as well.

As one of the New Deal's most expensive ventures in unemployment relief, the CCC's accomplishments were many and significant. The men of the CCC planted more than two billion trees, earning the nickname Roosevelt's Tree Army. They also built more than thirty thousand wildlife shelters, installed twelve thousand miles of telephone lines, constructed national park facilities, refurbished historic sites, fought forest fires and predatory insects, and improved the nation's reservoirs.

BIBLIOGRAPHY

Biles, Roger. *A New Deal for the American People.* 1991.

Freidel, Frank. *Franklin D. Roosevelt: A Rendezvous with Destiny.* 1990.

Salmond, John A. *The Civilian Conservation Corps, 1933–1942: A New Deal Case Study.* 1967.

NICHOLAS AHARON BOGGIONI

CIVIL LIBERTIES. The President of the United States has an enormous opportunity to protect and expand individual liberties and rights. Judicious use of presidential authority under the Constitution together with the President's political power provide a broad foundation for positive intervention or, sadly, for rejection or neglect. This article examines presidential actions related to First Amendment freedoms of speech, press, and religion as well as to some criminal justice matters.

The Bill of Rights. During the 1789 debates over ratification of the Constitution, numerous demands were voiced for a number of amendments protecting noneconomic freedoms. To fulfill ratification pledges, the First Congress recommended a number of amendments, ten of which, known as the Bill of Rights, were ratified by November 1791. They did not spell out the precise meaning of civil liberties such as freedom of the press, religion, and speech, and separation of church and state, and in the Constitution's first decade differences over the scope of press and speech freedoms threatened the prospects of meaningful two-party competition, as yet an untried experiment. President George Washington's condemnation of western Pennsylvania's Democratic and Republican Societies as fomenters of the WHISKEY REBELLION precipitated a major congressional debate over the legitimacy of strong public criticism of government policies. The legislative debates of 1794 initiated serious disagreement over the then-accepted common law conception of press freedom as absence of prior governmental restraint. James Madison's success in 1794 in defeating Federalist efforts in the House of Representatives to censure the western societies harbingered a more serious confrontation in 1798.

In that year, President Adams's Federalist partisans attempted to prohibit opposition by seriously limiting immigration and curtailing freedom of speech and the press in the ALIEN AND SEDITION ACTS. The Sedition Act equated opposition to laws with conspiracy (penalized as a high misdemeanor) and held illegal "any false, scandalous and malicious writing . . . against" the U.S.

government, the Congress, or the President. The Sedition Act, however, liberalized the common law by allowing the defendant to prove the truth of an assertion as a valid defense and the jury to decide whether the publication was libelous. The Adams administration vigorously enforced the act, however, ultimately gaining fifteen indictments and ten convictions. The Federalist-dominated judiciary rejected all constitutional challenges, precipitating a major constitutional challenge by Madison and Thomas Jefferson. Because attacks on the government were indictable under the act, Madison and Jefferson anonymously wrote resolutions criticizing the act that were introduced in the legislatures of Kentucky and Virginia. These resolutions asserted that Congress had exceeded its constitutional authority and infringed state power to do what was forbidden to Congress by the First Amendment.

The Democratic-Republican victory in the presidential election of 1800 marked a turning point. Although Jefferson's Democratic-Republicans subsequently prosecuted Federalist critics in federal as well as state courts for seditious libel, and although Jefferson was occasionally inconsistent in the application of his principles, the concept that the First Amendment freedom of the press was limited to an absence of prior restraint was deemed insufficient. Postpublication federal punishment became constitutionally unacceptable when applied to expressions of opinion or strong criticism but remained acceptable when applied to prohibited action. The Supreme Court in *United States v. Hudson and Goodwin* (1812) held against the existence of a federal common law of crimes. Probable violations of the Fourth Amendment's prohibition against unreasonable searches and seizures under Jefferson's Embargo [see EMBARGO ACTS] were struck down in a circuit court decision, *Gilchrist v. Collector of the Port of Charleston*, by Jefferson's first appointee to the Supreme Court, William Johnson (while circuit-riding), on the ground that executive actions must be authorized by law. James Madison, Jefferson's successor, judiciously avoided civil liberties infringements during the WAR OF 1812.

Like many nineteenth-century civil liberties controversies, the debates over the Sedition Act and federal common law were about the boundaries of state and federal authority as well as the civil liberties of individuals. In balance, and despite the occasional inappropriate actions taken by Jefferson and his administration, the main civil liberties contributions of the Democratic-Republicans were the expansion of free press and free speech and the establishment of the legitimacy of wide-ranging political dissent.

Slavery and Civil War. Issues related to SLAVERY evoked southern attempts to curtail free political discussion. In the 1830s, southern proslavery efforts to thwart delivery of abolitionist mail received President Andrew Jackson's support, despite his efforts to mute the slavery issue wherever possible [see ABOLITION AND ANTISLAVERY]. In December 1835, Jackson recommended a federal censorship act, clearly in conflict with the First Amendment. Ultimately, Congress adopted a law prohibiting the refusal to deliver mail. But when southern postmasters refused on STATES' RIGHTS grounds to acquiesce, the Jackson administration simply refrained from enforcing the law. In contrast, John Quincy Adams, after his defeat by Jackson in 1828, consistently and vigorously opposed the infamous gag rule of the House of Representatives. The rule prohibited petitions protesting slavery in the District of Columbia or discussion thereof. As a longtime member of Congress, Adams in 1844 finally succeeded in defeating this obvious violation of the First Amendment right to petition. Adams had helped focus public attention on the inequities of domestic and foreign slavery as counsel for the Africans in the dramatic case of *United States v. The Amistad* (1841), in which President Martin Van Buren's Attorney General unsuccessfully supported the international law claims of the Spanish government and its slave traders.

President Abraham Lincoln's determined and ultimately successful defense of the Union offended many contemporary and subsequent critics, who accused him of violating the civil liberties of both southern sympathizers and the northern political opposition by authorizing the federal military to impose martial law and detention of suspected supporters of the Confederacy. His initial suspension of the writ of habeas corpus (there were several) was met by a constitutional challenge by Chief Justice ROGER B. TANEY in the circuit court decision of EX PARTE MERRYMAN (1861) [see HABEAS CORPUS, SUSPENSION OF]. Lincoln and his military commanders ignored Taney's decision. Two years later, Congress, in the Habeas Corpus Act of 1863, authorized the President to perform all the actions that Taney had deemed required congressional approval. Lincoln's first rationale for suspending habeas corpus and for preventive detention was presented in a special message to Congress on 4 July 1861. He argued that the former was permitted by the Constitution during rebellions and that the latter was needed on grounds of military necessity and public safety. In the context of the Baltimore riots over the presence of federal troops in that city, Lincoln's argument that suspension and detention were necessary to ensure the defense of Washington was plausible. But the extensive use of military arrests of civilians, the imposition of martial law outside areas of combat, and trials of civilians by military tribunals in such noncombatant regions often went beyond the scope of Lincoln's rationale. The sweeping language of Ex parte Milligan (1866) sums up many of the current, as well as original, critiques of the Lincoln administration, but such critiques often omit one critique—court abolition. Milligan emphasized that "martial rule can never exist where courts are open." In fact, Lincoln and the Republican-controlled Congress abolished the Circuit Court for the District of Columbia (the sole survivor of the Jeffersonian abolition of the courts created by the Federalists in 1801). In the Congressional Act of 3 March 1863, the old circuit court was replaced by a new Supreme Court for the District of Columbia. Judges' life tenure on good behavior, guaranteed by Article III, Section 1, of the Constitution, could not save the three incumbents of the now-abolished circuit court. The new court, with exactly the same jurisdiction as the old, was quadruple the size of its predecessor and was rapidly filled with Republican appointees. In a political system where protection of civil liberties is heavily dependent on the independence of the judiciary, this action deserves greater emphasis in the examination of the dark side of Lincoln's civil liberties policies.

In an address to the Army of the Tennessee in 1875, President Ulysses S. Grant, supporting the separation of church and state by the First Amendment's establishment clause, made an unequivocal recommendation to "encourage free schools, and resolve that not one dollar appropriated for their support shall be appropriated to the support of any sectarian school." Grant repeated this in his message to Congress in December of the same year, and Representative James G. Blaine of Maine introduced a constitutional amendment embodying this proposal shortly thereafter. It passed the House by a substantial margin but failed to get the necessary two-thirds majority in the Senate.

In the Pullman Strike of 1894, President Grover Cleveland's Attorney General, Richard Olney, sought and received federal court approval for an unusually comprehensive omnibus injunction prohibiting not only force and violence in obstructing interstate commerce and the mails, but spoken and printed persuasion as well. Subsequently underscored by the fate of the socialist Eugene V. Debs and his associates, the omnibus injunction became a potent weapon for the suppression of free expression as well as action.

The World Wars. U.S. involvement in World War I brought a dramatic, negative shift in both government policies and public attitudes toward free press and speech. While President Woodrow Wilson in 1917 indicated that this administration would not suspend the Bill of Rights during the war, many of his policies, and their enforcement by overzealous subordinates, made this era a civil liberties disaster. The all-embracing scope of the Espionage Act of 1917 and successive legislation and these laws' enthusiastic enforcement and the generally broad constructionist judicial interpretation given them were portions of the problem. Enforcement of these and other acts, such as the Alien Act of 1918, was carried out with increasing severity after the armistice. The policy of extensive raids pursued by Attorney General A. Mitchell Palmer while President Wilson was ill was the worst episode in this period, but it was emulated by state prosecutors, executives, and legislators adopting or vigorously enforcing state criminal antisyndicalism and/or antisedition acts [see Palmer raids]. In addition to the Department of Justice, the Postmaster General (mail censorship) and the Immigration Bureau of the Department of Labor (deportation of radical aliens) were the most significant violators of civil liberties in the Wilson era. In the 1920s, Presidents Warren G. Harding and Calvin Coolidge released those federal prisoners convicted under the wartime Espionage Acts who were still in prison, and in 1921 the Espionage Act was repealed. While the Wilson administration—unlike the Franklin D. Roosevelt administration, later—did not single out one ethnic group for preventive or protective detention, its war propaganda efforts as well as its actions contributed to the climate of intolerance pervasive during World War I.

The advent of World War II brought a different and dramatic civil liberties challenge. In a sweeping executive order, President Roosevelt authorized the Secretary of War and pertinent military commanders to designate military zones in which certain categories of people could be subjected to controls or outright removal [see Japanese Americans, treatment of]. Promulgated on 19 February 1942, Executive Order 9066 was adopted by Congress on 21 March. Western Defense Commanding General John L. DeWitt issued a proclamation declaring the entire West Coast subject to enemy attack. Another executive order established a nighttime curfew for German and Japanese nationals and all individuals of Japanese ancestry, clearly determining the first category by citizenship status and the second by race. Subsequent orders were contradictory but had the ultimate effect of removing all persons of Japanese origin (whether U.S. citizens or not) into detention camps located outside the Pacific coastal zone. These so-called relocation centers confined Japanese Americans for as long as four years despite the fact that they had not been convicted of any crime. Indeed, one of General DeWitt's bizarre rationales for detention was contained in his remark that the fact that Japanese-Americans had not committed acts of espionage or sabotage was evidence that they planned to do so.

The Supreme Court upheld the curfew order in *Hirabayashi v. United States* (1943). In 1944 the Court upheld the exclusion over the dissents of Justices Robert H. Jackson, Frank Murphy, and Owen J. Roberts in *Korematsu v. United States*. Both decisions found constitutional authority for these actions under the combined WAR POWERS of Congress and the President. The most serious civil liberties issue, that of the constitutionality of the detention-camp system of extended confinement, was not confronted by the Supreme Court. However, in 1946, after the end of hostilities, the Court in *Duncan v. Kahanamoku* voided the establishment of military tribunals by gubernatorial proclamation in Hawaii immediately after the attack on PEARL HARBOR. In 1948, Congress enacted a property-claims law for Japanese Americans who lost property because of compelled detention. In 1988, it awarded $20,000 in reparations to each person who had been held in a detention camp.

The Cold War. On the eve of World War II, President Roosevelt created a loyalty-review system of limited scope. Three years later, he established an Interdepartmental Committee on Loyalty Investigations. These initiatives provided the foundation for the expanded programs of Roosevelt's immediate successors, Presidents Harry S. Truman and Dwight D. Eisenhower [*see* LOYALTY-SECURITY PROGRAMS]. As COLD WAR tensions increased, President Truman sought to define the realistic dimensions of the problem. Accordingly, he created the Temporary Commission on Employee Loyalty in November 1946. On the basis of the commission's recommendations, Truman issued EXECUTIVE ORDER 9835, establishing a comprehensive loyalty program. This included loyalty checks by the FEDERAL BUREAU OF INVESTIGATION of all federal employees and the transmission of adverse information to departmental or bureau loyalty panels.

Determining the criteria for loyalty tests became a major issue in the civil liberties debates of the emerging cold war. When a person was accused of disloyalty, a loyalty panel would determine whether "reasonable grounds exist[ed] for belief that the person involved [was] disloyal to the United States." After the Alger Hiss and Julius and Ethel Rosenberg trials, the Joseph McCarthy and Richard M. Nixon exposés in Congress, and the intensification of cold war tensions had exacerbated public anxiety, President Truman promul-

gated a stricter executive order (10241). Under it, an accused person could be fired after a loyalty hearing if the panel found that there was a "reasonable doubt" of his or her loyalty. Even under Truman's first order, membership in an organization categorized as "totalitarian, Fascist, Communist, or subversive" was ground for dismissal. Under the second order, dismissal no longer required proof of disloyalty. By the end of the Truman administration, the Attorney General had identified more than two hundred "subversive" groups.

After President Eisenhower took office, he issued Executive Order 10450 (27 April 1953), which reduced the grounds for discharge even further—to a finding that continued federal employment "may not be clearly consistent with the interests of national security." All three of these orders involved hearing procedures that denied the investigated or accused person the opportunity to examine FBI files, to know the identity of his or her accusers, or to cross-examine them (the faceless-accuser factor); they allowed for persons to be on the basis of group membership (the guilt-by-association factor). The Eisenhower order extended the grounds for dismissal beyond loyalty considerations to include sexual immorality, perversion, drug addiction, and other criteria. Combined with even greater constitutional excesses by Congress and its most assertive committees, the manner in which the Truman and Eisenhower administrations handled the issue of loyalty among federal employees was a civil liberties disgrace.

Richard M. Nixon used the presidency as an instrument for several virtually unprecedented assaults on key constitutional protections. Nixon's most serious attack on civil liberties—and indeed the entire system of constitutional safeguards—was his attempt to create an extralegal program, without statutory approval, for the covert surveillance of any Americans deemed by the executive office to be a threat to internal security. Bypassing even the FBI and J. EDGAR HOOVER, Nixon approved a plan, drawn up at his request, that proposed warrantless searches of domestic and overseas mail, monitoring of cable and telephone communications, and theft of professional and private papers or files. In 1971, Nixon established an Intelligence Evaluation Committee to integrate undercover executive espionage. A special White House unit, called the Plumbers, also operated without statutory authority. It subsequently committed the lawless acts that led to Nixon's exposure and eventual resignation in August 1974 [see WATERGATE AFFAIR]. Indeed, in UNITED STATES v. UNITED STATES DISTRICT COURT (1972) the Supreme Court had rejected as inconsistent with the First and

Fourth Amendments the use of warrantless domestic surveillance by the Attorney General's office under an alleged INHERENT POWER of the President to protect NATIONAL SECURITY. Also of major significance was the Nixon administration's 1971 attempt to impose prior restraint to prevent the publication of the so-called Pentagon Papers. In NEW YORK TIMES CO. V. UNITED STATES (1971), the Supreme Court rejected the administration's arguments in a per curiam decision. In sum, the cumulative effect of the Nixon administration's assaults on constitutional civil liberties safeguards represents the most dangerous abuse of presidential power on record.

The emergence of the radical right as a powerful political force after the late 1970s brought a determined effort for the legislative adoption of an agenda of so-called social issues, including the curtailment of ABORTION and, among other recommendations, the reintroduction of prayer in public schools. Presidents Ronald Reagan and George Bush championed these proposals, albeit unsuccessfully. Both prohibited the dissemination of birth control and abortion information domestically and internationally under several federal or U.S.-funded aid programs. They also initiated and supported various legislative attempts at limiting procedural due process protections for criminal defendants. At the outset of his presidency, Bill Clinton, who supported freedom of choice on abortion matters, revoked the Bush gag rule against abortion counseling at federally funded clinics.

In sum, an overview of Presidential responses to civil liberties indicates that internal-security issues, whether real or ostensible, have consistently created the greatest pressures for ignoring or weakening civil liberties safeguards.

BIBLIOGRAPHY

Chafee, Zechariah, Jr. *Free Speech in the United States.* 1941.

Emerson, Thomas I. *The System of Freedom of Expression.* 1970.

Irons, Peter. *Justice at War: The Story of the Japanese American Internment Cases.* 1983.

Levy, Leonard W. *Jefferson and Civil Liberties: The Darker Side.* 1963.

Malone, Dumas. *Jefferson and the Ordeal of Liberty.* 1948.

Morris, Jeffrey Brandon. "The Second Most Important Court: The United States Court of Appeals for the District of Columbia." Ph.D. diss., Columbia University, 1972.

Murphy, Paul L. *The Meaning of Freedom of Speech: First Amendment Freedoms from Wilson to FDR.* 1972.

Neely, Mark E., Jr. *The Fate of Liberty: Abraham Lincoln and Civil Liberties.* 1991.

Smith, James Morton. *Freedom's Fetters: The Alien and Sedition Laws and American Civil Liberties.* 1956.

Stokes, Anson Phelps. *Church and State in the United States.* 1964.

JOHN R. SCHMIDHAUSER

CIVIL RELIGION, PRESIDENT AND. Civil religion is a scholars' term for the widely held set of fundamental political and social principles concerning the history and destiny of a state or nation that help to bind that state or nation together. It is a collection of beliefs, values, ceremonies, and symbols that gives sacred meaning to the political life of the community, provides the nation with an overarching sense of unity that transcends all internal conflicts and differences, and relates the society to the realm of ultimate meaning. It allows a people to look at their political community in a special light and thereby to achieve purposeful social integration and cohesion. Essentially, it is a general faith independent of the power of both the state and the institutional church, and it exists in a harmonious relationship with the existing churches.

In the American context, the elements that are comprised in civil religion include belief in such secular concepts as democracy, freedom, justice, equality, tolerance, opportunity, concern for others, the possibility of a new beginning, and the open future. This faith draws on various historical sources. The Puritan tradition provided the particularistic conception of the chosen, covenanted, and millennial nation, the "city upon a hill." From the Enlightenment came the universalistic ideas of human equality, freedom, progress, and peaceful persuasion and the emphasis on the tolerant, deistic "god of nature." The evangelical and revivalistic stream contributed the notions of democracy, the free individual, personal piety, and moral rectitude.

Throughout American history the leadership in the public faith has been provided by the President, who has functioned at various times as the nation's pastor, priest, and even prophet. In prophetic civil religion the President assessed the nation's actions in relation to transcendent values and called upon the people to make sacrifices in times of crisis and to repent of their corporate sins when their behavior fell short of the national ideals. As the national pastor he provided spiritual inspiration to the people by affirming American core values and urging them to appropriate these values. In the priestly role the President made America itself the ultimate reference point. He led the citizenry in affirming and celebrating the nation, while at the same time he glorified and praised his political flock.

At the very outset of his term, the first President, George Washington, stressed tolerance and national unity. Out of many peoples he hoped to see a nation forged that would transcend all social, geographical, and religious differences. Thus, in his inaugural address in 1789 he affirmed the "Invisible Hand" that upheld the American people through the revolution just past, enabled the building of a united government through the voluntary consent of so many distinct communities, and promised future blessings for the new nation. Clearly expressed was the belief that the United States was a chosen nation, one that was charged with providing an example to other peoples and fulfilling a mission to spread republican institutions. He also conveyed the hope that the blessing of the "Benign Parent of the Human Race" would be conspicuous in the deliberations and measures taken by the new government.

Washington also took on a prophetic tone in this speech. He insisted that in "the economy and course of nature" was "an indissoluble union between virtue and happiness; between duty and advantage; between the genuine maxims of an honest and magnanimous policy and the solid rewards of public prosperity and felicity." Therefore, "the propitious smiles of Heaven can never be expected on a nation that disregards the eternal rules of order and right which Heaven itself has ordained." This was vitally important because at stake in the experiment entrusted to the American people was "the preservation of the sacred fire of liberty and the destiny of the republican model of government."

In his famous FAREWELL ADDRESS (actually a published article), Washington assumed the role of a national pastor. He warned of the dangers of "the spirit of party" (factionalism), which could lead to despotism and the destruction of liberty. Seeing danger in the love of power, he stressed the need for checks and balances to divide and distribute power so that no individual could acquire too much of it. Then he added: "Of all the dispositions and habits which lead to political prosperity, Religion and Morality are indispensable supports." They are the "great pillars of human happiness" and the "firmest props of Men and Citizens." He stated that "virtue or morality is a necessary spring of popular government," and that to promote civic virtue the government should support "institutions for the general diffusion of knowledge," avoid national indebtedness, observe good faith and justice toward all nations, and cultivate peace and harmony with all. "Religion and Morality enjoin this conduct; and can it be, that good policy does not equally enjoin it?"

Washington himself became part of the American civil religion. The apotheosis as the Father of His Country began during his lifetime, and he was portrayed as a person larger than life who united Americans into one people. Locks of his hair were treasured, babies were baptized with his name, and legends circulated about his miraculous abilities as a war leader. Actors read speeches in his honor, and birthday celebrations for him were elaborate. The myths and images that grew up around Washington have frustrated biographers ever since.

Contemporaries, often skillfully blending biblical and Enlightenment imagery, compared Washington to Moses, who freed his people from bondage, or Joshua, who led them into the Promised Land, and even to the Roman hero Cincinnatus, who left his plow to fight for his country and returned to the farm once the task was done. His birth anniversary was made a holiday, the nation's capital and one of the states were given his name, and his face became a national icon. Biographers, most notably Parson Mason Locke Weems, glorified his death and ascension into a "civil religion heaven"; this adoration has even been enshrined in a ceiling painting in the Capitol dome.

Thomas Jefferson affirmed the deistic secular faith in his first inaugural address when he urged people "to unite with one heart and one mind" and to restore social harmony. Referring to the political strife then dividing the nation, he observed that "having banished from our land that religious intolerance under which mankind so long bled and suffered, we have yet gained little if we countenance a political intolerance as despotic, as wicked, and capable of as bitter and bloody persecutions." He then introduced the theme of chosenness by enumerating the blessings bestowed upon America:

> Kindly separated by nature and a wide ocean from the exterminating havoc of one quarter of the globe . . . ; possessing a chosen country, with room enough for our descendants to the thousandth and thousandth generation; entertaining a due sense of our equal right to the use of our own faculties, to the acquisitions of our own industry, to honor and confidence from our fellow-citizens, resulting not from birth, but from our actions and their sense of them; enlightened by a benign religion, professed, indeed, practiced in various forms, yet all of them inculcating honesty, truth, temperance, gratitude, and the love of man; acknowledging and adoring an overruling Providence, which by all its dispensations proves that it delights in the happiness of man here and his great happiness hereafter . . .

Only one thing was needed: a wise and frugal government that would leave people free to pursue their own work and not take from them what their labor had earned.

As time passed, the founding documents—the Declaration of Independence and the Constitution—took on the quality of sacraments, that is, like churchly sacraments, they became both the signs of power and simultaneously the embodiment of the goals set out for the faithful to achieve. Thus, John Quincy Adams exalted their teachings as Holy Writ when he declared in 1839: "Lay up these principles, then, in your hearts, and in your souls . . . cling to them as to the issues of life—adhere to them as to the cords of your eternal salvation."

Possibly the greatest practitioner of civil religion was Abraham Lincoln. In his first inaugural address he praised the wisdom of the people in a priestly sense: "Why should there not be a patient confidence in the ultimate justice of the people? Is they any better or equal hope in the world?" Whether "the Almighty Ruler of Nations, with His eternal truth and justice," is on the side of the North or the South, Lincoln intoned, still truth and justice "will surely prevail by the judgment of this great tribunal of the American people." The issue of civil war was in the hands of all Americans, Lincoln said, and he pleaded with southerners not to become enemies:

> Though passion may have strained it must not break our bonds of affection. The mystic chords of memory, stretching from every battlefield and patriot grave to every living heart and hearthstone all over this broad land, will yet swell the chorus of the Union, when again touched, as surely they will be, by the better angels of our nature.

But Lincoln moved increasingly into a prophetic mode of expression as the war between the states dragged on. In his annual message to Congress in 1862 he stressed that the resolution of the SLAVERY question would determine whether America as "the last, best hope of earth" would be saved or lost. In the GETTYSBURG ADDRESS (1863) he expressed the hope that those resting in the newly dedicated national cemetery there would not have given their lives in vain, but that "this nation, under God, shall have a new birth of freedom" and that popular government would survive. In his second inaugural address, Lincoln acknowledged that the scourge of civil war was a divine judgment upon America for allowing the sin of slavery to persist, and he called for national reconciliation.

Theodore Roosevelt introduced moralism into civil religion. On one occasion he said: "I am charged with being a preacher. Well, I suppose I am. I have such a BULLY PULPIT." A hallmark of his presidency was his repeated calls for repentance by evildoers, such as big business and corrupt politicians. In his 1905 inaugural address he maintained that upon the success of the American experiment depended "the welfare of mankind. If we fail, the cause of free self-government throughout the world will rock to its foundations, and therefore our responsibility is heavy, to ourselves, to the world as it is today, and to the generations yet unborn." But he reassuringly added, "We have faith that we shall not prove false to the memories of men of the mighty past" and said that Americans would show "the power of devotion to a lofty ideal" that made the founders and preservers of the republic so great.

Woodrow Wilson sounded similar themes of morality, service to humanity, and America's mission as the vehicle of global reform. He believed that all nations were capable of democracy, for, as he said in 1914, "when properly directed, there is no people not fitted for self-government." After the country's entry into WORLD WAR I, in his many speeches Wilson expounded upon the topics of democracy and national mission and elevated them to the realm of world redemption, but he failed to achieve his lofty goals in the peace settlement.

Franklin D. Roosevelt drew heavily on the theme of tolerance to bring various religious groups together and united them behind his efforts to combat the Great Depression and to conduct the global war effort. Typical was a speech in Cleveland, Ohio, in 1940 in which he talked about the "deeply ethical principles" on which America and its democracy was founded and the necessity for national unity that would make the country prosperous, free, strong, and "a light of the world and a comfort to all people." He presented a vision of America whose people were consecrated to peace because their body and spirit were secure and unafraid: "The spirit of the common man is the spirit of peace and good will. It is the spirit of God."

Dwight D. Eisenhower was the consummate national pastor who talked about faith as public virtue, the things of the spirit, the freedom and dignity of humanity, and organized evil (communism) challenging free people in their quest for peace. John F. Kennedy picked up on Eisenhower's themes in his own inaugural address when he underscored the "revolutionary" belief of America's forebears "that the rights of man come not from the generosity of the state, but from the hand of God." He then affirmed America's responsibility to ensure the survival and success of liberty. In Americans' hands, he exclaimed, "will rest the final success or failure of our course." Each generation of Americans has been summoned to testify to its national loyalty, Kennedy proclaimed, and now the trumpet sounds again for the current generation to carry on the "struggle against the common enemies of man: tyranny, poverty, disease, and war itself."

The last President to use civil religion in a prophetic fashion was Jimmy Carter. In his inaugural address he urged Americans to take on "moral duties" and to renew "our search for humility, mercy, and justice." More important was his speech in July 1979 in which he spoke of "a moral and spiritual crisis" and "a crisis of confidence" in national values and institutions. This crisis, Carter asserted, was one that "strikes at the very heart and soul and spirit of our national will" and was contributing to an erosion of confidence in the future that "is threatening to destroy the social and the political fabric of America." He chided his hearers for worshiping "self-indulgence and consumption" and called on them to "sacrifice" and "seize control of our common destiny."

Although Kennedy had set forth a prophetic vision of America that went beyond Eisenhower's bland emphasis on faith and spirit, Richard Nixon and Ronald Reagan introduced distinctly priestly elements into civil religion, particularly American exceptionalism and national mission. Nixon said in 1970 that America "is a nation under God" whose destiny was, not to conquer or exploit the world, but "to give to other nations of the world an example of spiritual leadership and idealism which no material strength or military power can provide." Reagan went even further, affirming in 1982 and 1983 that a "divine plan" had put the American continent here between the two oceans, where people who "had a special love for freedom" could come and create "something new in all the history of mankind—a country where man is not beholden to government; government is beholden to man." This country, Reagan claimed, was "set apart in a special way," and men and women from every corner of the world "came not for gold but mainly in search of God. They would be free people, living under the law, with faith in their Maker and in their future." The first settlers "asked that He would work His will in our daily lives, so America would be a land of fairness, morality, justice, and compassion."

Because most Americans are religious people, they have been able easily to transform an essentially secular civil religion into a particularistic form. This was clearly revealed in the addition of "under God" to the Pledge of Allegiance in 1954 and in the adoption of "In God We Trust" as the national motto in 1956. However, the fact remains that, although many have read their own religious views into the civil faith, it continues to be a secular set of values, with the President as its chief expositor.

BIBLIOGRAPHY

Barber, David James. *The Presidential Character: Predicting Performance in the White House.* 4th ed. 1992.
Bellah, Robert N., and Phillip E. Hammond. *Varieties of Civil Religion.* 1980.
Hutcheson, Richard G., Jr. *God in the White House.* 1988.
Mead, Sidney E. *The Nation with the Soul of a Church.* 1975.
Pierard, Richard V., and Robert D. Linder. *Civil Religion and the Presidency.* 1988.
Richey, R. E., and D. G. Jones, eds. *American Civil Religion.* 1974.
Rouner, Leroy S., ed. *Civil Religion and Political Ideology.* 1986.
Toulin, Cynthia. "American Civil Religion from 1789 to 1981: A Content Analysis of Presidential Inaugural Addresses." *Review of Religious Research* 25 (September 1983): 39–48.
Wills, Garry. *Under God: Religion and American Politics.* 1990.

RICHARD V. PIERARD and ROBERT D. LINDER

CIVIL RIGHTS ACT OF 1866. During the early years of RECONSTRUCTION the civil rights bill of 1866 became a critical point of contention and finally a deciding issue in a struggle for power between the legislative and the executive branches of the federal government. This struggle ultimately ended in a weakened presidency and an impeached President. The Thirteenth Amendment had ended SLAVERY but it provided no structure or guidelines for the implementation of emancipation. Under the lenient supervision of President Andrew Johnson, who came to office after the assassination of Abraham Lincoln, southern conservatives were returning to power and establishing black codes to control their former slaves. The civil rights bill was an attempt to provide legislative protections for individual rights without regard to race or color. It declared that every inhabitant of every state was entitled to equal privileges and protection of the Constitution, providing black people the same rights of citizenship that white Americans enjoyed. It guaranteed the right "to make and enforce contracts, to sue, to inherit, purchase, lease, sell, hold, and convey real and personal property, and to full and equal benefit of all laws and proceedings for the security of person and property." It also countered the 1857 opinion of the Supreme Court in the case of DRED SCOTT V. SANDFORD in which the Court denied American citizenship to African Americans.

President Johnson opposed the bill on grounds that it ignored the rights of states. "It is," he asserted, "another step, or rather stride, toward centralization and the concentration of all legislative powers in the National Government." A Tennessean, Johnson sympathized with the calls of those who wished to reestablish southern conservative authority as quickly as possible. Moreover he was committed to white supremacy and was not persuaded that the civil rights bill was needed to protect the rights of former slaves. During a White House meeting with a delegation of black leaders the President was cordial but restrained. Frederick Douglass, one of the delegation, contrasted Johnson's condescension with Lincoln's more respectful manner. Johnson, Douglass wrote, seemed more interested in protecting the strong and "casting down the defenseless."

Black leaders and white reformers argued that the civil rights bill should provide for black suffrage but the President would not discuss the issue. In an effort to compromise with the White House, congressional moderates successfully framed the bill so that voting rights were not included. Efforts to appease President Johnson failed, however. He vetoed the bill denouncing it as unconstitutional and claiming that by protecting rights for blacks, Congress was somehow depriving whites of their rights. The Congress, surprised and disappointed by Johnson's actions, promptly overrode his veto. The Civil Rights Act became law on 9 April 1866, the first major piece of legislation passed over a presidential veto. In 1868 the Fourteenth Amendment solidified the statutory rights protected in 1866.

Ultimately, Johnson's uncompromising manner hardened congressional resistance to his policies. In the spring of 1868 Andrew Johnson became the first President in American history to be impeached, and although he escaped conviction in the Senate by one vote, his presidency was weakened beyond repair [*see* IMPEACHMENT OF ANDREW JOHNSON].

BIBLIOGRAPHY

Benedict, Michael Les. *The Impeachment and Trial of Andrew Johnson.* 1973.

Foner, Eric. *Reconstruction: American's Unfinished Revolution, 1863–1877.* 1988.

Sefton, James E. *Andrew Johnson and the Uses of Constitutional Power.* 1980.

JAMES OLIVER HORTON

CIVIL RIGHTS ACTS OF 1875. The last of the RECONSTRUCTION era's major civil rights measures, the Civil Rights Act of 1875, originated in a bill introduced by Senator Charles Sumner of Massachusetts in May 1870. Prompted by the intransigence of white southerners who refused to abide by the Fourteenth Amendment, Sumner's bill prohibited racial discrimination in public conveyances, accommodations, and schools. The original bill mandated equal access to railroad cars, steamboats, hotels, theaters, churches, schools, and cemeteries licensed by state or federal authorities, but bitter Democratic opposition and Republican disunity led to the removal of the school and cemetery sections before the bill was enacted into law in February 1875. Following the electoral setback of the 1874 congressional elections, the Republican leaders of the lame-duck Forty-third Congress lacked

the votes and the resolve to pass the bill in its original form. Many Republicans were convinced that Reconstruction had become a political liability, and only a handful of diehard RADICAL REPUBLICANS regarded school and cemetery desegregation as critically important. Thus, when the Democrats in the House blocked the bill with several clever parliamentary maneuvers, Speaker of the House JAMES G. BLAINE and Representative James A. Garfield of Ohio were quick to arrange a compromise that facilitated the passage of a truncated version. President Ulysses S. Grant, who played an inconsequential role in the drafting of the bill, favored the Blaine-Garfield compromise and immediately signed the act into law. A month earlier, General Philip Sheridan's rough treatment of five defiant Democratic legislators in Louisiana had provoked widespread criticism of the Grant administration's Reconstruction policies, and Grant was in no mood to fuel the fires of conservative reaction.

Despite the deletion of the school and cemetery sections, the Civil Rights Act of 1875, in the words of the historian Eric Foner, "represented an unprecedented exercise of national authority, and breached traditional federal principles more fully than any previous Reconstruction legislation." On paper, the federal government now had the power to effect a broad reconstruction of southern society. Indeed, scrupulous enforcement of the new law would have revolutionized social relations throughout the nation. Unfortunately for African Americans, the Grant and Rutherford B. Hayes administrations made only a token effort to enforce the Civil Rights Act of 1875. Only a few black plaintiffs brought suit under the law, and they received little encouragement from federal officials. By the end of the decade the law, which had held so much promise, was all but forgotten. In the *Civil Rights Cases* (1883), the Supreme Court delivered the final blow with an 8-to-1 decision declaring the Civil Rights Act unconstitutional. Only Justice John Marshall Harlan dissented from the Court's assertion that the Fourteenth Amendment did not prohibit racial discrimination by private individuals. Ironically, all eight of the Justices who struck down the law had been appointed by Republican Presidents. Nearly a century later the basic principles of the 1875 law would find new life in the CIVIL RIGHTS ACT OF 1964, but this resurrection came much too late for the freedmen and freedwomen of the CIVIL WAR and Reconstruction era.

BIBLIOGRAPHY

Foner, Eric. *Reconstruction: America's Unfinished Revolution, 1863–1877.* 1988.

Franklin, John Hope. "The Enforcement of the Civil Rights Act of 1875." In *Race and History: Selected Essays, 1938–1988*. 1989.

McPherson, James. "Abolitionists and the Civil Rights Act of 1875." *Journal of American History* 52 (1965): 493–510.

Wyatt-Brown, Bertram. "The Civil Rights Act of 1875." *Western Political Quarterly* 18 (December 1965): 763–775.

RAYMOND ARSENAULT

CIVIL RIGHTS ACT OF 1957. The Civil Rights Act of 1957 established a Civil Rights Commission and empowered the Justice Department to bring suit against state officials who interfered with citizens seeking to vote in federal elections. The act reflected the ambivalent posture of the Eisenhower administration and Congress toward the growing civil rights movement of the 1950s. The 1957 legislation was the first federal civil rights bill since RECONSTRUCTION.

Civil rights policy under Dwight D. Eisenhower was shaped by often-conflicting influences. The Eisenhower administration was pushed toward greater activism in civil rights by the growing sophistication of the civil rights movement, with its landmark victory in the 1954 school-desegregation case *Brown v. Board of Education* and the increased efforts of civil rights activists to register black voters. The desire to present a favorable image of the United States abroad, particularly in the newly independent nations of Africa and Asia, and the need to satisfy a then still-substantial black and liberal Republican constituency, also helped push the administration toward supporting some civil rights efforts.

But the administration's policies also reflected Eisenhower's racial conservatism, which made him, at best, a reluctant supporter of desegregation measures, particularly when such measures required strong federal action that overrode the power of state governments. The administration was also constrained by its desire to win white votes in what had traditionally been the solid Democratic South.

The 1957 legislation reflected these diverse concerns. It was the outgrowth of recommendations made by Attorney General HERBERT BROWNELL partly in response to the massive southern resistance to court-ordered school desegregation and black efforts at voter registration. The bill concentrated on VOTING RIGHTS, one area where Eisenhower's support of the civil rights movement's agenda was relatively strong. Although Brownell had drafted the major provisions of the legislation in 1955, it was not introduced until 1957 in order to avoid jeopardizing Eisenhower's 1956 reelection bid in southern states. The legislation's introduction was spurred on by pressure from such civil rights leaders as A. Philip Randolph, Roy Wilkins,

Martin Luther King, Jr., and New York Congressman Adam Clayton Powell. Vice President Richard Nixon was one of the key supporters of the bill within the administration.

The bill's effectiveness was severely limited by a provision introduced in the Senate that allowed jury trials for officials accused of violating court injunctions against interfering with voter registration. That provision—a departure from normal procedure in injunction cases—was supported by a coalition of southern and some northern Democrats including Senate majority leader Lyndon B. Johnson and Massachusetts Senator John F. Kennedy. Despite administration opposition, particularly from Nixon, the measure became part of the bill.

Although the act had only a limited effect in attacking racial discrimination and protecting minority voter rights, it nonetheless represented the first major national legislative victory of the civil rights movement in the twentieth century. Its achievement, with the sponsorship of the relatively conservative Eisenhower administration, was an indication of national response to changing times.

BIBLIOGRAPHY

Burk, Robert Frederick. *The Eisenhower Administration and Black Civil Rights*. 1985.

Branch, Taylor. *Parting the Waters: America in the King Years, 1954–63*. 1988.

Garrow, David J. "Black Civil Rights during the Eisenhower Years." In *We Shall Overcome: The Civil Rights Movement in the United States in the 1950s and 1960s*. Edited by David J. Garrow. 3 vols. 1989. Vol. 1, pp. 269–281.

ROBERT J. COTTROL

CIVIL RIGHTS ACT OF 1960. Passed against a background of increased conflict over VOTING RIGHTS and school desegregation, the Civil Rights Act of 1960 (74 Stat. 86) was designed to augment the CIVIL RIGHTS ACT OF 1957. Major provisions of the 1960 legislation were designed to protect minority voting rights. Other provisions extended the Civil Rights Commission authorized by the 1957 act and granted the Justice Department authority to prosecute those who used explosives to intimidate civil rights organizations. The legislation also provided for federally sponsored education for children of members of the armed forces stationed in states where officials had closed public schools to avoid compliance with desegregation orders.

The 1960 legislation reflected both President Dwight D. Eisenhower's ambivalence toward civil rights and his desire to balance the demands of the REPUBLICAN PARTY's still large black and liberal constituency with the party's ambition to make inroads in the white South. The 1960 legislation, like its 1957 predecessor, also reflected the President's tendency to be reactive rather than proactive in civil rights. Spurred on by southern resistance to federal civil rights mandates and by a concern for the image of the United States abroad—particularly in the newly independent nations of Africa and Asia—Eisenhower was forced by events to take a more active stand than he would have preferred.

Despite his reluctance to use federal authority to enforce civil rights guarantees and despite his misgivings over the Supreme Court's decision in the school desegregation case *Brown v. Board of Education* (1954; 1955), events in the late 1950s forced Eisenhower to become more supportive of federal intervention. Faced in many southern states with illegal and often violent resistance to school desegregation and black voter registration, Eisenhower acted to curtail defiance of federal authority, most dramatically with his 1957 use of federal troops in Little Rock, Arkansas, to enforce court-ordered school desegregation [*see* LITTLE ROCK CRISIS].

Vice President Richard M. Nixon and Attorney General William P. Rogers were two of the prime supporters of the legislation within the administration. Nixon, who at the time had a considerable constituency within the civil rights community, believed that administration-sponsored legislation would help gain him a large number of black votes in the 1960 presidential campaign. Rogers, a longtime supporter of civil rights who had worked on a JUSTICE DEPARTMENT brief endorsing desegregation in *Brown*, had urged Eisenhower to support legislation which would strengthen the voting rights provisions of the 1957 act.

Like the Civil Rights Act of 1957, the Civil Rights Act of 1960 proved to be relatively ineffectual in protecting minority voting and other civil rights. Nonetheless the legislation stands as a telling monument to changing times. The turbulent struggle over civil rights in the South in the late 1950s forced action by the Eisenhower administration despite the President's reticence.

BIBLIOGRAPHY

Berman, Daniel M. *A Bill Becomes a Law: The Civil Rights Act of 1960.* 1962.

Burk, Robert Frederick. *The Eisenhower Administration and Black Civil Rights.* 1985.

Branch, Taylor. *Parting the Waters: America in the King Years, 1954–1963.* 1988.

ROBERT J. COTTROL

CIVIL RIGHTS ACT OF 1964. Reflecting the legislative efforts of both the John F. Kennedy and Lyndon B. Johnson administrations, the Civil Rights Act of 1964 was the most far-reaching piece of federal civil rights legislation since the passage of the ill-fated CIVIL RIGHTS ACT OF 1875. The landmark provisions of the 1964 statute included measures outlawing racial discrimination in public accommodations and voter registration. It extended the life of the Civil Rights Commission, originally authorized by the CIVIL RIGHTS ACT OF 1957, and also gave the ATTORNEY GENERAL the authority to bring suit against public school boards and state universities in order to bring about desegregation. Perhaps the most influential provisions of the legislation were those prohibiting discrimination in employment and training programs. Not only was racial discrimination on the part of employers, unions, and apprenticeship programs prohibited, but discrimination on the basis of religion, national origin, and, perhaps most significantly, sex was also outlawed. The measure remains the foundation of federal protection against private discrimination.

Little in either Kennedy's or Johnson's background suggested they would be radical innovators in the field of civil rights. Neither had been especially vigorous champions of civil rights in the Senate during the 1950s, although, as Senate majority leader, Johnson had played a critical role in passing the relatively ineffectual Civil Rights Act of 1957 and CIVIL RIGHTS ACT OF 1960.

During the 1960 presidential campaign Kennedy had made a concerted effort to increase his share of the African American vote. He criticized outgoing President Dwight D. Eisenhower for not acting more decisively on civil rights and at one point during the campaign called the Reverend Martin Luther King, Jr.'s family to express his concern when the civil rights leader was imprisoned in Georgia. Kennedy's efforts were rewarded: he received better than 68 percent of the black vote at a time when the Republican Party was still competitive with the African American electorate. This share of the black vote provided Kennedy's margin of victory in the election, but, despite this, it is fair to say that neither he nor his brother ROBERT F. KENNEDY (who served as his brother's and, later, Johnson's Attorney General) nor Johnson came into office prepared to make civil rights their top priority.

Events would push the Kennedy administration toward greater support for civil rights measures. The civil rights movement's increased demands in the early 1960s met with violent, lawless resistance to desegregation in many southern states. That such lawlessless—whether the refusal to admit black students to state universities in Alabama and Mississippi or the violence visited on civil rights workers—was often orchestrated and led by state and local officials sharpened the issue for the administration. The Kennedy JUSTICE DEPARTMENT became increasingly involved in protecting blacks and civil rights workers, and the administration became convinced of the need for greater civil rights protection.

By May 1963 the administration had proposed a measure that would ultimately become the Civil Rights Act of 1964. Initially, its prospects seemed dim because of extensive southern resistance in Congress and the Kennedy administration's generally poor record in getting legislation passed. In August of that year, the issue of civil rights was vividly focused by the March on Washington for Jobs and Freedom. The march, which brought some 250,000 civil rights supporters to the nation's capital, was initially viewed with skepticism by both Kennedys, who feared that the protest would complicate the administration's civil rights efforts, but, ultimately, Kennedy met with the leaders of the march and gave his endorsement to its goals.

Kennedy's assassination on 22 November 1963 helped to transform totally the prospects for civil rights legislation. As President, Johnson took up the cause of civil rights with a vigor and legislative skill that surpassed that of his predecessor. The presidency and perhaps the pressure of events helped transform Johnson, who as Senator from Texas had shown a pronounced caution on civil rights, into the most vigorous exponent of civil rights in the White House in the twentieth century.

Almost immediately, Johnson began framing the issue of the passage of the civil rights bill as a tribute to the assassinated Kennedy. Johnson made passage of the measure his administration's top priority. By the end of 1963, Johnson was meeting with civil rights leaders such as King, Roy Wilkins, A. Philip Randolph, and James Farmer in an effort to map out a strategy to ease passage of the legislation.

But it was Johnson's legendary command of the legislative process that played the decisive role in shepherding the civil rights bill through Congress despite often strenuous resistance from southern congressional delegations. Johnson managed to persuade enough congressional allies to develop a solid majority in support of the provision.

In February 1964 the measure passed the House of Representatives. But the Senate presented a greater challenge to Johnson and the administration, both because of the threat of a southern filibuster—and the reluctance of many Republicans and some Democrats to support cloture to curtail that threat—and because the possibility that the bill might be buried by a hostile committee was greater than it had been in the House. Johnson's previous experience as Senate majority

leader played a critical role in building the bipartisan support necessary to ensure the bill's passage.

Robert Kennedy, who remained Johnson's Attorney General through 1964, also played a critical role in shaping administration tactics in the Senate, as did the Senate majority whip, HUBERT H. HUMPHREY, who would later become Johnson's Vice President. The measure passed the Senate in June 1964, and on 2 July 1964 Johnson signed the measure into law.

BIBLIOGRAPHY

Civil Rights Act of 1964 with Explanation. 1964.

Taylor, Branch. *Parting the Waters: America in the King Years, 1954–1963.* 1988.

Whalen, Charles, and Barbara Whalen. *The Longest Debate: A Legislative History of the 1964 Civil Rights Act.* 1985.

ROBERT J. COTTROL

CIVIL RIGHTS ACT OF 1968. Although adopted at the urging of President Lyndon B. Johnson, this omnibus measure contained a number of provisions not submitted to Congress by his administration, some of which had little to do with civil rights. One of these, proposed by Rep. William Cramer (R-Fla.), made it a federal offense to travel from one state to another or to use any facility of interstate commerce with the intent to incite, promote, or participate in a riot. Other sections punished various kinds of conduct engaged in during civil disturbances and addressed numerous legal concerns of Native Americans, among other things guaranteeing to INDIANS living under tribal rule most of the rights enumerated in the Bill of Rights and the Fourteenth Amendment.

In addition to these provisions, the act contained three sections that emanated from the Johnson administration. Title VIII prohibited discrimination in the sale or rental of most housing, the principal exceptions being small, multiple-until dwellings with a landlord living on the premises and single-family residences whose sale or rental was not handled by a real estate broker [*see* HOUSING POLICY]. Title I increased the penalties for violation of the existing criminal civil rights statutes and, along with Title IX, criminalized violent or intimidating actions that interfered with enjoyment of a variety of benefits and activities provided for by the Constitution and federal legislation.

The provisions targeting anti–civil rights violence and intimidation were inspired by Johnson's outrage at the murder of Viola Liuzzo by Ku Klux Klansmen following the Selma, Alabama, VOTING RIGHTS march in April 1965. In his January 1966 state of the union message, Johnson had called for legislation to deal with this problem as well as with housing discrimination, racial bias in jury selection, and school desegregation. Congress proved resistant to the omnibus bill that the administration sent to Capitol Hill in April of that year, both because rioting in the black ghettos of the nation's large cities had eroded white support for civil rights legislation and because the housing proposal threatened northern as well as southern interests. The bill was weakened in the House, and it stalled in the Senate.

Pressured by civil rights groups, Johnson in 1967 submitted a revised version of his omnibus bill and reiterated his support for it in a special message to Congress in January 1968. The House Judiciary Committee, however, broke his proposal apart, leaving only a violence-and-intimidation bill and adding a separate anti-riot bill that was not backed by the administration. In the Senate the administration managed to defeat a substitute bill offered by Sam Ervin (D-N.C.), but reforms in Indian law that it contained became part of the legislation ultimately adopted. So did open-housing guarantees, in the form of a compromise crafted by Everett Dirksen (R-Ill.). Emotions aroused by the murder of Martin Luther King, Jr., helped the administration overcome a final roadblock in the House Rules Committee, and Johnson signed the bill into law on 11 April 1968.

BIBLIOGRAPHY

Belknap, Michal R., ed. *Civil Rights, the White House, and the Justice Department, 1945–1968.* Vol. 14: *Securing the Enactment of Civil Rights Legislation, 1965–1968.* 1991. Pp. 55–447.

Belknap, Michal R. *Federal Law and Southern Order: Racial Violence and Constitutional Conflict in the Post-Brown South.* 1987. Chapter 9.

Graham, Hugh Davis. *The Civil Rights Era: Origins and Development of National Policy.* 1990. Chapter 10.

Lawson, Steven F. *In Pursuit of Power: Southern Blacks and Electoral Politics, 1965–1982.* 1985. Chapter 3.

MICHAL R. BELKNAP

CIVIL RIGHTS ACT OF 1991. The Civil Rights Act of 1991 stands as the most far-reaching and controversial civil rights enactment since the CIVIL RIGHTS ACT OF 1964. Ranging from racial harassment to age discrimination to numerical proofs of discrimination (disparate impact) to attorney fees, the 1991 act covered most aspects of equal-employment legislation and litigation. The breadth of this legislation, not surprisingly, brought with it sharp divisions among civil rights, business, and governmental interests. Most significant, the Bush White House strongly opposed significant features of the legislative reform effort—resulting in a successful veto of a 1990 civil rights

package and marathon negotiations that preceded the President's eventual support of the 1991 act.

The 1991 act was a matter of great moment to the courts as well as to the White House and Congress. Through this legislation, nine Supreme Court decisions (decided from 1986 to 1991) were either modified or reversed. These decisions involved issues of statutory interpretation and, consequently, could be overturned by legislative enactment. That so many decisions were overturned, however, signaled strong displeasure with the Supreme Court. Most significant, the sponsors of the act sought to clarify and expand the scope and sweep of Title VII of the 1964 Civil Rights Act's provisions for employment-discrimination litigation in the wake of three controversial 1989 Supreme Court decisions. One decision, *Price Waterhouse v. Hopkins* (1989), held that an employer who engages in purposeful discrimination can nonetheless escape liability by proving that motives not prohibited by Title VII would have otherwise caused the adverse employment action. A second decision, *Martin v. Wilks* (1989), held that persons not parties to litigation can challenge the terms of court-approved agreements between defendant employers and plaintiff employees. Third, and most significant, *Wards Cove v. Atonio* (1989), required a disparate-impact plaintiff to bear the burden of persuasion both in identifying the challenged employment practice and demonstrating that the practice does not significantly serve "the legitimate employment goals" of the defendant employer. The focus of the battle over the 1991 act was how these and other Court decisions should be modified.

The battle proved to be an epic, lasting twenty months and including one presidential veto and countless counterproposals and compromises. The principal division centered on whether disparate-impact lawsuits would encourage employers to engage in quota hiring in order to stave off costly litigation rooted in numerical proofs of discrimination. President Bush vowed that he would not sign a "quota bill" and, in 1990, he vetoed proposed legislation for precisely this reason. Claiming in his veto message that "the bill actually employs a maze of highly legalistic language to introduce the destructive force of quotas into our Nation's employment system" and that "[i]t is neither fair nor sensible to give the employers of our country a difficult choice between using quotas and seeking a clarification of the law through costly and very risky litigation," Bush concluded that "equal opportunity is not advanced but thwarted."

Bush's antiquota attack was subject to doubt. Legislation that Bush sent to Congress contemporaneous with his veto was nearly identical to the legislation he vetoed on the disparate-impact issue. On race-exclusive scholarships, minority-business set-asides, and disparate-impact proofs contained in the Americans with Disabilities Act, moreover, Bush spoke of this longstanding commitment to AFFIRMATIVE ACTION. The President, nevertheless, was successful in his antiquota veto.

Bush persisted in opposing the 1991 Civil Rights Act as "a quota bill." Along with White House Counsel C. Boyden Gray, Attorney General Dick Thornburgh, and Chief of Staff John Sununu, the administration fiercely opposed the 1991 act. A compromise was eventually reached, however. On the rights of persons not parties to litigation, the availability of jury trials and punitive damages, and several other issues, the Bush administration acceded to congressional sponsors. On the disparate-impact issue, the act was purposefully opaque. While noting that Supreme Court decisions prior to the 1989 *Wards Cove* ruling would become the governing standard, ambiguities in these decisions made this a legislative compromise in which both sides could honestly proclaim victory. By not establishing a definitive standard, moreover, the judiciary will have broad latitude to redefine disparate-impact proofs.

The willingness of President Bush to sign the 1991 act is an outgrowth of events occurring in the weeks before the announced compromise. Specifically, former Ku Klux Klansman David Duke defeated incumbent Governor Buddy Roemer as Louisiana's Republican candidate for governor and, more significant, Clarence Thomas, Bush's choice to replace Thurgood Marshall on the Supreme Court, was subject to allegations of sexual harassment. A veto of civil rights legislation in the wake of these events would have proven difficult, especially since several moderate Republicans notified Bush that they would not support him in a veto-override fight.

The 1991 act is a by-product of compromise and circumstances. The purposeful ambiguity of critical provisions, moreover, reveals that two years of negotiation could not yield a definitive resolution of the conflicting desires of the elected branches. Ironically, legislation spurred on by dissatisfaction with Supreme Court decision making will only become clear in the wake of judicial interpretation.

BIBLIOGRAPHY

"Civil Rights Legislation in the 1990's." Symposium. *California Law Review* 79, no. 3 (1991).

"The 1991 Civil Rights Act: Theory and Practice." Symposium. *Notre Dame Law Review* 68, no. 5 (1993).

NEAL DEVINS

CIVIL RIGHTS POLICY. Originally used to designate a limited group of rights believed to be fundamental to full participation in civil society and initially primarily applied to the rights of former slaves after the CIVIL WAR, the term *civil rights* was gradually transformed to describe a general rule that people should not be discriminated against in important matters on the basis of what society views as arbitrary characteristics. Civil rights policy expanded from concern for equality for African Americans to include concern for equality for women, the elderly, and people with physical disabilities. The rights included within the definition expanded from the right to enter into contracts to the right to vote and the right to fair consideration in employment decisions and in housing. Presidential civil rights policy has been defined by the political imperatives facing each President and by each President's basic commitments on questions of equality.

The Era of Limited Policy. Presidential civil rights policy during and after the Civil War was extremely limited [see RECONSTRUCTION]. Neither Abraham Lincoln nor Andrew Johnson had a general civil rights policy. Gradually the Civil War was transformed from a struggle to restore the Union to a struggle to abolish SLAVERY (and thereby restore the Union), yet Lincoln had little reason to define a broad civil rights policy apart from abolition. Johnson faced the question regarding what policies were entailed by abolition and came to the conclusion that very little else needed to be done. He did not believe, for example, that the mere abolition of slavery meant that states had to give former slaves equal rights in criminal cases or that former slaves necessarily had the same rights as whites in making and enforcing contracts. Congress disagreed and quickly took control of setting civil rights policy. The CIVIL RIGHTS ACT OF 1866, enacted over Johnson's veto, sought to override the discriminatory Black Codes that some states had adopted after abolition and to protect the rights of freed slaves to enter into contracts and to testify in court. Johnson believed that even so limited an exercise of national authority was beyond the power granted to Congress by the Thirteenth Amendment, which abolished slavery. Johnson's impeachment trial ensured that Congress would control civil rights policy [see IMPEACHMENT OF ANDREW JOHNSON].

Under President Ulysses S. Grant, the DEPARTMENT OF JUSTICE tried to enforce congressional civil rights policy, bringing numerous criminal cases against southerners who interfered with attempts by African Americans to exercise their civil rights. Through narrow interpretations of the Constitution and of the statutes Congress enacted, the Supreme Court effectively nullified those efforts.

The Compromise of 1876 [see ELECTION, PRESIDENTIAL, 1876; ELECTORAL COMMISSION] took civil rights policy out of the national arena for two generations. Later, in 1901, Theodore Roosevelt invited the African American leader Booker T. Washington to a widely publicized dinner at the White House, but adverse comments led Roosevelt to abandon even mild gestures aimed at helping the REPUBLICAN PARTY attract African American voters in the South. One important shift did occur, however, during the early twentieth century. Before 1870, the term *civil rights* had referred to a rather limited set of equality rights and was understood not to include equality in political rights, especially voting. A separate constitutional amendment, the Fifteenth, was required to ensure VOTING RIGHTS for former slaves, even after the Fourteenth Amendment had barred states from denying any group equal protection of the laws. The earlier distinction between civil and political rights dissolved with the adoption of the Fifteenth Amendment. As late as *Plessy v. Ferguson* (1896), however, the Supreme Court had held that "social" rights were outside the scope of "civil rights." By the early decades of the twentieth century even that distinction had dissolved. "Civil rights" began to be used to refer to claims about not only discrimination by the government but also discrimination in housing and employment—well beyond the concept's initial scope.

As a Democrat and a southerner, Woodrow Wilson felt even less need than had Roosevelt to develop a national civil rights policy. His administration expanded racial segregation in federal workplaces and rebuffed all efforts during WORLD WAR I to temper racial discrimination in the armed forces.

A Changing Political Environment. Presidential civil rights policy began to change in response to the demands of partisan politics. African Americans had for decades supported the Republicans—the party of Lincoln—by heavy majorities. But the party rarely responded to their concerns, in part because its leaders retained the hope of building white support in the South and in part because they believed that as long as white southerners dominated the DEMOCRATIC PARTY, Republicans could count on receiving African American votes without having to do much to earn them. African American migration to the North during and after World War I began to change these calculations. Further, the African American community and its supporters began to organize more effectively as a presence on the national political scene. The National Association for the Advancement of Colored People

(NAACP), founded in 1909, developed a litigation program that brought civil rights issues to the courts and became the widely acknowledged Washington lobby for the African American community.

In the 1920s Democrats began to realize that they had a chance to capture the northern black vote and, by doing so, take northern states away from the Republicans. The economic trauma of the depression accelerated the growth of African American support for the Democratic Party. Franklin D. Roosevelt's NEW DEAL was not targeted at African Americans, but the African American community, as one of the society's hardest-hit segments, benefited from New Deal programs. The Roosevelt administration was not dramatically responsive to the expressed concerns of African American leaders, however. It did not act decisively against race discrimination in the operation of New Deal programs, and Roosevelt refused to intervene against filibusters that blocked enactment of anti-lynching legislation.

Roosevelt did appoint a few young African Americans, including Robert Weaver and Mary McLeod Bethune, to lower-level positions in his administration. These officials, sometimes referred to as the Black Cabinet, brought African American concerns to the administration's attention, and the mere existence of a prominent group of African American public officials was an important symbol of the new place African Americans had in national politics. Responding to a threatened protest march on Washington in 1941, Roosevelt created the wartime FAIR EMPLOYMENT PRACTICE COMMITTEE, which was given power to investigate charges of employment discrimination. Roosevelt regarded the FEPC's creation as merely a concession to political reality, though, and efforts to give it enforcement power and to extend its life did not succeed. The fact that New Deal economic programs had cemented African American voters to the Democratic Party was, in the long run, much more important.

Roosevelt's appointments to the Supreme Court also changed the political environment for civil rights. The pre-Roosevelt Court had invoked the Constitution to obstruct the implementation of New Deal policies. After 1937, the new, Roosevelt-appointed Justices developed a theory to explain why the old Court had misinterpreted the Constitution. According to their theory, courts should exercise the power of judicial review not only when a specific constitutional provision directs them to do so but, importantly, also when they can act on behalf of what Justice Harlan Fiske Stone called "discrete and insular minorities," who lack the political power to protect their interests in legislatures. The African American community in the

South was the prime example of such a minority, and the new Court regularly overturned discriminatory practices challenged by the NAACP's lawyers. The Court's actions gave civil rights policy greater prominence in the national political arena and reflected the broader understanding of civil rights as embodying general rules against discrimination.

Opposing Discrimination and Segregation. Political calculations shaped the Truman administration's civil rights policy as they had its predecessor's. There was, however, a significant difference in that Truman himself believed that morality required the government to take some action against racial discrimination. Facing a political threat from HENRY A. WALLACE on his left, Truman in 1946 created the presidential Committee on Civil Rights to demonstrate his commitment to civil rights. The committee's 1947 report, *To Secure These Rights*, recommended passage of a national antilynching law, federal enforcement of antidiscrimination rules in employment, and ending segregation in federally subsidized housing, all programs that would face southern filibusters that were sure to be mounted in the Senate if such legislation were introduced. Immediately after *To Secure These Rights* was released, the Justice Department intervened in pending Supreme Court challenges to the enforcement of racially restrictive covenants that prohibited blacks from owning or occupying property (*Shelley v. Kraemer* [1948]). In later university and public school desegregation cases Truman's Justice Department urged the Court to overrule the separate-but-equal doctrine derived from the 1896 *Plessy* case.

The 1948 Democratic convention adopted a platform plank, drafted by Minneapolis mayor HUBERT H. HUMPHREY, that strongly endorsed civil rights. This statement prompted southern Democrats, led by South Carolina governor STROM THURMOND, to abandon the national Democratic Party. Less than two weeks after the convention, Truman ordered the desegregation of the armed forces [*see* EXECUTIVE ORDER 9981]. Truman's civil rights policies attracted enough African American support to overcome feared defections to Wallace's PROGRESSIVE PARTY (1948), and many observers credited those policies as enabling Truman's surprising victory over his Republican opponent, New York governor THOMAS E. DEWEY.

Dwight D. Eisenhower's 1952 election did not significantly change the course of civil rights policy. Some Republicans believed that Eisenhower could erode Democratic domination of the South by tempering the national government's recent commitments to civil rights, and Eisenhower himself was not particularly devoted to civil rights issues. His first Attorney General, HERBERT BROWNELL, however, was a product of the eastern branch of the party and consistently supported antidiscrimination policies. The Justice Department continued to challenge the separate-but-equal doctrine in the *Brown v. Board of Education* cases (1954, 1955). Its lawyers developed the formula that desegregation should occur "with all deliberate speed," which helped the Supreme Court unanimously overturn school segregation.

Southern resistance to desegregation culminated in the LITTLE ROCK CRISIS of 1957–1958. Arkansas governor Orval Faubus, formerly a racial moderate, thought that local political pressures required him to resist the Little Rock school board's gradual desegregation plan. As the situation deteriorated, Eisenhower was compelled to send federal troops to Central High School in Little Rock to protect African American students who were attempting to desegregate the school. Eisenhower, who regarded desegregation as primarily a local issue, nonetheless found Faubus's challenge to the authority of the Supreme Court and the President to be intolerable.

Continuing pressure from the civil rights movement and concern that racial discrimination was likely to provoke repeated crises led the Eisenhower administration to seek a more permanent remedy. It proposed legislation that resulted in the CIVIL RIGHTS ACT OF 1957. The act also served the political interests of Senate majority leader Lyndon B. Johnson (D-Tex.), whose presidential aspirations required him to demonstrate his support for civil rights. The act elevated the status of civil rights enforcement within the Justice Department by creating the Civil Rights Division. It also expanded the federal criminal laws against civil rights violations and established the Civil Rights Commission to investigate and report on violations of civil rights; however, like the earlier FEPC, the Civil Rights Commission was given no enforcement power. The 1957 act's keystone was a voting rights provision, which supporters believed would expand African American voting in the South and thereby put the nation on the road to eliminating legally mandated racial segregation. To enact the statute, however, the bill's supporters were required to water it down, and it had little effect on voting rights.

Civil rights played a small but important part in the 1960 presidential election campaign. On 19 October 1960, Martin Luther King., Jr., was arrested in Atlanta, Georgia, for participating in a sit-in. Neither Eisenhower nor Republican presidential candidate Richard M. Nixon responded to pleas from King's associates for a statement denouncing the arrest. In contrast, Democratic candidate John F. Kennedy telephoned King's wife. This widely publicized gesture may have contributed to Kennedy's margins of victory in crucial northern states.

The Civil Rights Movement. Although during his campaign Kennedy had promised to move promptly against racial discrimination in federally assisted housing, his administration needed southern support for other domestic programs and so adopted a cautious civil rights policy. Kennedy nominated a number of segregationist judges to the federal bench in the South, where they predictably obstructed efforts to enforce desegregation rulings. Responding to "freedom rides" protesting segregation at bus stations serving interstate lines, the administration asked the Interstate Commerce Commission to ban such segregation, which it did in September 1961.

The Kennedy administration continued to face resistance to desegregation in the deep South. Governors Ross Barnett of Mississippi and GEORGE WALLACE of Alabama confronted the federal government over desegregation of their state universities. Kennedy restated the government's commitment to enforcement of court-ordered desegregation through the use of federal troops if necessary, and small-scale desegregation proceeded after some rioting and some carefully staged confrontations between the southern governors and Department of Justice officials [*see* MEREDITH CASE]. Southern resistance, particularly in the form of rioting, strengthened the political position of civil rights advocates.

The civil rights movement continued to press the administration for more forceful measures. The administration supported a constitutional amendment to eliminate poll taxes, which traditionally had been used to disfranchise African American voters. Pressed by liberals, the administration also proposed more comprehensive voting-rights legislation, but in the face of legislative defeats the administration retreated.

After further demonstrations and violence in the South, notably the bombing of a church in Birmingham, Alabama, in which four schoolgirls were killed, the administration proposed comprehensive antidiscrimination legislation. Its bill, ultimately enacted as the CIVIL RIGHTS ACT OF 1964, banned discrimination in public accommodations such as restaurants. The act prohibited also employment discrimination and created the Equal Employment Opportunity Commission, which was given power to enforce the ban. It also allowed the federal government to terminate federal aid to school districts that continued to practice racial discrimination. Although the administration was concerned about the participation of radicals in the massive civil rights march on Washington in August 1963,

the march did demonstrate substantial public support for civil rights.

After Kennedy's assassination, Lyndon Johnson made enactment of the Civil Rights Act his "first priority." Johnson, unlike his predecessor, had a visceral commitment to equal rights. In 1967, saying that it was "the right time" to nominate the first African American Justice, he appointed the noted civil rights lawyer Thurgood Marshall to the Supreme Court. In response to Kennedy's assassination, opposition to the 1964 Civil Rights Act diminished. After its enactment, gross segregation in public accommodations rapidly disappeared. Discriminatory employment practices persisted, and years of litigation to enforce the statute ensued. The Johnson administration—and, even more effectively, the Nixon administration—used the threat of funding cutoffs to bring about substantial desegregation in schools in the deep South. At the end of the Johnson administration, and after the assassination of Martin Luther King, Jr., in April 1968, Congress narrowly approved the CIVIL RIGHTS ACT OF 1968, banning discrimination in housing.

Johnson's most important civil rights legislation was the Voting Rights Act of 1965 [see VOTING RIGHTS]. Earlier civil rights statutes had failed because they relied on lawsuits to challenge discriminatory practices; those lawsuits required expensive and time-consuming investigations and rarely protected African Americans against violent retaliation for their attempts to register and vote. Young civil rights workers organized an intensive voting rights effort in Mississippi in 1964; the murders of three civil rights workers attracted national attention, and the campaign's attempt to unseat Mississippi's delegates to the Democratic national convention in 1964, though unsuccessful, embarrassed the Johnson administration. The administration took advantage of yet another violent reaction, this one to a voting rights march in Selma, Alabama, in 1965, to push the Voting Rights Act through Congress. The act changed the rules by which discriminatory practices could be overturned. Instead of relying on litigation to end them, the act suspended all but the most neutral voting rights requirements in the South and then required states to get prior permission to impose exclusionary "tests or devices." This new technique was a massive success, and African American registration expanded dramatically throughout the South.

From Intent to Effects. School desegregation and employment discrimination continued to be the focus of civil rights policy in the 1970s, but attention shifted away from eliminating policies that made race (and sex) an explicit reason for denying people jobs or for assigning students to certain schools and toward remedies for past discrimination or practices that resulted in segregated schools or workplaces. In *Green v. County School Board of New Kent County* (1968), the Supreme Court held that "freedom of choice" plans for school desegregation were unacceptable; in *Swann v. Charlotte-Mecklenburg Board of Education* (1971), the Court upheld plans that required substantial busing of students to achieve desegregation. Busing was highly controversial, particularly as northern school districts became subject to busing orders. The Nixon administration initially supported freedom-of-choice plans and Nixon frequently expressed his opposition to busing, although his Justice Department did not forcefully challenge busing orders after the Supreme Court's 1971 decision.

The controversy over busing, which took the form of concern about the scope or remedies for acknowledged segregation, obscured a deeper transformation in the concept of civil rights. Although the scope of civil rights had expanded since Reconstruction and the term had come to designate a general right to equal treatment in political and economic life, the meaning of equal treatment had been fairly constant. Equality was denied when a decisionmaker took race into account, either by designing rules that explicitly treated whites and African Americans differently or by adopting rules that were intended to produce different results for whites and African Americans. Under this reasoning, equal treatment was denied when there was an *intent* to discriminate.

Brown v. Board of Education expressed this notion of civil rights by barring states from separating whites and African Americans in schools pursuant to a rule that explicitly used race as a basis for school assignments. On the classic conception of civil rights, discrimination could be eliminated if schools adopted student-assignment policies (for example, neighborhood-school policies) that ignored race. Freedom-of-choice plans allowed each student to choose which school to attend and so seemed consistent with the classic conception of civil rights. The South's recalcitrance, however, made the Supreme Court impatient. When districts adopted freedom-of-choice plans, the Court observed, the effects were basically to perpetuate segregation. The Court found such plans inadequate because they failed to achieve desegregation. With this, the Court changed the focus of civil rights policy, abandoning its earlier focus on whether a school board or employer intentionally segregated students or workers, which ordinarily could be determined simply by examining the board or employer's express policies, and focusing instead on whether the

schools or workplaces were actually integrated—that is, on the *effects* of board or employer policies.

The transformation from intent to effects fit well with the interests of civil rights advocacy groups and with a deep pragmatic strain in American culture. For many people, public policy had no point unless it did something, that is, achieved certain effects.

The transformation was most dramatic in connection with employment discrimination. In 1961 President Kennedy had issued an executive order requiring employers holding federal contracts to engage in AFFIRMATIVE ACTION. At the outset, the term meant that employers had to take positive steps to ensure that they would attract African American job applicants. As attention shifted from intent to effects, affirmative action programs began to examine the proportion of African American employees in the workplace, and federal agencies began to require employers to set hiring "goals." Because employers feared that failure to meet their goals would lead to the loss of federal contracts, some began to treat hiring goals as rigid quotas.

President Nixon's political advisers revived a long-standing Republican interest in making inroads on Democratic political power in the South. They understood that vigorous enforcement of desegregation, particularly busing, was rapidly eroding Democratic support there. They also understood that the term *quotas* triggered intense concern among white workers about their job security. Even though his administration actually did rather little to undermine either busing or affirmative action, Nixon regularly blamed those programs on Democratic liberals in Congress and their allies in the federal courts. This strategy contributed to the dissolution of the New Deal coalition in presidential politics.

The shift from intent to effects in civil rights policy was but one major change that occurred in the 1960s and 1970s. Another found its origin with the inclusion of a ban on sex discrimination in employment in the 1964 Civil Rights Act. Although the ban was inserted almost as an afterthought and was proposed by Representative Howard Smith (D-Va.), an opponent of the legislation, it was actually the culmination of a long-standing, though until then not very vigorous, effort by lobbyists for women's organizations to expand the concept of civil rights to include women as a "protected class' in civil rights laws. Later legislation further increased the number of protected classes [*see* WOMEN'S RIGHTS].

The effects of this expansion became clear during Jimmy Carter's administration and after. Representing an important political constituency, women's groups were able to get federal antidiscrimination agencies to pay attention to their claims about discrimination. This exacerbated the political difficulties for the Democratic coalition and, perhaps more importantly, diffused the agencies' attention. Rather than concentrating entirely on race discrimination, the agencies had to devote resources to investigating and addressing discrimination against the larger group of protected classes. By the end of the Carter administration, the EEOC was nearly overwhelmed by the number of individual complaints it had to handle.

Against Expansive Interpretation. The administration of Ronald Reagan challenged the prevailing view of civil rights. The administration argued in the Supreme Court against expansive interpretations of civil rights statutes. In *Bob Jones University v. United States* (1983), the administration defended the granting of tax-exempt status to a university that prohibited interracial dating; the Supreme Court rejected its position, finding that the public policy against discrimination overrode the university's religious objections. In other cases the administration successfully urged the Court to require that plaintiffs in employment-discrimination cases identify precisely what practices led to differences in rates at which minorities and whites were hired and to adopt an employer-oriented standard for justifying such practices (*Wards Cove Packing Co. v. Atonio* [1989]). Congress and President George Bush engaged in a protracted struggle over the appropriate legislative response to these decisions. Eventually President Bush signed the CIVIL RIGHTS ACT OF 1991, which somewhat ambiguously eased the burdens the Court had placed on plaintiffs.

In affirmative action cases the Reagan and Bush administrations adopted the premise that race discrimination occurred whenever an employer took race into account in hiring. Both administrations believed that affirmative action programs that set targets and goals were discriminatory in that sense, because employers concerned about reaching their goals would inevitably make race-conscious hiring decisions. Opposing the civil rights vision that had dominated the preceding decades, the Reagan and Bush administrations, led on this issue by Assistant Attorney General William Bradford Reynolds, argued that government should respond to race discrimination only when employers had the intent to discriminate and should provide remedies only for individuals who had themselves been discriminated against. Affirmative action, they believed, should not attempt to address "societal" discrimination (i.e., the effects of social arrangements that in some diffuse sense resulted from race discrimination) nor the present effects of past explicit race discrimination, at least not in any large-scale way.

The Reagan administration's individual-oriented focus led it to oppose the extension of the 1965 Voting Rights Act, which in its view had been inappropriately interpreted to provide group-oriented remedies that attempted to ensure certain racial outcomes—to wit, the election of minority members to legislatures—rather than to ensure that minorities would have an equal opportunity to participate in the electoral process. When Congress renewed the Voting Rights Act in 1982 it rejected the Reagan administration's effort to limit the act to practices designed to discriminate, including an ambiguous provision saying that voting rights could be denied by practices that had a racially disparate impact on voting outcomes.

The individual-oriented focus affected the administration of civil rights statutes as well. The Equal Employment Opportunity Commission shifted resources from class action cases involving large numbers of employees to the resolution of individual claims of discrimination.

During the 1970s and 1980s, the concept of civil rights again expanded. The Age Discrimination in Employment Act (1967) and the Americans with Disabilities Act (1991) expressed the new understanding—that the concept of civil rights extended to protect a large number of groups whose members were able to secure legislative protection against a wide range of discriminatory practices. By the 1990s, these protected groups had become important participants in executive and legislative politics. In the process, the moral force that lay behind the term *civil rights* dissipated, and advocates of civil rights became lobbyists for what had come to be understood as special-interest groups.

BIBLIOGRAPHY

Amaker, Norman C. *Civil Rights and the Reagan Administration.* 1988.

Berman, William C. *The Politics of Civil Rights in the Truman Administration.* 1970.

Burk, Robert Fredrick. *The Eisenhower Administration and Black Civil Rights.* 1984.

Graham, Hugh Davis. *The Civil Rights Era: Origins and Development of National Policy, 1960–1972.* 1990.

Kaczorowski, Robert J. *The Politics of Judicial Interpretation: The Federal Courts, Department of Justice, and Civil Rights, 1866–1876.* 1985.

Sitkoff, Harvard. *A New Deal for Blacks.* 1978.

Stern, Mark. *Calculating Visions: Kennedy, Johnson, and Civil Rights.* 1992.

MARK TUSHNET

CIVIL SERVICE. In the United States, "civil service" is not a precise legal category or political term. It generally refers to civilian employees, who are not politically appointed officers, in the executive branch of government. The term may also encompass employees of legislative agencies, such as the GENERAL ACCOUNTING OFFICE, and some judicial employees. Legislative staff and judicial clerks are generally not considered civil servants. Further, the term typically connotes white-collar employment, although police and fire fighters are within its purview and public school teachers and public university professors usually are not. In some contexts, "civil service" is used to distinguish employees working under a merit system and enjoying formal job security from temporary, conditional, and politically appointed public employees.

Even if "civil service" is not precisely defined, the development of large and politically influential civil services has been of great importance to governments throughout the world. Civil services are repositories of expertise on which governments depend in formulating and executing public policy. In some countries, including France, Germany, and at times, China, the civil service enjoys considerable prestige. Elsewhere, as in the United States, it is often derided for inefficiency and incompetence. Virtually everywhere there is concern with the influence of the civil service on policy and the potential or reality of corruption within it.

Historically the U.S. federal government has faced difficulty in fully integrating the civil service into the SEPARATION OF POWERS and the dominant political culture. The constitutional scheme places the President at the head of the executive branch but makes the civil service highly dependent on Congress. Not only must the creation of all offices and the disbursement of all appropriations be pursuant to law, but Congress has constitutional authority to determine how civil servants will be appointed. In practice, Congress delegates considerable legislative authority to executive-branch agencies in establishing their missions. Overall, the legislature is deeply involved in the organization, staffing, and funding of the civil service and in overseeing its performance.

At various times, the model for the civil service has been one of responsiveness to executive leadership, politically neutral competence, or representativeness of the people. There tends to be a trade-off between managerial and political values in the civil service that thus far has not been resolved. The management approach emphasizes efficiency, economy, and effective hierarchical control, whereas the political approach values responsiveness, representativeness, and accountability to external bodies, such as the legislature. The tensions inherent in these approaches have been complicated since the 1970s by far greater judi-

cial involvement in public administration. The courts have required that civil-service procedures and the actions of civil servants incorporate appropriate constitutional rights and values, such as due process and equal protection. For example, in *Rutan v. Republican Party of Illinois*, the Supreme Court held that the First and Fourteenth Amendments prohibited the use of partisanship in the vast majority of ordinary civil-service hirings, promotions, transfers, and other personnel actions.

Organizing Concepts in the Past. Historians agree that by the early twentieth century the United States had developed three distinct organizing concepts for the civil service in three different periods.

First period. From 1789 until 1829, federal civil servants were selected and retained primarily on the basis of fitness of character. They were recruited from the upper class, and consequently, the period is generally referred to as the era of "gentlemen." For the most part, the civil service was the arm of the elite who controlled national politics. Some concern with civil servants' political leanings developed in the administration of John Adams and became more pronounced in the early years of Thomas Jefferson's presidency, but the service was characterized more by political stability than by change. Executive leadership was a pronounced organizing value.

Second period. The period from 1829 until the early 1870s was a reaction to the first. The inauguration of President Andrew Jackson ushered in a fundamentally different concept of the civil service. In his inaugural address, Jackson argued that reform was necessary because the upper-class basis of the civil service, coupled with the long incumbency of civil servants, had made the service indifferent to the public interest. He proposed that civil servants be selected from the broad spectrum of the white male population and that they be rotated in and out of office relatively rapidly. In other words, the civil service was to be socially and politically representative of the public. Although Jackson's own record in implementing such reforms was modest in comparison with his successors, he is generally credited with establishing the spoils system because he provided a compelling rationale for it.

By the 1840s, when the system was at its height, the civil service was best considered the arm of the political party (or faction) in office. Wholesale rotation of civil servants occurred upon the inaugurations of new Presidents. Superfluous positions were created to satisfy the demand for PATRONAGE. Tenure was short, business methods were haphazard, the separation between political parties and the government was blurred, and corruption was rife. The spoils system is generally credited with fostering the development of mass-based, competitive political parties and with breaking the upper class's dominance of the national government.

Third period. The period from the 1870s to the 1920s was a reaction to the excesses of the spoils system. Three CIVIL-SERVICE REFORM movements combined to organize the civil service according to a third set of concepts—merit, political neutrality, and scientific management. Early merit reforms were introduced in the 1870s, but it was not until the enactment of the CIVIL SERVICE ACT (1883) that the merit system became a permanent organizing concept of the federal civil service. The act placed only about 10 percent of all federal civil-service positions under the merit system, but it authorized the President to extend such coverage. By 1919, at least 70 percent of the civil service was in the competitive classified civil service (organized on the basis of merit). The act also sought to eliminate partisan coercion and partisanship generally from the civil service. Enforcement was by an independent Civil Service Commission, consisting of a chairperson and two members appointed by the President with the ADVICE AND CONSENT of the Senate. No more than two of the commissioners could be of the same political party.

Civil-service reformers had long favored taking the civil service out of politics and politics out of the civil service. The idea of a politically neutral civil service dates back at least to Jefferson's first administration. Additional limited efforts to restrict the political activities of federal civil servants were made in the 1840s and from the 1870s through the 1890s. But it was not until the Progressive Era that the first successful federal restrictions on the partisan activities of civil servants took hold. President Theodore Roosevelt amended Civil Service Rule I so that those in the competitive classified service were prohibited from taking an active part in political management or campaigns. Rule I was superseded by the HATCH ACT (1939), which placed similar restrictions on a statutory basis.

The reformers and Progressives valued civil-service reform for the efficiency and higher public morality it would bring. However, it was also instrumental to their larger interests in making fundamental political change. They sought to destroy the machine-based, spoils-oriented political leadership and culture that had developed in the period after the CIVIL WAR. Depriving the political bosses of patronage and the use of the civil service for partisan purposes was central to their objectives.

In order to make their case regarding depoliticization of the civil service, however, the reformers and Progressives had to convince the public and their elected representatives that the civil service should be organized on the principle of politically neutral expertise. To do so, they presented two main arguments. First, they argued that public administration and politics were separate endeavors and that, therefore, it was unnecessary (or even undesirable) for the civil service to be organized according to executive leadership or representativeness. Administrative questions were matters of business, not politics. Second, they argued that there was a developing body of administrative expertise that could efficiently, economically, and effectively replace the haphazard practices of the past. In making the latter argument, the Progressives were aided immensely by the advent of Frederick Taylor's scientific-management movement.

Taking the perspective of engineering, in the early 1900s Taylor argued that there was an applied science of job design, work flow, and employee selection and motivation. He reported tremendous successes in improving efficiency and productivity in a variety of manual-labor jobs. The scientific-management movement attracted adherents and interest worldwide partly because of its promise of greater efficiency and partly because it presented a blueprint for redistributing authority in the workplace. At the core of Taylorism was the belief that the functions of management should be enlarged to include job design and work flow. In the past, workers had determined how jobs would be performed, thereby giving them considerable leverage vis-à-vis management. Under scientific management, managers would take over the responsibility of structuring jobs and work flow. They would use science, rather than past practices or the workers' rule of thumb, as the basis for assuring the highest level of efficiency. Although it was not a necessary outcome, Taylorism in fact led to the "de-skilling" of jobs, thereby reducing the value of what workers had to sell in the labor market and making them more or less interchangeable. Hence, management gained greater control of workers.

The Progressives benefited doubly from scientific management in promoting their organizing principles for the civil service. On the one hand, they could present much of public administration—employee selection, job design, position classification, and pay plans—as a science, rather than a set of practices to be established according to changing political or popular preferences. On the other hand, many of the Progressives, including such leaders as Woodrow Wilson, were deeply concerned that the very large influx of immigrants during the 1890s and 1910s could corrupt the Anglo-American political culture if that influx were not channeled in appropriate directions. Immigrants and political bosses had established symbiotic relationships based on patronage and personal loyalty. Scientific management offered the same excellent prospect in the public sector as in private industry for making workers, many of whom were immigrants, thoroughly dependent on managers, who were much more likely to be well assimilated into the dominant political culture. Indeed, early merit examinations often asked questions about civic organization and history that were seemingly irrelevant to the jobs at hand. In the Progressives' view, however, civil servants should be concerned about the public and imbued with civic virtue, which included knowledge about the structure and operation of government.

Aside from the merit system and political neutrality, the organizing concepts developed by the reformers, Progressives, and scientific managers included position classification. By 1920, the federal civil service was thoroughly organized according to positions rather than around individuals, collective bargaining units, or work teams. Among the leading principles of position classification were the following: Positions, not individuals, should be classified (thus, rank has overwhelmingly been in the position, not the person). Positions should be classified according to the duties and responsibilities they require. The duties and responsibilities should determine the educational, experiential, and other qualifications required of applicants. The individual characteristics of incumbent employees have no bearing on the classification of positions. Persons holding positions with the same classification should be considered interchangeable. Today, the civil service includes several classification systems. The main one is the General Schedule, which includes most white-collar occupations and ranges from grade 1 (low) to grade 18. The U.S. POSTAL SERVICE, FOREIGN SERVICE, some other agencies, and blue-collar workers are under separate classification systems.

Although the organization of state and local civil services varied considerably, the spoils system and the reform period left their mark throughout the nation. By the mid twentieth century, merit, political neutrality, and position classification had become the dominant ideal, if not the actual reality, almost everywhere in the nation.

Organization after 1978. The federal civil service was substantially reorganized by the CIVIL SERVICE REFORM ACT (1978) (92 Stat. L. 1111).

Impetus for the 1978 reform act. In some respects, the act was a delayed outgrowth of political developments that occurred during the NEW DEAL. The size of the civil service had grown from about 610,000 in 1931 to 1,438,000 in 1941. In the 1990s it employed some three million personnel. This rapid growth placed considerable strains on the organization derived from the reform-Progressive period. The independent Civil Service Commission was no longer able to perform most personnel functions on a centralized basis. More and more authority for personnel had to be delegated to the departments and agencies, with the commission engaging in audits, investigations, and other policing functions. Increasingly this policing role, which was appropriate according to the neutral-competence model, was viewed as a barrier to strong executive leadership. A dynamic President appointed department and agency heads to develop and implement policies, only to see their work frustrated by civil-service rules and procedures designed for an earlier time in which spoils was perceived as a preeminent problem. In 1937 Roosevelt appointed the President's Committee on Administrative Management (also known as the BROWNLOW COMMITTEE after its chair, Louis Brownlow). Among many other recommendations, the committee called for the elimination of the Civil Service Commission in favor of an office of personnel under more direct presidential control. Although this proposal made little headway, the reformers of the 1970s looked at similar problems and reached similar conclusions.

The immediate impetus for the 1978 civil-service reform was threefold. First, public confidence in government had been severely shaken by the WATERGATE AFFAIR, culminating in President Richard M. Nixon's resignation in 1974. The Civil Service Commission had been tainted during the Nixon years by illegally favoring the applications of persons having White House backing. It had long been considered ineffective in helping the President to exert executive leadership, and by the mid 1970s it seemed to fail at policing as well. Second, the relatively clear-cut organizing principles of the earlier reform-Progressive period were challenged by new concerns and practices, including the growing importance of efforts to achieve equal employment opportunity and the development of widespread collective bargaining throughout most of the civil service. For instance, merit examinations, such as the Federal Service Entrance Examination and, later, the Professional and Administrative Careers Examination, had a disparate (and harsh) impact on the employment interests of African Americans and Hispanics. The pronounced managerial authority that was partly a legacy of scientific management, and position-classification practices, reduced the scope of bargaining available to unionized federal civil servants. Third, President Jimmy Carter strongly believed that the federal bureaucracy was bloated, inefficient, and badly in need of reform.

Provisions of the 1978 reform act. The Civil Service Reform Act included the following changes:

1. The Civil Service Commission was abolished. Its legal successor is the MERIT SYSTEMS PROTECTION BOARD (MSPB). The board consists of a chairperson and two members, appointed to seven-year terms by the President with the advice and consent of the Senate. No more than two of these appointees may be of the same political party. The MSPB is considered the watchdog of the merit system. It is responsible for ensuring that merit principles, laws, and regulations are not violated. It hears employee appeals of adverse actions, such as dismissals and demotions, and has specific authority to protect WHISTLE-BLOWERS, who expose waste, fraud, abuse, or gross mismanagement, against reprisals. Adjudicatory decisions by the MSPB can be appealed to the Court of Appeals for the Federal Circuit, which has upheld its decisions in about 90 percent of the cases. The MSPB also has responsibility for conducting special studies of aspects of federal personnel administration.

2. A Special Counsel was established, which was initially attached to the MSPB, appointed to a five-year term by the President with the advice and consent of the Senate. The Special Counsel is now an independent entity responsible for investigating allegations of violations of personnel laws, rules, and regulations. The Special Counsel can bring cases before the MSPB for adjudication. It reports suspected criminal violations to the Attorney General.

3. An OFFICE OF PERSONNEL MANAGEMENT (OPM) was created to take over most of the Civil Service Commission's managerial functions. It is headed by a director, appointed to a four-year term by the President with the advice and consent of the Senate. OPM is considered the President's arm for personnel management and is more directly responsible to him than was the commission. Its responsibilities include operating the retirement system, training, position classification, examining, and developing and overseeing merit pay procedures for upper-level federal managers.

4. The act included a section on labor-management relations (Title VII), which placed labor relations affecting most of the civil service on a comprehensive statutory basis for the first time. Title VII establishes a Federal Labor Relations Authority (FLRA), consisting of a chair and two members appointed by the President with the advice and consent of the Senate for five-year overlapping terms. No more than two appointees to the authority may be of the same political

party. The FLRA has general responsibility for oversight of the federal labor-relations program, including employee representational matters, determination of bargaining units, grievances, unfair labor practices, and definition of the scope of bargaining. Title VII provides for a relatively narrow scope of bargaining, which does not include pay and many personnel matters such as hiring, promotion, and position classification. A Federal Service Impasses Panel works under the authority's general direction in trying to aid employee organizations and management to resolve disputes. Title VII does not cover the Postal Service and several smaller agencies, including the General Accounting Office, the FEDERAL BUREAU OF INVESTIGATION (FBI), the CENTRAL INTELLIGENCE AGENCY (CIA), and the Tennessee Valley Authority (TVA). FLRA relies overwhelmingly on adjudication, as opposed to rule making, in carrying out its mission. Its decisions can be appealed to the federal Circuit Courts of Appeals, in which it prevailed in less than half the cases brought from 1979 to 1987. The authority's failure to do better in court resulted from a number of factors ranging from the competence of its decision makers to the difficulty it, the agencies, unions, and courts have in interpreting Title VII.

5. A SENIOR EXECUTIVE SERVICE (SES) was created out of positions in grades GS 16 to 18 (previously called supergrades). The SES is predominantly comprised of top-level, career civil servants, though by law 10 percent of the positions in it may be filled with political appointees. The SES is a kind of higher civil service long thought desirable for the federal government. It reflects the beliefs that first, there is a body of skill or professionalism called public management that can be transferred from agency setting to agency setting; second, it is politically desirable for top federal managers to move among bureaus and agencies in order to develop a more comprehensive view of the public interest; and third, political executives need greater flexibility in assigning and directing top, career civil servants. The SES differs from most of the federal civil service in that rank is essentially vested in the person, not the position. Consequently, reassignments, transfers, and changes in the content of their jobs are not treated as promotions or demotions subject to complicated personnel rules or adverse-action procedures. However, involuntary transfers between agencies are prohibited. Members of the SES are eligible for bonuses and cash awards based on performance. They retain fallback rights to positions at the GS 15 level.

6. A minority recruitment program was established within OPM. Unlike earlier equal-opportunity measures, which were mostly based on EXECUTIVE OR-

DERS, the reform act included the policy that the federal work force should reflect the nation's diversity and be drawn from all segments of society. It established the principle that there should be no "underrepresentation" of minority groups in any category of federal employment. Although not part of the act, the Civil Service Commission's adjudicatory functions and some oversight authority for equal employment opportunity within the civil service were transferred to the Equal Employment Opportunity Commission in 1979.

7.   The Office of Personnel Management was given authority to suspend many personnel regulations in order to permit the development and implementation of personnel research and demonstration projects. These can involve up to five thousand employees and last up to five years.

8.   The civil service was to make greater use of performance-appraisal systems and merit pay. The latter was for those in management positions in GS 13 to 15 (subsequently labeled "GM" positions). These provisions reflected the belief that the civil-service system was inadequate at motivating employees and punishing them for poor performance. Both performance appraisal and merit pay have been difficult to implement, however, and they have undergone almost continual revision.

Issues of Concern. The civil service has always been a matter of political concern. With some three million federal civil servants and approximately fourteen million state and local government employees in the 1990s, the size and cost of the civil service are constant issues. Efforts to control taxes and budget deficits often focus on reducing the size of the civil service and making it operate more efficiently. One leading strategy for so doing has been to "privatize" civil-service functions by contracting them out to private firms. Reducing government functions, either through DE-REGULATION or some other means, is a complementary approach.

The appropriate roles for legislatures, elected executives, and courts in regulating or directing the civil service is also an issue. In exercising its clear constitutional authority to oversee the executive branch, Congress can become deeply involved in civil-service decisions. When CONGRESSIONAL OVERSIGHT seems to be interference in legitimate agency decisions, it is often called micro-management. For instance, a member of Congress, chairing a committee or subcommittee of strategic importance to an agency, may try to convince the agency to relocate many of its employees to his or her district.

The President can also seem to overstep the legiti-

mate bounds of his authority over the civil service. For example, during the first administration of Ronald Reagan, there were well-publicized cases of members of the SES being involuntarily transferred geographically for political rather than administrative purposes. The number of political appointees within the executive branch also increased, and it was alleged that they were taking on functions that had previously been exercised by career civil servants.

Judicial decisions have had a major impact on civil-service examinations, hiring procedures, and dismissals. The courts have held that where civil-service rules provide job protection to civil servants they have a "property interest" in their jobs that is protected by constitutional due process, for example, *Cleveland Board of Education v. Loudermill* (1985). Examinations, hiring processes, and promotions are currently regulated by court decisions interpreting not only a variety of statutes but also the Constitution's equal-protection clause, for example, *United States v. Paradise* (1987).

Finally, the overall quality of the civil service has become an issue in the last few years. According to the National Commission on the Public Service (called the Volcker Commission, after its chair, Paul Volcker), the federal civil service is in need of "rebuilding." The main concern has been that after years of criticism by politicians and the press, low pay increases, limited training opportunities, and inability to recruit the talent it requires, the civil service has lost the capacity to serve the public interest as well as it should. Similar concerns, however, have often developed in the past. As a result, the civil service is almost always undergoing a variety of incremental reforms and has been subject to major reorganizations when these prove insufficient.

BIBLIOGRAPHY

Ingraham, Patricia, and David H. Rosenbloom. *The Promise and Paradox of Civil Service Reform*. 1992.

Mosher, Frederick. *Democracy and the Public Service*. 2d ed. 1982.

Shafritz, Jay, Norma Riccucci, David H. Rosenbloom, and Albert Hyde. *Personnel Management in Government*. 4th ed. 1992.

Skowronek, Stephen. *Building a New American State*. 1982.

Van Riper, Paul. *History of the United States Civil Service*. 1958.

DAVID H. ROSENBLOOM

CIVIL SERVICE ACT (1883). The Civil Service Act (22 Stat. 403), also known as the Pendleton Act, provided the legal foundation for much federal personnel administration until it was superseded by the CIVIL SERVICE REFORM ACT OF 1978. The 1883 act was largely the product of the CIVIL-SERVICE REFORM movement, which became an important political force in the 1870s and continued to exert influence until the 1890s, when it merged with the more comprehensive Progressive movement. The act was intended to depoliticize the federal CIVIL SERVICE and to promote efficiency.

The act created a Civil Service Commission in the executive branch to make rules for federal personnel administration, administer some aspects of the personnel system, and oversee the personnel activities of other federal agencies. The commission consisted of three commissioners, appointed by the President with the ADVICE AND CONSENT of the Senate. No more than two of them could be members of the same political party. In 1956 the commissioners were given six-year overlapping terms but remained subject to dismissal by the President.

The act required the commission to make rules for several specific objectives. The first was "for open, competitive examinations for testing the fitness of applicants" for positions in the "classified" federal civil service. At the time of its enactment, only about 10 percent of the approximately one hundred thousand federal positions were classified. (By 1932, the proportion reached about 80 percent, and in the 1990s it was close to 90 percent.) The examinations were to be practical, and entrance into the federal civil service through them could be at any rank, not just the bottom. Selection was to be from among those who scored highest on the examinations. In practice, for most positions, selection was made from among the top three scorers, under what is known as the rule of three.

The act also required rules to prevent partisan dismissals and partisan coercion to render services or contributions. An additional required rule was to provide for a system by which "appointments to the public service . . . in the departments at Washington shall be apportioned among the several States and Territories and the District of Columbia upon the basis of population" according to the latest census. Aside from the prohibition of partisan dismissals, the act did not regulate removals from the federal service. The prevailing theory was that if hiring officials could not choose replacements, they would have no incentive to fire and replace competent employees on a partisan basis. Moreover, it was recognized that elaborate procedural protections for employees could impede efficiency. Violations of the act were punishable by removal from office, three years imprisonment, and/or a $5,000 fine. Its constitutionality was upheld in *Butler v. White* (1897).

The Civil Service Act proved very durable. It provided the basis for systems of comprehensive merit examinations and the classification of positions. Ordinary civil servants were effectively shielded from political coercion or manipulation, and as time went on, the civil service became increasingly professional. The act was superseded after nearly a century, however, because the commission was never able to move comfortably beyond being a policing agency, and it was eventually viewed as a barrier to effective, modern, decentralized personnel practices. Also the merit system promoted by the commission created and maintained barriers to equal employment opportunity in the federal civil service. Furthermore, in the mid 1970s it became known that the commission had capitulated to pressures from the Nixon administration to give favorable treatment to some politically connected applicants.

BIBLIOGRAPHY

Rosenbloom, David H. *Federal Service and the Constitution.* 1971.
Skowronek, Stephen. *Building a New American State.* 1982.
Van Riper, Paul. *History of the United States Civil Service.* 1958.
White, Leonard. *The Republican Era.* 1958.

DAVID H. ROSENBLOOM

CIVIL-SERVICE REFORM. Federal personnel policy, like most American public policy, is the product of a long, incremental development process. From the passage of the CIVIL SERVICE ACT of 1883 (Pendleton Act), nearly one hundred years elapsed before a systematic analysis of personnel policies was undertaken. During that time, a complex system of laws, procedures, and regulations—as well as a "personnel manual" nearly six thousand pages long—had accumulated around the federal CIVIL SERVICE. President Jimmy Carter, who had declared during his election campaign that there was "no merit in the merit system," gave civil-service reform high priority on his domestic policy agenda. Despite his deep dissatisfaction with the "Giant Washington Marshmallow," as he called the permanent bureaucracy, Carter was convinced that comprehensive reform could make a difference. The CIVIL SERVICE REFORM ACT (1978) was the outcome of that conviction.

Background. From the 1960s, when the federal government created civil rights programs, new educational opportunities, new housing opportunities, jobtraining and employment programs, and health-care initiatives for the elderly and the poor, the federal bureaucracy became more visible and more critical to the well-being of ever larger numbers of citizens. This growth in the scope and size of government occurred in a bureaucratic system generally considered competent and relatively expert. In the 1970s, however, there was a marked deterioration in this assessment. This change was attributable to a number of factors: declining economic conditions, a growing awareness that the programs of the GREAT SOCIETY and the War on Poverty had not achieved their aims, the WATERGATE AFFAIR, and the VIETNAM WAR all contributed to a perceptible malaise and disenchantment with government and its employees. Virtually every President during the twentieth century had expressed dissatisfaction with the career bureaucracy. In fact, commissions had been appointed to examine the organization and effectiveness of the executive branch on an average of every seven years since 1900. For example, Franklin D. Roosevelt had appointed the BROWNLOW COMMITTEE; Harry S. Truman had approved the first of the HOOVER COMMISSIONS; and Richard M. Nixon had appointed the ASH COUNCIL. Carter, however, was the first President to make civil service reform central to his domestic legislative concerns. In his campaign speeches, he argued that "there is no inherent conflict between careful planning [and] tight management, . . . on the one hand, and compassionate concern for the plight of the deprived and the afflicted, on the other. Waste and inefficiency never fed a hungry child, provided a job for a willing worker, or educated a deserving student." In Carter's 1978 State of the Union message, he declared civil-service reform to be "absolutely vital."

Carter's initiative actually began during the presidential campaign, when he enlisted Jule Sugarman, a noted policy expert, to begin the difficult task of organizing the problem assessment and a set of possible policy options. Sugarman was joined by Alan Campbell, dean of the Maxwell School of Citizen and Public Affairs at Syracuse University, who became director of the Civil Service Commission. Almost immediately upon election, Carter created the Personnel Management Project (PMP) as one part of his larger reorganization effort. The PMP, while technically centered at the Civil Service Commission, was a joint effort of that organization and the OFFICE OF MANAGEMENT AND BUDGET (OMB). The PMP was divided into nine task forces and was supported by a staff of more than one hundred. Carter's charge to the PMP was summarized in his 1978 State of the Union message: to create a "government that is efficient, open, and truly worthy of our people's understanding and respect." The PMP produced a three-volume final report detailing the complex problems of the federal personnel system and proposing comprehensive reforms. These proposals were translated into the Civil Service Reform Act of 1978 (CSRA) and Reorganization Plan Number 2. Both were submitted to Congress early in 1978.

The Legislation. Reorganization Plan Number 2 proposed to abolish the Civil Service Commission if neither house of Congress disapproved the provisions of the plan within sixty days; when neither house took action, the Commission was abolished. According to the provisions of the CSRA, it was replaced with the OFFICE OF PERSONNEL MANAGEMENT (OPM), the MERIT SYSTEMS PROTECTION BOARD (MSPB), and the Federal Labor Relations Authority (FLRA). OPM was made responsible for human-resources management and planning and the MSPB for hearing appeals and for basic protection of the merit system. Within the MSPB, the Office of Special Council (OSC) was responsible for investigating federal employees' claims of abuse and for protecting WHISTLE-BLOWERS. The FLRA was given a statutory mandate—for the first time in federal personnel history—to govern federal labor-management activities and procedures.

Other, equally dramatic components of the legislation included the following:

First, creation of the SENIOR EXECUTIVE SERVICE (SES). Since the 1950s, there had been recurring calls for the creation of an elite cadre of higher civil servants, modeled after the British system. The SES was intended to create that cadre of mobile, flexible, policy-oriented managers. The SES was open to the highest echelons of the career service; 10 percent of the total number of SES members could be political appointees. Members entered through individual contracts that, while enabling managers to compete for financial awards and bonuses, also removed some of their traditional protections under the civil service system. SES members were also eligible for additional training and development opportunities.

Second, performance appraisal and merit pay. The CSRA provided that, beginning in 1981, mid-level managers would receive merit bonuses based on their performance appraisal. The system was designed to be revenue-neutral; all funding for merit pay would come from a "pot" created by pooling a unit's annual within step increases. Merit bonuses would be added to employees' base pay.

Third, abolition of veterans' preference. Since the creation of the federal civil service, there had been provisions giving preference to veterans of the armed forces in civil service hiring. This was generally accomplished by adding a certain number of points to the civil service examination score received by the veteran (until 1955 it was not even necessary for the veteran to pass the test to have the points added). The CSRA proposed to abolish this system.

Fourth, protection of whistle-blowers. Carter and others were convinced that much of the inefficiency of government could be attributed to what Carter called "dead wood"—employees who did not give their best, try their hardest, or spend public funds as carefully as possible. Because such behavior is difficult to uncover from outside an organization, Carter and the legislation's framers placed a premium on obtaining information from employees willing to "blow the whistle" on behavior that they believed contributed to waste, fraud, or abuse of public resources. To protect those who took such action, the CSRA created the Office of Special Counsel in the Merit Systems Protection Board; the legislation further specified that whistle-blowers be protected from reprisal for "providing lawful information."

Fifth, creation of research and demonstration authority. To encourage innovation and creativity in federal personnel management practices, the CSRA gave the Office of Personnel Management research and development authority to allow it to conduct demonstration projects aimed at testing and evaluating new techniques.

Legislative History and Outcomes. Despite Carter's strong support and an intensive national lobbying effort led by Alan Campbell, it was difficult to focus congressional attention on the proposed personnel reforms. Campbell characterized support for the reforms as "a mile wide and an inch deep". Most congressional and interest-group attention focused on the veterans' preference and labor relations provisions; unsurprisingly, the language eliminating veterans' preference was deleted from the legislation. This action was largely due to opposition in the House of Representatives; the Senate voted to limit preference by abolishing job preference for retired military officers.

The House also proposed that the Senior Executive Service be limited to a two-year experiment in three agencies rather than a permanent, across-the-board reform. There was substantial concern that the SES provisions would allow for politicization of the career service, and memories of Nixon-administration abuses of merit were fresh in the minds of many members of Congress. Liberalization of the HATCH ACT (1939) which prohibits political activity by members of the civil service, also became an issue. The House also added an AFFIRMATIVE ACTION component to the CSRA, which was intended to encourage the recruitment of minorities and women into the federal service. The intensity of the debate around these disagreements between the Carter administration and the House necessitated bringing the legislation to the full House

twice before action could be taken; Carter himself lobbied strongly for his reform package during this period.

Most components of the Carter reform proposals remained intact. Employee protections against abuse were strengthened slightly, a five-year sunset provision was added to the SES, and the term of the director of the OPM was set at four years, not necessarily coterminous with presidential elections. The final bill was approved by Congress and signed by the President in October 1978, about seven months after its introduction. It was heralded by the press as Carter's most impressive political victory.

The Reality of Reform. Despite its careful planning and consistent presidential support, the Civil Service Reform Act had a rocky implementation history; few of its impacts were as predicted. This was due in part to the design of the reform. In an effort to be comprehensive, legislators included provisions that were not internally consistent or that conflicted with other provisions of the reform. The performance appraisal and merit pay provisions were confounded from the beginning by provisions that forced them to be revenue-neutral. Congress, for its part, was actually more interested in the CSRA after its passage than during its consideration. Six months into the act's implementation, for example, Congress cut by half the number of members of the SES eligible for annual bonuses in each agency. Of equal significance, the act fell victim to the enormous turbulence of the 1980 presidential election and to the budget and staff cuts that followed the inauguration of Ronald Reagan.

Most evaluations of the Carter reforms indicate that their success has been limited. The provisions most often termed troublesome are those related to the SES and those creating performance appraisal and merit pay. Early evaluations of the SES chronicled a demoralized group rather than the spirited elite cadre envisioned by the designers of the reform. Many members of the SES left government service during its first five years; the largest bonuses available to its members were not widely awarded during its first decade. From the mid to late 1980s on, however, there was evidence that the experience of the SES was becoming more positive.

Merit pay, the other reform provision directly targeted at improving the efficiency and productivity of the career civil service, also had an unstable history. Although it was not implemented until 1981, the provisions of the program were changed by Congress in 1984, when the Performance Monitoring and Review System (PMRS) replaced merit pay. PMRS, too, had its share of difficulties. For instance, virtually all employees received high performance appraisals, and there were problems in establishing a clear link between the performance appraisal process and financial bonuses. In addition, financial awards were frequently perceived as too small to serve a motivational purpose. Evaluations performed after the first decade of experience with pay-for-performance in the federal government found that a majority of employees and managers believed that the reforms had not improved the operations of government.

These, of course, are the technical, personnel-oriented outcomes of the reform effort. From a presidential perspective, the reform had other objectives. In that sense, Carter's Civil Service Reform Act is but one part of a long and complex reform cycle. Particularly since Franklin D. Roosevelt's NEW DEAL, the relationship between the President and the permanent bureaucracy has been a consistent target of reform efforts. Roosevelt's Brownlow Committee set the stage for this debate when it noted that "good" administration was closely linked to strong presidential direction and management of the executive branch. Brownlow's unequivocal statement of positive presidential management and control was historic; it recast the relationships between the President, Congress, and the bureaucracy. It did not, however, settle the debate. The fundamental question of bureaucratic responsiveness and accountability has recurred in every subsequent administration.

Carter's approach to civil service reform was unusual, therefore, in that it comprehensively addressed some critical personnel-management problems. It was not unusual in that it combined structural and political-responsiveness objectives with these more technical reforms. That pattern had been proposed, and generally followed, since the first Hoover Commission, during the Truman presidency. The Nixon presidency, however, had provided the most immediate models for Carter's reforms. Nixon's proposals for reorganization were extensive and dramatic. His strategic use of political appointees as policy managers was unprecedented in the modern presidency. The Carter reforms and political management strategy built on all these lessons.

A decade's experience with the Civil Service Reform Act and related initiatives demonstrated, however, not only that the quest for solutions to the bureaucratic-accountability conundrum was far from over, but also how modestly even comprehensive civil service reform efforts address the central question regarding the proper role of public bureaucratic institutions in a complex democratic society.

BIBLIOGRAPHY

Arnold, Peri. *Making the Managerial Presidency*. 1986.
Campbell, Alan K. "Civil Service Reform as a Remedy for Bureaucratic Ills." In *Making Bureaucracies Work*. Edited by Carol Weiss and Alan Barton. 1980.
Ingraham, Patricia W. and David H. Rosenbloom, editors. *The Promise & Paradox of Bureaucratic Reform*. 1992.
March, James, and Johan Olson. "Organizing Political Life: What Administrative Reorganization Tells Us about Government." *American Political Science Review* 77 (December 1983): 281–296.
Moe, Ronald C. "Traditional Organizational Principles and the Managerial Presidency: From Phoenix to Ash." *Public Administration Review* 50 (1990): 129–140.

PATRICIA W. INGRAHAM

CIVIL SERVICE REFORM ACT (1978). The federal personnel merit system was created in 1883 by the CIVIL SERVICE ACT (Pendleton Act). At the time of its passage, that law covered only 10 percent of federal employees; its purview grew incrementally for nearly a century before federal CIVIL SERVICE issues were again targeted for serious presidential and congressional attention. Jimmy Carter was the only President in the twentieth century to give top priority to personnel reform. The product of this unprecedented presidential effort was the Civil Service Reform Act (CSRA) passed in 1978.

To prepare the legislation, Carter created the Personnel Management Project (PMP), charging it with comprehensively examining, and recommending solutions to, the problems of the federal civil service. The PMP prepared the reports that formed the basis of the legislation, which was sent to Congress in three parts: the Civil Service Reform Act itself, Reorganization Plan Number 2, and an additional title, Title VII, to the CSRA. Reorganization Plan Number 2 abolished the Civil Service Commission, replacing it with the OFFICE OF PERSONNEL MANAGEMENT (OPM), the MERIT SYSTEMS PROTECTION BOARD (MSPB), and the Federal Labor Relations Authority (FLRA). Title VII contained the labor-management provisions of the reform. The package contained provisions creating the SENIOR EXECUTIVE SERVICE (SES), providing a merit pay system for mid-level managers, protecting WHISTLE-BLOWERS, emphasizing research and development in personnel systems, and abolishing veterans' preference. Both the SES and the merit-pay titles introduced financial bonuses based on individual performance. The package also restated support for AFFIRMATIVE ACTION and codified federal labor-management relations.

Congressional consideration was speedy; the CSRA was passed six months after introduction (the provision to abolish veterans' preference was, however, removed) and was signed into law in October 1978. Implementation was swift, but so too was congressional alteration of the original package. Within the first year, Congress and the OPM had cut the number of SES members eligible for annual bonuses by more than half. Budget and staff cuts under the administration of Ronald Reagan created an environment that overwhelmed reform efforts. SES members, who had relinquished many civil-service protections and who were the most senior managers in the career civil service, were the target of "bureaucrat bashing" during the Reagan years, leading to a decline in morale; many left government service during this period.

Other difficulties encountered by the reform package included a delay of several years in the full funding of the Office of Special Counsel (OSC), the arm of the MSPB responsible for protecting whistle-blowers. After 1986, however, efforts were made to improve the operation of the SES. Difficulties in recruiting and retaining qualified personnel—particularly scientific and technical personnel—led to new efforts to make government service more attractive.

By the early 1990s the CSRA had shown itself to be neither a complete success nor a flat-out failure. The reform did demonstrate, however, that presidential interest and support are essential to bring about change in the civil-service system that so profoundly affects the quality of government.

BIBLIOGRAPHY

Ingraham, Patricia W., and David Rosenbloom, editors. *The Promise and Paradox of Bureaucratic Reform.* 1992.

U.S. Merit Systems Protection Board. *Federal Personnel Management since Civil Service Reform: A Survey of Federal Personnel Officials.* 1989.

U.S. Merit Systems Protection Board. *Significant Actions of the Office of Personnel Management.* Published annually.

PATRICIA W. INGRAHAM

CIVIL WAR. The Civil War was the greatest crisis in the history of the United States. The existence of the nation, imperiled by SECESSION, was not assured until a bloody conflict had claimed more lives than all other American wars—before and after—combined. Massive changes accompanied this struggle, including the destruction of SLAVERY and increased federal expenditure that soared, by 1865, to more than 26 percent of the gross national product. Over the course of the war, federal spending amounted to five times the total expenditure of the central government from its creation to 1861.

A crisis of such magnitude inevitably had a significant impact on the American presidency. Some of the war's effects on the institution of the presidency took place during the conflict and occasioned immediate and passionate debate. Others followed in the train of the enormous alterations brought about by the war. Still others were long-range and of a more subtle nature; these related to citizens' conceptions of the nation and the President's role in American life. Unquestionably, however, all tended to increase the power and importance of the presidency in the nation's system of government.

Executive Authority. One of the first—and most hotly debated—effects on the American presidency was a sharp increase in executive authority. Facing a pressing emergency, President Abraham Lincoln felt compelled to take action to preserve the government. Circumstances required that he proceed on his own authority, since Congress was not in session during the first weeks of his administration. One of his first steps, after calling for troops to suppress the rebellion, was to order a major shipbuilding program, which subsequently won the approval of Congress. More urgent still was the need to secure Maryland to the Union.

With Virginia facing Washington, D.C., on one side, it was vitally important that Maryland, which enclosed the capital on the other three sides, not secede. Yet secession sentiment was strong there, and troops from Massachusetts who passed through Baltimore on 19 April 1861 encountered mob violence. Prosecessionists in Maryland then destroyed railroad bridges and severed telegraph lines leading from Washington through their state. For a number of days anxious residents of the nation's capital were cut off from the Union and expected attack. On 22 April President Lincoln authorized General WINFIELD SCOTT and others to suspend the writ of habeas corpus in the area along the railroad line between Washington and Philadelphia, and on 27 April he suspended the writ in other portions of Maryland as well [*see* HABEAS CORPUS, SUSPENSION OF]. Arrests of suspected Confederate sympathizers in Maryland began. These continued until, in September, Lincoln had federal troops seize thirty-one secessionist members of the state legislature and other officials, who were detained until new elections in November put the state safely on the Union side.

Lincoln's strong action promptly encountered a high-level challenge when one of the arrested citizens, John Merryman, sought a writ of habeas corpus from the federal circuit court in Baltimore. Roger Taney, the Chief Justice of the United States Supreme Court, was also the presiding judge of that circuit court, and on 28 May 1861 he issued a ruling [*see* MERRYMAN, EX PARTE] that denied the President's power to suspend the writ. Arguing that the constitutional provision authorizing suspension appears in the article concerned with Congress's powers, Taney declared that only Congress could exercise such power, and he denounced the arrest and detention of citizens by army officers.

Unmoved, Lincoln refused to obey Taney's ruling. Constitutional lawyers supporting the President argued that suspension was an emergency measure and had to be exercised by the President during rebellion, especially when Congress was not in session. "Are all the laws, *but one*," Lincoln asked, "to go unexecuted, and the government itself go to pieces, lest that one be violated?" [emphasis in original]. With troops at his command, the President enforced his decision and met criticism with the assertion that his duty was to preserve the government.

Military arrests of disloyal elements or suspected traitors continued and spread over a wider area. Late in 1862, Lincoln denied the privilege of habeas corpus to all persons imprisoned under military order, and in 1863 Congress passed a suspension of the writ throughout the Union when state courts obstructed the new conscription law. Eventually the federal army arrested and imprisoned without charge at least fifteen thousand civilians. Hundreds of others stood trial in military courts.

Most of these arrests occurred in the border slave states or in occupied portions of the Confederacy and bore a close relation to actual military activities, but some individuals were arrested for speaking their minds in secure areas, such as Indiana. Military courts there delivered two notable convictions for treason. Clement L. Vallandigham, a Democratic candidate for governor, was banished to the Confederacy by President Lincoln, who wisely commuted his sentence of imprisonment for the duration of the war and chose to avoid making him a martyr. Another civilian, Lambdin P. Milligan, challenged his conviction through legal channels. After the war the Supreme Court overturned the ruling against Milligan [see MILLIGAN, EX PARTE] and declared that civilians cannot be tried by the military in areas where the regular civil courts are functioning.

Northern Democrats attacked Lincoln with bitter ferocity for his assaults on CIVIL LIBERTIES and strong use of executive authority. They charged that he was violating "the rights of the States and the liberties of the citizen" and "establishing a despotism." Branding the President a "TYRANT," they asserted that instead of preserving the Union he was attempting "to destroy free institutions in the North." Lincoln replied that the nation faced spies and informers for a "giant rebellion" who used appeals to constitutional liberties as a cover for their activities. He emphasized that he had to protect the army, which was keeping the nation alive. In an effective formulation of his dilemma, Lincoln also asked, "Must I shoot a simpleminded soldier boy who deserts, while I must not touch a hair of a wily agitator who induces him to desert?"

Vociferous criticism also greeted the EMANCIPATION PROCLAMATION, which was an unprecedented exercise of the President's powers as COMMANDER IN CHIEF in time of war. Charles A. Beard called this proclamation "the most stupendous act of sequestration in the history of Anglo-Saxon jurisprudence," and once again, it was a step that Lincoln chose to take on his own authority. Facing aggressively racist attacks from his Democratic opponents and struggling to preserve as much support as possible in the loyal slaveholding states, Lincoln had largely ignored the confiscation acts passed by Congress. Instead of enforcing these new laws, he carefully shaped his own policy on slavery by acting through PROCLAMATIONS and administrative measures. When he presented a draft of the proclamation to his Cabinet, he invited its members to advise him only on the language of the proclamation, not on its wisdom or substance.

In the abstract, Lincoln's emancipation proclamation was not clear and decisive. Potential legal questions remained after its issuance, and to Southern representatives at the Hampton Roads conference Lincoln himself observed that the courts might be asked to judge who was and was not affected by his proclamation. But in practice, the Emancipation Proclamation effectively identified the Union with an antislavery policy on the world stage, and, in conjunction with the Thirteenth Amendment, ended slavery in the United States.

As Commander in Chief, Lincoln also exercised executive authority with a steady hand. Engulfed in a war of massive proportions, Lincoln had virtually no military experience to guide him; in fact, he made light of his brief and uneventful service as a young man in a frontier conflict called the Black Hawk War. Nevertheless, as President, Lincoln studied works on military strategy with care and penetration and did not hesitate to give advice to his generals in the field. The scope and destructive firepower of the war forced all involved to modify established doctrines and learn new lessons, and Lincoln learned faster than many experienced military men. Long before the end of the war his telegrams and dispatches to the field showed a firm grasp of the imperatives of modern warfare.

Moreover, Lincoln acted without timidity to establish the supremacy of a civilian President over military commanders. Until Ulysses S. Grant and William Tecumseh Sherman emerged in the latter half of the war, the ineffectiveness of Union generals often proved frustrating and distressing, and the Army of the Potomac was a special problem. Its first commander, the young, distinguished, and politically influential General GEORGE B. MCCLELLAN, was popular with his men but slow to move and unaggressive. McClellan habitually underestimated his strength and opportunities and overestimated the dangers he faced. Despite intense criticism and political pressure, Lincoln twice removed McClellan (who would become the Democratic Party's nominee for President in 1864), shelving him permanently in November 1862. Lincoln then proceeded to remove a series of other generals from command of the Army of the Potomac. Ultimately he found men who could get the job done, demonstrating in the process the authority of the President in time of war.

Party Leadership. Lincoln frequently faced criticism and attacks within his own party, and his skill in parrying these preserved the President's power as a PARTY LEADER and head of the executive branch. Soon after taking office, Lincoln discovered that WILLIAM H. SEWARD, whose prominence in the REPUBLICAN PARTY predated Lincoln's, was presuming to manage the crisis as Secretary of State. The President made it clear that he would be in charge and enjoyed Seward's loyal support thereafter. A series of challenges to Lincoln's leadership then ensued from ambitious and dissatisfied elements of his party. RADICAL REPUBLICANS, particularly, bemoaned the slow progress of the war and despaired over the conservatism of Lincoln's policies. They saw their champion within the Cabinet in the person of Secretary of the Treasury SALMON P. CHASE, who was indeed ambitious for the President's chair. Lincoln wanted to promote unity among the factions of his young party and retain the financial skills of his talented Secretary, although he was fully aware of the machinations against him. He bided his time until efforts to nominate Chase in 1864 had came to nought. Then Lincoln accepted one of the periodic resignations from the surprised Secretary of the Treasury and cemented his position as leader.

In his relations with Congress, Lincoln did not attempt to be a dominating force or control the legislative agenda. His bold uses of EXECUTIVE POWER tended to focus on military and emergency matters flowing from the wartime crisis. Following much of the theory and practice of the WHIG PARTY from which he had come, Lincoln allowed congressional leaders to order their own business and adopt their own goals for implementing the platform of the Republican Party.

The legislative results, nevertheless, dramatically strengthened national power. As a consequence, they enlarged the role and influence of the President, the government's chief executive officer.

With Southern representatives absent from Congress, the balance of power shifted, releasing a cascade of important economic legislation. So influential was this legislation that one historian has called Congress's wartime enactments a "blueprint for modern America." These included certain key items long advocated by Republicans, such as the Homestead Act and the MORRILL LAND GRANT ACT. Among significant economic measures were a higher tariff, which encouraged industrial growth, and loans and land grants to spur completion of a transcontinental railroad. The national banking act dramatically reshaped the nation's banking system and, along with a legal tender act, put the federal government in control of the nation's currency. The costs of war also required Congress to pass new taxes. The Internal Revenue Act brought a large number of new federal taxes, including a progressive income tax. By increasing the power of the federal government, these measures enhanced the role and potential influence of the President.

Protecting Liberty. The historian James McPherson has argued that, under the leadership of President Lincoln, the Civil War also effected a transformation in American ideas about the government's role in protecting liberty. The heritage of the American Revolution was a fear of central power and a determination to protect individual liberties against the government. The Bill of Rights embodied this negative conception of liberty precisely—liberty was freedom from the interference of outside authority, or in the words of John Stuart Mill, "protection against the tyranny of the political rulers." Under Abraham Lincoln's leadership, liberty acquired a positive conception. It became the freedom to realize one's rights over the resistance of previously existing laws or disabilities. He spoke of a "new birth of freedom," and through the intervention of the federal government four million slaves gained their liberty. McPherson thus joins earlier historians in seeing in the Civil War a second American Revolution, this time one of "positive liberty achieved by overwhelming power."

From the founding of the Republican Party, influential elements within it had seen a need for the national government to act as the guarantor of individual rights. In their view, the federal government had to protect individuals against the states, which had annulled the freedom of speech of antislavery spokesmen or attacked wholesale the rights of free Negroes. During the Civil War and RECONSTRUCTION, their conviction entered the Constitution in a series of amendments. Through the Thirteenth Amendment, the federal government destroyed slavery and Congress gained power to enforce the amendment. The Fourteenth Amendment directly and specifically placed the federal government in the position of defender of individual liberties against the states. Whereas eleven of the first twelve amendments to the Constitution restrained the national government, six of the next seven expanded its powers at the expense of the states.

After the crisis was over and the Union preserved, Americans exhibited a tendency to gravitate toward their traditional expectations of the central government and the presidency. Quite noticeable in public opinion, this trend was not as pronounced in fact. For one thing, the war had altered rather permanently the size of the federal government. Two decades after the fighting ended, interest on the war debt still accounted for about 40 percent of the central government's budget, and pensions for Union soldiers consumed another 20 percent. After wartime spending came to an end, federal expenditures stabilized at twice the prewar level, or about 4 percent of the gross national product. Thus the government to be administered by any President was larger than before. Moreover, its connections to the economy of the nation, and especially to industrial enterprise, were firmly established. The massive expansion of industry in subsequent years, and the rise of controversy over economic forces the government had helped to create, implied the possibility of a corresponding increase in the role of the President.

The constitutional revolution did not escape revision at the hands of a traditional Supreme Court and shifting public opinion. During Reconstruction President Ulysses S. Grant intervened extensively in the affairs of certain Southern states, but his actions proved ineffective either in protecting black citizens or maintaining the power of local Republican organizations. Soon Northern opinion turned against activist Reconstruction policies, while the Supreme Court reasserted older conceptions of liberty. In the *Slaughterhouse Cases* (1873), *United States v. Cruikshank* (1876), and other decisions, the Court rejected the idea of federal authority acting as a "censor" on the states and insisted that the duty of protecting a citizen's rights remained where it had originally been placed: with the states.

But this reversion proved temporary. Although nineteenth-century Supreme Court decisions largely eviscerated the wartime and Reconstruction-era amendments, the twentieth century has witnessed a sweeping restoration of their power to protect individual rights. The power of the President to function as an instrument of positive liberty and assert the rights of individuals revived at the same time. As the nation faced new problems arising from unprecedented aggregations of private economic power, voters in the Progressive and New Deal eras embraced the idea of positive liberty promoted by an activist President. Lincoln had established the precedent, and his fame and place in history helped to legitimate subsequent expansions of presidential authority.

Effects on the Presidency. In the long run the Civil War had other intangible but highly important effects on the presidency. Because the war involved competing definitions of the American nation, the North's victory over the Southern challenge to the Union ensured that there would be an expansion of national power. The Civil War marked America's transition from a loose federation of states to a nation. It settled the question whether the United States was an entity or a collection of parts. Though the immediate effects of this change were indefinite, they were certain in the long run to enhance the role of the President, especially in light of the economic integration of the country that was proceeding apace.

In assessing other long-range or subtle effects of the Civil War on the American presidency, one must reckon with the powerful influence of Lincoln's personality and historical image. Widely criticized while he was alive, Lincoln himself had often despaired of his chances of reelection in 1864. In fact, it seems likely that he would have gone down to defeat except for timely military victories, particularly Sherman's major breakthrough in Atlanta and Sheridan's cheering campaign in the Shenandoah valley. Even so, Lincoln's margin of victory in the popular vote would have been razor-thin without the absentee soldiers' vote, which went overwhelmingly in his favor. During his presidency he was less than a dominating political presence.

The Union victory, however, ensured Lincoln's reputation as a great President, and assassination, viewed by many as martyrdom, conferred on the fallen leader a special place in America's memory. While raising Lincoln to a special status, these events at the same time focused attention on his personal qualities. People remember Lincoln as much for his humility, ideals, and compassion as for his policies. Moreover, since he lived in an era before television his written words carried special weight, and thus Lincoln's undeniable genius as a writer has greatly magnified his influence. His speeches and letters—notably the Gettysburg Address, the Second Inaugural Address, and his letters to bereaved mothers—have touched the feelings of countless individuals and forged a special kind of bond between them and him.

Probably no President stands as high in the respect and admiration of the public as Abraham Lincoln, and through this intangible influence he has strengthened the office of President. Because Lincoln's image is that of a caring, trustworthy, and accessible leader, citizens look more readily to other Presidents to provide leadership through crises and challenges. Like Andrew Jackson, Theodore Roosevelt, or Franklin D. Roosevelt, Lincoln inspired confidence through his actions, but his character and martyrdom nurtured a tendency to respect the person who holds the highest office in the land. In this way Lincoln's personality added substance to the formal powers of the presidency.

BIBLIOGRAPHY

Curry, Leonard P. *Blueprint for Modern America: Non-military Legislation of the First Civil War Congress*. 1968.

Curtis, Michael Kent. *No State Shall Abridge: The Fourteenth Amendment and the Bill of Rights*. 1986.

Kaczorowski, Robert J. *The Politics of Judicial Interpretation: The Federal Courts, Department of Justice, and Civil Rights, 1866-1876*. 1985.

McPherson, James M. *Abraham Lincoln and the Second American Revolution*. 1990.

McPherson, James M. *Battle Cry of Freedom*. 1988.

Neely, Mark E. *The Fate of Liberty: Abraham Lincoln and Civil Liberties*. 1991.

Thomas, Benjamin P. *Abraham Lincoln*. 1952, 1968.

Wills, Garry. *Lincoln at Gettysburg: The Words that Remade America*. 1992.

PAUL D. ESCOTT

CLARK, RAMSEY (b. 1927), Attorney General. Ramsey Clark joined the Justice Department as Assistant Attorney General of the Lands Division in 1961. President Lyndon B. Johnson appointed him Deputy Attorney General in 1965, Acting Attorney General in 1966, and Attorney General in 1967, where he served until 1969. His father, Tom Clark, was a longtime friend of Johnson's and served on the Supreme Court.

Clark pursued an independent path while at the Justice Department. He did not consult the White House before filing cases and ended the weekly practice of informing the President about departmental plans. He and Johnson clashed most often on how to handle political protest. Johnson opposed both the massive peace march on the Pentagon during the VIETNAM WAR in October 1967 and the Poor People's Campaign, setting up a "Resurrection City" near the Lincoln Memorial in May 1968. Clark believed that constitutional rights of assembly and expression were involved. Over Clark's objections, Johnson sent federal troops to Chicago at Mayor Richard Daley's request to block demonstrations at the 1968 Democratic national convention. Clark believed the police were responsible for the ensuing violence and had proceedings initiated against nine policemen. He ignored demands by Johnson and Congress that he prosecute the demonstrators; his legal staff argued there were no grounds.

He and Johnson agreed on gun control, social programs to alleviate sources of crime, and particularly civil rights. As Attorney General, Clark initiated the first school desegregation case in the North and urged passage of the CIVIL RIGHTS ACT OF 1968, dealing with open housing.

In criminal law, Clark instituted rehabilitation programs in federal prisons and supported the Court's *Miranda v. Arizona* (1966) decision. He banned ELECTRONIC SURVEILLANCE, except in NATIONAL SECURITY investigations, and opposed the death penalty and preventive detention. For these views, he became the target of Richard M. Nixon in 1968, who ran on a law-and-order campaign. After leaving office, Clark continued to champion civil rights and liberties, often in unpopular causes.

BIBLIOGRAPHY

Clark, Ramsey. *Crime in America*. 1970.

Harris, Richard. *Justice: The Crisis of Law, Order, and Freedom in America*. 1970.

NANCY V. BAKER

CLARK AMENDMENT (1976). Sponsored by Senator Dick Clark (D-Iowa), the Clark Amendment became law in January 1976. It prohibited COVERT OPERATIONS, that is, secret intervention, by the CENTRAL INTELLIGENCE AGENCY (CIA) in the West African nation of Angola. The law is sometimes referred to as the Tunney Amendment, after Senator John Tunney (D-Cal.) a sponsor of comparable legislation wending its way through Congress at the same time.

In 1975, the administration of President Gerald R. Ford had secretly planned—without congressional debate or consent—to assist the pro-Western side in the Angolan civil war against a minority Marxist insurgency. The administration's objectives were twofold. First, the President hoped to stop the Soviet Union's already ongoing military assistance to the Marxist insurgents. The Soviets had earlier gained a toehold in Africa in Guinea and Somalia, and now Angola offered them valuable port facilities on the continent's Atlantic seaboard. The administration's second goal was to seek a negotiated settlement of internal differences in Angola, one that would place moderate groups in power. The ostensible intention was to throw the Soviets out of Angola, at which point the United States would depart, too.

A majority in both houses of Congress saw matters differently. For them, the President's authorization of covert action in Angola (which under the HUGHES-RYAN ACT of 1974 the President was required to report to Congress, though the law required no formal congressional approval of the action) held the danger of repeating the mistakes of the VIETNAM WAR, that is, of getting the United States involved in another unwinnable war in the developing world.

Elements within the administration itself also viewed the covert intervention as a mistake. The Assistant Secretary of State for Africa resigned in protest. This disarray within the executive branch contributed to the passage of the law. On 19 December 1975, the Senate voted 54 to 22 in favor of the amendment, and the House followed suit on 27 January 1976, by a vote of 323 to 99. The prohibition against CIA covert action in Angola stood until 1986, when Congress repealed the law.

BIBLIOGRAPHY

Franck, Thomas, M., and Edward Weisband. *Foreign Policy by Congress.* 1979.
Johnson, Loch K. *American's Secret Power: The CIA in a Democratic Society.* 1989.
Weissman, Stephen R. "CIA Covert Action in Zaire and Angola: Patterns and Consequences." *Political Science Quarterly* 94 (1979): 263–286.

LOCH K. JOHNSON

CLASSIFIED INFORMATION. Classified information encompasses a massive and continually growing amount of official secrets of the federal government. The classification system is designed to prevent the unauthorized disclosure of information that could cause damage to NATIONAL SECURITY, broadly defined as the national defense and foreign relations of the United States. The contemporary system began in WORLD WAR II and expanded during the COLD WAR. Throughout much of the Reagan administration, the number of classification actions escalated dramatically. As of 1991, there were approximately seven million classification actions annually.

Secrecy in American History. The system has been dominated by the executive branch through a succession of EXECUTIVE ORDERS. Ronald Reagan's 1982 Executive Order 12356 governs the system. In addition, a number of public laws support it both directly—by requiring protection for specific types of information and by funding the system—and indirectly, by providing penalties for espionage and related crimes. The inherent tension between official secrecy and democratic values, along with problems in the classification system itself, has resulted in major conflicts between the government and the press, among others, and between the executive and legislature. With the end of the cold war, efforts to reduce the amount of classified information and change the system emerged in the executive, Congress, and the public.

Official secrecy has existed throughout the history of the United States. Presidents and other executive officials, particularly with regard to military matters and foreign diplomacy, have controlled access to national defense and foreign relations information based on constitutional authority, custom and experience, and perceived practical necessity. In discussing the President's power to negotiate treaties, for instance, JOHN JAY wrote in FEDERALIST 64 that "So often and so essentially have we heretofore suffered from the want of secrecy and dispatch that the Constitution would have been inexcusably defective if no attention had been paid to those objectives."

The INHERENT POWER of the President to classify information for national security purposes was affirmed by the Supreme Court in 1988: "The President, after all, is the 'COMMANDER IN CHIEF of the Army and Navy of the United States'. . . . His authority to classify and control access to information bearing on national security . . . flows primarily from this constitutional investment of power in the President and exists quite apart from any explicit congressional grant" (*U.S. Navy v. Egan*).

The contemporary system for controlling national security information, which began with Franklin Roosevelt during World War II, is more formalized and institutionalized than its predecessors. It was established and revised by executive orders issued by Presidents: Franklin D. Roosevelt (E.O. 8381 in 1940); Harry S. Truman (E.O. 10104 in 1950 and E.O. 10290 in 1951); Dwight D. Eisenhower (E.O. 10501 in 1953); Richard M. Nixon (E.O. 11652 in 1972); Jimmy Carter (E.O. 12065 in 1978); and Ronald Reagan (E.O. 12356 in 1982). The Bush and Clinton administrations also considered a revision but, as of mid 1992, had not issued a new order. These actual and contemplated revisions reflect differences in the Presidents' philosophies with regard to official secrecy, changes in the international environment, fluctuations in PRESIDENTIAL-CONGRESSIONAL RELATIONS, and competing pressures in the domestic arena coming from government agencies and private organizations.

Agencies and Categories. In addition to the executive controls, the classification system relies upon various public laws that require the protection of certain types of information, such as "restricted data," referring to NUCLEAR WEAPONS and special nuclear material (42 U.S.C. 2161–2169 and 2274). The NATIONAL SECURITY ACT of 1947, which created the CENTRAL INTELLIGENCE AGENCY, moreover, requires the Director of the CIA to protect "intelligence sources and methods from unauthorized disclosure" (50 U.S.C. 403(d)(3)). The FREEDOM OF INFORMATION ACT (FOIA) also lends support to the system, by recognizing an exemption for matters that are "to be kept secret in the interest of national defense or foreign policy" and are properly classified (5 U.S.C. 552(b)). The operational files of the CIA, furthermore, may also be exempted from FOIA by the CIA Director (50 U.S.C. 431).

Other statutes reinforce the system indirectly, by setting requirements and penalties related to the unauthorized disclosure of classified information. These are found in laws dealing with the theft of government property, espionage, and other unauthorized disclosures (e.g., 18 U.S.C. 792–799). Incidentally, although Congress is frequently blamed for leaks to the press and inadvertent disclosures of classified information, the overwhelming majority of them, according to studies, are attributable to the executive branch, particularly high-ranking personnel.

The information security system is presently implemented by about eighty federal agencies that classify and handle national security information. Based on fiscal year 1991 data, original classification—that is, an initial determination that the information requires protection—accounts for only about 7 percent of the 7.1 million classification actions, while derivative classification, which results in a new form of classified information based on original classified materials, for nearly 93 percent. Nearly all the classified information is generated by four agencies, led by the DEPARTMENT OF DEFENSE, which, in fiscal year 1991, accounted for 61 percent (higher than the previous year's 50 percent because of the PERSIAN GULF WAR). The Department of Defense was followed by the Central Intelligence Agency, accounting for 26 percent; the JUSTICE DEPARTMENT, 9 percent; and the STATE DEPARTMENT, 3 percent. Other organizations and entities which handle classified information range from the NATIONAL SECURITY COUNCIL (NSC) to the PEACE CORPS, from the Office of National Drug Control Policy to the Marine Mammal Commission, and from the DEPARTMENT OF ENERGY, which is responsible for the development of nuclear weapons, to the DEPARTMENT OF EDUCATION. All follow classification and declassification directives from the INFORMATION SECURITY OVERSIGHT OFFICE (ISOO). ISOO, in turn, receives its policy and program direction from the NSC, a part of the EXECUTIVE OFFICE OF THE PRESIDENT.

National security information is to be controlled and safeguarded at three successively higher levels under E.O. 12356: "confidential" covers information whose unauthorized disclosure could cause damage to the national security; "secret," if it could cause serious damage to the national security; and "top secret," if it could cause exceptionally grave damage to the national security. Of the 7.1 million classification actions in fiscal year 1991, "confidential" accounted for 20 percent, "secret" for 73 percent, and "top secret" for 7 percent.

Specialized categories of classified information also exist. One of the most important is sensitive compartmented information (SCI), which covers intelligence sources and methods and is governed by a directive from the Director of the CIA. Another separate category encompasses special access programs (SAPs), which refer to military programs and weapons systems and collectively account for an estimated 24 percent of the military budget. Within SAPs are "black" programs, regarded as so sensitive that their very existence and purpose are classified.

Individual access to classified information is controlled by two basic means: First, the appropriate security clearance (or clearances for special categories, such as SCI) determines eligibility to a level and category of information; second, the need-to-know principle governs immediate access to specific information for individuals with the appropriate clearance; they are to demonstrate a legitimate need to know the information.

Amount of Classified Information. The precise amount of classified information is unknown. Even annual data are based only on estimates of classification actions and not on a direct count of the actual amount of information that is classified. Each classification action can vary from covering a single word, a name, or a sentence to covering a paragraph, a page, or an entire document. Consequently, the resulting statistics may be misleading. It is possible that the actual amount of classified information may increase from one year to the next even though the number of classification actions holds steady or even declines.

The increase in classified information was, in part, attributable to the size and growth of national security programs, reflected in the dramatic escalation of the defense and intelligence budgets in the 1980s. Because such spending has since declined or held constant, the amount of classified information generated by it has also stabilized. President Reagan's executive order, moreover, expanded the standards and criteria for classifying information and made declassification more difficult, compared to previous executive orders.

In addition, the confidential level has long been criticized for being too vague, allowing for the classification of nonsensitive information. Another seemingly permanent condition—overclassification—adds to the amount of classified information and introduces its own set of problems. Since it refers to unwarranted or unnecessary classification in violation of the provisions of the executive orders, overclassification not only results in more information being classified than should be, but it also perverts the classification system, by using it to hide administrative defects, policy disputes and misjudgments, and even unethical or illegal activities. Some of these problems were exposed in the famous 1971 Pentagon Papers case, dealing with the publication of documents connected with the VIETNAM WAR; inquiries in the mid 1970s into INTELLIGENCE COMMUNITY abuses; and investigations of the 1985–1986 IRAN-CONTRA AFFAIR. Finally, a failure to declassify information on any set schedule contributes to the total amount of classified information continuing at an unnecessarily high level.

BIBLIOGRAPHY

Abel, Elie. *Leaking: Who Does It? Who Benefits? At What Cost?* 1987.

Edgar, Harold, and Benno C. Schmidt, Jr. "*Curtiss-Wright* Comes Home: Executive Power and National Security Secrecy." *Harvard Civil Rights–Civil Liberties Review* 21 (1986): 349–408.

Kaiser, Frederick M. "The Amount of Classified Information: Causes, Consequences, and Correctives of a Growing Concern." *Government Information Quarterly* 6 (1989): 247–266.

Relyea, Harold, ed. Symposium on "Protecting National Security Information: An Overview of Federal Policy and Practice." *Government Information Quarterly* 1 (1984): 113–208.

Rourke, Francis E. *Secrecy and Publicity: Dilemmas of Democracy.* 1966.

Shattuck, John, and Muriel Morisey Spence. *Government Information Controls: Implications for Scholarship, Science and Technology.* 1987.

U.S. House of Representatives. Committee on Government Operations. *Security Classification Policy and Executive Order 12356.* H.R. 97–731. 97th Cong., 2d Sess. 1982.

U.S. Information Security Oversight Office. *Annual Reports.* 1978–present.

FREDERICK M. KAISER

CLASSIFIED INFORMATION PROCEDURES ACT (1980).

Passed in 1980 to facilitate federal criminal prosecutions where CLASSIFIED INFORMATION bearing on NATIONAL SECURITY is involved, this legislation (CIPA) includes requirements for periodic reports to Congress about its implementation. It was supported by the Jimmy Carter administration and passed both houses of Congress by voice vote. CIPA is designed to reduce the likelihood of the government being exposed to "graymail," that is, the threat that defendants would disclose classified information in their trials, thereby compelling prosecutors to dismiss or reduce the charges against them.

Legislative proposals to combat this problem arose in the late 1970s in response to two distinct concerns. The most immediate and decisive came from the intelligence and law enforcement communities over the government's limited ability to prosecute espionage and other unauthorized disclosures of classified information. A second concern followed earlier revelations about illegalities and abuses of authority by intelligence agencies themselves; some of this misconduct could not be prosecuted effectively without disclosing classified information.

CIPA (18 U.S.C. Appendix) broadly defines classified information, as any information or material determined by statute, EXECUTIVE ORDER, or regulation to require protection against unauthorized disclosure for reasons of national security (i.e., national defense and foreign relations) and any restricted data, meaning information about atomic energy and nuclear weapons. The act establishes a series of pretrial and trial procedures relating to the discovering of and possible use of such information during the proceedings.

CIPA requires defendants to give notice that they reasonably expect to disclose or cause the disclosure of certain classified information; permits an in camera hearing on the admissibility of such information; allows the judge to bar disclosure (and to seal the record of a related hearing) or allow for limited disclosure of classified information; provides for alternatives to disclosure, by allowing the government to substitute a statement admitting to relevant facts that the information would prove or a summary of such information; and permits the government to object to defense examination of a witness if classified information would be disclosed.

CIPA caused concern regarding the authority of the ATTORNEY GENERAL to determine the availability of classified information as evidence in all federal criminal proceedings. This power intrudes on the control over prosecutions of executive officials and personnel by an INDEPENDENT COUNSEL, who operates under a special federal court (Ethics in Government Act, 28 U.S.C. 591–598). In 1989, for instance, the Attorney General's refusal to allow certain classified information in a case brought by the independent counsel in the IRAN-CONTRA AFFAIR resulted in the dismissal of charges against a CENTRAL INTELLIGENCE AGENCY (CIA) agent.

BIBLIOGRAPHY

Askin, Frank. "Secret Justice and the Adversary System." *Hastings Constitutional Law Quarterly* 18 (1990): 745–777.

Salgado, Richard P. "Government Secrets, Fair Trials, and the Classified Information Procedures Act." *Yale Law Journal* 98 (1988): 427–446.

Shea, Timothy J. "CIPA under Siege: The Use and Abuse of Classified Information in Criminal Trials." *American Criminal Law Review* 27 (1990): 657–716.

FREDERICK M. KAISER

CLAY, HENRY (1777–1852), Speaker of the House, Senator, Secretary of State, presidential candidate in 1824, 1832, and 1844. Born in Virginia, educated in local schools, and trained in law principally by Chancellor George Wythe, Henry Clay received his license to practice in 1797. He migrated to Kentucky, settled in Lexington, opened a law practice, and married. Clay established himself as one of Kentucky's leading lawyers and, starting in 1803, was elected to the state legislature, the U.S. Senate, and the U.S. House of Representatives, where he served intermittently as Speaker for ten years, the longest tenure of anyone in the nineteenth century. He was also appointed one of five commissioners to negotiate the TREATY OF GHENT, which concluded the WAR OF 1812. His efforts in working out the MISSOURI COMPROMISE won him the title of "The Great Compromiser." He was also mainly responsible for the Compromise TARIFF OF 1833 and the COMPROMISE OF 1850, both of which prevented serious problems from escalating into bloody sectional conflicts. An ardent nationalist, he favored government support for developing industry and proposed a program he called the AMERICAN SYSTEM, which advocated protective tariffs to assist domestic manufactures, government-sponsored internal improvements such as the building of roads, bridges, highways, and other transportation facilities, and a strong national bank to provide the nation with sound currency and credit.

His reputation as a statesman made him one of the most popular politicians in the country, but his driving desire for higher office and his apparent willingness to equivocate on issues alienated many voters. He was first nominated for President by his state for the election of 1824. In this four-man race, no one received a majority of electoral votes as required by the TWELFTH AMENDMENT; the election went to the House of Representatives, where the President was to be chosen from among the top three candidates. Because his electoral count was the lowest of the four, Clay was eliminated from contention. As Speaker and as the most powerful member of the House, Clay influenced the outcome of the contest. He threw his support to John Quincy Adams because of the similarity of their economic and political views. Elected on the first ballot, Adams named Clay his Secretary of State, whereupon they were charged with a "corrupt bargain" to control the election. The accusation hounded Clay for the remainder of his political career.

Andrew Jackson defeated Adams for the presidency in 1828. Clay returned to Congress as Senator and was nominated to run for President against Jackson in 1832 by the National Republican Party. He convinced the president of the BANK OF THE UNITED STATES to apply to Congress for an extension of the Bank's charter before the existing charter was due to expire, believing he could use the President's opposition to the Bank to defeat him in the election. Jackson wrote a stinging veto message to the bill after it passed Congress and, among other things, accused the Bank of interfering in elections. As the candidate of the DEMOCRATIC PARTY, he overwhelmingly defeated Clay in the ensuing election because the American people admired and trusted him, whereas any number of them distrusted Clay.

A founder and leader of the WHIG PARTY, Clay expected to be nominated for President in the election of 1840. Because of the panic of 1837, which brought economic havoc to the nation, any Whig candidate could have defeated the incumbent Democrat, Martin Van Buren. But Clay was denied the nomination because of his record as a presidential loser, and the nomination went instead to General William Henry Harrison, who won an easy victory over Van Buren. Clay attempted to enact legislation creating another national bank and other Whig measures but Harrison died after a month in office and was succeeded by John Tyler, a former Democrat, who opposed a national bank and vetoed all attempts to charter a new one. The Whigs nominated Clay for the presidency in the election of 1844 to run against James Knox Polk, the Democratic candidate. The leading question in that election was the ANNEXATION OF TEXAS, which Clay opposed because he thought it would lead to war with Mexico. In the campaign, Clay wrote two letters that appeared to favor both sides of the issue, and he was again accused of equivocation. Polk narrowly defeated him. A switch of only five thousand votes in New York would have made Clay President. In 1848, for the last time, he sought the presidential nomination, but the Whigs chose General Zachary Taylor, who subsequently won the election against LEWIS CASS. Clay died in Washington in 1852.

BIBLIOGRAPHY

Eaton, Clement. *Henry Clay and the Art of American Politics*. 1957.

Howe, Daniel Walker. *The Political Culture of the American Whigs*. 1979.

Remini, Robert V. *Henry Clay: Statesman for the Union*. 1991.

Van Deusen, Glyndon G. *The Life of Henry Clay*. 1937.

ROBERT V. REMINI

CLAYTON ACT (1914). Enacted in 1914 as one plank of President Woodrow Wilson's NEW FREEDOM platform and named for Alabama Senator Henry De Lamar Clayton, its leading sponsor in the Senate, the Clayton Antitrust Act prohibits a number of specific business practices whose effect "may be to substantially lessen competition or to tend to create a monopoly." In contrast to the generality of the SHERMAN ANTITRUST ACT, the Clayton Act is detailed in its proscriptions and addresses trends, tendencies, and probabilities rather than certainties. It targets specific practices that monopolization proceedings under the Sherman Act had earlier revealed to play a key role in paving the way to monopoly. The Clayton Act thus is designed to supplement the Sherman Act and to strengthen American ANTITRUST POLICY by arresting incipient anticompetitive practices before they produce full-blown monopoly problems requiring corrective Sherman Act surgery. Government responsibility for enforcing the Clayton Act is shared by the DEPARTMENT OF JUSTICE and the Federal Trade Commission. Private individuals and firms are also empowered to file suits under the Clayton Act.

Section 2 of the act prohibits price discrimination—variations in prices charged for the same product—where the effect may be substantially to lessen competition or to tend to create a monopoly. This section was originally enacted to prevent predatory pricing employed by large firms (Standard Oil, most notoriously) to amass and enhance market control by driving smaller competitors from the field ("primary-line" anticompetitiveness). As amended by the Robinson-Patman Act of 1936, section 2 was expanded also to encompass "secondary-line" price discrimination, where the effect of price differences for a seller's product threatens to lessen competition among its customer firms. In either case, price differences are permitted where they reflect only differences in costs or where they represent a "good faith" effort on the part of the seller to meet lower prices that are offered by its competitors.

Section 3 of the act prohibits tie-in sales and exclusive dealership agreements—again where their effect may be to lessen competition substantially or to tend to create a monopoly. Tie-in sales occur when a seller requires its buyers to purchase one product in order to be allowed to purchase another product, thereby tying the sale of the products together. Exclusive dealership agreements occur when a producer forbids dealers from distributing goods produced by its rivals, thereby excluding them from access to distribution channels.

Section 7 of the Clayton Act addresses mergers and acquisitions. As originally enacted, section 7 suffered from a number of fatal loopholes and soon proved ineffective. Later, concern over a sustained, rising trend toward higher market concentration induced by corporate mergers and the utter impotence of the Clayton Act to deal with the problem precipitated the Celler-Kefauver Amendment in 1950. As amended, section 7 now prohibits any acquisition of stock or assets where the effect may be to lessen competition substantially or to tend to create a monopoly in any line of commerce and in any geographic section of the country. It applies to "horizontal" mergers (between competitors), "vertical" mergers (between firms operating at different stages within the same industry), and "conglomerate" mergers (between firms producing unrelated products and services).

Finally, section 8 of the act proscribes interlocking directorships by prohibiting the same person from serving as a director or officer of any two corporations (other than banks) that are competitors and that have individually aggregated capital, surplus, and undivided profits exceeding $10 million.

The effectiveness of the Clayton Act crucially depends on executive enforcement by the President, the Justice Department, and the Federal Trade Commission, as well as on sympathetic interpretation of the statute by the courts. When the executive branch and its judicial and administrative appointees are hostile to antitrust and espouse an extreme laissez-faire philosophy, the Clayton Act can easily be nullified by denying that its targeted practices may have the proscribed effect of lessening competition or tending to create monopoly. This is most dramatically evidenced in the case of corporate mergers. During the Ronald Reagan years, the United States witnessed a massive corporate acquisition-consolidation movement unparalleled since the early 1900s, including megamergers between direct competitors in steel, airlines, oil, food processing, meatpacking, video entertainment, and department-store retailing as well as joint ventures between American auto giants and their major foreign rivals. In this climate, enforcement of section 7 of the Clayton fell victim to the prevailing laissez-faire philosophy and its antipathy to implementing antimerger legislation.

[*See also* BUSINESS POLICY.]

BIBLIOGRAPHY

Adams, Walter, and James W. Brock. *Antitrust Economics on Trial: A Dialogue on the New Laissez-Faire.* 1991.

Adams, Walter, and James W. Brock. *Dangerous Pursuits: Mergers and Acquisitions in the Age of Wall Street.* 1989.

Jones, Eliot. *The Trust Problem in the United States.* 1927.

Kovaleff, Theodore P., ed. "Symposium on the 100 Anniversary of the Sherman Act and the 75th Anniversary of the Clayton Act." *Antitrust Bulletin* 35 (1990).

May, James. "Antitrust in the Formative Era: Political and Economic Theory in Constitutional and Antitrust Analysis, 1880–1918." *Ohio State Law Journal* 50 (1989): 257–395.

WALTER ADAMS and JAMES W. BROCK

CLAYTON-BULWER TREATY. Ratified 4 July 1850, the Clayton-Bulwer treaty pledged the United States and Britain not to "occupy, or fortify, or colonize, or assume or exercise any dominion over . . . any part of Central America"; it demonstrated American nationalism under Secretary of State John M. Clayton and President Zachary Taylor against the desire of Britain to occupy the narrow places of world commerce (for example, Gibraltar, the Malay Straits, the Cape of Good Hope). Alarmed by the territorial accessions of the MEXICAN WAR, the British government was maneuvering for control of a route across Nicaragua. The American government countered with the treaty, signed by the British representative Sir Henry Bulwer.

The importance of the negotiation lay in the continuation of President James K. Polk's expansive policies by his Whig successor, Taylor. Those policies constituted a veritable national effort to turn American energies outward, away from the SLAVERY controversy. Facing up to Britain was part of the proposed strategy, as were acquisition of Central American and Caribbean protectorates or territories, and, in the Far East, the opening of Japan. Presumably national pride would obscure the slavery issue. Taylor's death and a succession of weak Presidents in the 1850s, together with the rival claims of southern plantation owners and northern manufacturers, and pro- and antislavery enthusiasts, made further expansion impossible. The withdrawal of Great Britain from the Islas de la Bahía off Honduras and the Mosquito Coast of Nicaragua in 1858–1860, however, despite its being triumph for the MONROE DOCTRINE, did nothing to counter the dismal domestic policies of President James Buchanan, who was unwittingly moving the nation toward the CIVIL WAR.

Half a century later the Clayton-Bulwer Treaty became a great public issue during the administrations of William McKinley and Theodore Roosevelt. By this time Americans wanted not merely sole control of an isthmian canal route but also the ability to fortify it. Roosevelt made that possible in the HAY-PAUNCEFOTE TREATY of 1901.

BIBLIOGRAPHY

Leonard, Thomas M. *Central America and the United States: The Search for Stability.* 1991.

ROBERT H. FERRELL

CLEVELAND, GROVER (1837–1908), twenty-second (1885–1889) and twenty-fourth (1893–1897) President of the United States. When Cleveland was elected President in 1884 he ended twenty-four years of Republican occupancy of the office. Old-time Republicans looked on this as a major catastrophe, but exultant Democrats hailed it with gun salutes and fireworks. The Republicans referred to Cleveland as "His Accidency," and there is some truth in the nickname. His climb to power was rapid and favored by fortune. Until 1881, his only political experience had been as a Democratic ward worker, an assistant district attorney, and sheriff of New York state's Erie County. Then in that year he became mayor of Buffalo, New York; one year later he was governor of New York; and two years later he was elected President.

Early Career. The son of a Presbyterian clergyman, Cleveland was born in the small town of Caldwell, New Jersey, on 18 March 1837. Several years later his family moved to Fayetteville, in western New York, and it was there and in nearby Clinton that he spent his boyhood. Shortly after his father died in 1853, Cleveland went to stay with his uncle in Buffalo, and this wealthy and influential relative was able to put him into one of the best law offices in that rapidly growing city. For the next twenty-seven years, from 1855 to 1882, Cleveland remained in Buffalo, rarely traveling outside it for business or pleasure.

Cleveland's Buffalo years are significant for his presidency in two ways: the parochial outlook that they fostered and the development of some of the more appealing character traits he demonstrated as President.

Since he seldom traveled beyond Buffalo, he had a limited understanding of economic and political matters in other parts of the state or country. Problems of unemployment, long work hours, and low pay were to him remote and unimportant. Like many other residents of Buffalo, Cleveland believed that other communities could, and should, take care of themselves as his own city was doing. Kind and sympathetic, Cleveland did help the needy, but his name never appeared on published lists of contributors to causes such as the Buffalo hospital or the Chicago Fire sufferers. He never served on the board of a charitable institution and did not appear to support the idea that charitable activity was a concern of government.

Cleveland's Presidency. On the other hand, in these same years, Cleveland displayed some of the qualities that Americans came most to admire about him as President—his dogged industry and reliability, his phenomenal physical energy, and his honesty, the last trait so dominant that, according to one member of the Buffalo bar, "Everybody felt it."

Though Cleveland was a Democrat, he shared the Whig-Republican view about the extent of federal power and the role of the President in domestic matters, which, it should be noted, was prevalent in his day. He disliked paternalism in government and thus opposed the idea of the social-service state. He believed Americans were entitled to economy, purity, and justice in their government, but nothing more. There was to be a fair field for all and favors for none. As President he was to prove a righteous watchdog, looking after other politicians and preventing them from giving and taking favors. Thus he opposed tariff favors to business, pension favors to veterans, and land favors to railroads. In this sense Cleveland was a "negative" President, believing it was more important to keep bad things from occurring than to make good things happen.

This does not mean Cleveland's presidency did not merit praise. Cleveland deserved commendation for his stiff-necked determination not to be stampeded by Congress into a clash with Spain over atrocities in CUBA in the mid 1890s. When a bellicose Congressman reminded the President that the Constitution authorized Congress to declare war, Cleveland rejoined, "yes, but it also makes me Commander-in-Chief, and I will not mobilize the army."

In a critical biography of Cleveland, Horace Samuel Merrill contended that "Cleveland was much more successful as a defender of the status quo than as a crusader for peace," and Rexford Tugwell, in his study of the Cleveland presidency, argued that Cleveland "was not a leader; he was a caretaker." Allan Nevins, in his book on Cleveland, maintained that Cleveland bequeathed the nation "an example of iron fortitude" and that this was "better than to have swayed parliaments or to have won battles or to have annexed provinces."

In line with Cleveland's dislike of paternalism in government was his strong opposition to the government's aiding anyone in distress. The best remembered illustration of this view was his veto of a Texas seed bill in early 1887. Some Texas counties had been

suffering from a drought and were in pressing need for seed grain. In response to their pleas, Congress enacted a measure appropriating $10,000 to enable the Commissioner of Agriculture to distribute seed. The amount was small, but the bill sharply challenged Cleveland's principles. He had just vetoed a bill for pensions for war veterans and dependent parents of soldiers who had died in service, and he regarded the Texas seed bill in the same light. So he returned the measure unsigned with a strong protest that it was wrong "to indulge a benevolent and charitable sentiment through the appropriation of public funds for that purpose." He went on to say that he could "find no warrant for such an appropriation in the Constitution, and I do not believe that the power and duty of the General Government ought to be extended to the relief of individual suffering which is in no manner properly related to the public service or benefit." Then he added significantly, "A prevalent tendency to disregard the limited mission of this power and duty should, I think, be steadfastly resisted, to the end that the lesson should be constantly enforced that though the people should support the Government, the Government should not support the people."

In another phrase from this memorable veto message, which has been quoted many times in behalf of the same philosophy, Cleveland reminded Americans, "Federal aid in such cases encourages the expectation of paternal care on the part of the Government and weakens the sturdiness of our national character." In his second inaugural address in 1893, Cleveland returned to this theme when he dwelt at length on the "unwholesome progeny of paternalism," and when he complacently added, "The lessons of paternalism ought to be unlearned and the better lesson taught that while the people should patriotically and cheerfully support their Government, its functions do not include the support of the people."

When Cleveland took office he knew nothing about being President and nearly nothing about the important national issues. Yet he said that he intended to surround himself with the best minds, which would shun "extravagance and waste." In his first inaugural address he asserted, "The people demand reform in the administration of the government and the application of business principles to public affairs." To help carry out this mandate he built a Cabinet of men successful in law, politics, and business. But nowhere in the Cabinet was there a representative of the farmers, who made up the largest segment of the population, or of labor, or of any minority group.

Compared with the enormous amount of staff assistance a modern President has in the EXECUTIVE OFFICE OF THE PRESIDENT (EOP), in Cleveland's day the President had almost no staff. There were no administrative assistants to carry out important tasks. There was no BRAIN TRUST that could supply the President with ideas or provide him with a friendly opposition. In short, even were the President to formulate important new policy, he had no one to help him work it out. So, as Cleveland recognized, the Executive Office was only capable of dealing with the routine affairs of government.

Cleveland's relationship with the press represented another major difficulty for him. Urged to invite friendly editors and publishers to dinner, he refused on the ground that he should not make himself familiar with them simply because they were personally agreeable. Neither was he much more cordial to reporters and correspondents.

As for Congress, Cleveland made little effort to bring the political branches of the government together as an effective unit. He had much reverence for the doctrine of the SEPARATION OF POWERS, and his early favorite political theme was the "independence of the executive." This view caused him trouble, however, and in the end he had to relinquish some of it. But his usual reluctance to interfere with Congress was the despair of his friends.

Cleveland's hands-off attitude toward legislation was in line with the prevalent Gilded Age view that the President should not attempt to shape legislation nor meddle in the affairs of Congress. He did not begin to influence the form of legislation until about halfway through his first term, and even then he did little to follow through. In his second term he leaned more to the view that the President should help push laws through Congress, but he continued to hold the opinion that the President should, if possible, work independently of Congress.

Like other Chief Executives, Cleveland had his own CONCEPTION OF THE PRESIDENCY. It was a mixed one—firmly adhering to the doctrine of the separation of powers yet wanting a strong executive who would exercise all his powers to protect the interests of the federal government. This is why he is sometimes called "a third kind of President" between the strong concept exemplified by Abraham Lincoln and the weak concept represented by James Buchanan. The Cleveland presidency thus shuttled between strength and weakness, although its distinctive trait was the view that the presidency's essential function was defensive. The presidency's power lay in the veto, in disengagement, in the negation of what others had put in motion, and in the use of only enough executive energy to maintain an existing equilibrium.

At times, Cleveland's contradictory views about the presidency clashed, and under provocation he acted more like a strong President than a weak one. He faced no crisis of the magnitude that had confronted his predecessors Andrew Jackson, Buchanan, or Lincoln, but on two occasions—in the PULLMAN STRIKE and the Venezuelan boundary dispute—Cleveland was not reluctant to expand the powers of the President, acting to preserve national order and to ensure American influence in the Western Hemisphere, respectively.

In his first inaugural address, Cleveland emphasized responsibility, conscience, and duty, and these became important in the tone and style of his presidency. This was clearly demonstrated by the long hours he put in, sometimes working until two or three o'clock in the morning, by his taking care of his own correspondence, and by his answering many White House telephone calls in person—not too heavy a burden at a time when there were probably no more than a few score telephones in all of Washington. It was also shown by his meticulous attention to detail, as in his scrutiny of private pension bills for CIVIL WAR veterans (which he vetoed), and by his compulsion to do just about everything himself, including minor tasks that a clerk could have handled. He was probably the hardest-working person in Washington in his day, some considered his attention to detail more a fault than a virtue, since this habit made it difficult for Cleveland to give enough attention to larger issues. His critics complained that it would be better for him to have a good night's sleep and then face the major matters the next day with a clear brain.

Cleveland's presidency was also characterized by honesty. He worked to maintain honesty in both major and minor matters. An unswerving loyalty to duty also marked his presidency. He saw his office as a covenant with the American people, and he sincerely believed he had a deep obligation to all Americans. Cleveland's sense of duty, however, made it nearly impossible for him to compromise. He seemed unable to meet agreeably with those who differed with him. He was suspicious of them and of their motives and was too easily moved to denounce them personally. What is now called Cleveland courage was in his own day thought in many quarters to be plain obstinacy.

Cleveland's sense of duty created an atmosphere of courage and loyalty, but it also fostered antagonism, bluntness, narrowness, negativism, and stubbornness. These prevented Cleveland from exercising effective leadership to promote positive programs and to take positive action to ameliorate difficult situations. Such was Cleveland's loyalty to duty that the *New York Times* on 2 March 1897, just two days before he finally left office, concluded that this dutifulness "has completely estranged powerful Democrats who were able to deprive him of the support of great States and to turn against him their Members and Senators. It has provoked implacable enmities potent enough to obstruct or thwart his greatest designs and highest policies." Harry Thurston Peck, commenting on Cleveland's sense of duty in a 1908 essay, wrote, "But it was Cleveland's lot to alienate in turn every important interest, faction and party in the United States; and he did this always in obedience to his own matured conception of his duty."

Cleveland was determined to be a President of the people. In an address he made in 1887 he reinforced this view when he said, "If your President should not be of the people and one of your fellow citizens, he would be utterly unfit for the position, incapable of understanding the people's wants and careless of their desires." And Cleveland wanted his presidency to be of all the people. "The President and the President alone," he maintained, "represents the American citizen, no matter how humble or in how remote a corner of the globe." Fully aware that the President is elected from all parts of the country while members of Congress are chosen from smaller geographical areas, Cleveland affirmed that he was the only elected political leader in the country who represented the American people as a whole, a view held by many other Presidents.

Impact on the Presidency. In view of the foregoing characteristics and assessments of Cleveland and his presidency, one can say a few things about his impact on the presidency, which was felt and evidenced in several ways. He was the first President to use the veto freely, going well beyond his predecessors' sparing use of it. George Washington vetoed only two bills, and his successors down to 1830 returned a total of only seven bills to Congress. Jackson, with twelve vetoes, made a bolder use of the power, which aroused intense opposition. Yet until Cleveland's accession in 1885, the total number of bills vetoed was only 204, including 108 regular and 96 pocket vetoes. Cleveland vetoed 414 bills in his first term (304 by regular, 110 by pocket veto); most of them were private pension measures, but on occasion he vetoed an important bill, such as one restricting Chinese immigration.

Cleveland's most notable impact on the presidency was his successful effort to restore the powers and initiative of the CHIEF EXECUTIVE that had been largely lost by Johnson in his fight with Congress during RECONSTRUCTION. There were some stirrings of presidential assertion between Johnson and Cleveland, and there had been some presidential victories, particularly by Rutherford B. Hayes and James A. Garfield. But the TENURE OF OFFICE ACT of 1867 remained in effect. Cleveland made a major contribution not only

by reasserting presidential prerogatives but also by achieving the repeal of the Tenure of Office Act and thus ending its protracted aggression on the presidency. This reversal of Republican theory and practice was the most important gain for the presidency in the post–Civil War years.

Cleveland also strengthened the presidency by his action in the controversy with Britain over Venezuela, bringing all the negotiations with another country into the presidential arena. He later told a friend that his "aim was at one sharp stroke to bring the whole matter into his own hands, compel England to yield to arbitration, and put Congress in a position where it could not interfere." In doing this, Cleveland advanced the presidency immensely by seizing the leadership in FOREIGN AFFAIRS that might have escaped him if he had temporized.

Beyond merely advancing the presidency, Cleveland exceeded its limits and introduced a new pattern of employing the military in squelching civil disorder when he used the army to "restore law and order" in the Pullman Strike of 1894, which he did over the opposition of Illinois governor John P. Altgeld. Since Cleveland was a lawyer it can be assumed that he was aware of his constitutional offense. Cleveland never consulted Altgeld on the necessity of federal intervention but instead took Attorney General RICHARD OLNEY's view that strikers' interference with the mails made it necessary for the President to see that the laws were faithfully executed. Some historians believe that Cleveland's decisions in the Pullman Strike and the Venezuelan boundary dispute were "unduly influenced" by Olney, "a tough-fisted and ultraconservative Cabinet member," and that in the Venezuelan matter "Cleveland had allowed Olney to take him far on the road to war."

One future President noted the importance of the changes that Cleveland had wrought on the presidency. Woodrow Wilson, in his critique of the American political system in *Congressional Government* (1885), had concluded after analyzing the decay in presidential power from Andrew Johnson through Chester A. Arthur that there was no hope for the presidency, that congressional supremacy would have to be recognized, and that that body would have to accept the responsibilities of leadership. But, after observing Cleveland in action, Wilson altered his view. In approving the President's conduct, he said that it had been direct, fearless, and practical and that it had "refreshed our notion of an American Chief Magistrate." Wilson noted that, in office, Cleveland had changed from being a President who had considered himself responsible only for administration to one who had become what a President should be—a policy maker and a shaper of opinion. Wilson praised Cleveland as the only President between 1865 and 1898 who had "played a leading and decisive part in the quiet drama of our national life."

Some historians contend that while Cleveland was an outstanding person, he was not an outstanding President. They claim that he was too provincial and narrow-visioned and that he was not in tune with the times. Thomas Bailey, for instance, points out that "he left office at the end of his second term with the economy panic riddled, the Treasury in the red, his party disrupted, his Republican opponents triumphant, and himself formally repudiated by his Democratic following." There is some merit in this assessment. Cleveland did act more as an overseer than as an initiator or organizer.

Cleveland's Reputation. Those of Cleveland's contemporaries who commented on politics and political leaders during the post–Civil War years gave him mixed reviews. He was not highly regarded by two of his most prominent contemporaries, James Bryce and Henry Adams, whose observations of the Gilded Age had influenced many who have written about this period of American history. But James Russell Lowell, then one of America's leading poets and essayists, regarded Cleveland as the most "typical" American since Lincoln. And Rutherford Hayes, who had himself been President in the 1870s and thus had knowledge and experience of the office, thought Cleveland did "extremely well."

The most meaningful basis on which to judge a President is what he achieved, or failed to achieve, while he held the office—not his popular standing, or what he said he hoped to do, or what he said or did before becoming President or after leaving the office. Despite what some scholars and contemporaries have thought of Cleveland, he was ranked as one of the United States' better Presidents in two polls on presidential greatness conducted by Arthur M. Schlesinger, Sr., in 1948 and 1962. In the first of these polls ten Presidents, and in the second eleven Presidents, were placed in the "great" and "near great" categories. Cleveland was placed in the "near great" category on both polls, ranking number eight on the first and number eleven on the second. According to Schlesinger, Cleveland achieved his greatness (or near-greatness) for his stubborn championship of tariff reform and for his honesty and efficiency in government. In a 1970 extension of the Schlesinger polls, Gary M. Maranell, a University of Kansas sociologist, conducted an evaluation of the Presidents by polling the membership of the Organization of American Histo-

rians. Again Cleveland did well, coming in between twelfth and fourteenth among Presidents in categories of general prestige, strength of action, activeness, idealism and accomplishments.

Cleveland has also continued to receive favorable treatment in a number of college textbooks in American history. In a sampling of some of these textbooks Cleveland is portrayed as the ablest President between Lincoln and Theodore Roosevelt, the only outstanding President in the post–Civil War generation, a President who used his powers forthrightly and who worked fully within the tradition of the strong presidency, and a President who exercised more vigorous leadership than any of his predecessors since Lincoln.

Not all historians or college textbooks share these views about Cleveland, however. Some maintain that he failed to provide leadership for Congress or for the country. They contend that he had too narrow a conception of his powers and duties to be a successful President and that he had no broad comprehension of the political and economic forces then transforming the country. Further, they argue that he was not a skillful political leader and that his presidency was associated with little significant legislation.

Difficulties of Assessment. There are several major problems in attempting to assess Cleveland or, for that matter, any President of the American Gilded Age. For one thing, during these years politics and politicians were under heavy censure by many ordinary Americans as well as by thoughtful observers such as Adams and Bryce.

Another problem in evaluating Cleveland is that he was President when the presidency was at a low ebb in both power and prestige and when national political power was largely vested in Congress. In the post–Civil War years, congressional leaders had nearly overthrown Andrew Johnson, had gained almost complete control of Ulysses S. Grant, and had tried to put the Presidents of the Gilded Age at their mercy. In these years, the Whig theory of the presidency—which held that the President must confine himself to executing the laws enacted by an omniscient Congress—prevailed. So ineffective were the Presidents of this era that many observers, forgetting the greatness of some past Presidents, began to think of the presidency as a merely ceremonial office, if not simply a sinecure.

Considering the parlous condition of politics—and particularly the presidency—in the Gilded Age, how can one evaluate Cleveland (or any President of the era)? Cleveland's reputation rests not so much on his brilliance nor his accomplishments, considerable as some of them might have been, but rather on his character. Many historians believe that Cleveland's character awards him a special place in the history of the presidency. Many have praised Cleveland for his courage, firmness, uprightness, sense of duty, and common sense. They emphasize his steely stubbornness, his rugged independence, his courage in scorning popularity, his ability to rise above the needs of the party and to keep the needs of the country inerringly in view, his refusal to be be bought or bullied, and his truculent honesty. As Cleveland asked one Democratic politician seeking handouts for his followers, "Well, do you want me to appoint another horse thief for you?"

So Cleveland was thought of as a fearless and heroic figure who hewed to a strict moral line. He was also considered to be stolid, unimaginative, obdurate, and brutally forthright. Though he came to the White House with the reputation of a reformer, not many believed he would put forth a bold, progressive program or display vigorous leadership. During the presidential campaign of 1884, Cleveland had emphasized a new moral attitude in government and the need for corrective action over that of constructive action. Many Americans agreed with him.

Cleveland was also a thoroughgoing conservative, a believer in sound money, and a defender of property rights. In his first inaugural address in 1885 he promised to adhere to "business principles," and his Cabinet had a number of conservative and business-minded Democrats. His administration indicated no significant break with his Republican predecessors on fundamental issues. Yet he appealed to many Americans because he seemed to be a plain man of the people and because he consistently appeared to do what he believed was right. The public admired him for what was called his "you-be-damned-ness," and it loved him for the enemies he made. "What the people desired just then with a furious passion was a vigorous, uncompromising man . . . who would save the State from its statesmen," wrote William Allen White some years later. "The times crying out for an obstructionist to stern corruption found young Grover Cleveland."

Yet, for all his faults and limitations, Cleveland is still generally regarded by historians as one of the country's ablest Presidents. This is because he showed a degree of independence and courage rare in public life, and particularly rare in the Gilded age. Fidelity to the law and to duty enhanced Cleveland's reputation as a President who checked abuses, restrained bad men from carrying out their schemes, warded off impending calamity and stopped foreign aggrandizement in the Western Hemisphere. He always did what he thought was right and performed his task so well that, for his generation and the ones that followed, he came to embody the idea of the honest, dutiful President.

BIBLIOGRAPHY

Cleveland, Grover. *Presidential Problems.* 1904.

Ford, Henry J. *The Cleveland Era.* 1919.

Hollingsworth, Joseph R. *The Whirligig of Politics: The Democracy of Cleveland and Bryan.* 1963.

Marszalek, John F. *Grove Cleveland, A Bibliography.* 1988.

Merrill, Horace S. *Bourbon Leader: Grover Cleveland and the Democratic Party.* 1957.

Nevins, Allan. *Grover Cleveland: A Study in Courage.* 1932.

Nevins, Allan, ed. *Letters of Grover Cleveland, 1850–1908.* 1933.

Parker, George F. *The Writings and Speeches of Grover Cleveland.* 1892.

Tugwell, Rexford G. *Grover Cleveland.* 1968.

Welch, Richard E., Jr. *The Presidencies of Grover Cleveland.* 1988.

VINCENT P. DESANTIS

CLIFFORD, CLARK (b. 1906), presidential special counsel, foreign policy adviser, Secretary of Defense. Clark McAdams Clifford was born on 25 December 1906 in Fort Scott, Kansas. He attended Washington University in St. Louis, Missouri where in 1928 he received his law degree. Upon graduation he entered private practice and became a successful trial attorney. In 1945 he became the assistant to James K. Vardaman, President Harry S. Truman's naval aide. In 1946 Clifford replaced Vardaman and also assisted Truman's special counsel, SAMUEL ROSENMAN. After Rosenman's retirement, Clifford became Truman's special counsel.

During his years in the Truman administration, Clifford was instrumental in establishing many foreign policies and domestic programs. He prepared the study on universal military training and helped establish the National Intelligence Agency, the predecessor to the CENTRAL INTELLIGENCE AGENCY. During the strike by the United Mine Workers led by John L. Lewis, Clifford convinced President Truman to stand up against the strikers. Clifford was also instrumental in the development of Truman's foreign policy known as CONTAINMENT. He led the inside campaign for the recognition of ISRAEL, arguing that Truman would need the Jewish vote in the election of 1948. Additionally, Clifford wrote many of the speeches that Truman delivered, helping to clarify the President's positions on Greece and Turkey, the state of the union, and the "do-nothing" Eightieth Congress.

Returning to private practice in Washington after the Truman administration, he became one of the most influential and wealthiest attorneys in the city. He returned to public life as one of the most trusted advisers to both Presidents John F. Kennedy and Lyndon B. Johnson, although Clifford declined a Cabinet position in the Kennedy administration and, instead, headed the President's transition team. Additionally, he served on and then chaired the PRESIDENT'S FOREIGN INTELLIGENCE ADVISORY BOARD. Clifford continued to serve on PFIAB until 1968 when he was tapped by President Lyndon B. Johnson to be Secretary of Defense replacing ROBERT S. MCNAMARA. While initially committed to the bombing of North Vietnam, Clifford urged de-escalation of the VIETNAM WAR. In 1969, he returned to private practice in Washington, D.C.

BIBLIOGRAPHY

Clifford, Clark., with Richard Holbrooke. *Counsel to the President: A Memoir.* 1991.

Gauhar, Altaf. "Clifford Clark: An Interview." *Third World Quarterly* 6 (1984): 1–12.

JEFFREY D. SCHULTZ

CLINTON, BILL (b.1946), forty-second President of the United States (1993–). Bill (William J.) Clinton, elected President on 3 November 1992 at the age of forty-six, ran an unconventional campaign for the presidency, and some of his actions during the transition period, before he took office on 20 January 1993, suggested that his would be an unconventional presidency. He was elected amid high expectations that he would overhaul an ailing economy, make America more productive and competitive, and shake up Washington. In his campaign, Clinton tried to lower expectations—knowing the dangers of not meeting them—even as he raised them. Clinton is one of the smartest and best-informed men ever to be elected President, and he demonstrated substantial political skills in reaching his long-sought office. But his victory was less than a smashing one—he won with 43 percent of the vote, against George Bush's 38 percent and H. ROSS PEROT's 19 percent. Immediately upon his election, Clinton set out to consolidate his position, working to build a coalition that would enable him to both govern and be reelected.

Early Career. William Jefferson Clinton, who chose to go by the more familiar name Bill, was born in the small town of Hope, Arkansas, on 19 August 1946 and had a turbulent childhood. His father, William Jefferson Blythe, an itinerant salesman, died in an automobile accident about three months before Clinton was born. When he was very young, while his mother was away at nursing school, Clinton lived with his grandparents; his grandfather, who had only a grade-school education, ran a small grocery store. His stepfather,

Roger Clinton, whom Clinton's mother, Virginia, married in 1950, was a temperamental alcoholic. When Clinton was seven, his mother and his stepfather moved him to Hot Springs, Arkansas, a town heavily dependent upon its mineral baths, its racetrack, and its gambling casinos. Bill's mother was an inveterate gambler. Clinton's early life probably contributed to the remarkable resilience he showed during his campaign for the Democratic nomination and may lie behind his apparent need to please everyone.

The precocious, ambitious, and competitive young man with the modest background got himself to Georgetown University, where he majored in international studies. In the summer of 1963, before his senior year of high school, Clinton had been elected to Boys Nation and met President John Kennedy in the Rose Garden. (The Clinton campaign in 1992 made prominent use of a piece of film showing Kennedy shaking hands with an awed Clinton.) It was after that event that Clinton reportedly told his mother that he wanted to devote his life to public service. Clinton's winning a Rhodes scholarship, a much-coveted award for two years at Oxford University, had a big impact on his life. At Oxford, he formed friendships with several people who became close advisers during his presidential campaign, some of them joining his administration. After Oxford, Clinton attended Yale Law School, where he formed additional lasting friendships and met his future wife, fellow law student Hillary Rodham. Bill and HILLARY RODHAM CLINTON developed a pattern of establishing long-standing friendships and networking, with the result that by the time Clinton ran for the presidency, a wide pool of advice and talent was available to him. These people became known as FOBs—Friends Of Bill.

One sign of Clinton's long-standing political ambition was a letter he wrote while at Oxford to Col. Eugene Holmes, director of the ROTC program at the University of Arkansas, which came to light during the presidential campaign during the controversy over Clinton's attempts (which were successful) to avoid being drafted to fight in the VIETNAM WAR. (Clinton eventually submitted to the draft lottery but drew such a high number that he was not called.) In the long letter, Clinton, then twenty-three, agonized about the rights and wrongs of staying out of the draft and said, "I decided to accept the draft in spite of my beliefs for one reason: to maintain my political viability within the system." Clinton's avoidance of the draft and his participation in the antiwar movement while at Oxford became issues in his presidential campaign as much because Clinton told conflicting stories about these incidents as because of the incidents themselves.

When Clinton became governor of Arkansas at the age of thirty-two, he was a "boy wonder," and the Arkansas voters' rejection of him two years later was an educating trauma for him and his wife. Several changes ensued: Clinton took to heart the criticism that he had been too arrogant and too cut off from the public, and from then on he took considerable time to make contact with the voters and to listen to them and to the state legislators, with whom he had had a number of fights. He became more cautious. His wife, who had maintained her maiden name, became Hillary Clinton. Two years later, Clinton regained the governorship, and his friends knew that it was only a matter of time before he ran for the presidency. (At one point, Clinton considered running for the Senate but decided that he could not defeat the incumbent Democratic Senator, Dale Dumpers.) Clinton was a progressive governor who tried, with mixed results, to move Arkansas, a poor, largely rural state, to improve its standings in education and the environment. He also had the reputation of being something of a trimmer; so concerned with pleasing Arkansas's various factions that he achieved less than he might have. He was progressive on racial issues, but he did support the death penalty and approved three executions.

From the outset, Clinton and his wife were a political team. Hillary Clinton took up the private practice of law in Little Rock and also involved herself in several of her husband's issues—in particular, education. She also became involved in the Children's Defense Fund, a Washington-based organization founded to pursue educational and health benefits for poor children. Mrs. Clinton was chairman of the board of CDF by the time her husband ran for President—and had to resign since CDF is a nonpartisan organization. But children's issues remained high on her agenda, and her first public performance after the election was at the annual CDF dinner in Washington, where she spoke about her continuing interest in the subject.

The Campaign for the Nomination. When Clinton announced, on 3 October 1991, that he would seek the Democratic nomination for the presidency, he was widely considered a second-tier candidate who was in it for the experience—so that he would be ready when the real opportunity came around four years later. When Clinton entered the race, George Bush was still enjoying high ratings in the polls—a phenomenon based very largely on his victory over Iraq in the GULF WAR earlier in the year. Some of Clinton's friends insist that he was running for the presidency in 1992. As things turned out, none of the presumed first-tier candidates chose to run—because of Bush's popularity and the unlikelihood that the voters would turn an incumbent President out of office. Very few people thought that the Democrats had a chance in 1992, though one or two long-sighted Democrats foresaw the public's attention turning increasingly to domestic issues, Bush's weak point. Bush and his people were counting on the economy's recovering sufficiently to assure him of reelection.

By the time that Clinton announced his candidacy, he had carefully thought through—perhaps more thoroughly than any candidate before him—how to position himself to win both the nomination and the presidency. Many Democrats—shut out of the White House since 1980—found this appealing, even if they were not particularly drawn to Clinton, and they made their accommodation and backed him. Other Democrats were put off by the calculated nature of Clinton's candidacy (but later most of them, espying victory, came around). Clinton's campaign strategy reflected his own thinking and that of the Democratic Leadership Council, of which he was a founder in 1985. The idea behind the DLC was that the Democrats could not win the White House as long they nominated liberals who were too identified with the party's interest groups—especially with the poor and blacks—and who came across as taxers and spenders and as insufficiently muscular on the subject of defense.

Clinton ran as "a different kind of Democrat," and many of his ideas came from work done by the DLC, and its research offshoot, the Progressive Policy Institute. One of the themes of his candidacy was personal responsibility—for example, that welfare recipients, having been given training, should go off the rolls after two years (the feasibility of this, and the availability of jobs, remained to be tested); that, in exchange for government-provided tuition, college students either pay back the funds or perform two years of national service. On the subject of taxes, Clinton proposed to raise them only on the wealthy and remained obscure about how he would cut the mammoth budget deficit—then running at an estimated $330 billion a year. (After the election, the total deficit for the next several years was estimated to be $300 billion higher than previously projected. The Clinton campaign had been aware of most of this differential.)

Clinton aimed his campaign at the middle class: people who had had a hard time during the Reagan-Bush years, as the rich got richer and the middle class suffered a decline in real income. (The poor had done badly, too, but were not politically fashionable in 1992 and presumably would vote for the Democrats anyway.) Many of these people had been Democrats but had voted for Reagan and Bush because of the social issues—crime, patriotism, loose lifestyles, and race—

that the Republicans had been adept at exploiting. But the economy turned out to be a bigger issue for these Reagan Democrats in 1992, and Clinton neutralized a number of the other issues that previously had worked against the Democrats. At the beginning of 1992, unemployment was running at about 7 percent, and the polls registered widespread anger at the long recession, which had begun in the summer of 1990, and at Washington's seeming inability to do anything about issues of importance to the American people, such as the availability and cost of health care and the condition of American schools. (Bush had mistakenly thought it was good politics to veto a large number of bills passed by the Democratic Congress and not to try to work out compromises. Thus, Bush's attempt to make the gridlock between Congress and the White House an issue backfired on him.) Clinton ran as an "outsider"—though he and his wife were members of several elites. He was polished—too polished for some people's taste—leaving the question of who he really was or what he really believed in.

Clinton's campaign nearly came undone in New Hampshire, leading to one of the oddest episodes in American politics. The sometime rockiness of the Clintons' marriage was no secret to a lot of people, and there were scores of rumors about Bill Clinton's extramarital activities. Rather than try to deny the whole thing, in September 1991 the Clintons appeared before reporters at a breakfast in Washington and said that, while there had been trouble in their marriage in the past, it was behind them and that they would have nothing further to say on the matter. Several of Clinton's advisers thought that this formulation should hold for the rest of the campaign, but it collapsed in the wake of an article that appeared in late January in a supermarket tabloid, in which a woman, Gennifer Flowers, alleged that she had had a twelve-year affair with Clinton. Flowers, a sometime lounge singer and then an employee of the state of Arkansas, later held a press conference. Clinton, perhaps in panic, denied the affair, thus taking him beyond the line that he and his wife had drawn.

The uproar led the Clintons to decide that he could not be heard on any other subject until he put this matter to rest—the press would continue to ask questions—and so the couple made an extraordinary appearance on CBS's "60 Minutes," after the Super Bowl, and talked about it—if in an elliptical way. This was a great many Americans' introduction to Bill Clinton. In time the subject died away—in part because the press felt guilty about pursuing it and in part because the people of New Hampshire were demanding that they be given their primary back and that it

should be about the economy. During the controversies over Flowers and Clinton's draft record, his poll ratings went into a free-fall; he had been leading but then proceeded to plummet. Many Arkansans arrived to express their support of him, and, after a few days of being in a funk, Clinton campaigned strenuously. His second-place showing—after former Sen. Paul Tsongas of Massachusetts—was transformed by his campaign staff into a victory by having Clinton go before the television cameras first and declare himself "the comeback kid."

Clinton was widely, and deservedly, credited with running a smart campaign for the nomination. Time and again, he escaped serious trouble—but he also prevailed over a weak field. His next most serious challenge was in New York, where the primary was held 7 April. By this time, all the other candidates except the eccentric former California governor Jerry Brown were out of the race. (Tsongas had "suspended" his campaign after placing third in Connecticut but remained on the ballot). Thus Brown became the vehicle of protest—against the status quo and against the front-runner. Clinton, overconfident as a result of his strong victories in Michigan and Illinois on 17 March, had just lost Connecticut to Brown. His staff feared the internecine New York politics and the raucous New York City tabloids. Clinton stayed as far as he could (at least, publicly) from the tribal wars in New York and tried to avoid appearing to be pandering to its demanding interest groups. And Clinton and his staff took a decision to appear on every conceivable talk show, to try to work around the tabloids. In the end, Clinton won New York. Although Tsongas and Brown won substantial percentages, from this point on, Clinton was considered the inevitable nominee.

The Election of 1992. Clinton's prospects for the general election looked cloudy. In the spring and early summer, Clinton, Bush, and Perot each held about a third of the vote in the polls, with Clinton coming in third in some. Many Democrats were gloomy, figuring that they were about to nominate a political dead man, and considered a movement to draft someone else. Three events then changed Clinton's prospects: his selection of AL GORE, a smart and attractive forty-four-year-old Senator from Tennessee, which turned out to be very popular; the Democrats' smooth and successful convention; and Ross Perot's pulling out of the race on the last day of the convention. Initially, a substantial bloc of Perot's voters went to Clinton. (Perot got back in the race on 1 October.)

Clinton also benefited from the fact that Bush ran an abysmal reelection campaign. With the help of hindsight, many people will conclude that the result of the 1992 election was foreordained all along, but it wasn't. The Bush campaign pounded away at Clinton's "character"—playing on doubts many potential voters had about his propensity for changing his story on such questions as how he had avoided the draft and whether he had smoked marijuana (his confessing, after dodging the question for some time, that he had but that he "didn't inhale" became a national joke). Bush also attacked Clinton repeatedly as a taxer. Though Bush's attempt to suggest a lack of patriotism on Clinton's part because he had traveled to Moscow while a student at Oxford backfired, the President continued to attack Clinton for participating in anti-war demonstrations in a foreign country. But Bush and his chief advisers—in particular JAMES A. BAKER III, who had run his 1988 campaign and reluctantly resigned as Secretary of State in August to become Bush's Chief of Staff—misread the year, the country, and their opponent. The attack tactics that had worked in 1988 were incompatible with the political climate of 1992. Bush's failure to focus on domestic issues, as President and candidate, sunk him.

Clinton ran a cautious but smart campaign, keeping the focus, to the extent he could, on the economy. He showed a grasp of a large number of issues, but he was vague on what he would actually do if elected. He did pledge a more activist government that would try—through a new emphasis on education and training—to make America more competitive in the world market and that would overhaul the nation's health care system. The Clinton campaign's "rapid response team," formed in reaction to MICHAEL DUKAKIS's failure to respond to attacks in 1988, and to make it clear to the Bush campaign that there would be a response from the Clinton camp within the same news cycle, was highly effective but also sometimes had Clinton dealing with Bush's issues rather than his own. Clinton was careful to stay one step ahead of Bush on such foreign policy issues as the violent breakup of Yugoslavia and aid for Russia.

The team of Clinton and Gore, who often appeared together, had a synergy to it, as did the foursome of Bill and Hillary Clinton and Al and Tipper Gore. The innovation of sending the two couples out on a bus trip immediately after the Democratic convention, going through small towns, caused a sensation, and the device was repeated several times in the course of the campaign. In fact, the 1992 campaign marked the beginning of several new forms of communication between candidate and public—including multiple appearances on the "soft" talk shows. (Bush, who had said such a thing was unpresidential, followed Clinton's—and Perot's—path.)

Though Clinton was not outstanding in the three presidential debates—he smoothly and competently restated his positions on issues—Bush was below par (except for the last debate, when it was too late), and Perot's homilies became tiresome. Though the race narrowed toward the end, it widened again in the final days, and Clinton ended up with a landslide in the ELECTORAL COLLEGE (370 votes to Bush's 168), but only a narrow victory in the popular vote. Turnout was higher than ever, the Reagan Democrats went home to their original party, and Clinton won several states that no Democrat had carried since Lyndon Johnson in 1964.

Following his election, Clinton became engaged in selecting his Cabinet and in the hard work of translating his campaign promises into legislative proposals. He understood well that his biggest tests were yet to come.

BIBLIOGRAPHY

Clinton, Bill, and Al Gore. *Putting People First: How We Can All Change America.* 1992.

ELIZABETH DREW

CLINTON, DEWITT (1769–1828), governor of New York, presidential candidate in 1812. Clinton is best known for his successful advocacy of building the Erie canal, his service as New York's governor, and his support for educational, social, and cultural institutions in New York.

A graduate of Columbia College, Clinton entered politics in 1787–1788, when he published a series of Anti-Federalist essays, "Letters from a Countryman." He quickly became a Jeffersonian Republican, serving in the New York legislature (1797–1802), where he helped pass legislation to end SLAVERY in the state. In the United States Senate (1802–1803) he introduced the TWELFTH AMENDMENT. He left the Senate in 1803 to become mayor of New York City, a post he held from 1803 to 1806, 1809, and 1812 to 1815. While mayor he helped establish New York City's public school system, providing mass education for poor children under the Lancasterian system, in which older children taught the younger ones under the supervision of a teacher. He also organized the New-York Historical Society (1804), worked for the construction of the Erie Canal, and worked to remove the last political disabilities of New York State's Roman Catholics.

By 1804 Clinton was one of New York's most powerful politicians, and helped engineer the choice of his uncle, GEORGE CLINTON, as Jefferson's running mate. In

1808 DeWitt Clinton was a firm supporter of Jefferson's embargo. In 1812 he ran against James Madison in the presidential contest. Clinton still considered himself a Jeffersonian Republican, but he argued for the importance of cities, international trade, and INTERNAL IMPROVEMENTS. Although he was always an opponent of the Federalists, the existing remnant of that party supported him. These Federalists were motivated less by their love for Clinton than by their distaste for the Virginia Democratic-Republican hegemony that Madison represented. Clinton's policies were unclear. In New England his Federalist supporters argued he would end the WAR OF 1812, but in the rest of the nation his advocates claimed he was a staunch Democratic-Republican who would prosecute the war more vigorously than Madison. Clinton's candidacy represented an end to the sectional cooperation of the Democratic-Republicans. He won 89 electoral votes to Madison's 128. However, the election was closer than this vote would indicate. Clinton carried every northern state but Pennsylvania, Vermont, and Ohio. If Clinton had carried Pennsylvania, he would have defeated Madison.

After the 1812 election, Clinton returned to New York, where he spent most of his energy working for the construction of a canal linking Albany with Buffalo. In 1817 Clinton won a landslide victory in a special election for the governorship of New York. Avoiding presidential politics, he focused almost all his energies on building the canal and on educational and social reform. Clinton advocated state funded public schooling for women and well as men and also for blacks and Indians. Under his administration New York established an institution for the instruction of the deaf and dumb, a more modern and humane prison system, a state asylum for "lunatics," and the segregation of juvenile criminals from adults. In 1820 Clinton narrowly won reelection over DANIEL TOMPKINS, who was then Vice President of the United States. Clinton declined to run for reelection in 1822 but remained on the canal commission until Van Buren Democrats forced him from the post. He was elected governor again in 1824, and was thus the state's chief executive when the Erie Canal was completed.

Clinton declined President John Quincy Adams's offer to appoint him as minister to Great Britain and in 1826 he once again won the governorship. In 1828 he explored the possibility of running for President, but he had little support outside of New York. Moreover, his politics were uncertain and confused. Clinton portrayed himself as a STATES' RIGHTS Democrat, but he had advocated federal support for internal improvements and had made a career of opposing the Albany Re-

gency in his own state and the Virginia Democratic establishment nationally.

BIBLIOGRAPHY

Fitzpatrick, Edward A. *The Educational Views and Influence of DeWitt Clinton.* 1911.

Fox, Dixon Ryan. *The Decline of Aristocracy in the Politics of New York.* 1919.

Siry, Steven E. *DeWitt Clinton and the American Political Economy: Sectionalism, Politics, and Republican Ideology, 1787–1828.* 1989.

PAUL FINKELMAN

CLINTON, GEORGE (1739–1812), governor of New York, fourth Vice President of the United States (1805–1812). George Clinton served as New York's first governor from 1777 to 1795, and again from 1801 to 1804. He was arguably the most popular and effective governor in America during the revolutionary era. His leadership of New York's ANTI-FEDERALISTS during the debate over the ratification of the Constitution catapulted him onto the national scene as the most prominent Anti-Federalist candidate for VICE PRESIDENT in 1788. George Washington would have been comfortable with Clinton as his Vice President, but ALEXANDER HAMILTON, who opposed Clinton's postwar policies in New York, encouraged nationwide Federalist support for John Adams as Vice President. Clinton received only three electoral votes, all from Virginia.

Clinton again seemed to be a logical vice presidential opponent to Adams in 1792. Thomas Jefferson and James Madison supported Clinton's candidacy as did Democratic-Republican leaders from several states. But his candidacy was damaged by his controversial gubernatorial reelection in the spring of 1792. He lost the election to Adams by a vote of 74 to 50.

Clinton retired to private life in 1795. A year later, he refused an offer by Democratic-Republican leaders to stand for Vice President. In the spring of 1800, however, they coaxed him out of retirement with the argument that the presidential election later in the year would be determined by New York's presidential electors. Reluctantly, Clinton stood for office and was elected an assemblyman from New York City. In 1800, AARON BURR gained the nomination for Vice President over a reluctant Clinton. When Jefferson and Burr, however, received the same number of electoral votes, Clinton and Hamilton, both of whom distrusted Burr, joined in opposing Burr's election by the House of Representatives.

In 1801 Burr seemed ready to run for governor of New York. To thwart him, Clinton agreed to stand for governor again and was elected. After a caretaker three-year term dominated by his nephew DEWITT CLINTON, George Clinton retired for a second time. President Jefferson asked Clinton to forego retirement again to serve as his Vice President, thus preserving the important Virginia-New York coalition that had been crafted in the early 1790s. In June 1804 the TWELFTH AMENDMENT to the Constitution was adopted and Clinton became the first candidate specifically to run for the vice presidency, as the Democratic-Republican ticket overwhelmed its Federalist opponents by an electoral vote of 162 to 14.

From the beginning of Jefferson's second term, Secretary of State James Madison and his allies attempted to isolate the Vice President, thereby lessening Clinton's chances of succeeding Jefferson. Some even suspected that Jefferson's choice of Clinton as Vice President in 1804 was a Machiavellian maneuver to assure the presidential nomination of Madison four years later.

In January 1808, the Democratic-Republican congressional caucus nominated Madison for President and Clinton for Vice President. Clinton's supporters, most of whom boycotted the meeting, condemned the caucus and, sensing an inevitable Madison victory, failed to campaign vigorously for Clinton. Although ardently opposed to the administration's foreign policy and its failure to mobilize for war, Clinton himself remained silent, pledging to refrain from partisan presidential politics while Congress considered legislation strengthening the country's defenses. Consequently, Clinton did not declare himself a candidate for President, but he did not withdraw his name from consideration. At the same time, he neither accepted nor declined the caucus's vice presidential nomination. New England Federalists considered endorsing Clinton as their presidential candidate, hoping that he would end the embargo on American trade. Democratic-Republican electors, particularly in Virginia, had qualms about voting for Clinton as Vice President, because, according to their judgment, he had turned his back on the party's nomination. Not wanting to diminish respect for the congressional caucus, however, Madison's backers supported Clinton. Madison won the presidential election defeating the Federalist CHARLES C. PINCKNEY. Clinton was reelected Vice President.

Throughout his tenure as Vice President, Clinton opposed the foreign and defense policies of Jefferson and Madison. Opposition clustered around Clinton, but he was too old and ill to provide effective leadership. Clinton was ill-suited to be Vice President. He knew little about the protocol of presiding over the Senate, and his performance paled when compared with his masterful predecessor, Aaron Burr. On several occasions he cast the tie-breaking vote in the Senate, most significantly on 20 February 1811, when he voted against rechartering the BANK OF THE UNITED STATES. Clinton died in office on 20 April 1812.

BIBLIOGRAPHY

Hastings, Harold, ed. *Public Papers of George Clinton.* 1899–1911.
Kaminski, John P. *George Clinton: Yeoman Politician of the Young Republic.* 1993.
Spaulding, E. Wilder. *His Excellency George Clinton: Critic of the Constitution.* 1938.
Young, Alfred F. *The Democratic Republicans of New York: The Origins, 1763–1797.* 1967.

JOHN P. KAMINSKI

CLINTON, HILLARY RODHAM (b. 1947), First Lady, wife of Bill Clinton. Hillary Rodham Clinton was the first presidential spouse to bring an outstanding professional career of her own to the White House. A 1969 graduate of Wellesley College, where she was president of the college government, and a 1973 graduate of Yale Law School, where she served on the board of editors of the *Yale Review of Law and Social Action,* she worked briefly in Washington, D.C., for the House Judiciary Committee during the WATERGATE AFFAIR, before moving to Arkansas, where she taught law at the University of Arkansas and became a partner in the Rose Law Firm of Little Rock. She was twice voted to a list of "The 100 Most Influential Lawyers in America" by the *National Law Journal* and was singled out by a leading columnist as "one of the more important scholar-activists of the last two decades."

Such a record of achievement prompted reports that she would assume a paid title in her husband's administration, and the President repeatedly voiced his belief that she was qualified for one. But Public Law 90-206, passed by Congress in December 1967, prohibits the employment of relatives by members of either the executive or the legislative branch. Hillary Clinton's training, her expertise, and her extensive contacts among activists in several fields, especially among those working for the legal rights of minors (including the Children's Defense Fund and the Children's Television Workshop) and the rights of women (she had chaired the American Bar Association's Commission on Women in the Profession) promised that she would be an activist First Lady. Her husband and others singled her out as one of Clinton's most trusted advisers, and he named her to head the Task Force on National Health Care Reform.

BIBLIOGRAPHY

Ratcliffe, Donnie. *Hillary Clinton: A First Lady for Our Time.* 1993.
Warner, Judith. *Hillary Clinton: The Inside Story.* 1993.

BETTY BOYD CAROLI

COATTAILS EFFECT. Ever since Representative Abraham Lincoln first popularized the metaphor in 1848 in his references to Zachary Taylor and Andrew Jackson, presidential coattails have been part of the lore of American politics. Politicians project them, journalists attribute them, historians recount them, and political scientists analyze them. Yet we know little about coattails. Most significantly, we have a limited understanding of how they affect the outcomes of congressional elections.

Coattails votes occur when voters cast their ballots for congressional candidates of the presidential candidate's party because the voters support the presidential candidate. There may have been substantial coattail voting prior to WORLD WAR II, but most studies show a diminishing connection between voting for President and for members of Congress.

One indicator of this attenuation is the considerable increase in split-ticket voting. Typically the voters in at least one-third of House districts cast a majority of their ballots for a presidential candidate of one party and a candidate for the House of the other party. This figure is not much below the 50 percent mark we would expect for split results if voting were random and there were no connection whatsoever between the votes for President and Congress. Nevertheless, the percentage of the congressional vote attributable to the President's coattails is not insignificant. Coattail effects are most likely to be seen where party-column ballots are used, since they encourage straight-party voting.

A coattail victory is one for a congressional candidate of the President's party in which presidential coattail votes provide the increment of the vote necessary to determine the outcome in the election. If coattail votes determine which candidate wins a seat in Congress, they will be more significant than if they only raise a winner's percentage a few points. In the latter case the same person wins the seat, but does so by a wider margin.

If a large number of seats are determined by presidential coattails, the implications for public policy can be substantial. New members of Congress, who might be brought in on a President's coattails, are primary agents of policy change, because incumbents tend not to alter the voting patterns they have established in previous years. Franklin D. Roosevelt's NEW DEAL,

Lyndon Johnson's GREAT SOCIETY, and Ronald Reagan's shifts in taxing and spending policy depended on large changes in party seats.

Whether they bring in new members or preserve the seats of incumbents, coattail victories are important because representatives of the President's party generally support the administration's programs more than do opposition party members. Moreover, those members of the President's party who win close elections may provide him an extra increment of support out of a sense of gratitude for the votes they perceive they received as a result of the President's coattails, and members of both parties may be interested in responding to tangible indicators of public support for the President.

The effects of coattails on individual voters do not translate into aggregate election results in any straightforward manner. To have influence on congressional elections, presidential coattails have to be quite strong, that is, there has to be a large number of coattail votes in a constituency. However, most congressional seats are safe for one party because of the balance of party identifiers in the constituency and the power of incumbency. The only way for a presidential candidate's coattail vote to influence congressional election outcomes in these instances is usually for a large number of affiliates of the other party to vote for both the presidential candidate and a nonincumbent candidate of the presidential candidate's party based on their support for the presidential candidate. This number must be large enough to win the seat from the dominant party.

A presidential candidate's coattails may also save a seat for a representative of his party who previously won election in a constituency where the other party was dominant in terms of party identifiers. Finally, presidential coattails may make a difference in a highly competitive race in a constituency with a close balance between the parties. Since these conditions do not occur very often, there are relatively few presidential coattail victories. Presidents cannot expect their coattails to carry many like-minded running mates into office to provide additional support for their programs.

BIBLIOGRAPHY

Calvert, Randall L., and John A. Ferejohn. "Coattail Voting in Recent Presidential Elections." *American Political Science Review* 77 (1983): 407–419.
Campbell, James E., and Joe A. Sumners. "Presidential Coattails in Senate Elections." *American Political Science Review* 84 (1990): 513–524.
Edwards, George C., III. *The Public Presidency.* 1983.

GEORGE C. EDWARDS III

COHEN, BENJAMIN V. (1894–1983), presidential adviser, counselor to the State Department. A successful Wall Street lawyer and investor, Benjamin Victor Cohen went to Washington, D.C., in 1933 to work with James Landis, who was later appointed to the Federal Trade Commission, on the Securities Act of 1933. Later, Cohen exercised power far afield from his official position as counsel to the National Power Policy Committee and, along with THOMAS CORCORAN, with whom he often teamed up, became a key NEW DEAL insider. Cohen was responsible in whole or in part for many important pieces of legislation, including the Securities Exchange Act of 1934 and the PUBLIC UTILITY HOLDING COMPANY ACT of 1935. Cohen and Corcoran wrote speeches for President Franklin D. Roosevelt, lobbied Congress, and defended the New Deal in court.

Cohen had a well-deserved reputation as a legal genius and as a legislative draftsman par excellence. New Deal critics unfairly regarded Cohen and Corcoran as mere cheerleaders for FELIX FRANKFURTER and inaccurately saw them as wild-eyed liberals. In fact, Cohen's political philosophy was a complex and evolving liberalism, blended with dashes of pragmatism, noblesse oblige, and centralized planning for good measure.

As WORLD WAR II approached, Cohen became increasingly concerned about foreign affairs. He developed the legal arguments to justify the DESTROYERS FOR BASES agreement of 1940 and played a role in the passage of the LEND LEASE ACT (1941). After a brief stint in London as an adviser to the American ambassador, Cohen served as an assistant to JAMES F. BYRNES at the OFFICE OF WAR MOBILIZATION (OWM). Toward the end of the war, Cohen's work involved various aspects of postwar planning, and in 1945 he moved with Byrnes to the State Department, as counselor. Later he served as a delegate to the UNITED NATIONS and argued the first case involving the United States at the International Court of Justice in The Hague.

BIBLIOGRAPHY

Lash, Joseph P. *Dealers and Dreamers: A New Look at the New Deal.* 1988.

WILLIAM LASSER

COINS, PRESIDENTS DEPICTED ON. Presidents of the United States are featured on six circulating coins and fourteen commemorative coins issued by the U.S. Mint. Twelve foreign countries have also commemorated American Chief Executives on coins.

The first American coin to bear a likeness of a President was the Lincoln penny, which was issued on 2 August 1909. Three decades later, on 15 November 1938, the Thomas Jefferson five-cent coin was released. The George Washington quarter, Franklin D. Roosevelt dime, John F. Kennedy half dollar, and Dwight D. Eisenhower dollar were first produced respectively in 1932, 1946, 1964, and 1971.

Legislation approved by Congress led to the adoption of the Washington quarter, Kennedy half dollar, and Eisenhower dollar. President Theodore Roosevelt provided the impetus for the Lincoln penny. The Jefferson nickel resulted from a decision by Treasury Department officials to replace the buffalo nickel that had been in circulation for a quarter of a century. Franklin D. Roosevelt's sudden death in 1945 prompted Treasury officials to place the late President's image on the dime.

Although commemorative coins are also legal tender, they are not meant for circulation. They are designed instead to be souvenirs as well as profit-makers for their sponsors. The first commemorative depicting a President was struck in December 1899. The Lafayette silver dollar, which featured the likeness of George Washington and the Marquis de Lafayette, was issued to help defray the cost of a monument to the French general at the 1900 Paris Exposition. A commemorative silver dollar, issued ninety years later, carried a bust of Dwight D. Eisenhower (Eisenhower Centennial, 1990) on the obverse. A one-dollar silver coin, portraying James Madison, was approved by Congress in May 1992.

Two distinct gold dollars were issued in 1904 as fund-raisers for the Louisiana Purchase Exposition. The first honored Thomas Jefferson, who was President when the United States purchased the Louisiana Territory from France. The other showed President William McKinley, who had recently been assassinated. Subsequent gold dollars recognized William McKinley (McKinley Memorial, 1916–1917), and Ulysses S. Grant (Grant Memorial, 1922).

Silver commemorative half dollars have featured Abraham Lincoln (Illinois Centennial, 1918), Ulysses S. Grant (Grant Memorial, 1922), James Monroe and John Quincy Adams (MONROE DOCTRINE Centennial, 1923), George Washington and Calvin Coolidge (Sesquicentennial of the Declaration of Independence, 1926), and George Washington (250th anniversary of his birth, 1982).

Three commemorative coins celebrating the fiftieth anniversary of MOUNT RUSHMORE were issued in 1991. These included a five-dollar gold coin, a one-dollar silver coin, and a copper-nickel fifty-cent piece.

All three coins show on the obverse the faces of the four Presidents (Washington, Jefferson, Theodore Roosevelt, and Lincoln) as depicted in the memorial.

BIBLIOGRAPHY

Giedroyc, Richard. "Presidential Portraits Popular Topic on Coins." *Coin World* (7 August 1991): 74–75.
Reed, Mort. *Coinology*. 1985.

STEPHEN W. STATHIS

COLD WAR. Running from about 1947 to about 1989, the cold war represented a worldwide competition between the United States and its allies, on one hand, and the Soviet Union, other communist nations, and various communist and other revolutionary groups, on the other hand. Managing relations with the Soviet Union became the principal objective of American foreign policy, and every President from Harry S. Truman to Ronald Reagan practiced some form of CONTAINMENT of communism and Soviet power. Throughout the cold war, Presidents also occasionally pressed for DETENTE a relaxation of tension, between the two so-called superpowers. Most animosity between the United States and the Soviet Union ended in the late 1980s, although American officials did not acknowledge that the cold war had ended until the beginning of the administration of George Bush. Bush forged a close personal friendship with Mikhail Gorbachev, the Soviet leader. Sweeping revolutions eliminated communism in Eastern Europe and the Soviet Union from 1989 to 1991, and the Soviet Union ceased to exist at the end of 1991.

Origins. The cold war represented a clash between both rival ideologies—communism and capitalism—and national interests. Its roots ran back to the challenges to the existing order posed by the 1917 Bolshevik revolution in Russia and the Western efforts to thwart communism after that revolution. The cold war fully emerged after WORLD WAR II. In the two years following the surrender of Germany, lines were drawn between Washington and its allies in Western Europe, on the one side, and Moscow on the other. The parties disagreed sharply over a variety of international issues: the occupation and eventual division of Germany, the nature of Eastern European governments, the borders of Europe, Soviet security concerns, economic questions, and the role of communist parties in nations outside the region of direct Soviet military control. By 1947 American officials had concluded that Joseph Stalin, the Soviet leader, did not want to cooperate with the Western powers, and that the Soviet Union represented a threat to Western interests as grave as that posed by Nazi Germany in the late 1930s.

In the remainder of the Truman administration the United States confronted the Soviet Union and the threat of communism in Europe, Asia, the Middle East, and the Western Hemisphere. Truman pressed for the adoption of an exceptionally large array of new initiatives: the MARSHALL PLAN, or European Recovery Program (1948–1953); the NATO TREATY (1949); the POINT FOUR PROGRAM for peacetime foreign aid (1949); involvement in the KOREAN WAR (1950–1953); and support for the French war against the communist forces of Ho Chi Minh in Vietnam. Truman also acknowledged that the competition with the Soviet Union and communism would be prolonged by modernizing the management of FOREIGN AFFAIRS and NATIONAL SECURITY POLICY. The NATIONAL SECURITY ACT of 1947 created the CENTRAL INTELLIGENCE AGENCY (CIA) to gather information and conduct covert operations, the NATIONAL SECURITY COUNCIL to coordinate policy for the White House, and the JOINT CHIEFS OF STAFF and the Secretary of Defense [see DEFENSE, DEPARTMENT OF] to direct the military. The Selective Service Act of 1948 revived the peacetime draft. Such revolutionary changes made American foreign policy more assertive than it had ever before been during peacetime.

Nevertheless, many Americans criticized the Truman administration for not doing enough to counter Soviet and communist advances. During the 1952 presidential election campaign, the winner, Republican Dwight D. Eisenhower, ran on a platform of rolling back Soviet gains in Eastern Europe and ending the Korean War.

Containment and Confrontation. Eisenhower's actual conduct toward the Soviet Union and communism generally more closely resembled Truman's policy of containment than Eisenhower's campaign rhetoric suggested. After he ended the Korean War in July 1953, his administration searched for a way to lower the cost of the cold war to taxpayers while maintaining the pressure on the Soviets and communists. Eisenhower and Secretary of State JOHN FOSTER DULLES adopted the so-called New Look defense posture, which relied on air power and nuclear weapons rather than infantry and conventional arms, and the threat of massive retaliation to intimidate the Soviets. CIA-sponsored COVERT OPERATIONS became a tool against nationalists and revolutionaries in Iran (1953) and Guatemala (1954). The apparent success of these efforts to overthrow governments unfriendly to the United States led the CIA to begin planning an invasion of CUBA in the last months of the Eisenhower administration.

The death of Stalin in March 1953 presented the Eisenhower administration with opportunities for détente. Eisenhower conducted summit conferences with Soviet leaders in May 1955 in Geneva, Switzerland; in September 1959 at CAMP DAVID, Maryland; and briefly in Paris in May 1960. At the first two meetings, the United States offered measures designed to control the arms race between the two superpowers, but the proposals were so heavily weighted in Washington's favor that the Soviets rejected them. The last meeting, with Soviet Communist Party general secretary Nikita Khrushchev, broke up acrimoniously the day it began. Khrushchev angrily stalked out of the meeting after Eisenhower refused his demand for an apology for the overflights of Soviet territory by CIA U-2 spy planes [see U-2 INCIDENT].

The failure of the Eisenhower administration to end the cold war or at least to reduce tensions with the Soviets, became an issue in the presidential election of 1960. During the campaign, the Democratic nominee, Senator John F. Kennedy of Massachusetts, assailed the Republican administration for letting the communists seize the initiative in the cold war. Kennedy won, defeating Richard M. Nixon, who had been Eisenhower's Vice President. The first two years of the Kennedy administration, 1961 and 1962, saw some of the most intense American-Soviet confrontations of the entire cold war period. The new administration quickly increased the military budget for both conventional and nuclear forces, and Kennedy authorized the CIA to go forward with its ill-fated invasion of Cuba on 17 April 1961. After the failure of the BAY OF PIGS INVASION, Kennedy authorized the CIA to conduct a covert campaign against Fidel Castro, and also oversaw a substantial increase in American military personnel advising the army of the Republic of Vietnam (South Vietnam). Kennedy held an unfriendly summit conference with Khrushchev in Vienna in June 1961. He believed that Khrushchev wanted to test American resolve in Berlin, and a military showdown over that divided city was averted only after the Soviets authorized the communist German Democratic Republic (East Germany) to construct an ugly wall barring East Berliners citizens from traveling to the western zone [see BERLIN CRISIS (1961)].

Tensions between the United States and the Soviet Union reached their peak in the CUBAN MISSILE CRISIS of October 1962. The United States demanded that the Soviets remove their intermediate-range ballistic missiles from the Caribbean island, and the Soviets retreated in the face of overwhelming U.S. military force. After that showdown, the dangers of nuclear war between the superpowers encouraged the Kennedy administration to move toward détente. In June 1963 Kennedy encouraged Americans to "reexamine [their] attitude toward the Soviet Union." Two

months later, the superpowers signed a treaty banning NUCLEAR TESTING in the atmosphere, outer space, and under water. They promised progress on a subsequent treaty outlawing all nuclear testing. Yet Kennedy's death in November 1963 and the growing U.S. involvement in Vietnam interfered with further reductions in U.S.-Soviet tensions.

The growing VIETNAM WAR quickly consumed the foreign policy attention of the administration of Lyndon B. Johnson, leaving little time or energy for furthering détente. President Johnson and Secretary of State DEAN RUSK repeatedly justified U.S. participation in the war as a method of containing the spread of communism. For their part, the Soviets supported North Vietnam and concentrated on augmenting their own nuclear forces to avoid a repetition of their humiliation during the Cuban missile crisis. Nevertheless, the embers of détente remained. Johnson met Soviet prime minister Alexei Kosygin for a summit at Glassboro, New Jersey, in June 1967, and the two men promised to negotiate a treaty limiting the growth of ballistic missiles. Near the end of his term Johnson planned a visit to Leningrad (now St. Petersburg) to conclude an ARMS CONTROL pact, but the summit conference was scrapped after Soviet troops invaded Czechoslovakia in August 1968 to restore the authority of hard-line communists.

Prospects of Détente. From 1969 to 1980, détente with the Soviets became a major objective of U.S. policy. Richard Nixon had far more success than either Gerald Ford or Jimmy Carter in improving relations with Moscow. Yet his reduction of cold war tension had badly frayed by the time Nixon was forced to resign the presidency. In 1972 Nixon concluded an Interim Strategic Arms Limitation Agreement (SALT-I) and a treaty sharply curtailing the number of antiballistic missiles each side could deploy [see SALT (STRATEGIC ARMS LIMITATION TALKS)]. The Nixon administration greatly expanded trade with the Soviets and promised that Washington and Moscow would cooperate to reduce tensions worldwide. Détente began to unravel in the fall of 1973, when the United States and the Soviet Union disagreed over the Yom Kippur War in the Middle East. The growing WATERGATE AFFAIR distracted Nixon in 1974, and little progress took place toward a full-scale Strategic Arms Limitation Treaty.

President Ford retained HENRY A. KISSINGER as his NATIONAL SECURITY ADVISER and Secretary of State, and Ford promised to continue Nixon's and Kissinger's efforts to improve relations with Moscow. Ford met Soviet leader Leonid Brezhnev in Vladivostok in November 1974, and the two leaders promised to conclude a full SALT treaty (SALT-II) by 1976. Domestic

American politics thwarted the achievement of that goal. Détente became increasingly unpopular in the United States. Ford was challenged for the Republican presidential nomination by former California governor Ronald Reagan, who denounced Kissinger's efforts at détente as sacrificing American interests. Jimmy Carter, the Democratic nominee and the eventual winner of the 1976 election, also criticized Nixon, Ford, and Kissinger for overlooking abuses of HUMAN RIGHTS in the Soviet Union.

For the first two and one-half years of the Carter presidency, the United States tried to improve relations with Moscow. In June 1979 the two powers signed a full SALT-II treaty, setting strict limits on each side's intercontinental and submarine-launched missiles and their long-range bombers. Carter considered SALT-II a significant achievement, but he withdrew it from consideration by the Senate at the beginning of 1980. The withdrawal represented one aspect of a revival of cold war tension after the Soviet Union asserted its power in Cuba, Africa, and the Middle East. Carter reacted angrily after Soviet forces invaded Afghanistan in December 1979, and the United States and its Western European allies began to augment their armed forces in preparation for another possible showdown with the Soviet Union.

Ronald Reagan won the presidency in 1980 partly on the basis of a promise to confront the Soviet Union more assertively. His administration quickly won congressional approval for the largest peacetime increase in military expenditures in history. Reagan also assailed the Soviet Union as an "evil empire" and denounced its leaders for reserving the right to "lie, cheat and steal" to achieve their aims of communist revolution. Reagan's anticommunism alarmed some Americans and Europeans who feared that war might erupt. The aging Soviet leadership also acted perplexed and intimidated by Reagan. In March 1985, however, the Soviet Union selected the younger, more pragmatic Mikhail Gorbachev to lead the Communist Party. Gorbachev quickly recognized that his nation's backward economy could not bear the cost of a new arms race with the United States. Gorbachev and Reagan moved slowly toward accommodation, with summits in 1985 in Geneva and in 1986 in Reykjavik, Iceland. Relations between the two men and two countries improved rapidly thereafter. In 1987 the two sides concluded the INF (INTERMEDIATE RANGE NUCLEAR FORCES) TREATY. The next year, Reagan traveled to Moscow to receive a hero's welcome. "They've changed," he said, in response to a question about whether he still considered the Soviet Union an evil empire.

During the presidency of George Bush, American leaders came gradually to a realization that cold war tensions had ended. Bush warmed slowly to Gorbachev, but by 1990 the two men had formed a close friendship. The United States welcomed the end of Soviet domination of Eastern Europe. Bush backed Gorbachev in 1991, even to the point of refraining from expressing support for democrats within the Soviet Union. Bush did, however, help Russian President Boris Yeltsin resist a coup by old-guard communist leaders in August 1991. This unsuccessful uprising represented the last gasp of a dying communist system. On 31 December 1991, the Soviet Union ceased to exist, and the cold war was generally acknowledged to be over.

BIBLIOGRAPHY

Gaddis, John Lewis. *Strategies of Containment.* 1982.
Gaddis, John Lewis. *The United States and the End of the Cold War.* 1992.
Gaddis, John Lewis. *The United States and the Origins of the Cold War.* 1972.
LaFeber, Walter. *America, Russia, and the Cold War.* 1992.
Paterson, Thomas. *On Every Front.* 1992.

ROBERT D. SCHULZINGER

COLE v. YOUNG 351 U.S. 536 (1956). *Cole* was one of several cases during the 1950s that tested the authority of executive officials to remove employees on grounds of NATIONAL SECURITY. Kendrick M. Cole, a food and drug inspector in the Department of Health, Education, and Welfare, had been charged with establishing and maintaining a close association with individuals "reliably reported to be Communists" and was dismissed from the department on the ground that his continued employment was "clearly not consistent with the interests of national security." The Civil Service Commission subsequently refused to hear his dismissal appeal. Cole, who was a WORLD WAR II veteran, had neither requested a hearing nor replied to the charges, but he contended that the charges constituted an invasion of his private rights of association. Cole had asked the federal district court for the District of Columbia for a declaratory judgment invalidating his discharge and holding improper the refusal of the Civil Service Commission to entertain the appeal. He requested a court order requiring his reinstatement. The Court of Appeals, however, upheld Cole's dismissal.

The Supreme Court reversed. The majority opinion, written by Justice John M. Harlan, an appointee of President Dwight D. Eisenhower, was based on the scope and meaning of the Summary Suspension Act of 1950. Harlan argued that EXECUTIVE ORDER 9835, as amended by Executive Order 10241, was all-embracing. The executive order thus provided that, where loyalty charges are involved, employee dismissals may be made regardless of whether the employee's job may be considered sensitive to national security. This was in conflict with congressional authorizing legislation because Harlan interpreted the 1950 legislation as clearly linking the nature of an employee's job to national security. Consequently, Harlan reasoned that if all positions in the national government did not affect the "national security" within the meaning of the 1950 act and that if no determination had been made that Cole's job as a food and drug inspector would adversely affect the "national security," it "necessarily" followed that Cole's discharge was not authorized by the 1950 act. Since his dismissal was not authorized by law, it was in violation of the Veterans Preference Act.

Justice Tom C. Clark, joined by Justices Stanley F. Reed and Sherman Minton, dissented on the grounds that Harlan had misinterpreted the intent of Congress, which intended to include all federal jobs as affecting national security. The dissenters went beyond disagreement over congressional intent. They argued that by striking down the President's executive order, the majority

> raises a question as to the constitutional power of the President to authorize the dismissal of possible disloyal executive employees. . . . This power might arise from the grant of executive power in Article II of the Constitution and not from the Congress. . . . [Thus,] the opinion of the majority avoids this important point which must be faced by any decision holding an Executive Order inoperative.

In the era immediately following World War II, doctrinal support for a broad interpretation of executive dismissal authority was, as in *Cole v. Young*, the hallmark of the Truman appointees. The Truman-appointed Justices treated alleged disloyalty dismissals as incidental to, in the words of Edward S. Corwin, the President's "overriding power of removal." In contrast, Harlan and the largely Roosevelt-appointed Court majority insisted that procedural safeguards against blanket executive dismissal policies be upheld because of the "stigma attached to persons dismissed on loyalty grounds." Subsequent congressional efforts to overturn *Cole* failed.

BIBLIOGRAPHY

Corwin, Edward S. *The President: Office and Powers, 1787–1957*. 1957.
Fisher, Louis. *Constitutional Conflicts between Congress and the President*. 3d ed. 1991.
Murphy, Walter F. *Congress and the Court*. 1962.

JOHN R. SCHMIDHAUSER

COLFAX, SCHUYLER (1823–1885), Speaker of the House of Representatives (1863–1869), seventeenth Vice President of the United States (1869–1873). Colfax moved from the WHIG PARTY into the REPUBLICAN PARTY via the KNOW-NOTHING (AMERICAN) PARTY, a not uncommon pathway in the political turmoil of the 1840s and 1850s. His multifaceted career as a journalist, state office holder, convention delegate, Congressman, Speaker of the House, and Vice President, meant that his connection to the presidency was extensive, peripheral, and covetous. In 1860, when Indiana Congressman Colfax was but four years into his first national elected office, friends began public discussion of him as a presidential nominee. In January 1864 he denied a newspaper report that he favored a second term for Abraham Lincoln, claiming that his post as Speaker of the House required strict neutrality. In fact, he was playing a very shadowy part in the movement on behalf of SALMON P. CHASE to replace Lincoln with a more radical Republican.

As early as 1866, Indiana newspapers began to promote him as the best candidate for 1868. He did not promote himself openly but did intimate that Ulysses S. Grant was not strong enough on RECONSTRUCTION to lead the ticket and that a preferable pairing would be Benjamin Wade for President and Grant for the second spot. He denied authorship of a widely published Indiana newspaper circular listing sixteen reasons why Grant would be a poor candidate. With Grant available, however, it was clear that Colfax could not be the presidential nominee, and as the convention approached, Indiana delegates pushed Colfax for Vice President. In this he happily acquiesced, thereby reversing his opinion of 1864, when he said that the speakership was more important than the vice presidency "except in the nearness of succession." He received the vice presidential nomination on the fifth ballot after Wade had led for four.

As Vice President, Colfax kept aloof from policy discussions, never became part of Grant's circle of advisers, and did not attempt to influence PATRONAGE decisions, which disappointed his longtime friends. In September 1870 he announced his intention to retire to private life at the end of his term. Beginning in early 1871 and continuing for a year, newspapers in Indiana and elsewhere supported him as a candidate to replace Grant. In the face of the growing Liberal Republican movement, Colfax appeared to some Republicans as a viable candidate to reunify the party. By November 1871 Colfax thought it advisable to assure Grant in writing of his loyalty; Grant responded the same day to assure Colfax that he put no stock in reports of a rift. Colfax also told Grant that disaffected Republicans who came to him went away without support: "I have abstained from criticism, even when I thought it deserved, so that no one should be able to use my comments in an unfriendly way." To this cryptic and somewhat backhanded pronouncement of fealty Grant did not respond.

Not until February 1872 did Colfax totally repudiate the movement to nominate him for the presidency, a decision so late that it may have left him with no hope of maintaining Grant's support. Indeed, a contemporary said of Colfax that he never declined any office until it was clear there was no hope of his receiving it. In consequence of Colfax's apparently firm determination to retire, Senator HENRY WILSON had made himself the front-runner for the vice presidential nomination. Now in an awkward situation, by November 1871 Colfax was claiming he had never said he would refuse a second vice presidential nomination if the party pressed it on him without his soliciting it. A movement now grew to keep him in the vice presidency, and the spring of 1872 saw Colfax and Wilson vying with each other in public defense of the Grant administration against charges of corruption and other criticisms. But there was no public nod from Grant, and when the Republican convention came Wilson won a clear, if close, first-ballot victory. It was the fourth occasion in American history when an incumbent President, for reasons other than death or resignation, campaigned for reelection with a different running mate.

A variety of factors led to Colfax's replacement. Grenville Dodge, the brilliant surveyor-engineer of western railroads, and other prominent contemporaries claimed in later years that Grant had dictated it. Even so, the retirement statement and its reconsideration, press reports of a rift with Grant, the hostility by Washington press correspondents (manifested by their jubilation during the convention), and Grant's opportunity to rebuke administration foe Charles Sumner by choosing Sumner's Senate rival, all undoubtedly played a part. Colfax was also caught up in the CREDIT MOBILIER SCANDAL, but, while this may have been known earlier at the White House, the list of names of government figures who had received favors did not become public until after the convention.

BIBLIOGRAPHY

Hollister, O. J. *Life of Schuyler Colfax.* 1886.
Ross, Earle D. *The Liberal Republican Movement.* 1919.
Smith, Willard H. *Schuyler Colfax: The Changing Fortunes of a Political Idol.* 1952.

JAMES E. SEFTON

COLONIALISM. Despite the origin of the United States as a nation that fought to free itself from colonial status, the attitude and policy of U.S. Presidents toward colonialism has not been predictable and unalterable. Until the end of the nineteenth century, however, Presidents generally reasserted the principle of the right of revolution, limited only by the realities of national interest.

During the early days of the republic, independence struggles in Latin America sorely tested principles. George Washington avoided giving any encouragement to Spanish American revolutionary leaders, recognizing the danger of the United States being drawn into the wider conflict among the European powers. In his FAREWELL ADDRESS, Washington advised against taking sides in Europe's wars and, by inference, in their colonial rivalries. To allay the criticism of those who believed that NEUTRALITY was morally bankrupt and who demanded action to assist struggles for independence, John Adams observed that good government did not necessarily follow the elimination of bad.

Nevertheless, early Presidents grappled with the issue of the recognition of the Latin American right of self-government. Although pragmatism caused early Presidents to delay recognition of Latin American states, they also sensed opportunity in the collapse of Spain's New World empire. While Presidents Thomas Jefferson and James Madison avoided direct involvement in independence movements in Spanish America, they acted to prevent other states from taking advantage of Spain's troubles. They formulated the no-transfer concept, whereby they were prepared to resist the passing of these territories from weak Spain to a stronger England or France. Similarly, President James Monroe, in the MONROE DOCTRINE of December 1823, enunciated the noncolonization principle, affirming that "the American continents . . . are henceforth not to be considered as subject for future colonization by any European power."

The Monroe Doctrine resolved the contradiction in U.S. attitudes toward nonentanglement and colonialism. During most of the nineteenth century, Presidents were content with this doctrine of the "two spheres." They were generally indifferent to the partitioning of Africa and the de facto dismemberment of China, being concerned mainly with trade access (the so-called OPEN DOOR).

This attitude changed at the end of the century, with America's rise to world power. Presidents adopted the prevailing racist sentiment of the "white man's burden." In deciding what to do with the PHILIPPINES after defeating Spain in 1898, President William McKinley concluded, "There was nothing left for us to do but . . . to educate the Filipinos, and uplift and civilize and Christianize them." But, as the United States built an empire in the Pacific and the Caribbean, dissent arose at home. Even Theodore Roosevelt, an advocate of the large policy, anguished over such criticism. He denied that the United States felt any land hunger and described the nation as an international policeman performing a duty with extreme reluctance. Roosevelt did not create a colonial ministry but turned over the responsibility for overseas dependencies to the WAR DEPARTMENT or relied on his personal troubleshooter, William Howard Taft. America's colonial experience was temporary, and no uniform policy emerged for the various holdings. As President, Taft tried to reduce the taint of colonialism further by substituting economic investment for military intervention.

Still, President Woodrow Wilson felt compelled to reassert traditional American values. In 1913, he stated that "the United States will never again seek one additional foot of territory by conquest." He repudiated Taft's DOLLAR DIPLOMACY in China and Nicaragua on the grounds that the terms of proposed loans by American bankers were "obnoxious to the principles upon which the Government of our people rests." Concluding that colonialism was one of the causes of WORLD WAR I, Wilson in January 1917 suggested to the warring parties that they accept a "peace without victory," based on the principle "that governments derive all their just powers from the consent of the governed."

After the United States entered the war, Wilson proposed the FOURTEEN POINTS, which included the "impartial adjustment of all colonial claims," and when the war ended, Wilson proposed a LEAGUE OF NATIONS that would create a system of mandates entrusted with the "well-being and development" of peoples "not yet able to stand by themselves."

Although the United States did not join the League of Nations, the administrations of the 1920s and 1930s embarked on a policy of liquidation of imperialism, recalling U.S. troops from the DOMINICAN REPUBLIC, HAITI, and Nicaragua and renouncing the right to intervene in CUBA and PANAMA. In 1934, President Franklin D. Roosevelt approved the Tydings-McDuffie Act, setting forth procedures for the complete independence of the Philippines. The United States' involvement in WORLD WAR II delayed Philippine independence until 1946, but the war itself hastened the end of colonialism.

In 1941, Roosevelt and British Prime Minister Winston Churchill issued the ATLANTIC CHARTER, which proclaimed certain common principles, among them to "respect the right of all peoples to choose the form of government under which they will live." In the charter of the UNITED NATIONS, Harry S. Truman subscribed to the principles of "equal rights and self-determination of peoples" and to ever tighter international controls over the administration of non-self-governing territories through the establishment of the trusteeship system. The principle of permitting peoples "to choose their own form of government" guided Truman's policy of assistance to Greece and Turkey (the TRUMAN DOCTRINE) in 1947 and the POINT FOUR PROGRAM of 1950. Extending assistance to the emerging nations of the Middle East in 1957, President Dwight D. Eisenhower reiterated "the full sovereignty and independence of each and every nation in the Middle East."

Despite these pronouncements, after 1950 the United States intervened in former colonial areas, frequently with overt military force but also covertly. United States policy in the COLD WAR opposed the expansion of the Soviet Union or the establishment of a communist government anywhere. Though accused of neocolonialism, the United States denied any interest in domination or territory; indeed, the Truman Doctrine and the EISENHOWER DOCTRINE affirmed the right of self-determination. The preoccupation of the United States with the ATLANTIC ALLIANCE, however, further muddied its stance on colonialism.

At the urging of British Prime Minister Harold Macmillan, Eisenhower in December 1960 instructed the United States' U.N. delegation to abstain from voting on a resolution calling for immediate independence for all colonial countries. John F. Kennedy, however, sought to recapture the high ground on the issue of colonialism, seizing the opportunity in January 1962 to support a U.N. resolution that condemned Portugal (a NATO member) for its conduct in Angola.

Between the end of World War II and Kennedy's election, thirty-seven new nations were born in Africa, Asia, and the Middle East. Even though colonialism was dead, the journalist Walter Lippman in April 1965 criticized Lyndon Baines Johnson's VIETNAM WAR policy as reflecting the offensive notion of the white man's burden. In the cold war era, Presidents tended to confuse the right of self-determination with teaching other nations good government. The actions of Presidents Ronald Reagan in GRENADA and Nicaragua and George Bush in Panama demonstrated that confusion still reigned, though subsequent events witnessed the triumph of the principles of 1776 on their merits without the need to intervene.

BIBLIOGRAPHY

Kennedy, Paul. *The Rise and Fall of the Great Powers.* 1987.

Link, Arthur S. *Woodrow Wilson and the Progressive Era, 1910–1917.* 1954.

Paterson, Thomas G. *Meeting the Communist Threat: Truman to Reagan.* 1988.

Perkins, Dexter. *A History of the Monroe Doctrine.* 1963.

Pratt, Julius W. *Expansionists of 1898.* 1936.

Whitaker, Arthur P. *The United States and the Independence of Latin America, 1800–1830.* 1954.

CHARLES D. AMERINGER

COMMANDER IN CHIEF. Article II, Section 2, of the Constitution provides that "the President shall be Commander in Chief of the Army and Navy of the United States, and of the Militia of the several States, when called into the actual Service of the United States." In YOUNGSTOWN SHEET & TUBE CO. v. SAWYER (1952), Justice Robert H. Jackson condemned as "sinister and alarming" the invocation of the Commander in Chief clause as a source of presidential "power to do anything, anywhere, that can be done with an army or navy." While stated in the context of reviewing President Harry S. Truman's invocation of the clause to support his seizure of the steel mills, Jackson's observations certainly anticipated the claims of later executives, from Lyndon B. Johnson to George Bush, who carelessly invoked the provision as justification for their military adventures. The clause also has become the principal pillar for those commentators who hope to vest the constitutional power of war and peace in the President. The title of Commander in Chief, however, confers no warmaking power whatever, nor does it afford the President any general foreign policy powers. Understood by the Framers of the Constitution in narrow terms, the title vests in the President only the authority to repel sudden attacks on the United States and to conduct war when so authorized by Congress. In this capacity, the President is responsible for directing those forces placed at his command by an act of Congress, which is vested by the Constitution with the sole and exclusive power to decide for war.

Separation of Powers. The CONSTITUTIONAL CONVENTION severed the authority to decide for war from the power to conduct it. The Framers' decision to withhold from the President the power to commence war signaled a marked departure from the existing models of government that placed the WAR POWER, indeed virtually all FOREIGN AFFAIRS powers, in the hands of the executive. In *The Second Treatise of Government* (1690), John Locke had described three branches of government: legislative, executive, and federative. According to Locke, the federative power, or what we today refer to as the power to conduct foreign affairs, encompassed "the power of war and peace, leagues and alliances, and all the transactions with all persons and communities without the commonwealth." The power, moreover, was "almost always united" with the executive. The separation of the executive and federative powers, Locke warned, would bring "disorder and ruin." Similarly, Sir William Blackstone, in his distinguished *Commentaries on the Laws of England* (1765–1769), had explained that the king enjoyed absolute power over foreign affairs and war: the authority to send and receive ambassadors, make treaties and alliances, make war or peace, issue letters of marque and reprisal, command the military, raise and regulate fleets and armies, and represent the nation in its intercourse with foreign governments.

Despite their familiarity with the English scheme of governance, the Framers granted Congress most of the nation's foreign affairs powers. Congress was vested with the sole and exclusive authority to initiate war. The Constitution withheld from the President the sole power to make treaties, making him share that power with the Senate. James Madison and ALEXANDER HAMILTON referred to this combination as a "fourth branch" of government, which they expected would manage most of the country's foreign policy responsibilities. The President was granted the authority to receive ambassadors, an act that entails important international legal obligations. But the founding trio of Hamilton, Madison, and Thomas Jefferson did not view the reception or "recognition" clause as a font of discretionary executive power to decide whether the United States would have relations with other nations or to determine unilaterally the tone and temper of those relations. Rather, the Framers understood the recognition power as a narrow, clerklike function or duty imposed as a matter of convenience on the President, rather than Congress, to carry out the nation's obligation under international law to receive ambassadors from sovereign countries. The President was granted the authority to send ambassadors abroad but only after the Senate approved his nominations. He was not vested with the monarchical power to issue letters of marque and reprisal; that power was granted to Congress. Nor was he given the authority to raise and regulate fleets and armies. That power, too, was left with Congress. Finally, Congress was also granted plenary authority over foreign commerce.

The Debate over the War Power. The Framers' decision to grant Congress the war power is illuminated by the debates at the Constitutional Convention. An early draft reported by the Committee of Detail vested Congress with the power to "make war." This bore sharp resemblance to the Articles of Confederation, which had placed the "sole and exclusive right and power of determining on peace and war" in the Continental Congress. Charles Pinckney, who expected Congress to meet only once a year, objected to the plan because he thought the legislative proceedings "were too slow" to protect the security interests of the nation. The draft also proved unsatisfactory to Madison and ELBRIDGE GERRY. In a joint resolution, they moved to substitute "declare" for "make," "leaving to the Executive the power to repel sudden attacks." The meaning of the motion is unmistakable. Congress was granted the power to make—that is, to initiate—war; the President, for obvious reasons, would be empowered to act immediately to repel sudden attacks without authorization from Congress. There was no quarrel whatever with respect to the sudden attack provision, but there was some question as to whether the substitution of "declare" for "make" would effectuate the intention of Madison and Gerry. Roger Sherman of Connecticut thought the joint motion "stood very well," saying, "The Executive shd. be able to repel and not commence war. 'Make' better than 'declare' the latter narrowing the power [of the legislature] too much." Virginia's George Mason "was agst. giving the power of war to the Executive, because [he was] not [safely] to be trusted with it; or to the Senate, because [it was] not so constructed as to be entitled to it. He was for clogging rather than facilitating war; but for facilitating peace. He preferred 'declare' to 'make.'" The Madison-Gerry proposal was adopted by a vote of 7 to 2. When RUFUS KING explained that the word "make" might be understood to authorize Congress to initiate as well as conduct war, Connecticut changed its vote so that the word "declare" was approved, eight states to one.

The debates and the vote on the war power make it clear that Congress alone possesses the authority to initiate war. The war-making power was specifically withheld from the President; he was given only the authority to repel sudden attacks. JAMES WILSON, who played a role only slightly less important than Madison's in the Constitutional Convention, told the Pennsylvania ratifying convention: "This system will not hurry us into war; it is calculated to guard against it. It will not be in the power of a single man . . . to involve us in such distress; for the important power of declaring war is vested in the legislature at large." Similar assurances were provided to other state ratifying conventions.

The Constitutional Convention's rejection of prevailing governmental models for foreign affairs is attributable to two principal factors. First, the Framers were attached to republican ideology, the core principle of which was collective decision making in domestic as well as foreign affairs. Second, the founding generation, influenced by its own experience under King George III and by its understanding of history, lived in fear of a powerful executive and was adamantly opposed to a President's unilateral control of foreign policy. History had its claims. In FEDERALIST 75 Hamilton stated, "The history of human conduct does not warrant that exalted opinion of human virtue which would make it wise in a nation to commit interests of so delicate and momentous a kind, as those which concern its intercourse with the rest of the world, to the sole disposal of . . . a President." In a letter to Jefferson in 1798, Madison observed "The constitution supposes, what the History of all Govts demonstrates, that the Ex. is the branch of power most interested in war, & most prone to it. It has accordingly with studied care, vested the question of war in the Legisl." The Framers' decision to create a radically new blueprint for the conduct of foreign affairs justified Wilson's remark that it was incorrect to consider "the Prerogatives of the British Monarch as a proper guide in defining the Executive powers. Some of these prerogatives were of a Legislative nature. Among others that of war & peace."

The separation of the power to initiate war from the power to conduct it reflected the interplay of different values. The decision to commence war requires the most solemn, deliberative debate. It emphasizes the values of collective decision making. But the decision actually to conduct a war, to determine strategy and tactics, pivots on a different value, that of efficiency. In *Federalist* 74, Hamilton adduced the basic reason for making the President Commander in Chief: the direction of war "most peculiarly demands those qualities which distinguish the exercise of power by a single hand." The power of directing war and emphasizing the common strength "forms a usual and essential part in the definition of the executive authority."

The English and Colonial Legacy. While the Framers rejected the Locke-Blackstone model for foreign affairs, they nevertheless drew their concept of the Commander in Chief directly from English history. As Francis D. Wormuth observed, "The office of commander in chief has never carried the power of war and peace, nor was it invented by the framers of the Constitution." The title of Commander in Chief was introduced by King Charles I in 1639 and was always used as a generic term referring to the highest officer in a particular chain of command. With the erruption of the English civil wars, both the king and Parliament appointed commanders in chief in various theaters of action. The ranking commander in chief, purely a military post, was always under the command of a political superior, whether appointed by the king, Parliament or, with the development of the cabinet system in the eighteenth century, by the secretary of war.

England transplanted the title to America in the eighteenth century by appointing a number of commanders in chief and by the practice of entitling colonial governors as commanders in chief (or occasionally as vice admirals or captains general). The appointment of General Thomas Gage as commander in chief from 1763 to 1776 caused the colonists grave concern, for he proceeded to interfere in civil affairs and acquired considerable influence over Indian relations, trade, and transportation. The bitter memory of his decision to quarter troops in civilians' homes spawned the Third Amendment to the Constitution. These activities and others prompted the colonists in the Declaration of Independence to complain of King George III that he had "affected to render the Military Independent of and superior to the Civil Power."

But the colonists had no reason to fear the governors who were given the title commander in chief, even though they controlled the provincial forces, since the colonial assemblies claimed and asserted the right to vote funds for the militia as well as to call it into service. In fact, grievances came from the governors, who complained of the relative impotence of their positions. The colonists' assemblies' (and later, the states') assertions of the power of the purse as a check on the commander in chief reflected an English practice that was instituted in the middle of the seventeenth century. By 1665, Parliament, as a means of maintaining political control of the military establishment, had inaugurated the policy of making annual military appropriations lasting but one year. This practice sharply emphasized the power of Parliament to determine the size of the army to be placed under the direction of the commander in chief.

The practice had a long influence, for, under its constitutional power to raise and support armies and to provide a navy, Congress acquired right that the colonial and state assemblies had had to vote funds for the armed forces. An additional historical parallel in the Article I, Section 8, clause 13 provides that "no Appropriation of Money to that Use shall be for a longer Term than two Years." The requirement of legislative approval for the allocation of funds to raise troops underscores the principle of political superiority over military command. It also constitutes a sharp reminder that a Commander in Chief is dependent on the legislature's willingness to give him an army to command.

Most of the early state constitutions followed the colonial practice of making the governor commander in chief under the authority of state legislatures. For example, article VII of the Massachusetts constitution of 1780 provided that the governor would be "commander in chief of the army and navy." In carefully circumscribing his power, the governor was to "repel, resist [and] expel" attempts to invade the commonwealth, and it vested him "with all these and other powers incident to the offices of captain general . . . to be exercised agreeably to the rules and regulations of the Constitution and the laws of the land, and not otherwise."

The Continental Congress continued the usage of the title in 1775, when it unanimously decided to appoint George Washington as general. His commission named him "General and Commander in Chief, of the Army of the United Colonies." He was required to comply with orders and directions from Congress, which did not hesitate to instruct the commander in chief on military and policy matters.

The practice of entitling the office at the apex of the military hierarchy as commander in chief and of subordinating the office to a political superior, whether a king, a parliament, or a congress, had thus been firmly established for a century and a half and was thoroughly familiar to the Framers when they met in Philadelphia. Perhaps this settled historical usage accounts for the fact that there was no debate on the Commander in Chief clause at the Convention.

In the plan he read to the convention on 29 May 1787, South Carolinian Charles Pinckney introduced the title of President and proposed, "He shall, by Virtue of his Office, be Commander in Chief of the Land Forces of U.S. and Admiral of their Navy." Presumably, Pinckney had drawn on the traditional usage of the title employed in the South Carolina constitution of 1776, which had provided for a "president and commander-in-chief," and that of 1778, which had included a provision for a "governor and commander in chief." There was no such provision in the Randolph (or Virginia) Plan, which was read to the convention on the same day. On 15 June William Paterson submitted the New Jersey Plan, which called for a plural executive. It provided that "the Executives . . . ought . . . to direct all military operations; provided that none of the persons composing the federal executive shall at any time take command of any troops, so as personally to conduct any enterprise as General, or in other capacity." The qualifying clause was meant to discourage a military takeover of the government. When Hamilton submitted a plan to the convention on 18 June he probably did not propose the title Commander in Chief, but he undoubtedly had it in mind when he said the President was "to have the direction of war when authorized or begun."

Hamilton's speech summarized the essence of the President's powers as Commander in Chief: when war is "authorized or begun," the President is to command the military operations of American forces. He elaborated on this theme and sharply distinguished the powers of the king and those of the President in *Federalist* 69. While the power of the king includes the power to declare war and to raise and regulate fleets and armies, those powers, explained Hamilton, would be vested in Congress "by the Constitution under consideration." The President, as Commander in Chief, was to be "first General and admiral" in the "direction of war when authorized or begun." But all political authority remained in Congress, as it had under the Articles of Confederation.

Nineteenth-Century Practice. Nineteenth-century presidential practice and judicial decisions reaffirmed this understanding of the war power and the President's role as Commander in Chief. Early Presidents often refused to initiate hostilities without prior authorization from Congress. In 1792 and 1793, President Washington received urgent requests for the use of military force from governors who feared impending attacks by INDIANS. Washington stated that he had no authority to order an attack and deferred the issue to Congress, "who solely are vested with the powers of war." Contrary to the charge that President John Adams acted unilaterally in the QUASI-WAR WITH FRANCE of 1798–1800, Congress, in fact, passed some twenty laws to authorize the war. In *Bas v. Tingy* (1800), the Supreme Court held that those statutes had authorized imperfect, or limited, war. In *Talbot v. Seeman* (1801), a case that involved issues raised by the quasi-war, Chief Justice JOHN MARSHALL held that since the "whole powers of war" are "vested in Congress," it is for that body alone to authorize perfect or imperfect war. In LITTLE v. BARREME (1804), Marshall emphasized that the President, as Commander in Chief, is subject to statutory restriction. One of the statutes passed by Congress during the Quasi-War with France authorized the President to seize vessels that sailed *to* French ports. But President Adams ordered American ships to capture vessels which sailed *to or from* French ports, and, in his opinion for the Court, Marshall held that Adams's order had violated the statute. Subsequent judicial rulings have reiterated that the Commander in Chief may be controlled by statute.

President Thomas Jefferson understood the limitations of the Commander in Chief clause. In 1801, in his first annual message to Congress, he reported the arrogant demands made by Joseph Caramanly, the pasha of Tripoli. Unless the United States paid tribute, the pasha threatened to seize American ships and citizens. In response, Jefferson sent a small squadron to the Mediterranean to protect against the threatened attack. He then asked Congress for further guidance, since he was "unauthorized by the Constitution, without the sanction of Congress, to go beyond the line of defense." It was left to Congress to authorize "measures of offense." Jefferson's understanding of the war clause underwent no revision. Like Jefferson, President James Madison was aggrieved by the punishment and harassment inflicted on United States vessels. In 1812, he expressed to Congress his extreme resentment of the British practices of seizing American ships and seamen and inducing Indian tribes to attack the United States. Madison complained but said the question of "whether the United States shall remain passive under these progressive usurpations and these accumulating wrongs, or, opposing force, to force in defense of their national rights" is "a solemn question which the Constitution wisely confides to the legislative department of the Government." Following his 1823 announcement of what has become known as the MONROE DOCTRINE, President James Monroe was confronted with international circumstances that seemed to invite the use of force, but Monroe repeatedly disclaimed any constitutional power to initiate hostilities, since, he maintained, that authority was granted to Congress. President James K. Polk may well have initiated war with Mexico in 1846 [*see* MEXICAN WAR], when he ordered an army into a disputed area on the Texas-Mexico border. But Polk understood the constitutional dimensions of the war power and offered the rationale that Mexico had invaded the United States, which, if true, would justify a response by the Commander in Chief. It is noteworthy that he did not adduce a presidential power to initiate war. None of President Abraham Lincoln's actions in the CIVIL WAR involved a claim to a presidential power to initiate war. In the PRIZE CASES (1863), the Supreme Court upheld Lincoln's blockade against the rebellious Confederacy as a constitutional response to sudden invasion, which began with the attack on Fort Sumter. In the opinion for the Court, Justice Robert Grier stated that, as Commander in Chief, the President "has no power to initiate or declare war either against a foreign nation or a domestic State."

Presidential Warmaking. Until 1950, no President departed from this understanding of the parameters of the Commander in Chief clause. But to justify President Truman's unilateral decision to introduce troops into the KOREAN WAR, revisionists purported to locate in the President a broad discretionary authority to commence hostilities. Emboldened by Truman's claim, subsequent Presidents have likewise unilaterally initiated acts of war, from the VIETNAM WAR to the incursions in GRENADA and PANAMA. But this claim is cut from whole cloth. It ignores the origins and development of the title, the clear understanding of the Constitution's Framers, the nineteenth-century record, and the history of judicial interpretation. The Supreme Court has never held that the Commander in Chief clause confers power to initiate war. In *United States v. Sweeny* (1895), Justice Henry Brown wrote for the Court that the object of the clause was to give the President "such supreme and undivided command as would be necessary to the prosecution of a successful war." In 1919, Senator George Sutherland, who later became an Associate Justice of the Supreme Court, wrote, "Generally speaking, the war powers of the President under the Constitution are simply those that belong to any commander-in-chief of the military forces of a nation at war. The Constitution confers no war powers upon the President as such."

While the Supreme Court has held that the President may not initiate hostilities and that he is authorized only to direct the movements of the military forces placed by law at his command, it has been contended that the existence of a standing army provides the President with broad discretionary authority to deploy troops on behalf of foreign-policy goals. Although the intrusion of a public force into a foreign country may well entangle the United States in a war, Presidents have often manipulated troop deployments so as to present Congress with a fait accompli. Given the broad range of war powers vested in Congress, including the authority to provide for the common defense, to raise and support armies, and to decide, in Madison's words, whether "a war ought to be commenced, continued or concluded," it seems clear that Congress may govern absolutely the deployment of forces outside U.S. borders. As a practical measure, Congress may choose, within the confines of the delegation doctrine, to vest the President with some authority to send troops abroad, but there is nothing inherent in the Commander in Chief clause that yields such authority.

BIBLIOGRAPHY

Adler, David Gray. "The Constitution and Presidential Warmaking: The Enduring Debate." *Political Science Quarterly* 103 (1988): 1–36.
Berger, Raoul. *Executive Privilege: A Constitutional Myth.* 1974.
Fisher, Louis. *Constitutional Conflicts between Congress and the President.* 3d rev. ed. 1991.
Henkin, Louis. *Foreign Affairs and the Constitution.* 1972.
Keynes, Edward. *Undeclared War: Twilight Zone of Constitutional Power.* 2d ed. 1991.
Koh, Harold. *The National Security Constitution: Sharing Power after the Iran-Contra Affair.* 1990.
Robinson, Donald L. *To the Best of My Ability: The Presidency and the Constitution.* 1987.
Schlesinger, Arthur, Jr. *The Imperial Presidency.* 1973.
Wormuth, Francis D., and Edwin B. Firmage. *To Chain the Dog of War: The War Power of Congress in History and Law.* 1986.

DAVID GRAY ADLER

COMMENTATORS ON THE PRESIDENCY. The tradition of critical commentary on the presidency begins in the Progressive Era (1900–1917) and is associated with the evolution of the modern presidency. At the opening of the twentieth century, widely regarded and influential academics and publicists argued that the demands of a modern society required government whose focus was presidential rather than congressional. These Progressive Era commentators argued for increased prominence for the presidency in the American constitutional system.

An Unbalanced System. Nineteenth-century government reflected a Whig doctrine of legislative supremacy at the national level and the decentralization of authority to the state level. For the Presidents of this period, Congress set the tone of government and specified its directions. Presidents were without responsibility for proposing policy directions for government or for directing government's administration of policy. Congress controlled both policy and administration, and it, in turn, reflected the interests of PATRONAGE-seeking political party machines. Increasingly, middle-class Americans viewed the patronage-ridden, congressionally dominated national government as woefully inadequate. These citizens comprised a natural audience for critics of the presidency, who proposed substantial reform in government.

In 1885 Woodrow Wilson, then a professor at Bryn Mawr College, published *Congressional Government*, which argued that congressional committees dominated the national government. Wilson saw the presidency as a neutered role, with Congress dealing directly with the DEPARTMENTAL SECRETARIES and, in effect, operating the executive branch. The President's only weapon was the VETO, and Wilson observed that this made the President, "powerful rather as a branch of the legislature than as the titular head of the Executive" (1965 ed., p. 173). Wilson even wondered whether it made any difference who was chosen as President. "Has the President any very great authority in matters of vital policy?" Wilson wrote (p. 214). Wilson's book contained two assumptions that would be shared by later critics. First, these writers all rejected a "literary," or mechanical, view of the Constitution in favor of an "organic" view that would admit the possibility of changing constitutional practice without changing the letter of the Constitution. Second, to one degree or another, their example of a properly organized government was the British parliamentary system with its unity of executive and legislative authority.

Progressive Era Commentators. Wilson's *Congressional Government* reflected the low state of the presidency in American government in the two decades after the CIVIL WAR. By the end of the century, however, Presidents' assertiveness had increased, but the office lacked a continuing institutional basis for maintaining strength. Many saw Theodore Roosevelt, who succeeded the assassinated William McKinley in the presidency, as a harbinger of a changing presidency.

For Princeton University professor Henry Jones Ford, the most pressing reason for redressing the constitutional imbalance between the presidency and Congress was the fiscal irresponsibility of the national government. Peacetime deficits were becoming regular occurrences, and control of spending lay in congressional committees with no overall authority for a governmental budget. In *The Cost of Our National Government* (1910), Ford prescribed arrangements that would give to the President powers of initiative and some control over congressional financial decisions. Writing more than a decade before the BUDGET AND ACCOUNTING ACT OF 1921, Ford concluded, "Committee government must be superseded by responsible government. . . . The signs of the times indicate that the people are . . . craving effective leadership" (p. 120). For Ford there was no doubt that the locus of such leadership lay in the presidency.

Two other Progressive Era commentators, Frederick Cleveland and William F. Willoughby, were not only prominent for their writing on American government but were also distinguished by their service during the administration of William Howard Taft. Cleveland was Taft's consultant on administrative efficiency and later chair of the TAFT COMMISSION on Economy and Efficiency; Willoughby was one of the members of that commission. Cleveland's criticism of the American system was that it removed from the President responsibility for what he called the "doing" part of government. In his view, the Constitution's system of CHECKS AND BALANCES muddled the crucial distinction between choosing policy and implementing policy. Consequently, government was hindered from properly addressing the problems that abounded in modern society. In *Organized Democracy* (1913), Cleveland wrote, "The chief executive is the only officer

who can represent the government as a whole" (p. 456). Later, writing with Arthur E. Buck, Cleveland asked whether congressional committees would continue to dominate government or whether "the popularly elected executive will be made responsible and accountable to the electorate" (*The Budget and Responsible Government*, 1920, p. 395). Cleveland's concern was that the President should have the capacity to direct the executive branch for the good of the people rather than, as he saw it, the executive branch being misdirected by numerous congressional committees reflecting narrow interests. His prescription was that, in an era of major demands on government, the Constitution must be read so as to make efficient government—meaning a robust presidency—possible.

While he was also critical of the state of American government, Willoughby had a perspective that was rather different from that of Cleveland. Willoughby admitted that the Constitution's checks-and-balances system granted Congress responsibility for administration, but he argued that Congress misused its legitimate authority over administration by attempting to direct administration itself. He wrote, "The evils resulting from the Congress intervening in executive and administrative matters are constantly in evidence" (*Government of the Modern State*, 1919, p. 267). Willoughby's prescription for change was for Congress to realize it could best fulfill its responsibility through after-the-fact CONGRESSIONAL OVERSIGHT of the executive branch, broadly delegating responsibility for direction of administration to the President.

In 1908 Woodrow Wilson published *Constitutional Government in America*, a reexamination of the presidency that presents notable evidence that the climate of ideas surrounding American politics had undergone a profound shift. Wilson wrote that the office had grown in response to new demands, vigorous Presidents, and changing ideas about the presidency. He argued that while the Constitution did not endow the presidency with great institutional strength, incumbents could strengthen the office by harnessing PUBLIC OPINION and calling forth partisan support. Wilson wrote, "The President is at liberty . . . to be as big a man as he can. . . . His capacity will set the limit; and if Congress be overborne by him . . . it will be from no lack of constitutional powers on its part, but only because the President has the nation behind him." (p. 70).

More widely read than any of the academic critics, Herbert Croly, editor of *The New Republic*, became the most prominent political thinker of the Progressive Era, and his work supplied a context for arguments in support of enhanced presidential power. In contrast to academic critics' focus on specifics of the presidency, Croly offered an overall vision of modern American society in which comprehensive national power and executive leadership were prerequisite to genuine progress. In his *The Promise of American Life* (1909), Croly argued for a democratized, Hamiltonian nationalism as the means for enhancing America's progress. For Croly, Theodore Roosevelt exemplified the appropriate role for the executive. Discussing the imbalance between the Congress and the presidency in the nineteenth century, Croly wrote, "Our legislatures were and still are the strongholds of special and local interests and anything which undermines executive authority . . . seriously threatens our national integrity and balance" (p. 69).

Later Commentators. The great accomplishment of the Progressive commentators was to win Americans over to the view that the presidency was the national government's primary means for leadership. This association of the presidency and competent government became a paradigmatic assumption of later critics of American government—the assumption on which modern scholarly interpretation of the presidency was founded. In that sense, the scholarly literature exhibits an institutional partisanship. Three examples of post-Progressive academic commentators—Louis Brownlow, James M. Burns, and Richard Neustadt—will serve to illustrate the point.

Louis Brownlow was a bridge figure between the Progressive Era and modern commentators. Beginning his career in public administration during the Progressive period, Brownlow served under Franklin D. Roosevelt in the late 1930s as chair of the BROWNLOW COMMITTEE, which proposed reforms to strengthen the presidency. In *The President and the Presidency* (1949) he exhibited his connection to the Progressive tradition by arguing that a transformation of the presidency had begun after the turn of the century. Brownlow proceeded to argue for the importance of increasing the President's authority to match modern expectations for executive leadership, calling for such additional capacities as the ITEM VETO for appropriations bills and increased power over executive-branch agencies. Echoing his Progressive predecessors, Brownlow argued that the President must be made responsible for all that government does, for the incumbent "is Manager-in-Chief of the Executive Branch just as he is Commander-in-Chief of the Armed Forces" (*The President and the Presidency*, p. 128).

Throughout his large body of work, James M. Burns focused on the centrality of leadership in democracy and particularly on the presidency. His *The Deadlock of Democracy* (1963) adopted the Progressive critique of the constitutional SEPARATION OF POWERS as weakening executive authority, and Burns analyzed the American system of POLITICAL PARTIES to show that, in reality, four parties had emerged, with both the Democratic and Republican parties having produced presidential and congressional wings. Burns saw the presidency as too often weakened by the interaction of separation of powers and party organization. Reflecting the ideas of Wilson's 1908 book, Burns observed that presidential strength could be enhanced by incumbents who are aware of the possibilities of public leadership of the presidential wings within both parties. In short, the basis of presidential strength lies in the support of public opinion and the proper leadership of partisan forces.

Richard Neustadt is an analyst whose viewpoint began in the Progressive tradition but who stepped beyond that tradition to create the modern framework for the study of the presidency. In *Presidential Power* (1960) Neustadt reflected a Progressive perspective in arguing that the President's ability to lead is the prerequisite for a healthy American political system. He wrote, "There is reason to suppose that . . . the power problems of a President will remain what they have been in the decades just behind us. . . . The President himself and with him the whole government are likely to be more than ever at the mercy of his personal approach" (p. 186). In a conceptual move beyond the Progressive tradition, which saw the presidency's weakness as a function of separation of powers, Neustadt conceived of the President as a strategic actor searching for resources within the fragmented political system and attempting to influence other salient actors within the governmental system. Beginning with a Progressive-like institutional analysis of the presidency, Neustadt built a post-Progressive model for the study of the presidency.

BIBLIOGRAPHY

Brownlow, Louis. *The President and the Presidency.* 1949.
Burns, James M. *The Deadlock of Democracy.* 1963.
Cleveland, Frederick. *Organized Democracy.* 1913.
Croly, Herbert. *The Promise of American Life.* 1911.
Ford, Henry Jones. *The Cost of Our National Government.* 1910.
Neustadt, Richard. *Presidential Power.* 1960.
Vile, M. J. C. *Constitutionalism and the Separation of Powers.* 1967.
White, Leonard D. *The Republican Era.* 1958.
Willoughby, William F. *Government of the Modern State.* 1919.
Wilson, Woodrow. *Congressional Government.* 1956.

PERI E. ARNOLD

COMMERCE, DEPARTMENT OF. The modern Department of Commerce was established under the administration of President William Howard Taft on 4 March 1913. Signed on Taft's last day in office, the act establishing the department was one of the final actions of his presidency. After more than a century of debate and deliberation, which consumed the thought and energy of Presidents from George Washington on, the commerce and manufacturing sectors in the United States finally had an executive department they could call their own.

Yet it was not a President in office but a President-to-be, Herbert Hoover, who, during his tenure as Secretary of Commerce in the 1920s, saw the potential of the post and of the department to have wide-ranging and significant impact on U.S. domestic and international policy. The Commerce Department, which became the primary government entity responsible for fostering and promoting U.S. agendas for international trade, economic growth, and technological advancement was molded into the vehicle for doing so through the vision and actions of the "domestic dynamo" Hoover.

Origins. As early as 1787, at the CONSTITUTIONAL CONVENTION, a recommendation was made that there be a secretary of commerce and finance to help the new government and new national executive administer and promote the commercial interests of the United States. This followed on the heels of ALEXANDER HAMILTON's proposition, cosigned by James Madison and Edmund Randolph at a historical meeting in Annapolis, that matters of trade and commerce be addressed comprehensively by the federal government.

The importance of commerce to the maturation of a young nation was clearly recognized. The Framers cited the promotion of the general welfare—in part another way of saying the promotion of commercial interests—as essential to the formation of a more perfect union. Washington, in his first inaugural address, said, "The advance of agriculture, commerce and manufactures by all proper means will not, I trust, need recommendation." Yet the question remained which department within the federal government should handle the new nation's commercial affairs. Ultimately, the charge went to the TREASURY DEPARTMENT, while a committee of commerce and manufacturing was established by the House of Representatives in 1795. It was not until almost a century later that substantive action was taken toward creating a formal department expressly devoted to commerce.

Largely owing to President William McKinley's policy of actively promoting exports (exports exceeded $1 billion for the first time during McKinley's presidency), Theodore Roosevelt was able to recommend and accomplish the creation of a combined Department of Commerce and Labor. On 14 February 1903, Congress approved legislation creating such a department,

Secretaries of Commerce and Labor[a]

President	Secretary of Commerce and Labor
26 T. Roosevelt	George B. Cortelyou, 1903–1904
	Victor H. Metcalf, 1904–1906
	Oscar S. Straus, 1906–1909
27 Taft	Charles Nagel, 1909–1913

[a] The Department of Commerce and Labor, established in 1903, was divided in 1913 into the Department of Commerce and the DEPARTMENT OF LABOR.

Secretaries of Commerce

President	Secretary of Commerce
28 Wilson	William C. Redfield, 1913–1919
	Joshua W. Alexander, 1919–1921
29 Harding	Herbert C. Hoover, 1921–1923
30 Coolidge	Herbert C. Hoover, 1923–1928
	William F. Whiting, 1928–1929
31 Hoover	Robert P. Lamont, 1929–1932
	Roy D. Chapin, 1932–1933
32 F. D. Roosevelt	Daniel C. Roper, 1933–1938
	Harry L. Hopkins, 1938–1940
	Jesse H. Jones, 1940–1945
	Henry A. Wallace, 1945
33 Truman	Henry A. Wallace, 1945–1946
	W. Averell Harriman, 1946–1948
	Charles Sawyer, 1948–1953
34 Eisenhower	Sinclair Weeks, 1953–1958
	Lewis L. Strauss, 1958–1959
	Frederick H. Mueller, 1959–1961
35 Kennedy	Luther H. Hodges, 1961–1963
36 L. B. Johnson	Luther H. Hodges, 1963–1965
	John T. Connor, 1965–1967
	Alexander B. Trowbridge, 1967–1968
	C. R. Smith, 1968–1969
37 Nixon	Maurice H. Stans, 1969–1972
	Peter G. Peterson, 1972–1973
	Frederick B. Dent, 1973–1974
38 Ford	Frederick B. Dent, 1974–1975
	Rogers C. B. Morton, 1975–1976
	Elliot L. Richardson, 1976–1977
39 Carter	Juanita M. Kreps, 1977–1980
	Philip M. Klutznick, 1980–1981
40 Reagan	Malcolm Baldrige, 1981–1987
	C. William Verity, Jr., 1987–1989
41 Bush	Robert A. Mosbacher, 1989–1992
	Barbara A. Franklin, 1992–1993
42 Clinton	Ronald H. Brown, 1993–

with Roosevelt nominating his personal secretary, George B. Cortelyou, as the first secretary. The Department survived in its combined form through the Taft term, but with markets expanding at home and abroad, and with labor interests demanding a department of their own the formulation of a separate and distinct Department of Commerce was accomplished.

The new restructured department, which Woodrow Wilson then presided over, was composed of the following entities: the Coast and Geodetic Survey; the Steamboat Inspection Service; and the bureaus of Corporations, Census, Lighthouses, Standards, Navigation, Fisheries, and Foreign and Domestic Commerce. The bureaus within the department were almost completely different by the time of the presidency of Bill Clinton, exemplifying both the growth of government and the commercial changes that the United States had undergone during the previous six decades. In 1993 the department comprised the Office of Secretary and the following units: the Bureau of the Census, the Bureau of Economic Analysis, the Bureau of Export Administration, the Economic Development Administration, the International Trade Administration, the Minority Business Administration, the National Oceanic and Atmospheric Administration, the National Telecommunications and Information Administration, the Patent and Trademark Office, the National Institute of Standards and Technology, the National Technical Information Service, and the U.S. Tourism Administration.

The Hoover Era. By far the most substantive changes to the department occurred during Hoover's years as Commerce Secretary. In 1924, Hoover summarized his ultimate goal as the restructuring of the department "to change the attitude of government relations with business from that of interference to that of cooperation." Believing that government should not meddle in corporate affairs and thus make itself a burden to business, Hoover saw in the Commerce Department a vehicle for promoting and encouraging commercial activity. He saw the department as a service center, with U.S. business as its primary customer.

Hoover's tenure at Commerce showcased many of his talents. Though he would, as President, be criticized for inaction and indecisive leadership in the face of the Great Depression, Hoover's Commerce years showed him to be a man of progressive ideas capable of engineering change. Always searching for "a middle way . . . between monopoly and state socialism," Hoover used the Commerce Department to experiment with the optimum bureaucratic structure ("associationalism") for the post–WORLD WAR I environment.

The first change Hoover accomplished was to gain President Warren G. Harding's promise to give the Commerce Secretary a voice not just in matters of commerce but in all economic issues of importance.

From this beginning, Hoover worked to elevate the stature of the department further. Recognizing that the scope of the department's activities was dictated by the size of its budget, Hoover lobbied for and received a larger share of the budgetary pie. Between 1921 and 1928, at a time when other departmental budgets were shrinking, Commerce's budget increased from $860,000 to more than $38 million. Staff rolls swelled as well, as Hoover hired more than three thousand new employees.

Hoover worked to limit red tape and the duplication of duties. Further, he filled posts with experts who understood the postwar situation. This new blood is credited with turning the Census Bureau into a first-rate statistical bureau and for enabling Commerce to carry out extensive public education programs. Hoover and his staff put forward a steady stream of ideas, both radical and practical. In recognition of Hoover's impact, the central Department of Commerce building, located between 14th and 15th Streets and Pennsylvania and Constitution Avenues in Washington, D.C., was renamed the Herbert Clark Hoover Building in 1982.

Retrenchment and Constant Revision. Under Hoover's presidency, the high-profile activities of the Department of Commerce continued, but Franklin D. Roosevelt's defeat of Hoover brought about a drastic reduction in department activities. Because the department was almost a Hoover invention, there was even talk during the beginning of the Roosevelt administration of abolishing it altogether, but, instead, Roosevelt transferred primary responsibility for his business recovery programs to other areas of government, effectively breaking up the bureaucratic empire that Hoover had organized. The Bureau of Air Commerce was transferred to the Civil Aeronautics Authority; the Bureau of Lighthouses was made part of the Coast Guard, under the authority of the TREASURY DEPARTMENT; and Domestic Commerce was even transferred to the DEPARTMENT OF STATE.

Roosevelt's and subsequent administrations continued the constant shifting of bureaus from one Cabinet-level department to another. In 1940, the Weather Service became a Commerce entity; the Civil Aeronautics Authority (renamed the Civil Aeronautics Administration) bounced back from its short-term home at Treasury. Under Harry S. Truman, the Bureau of Public Roads was moved to Commerce; the Maritime Administration followed in 1950. It was the Commerce Department that implemented Dwight D. Eisenhower's plan for an interstate highway system in the 1950s, but by the end of the 1960s highways and other land transportation had been moved to the newly created DEPARTMENT OF TRANSPORTATION. The CIVIL RIGHTS ACT OF 1964 installed a Community Relations Service as part of the department, but two years later the agency was shifted to the DEPARTMENT OF JUSTICE. In the early 1970s, Commerce claimed control of the National Fire Prevention and Control Administration, but in 1979 control of that agency shifted to the newly created Federal Emergency Management Administration (FEMA).

During the Nixon administration the department saw another period of significant change, with greater emphasis being placed on international issues and fervent cultivation of commercial opportunities abroad. This period also saw Commerce initiate a minority business program and establish an ombudsman for business.

The Department's role in international trade and domestic economic affairs was again pushed into the limelight during the Reagan administration, under the direction of Secretary Malcomb Baldridge. An extremely capable administrator, Baldridge championed quality in U.S. business. He was determined to keep America competitive internationally and used the Commerce Department to that end. He chaired a Cabinet-level Trade Strike Force to deal with unfair trade practices, and he made the department the lead player in supporting and implementing the Export Trading Company Act of 1982. Both the Reagan and George Bush administrations were champions not only of free trade, but of fair trade with other nations, painstakingly negotiating with the world community to exact a trade agenda that would be satisfactory to U.S. commercial interests in an increasingly global economy.

BIBLIOGRAPHY

Ambrose, Stephen B. *Nixon, Ruin and Recovery 1973–1990*. 1991.
Bartley, Robert L. *The Seven Fat Years*. 1992.
Bowers, Helen. *From Lighthouses to Lasers: A History of the U.S. Department of Commerce*. 1988.
Kennedy, Paul. *The Rise and Fall of the Great Powers*. 1987.
Smith, Richard Norton. *An Uncommon Man: The Triumph of Herbert Hoover*. 1984.
Wilson, Joan Hoff. *Herbert Hoover, Forgotten Progressive*. 1975.

PETER CHANDLER

COMMISSION ON ADMINISTRATIVE MANAGEMENT. See BROWNLOW COMMITTEE.

COMMISSIONS, PRESIDENTIAL. The need for impartial information for policy-making and polit-ical judgment has been a constant thread throughout the history of the presidency, and advisory commissions have been a part of the process of gathering information.

Commissions in History. President George Washington appointed a commission to investigate and attempt to mediate settlement of the WHISKEY REBELLION, a revolt of western Pennsylvania farmers against a federal tax on spirits. The fact that the commission was unsuccessful in settling the situation neither deterred Washington from praising the body's efforts nor kept future Presidents from turning to commissions for guidance.

President Martin Van Buren sent commissions to study European postal systems and armies, and President Andrew Jackson appointed a commission to investigate the Navy Department. When President John Tyler appointed a commission to examine the New York customhouse, in 1841, Congress challenged his action. Tyler claimed constitutional authority for the appointment of commissions under Article II, Section 3, which states that the President shall "take Care that the Laws be faithfully executed" and "give to the Congress Information of the State of the Union, and recommend to their Consideration such Measures as he shall judge necessary and expedient."

Early in the twentieth century Theodore Roosevelt imparted a visibility and vitality to the use of commissions, contributing to their evolution as a tool for policy development and public education. His commissions on conservation, public lands, inland waterways, and country life focused national attention on the intelligent use of natural resources. Roosevelt actually participated in some commission activities and vigorously promoted commission reports. In response to his appointment of extralegal, unsalaried commissions to study social and economic issues, Congress passed legislation in 1909 that prohibited the appointment of commissions that lacked legislative authority (35 Stat. 1023).

The administrations of Presidents Franklin D. Roosevelt, Harry S. Truman, and Dwight D. Eisenhower saw the appointment of noteworthy commissions on government management and organization, with former President Herbert Hoover chairing the two HOOVER COMMISSIONS, under Truman and Eisenhower, respectively.

The 1960s and early 1970s—a period of profound change, turmoil, and social questioning in the United States—saw the employment of commissions in the examination of deeply troubling national issues under the administrations of Lyndon B. Johnson and Richard M. Nixon. Some commission reports became, themselves, part of the national debate and influenced national thinking. The President's Commission on the Assassination of President Kennedy (referred to as the WARREN COMMISSION, after its chairman, Chief Justice Earl Warren), the National Advisory Commission on Civil Disorders (known as the Kerner Commission, for its chairman, Otto Kerner, governor of Illinois), and the President's Commission on Campus Unrest (the Scranton Commission, for chairman William Scranton, former governor of Pennsylvania) exemplified the highly visible, volatile nature of the commissions' subjects and their times. Other prominent commissions of the period explored crime, violence, obscenity and pornography, population growth, and drug abuse. In many cases these commissions offered unexpectedly provocative and controversial recommendations and critiques.

Controversy notwithstanding, use of commissions proceeded apace in subsequent decades, achieving attention during the Ronald Reagan presidency with investigations of the disastrous launch of the space shuttle *Challenger*, the IRAN-CONTRA AFFAIR (the TOWER COMMISSION), and the Presidential Commission on the Human Immunodeficiency Virus Epidemic (AIDS Commission).

Forms and Functions. Presidential advisory bodies take many forms, from specialized executive-level permanent committees and councils to task forces, White House conferences, and commissions. Presidential commissions are best known as investigatory bodies, established by the President or by Congress for the President's appointment, which within a defined area of inquiry seek out all relevant information, subject it to scrutiny and review, and arrange it in a written report containing considered recommendations for presidential, legislative, and/or social reform.

Commissions may be seen in a typological sense as situation-oriented, crisis-oriented, or procedure-oriented. Situation-oriented groups are directed at social conditions or phenomena, widely dispersed and of general relevance, for which new perspectives may be required. The President's Commission on Law Enforcement and the Administration of Justice (established 1965), the Commission on Population Growth and the American Future (1970), and the Commission on Obscenity and Pornography (1967) fall within this category.

Crisis- or event-oriented commissions are occasioned by specific, highly charged developments that may or may not reflect longer-term issues but that are seen as requiring immediate exploration. The Warren Commission (1963), the National Advisory Commis-

sion on Civil Disorders (1967), and the commission on the *Challenger* disaster (1986) are examples.

Procedure-oriented commissions are intended to evaluate the operation of extant organizations and agencies and make recommendations with respect to policy and procedure. They are generally of more limited scope and lower profile. The aforementioned Herbert Hoover–chaired Commissions on the Organization of the Executive Branch of the Government exemplified this category, which may also include bodies assigned a specific task such as arranging the celebration of the American Revolution bicentennial.

Presidents (and Congresses) appoint commissions to achieve four general goals, any combination of which may be at play in a specific case: commissions provide symbolic reassurance; they are a part of the process of policy development; they overcome organizational complexity; and they permit delay.

The modern presidency is expected to respond to virtually any situation of national political or social consequence. Often, Presidents may be under significant pressure—externally or from within—to act when it is not at all certain what, in fact, should be done. For example, the 1968 assassinations of Martin Luther King, Jr., and ROBERT F. KENNEDY raised disturbing questions for many Americans, including President Johnson, of why U.S. society is so violent. One response was appointment of the National Commission on the Causes and Prevention of Violence. Commissions are a high-visibility mechanism for demonstrating concern, awareness, and intent to address a subject. They offer a means of symbolic reassurance to the public that the President takes something seriously and is willing to listen.

Commissions may provide an informational foundation for the construction of national policy. They may increase public and governmental awareness and perspective on a wide scale. Their mission, in this respect, was best expressed by President Johnson's charge to the Kerner Commission: "Let your search be free. Let it be untrammeled by what has been called the 'conventional wisdom.' As best you can, find the truth, the whole truth, and express it in your report." Presidents may hope for commissions to lend an underpinning of legitimacy or confirmation to policy that has already been developed. And, as part of the policy process, a commission may represent a response to a specifically concerned group, for example, the Commission on Wartime Relocation and Internment of Civilians, which dealt (in the 1980s) with the TREATMENT OF JAPANESE AMERICANS interned during WORLD WAR II.

Commissions generally focus investigative energies and attention in a single vehicle and avoid duplication or overlapping efforts by competing bodies. The ad hoc nature of some commissions not only allows for greater efficiency and clarity of perspective outside organizational norms, it can permit investigations unburdened by the appearance of conflict of interest.

Finally, commission appointments may afford delay, a cooling-off period in an environment of turmoil during which conflict may be guided toward legitimate channels. Here there is a real potential for abuse, that is, for presidential evasion of substantive response and the dismissal by pundits of commissions as reflective of cynical presidential motives. While this has undoubtedly been the case, in certain instances, it is the exception rather than the rule. Most often, with respect to crises or superheated issues, commissions provide time for defusing tension, marshaling resources, and coalescing attention in an organized search for answers.

Creation and Procedures. Most high-level commissions follow relatively similar procedures. They require membership, staff, and funding; they must conduct an investigation; and they must prepare reports. Presidents are involved primarily in the initial stages of a commission's existence and, in widely varying degrees, in responding to commission findings and recommendations.

Advisory commissions are created either by presidential EXECUTIVE ORDER or by legislation. Operating funds have come from any number of executive branch sources, for example, emergency funds or executive agencies, or from congressional appropriations.

For the most part, commissioners are appointed by the President. In the case of commissions established by Congress, appointment authority may be shared by the two branches, with legislation requiring balance of partisanship or points of view among appointees. The designation *blue-ribbon commission* reflects the tendency for commissioners to be individuals with records of distinction in the public or private sectors who lend credibility to commission efforts. Persons with well-known proclivities in the area of commission inquiry are generally to be avoided although proportion is often sought through appointments from various racial, geographic, and ideological groups. Commission memberships range from as few as three to more than twenty members.

Of particular importance is the selection of the commission chair. Presidents give serious attention to this position, which sets the tone for and communicates the importance of the commission's task. This is a role for individuals of integrity, fairness, high intelligence, administrative skills, and objectivity. When commission work becomes contentious—and it often does—the chair is the person, above all others, who may make the difference between confrontation and conciliation. Chief Justice Earl Warren, Governor Otto Kerner, Johns Hopkins University president emeritus Milton Eisenhower, and Senator John Tower were all, in their time, examples of high-profile chairmen capable of lending stature to commissions.

While diversity of membership is considered an asset in pursuit of measured inquiry, trouble may arise from what may be called a partisan temptation on the part of the President, that is, a desire to influence the direction of a commission via the appointment of partisan commissioners. An egregious, albeit rare, instance took place on the Commission on Obscenity and Pornography, whose members were appointed by President Lyndon B. Johnson and who were still at work when Richard M. Nixon took office. When a vacancy occurred in the commission membership President Nixon chose to fill it with an antipornography crusader, Charles H. Keating, Jr. While the commission made efforts to accommodate its new member he nonetheless embarked on a campaign of obstruction and sabotage of commission work. Impartial inquiry is dependent, in the first instance, on presidential motivation.

Once a staff is selected and office space is procured a commission's work begins. Commissions may divide themselves into study areas or task forces to focus their efforts. Ad hoc commissions face time constraints (mandates vary from a few months to two or three years) and commissions often work with the knowledge that their independence may collide with the interests of the President and other relevant political actors. Depending on the nature and scope of a commission's subject, it may use any combination of investigative tools: information from government agencies, social-scientific consultation, contracted special reports, survey research, travel for on-site examination of situations, public hearings (open or closed), and specially sponsored conferences.

As data are gathered, examined, and disseminated by the staff, and then as full commission meetings are held, commissioners may go through a process of intellectual growth. In-depth exposure to information and new perspectives may significantly alter preconceptions and lead to commissioners' advocacy of positions they would previously have opposed.

Generally, commissions meet for a few days on several occasions. During the final stages of work the report must be compiled. At this point compromise and consensus are sought; provision must be made, if necessary, for concurring and dissenting statements;

decisions are made regarding the primary audience for the report; and choices are faced as to the strength and specificity of language to be used in the presentation of findings. Although appointed by the President, a commission may aim its conclusions and recommendations in many social and political directions, recognizing that the President's political imperatives—not to mention his personal opinions—may limit his response.

Final commission reports are presented to the President and, often, Congress. They are printed by the government and, in the case of commissions that have dealt with subjects of significant public interest, commercial publishers may release editions.

Goals and Milieus. The Federal Advisory Committee Act of 1972 establishes standards for the operation of advisory committees, inventories all such existing bodies, and requires a presidential response to reports. Prior to this legislation there was no such requirement, and, of course, nothing guarantees the quality of a response.

Presidents may welcome commission reports and seek implementation of their recommendations. In this respect lower-key procedure-oriented commissions and advisory committees may more successfully yield policy and organizational adjustments at the executive level, facilitated by the less contentious nature of their subjects and recommendations. Certain factors, however, mitigate against a warm executive welcome, particularly in the case of high-visibility situation- and crisis-oriented commissions.

The goals and milieus of commissions and Presidents are different and, not surprisingly, are not always compatible. The President's response is shaped largely by sensitivity to his own political needs and to the realities of the political environment. During the Johnson administration, recommendations of the President's Commission on Law Enforcement and the Administration of Justice were incorporated in the Safe Streets Act of 1968. Yet Johnson was deeply frustrated by the report of the National Advisory Commission on Civil Disorders, with its calls for massive federal outlays at a time of congressional resistance to spending and its strong language condemning the behavior of white society.

Considerations of personality also condition responses. The President may be limited in the degree to which he is intellectually or emotionally capable of entertaining ideas contrary to—or critical of—his own. This seemed to play a role in the response of the Nixon administration to the Commission on Campus Unrest, among others.

In addition, a commission that is appointed by one

President and that survives his term and reports to his successor risks a limited response due to partisan and policy differences and the unlikelihood of a new administration wanting to pass much credit to its predecessor.

Cabinet- and agency-level responses may occur, on a less publicized basis, which reflect commission recommendations even in the case of commissions that have not received a presidential endorsement. And, beyond the presidency, at times quite strong responses may come from Congress, the states, public and private organizations and institutions, and the press.

The lasting value of high-visibility blue-ribbon advisory commissions must be seen in their role as instruments of public education. Commissions affect the social climate: they help redefine issues, increase awareness, demythologize loosely held but unexamined theories, legitimize new or out-of-the-mainstream ideas, speak to the national conscience, and inspire. While not empowered, by themselves, to change anything, commissions contribute to attitudinal shifts in what is socially and politically acceptable. In the context of its own place and time, a commission may advocate and lend credibility to points of view that exceed anything coming from other bodies of government. Commissions have shown a flexibility and an openness to the exploration of new ideas and the possibilities of intellectual growth as a result of exposure to information that is both rare in the conduct of public affairs and essential to the health of democracy.

BIBLIOGRAPHY

Bledsoe, W. Craig. "Presidential Commissions." In *Guide to the Presidency*. Edited by Michael Nelson. 1989.

Flitner, David, Jr. *The Politics of Presidential Commissions*. 1986.

Marcy, Carl. *Presidential Commissions*. 1945, repr. 1973.

Popper, Frank. *The President's Commissions*. 1970.

Wolanin, Thomas R. *Presidential Advisory Commissions*. 1975.

DAVID FLITNER, JR.

COMPETITIVENESS COUNCIL. In response to criticisms of government regulation in the 1960s and 1970s, the Reagan administration instituted a regulatory review program based on Executive Order 12292 and Executive Order 12498. The program was directed by the Task Force on Regulatory Relief, chaired by the Vice President; the Office of Management and Budget's Office of Information and Regulatory Affairs was authorized to review major regulations and assess their compatibility with the administration's guidelines for regulation. The Bush administration continued the review process and established in 1991 the President's Council on Competitiveness. The council stated its primary goals to be: reduce regulatory burdens on the economy; develop strategies to improve American's human resources required for an effective work force; eliminate government-imposed burdens on scientific and technological progress that threatens the competitiveness of U.S. businesses; and facilitate the free flow of investment capital necessary for economic growth.

Vice President DAN QUAYLE chaired the council, which included the secretaries of the Treasury and Commerce, the Attorney General, the Director of the Office of Management and Budget (OMB), the Chairman of the COUNCIL OF ECONOMIC ADVISERS, and the CHIEF OF STAFF to the President. The Council oversaw OMB's regulatory review process, served as an appeals board for disputes between agencies over regulations, and provided a forum for parties to raise concerns they had about regulations with which they were expected to comply. The council also identified areas where it believed major policy changes could enhance competitiveness. During its first year it focused on streamlining federal regulation of energy production, reforming products liability laws, ensuring that the costs of clean air regulations stayed within the ceiling imposed by the President, simplifying the drug approval process, reducing costs and delays in federal courts, protecting property rights, and facilitating the competitiveness of biotechnology industries.

The council was widely attacked by Democratic members of Congress and public interest groups for encouraging agencies to pursue regulatory options that are inconsistent with congressional intent, displacing agency authority to determine the content of regulations, and relying on secret meetings with industry officials where arguments and complaints are raised without giving others the opportunity to rebut the contentions, thereby contravening the procedural protections provided for in administrative law. Defenders of the council argued that the President is constitutionally and politically responsible for regulatory process and that proposed regulations must be coordinated to eliminate duplication and overlap and be integrated with other policies such as economic growth and competitiveness.

Part of the debate ultimately lay in differences over whether more environmental, health, and consumer protection regulation was needed or whether more emphasis should be placed on economic growth. Part of the conflict was rooted in competing views of the nature of regulatory RULEMAKING POWER: Is the formation of regulations an executive-branch function, ulti-mately accountable to the President? Should congressional committees play the major role in guiding the formation of regulatory policy and ensuring compliance with legislative intent? Or should the process be insulated from politics?

President Bill Clinton abolished the council in January 1993.

BIBLIOGRAPHY

Clarke, David. "Point of Darkness: The White House Council on Competitiveness." *Environmental Forum* (January–February 1992): 31–34.

Rauch, Jonathan. "The Regulatory President." *National Journal* (11/30/91): 2904–2906.

Woodward, Bob, and David S. Broder, "Quayle's Quest: Curb Rules, Leave 'No Fingerprints'" *Washington Post* (9 January 1992): A1.

GARY C. BRYNER

COMPROMISE OF 1850. A group of laws passed by Congress to determine the status (slave or free) of the lands acquired by conquest in the MEXICAN WAR and to settle several other questions regarding SLAVERY that had caused friction between North and South made up the Compromise of 1850. As with the MISSOURI COMPROMISE of 1820 and the compromise of 1833 over South Carolina's NULLIFICATION of the tariff, the measures enacted in 1850 were expected to settle the sectional problem and to lay the basis for harmony between slave and free states.

The dispute centered on California and New Mexico. Extreme positions on the issue of slavery in the territories—requiring Congress to intervene by either banning slavery or protecting it—made agreement difficult. With the 1848 election to the presidency of Zachary Taylor, a military hero of the Mexican War and a Southern Whig, there was a good possibility that the acrimony of the last years of the expansionist, pro-Southern administration of James K. Polk might dissipate and thereby make an agreement possible.

Taylor, however, revealed in his inaugural address that he supported the immediate admission of California as a free state and that New Mexico should be treated similarly. Although this move sidestepped the question of slavery during the territorial stage, it caused great consternation in the South, not only because the two states would be closed to slavery but also because Taylor, a Louisiana slaveholder, had betrayed his Southern Whig supporters. Indeed, Taylor seemed to be under the control of Senator WILLIAM H. SEWARD, a New York Whig whose hostility to slavery was well known.

HENRY CLAY tried to resolve the crisis and challenge the inexperienced Taylor for the leadership of the

WHIG PARTY. With the concurrence of another leading Whig, DANIEL WEBSTER, Clay proposed a single "omnibus" bill that packaged eight sectional issues, addressing them all together. California would be admitted as a free state. Utah and New Mexico would be organized as territories without preconditions as to the status of slavery. The disputed Texas–New Mexico boundary would be settled in New Mexico's favor, with the federal government assuming the Texas state debt as compensation. The slave trade in the District of Columbia would be ended. And, finally, a new and stricter federal fugitive slave law would be enacted. The omnibus bill was defeated, however, and then President Taylor suddenly died.

With the crisis deepening, the new President, Millard Fillmore, and a rising Democratic Senator, STEPHEN A. DOUGLAS, rescued the situation by cooperating in a brilliant maneuver. Douglas saw that, although no intersectional majority favoring compromise existed, there were sectional majorities for each measure in Clay's bill. Moreover, a small bloc of compromisers was willing to vote for each to get them all passed. So he broke the "omnibus" down into five separate bills and pushed them through Congress by September 1850. Douglas was helped considerably by Fillmore, who calmed the situation in his inaugural address and who signed the bills into law. Very little compromise had really taken place, however: the bills were passed with majorities that were clearly sectional, and neither side had made concessions to achieve a mutually satisfactory resolution to any of the issues. These major sectional differences had not been settled by negotiation and compromise. Instead, they had merely been put on ice, only to reappear in the KANSAS-NEBRASKA ACT of 1854.

BIBLIOGRAPHY

Hamilton, Holman. *Prologue to Conflict: The Crisis and Compromise of 1850.* 1964.
Holt, Michael F. *The Political Crisis of the 1850s.* 1978.
Potter, David M. *The Impending Crisis, 1848–1861.* 1976.

MICHAEL PERMAN

COMPTROLLER GENERAL. The GENERAL ACCOUNTING OFFICE (GAO), an independent body that investigates executive-branch operations, is headed by the Comptroller General. The office of Comptroller General, which has antecedents dating back to the years of the Continental Congress, was created by the BUDGET AND ACCOUNTING ACT of 1921. The Comptroller General is appointed by the President with the ADVICE AND CONSENT of the Senate for a term of fifteen years. As a result of legislation enacted in 1982, when a vacancy occurs in the office of Comptroller General a commission composed of ten members of Congress recommends at least three individuals to the President, who nominates one for Senate confirmation.

The Comptroller General may be removed either by IMPEACHMENT or through passage of a joint resolution by Congress, a form of legislation (like a bill) that is passed by both houses of Congress and submitted to the President for his signature or veto. The Budget and Accounting Act of 1920 was vetoed by President Woodrow Wilson in part because the bill permitted Congress to remove the Comptroller General by passing a concurrent resolution, which does not go to the President. Wilson regarded the REMOVAL POWER as an "essential incident" to the APPOINTMENT POWER of the President. Congress changed the procedure to require a joint resolution and President Warren G. Harding signed the Budget and Accounting Act of 1921.

Comptrollers General have often been involved in disputes with Presidents. Beginning in 1921, Comptrollers General have regarded their opinions on the legality of government expenditures as binding on executive departments and agencies. From the very start, however, the DEPARTMENT OF JUSTICE challenged that assertion of power and insisted that the ATTORNEY GENERAL had independent authority to render legal opinions regarding executive departments' expenditures.

A typical collision occurred in 1969, when the Comptroller General, Elmer B. Staats, claimed that an AFFIRMATIVE ACTION plan devised by the Nixon administration violated the CIVIL RIGHTS ACT OF 1964. The Secretary of Labor promptly announced that the administration would continue to implement the plan, pointing out that the interpretation of the Civil Rights Act had been vested by Congress not in the GAO but in the Justice Department, which had approved the plan as consistent with the statute. A federal appellate court, in *Contractors Ass'n of Eastern Pa. v. Secretary of Labor* (1971), later upheld the legality of the plan.

The GRAMM-RUDMAN-HOLLINGS ACT of 1985 authorized the Comptroller General to cut federal spending if deficits exceeded the annual ceilings established by Congress. The Justice Department regarded these controls over federal spending as executive in nature and objected that such duties could be carried out only by an officer subject to the direct control of the President. The Supreme Court, in BOWSHER V. SYNAR (1986), agreed with that analysis and invalidated the Comptroller General's powers under Gramm-Rudman.

At almost the same time, the Comptroller General's

Comptrollers General[a]

President	Comptroller General
29 Harding	John R. McCarl, 1921–1936
30 Coolidge	John R. McCarl
31 Hoover	John R. McCarl
32 F. D. Roosevelt	John R. McCarl Fred H. Brown, 1939–1940 Lindsay C. Warren, 1940–1954
33 Truman	Lindsay C. Warren
34 Eisenhower	Lindsay C. Warren Joseph Campbell, 1954–1965
35 Kennedy	Joseph Campbell
36 L. B. Johnson	Joseph Campbell Elmer B. Staats, 1966–1981
37 Nixon	Elmer B. Staats
38 Ford	Elmer B. Staats
39 Carter	Elmer B. Staats
40 Reagan	Elmer B. Staats Charles A. Bowsher, 1981–
41 Bush	Charles A. Bowsher
42 Clinton	Charles A. Bowsher

[a] The Comptroller General is appointed by the President to a fifteen-year term. In this table, the dates of the Comptrollers' terms are given when the terms began; the Comptrollers' names are repeated for each subsequent President under whom they served.

powers under another statute were challenged in court by the administration. When President Reagan signed the Competition in Contracting Act in 1984, he objected to a provision that authorized the Comptroller General to stay (i.e., delay) the award of a contract in response to a protest by a disappointed bidder. Reagan said that the Comptroller General could not interfere with the operations of the executive branch. The Director of the OFFICE OF MANAGEMENT AND BUDGET (OMB), David Stockman, later directed all agencies of government to ignore that provision of the law. In *Ameron v. United States Army Corps of Engineers* (1986) and *Lear Siegler, Inc., Energy Products Div. v. Lehman* (1988) however, the Third and Ninth Circuits upheld the bid-protest procedure as a legitimate method by which Congress could encourage savings in the award of federal contracts.

BIBLIOGRAPHY

Mansfield, Harvey. *The Comptroller General.* 1979.
Pois, Joseph. *Watchdog on the Potomac: A Study of the Comptroller General of the United States.* 1979.

LOUIS FISHER

CONFEDERATE CONSTITUTION. In February and March 1861, Southern leaders convened a constitutional convention in Montgomery, Alabama, in order to draft and submit for ratification a permanent constitution for the states seceding from the United States. (A provisional constitution approximating the Articles of Confederation had previously been adopted to be in effect for one year.) In the course of the drafting process the Confederate framers resolved to use the U.S. Constitution as their model, remaining open to innovations designed to address constitutional disputes between the national and state governments. Toward that end, much of their attention was focused on the institutional structure of the executive branch and the chief executive's relationships to the respective states and to the Congress of the Confederate States of America.

The primary institutional reform was a six-year term for the president and vice president, with the president ineligible for a second term (Art. II, sec. 1, cl. 1). Jettisoning reelection politics from the president's agenda was the rationale for the term limitation, while the extension from a four- to a six-year term was designed to facilitate the implementation of the administration's public policy agenda. The other significant institutional reform gave the president more discretionary power to remove executive branch officers, thereby enhancing the chief executive's control over the C.S.A. bureaucracy. In effect, the C.S.A. president had augmented control over the executive branch through the dismissal of "problematical" executive branch personnel.

In deference to state sovereignty, executive and judicial federal officers were subject to IMPEACHMENT by a two-thirds vote of both branches of the state legislature in whose jurisdiction the federal officers resided and conducted their official responsibilities (Art. I, sec. 2, cl. 5). With conviction being the responsibility of senators who were elected by their respective state legislators, state impeachment of federal officials provided the states with supplemental influence over the implementation of national policies within their respective jurisdictions. Moreover, legally assembled conventions of any three states could summon a national convention of all the states (Art. V, sec. 1), a provision that facilitated regional obstructionism of national policies. The intended consequences of such deferences to the states was to deter or, failing that, to block the president from being indifferent to state policy preferences that went against the national norm.

The innovations designed to alter the role of the executive branch in the legislative process were more extensive. Congress was permitted to grant "to the principal officer in each of the executive departments a seat upon the floor of either house, with the privilege of discussing any measures appertaining to his department" (Art. I, sec. 6, cl. 2), a provision designed to facilitate communication between the legislature and the various executive departments over and beyond the traditional committee system. The president could exercise an ITEM VETO over appropriation bills. Congress could override the vetoed items with a two-thirds vote (Art. I, sec. 7, cl. 2). The president was the constitutionally recognized initiator of national fiscal policy; if an appropriation bill did not originate with the executive branch, a two-thirds recorded vote of both chambers was requisite for the bill to pass (Art. I, sec. 9, cl. 9), with that two-thirds vote subject to a presidential veto (Art. I, sec. 7, cl. 2). Additionally, the constitution mandated that "every law, or resolution having the force of law, shall relate to but one subject, and that shall be expressed in the title" (Art. I, sec. 9, cl. 20), a provision that outlawed riders. When considered in conjunction with other exceptions to congressional power, such as the prohibitions against protectionist legislation to "promote or foster any branch of industry" (Art. I, sec. 8, cl. 1) and against appropriating money "for any internal improvement to facilitate commerce" except for constitutionally sanctioned purposes (Art. I, sec. 8, cl. 3), these four provisions show that the Confederate framers were intent on increasing the checks on the congress; one effective way to curtail the congress was to enhance the role of the chief executive while simultaneously diminishing that of the house and senate. The constitutional context of the president strengthened the chief executive's role in the national legislative process but diminished the overall scope of national authority over the states.

The political context within which President JEFFERSON DAVIS (1861–1865) exercised his presidential powers was not the most favorable for a confederacy whose primary objective was to reduce the powers of the central government. The protracted American CIVIL WAR was not conducive to the curtailment of presidential powers by reinvigorated states but required its opposite. As commander in chief of the Confederate army, President Davis was constrained not by the institutional innovations, which actually strengthened his role in the national government, but by the commitment to states' rights that permeated Southern political culture. The Southern commitment to states' rights certainly enhanced the consensual basis of confederate policies; that enhancement, however, opened avenues for state obstruction of national policies that were not imaginable in the North. For example, states withheld state militias from the Confederate command, denied supplies to the Confederate commissary, and even threatened to secede from the Confederacy.

The Confederate constitution attempted to establish the executive branch with the requisite powers effectively to devise and implement national public policies while ensuring that those national policies would be based on the consensus of the states. The debate over whether to choose a unitary nationalism with the chief executive as its head or a federal model that would defer to the political processes of the states was the fundamental controversy among the Framers in 1787. The Confederate framers of 1861 revived that debate, opting for a strengthened chief executive vis-à-vis the C.S.A. congress but then qualifying the prerogatives of the chief executive by enhancing the powers of the states vis-à-vis the national government. As important as effective national government was to the Confederate framers, it did not supersede their commitment to their states.

BIBLIOGRAPHY

Davis, Jefferson. *The Rise and Fall of the Confederate Government.* 2 vols. 1881.

DeRosa, Marshall. *The Confederate Constitution of 1861: An Inquiry into American Constitutionalism.* 1991.

Stephens, Alexander H. *A Constitutional View of the Late War between the States.* 2 vols. 1868–1870.

Vandiver, Frank E. *Their Tattered Flags: The Epic of the Confederacy.* 1970.

MARSHALL L. DEROSA

CONGRESS, PRESIDENTIAL RELATIONS WITH. See PRESIDENTIAL-CONGRESSIONAL RELATIONS.

CONGRESS, WHITE HOUSE INFLUENCE ON. The notion of the dominant President who moves the country and Congress through strong, effective leadership has deep roots in American political culture. Those chief executives whom Americans revere, such as George Washington, Abraham Lincoln, and Theodore and Franklin D. Roosevelt, have taken on mythic proportions as leaders. Yet every President bears scars from his battles with the legislature. Many of the proposals from the White House fail to pass Congress, while legislators champion initiatives to which the President is opposed.

The peculiar sharing of powers by the two institutions established by the Constitution prevents either from acting unilaterally on most important matters. As a result, the political system virtually compels the President to attempt to influence Congress.

Contemporary processes, such as the preparation of an elaborate legislative program in the White House, have evolved in response to the system's need for centralization. Yet such changes only provide instruments for Presidents to employ as they seek support from the legislature. They carry no guarantee of success and are no substitute for influence.

The right to make proposals to Congress and to veto legislation are the only formal legislative powers given to the President by the Constitution. Since the VETO is rarely overridden, even the threat of one can be an effective tool for persuading Congress to give more weight to Presidents' views. Yet the veto is an inherently negative resource. It is most useful for preventing legislation. Much of the time, however, Presidents are more interested in passing their own legislation. Here they must marshal their political resources to obtain positive support for their programs.

The three most useful sources of influence for Presidents in Congress are their party leadership, public support, and their own legislative skills.

Party Leadership. Presidents are dependent upon their party to move their legislative programs. Despite the pull of party ties, all Presidents experience substantial slippage in the support of their party in Congress. Presidents can count on their own party members for support no more than two-thirds of the time, even on key votes.

The primary obstacle to party unity is the lack of consensus among party members on policies, especially in the DEMOCRATIC PARTY; members of Congress are more likely to vote with their constituents, to whom they must return for reelection. To create goodwill with congressional party members, the White House provides them with many amenities, ranging from photographs with the President to rides on Air Force One. Yet, party members expect such courtesies from the White House and are unlikely to be especially responsive to the President as a result. Despite the resources available to the President, if party members wish to oppose the White House, there is little the President can do to stop them. Political parties have become highly decentralized and national party leaders do not control those aspects of politics that are of vital concern to members of Congress: nominations and elections.

The President's party is often in the minority in Congress; moreover, the President cannot depend on his own party for support and must solicit help from the opposition party. Although the opposition is generally not fertile ground for seeking support, the President may receive enough votes to ensure passage of a piece of legislation.

Public Support. One of the President's most important resources for leading Congress is public support. Presidents with the backing of the public have an easier time influencing Congress. Presidents with low approval ratings in the polls find the going tougher. Members of Congress and others in Washington closely watch two indicators of public support for the President: approval in the polls and mandates in presidential elections.

Public approval. Members of Congress anticipate the public's reactions to their support for or opposition to Presidents and their policies. They may choose to be close to or independent from the White House—depending on the President's standing with the public, as shown by his PUBLIC RATINGS—to increase their chances for reelection. Representatives and Senators may also use the President's standing in the polls as an indicator of the ability to mobilize PUBLIC OPINION against presidential opponents.

Public approval also makes other leadership resources more efficacious. If the President is high in the public's esteem, the President's party is more likely to be responsive, the public is more easily moved, and legislative skills become more effective. Thus public approval is the political resource that has the most potential to turn a situation of stalemate between the President and Congress into one supportive of the President's legislative proposals.

Public approval operates mostly in the background and sets the limits of what Congress will do for or to the President. Widespread support gives the President leeway and weakens resistance to presidential policies. It provides a cover for members of Congress to cast votes to which their constituents might otherwise object. They can defend their votes as support for the President rather than support for a certain policy alone.

Lack of public support strengthens the resolve of those inclined to oppose the President and narrows the range in which presidential policies receive the benefit of the doubt. In addition, low ratings in the polls may create incentives to attack the President, further eroding an already weakened position. Disillusionment is a difficult force for the White House to combat.

The impact of public approval or disapproval on the support the President receives in Congress is important, but it occurs at the margins of the effort to build coalitions behind proposed policies. No matter how low presidential standing dips, the President still receives support from a substantial number of Senators and Representatives. Similarly, no matter how high approval levels climb, a significant portion of the

Congress will still oppose certain presidential policies. Members of Congress are unlikely to vote against the clear interests of their constituencies or the firm tenets of their ideology out of deference to a widely supported Chief Executive. Public approval gives the President leverage, not control.

In addition, Presidents cannot depend on having the approval of the public and it is not a resource over which they have much control. Once again it is clear that Presidents' leadership resources do not allow them to dominate Congress.

Mandates. The results of presidential elections are another indicator of public opinion regarding Presidents. An electoral mandate—the perception that the voters strongly support the President's character and policies—can be a powerful symbol in American politics. It accords added legitimacy and credibility to the newly elected President's proposals. Moreover, concerns for both representation and political survival encourage members of Congress to support new Presidents if they feel the people have spoken.

More importantly, mandates change the premises of decision. Ronald Reagan's victory in 1980 placed a stigma on big government and exalted the unregulated marketplace and large defense efforts. Reagan had won a major victory even before the first congressional vote.

Although presidential elections can structure choices for Congress, merely winning an election does not provide Presidents with a mandate. Every election produces a winner, but mandates are much less common. Even large electoral victories, such as Richard Nixon's in 1972 and Ronald Reagan's in 1984, carry no guarantee that Congress will interpret the results as mandates from the people to support the President's programs, especially if the voters also elect majorities in Congress from the other party (of course, the winner may claim a mandate anyway).

Legislative Skills. Presidential legislative skills come in a variety of forms. Some, such as bargaining, personal appeals, and consultation, are oriented toward what might be termed the tactical level. In other words, the President and his aides attempt to obtain one or a few votes at a time. Other times Presidents may employ skills such as setting priorities, exploiting political honeymoons, and structuring votes in an attempt to influence most or all members of Congress at the same time.

Bargaining. Presidents often bargain in the form of trading support on two or more policies or providing specific benefits for Representatives and Senators. Yet the White House does not wish to encourage this process, and there is a scarcity of resources with which to bargain, especially in an era of large budget deficits. In addition, the President does not have to bargain with every member of Congress to receive support. On controversial issues on which bargaining may be useful, the President almost always starts with a sizable core of party supporters and may add to this group those of the opposition party who provide support on ideological or policy grounds. Others may support the President because of relevant constituency interests or strong public approval. Thus the President needs to bargain only if this coalition does not provide a majority (two-thirds on treaties and veto overrides), or, if this is not the case, the President needs to bargain only with enough people to provide that majority.

Personal appeals. The President's personal efforts at persuading members of Congress take several forms, including telephone calls and private meetings in the OVAL OFFICE. Appeals to fellow partisans can be useful, but the President operates under rather severe constraints in employing his persuasive skills to lobbying one-on-one: appeals often fail; members of Congress often exploit appeals in attempts to obtain quid pro quos; the uniqueness of appeals must be maintained to preserve their usefulness; some Presidents dislike and therefore avoid making personal appeals; making appeals is time-consuming for the President. As a result, one-on-one lobbying by the President is the exception rather than the rule. The White House conserves appeals for obtaining the last few votes on issues of special significance to it. In addition, the White House is hesitant to employ the President when defeat is likely because it risks incurring embarrassing political damage.

Consultation. Members of Congress appreciate advance warning of presidential proposals, especially those that affect their constituencies directly. In addition, consultation can provide the White House with early commitments of support if members of Congress have had a role in formulating a bill, or it may help the White House anticipate and preempt congressional objections. At the very least, members of Congress will feel that they have had an opportunity to voice their objections.

Despite these advantages, presidential consultation with Congress is often nothing more than a public relations effort that follows the White House's initiation of a bill rather than preceding it. Consultation with Congress does not normally have a significant impact on a President's proposals.

Setting priorities. An important aspect of a President's legislative strategy can be the establishment of priorities among legislative proposals in order to set Congress's agenda. The President does not want his high priority proposals to become lost in the complex and overloaded legislative process, and Presidents and their staff can lobby effectively for only a few bills at a time. The President's political capital is inevitably limited, and it is sensible to focus it on the issues he cares about most.

There are, however, fundamental obstacles to focusing congressional attention on a few items of high priority. First, the White House can put off dealing with the full spectrum of national issues for several months at the beginning of a new President's term, but it cannot do so for four years: eventually it must make decisions. By the second year the PRESIDENT'S AGENDA is full and more policies are in the pipeline, as the administration attempts to satisfy its constituencies and responds to unanticipated or simply overlooked problems. Moreover, the President himself will inevitably be a distraction from his own priorities. There are so many demands on the President to speak, appear, and attend meetings that it is impossible to organize his schedule for very long around his major goals, especially if he has been in office for long.

Second, Congress is quite capable of setting its own agenda. The public expects Congress to take the initiative, and members of Congress have strong electoral incentives to respond. Finally, Presidents may not want to set priorities and concentrate attention on a few items. Lyndon B. Johnson, for example, was more concerned with moving legislation through Congress rapidly to exploit the favorable political environment.

Moving fast. Being ready to send legislation to the Hill early in the first year of a new President's term to exploit the favorable atmosphere that typically characterizes this HONEYMOON PERIOD is related to the setting of priorities. First-year proposals have a considerably better chance of passing Congress than do those sent to the Hill later in an administration. Yet the President may not be able to turn to a well-established party program and thus may have to take a long time to draft complex legislation. Alternatively, the President can choose simply to propose a policy without thorough analysis, as appears to have been the strategy of Ronald Reagan's White House regarding the budget cuts passed by Congress in 1981 and Lyndon Johnson's legislation to establish the War on Poverty in 1964.

Structuring choice. Framing issues in ways that favor the President's programs may set the terms of the debate on his proposals and thus the premises on which members of Congress cast their votes. Usually this involves emphasizing consensual features of a policy other than its immediate substantive merits. For example, federal aid to education had been a divisive issue for years before President Johnson proposed the Elementary and Secondary Education Act in 1965. To blunt opposition, he successfully changed the focus of debate from teachers' salaries and classroom shortages to fighting poverty, and from the separation of church and state to aiding children.

Although the structuring of choices can be a useful tool for the President, there is no guarantee that he will succeed. In addition, the White House must advocate the passage of many proposals at roughly the same time, further complicating its strategic position. Finally, opponents of the President's policies are unlikely to defer to his attempts to structure choices on the issues.

In general Presidents are limited in their ability to obtain support from Senators and Representatives. A President operates in a legislative forum that is outside his control.

Conditions for Success. The conditions for successful presidential leadership of Congress are interdependent. Strength in only one resource is seldom enough to sustain leadership efforts. Congressional party cohorts and public support are the principal underpinnings of presidential leadership of Congress. Whereas the party composition of Congress is relatively stable, public approval of the President may be quite volatile. When both are in the President's favor, he may accomplish a great deal, but in the absence of such fortuitous circumstances, stalemate is the most likely relationship with Congress. Party loyalty is not sufficiently strong to overcome public skepticism of the President, and members of the opposition party will only move so far in the President's direction in response to public support for the White House.

The interdependence of resources extends beyond the need for a sizable party base in Congress and public support. For example, public support makes the use of legislative skills more effective. A President high in the polls or who is viewed as having a mandate will find members of Congress more responsive to his personal appeals for support. When he is lower in the polls, he is less likely even to seek votes in such a manner. Similarly, only if the President has strong public approval is it sensible to employ the strategies of moving rapidly to exploit this resource or of structuring congressional decisions in terms of support for or opposition to the President.

A President who already has strong public approval is also likely to find it easier to move the public to support specific policies, and efforts to mobilize the public are likely to be most effective when the party and White House organize private sector interests that will communicate with Congress. In turn, constituent groups are most enthusiastic about applying pressure on behalf of the White House when the President is high in the polls.

A favorable environment makes some potential resources less effective and others more so. If a President is skilled at bargaining but enjoys a large majority of supporters in Congress, he will have less need to engage in exchanges. Similarly, legislative skills will have less utility if the President emphasizes mobilizing the public to move Congress rather than dealing more directly with legislators. Thus resources such as legislative skills have more relevance in some situations than in others.

Clearly, the conditions for successful presidential leadership of Congress are contingent, and the President's strategic position uncertain. If circumstances are not serendipitous, the potential for leadership is diminished. In such a context it becomes all the more necessary for the President to take advantage of whatever opportunities do appear.

[See also LEGISLATIVE LEADERSHIP; PRESIDENTIAL-CONGRESSIONAL RELATIONS.]

BIBLIOGRAPHY

Bond, Jon R., and Richard Fleisher. *The President in the Legislative Arena.* 1990.

Edwards, George C., III. *At the Margins: Presidential Leadership of Congress.* 1989.

Edwards, George C., III. *Presidential Influence in Congress.* 1980.

Fisher, Louis. *Constitutional Conflicts between the Congress and the President.* 3d ed., rev. 1991.

Jones, Charles O. *The Trusteeship Presidency.* 1988.

Light, Paul C. *The President's Agenda.* Rev. ed. 1991.

Peterson, Mark A. *Legislating Together.* 1990.

GEORGE C. EDWARDS III

CONGRESS, WHITE HOUSE LIAISON WITH.

Presidents have always had legislative responsibilities that require interaction with Congress. As these responsibilities have expanded, so have PRESIDENTIAL-CONGRESSIONAL RELATIONS. Today, the President is expected to be the chief legislator. He is expected to present annual legislative programs, lobby for these programs, and oversee their implementation. To meet these expectations, the President needs a responsive administrative structure, an appropriate style, and effective strategy for interacting with Congress.

Office of Legislative Affairs. The President's principal institutional mechanism for conducting liaison with Congress is the White House Office of Legislative Affairs. Established at the beginning of the Dwight D. Eisenhower administration, its initial objective was to inform members of Congress about the President's legislative priorities and positions. After 1954, when the Democrats gained control of both houses of Congress, it assumed an additional responsibility—to prevent Democratic legislative proposals, which the administration opposed, from being enacted into law.

With this new responsibility came a more active involvement in the legislative process. Eisenhower, however, was careful not to create the appearance of intruding into Congress's constitutional domain, and so he exercised political influence behind the scenes. In the words of the political scientist, Fred I. Greenstein, Eisenhower operated as a HIDDEN-HAND PRESIDENT.

Eisenhower's legislative staff operated in a similar manner. Conducting business primarily from their White House offices, they maintained a low profile on Capitol Hill. They were careful not to be heavy-handed, not to alienate the Democratic majority with a lot of partisan rhetoric and behavior, and not to get themselves bogged down in a lot of constituency-related tasks. It was a small office with three principal lobbyists and a few support staff.

The size of the office and the scope of its operations expanded considerably during the presidencies of John F. Kennedy and Lyndon B. Johnson. The operating style changed as well. With comprehensive legislative agendas and Democratic majorities in both houses of Congress, Kennedy and Johnson used their congressional offices to launch their legislative programs and steer them successfully through Congress. "I was up there [Capitol Hill] for fourteen years," Kennedy told Lawrence F. O'Brien, his (and later Johnson's) special assistant for congressional relations, "and I don't recall that Truman or Eisenhower or anyone on their staffs ever said one word to me about legislation."

To pursue his more ambitious legislative objectives, Kennedy increased the number of White House liaison aides and their staff support. He also had them utilize a more partisan approach. In meeting with Democratic members of Congress at the beginning of the administration, O'Brien told the group, "The White House certainly remembers who its friends are and can be counted on to apply significant assistance in the campaign." Presidential supporters were rewarded with PATRONAGE appointments, projects for their districts, and public praise from the President.

Both Kennedy and Johnson also became more actively engaged in lobbying efforts than Eisenhower had been. Neither shared Eisenhower's philosophical reluctance to intrude on Congress's prerogatives or his personal hesitation to engage in the political infighting that characterizes congressional politics. Kennedy devoted considerable time and energy to his relations with Congress, although his aides were careful to make sure he was not swamped by details. Johnson, however, displayed a fetish about details. He wanted to be informed about and involved in everything. He read a specially prepared summary of the *Congressional Record* on a daily basis. He demanded countless status reports on his legislative initiatives, sometimes four or five a day. He would go over weekly charts of his administration's proposals with the Democratic congressional leadership, always urging them to do more.

The amount of personal interaction between the President and members of Congress was quite extensive during this period. Weekly breakfast meetings with congressional leaders, first begun during the Eisenhower presidency, were continued during the Kennedy-Johnson era. There was an increase in the number of White House social events to which members of both parties were invited. Both Presidents followed a ritual of meeting with Democratic congressional leaders before introducing legislation.

The White House also began to coordinate executive-branch liaison with Congress on major administration policies. Most departments and agencies had their own congressional staffs to push their own agendas as well as to handle a growing number of constituency-oriented legislative requests. O'Brien believed that if the administration's programs were to be achieved and the White House Legislative Affairs Office to remain relatively small, then there was no alternative but to utilize the departments' liaison agents. This meant convincing every department liaison office that it had a stake in the President's program. To increase its clout, the White House became involved in the selection and removal of department liaison agents and required each department to submit weekly lobbying reports. These reports, distilled by the White House, were presented to the President prior to his meetings with congressional leaders.

In addition to overseeing the departments and agencies in some of their legislative activities, the White House began to perform a variety of services for members of Congress. These ranged from the trivial, such as distributing tickets for the guided WHITE HOUSE tour and sending letters and greeting cards to constituents, to the more complex, such as arranging for the President to speak at a congressional fund-raiser or to include a member's pet project in an administration bill, or even scheduling a meeting between a group of constituents and the President.

Nixon and Ford. The newly enlarged functions of the Office of Legislative Affairs during the Kennedy-Johnson period became the model for subsequent administrations. During the presidencies of Richard M. Nixon and Gerald Ford, the structure and operation of the Legislative Affairs Office remained about the same. It continued to perform the four basic functions that had come to be regarded as standard liaison activities: to provide the President with information about the likely disposition of legislation, to lobby members of Congress (particularly fence-sitters) to support the President's initiatives, to help members of Congress perform their representative functions, and to act as a conduit to channel congressional views into the White House policy-making apparatus and White House views into the legislative process. The office also continued to oversee loosely the liaison activities of the executive departments and agencies when presidential initiatives were involved.

But presidential-congressional relations did change because of the style of these Presidents and the manner in which they interacted with Congress. Nixon was standoffish; although he appreciated the need to have contact with members of Congress to try to persuade them to support his administration's proposals, he had difficulty actually doing so. He tended to call people he knew—mainly for small talk. Unlike Johnson, he could not bring himself to ask for votes. William Timmons, the head of the Legislative Affairs Office for most of the Nixon period, recalled that the President would frequently end meetings or telephone conversations with members of Congress by saying, "I know you're going to do what you have to do anyway and that's fine. Whatever you do is OK with me." After statements like this, the liaison officials found it difficult to twist arms for the administration. Nixon's style created difficulties for his liaison staff and limited its effectiveness in dealing with Congress. The growing political conflict between Congress and the President, culminating in the inquiries into the WATERGATE AFFAIR and Nixon's eventual resignation, exacerbated the problem.

Ford was much more open and accessible than his predecessor. A creature of Congress, he knew many members on a first-name basis and continued to socialize with them after he became President. On the other hand, he did not have the stature of an elected President, which undermined his ability to use his office to help him achieve his administration's policy goals.

Democratic control of both houses of Congress during this period eventually forced both Republican Presidents to rely on a veto strategy. Liaison aides in the Nixon and Ford administrations used the threat of a presidential veto to try to convince the Democratic majority to modify its legislative proposals so that they would be acceptable to the President. Timmons estimated that the Nixon administration's use of this strategy caused some twenty to thirty measures to be "cleaned up sufficiently" so that the President could approve them.

Carter's Problems. Jimmy Carter got off to a poor start in his relations with Congress. Organizational and stylistic problems hampered his liaison effort, particularly in its first six months of operation. The organizational difficulties stemmed from a decision to structure the Legislative Affairs Office according to issues rather than along traditional regional lines, which had allowed each liaison aide to get to know all the members from the same geographic area. As a consequence, some House members received no contact at all from the White House while others were besieged by presidential aides. The new system also failed to serve the Congress's constituency needs. Although it was scrapped after about six months and the old one restored, much good will had been lost. Similarly, a decision at the beginning of the administration to eliminate, without congressional consultation, a number of major public works projects—pork barrel legislation, that had been authorized and funded by Congress had much the same effect.

The difficulties that the Carter people encountered stemmed from the inexperience of the new President and his chief liaison aide, Frank Moore, and from the new administration's outsider style, which conflicted with the norms and behavior of Congress. Congressional Democrats were eager to benefit from their party's control of the White House after eight years out of power, and they inundated the White House with requests for jobs for their constituents, projects for their districts, and other favors. The Legislative Affairs Office was unable to cope with this large volume of communication or to satisfy the multitude of demands made on it.

Carter's liaison problems stemmed not only from unrealistic congressional expectations and inexperienced White House personnel but also had to do with the way he was nominated and elected and the philosophy he articulated during his campaign. Carter won by running against the Washington establishment. Once elected, he was determined to do what was right (and what he had promised to do), not what was expected of him politically. Thus he was reluctant to bargain with members of Congress, to engage in politics as usual. Nor did he enjoy socializing with Washington insiders. When members of Congress were invited to the White House, the President's attitude was strictly business. All of this made it difficult for Carter to build the personal rapport he needed to win support for his proposals in Congress.

Carter had another problem. He came into office

without a unified legislative agenda focused on key policy goals. His administration spent its first six months developing such an agenda and the next twelve months overwhelming Congress with it. It was not until mid-1978 that he was able to break the legislative logjam by modifying the way his administration interacted with Congress. Legislative priorities began to be more clearly articulated; the White House became more receptive to congressional input into its policy-making process; and the President and his staff made a greater effort to increase the public pressure on Congress. A White House office was established to help mobilize interest-group and community support behind key presidential initiatives. These changes, combined with better White House coordination of executive-branch congressional activities, improved the administration's legislative record although they did little to change Carter's legislative reputation.

The Reagan Success. The lessons of the Carter experience were not lost on those responsible for congressional liaison in the administration of Ronald Reagan. Understanding the need to hit the ground running, they used the HONEYMOON PERIOD to push the major economic components of Reagan's legislative agenda. Reagan's transition advisers also realized the importance of initiating contact with all members of Congress even before the President was inaugurated. During the postelection congressional session and first three weeks of the new Congress, a transition liaison team scheduled appearances by the President-elect on Capitol Hill, helped in the confirmation of his Cabinet, and made sure that all congressional communications were promptly handled. These early efforts bore fruit. The liaison operation was highly praised and contributed to the favorable congressional climate. A *U.S. News and World Report* survey of members of Congress in 1991 found that 93 percent rated Reagan as being very effective with Congress.

The liaison office under Reagan did not differ markedly from its predecessors. Somewhat smaller than Carter's, it included twelve professionals plus support staff. Initially, the office did not organize itself along either geographic or policy lines. The original intent was to have all the liaison aides accessible and responsible to all the members of Congress. Eventually, however, loose jurisdictional areas did develop along regional and, to a lesser extent, policy lines. The administration also took great pains to orchestrate its legislative efforts. A legislative strategy group, consisting of the principal presidential advisers and appropriate Cabinet secretaries, met on a regular basis to plan the administration's lobbying activities.

Reagan's personal style contributed to his effectiveness in Congress. He was more willing to involve himself in legislative matters, particularly in the first year in office, than Carter had been. Unlike his predecessor, Reagan was not adverse to considering political issues when he asked members of Congress to support his legislative initiatives although he tended to leave the actual deal-making to his principal aides.

The administration's strategy combined ideology and partisanship. Appeals to Democrats, particularly those from the South, tended to be ideological, focusing on the President's economic and defense objectives. As the first Republican presidential candidate in a long time to have emphasized his partisan affiliation—he had asked voters not to send him to Washington "alone"—Reagan was in a good position to make a successful partisan appeal to Republicans. The other principal components of the administration's legislative strategy included limiting the agenda to economic issues, packaging them into a few policy proposals, and then mobilizing support for them both in Congress and outside it.

Together, the experienced liaison staff, the President's accessibility and personal style, and the strategy that concentrated on a few issues and moved them quickly through the legislative process paid handsome dividends during the administration's first year. Major parts of Reagan's economic program were enacted; Reagan established his reputation as a skillful and successful legislator; and the Office of Legislative Affairs received high grades for its professionalism. That these successes were not equaled in subsequent years points to the unique opportunities that an administration may have when first in office and how difficult it later becomes to maintain cooperative relations with Congress.

Bush's Difficulties. Contrary to expectations, the liaison effort at the outset of the George Bush administration did not flow from the early Reagan experience. Lacking a discernible policy mandate and facing Democratic control of both houses of Congress, the Bush administration decided to downplay domestic legislative policy in favor of foreign affairs. Moreover, Bush's Legislative Affairs Office got off to a slow start. It was a little smaller than previous offices (there were seven congressional lobbyists out of a total staff of twenty) and had difficulty performing the usual start-up tasks—getting to know all the members of Congress, handling the many patronage and project requests, and providing information for the White House on potential or pending confirmations in the Senate.

The office's difficulties were complicated by indistinct lines of authority and communication between the White House and the Cabinet, on one hand, and the White House and Congress, on the other. Bush was an active President, meeting with more than four hundred members of Congress, individually or in small groups, during his first hundred days in office, and a number of department heads and presidential aides also had direct contact with Congress on a regular basis. But, unlike the previous administration, there was no legislative strategy group that coordinated this activity at the beginning of Bush's presidency. Moreover, the first WHITE HOUSE CHIEF OF STAFF, John Sununu, acted as an intermediary between the President and his aides, and this left the impression in Congress that the head of the congressional liaison office was not a member of the inner circle, thereby undercutting the influence of his staff on Capitol Hill. Sununu did have considerable contact with members of Congress on key presidential initiatives, but his abrasive manner irritated many of them. None of this helped the President's cause.

Bush, on the other hand, was well liked and made it a point to be extremely accessible to Congress. He socialized with members and frequently communicated with them. He also changed the harsh campaign rhetoric to a more measured, less partisan tone. Presidential pressure on Congress was also reduced by the absence of a comprehensive domestic program although a number of controversial presidential nominations inflamed legislative passions.

Bush's style was pragmatic, his tone conciliatory, and, until the 1992 election approached, his orientation was to compromise with the Democratic majority. Within this policy-making framework, however, he used the veto effectively to indicate how far he was prepared to go in meeting Congress's modifications to his policy initiatives. The veto functioned as the stick in his carrot-and-stick approach to Congress.

Institutionalized Liaison. White House liaison with Congress has become an integral and critical component in a President's exercise of his legislative role. Much of the organizational structure and operational responsibilities of this liaison effort have become institutionalized. Every President is expected to have a congressional office that handles routine business as well as provides information on congressional intentions and lobbies for congressional support for his proposals. What the office does, how it is organized, the type of people who work in it, and the tactics they use have become standard, although there are and will continue to be differences in how successfully the liaison office performs.

The more variable elements that affect presidential relations with Congress tend to be stylistic and strategic. They differ from President to President and according to the political climate in which Presidents find themselves. Of the two factors, legislative strategy seems more important than legislative style, although how Presidents interact with Congress does make a difference in the extent to which Presidents can achieve their priorities.

A successful presidential style for interacting with Congress requires accessibility combined with a recognition of the legitimacy of members' representational needs and policy concerns and a willingness to take these needs and concerns into account when formulating legislation and mobilizing support for it.

A successful strategy has to resonate with the politics of the times. Whether that strategy is partisan or bipartisan, ideological or pragmatic, visible or behind-the-scenes, depends on the composition of Congress, the nature of the President's requests, and the public mood. Presidents seem to benefit most when they limit and prioritize their proposals, move them quickly through the legislative process, and are increasingly amenable to compromise with Congress as their administrations progress. A President's skill as a political leader combined with his ability to fashion situations in which he can most effectively exercise that leadership are the keys to his legislative success.

[See also LEGISLATIVE LEADERSHIP.]

BIBLIOGRAPHY

Davis, Eric. "Congressional Liaison: The People and the Institutions." In *Both Ends of the Avenue*. Edited by Anthony King. 1982. Pp. 59–95.

Jones, Charles O. *The Trusteeship Presidency*. 1988. Pp. 99–124.

Wayne, Stephen J. "Congressional Liaison in the Reagan White House: A Preliminary Assessment of the First Year." *President and Congress*. Edited by Norman Ornstein. 1982. Pp. 44–65.

Wayne, Stephen J. *The Legislative Presidency*. 1978. Pp. 139–177, 211–213.

STEPHEN J. WAYNE

CONGRESSIONAL BUDGET AND IMPOUND-MENT CONTROL ACT (1974). Often referred to as the Congressional Budget Act (CBA), the Congressional Budget and Impoundment Control Act represented an ambitious attempt to increase congressional control of the federal purse strings and to counter growing presidential power in budgeting. The CBA created a new system for managing budget totals and sharply reduced the President's ability to impound (refuse to spend) monies appropriated by Congress. The CBA has had a mixed impact on the presidency, but since 1974 it has generally increased the ability of Congress to participate in the budgetary process as the President's coequal partner.

The Old Budget Process. Dissatisfaction with the old authorization-appropriations process, which had been dominant for nearly a century, was rampant by the early 1970s. The fragmented process divided the budget into more than a dozen separate parts that were never considered as a whole. The House and Senate were often unable to pass spending bills by the start of the fiscal year, leaving many executive agencies funded only by temporary measures. Federal spending and budget deficits increased and Congress seemed incapable of exerting any restraint. Congress was spurred to action not only because of dissatisfaction with its own processes but because members increasingly believed that their constitutional power of the purse would continue to be usurped by the President if they did not develop their own budget process. Congress was dissatisfied with the quality of its budgetary information and grew suspicious of the budget numbers provided members by the President's OFFICE OF MANAGEMENT AND BUDGET (OMB). President Richard M. Nixon lambasted the Congress as irresponsible and threatened that the presidency would exert spending control if the Congress proved incapable of doing so.

In 1972, Nixon demanded that Congress enact a spending ceiling of $250 billion, threatening to veto any spending bills that appropriated more than he requested. He vetoed a number of spending bills to emphasize his budgetary disagreements with Congress. The conflict continued after Nixon won reelection in a landslide in 1972. Thwarted by Congress and dissatisfied with the veto strategy, he turned to IMPOUNDMENT, refusing to spend money appropriated by Congress. As much as $20 billion in outlays was held back by the administration. These impoundments infuriated members of Congress, including many Republicans, who believed that Nixon's actions were unconstitutional. Resolved to create its own budget process and to restrict impoundment, Congress created the Joint Committee on Budget Control, which began work in early 1973.

Many diverse institutional and political interests were represented. Conservative Republicans wanted a process that required a vote on the size of the deficit, hoping that the political pressure would lead to a balanced budget. Liberal Democrats wanted a process that would allow debate over national priorities, such as the budget shares of defense as opposed to social programs. The appropriations committees wanted to protect their turf and ability to review agency budgets. The result was a hybrid system that, rather than replacing the old system, superimposed a new process over the old. The final bill had strong bipartisan support; the Congressional Budget and Impoundment Control Act passed the House by a vote of 401 to 6 and the Senate by a vote of 75 to 0, clearly veto-proof majorities. This consensus, however, proved fleeting; sharp partisan cleavages appeared as soon as the new process was implemented. The President and the executive branch had virtually no input into the CBA, but a beleaguered Nixon, facing IMPEACHMENT, signed it into law in July 1974, only a month before he resigned the presidency.

Provisions of the Act. The CBA instituted a new process to enable Congress to make decisions on the budget as a whole. It created the House and Senate budget committees, which were responsible for reporting budget resolutions to their respective houses and for ensuring that a strict timetable for legislative action would be followed. Concurrent resolutions were chosen as the vehicle for congressional budgets since they did not require the signature of the President to take effect, even though they were binding only on subsequent congressional actions. The first concurrent resolution on the budget, which is supposed to be enacted by 15 May, set targets for budget authority and outlays, spending by functional category, revenues, surplus or deficit, and public debt. Congress would still receive the President's budget in January and would still take testimony from administration officials, but the budget committees would report a separate congressional budget. During the summer months, the old authorization-appropriations process would take place, including testimony from executive agency officials on individual spending bills.

By 15 September, Congress was required to pass the second budget resolution, which would set binding totals. Those figures had to be reconciled with the actions of the appropriations committees in time for the start of the new fiscal year, which was moved from 1 July to 1 October. The process of reconciliation, largely ignored for several years, would prove critical to both the President and Congress in budget battles of the 1980s [*see* RECONCILIATION BILLS]. To provide analysis and information to members and committees, the act created the CONGRESSIONAL BUDGET OFFICE (CBO). Congress would no longer have to depend on the economic assumptions and budget projections provided to them by the OMB; CBO would provide independent estimates for members. Finally, the act imposed new controls on impoundment, creating a process whereby the President could request that Congress temporarily delay spending (deferral) or permanently eliminate spending (rescission). Deferrals automatically went into effect unless either house disapproved. Rescis-

sions were automatically rejected unless both houses approved within forty-five days.

The Congressional Budget and Impoundment Control Act has had important effects on the power of the President and on executive budget procedures. Gerald Ford, the first President to send a budget to Congress under the new process, learned how the House and Senate could use this new process to change his spending priorities. Congress altered Ford's spending requests by a total of 7 percent (high by historical standards), disagreeing on a host of domestic and defense priorities. Ford seemed disdainful of the new congressional process, and urged that Congress adopt a separate spending ceiling. With the election of Democrat Jimmy Carter as President in 1976, Congress showed that the congressional budget process could also accommodate a President of its own party. In 1977, Congress enacted a third budget resolution for the fiscal year to accommodate the President's proposal for a tax rebate. Carter angered congressional Democrats, however, when he withdrew the proposal without giving adequate notice to budget leaders in the House and Senate.

Reagan's Use of the Process. The potency of reconciliation and the ability of the process to shape the budget from the top down did not become clear until 1981, when President Ronald Reagan used the congressional budget process to enact a dramatic economic and budget plan. The most important component of the strategy was the use of the reconciliation process to make sweeping changes in taxing and spending in a single legislative package. Moving reconciliation to the beginning of the process, the administration was able to build a working majority in the House by attracting several dozen conservative Democrats, popularly referred to as the boll weevils. The administration was able to overturn the budget resolution and reconciliation bill reported by the House Budget Committee and supported by the Democratic leaders. In a single bill, literally hundreds of programs were cut back by rescinding authorizations and appropriations. In this case, the act designed in 1974 to strengthen congressional control over the budget was used by the President to gain approval of dramatic changes in federal taxing and spending policy.

This pattern would not be repeated. By 1982, both branches were deadlocked because of the massive budget deficits that followed adoption of the Reagan program. After the 1982 midterm elections which restored a large Democratic majority in the House, the President's budget was pronounced "dead on arrival" when received on Capitol Hill. Increasingly, taxing and spending measures were lumped together in massive omnibus budget bills; control of this must-pass legislation gave congressional leaders greater leverage in its policy disputes with the administration. The Congressional Budget and Impoundment Control Act was formally amended for the first time in 1985 with the adoption of the Balanced Budget and Emergency Deficit Control Act, more commonly known as the GRAMM-RUDMAN-HOLLINGS ACT. It provided that if Congress and the President could not agree on a budget that would meet specified deficit targets, automatic across-the-board cuts (called sequestrations) would be imposed on discretionary spending. The act was amended again in 1987 and 1990 as Congress attempted to deal with the deficits while protecting their influence in the budget process.

Although President Reagan was able to use it to his advantage in 1981, in most cases the 1974 CBA has allowed Congress to challenge the President's budget as a coequal partner. Since 1974, competing estimates and projections by CBO and OMB have led to disputes over the numbers. Some scholars argue that as a result, the influence of the executive budget has seriously declined. Throughout the Reagan-Bush era, budget totals were commonly determined through BUDGET SUMMITS between congressional and administration leaders. The balance of budgetary power between the branches will continue to evolve. Depending on the political conditions and party control of government, the CBA may alternately serve to curb or enhance presidential leadership in setting budget priorities.

BIBLIOGRAPHY

Gilmour, John. *Reconcilable Differences?* 1990.
Ippolito, Dennis. *Congressional Spending.* 1981.
LeLoup, Lance T. *The Fiscal Congress: Legislative Control of the Budget.* 1980.
Schick, Allen. *Congress and Money.* 1980.

LANCE T. LELOUP

CONGRESSIONAL BUDGET OFFICE (CBO).

The Congressional Budget Office was established by the Congressional Budget and Impoundment Act of 1974 to provide Congress with objective analysis of the federal budget and the economy and to furnish technical support for the new Congressional budget process. The creation of this 226-person (in 1992) office effectively ended the executive branch's virtual monopoly on timely budget estimates and policy analysis of pending legislative issues. With its own source of technical expertise, Congress could challenge the President on budgetary and economic matters more

effectively. The CBO has strengthened the capacity and independence of the legislative branch.

The perceived need for a nonpartisan Congressional budget agency reflected the various forces that led to the passage of the 1974 budget act. Congress's desire to reassert its role in budget making was motivated by frustration over the fragmented and decentralized way in which Congress had been dealing with the unified budget presented by the President. The budget act provided a central focus for Congress by establishing a new budget process, with its concurrent budget resolutions, and by creating the House and Senate budget committees as well as CBO. President Richard M. Nixon's use of IMPOUNDMENTS to control spending was a second impetus to the passage of the act, which required that Congress approve executive cancellation of budget authority. Finally, the OFFICE OF MANAGEMENT AND BUDGET (OMB), long viewed as a nonpartisan, highly professional organization, became increasingly politicized during the 1970s, leading many in Congress to distrust the budgetary information flowing from the executive branch. This distrust helped to create CBO, which, as Hugh Heclo has written, assumed the role of the "more or less objective purveyor of nonpartisan numbers and analyses."

CBO serves the majority and minority in both chambers, analyzing options without making recommendations. Because CBO does not attempt to promote a particular policy agenda, the media and the analytical community (which includes policy analysts in government, think tanks, universities, and private firms) have come to accept its analyses, budget estimates, and economic forecasts as standards against which the administration's claims should be compared. This factor has reduced the administration's ability to exaggerate both the benefits of its policy initiatives and the shortcomings of policies it opposes. Under the Balanced Budget and Emergency Deficit Control Act of 1985 (popularly known as GRAMM-RUDMAN-HOLLINGS ACT), the administration is required to explain the differences between certain of its budget estimates and those of CBO. Further, executive branch representatives are frequently asked to compare their estimates and analyses with those of CBO at congressional hearings and in other forums.

Since 1976, CBO has issued annual analyses of presidential budgetary proposals. In them, CBO examines the President's budget using its own economic and technical assumptions and presuming that all of the President's policy proposals are to be enacted promptly. At times, this exercise has revealed the administration's estimates to be extremely optimistic; at other times, CBO's analysis of the President's budgetary proposal has largely confirmed the administration's figures. Knowing that this analysis will be available a few weeks after release of the President's budget has undoubtedly tempered the hyperbole that used to surround the President's release of his budget proposal. CBO's economic forecasts and budget estimates were particularly important during that brief era (1986–1990) during which the budget was required to meet fixed deficit targets and, therefore, the administration had a strong incentive to produce highly optimistic economic forecasts.

Administrations have sometimes taken strong exception to CBO's estimates or analyses of specific presidential policy proposals. The Carter administration disagreed with CBO's critiques of its energy policy and WELFARE POLICY; the Reagan administration objected to CBO's estimate of the impact of its tax proposals; and the Bush administration took issue with CBO's projections of the affordability of its plans for military weapons, its analyses of changes in the distribution of income, and its estimates of the likely impact on economic growth of reduced taxes on capital income. Such disagreements are inevitable when a nonpartisan agency attempts to provide objective analysis of controversial issues in a highly charged political environment.

Although an administration may disagree with certain of CBO's estimates and analyses, a good deal of interaction and cooperation takes place at a technical level between the CBO staff and the professional analytic staffs of the executive agencies. Data and estimating models are often shared, and analysts in the two branches sometimes critique each other's work on an informal basis. That cooperation has improved the quality of the estimates and analyses available to both branches of government. It has also led to a more open and public discussion of how various estimates are generated.

In addition to its analysis of the President's budget, economic forecasts, and policy analyses, the Congressional Budget Office issues baseline budget projections, bill cost estimates, and deficit reduction options. CBO's baseline budget projects the future course of federal spending, revenues, and deficits, assuming current laws, regulations, and policies will not change. The baseline provides a neutral reference against which various broad policy changes, including those proposed by the President, can be compared.

CBO's bill cost estimates indicate the fiscal consequences over five years of enacting each spending bill reported by a committee of the Senate or House. At times, administrations have used CBO bill cost estimates in their arguments against certain legislative initiatives. CBO reports on deficit reduction options in an annual volume that provides brief descriptions of several hundred policies that would reduce the deficit by raising revenues or reducing spending. Some of the options analyzed reflect presidential proposals; others have their origins in congressional proposals or the work of policy analysts. The volume summarizes the arguments for and against each option and provides a consistent set of budget estimates.

CBO is also charged with keeping track of the budgetary decisions the Congress makes, a task known as scorekeeping. When the periodic scorekeeping reports issued by CBO indicate that the limits established by the congressional budget resolution will be breached, special procedures may be invoked on the House and Senate floor. In the end, however, OMB's scorekeeping estimates are more important because they govern the automatic enforcement mechanisms of the Balanced Budget Act and the BUDGET ENFORCEMENT ACT of 1990.

In his book *The Power Game* (1988), Hedrick Smith concluded, "CBO represents the most important shift of power on domestic issues between the executive branch and Congress in several decades." But because it is only a staff arm of Congress, with no independent source of political power, CBO's influence is fragile. For the office to remain influential, its economic forecasts, estimates, and studies must continue to be perceived as unbiased and authoritative.

BIBLIOGRAPHY

Collender, Stanley. *The Guide to the Federal Budget.* 1992.
Fisher, Louis. *The Politics of Shared Power: Congress and the Executive.* 3d ed. 1993.
Heclo, Hugh. "Executive Budget Making." In *Federal Budget Policy in the 1980s.* Edited by Gregory Mills and John Palmer. 1984.
Schick, Allen. *The Capacity to Budget.* 1990.

ROBERT D. REISCHAUER

CONGRESSIONAL INFLUENCE ON PRESIDENT.

Many foreign observers find the American system of SEPARATION OF POWERS hard to grasp. The idea of completely separated powers is difficult enough, but the reality—that powers are in fact intertwined in many respects and that the system is, in Edward Corwin's term, "an invitation to struggle" for power between the branches—is even more puzzling. While formal powers are an important part of this struggle, the real dynamic, whereby Congress and the President push and tug at each other in the process of making policy, often occurs on an informal level.

Formal and Informal Powers. Over the years, the President has gradually assumed more and more legislative power and responsibility, and, as a result, a complex relationship has evolved between Congress and the President. Congress has its own strategies for influencing the President's positions on various legislative issues.

Congress has the power to override a presidential veto and the responsibility of oversight of executive-branch agencies as they carry out the mandates of federal laws and statutes. In probably its most important check on executive power, Congress controls the federal purse strings.

In addition, the Senate has the power to approve or reject presidential nominations of ambassadors, Supreme Court Justices, DEPARTMENTAL SECRETARIES, and other federal officers, ministers, and consuls [see ADVICE AND CONSENT]. The Senate must also approve all treaties that the President negotiates and signs.

Congress's power in the area of foreign policy was strengthened considerably by important legislation passed during the 1970s. The WAR POWERS RESOLUTION (1973) required the President to consult with Congress before sending American troops into combat and mandated that such troops be withdrawn after a certain time if Congress did not specifically authorize an extended stay, or war. In 1974, Congress passed a law requiring the CENTRAL INTELLIGENCE AGENCY (CIA) to keep the House and Senate intelligence committees fully informed of its activities. As often happens, the relative influence of the branches vis-à-vis each other can wax and wane as events and circumstances change; both these pieces of legislation were passed at a time when the public's confidence and trust in the presidency were at a historically low level, in the wake of the VIETNAM WAR, the WATERGATE AFFAIR, and revelations about illegal operations by the CIA.

It is obvious, then, that the system of separated powers is actually a system of overlapping authority. Americans tend to believe that the President of the United States has unlimited power, but the reality is that there are certain areas where he simply cannot act independently of Congress. The relationship is reciprocal, a partnership characterized by conflict and cooperation.

The relationship between Congress and the President is not static. It varies according to the personalities involved, the President's popularity and the popularity of his legislative program, and Congress's strength and cohesion, not to mention Congress's party makeup. It may also vary from issue to issue.

Sources of Conflict. To make some sense of the relationship between Congress and the President, it is important to identify some of the inherent sources of conflict between the two branches. Besides the constitutional conflicts alluded to above, the differing inter-

nal structures of the two branches also make it hard for them to work in tandem. While the executive branch is hierarchically organized, with the President firmly at the helm, power in Congress is highly decentralized, and various power bases compete against each other. Some have argued that as a result of these structural differences, the President's policy directives emerge from a broad cross-section of viewpoints, which he is free to hear and then decide unilaterally while the dominant position coming out of a congressional committee, reflecting the prerogatives of the individual members, with the need to accommodate the narrow needs of each, will tend to be more narrow and parochial. Although this may make sense in theory, it rests on the assumption that the President actually exposes himself to a wide range of viewpoints and perspectives, which is not always the case.

The decentralization of power in Congress has actually become a means by which Congress has gained increased influence over the President. While Congress's authority increased as the scope of the federal government expanded, the congressional rules reforms of the 1970s were designed, in part, to make Congress more competitive with the executive branch. The committee and subcommittee reforms decentralized power, making it harder for the President to form majority coalitions in Congress. Furthermore, fragmented committee jurisdictions added more potential roadblocks to presidential initiatives. Finally, congressional staff and support agencies were expanded, giving the legislature more policy expertise and analytical capability. Therefore, Congress, at least for a time, assumed a greater role in formulating domestic policy programs and creating government regulations. Of course, power in a decentralized Congress is negative power—the power to block or delay. When Congress wants to act on policy or the public wants it to work with a President, that decentralization can become frustrating or counterproductive, as it was late in the presidency of George Bush.

In addition to these differences in internal structures, their different constituencies can serve as a source of conflict between Congress and the President. The presidents and the VICE PRESIDENT are the only elected officials who can claim a truly national constituency. Members of Congress represent states or smaller units within states, and so represent local concerns or, at most, regional interests. James Madison pointed to this as the greatest source of conflict between the two branches in FEDERALIST 46.

Critics of Congress argue that members are overly responsive to the narrow interests of their constituents and that as a result Congress is unable to represent the interests of the nation as a whole. This in turn may make it difficult for the President to push through legislation that he deems to be in the national interest. It is important to point out, however, that Presidents construct their own narrow coalitions in order to get elected, and their subsequent loyalty to the groups that make up those coalitions may often interfere with what others may judge to be the national interest.

A third source of conflict is the different time perspectives of the two branches. This has two components. First, a President's time horizon tends to be four years, the length of the presidential term; for members of Congress, the horizon is two years. Thus, only a year into a presidential term, members of Congress inevitably are already getting skittish about bad news or controversial political issues. This is particularly true of the lawmakers from the President's party, since midterm elections almost invariably produce losses in the House for the party of the White House.

Second, there is the career element of the time horizons. Since the TWENTY-SECOND AMENDMENT was added to the Constitution, a President has been limited to two terms in office (or ten years if he takes over the term of a predecessor). Members of Congress are not limited in the number of terms they can serve in office (although advocates of term limits would like to see that changed). It can be argued, therefore, that the President must pursue a much more activist policy agenda, while the "careerists" in Congress often lack the motivation to act swiftly. This can be a source of great frustration for Presidents who come impatiently into office with a clear legislative agenda or mandate for change. The situation is exacerbated when the majority in Congress is of a different party than the President [see DIVIDED GOVERNMENT]. But strong-willed and clever Presidents are able to use their popularity and political momentum to make things happen, even if many in Congress are reluctant to do so. This is particularly true early in a presidency—the so-called HONEYMOON PERIOD—and during times of perceived crisis.

Sources of Cooperation. While there are clearly sources of conflict between the Congress and the President, there are also many sources of cooperation. Roger Davidson discusses some of these in a 1984 article entitled "The Presidency and Congress." Davidson points out that, in spite of the built-in tensions, the branches do cooperate with one another on a host of issues. If they did not, the government would not be able to function.

Numerous examples of cooperation between the branches can be cited. Congressional input is often taken into account in the selection of White House personnel, and quite often the President's CABINET will include at least one former member of Congress. Presidential appointments are generally easily approved by Congress, with the rare exception of some highly sensitive or politicized positions.

On the legislative front, Presidents, even those with strong initiatives, will usually feel out the relevant congressional committees and leaders in Congress and accommodate their overriding needs in formulating policy initiatives. Cooperation is usually even greater between the President and members of his own party in Congress. In the 1990s, Democratic leaders in Congress served as liaisons between the executive branch and the legislature, conveying the President's agenda to their fellow members and informing the President and his staff of the views of the legislators, even as their Republican counterparts did between 1981 and 1993. Former Senate Majority Leader Howard Baker described the relationship as it existed under President Ronald Reagan as follows:

> The majority leadership of this body has a special obligation to see to it that the president's initiatives are accorded full and fair hearing on Capitol Hill. By the same token, we have a special duty to advise the president and his counselors concerning parliamentary strategy and tactics.

Congressional leaders advise the President on parliamentary strategy, often as it is being shaped. By cautioning Presidents about which issues have real support on the Hill and which don't, and by advising on (as well as determining) the timing of legislative initiatives, congressional leaders can play a major role in actually setting the President's agenda. Spending time with the President (and the opportunity this provides for persuading him to do—or not to do—something) is one of the most valuable things congressional leaders can do. Compromise and cooperation are a necessary element of successful governing, and members of both branches understand this.

Partisan Control. One of the most important factors affecting the relationship between Congress and the President, partisan control can also serve as a source of influence for one branch over the other. When the same party controls both branches, the President usually has more leverage over the legislature, although this is not always the case. For example, Democratic President Jimmy Carter had little success pushing his legislative program through a Congress overwhelmingly controlled by his fellow Democrats. Carter's failures had little to do with patterns of party control and were attributable more to his lack of legislative and leadership skills.

In situations of divided government, Congress's ability to influence the President often increases. If a

President in these circumstances is unable to assert strong and proactive policy leadership, however, Congress, which is more naturally reactive, may not fill the vacuum and the government as a whole may become crippled in its ability to tackle difficult policy issues.

There are three distinct patterns of interbranch control, each of which has different implications for the congressional-executive relationship.

First is what is commonly called party government, a situation in which the President and the congressional majority are of the same party; this has been the norm through most of American history, though not since 1945. Some party governments, including those led by Franklin D. Roosevelt and Lyndon B. Johnson, have proved extremely productive. It is important to point out, however, that party government alone is not enough to get things moving in Washington; a strong mandate for change or a crisis-driven sense of urgency among the public, combined with an assertive President and a healthy partisan majority in Congress, can help a great deal.

The second, less common, pattern of interbranch control is known as a truncated majority. This situation exists when the President's party has a majority in one house of Congress but not the other. According to Roger Davidson, this has occurred in only four Congresses in the twentieth century, most recently during the first six years of the Reagan presidency, when Republicans enjoyed a majority in the Senate. This arrangement worked well for Reagan in the early days of the 97th Congress, when he was able to force through a massive package of spending cuts designed to spur the stagnant economy. In addition to having a majority in the Senate, Reagan was also able to mold a coalition of Republican and conservative Democratic House members in support of his program.

The third pattern of interbranch control is divided government. It has been under this circumstance that Congress has been able to exert the greatest amount of influence over the President, for better or worse. Twelve of the twenty-three congresses between 1947 and 1992 were in the hands of the party opposed to the Presidents. In some cases relations between the branches under conditions of divided government have been relatively stable, but they have often been strained, and sometimes have been quite hostile. Tension was at its peak during the final two years of the Richard M. Nixon presidency, until IMPEACHMENT proceedings in the House of Representatives forced him to resign from office. Tension was also high at the end of the Reagan presidency and in the final stages of the Bush White House.

It is important not to overstate the case against divided government; much of the malaise of the Bush years may have had to do with the individual actors involved, as well as with social and economic factors beyond their control. And, in spite of the occasional tension, a real working relationship between the two branches has been sustained and even, in some respects, strengthened over the years. This can be seen, for instance, in the virtual institutionalization of the congressional liaison office in the EXECUTIVE OFFICE OF THE PRESIDENT (EOP).

In any discussion of executive-legislative relations, it is important to keep in mind the context in which the two branches operate. The state of the economy, international affairs, social unrest, the public mood—each of these factors can come into play and influence this very complex relationship.

Political scientists George Edwards and Stephen Wayne elaborate on this point in their book *Presidential Leadership* (1985), contrasting conditions during the 1960s to those of the 1970s and 1980s. As Edwards and Wayne write,

> The prosperity of the 1960s provided the federal government with the funds for new policies, with little risk. Taxes did not have to be raised and sacrifices did not have to be made in order to help the underprivileged. In the late 1970s and 1980s resources are more limited, helping to make the passage of new welfare or health programs, for example, more problematical. When resources are scarce, presidents are faced with internal competition for them and the breakdown of supporting coalitions. . . . It is not surprising that the relations of recent presidents with Congress are often characterized by stalemate.

Congress or President? Discussions about the relationship between Congress and the President are often framed in terms of one branch's influence over the other. A focus on congressional influence over the President inevitably highlights the reciprocal nature of the relationship. It is impossible to say, really, which branch wields the most power in the complex and multifaceted American policy-making process. The balance of power is affected by many internal and external factors—individual personalities, partisan control, economic factors, and world events, among others—and is constantly changing.

Discussions such as this are often shaped by a bias toward one branch or the other. Those who advocate a stronger presidency may find fault with the built-in influences that Congress has over the executive branch, often accusing Congress of meddling or micromanaging, for example. On the other hand, those who fear unbridled executive power and would prefer to see Congress have the final say on most policy matters sometimes accuse the President of circumventing congressional will or of going over Congress's head or behind its back. It is important to recognize these biases when studying the literature and to keep in mind that effective leadership and responsive government are both crucial and that neither should be neglected in a discussion of executive-legislative relations.

Despite the fact that government was united at the outset of Clinton's presidency, the struggles and conflicts between Congress and the President will undoubtedly continue. Each side will have victories, and each will suffer frustration and defeat. The hope is that, when a consensus does emerge on a given policy issue, the system of shared powers will respond accordingly, interbranch rivalries will be set aside, and the needs of voters will be addressed.

[see also PRESIDENTIAL-CONGRESSIONAL RELATIONS.]

BIBLIOGRAPHY

Congressional Quarterly. *Guide to Congress*. 4th ed. 1991.
Crovitz, L. Gordon, and Jeremy A. Rabkin, eds. *The Fettered Presidency*. 1989.
Edwards, George C. *At the Margins*. 1989.
Edwards, George C. *Presidential Influence in Congress*. 1980.
Edwards, George C., and Stephen J. Wayne. *Presidential Leadership*. 1985.
Nelson, Michael. *The Presidency and the Political System. 1984.*
Peterson, Mark A. *Legislating Together*. 1990.

NORMAN ORNSTEIN

CONNALLY AMENDMENT (1946). The Connally Amendment was a condition embodied in the declaration by which the United States accepted the compulsory jurisdiction of the International Court of Justice, or World Court. Pursuant to that declaration, which was signed by President Harry S. Truman on 26 August 1946, the United States accepted jurisdiction over legal disputes with any state accepting the same obligation; but the Connally Amendment provided "that this declaration shall not apply to . . . disputes with regard to matters which are essentially within the domestic jurisdiction of the United States of America as determined by the United States of America."

Under the Connally Amendment it was the United States itself that would determine whether the limitation on the court's jurisdiction applied. This "self-judging" feature caused many to doubt the efficacy and even the validity of the U.S. acceptance of jurisdiction. The amendment had the side effect of precluding the United States from making affirmative use of the World Court as claimant, since defendant states were entitled to invoke it on the basis of reciprocity. Although the executive branch had not solicited the self-judging feature (which was added in the Senate at

the insistence of Sen. Tom Connally), it was understood that the executive branch would make any determinations pursuant to the amendment. Accordingly, the Eisenhower administration invoked the Connally Amendment to block the World Court's jurisdiction in a case brought by Switzerland.

When the Ronald Reagan administration terminated the U.S. acceptance of the World Court's compulsory jurisdiction effective in 1986, the Connally Amendment also terminated.

BIBLIOGRAPHY

Damrosch, Lori Fisler, ed. *The International Court of Justice at a Crossroads*. 1987.

LORI FISLER DAMROSCH

CONSERVATION POLICY. Conservation, a term coined in 1907 by Gifford Pinchot, head of the U.S. Forest Service, directly involved the President beginning in the 1890s. By the 1960s presidential involvement had shifted from a concern with preserving and managing natural resources to a much broader concern involving consideration of the quality of life available in the United States. When Richard M. Nixon became President, the term conservation was largely replaced by the more encompassing term ENVIRONMENTAL POLICY, which was brought to national attention with the establishment of the Environmental Protection Agency in 1970.

Early Policies. The Forest Reserve Act of 1891 and other legislation permitted the President to set aside public lands with valuable timber as national forests. Every President from Benjamin Harrison to Theodore Roosevelt withdrew such lands. In 1907 when Congress began to nullify the forest withdrawal power of the President, over 300 million acres of public lands were in the forest reserves, in all 234 million acres were set aside during Roosevelt's presidency. However, with the passage of the Antiquities Act of 1906 Presidents were permitted to withdraw public lands with exceptional natural or historic characteristics as national monuments.

Theodore Roosevelt was the first President to take an active interest in conservation. In addition to taking advantage of legislative authorization, he started the system of bird and wildlife sanctuaries in 1903 by establishing a three-acre Pelican Island Bird Refuge in Florida, actively endorsed the Reclamation Act of 1902, and curbed withdrawal of water power sites, as well as mineral and coal reserves from the public lands. More important, he brought conservation to public attention first by appointing in 1907 an Inland Waterways Commission to prepare "a comprehensive plan for the improvement and control" of the nation's river systems. Its massive report in 1908 called for multipurpose river valley development. A National Waterways Commission was created in 1909 to carry on its work. Then in May 1908 he convened a White House Conference on conservation, followed a month later by the creation of a National Conservation Commission. The object of the conference was to arouse the public conscience to the unnecessary waste and destruction of natural resources. By January 1909, thirty-six states and territories had appointed conservation commissions and there were forty-one national organizations. The national commission directed the first inventory of the nation's natural resources. In February 1909, weeks before leaving office, Roosevelt met with the representatives of the president of Mexico and the governor general of Canada at a White House conference to discuss conservation in North America and to call for an international conference at the Hague. Besides the National Conservation Commission, Gifford Pinchot established the National Conservation Association to further Roosevelt's efforts in calling for wise and beneficial use of natural resources as the means of checking waste and private exploitation.

William Howard Taft, Roosevelt's successor, said that he could not be other than an earnest advocate of any measure calculated "to prevent the continuance of the waste which has characterized our phenomenal growth in the past." While he called for various measures and set aside further mineral and coal reserves, by removing Gifford Pinchot from his post as Chief Forester in a controversy involving the disposition of coal reserves in Alaska, Taft incurred the criticism of conservationists. His tenure of office as well as the tenures of the four succeeding administrations witnessed no bold new conservation initiatives on the part of the presidency.

Herbert Hoover claimed a long-standing interest in conservation. But his preference for voluntary cooperation combined with his reluctance to call for federal regulation reduced his effectiveness as a conservation leader. In 1929 he appointed a Commission on the Conservation and Administration of the Public Domain. Its report called for turning over to the states all of the public domain suitable as rangelands. If states were unwilling to accept the lands, they would be placed under a federal range administration. The proposal received mixed responses and was never acted upon by Congress. All Hoover's conservation programs had the dual goal of conservation and relief for depressed industries. All involved cooperation with private developers, many of whom in the early

1930s, facing economic disaster, sought to increase production rather than cut back or wisely manage the federal reserves they wished to develop in cooperation with the federal government. Like his predecessor Calvin Coolidge, Hoover was interested in promoting land use for recreational purposes, calling for cooperation among states, communities, and the federal government in creating national recreation areas. While he continued to set aside public lands and called for the creation by Congress of new national parks and for the expansion of other federal reserves, Hoover's conservation program based on cooperation and reduced federal intervention was impaired by the Great Depression, which in the 1930s provided unparalled opportunities for his successor in the White House.

The New Deal. Franklin D. Roosevelt's NEW DEAL launched what has been called "the golden age of conservation." Its primary emphasis was on land use. In 1933 the first New Deal measure approved by Congress at the President's request was the creation of a CIVILIAN CONSERVATION CORPS to work in the national forests, aid in soil conservation, plant seedlings, as well as other related efforts. Numerous other New Deal agencies as part of their mission furthered these and similar conservation measures. While willing to cooperate with private land owners, and to develop federal-state systems of regulating practices, Roosevelt also sought to expand the federal presence in furthering the wise use and development of natural resources. Moreover, Roosevelt in furthering land-use conservation programs recognized that people constituted one of the greatest resources. In rehabilitating the national domain, New Deal conservation programs also put needy citizens to work.

In his 1931 veto message of the Muscle Shoals bill, President Hoover said that for the government to embark on such a venture, "That is not liberalism, it is degeneration." Two years later, during Roosevelt's administration, the TENNESSEE VALLEY AUTHORITY ACT, in calling for the "conservation and development of the natural resources" of the entire Tennessee River valley, gave the President the authority to recommend to Congress legislation to achieve these ends. The act specifically called for the multipurpose development of the region, including "the economic and social well-being of the people living in said river basin." Multipurpose development—navigation, flood control, utilizing marginal lands, reforestation, recreation, generating electric power, and sustained yield—was involved in one way or another in the conservation approach championed by Franklin Roosevelt and the bureaus and agencies that were created. Centralization was not a key factor in conservation. During the

New Deal, through legislation and EXECUTIVE ORDERS, the remaining unreserved area of the public domain was withdrawn from entry to secure more efficient land management with a particular emphasis on soil improvement.

President Harry S. Truman, while continuing his predecessors' approach to conservation, launched no new initiatives. In 1946 Presidential Reorganization Plan No. 3 created a new Bureau of Land Management assigned the functions of the General Land Office (created in 1812) and the Grazing Service (created in 1934). It would henceforth manage all public lands and administer all laws providing for their disposition and use. Dwight D. Eisenhower was closer to Herbert Hoover in his views on conservation. He wished to establish greater cooperation with private endeavors as well as local and state governments in promoting new as well as in managing existing conservation program.

The Shift to Environmentalism. His successors, Presidents John F. Kennedy and Lyndon B. Johnson, launched vigorous new initiatives that marked the transition from conservation to environmentalism. In 1961, Kennedy announced that the traditional principles of retention, multipurpose, and sustained yield would be central to the policy of his administration. In this vein he sent Congress a ten-year Development Program for the National Forests. In another message, he called upon the Bureau of Land Management to formulate a multiple-use policy for the public lands. Both Kennedy and Johnson sent special messages to Congress devoted entirely to conservation. In 1962, emulating Theodore Roosevelt, Kennedy invited five hundred leading conservationists to the White House to formulate policies for resource problems in seventeen specific areas of development. At the request of both Kennedy and Johnson, Congress approved legislation establishing a land and water conservation fund earmarking receipts from various sources for the acquisition of new park and recreation areas. Presidents Kennedy and Johnson brought conservation into a new phase, namely purchasing private lands for public use. Kennedy called for the creation of several national seashores and by executive action created a Bureau of Outdoor Recreation as well as an Outdoor Recreation Advisory Council.

In a special message to Congress, President Johnson in 1965 called for a new conservation concerned not with nature alone, but with the total relationship between people and the world around them. This meant that "beauty must not be just a holiday treat, but a part of our daily life" available alike to "rich and poor, Negro and white, city dweller and farmer." This new approach found expression in the Highway Beautification Act. In 1968, Johnson described the 1960s as "truly an era of conservation in this country." He noted that 2.4 million acres had been added to the National Park System since 1961, compared to 30,000 acres in the previous decade. Included in that vast acreage, besides national seashores, was a system of national wild and scenic rivers and a nationwide system of trails, urban parks, national recreation areas, national seashores, all created chiefly in response to presidential initiatives. Johnson, responding to a Park Service Report that only 2.5 percent of the giant redwoods were protected, called upon Congress to purchase a huge acreage in northern California for a Redwood National Park.

Conservation in the 1960s under presidential leadership became a matter of "restoration and innovation" interlocked with beautification and concerned with improving the quality of life enjoyed by the American people. Beautification was a theme championed by both President and LADY BIRD JOHNSON. In 1965 they hosted a White House Conference on National Beauty and later the President made public a report on beautification efforts by the heads of several Cabinet departments and appropriate agencies. And both Presidents Kennedy and Johnson argued that given increasing demands for water, it was necessary to assure the best use of existing water resources through coordinated planning and development, which had been advocated by Franklin Roosevelt in 1937 when he called for "seven TVAs" and by Harry Truman in 1950 when he proposed the Water Resources Policy Commission.

In outlining his conservation and antipollution proposals, which President Johnson said would set a course to "a natural America restored to her people, whose promise is clear rivers, tall forests and clean air." The shift to environmentalism was evident when Congress responded by accepting administration proposals resulting in the Clean River Act and the Clean Water Restoration Act in 1966 and in the Water Quality Act in 1965. In 1968, at Johnson's urging, Congress created a National Water Commission. The shift to environmentalism was completed in the Nixon administration with the National Environmental Protection Agency in 1970.

BIBLIOGRAPHY

Clements, Kendrick A. "Herbert Hoover and Conservation, 1921–1933." *American Historical Review* 80 (1984): 67–88.

Gould, Lewis L. *Lady Bird Johnson and the Environment*. 1988.

Nixon, Edgar B., comp. and ed. *Franklin D. Roosevelt and Conservation, 1911–1945*. 2 vols. 1957.

Richardson, Elmo R. *The Politics of Conservation: Crusades and Controversies, 1897–1913.* 1962.

Swain, Donald C. *Federal Conservation Policy, 1921–1933.* 1963.

RICHARD LOWITT

CONSERVATISM. In appraising the role of conservatism in the American presidency, one runs into two major problems. First, America lacked a self-conscious conservative intellectual movement until the 1940s. Before then, a number of political leaders championed policies that would later be called conservative, but few spoke at length of an explicit and coherent conservative philosophy. The authors of the seminal commentary on American government, THE FEDERALIST, never used the words *conservative* and *conservatism*. Except for the most recent Presidents, therefore, this discussion must largely rely upon retrospective labeling.

Second, the reach of American conservatism has disputed borders: no single definition can cover all the contending schools that fly the conservative flag. The best one can do here is to speak of two broad, arbitrary categories: *situational* conservatism and *ideological* conservatism.

Situational conservatism seeks to temper changes to society's status quo. Its great spokesman, the British statesman and philosopher Edmund Burke (1729–1797), warned against instant utopias: "Time is required to produce that union of minds which alone can produce all the good we aim at. Our patience will achieve more than our force." Situational conservatism consists not of abstract ideas but is rather a general counsel of prudence. It preaches gradual change but says little about the direction that such gradual change should take.

Ideological conservatism does involve abstract ideas, among them civil liberty, equality before the law, free markets, and limited government. (Conservatives and liberals alike hotly debate the meaning and priority of such concepts.) When ideological conservatives see a status quo hostile to these ideas, they may call for fundamental change, thus parting with situational conservatives. As Republican presidential candidate BARRY GOLDWATER put it in 1964, "Extremism in the defense of liberty is no vice. . . . Moderation in the pursuit of justice is no virtue."

From Washington to Hoover. George Washington made a poor fit for the garments of a situational conservative. As a patriot general, he led a bloody revolution that marked a radical break with the tradition of Europe's feudal past. As the first Chief Executive, he had to set precedents, not follow them. But, although ideological conservatives could hardly lay an exclusive claim to Washington, his statesmanship does square with their beliefs: while asserting the prerogatives of his office, he refrained from seizing excessive power, either for himself or for the national government.

His successor, John Adams, ruled himself out as an ideological conservative by denouncing ideology "as the science of Idiocy." Though he professed to have differences with Burke, his writings bore a strong Burkean flavor. As he wrote to Josiah Quincy, "I cannot see any better principle at present than to make as little innovation as possible; keep things going as well we can in the present train." Adams's presidential actions may seem inconsistent with such beliefs, for he agreed to a sharp increase in military spending as well as passage of the ALIEN AND SEDITION ACTS, which dramatically expanded the federal government's power over speech. Adams, however, defended such innovations as ways of preserving the status quo against internal and external danger.

Adams and his followers thought Thomas Jefferson posed a threat to the status quo—and more. One Federalist writer put the case against Jefferson this way: "Are you prepared to see your dwellings in flames, hoary hairs bathed in blood, female chastity violated, or children writhing on the pike and the halbert?" Without doing violence to women and children, Jefferson did reverse many Federalist policies. Believing in limited government and a strict reading of the Constitution, Jefferson worked with Congress to slash federal spending, reduce the debt, and abolish most internal taxes. In light of his standing as a founder of the DEMOCRATIC PARTY, it is ironic that today's ideological conservatives could cheer his domestic accomplishments.

The next major political upheaval came in 1828, with the election of Andrew Jackson. Jackson was no situational conservative, for he sought to scrap the special privileges that had grown up around the closed circle of well-born men who had run national politics for decades. Like Jefferson, Jackson came to embody Democratic presidential activism, yet he, too, pursued policies that twentieth-century ideological conservatives could appreciate. He cut federal support for INTERNAL IMPROVEMENTS (later known as pork-barrel spending), tried to curb outlays, and decentralized economic policy by dismantling the BANK OF THE UNITED STATES. His belief in decentralization had its limits, however, and he fought South Carolina's attempt to nullify a national tariff law [*see* NULLIFICATION].

The South supplied the central issue of the campaign of 1860, in which Abraham Lincoln argued that the Framers had anticipated the eventual death of SLAVERY. While rhetorically addressing the South during his Cooper Union speech, he made a rare use of the word *conservatism*: "What is conservatism? Is it not adherence to the old and tried, against the new and untried? We stick to, contend for, the identical old policy in the point in controversy which was adopted by our fathers who framed the Government under which we live; while you with one accord reject, and scout, and spit upon that old policy, and insist upon substituting something new." In other words, he was casting himself as a situational conservative, while applying the label of radicalism to those who would extend slavery.

Far from preserving the status quo, of course, Lincoln's administration revolutionized America. Not only did Lincoln lead the nation through the CIVIL WAR, but he supported a host of domestic innovations, including a homestead act, a land-grant college act, and a Pacific railroad act. To this day, ideological conservatives disagree about Lincoln's legacy. Some contend that he diminished liberty through a dangerous expansion of national power. Many others say that he upheld conservative principles by killing the tyrannical institution of slavery and by fostering individual opportunity and free-market capitalism. Within the conservative movement, the latter group seems to have the advantage: for example, the 1992 Republican platform prominently featured his portrait and repeatedly quoted his words.

After the Civil War, no Democrat won the White House until Grover Cleveland's victory in 1884, and Woodrow Wilson later made the sarcastic suggestion that Cleveland did not count: "You may think Cleveland's administration was Democratic. It was not. Cleveland was a conservative Republican." Indeed, Cleveland held to the ideologically conservative belief that "the right of the government to exact tribute from the citizen is limited to its actual necessities, and every cent taken from the people beyond that required for their protection by the government is no better than robbery." But his use of federal troops against the PULLMAN STRIKE in 1894 represented a conflict between support of capitalism and devotion to limited government.

With William McKinley, prudence loomed large. In referring to financial laws in his first inaugural address, he said, "We must be both 'sure we are right' and 'make haste slowly.'" McKinley's domestic policies matched his rhetoric. Yet, despite his talking like a situational conservative, McKinley expanded America's international role by waging the SPANISH-AMERICAN WAR.

The next conservative presidency, that of William Howard Taft, gave the nation a pause between the liberal activism of Theodore Roosevelt and Woodrow Wilson. Following the WORLD WAR I, Warren G. Harding ran under a banner of situational conservatism, pledging "not heroics but healing, not nostrums but normalcy." After his scandal-ridden administration and mysterious death, he was followed by Calvin Coolidge, whose beliefs combined elements of both situational and ideological conservatism. In his autobiography, Coolidge wrote that tradition and experience show the way that "causes the least friction and is most likely to bring the desired result." At the same time, he also expressed a profound understanding of the philosophical ideals of the Framers.

Herbert Hoover blended reformism with the two versions of conservatism, and achieved sorry results. In the face of the Great Depression, he proposed some new spending programs, balked at radical economic remedies, and clung to trade protectionism, a measure that made matters worse.

The Rise of Ideological Conservatism. Franklin D. Roosevelt was no ideologue, and one could make a powerful argument that the NEW DEAL ultimately served the conservative purpose of averting far more radical innovations. But the changes that Roosevelt made in government began to galvanize Americans who had conservative tendencies. Harry S. Truman carried on Roosevelt's domestic policies, and the conservative opposition slowly continued to ferment. Meanwhile, the foreign-policy views of conservatives underwent a rapid transformation. Notwithstanding the Spanish-American War, conservatives had historically tended toward isolation in foreign policy. But, with the emergence of the Iron Curtain, they moved to the side of assertive internationalism.

Under Dwight D. Eisenhower, situational and ideological conservatism sharply diverged. Eisenhower was a pragmatic defender of the status quo. But, after twenty years of Democratic rule, the status quo displeased ideological conservatives, who saw the New Deal and FAIR DEAL as dangerous deviations from the principles of the Framers. Eisenhower scorned these conservatives: "Should any political party attempt to abolish SOCIAL SECURITY, unemployment insurance, and eliminate labor laws and farm programs, you would not hear of that party again in our political history." He knew of a "splinter group that believes you can do these things" but sneered that "their number is negligible and they are stupid." Except for agriculture, where he sought to reduce the federal government's role, he carried on the policies of the preceding Democratic administrations.

During the Eisenhower presidency, frustrated ideological conservatives systematically began to reach out to a wider audience. In 1955, William F. Buckley, Jr., launched the influential *National Review;* a few years later, a small band of Republican activists promoted Senator Barry Goldwater as a Presidential candidate.

The Goldwater boomlet proved premature: the 1960 nomination went to Vice President Richard M. Nixon, who lost to John F. Kennedy. Though he called himself a liberal, Kennedy had been a friend of Senator Joseph McCarthy [*see* McCarthyism]. In the White House, Kennedy fought communism and introduced legislation to cut income-tax rates, and conservatives had difficulty arousing popular indignation during his administration. And during the first two years of the Johnson administration, they appeared doomed, as Lyndon B. Johnson won a landslide victory against Goldwater in 1964 and won enactment of the Great Society, his liberal legislative program, the following year. But the Vietnam War and the perceived failure of Johnson's social program led to the election of Richard Nixon in 1968.

Nixon posed a dilemma for conservatives. On the one hand, he had made his name as a fierce anticommunist and often used harsh rhetoric to denounce liberal elites. On the other hand, he pursued liberal domestic policies, proposing a guaranteed income and imposing wage and price controls. He also signed legislation creating the Environmental Protection Agency and the Occupational Safety and Health Administration, two favorite targets of ideological conservatives in later years. Toward the end of Nixon's tenure, and throughout the Gerald Ford and Jimmy Carter years, conservatives looked forward to the rise of Ronald Reagan.

The Reagan Revolution and After. Reagan ran proudly, even defiantly, as an ideological conservative. Reagan was no situational conservative, for his supporters cheerfully spoke of the "Reagan Revolution," and he himself often quoted Thomas Paine: "We have it in our power to begin the world over again." In his first inaugural address, Reagan made his aims plain: "It is time to check and reverse the growth of government which shows signs of having grown beyond the consent of the governed. It is my intention to curb the size and influence of the federal establishment and to demand recognition of the distinction between the powers granted to the federal government and those reserved to the states or to the people." In his first year, Reagan persuaded Congress to enact substantial cuts in taxes and spending. He met with less success in his subsequent years, as taxes began rising again and spending increased even faster. Reagan blamed the Democrats in Congress, but his conservative critics argued that Reagan and congressional Republicans failed to sustain the attack against the federal leviathan.

Reagan also refused to accept the international status quo, and here he met with greater success. "I believe that communism is another sad, bizarre chapter in human history whose last pages are even now being written," he said in his "evil empire" speech of 8 March 1983. The Reagan years saw a massive buildup of national defenses, which increased spending but arguably also led to the destruction of the Iron Curtain.

George Bush bore a closer likeness to Eisenhower than to Reagan. He was consistently a situational conservative, and his oft-stated devotion to "prudence" became a staple of political humor. But he was only fitfully an ideological conservative. While he ran his 1988 campaign on a pledge to resist tax increases, his 1990 support of tax-increase package undermined his support among conservatives.

In the post-Bush years, ideological conservatives pondered the meaning of their creed. The collapse of Soviet communism removed a primary motive for international activism, and some conservatives began speaking of isolation. Social issues such as Abortion divided libertarians from social traditionalists. And on economics, conservatives argued the merits of deficit control versus policies to simulate growth.

BIBLIOGRAPHY

Buckley, William F., Jr., and Charles R. Kesler. *Keeping the Tablets: Modern American Conservative Thought.* 1988.

Huntington, Samuel P. "Conservatism as an Ideology." *American Political Science Review* 51 (1957): 454–473.

Jaffa, Harry V. *American Conservatism and the American Founding.* 1984.

Kirk, Russell. *The Conservative Mind: From Burke to Eliot.* 7th ed. 1986.

Nash, George H. *The Conservative Intellectual Movement in America since 1945.* 1976.

Reichley, A. James. *Conservatives in an Era of Change: The Nixon and Ford Administrations.* 1981.

Rossiter, Clinton. *Conservatism in America.* Rev. ed. 1982.

JOHN J. PITNEY, JR.

CONSTITUTION, PRESIDENT IN THE. The American conception of executive authority was initially a direct repudiation of the real or perceived excesses of King George III. Conceived in bloody revolution, American state constitutions in the latter part of the eighteenth century emphasized limitations on Executive Power rather than its expansion.

The Constitutional Convention. A variety of constitutional experiments designed to contain, weaken, or virtually eliminate executive power were adopted during the American Revolution. Pennsylvania replaced the office of governor with an executive council of twelve members. Several states required that the governor share power with a council of state. Most limited the number of successive years executives could serve. Gubernatorial influence on legislatures was limited. Executive power of appointment was often shared with the legislature while, in some instances, such power was bestowed on the legislature alone.

Because many of the colonial legislatures had led public opposition to governors who generally were the enforcers of the will of the British monarch and parliament, legislative influence and popularity increased significantly during the Revolution. But in the immediate postrevolutionary years, the perceived abuses of legislative power and concerns about the stability of property rights swung the pendulum toward control of legislative power. The mainstays of control of executive power—annual elections, rotation, and recall—were all abandoned at the national level when the new federal Constitution was debated and subsequently adopted by the delegates to the CONSTITUTIONAL CONVENTION of 1787. The movement from the legislative supremacy and executive limitations characteristic of 1776 to the more complex system ratified in 1788 was indeed viewed as a counterrevolution. But as far as executive authority is concerned, it was quite clear that the pendulum did not swing all the way back to the prerevolutionary status quo. The concept of a hereditary monarchy, for instance, was not even considered. Furthermore, the employment of state governors to impose central authority and safeguard national power, while suggested by ALEXANDER HAMILTON and GOUVERNEUR MORRIS, was far overshadowed by the convention's debate over proposals for a national legislative power to negate state legislative interference with the legitimate purposes of the national government or a supreme court role as impartial arbiter as well as defender of national supremacy underscored by Article VI, Section 2. The latter was ultimately adopted.

The acceptance of a concept of presidential power considerably stronger than that of the revolutionary and Confederation eras was politically and ideologically acceptable at the conclusion of the Philadelphia Convention debates because the two key elements in British constitutional control of executive authority were granted to the legislature: the power of the purse and the power to declare war. ANTI-FEDERALISTS, however, refused to believe that these safeguards were likely to thwart the institutional and personal aggrandizement of presidential power, thus initiating a fundamental constitutional debate that has become a recurring theme of American politics.

The Early Republic. Such political and constitutional arguments began as early as 1793, with the controversy over President George Washington's recall of French chargé d'affaires Edmond Genet. Alexander Hamilton proposed a broad-constructionist interpretation of the scope of executive power in FOREIGN AFFAIRS. The President, according to Hamilton, possessed authority to conduct foreign affairs and initiate policy as an independent policymaker. He wrote that the "executive power of the nation is invested in the President, subject only to the exceptions and qualifications which are expressed in the instrument [the Constitution]." Later in the same decade, the efforts of members of the House of Representatives to utilize the lower house's power to appropriate money to modify the controversial JAY'S TREATY were narrowly defeated by supporters of President Washington.

Constitutional interpretation and debate concerning the nature of executive power has necessarily reflected the objectives of successive Presidents, the determination of their critics and, in times of international or domestic crisis, the circumstances confronting the country. Consequently, while Thomas Jefferson, with James Madison, had led the Democratic-Republican attack on Hamiltonian aggrandizement of executive power, Jefferson as President developed effective executive leadership of the Congress by means of the party caucus and behind-the-scenes consultation. The LOUISIANA PURCHASE was a broad-constructionist exercise of Presidential power as was the oft-criticized policy embodied in the EMBARGO ACTS.

Jefferson also faced the challenge of Chief Justice John Marshall's assertion of the power of judicial review in MARBURY V. MADISON (1803). As President, Jefferson denied that the Supreme Court was the sole or primary interpreter of the Constitution. Instead, he asserted that each branch—executive, legislative, and judicial—possessed coequal authority, within itself, of functional jurisdiction to interpret the Constitution "uncontrolled by the opinions of any other department." This was not only a strong assertion of executive independence, but also an explicit rejection of judicial supremacy. The next strong President, Andrew Jackson, also asserted the Jeffersonian doctrine rejecting judicial supremacy, arguing that "the opinion of the judges has no more authority over Congress than the opinion of Congress has over the judges, and on that point the President is independent of both." But in contrast to Jefferson, Jackson also asserted himself as a tribune of the people by using the veto to defy Congress, as in the issue of the BANK OF THE UNITED STATES and in his six vetoes of internal improvements legislation.

The Civil War and After. The executive leadership of Abraham Lincoln during the CIVIL WAR embodied the broadest interpretations of presidential authority under the Constitution up to that era. As COMMANDER IN CHIEF, he called up seventy-five thousand Union volunteers to defeat what he defined as an insurrection by rebellious individuals (rather than by seceding states). His initial actions after the Confederate attack on Fort Sumter included calling Congress into extraordinary session, but he set a date eighty days after his call for the convening of the members. He also pledged a large monetary sum to pay for the military buildup and suspended the writ of habeas corpus [*see* HABEAS CORPUS, SUSPENSION OF] in several regions—all without the prior authorization of Congress.

Lincoln's successful assertion of executive authority was initially made in a Congressional vacuum because some members had chosen to support the Confederacy while many others had left Washington, D.C., to return to their states or districts. Since the Constitution specifically granted Congress the power to declare war, raise and support armies, maintain a navy, and govern and regulate such armed forces as well as such state militia called to national service, Lincoln's decisive actions in these and related areas were unprecedented. Like the Congress, the Supreme Court was sharply divided over the constitutionality of Lincoln's sweeping actions, but in the PRIZE CASES (1863) the Court narrowly upheld Lincoln's blockade of the Confederacy and, indirectly, all the earlier actions he authorized. The Court reasoned that when confronted by war the President was obliged to take all appropriate actions "without waiting for any special legislative authority."

Although Lincoln's strong assertion of executive leadership was followed by decades of congressional ascendancy, the precedents of the Civil War era were invoked with increasing frequency by several Presidents in the decades following WORLD WAR II.

Between Lincoln's and Woodrow Wilson's presidencies, three writers contributed analyses of the presidency that stimulated a good deal of debate. Henry C. Lockwood's *The Abolition of the Presidency* (1884) emphasized the long-term dangers to democracy of concentrating public trust in a single person whose (usually short-term) popularity dulled public perceptions of presidential aggrandizement and lawlessness. Lockwood's observations about such dangers had greater relevance in the late twentieth century than during his time. Wilson's own, more familiar *Congressional Government* (1885) identified Congress as the "dominant, nay, the irresistible power of the federal system" yet recommended a stronger role for the President. In contrast to Lockwood's suspicion of executive power, the editor Henry Jones Ford, in *The Rise and Growth of American Politics* (1898), enthusiastically applauded strong assertion of presidential power as an American democratic revival of "the oldest political institution . . . the elective kingship."

The Twentieth Century. The early twentieth-century presidencies of Theodore Roosevelt and Woodrow Wilson embodied, in their domestic emphases, a combination of neo-Jacksonian tribuneship of the people made more pervasive throughout the country by party leadership roles by both Presidents also heightened by their ideological commitments to Progressivism. In addition, Roosevelt and Wilson asserted stronger foreign-policy approaches than any of their predecessors after Lincoln. Wilson, because of WORLD WAR I, had a greater opportunity to try to expand the presidential foreign-policy role from that of effective defender of domestic America (initiated by George Washington), to that of defender of the Western Hemisphere's freedom from interference by the European powers (exemplified by the MONROE DOCTRINE and its subsequent applications), to that of world leader (exemplified by his efforts to gain ratification for the TREATY OF VERSAILLES and the LEAGUE OF NATIONS). While Wilson's attempt to gain U.S. support for the League of Nations failed, his world leadership effort was a model for Franklin D. Roosevelt's championing of the UNITED NATIONS.

Because modern Presidents have often dominated the making of foreign policy, the role of CHIEF EXECUTIVE in making both treaties and EXECUTIVE AGREEMENTS received greater legislative and judicial scrutiny after World War II. For example, in UNITED STATES V. BELMONT (1937), Justice George Sutherland referred to executive agreements with foreign nations, the Soviet Union in this instance, as situations in which "the Executive had authority to speak as the sole organ of the [national] government which had exclusive authority in external affairs. Further . . . the external powers of the United States are to be exercised without regard to state laws or policies." Discontent arose over Franklin Roosevelt's uses of presidential power to circumvent prewar isolationist opposition (such as the DESTROYERS FOR BASES agreement transferring fifty "overage" American ships to Great Britain for ninety-nine year leases on seven Caribbean and North Atlantic naval bases in September 1940), and in the postwar period there was considerable right-wing opposition to possible invocation of the new United Nations Charter allegedly to circumvent the treaty-ratifying role of the U.S. Senate. Opponents of expanding presidential power rallied behind a proposed constitutional amendment in the early 1950s. Proposed by Republican Senator John Bricker of Ohio, it was designed to limit both the TREATY-MAKING POWER and executive-agreement authority by making both effective as internal law only through legislation that would be valid (constitutionally) in the absence of a treaty. In 1954, the amendment fell one vote short of the required three-fourths vote in the Senate but thereafter lost support.

Ironically, after the 1960s presidencies of John F. Kennedy and Lyndon Baines Johnson, the strongest and most constitutionally dangerous assertions of presidential authority were made by Republican Presidents and were supported, often enthusiastically, by the right. To be sure, Johnson's uses of executive power were not models of restraint, but it was anticipated that his decision not to seek reelection in 1968 would weaken what had been increasingly described as the IMPERIAL PRESIDENCY. But the narrow victory won by Richard M. Nixon in 1968 did not result in a voluntary withdrawal of executive assertiveness in foreign and domestic policy. Instead, President Nixon aggressively sought to expand, often in unprecedented fashion, both spheres of activity. Despite often-vigorous congressional opposition, Nixon broadened the scope of military operations in the entire Indochina region during the VIETNAM WAR. Contrary to the 1971 congressional repeal of the GULF OF TONKIN RESOLUTION of 1964, which had constitutionally authorized U.S. military activities, Nixon's extension of the U.S. air war to Cambodia was continued solely under his authority as Commander in Chief. In June 1973, Congress stopped the Cambodian air attacks by eliminating all supplies for the air war. As in the 1980s, when elements within the Ronald Reagan administration refused to obey the BOLAND AMENDMENT prohibition on military aid to the Nicaraguan contras, the imperiousness of Nixon's assertion of war-making authority logically eliminated Congress's power to declare war, thus removing one of the two essential original constitutional safeguards against aggrandizement of executive power [see IRAN-CONTRA AFFAIR].

Nixon also attacked the other essential constitutional power of Congress. By large-scale impoundment of appropriated money originally earmarked for purposes designated in legislation, Nixon withheld unprecedented amounts from congressionally authorized and funded programs. Ultimately, Nixon left office to avoid IMPEACHMENT, but the legacy of his years as President was one of cumulative executive aggran-dizement at the expense of basic constitutional proprieties. In the years immediately after Nixon's resignation, Congress adopted legislation designed to guard against executive domination of foreign and domestic policy, notably the CONGRESSIONAL BUDGET AND IMPOUNDMENT ACT (1974), the WAR POWERS RESOLUTION (1973), and the NATIONAL EMERGENCIES ACT (1976). But the presidencies of Ronald Reagan and George Bush embarked on foreign policy iniatives that, like the policies of Nixon, directly contradicted the positions taken by conservatives of the 1950s, notably Senators John Bricker and Robert Taft. Furthermore, the proliferation of clandestine operations such as covert aid to Iran and the contras, the assertion of authority to initiate hostilities in GRENADA and PANAMA without meaningful Congressional consultation, and the curtailment of legislatively mandated programs clearly place these Presidents in the Nixon tradition. In short, as the twentieth century neared its conclusion, the trend toward executive domination reemerged as the single most serious threat to the American Constitution.

[See also PRESIDENCY, PRESIDENTIAL CONCEPTIONS OF; IMPERIAL PRESIDENCY.]

BIBLIOGRAPHY

Corwin, Edward S. *The President: Office and Powers, 1787–1957.* 1957.

Fisher, Louis. *Constitutional Conflicts between Congress and the President.* 1991.

Fisher, Louis, *Presidential Spending Power.* 1975.

Ford, Henry Jones. *The Rise and Growth of American Politics.* 1898.

Lockwood, Henry C. *The Abolition of the Presidency.* 1884.

Schlesinger, Arthur M., Jr. *The Imperial Presidency.* 1973.

Schulz, Richard H., Jr. "Covert Action and Executive-Legislative Relations: The Iran-Contra Crisis and Its Aftermath." *Harvard Journal of Law and Public Policy* 12 (1989): 449–482.

Wilson, Woodrow. *Congressional Government.* 1887.

Wood, Gordon. *The Creation of the American Republic, 1776–1787.* 1969.

JOHN R. SCHMIDHAUSER

CONSTITUTIONAL CONVENTION. The office of the presidency was created by the CONSTITUTIONAL CONVENTION, which met in Philadelphia between 25 May and 17 September 1787 to replace the existing Articles of Confederation. Five weeks after the convention adjourned, James Madison sent a lengthy letter summarizing its decisions to Thomas Jefferson, in which he noted that the subject of the presidency had proved "peculiarly embarrassing." "On the question whether it should consist of a single person, or a plurality of co-ordinate members, on the mode of appointment, on the duration in office, on the degree of power, on the re-eligibility, tedious and reiterated discussions took place." In political terms, the CREATION OF THE PRESIDENCY was not the most difficult issue the Framers faced: that honor went to the protracted struggle between large and small states over representation in the Senate. But as a problem of constitutional theory, decisions relating to the presidency were truly daunting. As orthodox republicans, the Framers inherited well-established fears that the greatest danger to liberty always lurked in the unchecked ambitions of the executive—whether power was personally vested in a king or dispersed (and thus concealed) among a coteries of ministers. Acting on these ingrained fears, the authors of the early stage constitutions had tended to strip the governorship of political influence as well as any of the formal powers—such as a veto over legislation—that resembled royal prerogatives. By 1787, however, such influential delegates to the Convention as Madison, JAMES WILSON, ALEXANDER HAMILTON, and GOUVERNEUR MORRIS, believed that a restoration of executive power was necessary to prevent unrestrained legislative power from corrupting the principles of republican government. The great theoretical challenge the Framers accordingly faced was to reconcile this expanded conception of executive power with republican norms.

In contrast to the debate over representation that preoccupied the delegates from late May until the so-called Great Compromise of 16 July, discussion of the executive proceeded episodically in three distinct phases. An initial round of debate in early June produced consensus on the merits of a unitary executive armed with a limited veto over legislation. In a second round of debate in late July, the delegates tackled the intertwined issues of election, term of office, and reeligibility for office, moving from one seeming solution to another until they came full circle to endorse the idea of a congressionally elected President who would serve a single term of six years. Dissatisfaction with this result percolated among the delegates during August, but not until the first week of September did the convention take the decisive actions that led both to the adoption of its great innovation, the ELECTORAL COLLEGE, and to the vesting in the President of significant authority over appointments and foreign relations.

Unitary Executive. The starting point for debate was the Virginia Plan, which EDMUND RANDOLPH read on 29 May. Under its provisions, the executive (whether plural or unitary) would be elected by the legislature for a single term of unspecified length and be vested with the power to execute national laws and to exercise a limited veto over legislation through a joint executive-judicial council of revision. Though many delegates were hesitant even to speak on this subject, a few were bold enough to formulate basic choices. While Roger Sherman argued that the executive was merely an agent of the legislature (and therefore might not even need to be provided for constitutionally) and Randolph warned that a unitary executive would prove "the fetus of monarchy," Wilson made a strong case for vesting the executive power in a single person. Doing so, Wilson argued, would combine the benefits of efficiency and decisiveness necessary for sound administration with the responsibility republican values required.

After the Constitutional Convention endorsed the principle of a unitary executive on 4 June, it turned to the issue of the veto and the council of revision. Madison had borrowed the latter provision from the New York constitution of 1777. In Madison's view, which was shared by Wilson, the expertise and legal knowledge that the executive and judiciary could jointly contribute to the process of lawmaking outweighed whatever injury the council would inflict on the principle of the SEPARATION OF POWERS. But as the ensuring debate made clear, a majority of delegates felt that judges should not be involved in lawmaking, in part because that was a political act but also because prior involvement would compromise their later ability to determine whether a given act was constitutional. Equally important, the convention agreed that a limited veto could be safely entrusted to the executive. It thereby retreated from the republicanism of 1776 by giving the executive significant legislative power in its own right.

Election and Tenure. So ended the first phase of debate on the executive. When the convention returned to the subject on 17 July, it quickly plunged into a maze of questions revolving around issues of election and tenure. During this stage, the debate was dominated by perceptions of flaws and disadvantages in the various proposals under consideration. On the issue of election, Wilson and Madison endorsed the idea of popular election, though Madison worried that it would preclude the selection of a southerner because the free white voters of his region would be a permanent minority in the national electorate that would thereby be created. For a great majority of the convention, however, the decisive argument against popular election was not that the American people would be swayed by demagogues but rather that in a dispersed provincial society no decisive choice would be possible because the people at large would simply not have adequate information about candidates.

No one would know more about potential candidates than members of the national legislature. But here other objections came into play. For if the delegates agreed on one principle, it was that the new executive should be relatively independent of legislative control. Thus an executive elected by the legislature would either have to be ineligible for reelection or given so long a term—perhaps even tenure during good behavior—as to conjure up images of incipient monarchy. Because many delegates believed that reeligibility would provide a valuable incentive for good conduct while a single term, conversely, would encourage executive misconduct, the idea of legislative election was also rejected on 19 July, to be briefly replaced by the first version of the scheme for an electoral college (also proposed by Wilson). Further debate, however, left the convention doubtful that sufficiently qualified individuals would be chosen for the college, and this in turn led it to restore the mode of legislative election. Such restoration, of course, reopened the problems of term and reeligibility. By 26 July—the date set for adjournment to allow the Committee of Detail to produce a polished draft of a constitution—the convention had come full circle to endorse the idea of a single president elected by the legislature for a term of seven years without prospect of reelection.

To this point little had been said about the powers this independent executive would exercise. Most delegates assumed that the Senate would be the dominant institution of national government and that its powers would include the direction of foreign relations and the appointment of major national officers. Such proposals were part of the 6 August report of the Committee of Detail; by contrast the President (as the executive was now called) had two basic duties: to execute the laws and to serve as COMMANDER IN CHIEF of the armed forces. But over the next few weeks, a reaction against the Senate worked to enhance the authority of the executive, while the persisting desire to render the executive independent of legislative control kept the issue of election subject to revision.

Objections against the Senate ran along several lines. Such large-state delegates as Madison, Wilson, and Morris still resented the decision to give each state an equal vote in the Senate, and they further worried that a body elected by the state legislatures would lack the cosmopolitan character required to think deeply about the national interest. Other delegates including George Mason fretted that the Senate might evolve into an aristocratic cabal. When the question of the TREATY-MAKING POWER came before the convention on 23 August, the range of objections voiced against the Senate signaled that a shift toward the executive was likely. The next day Morris roundly attacked the idea of legislative election, and in ensuing balloting the convention divided equally on an "abstract question" reviving the idea of an electoral college.

The Electoral College. At this point the locus of debate shifted to the Committee on Postponed Parts, whose eleven members included Morris and Madison. After apparently wide-ranging debates, the committee on 4 September presented a report that was notable in two respects. First, the committee vested the President with power to make treaties and to nominate and appoint ambassadors, justices, and other major officials, subject in both cases to the ADVICE AND CONSENT of the Senate. Second, the committee greatly refined the plan of an electoral college by proposing that the electors would assemble separately in their respective states—thereby obviating the possibility of their being subject to "cabal"—and by providing a scheme of voting that in effect replicated the Great Compromise of 16 July. Each state would have as many votes as it had members of Congress, thereby giving the large states the advantage in promoting candidates while overrepresenting the small states by counting senators. Should no majority be reached on the first ballot, the decision would revert to the Senate, where the smaller states would have the greater voice. And because a President seeking reelection would obviously be well known throughout the country, the Electoral College would have the effective decision about a subsequent term, thereby reducing the prospect of presidential subservience to Congress.

The flaw in this scheme lay in its recommendation that the Senate elect the President whenever the Electoral College failed to produce a majority—a result that many delegates predicted would occur far more often than not. Coupled with the other proposal linking President and Senate in treaty making and exercise of the APPOINTMENT POWER, this seemed a formula for turning a pliable President into an instrument of the "aristocratic" Senate. Three more days of debate (4–6 September) passed before Sherman hit upon the ingenious solution of placing the contingent election in the House of Representatives, with delegations voting by states, thereby preserving the political formula of the Great Compromise and, more importantly, enhancing the authority of the executive vis-à-vis the Senate, with which it would now be more closely linked. Much less controversial, however, was the proposal to have the President exercise the initiative in making treaties and appointments to major national offices.

Far from being a hybrid improvisation, then, the Electoral College was a pragmatic solution that neatly resolved most of the difficulties that had confounded the convention. It allowed the delegates to secure their overriding goal of rendering the executive relatively independent of the Congress, on which, many of them hoped, the executive would act as a useful restraint. Yet neither did the Framers believe that Article II of the Constitution marked a blueprint for monarchy. Even in the areas of war and FOREIGN AFFAIRS, the tenor of the discussions at the Philadelphia Convention suggests that the Framers envisioned a President who could both exercise discretion and be held accountable for the conduct of his duties but who would remain in many ways the agent *executing* measures significantly influenced or even determined by Congress. A President elected at best secondarily by the House and eligible for reelection after a substantial term of four years may have seemed a far cry from the republican orthodoxy of 1776, all the more so when the executive reclaimed powers historically associated with the prerogative of the British crown. But by linking the energy and efficiency of a unitary executive with a well-developed notion of responsibility, the Framers thought they were creating an institution that was more republican than monarchical.

In truth, the "tedious and reiterated discussions" of which Madison complained were required for the delegates to work out the implications of what was perhaps the single most creative aspect of their constitutional labors.

BIBLIOGRAPHY

Cronin, Thomas E., ed. *Inventing the American Presidency.* 1989.

Farrand, Max, ed. *The Records of the Federal Convention of 1787.* Rev. ed. 1966.

Lofgren, Charles. "War-Making under the Constitution: The Original Understanding." *Yale Law Journal* 81 (1972): 672–702.

Rakove, Jack N. "Solving a Constitutional Puzzle: The Treatymaking Clause as a Case Study." *Perspectives in American History* n.s. 1 (1984): 233–282.

Slonim, Shlomo. "The Electoral College at Philadelphia: The Evolution of an Ad Hoc Congress for the Selection of a President." *Journal of American History* 73 (1986): 35–58.

Thach, Charles C., Jr. *The Creation of the Presidency, 1775–1789: A Study in Constitutional History.* 1923.

JACK N. RAKOVE

CONSTITUTIONAL REFORM. The idea of constitutional reform operates at several levels in American politics. At the most basic level, the Constitution seems impervious to formal revision. Ever since the ratification of the Framers' design in 1788, its basic provisions for distributing political power have enjoyed almost universal approbation. At the same time, however, there have been numerous attempts, several of them resulting in ratified amendments, to adjust these arrangements at the margins: to perfect the electoral process for Presidents, to set a date constitutionally for the inauguration of a new administration, to clarify the Vice President's status when he assumes the presidency, and to establish a mechanism for ascertaining a President's disability and provide for the continuity of executive power. More profound and far-reaching critiques of the Framers' design have been rare. In fact, only twice in the two centuries under the Constitution—during the 1930s and again from the mid 1970s until the mid 1980s—have proposals for structural reform of the Constitution's basic political institutions drawn much attention. In both cases, it was concern over the presidency that gave rise to the call for revision.

The Framers' fundamental design for executive power, though perhaps the boldest innovation of the CONSTITUTIONAL CONVENTION of 1787, has enjoyed broad support ever since it was established. A few delegates would have preferred an executive chosen by the legislature, with powers assigned in statutes and subject to amendment as circumstances required. The prevailing view, however, was that the national government needed strong, independent executive power. Independence was sought from an electoral process that explicitly excluded members of Congress (Article I, Section 1, says that no member of Congress may serve as a presidential elector), and by the INCOMPATIBILITY CLAUSE (Article I, Section 6), barring any person who holds an administrative office from serving in Congress. The executive was intended to be strong, as well as independent, though its strength came not so much from explicit language as from the vagueness of the constitutional provisions, coupled with the fact that George Washington, a trusted man of energetic disposition, would, everyone assumed, be the first President and would set a precedent for vigorous exercise of the office.

Election and Succession. The Framers' design, though widely affirmed, was not regarded as sacrosanct. As early as 1796, a defect in the electoral process became evident. The first contested election for President produced a President and Vice President, John Adams and Thomas Jefferson, of opposite political tendencies, creating political instability at the center of the administration. Four years later, the arrangements outlined in Article II for the election of a President and Vice President produced an even more troubling result. The contest in 1800 ended in a tie when Democratic-Republican electors each cast one of his votes for Thomas Jefferson and the other for AARON BURR, the Democratic Republican candidate for Vice President. The Constitution directed that ties be settled by the House of Representatives. This gave the opposition Federalists, intent on keeping Jefferson out of the White House, an irresistible invitation to mischief. It was not until the thirty-sixth ballot in the House that the decision was made for Jefferson over Burr.

By then it was evident that the electoral machinery set forth in Article II had to be repaired. The TWELFTH AMENDMENT, ratified in 1804, provided that electors cast a single ballot indicating one person for President and another for Vice President and reduced to three (from five) the number of candidates for President who would be sent to the House of Representatives in the event that no one achieved a majority of electoral votes.

Over the years, there have been other reform efforts to clarify the text and tidy up its provisions. In 1933, the ratification of the TWENTIETH AMENDMENT established 20 January as the official date for presidential inaugurations and directed Congress to provide by law for a case in which neither a President- nor Vice-President-elect shall have qualified by inauguration day. The TWENTY-FIFTH AMENDMENT, ratified in 1967, provided methods for filling a vacancy in the vice presidency and for replacing a disabled President. None of these amendments affected the political operation of the presidency, except in the extraordinary circumstances anticipated by the Twenty-fifth Amendment. (Gerald Ford came to the vice presidency in December 1973, by way of the procedures established in that amendment.)

Term of Office and Veto. The most significant of the successful efforts to reform the constitutional foundations of the presidency resulted in the TWENTY-SECOND AMENDMENT, ratified in 1951. It limited a President to two full terms in office. George Washington's voluntary retirement after two terms had set a precedent (the TWO-TERM TRADITION) that held until Franklin Delano Roosevelt stood successfully for a third term, and then a fourth (in 1940 and 1944). Many have attributed the Twenty-second Amendment to unwise partisan revenge, warning that it makes a President, during his second term, a LAME-DUCK PRESIDENT. Others, noting the enormous powers of the modern presidency and the advantage that incumbents in recent elections have seemed to enjoy, are grateful for a provision that limits the time during which any person can remain in such an office. In any case, the amendment seems to have done little to weaken the presidency in the constitutional scheme.

There is another proposal relating to the presidential term of office that might have greater effect, if enacted: limiting a President to a single, SIX-YEAR PRESIDENTIAL TERM. The idea arises from concern that Presi-

dents and their aides spend too much time plotting their campaigns for reelection, to the neglect of their executive responsibilities. Advocates of this proposal contend that a longer term, with no prospect for reelection, would discourage partisanship and give stronger incentives for courageous leadership. Curiously, Andrew Jackson, remembered as a founder of the DEMOCRATIC PARTY and usually reckoned as one of the strongest political leaders ever to occupy the White House, was a strenuous advocate of the single-term limit. Modern backers also cite supporting statements from Presidents Dwight D. Eisenhower, Lyndon B. Johnson, Richard M. Nixon, Gerald Ford, and Jimmy Carter, as well as leading members of their administrations, and from respected congressional figures. Despite these impressive endorsements, the idea languishes. Most people believe that the presidency is centrally and inescapably a place of political leadership, and that a term of six years is both too long for a person who proves inept and too short for someone who is able to command broad support.

Another proposed reform with potentially large implications for the power of the presidency is the ITEM VETO (also called the line-item veto). The idea is to allow Presidents to veto specific items in an appropriations bill, as many state governors can. The appeal of the idea arises from a desire to curb public spending, but its principal effect would be to strengthen the executive's hand at the expense of the legislature, rather than encourage frugality in government. Not surprisingly, Presidents have tended to favor the idea, but Congress has so far been able to deflect it.

Separation of Powers. Besides these relatively marginal proposals for reform, there is another tradition that questions the extreme SEPARATION OF POWERS imposed by the Constitution between the legislative and executive branches. The earliest source of this deeper critique was Justice Joseph Story of the Supreme Court. Story's monumental treatise, *Commentaries on the Constitution of the United States*, published in 1833, was generally celebratory of the Framers' achievement, but it did suggest that the system might be improved if CABINET officers were regularly required to appear before Congress to answer questions and defend the policies of the administration. A generation later, during the CIVIL WAR, Rep. George Pendleton, Democrat of Ohio, made the idea more concrete by proposing that Cabinet officers be required by law to participate in congressional debates on matters affecting their departments and to be present in Congress twice weekly to answer questions. Concern about the constitutionality of such a statute led to proposals for the repeal of Article I, Section 6, making way for

Presidents to appoint sitting members of Congress to high positions in the executive branch. Advocates argued that it would produce greater cooperation between the political branches and improve the value of Congress as a forum for debating the nation's policy. The idea continues to draw support, but it has been defeated by the argument that the existing channels of informal contact and accountability between the branches are sufficient.

Perhaps the most profound critic of America's basic constitutional arrangements was Woodrow Wilson. The summer after he graduated from Princeton in 1879, he published an article arguing that the United States should adopt "Cabinet government," with Cabinet officers chosen from Congress and resigning (as in Britain) when they were no longer able to win legislative support for the administration's program. Wilson's mature writings as a political scientist (he is the only political scientist ever to serve as President) drop the advocacy of constitutional reform but continue the heavy emphasis on party responsibility and on the importance of presidential leadership of a governing party. As President of the United States, he sought to demonstrate this approach to political leadership, with mixed results.

The first attempts to promote ideas for fundamental constitutional reform began in the late 1930s. By then, the NEW DEAL had committed the national government to unprecedented efforts at positive governance. Many experienced and knowledgeable people, practitioners and scholars of politics and a few journalists, concluded that the governance of a modern industrial economy required political strength and accountability that would be impossible without basic institutional changes. Some (like the BROWNLOW COMMITTEE) believed that the necessary adjustments, though profound, could be made within the existing framework; others (like William Yandell Elliott, Henry Hazlitt, Thomas K. Finletter, and REXFORD G. TUGWELL) developed ideas that involved far-reaching constitutional revisions.

The reform impulse was overwhelmed first by WORLD WAR II and then by the challenges of building the UNITED NATIONS and containing communism. In the late 1970s, however, the interest in more radical approaches to constitutional reform resurfaced. C. Douglas Dillon and Lloyd Cutler, former public officials, and Charles Hardin, James L. Sundquist, and James MacGregor Burns, writers, organized a group, called the Committee on the Constitutional System, that encouraged consideration of basic changes in the American political system. The group argued that modern conditions had had the paradoxical effect of increasing the demands on government while weakening the capacity of government to act effectively and be held accountable for the results. Demands for more active popular participation in the internal workings of parties and the availability of technologies enabling candidates to communicate directly with the electorate through television, phone-banks, and direct mail altered the traditional role of party organizations and placed greater emphasis on the ability of individual candidates and their campaign organizations, rather than the parties, to raise funds.

Dealing with Divided Government. The weakening of parties contributed to the increasing incidence of DIVIDED GOVERNMENT, where a President of one party faces at least one house of Congress dominated by the opposite party. This phenomenon had been relatively rare in the years before World War II, but it has become the norm. Since 1968, only during the Carter and Clinton administrations did the same party control both branches. Critics contend that divided control reduces the ability of the government to frame and implement coherent policy and, perhaps even more important in a democracy, prevents voters from rendering a coherent judgment on the performance of those running for reelection.

To restore coherence to the system, reformers have suggested "team tickets," offering voters a choice between parties, rather than individual candidates. Thus, a vote for the REPUBLICAN PARTY would count as a vote for the Republican candidates for President, Vice President, Senator (if there were a vacancy that year) and Representatives. An alternative would be to require states to provide the option of casting a straight party ballot.

A less direct approach would be to coordinate the terms of office for federally elected officials. Under the current system of staggered elections (two-year terms for Representatives, four-year terms for Presidents, six-year terms for Senators), the typical pattern is for voters to reverse direction in off-year elections (that is, when the presidency is not at stake). Typically, a winning presidential candidate's COATTAILS EFFECT has helped his supporters to win seats in Congress, but two years later, with the President no longer at the head of the ticket, his fellow-partisans lose ground. Reformers have argued that this pattern undermines a President's ability to enact and implement a meaningful program. If terms were coordinated (four years, coterminously, for Presidents and Representatives, eight years for Senators; or three years for Presidents and Representatives, and six years for Senators), there would be less tendency for an electoral mandate to be foreshortened.

Abuse of Power. These ideas—team tickets, coordinated terms—are intended to increase the coherence of a governing majority behind a President's leadership of his party. There is, however, another source of recent proposals for constitutional reform: concern that we have no satisfactory way to discipline a Chief Executive who abuses his power or otherwise proves unfit to continue in office. The Framers in 1787 wanted the President to be secure in office during his term. Only if he were impeached and convicted of "treason, bribery, or other high crimes and misdemeanors" could he be removed from office. The Framers evidently intended that the President's tenure be immune to political assault for four years.

Under the provisions of the Twenty-fifth Amendment, a President may be replaced, either temporarily or permanently, if the Vice President and a majority of the Cabinet certifies that he is unable to discharge his duties. Some reformers believe there are other circumstances that would render a President unfit to continue in office. If a President loses the confidence of the nation, for example, whether by stubbornly pursuing failed policies or by tolerating criminal or corrupt activities without himself committing an impeachable offense, or if there is a deadlock between the executive and legislative branches that paralyzes the government in a time of crisis, some reformers argue that neither IMPEACHMENT nor the disability amendment would provide an adequate remedy.

One way to bring an incompetent or corrupt President to account would be to broaden and extend the list of offenses leading to impeachment. Even if this could be done, however, the proceedings might be unduly prolonged, and it could only result in the replacement of the President by his Vice President (unless the Vice President was replaced first under the Twenty-fifth Amendment, as happened in 1973). In any case, the critics argue, impeachment would be unlikely to produce the necessary cleansing or change of direction.

Thus, critics of existing arrangements conclude that we need a way to get a fresh electoral verdict on the available options, in the event of a failed presidency or extended deadlock. One way would be by providing for dissolution: either the President by proclamation or Congress by concurrent resolution might be authorized to call for national elections, in which case the presidency and vice presidency, all seats in the House of Representatives and at least half of the seats in the Senate (one from each state) would be at stake. The elections would have to be held expeditiously (perhaps within six weeks), and the winning candidates take office quickly (say, within one week

following the election). If a constitutional amendment provided for the possibility of dissolution and for elections out of the regular, four-year cycle, parties would have to adjust, having nominees ready to conduct campaigns on short notice. Advocates of this reform see such an adjustment in the behavior of American national parties as an advantage, as is the prospect for shorter electoral campaigns and a reduced period between elections and inaugurations.

Dissolution is, of course, one of the central features of the parliamentary form of government, but reformers insist that its incorporation into the American system would not necessarily undermine the separation of powers. Congress and the presidency would still be separately elected, Congress from 435 local constituencies, the President from a single, national constituency. The incentives for mutual checks would still remain in place, if in modified form.

War Powers. One other area of concern to constitutionalists relates to the exercise of WAR POWERS. The Framers intended that the power to take this nation to war be shared. Congress raises troops and declares war; the President conducts diplomatic relations and commands the armed forces. The practical operation of these arrangements changed after World War II, when the nation entered into a worldwide network of MUTUAL-SECURITY TREATIES and committed itself to a standing army. Since then, Presidents have had popular support to defend NATIONAL SECURITY against the threat of communism and the military forces to do it without appealing to Congress. Congress sought to restore its traditional role in war making by enacting, over President Nixon's veto, the WAR POWERS RESOLUTION of 1973. The resolution calls upon the President to "consult with Congress" whenever he intends to send military forces into potentially hostile situations, to report to Congress within forty-eight hours whenever he dispatches troops into such situations, and to withdraw those forces unless Congress explicitly affirms his decision within sixty days. However, the resolution has proved unenforceable. Presidents have consistently refused to acknowledge that mere legislation can limit their constitutional powers, and the courts have refused to enforce its terms judicially.

The problem remains. Abraham Lincoln summarized the Framers' intent, saying that "no one man" should have power to take this nation to war. Nevertheless, since 1950, Presidents have routinely made the decision for war after consulting only those who serve by their appointment and at their pleasure. Apart from granting Congress the power of dissolution, it is not clear how Presidents can be forced to share the power to take the nation to war.

BIBLIOGRAPHY

Hardin, Charles M. *Presidential Power and Accountability: Toward a New Constitution.* 1974.

Mayhew, David. *Divided We Govern: Party Control, Lawmaking, and Investigations, 1946–1990.* 1991.

Robinson, Donald L. *"To the Best of My Ability": The Presidency and the Constitution.* 1987.

Robinson, Donald L. ed. *Reforming American Government: The Bicentennial Papers of the Committee on the Constitutional System.* 1985.

Schlesinger, Arthur M., Jr. *The Cycles of American History.* 1986.

Sundquist, James L. *Constitutional Reform and Effective Government.* 1986.

DONALD L. ROBINSON

CONSULTANTS. Consultants are experts who provide advice and services to political candidates and parties, their campaigns, and other political committees. At one time party professionals analyzed the electorate and issues, determining strategy, raising funds, and mobilizing voters on election day. But as their methods proved less effective and they failed to adapt to new technologies, as campaigning grew more candidate centered, and as candidate image-making became more desirable for presentation particularly on television or through direct mail, various specialists began to transfer and adapt their talents to the political arena. Press agents, public relations professionals, advertising specialists, charitable fund-raisers, and others turned their attention to politics, at first part-time and later full-time.

As politics became a big business, consulting became a business affecting politics in numerous ways. Consultants were generalists at first, but later tended to specialize as techniques were developed and campaigns grew to sizeable proportions. Consultants generally work only for clients of one party. Although the 1952 presidential campaigns were not the first to use public relations and advertising people, accounts exist describing their heavy involvement in the campaigns of that year, and campaigns ever since.

Serious candidates for major office came to feel the need to employ a professional campaign manager, a public opinion pollster, media specialists, computer experts both for fund-raising and for targeting groups of voters, lawyers to navigate the complexities of election laws, and political accountants to meet the legal requirements of public disclosure of campaign funds. [*See* FEDERAL ELECTION COMMISSION.]

A major factor in triggering rising political costs has been the professionalization of politics. When contribution limits shifted the emphasis away from big individual donors and forced campaigns to broaden and upgrade their donor bases, professional computer and direct mail experts became highly valued allies in CAMPAIGN FINANCES. With television now a primary medium for direct communication with voters, paid political advertising consumes ever-expanding portions of major candidates' budgets, and the role of media consultants has grown accordingly. Time-buyers for television determine the demographics of audiences and purchase air time accordingly. The image experts groom the candidate's presentations and decide what the political advertisements will say, to whom they will be directed, and how they will attempt to achieve the goals of name recognition and victory.

Consultants have been called "hired guns," "modern-day Hessians," and political mercenaries. Often, the very act of hiring high-powered consultants confers credibility on a campaign. Just as lack of money reduces political competition, so does the professionalization of politics create one class of candidate with the necessary funds to have access to high-tech services, and another class—usually challengers—without the funds to purchase them sufficiently in abundance to impact the potential voters.

Reciprocal relationships exist between campaign consultants and political money. Consultants decide how to spend political money, and because of fees they receive for the advertising and direct mail they produce and direct to the electorate, they have a vested interest in high spending. Yet as campaign costs rise, so are political consultants employed to use the available money most effectively and efficiently.

There has been very little study of consultants' roles: often hired from out of state, without roots in the local political culture, introducing homogenized campaigns, having a vested interest in high spending, responsible only to the candidate or group hiring them, engaging in negative advertising designed to get the most for their money.

Despite the undeniable skills many consultants bring to politics, elections are complex and numerous variables affect the outcomes. Moreover, when professionals assist opposing candidates, some must win and others lose. Finally, social science has not informed us definitively of the differential effectiveness of various campaign techniques, yet consultants get credit or blame for victory or defeat.

While political consultants have filled the gap left by the decline of the political parties, some believe the consultants have hastened the demise of the parties, if not directly contributing to their decline. Many observers still believe that strengthened and renewed political parties offer the most hope of avoiding the excesses and negativity of some campaigns operated by political consultants.

Some political consultants have followed their clients into government positions where they continue to advise, provide services, and exercise their skills on behalf of incumbents in what has been called the permanent campaign.

BIBLIOGRAPHY

Agranoff, Robert. *The Management of Election Campaigns.* 1976.

Blumenthal, Sidney. *The Permanent Campaign: Inside the World of Elite Political Operatives.* 1980.

Kelley, Stanley, Jr. *Professional Public Relations and Political Power.* 1956.

McGinnis, Joe. *The Selling of the President 1968.* 1969.

Sabato, Larry J. *The Rise of Political Consultants: New Ways of Winning Elections.* 1981.

HERBERT E. ALEXANDER

CONTAINMENT. Containment, the idea that the United States should resist the expansion of Soviet, later communist, power without risking either a war with Moscow or pursuing the forcible rollback of Soviet domination of Eastern Europe, became the fundamental principle of United States foreign policy in the Truman administration. With modifications, containment remained the principal aim of succeeding administrations until the end of the COLD WAR. Containment was sometimes criticized for being either a recipe for endless and costly competition between the U.S. and the communist world or, alternatively, for allowing permanent Soviet domination of Eastern Europe.

The July 1947 issue of *Foreign Affairs* contained one of the most influential magazine articles ever published, "The Sources of Soviet Conduct." *Foreign Affairs* identified the author only as X, but newspapers soon revealed that X actually was George F. Kennan, formerly the counselor at the U.S. embassy in Moscow and at the time of the publication of the article, the director of the State Department's policy planning staff. Kennan articulated for the public ideas he previously had argued in an eight thousand word dispatch—the "Long Telegram"—from Moscow to Washington in February 1946. In both the Long Telegram and the X article, he argued that three reinforcing motives—traditional Russian nationalism, revolutionary Marxist zeal, and the paranoid personality of dictator Josef Stalin—explained the expansionist and domineering policies the Soviet Union had pursued since the end of the WORLD WAR II. Kennan, a self-styled "realist" who distrusted ideologies and considered the power of the traditional nation-state the primary factor in international relations, believed that, of the three, only Russian nationalism would endure. Stalin would not rule the Soviet Empire forever, and Kennan thought that Marxism would wither. In the meantime, however, Kennan recommended "the long-term patient, but firm and vigilant containment of Russian expansive tendencies."

Containment quickly became adopted as a shorthand slogan for the Truman administration's efforts to thwart the Soviets. For policymakers Kennan's explanations of Soviet conduct provided the rationale for a series of anti-Soviet and anticommunist measures. The TRUMAN DOCTRINE of 1947 pledged U.S. support to "assist free peoples" everywhere "in maintaining their freedoms." A year later the administration proposed the MARSHALL PLAN of $18 billion in economic aid to help the economies of Western Europe recover from the devastation of World War II. In 1949 Washington sponsored the North Atlantic Treaty Organization, a military alliance directed against the Soviet Union.

Containment drew criticism from the beginning. The journalist Walter Lippmann objected that the policy was likely to involve the United States in costly and endless conflicts and wars everywhere in the world to stop the spread of Marxism. Such global competition would leave the initiative to the Soviet Union and render the United States powerless to decide where its true interests lay. Twenty years after these objections first were raised, critics presented identical complaints against the Johnson and Nixon administrations' policies in the VIETNAM WAR. On the other hand, strident anticommunists in the late Truman and early Eisenhower administrations charged that containment did not go nearly far enough in forcing a rollback of Soviet forces from Eastern Europe. During the 1952 presidential election, Richard M. Nixon, the Republican vice presidential candidate, indicted ADLAI E. STEVENSON, the Democratic candidate, as an "appeaser . . . who got his Ph.D. from [Secretary of State] Dean Acheson's College of Cowardly Containment."

Despite criticism, containment guided U.S. foreign policy until the end of the Reagan administration. The eventual disintegration of the Soviet Empire and the Soviet Union followed almost exactly Kennan's original 1947 forecast. Many analysts concluded that the doctrine of containment had achieved its original objective, although some argued that the cost of confrontation had been too high.

BIBLIOGRAPHY

Gaddis, John Lewis. *The Long Peace: Inquiries into the History of the Cold War*. 1987.

Gaddis, John Lewis. *Strategies of Containment: A Critical Appraisal of Postwar American National Security Policy*. 1982.

Hixson, Walter. *George Kennan: Cold War Iconoclast*. 1989.

Mayers, David Allen. *George Kennan and the Dilemmas of United States Foreign Policy*. 1988.

ROBERT D. SCHULZINGER

CONTEMPT OF CONGRESS. Throughout the history of the United States, Congress has directed its investigatory powers at exposing corruption and maladministration in the executive branch. The first such investigation dates to 1792, when the House of Representatives appointed a special committee to investigate the defeat of Major General Arthur St. Clair by the INDIANS in the Ohio frontier. Since then, phrases such as "Teapot Dome," "Watergate," and "Iran-contra," have become part of the popular vernacular as a result of highly publicized CONGRESSIONAL INVESTIGATIONS.

Among the most important of the tools of inquiry available to congressional committees in conducting investigations is the power to punish recalcitrant witnesses for contempt. Congress first asserted its power to punish for contempt in 1795, just seven years after the adoption of the Constitution. Prior to the adoption of the Constitution, the colonial assemblies and the Continental Congress exercised similar powers, as did England's House of Lords and House of Commons. From an early time, the power has been recognized by the Supreme Court as an inherent attribute of Congress's legislative authority.

These early exercises of congressional contempt were pursuant to Congress's inherent self-help contempt power. The self-help contempt power permits a house of Congress to order its Sergeant-at-Arms to arrest an offender for trial before the bar of that house. The contemptuous witness faces possible imprisonment, historically in the District of Columbia jail or the guardhouse in the Capitol basement. Imprisonment is limited to the duration of the pending session of Congress. Prisoners could challenge their confinement either in a suit for damages against the Sergeant-at-Arms or in a writ of habeas corpus.

In recent years, the self-help contempt power has become functionally obsolete; Congress last resorted to the procedure in 1934. This is so largely because an alternative, statutory contempt mechanism is available that renders time-consuming congressional trials unnecessary. The congressional criminal contempt statute, Title 2, Section 192, of the United States Code, provides that "every person who having been summoned as a witness by the authority of either House of Congress to give testimony or to produce papers upon any matter under inquiry before either House . . . willfully makes default, or who, having appeared, refuses to answer any question pertinent to the question under inquiry, shall be deemed guilty of a misdemeanor."

This criminal contempt statute applies to various kinds of willful failures to comply with congressional demands, including failure to appear, failure to produce pertinent items subpoenaed, refusal to take the oath, refusal to answer pertinent questions, and leaving a hearing before being excused. Because it is a criminal statute, the accused contemptor is entitled to all of the procedural safeguards accorded criminal defendants. Thus, the burden is on the prosecution to prove all of the elements of the offense beyond a reasonable doubt, the defendant is entitled to a jury trial, and, as with any criminal action, an acquittal cannot be appealed.

The procedure by which a witness is cited for contempt under the criminal contempt statute is as follows. First, the committee that issues the subpoena reports the witness's failure to comply to the full House or Senate. The president pro tem of the Senate or the Speaker of the House then certifies the contempt to the appropriate U.S. Attorney, "whose duty it shall be to bring the matter before the grand jury for its action."

An unsettled issue concerning the procedures for certification under the criminal contempt statute is whether the U.S. Attorney has discretion to refuse to prosecute contempt violations certified by a house of Congress. The literal language of the statute and scattered judicial dicta suggest that it is the U.S. Attorney's "duty" to present a contempt citation to the grand jury. However, this interpretation conflicts with the generally accepted view that prosecutorial discretion is a purely EXECUTIVE PREROGATIVE.

This potential conflict of interest in assigning prosecutorial control to the U.S. Attorney of an action against an executive branch official became a reality in 1982, when the House of Representatives failed to secure the contempt prosecution of the Administrator of the Environmental Protection Agency, Ann Gorsuch Burford. Burford appeared in 1981 before a House subcommittee and, under orders from President Ronald Reagan, refused to provide certain subpoenaed information concerning EPA enforcement activities. After the full committee reported a contempt citation, the House cited Burford for contempt, the first time a house of Congress ever held the head of an executive agency or department in contempt. The Speaker of the House certified the contempt resolution to the U.S. Attorney for the District of Columbia. However, relying on the prosecutorial discretion of the executive branch, the U.S. Attorney refused to present the contempt citation to the grand jury.

As the Burford controversy illustrates, the criminal contempt statute is ill-suited to securing executive branch compliance with congressional requests for information, because the power to control prosecutions rests squarely with the executive branch itself. (The Senate has a statutory mechanism for the civil enforcement of its subpoenas, which does not require the participation by the U.S. Attorney, but the statute expressly excludes from its coverage subpoenas directed at executive branch officials). Nevertheless, Congress is not without alternative measures to compel the executive branch to produce requested information. An administration's bill may be shelved in committee until relevant information is provided. Or Congress may exercise its power of the purse to reduce or deny appropriations sought by an administration until the information is produced. And Congress always retains the power to impeach an executive official, even the President, if political accommodation is not possible.

Since the administration of George Washington, disputes have frequently arisen between the President and Congress over the executive branch's obligation to respond to congressional demands for information. The use of the criminal contempt sanction to resolve these disputes between the two political branches is unsatisfactory—not only to the Congress, but also to the executive branch "contemptor" who, ordinarily, is simply carrying out the President's orders. In light of these inherent flaws in the criminal contempt procedure, ultimately the only effective means of resolving these interbranch disputes is to fashion a political compromise. In the Burford controversy, for example, the White House succumbed to political pressure, and after more than a year of delay, produced to the Congress the information sought.

BIBLIOGRAPHY

Dash, Sam. *Chief Counsel: Inside the Ervin Committee—The Untold Story.* 1976.
Grabow, John C. *Congressional Investigations, Law and Practice.* 1988.
Hamilton, James. *The Power to Probe: A Study of Congressional Investigations.* 1976.

JOHN C. GRABOW and COURT E. GOLUMBIC

CONTINUING RESOLUTIONS. Funding devices enacted whenever Congress is unable to pass one or more of the thirteen regular appropriations bills by the start of a fiscal year are known as continuing resolutions. Continuing resolutions—when first passed in 1876 and up to 1981—were noncontroversial interim spending measures designed to keep the government afloat until the enactment of the regular appropriations. Since 1981, however, the use, scope, and size of these measures have dramatically expanded. Today, continuing resolutions typically provide full-year funding for many (and sometimes all) federal operations and serve as a vehicle for unrelated legislation.

Continuing resolutions are extraordinarily controversial. Critics claim that this funding device disrupts the balance of power both within Congress and between Congress and the White House. Specifically, since continuing resolutions are not subject to the House of Representatives rule prohibiting the attachment of substantive legislation to an appropriations bill, appropriations committees gain power at the expense of authorizing committees. House and Senate appropriations committee members who negotiate the final terms of the continuing resolution wield enormous power. In fiscal year 1988, for example, these members negotiated a ban on smoking on domestic flights of two hours or less, a plan to allow states to raise the speed limit on rural highways to sixty-five miles per hour, an extension of the Clean Air Act, and a limitation rider prohibiting the Federal Communications Commission from modifying its regulations limiting the co-ownership of a television station and a newspaper in the same market.

Continuing resolutions also affect the President's veto power and, with it, the executive's role in shaping BUDGET POLICY. Critics of continuing resolutions argue that this funding device substantially undermines the veto power [*see* VETO, REGULAR]. By lumping together several (if not all) of the thirteen appropriations bills as well as unrelated substantive legislation, critics perceive that Presidents will be reluctant to disrupt so many programs (most of which they endorse) through a single veto. Moreover, since a continuing resolution prevents the shutdown of the federal government by providing necessary funding, critics view the costs of a presidential veto as extraordinarily high. Defenders of continuing resolutions, in contrast, argue that a President who is willing to use the veto power can help define the content of a continuing resolution. For example, in fiscal year 1988, President Ronald Reagan used his veto threat to preserve funds for antiabortion counseling [*see* ABORTION] as well as aid to the contra "freedom fighters" in Nicaragua.

Continuing resolutions, although maligned far more often than they are defended, are likely to remain a permanent fixture on the budget landscape. Only once in the 1980s did Congress enact all thirteen appropriations bills by the end of the fiscal year. Indeed, more than one hundred continuing resolutions were enacted from 1965 to 1990. The prevalence of continuing resolutions is a by-product of many interrelated phenomena, including the 1974 CONGRESSIONAL BUDGET AND IMPOUNDMENT CONTROL ACT, the GRAMM-RUDMAN-HOLLINGS ACTS, and policy conflicts between the White House and Congress. Whatever their cause, continuing resolutions dramatically affect both the shape and content of federal budget decision-making.

[See also PRESIDENTIAL-CONGRESSIONAL RELATIONS.]

BIBLIOGRAPHY

Fisher, Louis. "The Authorization-Appropriation Process in Congress: Formal Rules and Informal Practices." *Catholic University Law Review* 29 (1979): 51–105.
Devins, Neal. "Regulation of Government Agencies through Limitation Riders." *Duke Law Journal* (1987): 456–500.

NEAL DEVINS

CONVENTIONAL FORCES IN EUROPE TREATY. See CFU (CONVENTIONAL FORCES IN EUROPE) TREATY.

CONVENTIONS. See NOMINATING PRESIDENTIAL CANDIDATES.

COOLIDGE, CALVIN (1872–1933), thirtieth President of the United States (1923–1929). John Calvin Coolidge was born the son of a storekeeper and farmer in Plymouth Notch, Vermont. As a youth he took on what some observers have described as a trait of Yankee New England: a marked conversational inability and a withdrawn quality that seems to harmonize with the thin soil and granite hardness of the area. The odds of his reaching high national political office were slight; New England had had no President since Franklin Pierce.

Early Career. Coolidge was educated at St. Johnsbury Academy and Amherst College. On graduating from Amherst in 1895, he read law in Northampton, was admitted to the Massachusetts bar in 1897, and the next year was elected to Northampton's city council. Politics attracted him, and, by a combination of calculation and good fortune, he made his way up, step by

step. One of his later biographers, the politically well-attuned William Allen White, pointed out that few Presidents ran for office more often or more successfully. Counting the presidential campaign of 1924, Coolidge ran twenty times and was elected nineteen. The only time he failed was shortly after he married Grace Anna Goodhue, a teacher of the deaf, in 1905, when he failed to do sufficient canvassing in a campaign for school committeeman. Compared to Coolidge's electoral record, Warren Gamaliel Harding ran seven times and lost once, Woodrow Wilson ran and won three times, William Howard Taft won twice and lost once, Theodore Roosevelt won six times out of eight contests, William McKinley eleven out of fourteen. Coolidge achieved the offices of city solicitor, clerk of county courts, state representative, mayor, state senator, lieutenant governor, and governor. In 1920 he was elected to the vice presidency on the Harding ticket.

What attracted voters to the wispy, runty (he was five feet, nine inches tall), laconic, sometimes insultingly epigrammatic candidate? He seldom (if ever) made a false statement, and voters liked that. They liked his aphorisms and pointed wit. They liked his unpredictable brevity—as when in his inaugural address as president of the Massachusetts senate he told the other senators to tend to business and "above all things, be brief" in a few sentences totalling forty-four words. Voters even liked his more expansive oratory, though critics opined that Coolidge's speeches contained little beyond platitudes.

In office Coolidge displayed remarkably good judgment, and people liked that, too. As state senate president he was clearly the leader among the forty senators, for these experienced politicians knew he would make few mistakes. As governor of Massachusetts for two one-year terms (1919–1920) he again showed his understanding of the art of the possible, carefully watching over the concerns of all the state's citizens. He was no ideological conservative and pushed for womens' rights, protection of workers (particularly women and children), and the settlement of labor-management disputes.

As governor Coolidge gained attention with his statement about the Boston police strike of 1919, "There is no right to strike against the public safety by anybody, anywhere, any time." His response to the strike made him a national figure overnight and a favorite-son candidate for the presidential nomination at the 1920 Republican national convention. At the Chicago convention Senate insiders nominated their candidate, Senator Warren Harding, and sought to install another Senator as the vice presidential candidate—until a leather-lunged member of the Oregon delegation stood on a chair shouting for Coolidge and stampeded the convention.

Coolidge's vice presidency was completely undistinguished, save for providing occasions for a few of his witticisms. Observers noticed that every night the Vice President and his wife accepted a dinner invitation and went out to eat at the table of some distinguished host and hostess. Reporters inquired about this unwonted social activity. "Gotta eat somewhere," was the response.

The possibility of his becoming President does not seem to have crossed his mind. Whether Harding's worsening illness from cardiovascular disease ever caught Vice President Coolidge's attention is altogether unknown. Harding's death, of a heart attack, catapulted Coolidge into the presidency. Americans, shocked by his death, were quickly reassured by the simple, unaffected ways of his successor, and especially by description of the way Coolidge received the news that he had become the nation's Chief Executive. Vacationing in Plymouth Notch, the Vice President was sworn in by his father, who was a notary public, by the light of an oil lamp in the farmhouse living room.

Presidency. The Coolidge presidency presents a mixed record. Coolidge's largest failure came in his relations with Congress—at best a standoff and at worst a series of brawls. Congress went after the President's proposal for development of hydroelectric power at Muscle Shoals, Alabama, on the Tennessee River; insisted on pushing for a soldiers' bonus; advocated what Coolidge considered unwise farm legislation; and sought control of prosecuting the Harding administration scandals that emerged after Coolidge took office. The Senate abruptly turned down a Cabinet nomination. For the most part the unruliness of the legislative branch was not Coolidge's fault but resulted from Congress's memory of the Wilson administration, when that imperious President first dragooned Congress to pass a series of reform bills and then, during WORLD WAR I and the immediate postwar period, ignored Congress, in particular the Senate. To this difficulty was added the continuing farm problem of the 1920s, which led to the formation of a Senate farm bloc that pushed farm issues by threatening noncooperation on other matters. Lastly, Congressmen naturally pursued their local interests rather than national interests, relying on the President to provide whatever leadership he could and, sometimes, when congressional irresponsibility became notable, use his veto power. To these intransigences Coolidge added a confusion or two of his own. He often contented himself with stating his points of view in messages to the legislators, after which he seems to have believed he had done what was necessary—he had made his positions clear, and the legislative branch could make up its mind. This philosophy might have worked in Massachusetts but was of little value in the national Congress. Nor did he accompany his advice with intimate personal conferences with supporters or, at crucial times, enemies; he seems to have believed that White House breakfasts, unorganized affairs to which he invited friends and foes but to which he gave little or no guidance, sufficed to keep Congress in order.

Battles with Congress. For the first four months of his presidency Coolidge enjoyed a HONEYMOON PERIOD. Congress was not in session, but in December 1923, sessions resumed, and issues at once arose. One was the development of Muscle Shoals, begun by the Wilson administration during the war. Coolidge hoped to consign the development to private rather than public initiative. The danger of the latter, he maintained, was inefficiency, and his candidate for developer was the automobile magnate Henry Ford. The President may—perhaps no one will ever know—have made an arrangement with Ford that Ford would stay out of the presidential race in 1924 in exchange for Coolidge's sponsoring him for Muscle Shoals. Opposition to Coolidge, by Senator George W. Norris of Nebraska, held private operation of the project to be theft of public resources. The result was a delay for the Tennessee Valley project until the NEW DEAL era.

A second set-to with Congress arose over bonus legislation for World War I veterans, who had received little recompense for their service, unlike civilian war workers. The Bonus Bill was understandably popular. Coolidge believed that American soldiers and sailors had fought out of patriotism, not desire for money, and that no bonus could recompense them for their sacrifice. He vetoed the bill, and Congress overrode his veto by large majorities.

Then came a succession of farm bills designed to hold up domestic farm prices by buying excess production and dumping it abroad. Many Congressmen supported the McNary-Haugen dumping legislation. Here the President could hardly show his hand, for he, too, hoped to maintain support from the nation's farmers. Perhaps remembering his own flight from Plymouth Notch, he privately wondered why people who could not make a living out of farming wanted to remain on the farm. He opposed the farm bills, citing constitutional and economic reasons. That it was unfair for government to protect businessmen by tariffs and not to try, through subsidies if necessary, to protect farmers, was not one of his calculations. Nor did he, like many of his contemporaries (including his congressional opponents), understand that farming was in a deep economic trough: the value of farmland dropped constantly, in real terms, from 1915 until 1943, when it began a slow rise. An increase in agricultural prices in the latter part of Coolidge's presidency allayed the immediate problem.

The most difficult of Coolidge's negotiations with Congress came over the Harding administration scandals and involved the question of whether Congress or the President should handle them. The rivalry between legislative and executive branches naturally played a role in this controversy. It was exacerbated by contentions between Democratic Congressmen and a Republican administration. The huge margin by which Harding was elected to the presidency had irritated Democrats, as had the Republican claim, during the 1920 presidential campaign, that President Wilson had displayed too much idealism, especially over the LEAGUE OF NATIONS. When the Harding scandals came to light in the first year of the Coolidge administration, Democratic members of Congress could hardly avoid attempting to take leadership of any investigation. By that time they were looking to the presidential election of 1924.

Coolidge and his congressional critics squabbled over the mess the Harding administration had left—mostly the TEAPOT DOME SCANDAL, in which the Navy Department had turned over government oil reserves to the Interior Department, where Secretary Albert B. Fall, a former Senator, had leased them to private oil operators for a massive bribe disguised as a personal loan. There had also been bribery and conniving in the Alien Property Custodian's office and in the Veterans Bureau. Harding's Attorney General, HARRY M. DAUGHERTY, evidently had a hand in it, although no one could pin anything on him. Coolidge at first thought the talk of malfeasance was without foundation, but he came to see otherwise and accepted the resignations of Daugherty and Secretary of the Navy Edwin N. Denby and otherwise tried to clean things up. The Senate sought control, but, fortunately for the country, everyone moved slowly; the stretching out of Cabinet resignations and legislative and executive proceedings prevented panicky solutions, ensured justice, and resolved the mess that Coolidge had inherited.

In one totally unexpected way the Harding heritage redounded to the President's great discomfort, when the Senate refused to confirm the nomination of Charles B. Warren as Attorney General. This action marked the President's worst defeat in the Senate, the first time it had rejected a nominee since Henry Stanbery was rejected for Attorney General in 1868. When Daugherty had resigned, Coolidge had appointed Harlan F. Stone to head the Justice Department, but soon nominated Stone to the Supreme Court and wanted to replace him with Warren. The President failed, however, to invite the opinion of Senate leaders, to cultivate Senators, or really even to measure his man. The Senate defeated Warren's nomination by a vote of 46 to 39. Coolidge offered a recess appointment, which Warren wisely refused. The President then nominated John Garibaldi Sargent, a Vermont country lawyer who, like Coolidge, had attended Black River Academy. Sargent's nomination passed the Senate by acclamation.

Election of 1924. The acrimony with Congress was concentrated in the early part of the administration; the situation was made somewhat easier to bear by the President's victory in the election of 1924—which showed he had national popular if not congressional approval. At the outset he had reason to worry that Henry Ford or some equally popular figure might take the Republican nomination, but nothing like that happened. Serious Democratic candidates dropped from sight during the 103 ballots it took to nominate the Wall Street lawyer, JOHN W. DAVIS, whom the Democrats incongruously paired with Charles Bryan of Nebraska, the brother of WILLIAM JENNINGS BRYAN, the presidential candidate of earlier years. ROBERT M. LA FOLLETTE organized a third party, the PROGRESSIVE PARTY, which sought but failed to gather progressives of both old-line parties into a mighty host. The Republicans advised voters to "Keep Cool with Coolidge" and to think of their choice as one between "Coolidge or Chaos." The President campaigned little, for in July he and his wife suffered the tragic death of their youngest son, Calvin, Jr. With his death, so Coolidge later wrote, went the power and glory of the presidency. He could hardly savor his electoral triumph in November, in which he polled 55 percent of the votes cast.

Administrative expertise. Coolidge's presidential successes were substantial, though not describable in the usual terms of presidential achievement. Coolidge was a superb administrator, acting on the principle that he should never do himself what a subordinate could do for him. He passed responsibilities to his Cabinet members, whom he often described, privately, as "old men," as in Old Man Stone or Old Man Sargent or Old Man Mellon (Secretary of the Treasury ANDREW W. MELLON). Coolidge's Vice President, CHARLES G. DAWES, had been the first Director of the Bureau of the Budget, an office instituted under Harding. With the bureau's help Coolidge was eminently successful in his principal domestic program, which was the reduction of the federal debt. Moreover, he managed to reduce taxes twice, in 1926 and 1928.

Coolidge's relations with the third branch of government, the judiciary, were excellent. During his presidency the Chief Justice, former President William Howard Taft, was so enthusiastic over Coolidge (a man who behaved with dignity and was also a conservative after Taft's heart) that he could think of no reason to oppose the administration. Indeed, Taft was often a visitor to the White House, where, according to his later published letters, he did not hesitate to cross the bounds between the judicial and executive branches, offering political advice of all sorts. In return he doubtless hoped to get more control over the APPOINTMENT OF JUDGES. Taft was unsure whether the President took his advice, executive or judicial, but he continued to offer it.

Economy. The most important development during the Coolidge era was the "Coolidge boom" in the national economy, which in its later phase became not so much a boom as a speculative mania. The President captured the national mood in his pronouncement that "the chief business of the American people is business." He carefully qualified the statement, adding that "so long as wealth is made the means and not the end, we need not greatly fear it." Coolidge may have contributed negatively to speculative fever by usually avoiding the subject, doubtless because of his basic outlook toward politics. "When things are going along all right," he once wrote his close friend and supporter, Frank W. Stearns, "it is a good plan to let them alone."

Foreign affairs. In international affairs Coolidge was inactive, entrusting them to his able secretaries of State, CHARLES EVANS HUGHES and, after 1925, Frank B. Kellogg. ELIHU ROOT once said the President "did not have an international hair in his head," but if this was true, it was true of most Americans after the war. Americans did not think it necessary to intervene in Europe to maintain a balance of power favorable to the interest of the United States, which was world peace. Coolidge trusted to minor kinds of participation in European affairs, such as membership in the World Court, and, after that proved impossible after a Senate vote in 1925 that placed too many reservations on American membership, negotiation in 1927 and 1928 of the KELLOGG-BRIAND PACT for the renunciation and outlawing of war. In this negotiation he gave his Secretary of State few instructions and said little about the result, which seemed a minor success for international idealism. He took more interest in the possibility of reducing naval expenditures. Unfortunately, it failed at the Geneva Naval Conference of 1927, where the United States, Britain, and Japan got into contention over the size, armament, and tonnage of light and heavy cruisers. To Coolidge's irritation, in 1928 the British and French governments made a cruiser proposal that placed no limits on the type they desired but sought to limit the tonnage and armament of those ships desired by the United States—large cruisers with ten-thousand-ton displacement, armed with eight-inch guns and capable of holding their own in the Pacific against Japanese cruisers. The failed Geneva conference marked the end of arms limitation during the Coolidge administration.

On one point of international relations, collecting war debts (money lent to the Allies during and immediately after the world war), Coolidge was adamant, as were most Americans. No one has ever proved that the President said, "They hired the money, didn't they?" Still, his wife admitted it did sound like him. His administration renegotiated the loans by reducing interest rates and stretching out the years of repayment. It sponsored the Dawes Plan for reparations in 1924 and the Young Plan in 1929, which made it possible for private American bankers to lend money to Germany to pay reparations to the Allies, who passed the money back to the U.S. Treasury as war-debt payments. The arrangement broke down during the Great Depression, with the Treasury holding one bag, American bankers another.

Generally speaking, Coolidge favored peace over conflict. He approved Kellogg's efforts to avoid rising nationalism in China and to eliminate extraterritoriality and customs supervision. Coolidge ended a seemingly endless revolution in Nicaragua by sending a mediator, HENRY L. STIMSON. He resolved a dispute over foreign oil holdings in Mexico by sending his Amherst College boardinghouse friend, the financier Dwight W. Morrow. Stimson also went to the PHILIPPINES to quiet agitation for independence and obtain cooperation in local self-government.

Later Life. On 2 August 1927, the fourth anniversary of his assuming office, Coolidge astonished his press conference by handing out a statement, "I do not choose to run for President in nineteen twenty-eight." He could have had the nomination for the asking, but he had had enough, and he threw open the nomination, which went to his Secretary of Commerce, Herbert Hoover.

Coolidge lived nearly four years after leaving office in March 1929. He returned to the duplex house in Northampton in which he had spent many years, until sightseers ("Democrats," he called them) drove him to purchase a small estate within the city limits. Each morning he rode to his law office, but he refused to practice, for his ethical sense prevented him from taking the large retainers and cases that would have come because he was a former President and did not feel it dignified to accept the small cases—wills, estates, collections—that had once formed his practice. From the office he answered correspondence and for a year wrote a syndicated daily newspaper column, "Thinking Things Over with Calvin Coolidge." He traveled a little, including a trip to Florida, New Orleans, and the Pacific coast, where he visited the Hollywood studios and spent a week on the San Simeon estate of the publisher William Randolph Hearst. During that visit, and while PROHIBITION was yet in force, he drank two glasses of an excellent Tokay. But travel did not much attract him. He did accept a directorship in the New York Life Insurance Company and received fifty dollars for attendance at monthly meetings. He accepted the presidency of the American Antiquarian Society in Worcester, Massachusetts, and never missed a meeting. He offered few political judgments, and participated in President Hoover's campaign for reelection in 1932 only to the extent of giving a speech in New York's Madison Square Garden. For reasons of health he did not follow up with a promised speech in Chicago. "The fact is," he wrote a correspondent, "I feel worn out. . . . I know my work is done." One morning early in January 1933, alone in his upstairs dressing room in the Northampton house, he died of a heart attack.

BIBLIOGRAPHY

Coolidge, Calvin. *The Autobiography of Calvin Coolidge*. 1929.
Coolidge, Calvin. *Your Son, Calvin Coolidge: A Selection of Letters from Calvin Coolidge to His Father*. Edited by Edward Connery Lathem. 1968.
Fuess, Claude M. *Calvin Coolidge: The Man from Vermont*. 1940.
McCoy, Donald R. *Calvin Coolidge: The Quiet President*. 1967.
Quint, Howard H., and Robert H. Ferrell, eds. *The Talkative President: The Off-The-Record Press Conferences of Calvin Coolidge*. 1964.
White, William Allen. *A Puritan in Babylon: The Story of Calvin Coolidge*. 1938.

ROBERT H. FERRELL

COOPER-CHURCH AMENDMENT (1970).

In the course of the VIETNAM WAR, the Cooper-Church Amendment was passed in the U.S. Senate to force the withdrawal of U.S. forces from Cambodia. In spring 1970 President Richard M. Nixon ordered an attack of Cambodia by U.S. military forces. As Nixon explained on 30 April of that year, the "incursion," as he called the military action, had become necessary to clean out North Vietnamese and Vietcong troops who were launching forays against South Vietnam from sanctuaries inside Cambodia's borders. Critics suggested that the real reason, however, was to assist the government

of Cambodia in its resistance against a takeover by communist insurgents.

Whatever the reason, protests against the attack erupted across the United States. In response to demonstrations at Kent State University in Ohio, National Guardsmen in that state gunned down students on campus; other students were shot, this time by police officers, at Jackson State University in Mississippi. An avalanche of antiwar mail fell on Congress from an outraged citizenry—over 2 million letters and telegrams within three weeks of the invasion, the largest outpouring of direct constituent communications on a single issue in the history of the Congress, according to Post Office officials. Congress found itself besieged by busloads of citizen lobbyists from all over the nation, traveling to Washington to protest the spread of war in Indochina and the campus violence at home.

In response to the incursion and the public outcry, the Senate debated the wisdom of the military operation for seven weeks, to the exclusion of nearly all other business. Senators John Sherman Cooper (R-Ky.) and Frank Church (D-Idaho)—both senior members of the Foreign Relations Committee—introduced into the Senate a bipartisan measure that became known as the Cooper-Church Amendment of 1970. The purpose of the proposed law was to force the government to recall U.S. forces from Cambodia. For the first time in America's history, the Senate threatened to use its penultimate power (short of impeachment) against the President in order to curb his use of military force: the power of the purse. The amendment, which passed in June, was worded to cut off funding for support of U.S. troops in Cambodia if the President failed to withdraw them by 1 July 1970. Nixon did withdraw U.S. troops from Cambodia, claiming he had intended to do so all along regardless of the Cooper-Church Amendment. The VIETNAM WAR lingered on, however, for five more years.

BIBLIOGRAPHY

Dvorin, Eugene P., ed. *The Senate's War Powers*. 1971.
Johnson, Loch K. *America as a World Power: Foreign Policy in a Constitutional Framework*. 1991.
Karnow, Stanley. *Vietnam: A History*. 1983.

LOCH K. JOHNSON

COOPER v. AARON 358 U.S. 1 (1958).

President Dwight D. Eisenhower's dramatic action in the Little Rock crisis tested the Supreme Court's relation with the states. Defying the Court's desegregation decision, in *Brown v. Board of Education* (1954), Arkansas Governor Orval E. Faubus ordered the National Guard to prevent the desegregation of Little Rock's Central High School beginning 3 September 1957. Claiming that violence was imminent, he relied on vague police powers to justify his action. After a protracted confrontation lasting over two weeks, President Eisenhower ordered U.S. Army paratroopers to Little Rock to enforce the federal district court's order. Immediate compliance followed. Segregationist-inspired harassment however, disrupted the educational process, reducing from nine to eight the number of black students attending Central. In May 1958, the school board asked for, and a federal district court granted, a two-and-one-half-year delay in the continued implementation of its desegregation plan.

During the summer of 1958 the school board's suit coincided with Faubus's third-term gubernatorial race. He campaigned on a states' rights platform, contending that neither he nor other state officials were bound to follow the Supreme Court's desegregation decree. Faubus won a landslide victory, whereupon the legislature passed the measures he had called for. Meanwhile, the Supreme Court held a special August term to consider in *Cooper v. Aaron* the National Association for the Advancement of Colored People's (NAACP) appeal of the lower court's decision and the constitutional validity of Faubus's states' rights program.

The Court decided against the school board, holding that when disorder arose, its official duty was to defend rather than deny the constitutional rights established in *Brown*. The Court's rejection of the state's constitutional claims, moreover, was sweeping. It held that the interpretation of the Fourteenth Amendment pronounced in *Brown* was the supreme law of the land. Because Arkansas officials had taken an oath to uphold the Constitution, they were bound by Article VI, the supremacy clause. Accordingly, the Court declared, "No state legislator or executive or judicial officer can war against the Constitution without violating his undertaking to support it."

Critics questioned the decision's expansiveness. Precedents since MARBURY V. MADISON (1803), however, have supported the logic of the Court's opinion. Concerning the police power in particular, the issue involved primarily the threat of violence, which a FEDERAL BUREAU OF INVESTIGATION (FBI) probe later revealed did not exist until after Faubus's defiant stance. Nevertheless, the precedents were well established that in the face of threatened disorder it was the governor's and the legislator's duty to use their authority to preserve constitutional rights, not to deny them.

Ironically, Arkansas officials' actions were contrary even to the states' rights principles. According to theories of state sovereignty, a policy initiated by a local community's democratically elected representatives—in this case the Little Rock school board—embodied the highest expression of sovereign authority, and any lawful exercise of the police power must be in accord with this authority. According to states' rights logic, a lawful use of police powers would have required Faubus to assist the school board in the implementation of its desegregation plan.

Even so, the Court underlined the significance of its decision. All nine justices signed the opinion, though it had in fact been written primarily by Justice William J. Brennan. Moreover, the Court noted that even though several justices had joined the Court since the original *Brown* decision, the support for it continued to be unanimous.

President Eisenhower, however, failed to carry through the broad authority the Court declared. Faubus's defiance continued until a coalition of Little Rock's white moderate businessmen, a liberal women's organization, and blacks won a special school board election supporting desegregation during the spring of 1959. The civil rights victories of the 1960s, however, vindicated the significance of *Cooper v. Aaron*.

BIBLIOGRAPHY

Diamond, Raymond T. "Confrontation as Rejoinder to Compromise: Reflections on the Little Rock Desegregation Crisis." *National Black Law Journal* 11 (1989): 151–176.

Freyer, Tony. *The Little Rock Crisis*. 1984.

Schwartz, Bernard. *Super Chief Earl Warren and His Supreme Court: A Judicial Biography*. 1983.

TONY FREYER

COPPERHEADS. Also known as Peace Democrats, the Copperheads opposed the war policies of the Abraham Lincoln administration. Unlike those Democrats who supported the CIVIL WAR, some of whom even affiliated with the REPUBLICAN PARTY, the Copperheads—named by their opponents after the poisonous snake—denounced the war and demanded that it be brought to an end swiftly. By late 1863 they had become a threat to the war effort, capitalizing on Northern weariness with the war's prolongation and expansion.

Although they derived support throughout the North, the Copperheads' main base was in the rural areas of the lower Midwest—southern Illinois, Indiana and Ohio—where resistance to social change and opposition to governmental centralization were powerful. Also strongly Copperhead were traditional sources of Democratic support among immigrants and

Catholics in the cities. Mobilizing voters around the slogan "The Constitution as it is and the Union as it was," Copperheads challenged the introduction of the draft, the expansion of war aims to include emancipation (racism was a powerful ingredient in Copperheadism), and the restriction of CIVIL LIBERTIES, especially the SUSPENSION OF HABEAS CORPUS, which was aimed primarily at curbing the Copperheads themselves.

The civil liberties issue became the Copperheads' main challenge to Lincoln. They were able to make political capital out of what they considered arbitrary arrests and curbs on free speech, especially when their leader, Representative Clement L. Vallandigham, was arrested and exiled to the Confederacy in 1863.

Suspicion of Copperhead subversion was fed by the existence of a secret society called the Knights of the Golden Circle, with which Peace Democrats were believed to be associated, as well as by rumors of a plot to detach the Northwest from the Union and align it with the Confederacy, whose agents were known to be in touch with leading Copperheads. The extent of this kind of activity by the Copperheads is difficult to ascertain, but they did have political influence that the Republicans could not ignore. In 1863, they controlled the state legislatures of Illinois and Indiana; a year later, their agenda of peace at any price was the platform of the national DEMOCRATIC PARTY, and one of their leaders, George H. Pendleton, was its vice presidential nominee. The Copperheads' opposition to a long, inconclusive war that was generating threatening social and governmental change resonated powerfully with many Northern voters, especially traditional Democrats.

BIBLIOGRAPHY

Klement, Frank L. *The Copperheads in the Middle West*. 1959.
Neely, Mark E., Jr. *The Fate of Liberty: Abraham Lincoln and Civil Liberties*. 1991.
Silbey, Joel H. *A Respectable Minority: The Democratic Party in the Civil War Era, 1860–1868*. 1977.

MICHAEL PERMAN

CORCORAN, THOMAS

CORCORAN, THOMAS (1900–1981), presidential adviser and lobbyist. After graduating from Harvard Law School, Thomas Gardiner (Tommy "The Cork") Corcoran worked briefly on Wall Street before going to Washington, D.C., in 1931, staying on to become an important figure in the NEW DEAL.

Corcoran was a jack-of-all-trades in the Franklin D. Roosevelt administration. Working out of the RECONSTRUCTION FINANCE CORPORATION and frequently teamed with BENJAMIN V. COHEN, he helped write and steer

through Congress both the Securities Exchange Act of 1934 and the PUBLIC UTILITY HOLDING COMPANY ACT of 1935. He wrote speeches, planned political strategy, raised campaign funds, and took on whatever other tasks needed to be done.

As WORLD WAR II approached, Corcoran drifted away from the center of power. His relationship with both Roosevelt and FELIX FRANKFURTER, his two mentors, deteriorated sharply. In 1940 he left government service to head an organization called Independent Voters for Roosevelt; after the election he looked forward to an important post, perhaps SOLICITOR GENERAL. Meanwhile he began a private law and lobbying practice. In the end Frankfurter blocked Corcoran's appointment as Solicitor General.

Corcoran's career as a private lawyer and lobbyist was often controversial. He helped organize the Flying Tigers squadron, an American volunteer force that provided transportation services and air support to the Chinese army, and later worked closely with the Nationalist Chinese government in Taiwan. His clients included Sterling Products Corporation, a major drug company with ties to Nazi Germany, and the United Fruit Company. Corcoran's activities led to several congressional investigations, though no wrongdoing was ever conclusively proved.

Tommy Corcoran, once the quintessence of the New Deal, became permanently estranged from it. Many New Dealers regarded him as a traitor to his own cause; Corcoran broke with most of his former associates, excepting only Cohen. He remained an active force in Washington politics well into the 1970s.

BIBLIOGRAPHY

Lash, Joseph P. *Dealers and Dreamers: A New Look at the New Deal*. 1988.

WILLIAM LASSER

COUDERT RESOLUTION

COUDERT RESOLUTION. The GREAT DEBATE in 1951 over the President's power to send troops abroad was started by a resolution, introduced by U.S. Representative Frederic R. Coudert (R-N.Y.), forbidding the dispatch of troops abroad without congressional approval. Coudert's move occurred as the KOREAN WAR raged on inconclusively and NATO forces were being organized.

The resolution directed the President to send no additional troops anywhere outside the United States without the express authorization of Congress in each instance. If any new force was sent abroad without Congress's consent, the resolution called for the termination of appropriations necessary for the force's maintenance. An exception was made to facilitate the withdrawal of existing American forces in Korea.

On 4 January 1951, the day following the resolution's introduction, President Harry S. Truman, asked in a news conference whether he required congressional approval to send additional troops to Europe, replied, "No, I do not," implying that he need not seek the consent of the whole Congress except for a declaration of war. Truman asserted that his power to send troops abroad had already been recognized by Congress and the courts, and that, as President, he would uphold the UNITED NATIONS Charter, NATO, and other treaty obligations by sending the armed forces to wherever they were needed. The President noted that throughout the Korean War, he had invited both Republican and Democratic legislators to confer and would continue to do so in future conflicts.

Despite intense congressional debate, the Coudert Resolution remained bottled up indefinitely in the Armed Services Committee, to which it had been referred. On 1 March, Coudert wrote to the committee's chairman, Carl Vinson (D-Ga.), demanding immediate action on the resolution, saying that for Congress not to act on the troop issue would be "a shameless surrender" of its responsibilities.

While the resolution remained in committee, Coudert in July criticized Secretary of Defense GEORGE C. MARSHALL for announcing that 400,000 troops would be sent to Europe after an earlier statement that 200,000 would go. Marshall responded that the additional manpower was auxiliary troops needed to make the combat troops previously assigned field-ready. Coudert termed the episode "deceptive doubletalk" and moved to amend the armed services appropriation bill when it reached the House floor by limiting expenditure to 200,000 troops and barring use of appropriated funds to maintain any additional troops sent abroad without congressional authorization. Critics accused Coudert of substituting his judgment for that of the JOINT CHIEFS OF STAFF. The House rejected Coudert's amendment on 9 August, 84 to 131, in a standing vote. His original resolution died in committee.

BIBLIOGRAPHY

Corwin, Edward S. *The President: Office and Powers.* 4th rev. ed. 1957.
Donovan, Robert J. *Tumultuous Years: The Presidency of Harry S. Truman, 1949–1953.* 1982.

LOUIS W. KOENIG

COUNCIL OF ECONOMIC ADVISERS (CEA). The Council of Economic Advisers to the President was established by the Employment Act of 1946. The council is composed of three members appointed by the President with the ADVICE AND CONSENT of the Senate. One member is designated by the President to serve as chair. The act specifies that each member should be "exceptionally qualified" to (1) analyze and interpret economic developments, (2) evaluate programs and activities of the government in light of the policy objectives declared in the act, and (3) formulate and recommend economic policies to the President to promote the achievement of maximum employment, production, and purchasing power.

The council assists in the preparation the Economic Report of the President and makes a report on the economy, both of which are transmitted annually to the Congress within sixty days after the beginning of each regular session. It also gives testimony on the Economic Report before the Joint Economic Committee and is often invited to give testimony before other committees of Congress on legislative matters of importance to economic policy.

In addition to advising the President, the council and its staff of economists work closely with other government agencies and departments, particularly the Departments of the Treasury, Labor, Commerce, and Agriculture and the Office of Management and Budget (OMB).

Over the years the chair of the council has participated in meetings with the Secretary of the Treasury and the Director of OMB—the so-called Troika—to discuss economic issues. Occasionally, the Federal Reserve Board chair has participated in these sessions. In the 1950s the process was relatively informal, but it became more structured in the early 1960s. The weekly meetings of the group have played an important role in the formulation and management of economic policy ever since.

Among the three members of the council, the chair has traditionally acted as the principal adviser to the President. The chair's advice on economic matters is given both in regular meetings with the President and in brief memoranda. The other two members work closely with the chair and provide important input in the advisory process. Moreover, they function as specialists in certain policy areas, such as macroeconomic analysis, microeconomic and sectoral analysis, international trade, regulation, and agriculture.

In recent years, the council staff has consisted of about ten senior and seven junior economists. The senior economists are primarily professors of economics recruited from many of the nation's leading universities. They are usually granted one- or two-year leaves from their positions to serve as staff experts on a wide

Chairmen, Council of Economic Advisers

President	Chairman, Council of Economic Advisers
33 Truman	Edwin G. Nourse, 1946–1949 Leon H. Keyserling, 1950–1953
34 Eisenhower	Arthur F. Burns, 1953–1956 Raymond J. Saulnier, 1956–1961
35 Kennedy	Walter W. Heller, 1961–1963
36 L. B. Johnson	Walter W. Heller, 1963–1964 Gardner Ackley, 1964–1968 Arthur M. Okun, 1968–1969
37 Nixon	Paul W. McCracken, 1969–1971 Herbert Stein, 1972–1974
38 Ford	Alan Greenspan, 1974–1977
39 Carter	Charles L. Schultze, 1977–1981
40 Reagan	Murray L. Weidenbaum, 1981–1982 Martin Feldstein, 1982–1984 Beryl W. Sprinkel, 1985–1989
41 Bush	Michael J. Boskin, 1989–1993
42 Clinton	Laura D'Andrea Tyson, 1993–

variety of economic topics, such as macroeconomics, public finance, financial markets, banking, insurance, labor markets, agriculture, international trade, regulation, and energy. The seven junior economists are typically advanced graduate students who spend a one- or two-year internship at the CEA. In addition to performing economic research for the council, the staff participates in agency and interagency groups formed to study economic issues that may or may not be resolved at this level. A council member or a senior staff economist participates in these deliberations on issues requiring attention at the sub-Cabinet level. Topics that require higher-level attention or possible presidential action are referred to Cabinet-level bodies. The CEA chair participates in sessions that include Cabinet officials from those departments that have a particular interest in the economic topic being considered.

Legislatively, the council's mandate and responsibilities have changed very little since 1946. In its early years, there was some confusion about its policy role. One view held that its functions should be limited to providing professional economic advice to the President. Others believed that it was appropriate for the council to be an advocate of administration economic policies in public statements and testimony before congressional committees. This issue continued unresolved into the early 1950s, with some in Congress advocating the abolishment of the CEA. Nonetheless, in the early days of his administration, President

Eisenhower was successful in averting such action, and the council has played both advisory and advocacy roles ever since.

The CEA assumed an additional responsibility when the Full Employment and Balanced Growth Act (P.L. 95-523) was enacted in 1978. This legislation requires the President to include five-year economic forecasts in the Economic Report for employment, unemployment, production, real income, productivity, and prices. Such forecasts are also included in the President's annual budget. Because these macroeconomic forecasts have an important bearing on the administration's estimates for revenues and budget expenditures, the council works in close consultation with the Treasury Department and OMB in preparing its forecasts.

Ultimately, all administration policies affecting the economy are the responsibility of the President. In developing and implementing these policies, the President, in addition to receiving advice from the CEA chair, draws extensively on the advice of the Secretary of the Treasury and the Director of OMB. Heads of other federal agencies also provide economic counsel when the need arises.

Over the years it has been difficult to gauge the influence of the chair and the other council members on the policy-making process. Much depends on the extent to which the President is receptive to the views of the chair. For example, the chair played a visible and highly influential role in developing and promoting the adoption of a tax-cut strategy to promote economic growth during the Kennedy and Johnson administrations. In contrast, when the Reagan administration in early 1981 unveiled its economic program to promote economic growth, reduce unemployment and inflation, and balance the budget, the principal design work for the program was done during the latter stages of the 1980 presidential campaign. Moreover, in the early months of the administration, the Director of OMB and the Secretary of the Treasury were the most influential advisers and spokespersons for the program. The council chair, in this instance, did not appear to play a prominent role in the process.

Despite these different experiences, the CEA has always possessed the potential to offer influential economic advice to the President and to perform an important educational and analytical role in deliberations on economic issues at all levels of policy making within the administration. The council's influence, nonetheless, depends on the receptiveness of those government officials who have the power to shape economic policy, particularly the President.

BIBLIOGRAPHY

Feldstein, Martin. "The Council of Economic Advisers and Economic Advising in the United States." *The Economic Journal* 102 (September 1992): 1223–1234.

Hargrove, Erwin C., and Samuel A. Morley, eds. *The President and the Council of Economic Advisers: Interviews with CEA Chairmen.* 1984.

Naveh, David. "The Political Role of Academic Advisers: The Case of the U.S. President's Council of Economic Advisers, 1946–1976." *Presidential Studies Quarterly* 7 (Fall): 492–510.

Porter, Roger B. "Economic Advice to the President: From Eisenhower to Reagan." *Political Science Quarterly* 98, 3 (Fall 1983): 403–426.

Zwicker, Charles H. "The President's Council of Economic Advisers." In *The Presidency and the Economy.* Edited by James P. Pfiffner and R. Gordon Hoxie. 1989.

EDWARD KNIGHT

COUNCIL ON ENVIRONMENTAL QUALITY (CEQ). Created by an act of Congress as part of the National Environmental Policy Act (P.L. 91-190; 83 Stat. 852 [1969]) and located in the EXECUTIVE OFFICE OF THE PRESIDENT, the Council on Environmental Quality was established to formulate and recommend national policies aimed at improving the quality of the environment by issuing studies and reports for Congress and the President. The council consists of a three-member board appointed by the President subject to the ADVICE AND CONSENT of the Senate.

The CEQ was the brainchild of Senator Henry M. Jackson (D-Wash.), who had first proposed the idea in 1967. President Richard M. Nixon argued against the creation of such a special board, instead creating a CABINET-level Environmental Quality Council by executive order on 29 May 1969, in part to stave off Jackson's proposal. Jackson argued that Nixon's interagency council would be ineffective and that a special office was needed to coordinate the twenty-seven executive and independent agencies involved with environmental matters. When the Environmental Policy Act was presented to Nixon, it included creation of the CEQ. Nixon signed the bill on 1 January 1970. On 25 March 1970, Congress passed the Environmental Quality Improvement Act (P.L. 91-224; 84 Stat. 112), which included a provision to create and staff an Office of Environmental Quality to support the CEQ's activities. The council delivered its first report to Congress in August 1970. Nixon's first nominee to head the CEQ was Undersecretary of the Interior Russell E. Train.

Throughout the 1970s, the CEQ was a relatively active force in advancing a wide variety of environmental issues. The Nixon administration lost some of its enthusiasm for environmental concerns as it shifted toward a more strongly pro-industry stand, a trend accelerated by the energy crisis of the early 1970s. This pattern continued during the administration of Gerald Ford.

The CEQ acquired a more aggressive voice and extended influence during the administration of Jimmy Carter. It researched and issued reports on subjects as diverse as water quality and farmland loss. Two weeks after Carter signed a bill extending the deadline for some cities to meet federal clean-water standards in 1980, for example, the CEQ issued a report citing evidence linking water additives with rising cancer rates. Land-use planning received a boost from CEQ research on the conversion of farmland to shopping centers, public works projects, and other activities that diminished the nation's available farmland.

In 1981 and 1982, Congress acceded to requests by the administration of Ronald Reagan to cut the budget and staff of the CEQ dramatically. As part of the Reagan administration's move to reduce environmental regulations, the CEQ budget was cut by 72 percent, its staff was reduced from forty-nine to fifteen members, and its influence within the Executive Office was drastically diminished. CEQ reporting activities were also cut back, and the agency focused its attention on the economic costs and effectiveness of existing environmental efforts. This diminished role for the CEQ continued through the administration of George Bush.

BIBLIOGRAPHY

Congress and the Nation, 1981–1984. 1985.
Goodwin, Craufurd D., ed. *Energy Policy in Perspective.* 1981.

ROBERT J. SPITZER

COURT-PACKING PLAN. Following Franklin D. Roosevelt's decisive victory over incumbent Herbert Hoover in 1932, the popular new President acted swiftly to deliver on his campaign promises. The lingering and pervasive depression had been the only issue of real significance in the campaign, and Roosevelt had promised a wide range of remedies, from agricultural assistance to strict regulation of industry and the economy. In the "Hundred Days" following his inauguration [*see* HONEYMOON PERIOD], Roosevelt proposed a variety of measures designed first to alleviate the effects of the depression and then to attack its causes. Congress readily approved the program, willing and even eager to countenance unprecedented governmental experimentation to meet the nation's dire needs.

Although Roosevelt's initiatives originally enjoyed support across all sectors of society, by late 1934, despite a discernible amount of economic recovery, a vocal minority had begun to coalesce in opposition to the policies. Conservative business leaders who had initially supported innovative measures like the NATIONAL INDUSTRIAL RECOVERY ACT (NIRA) now considered such regulations inefficient and burdensome to industry. These NEW DEAL opponents found a strong ally in the Supreme Court, which boasted a formidable record of antagonism to governmental economic experimentation long before the stock-market crash of 1929, having almost consistently struck down as unconstitutional numerous attempts by states to regulate business and industry. Conservatives thus looked to the Court as their last and best hope to thwart once again what they considered to be unjustified intrusions into the free market. In fact, well before the Court adjudicated any of the Roosevelt program, advocates for business, including former President Hoover, had begun to charge that the New Deal represented an unconstitutional abuse of national power.

Roosevelt and his administration knew from the outset that their bold initiatives would sooner or later face judicial challenge. In January 1935, an unyielding Supreme Court reviewed its first piece of New Deal legislation, declaring section 9(c) of the NIRA an illegitimate delegation of legislative power to the executive. Over the next sixteen months, the Court rejected almost every New Deal provision it considered, including the AGRICULTURAL ADJUSTMENT ACT, the Bituminous Coal Act, and the rest of the NIRA.

These numerous challenges to Roosevelt's authority emanated from a deeply divided Court. Justices Louis D. Brandeis, Harlan F. Stone, and Benjamin N. Cardozo generally voted to uphold New Deal policies, while the conservative "Four Horsemen" (Justices Willis Van Devanter, James C. McReynolds, George Sutherland, and Pierce Butler) almost universally opposed them. In the middle were Justice Owen J. Roberts and Chief Justice CHARLES EVANS HUGHES, who more often than not sided with Roosevelt's opponents. Some New Deal measures were so controversial and unprecedented, however, such as the NIRA's codes of fair competition, that the polarized wings of the Court united to reject them unanimously.

As Roosevelt approached the election of 1936 with his policies consistently being struck down, he seemed resolved to force a confrontation. Despite the Court's repeated rebuffs, Roosevelt forged ahead, submitting and gaining Congress's approval of new legislation that seemingly defied the Justices' rulings. Roosevelt even counseled legislative leaders to enact his proposals regardless of doubts they might have about their constitutionality. Such actions elicited charges during the 1936 campaign that the President favored disregarding the Constitution. But with the Republicans largely confined to attacking New Deal initiatives and unable to offer any positive program of their own, Roosevelt won the election by a landslide.

With this huge reelection mandate, and no sign yet of his first Supreme Court appointment, Roosevelt announced on 5 February 1937, a plan to reorganize the federal judiciary. The centerpiece of his proposed bill was a provision that allowed the President to appoint one judge to sit on the same court for every federal judge who, having served at least ten years, refused to retire within six months after reaching his seventieth birthday. The plan set the Supreme Court's maximum size at fifteen, and allowed up to fifty new judges to be appointed nationwide.

Roosevelt's purported justification for the plan was disingenuous at best. He claimed that the courts were overburdened due to insufficient personnel, and that aging jurists were unable to evaluate competently the social problems of a younger generation. Chief Justice Hughes was so disturbed at these patently false allegations that, at the urging of the even more-incensed Justice Brandeis (at eighty-one the oldest and yet most liberal member of the Court), Hughes wrote a letter to the influential Senator Burton K. Wheeler (D-Mont.) convincingly demonstrating that the Court had no problems handling its caseload. Roosevelt's actual motivation was clear to all: he hoped to gain control over a consistently hostile Supreme Court, and the terms of his plan would have conveniently allowed him to appoint to it six new Justices.

Despite Roosevelt's sweeping reelection victory, and although his proposal was clearly constitutional, given Congress's power to set the size of all federal courts, opposition emerged immediately from diverse sources. Conservatives saw the proposed bill as only the most recent and blatant example in a series of attempts to subvert the Constitution, but even liberals sympathetic to the New Deal were uncomfortable with what was widely viewed as a dangerous assault on the Court. Citizens across the political spectrum held what has proved to be an enduring impression of the Court as above politics, almost sacred, and Roosevelt's bold move threatened to shatter that image.

The Democratic majority in the Senate soon split over the plan, with Wheeler among those leading the opposition. But two other factors were even more important in sealing the fate of the proposal. Within one month after Roosevelt's announcement, the Supreme Court began to uphold, in a series of cases, major pieces of both state and federal regulatory legislation. This "switch in time that saved nine" materialized due to the changed positions of Justice Roberts and Chief Justice Hughes, who began to side with the Court's liberal wing. In addition, with the threatening plan pending in Congress, Justice Van Devanter resigned in May 1937, assuring Roosevelt his first appointment to the Court. The political urgency for Roosevelt's proposal thus dissipated, and the Senate finally rejected the bill on 22 July by a vote of 70 to 20. The legitimacy of the Court had been preserved, but the accompanying social forces ushered in an unprecedented era of constitutional law in which the federal government was granted nearly absolute discretion over economic regulation.

BIBLIOGRAPHY

Alsop, Joseph, and Turner Catledge. *The 168 Days*. 1938.
Baker, Liva. *Back to Back: The Duel between FDR and the Supreme Court*. 1967.
Brant, Irving. *Storm over the Constitution*. 1936.
Corwin, Edward S. *Constitutional Revolution, Ltd.*. 1941.
Jackson, Robert H. *The Struggle for Judicial Supremacy*. 1941.
Pearson, Drew, and Robert S. Allen. *The Nine Old Men*. 1936.
Pusey, Thomas R. *The Supreme Court Crisis*. 1937.
U.S. Senate, Committee on the Judiciary. *Reorganization of the Federal Judiciary*. 75th Cong., 1st sess. 1937.

HENRY J. ABRAHAM

COVERT OPERATIONS. Covert operations are activities conducted in support of national foreign-policy objectives abroad which are planned and executed so that the role of the United States government is not apparent or acknowledged publicly. Such activities are distinguished from the collection and production of intelligence in that they are designed to influence the actions of foreign governments. Covert operations cover a broad spectrum of activities in foreign countries and include propaganda, providing political advice to foreign persons or organizations, financial support and assistance to foreign political parties, and conducting paramilitary operations designed to overthrow or support a foreign government.

United States policymakers and scholars have engaged in an ongoing dialogue for several decades about the proper role of covert operations in a democratic society. In 1974, and again in 1986, the public disclosure of major covert operations—the former against the democratically elected government of Chile and the latter involving what became known as the IRAN-CONTRA AFFAIR—led to important congressional investigations questioning whether these operations were appropriate or lawful, and whether Con-gress should exercise more supervision over presidentially authorized covert operations.

Historical Overview. The practice of presidential use of secret agents (also called PRIVATE ENVOYS) to accomplish foreign-policy objectives abroad dates back to the founding of the Republic. President George Washington maintained a pool of agents whose activities remained secret and were paid for by a secret contingency fund authorized by Congress. President James Madison secretly sent Joel Poinsett to South America. Upon his arrival in Chile, Poinsett broadly construed his instructions to include actively aiding the revolutionary leaders of Argentina and Chile in their revolt against Spain. American agents were covertly utilized to help wrest Florida from Spanish control in the early 1800s and again to foment the Texan revolt from Mexico in the 1830s. However, these early covert activities were small and generally carefully circumscribed.

The onset of the COLD WAR in the 1940s and 1950s brought a dramatic increase and change in the role of covert operations in U.S. foreign policy. Cold war ideology led U.S. policymakers to turn to covert action as an important means of influencing foreign events. A 1954 high-level governmental report expressed the underlying philosophy that

> we are facing an implacable enemy whose avowed objective is world domination by whatever means and at whatever cost. There are no rules in such a game. Hitherto acceptable norms of human conduct do not apply. . . . We must learn to subvert, sabotage and destroy our enemies by more clear, sophisticated and more effective methods than those used against us.

Covert action was one of those "more sophisticated methods."

This perception of crisis abroad led to the view that traditional SEPARATION OF POWERS principles had to yield to strong EXECUTIVE POWER. Presidential initiation of covert operations without any constitutional check provided by Congress was justified by many as necessary to maintain United States preeminence in the world.

In July 1947, the NATIONAL SECURITY ACT established the CENTRAL INTELLIGENCE AGENCY (CIA). While the act nowhere explicitly authorized covert operations, the executive has interpreted the act as implicitly authorizing the CIA to engage in such activities. In June 1948, the NATIONAL SECURITY COUNCIL approved a document (NSC 10/2) that allowed the CIA to undertake propaganda, economic warfare, and direct action including sabotage and subversion against hostile states.

There are different kinds of covert operations. One prominent form is known as *political action programs*.

Beginning in the late 1940s the United States gave considerable covert aid to the Italian and French Christian Democratic parties, and in the 1960s and 1970s provided aid to political parties in Chile opposed to Salvador Allende. The United States has also secretly provided funds to friendly politicians, bureaucrats, and labor unions in such countries as Jordan, Greece, the Federal Republic of Germany, Egypt, Sudan, Suriname, Mauritius, the Philippines, Iran, and Ecuador. Closely related to covert political actions are *propaganda operations* such as Radio Free Europe and Radio Liberty, which until the 1970s were run covertly by the CIA. The CIA has also initiated covert *economic destabilization efforts*, such as that utilized against the Allende government in Chile, which seek to create popular discontent within the target country. Experts surmise that about one-third of all covert actions conducted by the United States since World War II have been political operations, almost 40 percent have been propaganda campaigns, 10 percent economic destabilization efforts, and 20 percent paramilitary operations.

Probably the most controversial form of covert action involves paramilitary operations. In 1953 the CIA engineered the forcible overthrow of the Iranian prime minister, Mohammed Mossadeq, and the next year the downfall of the democratically elected Arbenz government in Guatemala. Between 1953 and 1973, the CIA used paramilitary troops in at least eight major efforts against foreign governments.

By the late 1960s, the CIA had hundreds of covert operations underway consuming over half of the agency's budget. The end of the Vietnam War and the public exposure and criticism of such dubious CIA operations as aiding the overthrow of the Allende government and plotting to assassinate Castro and other foreign leaders led to severe cutbacks in covert operations. By 1978 only 5 percent of the intelligence budget was allotted to such operations.

The Reagan years witnessed a dramatic expansion of covert operations. Under President Ronald Reagan, the CIA mounted major paramilitary operations in Nicaragua, Afghanistan, Cambodia, and Angola. Budgetary allocations for covert operations increased significantly over mid-1970s levels. These activities were a key component of Reagan's effort not merely to contain, but to roll back communism around the world.

Statutory Framework. Throughout the 1950s and 1960s, Congress provided virtually no oversight over the CIA's covert operations. With the cold war at its height Congress was willing to give the President unfettered discretion in conducting clandestine oper-

ations. Most members of Congress preferred, in the words of one Representative, "deliberate ignorance."

The public allegations of CIA wrongdoing in the early 1970s, coupled with the reassertion of congressional powers in the aftermath of the Vietnam War led to increased congressional attention on the CIA's covert activities. In December 1974, Congress enacted an amendment (the Hughes-Ryan Act) to the Foreign Assistance Act, which provided for the first time, congressional oversight by prohibiting the expenditure of funds for CIA covert operations:"unless and until the President finds that such operation is important to the national security of the United States and reports, in a timely fashion, a description and scope of such operation to the appropriate committees of Congress." The President could engage in covert operations without congressional approval, but only if he made the required Presidential finding and reported those actions to Congress in a timely fashion.

The widespread perception that the CIA was, in Senator Frank Church's words, "a rogue elephant on the rampage," also led to the establishment of Senate and House Special Committees to investigate intelligence activities. The Church Committee (Senate), chaired by Frank Church, recommended adopting an intelligence charter to ensure legislative control, publishing the overall intelligence budget figure, prohibiting all efforts to subvert democratic governments, and creating a permanent Senate Committee on Intelligence. The Pike Committee (House) proposed even stronger solutions such as prohibiting CIA paramilitary operations altogether except in time of war.

Congress also began to exercise its budgetary powers to prohibit specific covert operations when in 1975 it barred the expenditure of funds to covertly assist anticommunist guerrillas in Angola. In 1976 and 1977 the Senate and House acted to establish permanent intelligence oversight committees.

The Senate Committee on Intelligence drafted an elaborate charter for the intelligence community in 1978, which contained a detailed regulatory structure for covert operations, including prohibitions on the assassination of foreign leaders. Administration officials objected to the bill as too restrictive, other critics complained it was too permissive, and the new charter failed to pass the Senate. Instead, Congress enacted the short Intelligence Oversight Act of 1980 that required the President generally to give prior notification of any anticipated covert actions.

This oversight regime was tested during the Reagan escalation of covert operations, that actually began in the waning years of the Carter administration. In 1984, the Senate Intelligence Committee accused the

CIA of failing to notify it adequately about the covert mining of Nicaraguan harbors. In 1987, the Iran-contra affair raised questions of whether the Reagan administration had complied with the Intelligence Oversight Act and the BOLAND AMENDMENT, which had prohibited the CIA, the Defense Department, or any other agency or entity of the United States involved in intelligence activities from spending funds in fiscal year 1985 to support paramilitary activities in Nicaragua.

The majority report of the special congressional committees investigating the Iran-contra affair argued that the covert arms sales to Iran violated the spirit and letter of the notification provisions of the oversight act in that neither prior nor even subsequent notice in a "timely fashion" was provided the committees. The majority criticized the President's failure to authorize beforehand in writing the sale of arms to Iran and diversion of funds to the Nicaraguan Contras. The report also challenged the use of the National Security Council (NSC) to evade the Boland Amendment's restrictions on the CIA, finding that when the NSC began to engage in covert activities, it fell within the Boland Amendment's prohibitions. The minority report contested the majority's conclusions on each of these issues.

In the aftermath of the Iran-contra affair, a host of congressional initiatives sought to reform the oversight regime to provide for a definite period of time within which the President must report all covert actions to the congressional committees, to prohibit covert tactics that are inconsistent with the publicly avowed foreign policy of the United States (as in the Iranian case), and to provide mandatory penalties for deceiving Congress. Ultimately, as in the 1970s, none of the broader changes were enacted. Instead, the Intelligence Authorization Act for fiscal 1991 made certain clarifications in the definition of covert operations and codified certain procedures that had been agreed upon by Congress and the President for reporting covert operations.

Covert Action and the Constitution. Covert operations raise serious legal and moral problems. Democratic governance under the Constitution requires executive accountability, public debate of important policy matters, and a balancing of legislative and executive power. Covert actions collide with these principles. Moreover, to intervene secretly in another nation's internal affairs often violates international law and morality and questions our acceptance of a just and democratic world order.

The ethical and political problems posed by covert operations have led some to question their utility altogether. Former Attorney General NICHOLAS deB.

KATZENBACH called for the abandonment of all covert operations, stressing that the need for open, public debate in deciding important issues of foreign policy outweighed any potential advantages gained by executive use of covert operations. George Kennan argued that covert action does not accord with the character or traditions of this country while former State Department official George Ball suggested that generally we ought not fight secret wars or "initiate most covert actions." Morton Halperin, an official of the American Civil Liberties Union, was less equivocal: because secrecy is inimical to the democratic process, "the United States should not conduct covert action."

Some American policymakers believe, however, that covert action ought to remain one of the executive's foreign-policy options. They argue that certain covert operations have been successful, and that covert action presents a middle option between diplomacy and open warfare. To them, covert operations are less intrusive than open military attack. As former Secretary of State and National Security Adviser HENRY KISSINGER once argued, CIA covert operations can "defend the American national interest in the gray areas where military operations are not suitable and diplomacy cannot operate."

For those who support covert operations in some situations, it is a question of deciding which activities the President should engage. For some, such as former Secretary of State Cyrus Vance, covert operations should only be used as a last resort, "when doing so was 'absolutely essential to the national security' of the United States, when no other means would do." Others would support a lower standard that would look more broadly at whether any particular activity furthers the national interest. Some scholars have focused strongly on how intrusive into the affairs of another country the activity would be, with assassination plots and major secret wars being the most suspect, and low-level funding of friendly groups abroad an example of a relatively unobtrusive activity.

Covert operations have also engendered strong debate on the constitutional division and sharing of power between Congress and the executive. Post-WORLD WAR II Presidents have relied upon the President's broad constitutional authority over foreign affairs to assert that the Constitution limits congressional authority to restrain the President from initiating covert operations. The Carter, Reagan, and Bush administrations all claimed that an absolute requirement of prior notification, or even notification "within several days" of a covert operation would, as President George Bush claimed when he killed the Intelligence Authorization Act of 1991 by POCKET VETO, "unconstitutionally infringe on the authority of the President."

Bush also claimed that regulating requests by the U.S. government to a foreign government or citizen to conduct covert actions abroad would unconstitutionally "regulate diplomacy by the President."

Congress's constitutional understanding of covert operations is based on the notion of shared power over foreign affairs. Accordingly, Congress has responsibility to oversee, if not approve, covert operations. Notification to the congressional committees is crucial for Congress to perform its constitutional role. Moreover, if Congress disagrees with a planned covert operation, it may exercise its budgetary powers to prohibit the expenditure of funds on certain activities, as was done with respect to Angola in the mid 1970s and Nicaragua in the mid 1980s.

Paramilitary covert operations appear to raise even more substantial constitutional questions, especially regarding Article I of the Constitution and the delegation of war powers. Secret wars, like public wars, ought to be approved by Congress. Major paramilitary actions cannot remain secret for long—as the broad public exposure of the Nicaraguan, Afghanistani, Angolan, and Cambodian operations in the 1980s demonstrated. These operations are not a secret from the enemy; their "covertness" only precludes the American public's ability to debate openly the policy.

Thus far, Congress has not been willing to treat covert warfare as akin to overt warfare requiring congressional approval and not merely notification. An effort by Senator Thomas Eagleton to bring CIA paramilitary operations within the scope of the WAR POWERS RESOLUTION of 1973 was rejected by the Senate, primarily for procedural reasons. While it has been argued and accepted by a federal district court in California that the Neutrality Act (1794) prohibits certain covert paramilitary activities unless authorized by Congress, thus far Congress has not asserted its constitutional war powers to require prior congressional authorization of paramilitary action and not merely notification.

The end of the cold war has removed one of the major rationales for the growth of presidential covert operations: the Soviet Union. While new threats and enemies will no doubt arise to replace the Soviet Union, the all-encompassing obsession that led American officials to justify authorizing secret operations that utilized dubious methods is no longer with us.

BIBLIOGRAPHY

Johnson, Loch K. *America's Secret Power: The CIA in a Democratic Society.* 1989.
Prados, John. *Presidents' Secret Wars: CIA and Pentagon Covert Operations Since World War II.* 1986.
Reisman, W. Michael, and James Baker. *Regulating Covert Action: Practices, Contexts, and Policies of Covert Coercion Abroad in International and American Law.* 1992.
Treverton, Gregory. *Covert Action: The Limits of Intervention in the Postwar World.* 1987.

JULES LOBEL

COX, JAMES M. (1870–1957), governor of Ohio, Representative, Democratic presidential nominee in 1920. Born in rural Ohio, James Middleton Cox came to politics after a career in journalism. Prior to his election to the United States House of Representatives in 1908 Cox built and operated a small chain of newspapers in Ohio. Senator Warren G. Harding, the victor in 1920 also had worked as a journalist, editing a small town newspaper in Marion, Ohio, before turning to politics. The election of 1920 harkened back to the nineteenth century, when journalists often sought political office.

Cox was a three-term governor of Ohio (1913–1914; 1917–1920). Able to win reelection in 1918 when Democrats all over the country were going down to defeat, Cox emerged as a viable candidate for President in 1920. At the deadlocked San Francisco convention, he won the nomination on the forty-fourth ballot with the support of a coalition of urban-industrial delegations from the Northeast and the Midwest and with the second-choice pledges of many delegates who favored other candidates. Since Cox was not associated with the Wilson administration, he chose Assistant Secretary of the Navy Franklin Delano Roosevelt of New York as his vice presidential running mate.

The campaign rhetoric in 1920 came down to the issue of whether the United States should return to "normalcy" as Harding advocated or whether the federal government should play an activist role and shape the postwar reconstruction as Cox proposed. Cox used the language of the liberal-conservative model to describe American politics. Characterizing himself as a progressive and his opponent as a reactionary conservative, Cox promised rational change. He defined Republican Warren G. Harding as the candidate of a small senatorial cabal who sought to turn the country over to wealthy special interests. Convinced that domestic policy and foreign affairs could not be separated, he viewed the LEAGUE OF NATIONS as an extension of progressivism into world affairs. He believed U.S. participation in the League was the surest way to end "world anarchism." Nevertheless, during the early stages of the campaign Cox emphasized domestic issues. With the economy in turmoil as the wartime boom turned to bust and un-employment mounted, Cox proposed changes in the tax structure to ease the transition to a peacetime economy. He called for the end of the excess profits tax and proposed to replace it with a "one or one-and-a-half percent" value added tax similar to one then being introduced in western Europe. The tax cut would curb inflation and promote economic growth. To defuse the social and political unrest permeating much of the nation, Cox proposed labor-management relations legislation to facilitate orderly collective bar-gaining between representatives of capital and labor. On the PROHIBITION issue, although he was perceived as a "wet," Cox pledged to enforce the law. In an effort to counteract the hostility among immigrant groups, which the wartime social-control policies and the post-war PALMER RAIDS engendered toward the Democrats, Cox called for expanded Americanization programs and appealed to immigrant groups for loyalty to the United States.

While Harding ran a front-porch campaign, Cox took his message to the people. Visiting thirty-six states he traveled twenty-two thousand miles and delivered 394 speeches to an estimated two million people. As he crisscrossed the country, the Ohio Democrat tailored his message to his audiences by focusing upon regional concerns. But his program failed to capture wide-spread support. Unable to raise sufficient campaign money, by the end of September there was serious talk of closing campaign headquarters in New York. Lead-ing Wilsonians believed Cox erred by not emphasizing the League of Nations issue.

Despite Cox's energetic and tireless campaign the Democrats suffered an overwhelming defeat in 1920. Warren G. Harding received 16,181,289 popular votes to 9,141,750 for Cox, while the Socialist EUGENE V. DEBS garnered 902,310 votes even though he was a prisoner in a federal penitentiary. The Wilson coali-tion created in 1916 could not contain the postwar resentments. In an election with a 54 percent turnout many voters simply stayed home. Others returned to traditional loyalties as the Republicans maintained their dominance in the Northeast, Midwest and the West, and regained dominance in California and Ohio, two traditionally Republican states they had lost in 1916. In addition the Republicans cut into the solid Democratic South by carrying Tennessee. Analyzing the result Cox concluded that "The war brought so many reactions that the landslide was inevitable." As an elder statesman Cox continued to play a role in Democratic Party politics. He published his memoir *Journey through My Years* in 1946. Cox died of heart failure on 15 July 1957 in Dayton, Ohio.

BIBLIOGRAPHY

Bagby, Wesley M. *The Road to Normalcy: The Presidential Campaign and Election of 1920.* 1962.

Cebula, James E. *James M. Cox: Journalist and Politician.* 1985.

JAMES E. CEBULA

COXEY'S ARMY. Emerging from the depression of the early 1890s, Coxey's Army became one of the most visible antipoverty protest movements of the late Gilded Age. Jacob Sechler Coxey, of Massillon, Ohio, and Carl Browne attracted several thousands of ad-herents nationwide, particularly from the West.

Coxey, the intellectual leader of the movement, advocated a massive federal program of road con-struction to employ the jobless.

Beginning on Easter Sunday, 1894, in Massillon, Ohio, with nearly five hundred men, Coxey and Browne set out for Washington, D.C., on their "Petitions in boots." Arriving in late April amidst much national attention, Coxey planned to give a May Day address at the Capitol. President Grover Cleveland and Attorney General RICHARD OLNEY, apprehensive about this "crank army," had already prepared to constrain Coxey: undercover SECRET SERVICE men had traveled with him from Ohio; and Cleveland had placed the U.S. Army on alert in Washington. As Coxey walked up the steps of the Capitol, he was arrested for disor-derly conduct.

Followers of Coxey came from Los Angeles and San Francisco and attempted to travel free on the railroads to Washington. Olney responded by using a court injunction against the armies. Taking his constitu-tional authority from the interstate commerce clause, he maintained that the U.S. mails must continue and, therefore, the disruptions of the rails by Coxey's fol-lowers must desist. United States marshals and the army, under federal court injunction, forcibly re-moved Coxeyites, often acting in concert with railroad management. Olney applied the same labor injunction against the American Railroad Union in the PULLMAN STRIKE. The Supreme Court upheld the injunction's use in IN RE DEBS.

Coxey's direct action protest movement was a polit-ical failure. The Cleveland administration refused to listen to his relief plans, believing his armies to be a danger to property rights.

BIBLIOGRAPHY

McMurry, Donald, *Coxey's Army: A Study of the Industrial Army Move-ment of 1894.* 1929.

Schwantes, Carlos. *Coxey's Army: An American Odyssey.* 1985.

JOHN F. WALSH

CRAWFORD, WILLIAM H. (1772–1834), judge, Senator, minister to France, Secretary of War, Secretary of the Treasury, presidential candidate in 1824. Born in Nelson County, Virginia, Crawford emigrated with his parents to South Carolina and then to Georgia, where he became a successful planter. He taught school, studied the law and was admitted to the bar. He won election to the state legislature in 1803 and in 1807 was elected to fill a vacancy in the U.S. Senate.

A conservative in his politics and admired by other congressmen on account of his affability, good humor, and intelligence, Crawford resigned his seat to become the U.S. minister to France during the WAR OF 1812, although he did not distinguish himself as minister and returned home when the war ended.

Appointed Secretary of War by President James Madison, Crawford served a year before agreeing to head the Treasury Department. He continued in that post for the next eight years. With an eye sharply focused on winning the presidency, he used the enormous Treasury patronage to build up a political organization committed to his elevation. His commitment to STATES' RIGHTS and budgetary limitations upon the federal government endeared him to the more conservative wing of the Democratic-Republican Party.

However, James Monroe, the Secretary of State, also wanted the presidency, and Crawford proved reluctant to challenge him. Monroe had a long record of public service and his position as Secretary of State placed him in line for the succession. Furthermore, he had the support of President Madison.

The usual nomination of a presidential candidate at this time fell to a congressional caucus, that is a meeting of all members of the same party who served in Congress. Because of his popularity and the support of many rising young Democratic-Republicans, Crawford might have won the caucus nomination if he had fought for it. But, fearful of splitting the party, convinced of Monroe's prior claims to the presidency, and wrongly supposing that he would have Monroe's support eight years later, he informed several supporters that he wished to withdraw from the contest. Even so, when the caucus met, fifty-four members cast their ballots for Crawford. Monroe, who received sixty-five votes and with it the nomination of the Democratic-Republican Party, won the presidency.

Crawford continued as Secretary of the Treasury in the Monroe administration, working assiduously to win the Republican caucus nomination. The steady decline of the FEDERALIST PARTY on the national level during this so-called ERA OF GOOD FEELINGS virtually guaranteed that whoever won that nomination would be elected President in 1824.

To Crawford's dismay, the election of 1824 attracted a host of candidates, including John Quincy Adams, the Secretary of State; HENRY CLAY, the Speaker of the House of Representatives; JOHN C. CALHOUN, the Secretary of War; and General Andrew Jackson, the hero of the Battle of New Orleans.

Unfortunately, in the fall of 1823, Crawford suffered what appears to have been a severe stroke. He was paralyzed, almost blind, and incapable of carrying out his responsibilities as Secretary of the Treasury, much less as President of the United States. Nonetheless, his fiercely loyal supporters called a congressional caucus on 14 February 1824 and cast sixty-four votes in his favor for the nomination. John Quincy Adams received two votes, and Jackson and Nathaniel Macon one each. A majority of Congressmen—some 261—refused to attend the meeting and criticized the method of nomination as undemocratic and outmoded.

The fall election ended with Crawford in third place in electoral votes. Adams became President when Clay threw his support to him.

Crawford refused Adams's invitation to continue as Secretary of the Treasury and retired to his home in Georgia. He was appointed by the governor of Georgia as a judge in the superior court of the northern circuit where he served until his death.

BIBLIOGRAPHY

Hopkins, James F. "Election of 1824." In vol. 1 of *History of American Presidential Elections, 1789–1968*. Edited by Arthur M. Schlesinger, Jr., and Fred Israel, 4 vols. 1970. Pp. 349–381.

Mooney, Chase. *William H. Crawford*. 1974.

Remini, Robert V. *Martin Van Buren and the Making of the Democratic Party*. 1959.

ROBERT V. REMINI

CREATION OF THE PRESIDENCY. The Presidency was, in every sense of the word, a creation of the CONSTITUTIONAL CONVENTION of 1787. Convention delegates regarded no other country's executive as a useful model on which to base their own. Nor have subsequent constitutional amendments fundamentally altered the character of the presidency. The delegates built virtually from scratch, but they built for the ages.

The presidency developed along two major lines during the course of the Constitutional Convention. First, the relatively unformed notions about the executive that most delegates had took on greater clarity and specificity. Second, the presidency grew stronger as an institution as the convention wore on. These two developments were made manifest in six specific areas of executive design: the *number* of the executive, the process of presidential *selection*, the President's *term*, procedures for presidential *removal* prior to the expiration of the term, the enumerated *powers* of the presidency, and the executive's *institutional separation* from Congress.

The Constitutional Convention. The Constitutional Convention that labored in Philadelphia from 25 May to 17 September 1787 can be described, in John Roche's phrase, as a "nationalist reform caucus," or a meeting of relatively like-minded political leaders whose purpose was to develop a plan of government that "would both bolster the 'National Interest' " by being strong but not oppressive, and "be acceptable to the people" who would have to ratify and live under it. Most of the convention's great battles were not about the power of the new government—that issue was largely settled in the first week when the delegates accepted James Madison's highly nationalistic Virginia Plan as their working draft—but rather about how power within that government should be allocated. More often than not, the issues in dispute lent themselves to compromise solutions: small states split the difference with large states and provided for a Congress with two differently apportioned houses, North and South worked out the three-fifths rule for counting the slave population, and so on.

But when it came to designing the executive, the convention labored in a realm of such intellectual and political uncertainty as to render the politics of compromise largely irrelevant. Few delegates had any clear ideas about what a strong but nonoppressive executive would be; the British king and his colonial governors, whom Americans had lived under as colonists until 1776, had seemed to most delegates to be tramplers of liberty. Almost all the state constitutions written after independence provided for unthreatening governors but also rendered them weak to the point of impotence. The national government of the Articles of Confederation, such as it was, had no executive at all. Although the New York governorship seemed to offer a model of strong but safe executive power, its influence was slow to take hold at the convention, in part because New York's delegates were absent during most of the convention.

Nor was it clear what the public would accept. On the one hand, Americans were strongly opposed to monarchy, on the other, many Americans longed to make George Washington king. As Seymour Martin Lipset has shown, Washington was a classic example of what the German sociologist Max Weber called a charismatic leader, someone whom the people "treated as endowed with supernatural, superhuman, or at least specifically exceptional powers or qualities." But the popular longing for Washington, who was appalled by such antirepublican adulation, was just that: a longing for Washington, not for a hereditary monarchy.

The lessons that the delegates drew from their observations and experiences differed widely. To Roger Sherman of Connecticut, history taught that the best national executive would be "nothing more than an institution for carrying the will of the legislature." ALEXANDER HAMILTON of New York wanted a powerful "Governour" selected for life by "electors chosen by the people." Some other delegates had ideas of their own; most had no firm ideas at all. But as their ready acceptance of the Virginia Plan shows, with its provision for a one-term executive chosen by the legislature, a plurality of delegates began the convention as "congressionalists." They were ready for strong national government, but only if it was dominated by the legislature.

As the convention proceeded, many delegates' minds slowly changed, influenced by the powerful arguments and political shrewdness of "presidentialists" such as GOUVERNEUR MORRIS and, especially, JAMES WILSON, both of Pennsylvania. Tentative decisions made in the early summer months of the convention concerning number, selection, term, removal, and powers were revised in August and September in ways that made the presidency ever stronger.

Number. Madison's Virginia Plan left unresolved the issue of whether the executive would be single (an individual) or plural (a committee). The practical wisdom of his decision became clear after the convention began its work by reconstituting itself as a Committee of the Whole to tinker with the plan. When Wilson moved that "the Executive consist of a single person," Virginia's EDMUND RANDOLPH instantly rose to argue for a three-person executive on the grounds that a single executive would constitute "the foetus of monarchy." Others offered equally dire predictions. But on 4 June the convention accepted Wilson's defense of "a single magistrate, as giving most energy, dispatch, and responsibility to the office" and passed his motion. The delegates resisted Wilson's recommendations concerning number only when he urged them to add to the single executive the Virginia Plan's proposed Council of Revision, a committee of judges with which the executive would share the decision to veto legislation and which consequently would help to legitimize such decisions and buttress executive power. Proposals for a council—some intended to weaken, others to strengthen, the executive—surfaced frequently, but none attached a majority.

Wilson's list of purported single-executive virtues—energy, dispatch, and responsibility—demonstrated the political shrewdness that he, Morris, and their allies displayed throughout the convention. Their own desire was for as powerful an executive as possible, within the bounds of republican government. But realizing that they held a minority position in the convention, the presidentialist delegates advanced their ideas in terms that reluctant colleagues might accept. Responsibility for corrupt or incompetent actions could be assigned to a single executive, Wilson noted; not so with a plural executive, in which each member could blame the others. As for energy and dispatch, Wilson's arguments spoke in part to the widespread concern of the delegates—most of them personally prosperous—that the new government be able to protect their property in the event of an insurrection. In 1786, Shays' Rebellion and the national government's inability to end it had alarmed Washington and many others. A single executive, Wilson argued, could act quickly and decisively to protect property in such situations; a committee could not.

Selection. The convention's decisions concerning executive selection were influenced by the political shrewdness of the presidentialists. In June, July, and again in August, the delegates reaffirmed Madison's initial proposal for selection of the executive by the legislature. Wilson and Morris regarded this provision as a serious problem: a President who owed the job to Congress, they believed, would be subordinate to it. Their efforts to enact "election by the people at large" were unavailing. George Mason of Virginia, for example, scoffed that to allow the people to choose the President would be to "refer a trial of colours to a blind man." Failing direct election, the presidentialists still wanted to secure a provision for selection that would give the President an independent national constituency.

As it happened, two other developments at the convention—one political, the other philosophical—furthered their cause. The political event occurred on 24 August, when the delegates defined legislative selection to mean that the House of Representatives and the Senate would vote jointly for President, with each member of Congress having one vote. This convinced the small-state delegates that their interests would be ignored. Their own plan for a concurrent vote of the two houses, of course, would have alienated the large-state delegates if it had been passed.

The philosophical change was more gradual. Virtually every convention vote in favor of legislative selection of the President had been accompanied by a vote for a one-term limit. The delegates' assumption was that a President eligible for reelection would improperly trade favors for votes in Congress. But, some delegates began to argue, the President would have little incentive for excellence in office if there was no hope for another term. Their reasoning, in combination with the small-states' defection from legislative selection, eventually carried the convention.

The task then became to develop a nonlegislative method of selection that would neither invite corruption nor alienate any part of the country. The people, the state governors or legislatures, and even a randomly-chosen group of national legislators all had their champions, but the only widely acceptable solution—the ELECTORAL COLLEGE—was not provided to the weary delegates until the Committee on Postponed Matters reported on 4 September.

The Electoral College entrusted presidential selection to a group of electors chosen by their states by whatever methods the various states provided. The presumption was that most states would entrust the choice of electors to the voters. Each state received electoral votes equal to the number of its senators (two) and representatives (different according to population) in Congress. The convention enacted the plan swiftly. After months of struggle, Wilson and his allies had won all that they had wanted short of direct popular election. The presidency would have an electoral base all its own, the only office in the new government with a truly national constituency.

Interestingly, many delegates who still favored legislative selection went along with the Electoral College. One reason was that the committee had spun off supplementary proposals to prevent voters from selecting as President anyone younger than thirty-five, fewer than "fourteen Years a Resident within the United States," or not a "natural born Citizen." The age requirement would limit the choice to those old enough to have proven character and ability. The apparent xenophobia of the residency and citizenship requirements was meant to prevent rash popular choices of celebrated foreigners, such as the revolutionary war hero Baron von Steuben of Prussia.

A more important reason that legislative-selection proponents suffered defeat gladly on the Electoral College was that many thought they had actually won a victory. Their assurance was based on the committee proposal's provision that if no candidate received a majority of electoral votes, the House, voting by state, would elect the President from among the highest vote getters. Mason guessed that, in practice, the House would end up choosing the President "nineteen times in twenty."

One residue of the plan for an Electoral College was

the vice presidency. To dilute favorite-son voting by electors, the convention had accepted the committee's proposal to award each elector two votes for President and require that one of them be cast for a candidate from a different state. The candidate with the greatest number of votes, assuming it was a majority, would be President; to assure that electors would not throw away their second vote for tactical reasons, the runner-up would be VICE PRESIDENT. By creating this office, the convention also settled the question of who would act as President if the President died, resigned, was impeached and removed, or became disabled: the Vice President replaced the leader of the Senate in this role. However, the only ongoing constitutional task that was assigned to the Vice President was trivial—to preside over the Senate, not voting except to break ties—and the reason for allowing even that power seems to have been the one offered by Sherman: without it the Vice President "would be without employment."

Neither Mason nor the inventors of the Electoral College anticipated the early rise of a two-party system in which each party nominated candidates for President and Vice President. One advantage of the two-party system was that it greatly increased the likelihood that one party would win a majority of electoral votes. A disadvantage was that it upset the presumption that electors would be choosing exclusively among candidates for President. The TWELFTH AMENDMENT, which was adopted in 1804, redefined the electors' role by requiring that instead of casting two votes for President, they would each vote for one presidential and one vice presidential candidate.

Term. Questions of term, reeligibility, and method of selection were interwoven in the minds of the delegates [see TERM AND TENURE]. Underlying the complexity, however, was a basic choice: Which did the delegates care about more, legislative selection of the President or eligibility for reelection? As Max Farrand summed up the issue:

> If the executive were to be chosen by the legislature, he must not be eligible for reelection lest he should court the favor of the legislature in order to secure for himself another term. Accordingly the single term of office should be long. But the possibility of reelection was regarded as the best incentive to faithful performance of duty, and if a short term and reeligibility were accepted, the choice by the legislature was inadvisable.

Because, during most of the convention, legislative selection was favored by the majority of delegates, so was a long single term. Later, when the relative virtues of reeligibility rose in the delegates' esteem, they shortened the term and changed the mode of election to the electoral college. At various times, proposals for terms of three, six, seven, eight, eleven, fifteen, and twenty years were offered, along with Hamilton's idea for tenure "during good behavior." Four years eventually was accepted as being neither too long nor too short. In 1792, by law, the beginning of the four-year term was established as the 4 March following the election; in 1933, the TWENTIETH AMENDMENT moved the date to 20 January.

Despite the delegates' intention that the President always be eligible for another election, an unwritten rule that no President should serve more than two terms was established by President Thomas Jefferson. The tradition lasted until 1940, when Franklin D. Roosevelt was elected to a third term. Two years after Roosevelt's death in 1945, after he had been elected to a fourth term in 1944, Congress approved the TWENTY-SECOND AMENDMENT, which limited Presidents to two terms. The amendment was ratified in 1951.

Removal. In establishing a term of fixed length for the President, the convention did not neglect to provide for the President's premature removal under extraordinary circumstances. One such circumstance—IMPEACHMENT—was considered carefully; the other, disability, was not.

Provisions for presidential impeachment were a part of the Constitution in all its working drafts. Although Morris initially claimed that impeachment would open the door to legislative encroachment, most presidentialists defended it by arguing that unless the Constitution included some method to remove a President who behaved badly, they would never be able to convince their fellow delegates to accept a strong presidency.

Throughout the convention, the delegates tinkered with both the mechanism and the grounds for impeachment. The mechanism grew ever more political, moving at successive stages of the convention from the Supreme Court alone to the Court and the House of Representatives, then finally to the House and Senate: the House to impeach—that is, to indict—and the Senate to try, with a two-thirds vote needed to convict and thus remove the President from office. Simultaneously, the grounds for impeachment grew less political and more legal. The Committee of the Whole had offered "malpractice or neglect of duty," a broad standard. This was replaced in one later vote by "treason, bribery, or corruption" and finally by "treason, bribery, or other High Crimes and Misdemeanors," an obscure term borrowed from English law. "Corruption," they held could be perverted to mean just about anything by a hostile Congress; "High Crimes and Misdemeanors," although not confined to criminal offenses, clearly referred only to serious abuses of power.

Although the convention considered impeachment carefully, it treated the matter of presidential disability sloppily. The Committee of Detail, appointed by the delegates in late July to write a draft of the Constitution, proposed language that was so vague as to be meaningless: "In case of his . . . disability to discharge the powers and duties of his office, the President of the Senate shall exercise those powers of his office, until another President of the United States be chosen, or until the disability of the President be removed." John Dickinson of Delaware rose on 20 August to ask, "What is the extent of the term 'disability', and who is to be the judge of it?" No one answered him. Indeed, the only serious change that the convention made in the Committee of Detail's disability provision was to make the Vice President the President of the Senate.

In 1967, Dickinson's question finally was answered by the enactment of the TWENTY-FIFTH AMENDMENT. The amendment created procedures that the President, Vice President, Cabinet, and Congress could follow when the issue of presidential disability arose.

Powers. The power of the presidency consists of a great deal more than the sum of the enumerated powers—COMMANDER IN CHIEF, receiver of ambassadors, and so on—that are listed in the Constitution. Number, selection, term, removal—these structural characteristics of the office also carry with them important implications for EXECUTIVE POWER.

The delegates, or at least the presidentialists among them, seem to have understood this well. Shortly after Madison's Virginia Plan was offered, Wilson made a countermotion pertaining to the executive. Madison's proposal was regarded as a plan for executive weakness, Wilson's as one that would make the executive equal or superior to the legislature. In truth, the two plans differed greatly in their provisions for how the executive should be structured. The Madisonian executive would have been elected by the legislature for a single term and perhaps have been plural in number; Wilson's single executive was to be eligible for continuing reelection by the people. When it came to the stated powers of the executive, however, Wilson virtually copied the provisions of the Virginia Plan: "a general authority to execute the National Laws": a veto, to be shared with a council of judges; and the rather insubstantial "Executive rights vested in Congress by the [Articles of] Confederation."

But this proposal by Wilson rested on his assumption that the powers of the legislature also would be loosely defined, thus creating a constitutional "free-fire zone" in which the two branches would contend for dominance in policy-making. The Committee of Detail, of which Wilson was a member, invalidated this assumption. Against Wilson's wishes, the committee decided to enumerate the powers of the legislature, which it christened "Congress." This decision altered the presidentialists' strategy: if powers were to be enumerated after all, the presidency (which also got its name from the committee) would suffer if it was not included.

In the end, the Committee of Detail gave the presidency its share of enumerated powers in both senses of the word. For example, if Congress was empowered to "make all Laws," the President could still report to it on "the State of the Union," recommend "such Measures as he shall judge necessary and expedient," convene Congress on "extraordinary Occasions," and veto the laws it passed, subject to override by two thirds of each legislative house. If Congress was charged "to make war"—later changed to "declare"—and "subdue a rebellion in any State," the President, nonetheless, was commander in chief of the army, navy, and militia that would actually do the warmaking and subduing. Congress was to create the EXECUTIVE DEPARTMENTS and appropriate their funds, but the President had the power to appoint executive officers.

The presidentialists' general satisfaction with the report of the Committee of Detail was tempered by their dislike of the preeminent role that the Senate was ordained to play both in foreign affairs (where it could "make treaties" and appoint ambassadors) and in the courts, whose judges the Senate was to appoint. In this concern they found common cause with large-state delegates, who felt that the committee had gone too far in its effort to accommodate the small states by excessively empowering "their" part of the government. In September the presidentialists helped the large-state delegates pry loose exclusive control of the TREATY-MAKING POWER and APPOINTMENT POWER from the Senate. The large-staters returned the favor by helping to turn initiative in the exercise of these powers over to the President.

Institutional Separation. The various decisions that blurred the powers of the President and Congress were preceded by related decisions, made at the outset of the Constitutional Convention and substantially unaltered, to keep inviolate the institutional boundary between the two branches. The main constitutional provision was clear: no member of Congress could simultaneously hold an executive office, and vice versa. In the same spirit, Congress could not raise or lower an incumbent President's salary. So was the reason for the provision: fear of corruption such as that the delegates had observed in Great Britain, which drew no such boundary between crown and

Parliament. Pierce Butler of South Carolina, for example, "appealed to the example of G.B. where men got into Parlt. that they might get offices for themselves or their friends" and where George III, to further his goals, "put some of [his opponents] out of the house of commons and made them lords."

The Constitutional Convention began its work knowing much about what it did not want in an executive (a too-strong king or an ineffectual figurehead) but knowing little about what it did want. The convention ended its labors by presenting the waiting American public with a one-person President; chosen by the entire country for a term that was, except in the most unusual circumstances, fixed in length and renewable; and as immersed with Congress in exercising the powers of the new national government as it was institutionally distinct. The constitutional presidency has been criticized over the years for many reasons, most of them (the presidency is too strong, the presidency is too weak) contradictory. On four occasions, it has been amended. More than anything, however, the constitutional presidency of 1787 has endured.

BIBLIOGRAPHY

Lipset, Seymour Martin. *The First New Nation.* 1963.

Milkis, Sidney M., and Michael Nelson. *The American Presidency: Origins and Developments, 1776–1990.* 1990.

Nelson, Michael, ed. *Historic Documents on Presidential Elections, 1787–1988.* 1991.

Nelson, Michael, ed. *Historic Documents on the Presidency, 1776–1989.* 1989.

The Records of the Federal Convention of 1787. Vols. 1–3. Edited by Max Farrand. 1913.

The Records of the Federal Convention of 1787. Vol. 4. Edited by James Hutson. 1987.

Roche, John P. "The Founding Fathers: A Reform Caucus in Action." *American Political Science Review* 55 (December 1961): 799–816.

Thach, Charles C., Jr. *The Creation of the Presidency, 1775–1789.* 1923.

MICHAEL NELSON

CRÉDIT MOBILIER SCANDAL. Crédit Mobilier remains the most notorious scandal of the nineteenth century, and the most misunderstood. It tarred the name of a Vice President, a future President, and several prominent Congressmen even though most Americans never grasped what the fuss was all about.

Crédit Mobilier of America was a construction company organized in 1864 to complete the Union Pacific Railroad. Its inner machinations—a byzantine mix of legitimate and dubious activities—led to several acrimonious lawsuits among its quarreling directors, who were locked in a struggle for control. In September 1872 Charles A. Dana of the New York *Sun*, a liberal Republican disillusioned with the Grant administration, seized upon some testimony given fifteen months earlier in one of these suits to launch a smear campaign in hopes of helping HORACE GREELEY defeat Grant.

Although Dana failed to prevent Grant's reelection, the charges he raised were lurid enough to trigger two congressional investigations. Congressman Oakes Ames of Massachusetts, who had long been a mainstay of the Union Pacific along with his brother Oliver, was accused of gaining support for the railroad in Congress by bribing members with shares of Crédit Mobilier stock. The alleged recipients included Vice President SCHUYLER COLFAX, House Speaker JAMES G. BLAINE, James A. Garfield, George Boutwell, and other prominent Republicans, but not a single Democrat. Ames and his friends were also suspected of raking in huge profits from the stock.

The hearings that followed gave rise to sensational revelations, wild distortions of fact, and a barrage of charges and countercharges. Oakes Ames admitted selling Crédit Mobilier stock to friends in Congress, but denied any wrongdoing. Many of those friends denied receiving any stock until Ames, in exasperation, showed the committee his notebook itemizing the transactions. The final committee reports demonstrated convincingly how little either body understood of what had transpired. One committee concluded that Oakes was guilty of offering bribes but that no one was guilty of accepting them.

The House rejected a recommendation that Oakes and another member, James Brooks, be expelled and settled instead on censuring them. Within two months both men died, broken in part by the ordeal. The political shadow of the scandal extended well into the next decade. It ruined the ambitious Colfax, who never again held office. While Garfield managed to gain the presidency, Blaine's bid was thwarted by several brushes with impropriety, of which Crédit Mobilier was one. The term itself lingered on as a popular catchword for other scandals, much as "Watergate" later did.

In retrospect, the original charges were wildly distorted and exaggerated, the facts of Crédit Mobilier badly mangled, and the real issues of wrongdoing largely overlooked. From its origins as a blatantly partisan political tool in a presidential campaign, Crédit Mobilier mushroomed into an enduring symbol of corruption in part because it appeared on the scene during the most corrupt administration yet to grace Washington.

BIBLIOGRAPHY

Klein, Maury. *Union Pacific: The Birth, 1862–1894.* 1989.

MAURY KLEIN

CRIME, POLICY ON. While public concern over crime and disorder is as old as the Republic, crime control was not a major concern of American Presidents or a subject of presidential politics throughout most of the nation's history. Law enforcement and criminal justice were regarded as local concerns and exclusively state and local government responsibilities until the twentieth century. For most of U.S. history the federal government did not have a general-jurisdiction police force or, until 1891, a prison system.

Political pressure for federal involvement in law and order dates from the 1920s. The national experiment with alcohol PROHIBITION created what many citizens regarded as a crime wave and also a nexus between the federal government and the crime problem. Presidents Calvin Coolidge and Herbert Hoover set important precedents when they appointed national crime commissions as a federal response to this public concern. A commission could deal broadly with questions of criminal justice without directly threatening any of the boundaries of responsibility associated with the federal system. Federal crime commissions have since been frequently appointed.

The victory of Franklin D. Roosevelt in 1932 generated growth in federal criminal justice activity and led to new federal responsibilities in crime-related areas. The FEDERAL BUREAU OF INVESTIGATION (FBI) and federal prison systems were launched in their modern forms. Gun control was added to drug control as a special federal government responsibility in crime control. However, the federal government remained responsible for only a small share of criminal justice activities; law and order as a political issue did not become an important part of presidential politics until 1964.

BARRY GOLDWATER'S 1964 campaign was the first to give law and order a central position, and the appeal of the issue was apparent from the beginning. The response of President Lyndon B. Johnson to the crime issue was eventually two-pronged. He appointed a Commission on Law Enforcement and the Administration of Criminal Justice to consider the entire field. Additional programs of federal technical and financial aid to local crime enforcement agencies were also launched in the wake of the 1964 campaign. The federal-aid program became the Law Enforcement Assistance Administration and was a prominent program from the late 1960s until the late 1970s. It was all

but discontinued in 1981, but financial- and technical-aid programs then appeared again in the late 1980s as part of the federal war on drugs [*see* DRUG POLICY].

The law-and-order issue has become a permanent feature in presidential politics since the 1960s so that no national PARTY PLATFORM can ignore the topic. Appeals to hard-line sentiment on crime and law enforcement were particularly prominent in the Nixon campaign in 1968, the THIRD PARTY candidacy of GEORGE WALLACE in 1972, and the 1988 campaign of George Bush.

But if the crime-control issue is a presidential candidate's dream, it is a President's nightmare. The federal government is only a 10 percent partner with the states and localities in direct crime control. This provides scant opportunities to address crime problems. But federal responses to crime have become a political necessity, resulting in four different types of federal involvement.

First, there is the commission of inquiry. The Commission on Law Enforcement and the Administration of Criminal Justice reported to President Johnson in 1967. It has been followed by commissions on standards and goals in criminal justice, on organized crime, on juvenile justice, on drunk driving, on drugs, and on pornography. The appeal of a commission is that it can urge policy change without spending money or encroaching on state and local governmental responsibilities.

Second, federal leadership in the federal criminal justice system can offer an example to state and local government by, for instance, proposing an expansion of crimes covered by the death penalty in federal law or the creation of new standards for federal prisons.

Third, federal financial and technical assistance can be given to state and local government. This is the Law Enforcement Assistance Administration model. Such a program is popular with those levels of government that receive the money. These programs can be put in place shortly after similar programs have been abolished, as was the case when state drug-control aid began shortly after special LEAA revenue sharing was ended in 1981.

Fourth, the political pressure of the crime issue may lead to proposals for the federal government to take primary responsibility for certain types of criminal justice policy. Two examples of subjects where larger federal responsibility is frequently sought are gun control and drug control. The federal prison system in 1986 had only 4 percent of all nondrug-offender prisoners in the United States, but had 30 percent of the nation's drug-offense prisoners.

Political ideology plays an important part in the

attitude of Presidents toward crime control, but not in the choice of organizational strategy for federal involvement. Conservatives favor hard-line ad hominem approaches to criminals but oppose impersonal strategies like gun control and the exclusionary rule, while liberals favor environmental and situational approaches to crime problems. But conservatives have been as likely to favor direct federal involvement in aspects of criminal justice in recent years as well as federal aid programs that were once considered the distinctive cachet of liberals. Crime policy programs are usually created in quick reaction to political pressure and are not usually either well crafted or well explained.

BIBLIOGRAPHY

Cronin, Thomas E., Tania Z. Cronin, and Michael E. Milakovitch. *United States v. Crime in the Streets.* 1981.
President's Commission on Law Enforcement and Criminal Justice. *The Challenge of Crime in a Free Society.* 1967.
Zimring, Franklin E., and Gordon Hawkins. *The Search for Rational Drug Control.* 1992.

FRANKLIN E. ZIMRING and GORDON HAWKINS

CRISIS MANAGEMENT. The word *crisis* is applied to a situation that occurs suddenly, heightens tensions, carries a high level of threat to a vital interest, provides only limited time for making decisions, and possesses an atmosphere of uncertainty. Crisis management involves both precrisis planning and the handling of the situation during a crisis.

In normal times, the CHECKS AND BALANCES of the U.S. political system can be quite formidable, severely limiting presidential initiatives. But in a political crisis, most of these checks evaporate, and the President is given wide discretionary leeway in the exercise of EXECUTIVE PREROGATIVE or EMERGENCY POWERS. While the Constitution contains no explicit provisions for government during a crisis, in an emergency a President can invoke emergency statutes or merely assume power and become the nation's crisis manager in chief (as did Abraham Lincoln in the CIVIL WAR, Franklin D. Roosevelt during the Great Depression, and John F. Kennedy during the CUBAN MISSILE CRISIS).

As Alexander George points out, "Optimal strategy for crisis management is extremely context-dependent. While all crises share some characteristics in common, the precise configuration of each crisis varies in ways that have different implications for the selection of an approach strategy. In consequence, there is no single dominant strategy that is equally suitable for managing every crisis" (*Avoiding War*, p. 378). But there are lessons to be derived from past crises, dos and don'ts that can help guide decision makers. Successful crisis management requires the President's capacity to manage crises, an effective process for making decisions, and policies for avoiding capitulation or war.

One of the most important features of crisis management relates to the personality of the President. In a crisis, everything is heightened: stress, intensity of feelings, sense of loss of control, and feelings of powerlessness. All these have an impact on the decision maker. Thus the President's personality, style, interaction with senior staff, manner of processing information, and way of thinking are of great importance. In crisis situations, the combination of uncertainty, high stakes, shortness of time, high levels of stress, lack of sleep, and so on make for intense pressure. These pressures may lead to a variety of dysfunctional forms of behavior. Some Presidents have tended to overpersonalize events (during the Cuban missile crisis, Kennedy is reported to have exclaimed, "How could he [Khrushchev] do this to *me*?"), often leading to inappropriate judgments and actions.

Given the shortness of time and the perceived need to respond quickly, Presidents may rush to judgment, acting without adequate information, making too-limited a review of options, or overreacting by seeing the adversary's actions as a personal challenge. Likewise, high levels of stress may cause fatigue and inhibit the ability of the President to make realistic judgments. While, at the early stages of a crisis, stress can heighten concentration, as time goes by stress inhibits performance and may lead to perceptual problems, exaggerated coping and defense mechanisms, fear, aggressiveness, cognitive processing problems, premature decision making, and rigidity. ROBERT F. KENNEDY noted the impact of prolonged stress on the members of the EXCOMM (Executive Committee) during the Cuban missile crisis: "For some there were only small changes, perhaps varieties of a single idea. For others, there were continuous changes of opinion each day; some, because of the pressures of events, even appeared to lose their judgment and stability."

During crises, Presidents tend to screen out information that does not fit their preconceptions: new information is often not processed or is fit into preexisting mental constructs, and outright misperception is likely, leading to decisional problems. As Secretary of State HENRY KISSINGER noted, "During fast moving events those at the center of decisions are overwhelmed by floods of reports compounded by conjecture, knowledge, hope and worry. . . . Only rarely does a coherent picture emerge; in a sense, coherence must be imposed on the events by the decision-maker."

During crises, Presidents are likely to feel powerless or victimized. They are likely to have an exaggerated view of the control an adversary has over events and to overestimate the adversary's hostility and capabilities. How a President copes with this wide range of pressures will vary based on personality factors, but the tendency of crises to evoke dysfunctional individual response is clearly powerful.

The characteristics of the decision-making process also play a significant role in managing crisis. Each President will choose a crisis-management structure with which he is comfortable (e.g., Kennedy and EX-COMM, George Bush and a small group of advisers), but it is clear that there are several potential structural hazards that may impair decision making during the fog of crisis. How a President organizes and interacts with top staff during a crisis matters greatly. The first presidential decision involves whom to bring into the inner decision circle. There are a wide range of options, but it is important that the President solicit a wide range of ideas and opinions, avoid yes-men or groupthink, and insist on the presence of a devil's advocate within the proximate decision-making structure.

Good decisions require good information that is properly presented and clearly understood. Given the time pressures in a crisis, such information is extremely difficult to come by. It is hard to check the validity of information, difficult to wait for more information, easy for bias and misperception to replace information. Quantity of information can easily overwhelm quality and may lead to information overload and decisional paralysis. Decisional processes are prone to several common errors: omission of alternatives, confusion regarding objectives, failure to assess risks, reliance on poor information, bias in processing information, failure to examine choices critically, and weakness in implementing and monitoring decisions.

While bureaucratic routines and roadblocks are reduced in a crisis, Presidents must still be cognizant of problems that may arise if the President's decisions are not fully implemented. No policy gets implemented automatically, and during a crisis it is especially important that the President's orders are clearly communicated and faithfully executed. Additionally, it is wise for a President to use senior civil servants as part of his core decision group because it is so important to maintain institutional memory in crisis situations. As Presidents are only temporary holders of power, an ability to tap the memory of people who were there during past crises can be especially useful.

It is vitally important to give the decision makers as much time as possible to make decisions. Therefore, Presidents must attempt to slow the pace of crises, creating pauses and giving both sides time to collect their thoughts. The perception that there is no time is one of the leading causes of misjudgments during crises.

In deciding which policy to pursue, a President must first assess the situation and threat facing the nation. What has happened? Does it threaten a vital or a secondary national interest? What can the President realistically hope to achieve and how can he best pursue his goals? As Presidents attempt to solve crises, there is a tendency for short-term needs to drive out long-term considerations. In their need to devise policies that avoid both war and U.S. capitulation, Presidents must always calibrate decisions against the likely response of an adversary. Crisis decisions are not made in a vacuum, and the President must therefore be sensitive to a variety of complex factors when developing crisis policies.

Given the complexity of crisis management, what steps should a President take to improve the quality of crisis decision-making? While there is no solution that applies to all cases, there are things a President can do to make sound decision-making more likely. First, Presidents must be aware of the traps a crisis may contain. Crises produce pathological responses against which Presidents must be on guard. President Kennedy, having read the historian Barbara Tuchman's book *The Guns of August* just prior to the Cuban missile crisis, was determined not to repeat the mistakes that led to WORLD WAR I.

Second, several precrisis steps can be taken. Good anticipation, prediction, and intelligence skills are required so that the country is not caught by surprise. Presidents and their top staff should study past crises, engage in simulations of crises, learn about negotiation, and become familiar with the crisis-control mechanisms of government.

While precrisis preparation is useful, once a crisis begins it is important to introduce pauses wherever possible to give leaders more time to think. Presidents must also limit their crisis means and objectives and avoid taking excessively threatening postures or making ultimatums. Presidents must also engage in other-shoes exercises, seeing the crisis from the adversary's perspective, and must always give the adversary a "golden road" to retreat on, never sealing off the escape route but offering opportunities to disengage. Also, Presidents must be ever cautious about information received, options discussed, and decisions made. It is vital for a President to view every assumption, every piece of information, and every bit of advice with skepticism. Presidents must also keep all lines of communication with the adversary open. And it is often useful to bring an outside third party into negotiations.

A President bears a heavy burden during a crisis. While there is no magic formula for successful resolution of crises, Presidents can take steps that will make war or U.S. capitulation less likely.

BIBLIOGRAPHY

Allison, Graham. *Essence of Decision: Explaining the Cuban Missile Crisis.* 1971.
Fisher, Roger, and William Ury. *Getting to Yes: Negotiating Agreement without Giving In.* 1981.
Genovese, Michael A. "Presidential Leadership and Crisis Management." *Presidential Studies Quarterly* 16 (1986): 300–309.
Genovese, Michael A. "Presidents and Crisis: Developing a Crisis Management System in the Executive Branch." *International Journal on World Peace* 4 (1987): 81–101.
George, Alexander L. *Presidential Decision-making in Foreign Policy: The Effective Use of Information and Advice.* 1980.
George, Alexander L. *Avoiding War: Problems of Crisis Management.* 1991.
Janus, Irving L. *Crucial Decisions: Leadership in Policymaking and Crisis Management.* 1989.
Rossiter, Clinton. *Constitutional Dictatorship: Crisis Government in the Modern Democracies.* 1963.

MICHAEL A. GENOVESE

CRISIS OF CONFIDENCE SPEECH (CARTER).

By the summer of 1979, the Jimmy Carter administration was faced with a national sense of crisis, in part the result of a worsening economy, particularly the severe gasoline shortages and huge increases in oil prices, and in part the result of a growing public perception of presidential ineptitude in dealing with this and other problems facing the nation. This crisis of confidence in the White House reached a new level of intensity after President Carter canceled a planned speech on energy on 5 July and then secluded himself for eleven days at CAMP DAVID, where he met with various groups of leaders in and out of government.

The President had intended to address the nation after the Organization of Petroleum Exporting Countries (OPEC) announced its fourth, and largest, price increase in five months. But he was dissatisfied with the drafts of the speech he had received, which reflected disagreement among his advisers over the content and tone of the message. As a result of these differences and his own belief that he needed to stress a broader theme than energy (a position that his pollster, Patrick Caddell, had urged), Carter decided to postpone his speech and to undertake a complete reassessment of his administration before addressing the country.

When he finally spoke to the American people on 15 July, after having met with dozens of Americans from all walks of life, he subordinated the energy crisis to the "crisis of confidence," which, he maintained, was the country's most pressing problem. Resolving the energy crisis, he said, was crucial to the health of the American economy. But it was also important because it involved a test of the American will that the American people needed to pass if the United States was to remain a vibrant nation. "All the legislation in the world can't fix what's wrong with America," he concluded. "What is lacking is confidence and a sense of community."

Carter's speech was well received. Rumors about his physical and mental well-being during the preceding eleven days ensured that there would be a large audience for his address, and most Americans who heard him were impressed by his apparent determination to deal with the energy crisis and the larger crisis of spirit afflicting the nation. Yet, just a few days later, the President undermined his small improvement in the polls by accepting the forced resignations of five members of his Cabinet. This purge of the Cabinet made it appear that Carter's administration was falling apart, thereby causing a further erosion of public confidence in the President's leadership.

BIBLIOGRAPHY

Carter, Jimmy. *Keeping Faith: Memoirs of a President.* 1982.
Holland, J. William. "The Great Gamble: Jimmy Carter and the 1979 Energy Crisis." *Prologue* 22 (Spring, 1990): 63–69.
Kaufman, Burton I. *The Presidency of James Earl Carter, Jr.* 1993.

BURTON KAUFMAN

CUBA.

The island of Cuba has occupied a central place in the strategic calculations of every U.S. President since the early years of the Republic. The proximity of the island to the U.S. South, the dramatic growth of U.S. commerce with Spanish Cuba in the nineteenth century, and the North Americanization of Cuban elites dictated that the "Cuban question" would be of critical importance in the formative years of U.S. foreign policy. In 1823, Cuban revolutionaries were heartened by U.S. professions about New World States' inevitable independence from European powers, but President James Monroe simultaneously expressed a cautionary note about revolutionary movements in the Caribbean, especially in Cuba. His successor, John Quincy Adams, agreed. One day, he predicted, the island would inevitably fall under the sway of the United States.

The Cuban link to the United States, then, seemed to validate President William McKinley's comment about "ties of singular intimacy"—as if Cuba's destiny were bound to that of the United States. From the perspective of Cuban revolutionaries, however, the U.S. connection was a bond that often frustrated insular demands for independence and nationhood. In the 1830s, President Andrew Jackson aggressively promoted U.S. commercial ties with the island. A decade later, President John Tyler became concerned about British abolitionist efforts in Cuba, a reflection of SLAVERY's influence on U.S. policy. His successor, President James K. Polk, tried to purchase the island. Concurrently, Cuban revolutionaries began a campaign to liberate the island from Spain. The Spanish crushed the rebellion in 1851, but Southern political leaders' dream of "tropical empire" did not perish. President Millard Fillmore's Democratic successor, Franklin Pierce, tried to bully the Spaniards into selling the island. But Northern newspapers protested that the attempt was a plot to add more slave territory to the United States. On the eve of the CIVIL WAR, antisecessionist Democrats hoped to placate the South by proposing Cuban annexation.

In 1868, Cuban revolutionaries plunged the island into a devastating conflict, the Ten Years' War. Annexationist sentiment ran strong on Capitol Hill. Within the Ulysses S. Grant administration, Secretary of State HAMILTON FISH's effort to mediate the conflict failed, and relations between the United States and Spain deteriorated. In 1873, a crisis occurred when the Spanish executed American gunrunners in Santiago de Cuba (the *Virginius* incident). In the aftermath of the Ten Years' War, U.S. private investments in Cuba's sugar industry expanded considerably, and by the early 1890s trade between Cuba and the United States had reached significant levels, especially because of the 1890 McKinley tariff, which benefited Cuban producers. This ended with the Wilson-Gorman tariff of 1894, however, and the following year Cuban revolutionaries commenced another phase in their long struggle. Their cry was "Cuba Libre!" ("Free Cuba!"), a nationalism brilliantly articulated by José Martí. The intent of the revolutionaries was true independence, not only from Spain but from North American economic dominance, but that would have required ending the dominance of sugar in the Cuban economy and a radical alteration in Cuba's social structure. President Grover Cleveland condemned the brutal counterrevolution waged by Spain, but he resisted American intervention. His successor, McKinley, was more calculating. McKinley's intent was to preserve U.S. economic interests and (though historians sharply disagree on this point) lay the foundation for a de facto U.S. annexation of the island. Thus, U.S. intervention in 1898 was designed to defeat, not sustain, Cuba Libre. The United States did not recognize the Cuban republic; it entered the SPANISH-AMERICAN WAR as conqueror, not only of Spanish Cuba but PUERTO RICO and the PHILIPPINES as well.

Cuban annexation was not forthcoming but neither was independence. Instead, Cuba occupied a "special place" in the U.S. empire—a stunted republic subjected to military occupation from 1899 to 1902 and again from 1906 to 1909. Cubans had to acquiesce in the Platt Amendment of 1902, which limited national sovereignty and provided for U.S. intervention to "guarantee" Cuban independence. U.S. troops intervened in 1912 and again in 1917. By the mid 1920s, U.S. investments had escalated to $1.5 billion.

Despite the overpowering U.S. economic and cultural presence, Cuban nationalism thrived. In 1933 a reformist junta took power and might have achieved much had not the U.S. emissary, Sumner Welles, dispatched by President Franklin D. Roosevelt, effectively undermined this junta by recommending against recognition and dealing with the new power in the Cuban military, Fulgencio Batista. In the crisis, Roosevelt surrounded the island with U.S. warships, but Secretary of State CORDELL HULL committed the administration to nonintervention. A short time later, Batista (formerly a sergeant in the Cuban army) became the de facto ruler of Cuba. The Platt Amendment was officially terminated, but Cuba's economic dependence on the United States remained in place.

Cuba in the 1950s was the classic dependent state, with a veneer of prosperity and progress in the cities and poverty in the countryside. As the COLD WAR deepened, the corruption of the Batista regime embarrassed the Dwight D. Eisenhower administration, and liberals in the United States heartened to the guerrilla war begun by Fidel Castro. A few warned of Castro's Marxist ideology, but U.S. leaders were confident he could be controlled.

Castro, however, had his own agenda, which called for the restructuring of Cuba's economy and society and the de-Americanization of the island's culture. He was convinced that the United States would have to act against him but would not use its own troops to do so. The socialist revolution commenced, as did U.S. planning to move against it. The first of several waves of disaffected Cubans came to the United States. In 1960, their leaders organized, their efforts subsidized by the

U.S. government. In Miami, the CENTRAL INTELLIGENCE AGENCY (CIA) began training some of the exiles.

In the 1960 presidential campaign, John F. Kennedy sounded a militant cry against the loss of Cuba. As President, he pursued a dual course in Latin America, supportive of the ALLIANCE FOR PROGRESS and democratic government while simultaneously aiding counterinsurgency and supporting plans to overthrow Castro's government. But the collapse of Cuban institutions historically dependent on U.S. power and the migration of Cubans who were at odds with Castro virtually doomed any success of an internal counterrevolution. The BAY OF PIGS INVASION of April 1961 was quickly defeated, and Castro exploited the victory to gain sympathy for the revolution.

Cuba suffered economically from the trade embargo imposed by the United States, becoming virtually dependent on the Soviet bond. But the revolutionary commitment abroad was sustained, and Cuba became a leader in the developing world. There was no lessening of U.S. hostility toward Cuba. The determination to punish the Cubans for choosing a revolutionary course, as well as the presence of a million Cubans in the United States, obviated any possibility of a normalization of relations. Relations did briefly improve during the presidency of Jimmy Carter, but then deteriorated again.

Mutual hostility characterized Cuban–United States relations in the 1980s, as the Ronald Reagan administration identified Cuba as fomenting revolutions in Central America. The United States tightened the economic and political sanctions against the Cuban government. Several Latin American countries, however, had already moved to normalize relations with Cuba. In 1987, Cuba and the United States signed an immigration agreement whereby the United States would accept twenty thousand Cubans annually in return for the right to deport twenty-five hundred refugees deemed "excludable" back to Cuba.

The collapse of the Soviet Union in 1991 and the cessation of Soviet economic subsidy brought harsh times to Cuba. In both the United States and Cuba, there were expectations that relations would change, but as of 1992 neither President George Bush nor Fidel Castro had signaled a willingness to abandon the policies established in the early 1960s.

[*See also* CUBAN MISSILE CRISIS.]

BIBLIOGRAPHY

Langley, Lester D. *The Cuban Policy of the United States: A Brief History.* 1968.
Morley, Morris. *Imperial State and Revolution: The United States and Cuba, 1952–1986.* 1987.
Pérez, Louis A., Jr. *Cuba and the United States: Ties of Singular Intimacy.* 1991.
Pérez, Louis A., Jr. *Cuba between Empires, 1898–1902.* 1983.
Pérez, Louis A., Jr. *Cuba: From Reform to Revolution.* 1984.
Welch, Richard E., Jr. *Response to Revolution: The United States and the Cuban Revolution, 1959–1961.* 1985.

LESTER D. LANGLEY

CUBAN MISSILE CRISIS. The sudden, stealthy installation of Soviet nuclear missiles in CUBA confronted President John F. Kennedy with the most wrenching test of his presidency. The crisis of October 1962, a thirteen-day ordeal, steeled the President's determination to force the withdrawal of Nikita Khrushchev's missiles without war. It was Kennedy's first, and most dangerous, foreign-policy success.

Ever since his June 1961 meeting with Khrushchev in Vienna, the President had expected a challenge in Berlin, not Cuba. The Soviet leader served notice of his "firm and irrevocable" decision to sign a German peace treaty within six months—even at the risk of war. If Kennedy refused, the Western allies would forfeit their occupation rights, including their right to maintain troops in West Berlin and the Potsdam guarantee of access to the surrounded city. "If that is true it's going to be a cold winter," the President responded.

Khrushchev did not wait until winter. On 13 August, his East German protégés sealed off East Berlin, and eventually the rest of the German Democratic Republic, from the West with a barbed-wire barrier, soon to be replaced by a concrete wall. Although tensions ran high and morale sank in West Berlin, Kennedy rejected advice to take a hard line with the Soviet Union.

To his aides, though not in public, the President said: "It's not a very nice solution, but a wall is a hell of a lot better than a war." Kennedy nonetheless fretted over Berlin's exposed position long after Khrushchev's six-month ultimatum had expired. He quickly approved a $3.5 billion increase in the military budget. The President also decided to make known the naked facts of America's nuclear dominance—in refutation of both Khrushchev's claims to rocket supremacy and his own missile-gap speeches of the 1960 campaign. If a missile gap existed, he now realized, the Soviets were at the short end.

Roswell Gilpatric, then ROBERT S. McNAMARA's deputy at the Pentagon, bluntly recited the details of America's armed strength, including "a second-strike capability which is at least as extensive as what the Soviets can deliver by striking first." Khrushchev's subsequent decision to plant Soviet missiles in Cuba can be traced, in part, to his pained awareness that the

United States possessed a 17 to 1 edge in nuclear warheads. His main motive, according to Georgi Shaknazarov (one of three knowledgeable Russians who exchanged information and retrospective insights on the missile crisis with American scholars and surviving members of the Kennedy team in Cambridge, Massachusetts, in 1987), was to give the impression of military parity with the United States, not real parity.

Fyodor Burlatsky, once Khrushchev's speech writer and later an aide to Mikhail Gorbachev, believed that the missile deployment was "more an emotional than rational decision," and that the deployment was poorly planned and sloppily executed, by an impulsive politician who was also a gambler. At the time of the missile crisis, the United States had more than three times the number of Soviet intercontinental ballistic missiles, one and a half times the number of sea-launched missiles, and more than eight times the number of heavy bombers. If Khrushchev's secretive plan were to have succeeded, in spite of these strategic disadvantages, its execution would have had to be flawless. It was, in fact, deeply flawed.

In their haste to deliver troops and weapons to Cuba undetected, the Soviet high command sent so large a stream of ships across the ocean that U.S. intelligence could not fail to warn the White House that "clearly something new and different is taking place." According to Sergo Mikoyan, the son of Soviet deputy premier Anastas I. Mikoyan and himself a Latin America specialist, the mistake was "absolutely Russian. We had to do it speedily, so too many ships were used and the Americans noticed." A second mistake came to light with the deployment of surface-to-air missiles (SAM) in western Cuba. The Russians neglected the need for camouflage. On 29 August, a U-2 reconnaissance plane captured the first photographic proof of two SAMs in position. There were more menacing weapons to come, but the cloak of secrecy was wearing thin.

What that initial deployment meant was the question troubling John McCone, the new CENTRAL INTELLIGENCE AGENCY (CIA) chief. McCone doubted the value to the Soviet Union of installing SAMs unless their purpose was to protect something else, possibly offensive missiles trained on the American mainland. Through Anatoly Dobrynin, the Soviet ambassador in Washington, Khrushchev sent soothing assurances that no offensive missiles would be sent to Cuba. There were skeptics in the White House who dismissed McCone's surmise. McGeorge Bundy, for example, doubted that Khrushchev "would do anything as crazy, from our standpoint, as to install nuclear weapons in Cuba."

Ambassador Llewellyn Thompson, just returned from Moscow to advise the President on Soviet affairs, later recalled his own incredulity: "I just didn't believe the Russians would do it. They had never trusted their own [European] satellites with missiles. Though, once the missiles were there, my immediate reaction was to relate it to Khrushchev's repeated assurances that he would do nothing about Berlin until after our election. I figured that he was planning to come to the U.N. with those blue chips in his pocket."

Alexander Alexeyev, then Soviet ambassador in Havana, later confirmed that Khrushchev had a plan of just that sort. He believed, Alexander said, that the Soviet missiles would remain undetected until 6 November, election day in the United States, "when we would announce openly our measures." Then the Americans would learn, Khrushchev later said, "what it feels like to have enemy missiles pointing at you."

All the guessing about Khrushchev's intentions ended abruptly on 14 October, when two U-2 pilots returned from a Cuban overflight with compelling evidence of a medium-range missile base under construction near the town of San Cristobal. Now it was the Americans who shrouded their discovery in official secrecy—until Kennedy and his advisers decided how to respond. On 22 October, after seven days of intensive debate, Kennedy broadcast a demand that Khrushchev "move the world back from the abyss" by withdrawing his missiles from Cuba. He declared that any missile launched from Cuba would warrant a full-scale retaliatory attack upon the Soviet Union and imposed a naval blockade to turn back any vessels carrying offensive missiles.

On 24 October, at least a dozen Cuba-bound ships did turn back rather than risk boarding and inspection by the U.S. Navy. Four days later, following a difficult negotiation by exchange of letters between Moscow and Washington, Khrushchev agreed to remove his missiles from Cuba and to dismantle the launch sites. Kennedy gave written assurance that there would be no American invasion of Cuba.

Thus history's first and only nuclear confrontation ended peacefully over Fidel Castro's protest that Khrushchev had failed to consult him before retreating. Kennedy had turned the most difficult corner of his brief presidency. He directed that there was to be no gloating at Khrushchev's expense. The President understood how difficult it must have been for the Soviet leader to back down.

BIBLIOGRAPHY

Abel, Elie. *The Missile Crisis*. 1966.
Allison, Graham T. *Essence of Decision*. 1971.
Beschloss, Michael R. *The Crisis Years: Kennedy and Khrushchev, 1960–63*. 1991.

Blight, James G., and David A. Welch. *On the Brink: Americans and Soviets Reexamine the Cuban Missile Crisis.* 1989.

Kennedy, Robert F. *Thirteen Days: A Memoir of the Cuban Missile Crisis.* 1969.

Khrushchev, Nikita S. *Khrushchev Remembers.* 1970.

Sorensen, Theodore. *Kennedy.* 1965.

ELIE ABEL

CUMMINGS, HOMER (1870–1956), Attorney General. Homer Stillé Cummings entered the Franklin D. Roosevelt administration after a lengthy career in politics and law enforcement in Connecticut. In 1932 he acted as Roosevelt's floor manager at the Chicago convention. Originally designated governor-general of the PHILIPPINES, he became Attorney General when Senator Thomas Walsh died just two days before Roosevelt's inauguration. He held the post until 1939.

Cummings was an excellent organizer who managed the DEPARTMENT OF JUSTICE with efficiency and dispatch. He played a major role in strengthening federal law enforcement to combat the mob wars and crime waves of the 1930s, supporting legislation that extended federal police powers to kidnapping, bank robbery, firearms regulation, and the interstate transportation of stolen property. He strengthened the FEDERAL BUREAU OF INVESTIGATION and was responsible for retaining J. EDGAR HOOVER as head of that organization when LOUIS MCHENRY HOWE and others argued for his removal. In 1934 Cummings assembled an Attorney General's Conference on Crime to promote national standards and support for law enforcement, an effort that was overlooked in the national attention accorded the FBI.

Cummings believed law should cement the unity of society rather than protect the rights of the individual. He recommended putting down the San Francisco general strike of 1934 by force. His jurisdictional interpretations prevented the Justice Department from enforcing the labor provisions of the NATIONAL INDUSTRIAL RECOVERY ACT. He cooperated with Roosevelt to broaden the powers of the FBI to investigate subversive activities in cooperation with military intelligence.

Cummings had the responsibility of developing a constitutional support for NEW DEAL legislation. The history of constitutional interpretations' changing with new social and economic conditions convinced him that there could be no single, unvarying construction of the Constitution. He invoked the "presumption of constitutionality" doctrine that the Supreme Court should presume that Congress was acting constitution-ally, especially when the President had provided it with evidence of an economic emergency and reason to believe that a given act was the only way to deal with it.

A series of Court decisions that invalidated much New Deal legislation caused Cummings to conclude that the problem was not with the Constitution but with the judges who interpreted it. Frustrated and angered by the Court's decisions, he collaborated with President Roosevelt to propose enlarging the Court's membership in order to outvote its conservative core. The so-called COURT-PACKING PLAN, however, proved a major political blunder that strengthened conservative opposition to the New Deal and all but destroyed Cummings's credibility with Congress.

BIBLIOGRAPHY

Irons, Peter H. *The New Deal Lawyers.* 1982.

Powers, Richard Gid. *Secrecy and Power: The Life of J. Edgar Hoover.* 1987.

Swisher, Carl Brent. *Selected Papers of Homer Cummings.* 1972.

GEORGE MCJIMSEY

CURTIS, CHARLES (1860–1936), thirty-first Vice President of the United States (1929–1933). In many respects, Charles Curtis experienced one of the least successful vice presidencies of the twentieth century. He was unable to establish influence with the President, Herbert Hoover, or the Senate. Yet his incumbency was significant in several respects. He was the first person of American INDIAN descent and the first person from west of the Mississippi to hold that office.

Born on 25 January 1860 near North Topeka, Kansas, Curtis served in the House of Representatives from 1893 to 1907 and in the Senate from 1907 to 1929. From 1915 to 1924 he was the Republican whip of the Senate; he became majority leader in 1924 upon the death of Sen. Henry Cabot Lodge. In that position, he repeatedly attacked the Senate's tolerance of filibustering.

Curtis had been the preferred vice presidential candidate of the Republican legislative leadership in 1924 after Gov. Frank Lowden rejected the nomination, which the convention had voted him on the second ballot. The convention then disregarded urgings of the congressional leaders who supported Curtis and of the administration representatives, who favored Herbert Hoover, and nominated CHARLES GATES DAWES instead.

Four years later, Hoover and Curtis again were adversaries, this time for the presidential nomination. Curtis finished a distant third in the balloting for the Republican presidential nomination, behind Hoover and Lowden. Much to the chagrin of the Hoover camp, Sen. William E. Borah pushed Curtis for the second spot on the ticket. Resentful of Curtis's energetic opposition to Hoover, yet fearful of the consequences that objecting would engender, the Hoover forces reluctantly acquiesced, and Curtis was nominated with all but 37 of 1,089 votes. The selection unified the rival wings of the party and placated the legislative leadership, which was supportive of Curtis. In addition, Curtis was thought likely to help the ticket in the farm states. At sixty-eight, he was one of the oldest men ever elected Vice President.

Curtis's experience illustrated the difficulties inherent when the Vice President was selected by party leaders, not the presidential candidate, from an opposing wing of the party. Hoover and Curtis had little regard for each other. Although, at Hoover's invitation, Curtis occasionally attended Cabinet meetings, he played little role in the administration. Owing to the cool relationship between Hoover and Curtis and to the limited legislative aims of the Hoover administration, Curtis's advice was rarely solicited. In his memoirs, Hoover mentions no substantial contribution of Curtis during his vice presidency.

In view of his lengthy legislative experience, particularly as Senate majority leader, one would have expected Curtis to slip easily into his role as the Senate's presiding officer. Although he did enjoy better relations with his former colleagues than had his predecessor, Dawes, who had attempted to reform the Senate from the presiding chair, Curtis was something of a disappointment in the role for which he had seemed so suited. As Vice President, he apparently underwent a metamorphosis; no longer the informal Senator who had answered easily to "Charley," he became somewhat officious.

There was some uncertainty as to whether Curtis would seek a second term as Vice President or run instead for the Senate. Some party leaders favored other candidates, believing that the ticket needed a new face. Curtis deliberated at some length before deciding to run again with Hoover. He was renominated but only after twelve opponents also received support. Neither Hoover nor Curtis greeted the other's nomination with any visible celebration. The Republicans were, of course, soundly defeated in the 1932 election, a campaign marked by division between Hoover and Curtis on various issues, including PROHIBITION.

Curtis thereafter retired from electoral politics. He died on 8 February 1936, less than four years after leaving office.

BIBLIOGRAPHY

Ewy, Marvin. *Charles Curtis of Kansas: Vice President of the United States 1929–1933*. 1961.

Unrau, William E. *Mixed Bloods and Tribal Dissolution: Charles Curtis and the Quest for Indian Identity*. 1989.

Williams, Irving G. *The Rise of the Vice Presidency*. 1956. Pp. 141–147.

JOEL K. GOLDSTEIN

CUSHING, CALEB (1800–1879), Attorney General. A Harvard-trained Massachusetts lawyer, in the 1830s Cushing served four terms in the House of Representatives as a Whig. In 1840 he wrote the campaign biography for William Henry Harrison's successful Whig presidential campaign. After Harrison's death Cushing became a congressional supporter of John Tyler, and thereafter was aligned with the Democrats. Tyler nominated Cushing for Secretary of the Treasury but the Whig-dominated Senate refused to confirm him. From 1843 to 1853 Cushing held various public positions as a diplomat, general during the MEXICAN WAR, and member of the Massachusetts supreme judicial court. In 1852 he helped engineer Franklin Pierce's presidential nomination and became Pierce's ATTORNEY GENERAL in 1853. In that office he supported the KANSAS-NEBRASKA ACT, a vigorous enforcement of the Fugitive Slave Law of 1850, and the argument, ultimately successful in DRED SCOTT V. SANDFORD (1857), that the MISSOURI COMPROMISE unconstitutionally prohibited slavery in the territories. Once a moderately antislavery Whig, by the 1850s Cushing was a doughface, an active supporter of the South in national and DEMOCRATIC PARTY politics. Cushing presided over the 1860 Democratic national conventions in Charleston and Baltimore, but he joined Southerners in walking out to protest STEPHEN A. DOUGLAS's nomination. Always a Unionist at heart, Cushing opposed SECESSION, and when the CIVIL WAR began he offered his services to the Union cause. Cushing's proslavery past made him unacceptable as an officer to Massachusetts Governor John A. Andrew. Abraham Lincoln, however, willingly made use of his diplomatic and legal skills. Cushing worked with the administration in developing its foreign policy and in 1864 campaigned for Lincoln. He later served the Grant administration as a diplomat helping to negotiate the TREATY OF WASHINGTON (1871) and the *Alabama* claims dispute. In 1873 Grant appointed him to the Supreme Court, but a lifetime of accumulated political opposition forced him to withdraw his name from consideration.

BIBLIOGRAPHY

Fuess, Claude M. *The Life of Caleb Cushing*. 2 vols. 1923. Repr. 1965.

PAUL FINKELMAN

CYCLES, PRESIDENTIAL. The effectiveness and leadership capacity of Presidents, their popular and political support, and even their eventual reputations rest, to some degree, on the opportunities and constraints offered by history. These patterns produce cycles that vary in length and regularity. It is often difficult to distinguish an ephemeral trend from a long-term cycle. Much depends on the lenses through which we read history.

We can recognize three types of cycles by how long they last: term cycles, metacycles, and historic cycles. The shortest, *term cycles*, coincide with the fixed term of the presidency. The four-year presidential term regularly brings forth a set of activities timed to both the results and the onset of elections. *Metacycles* can influence more than a single presidency: the business cycle, for example, has an unpredictable pattern of highs and lows, and an important question for any sitting President involves how the business cycle meshes with the electoral cycle. *Historic cycles* tend to affect many presidencies within an entire epoch in similar ways. The ebb and flow of congressional challenge to Presidents, for example, affects the capacity of Presidents to exercise policy leadership.

Term Cycles. There are several key elements to the presidential term. The first is the election aftermath, during which Presidents tend to be at the height of their political power. Observers frequently refer to this period as the HONEYMOON PERIOD. A newly elected President comes into office with his political coalition intact and, usually, enjoys a level of political goodwill higher than it is likely to be later in his term. These conditions encourage a President to put forth a policy agenda relatively early, before the presidential coalition begins to deteriorate. While presidential influence tends to decrease over time, a President's knowledge of the office and effectiveness in it can improve as a President learns from his mistakes. This intersection of declining influence and rising effectiveness produces an irony: While Presidents are less likely to have major legislative successes later in their terms, they are more likely to manage the presidency effectively.

The *electoral cycle* dictates presidential attention at two points in the presidential term. The first is the midterm congressional elections, usually perceived as a referendum on the incumbent President. The extent to which the President's party loses or gains seats in Congress affects both the incumbent's reputation and, even more importantly, the arithmetic of putting together legislative majorities on behalf of presidential goals. The second point is the President's own reelection campaign. Late-twentieth-century Presidents have turned their attention to reelection much earlier, partly because of financial and logistical requirements. Challenges within their own parties also have required Presidents to respond earlier than they might have preferred. The onset of the campaign mentality tends to place a partisan gloss on much of what a President does during the election year. While this does not make a political cooperation between parties impossible, it does complicate the task of building governing coalitions, a problem aggravated by DIVIDED GOVERNMENT. These patterns play themselves out again in a second presidential term. Typically, however, the presidential party's losses of congressional seats are larger in the second midterm election than in the first. The fact that the sitting President cannot run again after eight years in office diminishes the incumbent's personal stake in the presidential election at the end of the second term and can make political cooperation somewhat more likely than at the end of a first term when a President is seeking reelection.

A newly elected President may try to adopt a distinctive trademark to distinguish his administration from the preceding one. This is a *succession cycle*. The differentiation may be stark—Franklin D. Roosevelt's NEW DEAL; Ronald Reagan's New Beginning—or mild—George Bush's "kinder, gentler nation"—but a new administration's theme is rarely "let us continue." That slogan, intoned by Lyndon Baines Johnson after the assassination of John F. Kennedy, is usually reserved for rare, tragic moments. The succession cycle, fueled by electoral victory, provides opportunities for leadership and policy change.

Metacycles. The most basic metacycle with which Presidents must grapple is the *business cycle*. When times are bad, Presidents also suffer. Presidents tend to prosper in flush times, although not as much as they suffer when economic conditions decline. Presidents have a keen stake in trying to lengthen the prosperity side of the business cycle or to move out of the downside of the cycle. Although the capacity of a President to affect the economy may be severely limited, few Presidents are inclined in bad times to do nothing. The timing of the business cycle is thus crucial to presidential prospects and will typically affect more than one presidency. Presidents want the downside of the business cycle to be as far removed from the electoral cycle as possible and the upturns to coincide with it. But this is not a matter that Presidents can fully control.

Another metacycle is the *presidential management cycle*. Much like sartorial fashion, philosophies of managing the White House tend to change seasonally. When White House staffing is hierarchical and formal, it is apt to be followed by arrangements that emphasize accessibility and informality. Dwight D. Eisenhower, for example, liked formality; Kennedy preferred ad hoc arrangements. Generally, Presidents who are highly involved in their administrations prefer a management style that is more informal, less hierarchical, and that relies more on the spoken than on the written word. Presidents who are less inclined to intervene in the workings of their administrations prefer more formal and hierarchical arrangements that rely more on the written spoken word. Adverse than on the reactions to one style of White House management promote its opposite (too authoritarian and closed versus too diffuse and chaotic).

Historic Cycles. A succession of Presidents is affected in similar ways by a historic cycle. The length of a historic cycle often makes it difficult to recognize from a contemporary perspective. Two long-term, or historic, cycles importantly affect Presidents' ability to exercise power and leadership. The first is the *cycle of* PRESIDENTIAL-CONGRESSIONAL RELATIONS. The other is the *electoral alignment cycle*. There is considerable debate, however, about whether these cycles even exist, and, if so, how regularly (or irregularly) shaped they are.

The relationship between Presidents and Congress is formed by a number of factors. A crucial factor is the number of Representatives and Senators belonging to the President's party, which is a function of the electoral alignment cycle. A second factor reflects the extent to which the Congress and the presidency are inclined to stake out territory in constitutional struggles to expand their own powers. Congressional dominance characterized the first century of the Republic. By the second half of the nineteenth century, after the CIVIL WAR, congressional dominance became even greater and Congress turned itself into a more professional, partisan, and centralized body. By the time of the Woodrow Wilson administration, however, presidential assertiveness was becoming more prominent and provided a pattern that for the most part has been followed since. The end of the first decade of the twentieth century brought a deterioration in the central leadership capabilities of Congress, especially by weakening the powers of the Speaker of the House of Representatives. Thus, a period of a generally assertive presidency and a more decentralized Congress followed.

The Great Depression, WORLD WAR II, and the COLD WAR led to an increasingly dominant presidency, at least in matters of FOREIGN AFFAIRS, fostering the expectation that Presidents had to provide leadership for the nation and for the world. During the mid 1960s, however, Congress began to reassert itself in areas, such as foreign policy, that had been thought to be EXECUTIVE PREROGATIVES. Congressional reforms and divided government later followed. These reforms simultaneously led to greater centralization and decentralization of Congress, creating considerably more staff, policy analysis, and oversight capabilities. Divided government contributed to increased mistrust between the branches. Both President and Congress pushed expansive ambitions in a largely adversarial climate.

The electoral alignment cycle interacts to some degree with the presidential-congressional relations cycle. While there is some controversy as to whether the alignment cycle persists, historical evidence provides support. Longer-term changes in the underlying electorate, when fused with a powerful stimulant to political change, can generate new political majorities. Such a period of political realignment offers the potential for substantial policy change. Over time, the coalition that helped create the new majority experiences a degenerative phase, at the end of which a new political majority is being constructed. The high tide of realignment politics generates great potential for Presidents. The strongest periods of realignment, however, tended to be in the nineteenth century, before presidential power was ascendant. Among modern Presidents, only Franklin Roosevelt seemed to have a sustained period of strong congressional majorities largely mobilized on behalf of a party political agenda. The similar majorities marshaled by Johnson in 1964 and 1965 and Ronald Reagan in 1981 proved to be only momentary. Consequently, in the absence of a massive national political shift, such as that of the 1930s, Presidents and Congress, even when of the same party, are not apt to respond to the same political forces. The consequence is that Presidents are apt to reach for more and get less.

BIBLIOGRAPHY

Bunce, Valerie. *Do New Leaders Make a Difference? Executive Succession and Public Policy under Capitalism and Socialism.* 1981.

Grossman, Michael B., Martha Joynt Kumar, and Francis E. Rourke. "Second Term Presidencies: The Aging of Administrations." In *The Presidency and the Political System.* 3d ed. Edited by Michael Nelson. 1990.

Light, Paul C. *The President's Agenda.* 2d ed. 1991.

Neustadt, Richard E. *Presidential Power: The Politics of Leadership.* 1960.

Rockman, Bert A. *The Leadership Question: The Presidency and the American System.* 1985.

Skowronek, Stephen. "Presidential Leadership in Political Time." In *The Presidency and the American Political System*. 3d ed. Edited by Michael Nelson. 1990.

                                         BERT A. ROCKMAN

CZOLGOSZ, LEON F. (1873–1901), assassin of President William McKinley. Czolgosz shot President William McKinley while the President greeted visitors at the Pan American Exposition in Buffalo, New York, on 6 September 1901. McKinley died eight days later of a gangrenous infection from the two bullets. Czolgosz shot the President at close range because normal security arrangements were changed to accommodate the dignitaries accompanying the President. The assassin was arrested at the scene, convicted of first-degree murder, and executed on 29 October 1901.

Czolgosz insisted that he killed the President "because he was the enemy of the good people—the good working people." The assassin, who espoused an anarchist ideology, had a long history of class-oriented political action and antagonism to the prevailing economic system. Investigations failed to uncover any other participants or a conspiracy. Nonetheless, Czolgosz's beliefs and foreign parentage (he was born in Detroit one month after his parents arrived from Czechoslovakia) led to new security procedures to keep track of "anarchists" and to new legislation (the Immigration Act of 1903) to keep out aliens who were anarchists.

BIBLIOGRAPHY

Clarke, James W. *American Assassins: The Darker Side of Politics*. 2d rev. ed. 1990.

Kaiser, Frederick M. "Origins of Secret Service Protection of the President: Personal, Interagency, and Institutional Conflict." *Presidential Studies Quarterly* 18 (1988): 101–127.

Sherman, Richard B. "Presidential Protection during the Progressive Era: The Aftermath of the McKinley Assassination." *The Historian* 46 (1983): 1–20.

                                    FREDERICK M. KAISER

D

DALLAS, GEORGE MIFFLIN (1792–1864), Senator, minister to Russia and Great Britain, eleventh Vice President of the United States (1845–1849). In 1844 newly elected George M. Dallas wryly commented to a friend, "I have become Vice President willy nilly, and anticipate the necessity of enduring heavy and painful and protracted sacrifices, as the consequence." His observation proved correct as Dallas struggled unsuccessfuly for the next four years to build a national reputation that would thrust him into the White House.

The scion of a Philadelphia family that enjoyed both modest wealth and social position, Dallas had served his state and nation briefly and with little distinction as U.S. Senator and diplomat in the 1830s. A northeastener was needed to balance the Democratic ticket in 1844 with Tennessean James K. Polk. As a loyal Jacksonian, Dallas appeared as an asset to the ticket in Pennsylvania. There the Democrats campaigned on a platform of territorial expansion and maintaining the protective tariff of 1842. By a narrow margin the Keystone State remained in the Democratic camp in 1844, but it is uncertain whether Dallas played any role in influencing the outcome.

Dallas, a man of ambition tempered by a sense of noblesse oblige, perceived from the outset that his office would force him into an ongoing struggle with his old nemesis, Secretary of State James Buchanan. Since Polk had declared himself a one-term candidate, "presidential fevers" infected both Pennsylvanians seeking to build their images, reputations, and political bases in preparation for 1848. Polk quickly became ensnared in the patronage wars between his two lieutenants. When the smoke cleared, Dallas had been defeated. Always the Quaker City patrician, he lacked the energy and forcefulness to press his case with Polk, yet he retained the sensitivity and honor to harbor a lingering resentment at White House rejection. The PATRONAGE squabbles were a harbinger of the tenuous relationship Dallas enjoyed with the President for four years. Unswervingly loyal to his party and chief, Dallas, nonetheless, never ingratiated himself as an ongoing confidant.

By the fall of 1845, the Vice President determined to impress the President and the nation through his service as presiding officer of the Senate. Unfortunately, the tariff dispute of 1846 placed him in an unenviable position. The reductions proposed by Secretary of the Treasury R. J. Walker conflicted with Pennsylvania coal and iron interests. When Dallas faced a tie vote in the Senate in July, he cast a painful "aye" for the measure. While pleasing Polk and enhancing his White House hopes in some quarters of the factious DEMOCRATIC PARTY, the ballot destroyed his credibility and base in Pennsylvania. Dallas rendered the vote, however, motivated by a combination of personal opportunism and a sincere belief that his action benefited the broader union and the American economy.

As a committed nationalist and champion of MANIFEST DESTINY, Dallas hoped to expand American hegemony into Texas, Oregon, the Southwest, and CUBA. He backed the ANNEXATION OF TEXAS, resulting in Lone Star residents naming a county in his honor. Democratic Senate majority leaders wanted to avoid selecting a president pro tempore and instead kept the Vice President in the chair. The expansionist Dallas then appointed avowed "Fifty-four Forty or Fight" men, who shared his vision, to the Foreign Relations Committee. Polk's compromise with Great Britain in the OREGON TREATY in 1846 disappointed Dallas. The Vice President quickly transferred his passions to the MEXICAN WAR, desiring to add Mexico's northern provinces to the United States. He also advocated obtaining a canal route across the Isthmus of Tehuantepec. The President rejected such extreme objectives, settling more modestly for California and the Southwest.

Dallas hoped that his views on the tariff, expansion, and SLAVERY would enable him to emerge as the Democratic choice in 1848. The President offered no assistance. Dallas's relationship with Polk had declined sharply during the war years and the two men were barely on speaking terms. The Philadelphian now adjudged the President as cold, devious, and two-faced. Supplementing his political portfolio by seizing the slave issue, Dallas, almost simultaneously with LEWIS CASS, arose as an exponent of popular sovereignty for the territories. His enemies, however, outmaneuvered him both at the state and national conventions and he temporarily withdrew into private life.

Dallas reappeared in 1856 as a potential rival to the doomed incumbent, Franklin Pierce. The President removed this threat by appointing Dallas as minister to Great Britain, but Pierce could not ward off the onslaught of the other Pennsylvanian, James Buchanan. Dallas retired from public life in 1861. A lifelong STATES' RIGHTS Unionist, his traditional remedies for the problems that plagued the nation now seemed unrealistic in the heated partisan climate of the new decade.

BIBLIOGRAPHY

Ambacher, Bruce. "George M. Dallas and the Family Party." Ph.D. diss. Temple University. 1970.
Belohlavek, John M. *George M. Dallas: Jacksonian Patrician.* 1977.
Bergeron, Paul. *The Presidency of James K. Polk.* 1987.
Klein, Philip S. *President James Buchanan.* 1962.
Snyder, Charles M. *The Jacksonian Heritage: Pennsylvania Politics 1833–48.* 1958.

JOHN M. BELOHLAVEK

DAMES & MOORE v. REGAN 453 U.S. 654 (1981). *Dames & Moore* upheld the EXECUTIVE AGREEMENT and EXECUTIVE ORDERS through which President Jimmy Carter settled the fourteen-month IRANIAN HOSTAGE CRISIS. Unlike earlier international agreements upheld by the Supreme Court despite the lack of Senate approval, this negotiation was not integral to recognizing or establishing diplomatic relations with another government. The Court's approval of this agreement thus marked an important extension of the President's FOREIGN AFFAIRS powers.

In November 1979 Iranian revolutionaries seized the U.S. embassy in Tehran, capturing U.S. diplomatic personnel. In response, Carter declared a national emergency and blocked the removal from the United States of all property and interests within U.S. jurisdiction of the Iranian government or of its controlled entities, including the Central Bank of Iran. The President and Treasury Department did, however, license U.S. litigants with claims against Iran to seek so-called prejudgment attachments against specific Iranian property. These attachments, in effect, would prevent Iran's removal of that property from a court's jurisdiction until the party's dispute with Iran was finally brought to judgment.

On 19 January 1981, the Iranian and U.S. governments entered into an agreement to secure the hostages' release. The agreement called for establishing an Iran–United States claims tribunal that would arbitrate any claims between U.S. nationals and the Iranian government or its entities. Carter also agreed

> to terminate all legal proceedings in United States courts involving claims of United States persons and institutions against Iran and its state enterprises, to nullify all attachments and judgments obtained therein, to prohibit all further litigation based on such claims, and to bring about the termination of such claims through binding arbitration.

The United States promised to "unblock" previously frozen Iranian assets, $1 billion of which were deposited in an escrow account to satisfy awards rendered against Iran by the claims tribunal.

On the same day, Carter implemented the agreement through executive orders that revoked all licenses permitting the exercise of judicial power over Iranian assets and "nullified" all non-Iranian interests in such assets acquired subsequent to the blocking order. On 24 February 1981, President Ronald Reagan issued an executive order ratifying the Carter orders, suspending all claims in U.S. courts that might be presented to the claims settlement tribunal and directing the pursuit of those claims in that tribunal, unless the tribunal determined that it lacked jurisdiction.

In *Dames & Moore* the Supreme Court determined that a portion of what Carter accomplished has been squarely authorized by the International Emergency Economic Powers Act (IEEPA), enacted to give the President certain EMERGENCY POWERS over foreign assets during periods of national crisis. In particular, the IEEPA authorized the licensing system under which Dames & Moore, and other U.S. nationals, had obtained prejudgment attachments against Iranian assets. Under the terms of that statute the President was authorized to make the licenses revocable.

The IEEPA, however, did not authorize the suspension of the claims against Iran already filed in U.S. courts. The Court likewise could identify no statutory authority for Carter's agreement in the Hostage Act, an 1868 statute generally authorizing Presidents to engage in diplomatic efforts to secure the release of U.S. hostages abroad.

The Court nonetheless concluded that the presidential orders were lawful in this respect because Congress's legislative activity in the area of international claims settlements reflected a long-standing expectation that the President would use his executive-order power to settle claims as a means of furthering U.S. foreign relations. The settlement was consistent with a congressional policy of seeking the peaceful release of international hostages, and Congress had not attempted to block the President's orders through subsequent legislation. The court said it was "[c]rucial to [its] decision . . . that Congress [had] implicitly approved the practice of claim settlement by executive agreement."

Dames & Moore enjoys a twofold importance in the delineation of the President's foreign-policy powers. First, the Court gave the IEEPA a broad, literal reading, although Congress's purpose in enacting that statute in 1977 had been to limit what had been perceived as too broad a delegation of emergency powers under an earlier statute, the Trading with the Enemy Act (1917), which still applies in wartime. Following *Dames & Moore*, it appears that a valid declaration of a peacetime national emergency under the IEEPA's somewhat more specific standards confers on the President essentially the same generous range of powers as did the Trading with the Enemy Act.

Second, it is important that the Court upheld an executive agreement negotiated without Senate approval in a context that did not involve the exclusively presidential RECOGNITION POWER or the power to establish diplomatic relations. Yet the Court did so cautiously. Rather than approving agreements of this type categorically or based on implicit understandings of the President's inherent constitutional authority, the Court relied explicitly on Congress's implied authorization of the President's actions. This interpretation stressed the importance of institutional history in assessing the legality of independent presidential initiatives.

BIBLIOGRAPHY

Glennon, Michael J. *Constitutional Diplomacy.* 1990.
Henkin, Louis, Michael J. Glennon, and William D. Rogers. *Foreign Affairs and the United States Constitution.* 1990.
Marks, Lee R., and John C. Grabow. "The President's Foreign Economic Powers after *Dames & Moore v. Regan*: Legislation by Acquiescence." *Columbia Law Review* 68 (1982): 68–103.

PETER M. SHANE

DARK HORSES. Relatively unknown political candidates who seem unlikely to win a party's nomination are called dark horses. Up until the mid 1900s, a dark horse could adopt a strategy of avoiding open campaigning and could seek to become the second or third choice of delegates while antagonizing as few as possible. In 1860 Abraham Lincoln described such a strategy: "My name is new in the field, and I suppose I am not the first choice of a very great many. Our policy, then, is to give no offense to others—leave them in a mood to come to us if they shall be compelled to give up their first love."

The best chance for such a candidate lay in a deadlock between the leading candidates at the party's nominating convention. The dark-horse candidate would first combine with others to oppose the front-runner and then present himself as the one to unify the party after its divisive convention. James K. Polk (1844), Franklin Pierce (1852), Rutherford B. Hayes (1876), Warren Gamaliel Harding (1920), JOHN W. DAVIS (1924), and WENDELL WILLKIE (1940) are examples of candidates who won nomination in this manner. All but Davis and Willkie went on to be elected President.

Under the democratizing reforms of the major parties in the late twentieth century, it has become increasingly unlikely that a dark horse can be nominated for President. Nominations are typically decided before the convention meets, so there is little role for a dark-horse candidate. Most delegates are pledged to those who have competed in PRESIDENTIAL PRIMARIES or state conventions, leaving dark horses with too few delegates to matter. The Democrats' decision in 1936 to abolish the rule requiring a candidate to obtain the support of two-thirds of the delegates has also decreased the probability of a convention deadlock.

If a convention should become deadlocked, however, it is still possible for a dark horse to emerge, but it is unlikely that a candidate would adopt a dark-horse strategy. It is also possible for a relatively unknown candidate to emerge from the primaries, as Jimmy Carter did in 1976.

BIBLIOGRAPHY

Davis, James W. *Presidential Primaries.* 1980.

GEORGE C. EDWARDS III

DAUGHERTY, HARRY M. (1860–1941), Attorney General. A key figure in securing Warren G. Harding's election in 1920, Harry Micajah Daugherty was a controversial appointment as Attorney General. Over the years he had earned a reputation less as a practicing lawyer than as a political wheeler-dealer and a crony of Harding, to whom he was fiercely loyal and whom he served as a close confidant.

From the beginning of the Harding administration, the public was willing to believe the worst about Daugherty. Moreover, Daugherty harmed his own reputation through his abrasive and contemptuous personal style and by a handful of ill-considered actions. The worst was his handling of the railway strike of 1922. With the President's (at least partial) approval Daugherty obtained the most sweeping antilabor injunction in American history. He was also roundly criticized for his failure aggressively to pursue fraud claims arising from WORLD WAR I.

All the controversy that swirled around Daugherty has obscured his genuine contributions as Attorney General. Despite a record of red-baiting, he was instrumental in arranging for Harding's pardon of wartime political prisoners, including EUGENE V. DEBS. His handling of the routine business of the Justice Department was generally competent, and his recommendations for judicial appointments were better than was generally assumed.

Still, Daugherty's close association with all the key figures involved in the Harding administration's widespread scandals forever sealed his reputation. Daugherty himself stood trial in 1926 on charges that he had illegally siphoned money into a bank account for political purposes. He and his brother destroyed bank records relating to the account, and Daugherty refused to testify on the subject. Though he was never convicted, his motives for these damning actions are still the subject of much speculation. Most likely, they were an attempt to protect Harding's reputation.

BIBLIOGRAPHY

Murray, Robert K. *The Harding Era: Warren G. Harding and His Administration.* 1969.

Russell, Francis. *The Shadow of Blooming Grove: Warren G. Harding and His Times.* 1968.

WILLIAM LASSER

DAVIS, JEFFERSON (1807–1889), president of the Confederate States of America (1861–1865). One of the most prominent men of the antebellum South, Jefferson Finis Davis enjoyed a close relationship with the presidency long before he assumed such an office.

He served as Secretary of War under Franklin Pierce (1853–1857) and was thought by many to wield undue influence on that President, though accusations of his being the "power behind the throne" were exaggerated. He did, however, exert considerable influence in maneuvering Pierce into making the repeal of the MISSOURI COMPROMISE in 1854 an administration measure. Davis was spoken of as a possible Democratic nominee in 1856 and 1860, but he never sought the presidency of the United States. When the Democrats split in 1860, ensuring the election of Abraham Lincoln, Davis did make a vain effort to secure the withdrawal of STEPHEN A. DOUGLAS, John Bell, and JOHN C. BRECKINRIDGE in order to unify their supporters on a compromise candidate.

Once the southern states seceded, Davis was immediately assured some high place in the new Confederacy. He told friends that he did not wish to be chief executive—preferring an army command—but on 9 February 1861, the convention meeting in Montgomery, Alabama, selected him as the future president of the Confederate States of America. He was a compromise candidate—a strong enough supporter of secession to appease the "fire-eaters" but not so extremist that he would alienate the large number of Unionists in the South.

Though he had previously been a consistent opponent of a strong executive, Davis took over almost immediately and had a hand in every aspect of the new government. He had little choice, since the Confederate government had to be built overnight from virtually nothing. Moreover, the South was not gifted at this time with an abundance of able administrators. Forced to make cabinet choices based on patronage rather than ability, Davis went through a succession of mediocre secretaries, finding only a few of lasting quality. Meanwhile, he had to—or chose to—oversee much of their work personally. Indeed, the chief criticism of him as an executive hinged on his unwillingness or inability to delegate authority and to keep out of matters too unimportant to occupy his limited and precious time.

In the end, Davis focused his attention where the CIVIL WAR forced him to concentrate—that is, on military affairs. After 1862 he gave up on foreign recognition of the Confederacy and paid scant attention to diplomatic matters. He left fiscal policy to his treasury secretaries. Even naval affairs he left largely to his secretary of the navy, but military policy and the strategy pursued by the armies of the Confederacy consumed him. It is testament to his in-depth interference that he went through six war secretaries, most of them men of limited capacity, although some were capable men who resigned in frustration at Davis's interference.

Nevertheless, as commander in chief his strategic thinking was mostly sound, and, given the limited resources of the South, his success in raising and equipping the Confederacy's armies surpassed expectations. His adoption of an "offensive-defensive" strategy—allowing the enemy to invade and attack while Confederates fought defensively on their own ground, always ready for an offensive counterblow into the North—was the wisest use of his limited means. It also addressed the political requirement to hold as much Confederate territory as possible.

Davis was less successful in his dealings with the Confederate congress and the governors; both the legislature and the state executives failed to share his ever-growing sense of Confederate nationalism. Still, though constantly at odds with congress, he only had one minor veto overridden and saw virtually all of his war legislation passed. With the governors, he alternately cajoled and threatened and in the end got the men and material that he demanded, though at great cost to his popularity and prestige.

The final judgment on Davis's presidency is uneven. By concentrating too much attention on events in Virginia he prolonged the war in that sector; he paid too little attention to developments west of the Appalachians, especially in the Mississippi Valley, and adhered to a string of failed and inadequate commanders, thus shortening the Confederacy's life in that region. On balance, however, he certainly performed the impossible task facing him as well as, and probably better than, any other southern leader could have.

[*See also* CONFEDERATE CONSTITUTION.]

BIBLIOGRAPHY

Crist, Linda Lasswell, Mary Seaton Dix, James T. McIntosh, and Haskell M. Monroe, eds. *The Papers of Jefferson Davis.* 7 vols. to date. 1971–1992.

Davis, William C. *Jefferson Davis, The Man and His Hour.* 1992.

Rowland, Dunbar, comp. *Jefferson Davis, Constitutionalist.* 10 vols. 1923.

WILLIAM C. DAVIS

DAVIS, JOHN W. (1873–1955), Democratic presidential nominee in 1924 and a leader of the American bar. John William Davis was born in Clarksburg, West Virginia. His father, a leader of the state bar, was a two-term Democratic U.S. Representative. Davis graduated from Washington and Lee University in 1892 and from its law school in 1895. Following a term in the West Virginia legislature, Davis developed an extensive corporate law practice. He was elected to Congress in 1910 and reelected in 1912. Acclaimed as the ablest lawyer in the House, he opposed tariff increases, drafted the liberal labor provisions of the CLAYTON (Antitrust) ACT, and otherwise supported President Woodrow Wilson's NEW FREEDOM, though usually with private reservations. He became SOLICITOR GENERAL of the United States in 1913.

Davis's arguments in many of the most important Supreme Court cases of the Progressive Era earned him a reputation as perhaps the finest Solicitor General in history. He won rulings outlawing Oklahoma's antiblack grandfather clause and Alabama's convict lease system while successfully defending Congress's right to regulate oil pipelines and, under certain conditions, the hours of railroad workers. He lost the first child labor case (*Hammer v. Dagenhart*, 1918) and failed to win a dissolution order against the United States Steel Corporation. In 1918 Davis succeeded Walter Hines Page as ambassador to the Court of St. James's, in which post he served with grace and distinction until the end of the Wilson administration. In 1920 he refused to encourage a boomlet for his nomination for President.

By 1924, when Davis reluctantly emerged a serious presidential candidate, he suffered the political onus of leadership of a prestigious Wall Street law firm that numbered J. P. Morgan and Company among its principal clients. Yet his image as a progressive Congressman and Solicitor General persisted in many quarters, and he went into the Democratic convention with considerable second-line support. The prolonged deadlock imposed on the convention by the progressive forces of William G. McAdoo and the conservative supporters of ALFRED E. SMITH gradually pushed Davis to the fore, and on the 103d ballot he became the party's compromise choice.

Davis understood that prosperity and the lingering resentment of WORLD WAR I and the TREATY OF VERSAILLES by isolationists, German-Americans, and several other ethnic groups made victory virtually impossible. "Thanks," he said to a friend who congratulated him on the nomination, "but you know what it's worth." Conceiving it his duty to hold the party together, he selected Governor Charles Bryan of Nebraska, the brother of WILLIAM JENNINGS BRYAN, as his running mate. Moreover, in spite of his desire to call unequivocally for American membership in the LEAGUE OF NATIONS and the World Court, Davis confined himself to an educational campaign. Even so, his internationalist background caused a great many isolationists and anti-British voters to support ROBERT M. LA FOLLETTE, who ran as an independent Progressive.

Davis's mild denunciations of the KU KLUX KLAN also drove many Democrats to Calvin Coolidge, who remained silent, or to La Follette, who referred to the Klan but once. Davis failed, furthermore, to present a progressive alternative to Coolidge. As a White House memorandum noted late in the campaign, the Democratic candidate had endorsed everything of importance that the President himself had advocated. Moreover, Smith gave Davis only nominal support and McAdoo gave him almost none at all. Davis received a little more than 8 million votes to Coolidge's 16 million and La Follette's roughly 5 million. He carried only the Old South and Arkansas, Oklahoma, Tennessee, and Texas in the ELECTORAL COLLEGE, and he trailed La Follette in the popular vote in twelve northern states.

Davis made no effort to assume leadership of the party after the election. He spoke eloquently for Al Smith and religious freedom in the campaign of 1928. But in 1936 he joined Smith, the du Ponts, and other conservatives in forming the anti-NEW DEAL Liberty League. He also attacked the New Deal through a half dozen law suits, including a Supreme Court test of the National Labor Relations Act (WAGNER ACT). As he aged, Davis became less critical than ever of the existing social and economic order, despite a vestigial commitment to CIVIL LIBERTIES. He deplored President Harry S. Truman's progressive domestic agenda but supported the UNITED NATIONS and most of the Truman-Eisenhower COLD WAR policies. Davis ended his distinguished career at the appellate bar with two epochal Supreme Court cases in the early 1950s: YOUNGSTOWN SHEET & TUBE CO. V. SAWYER (1952) and *Brown v. Board of Education* (1954). In the first, he won a 6 to 3 ruling that Truman's seizure of the steel industry was unconstitutional; in the second, he argued unavailingly against Thurgood Marshall that school segregation was constitutional.

BIBLIOGRAPHY

Harbaugh, William H. *Lawyer's Lawyer: The Life of John W. Davis.* 1973.

Murray, Robert K. *The 103rd Ballot.* 1976.

WILLIAM H. HARBAUGH

DAWES, CHARLES GATES (1865–1951), thirtieth Vice President of the United States (1925–1929), Comptroller of the Currency, Budget Director, ambassador to Great Britain, director of the Reconstruction Finance Corporation. Dawes was principally noted for the Dawes Plan restructuring German war reparations.

Born in Ohio, Dawes was educated at Marietta College and Cincinnati Law School, began law practice in Lincoln, Nebraska, and earned a reputation as the "people's advocate" in the Nebraska railroad rate cases. Subsequently, he acquired extensive interests in gas and electric companies, moved to Chicago to manage them, and entered politics as a supporter of and campaign manager for William McKinley. His reward was appointment as Comptroller of the Currency, an office that involved him in efforts to reform bank examination, closure, and reorganization practices. In 1902, after failing in a bid for the United States Senate, he became a bank president and over the next fifteen years spoke and wrote extensively on financial and antitrust questions. During WORLD WAR I he became chief purchasing agent for the American Expeditionary Force and rose to the rank of brigadier general. He gained a reputation for sharp-spoken bluntness and colorful eccentricity; cartoons accentuated his outthrust jaw and underslung pipe.

Dawes's major contributions to shaping the modern presidency came in the early 1920s, initially as the nation's first budget director and then as chair of an international committee of experts empowered to investigate German finances and devise a way out of the postwar reparations tangle. Long an advocate of governmental budgeting, Dawes had promised President-elect Warren Gamaliel Harding that if the Budget and Accounting Act passed, he would devote a year to the task of seeing that it was properly implemented. Harding held him to this promise, and the result was a new budgetary system credited with "saving the nation a billion dollars," bringing business methods and rational planning to governmental finance, and enhancing the President's managerial capacity. Dawes's other major achievement came shortly thereafter, when his solution to the German reparations problem helped to legitimize an executive-based business internationalism that largely bypassed Congress and pursued diplomatic ends through "industrial statesmen" drawn from the private sector. Acting as a private citizen yet in conjunction with procedures suggested and promoted by Secretary of State CHARLES EVANS HUGHES, Dawes was eventually able to gear German reparations payments to a "capacity to pay" principle, arrange for loans to reestablish the soundness of the German currency, and thus provide a temporary means of accommodating the competing demands of French security and European economic reconstruction. His achievements made him a popular choice as Calvin Coolidge's running mate in 1924 and earned him a share of the Nobel Peace Prize in 1925.

From 1925 through 1932, Dawes remained in the public eye and was among those thought of as potential Presidents, but his public service yielded no other major achievements. As Vice President, he helped to pilot the KELLOGG-BRIAND PACT and a new cruiser-building bill through the Senate but had no success in his strenuous efforts to reform senatorial rules and procedures, especially those permitting the practice of filibustering. As ambassador to Great Britain, he was famous for his hospitality and was actively involved in the negotiations leading to the London Naval Treaty of 1930, the Hoover debt moratorium in 1931, and the American response to the Manchurian crisis of 1931–1932. But in none of these negotiations did he play more than a supplemental role. And as a director of the RECONSTRUCTION FINANCE CORPORATION in 1932, his service lasted only four months and was subsequently clouded by an RFC loan to save his Chicago bank. After 1932 he largely withdrew from public life but remained active in the business world and in numerous philanthropic endeavors.

BIBLIOGRAPHY

Barzman, Sol. *Madmen and Geniuses: The Vice-Presidents of the United States.* 1974.
Carroll, John M. "The Making of the Dawes Plan, 1919–1924." Ph.D. dissertation, University of Kentucky. 1972.
Dawes, Charles Gates. *Journal of the Great War,* 1921; *First Year of the Budget,* 1923; *Notes as Vice-President,* 1935; *Journal of Reparations,* 1939; and *Journal of the McKinley Years,* 1950. Published versions of Dawes's diaries.
Leach, Paul R. *That Man Dawes.* 1930.
Timmons, Bascom N. *Portrait of an American: Charles G. Dawes.* 1953.

ELLIS W. HAWLEY

DEBATES, PRESIDENTIAL. The American political system grew up with debate. Colonial assemblies debated revolution, the Constitutional Convention debated the Constitution, and Congress debates laws. These contests have produced memorable speeches and launched political careers. But debate was more than a political tool in early America; it was also a means of educating the young, honing professional skills, demonstrating personal worth, and enlightening the citizenry.

Prominent Americans have ascribed various benefits to debate. Thomas Jefferson named "free argument and debate" the "natural weapons" of truth, "errors ceasing to be dangerous when it is permitted freely to contradict them." Woodrow Wilson believed that debate discouraged demagoguery. In Britain, he observed, debate had produced decades of leaders, but few demagogues. In parliamentary debate, orators were judged by their "readiness of resource," "clearness of vision," "grasp of intellect," "courage of convic-tion," and "earnestness of purpose." Accordingly, at each of the universities where he taught, Wilson advocated debating societies patterned on the Oxford Union. Though political debate often fell short of these grand promises, prebroadcast debates in America contributed to the development and preservation of the political system and educated the electorate about the issues and personalities of the day.

Just as direct appeal to voters was considered unbecoming throughout much of the nineteenth century, direct clash with an opponent was deemed indecorous for the first half of the twentieth. Such clash at first was unthinkable to those not yet comfortable with carrying their own case to the voters directly.

Even when there was no incumbent, the presumed front-runner then as now had little to gain by legitimizing an opponent in a face-to-face exchange. When WILLIAM JENNINGS BRYAN took to the stump in 1896 delivering over six hundred speeches to voters in twenty-seven states, McKinley's manager, Mark Hanna, dispatched a Republican speaker to follow his trail, rebutting his speeches town by town. The structure of the debate suggested that Bryan was opposing the Republican "truth squad" rather than McKinley. Meanwhile, on his front porch, seated in a rocking chair, McKinley received delegations of well-wishers at his home in Canton, Ohio, and rocked his way to the presidency.

Broadcast Debates. As Calvin Coolidge's Secretary of Commerce, Herbert Hoover led the fight for passage of the Federal Radio Act of 1927. Hoover believed that radio would revolutionize "the political debates that underlie political action [by making] us literally one people upon all occasions of general public interest." He was partially correct.

The infant medium of radio simply carried to the nation's living rooms the form of debate that had earlier characterized town meetings and the U.S. Congress. In 1928 the League of Women Voters, which had been founded only eight years earlier, broadcast a weekly ten-month series of debates on important issues. Representatives of the political parties, reporters, and editors but not presidential candidates took part in their exchanges.

To fend off those who saw redistributing existing radio channels as a means of increasing educational programming, the National Broadcast Company Blue network instituted "America's Town Meeting of the Air" and NBC Red gave national time to what had been up to that point a local program, "The University of Chicago Round Table." In "America's Town Meeting of the Air," which debuted in March 1935, time limits and audience questions were a standard feature.

A forty-minute period was divided in classical debate fashion with each speaker receiving equal time. The final twenty minutes of the hour were reserved for audience questions.

By inviting partisans of each party to hear the other side's views as well, "Town Meeting" overcame the selective exposure that otherwise characterized the information seeking of Republicans and Democrats. "If we persist," noted moderator George Denny, "in the practice of Republicans reading only Republican newspapers, listening only to Republican speeches on the radio, attending only Republican political rallies, and mixing socially only with those of congenial views, and if Democrats . . . follow suit, we are sowing the seeds of the destruction of our democracy." The program met its objective. A survey of "Town Meeting" mail revealed that the program prompted family discussion, further reading, and, among 34 percent, a change of opinion.

As politicians became more familiar with self-promotion, political variables continued to rule out general election presidential debates. One candidate always saw greater minuses than pluses in such an endeavor. At no time in the glory days of radio did an incumbent believe it advantageous to engage the opposition party nominee in direct exchange from the same platform. As Franklin D. Roosevelt repeatedly demonstrated, the benefits of wrapping oneself in the presidency were simply too great. So, for example, in 1936 four presidential contenders spoke at Chautauqua, New York, each on a different date.

In the Oregon primary of 1948, Republican candidates HAROLD STASSEN and THOMAS E. DEWEY held radio's first "great debate." Stassen was ex-governor of Minnesota, and Dewey, New York's governor. The debate played a role in the undoing of Stassen's presidential bid. Held 17 May 1948, the debate was carried nationally by ABC, NBC, and Mutual Broadcasting to an audience estimated at between forty and eighty million. One of the largest audiences in radio history had abandoned the "Carnation Contented Hour" and Fred Waring to listen to the Republican aspirants.

Their debate on whether the Communist Party should be outlawed demonstrated the value of focusing on a single issue. The specifics of the Mundt-Nixon bill were explained; the experiences of other countries that had outlawed the Communist Party detailed; Mundt was cited to rebut Stassen's interpretation of the bill; and the constitutional ramifications of passage were probed. In rebuttal, Dewey proved precise, his indictments telling. Stassen foundered.

Because the debate was able to deal at length and in depth with a clearly defined issue of importance to the public, and because time was allotted for rebuttal, the format invited illumination of the issue and the candidates' stands on it. The candidates' differences on outlawing the Communist Party were clarified and defended, their intellects publicly exercised in revealing ways. Dewey won on issue and image and went on the win that primary and his party's nomination.

On 1 May 1952, the League of Women Voters and *Life* magazine co-sponsored a nationally telecast "Democratic and Republican Candidates Forum" moderated by the journalist John Daly. A poll of League members created a pool of questions. Two of these questions were asked of each candidate. After the candidates' replies, questions were asked by the audience. Neither ADLAI E. STEVENSON (1900–1965) nor Dwight D. Eisenhower participated. Paul Hoffman stood in for Stevenson. Appearing with him were former Governor W. Averell Harriman, Senator Estes Kefauver, Senator Robert Kerr, former Governor Harold Stassen, and Governor Earl Warren.

The next primary debate demonstrated the disadvantages in moving from the traditional debate form. In what was billed as a "discussion," Democratic contenders Adlai Stevenson and Estes Kefauver met before national television audience 21 May 1956. The discussion ranged across foreign and domestic policy. A moderator, Quincy Howe, phrased questions and apportioned time. Just as Dewey had expressed hesitance about engaging in a personal encounter, so too did Kefauver. Kefauver, who won the flip of the coin giving him the right to speak first, announced that the campaign must "not degenerate into a mere personal conflict" but should instead be waged on the issues. In the next hour, the two candidates found little about which to disagree.

Format of Debates. The Communications Act of 1934 posed a problem for those who hoped that presidential debates would be televised. "A licensee who permits a legally qualified candidate for public office to use a broadcasting station must afford equal opportunities to all other candidates for that office," said Section 315 of the act.

For the 1960 elections, Congress suspended the equal opportunity provisions of Section 315. The Kennedy-Nixon debates took place during the suspension. In 1964, 1968, and 1972 the candidate ahead in the polls used Section 315 as an excuse for not debating.

In 1975, the Federal Communications Commission (FCC) exempted from Section 315 debates that were bona fide news events between or among legally qualified candidates if initiated by nonbroadcast entities and covered in their entirety live. The broadcast debates of 1976, 1980, 1984, and 1988, sponsored by the

League of Women Voters, were made possible by the *Aspen* ruling.

In 1983 the FCC exempted debates sponsored by broadcasters. The debates hosted by the networks in the primaries of 1984 and 1988 occurred as a by-product of that decision.

Since their existence, general election broadcast debates have come to assume a predictable and much criticized form. In it, a panel of reports asks questions of the candidates who respond in agreed blocks of time. The result more closely resembles a parallel press conference than the direct, forward clash that is the mark of traditional debates.

Many analysts suggest that the central problem is that these "joint press conferences" are not really debates at all. Much can be said for this point of view. In the most common of the current formats, moderators and/or press panelists come between those who might otherwise argue directly among themselves. Sustained consideration of important issues is at best difficult when the topics shift rapidly, the emphases are determined by noncontestants, and the time is short. On the other hand, what we now know as candidate debates do provide politicians with a national forum in which to take their cases to the people. Debates in some senses and individual performances in others, these moderated confrontations defy simple classification.

Nor is the conventionalized format the developed argument. In the 1988 general election the candidates' answers were limited to one and two minutes, and an agreement reached by the candidates barred follow-up questions from the press panel.

The nation's experience with televised presidential debates dates from the 1960 election when John F. Kennedy faced Richard M. Nixon. The four sessions held in that year were not only the first televised presidential debates, but the first face-to-face debates of any sort between the nominees of the major parties. In 1976 there were three debates between Gerald Ford and Jimmy Carter and also a debate between vice presidential nominees Robert Dole and WALTER MONDALE. The number dropped to two in 1980, the first between Republican nominee Ronald Reagan and independent John Anderson, the second between Reagan and the Democratic incumbent Carter. In 1984, President Ronald Reagan defied conventional wisdom and agreed to debate a challenger, Mondale, who was behind in the polls. In that year the presidential nominees faced off twice. A debate was also held between a major party's first female vice presidential nominee, GERALDINE FERRARO, and her Republican counterpart, George Bush.

By 1988, most theorists believed debates had become such an expected part of a presidential campaign that the public could count on their occurrence. That year, as in 1984, there were three debates, one vice presidential, two presidential.

Assessing the Debates. Proponents of debates argue that they benefit the electorate by revealing candidates' communicative competence and habits of mind, by augmenting the candidates' accountability, by acting as a check on candidate manipulation, and by increasing the candidates' preparation for office. Candidates also benefit from the cost-free exposure and by being able to hold opponents responsible for their campaign rhetoric.

Not only do debates invite a focused attention uncharacteristic of advertisements but they also create a climate in which even those otherwise disposed to shun political messaging are expected to be able to converse about political data. "For days after the 1960 debates," recalled columnist David Broder before the 1980 debates, "there was intensive private conversation about the debates." After the first debate of 1976, for example, eight of ten people reported that they had discussed the exchange. The social pressure to take a sustained view of both candidates creates a climate more conducive to political learning than any other which the typical voter will seek or chance upon.

Critics contend that debates foster habits that ought not be reflected in a presidency, including a willingness to offer solutions instantaneously, an ability to simplify complex problems, and a talent for casting the world in Manichean terms. At their worst, debates invite candidates to make distinctions where only shades of difference exist and encourage simplifications that credit neither the candidates nor their audience.

And debates can lead presidential candidates to promise policies that as President they should not deliver. In 1976, for example, both Ford and Carter abjured secret presidential decision making.

Moreover, when an incumbent debates, sensitive national security information is put at risk, a factor that may invite a President to lie. So, after the final presidential debate of 1960, columnist James Reston breathed a sigh of relief. "It may not be in the national interest," he noted, "to get into strategic plans for dealing with Cuba, Quemoy, and Matsu on a presentation of this kind." In the same spirit, in 1986 former President Richard Nixon wrote the Twentieth Century Fund's Taskforce (convened to try to ensure that presidential debates would take place)

under no circumstances should Presidential candidates debate each other during wartime. It would have been highly irresponsible for Franklin D. Roosevelt to have debated Tom Dewey in

1944. And a very serious question could be raised as to whether it would have served the national interest for him to have debated [Wendell] Willkie in 1940 in view of the danger that Roosevelt's highly sensitive secret negotiations with the British might have been exposed and caused not only enormous controversy at home but also, even more troublesome, given aid and comfort to Hitler.

Indeed, in 1972 Nixon had used just such an argument to explain why he would not debate McGovern. A President was not in a position to reveal all that he knew of an issue, noted the former Chief Executive.

Televised presidential debates command large audiences including many individuals who seek out little other political information during the campaign. Where approximately fifteen thousand heard one of the senatorial debates between Lincoln and Stephen A. Douglas, more than a thousand times that number viewed each of the twentieth century's televised presidential debates. Over 60 percent of the adult population, about 77 million individuals, watched the first Kennedy-Nixon debate. Some believe that the viewership for the second and third debates of that year was even higher. Historically, other campaign messages have failed to attract comparable audiences. In 1964, for example, no message by either Lyndon B. Johnson or Barry Goldwater reached even a quarter the audience that watched the first of the 1960 Kennedy-Nixon debates.

Where six of ten adults watched in 1960, that number became seven of ten in the first two debates of 1976, dropping back to the 1960 average for the third of the Ford-Carter encounters. More than 120 million viewers saw the 1980 Carter-Reagan debates. But four years later, the numbers were down. In 1984, the general election debates drew 85 million viewers; in 1988, 80 million. Even with that drop, the debates reached more viewers than any other single campaign message.

But the decline raises concern, for alone among the messages of the campaigns the debates have given a large heterogeneous audience the chance to compare directly the major candidates for office. Although determining the influence of any single factor on voting is difficult, surveys consistently find that 20 to 25 percent of voters report that the presidential debates played some role in their voting decision.

BIBLIOGRAPHY

Bitzer, Lloyd, and Theodore Reuter. *Carter vs. Ford: The Counterfeit Debates of 1976.* 1980.

Jamieson, Kathleen Hall, and David Birdsell. *Presidential Debates: The Challenge of Creating an Informed Electorate.* 1988.

Kraus, Sidney, ed. *The Great Debates: Background, Perspectives, Effects.* 1962.

Kraus, Sidney, ed. *The Great Debate: Carter vs. Ford, 1976.* 1979.

KATHLEEN HALL JAMIESON

DEBS, EUGENE V. (1855–1926), labor organizer, socialist, presidential candidate in 1900, 1904, 1908, 1912, and 1920. Eugene Victor Debs was born and raised in the small midwestern city of Terre Haute, Indiana. Debs's parents, Alsatian immigrants, operated a retail grocery store. At age twenty, although himself a clerk in a wholesale grocer's office, Debs was elected secretary of the local lodge of the Brotherhood of Locomotive Firemen. His commitment to the organization, his ability, and his conservatism (he opposed participation in the national railroad strikes of 1877) drew the attention of national brotherhood officials.

By 1881 Debs was national secretary of the Firemen, increasingly its labor spokesman, and its most tireless organizer. Simultaneously, Debs also entered political life, speaking at "flag raisings" for the Democratic Party in his ward and, in 1879, winning the city clerk's race over both Republican and Greenback-Labor candidates. In 1885, as a Democrat, he won election to the Indiana state assembly with broad support from the wards of the city's working people and the business community. Terre Haute residents predicted that the young state representative would, in time, sit in Congress.

Initially, Debs's trade-union positions paralleled his political thought. He favored organization of workers by their craft, endorsed the hierarchical administrative structure in the Brotherhood, and opposed efforts by the Knights of Labor to organize all workers, regardless of craft or skill. In the decade following his election to the assembly, however, his thinking on both political and economic questions changed dramatically. In the assembly Debs grew disillusioned with legislative corruption and disregard of constituent needs. He therefore chose not to stand for reelection.

In the economic arena, a similar sea change began. The 1888 strike by railroad workers against the Chicago, Burlington, and Quincy Railroad precipitated a major revision in his thinking. Organization by craft was divisive, he argued, for it divided workers in their efforts to obtain fair wages and safe working conditions. Moreover, Debs now identified concentrated corporate power as the major threat to both traditional political rights and to the promise of economic opportunity. By 1893, he had resigned from the Brotherhood to organize the American Railway Union (ARU), an industrial union of all railroad workers.

For Debs, the ARU's 1894 Pullman strike against the Pullman Company of Chicago exemplified the central conflict of American industrial development. The unified power of railroad management—working in consort with other businessmen and with the active involvement of the federal government—threatened basic American liberties. Although Debs continued to support trade unions, he now doubted their ability to oppose successfully management's concentrated political and economic power. Debs therefore endorsed political action again, but this time as an advocate of a third political party.

In the 1896 presidential campaign, Debs stumped for WILLIAM JENNINGS BRYAN on the Populist ticket, disregarding that Bryan was also the candidate of the Democratic Party. On 1 January 1897, following the election of the Republican, William McKinley, Debs announced that he had become a socialist. Three years later he made the first of his five unsuccessful runs for the presidency.

The American socialist movement in 1900 was small and internally fractured, with little following among American working people. The election results suggested as much: Debs and his running mate, Job Harriman, received less than 100,000 votes. Debs decisively lost even the city of Terre Haute. Four years later the ticket of Debs and Benjamin Hanford, a New York City printer, did slightly better: garnering 400,000 votes, the socialist candidates achieved impressive percentile gains in a number of midwestern and southwestern states.

The Socialist Party of America (SPA), Debs expected, would continue its arithmetical progression in future elections. Despite the "Red Special," a train that took Debs and his entourage into more than 300 communities in thirty-three states (at a time when most presidential candidates still campaigned from their front porches), the SPA ticket failed miserably in 1908. Against Republican William Howard Taft and Democrat William Jennings Bryan, Debs and Hanford gained only 18,000 votes more than their 1904 total.

The 1912 campaign promised greater success. Within the past two years, Socialists in Milwaukee had elected a Congressman, and more than seventy communities elected socialist mayors nationally. Debs's essential critique of industrial capitalism—that concentrated power denigrated the tradition of citizenship and denied basic economic justice to working people—resonated among more Americans than ever, and the election results reflected this unsettled state. In a four-way race (Debs; Democrat Woodrow Wilson; Republican incumbent William Howard Taft; and independent Bull Moose challenger, Theodore Roosevelt), Wilson did unseat Taft, and the socialist vote almost doubled its 1908 tally by totaling 6 percent

of all votes cast. Upon closer scrutiny, however, it was clear that socialist votes declined in a number of states where previously strong, a reflection of sustained inroads made by reform candidates of the major parties; and in the West, where socialist strength did grow, the SPA would suffer its most serious factional disputes in the following years. Finally, the premise of the socialist hope—that four years of governance by a reform Democrat would swell the socialist vote in 1916—proved illusionary.

Sick and bedridden, Debs did not run for President in 1916. In 1918 a still-ailing Debs rose from his bed to attack American participation in WORLD WAR I. Arrested, tried, convicted, and sentenced to ten years for violating the Espionage Act of 1917, Debs surrendered to federal authorities in April 1919. Notwithstanding that he was then prisoner number 9653 at Atlanta Federal Penitentiary, Debs ran again for President in 1920. With his campaign activity limited to a weekly press release, the now-gaunt "old Gene Debs" nonetheless drew 919,000 men and, for the first time, women voters to the socialist ticket. Debs's total, 3 percent of all votes cast, was a heartfelt salute to an aging, jailed leader.

In an oft-repeated part of his stock speech, Debs argued with his audience not to follow him blindly. "If you are looking for a Moses to lead you out of this capitalist wilderness," he preached, "you will stay right where you are. I would not lead you into the promised land if I could, because if I could lead you in, some one else would lead you out. YOU MUST USE YOUR HEADS AS WELL AS YOUR HANDS, and get yourself out of your present condition." A strange sentiment, perhaps, for a politician trolling for votes, but one that for a time resonated with many members of a generation in transition to modern industrial society.

BIBLIOGRAPHY

Ginger, Ray. *The Bending Cross: A Biography of Eugene Victor Debs.* 1949.
Salvatore, Nick. *Eugene V. Debs: Citizen and Socialist.* 1982.

NICK SALVATORE

DEBS, IN RE 158 U.S. 564 (1895). This decision of the Supreme Court grew out of the massive railroad strike led by EUGENE V. DEBS and the American Railway Union (ARU) against the Pullman Sleeping Car Company (the PULLMAN STRIKE) in 1894. The strike began as a dispute with the Pullman Company but immediately broadened. The managers of thirty-three railroads, organized into the General Managers Association (GMA), quickly came to Pullman's support, establishing committees to coordinate strike activity and to pressure state and federal officials to intervene on their behalf. When the ARU shut down most major railroads west of Chicago in early July 1894, the Attorney General of the United States, RICHARD OLNEY, acted. He ordered the United States District Attorney's office in Chicago, which included on its staff Edwin Walker, formerly counsel to the GMA, to seek an injunction against the ARU. The injunction barred the officers and members of the ARU from interfering with the passage of the trains and the mail and commerce they carried, and prohibited any union member from urging another worker to join the boycott. Debs and the other officers of the ARU were arrested and, in January 1895, found guilty of violating the injunction. In removing the officials and curtailing the activity of the members the injunction effectively broke the power of the union in the epochal strike.

Justice David J. Brewer's majority opinion held that "[t]he strong arm of the National Government may be put forth to brush away all obstructions to the freedom of interstate commerce or the transportation of the mails." Although the Court did not rule on the merits of the SHERMAN ANTITRUST ACT in delimiting union activity, the decision *In re Debs* provided employers, working with a judicially conservative yet activist court, a quite powerful weapon in their struggles with unions. Debs himself served a six-month jail term, and the case became an issue in the 1896 presidential campaign. The Democratic Party platform of that year denounced "government by injunction" and accused the federal judiciary of acting as "legislators, judges, and executioners." "[B]eginning with the *Debs* case," Justice FELIX FRANKFURTER wrote in an extrajudicial essay in 1922, "the use of the labor injunctions has, predominately, been a cumulative influence for discord in our national life." Americans, the Justice thought, perceived "that the powers of government are perverted by and in aid of the employers, and that the courts are instruments of this partisan policy." The legacy of *In re Debs*, Frankfurter argued, was that "industrial conflict is uglier than ever." The issue of the injunction remained an important one for labor in presidential politics but it was not until the passage of the Norris-LaGuardia Act in 1932 that unions received legal relief.

BIBLIOGRAPHY

Frankfurter, Felix, and Nathan Greene. *The Labor Injunction.* 1930.

NICK SALVATORE

DECISION OF 1789. The so-called decision of 1789 was an early congressional attempt to determine whether the removal of executive-branch officials from office was a prerogative of the President or of the President and Congress together. When the First Congress elected under the Constitution created the departments of Foreign Affairs, Treasury, and War, the question arose as to how the principal officer in each department might be removed from office. Was the Senate's consent part of the APPOINTMENT POWER itself or merely a check on it? On 16 June 1789, the House of Representatives debated a bill to create the Department of Foreign Affairs that contained the provision, penned by James Madison, that the principal officer was "to be removable from office by the President of the United States." When the question to strike language vesting the REMOVAL POWER in the President was put to a vote, there were twenty yeas and thirty-four nays. On 22 June, Egbert Benson moved to amend the bill to recognize that the removal power was a presidential prerogative by inserting the provision that "whenever the said principal officer shall be removed from office by the President of the United States" the chief clerk would have custody of his records, books, and papers. This language was approved by a vote of 30 to 18, representing a coalition of those who thought removal was a presidential prerogative and those who thought removal might be legislated and wished in this instance to provide the President with the power. Benson then moved to strike out the words "to be removable by the President" in Madison's original language to quash the possibility that Congress might seem to be delegating a removal power of its own to the President. This motion was carried by a vote of 31 to 19. Later, language similar to Benson's was put in bills establishing the departments of Treasury and War. The Senate kept Benson's provision, 10 to 9. In dealing with the Treasury Department, however, the Senate initially voted to delete the language on removals, preferring to share the removal power with the President. On a motion that the Senate recede from its position and accept the House version (with Benson's implied presidential removal power), the Senate divided evenly, 10 to 10, and Vice President John Adams broke the tie and voted in favor of keeping the House language.

BIBLIOGRAPHY

Corwin, Edward S. "Tenure of Office and the Removal Power under the Constitution." *Columbia Law Review* 27 (1927): 353.
Fisher, Louis. *Constitutional Conflicts between Congress and the President.* 1991. Pp. 53–58.

RICHARD M. PIOUS

DECLARATION OF WAR. See WAR, DECLARATION OF.

DEFENSE, DEPARTMENT OF. The Department of Defense (DOD) grew out of two major events of the mid-twentieth century—WORLD WAR II and the emergence of the COLD WAR. When World War II ended in August 1945, the armed forces of the United States totaled over 12 million men and women. Although demobilization occurred rapidly, the U.S. experience in the conflict demonstrated the necessity for teamwork among the services and with allies.

Creation of the Department. Congressional action in 1947 creating a new NATIONAL SECURITY system resulted from an intense debate about service "unification" during the latter stages of World War II. At President Harry S. Truman's insistence, the secretaries of War and Navy agreed on a plan that became the basis for the NATIONAL SECURITY ACT of 1947. Title II created the National Military Establishment (NME), composed of the departments of the army, navy, and air force, and several other agencies, including the JOINT CHIEFS OF STAFF. Heading the NME was a civilian secretary of defense, with power to "establish general direction, authority, and control" over the services. The law established other new organizations, including the NATIONAL SECURITY COUNCIL and the CENTRAL INTELLIGENCE AGENCY (CIA).

A compromise between full unification and no change, the act fashioned a confederation—the military departments would be separate executive departments, retaining "all powers and duties . . . not specifically conferred upon the Secretary of Defense." President Truman selected as the first Secretary of Defense JAMES V. FORRESTAL, who immediately faced a succession of challenges in 1948—a Soviet-supported communist coup in Czechoslovakia, the Berlin blockade, the Arab-Israeli War, passage of the MARSHALL PLAN, and the creation of the North Atlantic Treaty Organization (1949). Sharp disagreements among the military services over roles and missions also preoccupied Forrestal.

Based on his proposals, which were supported by Truman, Congress amended the National Security Act in August 1949. The NME became the Department of Defense; the army, navy, and air force became military departments without cabinet status; and the Secretary of Defense gained "direction, authority, and control" over the military departments.

Three other men served as Secretary of Defense under Truman—Louis A. Johnson (1949–1950), Gen. GEORGE C. MARSHALL (1950–1951), and Robert A. Lovett

Secretaries of Defense

President	Secretary of Defense
33 Truman	James V. Forrestal, 1947–1949
	Louis A. Johnson, 1949–1950
	George C. Marshall, 1950–1951
	Robert A. Lovett, 1951–1953
34 Eisenhower	Charles E. Wilson, 1953–1957
	Neil H. McElroy, 1957–1959
	Thomas S. Gates, Jr., 1959–1961
35 Kennedy	Robert S. McNamara, 1961–1963
36 L. B. Johnson	Robert S. McNamara, 1963–1968
	Clark Clifford, 1968–1969
37 Nixon	Melvin R. Laird, 1969–1973
	Elliot L. Richardson, 1973
	James R. Schlesinger, 1973–1974
38 Ford	James R. Schlesinger, 1974–1975
	Donald H. Rumsfeld, 1975–1977
39 Carter	Harold Brown, 1977–1981
40 Reagan	Caspar Weinberger, 1981–1987
	Frank Carlucci, 1987–1989
41 Bush	Richard B. Cheney, 1989–1993
42 Clinton	Les Aspin, 1993–1994
	William Perry, 1994–

(1951–1953). Truman brought in General Marshall to provide leadership in the KOREAN WAR and the long-term buildup of the armed forces. Under Marshall the defense budget skyrocketed ($57 billion for fiscal year 1952) and the size of the armed forces doubled, to over 3 million. Marshall supported Truman's controversial dismissal of Gen. Douglas MacArthur, who wanted to broaden the conflict by bombing military installations in China. Marshall worked to improve the national security structure—by promoting NATO and new MUTUAL-SECURITY TREATIES with the Philippines, Japan, and Australia and New Zealand. One of Lovett's major contributions was a series of defense reorganization proposals that later influenced President Dwight D. Eisenhower.

Eisenhower was his own Secretary of Defense, but three men formally held the office during his term—Charles E. Wilson (1953–1957), Neil H. McElroy (1957–1959), and Thomas S. Gates, Jr. (1959–1961). Eisenhower's defense reorganization plan (1953) abolished some existing agencies and replaced them with six new assistant secretaries. The services worried about Wilson's efforts to control the defense budget and about what their roles would be in the use of air power and missiles.

Because of these emerging issues, the Department of Defense passed through difficult times during the first Eisenhower administration. Under McElroy, the department had to respond to the first satellite launch-

Secretaries of the Navy[a]

President	Secretary of the Navy
2 J. Adams	Benjamin Stoddert, 1798–1801
3 Jefferson	Benjamin Stoddert, 1801 Robert Smith, 1801–1809 Jacob Crowninshield, 1805
4 Madison	Paul Hamilton, 1809–1812 William Jones, 1813–1814 Benjamin W. Crowninshield, 1815–1817
5 Monroe	Benjamin W. Crowninshield, 1817–1818 Smith Thompson, 1819–1823 Samuel L. Southard, 1823–1825
6 J. Q. Adams	Samuel L. Southard, 1825–1829
7 Jackson	John Branch, 1829–1831 Levi Woodbury, 1831–1834 Mahlon Dickerson, 1834–1837
8 Van Buren	Mahlon Dickerson, 1837–1838 James K. Paulding, 1838–1841
9 W. H. Harrison	George E. Badger, 1841
10 Tyler	George E. Badger, 1841 Abel P. Upshur, 1841–1843 David Henshaw, 1843–1844 Thomas W. Gilmer, 1844 John Y. Mason, 1844–1845
11 Polk	George Bancroft, 1845–1846 John Y. Mason, 1846–1849
12 Taylor	William B. Preston, 1849–1850
13 Fillmore	William A. Graham, 1850–1852 John P. Kennedy, 1852–1853
14 Pierce	James C. Dobbin, 1853–1857
15 Buchanan	Isaac Toucey, 1857–1861
16 Lincoln	Gideon Welles, 1861–1865
17 A. Johnson	Gideon Welles, 1865–1869
18 Grant	Adolph E. Borie, 1869 George M. Robeson, 1869–1877

President	Secretary of the Navy
19 Hayes	Richard W. Thompson, 1877–1881 Nathan Goff, Jr., 1881
20 Garfield	William H. Hunt, 1881
21 Arthur	William H. Hunt, 1881–1882 William E. Chandler, 1882–1885
22 Cleveland	William C. Whitney, 1885–1889
23 B. Harrison	Benjamin F. Tracy, 1889–1893
24 Cleveland	Hilary A. Herbert, 1893–1897
25 McKinley	John D. Long, 1897–1901
26 T. Roosevelt	John D. Long, 1901–1902 William H. Moody, 1902–1904 Paul Morton, 1904–1905 Charles J. Bonaparte, 1905–1906 Victor H. Metcalf, 1906–1908 Trueman H. Newberry, 1908–1909
27 Taft	George von L. Meyer, 1909–1913
28 Wilson	Josephus Daniels, 1913–1921
29 Harding	Edwin Denby, 1921–1923
30 Coolidge	Edwin Denby, 1923–1924 Curtis D. Wilbur, 1924–1929
31 Hoover	Charles Francis Adams, 1929–1933
32 F. D. Roosevelt	Claude A. Swanson, 1933–1939 Charles Edison, 1939–1940 Frank Knox, 1940–1944 James V. Forrestal, 1944–1945
33 Truman	James V. Forrestal, 1945–1947

[a]The Secretary of the Navy was a member of the Cabinet from the Adams administration to the Truman administration. In 1947, the Department of the Navy and the DEPARTMENT OF WAR were subsumed into the National Military Establishment, renamed the Department of Defense in 1949.

ing by the Soviet Union (October 1957) and charges of a missile gap. McElroy ordered a speed-up in development and production of intermediate range ballistic missiles and their deployment in England and Europe. Charges of a missile gap persisted, and later, although erroneous, played a role in the presidential campaign of 1960.

Supporting President Eisenhower's interest, McElroy presided over another reorganization of the Defense Department in 1958. He created the Advanced Research Projects Agency, responsible for antimissile and satellite projects. The Defense Reorganization Act replaced the military secretaries in the chain of command with the Joint Chiefs of Staff (JCS) and strengthened the role of the JCS chairman. The act continued the trend toward centralization of power in the Secretary of Defense and diminishment of the roles of the service secretaries.

Gates further improved DOD organization by instituting regular meetings with the JCS, and he sought to eliminate disputes over control of strategic weapons between the air force and the navy. During Gates's term intercontinental and submarine-launched ballistic missiles became operational.

Dealing with Vietnam. Upon his election in 1960, John F. Kennedy chose ROBERT S. MCNAMARA, the president of Ford Motor Company, to be Secretary of Defense. During his seven-year tenure, McNamara worked closely with Presidents Kennedy and Lyndon B. Johnson in a difficult period for the Department of Defense, marked by involvement in the VIETNAM WAR. McNamara was an active manager who carried further the centralization of authority, much to the discontent of the military. He brought to the Pentagon a civilian group who used systems analysis in decision making. McNamara canceled the B-70 bomber and the Skybolt missile projects but supported the controversial TFX (F-111) aircraft. Because of McNamara's reliance on civilian advisers and decisions the services considered detrimental to their interests, his relationship with them deteriorated.

McNamara played a major role in developing defense policy, advising the President, and directing U.S. military forces in a series of crises—the BAY OF PIGS INVASION of CUBA (1961), the CUBAN MISSILE CRISIS (1962), the conflict in the DOMINICAN REPUBLIC (1965), and above all, the Vietnam War. While publicly supporting President Johnson's escalation of U.S. involvement in Southeast Asia, including rapid increases in U.S. combat forces and a bombing campaign against North Vietnam, McNamara became skeptical about the President's approach. As domestic opposition to the war increased after 1965, McNamara and the Pentagon became central targets for criticism of the administration's approach. He left the Defense Department in February 1968.

President Johnson then chose CLARK CLIFFORD to become Secretary of Defense. The war preoccupied Clifford during his eleven months at the Pentagon. He approved the last increase in U.S. troop strength in Vietnam, to 549,000, but he eventually adopted McNamara's final position—a halt to troop increases and the bombing in North Vietnam, and gradual disengagement from the war. Clifford appears to have strongly influenced President Johnson to adopt a deescalation strategy by the time the President left office in January 1969.

Elected in 1968 after a campaign in which he promised a solution to the war in Southeast Asia, Richard M. Nixon chose Rep. MELVIN R. LAIRD to preside over the Pentagon. Laird developed Vietnamization, a gradual shift of the burden of fighting to South Vietnamese troops, as a way to achieve the President's goal of "peace with honor." Although the war reached some critical moments during this period, Laird steadily withdrew U.S. troops, cutting the total to under 70,000 by May 1972. Continued negotiations with the enemy led to a settlement in January 1973, providing for the liberation of U.S. prisoners held by North Vietnam and the withdrawal of U.S. fighting forces. Laird immediately announced the end of the controversial draft and the creation of an all volunteer force.

Nixon later brought to the Pentagon James R. Schlesinger, an economist who had been a member of the ATOMIC ENERGY COMMISSION since 1971. Schlesinger had to deal with several crises with military implications for the United States—the Arab-Israeli War of October 1973, the Turkish invasion of Cyprus in July 1974, the final collapse of South Vietnam in April 1975, and the MAYAGUEZ INCIDENT with Cambodia a month later. Schlesinger wanted to build up U.S. conventional forces, which had declined gradually since the 1950s, as well as NATO's conventional forces. He had the support of President Nixon, but his relationship with Nixon's successor, Gerald R. Ford, deteriorated, especially over the issue of defense funding. His outspoken advocacy of budget increases irritated both Congress and the President, who dismissed him in November 1975.

Donald H. Rumsfeld, the next Secretary of Defense, accepted Schlesinger's strategic-policy initiatives and moved ahead with the development of new weapon systems, including the B-1 bomber, the Trident nuclear submarine, and the MX intercontinental ballistic missile. Ford supported Rumsfeld's priorities, including budget increases. Congress cooperated to an extent, but still the fiscal year 1977 budget was in constant dollars only a little over the 1956 level.

Reorganization, Buildup, and the End of the Cold War. President Jimmy Carter's Secretary of Defense, Harold Brown (1977–1981) instituted significant organizational change, including the full integration of women into the army. Supporting Carter's interest in controlling defense costs, Brown worked hard both to strengthen NATO and persuade its members to increase their defense spending, and he also pressured major allies such as Japan and South Korea to share more of the defense burden. Responding to crises in 1979, in Iran and Afghanistan, Brown and Carter began a defense buildup.

During the 1980 presidential campaign, Ronald Reagan spoke widely about the deterioration of the U.S. defense posture in the 1970s and the need for a significant defense buildup. His first secretary of defense, CASPAR W. WEINBERGER, supported Reagan's effort to increase the defense budget, with particular emphasis on improving the strategic capabilities of the United States, including production of B-1 bombers and MX missiles and development of a Stealth bomber and a new submarine-launched ballistic missile. Weinberger got big increases, although Congress never agreed to as much as Reagan wanted.

Weinberger's successor, Frank C. Carlucci (1987–1989), carried on his policy emphases but showed a willingness to adapt defense policy to the changing world situation. DICK CHENEY, appointed Secretary of Defense by President George Bush in 1989, faced the task of downsizing the military forces following the breakup of the Soviet empire and the diminishment of the nuclear threat. In spite of new military challenges, including an invasion of PANAMA in 1989 to unseat a dictator hostile to the United States, and the GULF WAR in 1991, brought on by Iraq's seizure of Kuwait in 1990, the pressure to cut the military establishment and the defense budget continued apace. A massive budget deficit, which settled on the United States during the 1980s, contributed significantly to this pressure.

After its establishment in 1947, it was almost inevitable that the Department of Defense would become one of the most important units of the federal government. The United States was increasingly concerned about its security as the cold war developed. U.S. military involvement in conflicts, such as the Korean War and the struggle in Vietnam, seemed to require the maintenance of large standing military forces, typically over 2 million in the 1980s, supported by a civilian staff of 1 million. The Defense Department, with the support of the Presidents, consumed a major portion of the federal dollar.

[See also WAR DEPARTMENT.]

BIBLIOGRAPHY

Caraley, Demetrios. *The Politics of Military Unification: A Study of Conflict and the Policy Process.* 1966.

Cole, Alice C., et al., eds. *The Department of Defense: Documents on Establishment and Organization, 1944–1978.* 1978.

Hammond, Paul Y. *Organizing for Defense: The American Military Establishment in the Twentieth Century.* 1961.

Huntington, Samuel P. *The Common Defense: Strategic Programs in National Politics.* 1961.

Rearden, Steven L. *History of the Office of the Secretary of Defense,* Vol. I: *The Formative Years, 1947–1950.* 1984.

Rees, John C. *The Management of Defense: Organization and Control of the U.S. Armed Services.* 1964.

Trask, Roger R. *The Secretaries of Defense: A Brief History, 1947–1985.* 1985.

ROGER R. TRASK

DEFENSE POLICY. The initial defense policy of the United States was implicit in the Declaration of Independence in 1776—to defend the nation's independence. In its first century, the United States relied on geographical isolation and the European balance of power to defend its independence. A traditional distaste for standing military forces dictated maintenance of a very small military establishment. George Washington's dictum against "entangling alliances" in his FAREWELL ADDRESS and the 1823 MONROE DOCTRINE warning European nations against further colonization or intervention in the Western Hemisphere were defensive policies.

As European countries expanded their colonial empires in the latter part of the nineteenth century, the United States began to develop a more active defense policy. The modern navy began to emerge in the 1880s; after the SPANISH-AMERICAN WAR of 1898, further attention was paid to the expansion of the navy. At the same time the United States continued to depend on the Monroe Doctrine as a defensive strategy.

For almost two decades after WORLD WAR I, defense policy depended on geographical isolation and the assumed lack of real enemies. But the rise of aggressive totalitarian governments in Japan, Italy, and Germany forced the United States to think more about defense policy. By 1940, during the administration of Franklin D. Roosevelt, this meant expanding the nation's armed forces and defending America by aiding its allies. Roosevelt portrayed such programs as the DESTROYERS-FOR-BASES deal with Britain and the lend-lease program [see LEND-LEASE ACT] as defensive. Brought into the war by the Japanese attack on PEARL HARBOR in December 1941, the United States led the UNITED NATIONS coalition to victory after almost four years of fighting.

The Cold War and Containment. In 1945, the United States and the Soviet Union, longtime political and ideological competitors, faced off against each other. By 1947, their disagreements had provided the early provocations for the COLD WAR. Defense became a central concern, causing President Harry S. Truman to insist upon development of a comprehensive national security system. The NATIONAL SECURITY ACT of 1947 created the National Military Establishment (renamed the DEPARTMENT OF DEFENSE in 1949), encompassing the Army, Navy, and Air Force departments, the JOINT CHIEFS OF STAFF, and several defense agencies. The law also established the CENTRAL INTELLIGENCE AGENCY and the NATIONAL SECURITY COUNCIL. The Secretary of Defense was to be "the principal assistant to the President in all matters relating to the national security." JAMES V. FORRESTAL, the first Secretary of Defense, described the National Security Act as "the most decisive and definitive step taken by this country in the formation of a national military policy since the foundation of the republic."

By 1947, the guiding principle of postwar defense policy had emerged—the principle of CONTAINMENT, derived in theory from the ideas of George Kennan, a State Department Soviet expert. The Truman containment policy ruled out concessions to the Soviet Union but looked to negotiations to win acceptance of U.S. positions and to attract support from allies. In the meantime the United States would provide economic and military aid to friends abroad and eventually rebuild its own military strength. Another element of this policy was collective security, manifested most notably in the North Atlantic Treaty Organization (NATO), established in 1949.

The United States also relied somewhat on its monopoly (until 1949) in NUCLEAR WEAPONS, but the navy and the air force differed about how to deliver such weapons. The navy insisted on aircraft carriers, while the air force touted strategic bombers. Questions surfaced also about whether the use of atomic weapons would make sense militarily. After the Soviet Union detonated its first atomic device in 1949, President Truman decided to develop the hydrogen bomb as a deterrent rather than as an offensive weapon.

When North Korea attacked South Korea in June 1950, the Truman administration, assuming that the Soviet Union had ordered the operation, began a long-range military build-up, causing the defense budget to skyrocket from the originally planned $13.5 billion to $48.2 billion for fiscal year 1951. To shore up Western Europe's defenses, the United States decided to send four to six divisions to join the NATO defense force and to push for West German rearmament and incorporation of West German forces into NATO. NSC-68 (April 1950), an analysis of the world crisis and a prescription for U.S. NATIONAL-SECURITY POLICY, much influenced the Truman administration at this time. After the intervention of Communist China in the KOREAN WAR, in response to the United Nations Command's intrusion into North Korea, the Truman administration adopted a limited-war approach.

Eisenhower's New Look. Defense policy shifted after Dwight D. Eisenhower became President in 1953. The new NATIONAL SECURITY POLICY, assuming that combatants in a large-scale limited war or general war would go nuclear, posited greater reliance on nuclear weapons, delivered by strategic air forces, as well as cuts in conventional forces, enhanced continental defense, and modernization of reserve forces. The second Eisenhower administration (1957–1961) emphasized the placement of intermediate-range ballistic missiles (IRBMs) in Europe to counter the intercontinental-range ballistic missiles (ICBMs) being deployed by the Soviet Union. The United States also began development of the Minuteman ICBM, destined for deployment in hardened underground silos in the United States. Soviet success in launching the first satellite (1957) and competition between the United States and the Soviet Union in missile development led by 1960 to the so-called missile gap, based on charges that the Soviet Union was ahead in the development of missiles. This issue played a prominent role in the presidential campaign of 1960, but the new President, John F. Kennedy, learned after he entered office that the missile gap was a fiction.

Flexible Response. A new era in defense policy, featuring flexible response, began with Kennedy's appointment of ROBERT S. MCNAMARA as Secretary of Defense in 1961. Kennedy wanted the United States to have strategic arms and defense mechanisms sufficient to deter the Soviet Union from launching a nuclear attack. Kennedy and McNamara discarded massive retaliation in favor of flexible response, giving the United States a choice, as Kennedy said, between "inglorious retreat or unlimited retaliation."

Countering communist wars of national liberation was a particular goal. This required training U.S. and allied military personnel for counterinsurgency operations. Also, conventional strength had to be increased; this policy, combined with the manpower needs in Vietnam after 1964, led to expansion of U.S. forces from 2,484,000 in 1961 to about 3,550,000 in 1968.

McNamara played a major role in the formulation of nuclear strategy. He espoused assured destruction, an effort to deter nuclear attack by maintaining the means to inflict massive damage upon aggressors, even after suffering a surprise first strike. The later-coined term *mutual assured destruction* suggested that each side's ability to inflict massive damage on the other would stand as an effective deterrent. To implement this strategy, McNamara pushed for the modernization of weapon and delivery systems—the Minuteman ICBM, the Polaris submarine-launched ballistic missile (SLBM), and the Titan II missile.

McNamara believed that the outcome of the CUBAN MISSILE CRISIS (1962) demonstrated the readiness of U.S. armed forces to meet an emergency. Similarly, McNamara, Kennedy, and President Lyndon B. Johnson all saw the VIETNAM WAR as an example of flexible response, a policy that assumed the necessity of calibrating means to needs. In Vietnam the nature of the means gradually escalated until the United States had nearly 550,000 troops there. But flexible response as originally conceived could hardly have reached this height, and carrying it as far as McNamara and Johnson did brought both political turmoil at home and military failure in Vietnam.

Strategic Sufficiency. Elected in 1968, President Richard M. Nixon, along with his advisers, developed a policy of strategic sufficiency. Sufficiency was to be the substitute for superiority, in the hope that both the United States and the Soviet Union, rather than trying to surpass each other's efforts, would be served by mutual restraint. Strategic sufficiency required the United States to have enough nuclear capacity to deter nuclear attacks by persuading a potential aggressor that it would suffer an unacceptable level of retaliatory damage. The policy stressed avoidance of mass destruction of civilians and the development of machinery to prevent nuclear escalation. The NIXON DOCTRINE, defined as "pursuit of peace through partnership" with allies, was related to this policy. U.S. allies would be prepared, through transfer of military aid and equipment, to bear a larger share of the defense burden. Signing of the SALT (STRATEGIC ARMS LIMITATION TALKS) I agreements with the Soviet Union in 1972, decreeing a five-year moratorium on expansion of each country's strategic nuclear-delivery systems, related to both strategic sufficiency and the Nixon Doctrine.

James R. Schlesinger, Secretary of Defense (1973–1975) under both Nixon and President Gerald R. Ford, questioned the assured-destruction policy; he thought that credible strategic nuclear deterrence had to be based on essential equivalence with the Soviet Union in force effectiveness. He argued that the United States should have the capacity to attack critical military targets without hitting urban areas and causing widespread collateral damage, in the hope that the enemy would not attack U.S. cities. Schlesinger adopted a partial counterforce policy, which emphasized hitting strictly military targets and mutually abstaining from attacks on population centers. He also denied any intention of developing a destabilizing first-strike capability against the Soviet Union.

Schlesinger worked to halt the decline in conventional strength because he considered conventional forces essential in the U.S. deterrence system, especially to deter limited threats. He also emphasized the need to strengthen NATO conventional forces and promoted burden-sharing among the NATO allies. He argued stridently for larger defense budgets, irritating both Congress and President Ford in the process and contributing to his dismissal from office late in 1975. By 1976 the Democrats were arguing for a substantial decrease in defense spending, and President Jimmy Carter (1977–1981) cut the defense budget recommended by the Ford administration for fiscal year 1978. By the time Carter left office, his administration, faced with heavy criticism from Republicans and serious challenges in the Middle East, Iran, Afghanistan, and elsewhere, was supporting substantial defense increases.

Equivalence and Countervalence. Harold Brown, Carter's Secretary of Defense, adopted the principle of essential equivalence in the nuclear balance with the Soviet Union to make sure that the U.S. nuclear capacity neither was seen as nor in fact was inferior to the Soviet Union's. The strategic triad—ICBMs, SLBMs, and bombers—had to be upgraded; thus he supported development of the new MX ICBM, the Trident nuclear submarine, and the stealth technol-

ogy (to produce aircraft with low radar profiles). Brown developed a countervailing strategy, announced by President Carter in June 1980. Brown explained that the policy of the United States was "to ensure that the Soviet leadership knows that if they choose some intermediate level of aggression, we could, by selective, large (but still less than maximum) nuclear attacks, exact an unacceptably high prices in things the Soviet leaders appear to value most—political and military control, military force both nuclear and conventional, and the industrial capability to sustain a war." At the same time Brown urged NATO members to broaden their defense spending, suggesting an increase target of 3 percent a year, and pushed arms control, including the SALT II treaty of 1979.

The Cold War Ends. President Ronald Reagan (1981–1989) believed that U.S. strategic capabilities had declined relative to Soviet forces. In 1981 he announced a five-point approach—improvement of communications, command, and control systems; strategic-bomber modernization; deployment of a new SLBM; improvement in survivability and accuracy of the new ICBMs; and improvement in strategic defense. This meant producing one hundred B-1B bombers and one hundred MX ICBMs and developing a stealth aircraft, the Trident II SLBM, enhanced air-surveillance systems, and an antisatellite system. Reagan's Secretary of Defense, CASPAR W. WEINBERGER, emphasized that these plans had been formulated with deterrence in mind but nevertheless argued that the United States had to prepare to fight a long nuclear conflict because the Soviet Union was doing so.

Weinberger succeeded initially in increasing the defense budget, but Congress consistently appropriated less than he wanted and became reluctant as time passed to approve large increases. Reagan and his successor, George Bush, elected in 1988, were more willing than their predecessors in the 1970s to use U.S. military force; Reagan sent troops to the Caribbean island of GRENADA (1983) to drive out a Marxist dictatorship and later bombed Libya, accused of international terrorism. Bush invaded PANAMA in 1989 to unseat a leader unfriendly to the United States and based on United Nations resolutions sent a military contingent of over 500,000 to Saudi Arabia in 1991 as part of a multinational force to expel Iraqi leader Saddam Hussein from Kuwait, which Hussein took by military force in August 1990 (see GULF WAR).

At the same time that he pushed military expansion, Reagan entered into START (STRATEGIC ARMS REDUCTION TALKS) negotiations with the Soviet Union. He and the Soviet leader, Mikhail Gorbachev, signed an INF (INTERMEDIATE RANGE NUCLEAR FORCES) TREATY in 1987 and soon thereafter undertook negotiations to limit long-er-range weapons; the Bush administration concluded two such treaties, one with the Soviets and another with the Russian Republic. This progress, coupled with the internal breakup of the Soviet Union and the collapse of Soviet control in Eastern Europe, signaled by 1991 the end of the cold war.

Defense Policy in the 1990s. The events of the early 1990s forced a wholesale rethinking of defense policy. Defense budgets, beginning with fiscal year 1992, began to go down. The Defense Department, under congressional pressure, decided to close hundreds of military bases and to cut substantially the number of U.S. forces stationed in Europe. The overall size of the armed forces, averaging over 2 million in the previous decade, began to decline. The Pentagon revised downward plans for production of newer weapon systems, such as the MX missile, the B-1B bomber, and stealth aircraft. The election of Bill Clinton to the presidency in 1992 presaged additional large cuts in the defense budget.

The end of the cold war did not mean an end to maintenance of a large military force by the United States; defense planners assumed that there would still be trouble spots in the world, particularly in developing nations, as well as in the former Soviet Union and its satellite nations. Smaller local or regional wars appeared to be more likely than major world conflicts, and the threat of nuclear confrontation diminished. The questions for the United States were how large a force to maintain, whether and how to proceed on the development of new weapon and defensive systems, and how much to spend. The answers to these questions would determine the defense policy of the United States as it approached the beginning of the twenty-first century.

BIBLIOGRAPHY

Brown, Harold. *Thinking about National Security: Defense and Foreign Policy in a Dangerous World.* 1983.
Enthoven, Alain C., and K. Wayne Smith. *How Much Is Enough? Shaping the Defense Program, 1961–1969.* 1971.
Freedman, Lawrence. *The Evolution of Nuclear Strategy.* 1981.
Gaddis, John Lewis. *Strategies of Containment: A Critical Appraisal of Postwar American National Security Policy.* 1982.
Hammond, Paul Y. *Organizing for Defense: The American Military Establishment in the Twentieth Century.* 1961.
Huntington, Samuel P. *The Common Defense: Strategic Programs in National Politics.* 1961.
Schilling, Warren R., Paul Y. Hammond, and Glenn H. Snyder. *Strategy, Politics, and Defense Budgets.* 1962.
Trask, Roger R. *The Secretaries of Defense: A Brief History, 1947–1985.* 1985.

ROGER R. TRASK

DELEGATION OF LEGISLATIVE POWER.

A traditional maxim of American constitutional law, *delegata potestas non potest delegari* (delegated power cannot be delegated), holds that since Congress exercises only powers delegated to it by the people, it cannot in turn delegate that power to others. The principle is an important one in recognizing the primacy of legislative power and in placing restrains on government that were central concerns in the creation of the American constitutional system. However, in practice, much of the legislative power delegated to Congress in the Constitution has come to be exercised by the President and administrative officials.

Reasons for Delegations. Congress began delegating some of its power as soon as it began passing legislation in 1789, finding justification in the necessary and proper clause (Art. I, Sec. 8) of the Constitution. Congress has regularly conferred on the executive branch the power to exercise legislative-like power in making public policy. The delegation of legislative power to the President and to independent regulatory agencies and commissions has become important to members of Congress whose ambitions for the exercise of governmental power outstrip their time and expertise. Delegations of authority can permit flexible and adaptive policy-making by administrative agencies. Some delegations, particularly those to INDEPENDENT COMMISSIONS, reflect an attempt to insulate the exercise of regulatory and other politically sensitive governmental powers from interference by Congress or the White House. Delegation can be good politics: Congress can pass broad mandates that engender widespread support and defer the difficult decisions that will likely generate controversy to others.

Can the nondelegation principle be reconciled with the practice of broad delegation of legislative power? The Supreme Court has reviewed a number of these congressional delegations of power and has almost always upheld them, requiring only some minimal provision of congressional standards to guide administrative discretion. It has been particularly supportive of broad delegations in foreign affairs, because of the nature of executive power. In UNITED STATES V. CURTISS-WRIGHT EXPORT CORP. (1936), the Court has acknowledged that Congress can give to the President in this area a "degree of discretion and freedom from statutory restrictions which would not be admissible were domestic affairs alone involved," given the nature of executive power in foreign relations. The President's inherent foreign policy powers have encouraged the Court (in *Rostker v. Goldberg* [1981]) to accept broad delegations of legislative powers in areas of military affairs and international relations. Congress's delegation during World War II to the President and other executive branch officials to set prices for commodities, wages, and salaries, a particularly expansive delegation of power, was approved by the Court in Yakus v. United States (1944).

Delegations in domestic legislation have been almost as broadly crafted. Legislation transferring power and discretion to the President and administrative agencies has been upheld as long as some minimum guidelines are provided either in the statute itself or in its legislative history. In *Brig Aurora v. United States* (1813), the Court endorsed a delegation to the President to determine when trade restrictions were to be imposed; Congress could legislate conditionally and leave factfinding responsibilities that would trigger legislative-like judgments to the President. In 1825 the Court ruled in *Wayman v. Southard* that Congress could enact general legislation and have others "fill in the details." The Court, in *J. W. Hampton, Jr., and Co. v. United States* (1928), ruled that Congress need only provide an "intelligible standard" to guide administrators in order for its delegation to pass constitutional muster. In *N.Y. Central Securities Co. v. United States* (1932), mandates as vague as requiring agencies to act in the "public interest" have been found sufficient to satisfy the Court's requirement of legislative standards.

Court Interpretation. The only real controversy surrounding the delegation of power arose in the 1930s in response to enactment of the National Industrial Recovery Act of 1933 (73 Stat. 195), an extremely broad and ambitious law that created in the National Recovery Administration the power to stabilize markets, soften competitive pressures, and reduce the number of failed businesses. In two 1935 cases the Supreme Court rejected parts of the act that failed to include in their delegated powers guidelines to limit administrative discretion. A section of the act that provided for presidential controls on petroleum production was rejected in Panama Refining Co. v. Ryan (1935), because the law provided no criteria to govern the President's actions: Congress, the justices complained, "has declared no policy, has established no standard, has laid down no rule." In Schechter Poultry Corp. v. United States (1935), the Court voided another section of the act because Congress had failed to provide criteria to guide the executive branch in the formulation of codes of fair competition that were binding on specific sectors of the economy.

In 1936 the Court rejected another New Deal statute, the Coal Conservation Act of 1935, because it delegated power to representatives of the coal industry to write binding regulations for their industry, a particularly "obnoxious" form of delegation, accord-

ing to the Court in *Carter v. Carter Coal Co.* because it empowered private persons to make public policies affecting themselves and their competitors. However, three years later, in *Currin v. Wallace* (1939), the Court abandoned its prohibition of delegation to private parties in permitting farmers to veto Agriculture Department marketing proposals.

No law has been struck down since these three New Deal–era cases for failing to provide adequate guidelines for its implementation. However, one member of the Supreme Court, Chief Justice William Rehnquist, has invoked the nondelegation doctrine. In two cases dealing with the regulation of occupational safety and health—*Industrial Union Dep't, AFL-CIO v. American Petroleum Institute* (1980) and *American Textile Manufacturers Institute v. Donovan* (1981), Rehnquist argued that Congress had improperly delegated to the Secretary of Labor authority to determine standards for worker exposure to toxic materials.

The nondelegation doctrine has also had some relevance in areas affecting fundamental personal liberties. In *Kent v. Dulles* (1958), the Supreme Court voided the power of the Secretary of State to deny passports to persons who refused to state whether they had ever been members of the Communist Party. One year later, in *Greene v. McElroy* (1959), it rejected a Department of Defense program for security clearance because it required that "decisions of great constitutional import and effect" be made by administrators without "explicit action by lawmakers." In *National Cable Television Ass'n v. United States* (1974), the Court interpreted an agency's power to impose a fee narrowly so that Congress was not otherwise guilty of an impermissible delegation of the power to tax to an administrative body. Rather than rejecting delegations as too broad, the Court has preferred instead to narrow the delegation by limiting what administrative officials can do under their enabling statutes.

The delegation of legislative power is also constrained by procedural safeguards provided in the 1946 Administrative Procedure Act (60 Stat. 237, sec. 10(e), 5 U.S.C. 500–706), which provides for notice to be given to affected parties of proposed rules, an opportunity for them to submit comments and materials to the agency, and publication of the final rule in the *Federal Register*. Many statutes provide additional procedural protections to ensure public participation and judicial review of agency regulations.

Critics. Critics of the delegation of power have warned that it jeopardizes important values that are at the heart of constitutional government. Theodore Lowi argues that the delegation of legislative power results in administrative discretion rather than clear rules of law that are binding on citizens. Delegation shifts policy-making authority from the more politically visible and accountable forum of Congress to the administrative process, dominated by interest groups that enjoy special, privileged access and influence in agency decision making. Bureaucratic discretion weakens formal democratic processes that are essential in ensuring that policy-making authority is accountable to the public. Ultimately, it threatens the idea of the rule of law, that the exercise of the coercive power of government will be stable, predictable, and applied consistently.

Lowi contends that the delegation of power ultimately produces sweeping expectations about the power of government that cannot be fulfilled. While expectations are stimulated, effective governing power is weakened as it is dissipated in the administrative process by officials who try to accommodate the variety of interests demanding their attention. With no clear standards to guide them, agencies are expected to do whatever interest groups demand. They are unable to plan, to achieve justice, or accomplish the other expectations held for them as they are captured and buffeted by private interests. They lack the independence and autonomy from narrow political interests that come from clear and specific delegations of goals and authority to accomplish them. He calls on the courts to resuscitate the rule from *Schechter* against broad, standardless delegation of power; the President to veto legislation that is so vague that it creates expectations that are impossible to satisfy; agencies to engage in rulemaking as a way to limit their discretion; and Congress to review regularly and codify legislation based on its ongoing review of the administration of those laws as a way to mitigate against the adverse consequences of delegation.

Alan Morrison argues that the nondelegation doctrine should be used by the courts to reject legislation that does not provide reviewing courts with sufficiently clear standards by which they can assess whether administrative actions comply with congressional intent. Statutes should be voided when reviewing courts cannot determine if particular administrative actions fall within the bounds delegated by Congress since it is impossible in these situations for the courts to determine whether or not the agency is complying with the law. If Congress is not in a position to delegate with specificity, it can appoint an advisory commission or some other body to come up with a set of proposals that members can then debate and vote on.

Morrison believes there may be political constraints on delegation even if constitutional checks are lacking.

The political outcry following Congress's efforts in 1989 to raise its pay without directly voting on the proposal appeared to spring from the way in which members of Congress tried to avoid making the decision as much as at the increase itself. Political pressure to force Congress to address some of the difficult choices confronting the nation may be more likely to encourage compliance with the nondelegation doctrine than debate over constitutional doctrine.

BIBLIOGRAPHY

Fisher, Louis. *Constitutional Conflicts between Congress and the President*. 3d rev. ed. 1991. Pp. 84–114.
Lowi, Theodore J. *The End of Liberalism*. 2d ed. 1979. Pp. 92–126.
Morrison, Alan. "A Non-Power Looks at Separation of Powers." *Georgetown Law Journal* 79 (1990): 281–311.
Tribe, Laurence. *American Constitutional Law*. 2d ed. 1988. Pp. 362–369.

GARY C. BRYNER

DEMOCRATIC PARTY. "If I could not go to heaven but with a party," Thomas Jefferson once told a friend, "I would not go there at all." Jefferson was not serious, of course, for he was the cofounder of the Republican (usually called the Democratic-Republican) Party that went through some name-changing until it became unabashedly Andrew Jackson's Democratic Party. But Jefferson was reflecting the Framers' distaste for political parties stemming from their experience between 1765 and 1775. They believed partisan politics had infected the mother country, and from their reading of history they discerned that factional struggles had hastened destruction of those ancient models of republican virtues.

These lessons were remembered when the Constitution was being shaped in 1787, as the thirty-nine signers were in common agreement that political parties must be eschewed if the struggling republic was to survive. Indeed, the first President was a host unto himself, and George Washington's own belief that parties were "baneful" and destructive led him into the camp of the rising FEDERALIST PARTY despite his protests. Jefferson, as Secretary of State in Washington's Cabinet, found he was increasingly at odds with ALEXANDER HAMILTON, the Secretary of the Treasury. They split over fundamental planks in Hamilton's formula for recovery, a funding act to redeem depreciated wartime Continental notes at par, as well as the creation of a national bank.

Still on friendly terms, the two Cabinet members cut a deal—Hamilton swung behind a bill that placed the nation's capital on the Potomac, and Jefferson told his friends to support the funding scheme. James Madison, who was a party to the compromise still opposed the bank bill, however. But the bill creating the BANK OF THE UNITED STATES passed Congress, and Washington signed it. The acrimony caused by the chartering of the bank helped solidify the political opposition.

The Jeffersonian Opposition. Jefferson quit the Cabinet, feeling his advice was ignored, and retired to MONTICELLO, until the bitter fight over JAY'S TREATY in 1795 created an unmistakable cleavage in Congress. Jefferson and his supporters denounced the pact as a betrayal to the archenemy Great Britain by making concessions on wartime debts and confiscated loyalist properties in order to extract a British promise to evacuate frontier forts that they still held. Republicans overlooked the favorable terms (including reopening of ports to U.S. ships in the British West Indies), but Washington's prestige offset their carping, and the treaty was narrowly ratified. The intense debate helped create a strong impression that the Federalists favoring the treaty were pro-British to the core, and Jefferson's partisans were already upset that the United States had backed out of its treaty obligations to France. Thereafter, the Federalists talked of their opposition as the "Jacobins," "Gallophiles," or worse. The Democratic-Republican Party rose out of the controversy over Jay's Treaty. In the 1796 election Jefferson came close to defeating John Adams for the presidency. As runner-up second in the ELECTORAL COLLEGE balloting, he therefore became Vice President.

Four years of turmoil ensued, as the young nation tried to guide a neutral course in the world war that erupted involving France and England. American ships became victims as both belligerents stopped vessels, seized cargoes, impressed Yankee seamen, and threw other American sailors into English or French dungeons. Federalist Adams steered clear of war, but Congress passed and Adams signed the notorious ALIEN AND SEDITION ACTS. Vindictive Federalists used their majority in Congress to make it illegal to criticize the administration, clearly violating the First Amendment to the Constitution. Some newspaper editors were indicted and convicted and were either fined or jailed, or both. Jefferson, working behind the scenes, encouraged Madison to write a protest and wrote one himself—the two statements became the Virginia and Kentucky resolutions, which called on states to act when unconstitutional laws were passed by Congress and asserted the doctrine of NULLIFICATION. The resolutions affirmed the necessity for union, but detractors of the resolutions focused on the nullification clauses.

The Virginia and Kentucky resolutions spelled out a platform for the Republican Party, as it was now being called. Alarmed Republicans warned citizens that their CIVIL LIBERTIES were endangered. Increased taxes reminded voters of the obnoxious whiskey tax that had caused so much grief in western Pennsylvania and Republicans played on fears that the pro-British faction in Congress was eager for a war with France. Republican rallies passed resolutions lauding the French for their own revolution. Scornful Federalists began to call the Republicans "Democrats."

The Democratic-Republicans. If there was any doubt as to what the Republicans stood for, Jefferson did his best to dispel it. He sent a letter to ELBRIDGE GERRY, who had asked Jefferson for his political creed, in which he said he was for lower taxes, a smaller army and navy, a reduced diplomatic establishment abroad, and the preservation of civil rights, including freedom of speech, press, and worship. On the issue of federal versus STATES' RIGHTS, Jefferson took a clear stand. "I am not," he told Gerry, "for transferring all the powers of the States to the General Government, and all those of that government to the executive branch." These "Principles of '98" welded to the Virginia and Kentucky resolutions, became the Democratic-Republican platform until 1836.

Jefferson's pronouncements were broadcast at party rallies and in the press. The number of newspapers had almost tripled since the ratification struggle over the Constitution in 1787–1788, when barely one hundred journals labored in the nation's first great political battle. By 1800 almost three hundred newspapers were aligned for either the Federalists or Democratic-Republicans, and political campaigns were carried on mainly in their columns until well into the twentieth century.

All the tools for campaigning were now in place—a political philosophy, a dedicated band of followers, and a press eager to promote the election of favored candidates. A series of tactical blunders by Federalists helped throw the election of 1800 into a political whirlwind. Jefferson and AARON BURR, both Democratic-Republicans, emerged with identical votes in the Electoral College. The dispute was settled, only days before the inauguration, when the House of Representatives chose Jefferson.

Jefferson called his election "the revolution of 1800." At his inauguration he called for an era of political color blindness. "We are all Republicans, we are all Federalists," he said by way of reconciliation. Jefferson's party had strong majorities in the House and Senate, and for most of the next eight years, Jefferson worked to cut taxes, eliminate the national debt, and cut the military forces drastically. True to his conviction, Jefferson pardoned all those convicted under the Sedition Act and had their fines refunded.

And, perhaps as part of a deal made during the presidential skirmish early in 1800, Jefferson did not fire as many incumbent Federalist officeholders as Democratic-Republicans desired, but the President was aware of officeseekers from 4 March 1801 onward. Democratic-Republicans eager for patronage thought Jefferson was not partisan enough, but the President defended himself and noted that after his first two years in the White House "of 316 offices in all the U.S. subject to appointment and removal by me, 130 only are held by Federalists."

Only the embargo laws that Jefferson sought to keep American shipping out of war zones marred an otherwise harmonious presidency. His handpicked successor, James Madison, finally had to call for a war against Great Britain after negotiations failed.

As the nation's first wartime President, Madison hewed to Democratic-Republican policies. He drew criticism for his patience with incompetent Cabinet members and generals. But a combination of good luck and skillful negotiating allowed the United States to emerge from the WAR OF 1812 with a heightened sense of nationhood and no loss of territory. The Federalists had offered token candidates in the presidential elections of 1812 and 1816. With the election of James Monroe in 1816, the Democratic-Republicans' opposition disappeared during the ERA OF GOOD FEELINGS. The party's problems were mainly internal for the next forty years, and only the specter of SLAVERY prevented the Democratic-Republicans from becoming a permanent and dominant political force in the nation.

The Democratic-Republicans' hold on the nation stemmed, in part, from the statehood system built into the Constitution. The LOUISIANA PURCHASE, made under Jefferson's watchful eye, created a vast public domain for public settlement. The trans-Mississippi West became a vast territorial bonanza, and its settlement was to become a political plum for the Democratic-Republicans and their successors, the Democratic Party, until their opponents came to power in 1861.

As each territory was created by Congress, the President was empowered to appoint a governor and other key officials, who would establish courts, maintain order, and prepare the citizenry for statehoood. These appointments became political rewards for defeated members of Congress, party hangers-on, and ambitious men ready to start a new life in the South or West. From the settlement of Mississippi Territory

until 1860, most of the territorial officials were Democrats who maintained their hold when statehood was granted.

Power thus rested in the hands of Democratic-Republican Presidents from 1803 onward. The first major disruption to the party's dominance came in 1819, when the balance being maintained in the Senate as new states were admitted (one slave, one free) was threatened by a northern effort to prohibit slavery in the new western territories. The MISSOURI COMPROMISE of 1820 allowed Maine and Missouri to come into the Union with the twenty-four states evenly divided, free and slave, but thereafter slavery was forbidden in the Louisiana Territory above 36°30' latitude (Missouri's southern boundary).

The crisis blew over. The National Republicans (the conservative, anti-Jackson faction) managed to elect John Quincy Adams President in 1824, but supporters of General Andrew Jackson never forgave Adams for making a deal with HENRY CLAY. Clay became Secretary of State under Adams, and thought he was in line for the presidency; but Jackson's managers challenged the caucus system of presidential nominations that had chosen nominees since 1796. (In fact, the 1824 caucus nominee had been WILLIAM H. CRAWFORD, but state or district caucuses raised the banners of Adams, Clay, Calhoun, and Jackson.) Now the Jacksonians proclaimed the death of "King Caucus" and held their own district or state nominating conventions to promote Jackson's candidacy. A tariff passed in 1828—the TARIFF OF ABOMINATIONS—was opposed by southerners and threatened a party split, but South Carolinian JOHN C. CALHOUN joined Jackson's ticket, and in the general election, which took predictable turns, New England went for Adams, the South and West along with the swing-state Pennsylvania chose Jackson. Jackson's electoral vote was 178 to 83 for Adams. The election, however, signaled the return of a two-party system. Clay took his followers into the National Republican camp, determined to oust Jackson in the 1832 election.

The Jacksonian Party. Jackson rejuvenated the party, giving it the name "Democratic" and amending Jefferson's philosophy. Jackson hated the Bank of the United States, favored low taxes, reduction of the national debt, and a broad-based suffrage for white men without property qualifications. Jackson was accused of starting a "spoils system" that rewarded loyal Democrats with federal jobs, but he only improved on the turnover scheme Jefferson had started [see PATRONAGE]. Jackson was furious when southerners talked about nullification (reacting to the 1828 tariff), and he broke with Calhoun as he made it clear that "the Union must and shall be preserved." The death of the caucus system came in 1832 when Jacksonian Democrats held a national nominating convention, as did the National Republicans and a new party, the ANTI-MASONIC PARTY. Jackson trounced Clay in the Electoral College, 219 to 49, with a handful of votes for the other candidates.

His successor, Martin Van Buren, inherited a financial panic that dragged down his candidacy for a second term and allowed the newly formed WHIG PARTY to elect a military hero, William Henry Harrison. The Democrats regrouped when a former Democrat, John Tyler, succeeded Harrison as President and took sides with southern slaveholders as the admission of Texas burst forth as an issue in 1844. Texas became a state through some legislative intrigue that aroused northern opposition. James K. Polk, the first DARK HORSE candidate carried the Democratic banner in 1844. Polk, who believed in MANIFEST DESTINY, provoked Mexico into a war that ended with a treaty, which (until the purchase of Alaska) completed the continental expansion of the United States. Now the United States stretched from coast to coast, and antislavery agitation increased as southerners hoped to make California a slave state. The COMPROMISE OF 1850 kept the western state free, but the KANSAS-NEBRASKA ACT of 1854 ruined STEPHEN A. DOUGLAS's hope for the presidency. Douglas's "squatter sovereignty" doctrine angered northerners opposed to slavery (and who feared its extension) and frightened southerners as a political device that could strangle slavery by congressional action. In the political melee that followed, dissident Democrats, joined by antislavery Whigs, created a new political party that was purportedly Jeffersonian in principle, hence their "Republican" party had ties to the past but no real support in the South.

The Civil War and After. The Democrats in 1860 were deeply divided over the slavery issue and split votes between Douglas and JOHN C. BRECKENRIDGE to ensure the election of Abraham Lincoln. Lincoln won with fewer popular votes than the combined votes of his opponents. The coming of CIVIL WAR in 1861 tore the country apart along sectional lines and made a shambles of old political alliances that had usually ensured Democratic victories in such key states as New York and Pennsylvania. Democrats were tainted with charges of treason, as clandestine COPPERHEADS who favored a Southern victory. Lincoln won as the Union candidate in the wartime election of 1864, defeating GEORGE B. MCCLELLAN in a hard-fought campaign (Lincoln won only 52 percent of the popular vote). Republicans favoring a harsh RECONSTRUCTION policy hoped to keep Democrats a permanent minority; they periodically "waved the bloody shirt" to remind voters that a

Union victory came under a Republican administration. After federal troops were removed from their Southern stations in 1877 (following the close and disputed election of 1876, when Democrat SAMUEL J. TILDEN won in the popular vote, but lost to Rutherford B. Hayes in the Electoral College vote), a so-called solid South emerged to support Democrats consistently for the next fifty years.

Democratic losses in the Midwestern states accentuated national trends. Once-strong Democratic majorities in Iowa, Illinois, Ohio, and Indiana melted, and but for a series of financial panics (starting in 1873) and widespread unemployment, the Democrats would not have won at either the national or state level. Republican majorities in Congress favored high tariffs, protection for heavy industries, and the building of railroads. Democrats continued to hold to their historic position of low tariffs, but only when aroused by searing depressions would voters respond favorably. Grover Cleveland broke the spell twice, but he was innately conservative, and his two terms were punctuated by the Republican victory in 1888. Immigration fed the nation's factories and the western states welcomed farmers from the East as well as from Europe. Relatively few of the immigrants went to the South, but the hundreds of thousands of Swedes, Norwegians, Germans, and British who came for the most part identified with the Republicans.

The Republican Ascendancy. The 1896 election proved that the Democrats were not moribund. Focusing on the Republicans' insistence on high tariffs and a deflationary gold standard, Democrats rallied behind the silver-tongued orator WILLIAM JENNINGS BRYAN. In his "Cross of Gold" speech, he called for a cheaper dollar that would help debtors pay off mortgages. But despite Bryan's popularity, the more staid William McKinley won in 1896 and again in the election of 1900 when the two were once more pitted against each other. Voters were suspicious of Democratic pleas for lower tariffs; moreover, Democrats warned against the ANNEXATION OF HAWAII and the former Spanish colonies. ALTON B. PARKER, a lackluster Democrat, was swamped by Theodore Roosevelt in 1904. Bryan made his last run for President in 1908 against William Howard Taft and lost.

The mood of the country was Republican, and it seemed that perhaps the Democrats had become the permanent minority party. This might have continued but for a Republican squabble in 1912, when Theodore Roosevelt came out of retirement to challenge Taft. Roosevelt ran as the candidate of the PROGRESSIVE (BULL MOOSE) PARTY, thus splitting the Republicans into two factions and allowing the Democrat, Woodrow

Wilson, to win 435 electoral votes to 88 for Roosevelt and only 8 for Taft. During Wilson's first term, banking regulation, tariff rates, antitrust laws, labor workhours, and farm credit were enacted. When WORLD WAR I began, President Wilson tried to preserve NEUTRALITY, even while German submarines threatened American shipping. In April 1917 Wilson abandoned neutrality and took the nation into a war that saved the Allied cause but ended his domestic reform program.

After the Allied victory in 1918, Wilson tried to bring Democrats along with his vision of a world free of war by promoting the LEAGUE OF NATIONS. Blocked by League opponents in the Senate, Wilson tried to rally citizens behind his cause but was felled by a stroke while on a nationwide speaking tour. He returned to Washington a broken man, and in some ways the spirit of the Democratic Party was also shattered. In the 1920 presidential election both parties chose Ohio newspaper publishers as candidates. Warren G. Harding's landslide victory over JAMES M. COX vindicated Republican calls for a rejection of the League and a return to "normalcy."

If the late nineteenth century saw the exploitation of America's natural resources on an awesome scale, the 1920s saw a shift in focus to finance through banking mergers, stocks and bonds, and easy credit terms on Wall Street that sent share prices soaring to new heights. And although both major political parties denied any sympathy for the KU KLUX KLAN, the Klan was a political force in several states. Calvin Coolidge easily defeated Democrat JOHN W. DAVIS, a Wall Street lawyer, in 1924, and Herbert Hoover swamped Catholic ALFRED E. SMITH in 1928. Although PROHIBITION was not a real issue in either contest, the hypocrisy of a nation that imbibed bootlegged whiskey while voting "dry" made the Eighteenth Amendment an issue in 1932; the nation by then was in the throes of the worst depression in United States history.

The New Deal. There were over nine million unemployed workers. Democrat Franklin D. Roosevelt promised a NEW DEAL and swept into office with 472 electoral votes to 59 for Herbert Hoover. Roosevelt had told voters he was a Democrat in the tradition of Jefferson and Jackson, meaning that he was trying to "help the little man." He started major public works programs that included the CIVILIAN CONSERVATION CORPS for jobless young men. He also initiated legislation for SOCIAL SECURITY, insurance of bank deposits, and reform of the stock market.

Roosevelt prevailed through four presidential campaigns and left the Democratic Party a legacy of vigorous action that included full participation by the federal government in economic recovery programs. His successor, Harry S. Truman, led the nation to victory in WORLD WAR II and kept inflation at an acceptable level. Republicans charged that Truman was not tough enough in the COLD WAR; nonetheless, Truman won a stunning upset over THOMAS E. DEWEY in the election of 1948. He offered the MARSHALL PLAN to Europe; at home he opposed anti-union legislation passed by Republicans, but the Republicans held a majority in Congress and overrode Truman's veto.

Twenty years in office had left the Democrats weary. In 1952 a new political era in American politics began. Republic Dwight D. Eisenhower, landslide winner over ADLAI E. STEVENSON in 1956 after a comfortable win in 1952, ushered in a period in which Republicans held the presidency while Democrats retained control of Congress. As suburbs gained in population, voting patterns changed; old allegiances in labor and farming groups also gave way. The South was no longer "solid" and the Midwest and Far West, where the New Deal was once embedded, went back to the Republican column.

Television changed the public perception of politics: the personality of the candidate received more attention than debate over substantive issues. Consequently, polls became harbingers of a party's success or defeat. Meanwhile both Democrats and Republicans alike searched for a guiding political philosophy. Lacking one, the importance of parties declined and the campaigns became embroiled in trivial matters.

The close election in 1960 of John F. Kennedy gave Democrats a respite. Kennedy appealed to young voters; he spoke of the nation's commitment to space exploration, CIVIL RIGHTS for minorities, and peace abroad. Lyndon B. Johnson assumed the presidency after Kennedy's assassination in November 1963. Johnson sought and got civil rights legislation, although America's social structure changed more than its attitudes on race. The unpopular VIETNAM WAR caused Johnson not to seek reelection in 1968. HUBERT H. HUMPHREY, the Democratic nominee, was defeated by Richard M. Nixon.

Republican Domination. By appealing to the expanding middle class and promising low taxes, the Republicans destroyed the once-solid South as a Democratic stronghold while creating a formidable Republican phalanx in the western states. Jimmy Carter broke the pattern after the WATERGATE AFFAIR but the election returns in 1980 through 1988 were evidence of the voters' disenchantment with a Democratic Party that lacked imagination and bold approaches.

Perhaps the liberal impulse in American politics that had produced Jefferson, Jackson, Wilson, Roosevelt, and Johnson had run its course.

BIBLIOGRAPHY

Binkley, Wilfred E. *American Political Parties: Their Natural History.* 1943.

Chambers, William N. *The Democrats, 1789–1964.* 1964.

Cunningham, Noble E., Jr., "The Jeffersonian Republican Party." In vol. 1 of *History of U. S. Political Parties.* 4 vols. Edited by Arthur M. Schlesinger, Jr. 1973.

Rutland, Robert A. *The Democrats, from Jefferson to Carter.* 1979.

ROBERT A. RUTLAND

DEMOCRATIC-REPUBLICAN PARTY (JEFFERSONIAN). For discussion of the Republican Party of the first decades of the United States, also called the Democratic-Republican Party and the Jeffersonian Republican Party, see DEMOCRATIC PARTY.

DEPARTMENTAL SECRETARIES. The departmental secretary is the highest ranking appointive position in the executive branch, being referred to in the Constitution as "the principal Officer in each of the executive Departments." In 1789 the Congress established the first three departments, the STATE DEPARTMENT, the WAR DEPARTMENT, and the TREASURY DEPARTMENT. Congress also provided for an attorney general, although the JUSTICE DEPARTMENT was not created until 1870. In 1793 President George Washington began to meet with his department heads collectively, and the group came to be referred to as the President's CABINET.

The distinction must be made between the role of departmental secretaries in the United States and the role of cabinet ministers in parliamentary forms of government. In a parliamentary system cabinet ministers are members of the parliament, and the role of prime minister is that of first among equals. In the U.S. system of SEPARATION OF POWERS, however, the EXECUTIVE POWER rests with the President, and departmental secretaries serve at his pleasure. Cabinet ministers have independent status and formal powers in parliament and their political parties that U.S. departmental secretaries do not have.

The Cabinet. Throughout the nineteenth century Presidents used their departmental secretaries as sources of advice as well as the administrators of the major departments of the government. The practices of individual Presidents, however, varied. President Andrew Jackson did not meet with his departmental secretaries collectively for the first two years of his administration, preferring to rely on his informal KITCHEN CABINET for advice. On the other hand, President James Polk convened his departmental secretaries 350 times during his one term. Some Presidents weighed very heavily the consensus among their departmental secretaries in Cabinet meetings, carefully polling the judgment of each member on major issues. President Abraham Lincoln, however, summed up the constitutional relationship of the President to departmental secretaries when he announced the vote in a cabinet meeting: "Seven nays and one aye, the ayes have it."

In the twentieth century the Cabinet has been expanded to include fourteen department heads who hold the CIVIL SERVICE rank of Executive Level I, the highest-ranking appointive executive branch positions. Occasionally the President may include other officials in his Cabinet, such as the Director of the OFFICE OF MANAGEMENT AND BUDGET or the U.S. Representative to the UNITED NATIONS, occasionally others may hold Executive Level I positions. But the Cabinet secretaries traditionally constitute the President's Cabinet, though it is not established in law or the Constitution.

The role of departmental secretary is Janus-like in that secretaries must face both the President as the person who appoints them and to whom they report, but also each must face downward to his or her department, the people whom they must lead. Thus Cabinet secretaries are often caught in a bind in that they must prove themselves loyal to the President and carry out his policies. But in order to be effective leaders they must also be advocates for the agencies and employees in the department and the programs they operate. Cabinet secretaries must also be attentive to the constituencies of their departments and programs for political support for themselves and for help with presidential priorities in Congress.

The Secretaries' Role. The role of departmental secretary is a complex one. Each must be a skilled manager of the department's many bureaus and programs, an effective campaigner for the President's reelection, an effective lobbyer with Congress for the administration's programs, a leader of the career and political officials in the department, and a visible symbol of the President's commitment to the policy area he or she represents. The role of the secretary within his or her department is to act as the general manager of what often amounts to a holding company of separate bureaus and agencies. The role calls for adept political use of budgetary, organizational, and personnel skills by the secretary. At times these levers are sufficient, but in other cases bureaus have ties to sympathetic members of Congress independent of the secretary that enable them to pursue bureau priorities that may be at odds with their departmental secretary's agenda. Secretarial authority can also be undercut by the White House which in recent administrations has centralized budget and personnel decisions formerly exercised by department secretaries.

A distinction is often made between the "inner" Cabinet secretaries of State, Defense, Treasury, and the Attorney General. These original four departments cover the core of the functions of the national government, were the first to be created, and their heads are often the closest political advisers to the President. This inner core is often contrasted with the more recent additions to the Cabinet: the DEPARTMENT OF THE INTERIOR and the DEPARTMENT OF AGRICULTURE were created in the nineteenth century, and in the twentieth the DEPARTMENT OF COMMERCE (1913), DEPARTMENT OF LABOR (1913), DEPARTMENT OF HEALTH AND HUMAN SERVICES (1953), DEPARTMENT OF HOUSING AND URBAN DEVELOPMENT (1965), DEPARTMENT OF TRANSPORTATION (1966), DEPARTMENT OF ENERGY (1977), DEPARTMENT OF EDUCATION (1979), and the DEPARTMENT OF VETERANS AFFAIRS (1989).

The "outer" departmental secretaries have the disadvantage that they are often not as close to the President personally, and they are subject to the pulls of powerful interest groups whose interests their departments serve. Part of the tension between secretaries and the White House is that secretaries are often seen by interest groups as their advocates inside the administration, and they are often chosen by Presidents because of their appeal to these interest groups. When they act as advocates, however, they are often seen as disloyal to the President.

The selection of Cabinet secretaries by Presidents is one of the first official acts of a new President and sends important symbolic signals about the nature of the new administration. Thus secretaries are often chosen not merely because they are loyal to the President but also to represent presidential political values. In addition to loyalty, Presidents often consider sexual balance, racial mix, geographical distribution, religious representation, or ideological balance.

Because of the pressures from departmental constituencies and the need to administer their programs, secretaries are sometimes charged with "going native," that is, putting their departmental interests before their loyalty to the President. But this is understandable if one considers that the reason that many are chosen to head departments is that they have spent their careers becoming experts in the policy areas they are now administering. In addition, they want to perform well during their secretarial tenure, and in order to do a good job for the administration they need the resources of money and personnel. It is thus

quite understandable they should be advocates for their departments. CHARLES G. DAWES, Calvin Coolidge's Vice President and the first director of the Bureau of the Budget, said: "Cabinet secretaries are vice presidents in charge of spending, and as such are the natural enemies of the President." This absence of absolute loyalty to the President is also inherent in the U.S. constitutional system, because departmental secretaries are legally bound to carry out the law and can be called to report to Congress on the policies their departments are carrying out.

Thus the centripetal forces pulling departmental secretaries toward the President are often counterbalanced by centrifugal forces in the political system. But it may also be in the President's best interest for departmental secretaries to act as advocates for their departments. They may win the support of their interest groups as well as their own employees when they appear to be advocates for the programs and policies within their jurisdictions. This support may help the President politically.

The White House Staff. But these understandable forces that pull departmental secretaries away from the President are also part of the reason for the rise of the WHITE HOUSE STAFF in the modern presidency. In the nineteenth century and first half of the twentieth, cabinet members were the primary advisers to Presidents; in the last half of the twentieth century that function has been largely taken over by the White House staff. The organizational apparatus of the presidency has been greatly expanded since the report of the BROWNLOW COMMITTEE in 1937 and the establishment of the EXECUTIVE OFFICE OF THE PRESIDENT in 1939.

The reason for the rise of the White House staff is that top-level White House staffers are chosen only for their loyalty to the President and not the symbolic reasons mentioned above. They do not answer to Congress, have no independent political standing, and no client other than the President. In addition they enjoy proximity and access to the President and they can respond immediately to his demands. They have no other legal obligations and are not responsible for the managing of programs. So it is no wonder that the White House staff has grown and become more powerful as the rest of the executive branch has become more fragmented.

The dominance of the White House staff has become institutionalized in several ways: on the foreign policy side by the development of the NATIONAL SECURITY COUNCIL (NSC) and its staff and on the domestic side by the domestic policy staff and Cabinet councils. The NSC was created in 1947 as a coordinating mechanism for foreign and defense policy, but it was not until the Assistant to the President for National Security Affairs became the President's primary adviser in the 1970s that the NSC staff came to eclipse the departments of State and Defense. HENRY A. KISSINGER's role in the Nixon Administration overshadowed Secretary of State William Rogers and Secretary of Defense MELVIN R. LAIRD. Control of NATIONAL SECURITY initiatives was centralized in the White House. The dominance of the White House staff was evident when President Reagan ignored the advice of his secretaries of State and Defense when he chose to sell arms to Iran in trying to get U.S. hostages released. The NSC staff's supplanting of cabinet secretaries went to the extreme when the profits from the sales of arms to Iran were diverted to the contras in Nicaragua by the NSC staff without the knowledge of the Secretaries of State or Defense [see IRAN-CONTRA AFFAIR].

The domestic-policy staff, led by the DOMESTIC POLICY ADVISER, grew out of the Domestic Policy Council created in 1970 and has played an important role in domestic-policy development in each presidency since then. The rise of the White House domestic-policy capacity has led to frequent conflict between departmental secretaries and White House staffers. Part of this is necessary when disagreements between departmental secretaries have to be settled. Not every dispute can be settled by the President, and only top level White House staffers have the perspective to settle disagreements short of the President.

One way to mitigate this conflict is a policy development device known as CABINET COUNCILS. Ad hoc groups of departmental secretaries and White House staffers had been used in several presidencies but the Reagan administration institutionalized the arrangement by creating seven cabinet councils in its first term. The intention was to bring together White House staffers and departmental secretaries in the policy areas that each was concerned with. In President Reagan's second term the seven-council structure was deemed to be too unwieldy and was replaced with two councils, one for economic policy and one for domestic policy. These two councils, in addition to the National Security Council, continued into the Bush administration.

Cabinet Government. Presidents from Nixon on have campaigned for office promising Cabinet government, by which they mean that they intend to use their departmental secretaries actively, solicit their collective advice, and delegate significant authority to them. As candidates they were critical of the centralization of power in the White House that had occurred since the Kennedy administration and intended to return to President Eisenhower's manner of actively using his departmental secretaries. But these hopes and promises have been uniformly dashed on the rocks of the reality of the modern presidency.

President Nixon began his first term intending to delegate domestic policy to his secretaries, but ended up replacing many of them and centralizing power in his White House staff, particularly H. R. Haldeman and John Ehrlichman. In reacting against the centralized Nixon administration both candidates Ford and Carter promised Cabinet government and tried to be their own chiefs of staff. Each was soon disillusioned and named a WHITE HOUSE CHIEF OF STAFF while increasing the authority of their White House staffs. The Reagan campaign also promised a Cabinet approach to government as had been used in California by Governor Reagan. But after winning the election the White House staff systematically took control of budget, political personnel, and policy development. The Reagan administration had one of the most dominant White House staffs in history.

The fragmenting forces in American politics have increased with the growth of the scope and size of government. The modern presidency has dealt with this fragmentation by increasing the size and power of the White House staff. Regardless of campaign promises, the reality of the modern presidency is that the White House staff will continue to compete with and often overshadow departmental secretaries.

BIBLIOGRAPHY

Cohen, Jeffrey E. *The Politics of the U.S. Cabinet.* 1988.
Fenno, Richard F. *The President's Cabinet.* 1959.
Hess, Stephen. *Organizing the Presidency.* 2d ed. 1988.
Laski, Harold J. *The American Presidency.* 1940.
Patterson, Bradley H., Jr. *The Ring of Power.* 1988.
Pfiffner, James P. *The Strategic Presidency.* 1988.
Polsby, Nelson W. *Consequences of Party Reform.* 1983.
Seidman, Harold. *Politics, Position, and Power.* 4th ed. 1989.

JAMES P. PFIFFNER

DEPARTMENTS. See EXECUTIVE DEPARTMENTS. For discussion of each of the departments of the executive branch, see the article on the particular department (AGRICULTURE; COMMERCE; DEFENSE; EDUCATION; ENERGY; HEALTH AND HUMAN SERVICES; HOUSING AND URBAN DEVELOPMENT; INTERIOR; JUSTICE; LABOR; STATE; TRANSPORTATION; TREASURY; VETERANS AFFAIRS; WAR). For discussion of relations between the departments and the President, see WHITE HOUSE–DEPARTMENTAL RELATIONS.

DEREGULATION. In the American context, deregulation means reducing or eliminating established governmental controls over private-sector behavior. Starting in the 1960s, a succession of Presidents attempted to pare back regulatory restraints on economic behavior and later in other areas as well. Especially in their early efforts, they were responding more to the appeal of an idea than to strong popular pressures for change. The key idea, mainly articulated by academic economists, was that in certain areas and at certain levels, regulation produced costs that exceeded social gains. When protected from competition, as in the case of domestic airlines, the prime beneficiaries of regulation were the regulated. Reformers sought to replace regulatory protection with the discipline of the marketplace. When sole reliance on markets was not feasible, it was important to keep costs in the appropriate relationship to benefits.

Serious consideration of deregulation as a policy began in the presidency of John F. Kennedy. In a special message to Congress on transportation in 1962, President Kennedy equated less regulation with an improved transportation system and proposed an end to minimum-rate regulation in certain spheres. Congress debated changes in rate regulation in 1963 and 1964, but took no action.

Following Kennedy's assassination, President Lyndon B. Johnson favored the policy of cutting back on the regulation of business activity. Stimulus for this was provided by the COUNCIL OF ECONOMIC ADVISERS. Several regulatory agencies took small but significant steps that can be characterized as deregulatory in nature. Johnson personally was involved in ending import controls on residual fuel oil. He supported legislation that introduced a competitive element in the interest rates paid by financial institutions on savings deposits. In 1967, Johnson was fully prepared to make a dramatic proposal for deregulation the centerpiece of his transportation program. It was set aside after careful soundings indicated that enactment was not possible.

However, Johnson, as well as most of the Presidents who followed him, promoted, or at least tolerated, a vast expansion in the regulatory might of the national government. For instance, his administration sponsored many new regulatory programs aimed at environmental and consumer protection and safeguarding public health and safety.

During the presidency of Richard M. Nixon, regulatory reform continued to receive attention, although there were no serious efforts to abolish regulatory programs. The ASH COUNCIL (President's Advisory Council on Executive Management, headed by Roy Ash) recommended structural changes that would have brought many of the functions performed by independent regulatory commissions into the executive branch proper. Presumably, this would strengthen the President's hand in regulation and allow one so inclined to lessen the burdens of regulation on business. Pending favorable action on the Ash Council proposals, which never came, by EXECUTIVE ORDER President Nixon established an interagency regulatory review process coordinated by the OFFICE OF MANAGEMENT AND BUDGET. Its purpose was to monitor regulatory activity and to provide an opportunity to address questions of over-zealous efforts at control.

The presidency of Gerald R. Ford was a turning point in deregulation. He continued the effort to moderate the rules produced by regulatory agencies through presidential-level review and added to that consideration of their effects on inflation, then emerging as a serious problem. More importantly, Ford was the first President to launch a major attack on prominent regulatory edifices. His focus was on transportation, and removing airlines from regulatory protection was the prime objective. Starting in 1975, Congress engaged the issue. Ford added impetus to the process by the appointment of a Civil Aeronautics Board chairman who was sympathetic to deregulation.

President Jimmy Carter was an active regulator in areas such as the environment and auto safety, but at the same time he was an active deregulator. He further strengthened presidential-level review of rules. Many of his appointees to regulatory commissions favored cutting back on regulation. With Carter's active support. Congress removed economic controls over the airlines and abolished the Civil Aeronautics Board. He also supported and Congress passed legislation that lessened restraints on motor carrier and rail transportation, depository institutions, and natural gas.

President Ronald Reagan was the most enthusiastic deregulator, although he emphasized administrative rather than legislative means. Through appointments and budget decisions, he sought to loosen regulatory controls across the board. The regulatory review process, still the responsibility of the Office of Management and Budget, became an even more potent force for reducing the costs imposed by regulation, whether economic or social. Presidential efforts to restrain regulation were reinforced by the Task Force on Regulatory Relief chaired by Vice President George Bush.

The most important deregulation legislation enacted by Congress during the Reagan presidency was the Garn-St. Germain Depository Institutions Act of 1982. It was essentially a bipartisan response to the growing problems of banks and savings and loans and was the joint product of Congress and the Reagan administration. Its major features were relaxed controls over interest rates paid on checking accounts and the lending practices of savings and loans.

As President, George Bush retained much of the machinery built by his predecessors for influencing the content of regulation through the review of rules. The COMPETITIVENESS COUNCIL, headed by Vice President DAN QUAYLE, was established to ferret out unnecessary regulation. In other respects, such as in appointments, the deregulation theme was less evident, although there was an increase in deregulation rhetoric when the Bush campaign for reelection began in early 1992.

It would be inaccurate to say that Presidents from Kennedy onward caused the deregulation idea to come to the forefront as a result of their advocacy of it. However, the public advocacy of Ford, Carter, and Reagan was extremely significant, and the numbers of new regulatory programs added since 1961, often with strong presidential support, created reactions that fueled deregulation sentiments. Nevertheless, only a handful of regulatory endeavors have been replaced by the market. There seems to be general agreement that presidential initiatives caused an increased sensitivity to the costs of regulation in decision making. In the Reagan and Bush presidencies, in particular, regulation became less restrictive in some areas, such as mine safety, and as a result of presidential policies, agencies were cautious in writing new rules.

To the extent that there has been deregulation, there remains the question as to whether or not it has been beneficial. Environmentalists, for example, tend to challenge air and water quality regulation that appears to be relaxed, whereas businesses subjected to it hold a different view. Uncertainty also clouds evaluation of transportation and financial institution deregulation. In the case of the former, critics point to such evidence as airline failures and to hub systems and the decline in the number of direct flights that emerged when the government ceased to regulate routes. Others argue that consumers have benefited from lower fares. As for financial institutions, some blame deregulation for the collapse of many savings and loans and banks, requiring expensive bailouts. An opposing argument is that the problems were caused by factors such as the souring of New England and southwestern economies and the increase in deposit insurance up to $100,000 per account, inviting lenders to take excessive risks.

Whatever the case, the debate over the proper scope of regulation in public policy can be expected to continue. Since the 1960s, Presidents have played an important part in that debate and will continue to do so into the future.

BIBLIOGRAPHY

Ball, Howard. *Controlling Regulatory Sprawl: Presidential Strategies from Nixon to Reagan.* 1984.

Breyer, Stephen. *Regulation and Its Reform.* 1982.

Brown, Anthony E. *The Politics of Airline Deregulation.* 1987.

Derthick, Martha, and Paul J. Quirck. *The Politics of Deregulation.* 1985.

Gerston, Larry N., Cynthia Fraleigh, and Robert Schwab. *The Deregulated Society.* 1988.

Tolchin, Susan J., and Martin Tolchin. *Dismantling America: The Rush to Deregulate.* 1983.

DAVID M. WELBORN

DESEGREGATION OF THE MILITARY. For discussion of Harry S. Truman's order desegregating the military, see EXECUTIVE ORDER 9981.

DESERT ONE. In November 1979, Iranian militants overran the United States embassy compound in Tehran, Iran, took more than fifty American citizens hostage and held them for the next 444 days [*see* IRANIAN HOSTAGE CRISIS]. After failing to secure the hostages' release by nonmilitary means, on 24–25 April 1980, President Jimmy Carter ordered a military raid into Iranian territory aimed at rescuing the hostages.

The mission envisioned the dispatch of eight American helicopters from aircraft carriers in the Gulf of Oman in the Arabian Sea to a remote staging area, known as "Desert One," in the middle of Iran. There the helicopters were to meet six C-130 cargo planes carrying ninety commandoes and fuel and supplies for a military incursion into Tehran. After the team was transferred from the cargo planes to the helicopters, the helicopters were to fly a short distance northward to the nearby mountains to a site called Desert Two, where they were to hide during the following day. The next night, provided all went well, the rescue team was to be met by trucks driven by American agents from a warehouse on the outskirts of Tehran and carried to the U.S. embassy compound, where they were to overpower the guards and free the hostages. The helicopters were then supposed to pick up all Americans and carry them to an abandoned airstrip nearby, where two C-141's were to fly all of them to safety in Saudi Arabia.

The Desert One plan was approved by a team that included President Carter, Vice President WALTER F.

MONDALE, Secretary of Defense Harold Brown, national security adviser Zbigniew Brzezinski, Deputy Secretary of State Warren Christopher, General David Jones, Carter adviser Hamilton Jordan, and press secretary Jody Powell. Secretary of State Cyrus Vance disagreed with the policy, arguing that the Democratic and Republican leaders in the House and Senate should be advised before any military action was taken. In the end, President Carter decided to notify the leadership of the House and Senate only after the rescue operation had reached the point of no return, an apparent violation of the WAR POWERS RESOLUTION. That decision triggered Vance's resignation shortly before the rescue mission occurred.

Once the mission began, however, two of the helicopters developed mechanical trouble, and only six arrived at the Desert One staging site in good operating condition. After another helicopter broke down, and before any further action was taken, President Carter ordered the mission aborted. As the aircraft departed from the desert site, a helicopter and a cargo plane collided, killing eight Americans. Shortly thereafter, the International Court of Justice criticized the rescue attempt as action "of a kind calculated to undermine respect for the judicial process in international relations." President Carter was later defeated in his bid for reelection in 1980, in no small part because of his inability to secure the hostages' release. When asked what he would have done differently during his first term, Carter reportedly answered, "I wish I had sent one more helicopter."

BIBLIOGRAPHY

Carter, Jimmy. *Keeping Faith: Memoirs of a President.* 1982.
Smith, Gaddis. *Morality, Reason, and Power: American Diplomacy in the Carter Years.* 1986.

HAROLD HONGJU KOH

DESTROYERS FOR BASES. An EXECUTIVE AGREEMENT between President Franklin D. Roosevelt and Prime Minister Winston Churchill in September 1940 exchanged fifty aging U.S. destroyers for eight British naval and air bases stretching from Newfoundland in the Atlantic to British Guiana in the Caribbean. Concluded secretly and without congressional consent, the transaction greatly aided Britain in its fight against Germany, arguably enhanced American security, and moved the United States well away from strict NEUTRALITY in WORLD WAR II.

Soon after becoming prime minister in May 1940, Churchill cabled Roosevelt urgently requesting forty or fifty American destroyers to protect its Atlantic supply line from German U-boat attacks. Britain had lost thirty-two destroyers since the war had begun and needed its remaining sixty-eight to guard home waters against a German invasion. Churchill therefore pleaded "as a matter of life or death, to be reinforced with these destroyers."

Roosevelt initially hesitated at the prime minister's request, sensitive to isolationist opposition in Congress and Republican criticism in a presidential election year. But Churchill persisted in his appeal, writing on 21 July: "Mr. President, with great respect I must tell you that in the long history of the world this is a thing to do NOW." Added impetus came from a pro-British pressure group, the Committee to Defend America by Aiding the Allies, which marshaled public support for England and proposed trading the destroyers for British bases in the Western Hemisphere. Roosevelt finally agreed to act on 13 August, subject to Britain's added pledge to transfer its naval fleet to North America if Germany defeated England. The next day, an elated Churchill cabled his acceptance, writing that "each destroyer you can spare to us is measured in rubies."

After WENDELL WILLKIE, the Republican candidate in the forthcoming presidential election, agreed not to make the deal a campaign issue and Roosevelt's legal advisers found a way to bypass Congress, Roosevelt made the transaction public on 3 September. His message barely mentioned the transfer of destroyers and instead stressed the advantages to be gained by the United States.

Contemporary critics faulted the destroyer deal as "an endorsement of unrestrained autocracy in the field of our foreign relations" that "makes our official neutrality . . . [a] transparent cover for nonbelligerent cooperation on the side of Great Britain." Churchill himself characterized the transaction as "a decidedly unneutral act." But most Americans endorsed it as a measure necessary to stave off Britain's defeat. Negotiated at a time of intense crisis, it answered immediate needs while establishing a potentially worrisome precedent.

BIBLIOGRAPHY

Goodhart, Philip. *Fifty Ships That Saved the World.* 1965.
Heinrichs, Waldo. *Threshold of War: Franklin D. Roosevelt and American Entry into World War II.* 1988.
Kimball, Warren F., ed. *Churchill and Roosevelt: The Complete Correspondence.* 3 vols. 1984.
Langer, William L. and S. Everett Gleason. *The Challenge to Isolation, 1937–1940.* 1952.

BRIAN VANDEMARK

DÉTENTE. *Détente* is a French word meaning relaxation of tension. During the COLD WAR there were significant periods of détente in the administrations of Dwight D. Eisenhower, Richard M. Nixon, and Ronald Reagan. Relations between the United States and the Soviet Union improved in the 1950s after the death of Soviet leader Joseph Stalin. When Eisenhower met the new Soviet leadership in Geneva in 1955, it appeared that the two superpowers wanted to cooperate to avoid confrontation. The visit of Soviet Premier Nikita Khrushchev to the United States in September 1959 also improved relations between the two powers, but progress toward long-lasting detente stopped suddenly after the U-2 INCIDENT of May 1960.

Détente revived and became a principal focus of U.S. foreign policy in the Nixon administration. Working with National Security Adviser, later Secretary of State, HENRY KISSINGER, Nixon developed what he characterized as a structure of peace. The United States and the Soviet Union agreed not to let their ideological rivalry deteriorate into war, and they attempted to cooperate to resolve regional disputes in Central Europe and the Middle East. Nixon and Soviet Premier Leonid Brezhnev formed a personal bond at a series of summit conferences. The two powers agreed to limits on their intercontinental ballistic missiles and to restrict their anti-ballistic missile systems. Trade between the United States and the Soviet Union increased dramatically. Détente stalled, however, toward the end of the Nixon administration. Domestic critics charged that Nixon and Kissinger ignored Soviet human rights abuses and did not take seriously the Soviets' military buildup. President Gerald R. Ford initially attempted to continue Nixon's policies of détente. In August 1975 he signed the Final Act of the Helsinki Conference on Security and Cooperation in Europe, an agreement effectively ending the threat of war in Europe. Soon afterwards, however, critics such as Ronald Reagan accused Ford of being excessively accommodating toward Moscow. Relations between the United States and the Soviet Union declined dramatically from 1976 to 1984. The accession to power of Mikhail Gorbachev in March 1985 represented a major reversal. Détente between the United States and the Soviet Union revived in the second Reagan administration. Reagan and Gorbachev held regular summits and in December 1987 signed the INF (INTERMEDIATE RANGE NUCLEAR FORCES) Treaty removing U.S. and Soviet missiles from Europe. By the end of the Reagan administration the cold war had ended.

BIBLIOGRAPHY

Gaddis, John Lewis. *The Long Peace.* 1988.

Gaddis, John Lewis. *The United States and the End of the Cold War.* 1992.

Garthoff, Raymond. *Detente and Confrontation: American-Soviet Relations from Nixon to Reagan.* 1985.

ROBERT D. SCHULZINGER

DEWEY, THOMAS E. (1902–1971), governor of New York, Republican presidential nominee in 1944 and 1948. Born in Owosso, Michigan, Thomas Edmund Dewey was educated at the University of Michigan and Columbia University Law School, from which he graduated in 1925. For the next ten years, he practiced law in New York. In 1935, Democratic Governor Herbert Lehman appointed him a special prosecutor to investigate crime in New York City. In 1937, he was elected district attorney of New York County (Manhattan).

Dewey quickly became nationally famous as a fearless and incorruptible crime-fighter (he also went after Wall Street financiers and Tammany politicians) thanks to his location in the nation's media center, his organizational talents, and his flair for such dramatics as large-scale police raids and courtroom cross-examinations.

Dewey ran for governor against Lehman in 1938, calling himself "a New Deal Republican." He lost, but so narrowly that the effect of the defeat was to confirm him as a rising political star. In late 1939, still district attorney, he declared his candidacy for the Republican nomination for President.

A quintessential post–NEW DEAL moderate-to-liberal Republican, unwilling to quarrel with the fundamentals of President Franklin D. Roosevelt's social programs and espousing an internationalist outlook, Dewey was the front-runner until the defeat of France by Nazi Germany in June 1940 highlighted his inexperience in foreign affairs and destroyed his candidacy. The nomination went to WENDELL WILLKIE.

In 1942, Lehman having retired, Dewey swept to an easy victory for the governorship of New York, thereby giving himself a platform that would ensure continued national attention and front-runner status for the 1944 presidential nomination. Reelected governor in 1946 and 1950, he enjoyed a reputation for honest, efficient, and progressive administration. He supported civil rights and education, expanded social welfare programs, and improved New York's transportation infrastructure.

In 1944, with isolationism dead and Willkie controversial among Republicans, Dewey took the presidential nomination with little opposition. His campaign against a fourth term for President Roosevelt was unsuccessful largely because he faced a living legend against whom he could produce no compelling issues. He agreed with the President on the essentials of post–WORLD WAR II foreign policy and differed with him only in degree about the social welfare state.

Dewey agreed not to reveal that the United States had broken Japanese codes before PEARL HARBOR and was still intercepting them. The information would have added credibility to his charges of incompetence and unpreparedness, but, with the Pacific war at its bloodiest, he would have been exposed to charges of betrayal of American fighting men. Hence, he made generalized attacks on "the mess in Washington," lamely criticized the government's lack of preparedness for the war, and attempted to project a more vigorous personality than Roosevelt. Roosevelt's margin was the narrowest of his four presidential elections.

Dewey's strong showing against "the Champ" and his continued popularity as governor of the nation's largest electoral state won him a second Republican presidential nomination in 1948. Most political observers expected him to coast to an easy victory over incumbent President Harry S. Truman, who had low public-approval ratings and was bedeviled by splinter parties from the right and left wings of the DEMOCRATIC PARTY.

Underestimating his opponent, placing too much faith in flawed public opinion surveys, and wanting to avoid divisions in his own party, Dewey ran a vague, noncommittal campaign. Ignoring Truman's attacks on the highly conservative, Republican-controlled Eightieth Congress, he apparently assumed that the electorate would not take seriously Truman's charges that a Republican administration would repeal the New Deal. His efforts to remain above controversy came across to many voters as a demonstration of a cold and aloof personality, less appealing than Truman's. Truman won by a surprisingly decisive margin (49.5 to 44.5 percent), and Dewey received fewer votes than in 1944.

This second defeat ended Dewey's presidential aspirations but not his influence in presidential politics. In 1952, to the outrage of Midwestern isolationist Republicans, he played a key role in bringing Dwight D. Eisenhower into the Republican race, thus blocking his old rival, Robert Taft. Leaving the governorship of New York in 1955, he quickly established himself as a leading corporate attorney. In the 1960s, he facilitated Richard M. Nixon's move to New York and lent moral support to his political comeback.

Dewey was one of the most talented two-time losers in presidential electoral history. Conservative Republicans believed that he failed because he was a me-too candidate, but it is doubtful that one of their own would have done as well. It probably is more accurate to attribute his defeats to poor strategic decisions and an unattractive public personality that failed to project his private wit and warmth.

BIBLIOGRAPHY

Beyer, Barry. *Thomas E. Dewey, 1937–1947: A Study in Political Leadership.* 1979.
Ross, Irwin. *The Loneliest Campaign: The Truman Victory of 1948.* 1968.
Smith, Richard Norton. *Thomas E. Dewey and His Times.* 1982.

ALONZO L. HAMBY

DINGLEY TARIFF ACT (1897). Unlike the two preceding presidential elections, the election of 1896 did not focus on the tariff as the leading campaign issue. The new President, William McKinley, assumed office with the Treasury in deficit, a condition exacerbated by ongoing depression and by the Supreme Court's invalidation of the WILSON-GORMAN TARIFF ACT of 1894 income tax provisions. McKinley promptly called Congress into special session to pass legislation aimed at increasing revenues and, not incidentally, enhancing tariff protectionism. The resulting House bill, authored by the chairperson of the Ways and Means Committee, Nelson Dingley, increased most duties to levels between those imposed by the MCKINLEY TARIFF ACT of 1890 and those set by the Wilson-Gorman Act. It also increased revenues by reimposing wool duties.

Dingley's bill, quickly adopted by the Republican-controlled House, received greater scrutiny by Senate Republicans intent on increased protection for their home states' industries. The result, after the House accepted numerous Senate revisions, was a measure pushing most rates above those of the 1890 act.

McKinley's approach to tariff revision also revived the emphasis on reciprocity agreements favored by Benjamin Harrison and JAMES G. BLAINE. McKinley sought new trade agreements in Europe as well as in Latin America, focusing on enhancement of American industrial exports as American productive capacity outstripped growth in domestic demand. These efforts sought to counter protectionist measures directed against American exports by some European nations, especially France. McKinley also hoped to use the promise of American tariff reductions as a tool in his efforts to negotiate international bimetallism.

The Dingley Tariff permitted McKinley to negotiate reciprocal agreements reducing selected American tariffs up to 20 percent. However, the act conditioned the most important types of reciprocity arrangements on congressional approval. Although the effort was delayed by the SPANISH-AMERICAN WAR, the administration concluded a number of such agreements. However, following McKinley's assassination, congressional approval was not forthcoming, and reciprocity efforts faded under Theodore Roosevelt.

BIBLIOGRAPHY

Gould, Lewis L. *The Presidency of William McKinley.* 1980.
Stanwood, Edward. *American Tariff Controversies in the Nineteenth Century.* Vol. 2. Repr. 1967.
Terrill, Tom E. *The Tariff, Politics, and American Foreign Policy 1874–1901.* 1973.

RALPH MITZENMACHER

DIPLOMAT IN CHIEF. Of the manifold functions of the President one of the more important is that of serving as diplomat in chief. In this role of managing foreign relations, he determines fundamental national goals and concrete objectives, defines the nation's vital interests, frames and assesses optional courses of action to achieve them, refines policy precepts, wins congressional support and popular consensus, and supervises diplomatic representation to and negotiation with foreign governments.

Each President, though, is selective regarding the specific manner and degree of his involvement. Reasons for variation include their individual predispositions; the respective amounts of emphasis given to internal and external issues; technological developments in travel and communication; and the changing role of the United States in world affairs. Whereas Presidents' personal diplomatic activities were limited in the nineteenth century, with the emergence of the United States as a major power (and subsequently a superpower), they have come to pursue active, if not decisive, summit careers, at times even serving as their own Secretaries of State and ambassadors.

Since the days of George Washington, American Presidents have not only formulated and proclaimed foreign policy and directed the negotiation of treaties; they also have engaged in five summit diplomatic processes, which include: communicating directly with foreign chiefs of state and heads of government; sending special emissaries (PRIVATE ENVOYS) to consult personally with them as his personal surrogates; receiving foreign leaders on official visits to the United States; visiting and conferring with them abroad; and participating in summit meetings and conferences.

Written Communications. When Washington sent a message to the Sultan of Morocco in 1789, only seven months after the birth of the Republic, he set an important diplomatic precedent. The transmittal of written communications—at the presidential level, and bearing his signature—has since become well-established American practice.

Congratulatory, condolatory, and other ceremonial messages have proliferated with the expansion of nations. Mediatory messages, whereby the President assumes the mantle of peacemaker, are exemplified by those of Theodore Roosevelt during the Russo-Japanese War, Woodrow Wilson during WORLD WAR I, Franklin Roosevelt during the Sudetenland and Danzig crises in the 1930s, and late-twentieth-century Presidents in the Cyprus, Israeli-Arab, inter-American, and other international disputes.

Some twentieth-century exchanges warrant special attention, such as the more than twenty-five hundred WORLD WAR II messages generated by Roosevelt and the British, Chinese, and Soviet leaders that focused on defeating the Axis powers. The Eisenhower-Kremlin "correspondence diplomacy" from 1955 to 1960, featuring seventy-two communications of more than 100,000 words, dealt with arms reduction and summit conferencing. Published immediately, they tended to amount to little more then diplomatic speechifying. On the other hand, the five Kennedy-Khrushchev "eyeball-to-eyeball" summit notes during the CUBAN MISSILE CRISIS constituted the diplomatic nexus for defusing nuclear confrontation in 1962.

Initially, presidential messages were communicated by written instruments transmitted via traditional diplomatic channels or oral statements conveyed by special emissaries. Telegraphy and transoceanic cables expedited transmission. During World War II President Roosevelt, in communicating with Prime Minister Churchill, introduced the use of teleconferences; and after 1940 he had a direct phone line to Churchill. Following the Cuban missile crisis, these techniques were supplemented with direct White House–Kremlin contact, established by the 1963 HOT-LINE AGREEMENT and first used during the Six-Day War in the Middle East in 1967. Dozens of summit communications may be sent and received by the President each year. They bypass the normal bureaucracy and diplomatic channels, and reflect the degree to which the President is disposed to become his own ambassador.

Travel. In an age of rapid travel, it is not surprising to see heads of government crisscrossing the globe to meet, consult, and bargain with one another as they ply their statecraft. The earliest summit visit to the United States, in 1806, brought the Bashaw of Tunis to negotiate a claims settlement for the depredations of Barbary pirates, and in 1874 King Kalakaua of Hawaii came to the United States on an informal visit for twelve days. His stay was technically the first summit visit to this country.

Foreign leaders come for a variety of official and unofficial reasons. Whereas only twenty-three such visits occurred prior to Franklin Roosevelt's term, since then visits have increased, annually averaging approximately twenty, but numbering more than thirty-five per year during the 1980s and 1990s and occasionally mounting to forty-five to fifty. Summit visitors have come from some 150 nations on more than a thousand visits. The countries with the largest number of summit visitors are the United Kingdom, neighboring Canada and Mexico, West Germany, Israel, Italy, and, in the Far East, Australia, Japan, and New Zealand.

Matters of timing, intent, ceremony, agenda, PRESIDENTIAL PROTOCOL, and mechanics of individual visits are designed in advance by mutual agreement. They serve various purposes, ranging from purely ceremonial and formal state visits to informal consultation, working sessions, and deliberative meetings concerned with major issues of public policy. Usually, foreign guests focus on Washington, D.C., for one or two days, but sometimes they tour other parts of the country and remain as long as ten to twelve days. If a President hosts twenty-five to thirty such visits per year and each visitor averages two days in Washington, this time may amount to 20 percent of the President's normal workdays. Moreover, as the quantity increases, there is the risk that they become so routine that government leaders and the American people tire of them. Techniques are devised, therefore, to give key visits some air of individuality.

Early tradition established the precedent that the President should not leave American territory during his incumbency. Theodore Roosevelt was the first to break with tradition by visiting PANAMA in 1906. After World War I President Wilson headed the American delegation to the Paris Peace Conference and was lionized in Paris, Brussels, London, and Rome. To the time of Franklin Roosevelt, only five Presidents set foot on foreign soil and, with the exception of Herbert Hoover, all Presidents since 1918 have visited foreign lands, with the frequency of these visits accelerating substantially during and since World War II. For example, Roosevelt went abroad fourteen times on thirty-six visits, including his wartime meetings with Winston Churchill, Joseph Stalin, and other Allied leaders. Harry S. Truman was the first to be received abroad on formal state visits (Mexico and Brazil, 1947).

Other firsts include Dwight D. Eisenhower's partic-

ipation in multipartite East-West conferences convened abroad (Geneva, 1955, and Paris, 1960) and the introduction of the grand tour ("Quest for Peace" mission to Asia and Europe, 1959); Lyndon B. Johnson's attendance at the Manila Conference and sweep of seven Far Eastern allies (1966) and his circumnavigation of the globe (1967); Richard M. Nixon's historic trips to Beijing and Moscow (1972 and 1974); Gerald R. Ford's participation in the first annual conclave of the leaders of the major industrial powers (Rambouillet, 1975); Jimmy Carter's trip to Panama to exchange Panama Canal Treaty ratifications (1978); and Ronald Reagan's attendance at the North-South conclave at Cancun (1981).

Presidential trips abroad were commonplace by the early 1990s. Nearly 60 percent have been to a single country. In a half century Presidents made approximately 100 trips consisting of some 235 separate visits—an average of four to five per year. Some were formal state visits, 40 percent were devoted to informal consultation, and less than one-fourth entailed international conferencing.

The consequences of presidential trips vary with the objectives sought. Aside from purely ceremonial and formal state visits are many goodwill and conferral missions, some negotiatory conclaves, and occasional limited-purpose ventures. The issue is not whether the President will go abroad on summit trips, but whether a particular visit is best suited to achieve his objectives and those of the nation.

Summits. The form of presidential diplomacy that receives the greatest amount of popular, journalistic, and official attention is the summit meeting and conference. Although such gatherings were not untried previously, presidential involvement in conferencing began with Theodore Roosevelt's indirect role as mediator in the Portsmouth Conference during the Russo-Japanese War in 1905, followed by Wilson's participation in the Paris Peace Conference.

Since then every President has become involved personally in some conferencing capacity, ranging from purely ceremonial functions—such as Coolidge's address to an inter-American conference at Havana (1928) and Truman's address to the San Francisco Conference convened to produce the UNITED NATIONS Charter (1945)—to serious deliberation and negotiation. To illustrate the latter, during World War II Presidents Roosevelt and Truman confined their conferencing primarily to solidifying policy alignments with the leaders of five friendly countries: Australia, Canada, China, and especially the United Kingdom and the Soviet Union. Roosevelt engaged in twenty-one summit gatherings in less than six years from 1940 to 1945, including those at Casablanca, Cairo, Tehran, and Yalta; Truman continued this series at Potsdam in 1945.

Subsequent Presidents have engaged extensively in summit conferencing, largely of a bilateral nature. These meetings include periodic East-West summits with the leaders of the Soviet Union and China, and frequent meetings with the leaders of Britain, Mexico, and other allied countries and friendly nations. However, one in four meetings has been multilateral, such as the Western four-power conferences (including the United States, Britain, France, and Germany) to align policy on the German and Berlin questions and East-West relations, occasional NATO sessions, the seven-nation Manila Conference concerned with Southeast Asia (1966), several inter-American gatherings and, since 1975, the annual conclaves of the major industrial powers.

Official publications and the media describe such conferencing as "discussions," "conversations," "exchange of views," "conferral," or just plain "talks." All these descriptions denote face-to-face oral exchanges. Normally, the President explicates United States objectives and policies, solicits understanding of American interests, and seeks agreement on basic principles. Occasionally, serious negotiation is necessary, but rarely is the President subjected to the tortuous hammering out of the details of an important treaty or agreement. This work usually is delegated to foreign ministers and diplomats.

Presidential participation in summit conferencing has become an expanding, though controlled, technique of American diplomacy. Generally the President avoids formal multilateral conferences that entail detailed bargaining. He prefers those meetings that are intended to establish unity of purpose embodied in an impelling "spirit" or a declaration of mutual policy. Presidents favor smaller, less ostentatious, usually bilateral meetings or businesslike "working sessions" to exchange views, align positions, achieve understanding, or defuse a crisis.

Since World War II, such presidential personal involvement in summitry has become an accepted, highly visible, vital, and potentially expedient component of contemporary diplomatic practice. In part, America's central role in world affairs, which may require leadership as well as rapid and significant accommodation at the highest level, appears to justify, if not require, diplomacy at the summit; it is a viable supplement to—not replacement for—traditional and ministerial diplomacy.

Presidents generally prefer to communicate and confer than to negotiate in detail at summits. They realize that summitry—enriching and personally gratifying though it may be—is no substitute for sound policy and patient, skillful diplomacy. A few Presidents are historically remembered for their concrete contributions to the initiation, development, and utilization of summitry. As the first President, Washington employed the summit techniques available at the time. In the twentieth century the two Roosevelts, Wilson, Truman, Eisenhower, and Nixon contributed most to the expansion and refinement of presidential participation in summit practices.

The functioning of the President as diplomat in chief, although time-tested, widespread and newsworthy, is by no means a magic cure-all for international differences, problems, and crises. It is but one of several alternative diplomatic processes, is limited in potentiality, entails inherent costs and possible risks, and can be overemployed. Like other institutions and procedures, its value is determined by the willingness of the President and other world leaders to make it succeed in achieving mutual national objectives and ameliorating or resolving difficulties. Still, it needs to be wisely employed lest it lose its impact, and care needs to be exercised that it does not become a popular fetish or be regarded as an end in itself.

BIBLIOGRAPHY

Eubank, Keith. *The Summit Conferences, 1919–1960.* 1966.

McDonald, John W., Jr., ed. *U.S.-Soviet Summitry: Roosevelt through Carter.* 1987.

Plischke, Elmer. *Diplomat in Chief: The President at the Summit.* 1986.

Plischke, Elmer. *Presidential Diplomacy: A Chronology of Summit Visits, Trips, and Meetings.* 1986.

Plischke, Elmer. "The President's Right to Go Abroad." *ORBIS* 15 (1971): 755–783.

Plischke, Elmer. "Rating Presidents and the Diplomats in Chief." *Presidential Studies Quarterly* 15 (1985): 725–742.

Putnam, Robert D., and Nicholas Bayne. *Hanging Together: The Seven-Power Summits.* 1984.

Weihmiller, Gordon R. *U.S.-Soviet Summits: An Account of East-West Diplomacy at the Top, 1955–1985.* 1986.

ELMER PLISCHKE

DIRTY TRICKS. This umbrella term for under-handed efforts in election campaigns to prevent the election or disrupt the campaign of a candidate for office is borrowed from the worlds of warfare and espionage. It entered the lexicon of presidential politics as the WATERGATE AFFAIR came to light in 1973. The reelection campaign organization of President Richard Nixon had created a "dirty tricks department" to harass prospective Democratic rivals.

Cynical intervention in a rival's campaign for office is as old as elections and was practiced in Republican

Rome. Thus it is hardly surprising that dirty tricks appeared in U.S. presidential politics in the first contested election, in 1796. Rare indeed are subsequent campaigns in which they did not also figure.

This kind of political mischief falls into two broad categories. One, often called vote fraud, includes tactics affecting the casting and counting of votes. Among these are manipulation or intimidation of voters, prospective voters, and officials at the polling place; falsifying the count (stealing votes), and paying voters to vote a particular way or not at all (buying votes).

The other general category, often styled dirty campaigning, embraces tactics meant to discredit or disrupt the campaign of an opponent. Examples are vilification or old-fashioned mudslinging, depicting the opponent's character as gravely flawed, appeals to racial or religious bigotry, distortion or outright falsification of an opponent's record or actual position, raising spurious issues of loyalty or patriotism, and harassment or sabotage of the rival's campaign.

In 1796 Vice President John Adams and Thomas Pinckney ran against Thomas Jefferson and AARON BURR to succeed George Washington as President. The campaign saw the full range of dirty campaigning. Invective hurled against Adams accused him of excessive vanity, extreme jealousy, dreams of founding an Adams dynasty, a wartime plot against Washington, toadying to England, and scheming with her archenemy, France. To Jefferson was attributed drunkenness, atheism, cowardice, Negro blood, and secretly supporting the French Jacobins (tantamount to treason).

Sabotage figured too. Hamilton tried to maneuver the ELECTORAL COLLEGE into a tie so his allies in the House of Representatives might put Pinckney into the White House, leaving Adams Vice President. The French minister, Pierre-Auguste Adet, secretly worked for Jefferson so effectively that Adams won by only three electoral votes.

Apart from personal vilification, dirty campaigning is generally seen as unfair and dishonest. When serious mental or moral deficiencies are imputed to a candidate, such as insanity, drunkenness or other drug addiction, criminality, or sexual promiscuity, the citizen may reasonably expect the accusation to be accompanied by reputable evidence.

However, such evidence is not always available until decades after the campaign, which complicates the issue and only enhances the plausibility of the accusation. Abraham Lincoln, HORACE GREELEY, WILLIAM JENNINGS BRYAN, both Roosevelts, and BARRY GOLDWATER have been among the candidates assailed as crazy. Washington, Jefferson, Andrew Jackson, and Woodrow Wilson were the butt of heavy sexual innuendo

without incontrovertible evidence. So was Grover Cleveland, who denied paternity of an illegitimate child, but acknowledged past intimacy with the mother and helped support the child. Yet Warren Harding and John F. Kennedy, whose ardors in and out of the White House have been abundantly documented, were subject to little more than admiring snickers.

Rallying religious and racial bigotry in the electorate has been popular with political smear artists since the beginning. Lurid tales of Jefferson's sexual involvement with his slave Sally Hemings scandalized voters. Black ancestry was falsely imputed to him as well as to Jackson and Harding.

Anti-Semitic campaigners attributed Jewishness to both Roosevelts. Orthodox Christians assailed Jefferson, Lincoln, and Taft as anti-Christians who considered Jesus Christ "a common bastard." Anti-Catholicism was one of the major factors in ALFRED E. SMITH's defeat in 1928, and it was a serious problem for John F. Kennedy in 1960. Kennedy's deft handling of the issue largely defused it, but it later came to light that his Wisconsin primary campaign covertly circulated anti-Catholic literature in Catholic districts to get out the vote.

Distortion of a rival's actual record is a staple. Partial quotations, "yes" votes that in their parliamentary setting meant "no," and other facts out of context, are raw material for the slick and dishonest campaigner. This approach to deception is popular because a semblance of accuracy clings to any citation "from the record" and researching the original meaning is tedious at best.

The bolder practice of actually lying is also common. One of its oldest forms is the whispering campaign to spread a false and inflammatory story. Modern variations include editing audio and video recordings to reverse the original meaning, thus using the candidate's own voice or image to falsify his or her own words. Fake photographs and spurious publications or forgeries of legitimate ones also appear from time to time.

One of the most famous campaign lies gave a name to its technique. In 1844 an Ithaca, New York, newspaper published a fictitious account by one "Baron Roorback" of watching the Democratic candidate, James K. Polk, purchase forty-three slaves at auction. The story appeared shortly before the election, with time enough for wide reprinting but not for rebuttal. The timing was as important as the falsity; "roorback" defines a false and damaging story published too late to refute.

Loyalty and patriotism always have been important elements of dirty campaigning. As the French Revolution was beginning, reports of its bloody excesses filled conservative Americans with horror. "Jacobin" was a lethal political epithet in the 1790s, analogous to "Communist" at the height of the COLD WAR. Jefferson and his fellow Democratic-Republicans were Jacobins to many Federalists in their day, as Democrats from ADLAI E. STEVENSON (1900-1965) to HUBERT H. HUMPHREY—and even the Republican President Dwight D. Eisenhower—were communists to right-wing Republicans in the era of MCCARTHYISM. In the notorious 1950 U.S. Senate campaign in Florida, Republican George Smathers defeated Senator Claude Pepper in a campaign that labeled the incumbent "Red Pepper," a procommunist. (Tradition has it that back-country sexual innuendo called Pepper's sister a Thespian [pronounced "Thez-bian"] and his brother a "practicing homo sapiens." Probably, however, these were joking coinages by bored reporters.)

Antiwar Democrats in the CIVIL WAR era were widely labeled COPPERHEADS, an epithet that bespoke treason to regular or war Democrats. Similar tensions introduced such slurs as "Hun" and "Nazi" into presidential politics during the two world wars.

Harassment of the opposition's campaign may be as simple as dispatching hecklers to disrupt a rally—a tactic used after the 1960s more by special-interest groups than by party or candidate operatives. More elaborate measures were taken by Republican officials in Louisville, Kentucky, who caused the heating plant at the municipal auditorium to be turned up full for a campaign speech by Al Smith in the summer of 1928. It grew hotter as he spoke, and when he was done both he and the audience were soaked with sweat.

Dick Tuck, a Democrat, once rigged welcome signs for a Nixon visit to Chinatown with an embarrassing question in Chinese. In the Democrats' 1964 campaign against Barry Goldwater, he planted an agent on a Goldwater campaign train with a supply of special "newspapers" ridiculing the Republican candidate and emphasizing Democratic themes that he was out of touch with the times.

Certain elections have become notorious for particular dirty tricks. Both 1824 and 1864 saw outrageous levels of personal vituperation, the former against Jackson, the second against Lincoln, who may have been the most vilified American President.

The 1876 election, as RECONSTRUCTION was waning, was remarkable not only for the murder of many black voters and poll watchers but also for the maneuvers by which Republicans stole the presidency for Rutherford B. Hayes from the Democrats and SAMUEL J. TILDEN. Tilden narrowly won the popular vote and had 184 undisputed electoral votes from seventeen states, to 163 votes from seventeen states for Hayes. Tilden also carried Florida, Louisiana, and South Carolina, but Republican election officials there disqualified many Democratic votes, and each of the states sent two rival delegations to the Electoral College. Oregon had gone Republican, but its Democratic governor illegally replaced one Republican elector with a Democrat.

Congress created an ELECTORAL COMMISSION with seven members from each party, with the understanding that the fifteenth man would be an Illinois jurist famous for his impartiality. But the Republican-controlled Illinois senate elected him to the U.S. Senate instead. The four Supreme Court Justices on the commission picked a Republican colleague, and the election went to Hayes on a straight party-line vote, 8 to 7.

The campaign of 1884 was remarkable for the famous Mulligan Letters, detailing the duplicity and corruption of the Republican nominee, JAMES G. BLAINE, as well as for questions about the paternity of a bastard son laid to the Democrat, Grover Cleveland, a bachelor. The election ultimately turned on a gratuitous slur about "Rum, Romanism, and Rebellion" by a supporter in Blaine's presence. Overheard by a reporter, it enraged New York's large Catholic vote and carried the state and the country for Cleveland.

A brazen Republican plot to steal the 1888 election for Benjamin Harrison came to light when a Democratic spy filched the notorious "blocks of five" letter from the U.S. mails. In it, a Republican expert spelled out his procedure for buying the votes of enough "floaters" to carry Indiana for Harrison.

Determination to do anything necessary to win the 1972 election by a historic landslide lay at the bottom of the Watergate affair. Its dirty tricks were intended to ensure the nomination of the Democrat farthest to the left, GEORGE MCGOVERN. These efforts were not only petty and sophomoric, but unnecessary, for the Democrats were doing to themselves what the Nixon plotters aspired to do. Divisions over civil rights, school busing, and egalitarian reforms of the McGovern Commission after the 1968 convention had sundered any semblance of party unity, and rightist and centrist candidates canceled one another out in the primaries. A month before the 1972 convention McGovern's nomination was assured. Beyond ruining the Nixon presidency, the Watergate affair significantly altered the composition and organization of Congress, the balance of power between Congress and the President, and public confidence in government and politics, as well as building persistent hostility toward politics in the news media.

With this heightened cynicism has come a fallacious equation of two venerable and useful campaign practices with dirty tricks. One is presenting a candidate in the best possible light, now widely disdained as "selling" or "marketing" politicians. The other is candid criticism of an opponent's judgment, record, or stated positions, or "negative campaigning," which is seen as naughty and unfair.

The political parties, which once could either dictate or prevent dirty tricks in campaigns, lost that power with the decline of their role in selecting and disciplining candidates. State election laws have been able to regulate vote fraud and related activities with generally good effect. The introduction in the 1890s of the Australian ballot, provided by the state instead of the party, was a big step. Voter identification and registration requirements helped. So did the advent of mechanical, then computerized, voting machines. Still, every such reform opens the door to some new corruption.

Dirty campaigning is more difficult to control, because there are no generally accepted standards and definitions of fair and unfair campaign conduct. Laws prohibiting libel, slander, and anonymous literature have been tried at federal and state levels, but every such effort is both difficult and constitutionally suspect.

Efforts to employ publicity and moral suasion have usually involved legally toothless "watchdog" entities like the Fair Campaign Practices Committee (FCPC), which operated on a national level from 1954 to 1978. That group had a bipartisan board of directors and a small professional staff that enjoyed considerable cooperation from party organizations and the news media. It promulgated and publicized a Code of Fair Campaign Practices committing candidates to avoid personal vilification, distortion, appeals to bigotry, and the like, which had been proposed by the Senate Subcommittee on Privileges and Elections in addressing dirty tricks in the McCarthy era.

The FCPC sought to make campaign tactics a campaign issue and conducted a general public education effort through the media, schools, and civic groups. It was tax-exempt and existed on tax-deductible contributions from individuals, businesses, labor unions, and foundations. It eventually succumbed to lack of financial support, but proposals to resuscitate it arise from time to time.

BIBLIOGRAPHY

Abels, Jules. *The Degeneration of Our Presidential Election.* 1968.

BRUCE L. FELKNOR

DISABILITY, PRESIDENTIAL.

At the CONSTITUTIONAL CONVENTION of 1787, one delegate noted ambiguities in the presidential succession clause, inquiring "what is the extent of the term 'disability'?" and "who is to be the judge of it?" His questions were not answered. The Framers of the Constitution undoubtedly thought that they had dealt adequately enough with the subject of presidential succession by creating an office of Vice President and by providing that its occupant should discharge the powers and duties of President in the event of death, resignation, removal, or inability. The Framers also placed in Article II, Section I, clause 6, a provision authorizing Congress to establish a line of succession beyond the Vice President.

Disability in History. The inherent ambiguities in these provisions were not readily manifested until the assassination of President James A. Garfield in 1881. For eighty days he hovered between life and death, suffering relapses and hallucinations. Many doubts were expressed during that period concerning the meaning of Article II, Section I, clause 6. There was a wide divergence of opinion concerning who had the power to declare a President disabled and whether a Vice President became President in such an event for the remainder of the term. The latter construction was suggested because when President William Henry Harrison died in 1841, Vice President John Tyler had assumed the presidential office for the balance of Harrison's term. This TYLER PRECEDENT was then followed by Vice President Millard Fillmore when President Zachary Taylor died in office on 9 July 1850; and again by Vice President Andrew Johnson upon the death of Abraham Lincoln on 15 April 1865.

Some protested at the time of Tyler's succession that his correct status was Acting President, pending a special presidential election. Tyler rejected such claims on the ground that the Vice President becomes President when a President dies in office, and serves for the balance of the term. Since the Constitution did not distinguish among cases of death, resignation, removal, and inability, it was argued in 1881 that the Vice President also assumed the presidential office in a case of inability—based on the Tyler precedent. Even more perplexing was whether the President, Vice President, or Congress had any role in determining the question of presidential inability. The end result was that, as Garfield lay unconscious, the affairs of state were practically suspended. His only official act during the eighty-day period of his inability was the signing of an extradition paper. His doctors forbade other functions, believing that his isolation was crucial to his survival. Some steps, however, were taken by the President's Cabinet in administering the government, but there was much that the Cabinet could not do.

Wilson. The unanswered questions concerning the succession provision resurfaced in 1919 when President Woodrow Wilson suffered a paralyzing stroke. For all practical purposes, he was rendered incapable of functioning as President for the remainder of his term. During the interim period his wife, EDITH WILSON, his doctor, and his close friends sought to take care of the work of the presidential office. They determined what should be presented to him and who could see him. Vice President THOMAS R. MARSHALL refused to get involved, fearing that he might be seen as a usurper and "incur the wrath" of Mrs. Wilson. The Cabinet, on the other hand, sought to play a helpful role. But, upon recovering from some of the effects of his disability, Woodrow Wilson dismissed his Secretary of State, Robert Lansing. He believed that Lansing had wrongfully sought to exercise presidential power.

Unfortunately, much public business was unable to be transacted because of the condition of the President. United States participation in the LEAGUE OF NATIONS was defeated in the Senate; numerous bills became law in default of any action by the President; governmental vacancies went unfilled; foreign diplomats were prevented from submitting their credentials to the President; and letters and notes to the President went unanswered.

Wilson's disability produced numerous proposals for dealing with a crisis of presidential succession. Interest in the subject of reform, however, declined once a new administration was installed in the White House.

Eisenhower. But the nation was once again to endure confusion over the meaning of the succession provision when Dwight D. Eisenhower suffered several disabilities. In September 1955, he suffered a heart attack that left him in a weakened condition for a significant period of time. In 1956, he experienced an attack of ileitis that required surgery and a period of recovery, and in 1957 he sustained a stroke that affected his ability to speak. Vice President Richard M. Nixon and Eisenhower's Cabinet and WHITE HOUSE STAFF handled the daily affairs of government during each of these disability crises.

Concern over the gaps in the succession provision led Eisenhower to propose in 1957 a constitutional amendment to address the subject. As Congress analyzed his and other proposals at congressional hearings, the President took a major initiative of his own by developing an informal arrangement with Vice President Nixon to cover any future cases of inability in his administration. Under the arrangement, the President would, if possible, inform the Vice President of his inability. If the President were unable to do so, the Vice President would be empowered to declare the President disabled, after such consultation as might be appropriate. In either case, the Vice President would simply act as President, and the President would be able to resume his powers and duties upon his own declaration of recovery. Fortunately, Eisenhower suffered no additional disabilities that required the arrangement to be implemented.

Minor disabilities. While the temporary disabilities of Eisenhower, Wilson, and Garfield were the most prominent in the history of the country, other Presidents experienced disabilities that were hidden from the public. Chester A. Arthur was diagnosed in 1882 as having a disease that produced spasmodic nausea, mental depression, and indolence. President Grover Cleveland underwent two operations during his term of office to remove cancerous tissue from the roof of his mouth. Both operations took place on a yacht cruising through Long Island Sound so that the public would be kept in the dark. The available evidence indicates that during his last year in office, President Franklin D. Roosevelt suffered heart disease and hardening of the arteries that sapped his energy, reduced his attention span, and affected his reasoning powers.

The Twenty-fifth Amendment. When President John F. Kennedy was assassinated in 1963, the subject of presidential inability reappeared. As James Reston noted in the *New York Times* of 23 November 1963, "for an all too brief hour today, it was not clear again what would have happened if the young President, instead of being mortally wounded, had lingered for a long time between life and death, strong enough to survive but too weak to govern."

The pressure and emotions generated by Kennedy's assassination led Congress to propose the TWENTY-FIFTH AMENDMENT to the Constitution in 1965. The amendment, which was ratified on 10 February 1967, sets out a procedure for dealing with future cases of presidential inability. The procedure reflects, for the most part, the recommendations developed during the Eisenhower administration. The President is empowered to declare his own inability as well as its termination. In the event that he is unable or unwilling to do so, the amendment authorizes the Vice President and a majority of the principal officers of the EXECUTIVE DEPARTMENTS (popularly known as the CABINET) to declare the President disabled. If the President disputes the declaration, the amendment provides for both houses of Congress to resolve the issue. It takes a two-thirds vote of each house to prevent the President from resuming his powers and duties in such an event.

Congress has twenty-one days to resolve the issue, during which time the Vice President serves as Acting President.

The Twenty-fifth Amendment also sets forth a procedure for filling a vacancy in the Vice Presidency. The President is authorized to nominate a successor who takes office upon confirmation by a majority of both houses of Congress. This section of the amendment was applied for the first time in 1973 when SPIRO T. AGNEW resigned as Vice President. He was replaced by Gerald Ford and when President Nixon resigned during the WATERGATE AFFAIR of 1974, Ford became President and thereafter nominated NELSON A. ROCK- EFELLER to be his Vice President. Thus, for a period of more than two years, the nation's highest officers were appointed under the provisions of the Twenty-fifth Amendment.

The presidential inability provisions of the amendment have not yet been formally implemented. On two separate occasions, President Ronald Reagan suffered temporary disabilities that prevented him from discharging the powers and duties of his office for a period of time. In March 1981, he was shot by a would-be assassin and underwent surgery to remove the bullet and to stop internal bleeding. In 1984, he had an operation to remove cancerous tissue in his colon. At the time of the latter disability, upon entering the hospital, he sent a letter to the Speaker of the House of Representatives and the President pro tem of the Senate informing them of his transfer of presidential power to Vice President George Bush. Shortly after the operation, he sent another letter announcing that he was resuming his powers and duties. Although President Reagan refused to acknowledge that he had a disability or was invoking the Twenty-fifth Amendment, he effectively did so by his letters to the legislative leaders. During his campaign for the presidency in 1988, President George Bush admitted that this was the case.

On two occasions during his term in office, President Bush encountered health difficulties that focused attention on the presidential inability provisions of the Twenty-fifth Amendment. Fortunately, their application was not necessary. Their availability, however, will provide comfort to the nation in a future case of presidential inability.

[See also HEALTH, PRESIDENTIAL.]

BIBLIOGRAPHY

Abrams, Herbert. *The President Has Been Shot.* 1992.
Bayh, Birch. *One Heartbeat Away.* 1968.
Crispell, Kenneth, and Carlos Gomez. *Hidden Illness in the White House.* 1988.
Feerick, John D. *From Failing Hands: The Story of Presidential Succession.* 1965.
Feerick, John. *The Twenty-Fifth Amendment.* 1976.
Hansen, Richard H. *The Year We Had No President.* 1962.
Miller White Burkett Center of Public Affairs at the University of Virginia. *Report of the Miller Commission on Presidential Disability and the Twenty-Fifth Amendment.* 1988.
Silva, Ruth C. *Presidential Succession.* 1951.

JOHN D. FEERICK

DIVIDED GOVERNMENT. The term *divided government* denotes a condition in which one political party controls only one of the major institutional components of the two political branches: the House, the Senate, or the presidency. The system of SEPARA- TION OF POWERS designed by the Constitution makes national policy-making difficult without a significant degree of cooperation between the President and Congress. Though the Framers did not foresee the development of political parties, partisan conflict and cooperation have played an important role in the development of national policy-making. Because of differing constituencies and the institutional struggle over national priorities, there has been a natural friction between the branches, but one of the system's unifying factors has been the alliance between the President and members of the President's party in Congress, who presumably share similar political and policy goals.

Since the time of Andrew Jackson the national government has been divided about 40 percent of the time. In the nineteenth century, however, periods of divided government occurred primarily when a midterm election gave the opposition party one or both houses of Congress.

The first half of the twentieth century was characterized primarily by unified party government, with only eight years of divided control. From 1968 to 1992, however, the national government was divided in all but the four years of the Jimmy Carter administration (1977–1981). More significantly, the character of divided government changed from an off-year election phenomenon to prevalence in presidential election years as well. Dwight D. Eisenhower's reelection in 1956, accompanied by Democratic control of both houses of Congress, marked the first time (in a two-way presidential race) that the President's party failed to carry the House and only the second time that it failed to carry the Senate. From 1968 to 1992, with the exception of the Carter years, the President's party never controlled Congress. Republicans controlled the White House (except for Carter's term) and Demo-

Divided Government: Presidents and Congress, 1798–1993ª

President	Congress		Senate			House		
			Maj	Min	Other	Maj	Min	Other
Washington, F	**1st**	**1789–91**	**17 Ad**	9 Op		**38 Ad**	26 Op	
Washington, F	**2d**	**1791–93**	**16 F**	13 DR		**37 F**	33 DR	
Washington, F	3d	1793–95	**17 F**	13 DR		57 DR	48 F	
Washington, F	**4th**	**1795–97**	**19 F**	13 DR		54 F	52 DR	
J. Adams, F	**5th**	**1797–99**	**20 F**	12 DR		**58 F**	48 DR	
J. Adams, F	**6th**	**1799–1801**	**19 F**	13 DR		**64 F**	42 DR	
Jefferson, DR	**7th**	**1801–03**	**18 DR**	13 F		**69 DR**	36 F	
Jefferson, DR	**8th**	**1803–05**	**25 DR**	9 F		**102 DR**	39 F	
Jefferson, DR	**9th**	**1805–07**	**27 DR**	7 F		**116 DR**	25 F	
Jefferson, DR	**10th**	**1807–09**	**28 DR**	6 F		**118 DR**	24 F	
Madison, DR	**11th**	**1809–11**	**28 DR**	6 F		**94 DR**	48 F	
Madison, DR	**12th**	**1811–13**	**30 DR**	6 F		**108 DR**	36 F	
Madison, DR	**13th**	**1813–15**	**27 DR**	9 F		**112 DR**	68 F	
Madison, DR	**14th**	**1815–17**	**25 DR**	11 F		**117 DR**	65 F	
Monroe, DR	**15th**	**1817–19**	**34 DR**	10 F		**141 DR**	42 F	
Monroe, DR	**16th**	**1819–21**	**35 DR**	7 F		**156 DR**	27 F	
Monroe, DR	**17th**	**1821–23**	**44 DR**	4 F		**158 DR**	25 F	
Monroe, DR	**18th**	**1823–25**	**44 DR**	4 F		**187 DR**	26 F	
J. Q. Adams, C	**19th**	**1825–27**	**26 Ad**	20 J		**105 Ad**	97 J	
J. Q. Adams, C	20th	1827–29	28 J	20 Ad		119 J	94 Ad	
Jackson, D	**21st**	**1829–31**	**26 D**	22 NR		**139 D**	74 NR	
Jackson, D	**22d**	**1831–33**	**25 D**	21 NR	2	**141 D**	58 NR	14
Jackson, D	23d	1833–35	20 D	20 NR	8	147 D	53 AM	60
Jackson, D	**24th**	**1835–37**	**27 D**	25 W		**145 D**	98 W	
Van Buren, D	**25th**	**1837–39**	**30 D**	18 W	4	**108 D**	107 W	24
Van Buren, D	**26th**	**1839–41**	**28 D**	22 W		**124 D**	118 W	
W. Harrison, W **Tyler, W**	**27th**	**1841–43**	**28 W**	22 D	2	**133 W**	102 D	6
Tyler, W	28th	1843–45	**28 W**	25 D	1	142 D	79 W	1
Polk, D	**29th**	**1845–47**	**31 D**	25 W		**143 D**	77 W	6
Polk, D	30th	1847–49	**36 D**	21 W	1	115 W	108 D	4
Taylor, W Filmore, W	31st	1849–51	35 D	25 W	2	112 D	109 W	9
Fillmore, W	32d	1851–53	35 D	24 W	3	140 D	88 W	5
Pierce, D	**33d**	**1853–55**	**38 D**	22 W	2	**159 D**	71 W	4
Pierce, D	34th	1855–57	**40 D**	15 W	5	108 R	83 D	43
Buchanan, D	**35th**	**1857–59**	**36 D**	20 R	8	**118 D**	92 R	26
Buchanan, D	36th	1859–61	**36 D**	26 R	4	114 R	92 D	31
Lincoln, R	**37th**	**1861–63**	**31 R**	10 D	8	**105 R**	43 D	30
Lincoln, R	**38th**	**1863–65**	**36 R**	9 D	5	**102 R**	75 D	9
Lincoln, R **A. Johnson, R**	**39th**	**1865–67**	**42 R**	10 D		**149 R**	42 D	

ª Division in each house of Congress between the majority party, the principal minority party, and other members (independents and members of minority parties) at the beginning of each Congress. When the majority party is the party of the President, it is printed in boldface. When the majority party in both houses is the party of the President, the President's name and the number of the Congress are also printed in boldface.

Abbreviations: Ad, administration; AM, Anti-Masonic; C, coalition; D, Democratic; DR, Democratic-Republican; F, Federalist; J, Jacksonian; Maj, majority party; Min, principal minority party; NR, National Republication; Op, opposition; R, Republican; U, Unionist; W, Whig.

Divided Government: Presidents and Congress, 1798–1993 (Continued)[a]

President		Congress	Senate			House		
			Maj	Min	Other	Maj	Min	Other
A. Johnson, R	40th	1867–69	42 R	11 D		143 R	49 D	
Grant, R	41st	1869–71	56 R	11 D		149 R	63 D	
Grant, R	42d	1871–73	52 R	17 D	5	134 R	104 D	5
Grant, R	43d	1873–75	49 D	19 D	5	194 R	92 D	14
Grant, R	44th	1875–77	45 R	29 D	2	169 D	109 R	14
Hayes, R	45th	1877–79	39 R	36 D	1	153 D	140 R	
Hayes, R	46th	1879–81	42 D	33 R	1	149 D	130 R	14
Garfield, R Arthur, R	47th	1881–83	37 R	37 D	1	147 R	135 D	11
Arthur, R	48th	1883–85	38 R	36 D	2	197 D	118 R	10
Cleveland, D	49th	1885–87	43 R	34 D		183 D	140 R	2
Cleveland, D	50th	1887–89	39 R	37 D		169 D	152 R	4
B. Harrison, R	51st	1889–91	39 R	37 D		166 R	159 D	
B. Harrison, R	52d	1891–93	47 R	39 D	2	235 D	88 R	9
Cleveland, D	53d	1893–95	44 D	38 R	3	218 D	127 R	11
Cleveland, D	54th	1895–97	43 R	39 D	6	244 R	105 D	7
McKinley, R	55th	1897–99	47 R	34 D	7	204 R	113 D	40
McKinley, R	56th	1899–1901	53 R	26 D	8	185 R	163 D	9
McKinley, R T. Roosevelt, R	57th	1901–03	55 R	31 D	4	197 R	151 D	9
T. Roosevelt, R	58th	1903–05	57 R	33 D		208 R	178 D	
T. Roosevelt, R	59th	1905–07	57 R	33 D		250 R	136 D	
T. Roosevelt, R	60th	1907–09	61 R	31 D		222 R	164 D	
Taft, R	61st	1909–11	61 R	32 D		219 R	172 D	
Taft, R	62d	1911–13	51 R	41 D		228 D	161 R	1
Wilson, D	63d	1913–15	51 D	44 R	1	291 D	127 R	17
Wilson, D	64th	1915–17	56 D	40 R		230 D	196 R	9
Wilson, D	65th	1917–19	53 D	42 R		216 D	210 R	6
Wilson, D	66th	1919–21	49 R	47 D		240 R	190 D	3
Harding, R	67th	1921–23	59 R	37 D		301 R	131 D	1
Coolidge, R	68th	1923–25	51 R	43 R	2	225 R	205 D	5
Coolidge, R	69th	1925–27	56 R	39 D	1	247 R	183 D	4
Coolidge, R	70th	1927–29	49 R	46 D	1	237 R	195 D	3
Hoover, R	71st	1929–31	56 R	39 D	1	267 R	167 D	1
Hoover, R	72d	1931–33	48 R	47 D	1	220 D	214 R	1
F. Roosevelt, D	73d	1933–35	60 D	35 R	1	310 D	117 R	5
F. Roosevelt, D	74th	1935–37	69 D	25 R	2	319 D	103 R	10
F. Roosevelt, D	75th	1937–39	76 D	16 R	4	331 D	89 R	13
F. Roosevelt, D	76th	1939–41	69 D	23 R	4	261 D	164 R	4
F. Roosevelt, D	77th	1941–43	66 D	28 R	2	268 D	162 R	5
F. Roosevelt, D	78th	1943–45	58 D	37 R	1	218 D	208 R	4
F. Roosevelt, D Truman, D	79th	1945–47	56 D	38 R	1	242 D	190 R	2
Truman, D	80th	1947–49	51 R	45 D		245 R	188 D	1
Truman, D	81st	1949–51	54 D	42 R		263 D	171 R	1

Continued on next page

Divided Government: Presidents and Congress, 1798–1993 (Continued)[a]

President	Congress		Senate			House		
			Maj	Min	Other	Maj	Min	Other
Truman, D	**82d**	**1951–53**	**49 D**	47 R		**234 D**	199 R	1
Eisenhower, R	**83d**	**1953–55**	**48 R**	47 D	1	**221 R**	211 D	1
Eisenhower, R	84th	1955–57	48 D	47 R	1	232 D	203 R	
Eisenhower, R	85th	1957–59	49 D	47 R		233 D	200 R	
Eisenhower, R	86th	1959–61	64 D	34 R		283 D	153 R	
Kennedy, D	**87th**	**1961–63**	**65 D**	35 R		**263 D**	174 R	
Kennedy, D **L. Johnson, D**	**88th**	**1963–65**	**67 D**	33 R		**258 D**	177 R	
L. Johnson, D	**89th**	**1965–67**	**68 D**	32 R		**295 D**	140 R	
L. Johnson, D	**90th**	**1967–69**	**64 D**	36 R		**247 D**	187 R	
Nixon, R	91st	1969–71	57 D	43 R		243 D	192 R	
Nixon, R	92d	1971–73	54 D	44 R	2	254 D	180 R	
Nixon, R Ford, R	93d	1973–75	56 D	42 R	2	239 D	192 R	1
Ford, R	94th	1975–77	60 D	37 R	2	291 D	144 R	
Carter, D	**95th**	**1977–79**	**61 D**	38 R	1	**292 D**	143 R	
Carter, D	**96th**	**1979–81**	**58 D**	41 R	1	**276 D**	157 R	
Reagan, R	97th	1981–83	53 R	46 D	1	243 D	192 R	
Reagan, R	98th	1983–85	54 R	46 D		269 D	165 R	
Reagan, R	99th	1985–87	53 R	47 D		252 D	182 R	
Reagan, R	100th	1987–89	55 D	45 R		258 D	177 R	
Bush, R	101st	1989–91	55 D	45 R		260 D	175 R	
Bush, R	102d	1991–93	57 D	43 R		266 D	166 R	1
Clinton, D	**103d**	**1993–95**	**57 D**	43 R		**258 D**	176 R	1

[a] Division in each house of Congress between the majority party, the principal minority party, and other members (independents and members of minority parties) at the beginning of each Congress. When the majority party is the party of the President, it is printed in boldface. When the majority party in both houses is the party of the President, the President's name and the number of the Congress are also printed in boldface.

Abbreviations: Ad, administration; AM, Anti-Masonic; C, coalition; D, Democratic; DR, Democratic-Republican; F, Federalist; J, Jacksonian; Maj, majority party; Min, principal minority party; NR, National Republication; Op, opposition; R, Republican; U, Unionist; W, Whig.

ADAPTED FROM: Congressional Quarterly *Guide to the Presidency* (1989); Congressional Quarterly *Guide to Congress*, 4th ed. (1991).

crats controlled both houses of Congress except from 1981 to 1987, when Republicans controlled the Senate.

The proximate cause of divided government is ticket splitting, when voters elect a congressional candidate from one political party but cast their votes for the presidential candidate of the other party. The percentage of congressional districts splitting their ballots remained relatively low in the early years of the twentieth century and was generally in the 10 to 30 percent range from 1920 to 1960; it increased to the 30 to 45 percent range from 1960 to 1990, with a high of 45 percent in 1984.

Those who favor the model of American democracy characterized by responsible party government have pointed with alarm to the increasing incidence of divided government, arguing that divided government exacerbates the tensions inherent in the separa-tion-of-powers system by reinforcing institutional rivalry with ideological and partisan antagonisms. Such critics argue that political parties are the glue that holds together what the Constitution has divided and creates a common interest between the two branches in passing legislation. When political parties divide the two branches, the strategic interest of the leadership of Congress is to frustrate the initiatives of the President's party, and it is in the interest of the President to veto congressional initiatives so as to deprive the opposition party of political victories.

Those who see divided government along these negative lines have proposed a number of constitutional reforms that, they argue, would reduce the negative effects of divided government and push the U.S. government toward a more parliamentary form. These proposed reforms include team tickets (forbidding split-ticket voting); four-year terms for House members and eight-year terms for Senators (eliminating midterm election changes), allowing concurrent service in Congress and the executive branch, and allowing special elections in times of policy deadlock.

Others, however, have argued that divided government is not an indication that the constitutional system of separated powers is broken and thus does not need to be fixed. An empirical examination by the political scientist David Mayhew of the passage of major legislation and the conduct of investigations of the executive branch by Congress between 1946 and 1990 shows no significant differences between divided and unified government. Thus, some conclude that the cause of problems of policy stalemate in some areas is not divided government.

While divided government was nearly a constant in the U.S. political system in the late twentieth century, leading to periods of stalemate in significant policy areas, there is no scholarly or political consensus that divided government is a problem that can be solved by structural changes.

[*See also* CONSTITUTION REFORM.]

BIBLIOGRAPHY

Cox, Gary W., and Samuel Kernell. *The Politics of Divided Government.* 1991.

Fiorina, Morris P. "An Era of Divided Government." In *Developments in American Politics.* Edited by Bruce Cain and Gillian Peele. 1990.

Mayhew, David R. *Divided We Govern: Party Control, Lawmaking, and Investigations, 1946–1990.* 1991.

Thurber, James A., ed. *Divided Democracy.* 1991.

JAMES P. PFIFFNER

DOCKERY-COCKRELL COMMISSION. The commission was created by Congress on 3 March 1893, and officially named the Joint Commission to Inquire into the Status of the Laws Organizing the Executive Department. It conducted the most comprehensive and far-reaching of the several congressional investigations of administration initiated during the nineteenth century. As was the case with previous investigations, it conducted its work without reference to, or participation by, the President.

Congress instructed the commission to investigate the laws organizing the executive agencies, the rules and procedures instituted by those agencies, and the behavior of their employees, in an effort to achieve greater economy and efficiency in government. However, to protect the inefficiencies of the most politically important government program, Congress barred the commission from inquiring into the administration of the veterans' pension.

The commission had six members, three each from the House and the Senate. Its Senate members were Francis M. Cockrell (D.-Mo.), Shelby M. Cullom (R.-Ill.), and James Jones (D.-Ark.). Members from the House were Alexander Dockery (D.-Mo.), who chaired the commission, Nelson Dingley, Jr. (R.-Me.), and James D. Richardson (D.-Tenn.). Senator Cockrell had chaired an extensive but less effective investigation of administration, the Cockrell Committee, between 1887 and 1889, that presented to Congress bills to enact its recommendations. The commission was the first congressional investigation of administration authorized to employ staff to aid in its investigation, and three distinguished accountants were employed to serve as staff for the commission.

The commission ended its work on 4 March 1895. In its two years of activity it issued twenty-nine reports on different aspects of federal administration, and spent $41,264. Accompanying these reports, the commission presented Congress with bills to enact its recommendations into law. The commission's first report was a compilation of laws that shaped the organization of the administrative agencies. This report was followed by another detailing the positions and salaries of each administrative agency. The commission then focused on individual departments and achieved substantial changes in their accounting and work methods. For example, the commission reformed the Post Office's handling of money orders, modernized the accounting and auditing procedures of the Treasury, and introduced the typewriter and carbon paper to facilitate the issuance of land patents and the maintenance of the patent records of the Interior Department.

The Dockery-Cockrell Commission represented the end of the era of congressional dominance of administration. In the twentieth century Congress would lose its monopoly over the investigation of administration, and increasingly, Presidents would dominate the reform of administration.

BIBLIOGRAPHY

Keller, Morton. *Affairs of State: Public Life in Late Nineteenth-Century America.* 1977.

Kraines, Oscar. *Congress and the Challenge of Big Government.* 1958.

White, Leonard. *The Republican Era: 1869–1901.* 1958.

PERI E. ARNOLD

DOLLAR DIPLOMACY. During the administration of President William Howard Taft, Secretary of State PHILANDER C. KNOX developed a new U.S. policy toward Central America and the Caribbean region.

Stressing political reform through loans and customs receivership rather than direct military intervention, Taft proclaimed that dollars would be substituted for bullets as the instrument for advancing American interests abroad. This effort to foster cooperation between the U.S. government and bankers and commercial interests soon became known as dollar diplomacy. The Taft administration pursued it in Central America, the Caribbean, and to, a lesser extent, China. President Woodrow Wilson and Secretary of State WILLIAM JENNINGS BRYAN later criticized dollar diplomacy as concealing self-interested greed, but Wilson's actual policies continued the course set by the Taft administration. Advocates considered dollar diplomacy a humane advance in American foreign policy, preferable to the overt military interventions pursued by the administration of Theodore Roosevelt.

In Central America. During the Taft administration the State Department pressured the governments of Nicaragua, Honduras, Guatemala, and HAITI to refinance their European-funded foreign debt with loans floated in New York. In Nicaragua and Honduras the loan projects went further and resulted in the establishment of U.S. collectorship of customs receipts. The United States continued the practice, begun during the Roosevelt administration, of collecting import duties in the DOMINICAN REPUBLIC. These customs receiverships, in turn, led to direct military intervention by U.S. forces—precisely the sort of direct rule that dollar diplomacy had been developed to supplant.

Military interventions varied in scope and intensity. A revolution in the Dominican Republic in 1912 forced the closure of several customhouses. In September 1912 Taft sent 750 Marines and a commission to restore order and force the resignation of a corrupt president by cutting off his customs revenue. The commissioners and most of the marines were withdrawn in December, but the country remained unstable. In 1916 the Wilson administration sent the U.S. Navy back to the Dominican Republic, where it remained until 1922. In neighboring Haiti, the Wilson administration used the presence of two thousand Marines to collect the customs, imposing a protectorate on the country. The Marines remained the effective rulers of Haiti until 1934.

The Taft and Wilson administrations' supervision of customs receipts in Nicaragua led to repeated military interventions. In 1909 Taft broke diplomatic relations with the government of José Santos Zelaya and ordered U.S. Navy ships to support the rebels in a decisive battle in Nicaragua's civil war. Secretary of State Knox negotiated a treaty with the new government of Adolfo Díaz under which the United States controlled Nicaragua's custom houses. Knox encouraged U.S. banks to loan money to the Díaz government, but civil war continued in Nicaragua, and in 1912 Taft ordered U.S. Marines into battle alongside Díaz's forces. After defeating the rebels, the United States kept a symbolic contingent of one hundred Marines in Managua. The Wilson administration continued to encourage American bankers to lend money to Díaz's government; American warships continued to sail offshore to impress Nicaraguans with Washington's interest in their political affairs; and Nicaragua remained a U.S. protectorate until 1933.

In China. Under Taft the United States employed dollar diplomacy to penetrate China, a market he characterized as "one of the great commercial prizes of the world." Following the advice of Willard Straight, the acting chief of the State Department's Far Eastern Bureau, Taft encouraged a group of New York banks to demand participation in a European-sponsored consortium lending money for railroad construction in China. Taft himself wrote to the regent of China insisting on "equal participation by American capital" in the financing of China's railroads. The British, French, and German governments eventually agreed to participation by an American banking group headed by John Pierpont Morgan, and the loan was floated in June 1911. Shortly afterwards, however, revolution broke out in China, and the start of new railroad construction was delayed until 1913.

After the revolution, the Taft administration persisted in trying to use foreign loans to influence events in China. In 1912 Secretary of State Knox responded to desperate pleas from the new republican government of China for financial assistance by adding Japanese and Russian banks to the existing international consortium formed by France, Germany, Great Britain, and the United States. Knox hoped that the inclusion of Japan and Russia would restrain their appetite for Chinese territory. Instead, Tokyo and Saint Petersburg used their bankers to demand that China surrender some of its sovereignty over Mongolia and Manchuria. Surprisingly, the Taft administration sided with Japan and Russia and withheld full diplomatic recognition from the new Chinese republic until it acceded to the demands. The transformation of the loan consortium from something that would benefit China into an instrument of foreign domination provided ammunition to the critics of dollar diplomacy. Less than two weeks after Woodrow Wilson became President he abruptly canceled American participation in the international consortium.

Effects. Dollar-diplomacy advocates' hopes of making U.S. foreign policy in the Western Hemisphere and China more helpful to people in these lands proved illusory. Although the policy was designed to foster economic development and political stability, little of either followed. The United States continued to send troops to nearby countries despite the expectations of dollar diplomacy's sponsors that supervision of foreign customhouses would eliminate the instability that had triggered earlier interventions. The U.S. banks and businesses recruited by the government to invest abroad made little money. The most enduring effect of dollar diplomacy was a legacy of bitterness toward the United States. People in areas where the policy had been tried believed that Washington had acted to dominate the political life and economy of poor states. Wealthy Europeans also resented the U.S. government's efforts to take control of the finances of poor, small Western Hemisphere states, since in the process U.S. banks replaced European banks as the lenders to the countries involved.

BIBLIOGRAPHY

Hunt, Michael H. *The Making of a Special Relationship: The United States and China to 1914*. 1983.
Munro, Dana G. *Intervention and Dollar Diplomacy in the Caribbean, 1900–1920*. 1964.

ROBERT D. SCHULZINGER

DOMESTIC POLICY COUNCIL. See OFFICE OF POLICY DEVELOPMENT.

DOMESTIC POLICY ADVISER. Each President has used either formal or informal advisers on domestic policy. The variegated nature of domestic policy issues and their changing priority on the political agenda, as well as differing presidential management styles, have resulted in various roles and forms of domestic advising. Ad hoc advisers, often CABINET officials or friends of the President, were standard into the early twentieth century. As domestic policy became an increasing concern of the modern presidency, however, the position of domestic policy adviser began to emerge.

In the Harry S. Truman White House, domestic policy coordination was associated with the Special Counsel—SAMUEL ROSENMAN, CLARK CLIFFORD and, later, Charles Murphy—working in cooperation with the Bureau of the Budget. Under Dwight D. Eisenhower, domestic policy advice became more diffuse, drawing on Cabinet members and various White House staff and channeling information through the WHITE HOUSE CHIEF OF STAFF, SHERMAN ADAMS. President John F.

Kennedy turned to his friend and Special Counsel, THEODORE SORENSEN.

President Lyndon B. Johnson initially relied on presidential assistant Bill Moyers to coordinate the development of Hooveresque task forces on domestic policy issues [*see* HOOVER COMMISSIONS]. After 1965, Joseph Califano established the first distinct and stable domestic policy operation within the White House, setting the stage for the establishment of the Domestic Council (DC) under President Richard M. Nixon and Nixon's formal appointment of an Assistant to the President for Domestic Affairs in the person of John Ehrlichman. Ehrlichman used the Domestic Council apparatus to oversee domestic policy formulation, coordination, and implementation for the President, at times dominating even Cabinet members [*see* OFFICE OF POLICY DEVELOPMENT (OPD)].

President Gerald Ford named NELSON A. ROCKEFELLER vice chairman of the DC and placed the council staff under his direction, with an expectation that the Vice President would serve as the primary domestic policy adviser. Delays in Rockefeller's confirmation helped to impede this plan, however.

Stuart Eizenstadt, President Jimmy Carter's Assistant for Domestic Affairs, served as an information broker in the domestic policy area, collecting and assessing domestic policy information and advice from many sources and then analyzing and passing it on to the president.

Under President Ronald Reagan the domestic policy adviser lost influence and access and faced stiff competition from other presidential staff and offices. Instead of dealing directly with the President, the domestic policy adviser reported through Presidential Counselor EDWIN MEESE III. Chief of staff JAMES A. BAKER III coordinated legislative strategy aspects while David Stockman, director of the OFFICE OF MANAGEMENT AND BUDGET (OMB), essentially set the pace for domestic policy as part of the budget process.

While President George Bush continued Reagan's pattern of reliance on Cabinet officials for advice, he also relied on White House advisers, notably Roger Porter and Richard Darman. Porter had the knowledge, access, and experience to serve as a focal point for administration policy-making, and he chaired a number of working groups and councils on domestic policy issues. But the budget office generally took the lead in domestic policy via the budget process, with the domestic agenda having less presidential priority that FOREIGN AFFAIRS.

The initial indications for the Clinton presidency suggest that there will not be a primary domestic policy adviser. Rather, the President seems likely to turn to various officials to take the lead in specific domestic-policy areas, using a variety of advisory structures. For example, he has relied on department heads, such as Secretary of Education Richard Riley, to articulate the administration's EDUCATION POLICY, and Secretary of Labor Robert Reich to take the lead on LABOR POLICY. Alternatively, he has asked Vice President AL GORE to form a six-month National Performance Review task force, while the First Lady, HILLARY RODHAM CLINTON, orchestrates a comprehensive health-care task force.

BIBLIOGRAPHY

Burke, John. *The Institutional Presidency.* 1992.
Cronin, Thomas E. *Presidents and Domestic Policy Advice.* 1975.
Moe, Ronald. "The Domestic Council in Perspective." *The Bureaucrat* 5 (1976): 251–272.
Wyszomirski, Margaret Jane. "The Roles of a Presidential Office of Domestic Policy: Three Models and Four Cases." In *The Presidency and Public Policy Making.* Edited by George Edwards III, Steven Shull, and Norman Thomas. 1985.

MARGARET JANE WYSZOMIRSKI

DOMESTIC PROGRAM INNOVATION. The Constitution in Article II, Section 3, provides that the President "shall from time to time give to the Congress Information of the State of the Union and recommend to their Consideration such Measures as he shall judge necessary and expedient."

History of Innovation. The earliest precedents involving administration recommendations were the comprehensive set of proposals for the development of the American economy submitted to Congress in 1790 by the first Secretary of the Treasury, ALEXANDER HAMILTON, who then organized a faction in Congress to pass his measures. When President George Washington supported them some of the proposals went through; others died when Washington showed lack of interest. After Washington, however, Presidents simply listed subjects on which new legislation might be required in an annual message to Congress. The most important role in domestic policy formation for nineteenth-century Presidents was to serve as guardian of the Treasury against predatory raids by legislators. The WHIG PARTY, whose candidates competed for the presidency from 1836 through 1856, wished to eliminate any presidential role in domestic policy-making. Whig Presidents played no leadership role with their congressional parties, and their STATE OF THE UNION MESSAGES were written by congressional leaders. Moreover, no Whig President vetoed legislation passed by Congress except on grounds of unconstitutionality.

During the CIVIL WAR, while Abraham Lincoln demonstrated the vast constitutional powers of the presidency in national emergencies, Congress played the major role in domestic policy-making, creating a complete new financial system, establishing land-grant colleges, and creating the DEPARTMENT OF AGRICULTURE. After the war the House of Representatives voted the IMPEACHMENT OF ANDREW JOHNSON for his interference with its domestic policies of RECONSTRUCTION.

Presidents in the early twentieth-century Progressive Era argued that the committee–department–interest group nexus produced policies at variance with the public interest. The muckraking press laid bare the shortcomings of congressional government and turned public opinion against it. Theodore Roosevelt established the twentieth-century practice of making the annual message a statement of new domestic and foreign-policy goals, including requests for new legislation to implement programs favored by the President. According to the Progressive vision, the President would rely on the scientific and technical expertise of a new generation of civil servants, chosen by the merit system and imbued with a new ethic of the public interest; PRESIDENTIAL COMMISSIONS and task forces would promote new programs, such as conservation or an end to child labor; and Presidents would use the BULLY PULPIT of public opinion to fight for their programs. Policy would become a set of compromises between a President dominating the national agenda and asserting the national interest and legislative leaders fighting a rearguard action to protect narrower, more parochial interests.

Since Theodore Roosevelt's SQUARE DEAL, Woodrow Wilson's NEW FREEDOM, and Franklin D. Roosevelt's NEW DEAL, Congress has expected the President to initiate program proposals to which it then reacts. Wilson revived the custom that Thomas Jefferson had abandoned in 1801 and delivered his STATE OF THE UNION MESSAGE in person, calling for the enactment of a number of New Freedom measures. Since 1945 this presidential speech has been known as the State of the Union address, and preparation of the address has become an action-forcing process. The President asks department secretaries to make suggestions for new programs. Congress has passed laws that require the President or departments to submit proposals or annual reports: the BUDGET AND ACCOUNTING ACT of 1921 requires the President to submit an executive budget, prepared for the President by the OFFICE OF MANAGEMENT AND BUDGET (OMB); the EMPLOYMENT ACT of 1946 requires the President to submit an annual economic report outlining proposals for economic growth, price stability, and maximum employment consistent with growth and stability, which is prepared for the President by the COUNCIL OF ECONOMIC ADVISERS (CEA). Other laws require reports on subjects such as civil rights, energy, and the environment.

To meet the President's enlarged responsibilities as program innovator and manager of the administrative establishment, Franklin Roosevelt won congressional approval in 1939 for a reorganization plan that created the EXECUTIVE OFFICE OF THE PRESIDENT, an entity that encompasses presidential staff agencies such as the OMB, the CEA, the COUNCIL ON ENVIRONMENTAL QUALITY (CEQ), and the NATIONAL SECURITY COUNCIL (NSC). Of these agencies, the OMB plays the most important role in domestic program innovation. First, it prepares the executive budget, and in doing so it may work with departments and bureaus to modify the substance of their program requests. Second, it may be given the responsibility of organizing, coordinating, and even chairing interdepartmental task forces that develop new program proposals. Third, its legislative clearance function allows it to incorporate departmental proposals into the "program of the President," endorse proposals as "in accordance with the program of the President," or prohibit departments from attempting to win congressional approval for their proposals. Fourth, when programs have been legislated and funded, OMB regulatory clearance (instituted in the 1980s) allows it to control the process by which agencies promulgate regulations to implement programs and to "veto" regulations not in accordance with presidential priorities. Finally, the OMB performs a veto-clearance function for the President, considering all measures passed by Congress and flagging those it thinks the President ought to veto.

Influences on Innovation. Many factors influence the timing and content of presidential program proposals. Political scientists who have done quantitative studies on innovation have argued that the larger the President's election victory and the greater his margin of party control in the House and Senate, the more likely he is to submit a large number of program proposals to Congress—and the more likely he is to get a large percentage of them passed. Landslide victories like those won by Roosevelt in 1932 and Lyndon Baines Johnson in 1964 may result in breakthroughs in domestic policy, in which significant programs—for example, the New Deal or the GREAT SOCIETY—are passed within a short period of time. When a President's popularity is high or rising, he is more likely to appeal for public support for his proposals, to win over public opinion, and to gain additional votes in Congress for his proposals.

Partisan politics, and the tendency since 1952 for voters to give themselves DIVIDED GOVERNMENT by electing Republican Presidents with Democratic Congresses, may override other factors. Often Republican Presidents come into office with a limited domestic agenda and little inclination to propose a large number of new programs, even early in their first term. In the aftermath of the 1991 PERSIAN GULF WAR with Iraq, President George Bush capitalized on an unprecedented public approval rating of 91 percent by appealing to Congress to pass a crime bill and a transportation measure—hardly the sign of energetic domestic policy leadership. Republican Presidents win personal and not party victories, rarely capturing the Senate and (since the 1950s) never winning control of the House of Representatives. Their party also tends to lose ground in the midterm elections. Since the major determinant of legislative success for a President is the number of congressional seats his party controls, these Republicans may find that their popularity does not translate into successful program innovation. They find themselves confronting Democratic Congresses with their own agendas and must often resort to the veto.

Since the late 1970s, large budget deficits and the burden of the national debt have limited the ability of both Democratic and Republican Presidents to propose new programs that require large new expenditures. Instead, Presidents from Jimmy Carter on have often acted as "curtailers in chief," proposing to retrench on expenditures by downsizing or eliminating programs. Carter presided over the first reductions in the funding for intergovernmental programs. Ronald Reagan used the budget process in 1981 to gain congressional passage of a program that eliminated or curtailed many social programs and was later able to eliminate entirely many programs aiding central cities and to tighten eligibility for welfare, food stamps, and school-lunch and public housing programs. Most of President Bush's initiatives, though they involved setting national standards or goals, required the states to pay for programs. His budgets proposed eliminating dozens of programs he considered wasteful, though Congress rarely approved his requests.

Presidents often seem to be the initiators of new programs because media attention is focused on the White House and the work of Presidents is more dramatic and understandable to the public than the work of Congress. Yet Congress often plays the major role in domestic policy-making, especially when the President is not interested in an issue or is preoccupied with international crises. A study by Paul Light in 1982 found that more than half of the President's program ideas were influenced by Congress, slightly less than half by executive-branch agencies, and only a very small percentage by parties or interest groups. And Congress itself plays a more important role in domestic program formulation than does the White House. A 1946 study conducted by Lawrence Chamberlain of ninety major laws passed by Congress in the twentieth century found that only one-fifth were initiated by the White House, while two-fifths were developed primarily by Congress, three-tenths were shared efforts, and one-tenth came from pressure groups. Congressional committees and their staffs, working with congressional agencies such as the Office of Technology Assessment and the GENERAL ACCOUNTING OFFICE, are frequent sources for new policy ideas.

[*See also* AGENDA, PRESIDENT'S.]

BIBLIOGRAPHY

Chamberlain, Lawrence. *President, Congress and Legislation.* 1946.

Cronin, Thomas, and Sanford D. Greenberg, eds. *The Presidential Advisory System.* 1969.

Edwards, George, Steven Shull, and Norman Thomas, eds. *The Presidency and Public Policy-Making.* 1985.

Heclo, Hugh, and Lester M. Salamon, eds. *The Illusion of Presidential Government.* 1981.

Kessel, John. *The Domestic Presidency.* 1975.

Light, Paul. *The President's Agenda.* 1982.

Pious, Richard. *The American Presidency.* 1979. Chapter 5, "Domestic Program Innovation."

Sundquist, James. *Politics and Policy.* 1968.

RICHARD M. PIOUS

DOMINICAN REPUBLIC. Generally, U.S. Presidents have not paid a great deal of attention to the Dominican Republic, but four Presidents have taken the situation in this Caribbean nation very seriously. Ulysses S. Grant tried to annex the territory but received instead a shattering rebuke from leaders within his own party; Theodore Roosevelt stretched the Constitution and established a corollary to the MONROE DOCTRINE based on his relations with the Dominican Republic; and Woodrow Wilson and Lyndon B. Johnson intervened militarily in the island, causing serious damage to their respective reputations and adversely affecting their overall foreign policies.

The Dominican Republic and Haiti share the Caribbean island of Hispaniola but little else, being deeply divided by culture, language, and race. For most of the nineteenth century, the Dominican Republic experienced political instability and economic distress.

Under Grant. In 1869, President Grant became convinced that he might save the Dominican Republic by annexing it. Approached by the Dominican dictator

Buenaventura Báez, who was willing to cede his country and pocket the purchase price, Grant bypassed diplomatic channels and sent his private secretary to Santo Domingo to conclude a treaty of annexation. Naively, Grant pledged "to use all his influence" to win Senate approval of the treaty. But, although the navy wanted to acquire the Dominican Bay of Samaná, sentiment in the United States was antiexpansionist, and not enough Senators were willing to enter into a deal with the unsavory Báez.

Charles Sumner, Republican Senator of Massachusetts and the Chairman of the Senate Foreign Relations Committee, led the opposition to Grant, also a Republican. Sumner protested Grant's treaty "in the name of Justice outraged by violence, in the name of Humanity insulted, in the name of the weak trodden down, in the name of Peace imperilled, and in the name of the African race." Grant, who took the attack personally, carried on a feud with Sumner, eventually having him removed from his committee chairmanship, but Grant's pet project failed.

Under Theodore Roosevelt. The Dominican Republic remained independent and insolvent. In 1904, Theodore Roosevelt grew concerned over the size of the Dominican external debt and the threatening attitude of European creditors. Believing that debts must be paid but unwilling to allow European gunboats to do the collecting, Roosevelt felt obliged to perform the task himself. Proclaiming the "Roosevelt Corollary" to the Monroe Doctrine, he explained that though "chronic wrongdoing" could not go unpunished, the United States would have to exercise "international police power" in the Western Hemisphere because of the Monroe Doctrine.

Roosevelt arranged with the Dominican Republic to collect all customs and use a portion of the receipts to service the foreign debt. The Senate delayed approving this settlement for two years, until 1907, but in the meantime Roosevelt went ahead under the terms of an executive agreement. Roosevelt was one of the first Presidents to use EXECUTIVE AGREEMENTS repeatedly in the conduct of foreign affairs. In this case, congressional Democrats labeled the action as "unconstitutional and tyrannical."

Under Wilson. The customs receivership provided only temporary relief. In 1916, on the pretext of turmoil in the Dominican Republic and general unrest in the Caribbean, Woodrow Wilson ordered the U.S. Marines to occupy the country and the Navy Department to establish law and order. Although Wilson condemned imperialism in his speeches, in practice he wielded the "big stick" more often than Roosevelt. The "moral" President tarnished his reputation by intervening in the Dominican Republic. The occupation improved finances, education, and sanitation, but the effort to promote democracy by undergirding it with a professional constabulary force backfired, and the legacy of Wilson's intervention was tyranny, not democracy.

When the Marines withdrew in 1924, Rafael Trujillo, the commander of the Dominican Republic's National Police, emerged as the strong man. He seized power in 1930 and ruled tyrannically for three decades. Trujillo survived by astutely playing the anticommunist card. Dominican specialists insist that he is the political figure to whom Franklin D. Roosevelt was referring in his famous (though alleged) remark, "He may be an S.O.B., but he's our S.O.B."

Under Lyndon Johnson. Trujillo became too much of a liability after the rise of Fidel Castro in CUBA, and the CENTRAL INTELLIGENCE AGENCY clearly encouraged the cabal of military officers that assassinated him in 1961. The administration of John F. Kennedy assisted in the Dominican Republic's transition to democracy and supported the election of the liberal Juan Bosch in 1963. Bosch lasted only seven months, failing to root out the entrenched *Trujillista* elements in the armed forces, who overthrew him. In 1965, the pent-up rage of the Dominican people finally exploded into the streets in a kind of delayed-reaction revolution.

Stating his concern for the safety of Americans in the Dominican Republic but also worried about a pro-Castro takeover, President Johnson ordered the landing of U.S. forces, which eventually exceeded twenty-two thousand. Smarting from criticism for intervening unilaterally and suppressing a popular revolution, Johnson appealed to the ORGANIZATION OF AMERICAN STATES (OAS) to help achieve a cease-fire and restore legitimate government. The OAS agreed to organize an inter-American force and send a peace mission to Santo Domingo. That Brazilian troops comprised the bulk of the inter-American force (Brazil was then under a right-wing military regime), supplemented only by token forces from other countries, did little to help Johnson save face. The perception that Johnson overreacted in the Dominican Republic, resulting in the death of twenty-six U.S. soldiers, accelerated his already deteriorating position with regard to conduct of the VIETNAM WAR.

After 1965, with order restored and with U.S. economic assistance, the Dominican Republic enjoyed relatively stable government, avoiding extremes of right and left, with competitive elections and peaceful presidential transfers. In the 1990 national elections, former President Jimmy Carter led a team of observers that attested to the Dominican Republic's progress toward democracy.

BIBLIOGRAPHY

Atkins, G. Pope. *Arms and Politics in the Dominican Republic.* 1981.
Crassweller, Robert D. *Trujillo: The Life and Times of a Caribbean Dictator.* 1966.
Martin, John Bartlow. *Overtaken by Events: The Dominican Crisis from the Fall of Trujillo to the Civil War.* 1966.
Tansill, Charles C. *The United States and Santo Domingo, 1798–1873.* 1938.
Welles, Sumner. *Naboth's Vineyard: The Dominican Republic, 1844–1924.* 1928.

CHARLES D. AMERINGER

DORR WAR. In 1842, a reform coalition in Rhode Island led by the lawyer and politician Thomas Wilson Dorr sought to implement a constitution ratified by a majority of white, adult males without the consent of the existing state government. That effort followed years of patiently trying to reform the government that operated under the revised colonial charter of 1663, which was altered at independence in 1776 and ratification of the federal Constitution in 1790.

Attempts to change or replace Rhode Island's government had aborted largely because of nativist concerns about immigration and the refusal of established groups to share power. In the spring of 1842, reformers and charter supporters selected state officers in separate elections, and, as a result, the state had two governments claiming authority. The charter government, however, retained possession of all the accoutrements of power and maintained a recognized, official presence in Washington, D.C. Neither side evinced a willingness to withdraw, and many feared a resort to force.

Both sides appealed to Washington for recognition and support. Despite his personal desire to remain aloof, President John Tyler announced that he would act, if required, in defense of the recognized charter government under the provisions of the federal Enforcement Acts adopted in pursuance of Article IV, Section 4, of the Constitution, which guarantees to all states a republican form of government and protection against domestic violence. While no federal troops ever took the field to defend the state against the reformers, the President ordered measures to prepare for all contingencies.

In this context, Dorr vainly attempted to seize the state's government facilities, and his supporters abandoned him. In response, the charter government invoked martial law over the state, restored order within three months at the expense of the CIVIL LIBERTIES of a considerable number of people, and authorized a constitutional convention. In the sequel, the people ratified the new constitution and Rhode Island entered the modern age—finally discarding its colonial charter—in 1843, despite or perhaps because of the near-chaos of 1842.

The Supreme Court case of *Luther v. Borden* (1849) grew out of the Dorr War. It arose when Luther M. Borden and a group of charter militiamen, acting under cover of martial law, forcibly entered the home of the mother of reformer Martin Luther to arrest him. Chief Justice ROGER B. TANEY held that the continuance of the representatives of the charter government in Congress settled the political issue of the legitimate government of Rhode Island, and that President Tyler had acted appropriately under the Constitution and relevant law when he supported the charter government. Further, he ruled that every government—including state governments under the Constitution—has the authority to protect itself against domestic violence, even if from a majority of its own citizens and under martial law. Thus, the reformers lost on every count. These constitutional rulings gave accepted meaning to the doctrine of political questions and the law of emergency powers until well into the twentieth century.

BIBLIOGRAPHY

Coleman, Peter J. *The Transformation of Rhode Island, 1790–1860.* 1963.

Conley, Patrick T. *Democracy in Decline: Rhode Island Constitutional Development, 1776–1841.* 1977.

Dennison, George M. *The Dorr War: Republicanism on Trial, 1831–1861.* 1976.

Gettleman, Marvin E. *The Dorr Rebellion: A Study in American Radicalism, 1833–1849.* 1973.

GEORGE M. DENNISON

DOUGLAS, STEPHEN A. (1813–1861), United States Senator, Democratic presidential nominee in 1860. Born in Vermont, apprenticed as a carpenter, Stephen Arnold Douglas migrated to Illinois and in 1834 began practicing law. Nicknamed the "little giant" for his small physical size and his looming political power, Douglas led the Illinois DEMOCRATIC PARTY, serving in various offices, including Illinois supreme court justice and U.S. Representative. In 1847 he was elected to the Senate, where he remained until his death. There Douglas supported the MEXICAN WAR, western settlement, and annexation of CUBA. Unlike the older Jacksonian Democrats, Douglas favored federal support for INTERNAL IMPROVEMENTS. He chaired the powerful Senate Committee on the Territories and put the COMPROMISE OF 1850 back together after the Senate initially defeated the package.

In 1851 Douglas brazenly sought the 1852 presidential nomination, representing his party's "Young America" faction. A midwesterner born in the Northeast, with a southern slaveholding wife, Douglas tried to appeal to all Democratic factions and all regions of the country. Breaking with precedent, he chose his own running mate—Senator R. M. T. Hunter of Virginia—before he had the nomination. Douglas's 1851 unorthodox campaign began too soon, peaked too early, and offended too many party leaders. Although at one point he led the convention, after forty-nine ballots the Democrats nominated Franklin Pierce, who like Douglas, represented "Young America."

Douglas declared the Compromise of 1850 ended all debate over SLAVERY at the national level. In an 1851 speech he articulated his view that slavery should be kept out of politics and dealt with "by every man minding his own business, and abstaining from all interference with the concerns of his neighbor." But in 1854 Douglas undermined the compromise with his KANSAS-NEBRASKA ACT, which opened western territory to slavery on the basis of popular sovereignty. The act, part of a plan to build a transcontinental railroad, illustrates Douglas's obsession with western settlement and internal improvements and his moral obtuseness on slavery. Douglas always claimed he did not care if slavery was voted up or down. That view ultimately helped undermine his presidential ambitions.

In 1856 Douglas again sought the Democratic nomination. Douglas had strong southern support, but most of his own section, the old Northwest, opposed him because popular sovereignty in Kansas made Douglas unpalatable to many voters. Neither candidate could achieve the necessary two-thirds majority to win the nomination, but Douglas withdrew from the contest to guarantee party unity, giving the nomination to James Buchanan.

In 1857 Buchanan asked Congress to admit Kansas into the Union under the proslavery Lecompton constitution. This constitution, written and ratified through fraud and intimidation, lacked support of the free-state majority in Kansas. Douglas opposed Kansas admission, arguing the Lecompton Constitution was a dishonest implementation of popular sovereignty. Douglas's opposition cost him his chairmanship of the Committee on the Territories, but set the stage for his 1858 reelection to the Senate from Illinois. There he barely won a difficult race over Abraham Lincoln. During this race Douglas persistently declared that he did not care whether slavery was "voted up or down" and that blacks were not only inferior to whites, but, unlike Lincoln's position on the issue, they were not entitled to the natural rights articulated in the Declaration of Independence.

The Lincoln-Douglas debates enhanced the national reputation of both men. Lincoln campaigned against popular sovereignty, arguing that the decision in DRED SCOTT v. SANDFORD prohibited territories from banning slavery. Challenged to explain how popular sovereignty could prevent slavery, Douglas offered the "Freeport Doctrine," a de facto rejection of *Dred Scott,* which asserted that without positive legislation, which the people of a territory could not be compelled to enact, slavery could not survive. Douglas had previously made this point, but the national publicity from the debates undermined Douglas's remaining southern support, which was already severely damaged by his opposition to the Lecompton Constitution.

At the 1860 Democratic convention Douglas had a majority of the delegates, but he lacked the two-thirds support necessary for the nomination. The deadlocked convention adjourned. Reconvening in Baltimore, without the South, the Democrats nominated Douglas. Douglas ran second to Lincoln in popular votes, a half million votes ahead of the third candidate. Douglas was the only candidate to carry substantial numbers of votes nationwide but ran a distant fourth in the ELECTORAL COLLEGE, carrying only Missouri and splitting New Jersey. After the election Douglas worked for compromise and opposed SECESSION. When the CIVIL WAR began Douglas toured the old Northwest, speaking in favor of the Union and supporting the war effort. Exhausted from the presidential campaign, he became ill in May and died in early June.

BIBLIOGRAPHY

Angle, Paul M., ed. *Created Equal? The Complete Lincoln-Douglas Debates.* 1958.

Johannsen, Robert W. *Stephen A. Douglas.* 1973.

Wells, Damon. *Stephen Douglas: The Last Years, 1857–1861.* 1971.

PAUL FINKELMAN

DRED SCOTT v. SANDFORD 60 U.S. (19 How.) 393 (1857). One of the most significant and controversial cases in the history of the Supreme Court, the *Dred Scott* decision also involved charges of collusion between members of the Court and President-elect James Buchanan. By the winter of 1856 the case, originally a dispute between Dred Scott and his owner (Mrs. John Emerson, represented by her brother, John F. A. Sanford; the official record misspelled his name) over Scott's freedom, had escalated into a full-scale review of the status of SLAVERY in the territories and the legality of restrictions upon it. The Democratic platform of 1856 on which Buchanan campaigned had affirmed the COMPROMISE OF 1850 as a final settlement and also the principle that Congress could not interfere with slavery in the territories. Buchanan's solution was local control, or popular sovereignty. In December 1856 the Court heard final arguments in the case, including the entire territorial issue. Newspapers carried reports of the arguments, and popular pressure on the Court to settle the issue was strong. Buchanan also hoped that the Court would resolve the issue comprehensively, and preferably before his inauguration in March. While working on his INAUGURAL ADDRESS, he initiated a correspondence with Justice John Catron that continued throughout most of February, just as the Court was discussing the case in conference. Catron, a longtime acquaintance of Buchanan's, was more receptive to such inquiry than the circumspect Chief Justice, ROGER B. TANEY.

Buchanan began by asking if the case would be decided before the inaugural. Catron responded that he did not know but would find out. Four days later, on 10 February, Catron reported that the case was set for decision at a conference on the fourteenth, but that because of divisions within the Court, the larger question of slavery in the territories might not be decided. Such an outcome would have made the case much less useful to Buchanan's inaugural address, as well as frustrating to the expectations of the country. On the fourteenth, the Court decided to settle the matter on very narrow grounds, without going into the issue of slavery in the territories, and assigned to Justice Samuel Nelson of New York the task of writing the opinion.

During the next five days the Court, for a variety of reasons, reconsidered its action. The new course would be to examine fully the power to restrict slavery in the territories and to have the Court's opinion written by Chief Justice Taney, who had wanted to cover all the issues in the first place. Catron passed this new information along to Buchanan and offered a specific text for his inaugural address. Buchanan ought to say that the question of congressional limits on slavery in the territories was now before the Court, where it should be, and that "It is due to its high and independent character to suppose, that it will decide and settle a controversy which has so long and seriously agitated the country: and which *must* ultimately be decided by the Supreme Court." Catron also urged Buchanan to add that until the present case is disposed of, "I would deem it improper to express any opinion on the subject."

Catron had not specifically said what the vote would be. However, knowledge that the Court would review the larger issues would have led any informed citizen to predict at least a 5 to 4 holding that Congress lacked power to prohibit slavery in the territories, since five justices were southerners. There would be two northerners dissenting and the other two northerners, Nelson and Robert C. Grier, would be uncertain. Buchanan wrote again to Catron, pressing for settlement before the inauguration. Catron responded that the key was Justice Grier, and that Buchanan should write to his fellow Pennsylvanian to urge his speedy assent. Buchanan did so; Grier showed this letter to Taney and to Justice James M. Wayne, both southerners. As a result, Grier informed Buchanan on the twenty-third that he would join the majority in order to prevent a purely sectional split on the Court, and also that the opinions would not be publicly announced until 6 March at the earliest, two days after the inauguration. All of this correspondence, Grier admitted, was against the Court's normal practice, but he and his two colleagues thought Buchanan had a right to know.

At the inauguration, Taney and Buchanan had a brief private conversation, in public view, which was doubtless upon some commonplace subject but which quickly became sinister to the antislavery Republicans. For Buchanan's address inserted a brief reference to the *Dred Scott* case into a longer paean to popular sovereignty in the territories as a manifestation of the excellence of American popular government generally. Two days later, when Chief Justice Taney announced the Court's opinion, holding that blacks were not citizens of the United States and striking down as unconstitutional the congressional restrictions on slavery in the territories in the MISSOURI COMPROMISE of 1820, leading antislavery politicians made collusion one of the principal assertions in an attack that would carry on for years.

BIBLIOGRAPHY

Auchampaugh, Philip. "James Buchanan, the Court, and the Dred Scott Case." *Tennessee Historical Magazine* 9 (1926): 219–238.

Fehrenbacher, Don R. *The Dred Scott Case: Its Significance in American Law and Politics.* 1978.

Swisher, Carl B. *Roger B. Taney.* 1935.

Warren, Charles. *The Supreme Court in United States History.* 2 vols. 1926.

JAMES E. SEFTON

DRUG POLICY. Since the late nineteenth century, the federal government has played a central and growing role in efforts to discourage the nonmedical use of narcotics and other dangerous drugs. Although the states continue to be responsible for many law enforcement and prevention and treatment aspects of such efforts, federal involvement has expanded steadily, especially since the 1970s. In addition to more traditional concerns—monitoring of importation, participation in multilateral activities for international control, regulation of the pharmaceutical industry, and research—the government makes grants to states and localities for a variety of drug abuse prevention and control purposes, provides drug control aid to individual foreign countries, and makes the resources of the armed services available for drug law enforcement under certain circumstances. The executive branch has played an essential role in this expansion.

Before 1914. An explicitly anti-opium statute was enacted in 1887, but the first significant federal efforts were made after the turn of the century. The Food and Drugs Act (1906), although not focused on addiction prevention, established federal authority over certain basic aspects of drug commerce. Soon thereafter, the abuse problem itself was addressed through separate measures.

Responding to concerns about China's opium problem as well as widespread use in the new U.S. colony of the PHILIPPINES, President Theodore Roosevelt charged the State Department with finding solutions. The department took the lead role in convening and planning for the 1909 Shanghai Opium Commission. Under the leadership of President William Howard Taft and Secretary of State PHILANDER KNOX, its work led to the Hague Conference on Opium in 1911.

From the Hague Conference emerged a convention requiring signatories to adopt domestic antinarcotics legislation. In the United States, the result was enactment of the Harrison Narcotics Act of 1914. The history of U.S. drug control has often followed such a pattern: an international forum in which certain conclusions are reached or resolutions taken, then the use of those conclusions at home to press for appropriate domestic measures.

1914–1961. To avoid constitutional difficulties, the Harrison Act was written as a tax measure. It required the registration of anyone dealing with narcotics other than an ultimate user; and all transactions involving such drugs, except direct administration by a physician, became subject to taxation and restrictive order-form requirements. Significantly, "narcotics" was defined to include coca-based drugs as well as opium derivatives.

The system of international controls continued to be refined, often as a result of U.S. diplomacy. High points included the Geneva Conferences of 1924–1925, which resulted in establishment of the Permanent Central Opium Board (shifting the focus of drug control from domestic regulation to international mechanisms) and, in 1961, the consolidation of previous international concords into one governing treaty, the Single Convention on Narcotic Drugs.

Domestically, the progress of drug-control policy during the first fifty years after the Harrison Act could be characterized as a further development of that statute's essential themes. It was marked particularly by passage of the Marihuana Tax Act of 1937, almost a replica of the narcotics statute, and in the 1950s by a series of substantial penalty increases both for illicit distribution and unauthorized possession of a controlled drug.

The Treasury Department's Bureau of Narcotics was created in 1930; its commissioner until 1962, Harry J. Anslinger, dominated the formation and implementation of a drug policy concerned almost entirely with regulation or "law enforcement." A reaction against this approach contributed, in the early 1960s, to growing emphasis on addict rehabilitation.

1961 and After. Underlying the development of drug-control policy in the United States have been not only concerns for the moral health of society but also the widely held belief in a strong relationship between drug use and crime. During the 1960s, as the crime rate rose substantially, this belief was reinforced. Moreover, the country's drug problem began to take on new dimensions, not only in terms of a rapid increase in users and of drugs being used but also in the age range of the using population. The development of a "drug culture" among young middle-class Americans further alarmed the public and policy-makers.

In his first year in office, President John F. Kennedy convened a White House Conference on Narcotic and Drug Abuse, the first such gathering ever and a sign of growing American concern over the post-WORLD WAR II increase in drug use. As a follow-up, he established the (Prettyman) Advisory Commission on Narcotic and Drug Abuse; its report, issued in 1963, was the source of many of the concepts underlying later administrative and legislative action, especially in the call for a larger federal role in the treatment and rehabilitation of narcotics addicts.

The new concern with rehabilitation was first reflected in the Community Mental Health Centers Act of 1963, which defined "mental illness" to include narcotic addiction, thus allowing its treatment in the facilities funded. The Narcotic Addict Rehabilitation Act of 1966 (P.L. 89-793), based on a Johnson administration proposal, authorized civil commitment (for treatment) of addicts charged with federal offenses,

thus introducing a new concept in the federal criminal justice system and further promoting the development of a treatment network. A 1968 enactment established a program of grants, expanded rapidly during the early 1970s, specifically for addict treatment (P.L. 90-574). Also during those years, Congress overrode general administration scepticism by initiating various programs designed to prevent the initiation of drug taking or to intervene in adolescent drug use before the development of dependency.

In the area of regulatory law, stimulant and depressant drugs, along with hallucinogens, were brought under special control in 1965 (P.L. 89-74), in line with a Prettyman Commission recommendation. However, the period's major event was the 1970 enactment of the Controlled Substances Act and its companion, the Controlled Substances Import and Export Act (P.L. 91-513, Titles II and III). Built on a proposal conceived by the Johnson administration but refined and submitted under President Richard M. Nixon, these statutes were originally intended only to consolidate the many dangerous–drug-control laws passed since 1909. However, the final version made significant changes in existing penalty schemes and strengthened regulation of the pharmaceutical industry. A complementary model state law was promulgated by the Drug Enforcement Administration (DEA) and, with variations, universally adopted.

Other significant legislative developments of the period were the establishment of an aid program under the Foreign Assistance Act (P.L. 92-226) to encourage the reduction of overseas drug production and international control of narcotics generally and clarification of the Posse Comitatus Act to allow appropriate support by the armed services for civilian enforcement of drug-control laws, particularly outside the United States (P.L. 97-86). The first, supported by President Nixon, could be seen as a major alteration of policy on drug-control efforts overseas, a turn to greater emphasis on bilateral arrangements with producer countries. The second, endorsed by President Ronald Reagan, reversed long-established military policy.

Important actions taken by the executive branch between 1965 and 1984 included establishment of the following: by President Lyndon B. Johnson, the Bureau of Drug Abuse Control in the Food and Drug Administration (1966), followed by its merger with the Bureau of Narcotics into a new Justice Department agency, the Bureau of Narcotics and Dangerous Drugs (1968); by President Nixon, the Special Action Office for Drug Abuse Prevention (1971), the Office of Drug Abuse Law Enforcement (1972), and the Drug Enforcement Administration (DEA, Justice Department) combining five existing agencies (1973); by President Gerald Ford, the Alcohol, Drug Abuse, and Mental Health Administration in the Department of Health and Human Services, and thus the National Institute on Drug Abuse as a separate entity (1973); and by President Reagan, the Organized Crime Drug Enforcement Task Force program (1982) and the National Narcotics Border Interdiction System (1983).

The first "war on drugs" was declared by President Nixon. Aside from appointing a "drug czar," his administration presided over the breakup of the Turkish-French heroin trafficking network, an agreement by the Turkish government to ban the production of poppies, "Operation Intercept" to halt the inflow of drugs across the Mexican border, and the rapid expansion of treatment services for heroin addicts—including, in a major policy change, maintenance on the substitute drug methadone.

Although the broad outlines of an antidrug strategy were in place by the early 1970s, subsequent policies have reflected changing emphasis. Generally, later administrations continued and expanded upon the aggressive and multifaceted policies formulated during the Nixon years. The exception was the administration of President Jimmy Carter, which proposed "decriminalization" of marihuana possession and was perceived as deemphasizing the law enforcement side of drug control.

Beginning in 1984, a new legislative pattern emerged: the enactment in each Congress of an omnibus, far-ranging bill for purposes of either drug control specifically or the control of crime generally. These measures, with provisions originating both in the executive branch and Congress, have added substantially to federal criminal and drug laws as well as the scope and level of federal treatment, prevention, and international control efforts: the Comprehensive Crime Control Act of 1984 (P.L. 98-473, Title II), Anti-Drug Abuse Act of 1986 (P.L. 99-570), Anti-Drug Abuse Act of 1988 (P.L. 100-690), and Comprehensive Crime Control Act of 1990 (P.L. 101-647). Their impact may be judged in part by the great increase in antidrug spending, especially after the 1986 enactment.

President Reagan, although insisting that the drug problem's solution lies ultimately in demand reduction, particularly through education and legal and social pressure on the user, resumed the campaign to enhance supply-control efforts. Among other early moves, he pushed for major increases in forfeiture cases against drug-trafficker assets, expansion of activities to curb money laundering, stepped-up border interdiction, and vigorous overseas efforts to curb production and traffic. He brought the FEDERAL BUREAU OF INVESTIGATION more definitively into drug-law enforcement by giving it concurrent jurisdiction with the DEA. In 1986, he called for a "national crusade" against drugs, striving for elimination of all drugs from workplaces and schools. He supported increased testing for drug use, expanded treatment programs, and greater public intolerance of drug misuse.

The administration of President George Bush for the most part pursued the Reagan objectives, further emphasizing "user accountability" themes and implementing a number of new initiatives. Under Bush, total spending on drug control increased from $4.7 billion to $12 billion (fiscal year 1992). Through the statutorily mandated Office of National Drug Control Policy, his administration formulated and annually revised a "National Drug Control Strategy" and submitted a "Consolidated National Drug Control Program" budget as required by law. Diminished emphasis on interdiction was reflected in his budget requests.

The overall federal budget for drug control has been generally increasing since fiscal year 1969, the first year such figures were compiled, when it was $82 million. The exception was a period during the Ford administration, after the rapid rise of the Nixon years. Static under Carter, spending rose substantially under Reagan, especially after the Anti-Drug Abuse Act of 1986, and more so under the Bush administration. Relative supply-side and demand-side spending, currently about 70 to 30, has been weighted in favor of supply since fiscal year 1977, when it was approximately 50 to 50. At the peak of the Nixon years, the demand side accounted for roughly 65 percent.

How effective have U.S. drug control efforts been? Of approaches taken, which if any have succeeded? Available data seldom provide clear answers, and a central policy issue concerns the reliability of drug-use statistics. Although certain indicators showed favorable general trends in the early 1990s, some policymakers and analysts disputed them, pointing to continued chronic use among particular population groups. Even more problematic for strategy assessment may be the difficulties in making allowance for the effects of general cultural developments.

BIBLIOGRAPHY

Besterman, Karst. "Federal Leadership in Building the National Drug Treatment System." Courtwright, David T. "A Century of American Narcotic Policy." In vol. 2 of *Extent and Adequacy of Insurance Coverage for Substance Abuse Services.* 1992.

Morgan, H. Wayne. *Drugs in America: A Social History, 1800–1980.* 1981.

Musto, David F. *The American Disease*. 1973.

Taylor, Arnold H. *American Diplomacy and the Narcotics Traffic, 1900–1939*. 1969.

Terry, Charles E., and Mildred Pellens. *The Opium Problem*. 1925.

U.S. National Commission on Marihuana and Drug Abuse. *Drug Use in America: Problem in Perspective*. Vol. 3: *The Legal System and Drug Control*. 1973.

HARRY L. HOGAN

DUKAKIS, MICHAEL S. (b. 1933), governor, Democratic presidential nominee in 1988. As the Democratic nominee for President in 1988, Governor Michael Dukakis of Massachusetts became the target of searing Republican attacks and his campaign the symbol of unrivaled ineptitude. The son of Greek immigrants and a product of Harvard Law School, Dukakis developed an impressive command of public policy issues and the operations of state government. Yet his rigid self-reliance, impassive temperament, and legalistic approach to political issues made him vulnerable in an era of packaged candidates and electronic campaigns.

During his three terms as governor, Dukakis presided over an economic boom. The "Massachusetts miracle" became the rationale for a presidential campaign. Dukakis's rigorous policy analysis and his prescriptions for economic development appealed to young professional voters, while his outrage over the IRAN-CONTRA AFFAIR rallied traditional Democrats.

Recognizing that "money is the first primary," Dukakis amassed a war chest that more than doubled those of his primary opponents. This financial superiority gave him a significant advantage in field organization as well as advertising.

The political calendar and the combined field of candidates also worked to Dukakis's advantage. Although winning the Iowa caucuses was vital to both midwestern candidates Representative Richard Gephardt and Senator Paul Simon, Dukakis had the luxury of lower expectations. Finishing third was hailed as a victory, while Simon's second place constituted a major defeat. A week later, Dukakis's win in neighboring New Hampshire enabled him to emerge as the Democratic front-runner. He consolidated his lead in the nineteen state contests on Super Tuesday. His closest rival, Gephardt, collapsed under a withering barrage of negative commercials aired by Senator AL GORE and Dukakis. Only the latter two and the Reverend Jesse Jackson survived the subsequent midwestern primaries, and Dukakis's victory in New York finished Gore. A subsequent series of lopsided primary wins over Jesse Jackson cast Dukakis as a moderate and secured his nomination.

Yet Dukakis's presidential drive stalled just when it should have accelerated. An illusory seventeen-point lead in the polls over Vice President George Bush lulled the Boston-based campaign into a debilitating overconfidence. Insulated from the Democratic leadership and without the involvement of the party's most experienced professionals, the Dukakis hierarchy viewed the fall campaign as merely a continuation of the primary marathon. In the absence of a general election strategy, they relied too heavily on transplanted field operatives who frequently clashed with local Democrats.

Even more detrimental was the failure of communications. The advertising component, without strong, experienced coordination, lapsed into disarray and internal squabbling. Photo opportunities were so inept that one was even recycled as a Bush commercial. Dukakis's candidacy projected no central message, while garbled themes confused voters. By failing to define himself to the electorate, Dukakis allowed the Republicans' caricature of him as an incompetent liberal to prevail.

Through the use of negative research and focus groups, the Bush campaign mounted a devastating advertising campaign against Dukakis. One ad blamed him for Boston Harbor's pollution, while others ridiculed his lack of experience in foreign policy, his weakness on national defense issues, and his stewardship of the Massachusetts economy. Even his patriotism and the state of his mental health were questioned. The most telling assault branded Dukakis as soft on crime. By dramatizing the case of Willie Horton, a furloughed murderer who had terrorized a Maryland couple, the Republicans stirred racial fears and exposed one of Dukakis's greatest weaknesses—his inability to admit mistakes. After failing to respond to the attacks, Dukakis himself administered the coup de grace with an emotionless response to an explosive question during the second presidential debate. Asked if he would favor the death penalty if his wife were raped and murdered, he dryly recited his opposition to capital punishment.

Although Bush's victory was decisive, many political observers believed that with a more competent campaign and a more experienced candidate, the Democrats could have won.

BIBLIOGRAPHY

Black, Christine M., and Thomas Oliphant. *All by Myself: The Unmaking of a Presidential Campaign*. 1989.

Nyhan, David. *The Duke: The Inside Story of a Political Phenomenon*. 1988.

MICHAEL L. GILLETTE

DULLES, JOHN FOSTER (1888–1959), Secretary of State. John Foster Dulles, son of a clergyman, was born in Watertown, New York, and was named after his grandfather, John W. Foster, who was Benjamin Harrison's Secretary of State. Dulles was the nephew of President Woodrow Wilson's Secretary of State, Robert Lansing, and seemed destined for diplomacy but spent most of his life as a Wall Street lawyer. In international outlook he was a Wilsonian; he had been a student at Princeton University when Wilson was president of the university. In politics he was a Republican.

Dulles had little opportunity to deal with diplomacy until after WORLD WAR II, although he did attend the second Hague Peace Conference (1907), where he assisted his grandfather, and serve on the American delegation to the Paris Peace Conference of 1919, where he dealt with German reparations. He was also THOMAS E. DEWEY's principal adviser on foreign policy during the presidential campaigns of 1944 and 1948. Under President Harry S. Truman, Dulles served as a delegate to international conferences. At first Truman did not like him, and when Secretary of State DEAN ACHESON proposed him as special ambassador to negotiate the Japanese peace treaty, Truman objected. Eventually, Acheson prevailed. Dulles scrapped a huge draft treaty and then traveled to the capitals of the primary nations involved, seeking suggestions. The peace conference of 1951 at which the treaty was signed was largely his triumph.

The year after he finished the Japanese peace treaty Dulles wrote the foreign policy planks for the Republican platform, in which he excoriated the Democrats for, among other sins, the YALTA CONFERENCE agreement.

In his first months as Secretary of State under President Dwight D. Eisenhower, Dulles erred in not taking more interest in administration, believing that he could handle policy while staff managed the department. The result, however, was a series of resignations and removals, notably of officials connected with China policy.

The most interesting aspect of Dulles's six years as Secretary of State—he resigned early in 1959 and died of cancer shortly thereafter—was his relationship with President Eisenhower. Although Eisenhower and Dulles worked closely, Eisenhower, a very strong President, managed his appointees, including Dulles, and maintained a keen interest in foreign policy. Dulles spent much time setting out his opinions and waiting for presidential acceptance; at the same time, he sought the President's ideas and elucidated them. He became the veritable agent of presidential diplomacy, flying to the corners of the world to advance policy. It was said that the airplane was not merely a convenience, it was a temptation for Dulles, who logged hundreds of thousands of miles.

During his tenure, Dulles saw the formation of the CENTO alliance in the Middle East and the SEATO alliance in East Asia to complement the OAS in Latin America and NATO in Western Europe. Both Eisenhower and Dulles supported the West German government of Chancellor Konrad Adenauer. Dulles's only failure was the Suez Crisis of 1956 which he unwittingly precipitated; by refusing publicly to assist the Egyptian government in construction of the higher dam at Aswan, he encouraged that government to seize the Suez Canal and pay for the dam from canal revenues. The crisis angered Eisenhower because it coincided with the American presidential election. Eisenhower, however, considered the crisis as the failure of Great Britain and France to use peaceful means to maintain transit of the canal. Dulles and his chief, Eisenhower, proved especially competent at controlling the growing nuclear threat posed by the Soviet Union.

BIBLIOGRAPHY

Ambrose, Stephen F. *Eisenhower the President.* 1984.
Ferrell, Robert H., ed. *The Eisenhower Diaries.* 1981.
Gerson, Louis L. *John Foster Dulles.* 1967.
Hoopes, Townsend. *The Devil and John Foster Dulles.* 1973.

ROBERT H. FERRELL